$20 New User Discount

Valid to September 30, 1997

The ***Canadian Internet Handbook*** is pleased to announce that new users of the Internet can obtain a discount on their sign-up to the Internet. The Internet Service Providers listed on the reverse will provide a discount of $20 off your first month's usage, sign-up fee or some combination of both.

This offer applies to new, original Internet subscriptions only. Duplicates or copies of this form are not acceptable. Proof of purchase of the Canadian Internet Handbook *may be required at the discretion of the Internet service provider. This offer cannot be combined with any other offer. Certain restrictions may apply depending on the particular Internet service provider.*

Coupon Participants

Achilles Internet Ltd.
AEI Internet
Age.net
Alberta Supernet Inc.
Astra Network Inc.
Atlantic Connect
Atréide Communications inc.
Autobahn Access Corporation
autoroute.net inc.
Axion Internet Communications Inc.
Aztec Computer Inc.
Babillard Synapse Inc.
Barrie Internet
Binatech Information Services Inc.
British Columbia Business Connections Ltd.
Burlington Network Services
Central Ontario Internet Services Inc.
CIMtegration Ltd.
CitéNet Telecom Inc.
ClicNet Télécommunications, Inc.
Communication Inter-Accès
Communications Accessibles Montréal
CompuTECH Internet
Connection MMIC Inc.
ConsuLan
CSI Group of Companies (Cyberstore Systems Inc.)
CSP Internet (Pacific Interconnect)
Cyberspace Online Information Systems
CYBERStream Inc.
Cybersurf Information Access
Cyberus Online Inc.
Data Link Canada West (DLC-West)
DataCom Online Services
Dtronix Internet Services
Easynet Inc.
Electro-Byte Technologies
Escape Communications Corp.
Fleximation Systems Inc.
FrancoMédia
generation.NET – Total Internet Solutions
Global Linx Internet Inc.
Globale Internet Canada
Globalserve Communications Inc.
Grant Internet Communications Corporation
Helix Internet
HMT INTERNET Inc.
HookUp Communications
Huron Internet Technologies
HuronTel
HyperNet
Hypertech North Inc.
Infinity Internet Communications
IGS (Information Gateway Services)
Information Gateway Services (Kitchener-Waterloo) Inc.
Information Gateway Services Windsor
InfoTeck Internet
Inline Information Services, Inc.
Interactive Online Ltd.
Inter*Com Information Services
Interhop Network Services Inc.
InterLog Internet Services
Internet Access Inc.
The Internet Centre
The Internet Companion
Internet Connect Inc.
Internet Connect Niagara
Internet Direct Canada Inc.
Internet Front Inc.
Internet HTL
Internet Innovations Inc.
InterNet Kingston
Internet Light and Power™
Internet Mégantic
Internet NNT
Internet North
Internet Portal Services
Internet Québec IQ inc.
Internet Solutions Inc.
Internet XL
Internet—BBSI Inc.
Island Services Network
iSTAR Internet Inc.
Kingston Online Services
Kneehill Internet Services
Lands Systems Ltd.
Lanzen Corporation
Le Cybernaute
Learn-Ed Internet Services
Lexicom Ltd.
Log On Internet Solutions
Magic Total Net Inc.
Mag-Net BBS Ltd.
Maritime Internet Services Inc. (MIS)
Matrox SphereNet
Metrix Interlink Corporation
Metrolinx
MGL Systems Computer Technologies Inc.
MicroAge Computer Centres
Mortimer Online
Mountain Internet (Division of Tantalus Technologies Inc.)
Muskoka.com
NavNet Communications
NBTel
Net Communications Inc.
The Net Idea Telecommunications Inc.
Netcom Canada Inc.
NetCore Global Communications
NetMatrix Corporation
NetReach International
NetSurf Inc.
Netway Internetworking Technologies
Network Enterprise Technology Inc.
Network North Communications Ltd.
Networx Internet System
Norfolk Internet Services
Norlink Communications and Consulting
North Shore Internet Services
Northern Telephone Ltd.
NorthStar Communications
Northumberland Online Ltd.
Octonet Communications Corporation
Odyssey Internet
Odyssey Network Inc.
Okanagan Internet Junction, Inc.
ORCCA Networks Ltd.
Oricom Internet
Osiris (Software) Inc.
Pacific Coast Net Inc.
Pangea.ca Inc.
Pathway Communications
Peterboro.Net
P.G. DataNet Inc.
Prisco interNET
Réseau Virtuel d'Ordinateurs RVO
Resudox Online Services Inc.
RGS Internet Services Ltd.
Les services télématiques Rocler
Sakku Arctic Technologies Inc.
Sentex Communications Corporation
Serix Technologies
SOHO Skyway
Sunshine Net Inc.
Suntek Software
Super i-Way
T-8000 Information Systems
Tamarack Computers Ltd.
Telnet Canada Enterprises, Ltd.
TNC–The Network Centre
TotalNet Inc.
TransData Communications
Travel-Net Communications Inc.
Trytel Internet Inc.
UUNorth International Inc.
VIF Internet
Web Networks/NirvCentre
Webster Internet Communications Inc.
Weslink Datalink Corporation
WestLink Internet
Wiznet Inc.
WorldCHAT™ Internet Services
WorldGate Inc.
WorldLink Internet Services
Worldwide Data Communications Inc.
Xenon Laboratories
ZooNet Inc.

Jim Carroll

Rick Broadhead

Prentice Hall Canada Inc.
Scarborough, Ontario

Canadian Cataloguing in Publication Data

Main entry under title:
Canadian Internet handbook

1994 ed.–
ISSN 1204-9034
ISBN 0-13-574146-7 (1997)

1. Internet (Computer network).

TK5105.875.157C37 004.6'7 C96-900997-6

Prentice-Hall, Inc., Upper Saddle River, New Jersey
Prentice-Hall International (UK) Limited, London
Prentice-Hall of Australia, Pty. Limited, Sydney
Prentice-Hall Hispanoamericana, S.A., Mexico City
Prentice-Hall of India Private Limited, New Delhi
Prentice-Hall of Japan, Inc., Tokyo
Simon & Schuster Asia Private Limited, Singapore
Editora Prentice-Hall do Brasil, Ltda., Rio de Janeiro

ISBN 0-13-574146-7

Managing Editor: Robert Harris
Production Editor: Avivah Wargon
Copy Editor: Betty Robinson
Production Coordinator: Julie Preston
Cover/Interior Design: Olena Serbyn
Cover Image: Masterfile, Rick Fischer
Page Layout: Michael Kelley/Hermia Chung

1 2 3 4 5 00 99 98 97 96

Printed and bound in Canada

Visit the Prentice Hall Canada Web site: **www.phcanada.com**

Every reasonable effort has been made to obtain permissions for all articles and data used in this edition. If errors or omissions have occurred, they will be corrected in future editions provided written notification has been received by the publisher.

Praise for the Canadian Internet Handbook

...the 1996 Canadian Internet Handbook is a precise but friendly guide to the Net. It will get you through the basics and still leave you with plenty of interesting reading material when you've thrown off the shackles of newbie-hood....there's no question that it's the best buy of the year. Karl Mamer, December 24, 1995

With the release of the 1996 edition, the Canadian Internet Handbook remains the most authoritative book about the Internet for Canadians. With the 1996 Canadian Internet Handbook, it is possible to become Net-savvy without even having a computer. Carroll and Broadhead have done it again, producing one of the very few computer books that should be considered a must-have for any Internet-surfer's bookshelf.
Keith Schengili-Roberts, *The Computer Paper*, March 1996

If you are to buy only one Internet reference book this year, get the 1996 edition of the Canadian Internet Handbook by Jim Carroll and Rick Broadhead.
Marg Meikle, *Canadian Living*, December 31, 1995

If you're at all serious about taming the Net, you won't want to venture into the cyber frontier without the 1996 Canadian Internet Handbook. If there is something you want to know about the Internet in Canada that is not in this book, my guess is the only place you'll find it is on the Net. Gerry Blackwell, January 6, 1996

For Canadians who are intrigued by the Internet, the Canadian Internet Handbook is a very useful tool — even for those of a certain age, like me, who are sometimes daunted by the rapidly changing technologies we see all around us.
Jean Chrétien, Foreword to the *Canadian Internet Handbook*, 1996, p. xiii

This book is highly recommended, not only as a primer for novices, but as an exceedingly complete, mostly Canadian, easy-to-understand reference tool for anyone who uses a computer to communicate. Saul Chernos, *Toronto Computes*, February 29, 1996

The updated 1996 Canadian Internet Handbook gives you an excellent springboard to take advantage of the new information technology that is sweeping the world.
Tim Philp, *The Brantford Expositor*, March 9, 1996

This widely available, national best-seller is quickly becoming the definitive text on Canadian internetting. Robb Cribb, *The London Free Press*, August 21, 1995

An exhaustive compendium of WWW services, software information and common-sense advice makes this book so important it should be placed right next to the monitor.
Jack Kapica, *The Globe and Mail*, June 30, 1995

It's the most comprehensive roadmap for the electronic highway I've seen for Canadians. I highly recommend it. Richard Morochove, March 7, 1994

I highly recommend this book to both new and experienced Internet users. The Canadian Internet Handbook has joined Newton's Telecom Dictionary as a key reference which I keep right beside my computer. Ian Angus, Editor, *TELEMANAGEMENT Magazine, The Angus Report on Communications Systems, Services, and Strategies,* February 1995

...a comprehensive, near-invaluable guide for Canadian cybernauts.
Kevin O'Connor, *The Regina Leader Post,* February 11, 1995

This is a good book: well written, nicely organized and attractively illustrated. The Canadian Internet Handbook is for newbies and 'Net vets alike, and the appendices are a mother lode of 'Net information.
Paul Williams, *The Chronicle-Herald/Mail-Star,* Halifax, February 8, 1995

The Canadian Internet Handbook calls itself the "Definitive Guide to the Internet in Canada." It is. For most people who are using or planning to use the Internet, this is probably the only book they'll ever need.
Keith Schengili-Roberts, *The Computer Paper,* December 1994

If you are into using your computer for information, this book is for you. Bravo to its authors! Allan Gould, "Books Today," Thomson News Service, July 17, 1994

Once reserved for students, researchers, and computer nerds, the Internet is now attracting attention as a tool for business people, activists, and just plain folks who crave discussing their favourite topics with like-minded people, even if they live halfway around the world. This is the real promise of the information highway — and the Canadian Internet Handbook is essential reading for anyone curious about it. *Quill & Quire,* May 1994

For Canadians, or for anyone who needs access to Canadian Internet resources, this book is a goldmine. *Matrix News,* April 1994

...[The Canadian Internet Handbook] is quickly becoming the bible of Internet users.
The Evening Telegram, St. John's, April 4, 1994

If you're wondering what the Net is really all about, pick up a copy of the Canadian Internet Handbook by Jim Carroll and Rick Broadhead. It's a good introduction to how the Internet evolved, what you need to get on the network, and what you can do once you're logged on. *Marketing,* April 4, 1994

...tells you step by step exactly what you have to do to start surfing the Internet. And it does it in a language that even the rawest of computer users can understand. It not only tells you what the Internet is and how rapidly it's growing but takes you by the hand and leads you there. Connie Woodstock, *The Toronto Sun,* April 3, 1994

...a concise, straightforward, thorough look at the Internet in Canada.
The Halifax Daily News, March 15, 1994

Contents

What's Your Fred?

by Douglas Coupland

Author of *Generation X* and *Microserfs*

I'm not too sure about the Internet. How many years are we into it now?— not just university folks, but your *parents* knowing about the Internet and actually *caring* about it? A few years, I guess, but it feels like *always.*

Doesn't it?

A month ago, while visiting the studio of an artist friend, I noticed that the office next door was being renovated. The new tenants had left piles of scrapwood outside in the hallway as well as two IBM Selectric typewriters (with auto-correct!) with a big sign above saying, "FREE." When I returned a week later, all the wood was gone, but the typewriters still sat there, unloved and forlorn. I doubt there's ever been a technology rendered so obsolete so quickly as the typewriter. Unless it's the fax.

I remember a time around, say, 1988, when giving somebody your fax number was sexy groovy cool and intimidating. Then it became everyday. Your mother or pet may well have a fax number these days. And then suddenly having a fax number was kind of – er – uh – loser-ish — all of the hip, with-it, in-the-know folks had *Internet* addresses. I remember while doing some work at *Wired* magazine in San Francisco in the summer of 1995 how receiving a fax was the acme of loserdom. "Hey Doug," someone might say, "here's your *fax,*" (*snigger snigger*). Suddenly all the swells sent information digitally.

And now it's 1996 and suddenly Internet addresses are a given. To have your Net address on a business card is simply assumed these days. Suddenly the sexy groovy cool and intimidating thing is to have an *URL.* Oh God, will this *ever* end? Doubtless, five years from now people will snigger if you give a Web address. Instead the cool thing will be to have a – oh – I don't know – a *FRED.* "Hey, what's your FRED?" "I'm working on a FRED 'zither-spoke' for Geffen Records." "Cool!"

* * *

I think that these days most people have a sense of time moving too quickly. It's such an all-pervading sensation that like fish in the sea, we're almost unaware of its all-pervasiveness. Likewise, many people are feeling atomized lately — less connected to humanity in a way they *know* they once felt. I suspect the culprit in the above two syndromes is information — the daily information we receive and its profound effect on the texture of our lives — the rate at which we sense the passing of time and the way we interact with others.

I got rid of my fax machine six months ago and it was one of the smartest decisions I ever made. I realized that people never send somebody a fax unless they want work from them — or a favor, or a phone call. Nobody ever faxed me a Far Side cartoon or a poem. Faxes = Labor became the equation, and once the machine was gone, chunks of my time opened up and life moved at a more sane clip.

Currently I'm getting the sense that e-mail is colonizing my life in a manner whose texture I have yet to fully determine. I feel porous, like an unglazed pot, losing its water through its microscopic clay sieve. Everyday I "speak" casually with friends around the world — friends with whom I might never have spoken to or seen again — and what do we talk about? Things like, how our days went; something their boss did to drive them nuts; last night's Simpsons episode. These global conversations are at once astounding and banal. I wonder if *not* having e-mail might help re-install the magic of geographical distance. Maybe the tyranny of distance is over forever. Whatever the answer is, we'll probably know in three years when we're all busy handing out our FREDs to people.

As for Web sites, well, I *do* have one. Please do visit (**www.coupland.com**, yeah, yeah, yeah...). But I have an addictive personality and I know that once I allow a Web browser into my life, I'll pretty well stop having a life. It's happened to not a few people I know.

Web sites allow you to see interior dimensions of people you would never have known existed otherwise, and that's always interesting. People tend to really spill the dirt on themselves when given a Web site. You get to learn about their love of dressing up like Sir Lancelot, the food preferences of their eleven cats or the stories behind their tattoos you didn't even know they had. And we've all heard stories — not urban legends but *real* stories — of people who met on the Net who then flew to meet their "other," only to sit with an unattractive stranger in a smoky airport lounge awkwardly eating bar nuts and trying to figure out a way to tell them that you really like their mind but not, perhaps, their *body*. Natural selection: cruel yet sometimes –amusing.

Anyway, if nothing else, it's fairly obvious that in the near future, for at least a while, most everybody will have their own Web site. It's like everybody in the world being publisher of their own magazine called "ME." Distribution is cheap and easy, as is production. Content is, well, we'll find *that* out soon enough. And I suppose we'll also be finding out soon enough who or what FRED is going to be; in a clap, URLs will soon be toast. Long live FRED.

What's New in the 1997 Edition

This is, once again, almost a brand new book when you compare it to our previous editions.

There are a significant number of completely new chapters. We have updated and modified older material. The result? You won't find much in here that is the same from prior years.

What's new in this book? Almost everything — let's take a look, chapter by chapter.

- The **Foreword** by Douglas Coupland, author of *Generation X, Microserfs*, and other international bestsellers. If there is one individual worldwide who symbolizes cyberculture, it has to be Douglas, and so we are thrilled to have him on board.
- Chapter 1, **Do We Need to Care About the Internet?**, is a brand new chapter. Each year, we set the tone for the book by offering our observations on the "state of the Net." Given the number of statements that are being made about the significance of the Internet, we decided to take a look back in time at other predictions that have been made about technology, events, and people, in order to appreciate the nature of the phenomena before us.
- Chapter 2, **What Can I Do on the Internet?**, is a brand new chapter which examines the many different ways that the Internet is shaping our world.
- Chapter 3, **The Internet in Canada,** contains brand new case studies that describe how various organizations and people are using the Internet in Canada, including Tip Top Tailors, the Ontario Corn Producers Association, and the Miniature Schnauzer Club of Canada.
- Chapter 4, **Connecting to the Internet in Canada,** explores how individuals and organizations can join the Internet. We walk you through five examples and offer a handy check-list of things to think about when you are choosing an Internet service provider. Updated for 1997.
- Chapter 5, **How Does the Internet Work?**, includes a discussion of Internet domain names and an explanation of TCP/IP—the technology that underlies the Internet. Revised for 1997.
- Chapter 6, **Internet Electronic Mail,** will tell you everything you need to know about the most popular application on the Internet—e-mail. Revised for 1997.
- Chapter 7, **The World Wide Web**, is almost a brand new chapter. So much has happened with the Web that we decided we had to throw out last year's material and

start fresh, in order to adequately describe what a marvel the Web has become! Use this chapter to learn about the latest Web trends (for example, did you know that you can use the Internet to play Monopoly with other people around the world?).

- Chapter 8, **Off-line Web Readers**, is a brand new chapter that describes how you can use offline readers to capture and automatically download your favorite Web sites, even in the middle of the night! Off-line readers will allow you to monitor your favourite Web sites for changes. You can even take your favourite sites with you when you're travelling. Definitely a must-read for anyone serious about using the Web!
- Chapter 9, **Undertaking Research on the Internet**, is a brand new chapter. One of the most important skills in today's information age is the ability to search the Internet. This chapter provides helpful tips and information to help you uncover information on the Internet.
- Chapter 10, **Personalized News Services**, is a brand new chapter that examines the many new services emerging on the Internet that allow you to receive customized news stories on your personal computer. This chapter will change the way you read the news!
- Chapter 11, **Knowledge Networking**, discusses how you can use Internet "discussion groups" and "mailing lists" to link up with communities of people around the world. Revised for 1997.
- Chapter 12, **Interactive Communications On-line,** reviews interactive applications on the Internet such as Internet Relay Chat, videoconferencing, and Internet phone products. It has been revised and updated for 1997 to reflect developments in collaborative communications on the Web.
- Chapter 13, **Older Internet Applications,** looks at some of the older, lesser-used Internet applications including "telnet" and "FTP". Revised for 1997.
- Chapter 14, **Setting Up a Web Site,** is a brand new chapter that examines what is involved in building a Web site.
- Chapter 15, **Web Development Software**, is a brand new chapter that examines some of the many new software programs that are available to help Canadians publish information on the World Wide Web.
- Chapter 16, **Thinking Strategically About the Internet**, is a brand new chapter that reviews how the Internet can be used as a business tool.
- Chapter 17, **Dealing With Offensive Content on the Internet**, is a brand new chapter that describes many of the Internet filtering programs that can help parents and educators restrict access to offensive Web sites. We review popular Internet programs such as NetNanny, SurfWatch, and CyberPatrol.
- Chapter 18, **Intranets**, is a brand new chapter that discusses one of the hottest new trends on the Internet—internal Web sites. It includes case studies that describe how many Canadian organizations are using intranets to improve communications and cut costs.

- Chapter 19, **Intellectual Property on the Internet,** is a brand new chapter that examines one of the most-talked about challenges facing the Internet—trademark and copyright infringements. We provide a series of questions and answers to help clarify how Canadian copyright and trademark law applies to the Internet. We also examine how freelance writers in Canada are struggling to protect their rights in this new electronic age. Don't miss this chapter!
- Chapter 20, **The Changing Face of the Canadian Internet Industry,** is a brand new chapter that summarizes some of the changes taking place within the Canadian Internet industry. We also take a critical look at the issue of high-speed access to the Internet in Canada.
- Chapter 21, **We Need to Protect the Internet,** is a brand new chapter that examines issues surrounding freedom of speech and the Internet.
- Appendix A, **Top 25: Rick and Jim's Picks for the 25 Most Memorable Internet Events of 1996,** is a brand new appendix that highlights some of the most noteworthy Internet events of 1996. A trip down memory lane!
- Appendix B, **Good Surfing Spots on the Web,** is a substantially updated appendix that summarizes the Internet's most popular search engines and directory services. Get your surfboard ready!
- Appendix C, **Telephone and E-Mail Lookup Services,** is a brand new appendix that details methods of looking up business and residential telephone numbers using the Internet. You'll never have to use directory assistance again.
- Appendix D, **Identifying Countries on the Internet,** explains the meaning of the two-letter codes at the end of Internet addresses. Keep this list near your desk as you're surfing the Web. Updated for 1997.
- Appendix E, **Canadian USENET Newsgroups,** is a directory of Canadian-oriented USENET newsgroups. Updated for 1997.
- Appendix F, **Guide to Canadian Government Internet Domains,** provides a comprehensive list of domain names for Canadian government departments and agencies. Updated for 1997.
- Appendix G, **Directory of Canadian Internet Access Providers,** is a revised and updated directory of companies that sell access to the Internet in Canada. It includes a handy town/city index to help you identify Internet access providers in your area.

About the Authors

Jim Carroll, CA, is a Chartered Accountant who excels at assisting organizations to understand the strategic business potential of the Internet through his Mississauga-based consulting firm, J.A. Carroll Consulting. As a Chartered Accountant, Mr. Carroll has unique insight into the emerging world of personal finance on the Internet. Mr. Carroll is a prolific writer and contributor to many popular publications, and has written for *The Globe and Mail, Computing Canada, EnRoute, Strategy* and the *Toronto Star* to name but a few. He is the "star" of the *IBM Family Guide to the Internet*, a video that puts the Internet into perspective for families. Mr. Carroll speaks extensively across North America on the topic of the Internet, and is a popular keynote speaker for many annual conferences and meetings. Mr. Carroll is represented nationally and internationally by the National Speakers Bureau of Vancouver, B.C., which can be reached at 1-800-661-4110 or 1-604-224-2384, or by sending a message to **jcarroll@jacc.com** or **speakers@nsb.com**

Rick Broadhead, MBA, is one of Canada's leading Internet experts, advocates, and commentators. A popular speaker, Mr. Broadhead regularly gives presentations at conferences, annual meetings, and seminars across North America on the topic of the Internet and its impact on organizations. He also teaches courses on the Internet at York University's Division of Executive Development in Toronto, where he has instructed and educated senior management from many of North America's leading companies. His clients have included many government, non-profit, and corporate organizations, including VISA International, the Government of Alberta, the Financial Management Institute of Canada, the Pipe Line Contractors Association of Canada, the Canadian Wood Council, the Confectionery Manufacturers Association of Canada, the Association of Registered Interior Designers of Ontario, and the Canadian Paint and Coatings Association. He can be reached at **rickb@inforamp.net** or visit his World Wide Web site at **http://www.intervex.com**

Our Books

This is not our first book.

In fact, it is our eleventh! This is perhaps one of the reasons why the *Winnipeg Free Press* described us as the "Lennon and McCartney of the Canadian Internet"!

The *Canadian Internet Handbook* has now been updated annually since 1994, and has sold 250,000 copies in Canada alone, an absolutely stunning number.

Shortly after the *Canadian Internet Handbook* was released, we began hearing from school teachers and university professors who were using our book in their classrooms. To further meet the needs of organizations teaching Internet courses across Canada, we have released an *Educational Edition* of the *Canadian Internet Handbook* in collaboration with Professor Don Cassel at Humber College in Toronto. The book includes true-false exercises, multiple-choice questions, chapter objectives, glossaries, and teaching supplements. It is being used as a primary and supplemental textbook in Internet and technology courses at colleges and universities across Canada.

We have written many other books as well. To help Canadians surf the Internet, we have a companion product called the *Canadian Internet Directory* that provides descriptions of thousands of Canadian World Wide Web sites. If you are new to the Internet, you will find this book to be a great guide to some of Canada's best Internet resources.

Our newest book, *Canadian Money Management Online — Personal Finance on the Net,* discusses how Canadians can manage their personal finances using the tools of the Internet. It covers virtually every aspect of financial management including banking, credit cards, insurance, retirement planning, taxation, and mortgages.

To help Canadians who are intimidated by the Internet, we have written the *Canadian Internet New User's Handbook.* It provides a concise, easy-to-read introduction to the Internet for Internet novices across Canada.

Interested in doing business on the Net? We have written a book that describes how businesses, government organizations, and not-for-profit associations can use the Internet for competitive advantage. It is called *The Canadian Internet Advantage — Opportunities for Business and Other Organizations* and focuses on the strategic use of the Internet.

All of our books, with the exception of the *Canadian Internet Handbook Educational Edition,* are available at bookstores across Canada. We encourage you to use our other books, should this book whet your appetite for more in-depth, comprehensive information about the Internet in Canada.

Acknowledgments

We owe a huge debt of gratitude to many people at Prentice Hall Canada who are responsible for making this book possible. They include Robert Harris, our Managing Editor; Sara Borins, our Acquisitions Editor; and Avivah Wargon, our Production Editor. We are also grateful to Hart Hillman and his sales and marketing team: Andrea Aris, Suzanne Holick, Linda Voticky, and the many others who have relentlessly promoted and marketed our books. On the production side, Jan Coughtrey, Kelly Dickson, David Jolliffe, Erich Volk, and many others have now worked on eleven book projects with us, making each and every project just that much easier. We would also like to thank Sharon Sawyer and Judy Bunting for helping to coordinate much of our interaction with Prentice Hall.

We would like to express our appreciation to Betty Robinson, our editor, for working with us once again. It's a pleasure to exchange edits directly by e-mail, rather than having to wait for couriers! Betty has always been a true pleasure to work with.

For providing us with Internet accounts, we would like to thank iSTAR Internet, Sympatico, NETCOM Online Services, and Internet Light and Power. For hosting our Web sites, we are grateful to i*STAR Internet, e-Commerce Inc., and Cybersmith Inc.

Additional thanks go to Bell Canada for providing us with an ISDN line that we used to access the Internet at high speeds. Thanks to George VanderBunte of Zyxel for providing us with a Zyxel 2864IU ISDN modem and to Mike Pun of Motorola for providing us with a Motorola BitSURFR PRO ISDN modem. Both were excellent products, and we highly recommend them.

We would like to single out a number of people who assisted in this book's preparation by supplying information, research findings, or other assistance. They include Jamieson Yeates, for helping to organize the many screen shots appearing in the book; Internet Light and Power, specifically Tristan Goguen and James Brown; James Saunders of iSTAR Internet; Harry Jarvlepp, a Toronto-area lawyer specializing in information technology law; and Wayne Chung — our principal research assistant this year. Thanks also to Joyce Leblanc at Government Telecommunications and Informatics Services for supplying information about the Canadian government domains.

A special word of thanks to Lesley Ellen Harris, author of *Canadian Copyright Law,* who generously reviewed sections of Chapter 19 dealing with Canadian copyright law. Ms Harris is an authority on Canadian copyright law, and we are grateful for her assistance.

To the Internet software vendors who supplied us with review copies of software for this book — thanks. We also appreciate the cooperation of Internet service providers across the country. Thanks for completing our questionnaires and supplying information for inclusion in this book.

We also owe a big thank-you to our families. Jim would like to thank his wife Christa for her assistance with the manuscript preparation. Rick is grateful for the ongoing support of his family: Richard, Violet, and Kristin Broadhead, and to Ya-Ya. Jim would also like to thank John, Allan, Alar, Matti, Mathew, Jeff x 2, and the rest of the construction crew for managing his home renovations while this book was being written. Jim is absolutely thrilled with the new office! Only once did a piece of plaster fall from the ceiling onto the keyboard!

Finally, we appreciate the ongoing support of our readers and Internet users across Canada, many of whom have taken the time to send us messages of encouragement and thanks. This book would not be possible without you!

Contacting Us

We are always interested in hearing from our readers — we welcome comments, criticisms, and suggestions. We do try to respond directly to all e-mail sent to us. Drop us a line and let us know what's on your mind.

If you have found the Internet useful, let us know about it! We might use your experience in a future case study. Furthermore, if you are aware of any new or significant Canadian Internet initiatives that you believe are worthy of inclusion in future editions of this book, please contact us.

Contacting the Authors Directly

Here is how to contact us on the Internet:

authors@handbook.com	To reach both Jim Carroll and Rick Broadhead
jcarroll@jacc.com	To reach Jim Carroll
rickb@inforamp.net	To reach Rick Broadhead
info@handbook.com	To receive an automatic message about our books

Our World Wide Web Sites

The World Wide Web site for all our books is **http://www.handbook.com**. Visit this site for the latest information about all of our book projects.

Jim Carroll maintains a World Wide Web site at **http://www.jacc.com**. It features articles that he has written about the Internet and the "information superhighway," including articles from *The Globe and Mail*, *Computing Canada*, the *Toronto Star*, *EnRoute*, *Strategy Magazine*, and other publications.

Rick Broadhead maintains a World Wide Web site at **http://www.intervex.com**. It contains information about his work, his client list, and pointers to World Wide Web sites gathered from his presentations and speeches about the Internet.

Conventions Used in This Book

Throughout this book, we provide pointers to sites or discussion groups that can be found on the Internet — for example, World Wide Web sites or USENET newsgroups. These addresses are bolded. For example:

http://.....

e.g., **http://www.handbook.com**

Sometimes we omit the **http://** prefix and the address will start like this:

www.....

e.g., **www.handbook.com**

Keep in mind that the Internet is in a constant state of flux. All of the addresses cited in this book were verified at the time of printing, but inevitably some sites will change their location or just disappear. Unfortunately, we cannot guarantee that the addresses published in this book will last forever. If you find an address that does not work, please let us know about it. We will try to track down the correct address and update the information in subsequent editions.

CHAPTER 1

Do We Need to Care About the Internet?

A global computer is taking shape, and we're all connected to it.

Stuart Brand, *The Media Lab* (Penguin Group, New York, 1987)

When it comes to computer technology, brilliant predictions and statements are often a dime a dozen — and often incorrect. Let's look at some classics:

- "Where a calculator on the ENIAC is equipped with 18,000 vacuum tubes and weighs 30 tons, computers in the future may have only 1,000 vacuum tubes and perhaps weigh one and a half tons." *Popular Mechanics*, 1949. Imagine the scene. It is 1949, and the first computers have just been reported upon in the popular press. It is the dawn of the computer age, and the media writes excitedly about robots and computers and all kinds of technology that will make our lives so much easier in the future. It is the era of "future city": Cars that fly in the air, cities that never sleep, and people who choose their dinner by pressing a button on their ultimate in-home automatic dinner-maker. It is the golden age of technology; anything seems possible.

DO WE NEED TO CARE ABOUT THE INTERNET?

1. Many brilliant — and incorrect — predictions have been made in the past about computer technology.
2. Technology can do amazing things — but it takes time for people to change their behaviour.
3. The Internet is part of a trend by which our world is becoming digital — but this trend will take time to evolve.
4. Regardless of the many predictions made about the Internet — some of which may be incorrect — no one can deny that "something big is happening" with its arrival.

And the first computers? Indeed, they did weigh several tons and filled entire rooms with their arrays of vacuum-tube racks. Massive and complex, they generated enormous amounts of heat and sucked up huge amounts of energy, so much that it was said that the lights of Philadelphia dimmed when an early computer in that city was turned on.

But in 1949 the concept of a computer was so new, so different, and so far-reaching that few people really appreciated that a little more than forty years hence, computer circuits found on computer chips would be so small that they were invisible to the human eye and that the average microwave or automobile contained more computing intelligence than found in all the computers in 1950. No one prognosticated that computers would not need vacuum tubes but instead would use tiny computer chips based on silicon. No one foresaw the incredible shrinking act that computer technology would soon undergo.

- "I think there is a world market for maybe five computers." Thomas Watson, Chairman of IBM, 1943. It just goes to show that even the guys in charge do not know what the heck the future holds. The next person in charge of IBM, of course, was the son of the fellow who made the above statement. Thomas Watson, Jr., went on to steer IBM to becoming a company so large that competitors shuddered at its every move. And even as it succeeded, it soon found itself humbled by the rapid growth and adoption of personal computers around the world, because it had been focusing on its cash cow business, the sale of computer mainframes. It then took IBM several years to change its business focus from the sale of mainframe computers in order to become a force in the PC industry itself.

  And it is funny how history repeats itself: As late as 1993 or 1994, Bill Gates dismissed the Internet as nothing more than a playground for academics before finally realizing late in 1996 the significance of what it had become.

- "There is no reason anyone would want a computer in their home." Ken Olsen, President, Chairman, and Founder of Digital Equipment Corp., 1977. Ah, yes, another brilliant visionary, making another classic mistake that would end up costing Digital several billions of dollars in revenue. Because Olsen blindly missed the PC revolution, he cost Digital a chance to play in the personal computer market in its infancy, a mistake from which Digital has never truly recovered.

  The problem with predictions about technology is that all too often companies and organizations are caught up by the sheer arrogance and ego of their leaders, who refuse to believe that change is imminent and that it will be far-reaching in its nature. Sadly, there are many Ken Olsens in the world.

- "I have traveled the length and breadth of this country and talked with the best people, and I can assure you that data processing is a fad that won't last out the year." The editor in charge of business books for Prentice Hall, 1957. Take a look at the title page near the front of this book. Who is the publisher? Why, it's Prentice Hall! Indeed, the organization, now part of McMillan Publishing, one of the world's largest publishers of books, also happens to print one heck of a lot of computer books. So much for fads.

- "This 'telephone' has too many shortcomings to be seriously considered as a means of communication. The device is inherently of no value to us." Western Union internal memo, 1876. Oops! Western Union, of course, decided not to become involved in the telephone business and instead focused on the ever-declining telegraph business. Talk about a blunder, in fact, a multibillion dollar blunder. You cannot make a bigger mistake than this, can you?

- "640K ought to be enough for anybody." Bill Gates, 1981. We don't mean to pick on Bill, but in the early days of computers he made this comment about the amount of memory needed by computers. And of course today, to run a system like Microsoft Windows 95, you need at least 16 megabytes of memory, which translates to about 16,000 kilobytes (K). And to really run it properly, you should have 32,000 K or 48,000 K. Talk about a blunder.

You probably get the drift. There is a danger in talking with the experts and obtaining their predictions. Certainly, when it comes to the Internet, this is true. Anyone who offers definite predictions of where something like the Internet will be five years hence is kidding him/herself, in the same way that it is impossible for anyone to predict the weather in Flin Flon, MB, on December 21, 1998. It is a good guess that it will be cold and that it might be snowing in Flin Flon in 1998, but we cannot be sure about it. And five years out on the Internet? It is a safe bet that it will still be with us and that it will be even more significant than it is today, but we would be foolhardy to predict exactly what it will be and what you might be able to do on it.

Mistakes Abound

When something new comes along, it is all too easy to dismiss it. New "things" are, well, new. And because they are new, they often cause people discomfort or concern and make others blind to how rapidly things might change. This is certainly the case with the Internet; a new technology that in many ways has been with us for less than five years (even though it is "really" 25 years old), it is often dismissed as a fad, a trend, the "CB radio of the 1990s." Let's put such comments in the context of what others had to say about new developments in earlier years:

- "The wireless music box has no imaginable commercial value. Who would pay for a message sent to nobody in particular?" David Sarnoff's associates in response to his urgings for investment in the radio in the 1920s. David Sarnoff would go on to found CBS and become one of the largest pioneers of radio in the world. We wonder what happened to his associates.
- "The concept is interesting and well-formed, but in order to earn better than a 'C,' the idea must be feasible." A Yale University management professor in response to Fred Smith's paper proposing reliable, overnight delivery service. Fred Smith went on to found FedEx, which spawned many imitators and gave birth to a huge, multibillion dollar express delivery industry.
- "Who the hell wants to hear actors talk?" H.M. Warner, Warner Brothers, 1927. It was the era of silent movies, an era that ended soon after the arrival of "talkies."
- "I'm just glad it'll be Clark Gable who's falling on his face and not Gary Cooper." Thus said Gary Cooper when he turned down the leading role in *Gone With The Wind.* And of course, his acting career began to falter, while Clark Gable went on to become perhaps the most famous actor of all time.

- "A cookie store is a bad idea. Besides, the market research reports say America likes crispy cookies, not soft and chewy cookies like you make." Response to Debbi Fields' idea of starting Mrs. Fields' Cookies.
- "We don't like their sound, and guitar music is on the way out." Decca Recording Co. rejecting the Beatles, 1962. Talk about a bad decision! In fact, several music labels turned the Beatles down at the time, missing an opportunity to partner with what many consider to be the most influential musical act of the twentieth century.
- "Heavier-than-air flying machines are impossible." Lord Kelvin, President, Royal Society, 1895. We marvel at the brilliance of this statement every time we look out the window at the Rocky Mountains as we fly to Vancouver, or when we see Parliament Hill as we begin our descent into Ottawa.
- "So we went to Atari and said, 'Hey, we've got this amazing thing, even built with some of your parts, and what do you think about funding us? Or we'll give it to you. We just want to do it. Pay our salary, we'll come work for you.' And they said, 'No.' So then we went to Hewlett-Packard, and they said, 'Hey, we don't need you. You haven't got through college yet.'" Apple Computer Inc. founder Steve Jobs on attempts to get Atari and Hewlett-Packard interested in his and Steve Wozniak's personal computer. Atari, Hewlett-Packard, and many others went on to miss the opportunity to become participants in the early years of the personal computer. Jobs and Wozniak went on to launch a new and significant industry with their invention of the personal computer.
- "Professor Goddard does not know the relation between action and reaction and the need to have something better than a vacuum against which to react. He seems to lack the basic knowledge ladled out daily in high schools." *New York Times* editorial, 1921, about Robert Goddard's revolutionary rocket work. Goddard, of course, would go on to define much of the groundwork that led some 50 years later to men walking on the moon, an event that the *New York Times* and countless other newspapers breathlessly reported.
- "Drill for oil? You mean drill into the ground to try and find oil? You're crazy." Drillers who Edwin L. Drake tried to enlist to his project to drill for oil in 1859. Perhaps you have to be crazy to make the right predictions.
- "Stocks have reached what looks like a permanently high plateau." Irving Fisher, Professor of Economics, Yale University, 1929. Days later, the stock market completely crashed.
- "Everything that can be invented has been invented." Charles H. Duell, Commissioner, U.S. Office of Patents, 1899. We can't even bear to make a comment on the sheer brilliance of this fellow.

Need we go on? The point we want to make is that it is difficult for anyone to clearly and accurately predict the future. The problem is that, quite often, even the best people don't know where the future is headed. Certainly, this is true with the Internet. When it comes to predicting the Internet, the best anyone can hope to do is infer where it might be headed, based on current facts and observations of where it is today.

Our Own Prediction About the Internet

These comments, of course, bring us front and square to a comment that we made in our first edition, the 1994 *Canadian Internet Handbook.* Written in December/January of 1993/1994 and released in March 1994, the book was a simple, stripped-down guide to the Internet, of some 400 pages.

In the opening pages of the book we made the observation that "each time someone signs into the Internet, they are participating in a development that is so unique and far reaching, that many people believe it is a development in human communications equal to the invention of the printing press, the telephone and television." Whoah! Is this one of those classic predictions like those we discuss above? Might we and many millions of others who say the same type of thing about the Internet be exposed in the future as a fraud, guilty of greatly overstating the significance of this global network of computers? It's a good question.

The Myth of the Paperless Office

Let's try to answer it by dealing with the myth of the paperless office. We opened this chapter with many of the silly mistakes and statements that people made in the past, some of which involved computer technology and others that did not. Want to know the most brilliant mistake of all time? It has to be attributed to the person who first said that computers would result in a "paperless society" or a "paperless office."

The paperless office? Hardly! The *Financial Times Review*, a European publication, reported on November 1, 1995 that "in the past 25 years, the volume of paper used in offices has soared by 600 per cent, despite early promises that technology would create a "paperless office." Today's staff often spend 60 per cent of their time working with printed documents..." If you think that paper is doomed, we suggest you take a look around you. Look at the books that you have read in the last few days. Watch the mail and magazines that arrive in your mailbox. Look at the newspapers that you read.

The *Financial Times Review* article also stated that "most industry estimates suggest that at least 95 per cent of the information used in the office is still stored on paper, rather than electronically, despite tumbling hardware prices. One reason for this is that paper, for all its limitations, remains a particularly user-friendly medium for transmitting and reading information — most people would still rather plow through and annotate a long physical report than read it on the screen."

The computer revolution is some 40 years old, and personal computers have been with us for over 15 years. So why has paper not disappeared? Clearly, computers are much more efficient at dealing with information and do a far better job in helping people find things. And those who work with computers have come to realize they truly are a magical tool. Why indeed? To answer that question, we will use two simple words: behavior and complexity.

Behavioral Change Takes Time

Sit back and think about why the paperless office has failed. Certainly it cannot be the technology; after all, companies have spent billions if not trillions of dollars on computer technology. They have implemented sophisticated systems to process invoices, pay bills, process inventory, and handle electronic mail. And certainly they are not lacking in people who know how to use those computers: There are over 100 million computers in North America alone, found in homes and offices. In Canada over 41% of the population has a computer in the home, and 58% use one at work, according to an Angus Reid survey. We are, it seems, on our way to becoming a highly computer-literate society.

And yet companies still have mailrooms with mail clerks who spend a lot of time delivering — paper. Paper abounds: There are paper files and boxes full of paper, and paper invoices and cheques and legal documents and letters — all on paper. Paper, paper, and more paper! So whatever happened to the paperless office, and what about the paperless society? Why are we using more paper than ever before?

Aside from the fact that computers have made it very easy for anyone to churn out large volumes of information in paper form, the simple fact is that we still use a lot of paper because we are used to it, we like it, and we are comfortable with it; it will take a long time for us to change our attitudes towards it. People are stubborn about change, and regardless of how good something might be, it will take time to change our day-to-day behavior. And when it comes to information, our behavior — the things that we do day-to-day with information — revolves around paper.

We have become accustomed to computers and are always discovering new and innovative things to do with them. But regardless of how wonderful they might be, they are up against a world in which people have 500 years of history in becoming accustomed to dealing with paper — ever since the invention of the printing press. You don't change 500 years of history overnight, do you? From our perspective, proponents of the paperless office missed this one simple fact.

The Complexity of Change

Not only are people reluctant to change — taking time to change their day-to-day behavior — the whole process of change itself is an extremely complex undertaking. Have you ever had a look inside a company and examined its system for purchasing supplies? It can be fascinating. For example, the mere process of ordering a stapler and paying for the purchase can often involve a long and complicated process, with various stages of approval and different types of forms being filled out at each stage along the way. What is a company, then? From this perspective, it is a place where a whole bunch of people do a number of things with information: it is a place of *processes and procedures.*

The thing about processes and procedures is that it is an extremely complex job to change them; you don't just toss out the old way of doing things one day and the next day adopt the new method. Try to get a switchboard operator to use a brand-new switchboard without proper training and without providing some motivating thoughts, and you are bound to experience some form of switchboard hell. Attempt to have a 55-year-old accounts payable clerk switch to a new automated order entry system, and you will get mumbles of complaint and a lot of mistakes along the way. Try to teach a chief executive officer to use a computer, and you will get extreme reluctance because she will not want anyone to see that she cannot type.

Change is complex. Ask any management consultant involved in assisting organizations to implement computer technology about the topic. They will tell you that changing the simplest and most straightforward tasks can become an extremely complex undertaking. And it is because of that behavior issue again: people do not like change. The simple process of changing their behavior or getting them to change the way they do things is often extremely difficult. The paperless office? It is going to take a long time, because it will be infinitely complex to implement.

So What Does This Have to Do With the Internet?

Lots. We started this chapter by observing some of the sillier statements that have been made about technology in the past. And if you get involved with the Internet today, you will hear all kinds of statements on what it is and predictions of the impact it may have. So what do we have to say to all these predictions? Remember the paperless office, and learn from it.

The fact of the matter is that because of the issues of behavior and complexity, the paperless office is no closer to reality than it was ten years ago. So when it comes to predictions about the Internet, we must realize that it is going to take time for it to change our world and the way we do things.

What the Internet Is Really All About

But the predictions above will likely come true, although not as soon as some people expect. And as they do, the change that the Internet will cause will be dramatic. Why? The Internet is but one piece of a massively complex puzzle, a puzzle in which the information in our world is rapidly being digitized. It is a significant trend. For years and decades and centuries information has existed in various forms: paper, records, tape, and film. But today, regardless of what format it is in, information shares a common characteristic: It is being converted into computer form. In a digital world all information is converted to 1s and 0s, the fundamental computer language that all computers speak. Consider what is happening:

- Music was once distributed on LPs and 45s, round discs made of plastic that were placed on a spinning turntable and the music on which was picked up by a diamond stylus. In 1980, LPs and 45s dominated the record industry, and by 1995 they were all but unknown except to a few diehards, as the compact disc (or CD) took the world by storm. The CD? Music is represented by digital 1s and 0s, the language of the computer age. The next step? Perhaps one day, those 1s and 0s will be purchased through the Internet. After all, it is already possible to hear music on-line.
- Cable companies are rushing to wire entire neighborhoods with higher capacity cable so that they can send digital television signals instead of analog television through the line. This will permit them to vastly expand the number of channels and services offered through your television, resulting in much talk about the so-called 500-channel universe. The era of digital television will soon be upon us; soon all television stations will be broadcasting a lot of 1s and 0s that make up television shows. And the next step? Those 1s and 0s will be accessed through the Internet, turning it into a massive television network.
- Entire highways are going digital. In Toronto, drivers traveling a new pay-to-use expressway will be digitally queried to see if they have purchased sufficient travel rights, a digital transaction between a computer chip in a device in the car and a device in the road. The computer chip in the car will be asked if it has enough 1s and 0s to complete the voyage without any additional charge being necessary. The next step? You will be able to buy those 1s and 0s by having your computer obtain them from another computer.
- Cameras are going digital. Kodak and other photography companies are finally discovering success with digital cameras as the world of photography makes a slow and

painful transition to a world in which there is no film, only a computer chip that captures a picture in a form of 1s and 0s. The next step? You will regularly send those 1s and 0s to others through the Internet.

- Newspapers used to set their type with lead type, small blocks of letters in different sizes, which were used to pull together the components of individual pages. Today, sophisticated computer networks transmit the current day's news layout directly to high-speed presses, making the process completely digital. The next step? You will get more of those 1s and 0s on your computer — through the Internet.
- In the old days assembling a movie was a slow and painstaking process. Editors would develop and go through miles and miles of acetate tape containing the movie film and painstakingly splice together bits of film into one 90-minute feature. Today most editing is done directly on high-speed computers that are complete editing systems so that the editor and producer are in essence manipulating the 1s and 0s found in massive computer files. Tomorrow perhaps those 1s and 0s will be sent to us in a really big electronic mail message on the Internet, allowing us to receive a movie directly to our PC as soon as it is available for general release.
- Individuals and organizations still exchange paper money and coins. But anyone in the Canadian banking industry will tell you that the rate of adoption of credit cards has been far faster than ever expected, resulting in a greater number of economic transactions that are based not on the exchange of actual physical money, but on the exchange of a series of 1s and 0s between different computers at different banks. Tomorrow your banking and monetary transactions may consist of your computer exchanging some 1s and 0s with computers at your bank and other locations through the Internet.

So what is the Internet all about? It is simply one of the central characters in the play, a play in which all the information around us is being converted into digital form and in which the digital 1s and 0s of that information are regularly exchanged. The vehicle by which they are exchanged? The Internet.

What is the Internet? We wrote this introductory paragraph to the 1996 *Canadian Internet Handbook* to try to explain:

> The Internet will one day plug together every computer chip in the world. The computer chip — that small piece of sand, glass, and metal containing the logic and hence the capability to process information — is a device that has already reshaped and changed our world. You will find computer chips everywhere — not just inside computers, but inside your car, your telephone, in some cases even your microwave and toaster ovens. The computer chip has become ubiquitous.
>
> And so far, for the most part, all these little computer chips have lived in splendid isolation. They've existed mostly by themselves, doing what they are supposed to do, and usually doing that quite well. That is about to change because of the Internet.
>
> What is the Internet? It is a trend that is making all of these little computer chips aware of each other and providing them the ability to link together.

Digitize the information of the world, add the Internet, and you have a global computer of massive proportions.

You Cannot Ignore the Fact That Something Big Is Happening

Take a look around, and it is obvious something is going on with the Internet. A lot of businesses are rushing to establish "home pages" on the area of the Internet called the World Wide Web. Certainly this is laudable; organizations need to get involved with the Internet to discover how it can be used as a marketing and customer support tool. Schools are becoming involved, teaching children how to research and publish on-line. Obviously this is important, for children should not grow up in a wired world without the basic skills needed to master that world. And government is involved with the Internet, viewing it as a means through which it can streamline the delivery of some government services and putting in place policies that encourage its adoption. Certainly this is worthwhile, for it helps to create a climate of acceptability for the Internet itself.

But what is really going on? Is something really happening? We offer an unequivocal *yes.* Once you read this book and see the many examples of how organizations and individuals are using the Internet, and once you understand the technology that is emerging, we believe you will become convinced of this fact as well.

The Significance of the Internet

There probably isn't an individual in Canada who does not believe that information technology and computers will cause substantial and profound change to our world. But many still do not recognize the central role that the Internet will play in effecting that change. One reality is that we are at a very early stage with the Internet: It is not yet the first inning, and the opening pitch hasn't even been thrown. But as the game is played out, we will come to see that the Internet will cause a significant change in the way we conduct business, the way we interact, and the way we live our lives.

When it comes to the Internet, there is a belief that we are on the crest of a huge new wave of computing, a new era in which the computers that we all have are reaching out to all the other computers on the planet, with the result being the emergence of one massive global network of computers, of unprecedented scale. The wired world will soon be upon us, a world in which each of us will soon be linked to everyone else through the computers that we use day by day.

To truly understand the Internet, you must understand that it is being quickly propelled into a future role that not even its inventors dreamed of. New hardware, software, standards, and initiatives are being established on the Internet so quickly that the Internet of today is completely different from the Internet of yesterday. We certainly are familiar with that fact; each year the *Canadian Internet Handbook* emerges as an almost completely new and different book, given the widescale changes that have occurred throughout the network. Certainly this year is no different.

What is the end game of this rapid rate of change? The technology is moving us to the point where in the near future (from one to five years) the technology of the Internet will become so pervasive and all-encompassing throughout the computer world that most of us will have a direct high-speed link to the Internet *at all times.* The Internet will simply be a part of our computer and part of the "operating system" of our PC or Macintosh. We will be plugged in all the time. Five years from now? We will turn on our computers, which will activate our CD ROM, our speakers, link us into our local area network, and will automatically link us into every other computer on the planet through the Internet.

What does that mean? Who knows? But we often make the observation that if we plug together all the computers in the world in such a way that all the newly digitized information at our disposal is easily exchanged, then something significant is bound to happen.

The Internet Changes Our Concept of Information

We remain convinced that the most significant thing that the Internet leads to is a world in which everyone is a publisher, a broadcaster, a journalist, a television and radio producer — a distributor of information. One result of the forthcoming widespread availability of the Internet is that we will not have the much-talked about 500-channel universe; instead, we will have a million-channel universe, or even a *500-million channel* universe.

Of course, television and radio stations, newspapers, and magazines will not become extinct, but they will have a heck of a lot of competition. In the future anyone in the world will be able to put up a digital file on their Web site. This file could contain a "television show," a movie, recording, or some other type of interactive media program *that they have created.* Remember: We are entering a digital world, and the Internet is the vehicle by which those 1s and 0s of the digital world are exchanged.

The real impact of the Internet is that we will no longer be just a world of "information consumers" (you and me) and "information producers" (newspapers, magazines, radio, television); we will be a world of "information consumer/producers," any of us able to publish on a global basis. Consequently, our entire global information paradigm is changing because of the Internet.

Aren't These More Predictions?

Yes, we are making predictions here, after poking fun at so many predictions from the past. And it is, at this point, certainly easy to be skeptical about such predictions when it comes to the Internet, since they sound so much like hype. But none of us can afford to be skeptical of what the Internet might mean. If we are doubtful about its impact, all we need to do is talk to some kids. Thousands — no, millions — of kids worldwide are growing up with the Internet and are learning about it at home and at school. By the time this young generation grows up, the Internet will be a fact of life for them.

And guess what? They will not be reluctant to change to the Internet way of doing things, because they will have grown up with it. There will not be complex issues of changing their behavior to deal with the Internet, because their behavior will have already been shaped by its existence. As the current young generation grows up, the Internet will come into its own. Give it time and watch what happens.

As you deal with the Internet and as you read this book, do not limit yourself to thinking that it is a place just for business or education or government. Realize instead that there is much more underway here: *Something big is happening.* Take the time to comprehend and understand what it means for you and what you do. Think about the longer-term aspects of the Internet, rather than looking for any definitive answers to what it is today. And finally, keep in mind that the Internet is whatever you want it to be. The Internet is just the fuel; you are the spark.

For some, the Internet is a form of entertainment, while for others it is a serious business tool. Some people form lasting global friendships on-line, while others discover it to be a place to access useful information about particular ailments from which they suffer. For many more it is a place to access updated news and weather information. And for others it is a place to explore the latest and greatest computer software or to undertake important research into particular topics. There are many millions of people on the Internet, and for each of them the Internet has proven to be something different. To you, the Internet will be whatever you want it to be.

CHAPTER 2

What Can I Do on the Internet?

For a technology visionary, Gates admitted last night he was surprised how fast the Internet has caught on and reached critical mass. The Internet now is the so-called information highway. "A few years ago, I wouldn't have expected that," Gates said. "A lot of people were caught by surprise." But now Gates calls the Internet "the greatest change in the way people do business probably since the phone came along."

Gates predicts lag in Internet growth, *The Toronto Star*, July 26, 1996

Yet, for many people, the information highway doesn't consist of home banking, electronic shopping or video on demand. The information age doesn't necessarily mean that everyone wants to play video games — nor do they want to passively watch new television capabilities or shop at home. Instead, many people are indicating that they see a different vision of the information highway. Through the highway, they want to be able to communicate with people, to explore new electronic frontiers, to enhance their working and professional skills, to debate topics in global conferences or to seek information. For many, the global information highway is already here in the form of the Internet.

Jim Carroll and Rick Broadhead, *The Canadian Internet Handbook* (Prentice Hall, Scarborough, ON, 1994)

There is no doubt that the "information age," or the "digital age" (and what some may call the "metaphor age"), has arrived, with the Internet at the forefront. In essence, as we move into this new era, all kinds of individuals — including yourself — are asking, "What can I do with this thing called the Internet?" There are several ways, of course, to answer this question. We could tell you what other people and organizations are doing on-line. Or we could describe their day-to-day activities. Or we could look at the tools that are available to them. But that would not be enough, because asking what you can do on the Internet is very much like asking what you can do with

WHAT CAN I DO ON THE INTERNET?

1. The Internet is taking on an important role in business, politics, entertainment, news, weather, and sports, as well as in healthcare and the computer industry.
2. People and organizations are using the Internet to access information, research information, and to publish or communicate on-line.
3. There are many Internet "tools" that people use, including the World Wide Web and Web browsers, electronic mail, discussion groups, and other technologies.

a piece of paper. After all, what is paper used for? Millions of things: it is used to print the news, to write a cheque for a product purchase, to type or print a letter, to publish a book, to create an airplane. Count the number of ways that paper is used, and you quickly realize there is only one way to define paper: it is an object used to convey information.

Try to define the role of the Internet, and you will encounter the same challenge. You might use it to read the news, to purchase a product, to send a message to a friend, to read the contents of a book (including chapters of past editions of this work), or to find instructions on making a paper airplane. (There are some things you cannot do with the Internet yet.) What can you do with the Internet? Lots. Let's take a look.

What Is the Role of the Internet?

One way to determine the role of the Internet is to look at the diversity of organizations and individuals involved with the Internet and then consider what they do and examine the role that the Internet plays for them. In the next chapter we will look at stories of how average Canadians and organizations are using the Internet. But for now, we will simply give you a taste of what is occurring on the Internet.

From this perspective, the Internet seems quite straightforward; it defines a lot of interaction between individuals and organizations, whether for the simple exchange of information or for some business or social reason. Consider the areas in which the impact of the Internet is being felt:

- Business. The Internet now defines the tools of "electronic commerce," that is, the financial standards and methods with which organizations and consumers will interact and do business transactions on a secure basis. Whether for business-to-business or consumer-to-business interaction, the Internet is, many believe, emerging as the foundation of the economy of the twenty-first century.

  This is not an overstatement, and examples abound as proof, for instance, an increasing number of financial institutions are providing the capability for individuals to undertake some type of financial activity on-line. Canada Trust allows its customers to access details of their bank balances and other financial information through the Internet, and like all banks, is aggressively pursuing the concept of personal banking on-line.

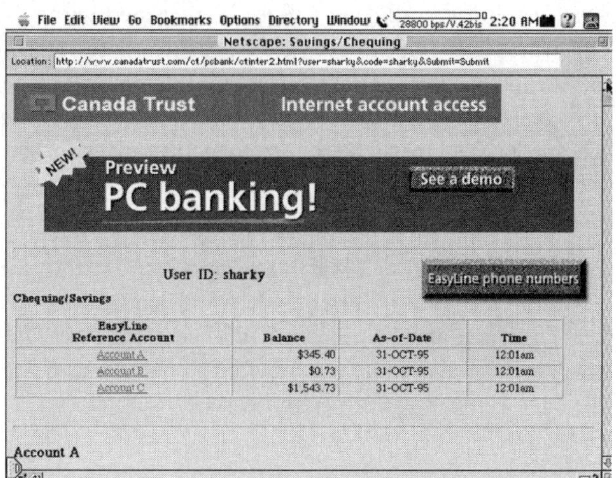

The future? Large portions of the global economy will migrate to the Internet as the transactions and infrastructure that drive business today migrate to this global computer network. Increasingly, Canadians will find themselves turning to the Internet in order to find information with respect to a product or service in which they are interested, and over time will purchase that product or service on-line.

- Politics and social activism. Everyone from political parties to candidates to government organizations is using the Internet to convey his/her message to an ever-weary, ever-skeptical electorate. Not only that, but opponents of established political organizations and grassroots organizations are using the Internet to get their perspectives out, making the Internet the new battleground for the hearts and minds of voters and consumers. Take, for example, Greenpeace: This international environment movement has long used the Internet to encourage consensus and adoption of its views on how to deal with the global environmental crisis.

The future? Savvy political candidates will realize that the Internet is a significant forum through which they can express their views directly to voters. But they will come up against equally savvy special interest groups, who will try to destroy their credibility. Cyberspace politics will become a significant and growing force on our political landscape; perhaps it will help to make politicians more accountable for their promises.

- Entertainment. Check any movie listing in the paper today, and you will see a World Wide Web (or Web) address listed. Watch a television show, and you will likely see an e-mail address at the end. Buy a CD, and you will be encouraged to visit the Web site of the band. The Internet now provides artists and entertainers with a new, direct method to reach the audience and fans, providing a new form of two-way communication and dialogue between performer and viewer.

Are you old enough to remember the Stampeders? Young enough to be into retro and have an interest in a classic band from the 1970s? The Stampeders live on, on the Web, where you can read about their music, their awards, their history, and sample a few of their tunes, if you wish:

The future? The Internet will become an entertainment medium; it will be a 500-million channel universe, with entertainment content available with the click of a mouse. Television and computers will merge, and the Internet will become the conduit for future products. Want a new CD? Visit a site, sample the tunes, and download the bits and bytes onto your brand-spanking-new 25 gigabyte personal audio stereo computer.

◆ News, weather, and sports. All kinds of news organizations, from the CBC to the Weather Network to the *Halifax Chronicle Herald*, are setting up shop on the Internet, using it as a means to deliver news, weather, and sports information. The Internet is being used to deliver news on-line as an alternative to traditional distribution methods. In other cases it is being used to enhance the news services offered by these organizations: Want more details about a particular news story? Just check an on-line Web site. For many news organizations the Internet is being explored as a means by which brand new profitable business ventures may be established.

Indeed, the area of news delivery on the Internet is evolving at breathtaking speed, with new, sophisticated technology emerging regularly. For example, CANOE, the Canadian Online Explorer (**http://www.canoe.ca**), a joint venture of the Toronto

Sun Publishing Corporation and Rogers Multi-Media, provides a Web site containing regularly updated news stories from the news wires:

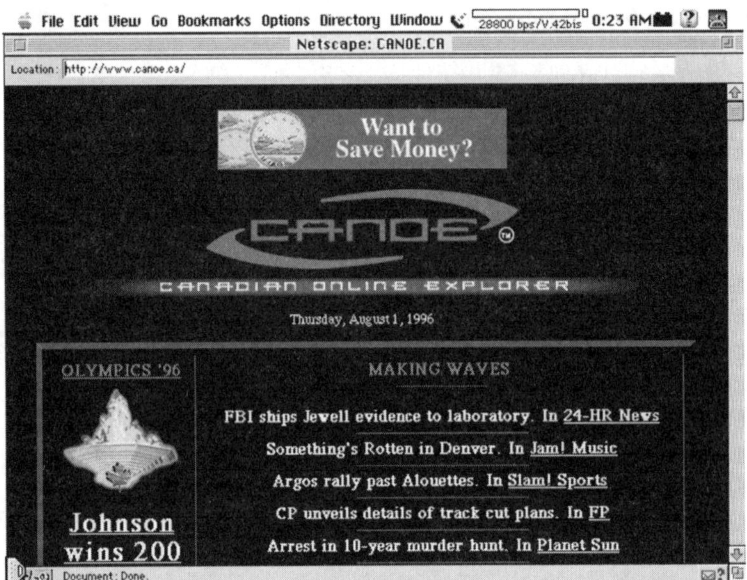

But you do not have to be a major media organization to take part. The *North Shore News* of North Vancouver, BC, for example, publishes some of its information on-line:

The future? You will receive a daily personal "newspaper" that contains only the news stories that interest you. The computer chip in your furnace will be directly linked into the Weather Network and will automatically start itself up once the network warns of an upcoming cold snap.

- Health care. Many medical institutions and health care professionals have adopted the Internet to share valuable and cutting-edge medical knowledge or to publish and make accessible important health care information to patients and other institutions. There is an increasing number of patients looking to the Internet to access medical information in advance of, or after dealing with, the Canadian health care system.

  Certainly there is no shortage of medical information on-line as the health profession and medical industry discover the Internet. For example, Vancouver's Sunny Hill Health Centre For Children makes available information about its services, facilities, and areas of specialty, as well as access to information about "Child Development and Rehabilitation":

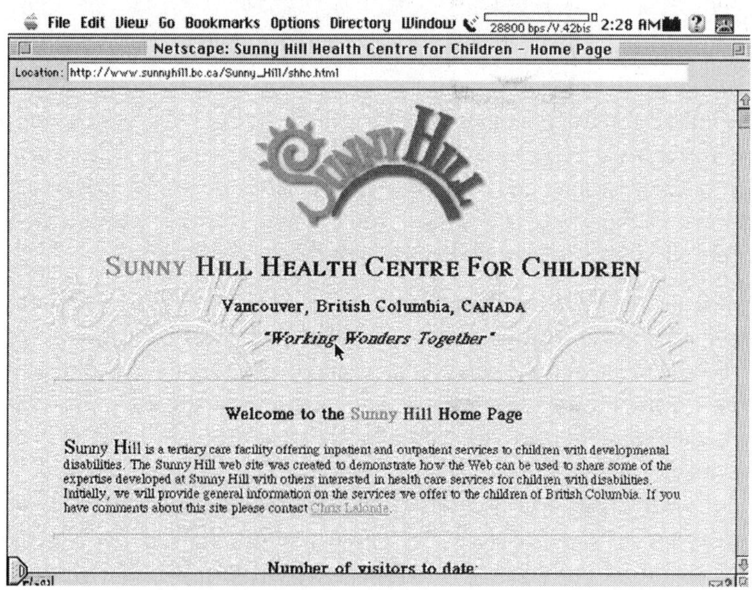

The future? The health care industry will come to recognize the potential cost savings to be found by providing medical information on-line. Medical professionals will share diagnoses on-line by zipping x-rays to experts at the other end of the country through the Internet. And you will receive automated e-mail notices from your doctor reminding you of your annual checkup.

- Government. Take a look around, and you can see municipal, provincial, national, and even international governments and government bodies exploring how to use the Internet in the delivery of government services or as a means of reaching out to constituents. Even the Mississauga, ON, Fire Department has a Web site, with information for residents about the department, fire prevention information, and safety tips:

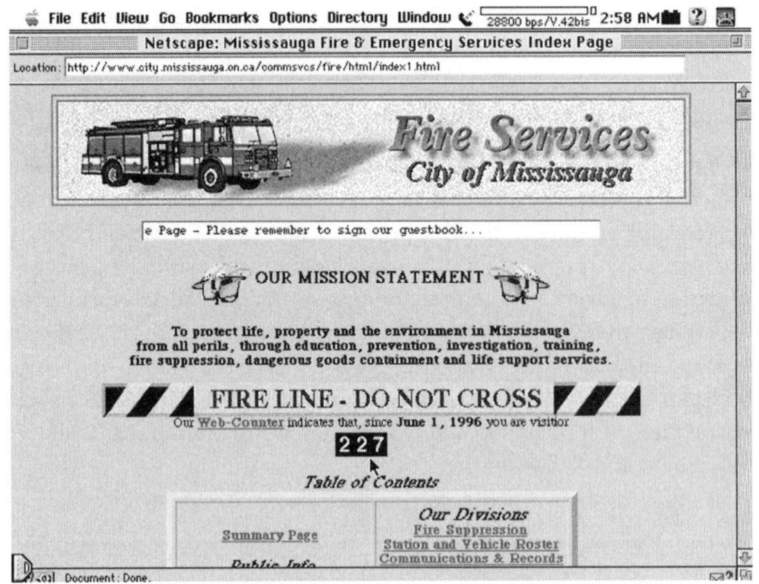

The future? You will link directly to Revenue Canada to file your tax return on-line, and after a few seconds you will be advised that your refund has just been deposited to your bank account. You will contact a government department and actually get an answer back the same day by e-mail. You will apply for your passport on-line and still get the physical document in the mail, but much sooner.

- Associations and not-for-profit organizations. Many associations, not-for-profit organizations, and charities are exploring how they can use the Internet to reach out to their members and the public at large and how it might be used to assist in the achievement of their core mandates. The Internet is a natural fit for such organizations, given that for many, they are first and foremost in the business of providing information.

  It is a marriage made in heaven. Take, for example, the Periodical Writers Association of Canada. Made up of freelance writers, PWAC uses the Internet to fight what it believes are unfair contract demands and what it labels "the theft of copyright of freelance writers" by leading media organizations such as Thomson Newspapers, Southam, *Macleans* magazine/Rogers Communications, and others:

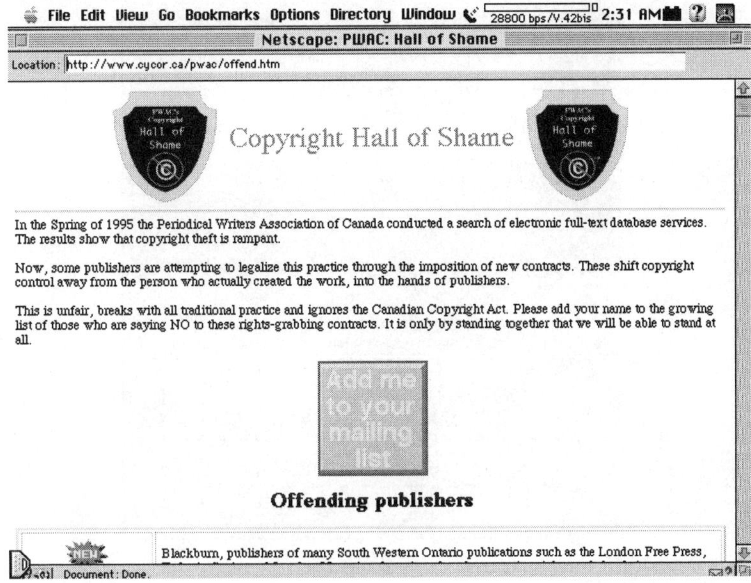

The future? Fund-raising drives will begin to exploit the reach and power of the Internet. Members of associations will obtain a higher level of interaction with each other through the Internet.

- Computer industry. Needless to say, the entire global computer industry has been galvanized by the concept of the Internet. Software organizations are using the Internet as a new revenue market, developing all kinds of new software. Computer hardware companies such as Oracle are designing new products that allow access to the Internet. Computer consultants and programmers are finding new opportunities and possibilities in the nascent and emerging marketplace of the Internet.

  One result of the Internet is a renewed sense of creativity within the computer industry, with involvement by major and minor players alike. Even though industry titans such as Microsoft and IBM are playing a major role, small, one-person operations such as Vancouver-based Locutus Software can play in the game, with their release of a small program for Windows 95 that automatically grabs recent weather conditions for a specified city from the Internet and updates it regularly throughout the day. So far, the program is only available for American cities:

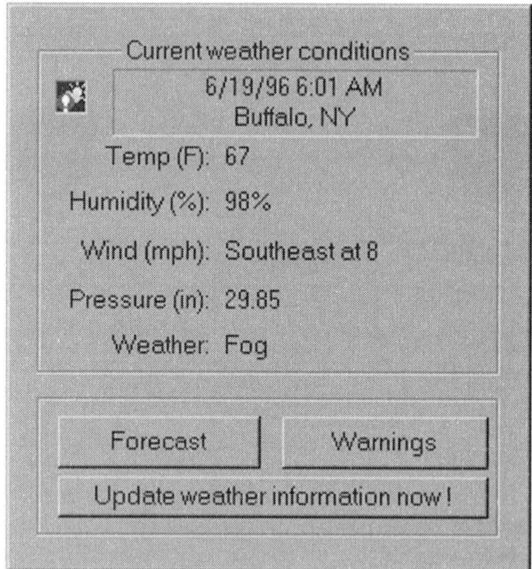

- Individuals. Of course, you do not have to be a big business or organization to discover your role on the Internet. Since anyone can, with a little bit of effort, figure out how to put a page up on the Web, the result is a global network that displays, in raw and often fascinating form, the diversity of the human condition. Sites abound on all kinds of topics, issues, subjects, and areas of interest; you name it, you can likely find it out there. Even The Anchormen, a barbershop singing group from St. John's, NF, has put up a site to describe what they do:

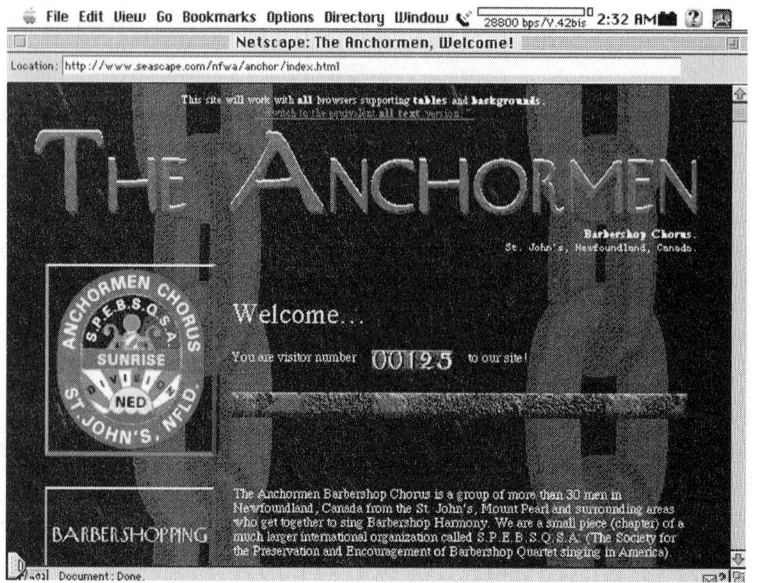

It is clear that the Internet is fast emerging as a significant force in our day-to-day lives and promises to help us in much of our day-to-day activities. But we will still go to grocery stores, we will still plant flowers in the garden, and we will still go and visit friends and have a conversation. The Internet will be a useful tool in our lives, but we will still have a life. We will read with mirth, humor, and wonderment the ever-present stories about the negative aspects the wired world will have on our day-to-day lives.

What Do People Do On-line?

Of course, classifying the Internet by the types of organizations that are involved and the activities that they have underway is one method. It is also useful to examine what these individuals and organizations do while they are on-line.

Access Information

In the space of just a few years, the Internet has become a storehouse of vast amounts of human knowledge. This is because anyone in the world can become a publisher of information on the Internet. The technology behind this development is something called the World Wide Web, an absolutely massive system of interconnected information resources from all over the world.

The World Wide Web has become the place to be on the Internet. Through the Web you can access thousands of "sites," each containing page upon page of information. These pages can contain text, sound, pictures, images, and even video (if you have a fast enough link to the network). We saw examples of many "pages" of Web sites in the previous section. The magic of the Web is that any page can be linked to any other page on the planet, hence the name "Web."

Experiencing this linking between Web sites for the first time is something that most people never forget. You can start out on the Web in Paris, France, one minute and then the next minute be in Halifax, NS, Australia, Russia, or the United States; with a click of the mouse you travel the globe from location to location, from information site to information site. Since everything is interconnected, you could suddenly find yourself in a location completely unrelated to what you were looking at two minutes ago.

What is happening is that people are increasingly turning to the Web for information. They might watch a television show, see a Web address in a commercial, and travel to that Web site. They might look at a magazine, read an article, and be told that more information can be found on-line at the Web site for the magazine. They might get their bank statement and see a notice that they can find up-to-date interest rates and service charges at the Web site for the bank. They might receive a business card and notice that it has a Web address — then visit there to find out more about the company. They might meet a new friend and visit his/her Web site to learn a bit more about that person. The uniqueness of the Internet is the sheer diversity and range of Web sites that are out there.

Rob Davison, for example, is a competitive figure skater from Calgary, AB, and has his own page on the Web. Why? As he notes, "this page is aimed at giving you the skating fan an idea of what it is like to be a competitive athlete in this highly competitive sport. It is also here to help publicize our up and coming Canadian talent. In the future I hope to include results from more competitions, profiles of my friends, and some of the world's best skaters."

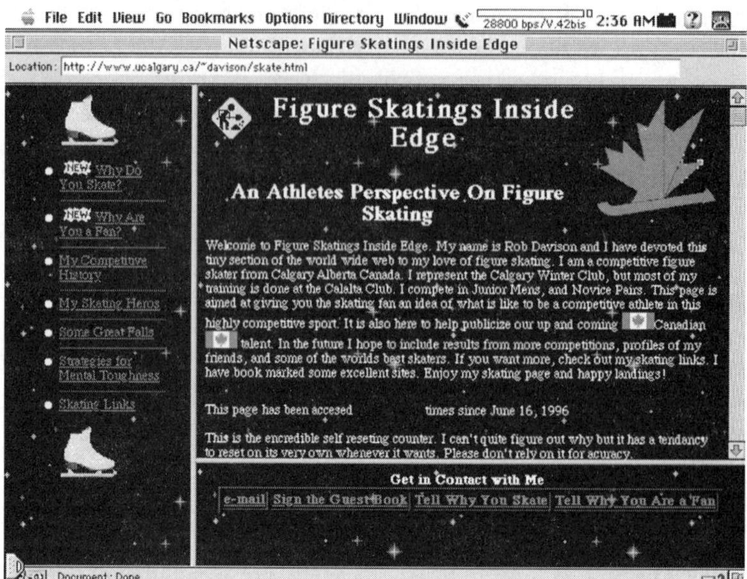

In effect, it is his own little spot where he can make available information to the world. This is where the power of the Internet surfaces, for as he notes on his page, "if you want more, check out my skating links. I have bookmarked some excellent sites. Enjoy my skating page and happy landings!" What does he mean by "check out my skating links"? Click on the "skating links" button to find out. This takes you to a page of information that points to all kinds of other sites that are related to the subject of skating:

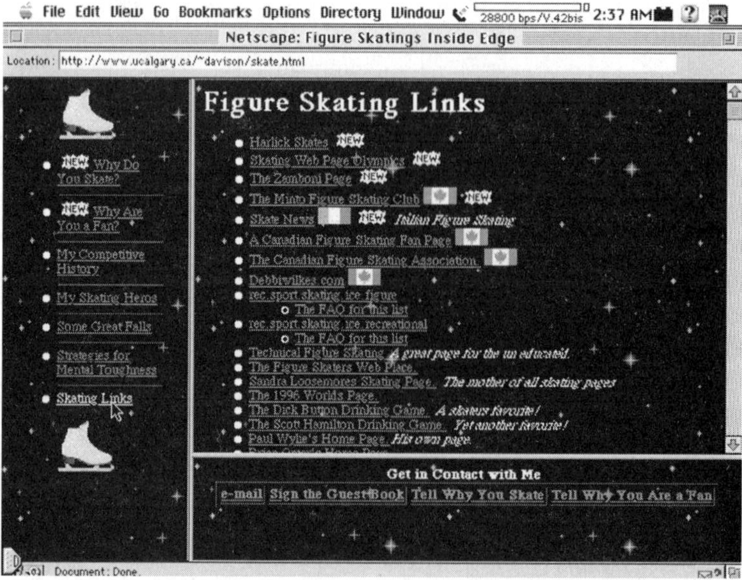

From here, Davison has made it easy to travel to sites such as "The Minto Figure Skating Club," "Skate News," something called "A Canadian Figure Skating Fan Page," "The Canadian Figure Skating Association," "The Figure Skaters Web Place," "The 1996 Worlds Page," and, of course, "The Mother of All Skating Pages." Want to travel to any of these? Simply click with your mouse, and you will leave Davison's place in Calgary and travel somewhere else on . . . the planet.

Whatever the case may be, the Web has quickly emerged as the means of accessing information from all kinds of individuals and organizations. In this way, it has become the paper of the information age.

Research Information

While many use the Web to entertain themselves and to retrieve information from a particular organization or company as we described above, many also use the Web to undertake research into a specific topic or subject. One impact of the continuous, ongoing evolution of Internet technology has been the arrival of a number of "tools" that help you to perform such a search among the millions of pages that make up the Internet, or to draw upon the river of information constantly flowing through it. These tools help you to find particular documents, topics, words, or phrases from the Internet; in essence, you use them to find information on-line. People are turning to these tools when they have a question that needs to be answered, so they are teaching themselves how to conduct "electronic research" on the Internet.

How can you use the Internet to find information? Let's say the Cirque du Soleil (a popular "circus" featuring all-human performers) is coming to town, and you wish to find out when and where they will be playing. An easy enough order. You can travel to a Web site on the Internet called Yahoo!, a giant directory of sites found on-line. When you get there, type in the "search" box the object of your search:

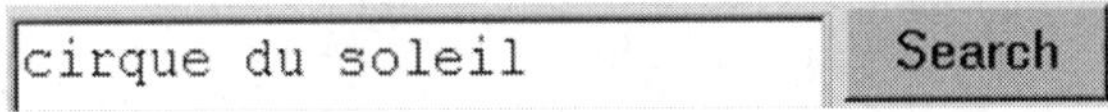

Yahoo! thinks for a moment or two and then comes back with a list of the sites containing that name:

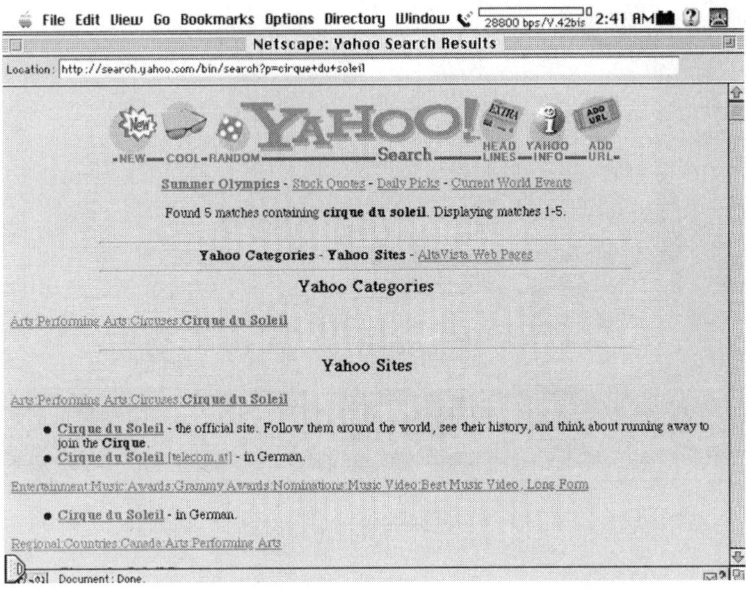

You click on the first item and in seconds find yourself at the official site for the Cirque du Soleil, a site that contains everything that you need to know:

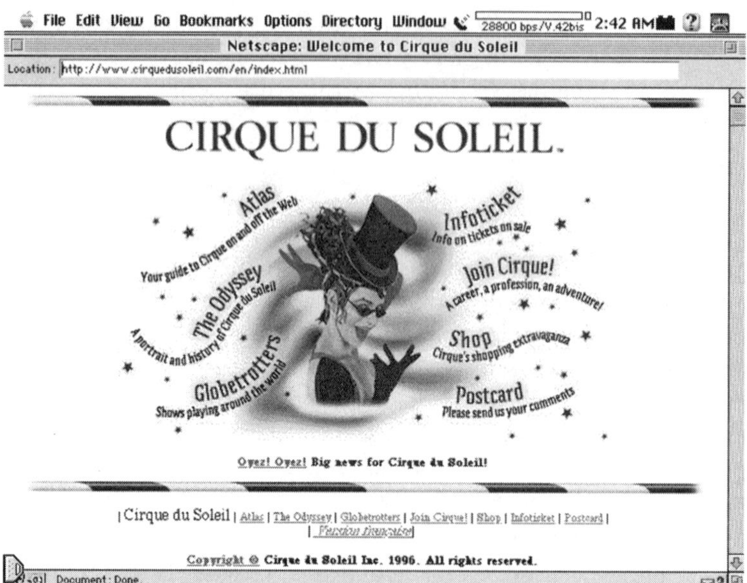

Of course, you can do much more than simply use the Internet to find a person, company, or organization such as the Cirque. Let's say you wanted to find a review of their performances. That is easy: Travel to one of many "search engines" on the Internet, sites that are designed to help you find information. Type in what you are looking for: "reviews about Cirque du Soleil," and the site we visited, known as HotBot, comes back with a list:

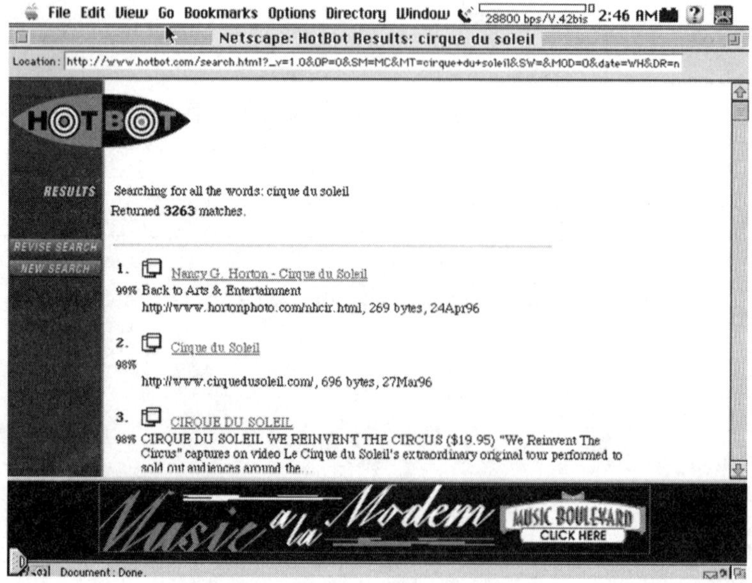

Picking the first item, we discover an electronic "magazine" about reviews of the arts. Exactly what we needed:

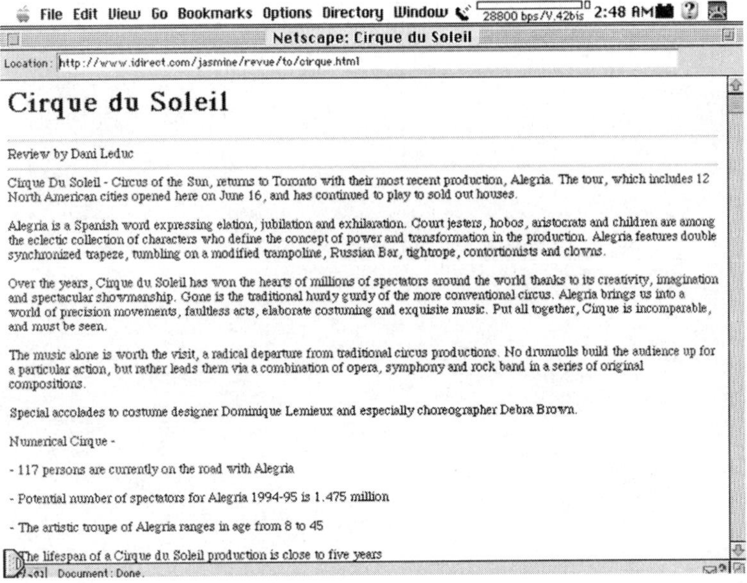

Cirque du Soleil

Review by Dani Leduc

Cirque Du Soleil - Circus of the Sun, returns to Toronto with their most recent production, Alegria. The tour, which includes 12 North American cities opened here on June 16, and has continued to play to sold out houses.

Alegria is a Spanish word expressing elation, jubilation and exhilaration. Court jesters, hobos, aristocrats and children are among the eclectic collection of characters who define the concept of power and transformation in the production. Alegria features double synchronized trapeze, tumbling on a modified trampoline, Russian Bar, tightrope, contortionists and clowns.

Over the years, Cirque du Soleil has won the hearts of millions of spectators around the world thanks to its creativity, imagination and spectacular showmanship. Gone is the traditional hurdy gurdy of the more conventional circus. Alegria brings us into a world of precision movements, faultless acts, elaborate costuming and exquisite music. Put all together, Cirque is incomparable, and must be seen.

The music alone is worth the visit, a radical departure from traditional circus productions. No drumrolls build the audience up for a particular action, but rather leads them via a combination of opera, symphony and rock band in a series of original compositions.

Special accolades to costume designer Dominique Lemieux and especially choreographer Debra Brown.

Numerical Cirque -

- 117 persons are currently on the road with Alegria

- Potential number of spectators for Alegria 1994-95 is 1.475 million

- The artistic troupe of Alegria ranges in age from 8 to 45

The lifespan of a Cirque du Soleil production is close to five years

Research on the Internet is easy enough to do, but it is also infinitely complex. Anyone introduced to the Internet can quickly learn how to do it, but becoming a good, effective searcher is a skill that is only developed after careful trial. In fact, research on-line has become such an important topic that we have devoted an entire chapter in this book to it: Chapter 9, "Undertaking Research on the Internet." In that chapter we will walk you through some of the issues that you need to think about as you learn to take advantage of the vast information resources of the Internet.

Publish

Another reason for so much interest in the Internet is that it allows anyone, anywhere, to become a global publisher. Anyone with a little bit of time and inclination can figure out how to put up their own Web site with information that interests them. Want to build an on-line shrine to Englebert Humperdinck, celebrating the man and his music? Go for it! Is there a need for people to become aware of some social cause you believe in? Put it on-line. Think there should be a site on the Internet that contains the life story of your pet hamster? Publish it!

Here is a page by Jeffrey; he is an 11-year-old who lives in Gagetown, NB, and is, in effect, an international publisher with his own story about his hamster:

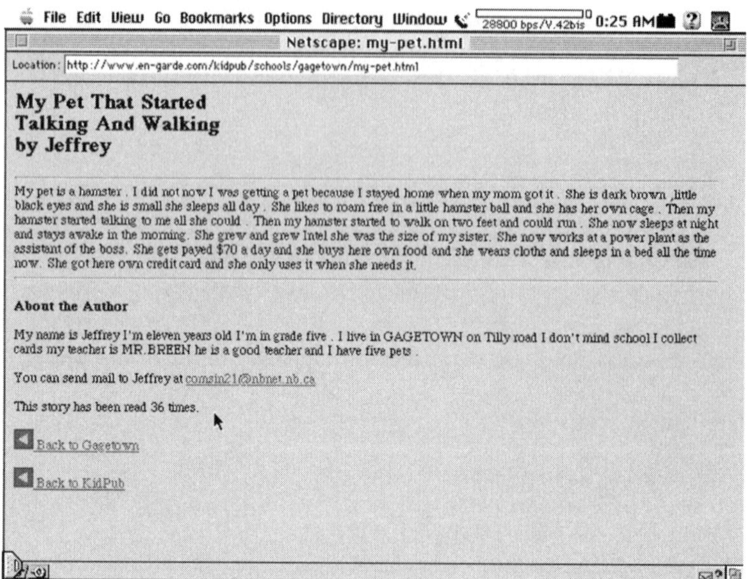

And here is a page for Pickles, a hamster who lives in Japan:

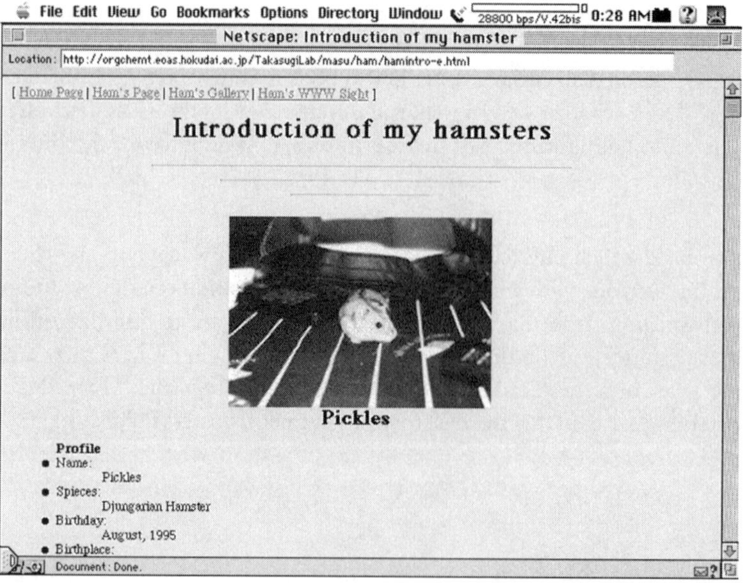

Both hamsters join several hundred others in having their own pages on the Internet.

Establishing a Web site has, in some ways, become the fad of the 1990s. (In Chapter 14, "Setting Up a Web Site," we describe what is involved in setting up your own Web site.)

Communicate One-to-One

It is also true that the Internet has emerged as the fax machine of the1990s, for it is a system that permits people to communicate with friends, relatives, business associates, lovers, or complete strangers worldwide, instantly, and for a fraction of a penny.

One of the most popular uses of the Internet is electronic mail (e-mail). The Internet has quickly become the world's largest global e-mail system. Anyone joining the Internet from home or work is provided with an Internet e-mail address. In addition, many organizations are providing employees with Internet e-mail capabilities by linking their corporate e-mail networks to the Internet.

The result is an ever-increasing exchange of e-mail through the network. Many have adopted this way of communication, as evidenced by the number of e-mail addresses appearing on business cards, corporate stationery, in advertisements, and in television shows, newspapers, and magazines. People now exchange Internet e-mail addresses like they exchange fax and telephone numbers, and they are now widely recognized throughout the Canadian population.

Why are so many people adopting Internet e-mail? Because it is fast, efficient, and cost-effective. As we will explain in Chapter 6, it is also the application on the Internet with the farthest reach and the greatest number of participants. It is easy to create an e-mail message and send one, particularly when in a hurry:

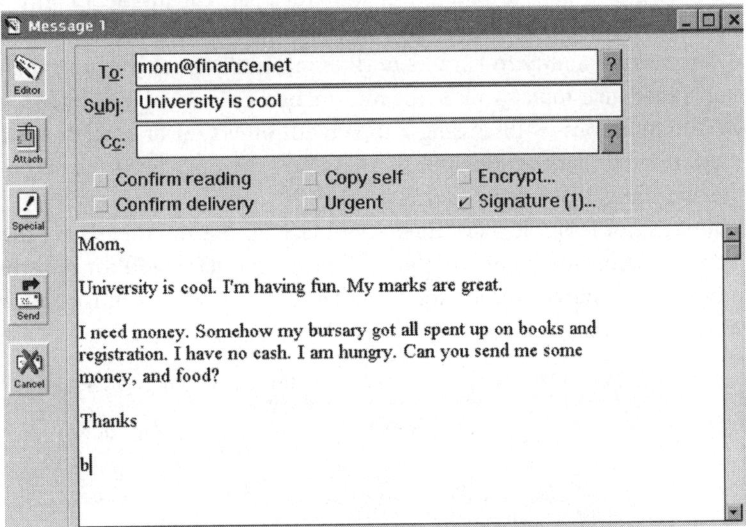

It is not just e-mail that is used for one-to-one communication; an increasing number of Internet telephone products have surfaced that allow you to make "phone calls" through the Internet. We take a look at this in Chapter 12, "Interactive Communications On-line."

Communicate One-to-Many

Although the Internet is a large and massive global system, it is also a place that consists of thousands of small "communities" (known as USENET newsgroups and electronic mailing lists), where people with a common interest exchange information and ideas. For example, there is a place on the Internet where people who are interested in the art of bonsai trees "hang out." They have their own spot (or "community") on the Internet where they exchange information about the topic. They go on their way and do their own thing, without bothering anyone. On any given day you might see discussions on any number of topics related to bonsai trees, if you choose to join that topic and participate. With tens of thousands of topics, there is an area of interest for everyone.

The Internet is used heavily throughout the global business, scientific, and research communities and has quickly become the method by which leading-edge public research is shared among these organizations. The Internet permits global collaboration on research projects between many disparate organizations to an extent not previously possible, a development that many believe to be fundamentally reshaping the manner in which public and private research is conducted. Since anyone can participate in these research groups, the Internet opens up a new wealth of information to its users.

Elsewhere, on a less serious note, Internet discussion groups are used by people to discuss and debate all kinds of topics, such as popular television shows and soaps; musical bands and entertainers; sports, recreation, or leisure activities; and thousands of other topics. The range of topics available is extensive, serious, and bizarre all at the same time; you can exchange information about leading biological research or track the postings by people who sincerely believe they were abducted by aliens.

For what purpose can you use Internet "discussion groups"? You can "knowledge network," that is, use the discussion groups to gain information on a particular topic, to bring yourself up-to-date on a certain issue, or to find an answer to a question. We use the term "knowledge networking" to describe the ability to harness on-line information, either by regularly tracking information on a particular topic by receiving information on that topic or by seeking information or answers to questions by discussing a topic with others on-line. Since the Internet has broken itself down into so many thousands of topics, you can quickly narrow in on a particular topic that interests you.

Kite enthusiasts, for example, have their own place on the Internet where they can share information about the intricacies of kite flying. One person has asked for information about whether you can use a 4-line conversion for a Zip-Tip Peel (whatever that is), and someone else has volunteered an answer:

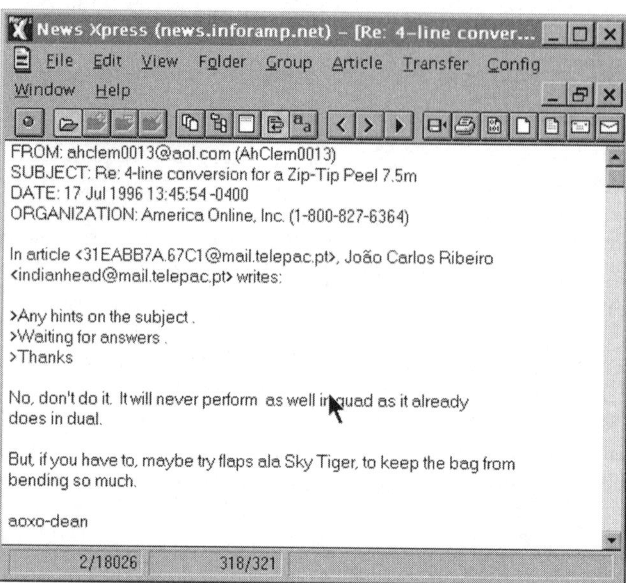

One-to-many communications do not occur only with USENET and electronic mailing lists; the whole area of "on-line" chat is growing on the global Internet. On-line chat programs allow you to type something onto your computer screen and then have tens, hundreds, or even thousands of people see what you type. Electronic "whiteboard" technology allows you to share your computer screen with others who choose to "tune in." Interactive presentation programs allow others to watch presentations running on your computer systems. Everywhere you turn, companies are releasing products that allow for a new level of one-to-many interaction through the Internet, and from that perspective, we are simply at the early stages of a new level of communication between the inhabitants of this planet.

The Tools of the Internet

The third way to think about what you can do on the Internet is to consider it from the perspective of the technology that you can use. We talked about a lot of "tools" in this chapter; let's describe the key tools, one by one.

World Wide Web and Web Browsers

The undisputed heavyweight of the Internet — the "killer application," as the business and computer press like to call it — is the World Wide Web. The Web is the place on the Internet where individuals and organizations publish information, whether it be text, audio, video, or some type of multimedia animated computer file. This information is accessed with Web browsers, programs that allow you to "browse" the Web. Given its importance, we devote several chapters to the Web, starting at Chapter 7, "The World Wide Web."

Electronic Mail

Electronic mail, or e-mail, is probably the most useful but perhaps least exciting Internet application; it does not have the glamor and cachet of the World Wide Web. But it is an application that seems to benefit the most in terms of cost savings, the immediacy of communications, and global reach. We will take a look at it in Chapter 6, "Internet Electronic Mail."

Discussion Groups: USENET and Electronic Mailing Lists

People knowledge network through USENET discussion groups and electronic mailing lists. In Chapter 11 we take a look at how you can join discussions in any one of several thousand topic areas. The world has never seen anything like the information exchange that has become possible on a global basis through USENET and electronic mailing lists.

FTP, Gopher, Telnet

The Internet goes back some twenty-five years, and programs like FTP, Gopher, and Telnet are the historical remnants of the earlier days of the Internet revolution. We examine them and how you might use them in Chapter 13, "Older Internet Applications."

IRC

IRC (Internet relay chat) is an application that allows you to converse — in "real time" — through your computer keyboard with others around the world. There are many other "chat programs" emerging on the Internet providing similar capabilities, some involving voice and video transmission, such as CU-SeeMe and Internet Phone. We take a look at this area in Chapter 12, "Interactive Communications On-line."

New Tools, New Capabilities

The sheer nature of the Internet is that it is simply the technical underpinning for a lot of fancy, interesting, new computer "stuff." It is becoming more difficult to categorize the tools of the Internet, given that so many unique ones are emerging. For example, consider EarthTime, a simple, straightforward program that shows you the time in various parts of the world and the progression of the sun across the face of the earth. When you want it to be "right up-to-date," it will go off to an "official government computer" to get the most recent time:

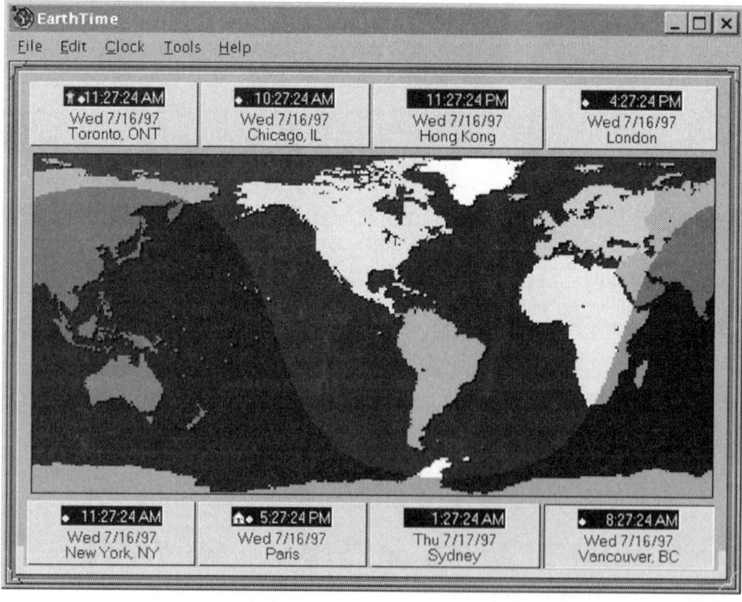

How do we classify EarthTime as an Internet tool? We cannot; it is unique, and it is different, but it is an example of a new breed of computer software, software that relies upon the existence of the Internet to do something special.

Let's Be Real About What People Do on the Internet

There is an incredible amount of hype about the Internet, and its real impact is sometimes oversold. You should be cautious in your expectations of how long it will take you to "master" the Internet. It might take you no time at all to get "on" to the Internet, but it will take time to learn to use it effectively. Because the Internet is a brand-new means of communication, very different from paper, the telephone, and fax machines, what you are really doing when you encounter the Internet for the first time is learning all over again: learning how to communicate, how to interact, how to perform research, how to publish information.

The Internet is also a new technology on the computer scene. Some joke that the technology that supports the Internet is evolving so fast that 6 months in Internet years is similar to 20 human years. And indeed, the Internet of today will be completely different from that of tomorrow. Hence, when you learn about the Internet, you must understand that you will be learning about something that is continually changing and expanding.

The Internet is a massive network with all kinds of people, information, and organizations; it can be a wonderful place to explore. It is also a frustrating, disorganized, anarchic network that sometimes will cause you to shake your head in anger. Sometimes you will wonder why you ever chose to become involved. The Internet is not a magic solution. Sometimes you will look for information on the Internet and you will not find it. You will hope to use the Internet for one purpose, only to discover that it cannot be done. Sometimes you will encounter people and information on the Internet that you will not like.

But you will also discover on the Internet something that you have never seen before: A global sense of community; information riches of untold depth; fascinating and ongoing developments in business activities; people who share your interests; knowledge about topics that you never knew existed. Over time, you will be stunned by what you discover. We are willing to bet that you will not be able to walk away from it.

It is obvious that there is a lot you can do on the Internet. In the next chapter we will take a look at what everyday, average Canadians have been doing with the Internet. This is the best way to understand what the Internet is all about.

CHAPTER 3

The Internet in Canada

The global network of interconnected computers and telecommunications links is already the biggest machine ever built. But it will likely become many times bigger and more powerful in the coming decades. This monster machine will fundamentally transform human life as we know it today...Human activities—both personal and institutional—will be globalized. Cheap, user-friendly telecommunications are dramatically reducing distance as a barrier to people doing things together. People thousands of miles apart are now finding ways to work together, buy things from each other, and form groups for common purposes.

We are moving toward an era when individuals and organizations will operate almost as if national borders and natural boundaries did not separate them.

The cyberfuture: 92 ways our lives will change by the year 2025
Futurist, January/February, 1996

Speak to those unfamiliar with the Internet, and they will probably have the typical Hollywood image of strange little geeky teenagers with greasy hair and plastic pocket protectors, poking away at their keyboards, never seeing the light of day as they try to figure out the best way to hack computers at the Pentagon. Either that or ultracool, beautiful, intelligent *beings* with perfect teeth, great hair, and IQs that are well over 200 — masters of the Internet. Right.

THE INTERNET IN CANADA

1. How various Canadians and organizations are using the Internet.
2. The case studies are about individuals making use of the Internet in a variety of ways, such as distributing music, publishing information about gardening, making family trees available, and maintaining indexes of children-friendly sites.
3. Canadian organizations using the Internet that we profile include the Miniature Schnauzer Club of Canada, the Gathering of the Clans, Jaymar Music Limited, CharityVillage, the Ontario Corn Producers Association, and Tip Top Tailors.

Let's forget Hollywood for a moment and come back to reality. In this chapter we take a look at some of the individuals and organizations who are using the Internet on a day-to-day basis across Canada. Have a look around and you will discover that it is being used by your friends, neighbors, co-workers, parents, children, and grandparents. Basically, the Internet is used by a lot of average, everyday, normal human beings. If you want to read a few more case studies like the ones that follow, take a voyage to our Web site (**http://www.handbook.com**). There we have posted many of the case studies from the 1994, 1995, and 1996 editions of the *Canadian Internet Handbook.*

John Himpe and The Game Show Web

John Himpe is a 15-year-old who lives in Yorkton, SK, and has a site on the Internet called "The Game Show Web." It is, of course, about game shows. Himpe notes that he has been a fan of game shows ever since he was a kid. Once he joined the Internet in May 1995, he quickly discovered the **alt.tv.game-shows** USENET newsgroup, a place where individuals from around the world post information about game shows. He established the Game Show Web site (**http://www.hmtnet.com/users/jhimpe/main.html**) in December 1995 after learning how to create a Web site through his own initiative:

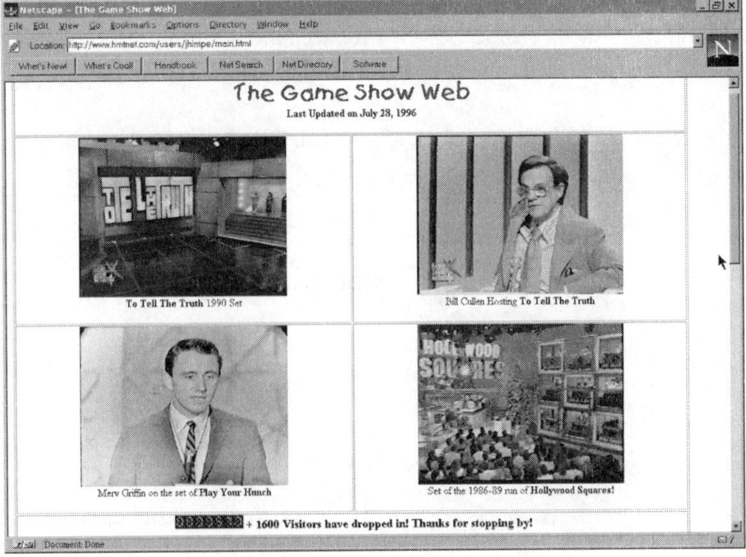

The site features all kinds of information about game shows: trivia, background, links to other Web sites about game shows, and more. Himpe also provides a listing of the game shows of which he has copies on tape:

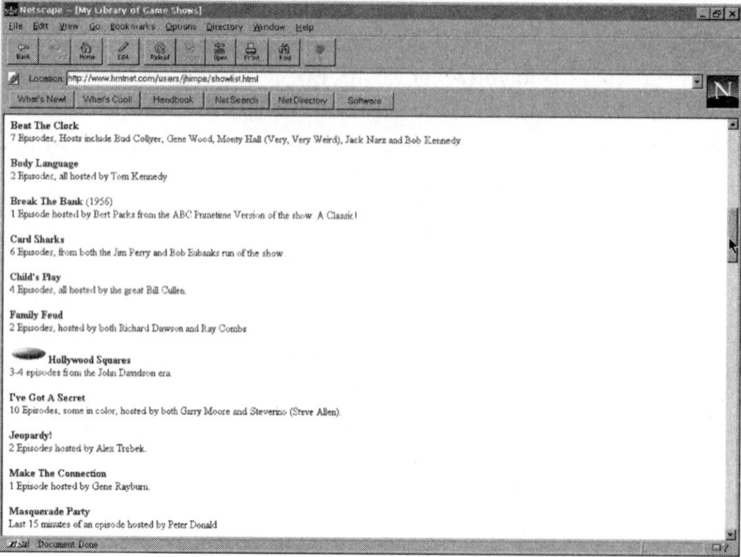

His level of interest in game shows is high, so much so that at this point, he has over 130 game show episodes on tape. What does this have to do with the Internet? Quite a bit. Explore the world of game shows on the Internet, and you will discover an entire group of game show enthusiasts who exchange and trade such episodes. At the time we visited Himpe's site, he had details of his complete collection on-line, as do many of these people:

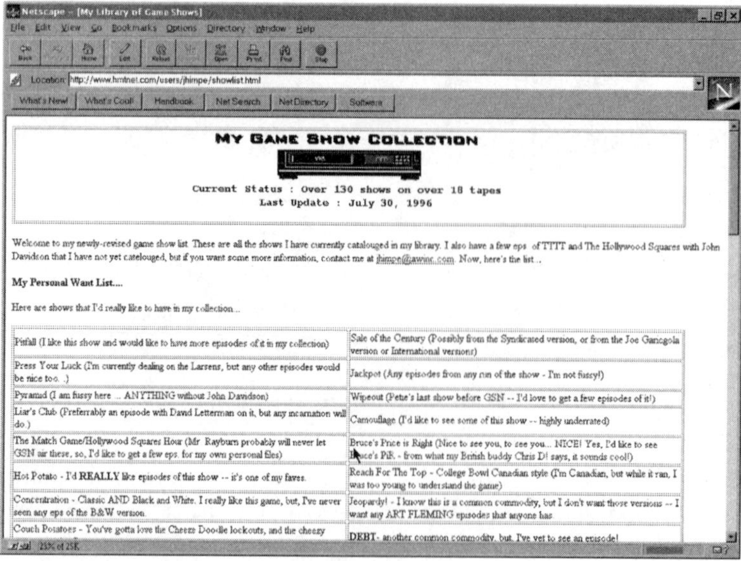

Game show enthusiasts around the world also use the Internet to undertake their own games on-line; at the time we visited Himpe's site, it was evident that he had just concluded a "Tournament of Champions" competition. How does it work? John posts a series of questions on his Web site and accepts submissions by e-mail:

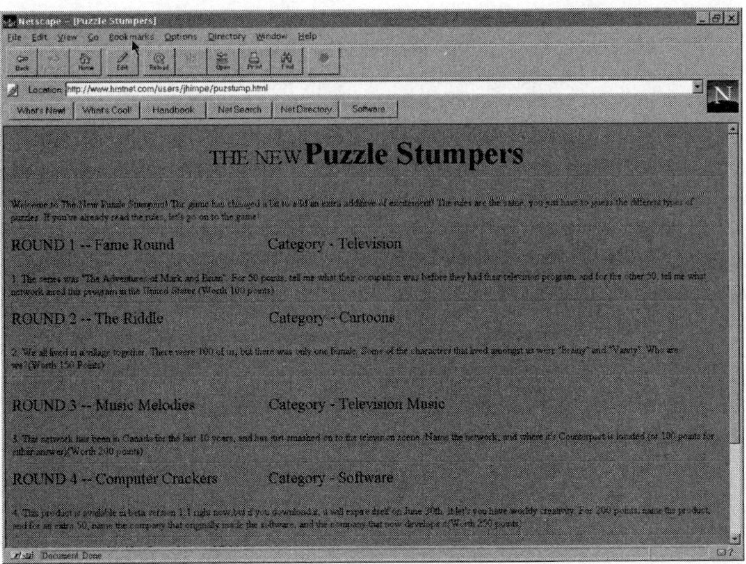

He also provides links to a number of other similar on-line game show sites around the world.

Why does he do this? He indicates that it started out as a hobby. After being on the Internet for a few months, he decided he wanted to have a Web site. The question became, about what? Naturally, the thing he was most interested in — game shows. His plans for the future include more games on-line. He notes: "This fall, there will be 6 games played at the Game Show Web. The only remaining game from this previous season will be 'Match-Ups' a game played in verisimilitude to the Match Game end-game, where contestants had to match the most popular answer — hence the idea for a little show called 'Family Feud' was born."

When he talks about the new games on-line, he talks of the "fall season"; here is the announcement he put out to participants:

NEW GAMES TO THE GAME SHOW WEB

1. GSW Links

Played by our contestants during the tournament of champions, this Web based game will be one of our new favorites. Guess what will come next in the link, and win the points! It is based on the game show "Chain Reaction" which was produced in Canada.

2. Trivia Busters

This is a brand new game to the Game Show Web that will be played quite differently — via E-MAIL AND IRC! It will become one of the signature games of the Game Show Web. Three contestants will be playing throughout the week via e-mail with questions for some mild points. Then, in front of a live studio (IRC) audience each Saturday morning, our contestants will play for big points and the champ will continue on to play the next week, and so on and so on — kinda like a Winner Take All set up, but, the trivia will be not easy, and not hard — it'll be kinda funny though! Watch out for this new game!

3. First Person

This is a new web based game that will feature "Who Am I" questions. The game will feature questions about people, places and things. This game is currently in the planning stage.

4. Acronym Attack!

This, hopefully, will be one of the new signature games of the new fall season! Acronym attack will be a web based game where contestants will have to guess famous and infamous acronyms! Big points will be awarded for the harder acronyms, and there will be some humor along the way! Join us, won't you?

5. SuPeR SlOgAnS

This is going to be one of the most nostalgic games on the GSW this fall. Super Slogans will be a web based game where contestants will have to match slogans with products or companies. Cool game board will be used in this game, so check it out this fall!

In this way, he and others like him are really establishing a new form of on-line entertainment. He also notes that in addition to the above there will be more game show trivia and tidbits added to the Web site. He has had a lot of success: "As of now, 2,175 people have visited the Web site." Is it worth it? Definitely, he says: "I enjoy being connected to the net. I find that being on the Internet has allowed me to communicate more freely with people I probably would have never got a chance to meet under any other circumstances. It is truly an experience that you must see to believe!"

Andrew McCallum

Andrew McCallum goes by the stage name Mental Floss. He is a 20-year-old who lives in Richmond Hill, ON. His claim to fame? He creates music on a computer and releases it on the Internet for free (**http://www.io.org/~org**). As a result, he has heard that one of his tunes has been featured regularly in a nightclub in Turkey, and he has attracted a worldwide audience for his efforts. This is all part of a new culture emerging on the Internet, where the youth of the world use the Internet to explore and discover new capabilities. Travel to McCallum's Web site, and you can obtain his songs and the appropriate software to listen to them:

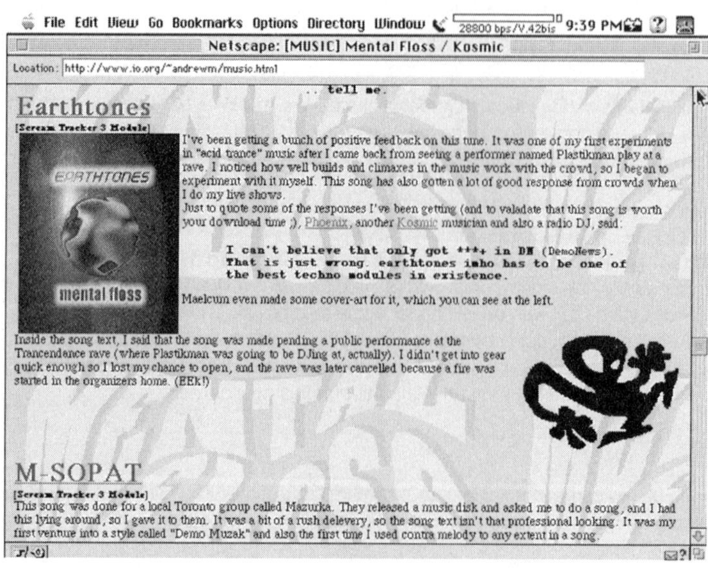

For those who do not want to go through the hassle of downloading his songs, he also makes the compilation available for sale on cassette tape through the site known as "Grey Matter":

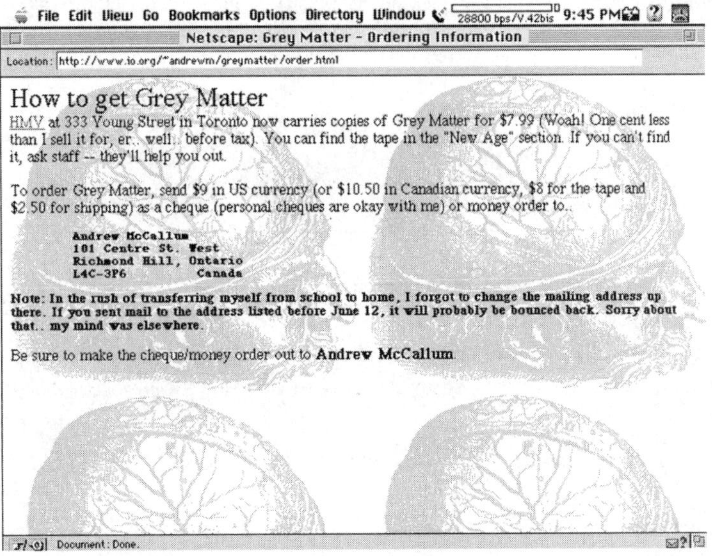

McCallum has actually been recording and making his music available electronically for over six years, well before the Internet came into vogue. He believes it is a good venue through which creative talent can get their works out to individuals, without the difficulty and hassle of trying to convince a recording label that there is a market for the product. In so doing, he is one of many thousands of youths around the world, in effect, rewriting the rules of the music industry.

Eric Sansom

From music to cartoons — let's continue with this creative angle and explore how another individual is reaching fans directly. Eric Sansom is a cartoonist who lives in Stratford, ON. You may have seen some of his work in various newspapers; one cartoon, "Green Earth Guardians," is circulated widely and is reprinted in newspapers such as the *Baltimore Sun* and the *Atlanta Journal.* From his perspective newspapers are slowly dying off, and with the consolidation occurring in the industry, fewer and fewer opportunities exist to place new comic strips in newspapers. For many years it has been extremely difficult for any new strip to replace the "old faithfuls": Beetle Baily, Blondie, and Peanuts.

He has been putting together a cartoon for years called "Toy Trunk Railroad" and has attempted to syndicate it to newspapers, to no avail. "I have to try something new," he thought after yet another rejection letter. Then he saw the Internet and thought that if he couldn't get the strip syndicated to newspapers, perhaps he could generate an interest for it on-line. So he created the Toy Trunk Railroad Web site, an on-line comic strip about trains. You can find it at **http://www.cyg.net/~sansom/**:

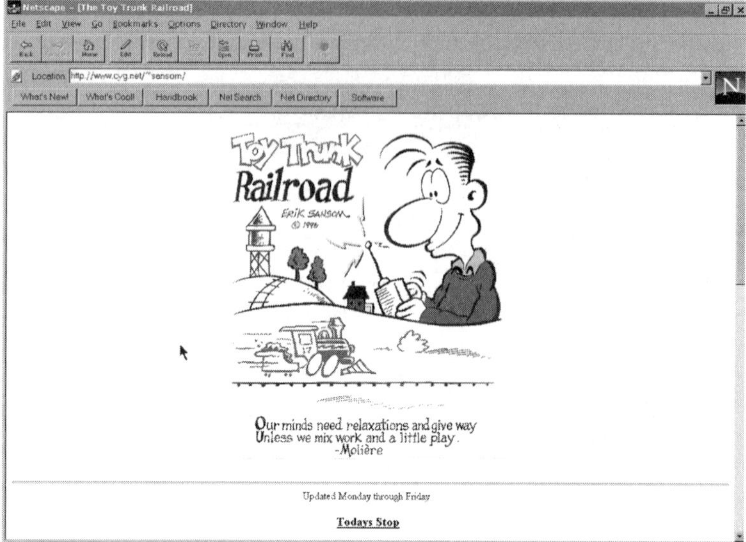

Through the site the comic strip is now available worldwide on a daily basis:

It has proven to be an exhilarating experience for him. The problem with newspapers, Eric notes, is that their market is too broad, meaning that they do not cater to niche markets when it comes to cartoons. In fact, many reacted to the idea of a cartoon specifically about trains as being far too broad a topic.

But what he has discovered about the Internet is that it is a unique way to reach specific markets. He notes that he has discovered that a market for a cartoon specifically for train enthusiasts exists worldwide, the natural market for Toy Trunk Railroad. The result is that he is achieving his primary goal of getting the strip noticed by his exact audience, but is now doing so worldwide, not just in a few local newspaper markets. Much of this is occurring as the result of the USENET newsgroup **rec.models.railroad**, an area on the Internet where model train enthusiasts from around the world "hang out."

His objective with the Internet was to "build an audience," ultimately hoping that revenue would flow from ancillary products related to the cartoon, such as T-shirts, books, posters, and other products. And through the Internet he is discovering that he can accomplish this goal. He notes, however, that he went in with his eyes open and was reasonably cautious about the chance for success.

From his perspective it has been a success: "I have certainly made some interesting contacts," he says. A good example is found with a fellow in Cleveland, who will be selling some posters based on his comic strip, after discovering him on the Internet. "When I went into this, I originally said I would give myself a year. I now figure I will make some money in a month or two, so I'm far ahead of my expectations." His whole attitude in getting involved with the Internet might be labeled as one of cautious optimism. "I didn't know what it would lead to, but I knew it would lead to something."

Tom and Donna Dawson

You can find Tom and Donna Dawson's ICanGarden Web site, a joint effort of this couple from St. Alberta, AB, at **http://www.icangarden.com**. Started in February 1996, it is already one of the largest sites about gardening in Canada available on the Web and boasts what must be the only major collection of information about gardening catalogues available in Canada:

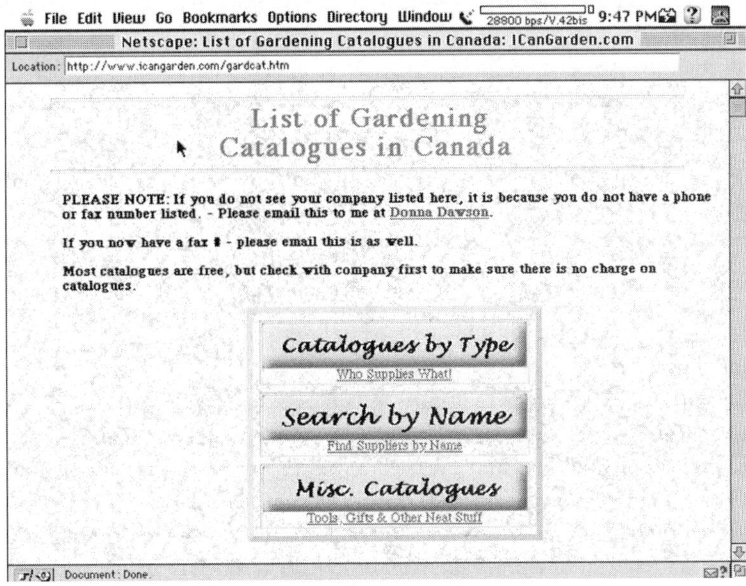

You can access a list of catalogues by type of product or search the list by keyword:

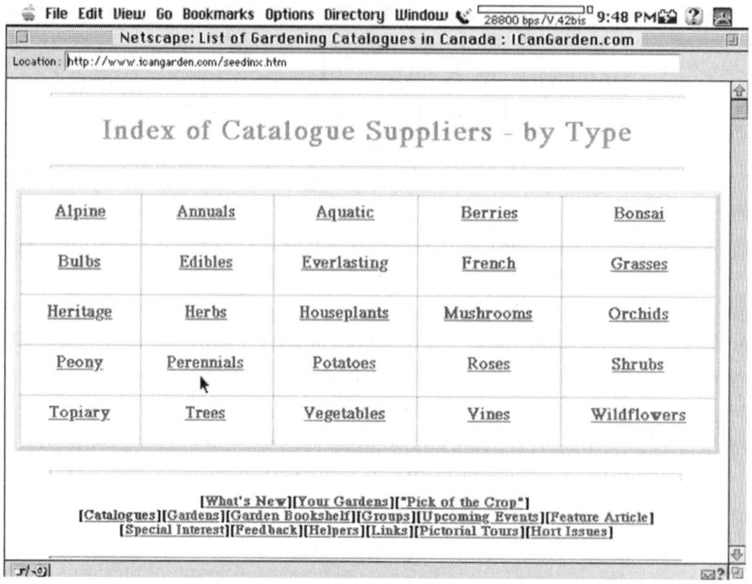

File Edit View Go Bookmarks Options Directory Window 9:48 PM

Netscape: List of Gardening Catalogues in Canada : ICanGarden.com

Location: http://www.icangarden.com/seedinx.htm

Index of Catalogue Suppliers - by Type

Alpine	Annuals	Aquatic	Berries	Bonsai
Bulbs	Edibles	Everlasting	French	Grasses
Heritage	Herbs	Houseplants	Mushrooms	Orchids
Peony	Perennials	Potatoes	Roses	Shrubs
Topiary	Trees	Vegetables	Vines	Wildflowers

[What's New][Your Gardens]["Pick of the Crop"]
[Catalogues][Gardens][Garden Bookshelf][Groups][Upcoming Events][Feature Article]
[Special Interest][Feedback][Helpers][Links][Pictorial Tours][Hort Issues]

Provided for each catalogue supplier is their phone number, details on what is sold, and other contact information, if any. The site also contains information about books, gardening groups and clubs, events, and all kinds of other information. If you are a gardener, or even if you are not, this site is worth a visit.

It is fascinating to see how the site came about. The first thing Donna admits is that she was not very computer-literate at the beginning of 1996 and had only heard others talk about the Internet. Today, she and her husband maintain what is arguably the largest site about gardening in Canada on the Internet. What brought it about? Donna explains: "I've always been into gardening; I belong to a lot of clubs, participate in competitions, and I'm the secretary for the Alberta Horticultural Association."

When they joined the Internet in early 1996, Donna immediately tried out a system that searches the Internet to discover what type of information could be found on-line about gardening and found very little specific Canadian information. At the time, her husband, Tom, already dealing with the Internet in his job as the Vice-President of Product Development for a software firm, was struggling to understand in greater depth the technical underpinnings of the network. The two of them talked and the idea gelled. She would pull together information necessary to building a site about gardening in Canada, and he would use it as an opportunity to learn more about the Internet and what was involved in building a Web site.

Coming up with information was no problem: "I've always had access to a lot of information, and have had a pretty extensive library of catalogues," says Donna. That is an understatement, since there are now several hundred catalogues on-line as well as other extensive information resources. The impact has been tremendous. "The seed companies are really excited," notes Donna. "They tell me they are getting calls from customers who say, 'I saw you on the Internet.'" She notes that for some of them the news they were found on the Internet came as a surprise.

The site is getting a lot of visitors and a lot of feedback, much of which you can view on-line. "Not only that, but people are starting to send in information or are asking to be listed," says Donna, "wanting to be included on the site." And the site was profiled in the spring in a three-minute feature on the popular morning TV show *Canada AM.*

Donna also participates in several on-line "discussion groups" related to gardening topics and spends perhaps four to five hours a week on-line. Not bad for someone who wasn't even on the Internet at the beginning of 1996. How does she react to people who aren't quite sure what the Internet is all about? She laughs: "Once you get on it, you won't know how you did without it. It is incredible."

Tom does all the maintenance of the Web site. "I've been involved with computers since 1995," he says, "and several years ago, took a crash course in programming to teach myself some of the fundamentals." He views his involvement today in building, enhancing and maintaining the ICanGarden Web site as a benefit both personally and from the perspective of his career. "It helps me understand from a business perspective what the Internet is all about and helps me add some useful skills to my background." He spends some 10 to 12 hours most weeks on the site, and some weeks 20 to 30 hours. All his experience is self-taught, by looking at a few books and by examining what others are doing on their sites.

The next step? He plans on linking the site to a database so that he can build up and more easily maintain the volume of information in the site. And he wants to provide suppliers the capability of adding their own information on-line as well as allowing visitors the ability to request catalogues and product directly from suppliers on-line. The goal of both? "We want to make it the most complete resource site of gardening information for Internet users in Canada." They are well on their way!

Miniature Schnauzer Club of Canada

It seems there are many husband and wife efforts with respect to the Internet. Just take a look at the Miniature Schnauzer Club of Canada, a Web site that is the result of efforts of Sharon and Tom-Lau Wiffin of Kitchener, ON (**http://www.kw.igs.net/~wiffers/**):

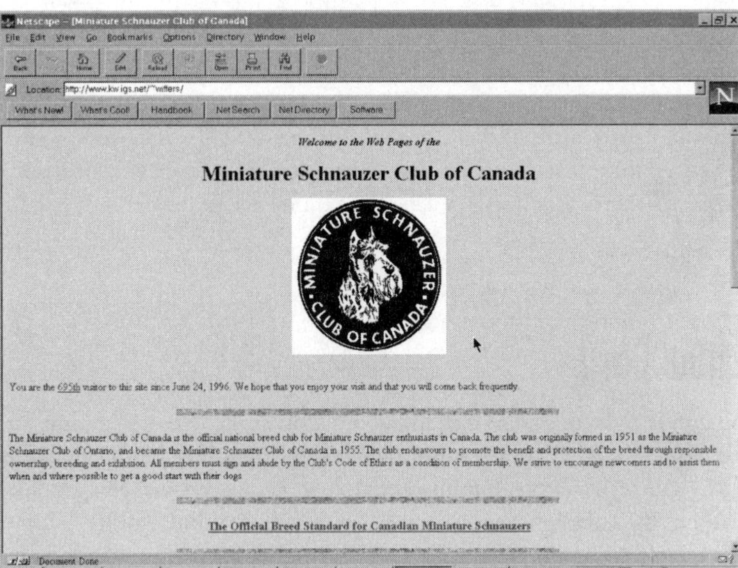

Like the Dawsons, they are relatively new to the Internet, having joined in December 1995. Sharon remembers what they found: "One of the first things we did was do a search; I typed in 'miniature schnauzer' and came up with a bunch of American sites." Although fascinated by what she found, she was concerned about the lack of Canadian information, so we can strike another notch for Canadian initiative. Sharon remembers thinking: "This is neat, but we can do something just as good or even better!"

She and Tom started finding out what was involved in creating their own Web site and turned first to their Internet service provider, who provided them with information on what was involved in building Web pages. Tom spent a lot of time looking at on-line sources of information about the "language of the Web," HTML, discussed in Chapter 14. The on-line result is that, like many Web sites, what Tom has accomplished is entirely self-taught.

Sharon does not get involved in issues of building the Web site, but is an extremely enthusiastic user of the Internet. She notes, for example, that she is now using e-mail extensively to exchange documents containing the club newsletter before it is finalized, which saves all kinds of time. She does note that there are, at this time, only a few club members on-line, one challenge being the fact that many club members are from an older generation not entirely comfortable with the use of a computer.

She is also quick to indicate that the primary purpose of the site is not to use it as a tool to reach club members, but to serve the public. One issue having to do with miniature schnauzers, as with many dog breeds in Canada, is that the public needs to be certain that they are purchasing a good, healthy, strong dog. With the growth of "puppy mills" in Canada, organizations specializing in breeding dogs, this is not always the case. And it is Sharon's belief that the established pet industry in Canada is not as forthcoming with the truth about breeding in Canada as it should be. She passionately believes in the Internet for this reason, because it is a tool that can help the general public bypass the traditional information structures in the country and get to truthful information, particularly related to the purchase of a pet.

Sharon cites an example of how the site was used in one recent case. A family was about to buy a pet. They checked the club Web site and learned about the potential hereditary problems as well as background on what to look for when purchasing a pet; they sent a message indicating that they believe they made a much better purchase as a result of visiting this site.

"People are education crazy," Sharon says, "and they are starting to look for information about dogs on-line, particularly if they are about to spend $800." Hence her goal is to use the Web site to help educate them on what they should really be aware of when purchasing a dog and in this regard, believes that it will make a huge difference to the pet industry in Canada. We believe her.

George Bouchard

Certainly Sharon is right in saying that many individuals in older generations, who have not grown up with computers, are somewhat intimidated by them and, hence, are not heavy users of the Internet. Certainly this is true, but that's not to say that we are not seeing many grandparents appearing on-line, discovering their own magic in this new on-line world.

A good example is George Bouchard, a 68-year-old father of five who lives in Salem, MA. What is the connection with Canada? His roots are in Quebec; he has traced his family tree back eleven generations. And he makes this information available, in quite a bit of depth, on his Web site, along with an extensive listing of links to sites in which he is interested, at **http://www1.shore.net/~glb/glbhome2.htm:**

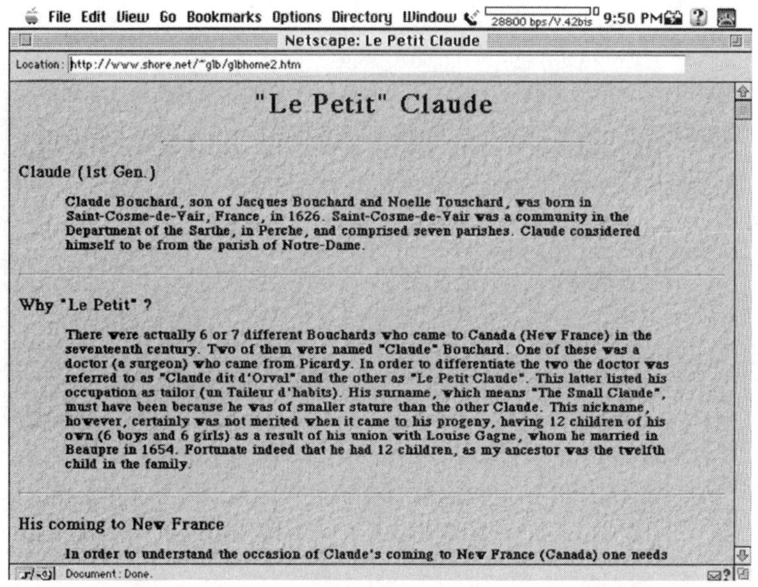

It is a fairly complex overview; for example, we are still trying to figure out this comment on one page: "the above in effect means that Danielle and Jared are 8th cousins to their own mother (from their father's side), and 7th cousins, twice removed, to their own father (from their mother's side). To press it (!!) one step further, they are their own 8th cousins once removed."

It is also a good example of the fact that genealogy has become a huge area of interest on the Internet. Like Bouchard, thousands of people worldwide are establishing Web sites providing details about their family tree and history for access by others.

Bouchard is retired, after a long career with the John Hancock organization. It was there, in the mid-1980s, that he first began using personal computers. He was, for a time, regarded as the PC guru in his division, which in his opinion meant that he knew just a little bit more than the others who didn't know very much. He is self-taught in everything he does with PCs and the Internet and obtained a home PC when he retired in 1987. He started using the Internet about 1992 or 1993 on a "shell account"; this was back in the days when you had to learn a lot of UNIX commands to access information on the Internet.

His Web site was only a few months old when we contacted him, and true to form with his experience with computers in general, he figured out what was involved in building it on his own. "I learned how to program in BASIC," he notes, "and it was the same for the Web site. I was intrigued by it; I wanted to figure it out, and so it seemed like the best way to learn about it was just to build a site."

For Bouchard it is just a hobby, but one in which he has become quite involved. The next step? On the very day we called him he was about to sign into the Internet to begin learning how to access some of the genealogy newsgroups so that he could begin contacting others around the world involved in tracing their roots.

John Religa

We also discovered another retired gentleman, John Religa, 62 years old, who has a Web site featuring stories of his career as a member of the RCMP constabulary in Newfoundland (**http://www.wp.com/JR/**):

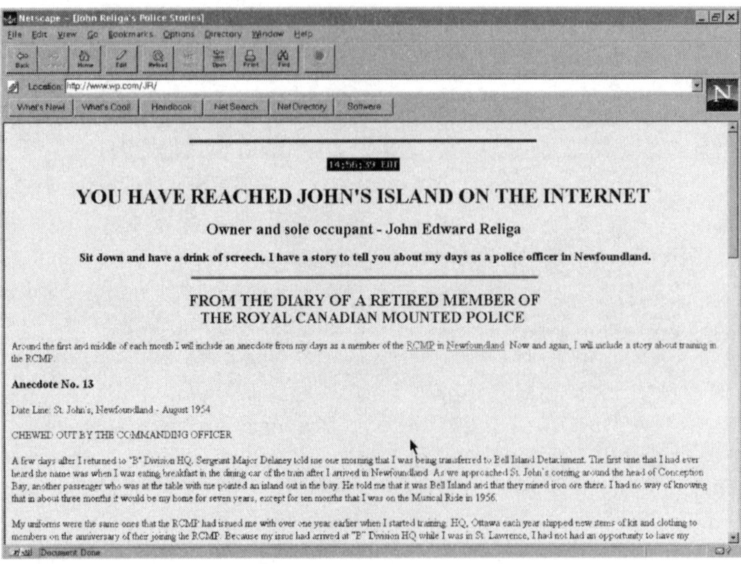

How did he get involved in doing this? After retiring, he started writing two books about Newfoundland and finally realized after many attempts at trying to get a foot in the door of publishers that his work might never be published. When the Internet came along, he jumped at the opportunity to make selected information from what he had written available on-line. He isn't new to the world of computers; while with the RCMP he worked at various times as a senior analyst and programmer and was quite involved in computer security for some time. For computer veterans, much of this experience began in the time when punch cards were quite common.

His reaction to the Internet and computers in general? He thinks that "they are the simplest thing in the world, once you get over the intimidation." He got on with the help of a friend. "Getting the mystery out of the way was the biggest challenge," he notes, indicating that for many people, just getting an understanding of what the Internet is and what people do there is perhaps the biggest problem they might have. "And once you are into it," he says, "you go exploring." Soon after joining the network he decided to build his own Web site, so he bought a few books on HTML, visited the local library, and was soon well on his way. He uses the Internet for other purposes as well. Recently, he has been having "phone conversations" through the Internet with another retired RCMP officer in BC as well as an old friend in Newfoundland. His plans? He wants to learn more about building Web sites and wants to put more of his stories on-line. "It gives me something to do," he says with a chuckle.

Howard's Links for Kids

From the topic of retirees using the Internet, we turn to the topic of kids on-line. Many parents are concerned that if they plug into the Internet, their kids will suddenly be introduced to a cesspool of depravity. It is not quite true; there is offensive content on-line, but you have to go looking for it. And in Chapter 17 of this book we take a look at several programs that can be used to prevent access to such sites.

There are many thousands of parents worldwide who are taking their children on-line; they recognize that the Internet is going to become a true force to be reckoned with in our future world and want to help the kids understand it, just as they might teach them to use a library. And in their own adventures on-line they have discovered that there is a lot of useful, kid-friendly information on-line.

Which brings us to Howard Lavitt, an employment officer in Winnipeg with Human Resources and Development Canada. He joined the Internet about two years ago and, having a 6-year-old and 2-year-old, began to look around to see what he could find for kids on-line. Every time he found a great site, he bookmarked it, which means that he added it to a special list so that he could quickly go back to the site at any time. His list of kid sites began to grow and grow and grow, so much so that one day he decided to try to turn it into a site on the World Wide Web. He now has a list of about 400 items, which can be found on the page "Howard's Links for Kids." It is a marvelous place to start for any parent taking their children on-line (**http://www.geocities.com/Heartland/1143/index.html**):

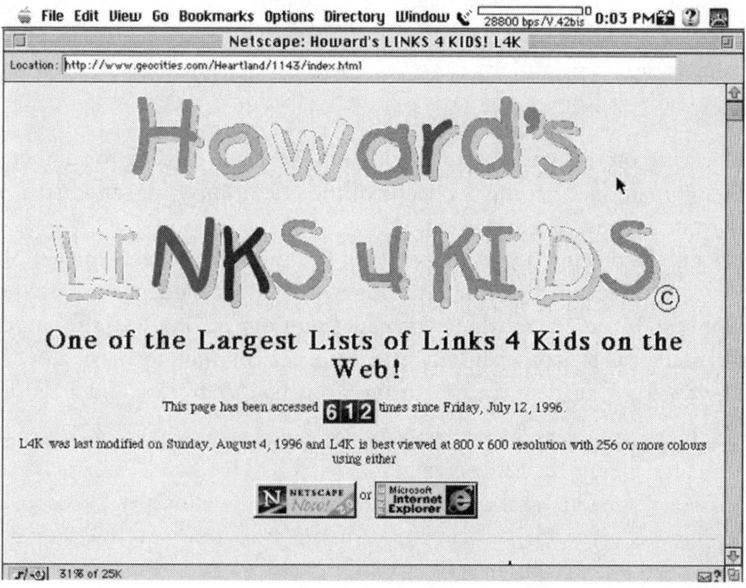

Through the site you can easily discover and travel to all kinds of "kid-friendly locations," such as Alice's Adventures in Wonderland, Alley Oop, Calvin and Hobbes Archive, Magic School Bus, and the Geometry Forum Online. And the site is being used: over 500 people from around the world had visited it on the weekend before we spoke to him, far exceeding his expectations.

Does he worry about children stumbling across some of the negative content to be found on the Internet? Not really. He believes that parents shouldn't hold back and should be involved in their child's use of the network. He is practical, however, as well: "We can't stop our kids forever from seeing everything," meaning that sooner or later they will discover both the positive and the negative aspects of the Internet. We spent a lot of time looking at Howard's site and then noticed near the middle something called the "Friendship Ring":

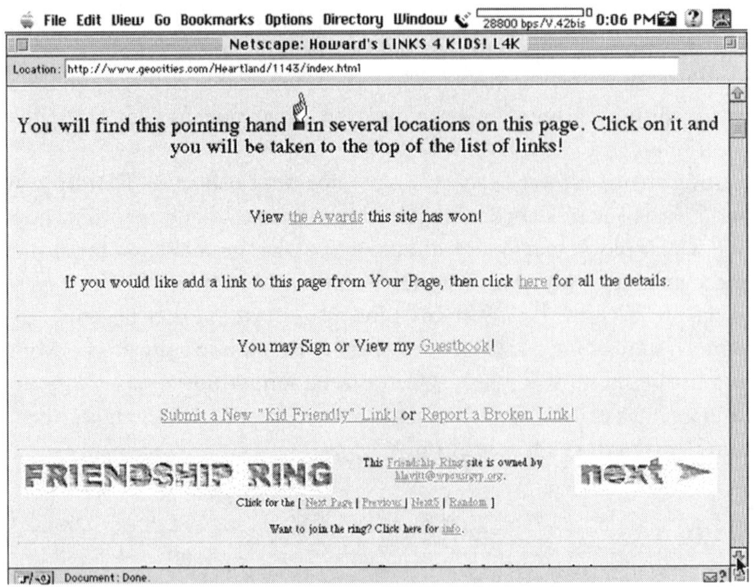

Curious, we clicked on the "next" button and found ourselves traveling to another Web site with kid-friendly information. That site also featured the Friendship Ring, and had a "next" button, which took us to the next site, and so on.

We had stumbled across something new on the Internet: "rings." In fact, one of the sites we visited listed a whole bunch of rings, making us aware that suddenly the Internet was sprouting a new concept. It was one in which you could start out on one Web site and use the ring to go to another and travel to another, helping you discover a common theme or area of interest along the way. There was a Canadian ring, featuring Canadian Web sites, and a World Ring and A Cool Site Ring:

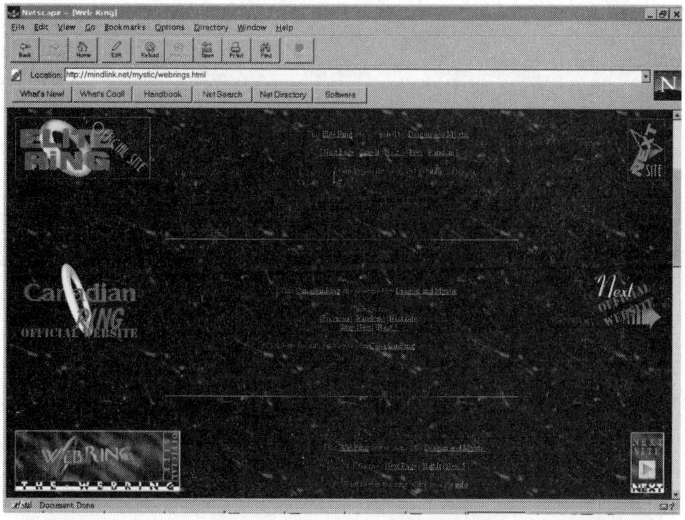

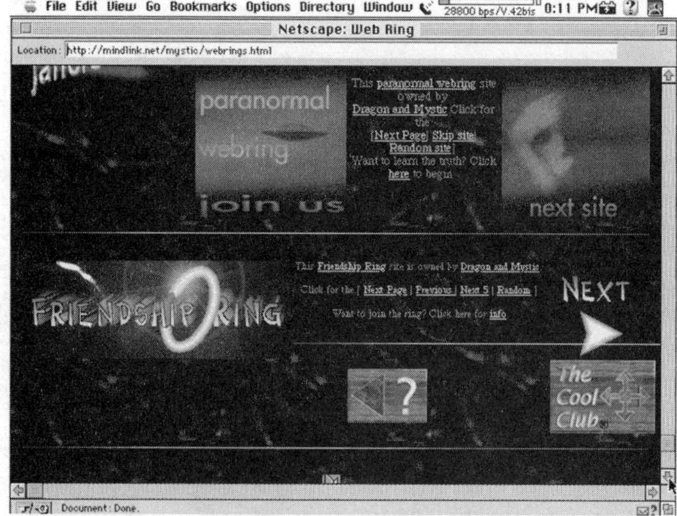

What we discovered was a new and unique method for people to link to other Web sites, and for encouraging people to visit their Web sites. And in the case of the Friendship Ring this was being done with a view to providing people another method of letting their kids visit sites that are considered safe. What was this "Friendship Ring," and who was behind it? We decided to find out.

Merlene Paynter Blacha and the Friendship Ring

It took only a second to discover who was behind it. We simply clicked on one button and found ourselves at a page that featured background information about the Friendship Ring and how a Web site could join the ring, at **http://www.wchat.on.ca/merlene/friendship/friendship.htm**:

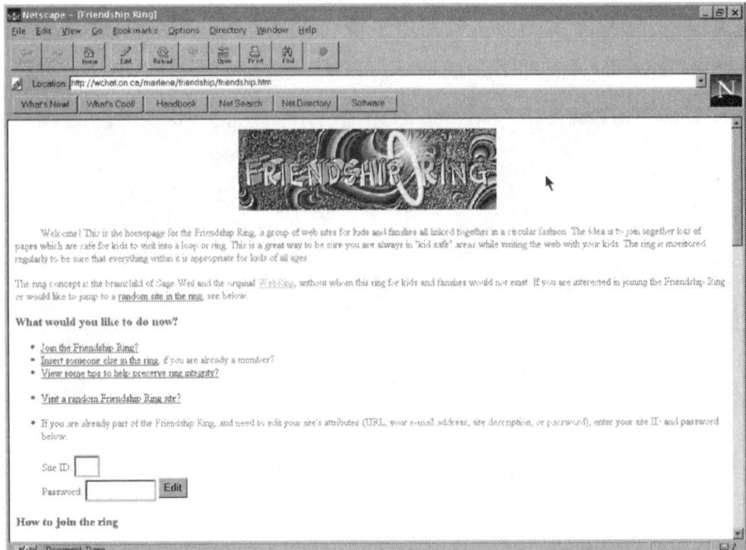

We dug a little deeper and discovered the home page of the owner of this site, which featured the curious opening phrases “I am WOMAN!”, “I am INVINCIBLE”, and “I am tired”:

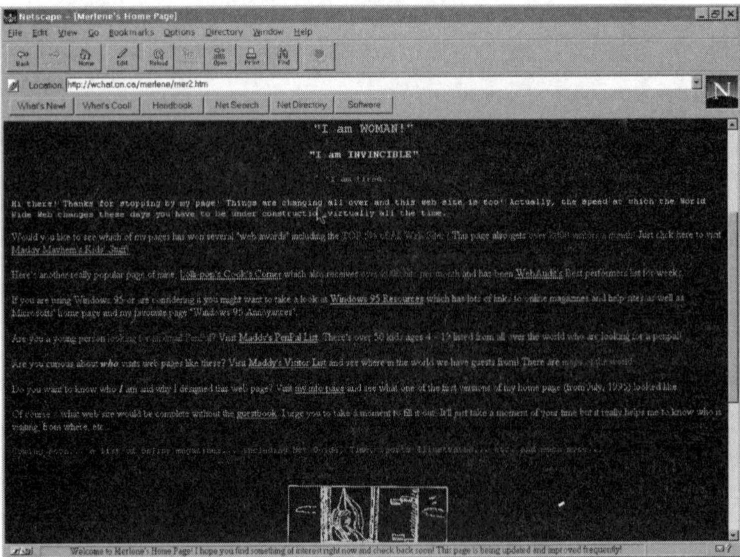

We explored a little and came to Maddy Mayhem’s Kid Stuff, the page for the 6-year-old daughter of the owner of this particular Web site. It, too, consisted of lists of some kid-friendly sites around the Internet:

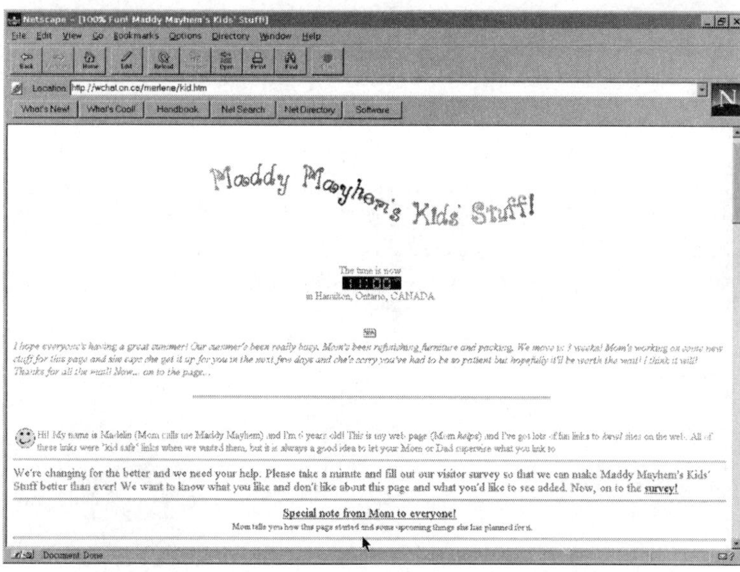

Curious, we made a telephone call to Merlene Paynter Blacha, the owner of the site. Why was she tired? She has a 19-month-old boy, a good enough reason for anybody to be tired! And therein unfolded the most fascinating story. "I'm a stay-at-home Mom," she says, "and a year and a half ago when my son was born, I was up all night. One night, I signed into the Internet, looked around, and got hooked. By October, I had decided to do a page with links to sites for kids."

And like many other people we talked to in this chapter, she is entirely self-taught. She and her husband initially bought a PC for their daughter and just bought another one because the first one is used so much.

Things happened quickly. Netscape put her site up on their What's New page, which is a huge coup for anyone who is involved with the Internet. "Suddenly, I was getting 5,000 visitors a week. And I was discovering that a lot of people wanted information on how to find pen pals and information for kids — parents, kids, educators and others." This led to the concept for the Friendship Ring, based on the ring concept rapidly appearing throughout the Internet at that time.

Things have been busy for Blacha ever since. On some weekends she gets up to 400 e-mail messages from people who have visited the site and she has nine different e-mail addresses used for various purposes. The reason for the ring? What she believes it says is that, "as a parent, these are safe places for your kids to visit." Sites that want to join the ring must request to be "validated," that is, she checks them to see if the content is OK for kids. At the time we spoke to her, 29 sites had been validated, another 19 were waiting to be checked, and 15 more enquiries were still pending. She could well have a hundred sites in the ring by the end of the year. And she is, in fact, about to participate in two other rings: one for gourmet cooking and another related to home budgeting. She recently won an Internet cooking award for some of the recipes on her site. Her husband? At first, he wasn't quite sure about her use of the Internet, since it was taking a good part of her time. But now, given that she has launched a small business on the side related to Web site design, he has come to understand it more.

Gathering of the Clans

We took a right turn at that point and found the site for the "Gathering of the Clans" (**http://www.tartans.com**):

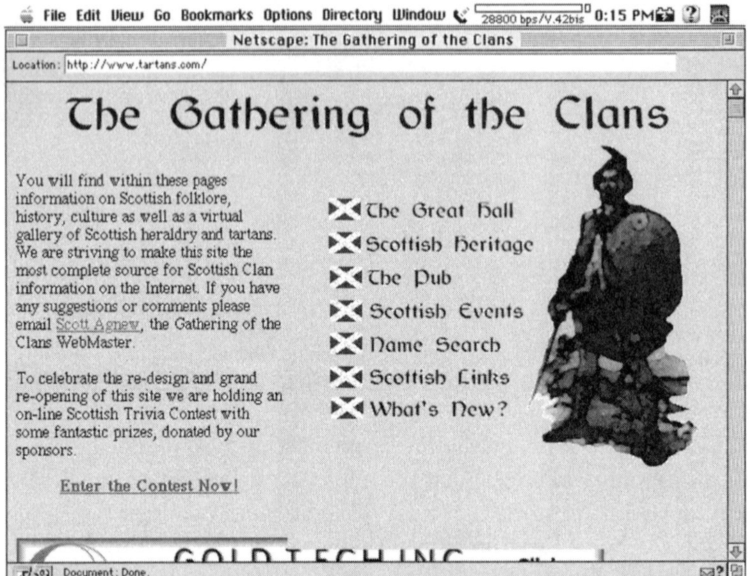

Touring through the site, we found it contained all kinds of information, including very detailed information about specific Scottish clans:

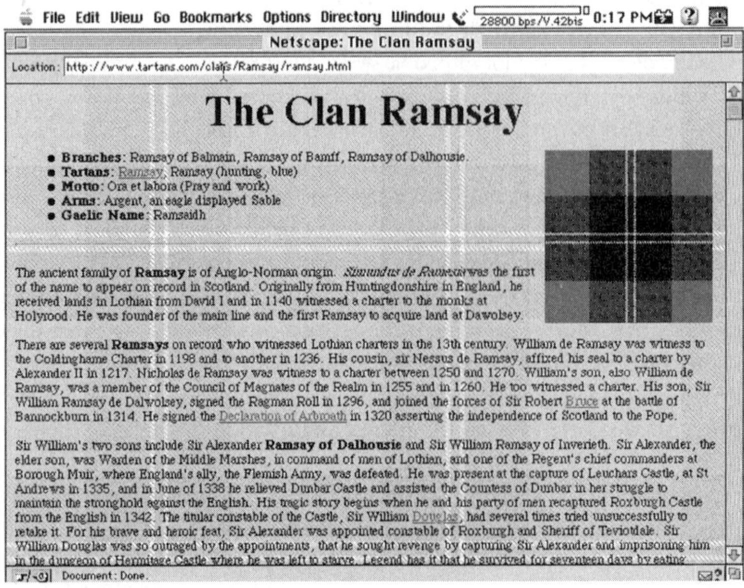

And like many other sites, it included extensive information on how to find other Scottish-related sites on-line:

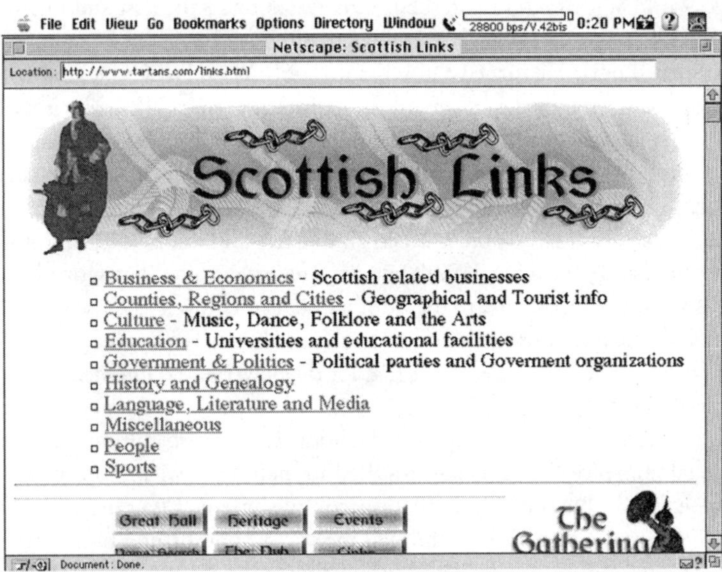

It also featured something called "the pub," which turned out to be an extensive discussion about everything Scottish:

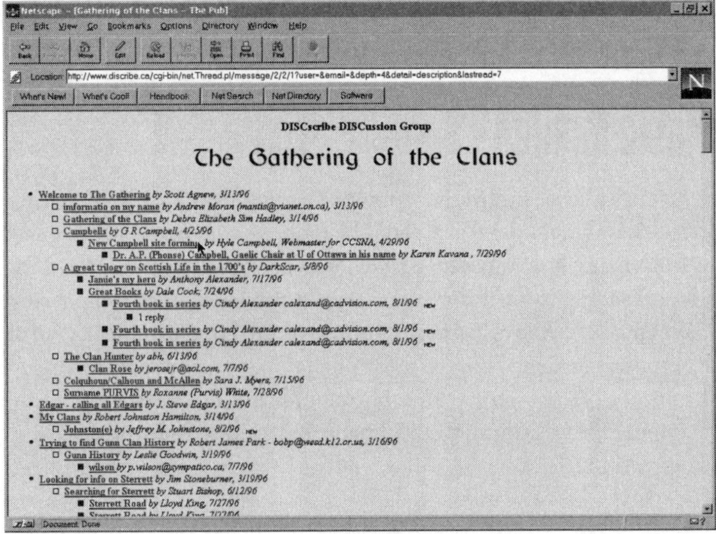

What does this very Scottish site have to do with Canada? The site is in New Brunswick, which is one of the primary homes worldwide for Scottish information on the Internet.

Curious about how this came about, we tracked down Scott Agnew, a 27-year-old chap who lives in Moncton, NB. After finishing university with a degree in anthropology and no job offers, he got a computer, learned about the Internet, built up his skills, and got a job — with DISCribe, a unique organization based in Saint John, NB (**http://www.discribe.ca/**), which describes itself as combining "instant conference and meeting documentation with the operation of a 6000+ page World Wide Web site on the Internet making us the first and foremost Webcaster in Atlantic Canada."

What happened next? He turned a hobby into a job. With DISCribe he spent time helping many businesses discover and take advantage of the Internet, since DISCribe initially focused on helping companies put up Web sites. In his spare time, though, he continued surfing the Internet looking for Scottish information resources. Seeing a scarcity of information on-line, he began to build the Clans site.

Before he knew it things took off, with an almost ten-fold increase in the number of visitors in a half-year period and generating 310,000 hits in a recent month. (The term "hits" is often used as a measure, sometimes inaccurate, of the number of visitors to a site.) It seemed that his hobby had suddenly become a serious initiative, so much so that the owner of DISCribe decided to allow him to pursue the site full time. How's that for the power of the Internet: a fellow who turned his hobby into a career!

Today, his objectives are to make the site the home for Scottish culture worldwide and to become the official home for Scottish clans on the Internet. He is well on his way; so far, 37 clan societies are located on his site, a significant accomplishment. Of course, his efforts must be funded, and the plan is to earn revenue through the sale of sponsorships or advertisements on the site. He hopes to make the site at least self-supporting and believes that he can do this within a year.

As for DISCribe, the attitude is that they want to be like an independent producer in the television world — what they call a Webcaster — producing entertainment and educational sites for the Internet. Given the drive to establish New Brunswick as one of the homes of hi-tech in Canada, we would not be the least bit surprised to see them pull this off.

Jaymar Music Limited

Scottish clans seemed like an innovative enough topic to find on the Internet, so we tried to find another one. Chamber music! What could be more unique than that? A quick search on the phrase took us to Jaymar Music Limited, a small, two-person operation located in London, ON, who seem to be managing to turn the Internet into the backbone of their current operation (**http://www.jaymar.com**). The organization is one of the largest publishers of sheet music for independent composers in Canada in the areas of chamber ensemble, instrumental, choral, and concert band music. They are similar to a book publisher in that they publish the music on behalf of the composer, for distribution in Canada and around the world.

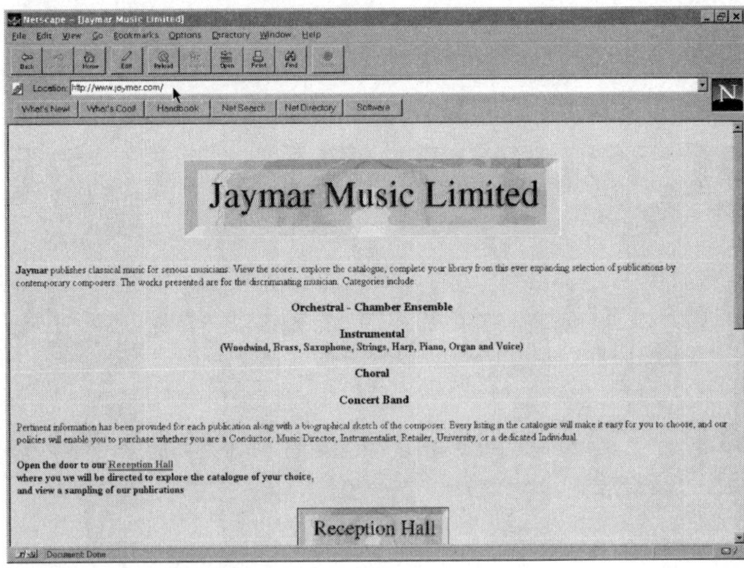

We spoke to Peter Martin, who filled us in on their story. Today, he is at the point that he receives sheet music from composers, scans the pages into a computer, and e-mails the resultant computer files to a company in Columbia, South America. There, the music is turned into a special computer format suitable for printing in sheet music format and is sent back to him by e-mail. This information is then transmitted to a local printer and made available for sale. He is also using the Internet to market the works of individual composers; to help with this, he makes available sample sheet music from each composer:

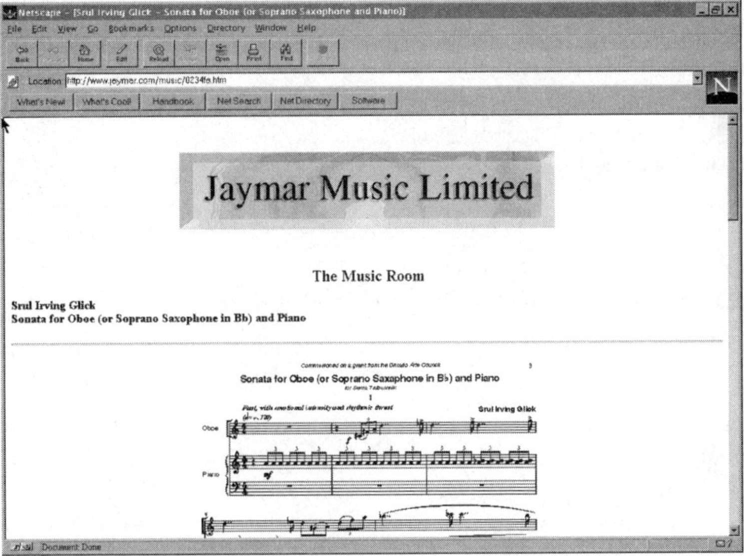

He also makes available the biography of every composer on the site:

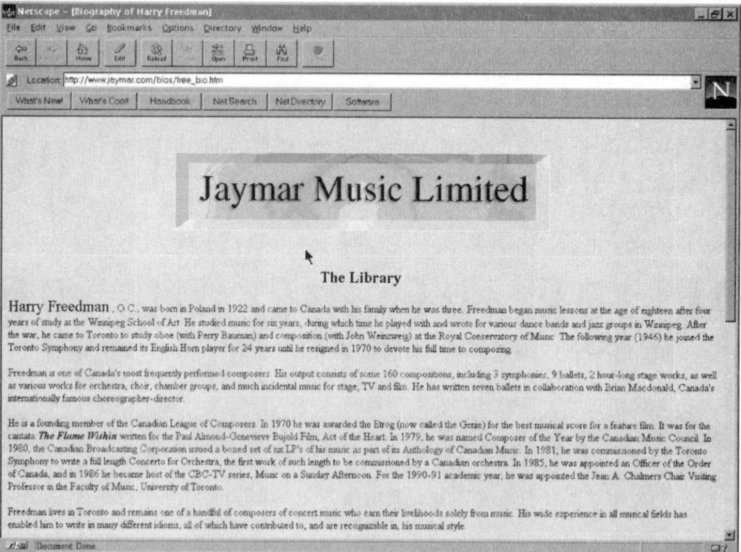

As well, he publishes review notes that include comments on the music and on when it has been performed, important information for those who may choose to purchase it:

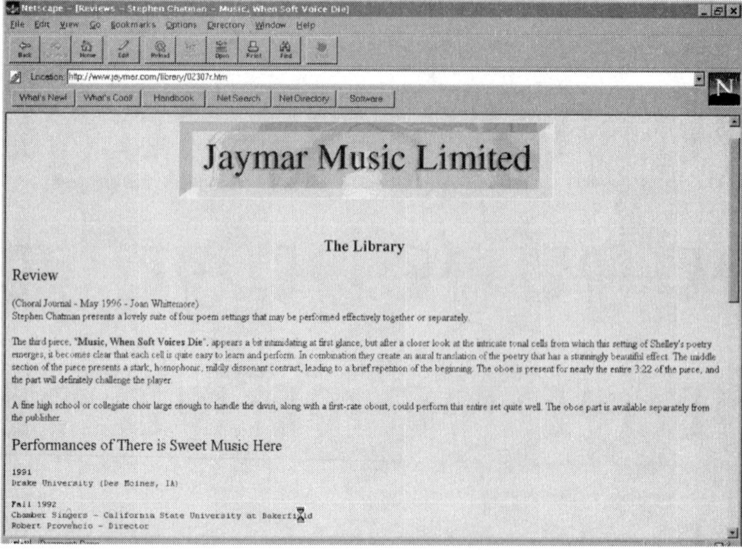

Who buys such music? In one case, universities, and given the use of the Internet throughout the academic community, there is a natural audience for the works sold by Jaymar. Musicians, choir directories, and various performance groups also form part of the audience.

Martin's site had been up for about four months by the time we visited him, and he rates it an unqualified success. He now gets at least four people a day joining a mailing list, which notifies recipients when new sheet music goes on the site, and has some 4,000 participants. He finds he is getting a lot of interest in the music from Asia, perhaps because both the Internet and the music are brand-new to them. And his belief is that the Internet is ideal as a tool to market the type of product he sells, since buyers can really see what they might be purchasing and get useful background information to help them decide whether to make the purchase.

And as for Martin, every time there is a sale of music on-line, there is a direct benefit. In Chapter 16 we will talk about a business trend called disintermediation; it is a trend in which the middleman in a transaction no longer plays a role. For Jaymar the direct benefit is this: if they sell the music on-line, they keep more of the sale proceeds, by not having to provide a discount to a store or retail agency. At this point he is making six to seven sales per week, not huge numbers, but given that he keeps more of the proceeds, a number that has a direct impact on his bottom line.

His goal? He is working hard, just like the Gathering of the Clans folks, to make his site the home for this type of music worldwide. To that end, when we spoke to him, he was just about to launch Adventures in Words-Music, a home for publishers of music from around the world (**http://www.words-music.com/**). This, perhaps, is a good indication of how quickly things move on the Internet: he started four months ago and is now prepared to significantly expand his strategy.

CharityVillage

Jaymar is an excellent example of a small business on-line, so we wondered about the not-for-profit sector. What was the state-of-the-art with those types of organizations, many of which had been experimenting with the Internet for quite some time? That led us to CharityVillage (**http://www.cyberplex.com/charityvillage/**), an initiative built with the intention of becoming a home for information for Canadian not-for-profit organizations:

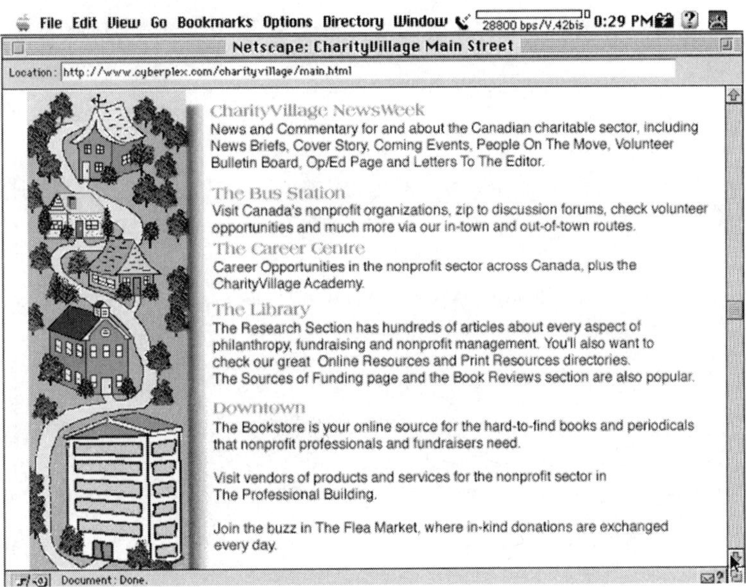

A quick tour reveals CharityVillage is succeeding; the site features a weekly news round-up of information of interest to the charity and not-for-profit sector, for example:

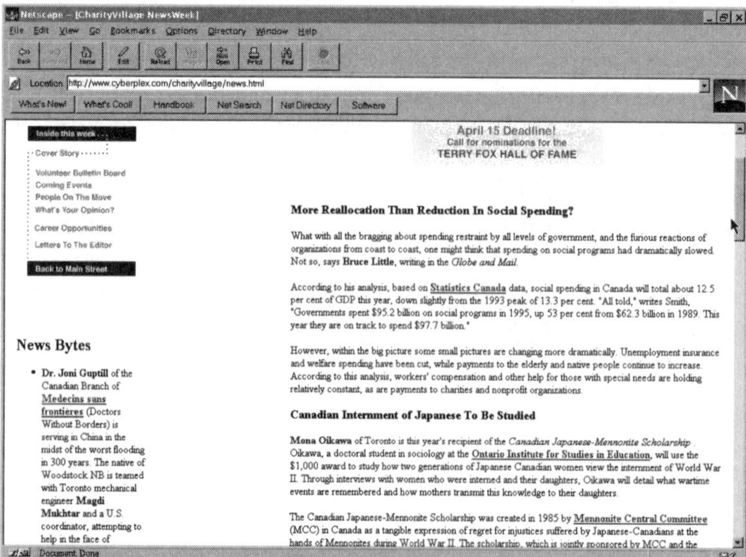

The site is also a career centre, featuring advertisements and notices for positions with charities throughout Canada. A review indicated a lot of activity:

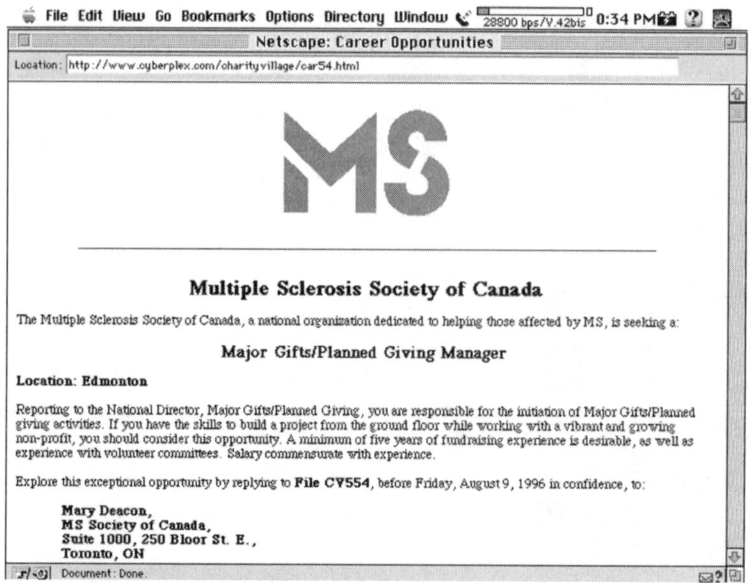

What else? A library, with reference information pertaining to the not-for-profit sector and all kinds of other stuff. There is also the "Flea Market," a site where not-for-profits post information about products or services that are needed. Anyone have a boat?

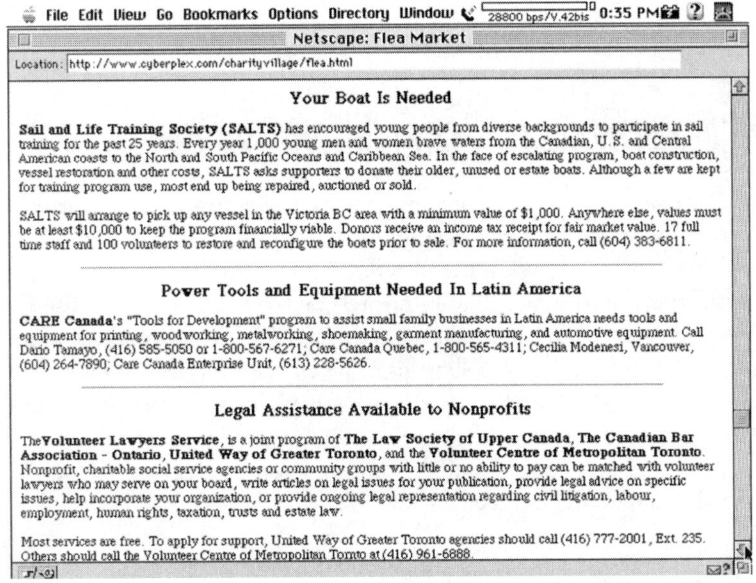

There are many other resources at this site, including what is probably the most extensive list of charities with Web sites throughout Canada. Who is behind this particular site? None other than the Hilborn Group, "Canada's publisher, in print and on-line, to the nonprofit sector." They have been the long-time publisher of the publication *Canadian Fundraiser*, "the journal of record for Canadian fundraising professionals." In that regard CharityVillage is an excellent example of how many organizations are attempting to respond to the arrival of this unique facility called the Internet; they are carefully and slowly determining how they can continue to play an important role as the world migrates from a world of print publications to the on-line computer world.

They are discovering that there are two types of people accessing the service: professionals from the not-for-profit sector, such as the executive directors of charities and other groups, and, perhaps the most surprising, interested volunteers and donors from the general public, who seem to be hungry for information about the not-for-profit sector on-line. Their experience has shown, for example, that the areas on-line in which people are volunteering services or are looking for volunteers have been some of the most active.

Why are they doing this? One objective is to see how they can use the on-line world to enhance their print publication; in this regard it is a promotional tool. And their goal, like many of the other groups we have talked to, is to at least make it a break-even proposition. And they do want to be the preeminent source for information about the not-for-profit sector in Canada, a goal that seems reachable, given the credibility they have already achieved in the marketplace and the sophistication of their on-line efforts.

They will admit that, so far, the site has not met the objectives in what they now call their "overly ambitious business plan"; they realized this within two months. But Doug Jamieson, the primary person behind the initiative, says that "on every other level it has exceeded our expectations.

The responses of people on-line, and the fact that we get many messages when we slip a day or two in keeping something up-to-date, tells us that people have a sense of belonging to the site. And that is success." Bottom line? They are convinced that something important is emerging on the Internet and definitely want to be a part of it. "And we're having a lot of fun," adds Jamieson.

Ontario Corn Producers' Association

The CharityVillage site is one example of how a not-for-profit organization or association can use the Internet. Another good example is the Ontario Corn Producers' Association (OCPA). Terry Daynard is the Executive Vice-President of the OCPA, a non-profit trade organization with a staff of 12 and a membership of some 21,000 farmers across Ontario. He is also their resident WebMaster and Internet expert. Although the OCPA established its Internet presence in March 1996, Daynard says that he had been polling his members every six months for at least a year prior to that, trying to figure out how the OCPA could best use the technology. Starting around January 1996, there was a "notable difference" in the number of OCPA members who were on the Internet. It was also around that time that pressure began to mount for the organization to publish its information on the Internet.

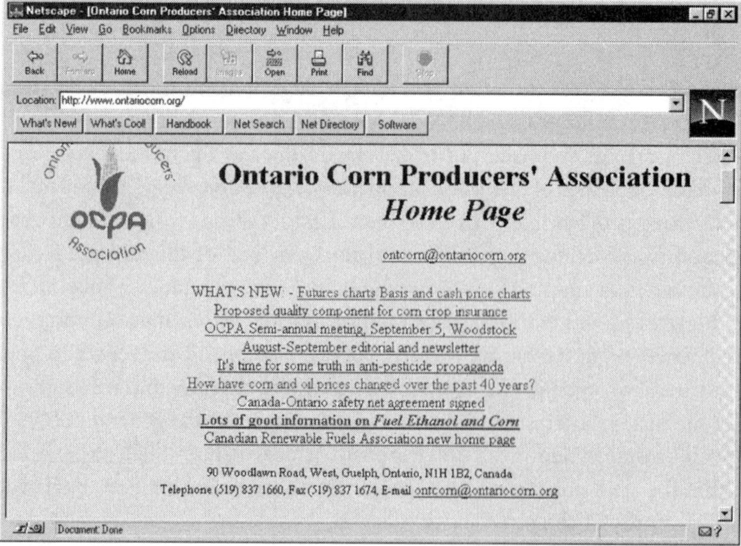

Daynard says he initially spent about 80 hours putting the site together. He says the real challenge is to keep users coming back, especially farmers, who he says are not inclined to tap into their computer on a daily basis for e-mail and other information. Daynard now spends about two hours a week — often from home — updating and maintaining the Web site. He wouldn't have it any other way. "I'm convinced the way to do this is to do it yourself," he says.

Having built the OCPA Web site himself, Daynard knows that you do not have to spend $100,000 to do a great job. With just a little time and effort, he says, your Web site can look as good as the one built by a multimillion dollar corporation. "The Web is a great equalizer. I look at all the sophisticated sites...there's no reason why anybody can't match just about anything else that's out there...all it takes is some imagination and thought to organize." OCPA pays less than $1500.00 per year for its Web page. This includes e-mail addresses for all its office staff. Is it worth it? "Oh, yes," says Daynard, pointing out that one of OCPA's primary functions is to communicate, an objective well-suited to the Web.

The OCPA's Web site has been designed with two audiences in mind: farmers and students. For farmers the site is primarily a resource for industry news and information. Daynard envisions farmers checking the Web site once a week to access market and pricing information and to keep current on OCPA activities. The organization's newsletter, the *Ontario Corn Producer*, is already published on the Web in addition to its print circulation of 25,000. One of the benefits of using the Internet to distribute the OCPA's news information is its speed. "We have our newsletter out to people two weeks faster on the Internet...as soon as it's done, we put it on the Internet...people who get the print version get it two weeks later."

While many farmers currently rely on satellite services for weather reports and other industry information, Daynard predicts that the days of a farmer using a satellite for information retrieval are numbered. "Satellite technology is on borrowed time," he says. "The Internet is far cheaper — everything that is on the satellite service is on the Internet."

Since the OCPA Web site is packed with educational content, it is a boon for students, teachers, and anyone who has even the slightest curiosity about corn and its origins. Daynard recognizes the growing importance of the Internet in Canada's school system. "It's just obvious that universities, public schools, and high schools are using the Internet as their libraries," he notes. Distributing its learning material through the Web is a natural fit for the OCPA, which works closely with the educational community to promote corn education in the schools. Adds Daynard: "I've come to the conclusion that it's more important to get our publications onto the Web in a readable, usable manner than publish them on paper, because this is obviously where the kids are going to get it from."

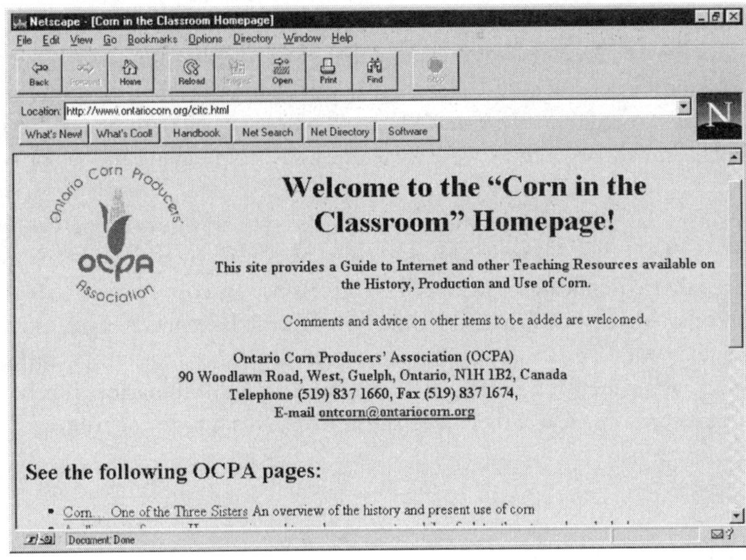

The OCPA now receives about a dozen e-mail messages a day from the Internet. They are received by the organization's clerical staff, who forward them to the appropriate office personnel. Eventually, Daynard hopes to train his clerical staff to maintain and update the Web pages as well. "If they can handle WordPerfect, they can handle HTML," he says.

The OCPA's Web site has brought its share of surprises. "I didn't anticipate how many foreign visitors we would get," explains Daynard. Since its Web site went live, the OCPA has been receiving messages from as far away as Japan with requests for Ontario corn. About 20% of the corn grown in Ontario goes into export markets. But the OCPA will not be selling corn over the Internet anytime soon. The OCPA acts only as a trade organization and does not have a mandate to sell corn itself. Instead, the OCPA acts as an intermediary, putting corn buyers in touch with corn sellers. To help foreigners who find OCPA on the Internet and want to buy Ontario corn, a list of corn exporters has been published on OCPA's Web site:

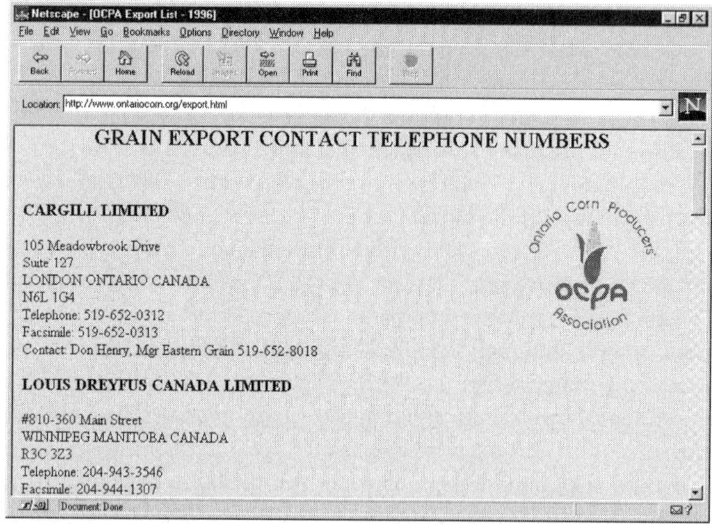

For the most part, sales still need to be initiated by conventional methods — telephone or fax, for example — but the OCPA is trying to change that. The organization would like to see all of Ontario's corn exporters obtain e-mail addresses. "I see the Internet as an obvious means to communicate pricing and specifications to foreign buyers," notes Daynard, but he is also quick to point out the Internet's limitations. "I think we're sometime away from buying and selling corn over the Internet."

Since corn is a large volume product, it is not the type of product you can purchase for overnight delivery by FedEx. International shipments usually go by boat and U.S. shipments by rail. There are other complications as well. For these reasons, corn transactions are not quite ready for the Internet, yet. But Daynard knows how fast the Internet changes, and he is careful not to rule anything out. "This business is moving so quickly; it's hard to anticipate what you might be doing in a year's time." The Ontario Corn Producers' Association can be reached at **ontcorn@ontariocorn.org** or visit their Web site at **http://www.ontariocorn.org**.

Tip Top Tailors

Finally, we thought that with the focus on business on-line, a topic we cover in Chapter 16, we should take a look at how one high-profile business is approaching the Internet. To do that, who better to visit than Tip Top Tailors, well known to Canadians as the operator of over one hundred men's retail clothing stores across Canada. They officially launched their Web site in May 1996 (**http://www.tiptop.ca**). The main thrust behind the site, according to Joan Donogh, Tip Top's Marketing Manager, is to use it as a communications vehicle with customers. But Tip Top recognizes that communication on the Internet is a two-way street. "Putting up a Web site without any interactive elements is just a waste of everyone's time," observes John Dawkins, Tip Top's Vice-President of Marketing. With this in mind the company created its Web site as an "electronic extension" of what it has already been doing through its traditional marketing: building relationships with its customers, for life. The Web site was backed up by a strong business case that initially emphasized communications rather than commerce.

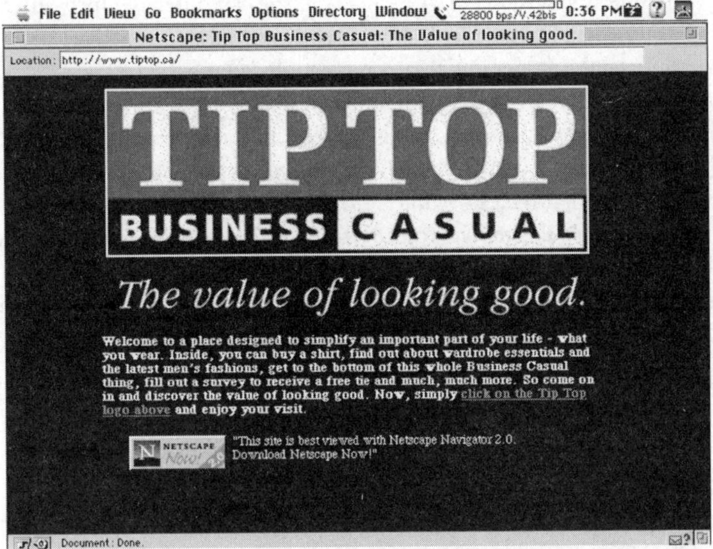

This philosophy is very apparent in Tip Top's Web site, where visitors are encouraged to leave comments for company management and fill out a survey that asks questions about their buying habits and clothing preferences. Tip Top monitors what customers are saying, and prompt responses are provided when necessary. Donogh says the feedback has been "tremendous." She says the information that Tip Top collects is used to reduce the risk of carrying merchandise that customers are not interested in. This means fewer markdowns, since stores can carry the merchandise that consumers really want.

Dawkins says that the Web provides a "very economical way" of doing qualitative research, since focus groups and more traditional forms of market research can cost thousands of dollars. Yet Internet surfers are no different than traditional customers; they are busy people. How do you get them to spend a few minutes filling out a questionnaire? Tip Top came up with a clever solution; they reward each and every person who fills out their on-line survey with a printable coupon for a free silk tie.

If you have any doubts about the Internet's ability to reengineer the delivery of customer service, consider Tip Top's experience with one customer in Western Canada. A distraught Edmonton resident used the Tip Top Web site to contact the company when he couldn't find any grey suits at his local Tip Top store. Upon receiving the message, Tip Top responded and asked the customer what price range he was interested in and what style of suits he liked. Based on the customer's responses, Tip Top selected a couple of fabrics and couriered some swatches to his home. Upon receiving the customer's approval of the swatches, the suits were shipped to Edmonton, and the customer picked them up at his local Tip Top store. The entire process was handled over the Internet, and Donogh says the client was "delighted."

With success stories like this one in the books, Tip Top is planning to "decentralize" its Web site and bring all its stores on-line. You will be able to talk with your local store manager, book a wardrobe consultation, check on the availability of your alterations, and even get some fashion advice if you have an important event coming up.

While customer communications is Tip Top's number one priority on the Web, the company has big plans to use the Internet as a distribution vehicle. This aspect of Tip Top's Internet strategy is already well underway. Visitors to Tip Top's Web site can purchase shirts and have them delivered overnight anywhere in Canada. While Tip Top says the results have been "very good," on-line sales volumes have not met initial sales projections. Donogh says the sluggish sales on the Web were not unexpected, but she has no doubt that on-line sales are going to "snowball" once Tip Top figures out the right formula. Dawkins agrees, and points out that the Internet's demographics are a perfect match for Tip Top's clientele. Many Internet users are educated males in the middle-to-upper income brackets, a natural fit for Tip Top.

To draw visitors to its Web site, Tip Top advertised its Internet presence on in-store flyers and newsletters and on large posters that were hung in its store windows. The company also placed an ad in *Maclean's* magazine's print Web directory and promoted the Web site through traditional media vehicles. To further increase traffic to its site, Tip Top looks for other organizations that will link to it. A good example is the Wool Bureau, based in New York, which has a site on the World Wide Web at **http://www.woolmark.com:**

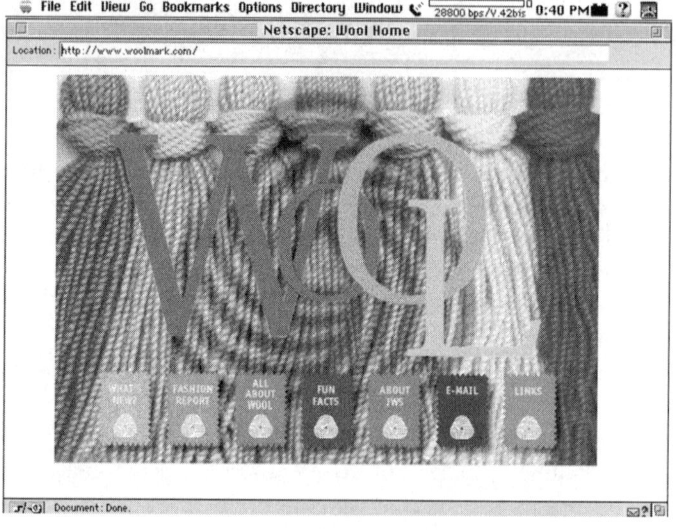

What does Tip Top have to do with the Wool Bureau? Tip Top's suits are wool. Therefore, both organizations have a common goal: to sell more wool. The Wool Bureau has linked its Web site to the Tip Top Web site, thereby generating more visitors for Tip Top and, hopefully, more sales of wool suits. A win–win situation.

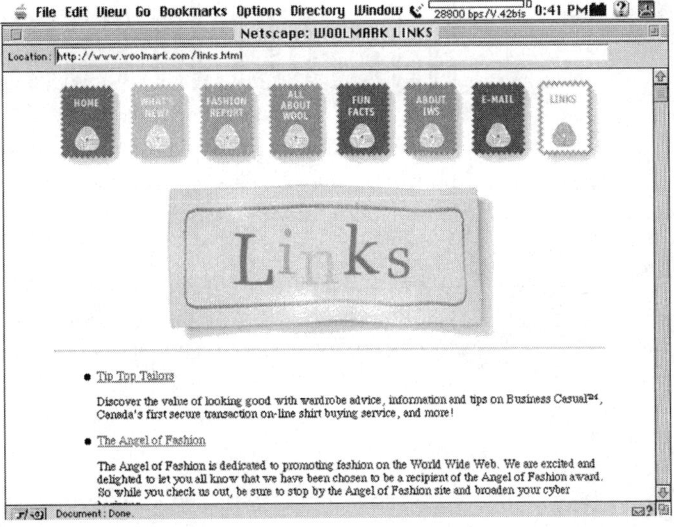

Tip Top's advertising agency, Padulo (**http://www.padulo.ca**), is also the company that designed its Web site. When Tip Top initially went looking for a partner to develop its Web site, they considered many options, including using a traditional Web development company. They eventually settled on Padulo for a number of reasons. First, since Padulo is Tip Top's advertising agency, it already has a strong knowledge of Tip Top's business. But perhaps more importantly, by allowing its ad agency to design the Web site, Tip Top was able to seamlessly integrate its marketing strategy with the Web site in a consistent manner.

What is the future for Tip Top on the Internet? The company will continue to push the interactiveness of the Web and bring all its store managers on-line to make them more accessible to customers. Tip Top also plans to use the Internet to manage more effectively its relationship with customers. Tip Top sees an opportunity to build a database of customers who prefer to receive notification of store sales and specials on the Internet rather than by Canada Post. Tip Top knows it has a lot at stake. "You have to be really careful if you're a big company," cautions Donogh. "You're showing your public face to customers; you have to have a professional, updated, and maintained site." If there is a Canadian model that Tip Tip does not want to follow, it is Eaton's, which prematurely rushed onto the Web and then shut its site down, a victim of overambitious plans.

Tip Top's strategy has been carefully executed, with a lot of attention to detail. "We're not going to put a plethora of product up on the Internet just for the sake of doing it," notes Dawkins. "What we want to do is keep it narrow and focused and test for awhile to figure out what customers really react to...It's not a matter of just duplication of services, it's a matter of how you build incremental added value services for Internet users...if we use that approach, then the Internet becomes something that's got real viability." Tip Top's goal? To "underpromise and overdeliver."

This has been just a sampling of who is using the Internet in Canada. Take a look around, and you will discover thousands of other stories. Let's move on and take a look at how you can get connected to this marvellous network.

CHAPTER 4

Connecting to the Internet in Canada

AT&T Corp. yesterday said it would offer Internet access service to consumers nationwide within a few weeks... The long-distance telephone giant is the latest big company to enter the fast-growing business of linking people to the worldwide network of computers... AT&T will give its own customers a reduced Internet rate for the first year — five free hours monthly, with each hour after that for $2.50. It will charge $19.95 for unlimited usage. The relatively low AT&T prices are expected to lower usage costs for Internet consumers industrywide, some analysts said.

AT&T to Begin Offering Access to the Internet; Company Faces Wide Range of Competitors *The Washington Post*, February 28, 1996

AT&T launched its new Internet access service, but had trouble keeping up with demand as 5,000 visitors to the company's headquarters in Bridewater, N.J., snapped up copies of its access software and wanted more. "Originally, we had anticipated that 60,000 to 70,000 people would sign up for service. It's almost triple that," said spokesman Ritch Blasi.

Digest, *The Washington Post*, March 15, 1996

We can provide you with everything you need to get started in the fastest growing business of our time. Internet Solutions for as little as $15,000 startup.

Posting, seen on USENET, August 1996

To access the Internet, you need an Internet service provider, also known as an Internet access provider. This is the company or organization that will either provide you with an account through which you can dial into the Internet or will provide your organization with a link to the network through some type of permanent connection.

In this chapter we will take a look at what you need to do to get the most popular type of connection to the Internet, a SLIP or PPP account, from your home or office computer. In Chapter 20 we will take a look at the Canadian Internet industry to help you understand the full range of companies that provide Internet services in Canada and to outline the many different methods of providing access to the network, above and beyond the basic account type that we discuss in this chapter. Then in Chapter 5 we will describe the way Internet service providers route you through the network, because like many people, you will want to understand how the Internet "works."

The Role of the Internet Service Provider

The first question many ask about the Internet is, "How do I get on?" This is the role of an Internet service provider (ISP), or Internet access provider, a company that sells access to the Internet. ISPs range in size from small companies that may be managed by one or two people, to medium-sized organizations that provide service in one or more cities or towns in Canada, to large national and multinational organizations. The latter group consists of companies such as iSTAR Internet, NETCOM, IBM, and Microsoft, which provide service across Canada and around the world, and major commercial on-line services such as CompuServe and America Online.

Many telephone and cable companies also provide access to the Internet. For example, there is a nationwide Internet access service called Sympatico, which is provided by Canada's major telephone companies such as BCTel, Bell Canada, and NBTel. There are even some newspapers that have become Internet access providers. In effect, there are many different types of organizations providing Internet access across Canada.

For our purposes, the definition of an ISP is simple: it is a company or organization that provides, for a fee or for free, access to all or part of the Internet. An ISP sells either accounts for use by individuals with modems or higher-speed "bulk access" through direct, permanent connections for use by individuals, companies, and other organizations. An ISP sells connectivity to the Internet. Consider what an ISP has put in place to get into the Internet business:

- It has bought the hardware and software necessary to support access to the Internet.
- It has purchased phone lines to accept inbound modem connections from individuals and companies.
- It has (hopefully) put in place a support system to take calls from customers.
- It has a billing and administrative system, used to charge customers for access to the system.
- It has hired staff to manage its services and has spent money promoting its services.

In other words, it has become a full-fledged business organization. Most importantly, an ISP has purchased one or more high-speed communication links to some other Internet service provider to support its connection to the rest of the world. Having done so, it has configured its computer system to access the rest of the Internet through use of what is known

CONNECTING TO THE INTERNET IN CANADA

1. To access the Internet, you need an Internet service provider — a company that will sell you access to the Internet.
2. As an individual, you can buy "dial-up" access to the Internet; as an organization, you can implement a full-time link to the network.
3. Up until the last few years, it was very challenging for people to join the Internet, from both a technical and logistical perspective.
4. It has become very simple to "plug into" the Internet today. In this chapter, we take a look at how five organizations have made it easy for anyone to sign on.
5. To use the Internet as we describe in this book, you should be using a computer that meets certain minimum specifications.
6. There are many things you should think about when considering how to choose an Internet service provider, including quality of service and support.
7. Many ISPs in Canada are struggling with reliability, technical support, service, and other problems.

as the Domain Name System and TCP/IP addressing, topics we cover in the next chapter. An ISP has plugged itself into the world and sells you the capability to use its connection. For now, do not worry about how all these ISPs plug together; that is the subject of the next chapter. Right now, we just want to give you an idea of where you can get access to the Internet.

ISPs Sell Expertise

Everyone always asks, when confronted with the Internet, "Where does the money go?" It goes to your ISP. In effect, what you are paying for when you buy your Internet account or high-speed Internet link is access to the equipment, knowledge, expertise, and support that the ISP has put in place. You are paying for the fact that your ISP has the technical staff who know how to configure their computers, routers, and software to support connectivity to every other Internet computer on the planet. Thus you are buying connectivity to every other individual and computer that make up the global Internet. Appendix G includes a detailed listing of ISPs in Canada. As you can see, there are quite a few of them right across the country.

The ISP Industry Is Constantly Changing

The ISP industry is perhaps the most volatile part of the Internet. We believe that the relationship you have with your ISP is as important as the one you have with your telephone company. It is important for you to understand how the industry is changing and to reflect on how these changes may affect you or your organization. Change is a constant in the Internet industry; we will focus on that topic a little more in Chapter 20. But consider for a moment what is going on with ISPs across Canada and, indeed, around the world:

- New players are entering the market. Newspapers, telephone companies, and cable companies across Canada are just some of the different types of companies that have entered the already crowded Internet access market, providing significant competition to the "established" players, organizations that have only been in the business three or four years themselves.
- The industry is consolidating. Many of the smaller ISPs are joining forces with other providers through mergers and alliances in order to compete more effectively against the television and cable companies. Even some of Canada's largest Internet providers have merged their operations in order to become stronger competitors in the industry.
- Internet access is becoming less expensive. Prices for Internet access keep dropping as competition becomes more intense. It is now possible to buy "flat rate" Internet access (i.e., unlimited access to the Internet for a flat monthly rate). Ongoing price cuts are causing severe margin and revenue pressures for many providers.
- Internet access is ubiquitous. With the introduction of the Sympatico Internet Service, run by Canada's provincial telephone companies, Internet access is now available virtually everywhere in Canada where basic telephone service exists.
- Internet access is easier than ever before. New software products are making it easier to sign up with an ISP and configure your computer for access to the Internet. This has made competition all that more intense.

- Internet access is more portable. Cellular telephone and paging companies are creating alliances with ISPs so that you can send and receive messages on the Internet when you are on the road.

What You Need to Buy

You should understand the two main types of Internet access that are available: casual (or temporary) dial-up access and dedicated (or full-time) access. Some ISPs sell only casual dial-up accounts, others sell only dedicated access, and many sell both. Other ISPs only sell Internet access to other ISPs, thus restricting their role to a particular segment of the industry. In this chapter we focus on what is involved in buying dial-up access to the Internet. We will take a closer look at dedicated access in Chapter 20.

Casual Dial-up Access

With casual (or temporary) dial-up access, you access the Internet using a "modem," a device that lets your PC "talk" to another computer. You join the Internet by purchasing a dial-up account with an ISP. The most popular type of account is called a SLIP or a PPP account. SLIP and PPP dial-up accounts are what most people use to access the Internet from home. They are also used by employees of companies and organizations that do not have a full-time link to the Internet.

A SLIP or PPP account will provide you with full access to the Internet and allow you to access electronic mail (discussed in Chapter 6), discussion groups (discussed in Chapter 11), and the World Wide Web (discussed in Chapter 7). When you obtain a SLIP or PPP account, you also have access to most of the other Internet services that we discuss in this book, including personalized news services, off-line Web readers, and audio and video.

Quite simply, SLIP and PPP have become the standard methods of access within the Internet industry. This means that when you call up an ISP and ask for an Internet account, they will almost always assume that you want a SLIP or PPP account. PPP is a better technology and is more common than SLIP, but you will find both types of accounts in use across Canada, and either technology should be sufficient for your purposes.

Once you have purchased your account, you can dial into the Internet when you like and use it at your leisure. With dial-up accounts you are only connected when you choose to be, and you only pay for the time you spend on-line.

Dedicated Full-time Access

Dedicated connections are generally used by organizations with many employees or by companies with large-scale Internet applications that require a fast connection to the Internet and want their employees to be "plugged into" the Internet at all times from their desktops. Dedicated connections are also used by organizations that want to set up and maintain their own World Wide Web sites (we discuss this in Chapter 14). A dedicated Internet connection is open all the time, 7 days a week, 24 hours a day. It can consist of a "dedicated high-speed line" or can simply be a

SLIP/PPP account that is "on" all the time. By using a dedicated connection, employees do not have to use a modem to dial into the Internet. They are always connected.

Dedicated access is definitely not recommended for individual Internet users, because it is prohibitively expensive and complicated — and often unnecessary. Unlike dial-up accounts, the cost of a dedicated Internet connection is not based on the amount of time that a person spends on-line, but is generally sold for a flat monthly rate. The faster the connection, the higher the cost.

Accessing the Internet in Canada

If you tried to join the Internet in 1993 or 1994, it was like trying to join a secret club. There were several dilemmas:

- It was difficult to get information about which companies actually sold access to the Internet, because the Internet was so new and no one was compiling that type of information. At that time there were very few ISPs in Canada, and of those that were in operation, most were based in metropolitan areas such as Toronto or Vancouver. Internet access was almost impossible to get if you did not live in a major city. At the beginning of 1994, when the first edition of the *Canadian Internet Handbook* was released, we counted just over 40 ISPs in Canada. Today, there are well over 400 companies, in every province and territory, many of them serving rural communities as well as big cities and towns.
- Aside from the few commercial organizations selling Internet access, universities, colleges, and research institutions were practically the only places where Internet access was available. Access was tightly controlled, however, and Internet accounts were generally only made available to staff, faculty members, and people undertaking special research projects that required use of the Internet. Unless you had a "connection" in a high place, it was virtually impossible to get an Internet account through any of these institutions.
- Another challenge was figuring out what you needed to actually link to the Internet. There were not many user manuals or other tools to help you sign on. Not only that, but there were few, if any, software packages available "off the shelf" that you could purchase to help you connect. Often, the only place this software could be found was on the Internet itself. Thus, if you were not already on the Internet, you were out of luck.
- If you were lucky enough to find a commercial ISP, the next challenge was to get help signing on. The problem was that many of these organizations were very small operations created by computer specialists. They were focused more on technical implementation rather than customer service and support, so they did not have a lot of friendly marketing information to help you understand the Internet and how to use it.

Still, some people managed to get over these hurdles and actually joined the Internet in the old days. Perhaps because of the challenges of the past, the perception painted by some is that getting on the Internet still remains a technical challenge, worthy of accomplishment by only the ultimate super-dweeb-cyber-punk-computer-hackers. Nothing could be farther from the truth.

Today, subscribing to the Internet is as easy as filling out a form on a computer screen, pressing a few buttons, and signing on. Most ISPs have become quite adept at the customer service and support game and have put together packages that contain everything you need to access and use the Internet. The result is that in most cases it should take you no more than a few minutes to get your link to the Internet working, assuming you have a fully functional PC or Macintosh, a modem, and a phone line.

What Type of Computer Do You Need?

If you plan on joining the Internet and using it in the way that we describe in this book, you must be using a computer that meets certain minimum specifications. Keep in mind that your local neighborhood computer geniuses might tell you that almost any computer can be used to access the Internet, and certainly they are right. Our recommendations are based on a certain philosophy: There are some things that you just should not do. Saying that any old computer can access the Internet is like saying that any four-wheeled vehicle can drive on a freeway, including the Crazy Coupe used by your kids or grandkids.

Here are our recommendations on buying a computer to use with the Internet:

- If you are thinking of purchasing a computer and can afford it, purchase the current top-of-the-line system; you will not regret it.
- If you cannot, buy as much computer as you can afford.
- If you must use an older, less powerful computer, recognize you will encounter limitations with your use of the Internet.

These are some pretty strongly worded recommendations, and many may accuse us of not recognizing that it is entirely possible to use the Internet with lower-end computer systems. Here we explain our suggestions.

First, the Internet is changing so quickly that even if you think you are spending too much on a computer today, you are probably not. The more bare-bones your computer, the shorter its lifespan. Two years ago, when one of the authors of this book bought a 486 computer with a 25 MHz processor and 450 megabytes (Mb) of disk storage space, he figured that would be sufficient for his Internet usage. Today, such a machine can barely keep up with some leading-edge Internet applications, some of which recommend, at a minimum, a Pentium computer (that is one step up from a 486 computer).

Many programs we review in this book require Windows 95, and the truth is that you need a pretty powerful computer to really use Windows 95 effectively. In addition, Internet applications are getting larger and larger, consuming more and more disk space, and requiring faster and faster processor speeds. The current versions of Netscape, which we mention throughout this book, have grown at least five or six times larger in disk space compared to the first version.

It is an undeniable rule that the evolution of the Internet will continually demand more and more computer power. Hence, if you make the investment in a fully featured computer today, you will save money in the long run, because you will not have to make as many upgrades to your computer over time, and you will hopefully be able to use most of the new Internet applications as they come onto the market.

The problem is this: it is difficult to look into the future and predict what type of computer you will need to make optimal use of the Internet at that time. The best advice we can give you is to invest in the best system you can afford. That way, it will not become obsolete so quickly.

Minimum Technical Specifications

Here are the minimum computer requirements you need to use the Internet as we describe in this book:

- Choose a computer than can run programs based on the Microsoft Windows/Windows 95 or Apple Macintosh operating systems, the basic set of programs that allow your computer to run. Why? Because the programs that we use throughout this book to use the Internet, such as Netscape Navigator, require the power and capabilities offered by these operating systems. Operating systems such as these usually come with the computer you purchase, that is, if you purchase an Apple Macintosh, it comes with the Macintosh operating system already installed.
- If you plan to use a computer based on Microsoft Windows or Windows 95, you should be using an IBM or compatible system with an 80486 or Pentium processor, at least 8 Mb of RAM, a VGA graphics adapter, and 100 Mb of free hard disk space. If purchasing a new computer, go for a Pentium; the 486 systems are just not worth the price. You can expect a base price of $1,000 to $1,500 for such a system. If you can afford 16 Mb or more of RAM, go for it; it will make a big improvement in the performance of your computer.
- If you plan on using an Apple Macintosh, you need a Power Macintosh or Macintosh computer. It must have a 68030 microprocessor or faster, the 68040; it must be running Macintosh operating system software version 7.5 or later; it must have 8 Mb of RAM and at least 21 Mb of hard disk space. You can expect a base price of about $2,000 for such a system.
- We recommend a 14,400 bps modem as a minimum. If you plan on buying a new one, go with a 28,800 bps modem. The modem is the device you use to link your computer to the Internet through your telephone lines. The baud rate is a close approximation of the speed at which your computer can get information from and send information to the Internet. The general rule of thumb is the faster the better.
- You need a phone line. You can use the phone line you already have in your home; you do not have to install a separate phone line unless, of course, excessive use of the Internet starts a lot of arguments in the home because no one can use the phone.
- There are all kinds of bells and whistles that you can add to your computer: speakers, microphones, CD ROMs, and more. We cannot hope to cover all the extra options here; for that, seek the guidance of your local computer whiz. Buy what you can afford. But remember, without speakers and multimedia capabilities, you cannot access audio and video on the Internet.

What is the best way to proceed when buying a computer? Keep the following Angus Reid statistic in mind: four of five Canadians on the Internet used the assistance of family or friends to help them to choose an Internet service provider. Seek the guidance of those same folks in your purchase of a computer.

Accessing the Internet

In this section we take a look at what is involved in signing on to the Internet through five different ISPs. We look at

- Internet Light and Power, an ISP in Toronto;
- iSTAR Internet, a national ISP;
- NETCOM Canada, a national ISP and subsidiary of NETCOM in the United States;
- AOL Canada, the Canadian arm of America Online, a large commercial on-line service;
- Sympatico, a national ISP operated by Canada's telephone companies.

Internet Light and Power

We will start our voyage by looking at Internet Light and Power, or, as it is known by its customers, ILAP. Toronto-based, it could be classified as a small ISP compared to the large-scale national ISPs such as iSTAR, NETCOM, and Sympatico. ILAP is proof that you do not have to be a huge organization to provide sophisticated, friendly, and easy-to-use Internet service with excellent customer support. Their solution to getting you on-line is their "kit": with your Internet subscription you get a kit that provides your link to the Internet as well as programs that you can use once you get on-line. They provide this kit for both Windows and Macintosh computers.

In terms of obtaining your connection to the Internet, it is a fairly straightforward process:

- You contact ILAP for an account and provide them with appropriate billing information.
- Once that is done, they ship to you their installation diskettes.

The installation routine itself is a model of simplicity. First, you choose which programs to install. They provide Netscape Navigator for the World Wide Web, Eudora for e-mail, NewsXpress for accessing USENET discussion groups, and Trumpet Winsock. (Trumpet is the software you use to dial in to the Internet from your computer.)

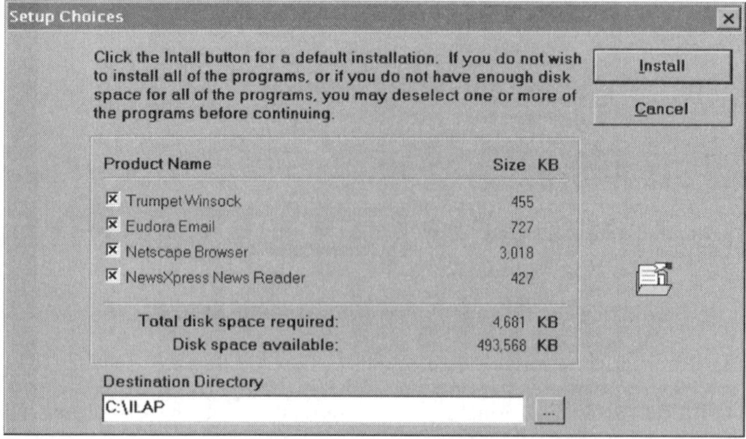

Once you have done that, you enter the account details that have been provided by ILAP:

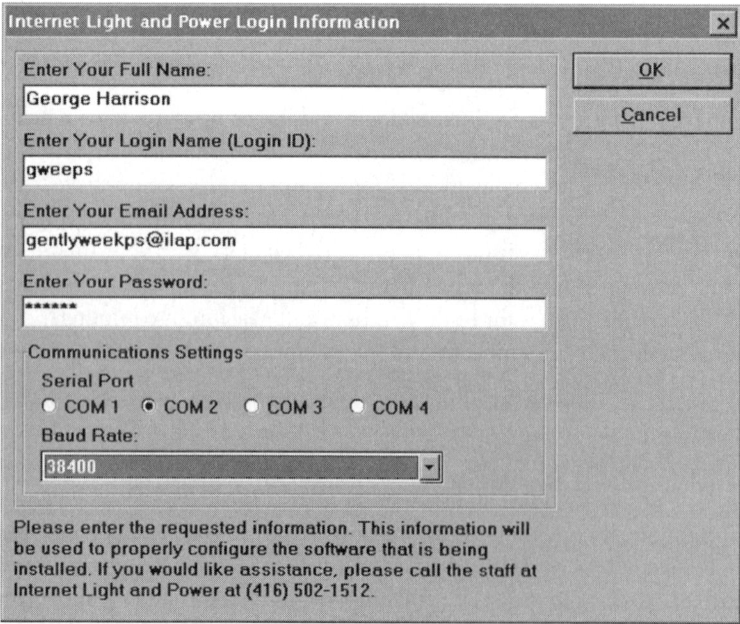

Seconds later, you load the Trumpet Winsock program, and you are linked into the Internet, at which point you could browse the Web, send or receive e-mail, and access USENET:

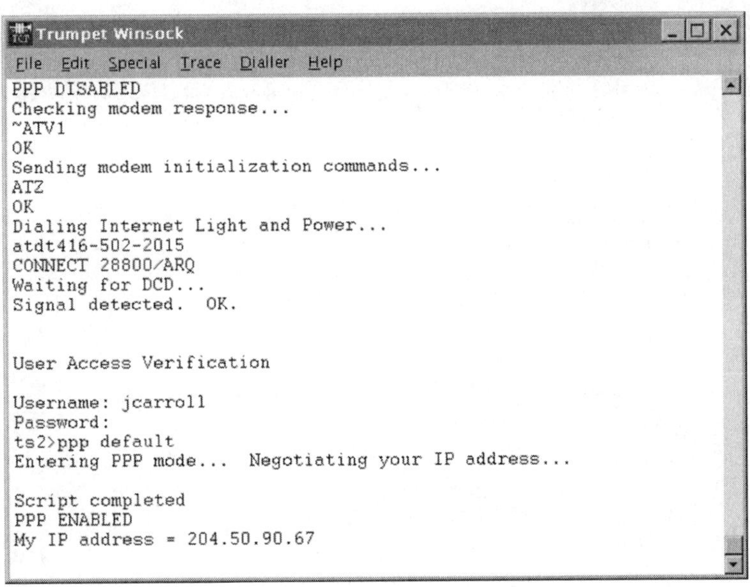

The elapsed time is perhaps a few minutes.

iSTAR Internet

iSTAR is one of Canada's largest national ISPs and is proof that big organizations can get it right when it comes to simple and straightforward Internet access. They make available their shrink-wrapped "Internet Access Kit" for users of Macintosh, Windows, and Windows 95 systems. The package features a fully functional version of Netscape as well as appropriate software to connect you to the Internet. Unlike ILAP, they do not provide a separate e-mail and USENET program, but suggest that you use the features within Netscape that support those activities. (You can still choose to use separate programs, such as those distributed by ILAP, since the beauty of the Internet is that once you are connected, you can mix and match the software you want to use to meet your needs. As we go through this book, we will describe where you can obtain much of that software on-line.)

Like ILAP, iSTAR requires that you first contact them through their toll-free number (1-888-Go-iSTAR) to arrange for an Internet account. You can provide your billing information over the phone. iSTAR will then generate a username and a password for you and mail their software package to you. Once you have received the software, the installation process is straightforward for all three of the above operating systems.

First, it copies the appropriate programs to your computer. Then you run the program to link into the Internet. On the Mac, a program known as "FreePPP" is used to establish the connection; the only thing you need to do is select the city in which you are located:

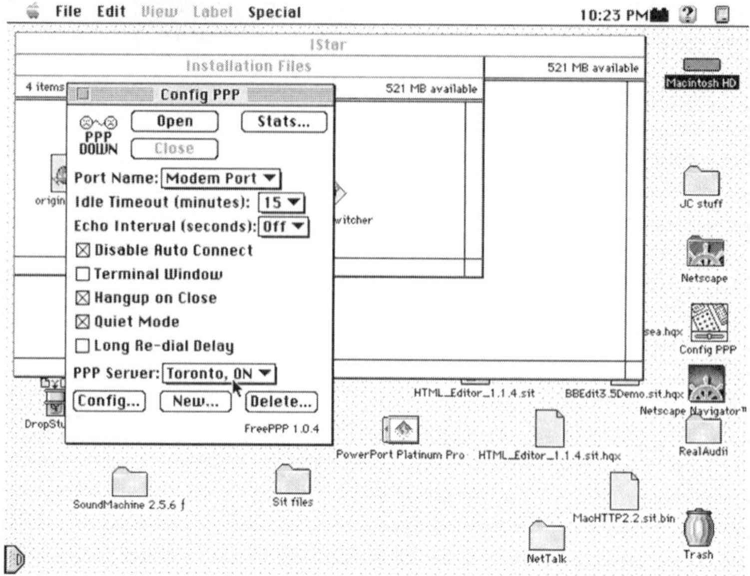

You then click on the open button to dial into iSTAR; if in Windows 95, you would click on the "Connect" button, as seen in the screen below:

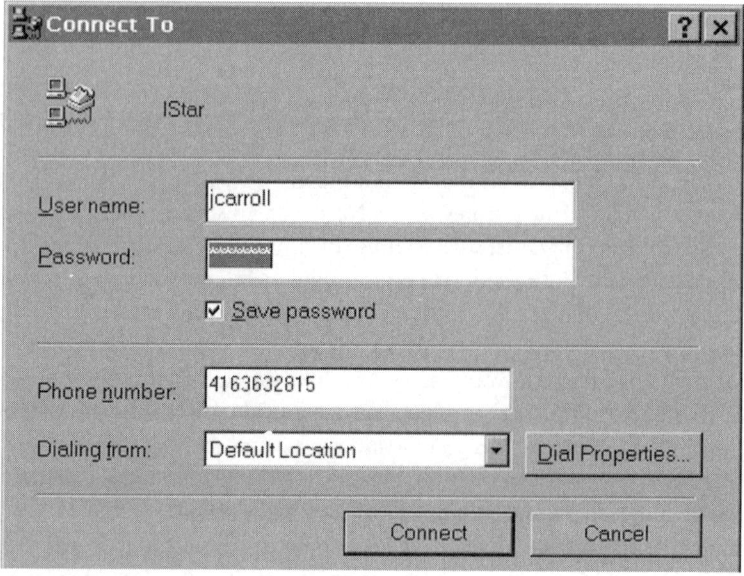

Once you have done that, you run Netscape and provide the program with your username and password, which you received during the telephone registration process. Then you are set to go. By providing Netscape to their new customers, iSTAR provides all you need to send and receive e-mail, participate in USENET news, and browse the World Wide Web. The time from start to finish, including installing the software and surfing the Web, is, once again, less than a few minutes.

NETCOM Canada

NETCOM Canada is a subsidiary of the large U.S.-based Internet provider NETCOM and provides access to the Internet in major cities right across Canada. NETCOM takes a different approach to the Internet: it provides users with its own special program to access the Internet, called NETCOM NetCruiser. The software provides electronic mail, a program to access USENET news, and its own Web browser. It is important to note that you are not restricted to this software; if you do not like NETCOM's Web browser, for example, you can use another Web program such as Netscape in conjunction with NetCruiser. You can obtain NetCruiser software by calling NETCOM Canada at 1-800-NETCOM-1. They will mail a copy to you. The software is available for both Windows and Macintosh computers.

NETCOM is very simple but differs from ILAP and iSTAR in that it provides for automatic, on-line sign-up to the Internet. Once you receive and install the software, it goes through a series of steps to configure itself for your computer.

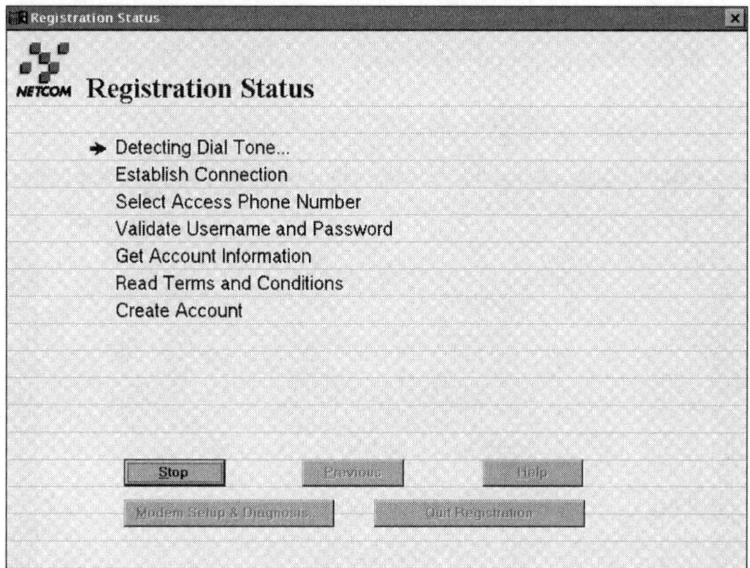

All you need to do at this point to get on-line is provide a valid credit card number. Once you do so, your Internet user ID is immediately created, once the NetCruiser software dials into NETCOM. During the installation process, NetCruiser will also offer to search your hard disk for any Internet programs you may already have and make these part of your NetCruiser setup:

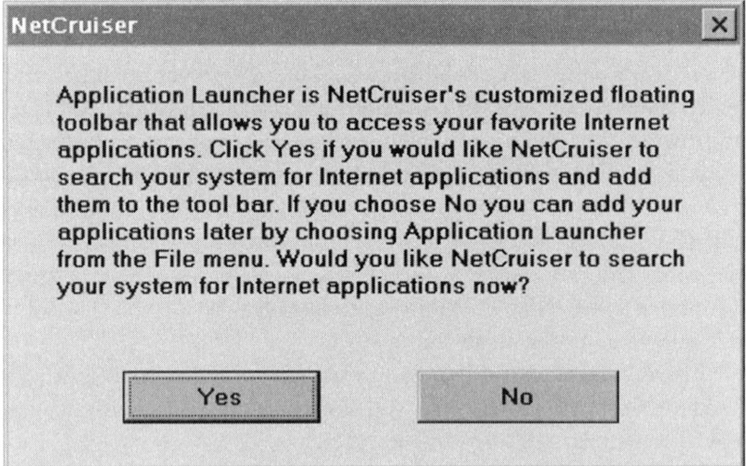

Once you are on-line, you are presented with the NetCruiser Web browser:

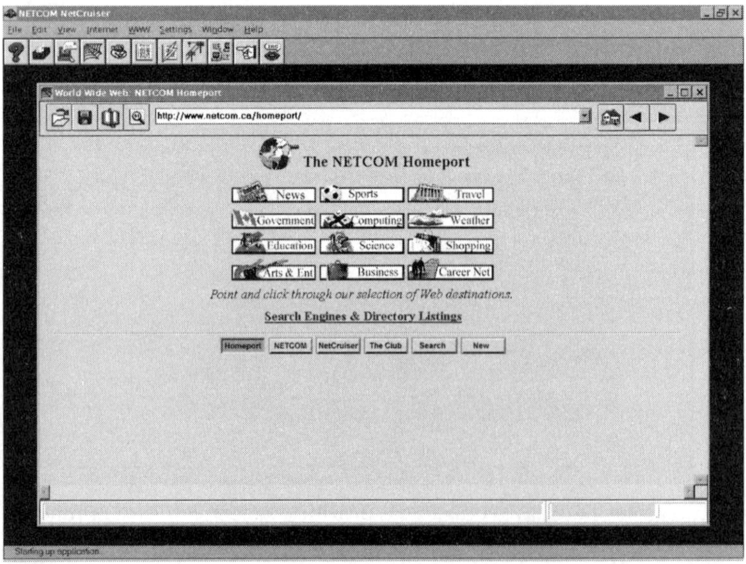

Once again, the elapsed time is no more than a few minutes.

AOL Canada

AOL Canada is the Canadian operation of America Online, one of the big commercial on-line services. In addition to Internet access, America Online provides access to a wide range of information services exclusively available to America Online subscribers. As with the three companies already discussed, signing on to America Online is a simple process. First, you call AOL Canada at 1-800-827-6364 and request their special software. It is available for both Macintosh and Windows computers. The software will be sent to you in the mail.

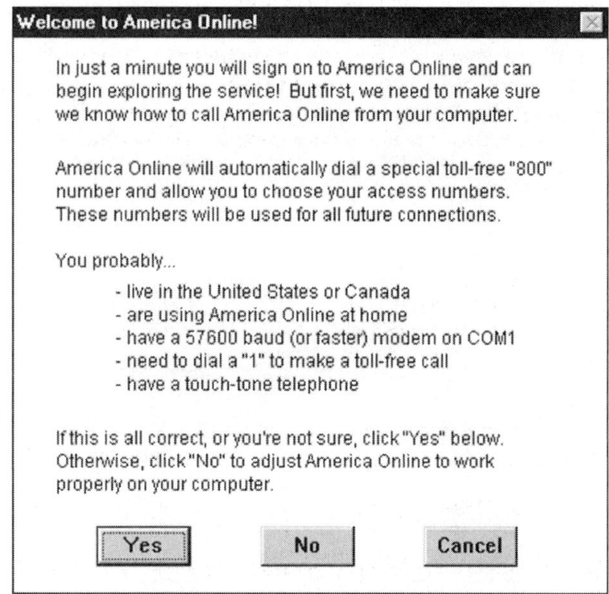

Once you receive the software and install it on your computer, you are ready to begin the registration process. America Online, like NETCOM, registers users on-line. First, your software will dial a special 1-800 line and help you find a local access telephone number:

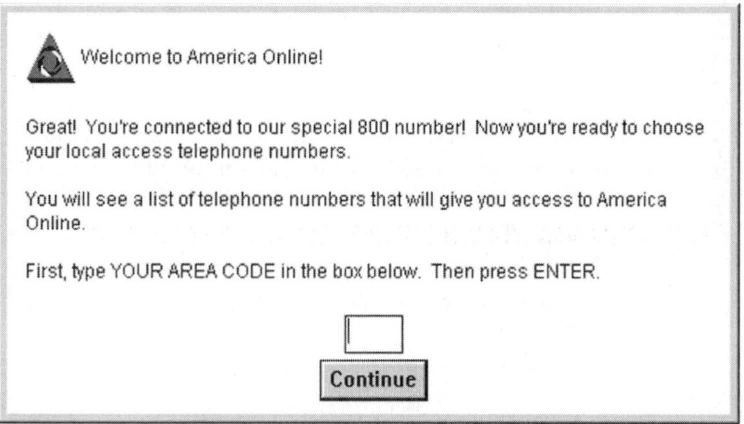

Next, AOL Canada will dial your local access number (the number you selected in the previous step). Once you are connected, you will be asked to type in the registration number and password that came with your software:

Welcome to America Online!

New Members:

Please locate the Registration Certificate that was included in your software kit and, in the space below, type the certificate number and certificate password as they appear on the printed certificate.

Existing Members:

If you already have an America Online account and are simply installing a new version of the software, type your existing Screen Name in the first field and Password in the second. This will update your account information automatically.

Note: Use the "tab" key to move from one field to another.

Certificate Number (or Screen Name):

Certificate Password (or Password) :

Cancel Continue

You will then be asked for personal information such as your name, mailing address, and telephone number. You will also need to supply a credit card number for billing purposes:

Please be sure to enter ALL of the following information accurately.

First Name: Rick **Last Name:** Broadhead

Address:

City: **State:**

Zip Code: **Daytime Phone:**

Country: UNITED STATES **Evening Phone:**

Note: Please enter phone numbers area code first, for example, 703-555-1212, and enter state with no periods, for example, VA for Virginia.

Cancel Continue

The last step is to select what AOL Canada calls a "screen name." This will be used to form your e-mail address. You can pick any name you like, as long as it is not in use by someone else:

Choosing a screen name

To choose a screen name, type the name in the box below and select "Continue". Keep in mind the following guidelines:

* The name must be at least 3 characters, but can be no longer than 10 characters.

* Names must begin with a letter, which will be capitalized, then any combination of letters, numbers, and/or spaces can be used, and will appear exactly as you enter them.

Cancel Continue

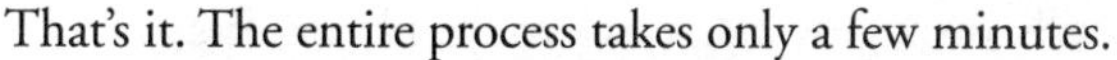

That's it. The entire process takes only a few minutes.

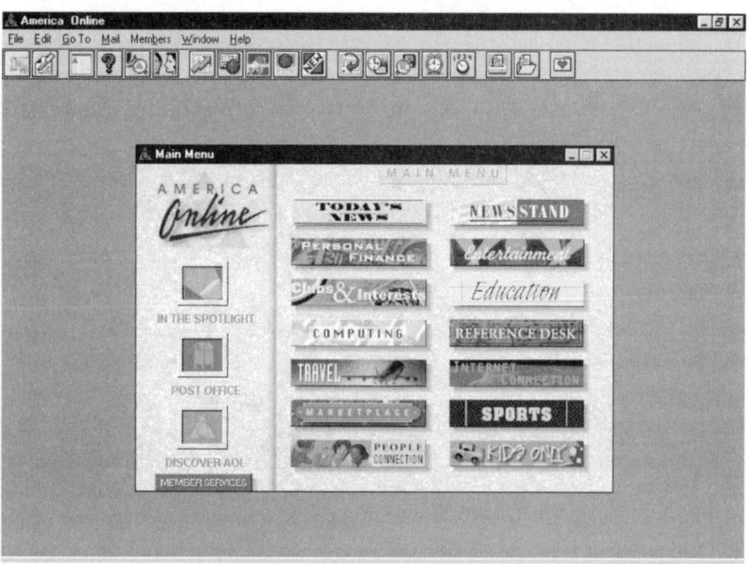

Sympatico

Finally, we come to Sympatico, the Internet offering from Canada's major telephone companies. Like iSTAR, the service is built around the Netscape Navigator program, and like NETCOM, it allows for immediate, automatic sign-up. It does so by using Netscape Registration Wizard, a program that helps you set up the software for your computer through which you can instantly obtain an Internet account. You can obtain a copy of the Sympatico software by calling Sympatico at 1-800-773-2121. It is available for both Macintosh and Windows computers:

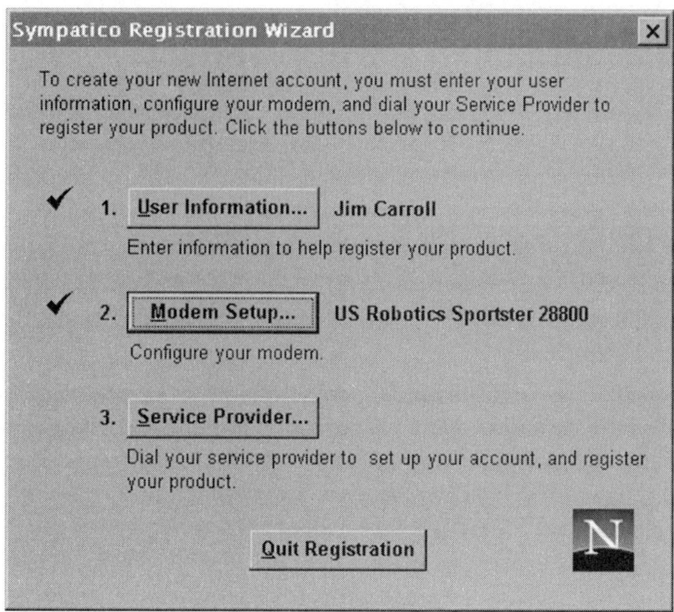

The registration takes place automatically through a direct link to the phone company. On the screen you provide your name, address, billing and credit card information:

Netscape - [Sympatico]

SympATico SYMPATICO™ SympATico

Serial Number

To register your **Sympatico** software you must enter your serial number. Your serial number is printed on the front of **Sympatico Setup Disk 1**.

Serial Number: 402992323438921100 *please use only the number keys to enter the number.

Click to continue

Personal Identifier

When you call Sympatico Member Services to request information about your account, you will be asked to provide your **Personal Identifier** before you receive any information.

Choose any personal word that you will easily remember and enter it below.

Personal Identifier: telephone

Click to continue

Address

Title: Mr. First Name: Alexander Graham Last Name: Bell

Company (if applicable): Private inventor

And that's it. Your account is immediately created and you are ready to go. Yes, we know — in less than a few minutes.

The point we are trying to make with all of these examples is that joining the Internet in Canada has become an almost trivial exercise. The process has greatly improved over the last few years. It should take most people no more than a few minutes, provided there are no special technical problems encountered (such as problems with your modem, phone line, or a computer with insufficient power).

How to Select an Internet Service Provider

Certainly, it has become very easy to join the Internet in Canada. So now the biggest issue for many is how to select an ISP. This is not always easy to do; it can be quite difficult to find a good, reliable ISP. And given the constant change within the Internet industry, it is possible that a good, solid, reliable provider can overnight become a disaster waiting to happen.

So the first thing that we think you should do is talk to people who are already on the Internet. Do not hesitate to ask around for references: friends, associates, and others who might be willing to share their experiences with you. Here is a checklist of some of the things to think about as you shop around for an ISP:

- Access lines. How many phone lines does the provider have in place to support connections from customers? Does the provider offer a no-busy-signal policy? (This means that they guarantee very few busy signals.) There is nothing more infuriating than dialing into the Internet and constantly getting a busy signal. Obviously, your best choice is an ISP that has a large pool of phone lines that are rarely, or never, busy.

- Roaming. To help make Internet access more portable for their subscribers, many ISPs have set up local telephone numbers for their service in many cities and towns across Canada. When you are traveling, you can use these numbers to access your Internet account without paying any long distance charges. This feature is called "roaming" and is supported by many of the large Internet providers that operate a national Internet service in Canada (such as iSTAR, Sympatico, and NETCOM Canada). "Roaming" will be of special interest to business travelers who want to be able to travel around the country and access their Internet account wherever they may be.

  If your travels frequently take you to the United States, you might want to look for an Internet provider that has roaming capability both in Canada and the United States. NETCOM Canada offers this service because of their affiliation with NETCOM in the United States. This means that you can use your NETCOM Canada account in most major U.S. cities without making a long distance telephone call. If you choose an ISP that does not offer this service, you will have to make a long distance call to connect to the Internet whenever you are outside of your local calling area.

- Speed of Internet connection. How fast is the ISP's connection to the rest of the Internet? In other words, what type of through-put do they support to the outside world? Are the links congested and slow? An ISP might proudly announce to the world that they have what is known as a "T1" connection to the Internet (1.544 Mbps), but it will not be of much use if they have so many customers accessing the Internet through that connection to such an extent that it is intolerably slow during certain times of the day.

  Another key issue is "redundancy." Does the provider have one link to the Internet, or two, or more? If you choose an ISP that has only one link, and that link goes down, you are out of luck until it is back up. Sometimes it does not make sense to do business with an organization that has a single point of failure.

- Quality of customer service. Ask around. Does the ISP have a reputation for poor customer service? How much help can you expect from them? Do they have a good support team? Is their staff knowledgeable? Do they have an on-line discussion group that you can read to determine if people are complaining about their service? Find out if you can take a tour of the provider's operations centre. Your best choice is a provider that acts, appears, and is professional at all times.

- Technical support. Does the provider offer technical support, and during what hours is technical support available? For example, what happens if you cannot get into your Internet account at 3:00 in the morning? Will technical support be available at that time, or would you have to wait until the next morning to get help? Some providers offer around-the-clock support for their customers.

- Cost. How much does the provider charge for an Internet account? Will you be charged per hour, or will you pay a flat fee for a certain number of hours per month? If the latter pricing structure is being used, what is the hourly charge beyond the maximum number of hours you are allotted per month? For example, if you pay $30.00 per month for 50 hours of on-line time, what happens when you go beyond 50 hours? Do they offer different plans, and are you allowed to switch pricing plans at any time? Can you pay on a monthly basis, or must you pay for a certain number of months up-front? Also ask if the provider has an "unlimited access" pricing plan. This type of pricing is becoming very popular across Canada; it means that the ISP provides unlimited access to the Internet for a flat monthly fee.

Keep in mind that your best choice is not necessarily the least expensive, taking into account the other factors outlined in this section. The pricing plan that is most suitable for you will depend upon your usage patterns. For example, if you expect to be a very heavy user of the Internet, you may want to search for an ISP that offers unlimited access to the Internet. On the other hand, if you expect your usage to be only a couple of hours per week, you will want to find a provider with a low-volume pricing plan.

Many ISPs have several pricing plans from which to choose. Find out if the provider will allow you to switch from one plan to another. For example, suppose you try out a package that includes 90 hours of access per month, and you later determine that your actual usage is much lower than that. How easy is it for you to change your account to a lower-volume pricing plan?

- Web sites. If you want to set up your own Web site, find out how much the provider will charge to maintain (host) a Web site. Are there different rates for personal and commercial pages (i.e., some providers charge more for Web pages if the Web site is being set up on behalf of a business)? Does the provider offer Web design services as well? In other words, can they help you design a World Wide Web site? If so, how much do they charge for design work? Many Canadian Internet providers include, as a bonus, a free basic Web page when you purchase an Internet account from them. By "basic" we mean the Web page is very limited: there are generally restrictions on what you can put on it and how much information you are allowed to display. Although these "free" home pages are extremely limited in their functionality, they can be useful for beginners and for experimental purposes. Find out if the provider offers free Web pages to its customers.

- Financial situation and track record. Is the provider financially stable, with a solid history in Internet services? How long has the provider been in business? Do they have sufficient resources to survive over the long term? What reputation does the company have in the local business community? Have the local media been reporting on the company? Have the reports been positive or negative?

- Alliances. Has the company made any alliances with other Internet providers or other companies to strengthen their competitive position in the industry? Is the company a member of any associations or industry groups such as the Canadian Association of Internet Providers?

- Customer base. How large is the provider's customer base? Do they have any "major" clients? This often speaks well in terms of the quality of service.

- Business experience. Who are the principals behind the firm? Do they have business experience, or is the company being run by technical wizards who have few business skills? If the principals of the company do not understand business fundamentals, how can they expect to keep the company afloat and respond to the needs of their customers?

- Business focus. What is the focus of the company? Do they classify themselves as a "corporate" Internet provider or a "consumer" Internet provider, or do they serve both markets equally? If you are seeking an Internet connection on behalf of an organization, you might be better off using an ISP that either specializes in or has dedicated specific resources to serving the business community.
- Ease of access. Does the provider offer easy-to-install software that helps you establish your connection to the Internet? Does the software come with a manual or other printed material to make your access easier?
- Range of services. Some providers offer more services and features than others. For example, does the provider allow e-mail forwarding in the event that you have multiple e-mail accounts and want to have all your messages redirected to a single account? How about mail vacationing? This is a handy feature that allows you to send an automatic message to anyone who sends you an e-mail message when you are on holidays or away from the office. iSTAR, for example, offers this service to their customers via the World Wide Web at **http://home.istar.ca**:

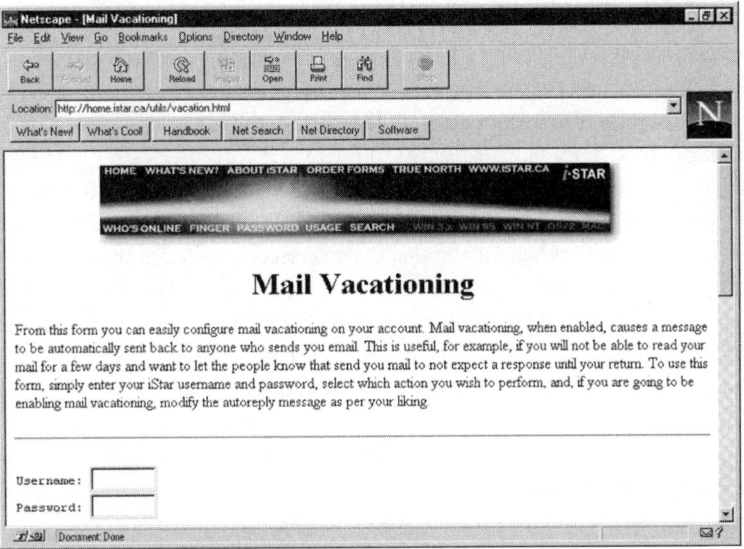

- Future. What are their plans for expansion? What new services do they plan to make available over the next six months to a year?

Taking the time to understand some of these issues will help you select the best possible vendor for your Internet requirements. Keep the following points in mind as you are making your decision:

- You could decide to purchase based on price and go with the lowest cost provider available and then discover that you get what you pay for. No support, no service, busy phone lines, and intense frustration. It might be inexpensive, but you will make up for it in time and effort.

- On the other hand, you could decide to purchase an account from a major national ISP and pay a premium on the theory that a big company provides excellent support. You may discover this theory is not true in practice.

It is difficult to find a happy medium. In the final analysis the best way to evaluate the performance and reliability of an Internet service provider, in addition to reviewing the checklist above, is through word of mouth. Speak to the people around you — your friends, family, and co-workers — to find out who they are using, but remember that everyone's experience with Internet providers will be different. It is not unusual to find someone who loves a particular Internet provider and then speak to someone else who despises the same company.

Many become frustrated with one Internet service provider and then switch to another, hoping for better service. Sooner or later the service deteriorates again, and the individual begins the search for yet another Internet provider. It is rare to find an ISP with which anyone is entirely happy. The bottom line is that no Internet provider will be perfect. It is an unrealistic expectation in an industry as turbulent as the Internet.

Should I Use a Commercial On-line Service?

As you shop around for an ISP, one of the questions you might ask yourself is this: "Should I use a company like CompuServe or America Online?" Commercial on-line services such as CompuServe and America Online were around long before the Internet became a mainstream business and consumer tool. They provided access to interactive forums, electronic messaging services, stock quotes, software files, databases, on-line shopping malls, and exclusive content provided by information suppliers such as broadcasters, newspapers, and special interest groups. By providing special access software to their customers, these services excelled at making on-line information "user-friendly" and easy to access. In most cases the content that you could find on these on-line services was not available anywhere else, since, in the early days, there was no competition from the Internet. The cost of accessing these services, however, was not inexpensive. In 1994, when the first edition of the *Canadian Internet Handbook* came out, the cost of an America Online account was U.S. $9.95 per month with an additional charge of U.S. $3.50 per hour if you used more than five hours in a month. There was also a whopping surcharge of U.S. $0.20 for every minute you stayed on-line.

Then along came the Internet. In the words of one investment analyst: "The Internet has thrown the on-line industry a curve ball." Although CompuServe and America Online have dropped their prices and they now provide their customers with full access to the Internet, many are questioning the value of using a large on-line commercial service such as CompuServe or America Online. There are a few reasons for this.

First, many of the services that used to be exclusive to large on-line commercial systems like CompuServe and America Online — stock quotes and news services, for example — can now be easily found on the Internet.

Second, many of the content providers that used to provide information exclusively on either CompuServe or America Online have now opened up their own Web sites on the Internet.

Third, both CompuServe and America Online now find themselves competing with hundreds of locally owned ISPs that offer access to the same types of on-line information that they do, but at significantly lower rates than they charge.

Despite these challenges, CompuServe and America Online still offer numerous benefits to prospective users, including an extremely friendly and well-organized user interface, local dial-up numbers in cities across North America (this means that you can access the Internet when you are traveling), and lots of local content in addition to Internet access. Prices are constantly fluctuating, so check with CompuServe and America Online for the latest information on their rates. If the price is right, and an easy-to-use visual interface is important to you, you really cannot go wrong.

What Can Go Wrong With an ISP?

In short, just about everything. As you try to decide on an ISP, you should be aware of the sorry state of the Internet industry in Canada. The good news is that we have an Internet industry. The bad news is that the Internet industry has a lot to learn about service and support.

If you watched Canadian television in the last few years in central Canada, you likely saw a commercial from Bell Canada in which the President and CEO indicated how they excel at providing the best possible customer support. He spoke eloquently about how customers were returning to Bell from other long distance providers due to the great service and support Bell provides. An interesting commercial and one that might certainly be believable, until one day, when the business telephone of one of the authors stopped working, and he was told that it would take until late the next day to send someone out to have a look at it. So much for great service and support.

Advertisements are wonderful, but they often do not speak the truth. Companies often promise wonderful customer service, but only if you happen to be a business big enough to warrant their attention do you get it. Sadly, the same type of problem exists within the Internet industry in Canada. Many ISPs are making loud promises that they provide only the best in service and support, yet fail to deliver. Talk to users of the Internet across Canada, and you will hear a litany of complaints and frustration. Stories of lengthy waits on hold when calling for customer assistance. Support calls that go unanswered, or support staff who are cranky, irritable, and lacking in manners, or who seem ready to tell the customer of their "stupidity." Of dropped Internet connections or unreliable connections. Of constant busy signals on both the dial-up line and customer support line. Of billing errors and problems. Of inconsistent and ever-changing usage policies.

Our perspective? While you might do all the right things in trying to choose an ISP, sooner or later you will regret your decision. We believe that you should clearly understand that as a user of the Internet, you should not come to expect the stellar customer service that you might receive in other industries. You should, in fact, expect that you will be infuriated, frustrated, and often angry. You will have to be prepared to accept mediocre customer service. We have experienced these frustrations ourselves. Consider what one of the authors went through in the space of two months:

- Inexplicably, early one Friday morning, his registered Internet domain (**jacc.com**) stopped working. Anyone sending e-mail to **jcarroll@jacc.com** or trying to connect to the Web site **http://www.jacc.com** received an error message. Any e-mail sent was automatically rejected or disappeared entirely. The situation continued into the weekend. Finally, on Sunday at 12:00 p.m., a call was made to the customer support desk of the provider. It was not until five hours later, after some complaints were made to the senior management of the organization, that someone finally tracked down the problem and fixed it. We never knew what it was. Strike one.

- A few weeks later the Toronto location of the organization disappeared off the Internet at 9:30 a.m. Although the modems answered the call, there was no access to e-mail, the Web, or any other type of Internet service at the provider. By 1:00 p.m. the recording on the customer technical support line reported that "we have identified the source of the problem and expect to have it fixed momentarily." But it was not until 9:30 p.m. that evening that the problem was fixed. The "official report" on the incident was that a wire was crossed at the company which provided the high-speed networking connection for the provider. And of course, promises were made that it would not happen again.

  The impact of a 12-hour disappearance? Not only were dial-up users of the service affected (including the authors), but entire Web sites of major organizations such as banks and financial organizations disappeared off the globe. Imagine being a big bank and seeing one of the tools that you use to provide customer service completely disappear for 12 hours. Strike two.

- Late one Friday afternoon, his e-mail account stopped working. He called the help line, and after a 15-minute wait on hold was told that someone would look into it. Of course, no one did. At 12:15 the following Sunday, he called the help desk. He again talked to a technical support representative (after a 25-minute wait on hold), who assured him that the problem would be fixed within the half hour. By 3:00 p.m., frustrated, he called back again, waited on hold for 35 minutes this time, and insisted that they look into the problem right away. He was assured that they would look into fixing the problem immediately.

  At 5:00 p.m. it still was not working, so he called the help line again only to be advised by the recording that the help line had shut down for the day. And of course, no one thought to call the customer to advise that they could not deal with the problem today. It was not until the next day at 10:45 a.m. that someone managed to solve the problem. Strike three.

Three events, within a month and a half, for one of Canada's largest Internet service providers. Such problems seem to be typical of many of the ISPs in Canada, regardless of their size. In fact, we do not want to single out one particular company with the example above, since most ISPs are guilty of having similar problems. Consider some of the events within the ISP industry throughout 1995 and 1996:

- Some ISPs began to disappear because of business or other problems. Internex Online, one of the largest (and one of the first) independent Internet service providers in Toronto, found itself unable to pay its telephone bill in late 1995. Bell Canada pulled the lines, and thousands of loyal customers found themselves without the ability to access e-mail, surf the Web, or do anything else on-line.

  Other providers across Canada have completely disappeared because of bankruptcy or other business problems. Similar situations have arisen in the United States. Remember, it is easy for anyone to create an Internet service provider, but it is inevitable that many will disappear as the ISP industry undergoes a shake-out. The chance always exists that a service that you have come to rely on could one day disappear.

- Network outages started to occur. Unfortunately, the incident we described above is not the only case in which a major ISP "completely disappeared." In the United States one of the largest dedicated ISPs in the world suffered a network outage in July 1995 that brought its entire national network down. Hundreds of thousands of customers found themselves without network access. In other cases e-mail systems supporting service for hundreds of thousands of people have suffered outages, resulting in lost mail or inordinate delays in the delivery of mail.
- ISPs started to rely on inadequate technical staff. There is not a lot of money to be made in the Internet business these days. Margins are razor thin, and price wars over the cost of providing access to the Internet rage. Many ISPs began cutting their operations and staff to the bone in 1996, with the result that many customer service departments have become short of staff and have inadequate resources to deal with the problems at hand.
- ISPs started to rely on inexperienced technical staff. The Internet is a highly complex technical topic, and the ability to resolve the many possible problems that might arise requires a highly skilled, very knowledgeable type of person. The reality is that many ISPs do not have or cannot afford the specialized expertise that is required and instead staff their help lines with individuals who have basic working knowledge of the Internet. Therefore, a lot of time is spent dealing with problems that are, in essence, trivial.

We have come to the conclusion that many of the ISPs in Canada — regardless of their size — provide only marginal support at best. It is our belief that notwithstanding their marketing claims, the entire issue of providing quality in terms of customer service and reliability of service seems to be but a concept to be attained one day in the future.

How to Decide?

Do not choose an ISP in haste; treat the decision with care, giving it an appropriate amount of consideration and thought. Do not let yourself be misled by unrealistic advertising claims. Above all, remember what we said earlier: you will never find a perfect Internet service provider. It is impossible for an ISP to guarantee that your Internet connection will never go down, just like it is impossible for your local hydro company to guarantee that your power will never go out.

Technical problems will inevitably occur. But when they do, it is important that you have chosen a provider that will deal with your problem promptly, efficiently, and politely. While there may be a valid explanation for a technical problem you encounter, there is certainly no excuse for poor service in dealing with that problem. We suggest that you talk with friends and family who are already using the Internet. Find out what provider they use, and ask them about the quality of service they receive. Word-of-mouth recommendations should weigh heavily in your final decision.

CHAPTER 5

How Does the Internet Work?

To paraphrase Arthur C. Clarke, any technology that is sufficiently advanced will appear to those unfamiliar with it as magic. This certainly seems to be the case with the Internet. Between the pooh-poohing and the pontificating lies a simple, understandable reality. Although a certain level of computer literacy is required to see it, many people's frustrations with the Internet stem from their belief that it is much more complicated than it really is.

Technopeasantry
Globe and Mail, February 8, 1995

When confronted with the concept of the Internet, most people first ask the question, "OK, so how does it work?"

Getting From Point A to Point B

It is funny that many people feel compelled to understand how the Internet works. Yet few of us have a strong desire to know how a telephone system works, or how our cable television network works, or how our can opener manages to open a can. We have come to take for granted the reliability of our telephone, electrical, and gas systems and other infrastructures across the land. And you should not have to worry about how the Internet works; you only need to be aware that it does (in most cases). It is truly a curious state of affairs; most of us are not interested in other *systems* that are part of our lives, but we do want to know how the Internet works. So, in this chapter, we will try to answer that question.

Telephone Protocols are the Heart of the Phone System

To begin explaining how the Internet works, consider the telephone system. You probably do not even give a second thought to telephone numbers. You simply pick up the telephone, punch in a number (unless you have an older rotary phone), and it connects to a telephone somewhere else in the world.

It is a massive system, the global telephone network. Today, you can pick up your telephone and dial any one of several hundred million telephones around the world. And when you call someone in Sydney, Australia, you do not think or worry about how the telephone system manages to figure out how to get from your telephone in Canada down to the one in Australia. You do not lose sleep wondering how the call is routed. In fact, you do not worry about whether the call goes via an undersea wire or an overhead satellite. All you care about is the fact that you can pick up the phone, dial a number, and the call is established within seconds.

Behind the scenes there is a system of amazing complexity. And what makes this global telephone network function correctly is agreement between many people and organizations on how this complex telephone system should function. The global telephone network works because of a common *protocol* and an accepted set of *standards*. These protocols and standards involve many things. They define, for example, the structure of telephone numbers, how telephone switches should connect, what the red wire and the green wire should do in your telephone handset, and how telephone systems can best figure out how to route a call anywhere in the world.

But we only see these standards in their simplest form. A North American telephone number, for example, of the form xxx-xxx-xxxx; the fact that you can call 604-555-1212 and get a long distance operator in British Columbia, and call 905-555-1212 and get a long distance operator in Ontario; the fact that 911 is being adopted as a standard emergency number and that 411 is directory assistance; the fact that England has the international code 44 and Canada and the United States share the code 1.

What makes the global telephone system work? Telephone companies around the world have agreed on standard methods on how they will interact. Conferences are held on a regular basis that deal with emerging technology issues. Special international committees and organizations such as the International Telecommunications Union deal with special technical standards. Technical specifications are agreed upon and are published for wide distribution. Telephone companies sign written contracts in which they agree to link to other telecommunications companies around the world.

All these activities provide the foundation for the global telephone network. Protocols, standards, and agreements are the foundation of the simple telephone number that we have come to know. And somehow, telephones just "work."

HOW DOES THE INTERNET WORK?

1. Computer protocols (accepted standards and interorganization agreements), primarily something known as TCP/IP (transmission control protocol/Internet protocol), are at the heart of the Internet.
2. The Domain Name Service (DNS) and IP figure out how to route you from your computer to another location/computer on the Internet.
3. Your seemingly simple link from your computer to another location on the Internet might actually take a long and convoluted route through the Internet.
4. Every computer directly linked to the global Internet has a unique "IP" address.
5. The domain Name System provides names to Internet computers and resources.
6. You can register your own corporate domain name either with a Canadian authority in the Canadian domain, with an international authority based in the United States, or in a more general domain.
7. Your choice of where to register will depend upon many issues.

Computer Protocols are the Heart of the Internet

A computer protocol is simply an agreed upon definition of how a particular piece of computer hardware or software should work. By having common protocols, hardware and software from different companies can still "talk" to each other. The Internet industry is no different than the global telephone industry: common protocols, accepted standards, and interorganization agreements determine how the Internet all fits together. These protocols define many things, including:

- how you link to a World Wide Web site in Australia from your dial-up connection in Iqaluit;
- how your e-mail message to the United Kingdom is routed from your dedicated Internet link in Halifax;
- how your USENET posting travels to most USENET sites around the world from your cable company connection in Kelowna;
- how you can be a unique name in the global Internet world.

There are many Internet protocols; we will take a look at a few of them in this chapter. We can by no means be comprehensive, nor can we cover these standards in a great deal of technical depth. Our objectives are to give you an idea of how the Internet works, and to raise some of the important issues related to your use of the Internet.

In this section we will take a step-by-step voyage, describing what it takes to get onto the Internet and how we can find ourselves traveling around the world. We will describe what happens in the background, within the Internet system, to make the Internet work.

TCP/IP

At the heart of the Internet is a common computer networking protocol called TCP/IP, which has quickly become the protocol used to link together millions of people and computers around the world through the Internet. *If TCP/IP is anything, it is the protocol that is defining how all the computers and computer-related devices in the world can eventually plug together. It is very, very significant for this reason.*

TCP/IP networking, and thus the technology and protocols that drive the Internet, involves many different components. TCP/IP in and of itself defines how computers can share information by turning that information into small, discrete chunks of information known as "packets." It essentially defines how different computers can share information through a wire.

There are many components that complement TCP/IP in addition to its basic hardware role of sharing information through a wire. For example, domain name servers exist throughout the Internet and know how to find and provide a route to computers and resources throughout the Internet. SMTP is the messaging, or electronic mail protocol, at the heart of many of the e-mail transfers that occur through the Internet. NNTP is a protocol that supports the distribution of information through USENET, a popular area of the Internet used for global "discussions." HTTP is a protocol that supports the exchange of information through the World Wide Web. There are many other such protocols that support some aspect of the Internet.

And these protocols are used regardless of how you might access the Internet. Today, most of us in Canada access the Internet using relatively slow modems, devices that permit our computer to link to other computers through the phone line. Some people in business, research, and educational organizations in Canada have what is known as "direct access" to the Internet, in that they have a full-time, "high-speed" link to the network from their corporate or organizational computer network to the Internet. And a very fortunate minority access the Internet at high speeds through the cable television wire that comes into their home. Regardless of how people are linked to the Internet, they are sharing the use of a common computer technology, or protocol.

What is happening through the global Internet is a quick adoption, by business, education, and government, of commonly accepted methods by which computers around the world can link together and by which information can be exchanged. Internet protocols are being adopted by computer hardware and software vendors around the world; developments in the computer industry are occurring at such speed that some people joke that six months in Internet years is like 20 human years.

An important thing to note about TCP/IP is that organizations are adopting it not only to link to the Internet, but as the foundation for their internal computer networks. As we wrote in our business strategy guide to the Internet, the *Canadian Internet Advantage*, "the Internet is important to anyone in business, government, or education, because it is the leading technology candidate to link all the computers in the world." In effect, we are seeing in the Internet the emergence of the first true standard to support global connectivity of computers.

Who Writes the Standards?

Any global cooperative effort of the size and scope of the Internet requires a high degree of coordination, standardization, and registration. The issue of the evolution of Internet standards is a complex one. There are many hundreds of organizations (including computing companies, research and educational organizations, government bodies, and corporations) and individuals involved around the world who debate, discuss, design, test, and implement the standards. The process is far beyond the scope of this book.

Suffice it to say that much of the design, debate, and discussion occurs through the Internet itself. For example, check the USENET newsgroup **comp.protocols.tcp-ip** for an ongoing discussion of issues related to the TCP/IP protocol.

There are also a number of organizations responsible for these activities, including the following:

- Internet Society, an organization dedicated to promoting the growth of the Internet. The key mission of the Society is "to provide assistance and support to groups involved in the use, operation and evolution of the Internet." Anyone can join the Internet Society. For a small fee you will receive a quarterly newsletter reporting on Internet issues; you can also participate in an on-line mailing list to which Internet news and developments are posted.
- Internet Architecture Board (IAB), an organization that coordinates research and development in Internet-related issues and standard setting for Internet activities. The IAB is responsible for the technical evolution of the network.
- Internet Engineering Task Force. A component of the IAB, this Task Force develops Internet standards for review by the IAB.
- The Internet Network Information Centre (InterNIC), run by AT&T and Network Solutions, Inc. InterNIC serves as a registrar for Internet domain names and network numbers and provides information and directory services concerning the Internet. If you want to register a domain name outside of the Canadian domain (as described below), you can do so through the InterNIC.

A good place to start exploring the world of Internet standards is the InterNIC at **http://www.internic.net** and the Internet Engineering Task Force at **http://www.ietf.cnri.reston.va.us**. A good source of information about Internet protocols and standards can be found at **http://netlab.itd.nrl.navy.mil/Internet.html**.

In Canada, organizations such as CA*net and the Canadian Association of Internet Providers (which we discuss below) are very involved in the standard-setting process as it might affect Canada. In addition, many Internet veterans within the Canadian academic community (many of whom have now migrated to commercial Internet service providers) remain very involved in all activities related to the Internet.

When you link to the Internet, you are using, in some way, TCP/IP and all the standards and protocols that make up the Internet. The extent to which you use these protocols depends upon the method used to link into the Internet. In most cases, these protocols work silently in the background, just as protocols work within the global telephone network, to route your requests for information and to move your e-mail around the world.

Internet Software

The next step in our voyage in understanding how the Internet works is to take a look at the software that you need to access the network. There are various technical methods through which you can establish a link to the Internet, each involving different types of communication software. We will go into those options in greater depth in a subsequent chapter. But basically, once you have an Internet account from an Internet service provider (ISP), to get onto the Internet you need, obviously, a computer, a modem (the faster the better), and communications software.

For now, since we want to concentrate on how the Internet works rather than how to get connected, we will make use of the most common type of Internet connection, a dial-up SLIP/PPP account.[1] This is a special type of TCP/IP connection that lets you link directly to the Internet using a dial-up modem. Hence your computer starts to talk TCP/IP and can *talk* to all the other computers in the world talking TCP/IP that are linked into the Internet. To use such an account, you will need communications software that supports a SLIP/PPP connection and software to support popular Internet services such as e-mail, the World Wide Web, and USENET.

You can buy such software in computer stores; products such as Internet in a Box, Quarterdecks' Internet Suite, Netscape's Personal Edition, and many others are available. For our example, we will use the services and software of InfoRamp, an ISP that sells access in the Metropolitan Toronto area.[2] They are part of i*STAR, one of Canada's largest Internet service providers.

Many providers provide software kits used to establish your SLIP/PPP connection to the Internet. InfoRamp, like many ISPs across Canada, provides new users with a kit that contains Netscape Navigator, which provides access to e-mail, USENET, and the World Wide Web. They provide this software for Windows, Windows 95, and Macintosh Systems.

---

1. SLIP and PPP are two different but very similar methods of establishing a link to the Internet using a modem. We describe in Chapter 4 what is involved in using such an account.
2. At this time, there are over 50 such providers who sell some type of access in Metro Toronto, compared to only 10 a few years ago, an indication of the rapid rate at which the Internet is growing.

Establishing a Connection

Now that you have software to link you into the Internet, you need to access a provider. To establish our link to the Internet, we run a program that establishes the modem connection to the InfoRamp Internet service. In our example, we are using Windows 95, which has been configured to connect to the provider we are using, InfoRamp. Once the connection has been established, our screen looks like this:

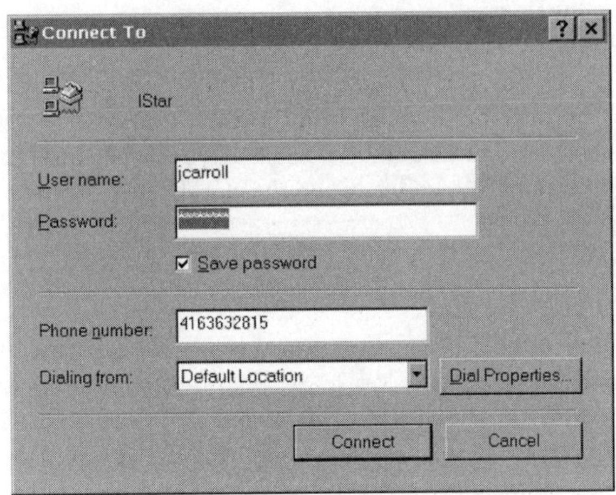

Some systems are configured so that all you have to do is run Netscape Navigator, your program to browse the Web. This will automatically start the program that connects you to the Internet.

In effect, our personal computer dialed InfoRamp through our modem and established a connection to a modem at InfoRamp. Once it had done so, it provided our username and password. Finally, InfoRamp provided us with an "IP address," which establishes us as a computer that is directly attached to the Internet.

At this point, we are connected to the Internet, we are running the TCP/IP protocol on our own computer, and we can begin to use other software to access popular Internet services. We could choose to use electronic mail, USENET, the World Wide Web, or any other Internet service using the Netscape software that InfoRamp has provided to us.

Traveling Through the Web

Now that we have our PPP connection to the Internet, we will access one of the areas on the Internet, the World Wide Web, using a "browser," in our case with the popular software program Netscape, to help you understand how the Internet works.

Say we want to use Netscape to get to the World Wide Web site of the Royal Bank of Canada. We load the Netscape software into our PC, and since we know the address is

http://www.royalbank.com, we key this into the location box of the Netscape software.[3] Within seconds we are taken to the introductory page (or "home page") of the Royal Bank Web site:

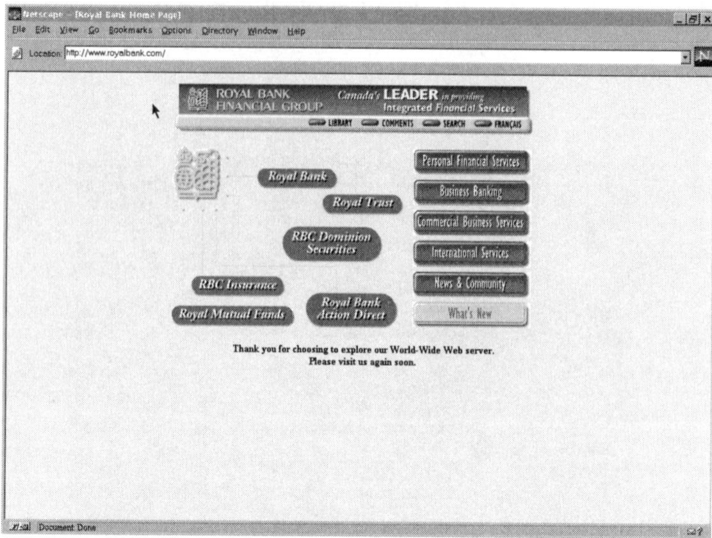

Voilà! The magic of the Internet, and the TCP/IP and other protocols that drive it, permitted us to connect directly from our PC to the Royal Bank.

How did the InfoRamp system know how to get us there? What route did it take through the Internet? Who and what was involved? These are the types of questions that many new users want to know, so to put the Internet into perspective, we will take apart our journey to the Royal Bank.

Domain Name System

The Domain Name System (DNS), part of the Internet protocol, determines how to establish a link from one computer to another on the Internet. Individuals do not interact with the DNS; it is the Internet software that interacts with it. We describe it here simply to help you in your quest to understand how the Internet works.

Essentially, in its simplest form, the DNS is a large, globally distributed database found throughout the Internet that provides a "route" to each company or organization on the Internet. When we indicate to our software that we want to go somewhere, it is the DNS that figures out how to get there.

To find out what happens when we indicate we want to use Netscape to go to the Royal Bank World Wide Web site, we used another program, called Trumpet Winsock, to dial into i*STAR. This program has a "trace" command so that we can see the query that it makes of the domain name server at i*STAR:

---

3. Later in this book we will talk about some of the methods to use to locate particular companies and information resources on the Internet.

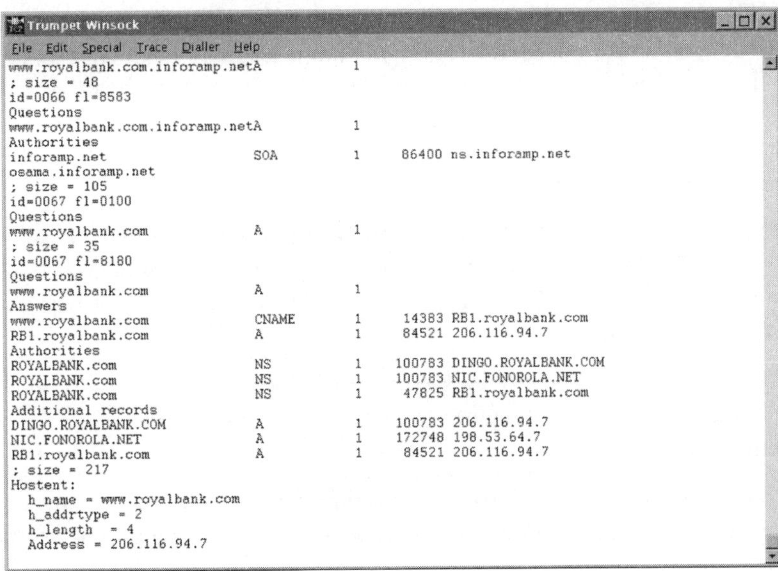
Trumpet Winsock
File Edit Special Trace Dialler Help
www.royalbank.com.inforamp.netA 1
; size = 48
id=0066 fl=8583
Questions
www.royalbank.com.inforamp.netA 1
Authorities
inforamp.net SOA 1 86400 ns.inforamp.net
osama.inforamp.net
; size = 105
id=0067 fl=0100
Questions
www.royalbank.com A 1
; size = 35
id=0067 fl=8180
Questions
www.royalbank.com A 1
Answers
www.royalbank.com CNAME 1 14383 RB1.royalbank.com
RB1.royalbank.com A 1 84521 206.116.94.7
Authorities
ROYALBANK.com NS 1 100783 DINGO.ROYALBANK.COM
ROYALBANK.com NS 1 100783 NIC.FONOROLA.NET
ROYALBANK.com NS 1 47825 RB1.royalbank.com
Additional records
DINGO.ROYALBANK.COM A 1 100783 206.116.94.7
NIC.FONOROLA.NET A 1 172748 198.53.64.7
RB1.royalbank.com A 1 84521 206.116.94.7
; size = 217
Hostent:
h_name = www.royalbank.com
h_addrtype = 2
h_length = 4
Address = 206.116.94.7

On the screen above we can see the Trumpet Winsock software asking the DNS "where is **www.royalbank.com**?" The DNS responds that the bank can be found at the "IP address" **206.116.94.7**, which is itself found via the **NIC.FONOROLA.NET** system. It also tells us that the **NIC.FONOROLA.NET** system can be found at the address **198.53.64.7**.

In effect, the DNS has told our system how to get to the system at the Royal Bank from our account at InfoRamp. It has told our system the route that we will take. Many voyages through the Internet are not direct, but take a number of steps to get from point A to point B. We can now take a look at the exact route taken in this case.

Traceroute

We do so using a UNIX command, "traceroute,"[4] or by using a program that can access the traceroute command. We are provided with the following detail from the traceroute command:

```
jcarroll@diane:[jcarroll] 23>traceroute www.royalbank.com
traceroute to www.royalbank.com (206.116.94.7), 30 hops max, 40 byte
packets
1 InfoRamp-fONOROLA.InfoRamp.Net (198.53.144.1) 5 ms 91 ms 10 ms
2 border3.toronto.i*star.net (198.53.252.3) 6 ms 3 ms 3 ms
3 royalbank-gw.Toronto.i*star.net (198.53.33.230) 5 ms 5 ms 5 ms
4 RB1.royalbank.com (206.116.94.7) 5 ms 4 ms 4 ms
jcarroll@diane:[jcarroll] 24>
```

4. Traceroute is a UNIX command that tells us the route that we have taken when traveling from the InfoRamp Internet service to another location on the Internet and thus helps us to understand where we are traveling in order to get there. Most users do not need to know how to use traceroute (and many will not have access to the command), but it is a fun way to take a look at how the Internet works. At a UNIX prompt in our InfoRamp account, we can simply key **traceroute www.royalbank.com** to get a snapshot of the route that we took from InfoRamp to get to the Royal Bank.

What does this tell us? Quite a bit. The information shows us the computers and hardware devices known as "routers" that we traveled through in order to get from InfoRamp to the Royal Bank. (Each step is counted as a hop, and as a general rule of thumb, the fewer hops the better, since it means the route is shorter and will happen quicker.)

Using the example above, we can put into perspective what happened when we keyed **www.royalbank.com** within Netscape:

- Our traceroute command showed that we started out at a computer at InfoRamp with the TCP/IP address 198.53.144.1. It took 5 milliseconds to get there. (The other two columns are the time it took for a second and a third try, that is, traceroute tries each step three times.)
- We then traveled through a few systems at i*STAR (a few milliseconds in all) and then went directly to a computer at the Royal Bank of Canada (another 5 milliseconds).

The time on the right of each "hop" represents the time that it took to get from the previous hop to that hop and is measured in milliseconds. Thus it took us 21 milliseconds to travel to the Royal Bank.

What is also apparent to us from this example is that the Royal Bank has purchased its link to the Internet from the ISP i*STAR. This means that we have made a very straightforward link from our computer directly to the Royal Bank system.

We can also take a look at the traceroute detail using a program called Trumpet Hop Check. In this case, the times are about 100 times higher than when we used the traceroute command above:

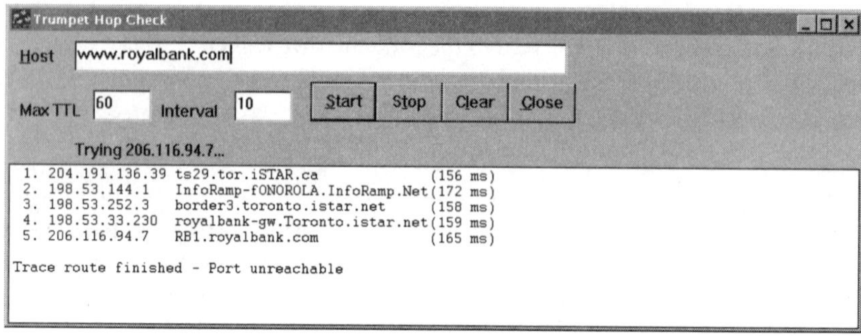

The reason it takes longer in this case is technically complex, but in a nutshell,

- When we used the traceroute command directly above, we were "closer" to the Internet, since we were using a computer at InfoRamp as the starting point.
- When we were using Trumpet Hop Check, we were a little farther away from the Internet, since we were using our own PC as the starting point.

Our modem link has slowed us down just a touch (i.e., 100 milliseconds, which is really not a big deal in the Internet).

Things Get Complicated

There are many ISPs in Canada, and thus our route is often not as direct as in the example above. For example, say we want to travel from our InfoRamp account over to the Canadian Airlines Web site (**http://www.cdnair.ca**). Once again, the DNS is queried, and a path is provided from InfoRamp over to Canadian Airlines in Vancouver. Taking a look at our traceroute results, we can see that the route was a little bit more complex :

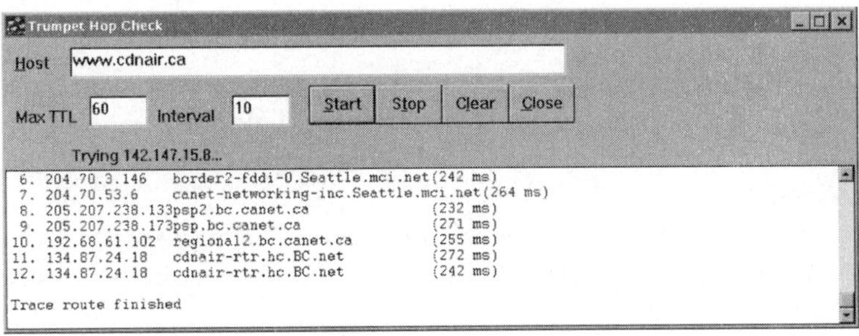

Interpreting this, we can see that Canadian Airlines has linked a computer located in Vancouver to the Internet through BC*Net, a major provider of Internet services in British Columbia. We can also see the path that we took, starting at the sixth step after Inforamp linked to a U.S. service, MCI. From there it linked to the CA*net backbone, which is the major Internet backbone in Canada today. CA*net routed us to one of its member organizations, BC*Net, and from there to Canadian Airlines.

Things Get Really Complicated

So far, both of our examples have involved some fairly straightforward connections from our account at InfoRamp over to another company, through one or more Canadian ISPs. But sometimes the route gets quite complicated, and you might not even be aware of it, particularly when you travel to sites outside Canada. For example, let's go to the primary site for information about

Singapore (**http://www.sg**). Running traceroute shows an almost completely different story compared to the examples we have had so far:

```
jcarroll@diane:[jcarroll] 28>traceroute www.sg
traceroute to www.sg (192.169.33.155), 30 hops max, 40 byte packets
1 InfoRamp-fONOROLA.InfoRamp.Net (198.53.144.1) 4 ms 50 ms 2 ms
2 border5-hssi1-0.WestOrange.mci.net (204.70.69.5) 18 ms 19 ms 19 ms
3 core2-fddi-0.WestOrange.mci.net (204.70.64.49) 19 ms 26 ms 20 ms
4 core1-hssi-4.NewYork.mci.net (204.70.1.97) 21 ms 37 ms 24 ms
5 border2-fddi-0.NewYork.mci.net (204.70.3.18) 112 ms 28 ms 202 ms
6 jvncnet-ges-ds3.NewYork.mci.net (204.70.45.10) 23 ms 23 ms 120 ms
7 waters-ser1/6.jvnc.net (130.94.45.249) 33 ms 33 ms 58 ms
8 ness-ser4.jvnc.net (130.94.17.250) 49 ms 57 ms 48 ms
9 goldengate-ser8.jvnc.net (130.94.15.65) 102 ms 106 ms 121 ms
10  technet-t1.jvnc.net (130.94.15.42) 310 ms 333 ms 311 ms
11  192.169.34.17 (192.169.34.17) 325 ms 328 ms 344 ms
12  www.sg (192.169.33.155) 2302 ms 308 ms 335 ms
jcarroll@diane:[jcarroll] 29>
```

In this case, something different happened: our link went south to the United States!

What the traceroute command shows is that InfoRamp linked to a system at MCI. It actually went through New York and then to an organization known as **jvnc.net.** From there it linked to a computer in Singapore.

The key in this case is that several ISPs all over the world are agreeing to exchange traffic. Behind the scenes, the DNS is operating as a massively distributed database, defining the route that should be taken in this case.

What to Keep in Mind

As a user of the Internet, you do not have to worry about such routing details. Your Internet software and the Internet service provider take care of the routing for you. All you need to know is the Internet address that you are trying to reach.

What is significant about the Internet is that the many thousands of organizations and millions of individuals involved have all agreed to use the TCP/IP and related protocols. Hence i*STAR has agreed to exchange information with other Internet service providers in the routing of your simple World Wide Web request. It really is no different from the global telephone companies agreeing to route telephone calls.

Many people ask, "Who owns the Internet?" This is like asking "Who owns the global telephone system?" No one does. There is no big, global, giant telephone company. Instead, there are several thousand telephone companies, all of which have agreed to work together to exchange telephone calls according to common protocols and standards. The Internet is no different. There is no big, global, giant Internet company. Instead, there are several thousand Internet companies, all of which have agreed to work together to exchange Internet connections according to common protocols and standards.

And the fascinating thing is that much of this Internet information is routed through the telecommunication networks of the telephone companies in the first place. As noted by *The Economist*, "The Internet's builders laid no cables and dug no trenches; they simply leased existing telephone lines."[5] Later in the article, the publication notes that "equally, it was not the telephone companies that built the Internet, although it uses their networks. They carry its data for a fee, just as they carry data from thousands of other sources. The companies that lease this capacity to bring the Internet to users around the world are mostly newcomers: Performance Systems International, Netcom, Pipeline, UUNet, Demon, Pipex. America alone has more than 600 of them. Almost all of them are under five years old." And as we noted in our previous chapter about ISPs, there are now well over 300 of them in Canada, including many of the major telephone companies who have finally come to realize the significance of the Internet.

In other words, the Internet runs through global telecommunication networks, mostly those of telephone companies, but really is a *separate system within that telephone system.*

What Is Next?

You do have some learning to do. Going back to our telephone analogy: you have learned to talk on the telephone, you have learned how to use voice mail, and you have learned how to call directory assistance on occasion. But you have not had to learn how telephone companies program their telephone switches. You trust it — it works.

In the same way, you will have to learn how to use your Internet software, how to obtain the addresses of companies on the Internet (e.g., **http://www.cbc.ca**), and how to navigate your way around an absolutely massive information network. But you will not have to learn how the ISPs program their systems or keep their domain name servers up-to-date, nor do you have to worry about how Netscape knows how to get from your computer to the CBC. Trust it — it works.

In the next two sections, we will take a look at the basics of TCP/IP addressing and the Domain Name System, since you will need some familiarity with these standards as you begin to use the Internet.

TCP/IP Basics

TCP/IP stands for transmission control protocol/Internet protocol. Every computer that is directly attached to the Internet has an IP address associated with it. IP addresses consist of four sets of numbers separated by periods. For example, the particular computer that has the Royal Bank's World Wide Web site has the IP address **206.116.94.7**. The address is unique throughout the Internet world and is used by individuals and by Internet applications to reach particular Internet applications on that computer at the Royal Bank. Think of an IP address as being the Internet equivalent to a telephone number, since it refers to the address of a specific computer on the Internet.

---

5. The Accidental Superhighway, *The Economist*, July 7, 1995.

However, you do not normally need to use IP addresses, since you can use domain names instead. Since people often remember names better than numbers, the people involved in the Internet came up with the Domain Name System. This permits each computer (referred to as a "host") on the Internet to be reached by a simple name rather than just by IP addresses. It is like using 1-800-GO-FEDEX instead of using 1-800-463-3339.

Internet applications such as the World Wide Web or FTP can be used with either an IP address or Domain Name System to reach a particular computer. Only in rare cases, however, is an IP address used instead of a domain name. In fact, you should always use the domain name to avoid any problems that might occur in case a particular Internet resource is moved from one computer to another, which results in a change to the IP address but not to the domain name.

An example of a name under the domain name system is **royalbank.com**, and to reach the World Wide Web site for the Royal Bank you would use **www.royalbank.com**.

Let's put this into perspective. To reach the Royal Bank on the Web, you could use the address **http://206.116.94.7**, or you could use the address **http://www.royalbank.com**.Try it! It is no wonder that people prefer to use the Domain Name System over IP addresses. The IP address and Domain Name System form the heart of the global Internet.

IP Addresses

The current IP numbering scheme allows for what are known as Class A, B, and C addresses. There is an upper limit on the number of potential A, B, and C addresses. Class A addresses (of which there are only 128) are allocated only to the largest organizations or networks in the world and are virtually impossible to get. Class B addresses are used by most large networks or organizations around the world, but new ones are not available to Canadian organizations due to a shortage of remaining available Class B addresses. Class C addresses are used by smaller or medium-sized organizations or networks and are the only addresses available to Canadian organizations that have not already obtained a TCP/IP address. In many cases, multiple Class C addresses are used by one organization.

How Do I Know if I Need an IP Address?

The decision whether you need your own IP address depends upon how you plan to access the Internet:

- If you plan on linking the computer networks in your organization "directly" to the Internet at some time, you will need an IP address. An IP address is fundamental to establishing this direct link, since it provides a unique identity for your network in the global Internet.
- If you plan on accessing the Internet through what is known as a SLIP/PPP account, you will need an IP address. However, this will usually be assigned to you automatically by your Internet service provider, and the software you use to access the Internet determines the TCP/IP address on your behalf. You do not need to obtain one on your own.

- If you access the Internet in any other way (i.e., through a bulletin board, through what is known as a "shell account," or through an "e-mail gateway"), you do not need an IP address. In this case, IP addresses will not be terribly important to you other than as a means of reaching certain Internet resources.

How Do I Get an IP Address if I Need One?

Until April 30, 1996, registered IP addresses in Canada were allocated from a group called the CA*Net IP Registry. However, with the increasing commercialization of the Internet in Canada, the Canadian Association of Internet Providers (CAIP) (**http://www.caip.ca**) began to take over many aspects of Internet administration issues in Canada. Hence for the most up-to-date information on how to obtain a registered IP address in Canada, contact the CAIP through their Web site. At this time, only Class C addresses are available for use in Canada.

Keep in mind that since there is an upper limit to the number of available IP addresses as mentioned above, and although solutions are in the works, the best advice is to plan ahead. Indeed, at one time, you could obtain sufficient Class C addresses for your organization in advance. Now, you must establish that you have a real need for such an address.

Internet Domain Names

Figures 5.1 and 5.2 give some examples of the registered names for several Canadian organizations. As we can see in Figure 5.1, several Canadian organizations have registered in what is known as the Canadian domain and have **.ca** at the end of their domain name. In Figure 5.2 we can see that a number of other Canadian organizations have domains ending in **.com**, **.org**, **.net**, **.edu**, and **.gov**.

FIGURE 5.1 Organizations in the "Canadian .ca Domain"

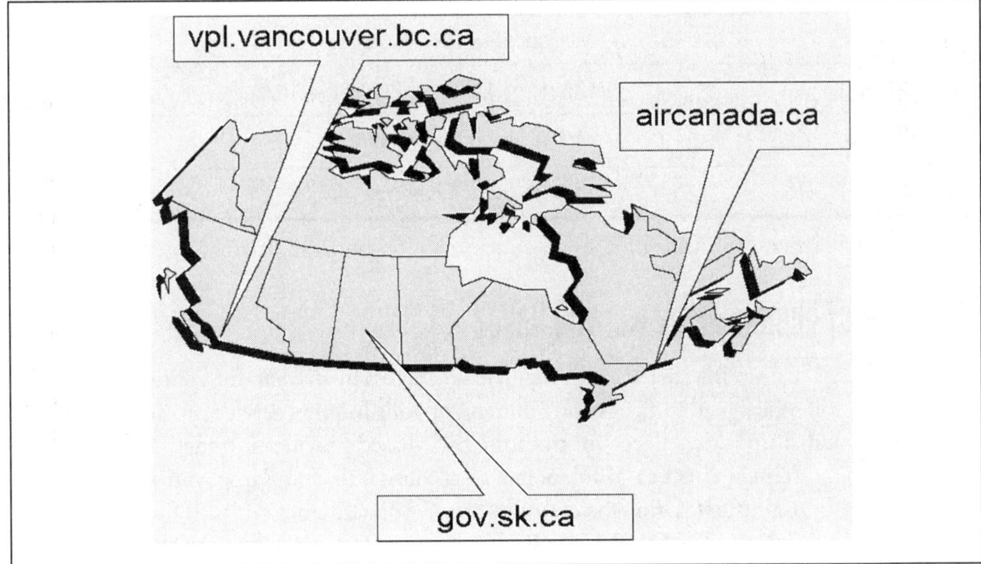

FIGURE 5.2 Organizations in the Top Level "Zone Names"

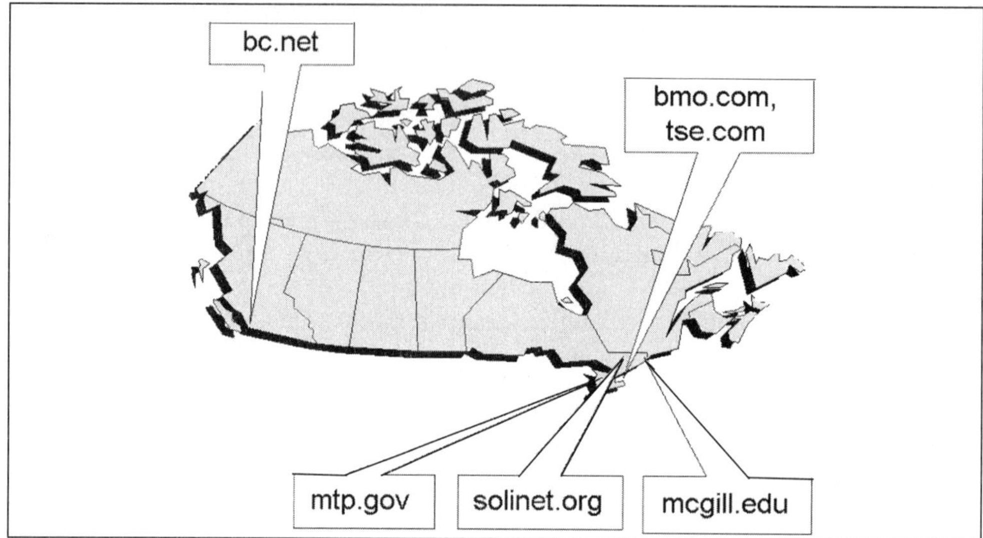

These organizations are listed in the table below:

DOMAIN NAME	ORGANIZATION
aircanada.ca	Air Canada
gov.sk.ca	Government of Saskatchewan
vpl.vancouver.bc.ca	Vancouver Public Library
bmo.com	Bank of Montreal
mtp.gov	Metropolitan Toronto Police
solinet.org	Canadian Union of Public Employees
mcgill.edu	McGill University, Montreal
tse.com	Toronto Stock Exchange

What Type of Domain Name Will You Have?

If you purchase a dial-up Internet account that you will access by modem for your own use, often your account will be assigned to the existing domain of your Internet service provider. For example, if you get a dial-up Internet account from the B.C.-based provider Internet Direct, you will be assigned to the domain **direct.ca**. If you obtain an account from InfoRamp, you will be assigned to the domain **inforamp.net**. Using the examples above, your Internet e-mail ID would look like **YOUR-NAME@direct.ca** or **YOUR-NAME@inforamp.net**, depending upon the provider you were using. **YOUR-NAME** will, of course, be replaced by your personal account name.

Your Own Domain Name

If you plan on linking your organization to the Internet, you can obtain an Internet domain name for your organization, usually for a small fee. This involves registering in either the Canadian domain or in one of the "descriptive zone names." You register for such a domain name through your Internet service provider.

You might want to have your own Internet domain name, primarily as a means of establishing to your customers, trading partners, business associates, or others, that you are serious about the role you plan to have the Internet play in your organization. In general, your own domain name helps to reinforce your corporate identity. It is easier for those doing business with you to remember how to reach you if you have your own domain name than if you simply exist under the domain name of an ISP. It also helps to protect your intellectual property.

Another good reason to have a domain name is that it is portable. For example, if you are **jsmith@provider.net** and decide to move to another Internet service provider, your e-mail address will change. If you are **jsmith@yourcompany.com**, you can take your domain name with you to your new provider, and hence your e-mail and Web addresses will not change.

Top Level Domains

As seen in Figures 5.1 and 5.2, at the extreme right of every Internet domain name is a top level domain, which is either a country code or a descriptive zone name. Country codes are two-character codes, as defined by the International Standards Organization. The country code for Canada is **.ca**. A list of country codes is included in Appendix D. Descriptive zone names include the categories shown in the table below:

ZONE NAMES	CATEGORIES
.com	Commercial, for-profit organizations.
.edu	Educational institutions or sites. New registrations are limited to colleges and universities with four-year programs.
.gov	Government institutions or sites. New registrations are limited to U.S. Federal Government departments.
.int	International organizations (e.g., NATO), established by international treaty or law.
.mil	U.S. military sites.
.net	Network organizations; most often used by organizations reselling Internet services.
.org	Other organizations, primarily not-for-profit.

Choosing Where to Register

The choice of whether your organization should register in the Canadian (**.ca**) domain or within one of the descriptive zone names as outlined above depends upon several factors, mostly having to do with the image your organization wishes to create with respect to its Internet domain name. If you wish to create an international image and do not necessarily wish to create an image of being a strictly Canadian organization, you would choose to register in one of the descriptive zone names. If, on the other hand, you mostly do business in Canada, you might choose to register in the Canadian domain. A few examples will help illustrate this:

- Delrina Corporation is a Toronto-based software company known internationally for its award-winning products, including WinFax Pro. Because Delrina has an international image as opposed to a strictly Canadian image, it chose to register as **delrina.com**.
- Air Canada does business around the world, but it wants to create the image that it is closely linked to its home base, Canada. As a result, it registered in the Canadian domain as **aircanada.ca**.

It is not just an issue of national or international image when it comes to registration. Looking at Figure 5.2, we can see that some organizations have registered outside of the **.ca** domain, when we might think they should have registered in the Canadian domain (e.g., McGill University, in the **.edu** domain).

Several Canadian organizations have chosen to register in the descriptive zone names for several reasons:

- Historical reasons. For example, several educational institutions registered in the **.edu** domain prior to the establishment of a Canadian (**.ca**) domain and have kept that domain name.
- It indicates the organization type. Some choose to register in the **.org** or **.gov** descriptive zone names instead of the Canadian domain name, because they believe it helps them indicate to the Internet community the type of organization they are. A commonly used zone name, **.net**, is used by many Internet service providers in Canada (e.g., **hookup.net**, **inforamp.net**).
- They could not register the name they wanted in the **.ca** domain. Some organizations chose to register in the descriptive zones because their proposed name was not accepted by the Canadian authorities. For example, the Addiction Research Foundation registered as **arf.org**, because the Canadian Domain Committee did not believe **arf.ca** to be an acceptable name.
- Frustration with the current Canadian Domain Name System. In particular, smaller organizations that are required to use provincial and municipal subdomains as described below often do not like the complex names that might arise, for example, **company.prince-rupert.bc.ca** versus **company.com**. As a result, some organizations turn to the InterNIC to register directly within a **.com** or **.org** domain.

When it comes to registration of a domain name on the Internet, diversity is certainly the watchword.

Registering Under the Canadian [.ca] Domain

Your organization is permitted only one registration under the **.ca** domain.[6] If your organization registers in the Canadian domain, your domain name might include provincial and municipal subdomains, depending upon the size and scope of your organization.

A company or organization name is also included. If the legal name of your organization includes both an English form and a French form, you may apply for a domain name for each form. For example, Consumers Distributing, the national chain of retail stores, has registered both **consumers.ca** and **dac.ca** (which stands for Distribution Aux Consommateurs Inc.). Similarly, the National Film Board of Canada has registered **nsb.ca** and **onf.ca** (the latter standing for Office National du Film du Canada).

Figure 5.1 shows examples of some organizations that have registered in the Canadian (or **.ca**) domain. The names used by two of the organizations use subdomains. In Canada, under the **.ca** domain, a geographically oriented subdomain hierarchy is used. This means the domain name that you can obtain will be determined by the scope or presence of your organization within Canada. Subdomains, when used, include

- a provincial code, for example, **.sk** for Saskatchewan in the example in Figure 5.1;
- a city or municipality name, for example, **.vancouver** in the example in Figure 5.1.

The following rules of guidance are used in determining what type of subdomain name an organization can obtain in Canada:

- If the organization is national in scope, that is, has presence in more than one province or is incorporated or chartered nationally, the name of the company is used with the .ca domain name. For example, Air Canada has the domain name **aircanada.ca**.
- If the organization owns a trademark that is registered with the Canadian Registrar of Trademarks and is being put forward in full as the organizational part of the subdomain name, the name of the trademark can appear within the domain name. For example, Teledirect Publications has registered **yellowpages.ca**.
- If the organization is based in only one province, but has multiple locations in the province, or is incorporated or registered provincially or territorially, the two-letter provincial or territorial abbreviation in the domain name is included (i.e., provincial or territorial governments, colleges, or universities). For example, the Government of Saskatchewan domain name is **gov.sk.ca**.
- If the organization is small and based in only one jurisdiction, the municipality name is included in the subdomain name. (Examples include local hospitals, libraries, municipal governments, small or local businesses, and schools.) For example, the Vancouver Public Library domain name is **vpl.vancouver.bc.ca**.

The codes in the table on the next page are used within Canadian subdomains for provinces and territories in Canada.

---

6. This was effective in 1995.

CODE	FOR ORGANIZATIONS REGISTERED IN
.ab.ca	Alberta
.bc.ca	British Columbia
.gc.ca	Government of Canada
.mb.ca	Manitoba
.nb.ca	New Brunswick
.nf.ca	Newfoundland
.ns.ca	Nova Scotia
.nt.ca	Northwest Territories
.nu.ca	Nunavut (possible)
.on.ca	Ontario
.pe.ca	Prince Edward Island
.qc.ca	Quebec
.sk.ca	Saskatchewan
.yk.ca	Yukon

Once Nunavut is carved out from the Northwest Territories as a new territory, it may be allocated the code **.nu**. In addition, there is a government domain, **gc.ca**, and a Canadian Government Domain Registrar, which handles all requests for Internet domains from Canadian government departments and agencies.[7]

You can find out the details of obtaining an address in the Canadian (**.ca**) domain at the Web site of the Canadian Association of Internet Providers (**http://www.caip.ca**). Registration requests from within the Government of Canada (**.gc**) domain are currently coordinated by the Government Telecommunications and Informatics Service in Ottawa. A listing of Canadian Government Internet domains can be found in Appendix F.

For Information on obtaining the Canadian (**.ca**) domain application form:

URL: **http://www.caip.ca** (Canadian Association of Internet Providers)

For information on obtaining the **gc.ca** application form:

email: **registry@gc.ca**

7. The reason **gc.ca** was chosen is because **gov.ca** does not translate well into French. "Government" in French is "gouvernement." Thus **gc.ca** was chosen because it can stand for Government of Canada and gouvernement du Canada.

Most Internet service providers in Canada offer domain name registration services and will fill out and submit the form for you for a nominal fee. Filling out the form on your own can be difficult, particularly if you are not familiar with the nuances of the Internet. Even if you retrieve either of these forms and fill it out yourself, you should not send a registration application directly. Instead, you should submit the form to your ISP.

Once an application is submitted through your provider or the **gc.ca** Domain Registrar, the application is reviewed and scrutinized by a domain name committee to ensure its compliance with the domain name policies and procedures.

Keep in mind that you should seek guidance from your Internet service provider about the name you plan on choosing, since they will be best able to let you know whether the name you have selected will be acceptable to the committee.

Registrations Under a Descriptive Zone Name

You follow a different process if you choose to register within one of the descriptive domain names (e.g., **.com**, **.edu**). In this case, you register directly with InterNIC Registration Services, a component of the Internet Network Information Center in the United States. You would usually do this through your Internet service provider. Much more flexibility in your domain name is possible, since it can consist of a domain name of up to 24 characters, followed by the 3-character descriptive zone name, for example, **.com**, **.edu**. If you would like to understand how to register directly in one of these descriptive zone names, you can visit the InterNIC web site at **http://rs.internic.net**.

Completion of these forms requires some technical knowledge about the Internet. We recommend once again that you get your Internet service provider to complete and submit the forms on your behalf. There is an annual fee of $50 for a descriptive zone name.

Other Issues Related to Domain Names

There are two other issues related to the Domain Name System:

- There are many organizations not yet directly on the Internet; that is, they do not have a computer that directly connects to the Internet and hence cannot be directly reached via the Internet. However, these organizations might desire to link their internal e-mail system into the Internet using their own domain name. In order to do this, they must have a name registered on the Internet.

  To get around this dilemma, the concept of an MX (mail exchange) record was introduced; this allows an organization to obtain and use a name for purposes of e-mail. Accordingly, as we examine the domain name scheme, keep in mind that any organization, even if it is not directly linked to the Internet, can have an Internet domain name.

- There is nothing to prevent an organization from registering within multiple domains. For example, the University of Toronto has the subdomain names **utoronto.ca** and **toronto.edu**. The media company Southam has registered **southam.ca** and **southam.com**.

  The continued rapid growth of the Internet means that many domain names are being claimed very quickly. As a general rule, you should plan on reserving a name for your organization as quickly as possible, even if you do not have plans to link your organization to the Internet in the near future. This will prevent some other organization with a similar name from reserving the name you might want.

  You might even consider reserving the name with both the Canadian Domain Registrar and with the InterNIC so that both options are available to you in the future. For example, if your company name is BIGTOOLS, and you are national in scope, you might consider registering both as **bigtools.com** and **bigtools.ca**, for two reasons. First, potential customers might try to find you on the Internet by using your company name within the **.com** and **.ca** extensions. Second, obtaining both will help prevent a circumstance in which some organization with the same corporate name registers and gets the name before you do.

You can register your domain name in advance of getting on the Internet. In fact, it is advisable to do so, before someone else does. Chapter 6, which is about electronic mail, describes different methods to find domain names registered on the Internet. You can use these procedures to determine if your desired domain name has already been taken.

The Next Step

We opened this book by commenting that "the Internet is, in some ways, nothing less than a trend that is making all of these little computer chips aware of each other and providing them the ability to link together." So far, the Internet has succeeded at linking together some computers around the world. However, it is still in its infancy; it has a long way to go before most computers around the world are linked. Some people believe that one day this will be the case.

Connectivity to the Internet need not be restricted to computers that have a keyboard and a screen. Some believe that one day your home burglar alarm system, house monitoring system, office lighting system, and indeed your toaster oven will be wired into the Internet.

Some also believe that it will be possible to query the microprocessor in your automobile via the Internet to download data about your trip yesterday. Or use the Internet to see if you turned the lights off in the house in the morning. Or for other day-to-day routines.

Quite simply, these people believe that the Internet is rapidly becoming the protocol and network that will link all devices of computing intelligence. Will it happen? Maybe yes, maybe no. The key thing is that there is no similar commonly accepted protocol like TCP/IP and the Internet.

One challenge, however, is that TCP/IP has an upper limit in terms of the number of computers that it can reach. Simply, we run the risk of running out of Class A, B, and C TCP/IP addresses. Some estimates have said that we will hit this limit globally as early as 1997, while others predict that it might still be some time off.

There is a solution in the works. The various groups and standards bodies involved in Internet protocols have designed IPng, which stands for IP addresses, next generation. The standard provides for many billions more possible computer chips, addressing the future potential of the Internet as one giant network of all computing intelligence on the planet.

CHAPTER 6

Internet Electronic Mail

E-mail is available anywhere you have access to a computer and modem. It's so simple that anyone who knows how to type can use it, and it's turning society on its ear. It provides us the same reach and immediacy of telephones, costs less than a stamp, and offers the immediacy of digital communications. Type a few lines, click a few icons and your thoughts fly anywhere in the wired world in minutes, even seconds.

E-mail boom means postman may not ring at all
The Hamilton Spectator, May 23, 1996

We're still reaching out to touch someone — but e-mail may soon become the choice mode of communication among friends and family members, leaving handwritten letters in its dust. Internet boosters say e-mail from those they love in far-flung places provides psychological comfort, stronger emotional bonds, long-distance savings and, perhaps most importantly, immediate gratification.

Yours sincerely: E-mail may be convenient, but it's nothing like getting a long, hand-written letter
The Halifax Daily News, June 16, 1996

A conference on the future of postal services says the mail will go on despite the spread of electronic communication.

Mail Will Go On Despite Wired World
The London Free Press, November 1, 1995

With all the excitement about the World Wide Web, electronic mail, or e-mail, might seem decidedly dull. Although it may be new to you, there are many people in Canada and around the world who have been using e-mail for several years to send messages within their company. Since it is a technology that has been with us for some fifteen years or more, many people just cannot get excited about it. And what is so fun about sending and receiving messages anyways, you might ask?

But establish a personal mailbox on the Internet and something magical happens — you discover that you can reach out to the world. Link a corporate e-mail network to the Internet, and an organization discovers that many of its business activities can be made more straightforward through the sheer efficiency of global Internet e-mail. Internet e-mail has established a new method for people and organizations to communicate around the globe. And as more and more people sign up to Internet e-mail, its use and value increase at an ever-spiralling rate.

Why Is Use of Internet E-mail Exploding?

Many organizations have discovered that a link to Internet e-mail is the most useful application of all Internet capabilities. The reason for this is that e-mail is the only application that extends well beyond the boundaries of the real Internet and involves many other e-mail systems and many different technologies. With a simple Internet e-mail address, it is said that you can reach an estimated 60 million people around the globe.

E-mail has entered the Canadian public consciousness. E-mail addresses appear on TV shows, from the CBC *National News* to the *Dini Petty Show.*

They appear in newspapers ranging from the national *Globe and Mail* to local community weeklies. They are appearing in advertisements, on product labels, on business cards, and on stationery. Many people recognize e-mail addresses, and more people are ensuring that they get one. One thing is for sure: the use of Internet e-mail across Canada is growing by leaps and bounds, with an ever-increasing use for all kinds of business, social, personal, and organizational communication. The trend is not slowing down.

It Has Gained Acceptance

In some ways, Internet e-mail has become the fax machine of the 1990s and has become an accepted means of communication between people, business, and government. As more and more people sign onto the Internet, there is a growing expectation that they should be able to expect e-mail communications with business associates and friends. The practical impact of the rapid adoption of Internet e-mail is that those individuals without an Internet e-mail address are feeling a little left out — and feeling compelled to get one. It is a self-feeding kind of growth that shows no signs of slowing down — as more and more people use Internet e-mail, more and more people want to get on.

It Saves Money

Cost savings are a big reason why many are so enthusiastic about Internet e-mail. Using it is dramatically less expensive than courier, fax, and telephone costs. And with more and more people putting Internet addresses on their business cards, and with more and more people joining the Internet at home, there are *tremendous* opportunities for cost savings.

Most Internet connections are based upon either a flat hourly fee or purchase of a certain amount of Internet access for a flat monthly fee. This fee includes the use of Internet e-mail. This means that the incremental cost to send a message from one location to another is practically nil.

INTERNET ELECTRONIC MAIL

1. Many organizations have discovered that a link to Internet e-mail is the one of the most useful applications of all Internet capabilities.
2. Internet e-mail has gained acceptance throughout many organizations as an accepted means of communication, offering cost savings, time savings, and strategic benefits.
3. Internet e-mail can be many things and is generally considered to be any e-mail system in the world that can send and receive e-mail to and from the Internet.
4. Internet e-mail addresses have become easily recognizable.
5. You should be cognizant of important e-mail etiquette issues.
6. There are a few methods by which to locate an e-mail address for someone else, but a "big database" of all e-mail addresses in the world does not exist.
7. There are some potential security problems with Internet e-mail.

The cost to send a message to several hundred people is, in most cases, the same as sending a message to one person.

Consider this example: let's say you had to send a two-page letter to someone in Halifax, Vancouver, and Winnipeg. If you sent a fax to those three cities, it would probably cost at least a couple of dollars. Sending paper mail will cost $1.32 each or more. Sending three courier packages might cost $15 or $20 each.

Sending that same information via the Internet will cost, at most, a penny, and in most cases, even less. And since you can send a message to many people all at once, you'll face the same cost whether you send a message to one person or to 200 people. The cost savings are tremendous and are a very good argument for why you want to be on the Internet.

It Is Easy to Use

Once people get on to the Internet, they discover that it is not all that difficult to send a message, nor is it difficult to read messages that have been sent to them. E-mail software is becoming more sophisticated all the time, and with the increasing dominance of software like Microsoft Windows, IBM's OS/2, and Macintosh computers, simple "point-and-click" e-mail software is becoming the rule rather than the exception.

Want to create a new message to send to someone? Click on the little envelope. Want to see if there is any new mail? Click on the post office icon. Want to attach a file? Click on the icon of the paper clip. Regardless of what you are doing, e-mail is becoming something that is easier and easier to use with each passing year, thus helping to encourage more people to try it out.

It Is a Time Saver

Once people get on to the Internet and discover e-mail, they realize the tremendous efficiencies in its use. Consider the "old-fashioned method" by which a company might communicate with a number of people at different companies. Someone

- types the letter;
- prints the letter;
- copies the required numbers by taking it to the photocopy machine;
- stuffs the letters into envelopes;
- runs the envelopes through the postage meter or completes multiple courier waybills;
- gets the messages to the post box or courier.

All in all, a time-intensive and, in effect, expensive process, particularly when there are many recipients of the letter.

A company might save a bit of time by sending the paper through a fax machine instead of sending it through the post or by courier, but in doing so runs up substantial telephone bills. In addition, lineups form at the fax machine — they have become the "water cooler" of the 1990s. All in all, a very inefficient process. (Some organizations are reducing some of the inefficiencies found with paper-based fax machines by using fax software, which lets them send faxes directly from their computers.)

Many organizations expend vast human resources in shuffling paper, when technology exists that can result in significant time and efficiency savings. The Internet represents a significant opportunity for substantial improvement in the efficiency of regular communications by a business. Compare the process above with electronic mail. Someone

- keys the memo into a computer;
- selects an e-mail address, which could be for one individual or could be an electronic "mailing list" of several hundred people;
- presses a button to send the message.

Messages through e-mail are sent within seconds of completion; there is no paper shuffling. They are sent instantaneously and often simultaneously to a large number of recipients combined in mailing lists. There is simply no comparison in terms of efficiency between paper/fax mail and e-mail.

Individuals at home using the Internet for non-business purposes discover that they can enjoy the same efficiencies. Indeed, we are seeing more and more people discover that they can reach friends, families, and other people around the world using Internet e-mail. Since it is easier to send someone a message via e-mail than it is via the post, in many instances people end up communicating through e-mail more than they might ever have using more traditional methods.

It Transcends Time Zones and Eliminates Telephone Tag

Those who use Internet e-mail discover that it is a particularly useful tool to use when communicating with people in other time zones. You can send a message to someone at the other end of the country while they are still sleeping. They will receive it when they get into the office in the morning. Or, if you are communicating with people in Australia, you do not have to coordinate a time to call when you are both available. You can just jot off a message to them at any time and send it. In addition, people find e-mail to be a particularly convenient method of communicating with someone without the annoyance of voice mail or the frustrations inherent in "telephone tag."

It Is Strategic

Many companies are gradually discovering the benefits of an internal e-mail system as an alternative to traditional phone, fax, and paper communication. E-mail is thus used to support communications between employees at many different locations throughout the company. But if your company only has an internal e-mail system, it's like having a telephone that cannot be used to call anyone in the outside world, hence the trend where Internet e-mail is becoming a critical business application for many organizations, as companies discover that the ability to establish an e-mail link with customers, business associates, and other third parties is an invaluable and strategic business use of technology.

Clearly, there is an increasing trend throughout the corporate world to adopt Internet e-mail as a means of providing intercompany communications. This in itself has helped to fuel the growth in Internet e-mail.

It Has No Alternative

What has happened is that Internet e-mail has become the primary method by which individuals and organizations communicate. Consider what is happening:

- Anyone who joins the Internet from home or through work is automatically provided an e-mail account through which he/she can send or receive messages.
- Organizations that have been using their own e-mail systems for years have linked them to the Internet in order to support interorganization communications. These organizations, which often use e-mail software products such as cc:Mail, MSMail, PROFS, or All-in-One, have come to view Internet e-mail as the best method of providing e-mail communications between different businesses.

Hence, if you use Internet e-mail, you can quickly find yourself exchanging messages with friends, family, and business associates from large and small organizations, ranging in size from only a few staff to tens of thousands of employees. Even the Prime Minister of Canada has an e-mail address: **pm@pm.gc.ca**.

Internet e-mail addresses are based on the Internet Domain Name System described in Chapter 5, which provides for standard format addresses to be used throughout the network. It is easy to recognize an Internet e-mail address; it is usually of the form **someone@somewhere**; for example, **jcarroll@jacc.com**.

What Is Internet E-mail?

A strict definition of Internet e-mail is that it consists of e-mail sent and received from computers directly connected to the Internet. Strictly speaking, it is e-mail based on SMTP (simple mail transfer protocol), the software that defines how messages should be sent between different computers on the Internet. However, that definition is unworkable today, given the number of other systems connecting to the Internet.

Quite simply, Internet e-mail, because of its easily recognized address, is increasingly used for interorganizational communications and is rapidly emerging as the backbone of a globally linked e-mail network.

Basically, all kinds of e-mail systems around the world are plugging together, by linking into the Internet. They do so through software that translates the e-mail format into the SMTP format used throughout the Internet. The software that does this is known as a "gateway."

Everyone Sees Something Different

When dealing with Internet e-mail, you must realize that everyone you deal with might read, send, and work with Internet e-mail in a way that is completely different from the way that you work with it. With so many different systems linked to Internet e-mail, it should come as no surprise that there is a wide variety of Internet e-mail software in use.

Given the wide number of possible methods by which people can access and use the Internet, it is not possible within this book to detail all the steps involved in dealing with your own Internet e-mail. For that, we suggest you refer to the manual of the particular e-mail software you use and discuss with your Internet service provider any special technical considerations that it might involve. We do suggest, at the end of the chapter, other e-mail programs that you might consider using.

Configuring Your E-mail Program

Internet e-mail is fairly straightforward to learn how to use; we will take a look at the structure of an e-mail message and outline what you can do within most e-mail programs in terms of sending and receiving messages. The first challenge that some may have, however, is configuring their e-mail program to work with the Internet. Your e-mail program may already be configured for you within the software provided to you by your Internet service provider, or you may have to do it yourself. In the latter case, you should have received a set of instructions from your ISP. If you did not, then you will need some key information from them, such as the POP3 name, SMTP name, and your Internet user ID and password.

Within Netscape you configure this information within the "Servers" section of "Preferences"; you get here by choosing "Preferences" and then selecting "Mail and Network Preferences." You can see how we provide the SMTP and POP3 server names of the Internet service provider used as well as the user name and other details:

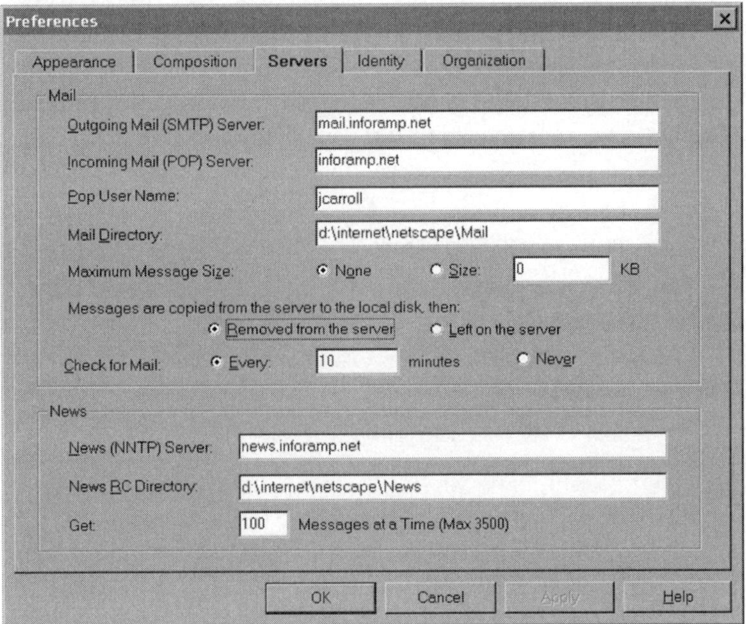

Within Pegasus Mail similar information is provided:

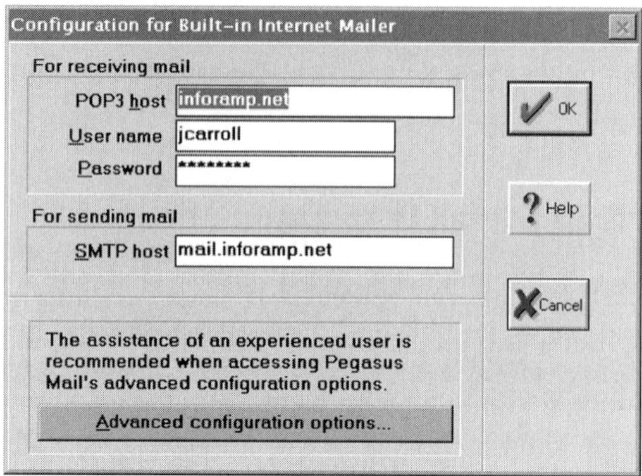

Again, if your e-mail is not already configured for you, then simply ask your ISP or check their home page for instructions on how to do so.

The Structure of an Internet E-mail Message

An Internet e-mail message has several distinct parts. Although any particular message might be more or less complex, a sample Internet message looks like this in plain text:

From: "Julian Sher" <sher@vir.com>
To: jcarroll@jacc.com
Date sent: Sun, 16 Jun 1996 11:38:34 +0000
Subject: Re: Internet search tips
Send reply to: sher@vir.com
Priority: normal

On 13 Jun 96, Jim Carroll wrote:
> Rick Broadhead and I are now working on the 1997 edition of the
> Canadian Internet Handbook....and I'm working on a chapter on "doing
> research on the Net."
>
> I would appreciate if anyone is aware of any really good documents out
> there that describe for novices how to go about doing research on the Net....
> that the chapter can point to.

Jim —

In response to your note. I teach journalism research on the Net to CBC journalists (and CAJ members) across the country so I might be able to be of some help.

My home page is used by about 2,000 journalists a month. Since journalists are in a hurry and need info fast, it is largely graphic-free and reads virtually as a research guide.

It is organized into sections such as How can I find experts? How can I hunt newsgroups? How can I find the best mailing lists? What newspapers are on line? Plus various story topics and Canadian government sites.

There is also a link to a section called "Teach yourself the net" which reproduces my columns from "Media" magazine. These articles are geared to introduce beginners to things like Start Pages, Mailing lists, etc.

I don't pass this info on to toot my own horn. Like you, no doubt, I spend a lot of time answering e-mail requests for guidance about the Net and you develop an expertise that you're eager to share.

I hope this will be useful for your book. By the way, we talked last year before publication of your last edition and I sent you some notes about how the Net is changing the face of journalism. Let me know if you're still interested in that topic and I can update my notes to you.

Keep in touch (and in separate e-mail I have sent you a proposal about the freelance battle.)

-Julian Sher

```
======================================================
                    WWW Home Page:
         "Investigative Journalism on the Net"
         .http://www.vir.com/~sher/julian.htm.
Julian Sher            1400 Boul. Rene Levesque East
Producer         Montreal, Quebec H2L 2M2
 "the 5th estate" Tel: (514)597-6390
 CBC-TV  Fax:            (514)597-4596
                 e-mail: sher@vir.com
             [Speaking only for myself...]
======================================================
```

Take a moment and examine the message. You will note that it includes the following components, or fields:

- From:
  The name of the sender and the full Internet address of the sender. In this case, the sender is **sher@vir.com**. The software has also included the sender's full name (Julian Sher).

- To:
  The intended recipient of the message.

  In this case, the message is being sent to the Internet ID **jcarroll@jacc.com**.

- Date sent:
  The date/time the message was created by the sender.

- Subject:
  Details the subject line entered by the sender. In some cases, if the message is in response to an earlier message, the e-mail software used might place a "Re:" in front of the original subject, and if the message has been "forwarded" by someone else, the software might place a "Fwd:" or similar indicator in front of the subject.

Depending upon the e-mail software you use, you might also see other fields, including

- cc:

  Messages can also include a cc:, or carbon copy field. This indicates that the message has also been copied to other people.

- In-reply-to:

  A field used by many e-mail systems to uniquely identify messages.

- Message-ID:

  A unique message address, generated by the e-mail system of the sender.

- Mime-Version: and Content-Type:

  This appears or is used if the sender of this message is working with the newest evolution of Internet e-mail, known as MIME (multipurpose Internet multimedia extensions), which provides interesting new e-mail capabilities. MIME significantly extends the capabilities of simple Internet e-mail and is discussed in greater depth later in this chapter.

- X-mailer:

  Internet messages also often include an X-mailer: field, which indicates the e-mail client software used to create the message.

Other fields might appear in the message, again depending upon the particular software that is in use. You might be using e-mail software that automatically shows you all kinds of other detail, known as the "headers."

Finally, the e-mail message above includes a "signature," or standard piece of information added to every message by the sender. Many e-mail software packages let you create a signature in which you can include your name, address, phone number, e-mail and World Wide Web addresses, and other information. Many messages do not include a signature.

In this case, the signature used by Julian Sher provides basic information on who he is, what he does, and how to reach his Web site.

It should also be noted that much of the software for the Internet strips an Internet message down to its fundamentals, by showing only To:, From: and Subject: fields. For example, this message, when viewed with Pegasus Mail for Windows,[1] appears as follows:

---

1. A shareware program, Pegasus Mail for Windows, is available from the URL **ftp://risc.ua.edu/network/pegasus**. Macintosh and DOS versions are available at the same location.

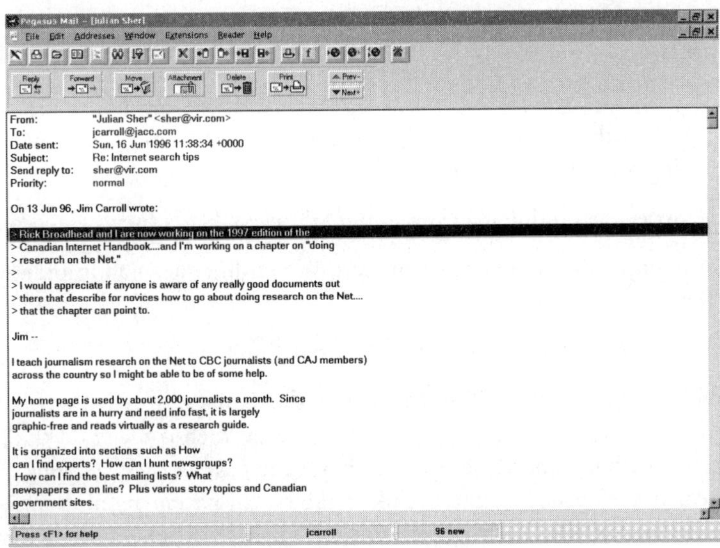

How Did This Message Get Here?

Since you are likely curious, we will explain how the message got from Julian to Jim. Some e-mail software hides certain details of e-mail known as the "full headers," so that you do not have to see all the information about how the message got from point A to point B. Some e-mail programs automatically show you these "full headers," while other software packages provide an option to view the headers. Using Pegasus, we can take a look at the full headers.

The start of the message now looks like this:

Received: from mail.inforamp.net (Mail.InfoRamp.Net [204.191.136.66]) by

diane.inforamp.net (8.7/8.7) with ESMTP id MAA14510 for <jcarroll@inforamp.net>; Sun, 16 Jun 1996 12:37:36 -0400 (EDT)

Received: from Vir.com (News.Vir.com [199.84.154.68]) by mail.inforamp.net

(8.7.3/8.7) with ESMTP id MAA18100 for <jcarroll@jacc.com>; Sun, 16 Jun

1996 12:31:37 -0400 (EDT)

Received: from ipdyne21.vir.com [199.202.197.21] by Vir.com (8.7.1/v1.1)

with SMTP id MAA26573 for <jcarroll@jacc.com>; Sun, 16 Jun 1996 12:36:32

-0400 (edt)

Message-Id: <199606161636.MAA26573@Vir.com>

Comments: Authenticated sender is <sher@pop1.vir.com>

From: "Julian Sher" <sher@vir.com>

To: jcarroll@jacc.com

Date: Sun, 16 Jun 1996 11:38:34 +0000

Subject: Re: Internet search tips

Reply-to: sher@vir.com

Priority: normal

```
X-mailer: Pegasus Mail for Windows (v2.23)
Content-Type: text
X-PMFLAGS: 33554560 0
```

The first few lines show the path that the message took as it went from Julian in Montreal to Jim Carroll. Interpreting this information tells us that

- Julian answered a posting made by Jim in USENET News (**news.vir.com**, in line 4);
- within seconds, **vir.com** opened a connection to Inforamp (**mail.inforamp.net**) and transmitted the message there;
- the message was eventually picked up by Jim Carroll.

All this occurred within minutes of Julian having sent the message, thus demonstrating the efficiency of Internet e-mail. The route was rather direct (as it often is today on the Internet), as computer systems at each ISP linked directly to each other to pass the message along. For example, the e-mail system at Vir opened a "direct" link to the e-mail system at InfoRamp to send the message to the ISP used by Jim. Years ago, the message might have gone through many different e-mail systems.

What Can You Do With E-mail?

Since there are many different types of e-mail software that people might use, the way that people create, read, and send messages will be different depending upon the software used. Regardless of what software is used, however, there are certain basic things that you will want to do with Internet e-mail.

Create a Message

Obviously, you will want to create a message and send it to someone. To do so, you will need to know the e-mail address, which is the subject of a separate section below. Once you know the address, there is usually some type of function in your e-mail software that lets you create a new message. For example, using the software Eudora, a Windows application, you can choose to create a new message. When you do so, you see a screen that looks like this:

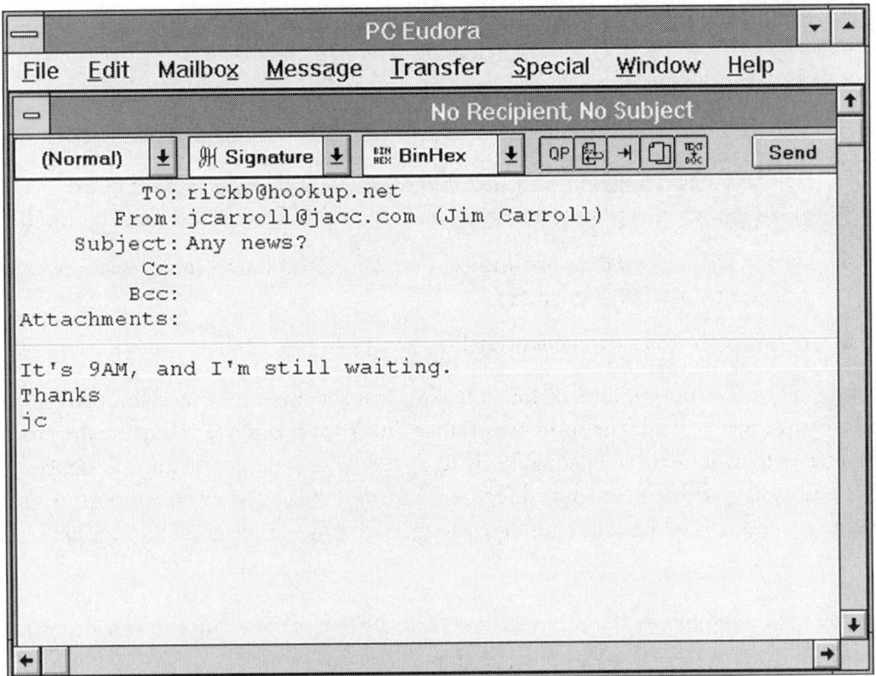

You can choose to do many different things with your message, depending upon the e-mail software that you are using, such as sending a computer file to someone, inserting text from a document from within your word processor, making an automatic copy of the message for yourself, sending the message with a receipt request so that you are told when the recipient reads the message, or "encrypting" the message to protect against prying eyes.

Read a Message

Your e-mail software will have an "inbox," or "new mail folder," a place where new messages are listed. You can usually choose to read any particular message, or you can read all messages. A new mail folder might look like the one in the screen below. In this case, the ✔ symbol indicates that a message has already been read. Here is the inbox for one of the authors:

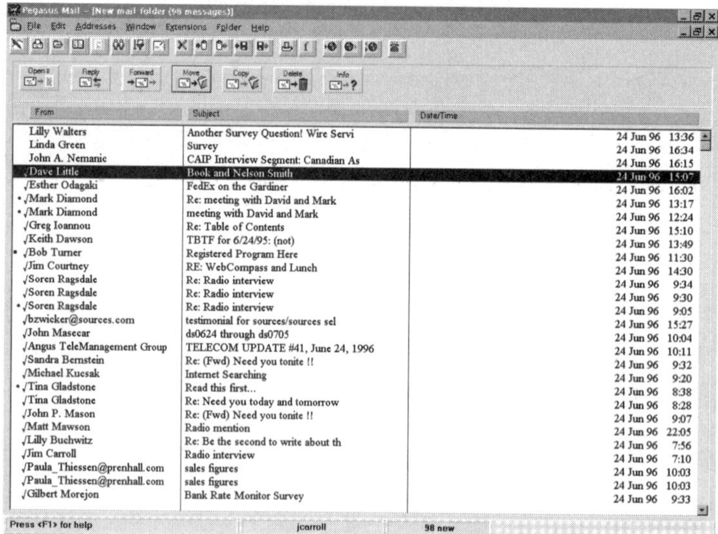

And here is the inbox for the other author. You can see some similarities in the way they are structured, even though there are two different programs in use:

Reply to a Message

When you read an e-mail message, you can usually choose to reply to a message sent to you by someone else. When you reply, to help that person remember what the message was about, many e-mail software programs will "quote" the original message within the body of the reply. For example, let's assume we are replying to our example message. When we do so, a new message box is opened up. The reply contains both the original text and our reply:

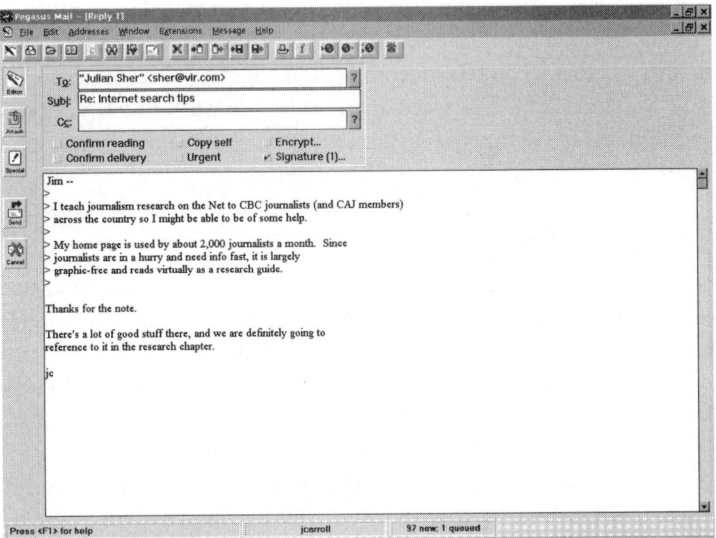

In the sample message a special marker has been placed by the software in front of the text of Julian's original message, a > symbol. (Many different types of markers are used.) This feature helps the recipient easily and quickly identify the original message in the message that he/she received from you and is a courtesy that is much appreciated by the Internet community. You will often see your original message quoted to you when you get replies to your message.

Forward a Message

Any message that you receive can also be forwarded to someone else. This makes it easy to get someone else involved in dealing with the contents of the message. It also means that any message you send to someone might be forwarded on to someone else without your knowledge.

Delete, Print, or Save the Message

When reading a message, you can also usually choose to delete the message, print it to your printer, or save the text of the message to your computer so that you can view it later. Many e-mail programs also support the use of folders, so that you can file your messages within the e-mail program according to folders that you define. These folders have proven to be very effective tools by which people manage their information; for example, people have subject folders, project folders, "to do" folders. It's an easy way to organize your e-mail according to your particular needs.

Send or Receive a Computer File

On occasion, you will receive a message that contains a "binary enclosure" or file. This means that someone has sent you an e-mail message that contains a program, a document or spreadsheet, or some other type of computer file. The enclosure or file is "encoded," that is, it is converted to a special format of text so that it can be sent through e-mail. On the Internet, binary files and enclosures are usually included in the message in one of three types: binhex, uuencode, or MIME. People usually find the issues of binary files/enclosures to be the most complicated issue related to Internet e-mail.

Why Does It Get So Complicated?

Computer programs and document files (such as Microsoft Word or WordPerfect documents) contain special codes that cannot be represented in the "plain text" that you normally see in an e-mail message. To be sent through e-mail, they must be "encoded" in some way and are therefore "attached" to a regular e-mail message. This means that when you receive such an e-mail message, it will be necessary for you to "extract" the file from your message and sometimes "decode" it. It is confusing, but once you do it a few times, you will get the hang of it.

You can deal with all three types if your e-mail software supports all types, and you might find that not to be the case. The result will be that your first encounters with trying to "extract" file attachments will be frustrating, until you and the sender can agree on a type of enclosure that you can both "extract."

When a computer file is turned into an attachment of one of these types, it is often turned into simple "text" that looks like gibberish. For example, if the file is "uuencoded," the binary file has been turned into rows and rows of text and is included in the body of the message that looks like this:

```
begin 644 config.sysM1$5624-%/4,Z7$1/4UQ(24U%32Y365,-"D1%5DE#13U#.EQ$3U<14U-,S@
VM+D5812!.3T5-4PT*0E5&1D524STS,"PP#0I&24Q%4STX,`T*1$]3/550@T*
```

The exact method that you will use to "extract" the file from the message, "decode" it, and save it to your computer will vary depending upon the e-mail software that you might be using. Some e-mail software automatically "decodes" enclosures when you read the message, while with others you will need to save the mail message in a file and then use a separate program to decode it. For example, Pegasus Mail lets you automatically "extract" most enclosures in order to save them on your computer:

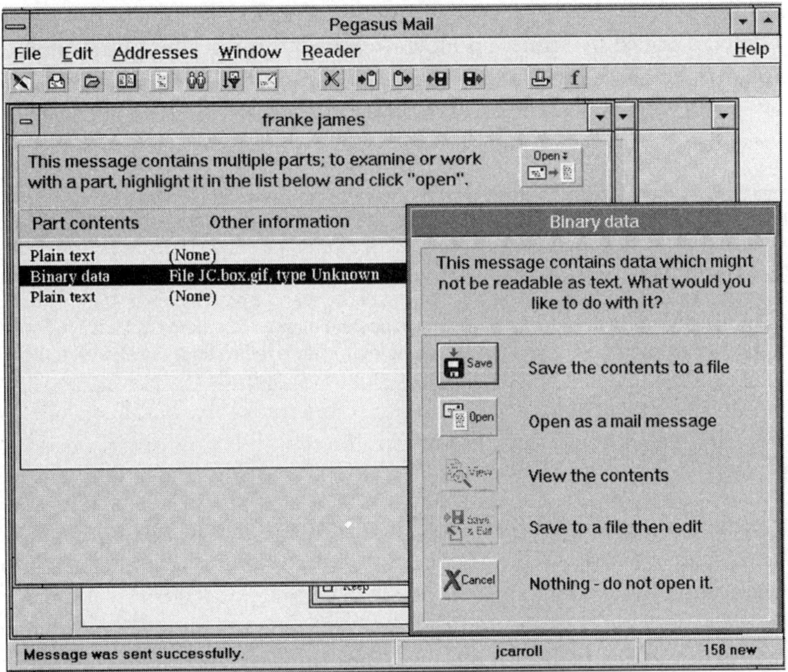

Older versions of Eudora recognize attachments in the binhex and MIME formats, but do not recognize uuencoded files. Hence the result is that if you read a message that contains a file attachment in uuencoded format, Eudora will not know what to do with it and will show you the gibberish within the text of the message.

Is there any hope on the horizon of making this complexity go away? Eventually. That is what MIME is all about. MIME is a rapidly emerging Internet standard to permit a more straightforward exchange of binary files and enclosures. MIME messages also look like uuencoded files if you receive them and do not have MIME-capable software. However, if the software you are using (and more and more e-mail software is supporting the standard) supports MIME, your software will automatically recognize the contents of the message as a file attachment. We talk more about MIME near the end of this chapter. If you are going to choose a new e-mail program, our advice is to make sure that it supports MIME.

Attach an E-mail Signature

Many e-mail software programs support the use of a signature but not everyone uses them. Accordingly, you should not always expect to see them in every Internet message.

Our sample message above from Julian Sher included an e-mail signature which provided further information concerning the sender. In this case, his signature includes his name, e-mail, Web, and paper addresses.

If your software supports signatures, you can automatically append one to the end of a message. Some software allows you to choose the signature that you wish to use from a list of several. If the software does not support signatures, you can still type one in manually.

In general, signatures should be concise and should not be overdone. In a document released on USENET called "A Primer on How to Work With the USENET Community," by Chuq Von Rospac, guidance is given with respect to how to structure signatures. Although the document is specific to the use of the USENET news system, the guidance is equally applicable to e-mail signatures.

> Signatures are nice.... Don't overdo it. Signatures can tell the world something about you, but keep them short. A signature that is longer than the message itself is considered to be in bad taste. The main purpose of a signature is to help people locate you, not to tell your life story. Every signature should include at least your return address relative to a major, known site on the network and a proper domain-format address. Your system administrator can give this to you. Some news posters attempt to enforce a 4 line limit on signature files — an amount that should be more than sufficient to provide a return address and attribution.

Filter Your Mail

With the growth in the use of Internet e-mail has come the inability for some people to deal with massive volumes of messages. One practical way to deal with this is through the use of e-mail filters, a feature found in a growing number of e-mail software packages.

You can think of a filter as an electronic program on your e-mail system or a computer that reads your e-mail before you do. It then acts upon those messages, depending upon a set of rules that you have defined beforehand. For example, you might belong to an Internet service that regularly sends you, via e-mail, a newsletter. You notice that the message always arrives with the subject "Newsletter- (YY/MM/DD)." Using a filter, you could specify that any messages that you receive containing the subject "Newsletter" should automatically be moved to a folder in your e-mail system called "newsletters." You can then choose to go to this folder at any time to read the messages stored there, rather than seeing this particular newsletter arrive with your regular messages.

Using filters, you can specify that certain actions should be performed on incoming messages based upon the contents of the To:, From:, Subject:, or other fields. These actions include

- automatically moving or copying the messages to a particular file folder or automatically deleting certain messages;
- replying to every message with an automatic response, for example, "I am a little behind on my e-mail, and it will take me about three days to respond — don't fret";
- automatically adding a person to an e-mail list within your e-mail system.

Mail Robots

Often the Internet solves unique problems through the simplest of methods. One problem on the Internet has to do with providing only those people who have an e-mail link to the Internet with the ability to retrieve files or documents. To solve the problem, the Internet came up with the concept of the "mail robot." E-mail filters can be used to implement a simple and effective mail robot, so that messages sent to a certain ID are automatically replied to with certain text.

A mail robot is a program that runs at the receiving e-mail location, takes apart an incoming message, and mails back some type of response automatically. Organizations are using e-mail robots to permit individuals throughout the Internet to easily request information from a company. Try one out: for an up-to-date message concerning the *Canadian Internet Handbook*, send a message to **info@handbook.com**. You will receive an automatic response via e-mail, usually within hours. Or send a message to the corporate mail robot **managingpartner@mccarthy.ca.**

Mail robots can be implemented quite easily with many popular e-mail systems and by many Internet service providers as well. Mail robots are close cousins to "listservs," which are discussed in Chapter 11.

E-mail Addresses

Internet e-mail uses the domain name style of addressing, based upon the Domain Name System. An Internet e-mail address usually consists of a name or some identifier, followed by an @ symbol, followed by the domain name. For example, **jcarroll@jacc.com** contains the user name (**jcarroll**) and the domain name (**jacc.com**, which stands for J.A. Carroll Consulting, and which is listed in the commercial, or **.com**, domain).

As seen in Chapter 5, the Internet Domain Name System results in e-mail addresses in Canada that use a **.ca** extension, if registered within the Canadian domain. The address might include a city/jurisdiction name and province, depending upon the size of the organization, and the location of that organization within Canada. Within the Canadian domain, some Internet addresses in Canada would appear with names such as **Pete_Smith@mediumcorp.ab.ca** for an organization in Alberta, **Tjones@smallco.ns.ca** for a company in Nova Scotia, or **Al_Stevens@bigcompany.ca** if the company is national in scope.

Other Internet addresses, within organizations that are not part of the Canadian domain but are registered directly with the Internet InterNIC, might have Internet addresses that end in **.com**, **.edu**, **.gov**, or other extensions. Such an address will usually include the name of the organization next to the extension, for example **TJones@Bigco.com**.

E-mail Styles

It is important to note that the information that appears in front of the @ symbol in an e-mail address will vary depending upon the particular e-mail system used, the Internet vendor, and the way that names are used within the organizational e-mail system:

- Some addresses will use some combination of the first name and last name, for example, **Pete_Smith** or **Psmith** or **pete.smith**. Since spaces are not allowed, the first and last name are separated, usually by a _ character or a dot.
- Other addresses might use alpha-numerical characters, for example, **76467.3502** for someone on CompuServe, or **aa123** for an address on a FreeNet.
- Other addresses might use nicknames or nonsense names.

In other words, there are no rules on what must be used in front of the @ symbol. Some sites will let you choose your own address. The result is an incredible diversity of addresses throughout the Internet.

Rejected Messages

On occasion, you will receive notification that a message sent to someone has been rejected or not delivered. A rejected message looks like this:

```
>Return-Path: MAILER-DAEMON
>Date: Sun, 21 Jul 1996 23:52:48 -0400
>From: Mail Delivery Subsystem <MAILER-DAEMON@hookup.net>
>Subject: Returned mail: User unknown
>To: <rickb@hookup.net>
>
>The original message was received at Sun, 21 Jul 1996 23:52:31 -0400
>from ts7-12.inforamp.net [198.53.144.232]
>
>Please contact postmaster@hookup.net for assistance.
>
>—— The following addresses had delivery problems ——
><kanata1@resudox.net> (unrecoverable error)
>
>—— Transcript of session follows ——
>... while talking to gabriel.resudox.net.:
>>>> RCPT To:<kanata1@resudox.net>
><<< 550 <kanata1@resudox.net>... User unknown
>550 <kanata1@resudox.net>... User unknown
>
>—— Original message follows ——
>Return-Path: rickb@hookup.net
>Received: from ts1-05.inforamp.net (ts7-12.inforamp.net [198.53.144.232])
by nic.wat.hookup.net (8.6.12/1.14) with SMTP id XAA23549; Sun, 21 Jul 1996
23:52:31 -0400
>Date: Sun, 21 Jul 1996 23:52:31 -0400
>Message-Id: <199507240352.XAA23549@nic.wat.hookup.net>
```

```
>X-Sender: rickb@noc.tor.hookup.net

>Mime-Version: 1.0

>Content-Type: text/plain; charset="us-ascii"

>To: kanata1@resudox.net

>From: rickb@hookup.net (Rick Broadhead)

>Subject: Re: MISA Conference

>X-Mailer: <Windows Eudora Version 2.0.2>

>

>[...]
```

The message usually includes the original message you sent.

Rejection messages come in all kinds of flavors and often look different depending upon where they originated. If you get a rejected message, carefully check the e-mail address to which you sent the original message. Quite often, a simple spelling mistake in the address will have been made. Other times, you should check with the person (by phone or otherwise, of course) to verify the address. When you have a rejected message, you can usually forward it to the correct ID, but be sure to edit out all the details in the rejected message header.

E-mail Etiquette

When sending and receiving e-mail on the Internet, you should keep in mind this simple rule:

> What you type and what you say in your e-mail messages could one day come back to haunt you. Be careful.

The use of Internet e-mail (or any e-mail system) requires an on-line etiquette, or a set of manners, that you should keep in mind.

E-mail Is Different

There are several characteristics about e-mail that should make you cautious in the way you use it:

- E-mail is fast. In the "good old days," before the arrival of computer technology, people were careful with paper letters. A response took time to prepare, was well thought out, and was probably reviewed a few times before being sent. There was no room for error on paper correspondence. That is not the case with e-mail. Within seconds of receiving a message, you can respond, often without thinking about what you have typed. Do you really want people to receive messages that you have not carefully thought about?

- E-mail is wide-reaching. Within seconds, you can create a message or response to a message that will reach one person, 20 people, or thousands of people (particularly if you are responding to a mailing list posting; if the mailing list is linked to a USENET newsgroup, your message will reach an even larger audience). If you write an e-mail message in anger, you might say something that you regret. Do you really want to send copies of your message to a lot of people?
- E-mail is easily saved. Computer technology permits people to easily store the e-mail messages they send or receive.[2] What this means is that any e-mail message you send to someone could end up in his/her personal data archive or even in an organizational archive. If you are posting to an Internet mailing list, your message could end up in several archives around the world that are open to public viewing. If you write something controversial or stupid, do you want to risk having your words come back to haunt you?
- E-mail is easily forwarded. E-mail technology promotes the easy distribution of information. What you write and send to someone can easily be forwarded by him/her to someone else or posted to a global mailing list or USENET newsgroup. The recipient of your message might not realize that you intended the message for limited distribution. Before you know it, your message could be sent all over the world. Do you really want a message that you intended for just one person to be forwarded to a number of people?
- E-mail is easily misinterpreted. The person reading your e-mail message cannot see your body language. He/she cannot see if you are smiling, frowning, or crying as you write. It is more difficult to interpret what you have written. Often this leads to misinterpretation. What the recipient thinks you mean is often not what you really mean. Do you want to run the risk of having someone misunderstand your message?

Flaming

The on-line world has come up with a term to describe what happens to people who ignore these risks and who write an e-mail message while their emotions are not in check. It is called flaming. Flaming is the tendency for someone to quickly key an e-mail message in anger without thinking the message through. As noted in a study entitled "The Human, Social, and Organizational Impact of Electronic Mail" from California Polytechnical University, "some laboratory and university research demonstrates that electronic mail can encourage overly emotional and negative messages."

It is all too easy to go overboard with e-mail. You might find that suddenly your emotions bubble over, and you start to send a really nasty message. Or that you feel you just have to straighten something out by being blunt. But such anger and bluntness do not work well with Internet e-mail due to the lack of body language. People might read the wrong thing into what you are sending. Remember this warning. At some time, you will regret sending an e-mail message. You will regret it a lot. You should always, always think before sending a message to someone in anger.

---

2. One of the authors has on file about 100 megabytes of messages, e-mail messages sent/received since October 1985.

E-mail Guidance

A few simple suggestions might make it easier for you to avoid problems sending e-mail messages:

- Do not use just capitals in your messages. This is called shouting. Imagine receiving a message that looks like this:

  GREG. WE NEED TO UNDERSTAND HOW TO REORGANIZE FOR THE JUNE 5TH MEETING. IT'S IMPORTANT THAT WE GET TOGETHER NOW. CALL ME SOON.

  Messages like this are difficult to read and cause others frustration with the messages you send them. Always be careful to use upper- and lowercase.

- Use a meaningful subject line. Remember that the person you are sending the message to might receive tens or hundreds of messages each day. To make it easier to deal with your message, provide a subject line that is meaningful and to the point.

- Take your time thinking about a response to a message, especially if the message makes you angry. The best advice is to get up, go for a glass of water, or have a cup of coffee. Or take a walk. Or go shopping, watch TV, or read a book. Never respond to a message when you are angry!

- Do not send a carbon copy of your message to the rest of the world, unless you have to. When sending an e-mail message, it is easy to send copies to a lot of people, including some who may have no interest in your message. Be judicious about the people who get a copy of the message.

- Summarize the message to which you are responding. If you are lucky, you are using an Internet e-mail software package that quotes the original message text in your response, as we discussed earlier in "Reply to a Message." Be sure to use this feature to make it easier for the recipient to remember what the message was about. Edit the message so that only the relevant text is kept. There is nothing worse than getting three pages of an original message with a few words in response at the end.

- Use special characters to label your emotion. To *highlight* a point, consider using >>>>>special<<<<<< characters. For example, rather than keying a message that looks like this:

  It is important that we meet as soon as possible.

  you might key

  It is !!!!!!important!!!!!! that we meet as soon as possible.

  This will help portray the urgency of the situation.

- Be careful when responding to messages received from a mail list (we discuss e-mail lists in the next chapter). With some mail lists the default is that any reply is sent to everyone on the list, while with others the reply is to the original message author only. You should check the reply address before sending the message to ensure that you are sending the reply to the intended recipient.

As you use the Internet, you will discover that people use all kinds of tricks to emphasize points within their messages. Carefully observe, and in time you will come up with your own distinctive Internet writing style.

Tips on E-mail etiquette (and other general "netiquette" issues) can be found at the following URLs:

http://www.webfoot.com/advice/email.top.html

http://www.fau.edu/rinaldi/netiquette.html

http://www.screen.com/understand/Netiquette.html

Smileys

The e-mail world has come up with an ingenious way of expressing emotion within a message by using special characters that some call "emoticons." Others call them "smileys." A smiley is a set of symbols that, when turned on its side, represents some type of character. For example, a (-: is a sideways smiley face; a (-; is a sideways smiley face winking, while)-: is a face with a frown.

A :-) is often used in a message to indicate that the preceding remark was made in jest. Smileys are important so that people do not misinterpret what you type. These characters can be used within e-mail messages to add additional emphasis. For example,

Pete, Your summary was interesting(-;. Have a good day. John

or

Pete, I didn't get the report finished.)-: Call me. John

There are so many possible smileys that a book has been written about them.

As you use the Internet, you will see a lot of smileys in messages. Accumulate your own special list. If you are looking for more, you can find a number of sites on the Internet that keep lists of smileys, for example, an on-line database of smileys at the Web site for the Electronic Freedom Foundation (**http://www.eff.org/papers/eegtti/eeg_286.html**):

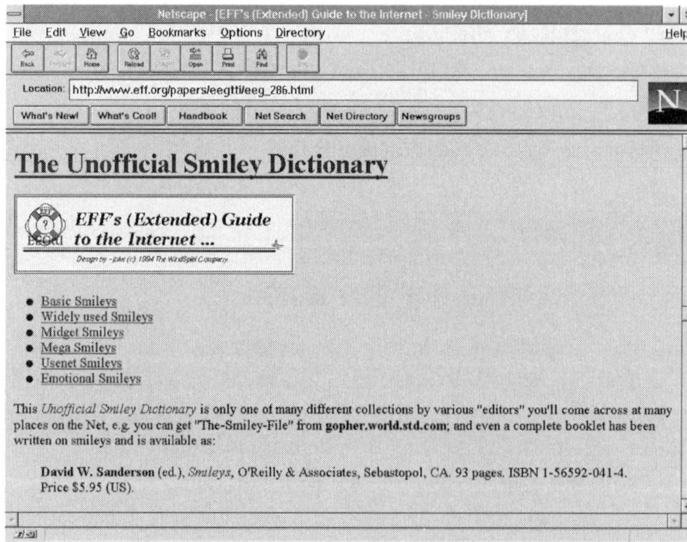

Listings of "smileys/emoticons" can be found online at the following URLs:

http://www.emoticon.com

http://www.eff.org/papers/eegtti/eeg_286.html

http://olympe.polytechnique.fr/~violet/Smileys/

How Do I Locate an Internet E-mail Address?

At some point you will want to determine how to obtain the e-mail address of a particular person or organization. Invariably, as you use various parts of the Internet, you will come across a message from someone that reads as follows:

> I am looking for Bob Smith in Toronto. Does anyone know his Internet address?

The question is silly, since there is no easy answer. Obviously, there are many Bob Smiths in Toronto, many of whom do not use the Internet.

The Internet does not have any central storage location that lists all possible users of the network, and such a directory will never exist, given the massive scope of the Internet. However, there do exist a number of smaller directories and query systems that you can use to try to locate the e-mail address of someone. However, such services are certainly not very comprehensive and are not really a good solution to your dilemma.

Fortunately, many users list their Internet addresses on their business cards, and addresses are beginning to gain as much acceptance on business cards and correspondence as fax numbers did in the mid-1980s. Hence sometimes the answer to the question is the obvious one. The easiest way to find out the Internet address of someone is probably simply to ask. Pick up the phone and call. Maybe he knows. If he knows he is on the Internet and knows how to send a message, but does not know his address, then ask him to send a message to your Internet address. You will then see what his address is and can respond to him in the future. If this does not work, then you can begin exploring the world of the Internet by trying to locate an address. Take a deep breath; there are many resources on-line.

E-mail FAQ

A good starting point is the document "How to find people's E-mail addresses," originally written by Jonathon Kames and now maintained by David Lamb at Queen's University in Kingston. It can be accessed through the Web site at Queen's University in Canada (**http://www.qucis.queensu.ca/FAQs/email/finding.html**):

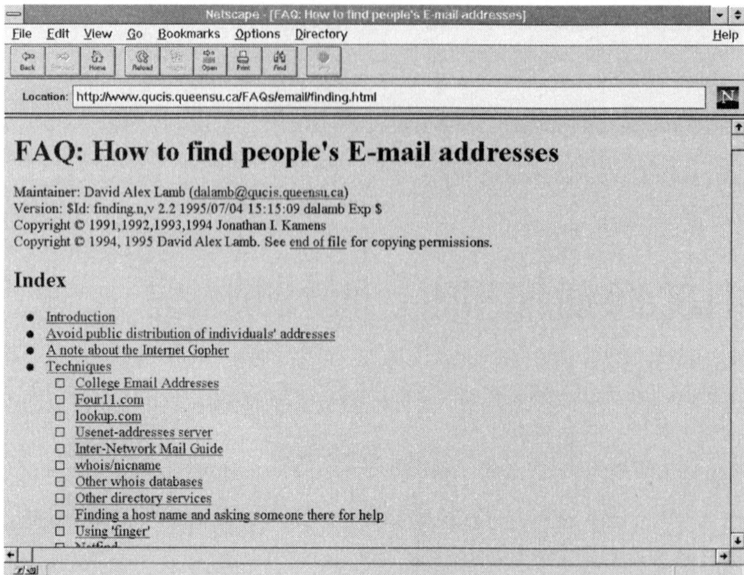

The document is posted on a regular basis to several USENET newsgroups, such as **news.answers**. You can also retrieve it on-line or through e-mail.

How to Obtain the "How to Find People's E-mail Addresses" Summary:
URL: **ftp://rtfm.mit.edu/pub/usenet-by-group/news.answers/finding-addresses** or
http://www.qucis.queensu.ca/FAQs/email/finding.html
By e-mail: Send a message to **mail-server@rtfm.mit.edu**. In the test of message, type (on one line): **send usenet/news.answers/finding-addresses**

The next step is to try to find the person directly through one of the various directories available on the Internet. If this does not work, see if the company or organization for which the person works is on the Internet. If so, you may be able to contact the company to determine the e-mail address for the person. Here are some of the ways in which you can search for e-mail addresses.

Methods of Finding E-mail Addresses

E-mail directories are appearing all over the Internet. In this section we outline some suggested methods by which you can locate someone. The easiest place to start is one of the large on-line e-mail directories, which is discussed below. But there are a lot of smaller directories as well. To find them, you must learn to become an effective Internet researcher. Hence much of the guidance that follows is provided in the spirit of our chapter "Undertaking Research on the Internet." To really master finding an e-mail address means that you must learn how to master undertaking research on the Internet in the first place.

Use an On-line E-mail Directory

You can try several on-line e-mail directories. These are large databases that try to catalogue as many global e-mail addresses as possible. When using such systems, keep in mind that none of them are comprehensive. They are often built from e-mail addresses found in USENET postings and on Web sites, in addition to those addresses added to the database by individuals.

- A good starting point is the Yahoo! People Search system (**http://www.yahoo.com/search/people/e-mail.html**). A search for Jim Carroll, for example, returned 24 listings:

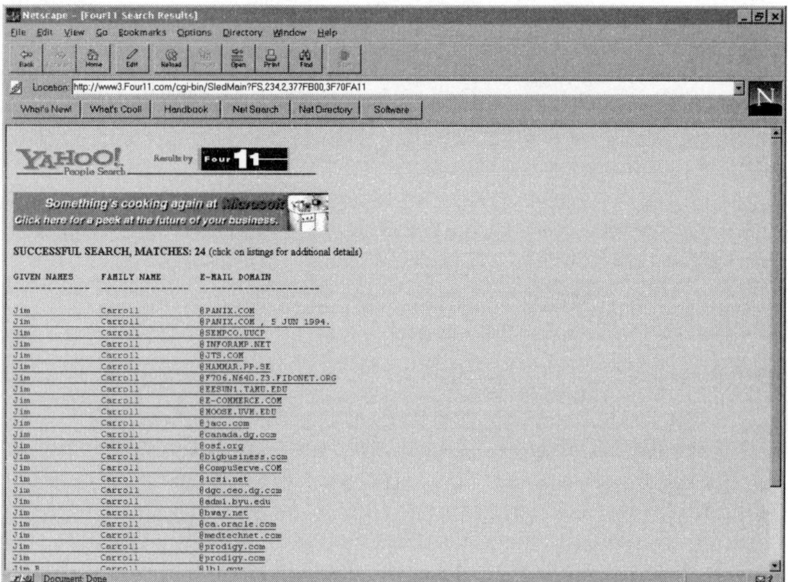

  The 'Yahoo!' system is based on Four11, one of the largest on-line e-mail directories (**http://www.four11.com**).

- The Internet Address Finder (**http://www.iaf.net/**) boasts in excess of 4 million e-mail addresses. It returned 30 items on Jim Carroll.

- OKRA: net.citizen directory service is another system (**http://okra.ucr.edu/okra**) that returned over 50 listings on Jim Carroll.

- The Bigfoot Directory promotes itself as the "Global Directory for the Online Community" (**http://bigfoot.com**) and returned 14 items.

It is of interest to note that many older, unused e-mail addresses were found by most of these systems; thus there is no guarantee that just because they know of an e-mail address it is going to work. You should take the time to add yourself to each of these systems to help others find you in the future. Most allow you to do so simply by filling out a form.

Look for a Web Site of the Company

If you know the employer of the object of your search, try the Web site of that company. Many Web sites now contain e-mail address directories. Take a look, for example, at the Web site for Holstein Canada, which lists the e-mail addresses for many employees (**http://www.holstein.ca/address2.htm**):

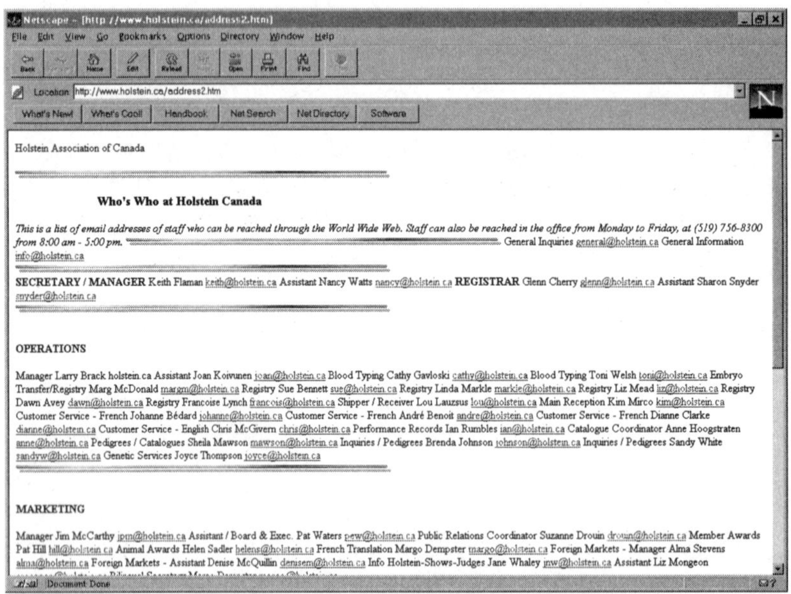

Some companies allow you to obtain a directory of e-mail addressees by e-mail. For example, send a message to **info@globeandmail.ca** to get a list of all *Globe and Mail* e-mail addresses.

If the company does not have a directory, try sending e-mail to the site's Webmaster (the person who maintains the Web site on behalf of the company) and ask if she can provide an e-mail address for the person you are trying to locate. Most Web sites contain an e-mail address for the Webmaster, or failing that, an e-mail address for general comments and questions where you can direct such questions as "What is the e-mail address for John Smith?"

Use a Search Engine to Look for the Person's Name on the Web

You can do a search in one of the many Internet search engines looking for mention of the person's name. For example, a search in either AltaVista, Excite, InfoSeek, WebCrawler, or OpenText is a good way to undertake such a search. Many of these systems allow you to search either Web sites or postings made to USENET, so this can be one of the best ways to find someone. This will often turn up his e-mail address or take you to his Web site in order to find it.

Learning how to use these particular systems can be easy yet challenging. As a result, we take a look at how to effectively use the Internet to do such research in our chapter "Undertaking Research on the Internet."

Look for a High School/University Alumni Site

If you know the person's old high school or university, try its Web site. Many high schools now contain e-mail directories of alumni. Northern Secondary School in Toronto, for example, (**http://www.vantage.net/northern/**) features an alumni listing:

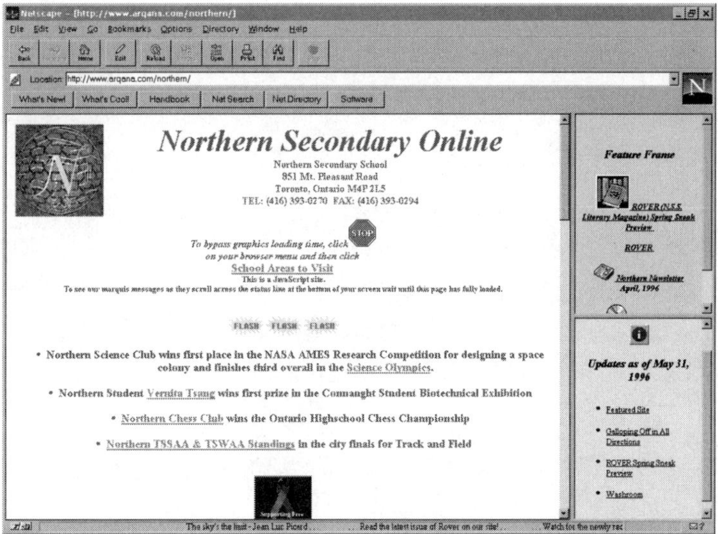

So does the Halifax West High School Unofficial Web Page (**http://www.ccn.cs.dal.ca/~ac829/HWHS.html**):

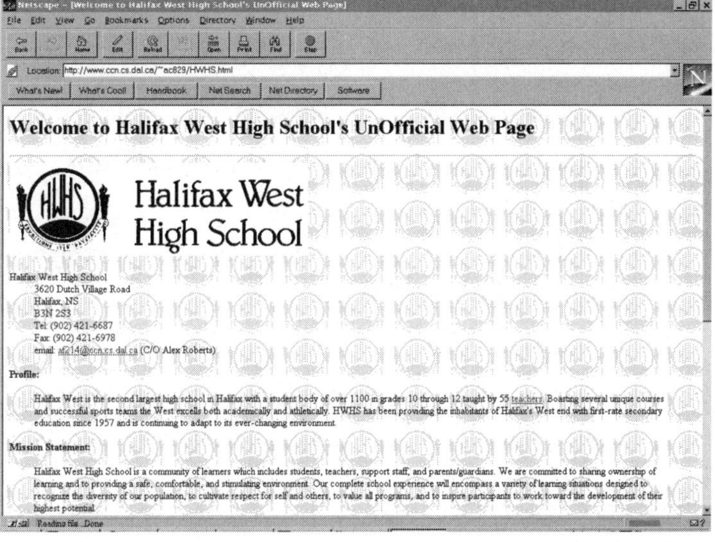

Use a Directory of Professionals

There are several sites on the Internet that index e-mail addresses by profession. For example, MineNet is a directory of professionals involved in the mining industry (**http://www.microserve.net/~doug/whitepg.html**).

Use a Regional Directory (City, Town, Province, State, etc.)

You might also discover directories that provide directories for particular geographic areas. The Yukon Internet Directory (**http://whitepages.yknet.yk.ca**) is a good example of this type of initiative:

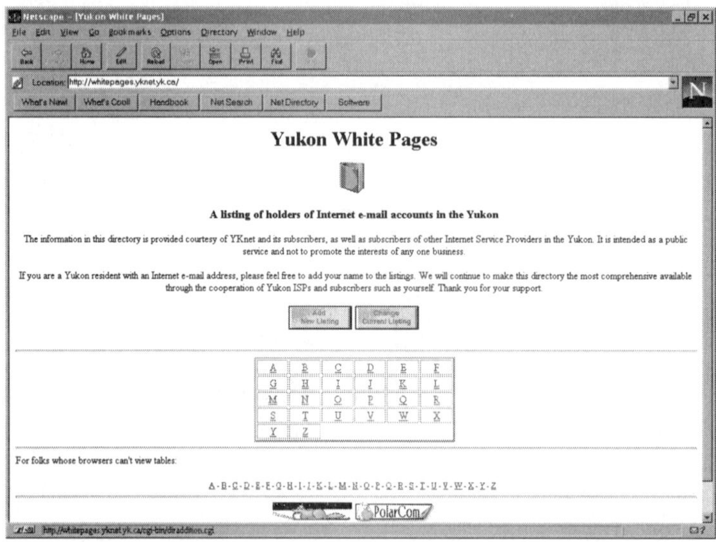

Use a Community-Oriented Directory

Many cultural communities are establishing e-mail directories, and are therefore a worthwhile place to check. The Filipino–Canadian Internet Directory (**http://www.terraport.net/baylon/filihome.htm**) is a good example of this type of initiative:

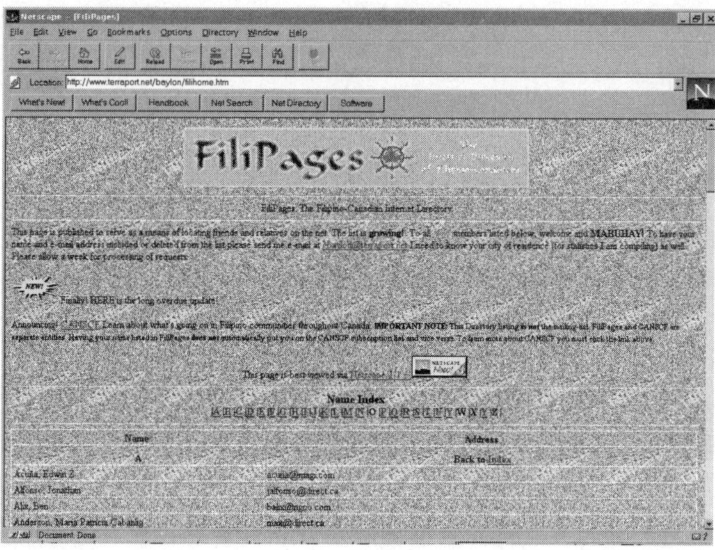

Could You Be Using a Better E-mail Program?

Many individuals using Internet e-mail do so through the e-mail program provided to them by their Internet service provider or included in the software package that they bought to access the Internet. Consequently, many people use packages such as Eudora Light, the e-mail component of Netscape Navigator, or the "Inbox" that comes with Microsoft Windows 95. While all these programs are good, using them could be likened to driving a Volkswagen Beetle when there are a lot of Porsches around. You might not have the full degree of flexibility that can be found with many e-mail programs. Hence, as you continue to explore the Internet, you might consider using another Internet e-mail program. Some of the better ones include:

PROGRAM	COMPUTER SYSTEM	LOCATION
Pegasus Mail	Mac, Windows, Windows 95	**http://www.pegasus.usa.com**
Email Connection	Windows	**http://www.connectsoft.com/corp/products/download.html**
Eudora (full version)	Mac, Windows	**http://www.qualcomm.com/ProdTech/quest/products.html**
Claris E-mailer	Mac	**http:://www.claris.com/support/products/ClarisEmailer**
JetMail	Windows, Windows 95	**http://www.netmanage.com**
Z-Mail	Mac, Windows, Windows 95	**http://www.netmanage.com**

Through many of these sites you can download a trial version of the software, in order to see if you want to purchase the particular product. In other cases the software may be available on a shareware or freeware basis.

Jim and Rick's Picks

When it comes to electronic mail, Jim and Rick have been using the same e-mail software for several years now. Some people ask what we use.

Jim

I use Pegasus Mail for Windows and have been since about 1993. There are several reasons. First off, it has very sophisticated e-mail filters, which "preread" my e-mail for me and file it off into a folder accordingly. These filters are a godsend; for example, any mail that I get from Rick automatically goes into a separate folder, as does e-mail for our radio show and any sent from people who read the book. I keep threatening Rick that I'll modify my filters one day so that any mail from him goes in the trash.

I also belong to a few e-mail lists, and the filters can be used to automatically store those messages in predefined folders. All of this helps me to manage the sometimes massive volumes of e-mail that I get. You can see these folders below:

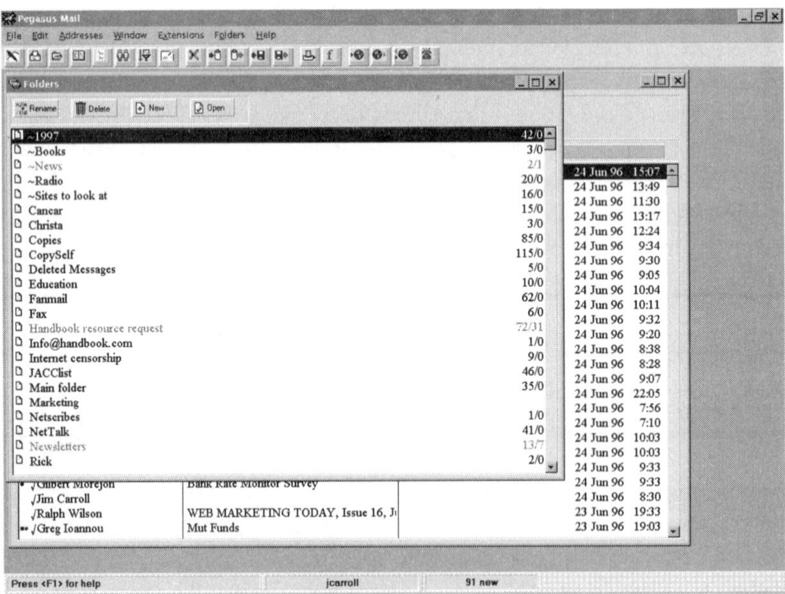

I also use these filters to manage my own custom mailing list, which people can join through my Web site. If you go to **http://www.jacc.com**, you will see you can join an e-mail list that I use to keep people posted about changes to my Web site. What happens when you do that is that a message comes to Pegasus Mail, which then automatically adds you to my mailing list. You also get a welcome message. That is handled by the e-mail filters in lines five, six, and seven of the screen below:

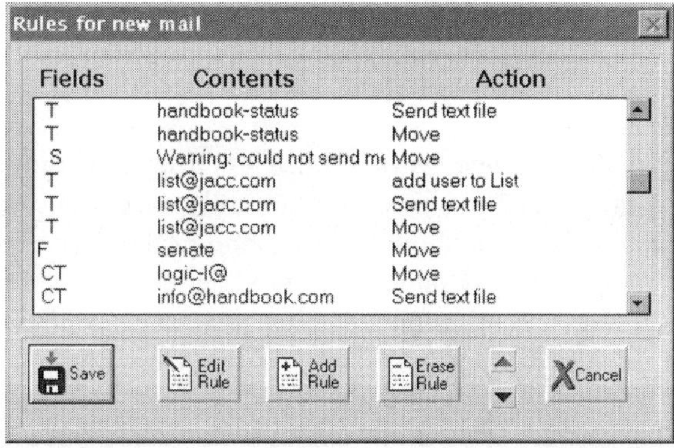

In effect, Pegasus Mail for Windows allows me to run any number of completely automated e-mail lists, which not only provides me a lot of flexibility, but saves me a lot of time. It's all totally automatic. The other thing I like about the program is that it provides folders to file mail in; I've got a bunch of folders:

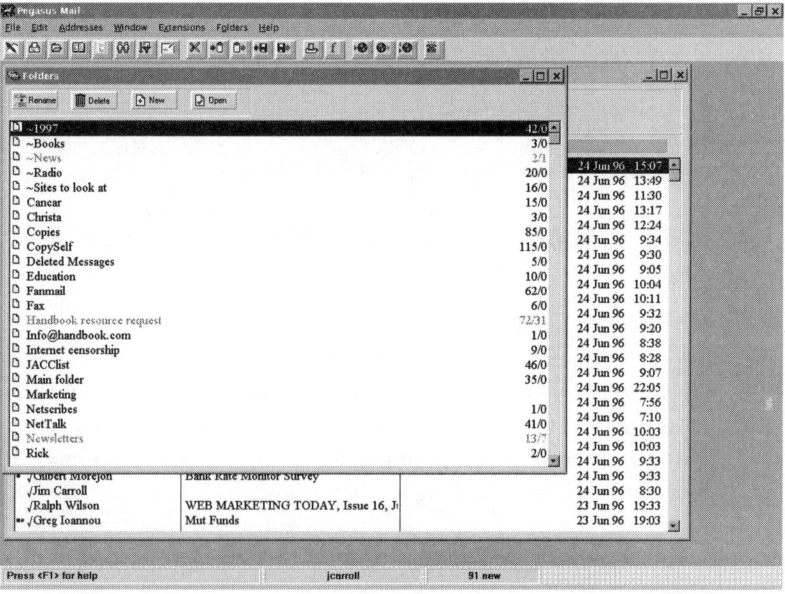

I should note that I've always been a bit of an e-mail nut. I have messages stored on my computer that I sent or received as far back as 1986. I probably keep about 60% of the messages that I send or receive, with the result that I now have over 200 megabytes of e-mail for the last twelve years. Send me something, and there is a good chance that I've kept it. It's become a wonderful reference source.

Finally, I simply like the spirit of the fellow who writes Pegasus Mail; he lives in New Zealand and does a wonderful job putting out new releases and bug fixes. I wrote an article about it, "Pegasus Mail Inspires Passion In Its Users," which can be found on my Web site. He has many enthusiastic fans worldwide.

Rick

I use Eudora Pro for Windows 95, and I've been using it ever since I got my first personal Internet account in 1993. Eudora is packed with useful features and can be customized to suit your needs. One of the most useful features is the ability to sort your e-mail into predefined folders based on the origin of the incoming message. I subscribe to IBM's infoSage — a newsclipping service — and that alone generates several dozen messages per day. I have configured Eudora so that it places all my news stories in a separate folder, so they don't clutter up my mailbox.

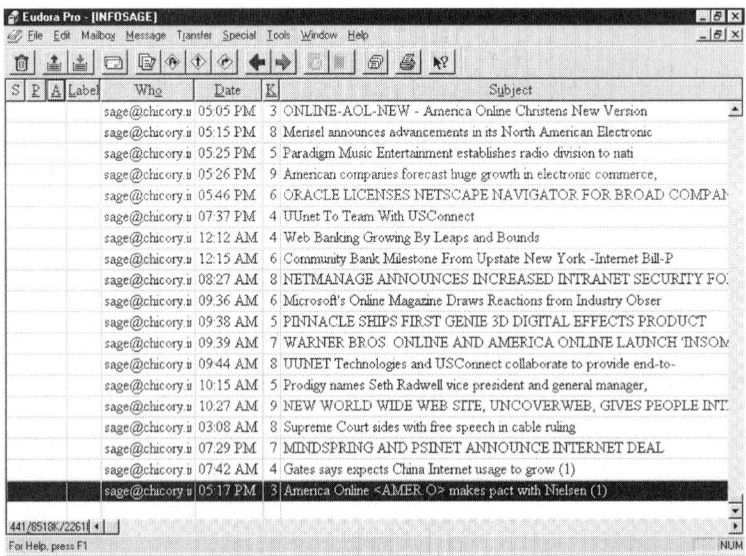

I have a sound card installed on my computer, and I have set up Eudora to alert me with a "chime" when I receive e-mail. This is particularly useful because I am often using other programs (Netscape, for example, or my word processor) when new mail arrives, and sometimes I don't notice that I've received an e-mail message from someone. When I turn the chime feature on, I don't have to worry about constantly checking for new e-mail.

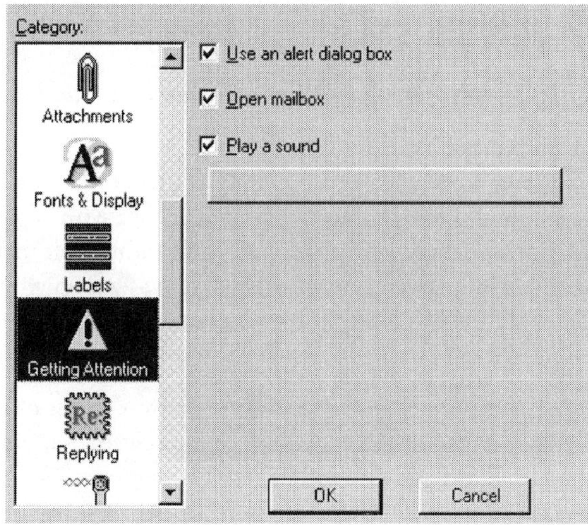

Finally, I travel frequently, and I like to be able to check my e-mail while I'm on the road. The problem is, I have two computers: a desktop computer for my office and a notebook computer for my business trips. I have Eudora installed on both. This means that some of my e-mail is on my notebook, and some of my e-mail is on my desktop, depending upon where I was when I picked up the messages. E-mail is difficult to manage when it's not all in one place.

Eudora solves this problem for me. When I am on a business trip, I can select an option called "Leave mail on server." I do this on the Eudora package installed on my notebook computer. This allows me to retrieve all my e-mail on my notebook, but also receive a copy of each message on my desktop computer when I get back to the office. Without this feature I would manually have to transfer my e-mail messages from my notebook computer to my desktop computer every time I return from a business trip.

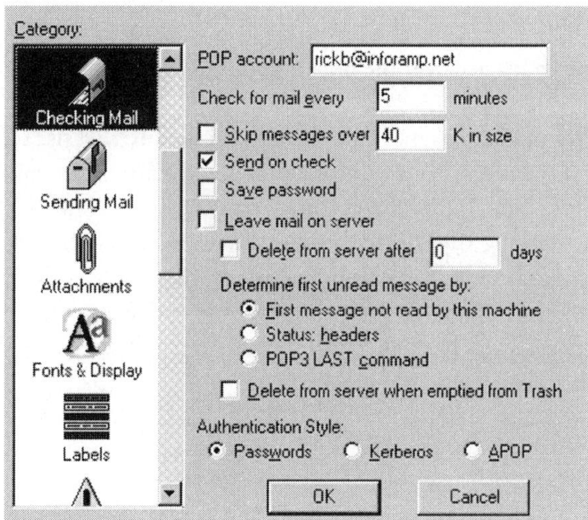

Problems With Internet E-mail

Finally, if you plan on using Internet e-mail in your organization, there are a number of important considerations:

- Internet e-mail is not necessarily secure nor is it private. The Internet is a cooperative global network, built upon a protocol (TCP/IP) that involves the routing of information through different paths in the network. This means that mail is sometimes routed through various systems on the network; at any point your e-mail message could be compromised. An Internet e-mail message is subject not only to possible access by third parties somewhere in its travels, but its contents could also be changed.
- Internet e-mail does not necessarily guarantee delivery nor is it necessarily fast. There is nothing to ensure that an Internet message is received. Sometimes systems disappear, and sometimes they go down. The result is that your message might not be sent. In some cases, you will be told of the failed delivery, and in other cases you might not. With some Internet e-mail systems you can request a "receipt" for messages that you have sent; however, you are not guaranteed that you will get such a receipt back. The result is that if you need a business application that guarantees delivery of e-mail with proof of delivery, the Internet is not the system for you.
- Internet e-mail can be forged. It is relatively easy for a person familiar with Internet e-mail protocols to forge e-mail. An experienced user could send you a message from **president@whitehouse.gov**, and you might be thrilled to receive such a message, but it is unlikely that Bill Clinton would decide to send you a message. There is no mechanism in Internet e-mail to prove the authenticity of the sender. However, the use of "digital signatures" is becoming increasingly commonplace on the Internet and will make forgery much more difficult in the future. With a digital signature it is possible to determine if the message has been tampered with and verify that the author is who he says he is. Some predict that digital signatures will become much more widespread on the Internet in the next 12 to 18 months.

These issues result in the reluctance by some organizations to use Internet e-mail for anything more than casual messaging.

To solve the security problem, some organizations on the Internet use software that encrypts inbound and outbound messages, both to protect their contents and to ensure their authenticity. Such a capability does exist, but involves some extra expense.

The reality is that, despite the shortcomings, the use of Internet e-mail continues to explode. In the same way that people continue to use cellular phones, people continue to use Internet e-mail. In your case, if you have a great deal of sensitive e-mail, you should encrypt it. If you do not, you should always be cognizant of these fundamental concerns.

Significant E-mail Trends

We close this chapter with some comments on how Internet e-mail will evolve in the future.

1. Internet E-mail Addresses Will Be Included in Print Telephone Directories

Sweden was the first country to announce such plans; the publishers of their telephone directories now allow one additional line of information for each telephone number to accommodate an e-mail address. As an indication of how widely accepted e-mail is as a standard means of communication, most of Canada's telephone companies plan to integrate e-mail addresses into their white and yellow page listings during the 1996/1997 season. For a nominal fee customers will be able to include an e-mail or Web address beside their telephone number in the *White Pages.*

In addition, on-line *Yellow Pages* will regularly highlight Internet e-mail addresses. A good example can already be found with the Manitoba *Yellow Pages,* all of which have been placed on-line (**http://www.mtsdirectory.com**). Each yellow page entry on-line can include an e-mail address for key company contacts.

The concept of including e-mail addresses in the phone book does, however, raise some interesting issues:

- Privacy concerns. Telephone companies are eager to find out how Canadians will respond to this new service. Because of concerns over junk mail, most Canadians may opt not to have their Internet addresses published in the *White Pages.*
- Technical obstacles. Many telephone directory publishers admit they may need to upgrade their computer systems to be able to accept and print the symbols found in many Internet addresses. For example, the ~ (tilde) symbol is a part of many Internet addresses, but some telephone directory publishers are not able to handle that symbol without changing all the computer keyboards in their offices.

We hope that by the time you read this book, many of these problems will have been worked out.

2. E-mail Will Include Video, Voice, and Other Data

Once individuals and organizations began to exchange Internet e-mail with others around the globe, they soon realized that there was no standard method to exchange computer files such as documents, spreadsheets, pictures, and other forms of data. This is why so many people become confused or have problems when trying to send e-mail "attachments." As a result, today e-mail on the Internet is still very much a technology that simply permits people to exchange plain text. Some have taken the time to learn how to master sending a computer file to someone else, but many others have not bothered.

That will soon change with the impact of a new form of e-mail that incorporates sound, images, video, and other forms of data called MIME (multimedia Internet mail extensions). MIME is an Internet standard that permits many different types of data to be included in e-mail. This will change our concept of e-mail.

Consider this example of where e-mail is headed. Voice E-Mail, a program from Bonzi Software (**http://www.bonzi.com**), supports "voice attachments" within e-mail messages. Bonzi works with the Eudora e-mail program as well as the e-mail component of Netscape 2.0 and a few other e-mail programs. Once installed, the program simply becomes a new menu item within Eudora which allows you to "play voice e-mail" and "create voice e-mail" within your regular e-mail messages. All you need on your PC are speakers and a microphone, accessories that are already becoming standard equipment on most PCs.

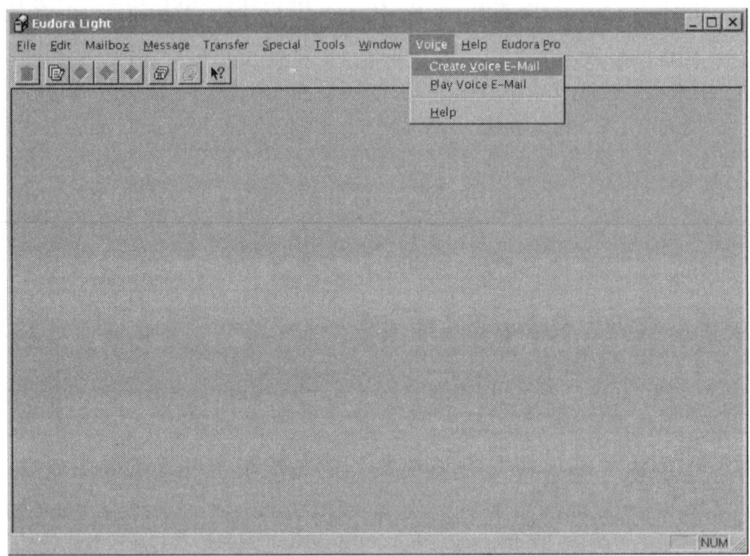

When you want to create a new voice e-mail message, a screen pops up in which you press the "Record" button. You then say your message. When finished, you press the "Stop record button," address the e-mail message, and send it. Your voice message is sent, buried within the e-mail message.

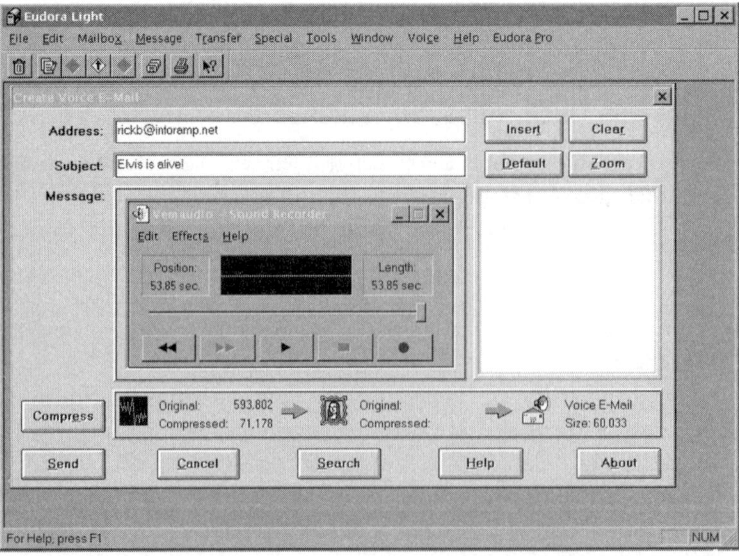

The software compresses the voice e-mail message automatically before sending it. The recipient, who must also be using the same software, will see the message automatically "decompress" when she goes to read it. Hence the software helps to deal with the fact that voice files are quite large compared to simple e-mail text messages.

The software from Bonzi is quite interesting, for it helps to demonstrate how in the future e-mail will consist of more than simple messages. People will routinely send each other messages that contain their spoken words. As video becomes more tightly integrated with computers, e-mail will be used to send actual video as well. Overall, e-mail will undergo a distinct and subtle shift through the next decade because of the capabilities presented by the MIME standard.

3. E-mail Will Happen Anywhere

Cellular telephone companies such as Nokia (**http://www.nokia.com**) are rolling out cellular products that provide access to the Net, allowing people to access their e-mail using a cell phone for the connection. And radio-based e-mail is already a reality: Infowave Canada (**http://www.infowave.net**) already provides the facility to send and receive e-mail messages from anywhere in most major cities and towns across Canada. Flip open your laptop in the middle of a park, type your message, and away it goes! Soon we will be sending and receiving e-mail from the darndest places. Restaurants will put up signs saying "No e-mail from your table" next to the signs forbidding people to use cell phones while eating dinner.

4. E-mail, Telephones, and Paging Services Will Integrate

In a more interesting development, Northern Telecom is developing telephones that incorporate Sun's Java technology, which allows telephones to directly access e-mail. As they noted in a press release, "by bringing the Java Technology™ advantage to the telecommunications industry, consumers will soon be able to access Internet services wherever they are, using a new breed of affordable, next generation client/server telephones."

Notes the press release: "the potential uses of these low-cost intelligent devices in accessing Internet services are many. For example, a realtor could use one of the new wireless or desk telephones to call into an Internet multi-listing database and have a brief description, price and even small photo of a property displayed on the telephone screen. Other innovative uses include travel reservations, directory services, efficient access to e-mail, fax mail and voice mail, and a wide variety of other applications." As telephones become married to the Internet, e-mail on the Internet will simply become more accessible.

Paging services, too, will become tightly integrated with the Internet. Many paging companies, including Cantel, Bell Mobility, and PageMart Canada, already allow their customers to be paged over the Internet. PageMart Canada, for example, allows you to send a page to someone through the World Wide Web (**http://www.pagemart.ca/send.html**):

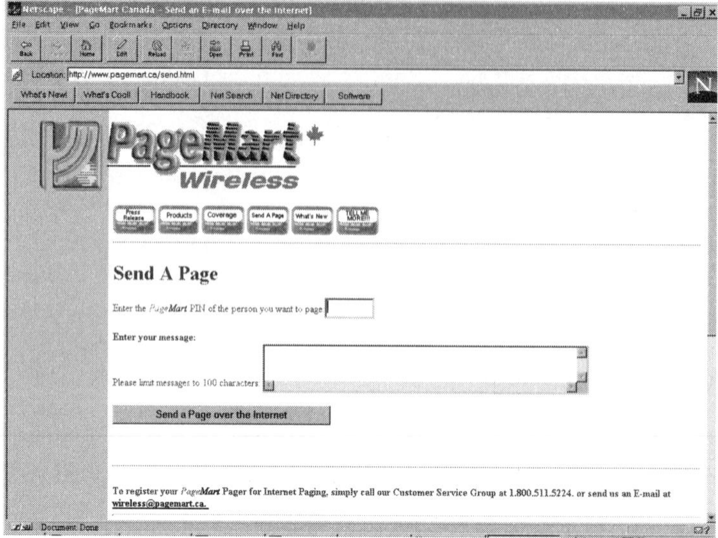

The next step? Paging companies are already linking their paging services to e-mail, so that you can send messages to any pager user directly from your e-mail software, the e-mail address of the pager being their PIN number. For example, in the case of PageMart Canada, the e-mail address of the recipient is **pinnumber@pagemart.net**.

As paging services integrate with the Internet, paging companies are beginning to offer their customers greater flexibility and control over their messaging options. For example, Bell Mobility's Epager™ service allows customers to customize how and when they receive pages from the Internet. Customers can configure their options on Bell Mobility's World Wide Web site, shown below.

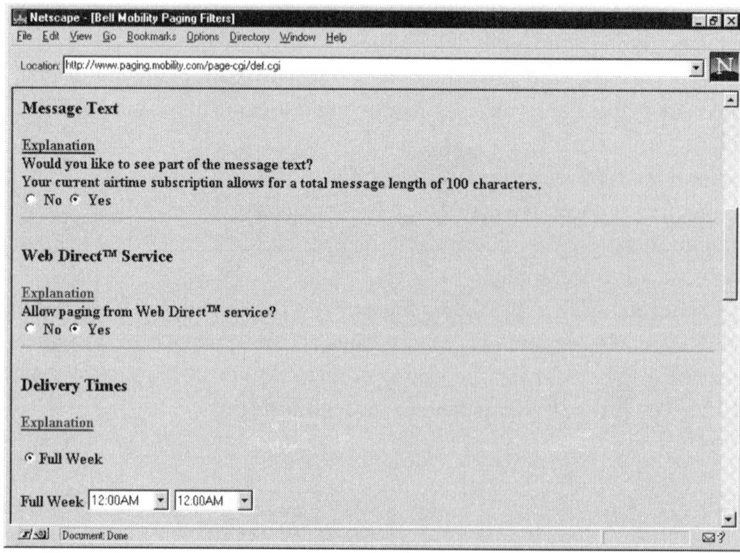

You can select the times of day you want to be paged, control how the sender is identified, and even block messages from certain people. If you receive a page from the Internet when you have asked not to be disturbed, the system will hold the message for you until you become available again.

5. Canada Post Will Become a Major Player in E-mail

Canada Post is not taking the Internet sitting down and, in fact, plans to become a significant player in the Internet in Canada. As they do so, they will help to make Internet e-mail accessible to more and more Canadians. For years, Canada Post has been the main method by which Canadians communicate. Jean-Maurice Filion, Manager of Media Relations for Canada Post, notes that "we plan to play the same role, by 'taming' the electronic highway and adapting the traditional post office to the new reality."

The size and scope of Canada Post are important factors in helping this realization: "Canada Post remains the only single organization that reaches all Canadians in all communities. We have to leverage the Internet to make everybody benefit, physically or electronically." Part of those plans includes exploring the opportunity of providing "kiosks" in Canada Post locations with which anyone can send and receive e-mail. Don't have Internet e-mail? No problem. Go to your local post office and sign on. In effect, Canada Post wants to take on the role of helping to ensure that all Canadians have access to the Internet, including Internet e-mail. In effect, the "kiosk" might help to extend Internet e-mail throughout Canada.

An important point is raised, however: will paper mail disappear because of the Internet? Not likely. Notes Filion, "the unique qualities of paper mail are more precious than ever. Mail is personal, tangible, private, secure, interactive..." In fact, even with the explosion of the Internet, volumes of paper-based mail are still increasing at rates of 1% to 3% per year, according to figures supplied by Canada Post (see the following illustration).

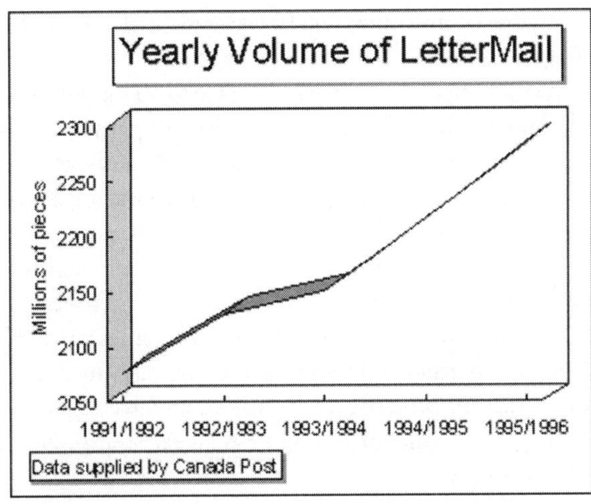

Quite simply, Internet e-mail and paper mail will come to coexist, simply because Internet e-mail has certain physical limitations. Filion makes this point rather succinctly: "Not all customers of these businesses are on-line. The target features of direct mail are still very important to businesses, as well as an efficient distribution service for the merchandise those same businesses will sell through the Internet." A good overview of Canada Post and its thoughts regarding e-mail can be found on-line, the "Welcoming Address – Postal Conference '95," featuring remarks by Georges Clermont, President and CEO, Canada Post Corporation (**http://www.mailposte.ca/english/whatsnew/speeches/clerm.html**).

6. Junk Mail Will Increase

One unfortunate reality of Internet e-mail seems to be that junk mail is destined to increase. Noted the *Seattle Post-Intelligencer* in an article on June 25, 1996 ("Junk-Mailers Discover The Internet"): "Direct-mail solicitors have discovered the Internet and the online world of electronic commerce. The chance that one's e-mailbox will remain a pristine file for personal communications has passed." The authors have noted the trend increasing throughout 1996, a slow but steady trend in which people send unsolicited e-mail.

What can you do when you get junk mail? One of the key things is to send e-mail to the postmaster of the offending organization or the company that provides Internet services to the junk mail sender, requesting that the account be shut down. Keep in mind that many people who send junk mail are abusing the terms and conditions of their Internet account. Sadly, the problem has become so severe that several large Internet service providers have set up special mailboxes to handle complaints about junk mail and other forms of Internet abuse. Examples are NETCOM (**abuse@netcom.com**), America Online (**abuse@aol.com**), and Earthlink (**abuse@earthlink.com**).

7. Internet E-mail Will Help to Drive New Forms of Corporate Organization

In an article in the June 18, 1989 issue of the *New York Times* entitled "Tomorrow's Company Won't Have Walls," it was noted that "for many companies, the classic forms of corporate organization no longer work very well." Instead, the article referred to the fact that "the perfectly competitive organization of the future will be an elaborate network of people and information..." In other words, the company of the future will be more of an electronic network than a physical place to where people go to work.

Internet e-mail is already helping to drive this change. The result is a growing belief that the organization of the future will look nothing like the company of today. Rather than a large head office with a massive staff, the company of the future will consist of a small group of key management, who have access to staff, contractors, specialists, and business partners around the globe. This management group will require sophisticated tools to keep in contact with these resources, so Internet e-mail (as well as other tools) will be fundamental to their working lives.

Changes in our economy are already driving the need for increased intercorporate communication, with the result being ongoing growth in the use of Internet e-mail. Quite clearly, our economy is seeing new levels of "partnership," in which companies increasingly work together on joint development or marketing projects. Such projects involve regular, ongoing communication, something that the global nature of Internet e-mail excels at providing.

8. Internet E-mail Privacy Issues Will Become Prominent

In February 1994 the Information and Privacy Commissioner/Ontario released a report entitled "Privacy Protection Principles for Electronic Mail Systems." The report outlined many of the complex and important issues related to the use of and access to e-mail within organizations and between organizations. One comment in the report caught the attention of the popular press, an observation that "e-mail has 'the same security level as a postcard.'" What the report managed to do was to make people aware that privacy was indeed becoming an important issue with e-mail.

With the explosion of Internet e-mail the privacy issue is now coming to the forefront. There are several risks:

- unauthorized access to employee e-mail, which might include Internet e-mail, by the employer;
- interception of e-mail by unauthorized persons as it travels through the Internet;
- access to Internet e-mail by the government in order to monitor its citizens or to track criminal activity.

People who use Internet e-mail should be aware, at a minimum, of the risks posed by the first two points. But it is the final point that is the most troubling.

When it comes to the Internet, it seems that different proposals are being floated by different governments around the world in which they suggest that they should be provided the capability to monitor e-mail sent by their citizens. And we, as citizens, are supposed to trust these people when they tell us they will only look at our e-mail if certain circumstances are met, that is, we are suspected of criminal activity. Right. And citizens believed them when they introduced taxes in 1917 as a *temporary measure*. Or that certain political parties would get rid of the GST if elected. For some strange reason we trust politicians. Perhaps we should all have our heads examined.

There is no doubt there will be an ongoing battle between government (who want to enshrine a legal right to monitor any form of digital communication) and citizens (who believe there are fundamental issues of freedom of speech) over the issue of electronic privacy. Internet e-mail is directly affected.

What can you do? Learn about the privacy topic at the Electronic Frontier Canada Web site (**http://www.efc.ca**) or at the Electronic Frontier Foundation (**http://www.eff.org**). Become involved. Stand up for your rights. Doubt the politicians when they issue their soothing words. *Trust no one.*

If you are interested in learning how you can "encrypt" your e-mail so that no one can access it (not even the government), you should learn about PGP (Pretty Good Privacy), a program that is quickly being adopted throughout the Internet as the standard for e-mail encryption. Although still a technically complex topic, the field of encryption is evolving rapidly. Check out the PGP Frequently Asked Questions summary for more information (**http://www.quadralay.com/www/Crypt/PGP/pgp00.html**).

9. E-mail Will Become Ubiquitous

As more Canadians adopt the Internet, the use of Internet e-mail will become even more ubiquitous than it is today. All the elements are there for a rapid and massive adoption of the Internet across Canada within the next five years. For example, consider the Sympatico Internet service offered by Bell Canada, which is available almost everywhere in Canada where local telephone service is available, effectively extending Internet capabilities to everyone. Combine developments like that with the ongoing marriage of the Internet to telephones, the arrival of $500 network computers and other devices, and you can see that it is not silly to realize that a majority of Canadians will soon be using Internet e-mail.

10. E-mail Will Be Acknowledged as a Legitimate Form of Communication

In 1996 the Prime Minister announced his e-mail address (**pm@pm.gc.ca**). What else can be said? The fact is that Internet e-mail has already been accepted by mainstream society.

CHAPTER 7

The World Wide Web

In 1844, Samuel Morse unleashed the era of instant communications by telegraphing four words from Washington to Baltimore: "What hath God wrought?" We ask that question every time a new technology sweeps across our culture. The latest example is the World Wide Web. Just five years ago at a lab in Switzerland, computer scientist Tim Berners-Lee devised a novel way for computers to share information. It would allow people anywhere on the globe to receive text, pictures, sounds — all in seconds, without complicated commands, no matter how far the distance. Not only that, the information would arrive containing electronic links to related material, so that after finding an item of interest, a person could move automatically to the next.

The Web was born. Today tens of millions of people are tapping into it and thousands more are initiated every day. A cross section of the human experience, good and bad, is swirling around the Web and other conduits of the on-line dimension known as cyberspace: religious texts, blackjack games, art exhibits, political manifestos, theater timetables, love letters, ads, wanted posters, scientific treatises, drafts of first novels, peep shows.

On the Internet, a Worldwide Information Explosion Beyond Words
The Washington Post, June 30, 1996

On the World Wide Web you can find a site that details the contents of Jeremy Wilson's wallet (**http://www.inforamp.net/~xeno**):

THE WORLD WIDE WEB

1. Millions of people around the world have become global publishers because of the existence of the World Wide Web.
2. You access information on Web "sites" found throughout the Internet by using Web browser software.
3. The Web has many different characteristics, making it an increasingly easy-to-use source of useful multimedia information.
4. Most of the information that you access on the Web is free, but there are a growing number of pay-per-access sites, as well as advertising-supported sites.
5. You can access sound and video through the Web, although the quality will depend on the speed of your Internet connection.
6. You can also access other special information formats through the Web, ranging from specially formatted documents to three-dimensional images and animation.

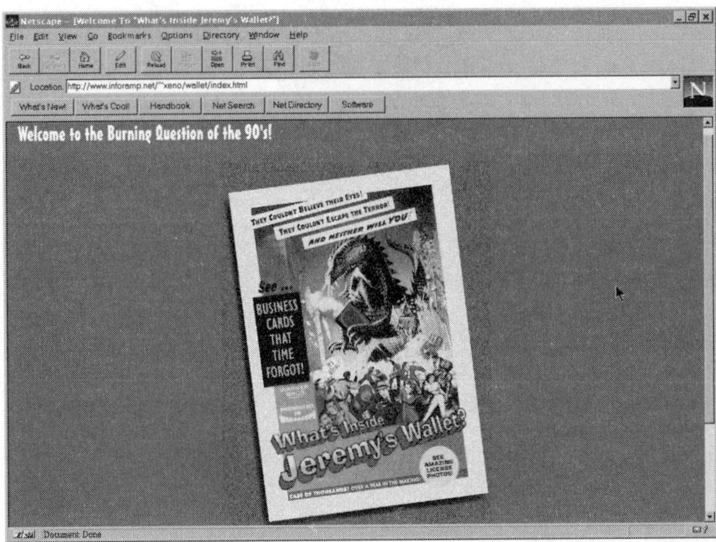

Visit the Web site, and you can take an actual tour of the details of his wallet, either by taking a "walking tour" or by viewing individual components of the wallet:

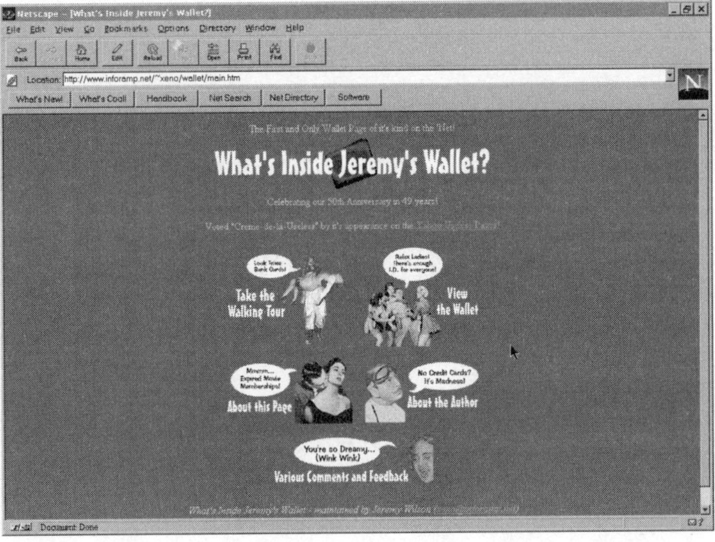

What can you see? Jeremy has taken the time to put in his Web site actual images of the credit and other cards from his wallet and provides a description of each. (Wisely, he has altered the number of each individual card.)

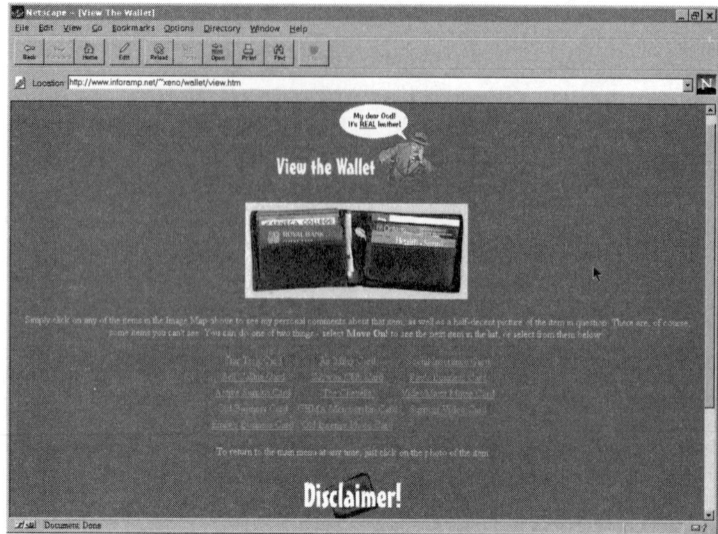

Here is a picture of Jeremy's "Sub Club Card," which gets him a free submarine sandwich every once in a while:

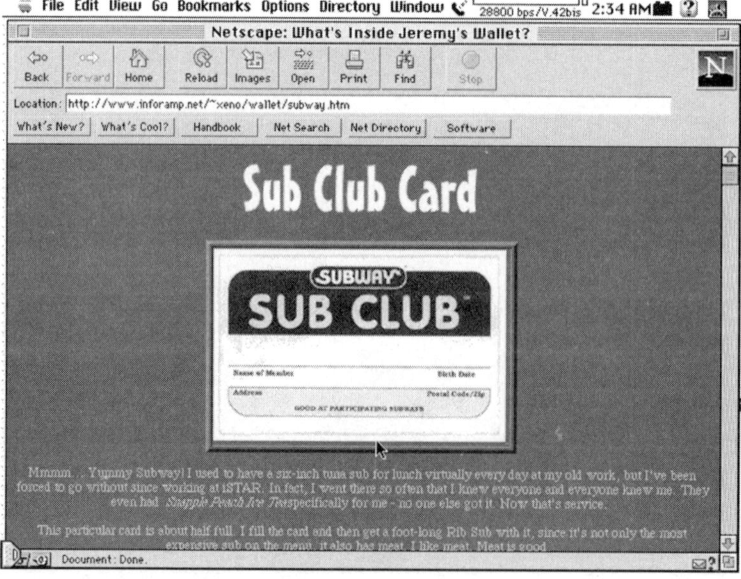

Who is Jeremy Wilson? Why did we tell you about his wallet? For that matter, why would Jeremy Wilson put up pictures from his wallet onto the World Wide Web? What is going on here?

The Nature of the World Wide Web

What is going on here is that millions of people around the globe are becoming international publishers through the World Wide Web. The Web is nothing less than a global digital printing press, a printing press that people are using like mad to make information available on anything imaginable. Including the contents of their wallets.

Jeremy Wilson has put his wallet up on the Web simply *because he can.* With the Web he has been given a global printing press, and he intends to use it for whatever he likes. He is simply a 23-year-old who has learned what is involved in putting a site up on the Web and has decided to use it to provide intimate details about his wallet. And why shouldn't he?

What is the Web?

Where do we start in describing the Web? We have to start somewhere, but the thing about the Web is that we can start anywhere and end up everywhere. The Web does not really have a starting point, and it does not have a finish line. And it changes on a daily, minute-by-minute, and even millisecond-by-millisecond basis. The Web of right now is different from the Web of a moment ago. It is kind of a fascinating place. And that is an understatement.

The Web Is Whatever You Want It to Be

Trying to define the Web is like trying to define a book. What is a book? It is simply a physical object that can hold information. Information on any topic imaginable, of any length from one or two pages to several thousand pages, from one volume to many volumes. Books can be updated each and every year, and books can be printed and instantly go out of print because of lack of interest in the topic they cover. Technical books, general interest books, kids' books, reference books, trash romance books, picture books — you name it, they exist.

It is the same with a "Web site," the term often used to describe a place on the Internet that contains information. Information on any topic and of differing complexity and depth. Of wide-ranging appeal to little or no intrinsic value whatsoever. From the contents of Jeremy Wilson's wallet to the contents of the Smithsonian Institution.

The Web is nothing less than a global publishing phenomenon. If you think about it, it is a tool that is quickly changing our entire global information paradigm. Everyone in the world can become a publisher through the Web. Anyone can put information on-line about any topic; there is no central authority, there are no rules, and there are no boundaries. Anyone can make his/her Web site "point" to any other Web site. Anyone can build an index of Web information, and anyone can list his/her favorite sites. The result is that through the Web there is an amazing amount of information available, which consists of text, sound, images, pictures, and even "movies" and three-dimensional animation. One estimate is that there are in excess of 75 million pages of information available, a number that is growing rapidly. Tomorrow, it will consist of much more. This, for a system that did not even exist until 1989 and did not really begin to take off until 1993.

The Web is becoming a system that is coming to rival traditional information distribution methods such as radio, newspapers, and television, since it has become possible to access live radio stations and other "broadcasts" from around the world. The Web is nothing less than the foundation for a new type of information distribution channel, unlike any the world has seen before. The reason? Everyone on the Internet is potentially a broadcaster through the Web.

The History of the Web

The Web is little more than seven years old and has come a tremendously long way in those years. Viewing its history is a good indication of how quickly the Internet moves when it comes to the development and implementation of new technology.

- In March 1989 a project proposal to build an Internet "hypertext" system was made at CERN, the European Laboratory for Particle Physics, an organization involved in the fledgling Internet in Europe. The proposal envisioned a system on the emerging Internet that would permit "interlinked documents" located anywhere in the world to permit the exchange of information and to allow the cross-linking of reference and research papers by different institutions. Discussions and research into the concept took place through the next year. The proposal was resubmitted in October 1990, and a prototype of the World Wide Web was built the following month.
- In August 1991 details of the Web server software and preliminary "browser software" (i.e., the tools you use to travel through the Web) were posted to various USENET newsgroups on the Internet, so that anyone in the world could begin experimenting with World Wide Web technology. Global mailing lists to support online discussion of the Web protocols started two months later, so that people could share their research results instantly. Web development began at a breakneck pace.
- Through 1992 more browser software was released, and more refinements to the server software took place. The Web began to gain a foothold in academic and research communities around the world, who realized that they had something significant on their hands.
- In February 1993 the first version of Mosaic was released for UNIX systems from NCSA, the U.S. National Center for SuperComputing Applications. Unlike previous Web browsers, Mosaic supports automatic display of images and pictures found in Web documents, multiple fonts, and many other enhancements that make the Web a dramatically different place.
- The next month Web traffic took up 0.1% of the total traffic on the main Internet backbone network in the United States (NSFNet). Within six months it grew to 1% of total traffic, as use of Mosaic opened up the Web to many people.
- NCSA released versions of Mosaic for Windows and Macintosh systems in September 1993. Interest in the Internet began to hit the mainstream, as many discovered its magic for the first time.
- Some 500 global Web servers were in existence around the world by October 1993. Growth increased, as the Web gained attention in the *Globe and Mail*, *New York Times*, and other leading media organizations.

- In March 1994 the original developers of Mosaic left the NCSA to form Netscape Communications Corp. They released Netscape in September 1994 for Windows, UNIX, and Macintosh systems. Netscape solved many of the technical problems encountered by users of Mosaic who access the Internet using dial-up modems. The result was a tidal wave in growth of use of the Web by people at home.
- The Web exceeded all other types of Internet traffic in March 1994. It has not slowed down since.
- By June 1994, 1,500 Web servers were known.
- Netscape went public in August 1995, almost tripling its share price in a matter of days. Web mania seemed to envelop the world. By October 1995 a popular index of Web sites had listed over 40,000 Web servers.
- In December 1995 Bill Gates announced to the world that he realized the future of computing focused around the Internet and the World Wide Web, and he announced plans to make Microsoft a major player in the global Internet marketplace.
- By July 1996 a popular index of Web sites listed over 90,000 Web servers, and another announced that it knew of 75 million pages of information. Web addresses were common on television shows, in the news, and on business cards. The Web had clearly arrived.

How Does the Web Work?

The basics of the Web seem straightforward enough: you use software known as a "Web browser" to travel to a Web server somewhere to access a page or pages of information on that server. You do this by loading your browser software (a program such as Netscape Navigator or Microsoft Internet Explorer) and then key in a Web address (e.g., **http://www.inforamp.net/~xeno**). In a few seconds you are at the site that contains the contents of Jeremy Wilson's wallet.

It seems straightforward enough. Behind the scenes there is a lot going on to accomplish the simple act of traveling to a Web site. To be honest, you really do not need to worry about how it works. The magic of the Internet is that even though it might be a long and circuitous route from your browser to the site containing the information, how it accomplishes this is not really your concern. All you have to do is simply key in the address of the place you want to go to, and you should arrive there (at least most of the time). However, like many people, you probably do want to know how the Web works. Basically, there are several things that happen on the Web that permit you to see a "page" of information anywhere in the world:

- You use software known as a Web browser to view information on the World Wide Web. The most popular Web browser is Netscape Navigator; however, the Web browser from Microsoft, Internet Explorer, is quickly gaining attention.
- You provide your browser with the Web address to which you wish to travel. The address is known as the uniform resource locator, or URL. The URL address consists of the Web server (or computer) that your browser should travel to on the Internet and the specific "page" of information that should be viewed at that server.

- Once your browser has opened up a connection to the Web server specified in the URL, the information on the Web page specified in your address is sent to you in HTML format, which is a type of computer code known as hypertext markup language. If you did not indicate a specific page, then a default page (known as the "home page") is sent to you.
- Your Web browser then interprets the HTML information being sent to you by the remote Web server and presents it to you in a friendly, simple fashion according to the instructions contained in the HTML code.

An important point when you use the Web is that your Web browser is told how to get to a particular site, or Web address, as described in the second point above, in one of two ways:

- Either you tell it where to go by typing an address directly into your Web browser, e.g., **http://www.inforamp.net/~xeno**. In general, at a very simplified level, the process works like this:

FIGURE 7.1
How the Web Works

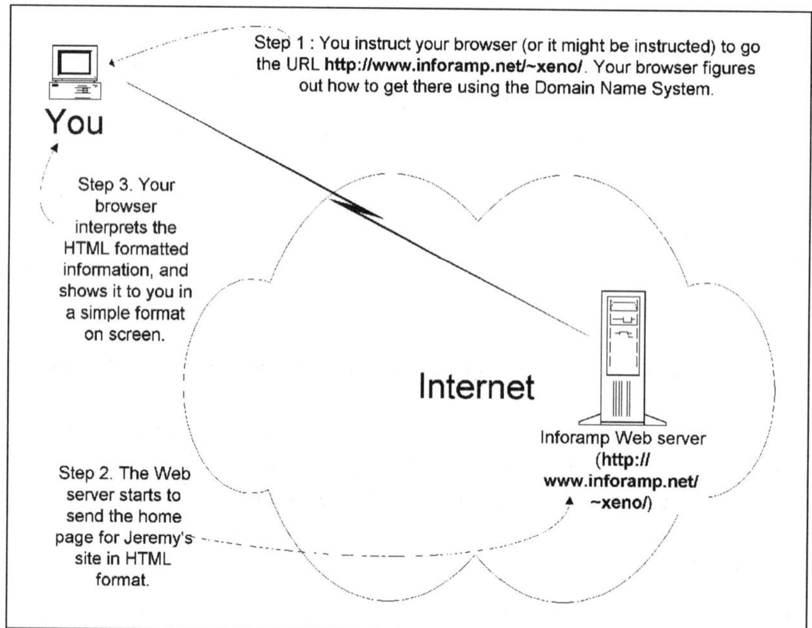

- Or it is told to go to that page by a "hypertext" link that you choose from a Web page that you are currently on. In this case an item on the Web page you are currently viewing is "linked" to another page somewhere on the Web, and the Web address of that page is automatically provided when you choose that link. The link is highlighted, so that you know if you click on it, you will be taken somewhere else on the Web.

> The real magic of the Web is this ability for "hypertext" links, for it means that any Web page can point to any other Web page on the planet, and to travel there, all you have to do is click on the highlighted link, which can be a word or an image.

In this section we will put into perspective

- the types of browsers that you can use
- and the components of a URL.

We will also take a look at the components of HTML in Chapter 14, "Setting Up a Web Site."

Web Browser Software

You travel through the World Wide Web using a browser. This is software that is designed to interpret the special code — known as HTML — that is sent to you by a Web server somewhere in the world. The browser, in most cases, can show images and pictures as well as text in many different formats. If you have configured your browser correctly (or if it is preconfigured), you can also listen to sound files and video files as well as other types of information. More on that later, when we talk about how to enhance your Web experience.

There are many different Web browsers, but from our perspective today, the only two Web browsers that really count are Netscape Navigator and Microsoft Internet Explorer, the former because of its market dominance and widescale recognition throughout the Internet, and the latter because of the formidable marketing and technical determination of Microsoft. We really cannot do a comparison of the features of Netscape Navigator to Microsoft Internet Explorer here, given that new versions of each program seem to be released almost monthly. And certainly there is enough industry hype about the battle between Netscape and Microsoft, much of it related to the features they are adding to their respective browsers.

When it comes to Web browsers, one of the most important things to keep in mind is that most people will see a different view of a particular Web page, depending upon the Web browser software and the type of computer they are using. Different computers have different capabilities, different fonts, and different screen sizes, and hence people may see something different depending upon the type of computer they use. But in many cases they may see something that is remarkably similar even though completely different software and different computers are used. For example, here is a site called "Hyperhistory" (**http://www.hyperhistory.com**), which allows you to view charts that put in perspective various historical events, as seen through Netscape on a Windows 95 system:

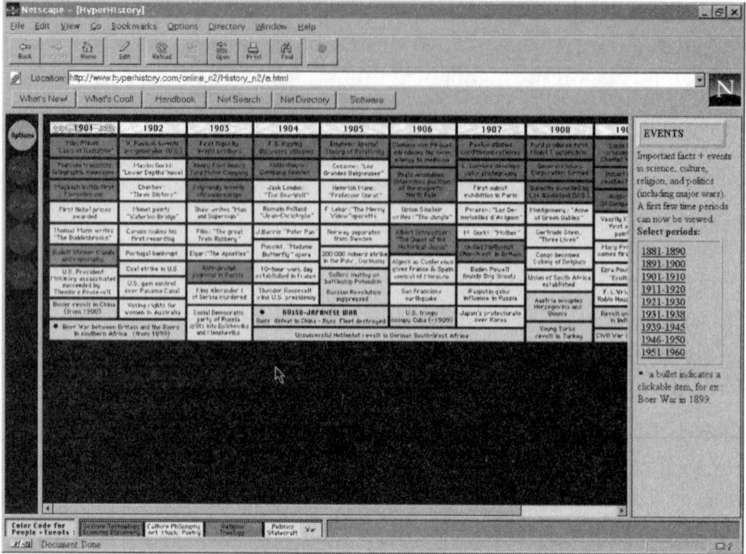

Here is the same thing through Internet Explorer on a Windows 95 system:

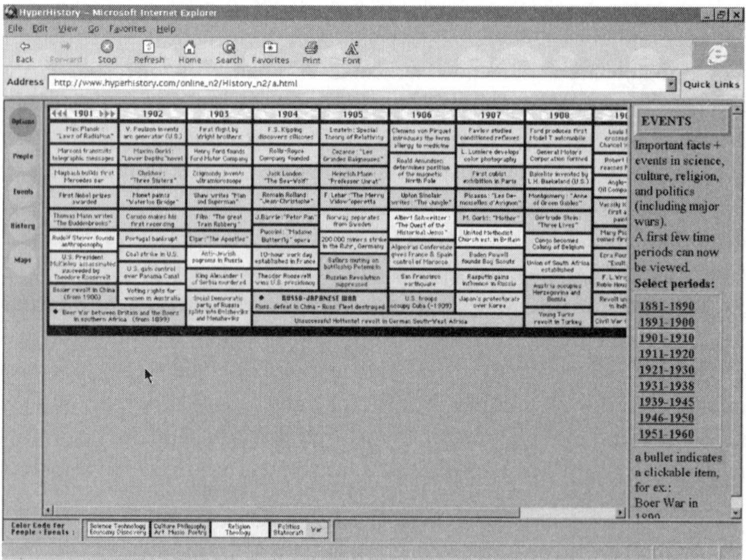

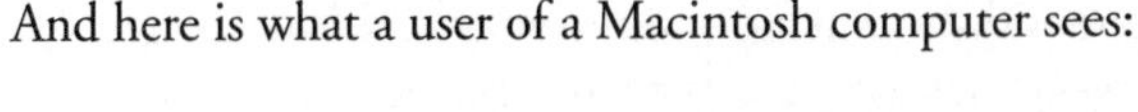

And here is what a user of a Macintosh computer sees:

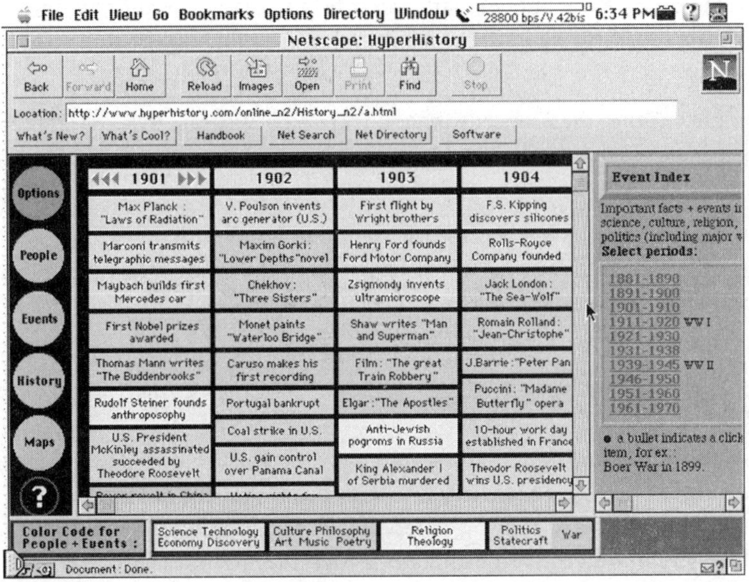

All three Web browsers pretty well show the information in the same format. The slight difference that does occur is a result of how each program interprets the HTML codes sent to it and the fonts and text styles that the program is configured to use. For example, the Mac that we used did not have as high a "screen resolution" as the PC we were using (although it might have) and hence shows only four columns of information.

You should keep in mind that most people access the World Wide Web using browsers on computers that work in "windowing systems," such as found with Microsoft Windows and Macintosh computers. But there are many who do not have computers with the power to run windowing software; they can only view plain text information. One popular software package available for basic MS DOS PCs is known as Lynx; individuals who use this program do not see any images at all. Hence like everything else you have encountered with the Internet, it is important to keep in mind that individuals accessing the Web are using all kinds of different computers and all kinds of different software. Thus everyone sees something a little different.

Browsers today share all kinds of basic features:

- Navigating within the browser is easy enough; there are buttons to take you one page forward and back, depending upon where you have been. There is also a "history" list of the sites you have visited, so that you can see where you have been.
- Most feature a series of buttons that take you to specific Web pages of the developer and provide help.
- Most support a "cache." This means that when you visit a Web site, a copy of the page that you are viewing as well as any images on that page are stored on your own computer. When you visit the site a second time, the page and images are retrieved from your hard disk, rather than from the Internet, meaning that the page will load

much quicker the second time around. Information from your cache is deleted depending upon rules you define with your software, such as every 30 days or so.

- You can have a series of bookmarks, a list of sites that you want to visit frequently, so that rather than typing in their address, you can simply choose them from a bookmark list.
- You can enhance the browser so that if you visit a Web site that contains audio or other information, it will run a separate program (either outside of the browser or within the browser window) to view that data.

The business of Web browsers has become such a serious business that new capabilities and software are released on a regular basis, so much so that in 1996 Netscape was already talking about what would be in its version 4.0, before 3.0 even became finalized.

How Does a URL Work?

We have been using the word "site" to indicate a place on the Web that contains information. A site is located on a Web server somewhere, a computer that almost always has a full-time connection to the Internet. The Web server runs "Web server software," which interprets incoming requests from Web browsers around the globe and sends back the appropriate page of information in HTML format.

The vast majority of Web servers are based on computers running the UNIX operating system. In addition, there are Web sites that run Web server software on systems running Windows 95, Windows NT, Macintosh, IBM OS/2, and other operating systems. Web server software is available from Netscape, Microsoft, and a host of other companies.

The Web server might be a computer actually located at the company to which you are linking. For example, Canadian Airlines has its own Web server located on its premises in Vancouver. In other cases the Web server might be a computer located at an Internet service provider or Internet presence provider; the company or person whose Web pages you are accessing might be renting space at that provider. For example, the Great Canadian Sports Fishing Club, a Woodbridge, ON, based site, "rents" Web space on a server located at the Internet presence provider Internet Direct Canada (**http://www.idirect.com**). Any requests to travel to the Web address for the Great Canadian Sports Fishing Club (**http://www.realfishing.com**) are actually redirected to a computer at Internet Direct Canada.

On the Web server is a collection of "pages of information" in HTML format. Each page has a unique identity known as the URL (URL is most often pronounced "you are el," but is also pronounced "earl"). We describe HTML format below. The URL is, in effect, the address of a particular page on the Web. Say you want to take a look at Billy Bob's Bait and Tackle, found on the Great Canadian Sport Fishing Club. The URL of this particular company is **http://www.realfishing.com/billybobs/billybobs.htm**. Let's take it apart to see what it means.

- The first part is the URL "service type." The most common type of service you will access is **http://**, which is a server running the hypertext transmission protocol. This is the protocol run by Web servers and is the protocol that supports the interlinking of documents (the interlinking is known as hypertext). Whenever you see an address starting with **http://**, you can assume that it is a Web address. As you will see later, there are other service types, so that you can access Gopher, FTP, and other resources through your Web browser. For purposes of our example in this section, we will concentrate on **http://** servers. "Service type" is required information.

- The next part is the "domain name" of the site where Billy Bob's Web page is stored. In our example, the Web site for Billy Bob's is at the domain name **www.realfishing.com**, which is actually a company that hosts and builds Web sites on behalf of people and companies.
- Next is the "directory path." In this case the directory where the HTML files will be found is **/billybobs/**. This is optional information.
- The last part is the file name containing the HTML information for this particular page, in this case, **billybobs.htm**. This is optional information. If a file name is not specified, the server will usually show a default file found in the directory specified, or a file directory listing will be shown.

Pulling all the parts together, it means that you are looking at the file **billybobs.htm**, in the directory **/billybobs/**, at the domain name **www.realfishing.com**. The actual file **billybobs.htm** contains instructions in HTML format regarding what information to show when you access that Web page.

There can be even more components to a URL. Sometimes you might see a "port number," which is extra information required by the server you are accessing. Or in other cases, particularly when using Web servers that perform a search of information, you might see a lot of other text or symbols in the URL, including text with a ? or a # throughout. Sometimes URLs can be very simple, and other times they can be very complex. However, the URL above is typical of many of the URLs that you will encounter throughout the Internet.

Home Pages

Closely related to URLs is the concept of the "home page." You will often see people refer to their home page: it is the first page that you access on a Web site or within the directory for a particular person or company. For example, if you key in the URL of the Great Canadian Sport Fishing Club without any directory and file information (i.e., **http://www.realfishing.com**), you get the "home page" for the organization:

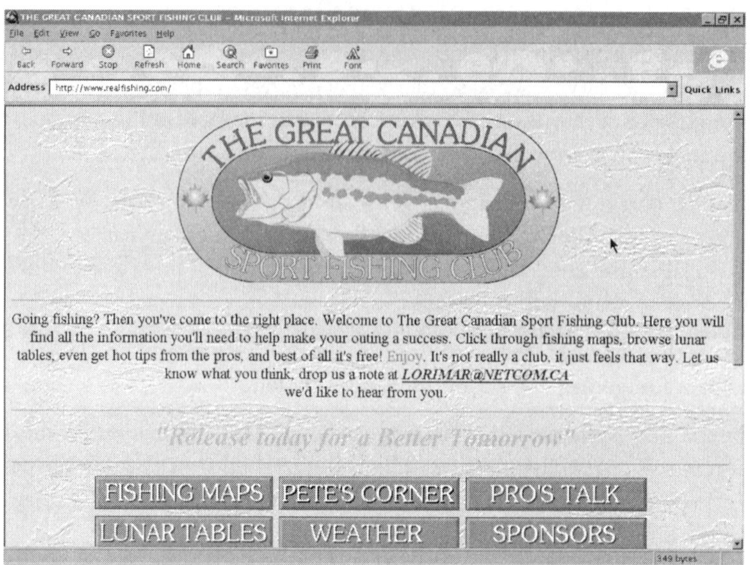

Types of Information You Can Access

Finally, you should keep in mind that a Web browser can access different types of information resources, beyond basic Web pages. You are not restricted to accessing information supported by hypertext transfer protocol servers that provide HTML format data (i.e., those with an **http://** in the URL). As mentioned earlier, you can also access information from Gopher sites, FTP, Telnet sites, and other information types. (We review these applications in Chapter 13, "Older Internet Applications.") Most Web browsers can access several different types of servers. The basic ones are

- **http://** for Web sites;
- **https://** for secure Web sites (we discuss credit card transcations in Chapter 16, which is where the **https://** server is most often used);
- **ftp://** for FTP locations;
- **gopher://** for Gopher servers;
- **telnet://** for Telnet locations;
- **news://** to access USENET news.

This means that you can use your Web browser to do many different things instead of having to use separate programs to accomplish separate tasks. For example, as you will see in Chapter 11, Netscape can be used to access USENET newsgroups using the URL format **news://newsgroup.name**. In Chapter 13 we will see how the same program can be used to access FTP sites using the format **ftp://ftpdirectory/filename**. Hence the typical Web browser is quickly becoming one of the only pieces of software that you need next to an e-mail program.

Key Characteristics of the World Wide Web

Have you ever seen the movie *The Wizard of Oz*? A few minutes into it, there is a scene in which Dorothy and her dog, Toto, are rushing back home, in order to avoid a terrifyingly real tornado that is sweeping towards their farm. The scene scared an entire generation of youngsters long before the special effects of the movie *Twister* awed another generation of kids. Noteworthy was the fact that the scene was filmed entirely in black and white, as most movies were at the time.

Minutes later, with Dorothy and Toto "safely" inside, the tornado lifts the entire house into the air and then returns it to earth once again, scenes that were also filmed entirely in black and white. Once the house is on the ground, Dorothy carefully makes her way to the door, opens it, and discovers a world of stunning and beautiful color. No one will forget what was probably the entertainment understatement of the century stated by Dorothy: "Toto, I don't think we're in Kansas anymore." The movie industry discovered color, and its birth was given dramatic impact in the *The Wizard of Oz*; movies were never the same. There could not have been a more dramatic way to signal the transition.

So it is with the Web. Before the Web came along, the Internet, already a world some twenty years old, was being used for the exchange of knowledge and research, e-mail, and for information publishing and distribution. Many millions worldwide discovered its power and reach and became convinced that it was something revolutionary and significant. But just as movies were filmed in black and white, the Internet rolled along with simple text being the primary form of information exchange. Then the Web burst onto the scene, bringing the full glory of text, images, pictures, and even sound and video to the Internet experience, resulting in a transition as dramatic as the wonderful voyage of Dorothy and Toto into the land of Oz.

There are many reasons why the Web has become so significant. Let's look at several of them, for it helps to put into perspective your understanding of the Web.

The Web Supports Many Different Types of Information

Today, when you look at a Web "page," a page of information located somewhere on the global Internet, you see text in different layouts and different fonts, and you can see logos, images, buttons, and pictures. You can hear sound, and if you have a fast enough link, rudimentary video. All kinds of data and information can be incorporated into a Web page. Consider what has become possible; here is the introductory screen from the Web site for the Weather Network, which is admittedly one of Canada's favorite TV stations. It incorporates pictures, text, and graphics (**http://www.weathernetwork.com**):

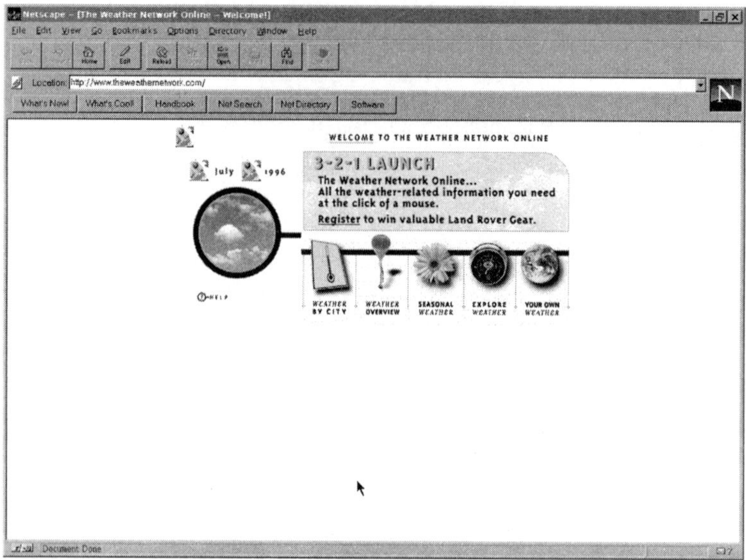

It Is Easy to Use

Before the Web came along, the Internet was a fascinating but sometimes technically challenging place. Systems like Telnet, FTP, and Gopher (which we review in Chapter 13) were used to discover and access information, but were not all that intuitive. Some people joked that the Internet was really "the revenge of the nerds," since it was so difficult to use. That changed with the arrival of the Web. Want to see the weather forecast for your city or town? From the Weather Network Web site above, simply click on the button "Weather by City"; it is a hyperlink such as we described before. A few more clicks of the button, and you have the information you need:

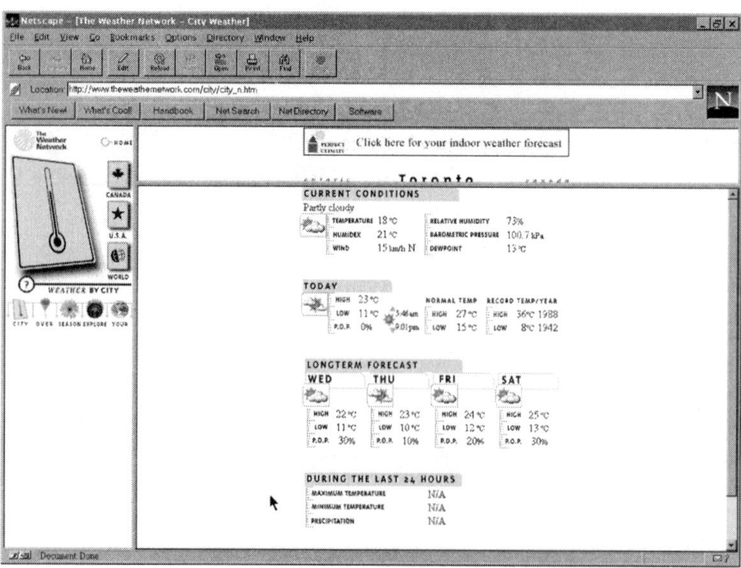

When the Web and Web browsers arrived on the scene, the Internet suddenly became much easier to use. Everyone with a computer, a modem, an Internet connection, and only a little computer experience could travel the world through the Web with just a click of the mouse. It was no longer necessary to learn arcane computer codes, UNIX file directories, or other technically challenging instructions to discover information on the Internet, as had been required in the past. Instead, using the "hypertext" features of the Web, when you see a word highlighted, you can double click on it with your mouse and be whisked away to another page of information. Images, buttons, anything on a Web page can be made "clickable." And using "clickable maps" means that you can click on various places within an image to choose another page of information. The result is that you travel through the Web simply by pointing and clicking with your mouse.

It Supports Interlinking Between Sites

A key fact of the Web is that much of the information throughout it is linked together through these hyperlinks. When you click on an item on a Web page, you are, in most cases, taken to another page of information, which could be on the same computer to which you are linked. Or it could be another computer somewhere else in the world. You might not even know where in the world you are.

Every page on the global Web can be linked to any other page on earth. Many individuals build pages that are linked to other pages. Follow a "link," and you will find yourself in New Zealand. Click again, and you are on a page in Timmins, ON. Click again, and you are in Madrid, Spain. As soon as someone establishes a Web site on the Internet containing pages, any other Web site in the world can link to it; hence it is a massive "web" of interlinked sites. Take a look at the Ottawa White Water Rafter page; its Web address is **http://www.synapse.net/~kayaker/**:

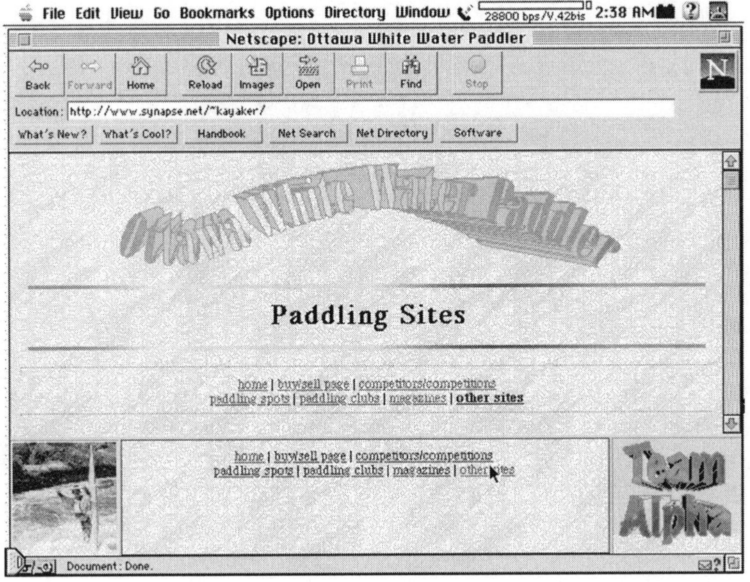

If you click your mouse on the phrase “other sites” on this page, you will then see another page of information listing information about other kayak-related sites found on the Web around the world. If you then click on “Norwegian Kayak Pages,” you are taken to a Web page in Norway all about kayaking in that country. Clicking on any of the other “links” takes you to other sites about kayaking around the world. It is this method of interlinking, which we call “hypertext,” or “links,” that provides the Web so much of its utility. Rather than reading a book from cover to cover, you now “browse” a source of information that quickly links you to other related (and often unrelated) information sources.

It is Practical and Useful

There has been a dramatic shift in the Web over the past year; its usefulness has increased significantly. In the early days of the Web, that is, before 1996, you could read a number of media reports on the uselessness or limited value of information found on the Internet, and specifically the Web. Quite often that was true; keep in mind that it was comparable to the days in which automobiles had just been invented, when there were not many destinations to drive to because there were not a lot of roads. That has changed significantly in the last several years, such that today you can find any number of useful information sources on-line, depending upon your area of interest. Not only that, but many major organizations are beginning to make available information on the Web, enhancing its value as a real, useful information utility.

Want to look up a telephone number anywhere in Canada? Visit Sympatico 411, a complete listing of all listed phone numbers across Canada from Canada's major telephone companies (**http://canada411.sympatico.ca**):

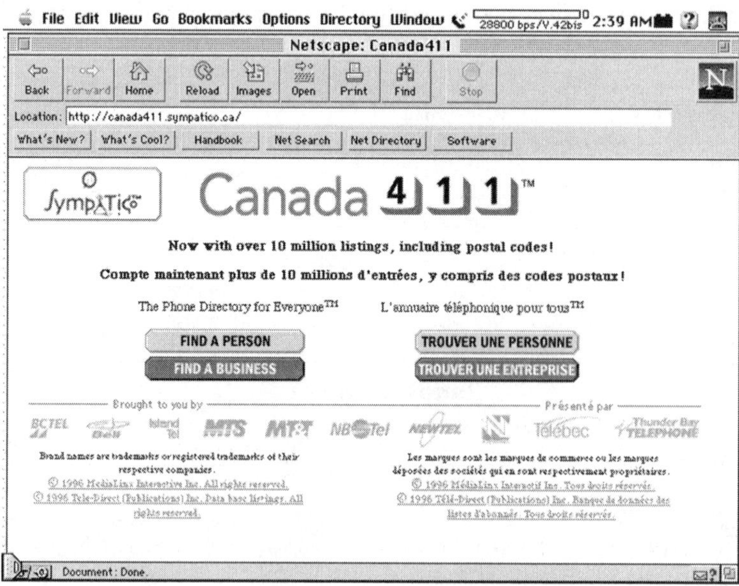

Just key in the name of the person or business you are looking for. You can also specify a city and province in your search, then wait a second or two, and you have what you need:

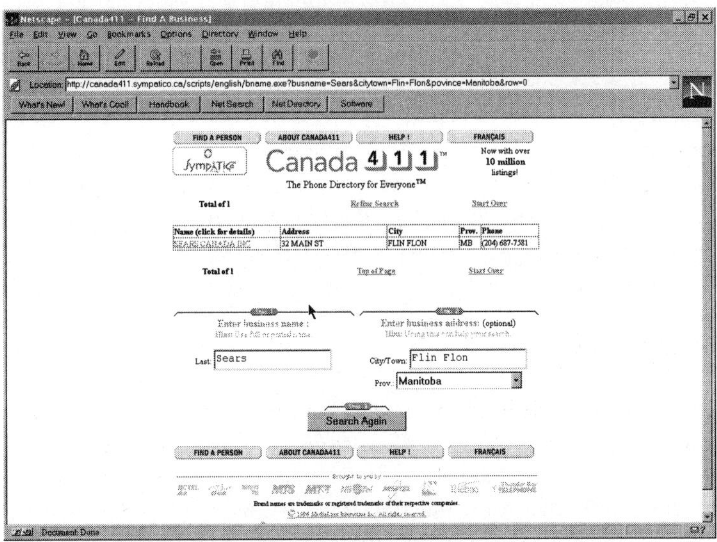

Need to know what it will cost to ship a parcel to another location in Canada? Take a trip to the Canada Post Parcel Rate Locator (**http://www.mailposte.ca/english/postrate/ratee.html**), key in the postal codes of where you are sending it to and from, and the dimensions of the package:

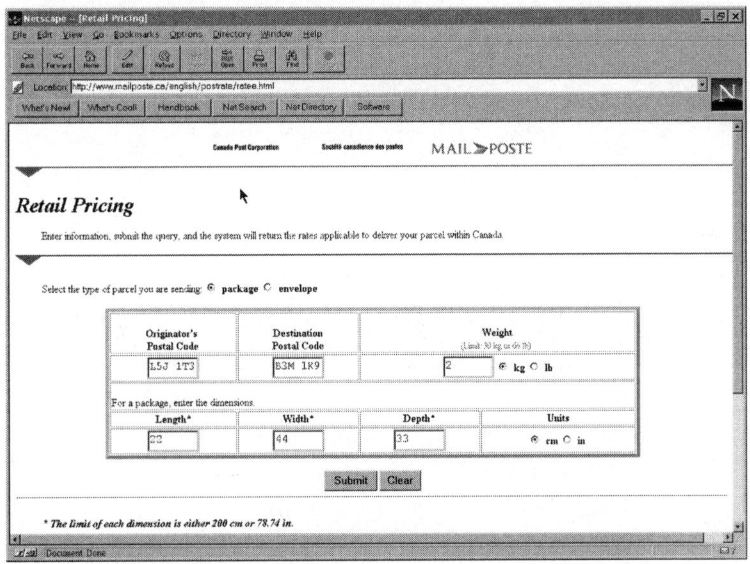

Canada Post will come back and tell you how much it will cost to send the package by regular post, Express Post, and Priority Courier:

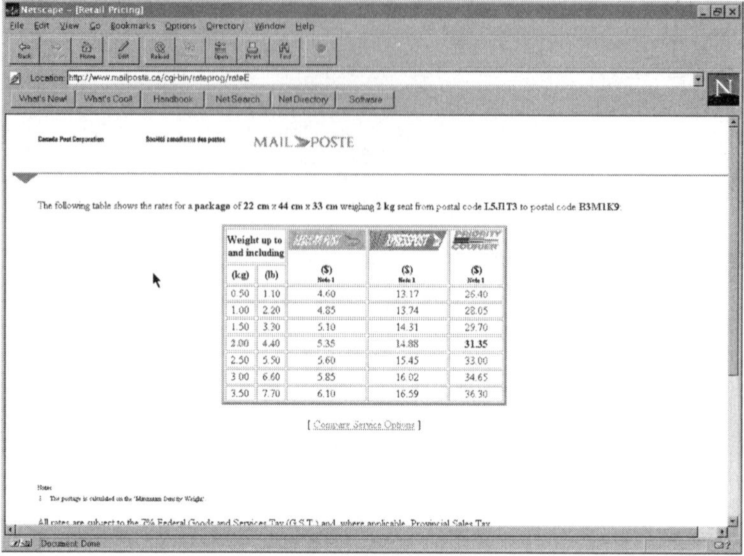

Press another button, and you can get a summary of the differences between these options:

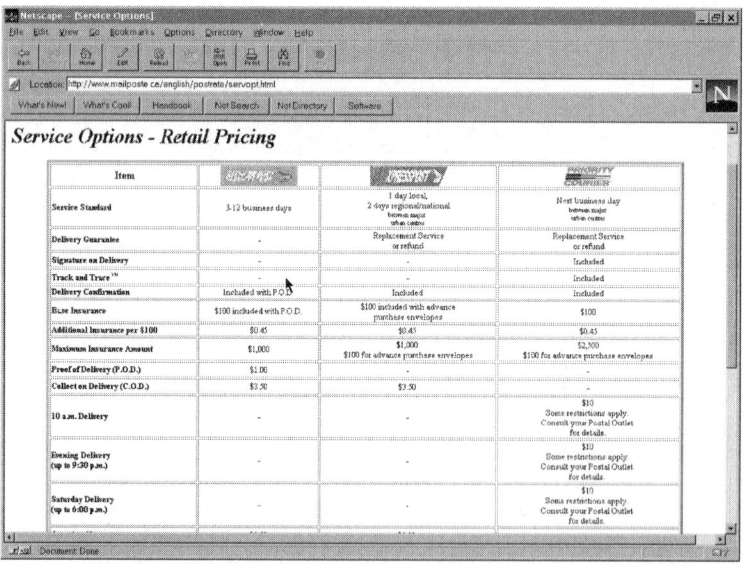

Want road reports for BC? Visit the BCHighways Road Reports (**http://www.bchighways.com/**) for up-to-date traffic conditions. Simply select the highway for which you want current reports:

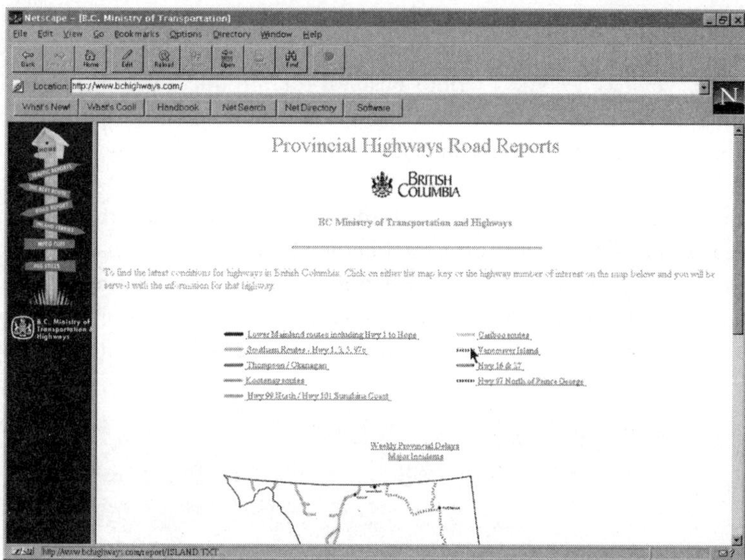

and you will get the latest report issued that day:

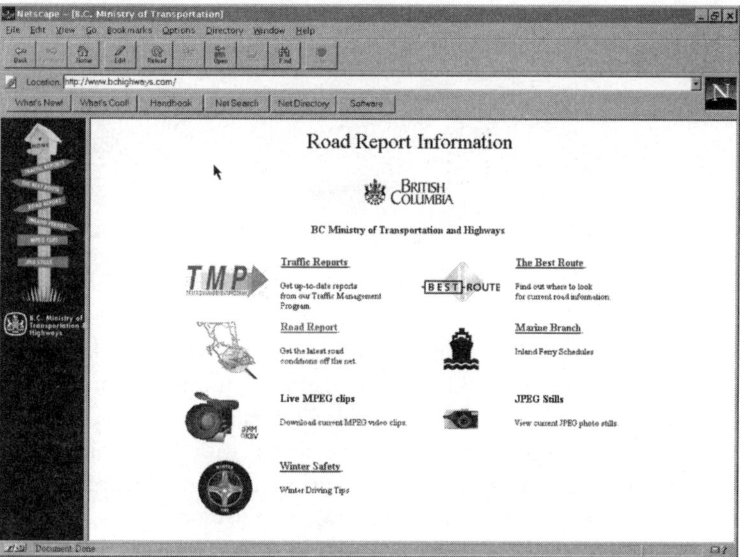

Is the Web full of useless information? Not anymore. Over the last couple of years, the Web has matured to the point that it has now become a source for real, practical, and useful information. And as more organizations become involved, its value and usefulness are only increasing.

It Is a Serious Business Tool

Quite clearly, the Web has become a serious business tool; in one way, the corporate world is quickly adopting the Web as a means to reach and deal with existing and potential customers. Everyone is trying to discover the secret and elusive "magic formula" that will help to gain some type of business advantage through the Internet.

Marketing on the Internet has become all the rage, with the result that there are tens of thousands of corporate Web sites found on the Internet. Some organizations are quickly moving beyond simple on-line marketing, which is often a dubious proposition at best, to using the Internet to fundamentally change the way they do business with their customers. A good case in point is Canada Trust, which is using the Web as a means of providing customer support:

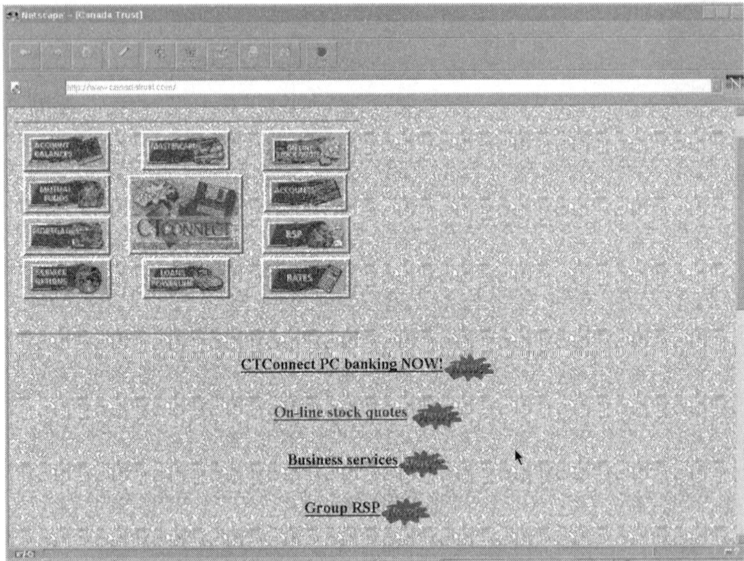

Governments are caught up in Web mania, too. Rather than waiting in line at some government office, today you can retrieve all kinds of government information on-line. An increasing number of government bodies are working to provide a full range of government services through the Internet. Already, you can register your displeasure directly with the Premier of a province concerning some new legislation, and you can take part in an on-line electronic poll. You can be electronic citizens of a network that is the ultimate form of democracy.

Everywhere you go in Canada and around the world, national, provincial and state, local and municipal governments are exploring how the Internet can be used. From a government perspective, the Web presents government with tremendous opportunities for the "reengineering" of services and hence offers efficiencies and cost savings in the way that governments deal with their citizens. It also presents a significant change to the political landscape by permitting citizens to band together in ways that have not previously been possible. The Web is coming to support electronic commerce, a sufficiently important topic that we look at it separately in Chapter 16, "Thinking Strategically About the Internet."

It Has Become a Serious Information Distribution Tool

Organizations with many decades of involvement with print publications are starting to abandon those efforts to become involved with the Internet or are making the Internet one of the fundamental components of their information distribution systems. Consider the venerable *Encyclopedia Britannica*, which has chosen the Web as the on-line platform for their encyclopedia service. Visit their Web site and you can search the entire updated contents of the publication; just key in a word or phrase to search:

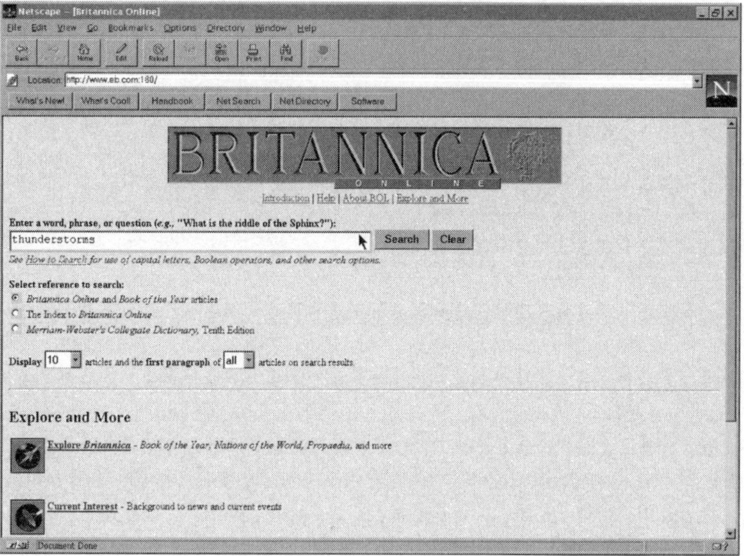

Within seconds, you have a list of matching items from the encyclopedia:

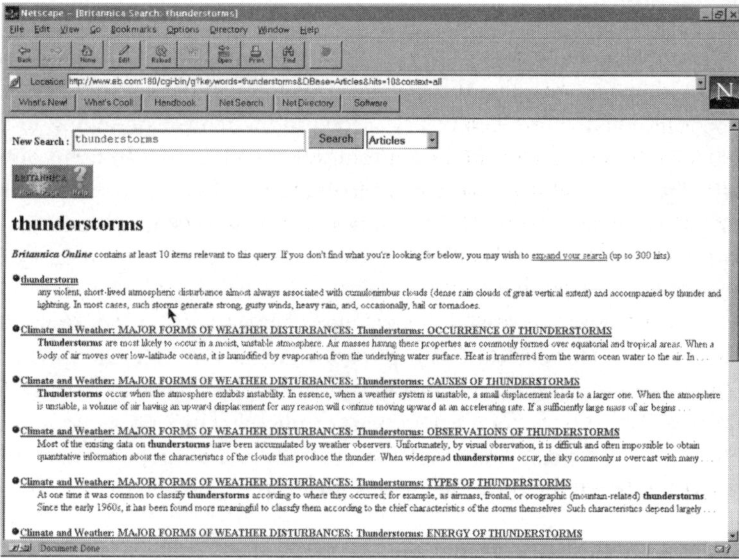

You can then choose to read any of the articles listed:

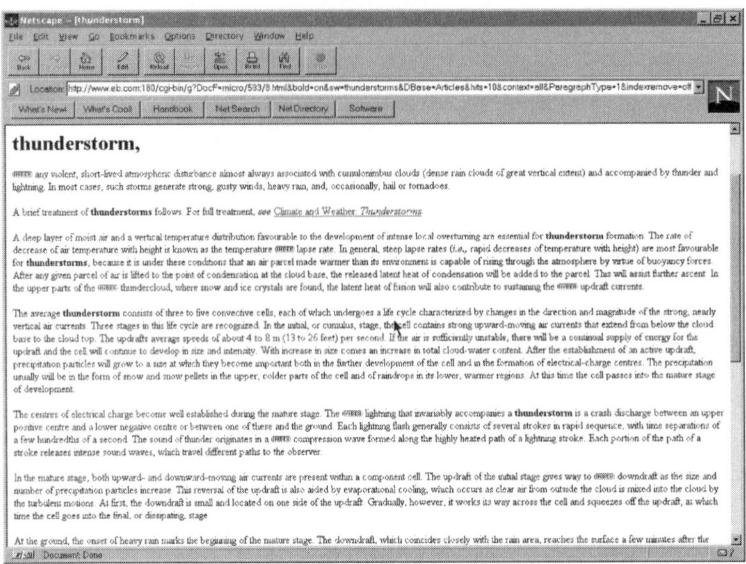

The *Encyclopedia Britannica* on-line is an example of a pay-to-access service on the Web; it costs $14.95 per month or $150 per year (U.S. dollars) to access. (We will talk about the economics of the Web later in this chapter.) Even so, it is a good example of the stunning diversity of information that can be accessed through the Web. Eventually, services like this could replace CD ROM drives, particularly when higher-speed access becomes available on the Internet. This is why some people, when talking about the World Wide Web, make comments to the effect that the whole of human knowledge is becoming available on the Web.

It Supports Audio and Video

The Web today is not limited to simply seeing text, pictures, and images. If you have the proper type of computer equipment, you can even listen to audio through the network, and if you have a fast enough connection to the Internet, you can access and watch video. Adding audio to your use of the World Wide Web is one of the easiest things that you can do. In terms of your computer, you need either a Macintosh with audio capability or a PC that has a sound card and speakers. And if you have that and use a Web browser such as Netscape or Internet Explorer, you are in business, since both of these Web browsers and many others come with the ability to play basic sound files.

Netscape, for example, supports what are known as **.au** and **.aif** sound formats. Travel to the Internet Underground Music Archives (**http://www.iuma.com**) site, where many independent Canadian musical artists promote their work. Look up a fellow named Jeff Bird, click on the button "AU EXCERPT," and wait for a few seconds or minutes (depending upon the speed of your Internet connection) for a short audio "clip" from one of his albums to be transferred to your PC. Once it has been transferred, a separate little Netscape program will run, and you will hear the audio clip:

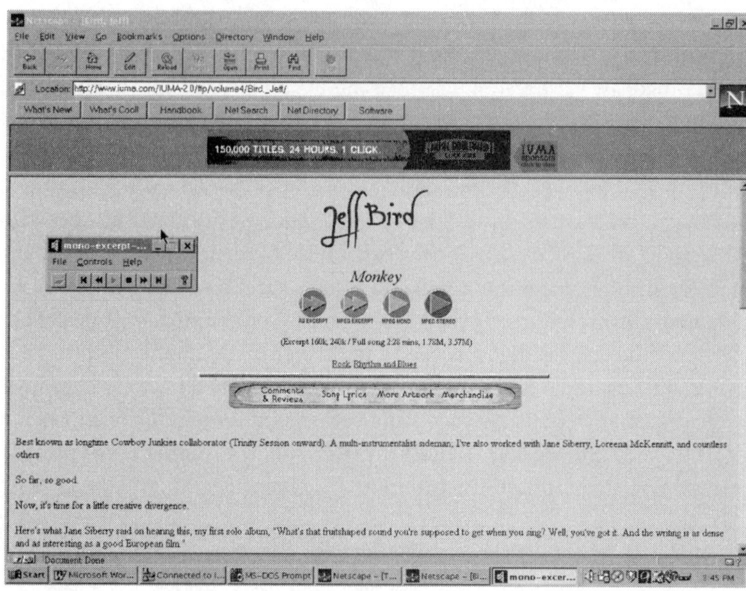

There are other sound formats that are available, and you can install all kinds of other software such as RealAudio (often referred to as "players") to access them. To watch video, you must download or obtain a program such as a QuickTime "player." Once installed, you access a Web site containing video, click on a link to a video file, wait a few minutes, and then watch it on your screen. For example, on the screen below we are watching a clip from the CBC video archives (**http://www.cbc.ca**), in which Pierre Trudeau is proclaiming the imposition of the *War Measures Act* in 1970:

It Supports Cybercasting

Another new and very significant activity on the Internet is "cybercasting," broadcasting on the Internet. In 1996 there were many significant events broadcast live on the Internet, often in audio form, and sometimes with associated video. In the field of entertainment in 1996 we saw cybercasts of the Tony awards (**http://www.tonys.org**) and the Juno Awards (**http://www.goodmedia.com/junos/**). It is not restricted to entertainment; Bell and Howell (**http://www.bellhowell.com**) broadcast its shareholders' meeting live in 1996.

At this point, audio broadcasting works quite well; there are a number of software programs available, and the quality of the on-line broadcast is not too bad (it improves greatly with faster Internet connections). However, the technology to support video on the Internet is still very much in its infancy; it is almost as if it is the late 1940s and television has just been invented. You have a huge television set that contains a tiny, fuzzy little black and white screen, and while you can watch a television show, it is not necessarily a pleasant and rewarding experience. That pretty well sums up state-of-the-art for video cybercasting on the Internet today. To really be able to participate in on-line video cybercasting, you need a fairly high-speed connection to the Internet. We will take a look at adding audio and video capability to your Web browser later in this chapter.

In terms of cybercasting events, they are fairly easy to find on-line. They are often heavily publicized in the media, and sites such as AudioNet (**http://www.audionet.com**) provide a listing of current broadcasts available through the Internet:

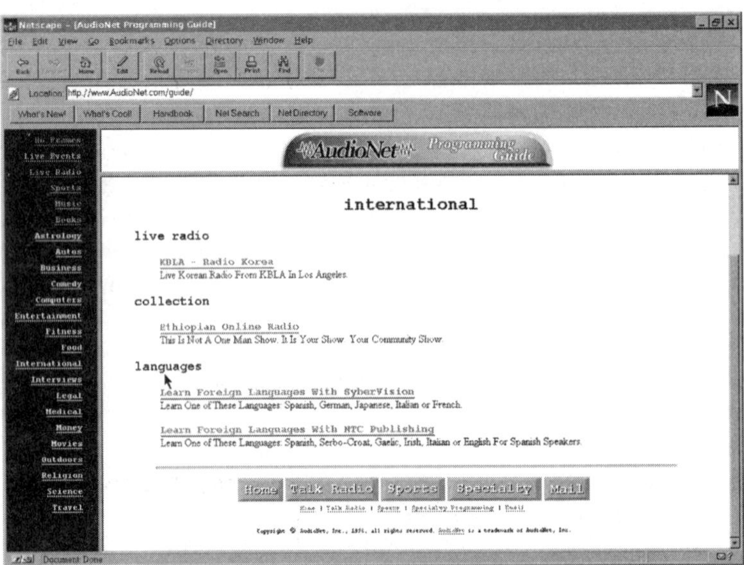

It Is Being Monitored Like Television

With the arrival of advertising on the Web (a trend we discuss later in this chapter), the Web is being monitored like television to help advertisers understand what target audience they are reaching. Web measurement also helps site owners understand how popular their sites are. Naturally, this type of feedback is important to anyone who spends hours and hours every week maintaining and updating a Web site. For example, Web measurement tools can help you determine what areas of your site are the most popular and what areas of your site are the least popular. Hence we have seen all kinds of organizations develop commercial software and Web tracking tools that examine how popular a Web site is and what demographic profiles the visitors fit into. In other words, they measure how people are using the Web in the same way that companies like A.C. Nielsen monitor which television shows people are watching.

Organizations Involved in Web Tracking	
PC Meter	**http://www.npd.com**
NetCount	**http://www.netcount.com**
Interse	**http://www.interse.com**
I/Pro	**http://www.ipro.com**

Many of these services are being offered by new start-up organizations, but some long-established organizations like the Audit Bureau of Circulation (**http://www.accessabc.com**), involved for many years in monitoring newspaper circulations, are also becoming involved. In fact, the industry is gaining significant attention, investment, and growth.

One type of Internet-monitoring device that is gaining a lot of attention is the concept of a "cookie." A cookie is a personal-information tracking mechanism that is deposited on your hard drive when you visit certain Web sites. Cookies allow Web site owners to track information about you, such as the the number of times you have been to the site and the names of files that you have viewed. Cookies can also store information about your age, your sex, your income, and your likes and dislikes if you voluntarily provide this information during the registration process for a Web site.

Before cookies came along, the only way a Web site could accurately track individual users on a visit-by-visit basis was by assigning each user a special ID and a password. Users would have to type in their ID and password every time they returned to the Web site. Web owners were therefore able to monitor user activity on an individual basis. Many fee-based Web sites still use passwords and IDs to keep out unauthorized users, the *Wall Street Journal*, for example (**http://www.wsj.com**):

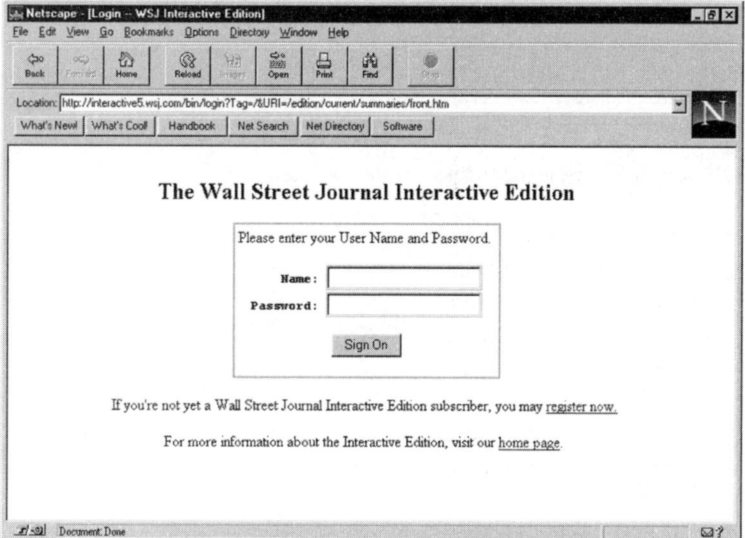

But there is one big problem with this approach. People often forget their passwords. Because most people cannot be bothered applying for new ones, they simply stop returning to Web sites that require them.

Many Web site owners favor cookies as a way to track individual Internet users. Let's look at an example of how cookies work.

InfoSeek Personal (**http://personal.infoseek.com**) is a popular custom news service that delivers news stories over the World Wide Web. To use the service, all you need to do is register; it's free! The first screen in the registration process is shown below:

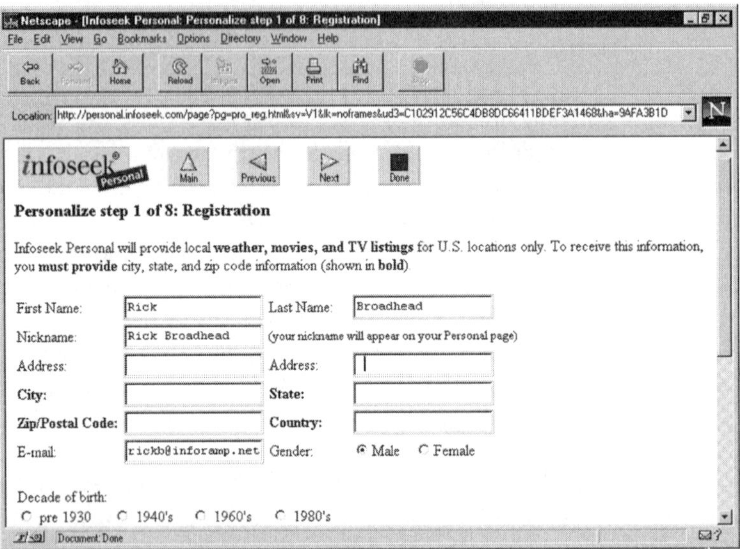

A couple of screens later, you tell the program what type of news stories you are interested in. You can list personal names, company names, product names…anything you want:

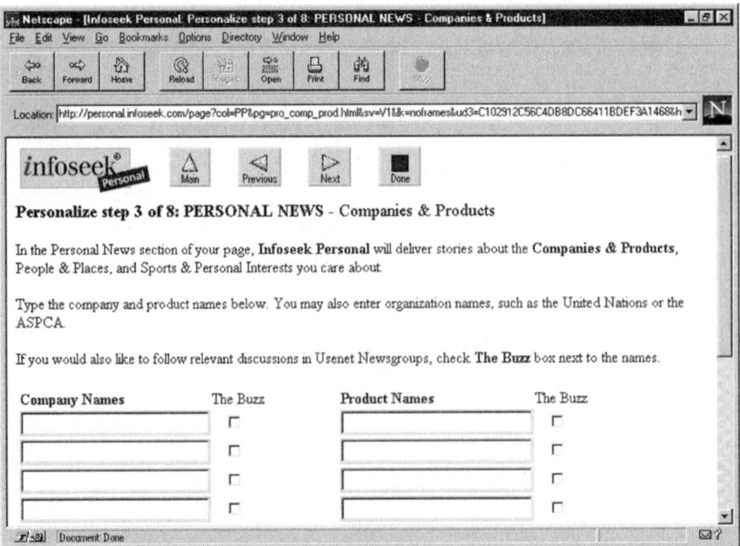

Once you are done with the registration process, return to the InfoSeek Personal Web site at **http://personal.infoseek.com** and watch what happens. Not only will the Web site remember your name, it will also remember the type of news stories you like to read, based on the information you supplied during the registration process. For example, take a look at the screen below. Notice that the heading says "Business News for Rick Broadhead":

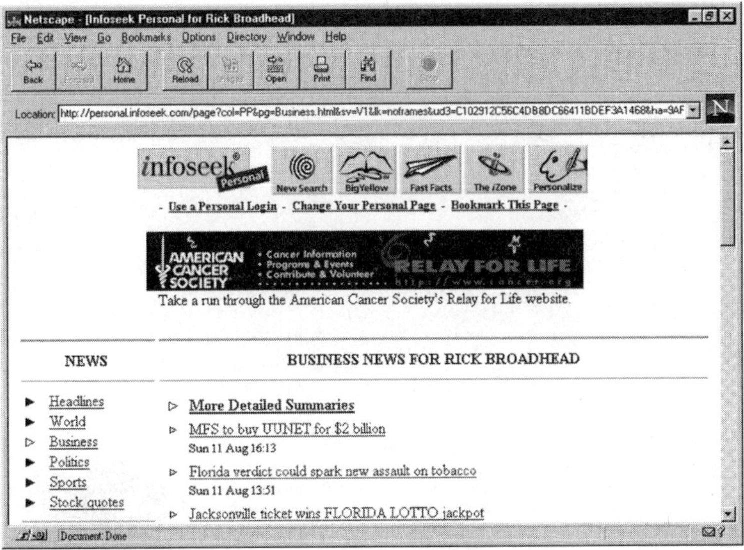

How did InfoSeek Personal know my name? It's actually quite simple. When a person registers for InfoSeek Personal, information about that person is automatically stored in a file (called a "cookie file") on the person's computer hard drive. The file contains information such as the person's name and his/her news preferences, information that was collected during the registration process described above. This process happens in the background and is completely transparent to the user. The next time the person returns to the InfoSeek Personal Web site, the cookie file is automatically retrieved from the person's computer. The information obtained from the cookie file (e.g., the person's name) is used to customize the Web page. Presto!

Because cookies uniquely identify Web users, they can be used to identify repeat visitors to a Web site. Most of the popular Web browsers, such as Netscape and Microsoft Explorer, support the use of cookies. But many people, especially privacy advocates, do not like cookies because they can operate quietly in the background, collecting information about an Internet user without the person's knowledge. But with applications such as InfoSeek Personal, where cookies are used to enhance a person's Web experience, the benefits likely outweigh the disadvantages.

Cookies can help Web site owners personalize the delivery of information. For example, if your local video store has a Web site, it could use cookies to store information about the types of movies you like. Every time you visit the video store's Web site, you would be greeted with a message that highlights new video releases suited to your tastes and interests. On-line grocery stores could use cookies in the same way. A grocery store on the Web could keep track of items you have purchased in the past and alert you to specials on similar products the next time you return. Even pizza companies, such as Pizza Hut, could use cookies to automate the process of placing an order over the World Wide Web. The first time you order a pizza over the Web, a cookie file would be placed on your computer with information about your order. The next time you visit the same pizza company on the Web, it would remember your previous order and greet you with a customized message like this: *"Hello Mr. Broadhead! Last time you ordered a medium pizza with mushrooms, green peppers, and onions. Would you like the same order this time?"*

The possibilities are limitless and quite exciting. Cookies are a rather complex subject and a topic of ongoing debate. If you are interested in reading more about them, we suggest Andy's Netscape Cookie Notes (**http://www.illuminatus.com/cookie**) and Malcolm's Guide to Persistent Cookies Resources (**http://www.emf.net/~mal/cookiesinfo.html**):

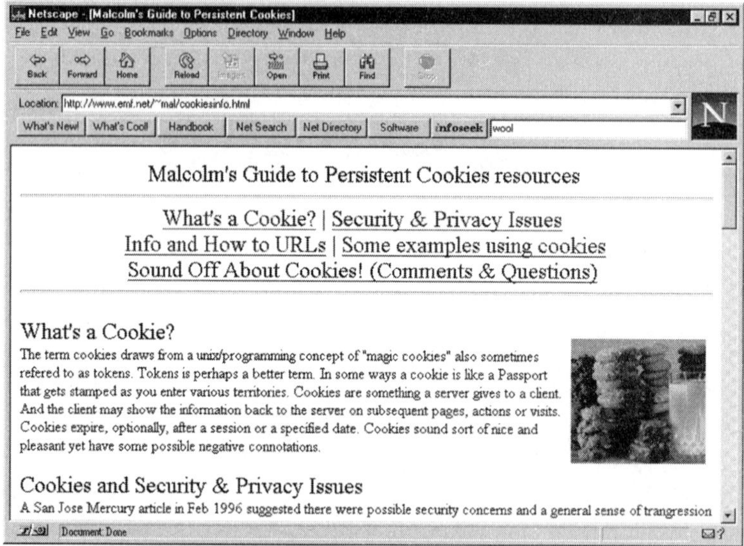

It Is Multilingual

The Web has also become multilingual. There is no doubt that English has become the predominant language of the global Internet, just as it has come to dominate global business. However, while English is the predominant language, it is not the only one in use on the Web. Certainly in Canada there are many pages in French, particularly for Web sites throughout Quebec, such as this index for restaurants in the province (**http://www.alteris.ca/th/**):

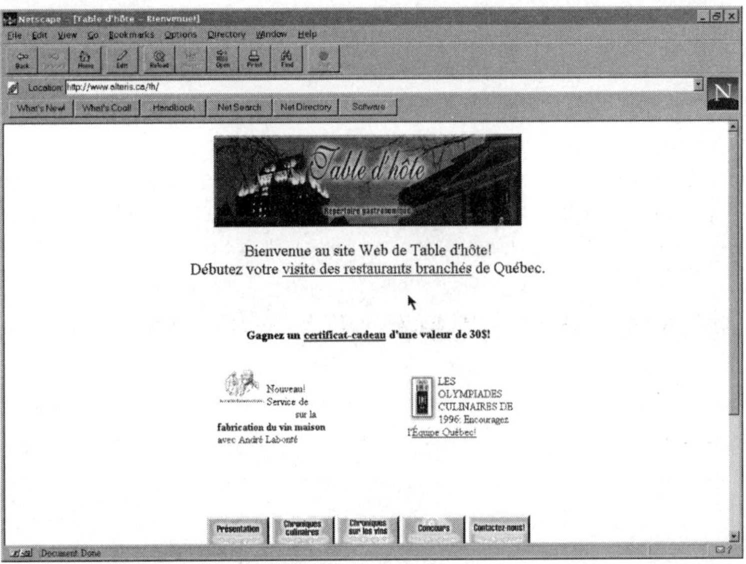

As the Associated Press noted in an article entitled "They're defying English domination — The French seek niche on the Net," "the goal…is to allow Francophone 'cybernautes' to use the Net without submitting to English, which dominates the worldwide computer network….For many Quebecers, Frenchifying the Net is a crusade." As a result of these initiatives, you can find a growing amount of French content on-line, such as "Lokace," a French search engine (search engines are discussed in Chapter 9) (**http://iplus10.iplus.fr/lokace**):

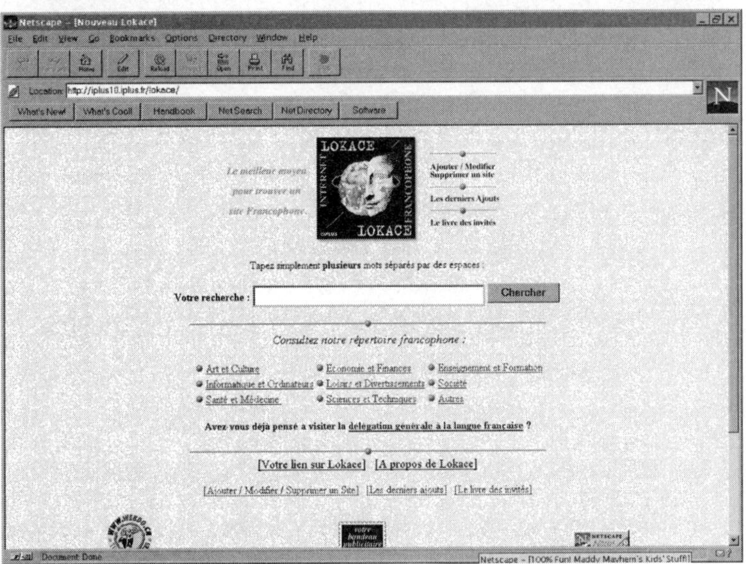

And the Toronto Dominion Bank is a good example of a business that caters to its customers in different languages — Chinese, French, and English — allowing its customers to access the Web site in their language of choice:

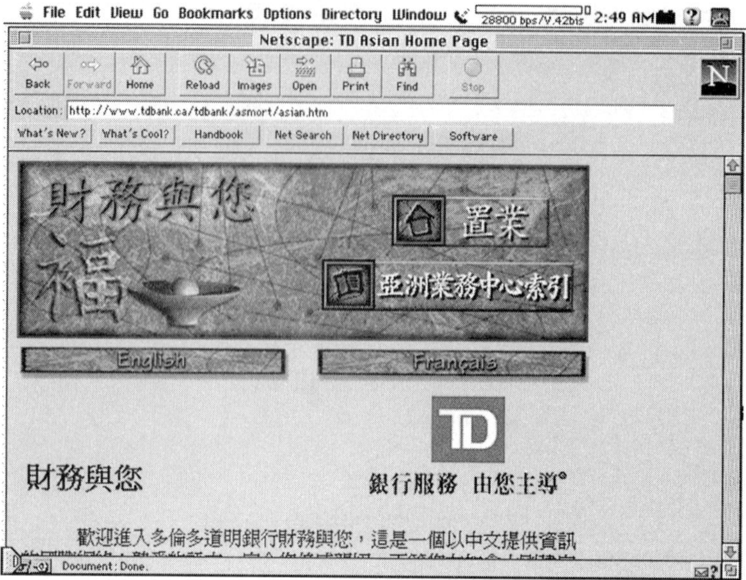

Both Netscape and Internet Explorer are available in different languages as well, in order to support the use of different character sets found in many other languages worldwide. For example, if you choose to download a copy of Microsoft Internet Explorer, you can choose one of several languages:

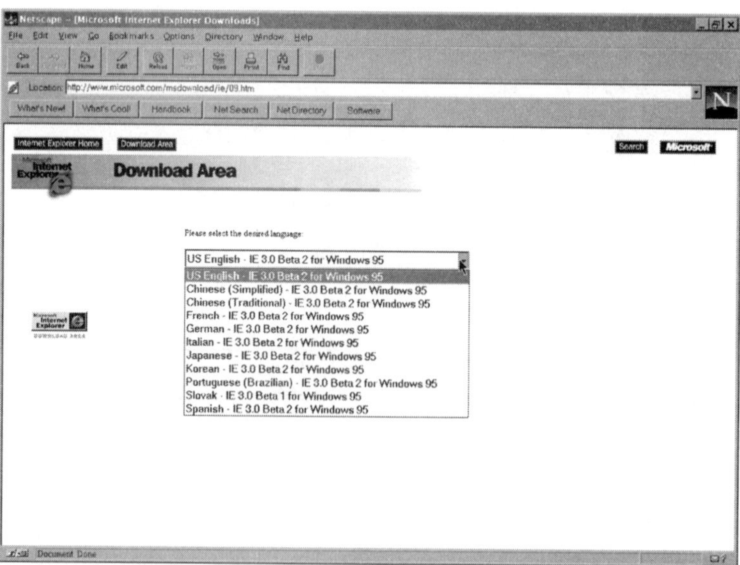

There are also Web browsers that are customized to support other languages. Internet With an Accent, for example, supports over thirty different languages. In the screen below we are using the program to access a site about Russian music in which the text appears in Cyrillic. We have also configured our Web browser menus and help screens to appear in Russian:

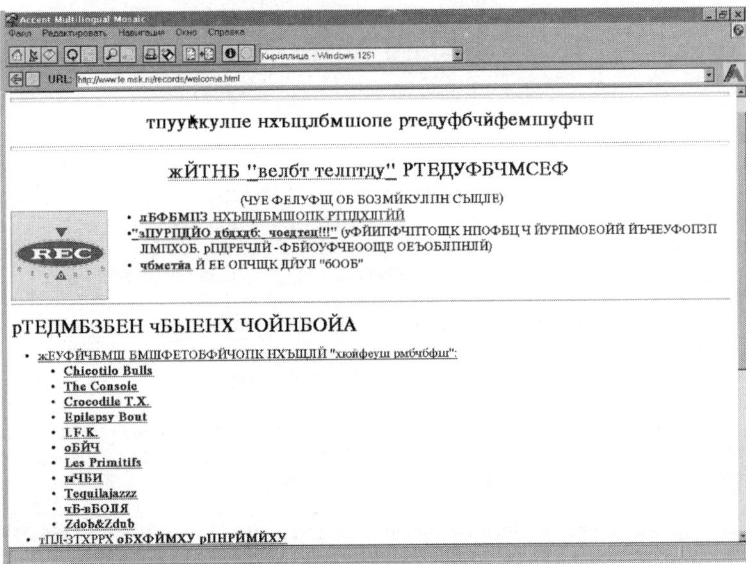

The program does this by supporting multiple "character sets," any of which can be chosen appropriate to the Web page you are visiting. A character set is the name given to the groups of symbols and non-English characters, Ó, ē, and ê, for example. And if the site you are visiting was actually created with Internet With an Accent, it will automatically configure itself to the appropriate character set; otherwise, you will have to select it yourself.

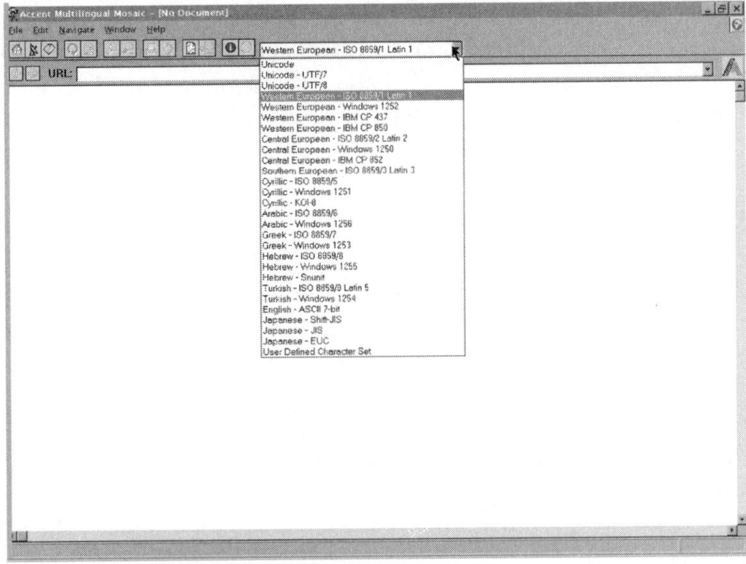

It has become a significant issue for many cultures and countries to ensure that local languages play a role on the Internet. During a recent meeting of Francophone nations, for example, the leaders of several countries expressed dismay at the ongoing dominance of English throughout the

Internet and talked of the need for concerted action to ensure that French has a role on the network. The nature of the concern is captured in an article that appeared in *Newsbytes*, a technology-specific publication available on the Internet (used with permission):

> The European Commission (EC) is urging its members to make sure that English, which already has a strong position on the World Wide Web, does not become the de facto language of European online services and Internet systems. According to Nana Mouskouri, Euro Member of Parliament (MP) and perhaps best known as the Greek singer of the smash hit of the 1960s, "Never on a Sunday," the danger is much more than simply seeing languages other than English falling into disuse on the Internet.
>
> Mouskouri argues that the lack of use of non-English European languages on the Internet would work against the international success of the information superhighway. By using only English, she notes, "there is a danger that EC citizens would be excluded from the information society."
>
> Mouskouri, one of the prime movers behind the EC's backswing against the use of English on the Internet, claims to speak — and sing — in six languages. The problem with using English on the Internet, to the exclusion of other European languages, is that it marginalizes smaller languages even more than before.
>
> "I think it's essential that we protect that cultural heritage and make sure that it's not destroyed by the information society which would then be an information society with no content," she said.
>
> So far, Mouskouri's campaign has received only the support from the EC, but there is a possibility that the EC could well turn the support into a full fledged campaign, backed by European legislation, something that could have some serious effects on the future of the Web in Europe.

With the ongoing growth of the Web, it has become a force by which nations and cultures will assert themselves into the future.

From the user's perspective, the multilingual nature of the Web presents some interesting challenges. For example, users get frustrated when they come across a site in another language that they cannot understand. A company called Globalink has come up with at least a partial solution to this problem. Globalink has released a program called "Web Translator," which translates Web pages on the fly, right in front of your eyes. It can translate Spanish, French, and German Web sites into English, or English Web pages into Spanish, French, and German. Best of all, it is really simple to use. Let's look at an example.

Once the program is installed, a small bar (shown below) appears on your monitor while you are browsing the Web:

Whenever you come across a Web page that you want to translate, simply click on the "Translate" button. For example, here is the Web page for the Québec Department of Tourism, in French. Suppose you want to translate this page into English. Click on "Translate" to start the translation:

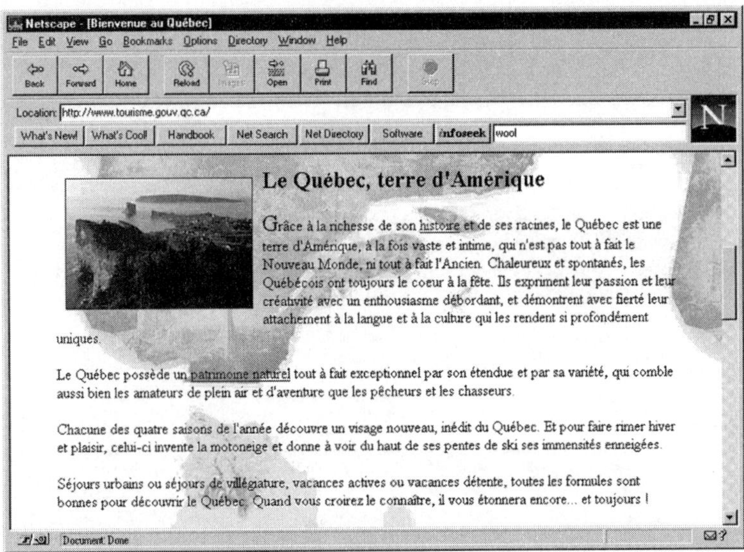

A screen will appear and ask you to choose which language you want to translate *from* and which language you want to translate *to.* In this example we want to translate from French to English:

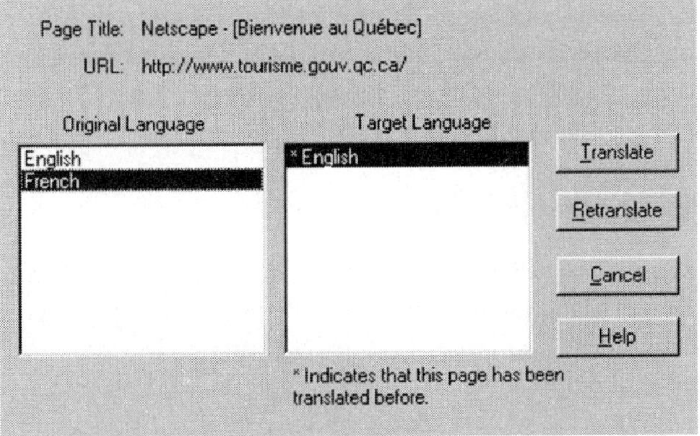

Next, click on the "Translate" button at the right of the screen. The translation process will start and may be complete as quickly as within 90 seconds. Here is the translated page for the Quebec Department of Tourism. Once the translation is complete, you can either save the translation to your hard drive or print it out:

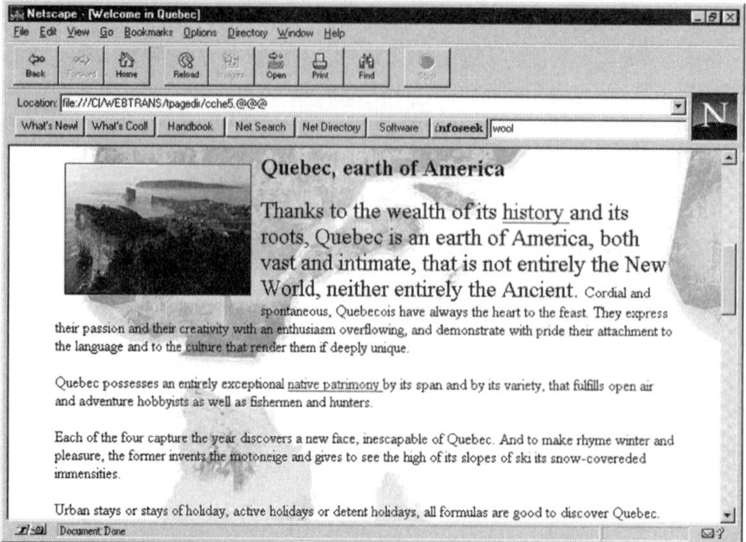

As you can see, the translation is not perfect. There are a number of rough spots. For example, the second sentence reads: "Cordial and spontaneous, Quebecois have always the heart to the feast. They express their passion and their creativity with an enthusiasm overflowing, and demonstrate with pride their attachment to the language and to the culture that render them if deeply unique." In spite of its inaccuracies, the translation is good enough to give you a fairly good feel for what the page is saying. Overall, it is a fun little program and a handy tool for people who use the Web. For more information about Web Translator, visit the Globalink Web site at **http://www.globalink.com**.

It Is Being Linked to Existing Data

There is a lot of information around the world that exists in digital, computer form. Organizations and individuals have learned to use word processors to prepare reports and to publish brochures. Massive databases of information on mainframe computers drive entire businesses. Movies are edited on computer, and radio shows are compiled on disk rather than tape. Even before the arrival of the Internet, our world was becoming wired by information becoming digital. This digital information can be made part of the Web; in fact, it is often easy to do so. Software tools are now available, for example, that convert information prepared in popular word processing programs into a format that can be used by the Web. Scanners can take pictures and convert them into digital form. Movies can be turned into digital bits and bytes so that they are accessible through a Web site. Organizations are suddenly discovering that the information they generate on a day-to-day basis in digital form can be easily converted so that it is accessible on the Web; just ask a newspaper owner. Throughout 1996 many newspapers, large and small, began efforts to publish their newspapers on-line, such as the *Halifax Herald*. The information is taken directly from their newspaper production system and is converted so that it can be put up on the Web (**http://www.herald.ns.ca/**):

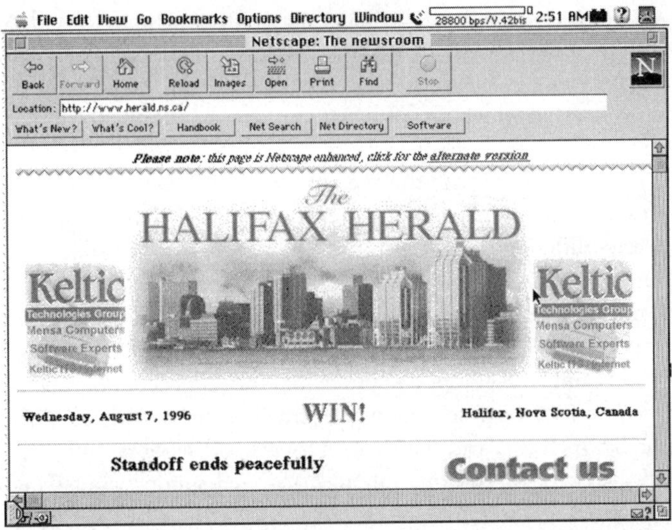

As a result, we have become a world in which digital information is turned into paper form for distribution in print, but is also available in digital, electronic form through the Web.

It Provides for Feedback

Because of the many technologies coming together in the Web, there is now a type of business–customer feedback that has not previously been possible. For example, the technology behind the Web supports the use of forms. Through these forms you can answer questions, provide information, fill out surveys, and any number of other things. When you are finished with the form, it is sent to the "owner" of the Web site. Here is a fairly sophisticated form, found at the site of Greenberg, Trister & Turner, a law firm. When the form is completed, it is sent to the law firm, where the responses are analyzed and the applicant advised of the likelihood of success of immigrating to Canada (**http://www.gttlaw.com/assessment.html**):

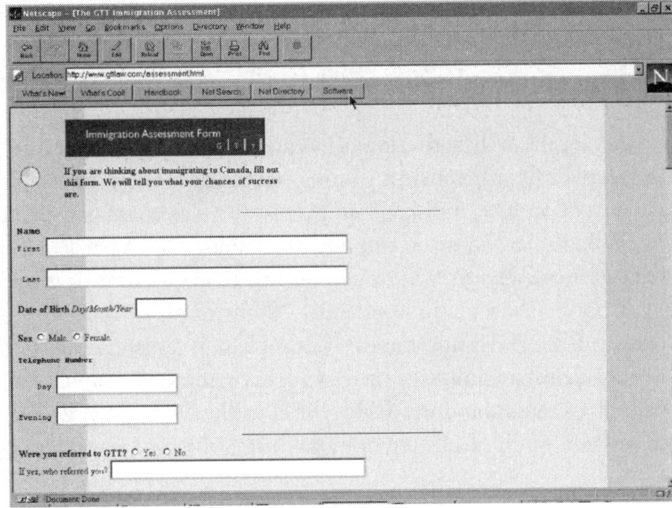

The companies and organizations that receive the information coming from these forms can integrate the data into their own computer systems. They can interface it to an order-entry system or have it perform an inquiry of an electronic catalogue. They can build sophisticated customer-based information systems in which the Web acts as a "front end."

The Web offers business a level of interactivity and customizability that is fascinating. Programmers are getting involved with the Web to integrate Web sites with corporate information systems. Software is emerging to make the whole process that much easier. Analysts are spending time clearly outlining the "architecture" of a complete customer interaction system. Corporate computer strategies are being changed to encompass the Web.

The Web is quickly becoming the window into the world of business. Sophisticated and not-so-sophisticated electronic catalogues are springing up to support on-line shopping. Credit card companies and mainframe computer system vendors are becoming involved and providing the tools of "electronic commerce." Elsewhere, small businesses are establishing outposts on the Internet through which they can sell their products and services. Other businesses are establishing sophisticated product information and customer support sites. The possibilities are intriguing — and endless.

It Reacts

Whenever a tragedy occurs or a major news story breaks, the Web responds with information, in some cases, almost instantly. Consider, for example, the "Great Flood of 1996" in Oregon and Washington States. As soon as the extent of damage became clear, individuals began setting up Web pages, providing both very specific news details about the disaster and the methods by which individuals could help (**http://www.teleport.com/~samc/flood1.html**). A similar exchange of information occurred with the Quebec flooding in mid-1996. The Web is beginning to take on a prominent role in many disasters as a tool with which information can be shared and distributed. With the San Francisco earthquake in 1994 the Internet played a key role in getting news of the extent of the disaster out to the world and in helping people to find out if friends and relatives in the area were affected, a role that was repeated a year later with the Kobe earthquake in Japan in 1995. The Web reacts not only to disasters; it has become a forum for users to publish opinions and information related to some current event.

It Is Leading to New Forms of Interactivity

When it comes to uses for the Web, software authors are limited only by their imagination in terms of the role that it can play. One area that is gaining particular interest involves the role the Web is taking on in the area of on-line "multiperson" games. Popular board games such as Monopoly and Clue are now finding a new home on computer technology and a particularly interesting new angle through the Internet. *Newsbytes*, a popular on-line news publication that reports on computer technology, reported the situation perfectly: "Want to play Monopoly, but your friends are spread between cornfields and exotic islands? No problem, Internet users can now meet up with game partners worldwide for an online game — with the additional graphical support of a CD-ROM." The role of the Internet and the Web? Travel to the Monopoly Web site (**http://www.monopoly.com**), and you can find a listing of individuals willing to play Monopoly through the Internet:

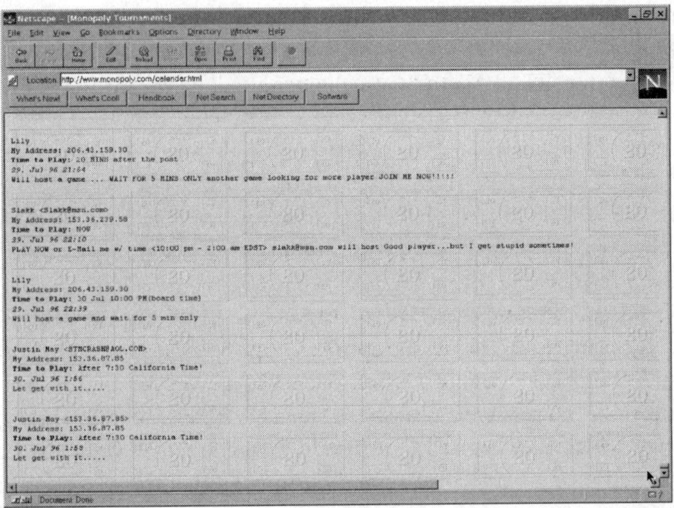

When playing Monopoly, you can choose to host a game or join a game that is already in progress out on the Internet, by providing your TCP/IP address:

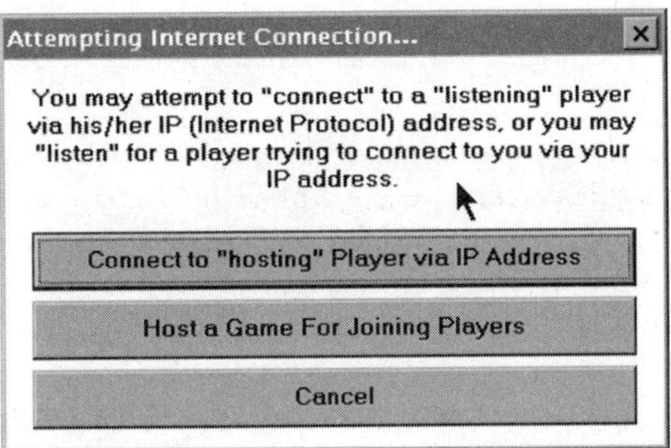

Or, if you are hosting a game, you can choose to add players to the game, whether they are on your computer or are out on the Web:

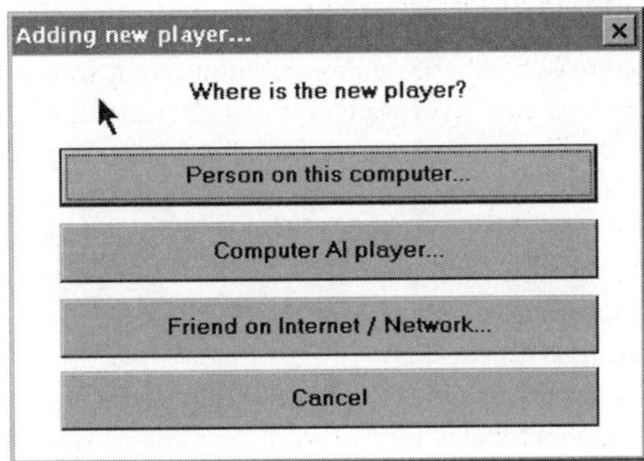

Interactivity is also found in systems that allow for a form of on-line, "real time" discussion. For example, the *Globe and Mail*'s National Issues Forum on the Web, in which anyone can participate, provides ongoing discussion (**http://www.globeandmail.ca/forum/index.html**):

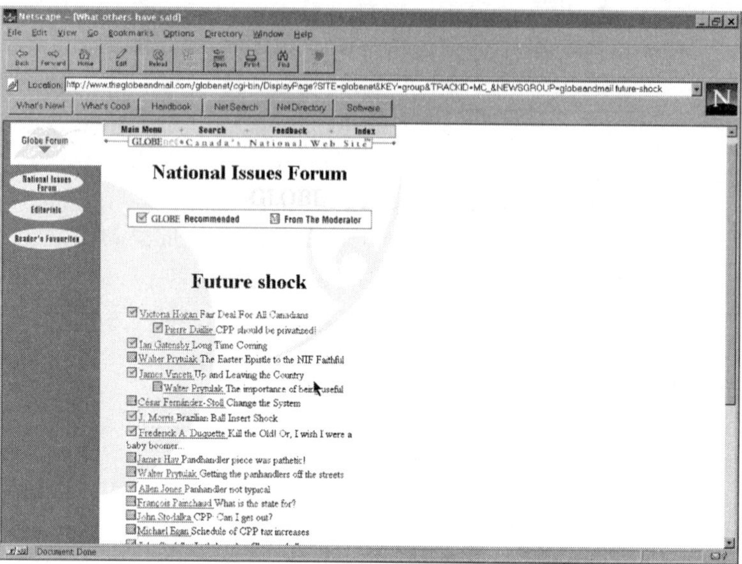

Software companies are exploring how this type of interactivity might be used for customer support; for example, on this screen, we are linked into a site at Corel Corporation (**http://www.corel.com**), in which we can seek live on-line interactive customer support using an application called IRC (which we discuss in Chapter 12):

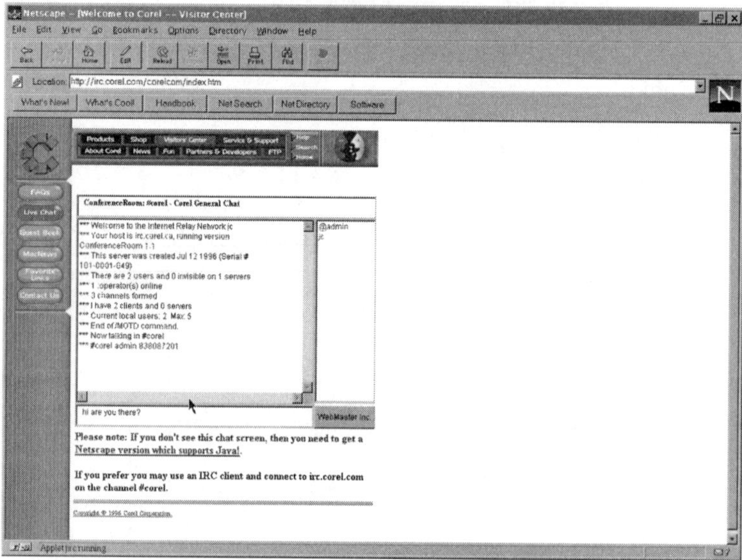

Hence the Web is quickly moving from being a system that supports mere access to information to a system that provides a form of communication between people.

It Provides for On-line Updating

Software companies are also discovering that the Web can play a role in providing updates of popular software. Corel's Movie Guide CD ROM, for example, is updatable directly from the Web on a quarterly basis. Users of the CD ROM can travel to the Corel Web site and obtain updates to the database on-line. The DeLorem AAA Map'n'Go software provides a dramatic example of the future role of the Internet with on-line updating. An extremely sophisticated program in its own right, developed with the participation of the American Automobile Association, it can be used to plot the route between any two points in the United States and much of southern Canada. Just provide a starting point and an ending point, and it draws the suggested route on the map as well as details for every highway in the route:

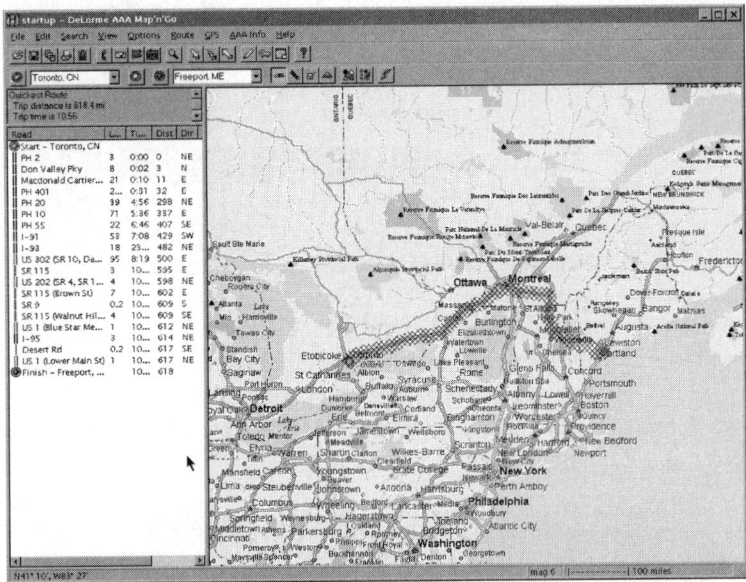

What is the connection with the Web? The program will connect to the DeLorme Web site on request and retrieve updated information about weather conditions, traffic delays, and local events that you can refer to in plotting your trip (or even while you are on your trip, we presume, if you use a laptop computer, retrieving updates along the way with a cellular modem). You choose the states for which you would like to receive updates. (Curiously, Canadian provinces are listed as states.)

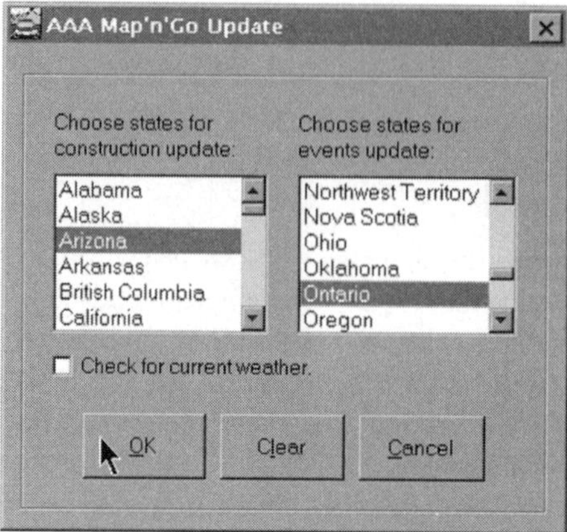

Once you choose what updates you want, you click on the update button, and the software goes off to the DeLorme Web site to retrieve the latest highway, weather, and event information:

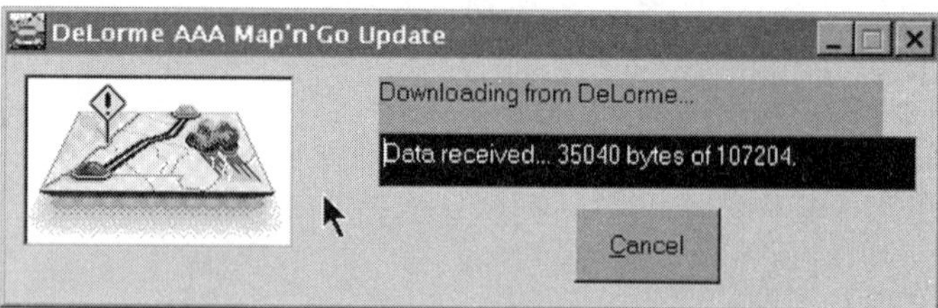

Once it has retrieved the up-to-date data from the Web, the map is marked with the locations for which information is available. This information then appears highlighted on the map. For example, below, we received a construction message (signified by a !) just before Butte, Montana, on a route from Toronto to Vancouver (And you might notice, according to the screen, DeLorme thinks Vancouver is in Ontario!):

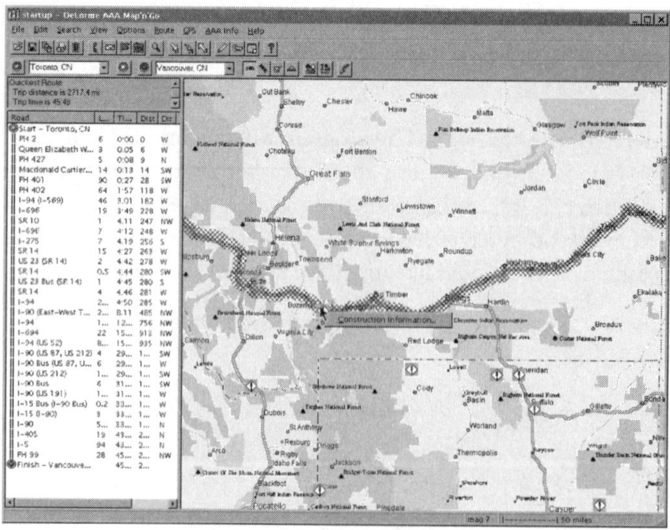

Just click with your left mouse button, and you will see the construction information that it just retrieved from the Internet for that specific location:

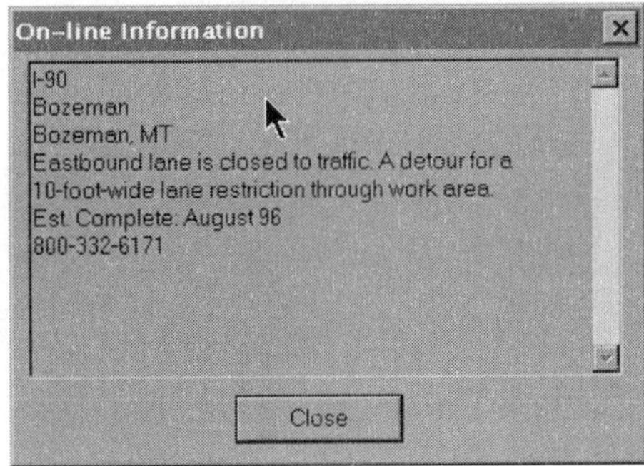

Or click with your right mouse button, and you can obtain the most recent weather report for a location en route:

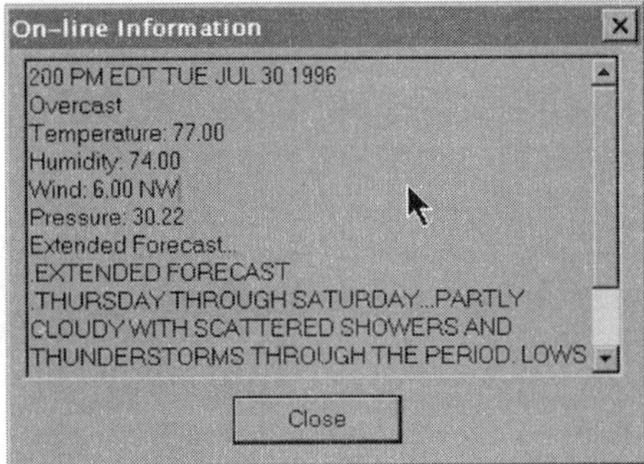

The role of the Web in this case? It has become a tool that has vastly expanded the capabilities of an already impressive software product, resulting in a significant enhancement to the functionality of the program.

As the computer industry expands in this way, by allowing users to obtain software updates through the World Wide Web, we will see major changes and upgrades in the basic functionality of just what a computer can be used for. The DeLorem AAA Map'n'Go software helps to demonstrate this fact.

It Can Be Linked to Devices

Just about everything can be attached to the Web. Consider, for example, Web cameras. Around the world individuals and organizations are linking digital cameras to the Internet. These cameras take a picture every minute or hour and make the picture available on a Web site. For example, this picture from Antarctica (**http://www.antdiv.gov.au/aad/exop/sfo/mawson/video.html**) captured the land of the midnight sun (so there isn't very much to see in the picture below):

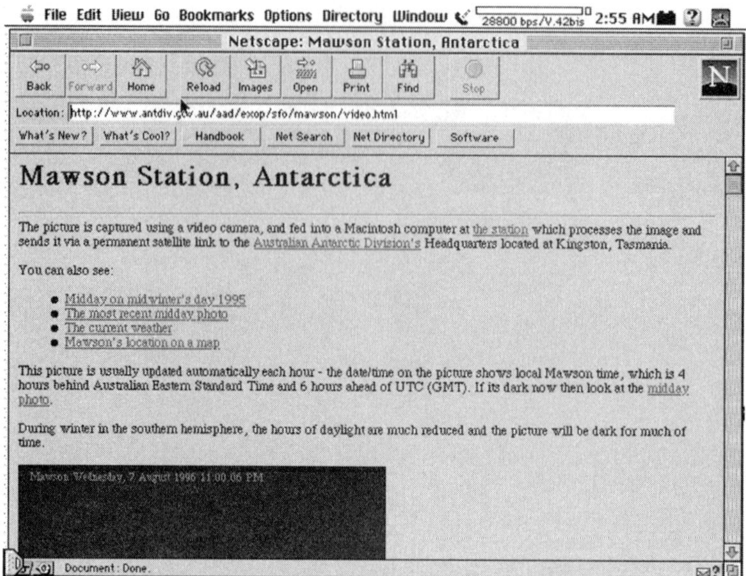

And this picture from the Prince Edward Island tourism site (**http://www.gov.pe.ca/islandcam/index.html**):

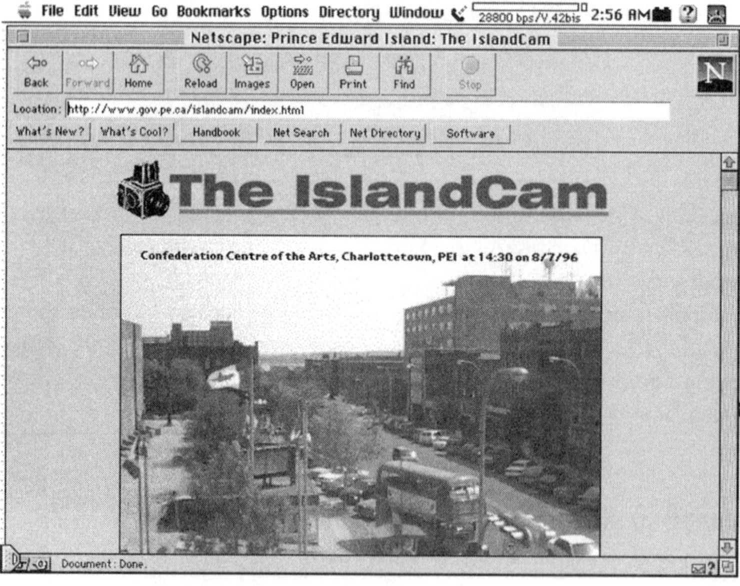

And, of course, the Internet would not be complete without an image from Niagara Falls (**http://fallscam.niagara.com/FallsCam/Live/Pictures**):

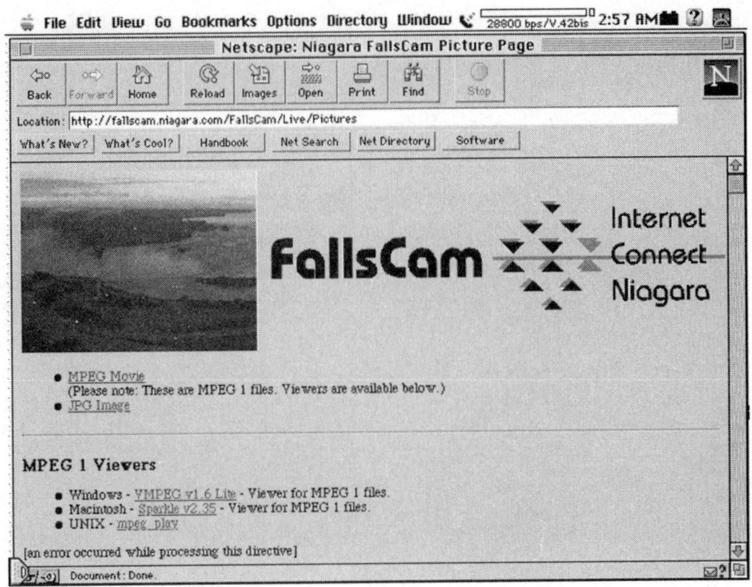

When it comes to linking devices to the Web, there are sometimes many silly things going on, so if you read a magazine or newspaper about the Internet, you are bound to hear about them. Things like

- the fellow who linked his telephone into the Internet, so that you can see the last time it rang.
- the "Amazing Fish Cam," a fish tank located at Netscape Communications Corporation. The camera takes a picture once a minute, and the picture is available on the Internet.
- a hot tub in California: you can find out how hot it is and whether the cover is on or off.
- innumerable drink machines that tell you how many cans of certain types of pop are left and coffee machines that tell you if they are on or off.
- CD players in dormitory rooms, which tell you what song is currently being played.
- Christmas trees that would tell you if their lights were on or off, and doors that would tell you if they were open or closed.

There is also the fellow who has set up a Web site in which you type a message. A speech synthesizer takes what you type and turns your message into speech in his office. You can say anything you like to him:

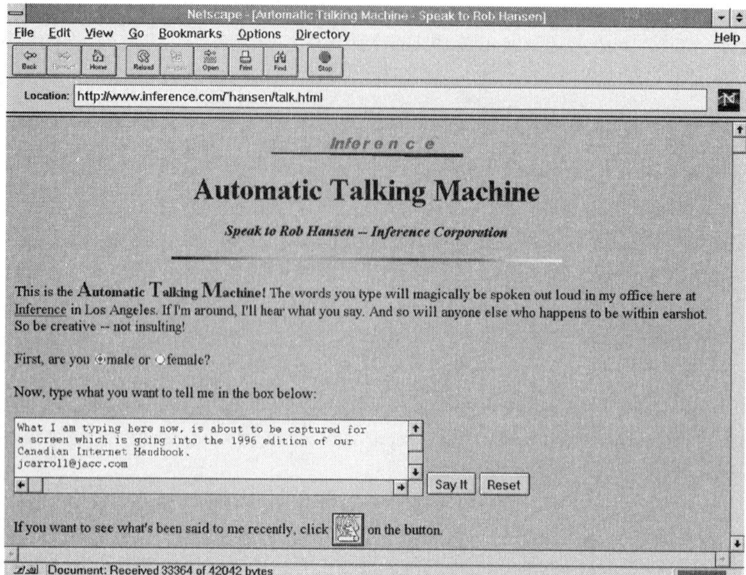

There is even a model railroad that you can watch and control in Germany:

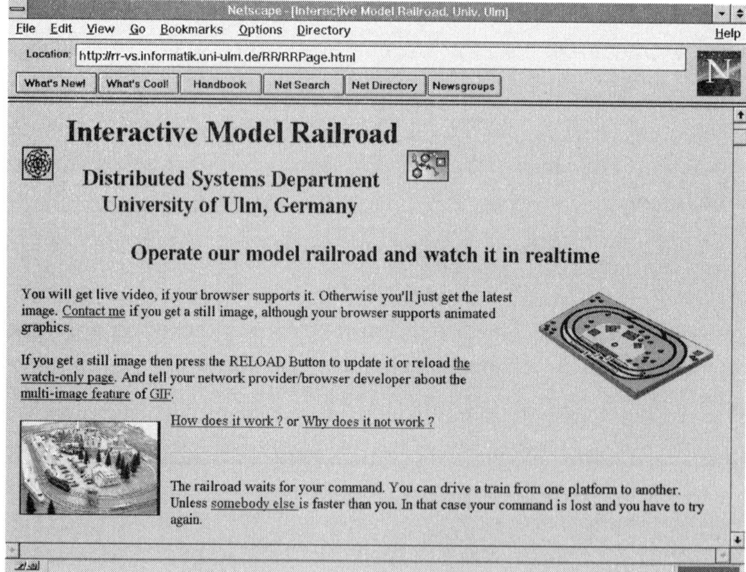

Throughout the world there are various technologies and an amazing number of devices that are linked into the Internet. A tour reveals a fascinating number of silly, inane, serious, amusing, and amazing things that are plugged into the Internet. You can end up spending hours and hours exploring this fascinating and bizarre side of the network.

It all seems dumb and a waste of resources; in fact, many people who are not Internet users and who are confronted with the idea of these devices for the first time come to the conclusion that much of the Internet is all a waste of time. But it really is not; in fact, all of these efforts to connect devices to the Internet represent leading-edge research, which is providing insight into the computer protocols and technology that will drive our wired world into the future. People working with these devices — brilliant computer techies — are discovering what is involved in linking mechanical devices to the all-important TCP/IP computer protocol that supports the Internet. They are determining how remote control via the Internet is possible. They are determining how to turn analog experimentation results into the digital bits necessary for transmission through the Internet. In effect, these "silly" folks are like so many Thomas Edisons around the world, discovering what it takes to establish a new type of computer network–machine interaction. Their efforts are already paying off. For example, consider devices that remotely monitor the water level and flow at various key locations in California. Members of the U.S. Geological Survey can remotely monitor sensor data regarding water flow to determine if there are any potential floods:

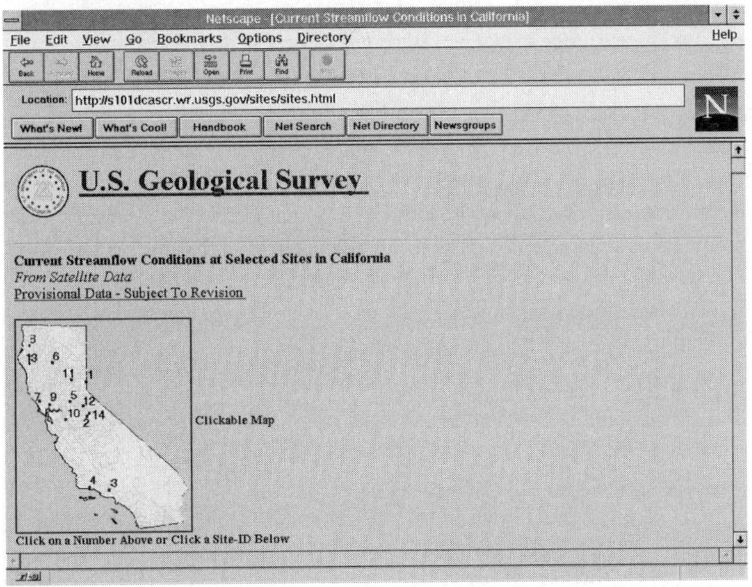

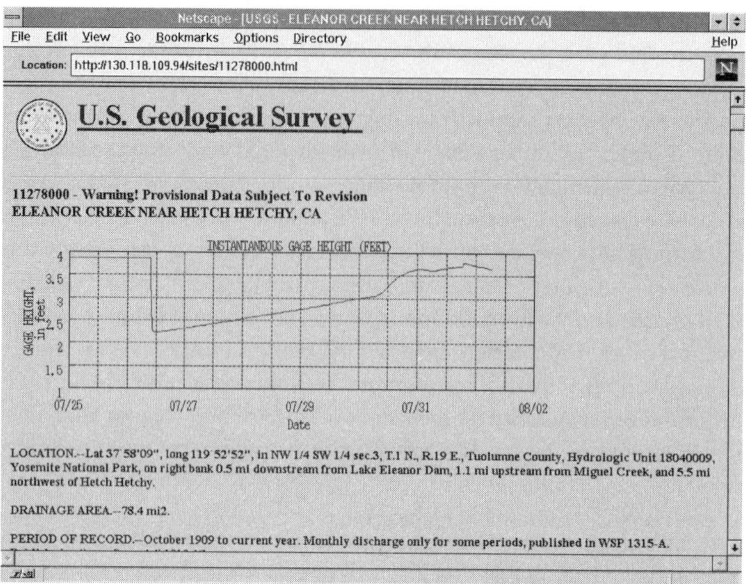

Consider another practical application: a number of cities are linking systems that monitor current road conditions to the Internet, in order to allow citizens to access continually updated traffic conditions. The Arizona Department of Transportation Freeway Management System (**http://www.azfms.com/**), for example, in addition to making available photos from its traffic management system, also allows people access to up-to-date traffic flow information:

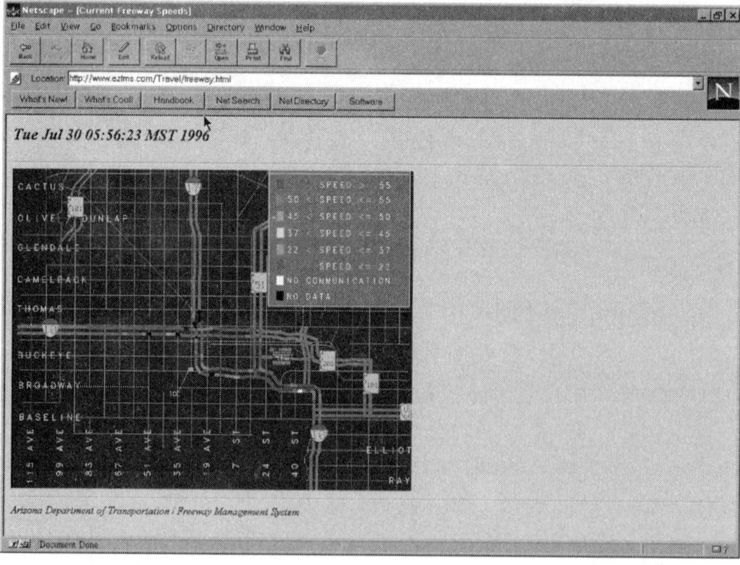

The use of such technology in this case is helping a government department perform a unique and valuable service, by providing an early warning about potentially dangerous conditions.

In the scientific field we are seeing the "device" concepts being used by scientists to remotely monitor and manipulate their experiments through the Internet. In other cases devices that monitor local traffic patterns in various cities are being linked to the Internet; people in these cities can check in before they leave work for the day to see the best route home. Seismographs in earthquake-prone areas are linked into the Internet to provide scientists and the general population with ongoing information about tremors and potential quakes. What is really happening as people around the world link "silly" devices into the Internet is another step forward in technological evolution. What is happening on the Internet, believe it or not, is research into the methods by which other technologies can be monitored, supported, manipulated, and accessed on a remote basis through the Internet. These silly experiments — granted, many are very silly — are in many ways helping researchers discover how computer technology can be used for remote purposes in many aspects of our day-to-day lives. Keep in mind that many of the everyday devices that we take for granted also contain computer chips: televisions, radios, fridges, stoves, stereos, alarm systems, inventory carts, automobiles, factory devices all contain increasing amounts of computer intelligence, all of which can be linked into the Internet. The Internet is plugging together all the computers in the world, and it doesn't necessarily have to be a full-fledged computer in order to plug in.

Where is this leading? The Internet is defining the future of our wired world. One day you will be able to check your home heating, air conditioning, and alarm system from a remote location through the Internet. You will be able to program your tape deck at home in order to be able to record a radio program from afar. Doctors and medical staff will be able to access medical monitoring devices at the other end of the country through the Internet. Staff at a mining company in Toronto might actually control an excavator in Northern Ontario through an Internet connection. It is not a far-fetched idea that at some point in time a farmer will be able to direct an overhead satellite to take an infrared picture of the farm, after providing longitude and latitude coordinates through a Web site, with the picture being sent back after credit card information is validated by the satellite company.

There is nothing wrong with the fact that this leading-edge research is fun and interesting and silly. In fact, maybe it helps to move it along a little quicker. Whatever the case may be, this is another area of the Internet that is providing a tantalizing glimpse into the future.

It Provides for Customization

We are seeing a trend towards increasing customization on the Web and what we refer to as "personalized Web pages." For example, consider the "personal Yahoo! service" (**http://my.yahoo.com**). Yahoo!, a popular search system on the Internet which we examine in Chapter 9, "Undertaking Research on the Internet," allows an individual to build a "custom Web page" based on the topics in which that person is interested. You first select the topics or subjects that interest you:

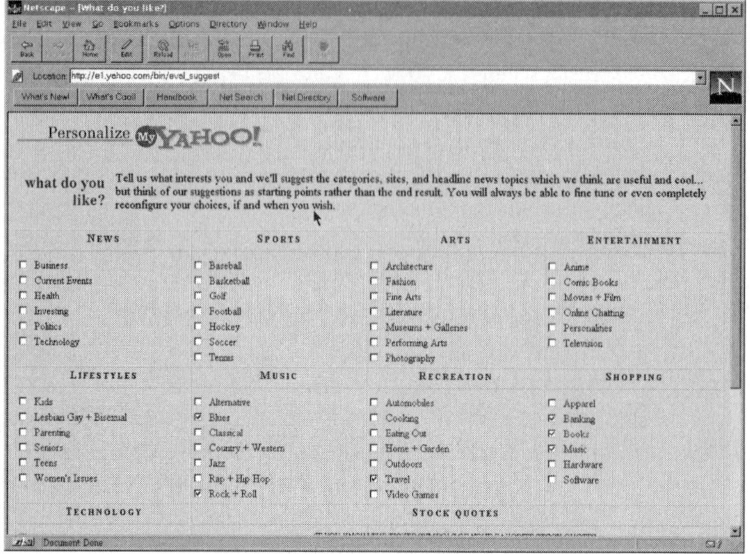

Once you have done that, Yahoo! builds a custom Web page with only your topics, to which you can return at any time:

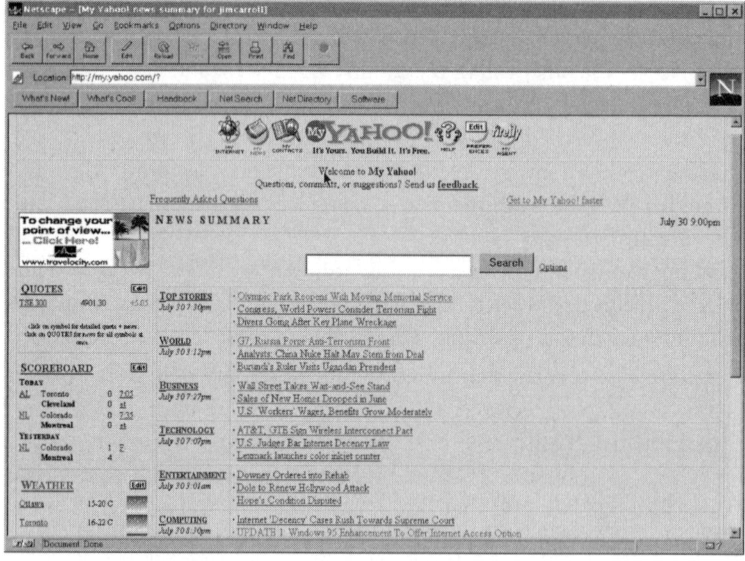

The level of customization on the Web has reached such a level of sophistication that we examine it separately in Chapter 10, "Personalized News Services."

The Economics of the Web

One of the most interesting things about the Web, and certainly one of the reasons for its massive growth, is the fact that *so far*, most of the information that you might access on it is free. Travel through the Web, and you will discover that 99% of the places you visit will let you in for absolutely no charge. You can access health information, news, sports, weather, personal and corporate Web sites, and even the contents of Jeremy's wallet, all without having to pay anything to the owner of the Web site. (Keep in mind, though, that in most cases, you are paying your ISP for your Internet account.)

Why is this so? Part of the reason lies in the historical roots of the Internet: emerging as a tool within the worldwide academic and research communities, many activities on the Internet evolved around the concept of global information-sharing. Researchers, teachers, students, and computer experts developed a unique on-line culture that encouraged individuals and organizations to contribute their knowledge, talents, and expertise to the Internet. Therefore, long before the Web came on the scene, the Internet had become a haven for information access, information that was shared freely, without restriction, and without charge.

When the Web exploded onto the scene in 1993, it became easier to access information through the Internet, and it provided a "user-friendly" view into global information sources, allowing people to view text, images, pictures, and other types of information. But the core culture of free information access remained. It also brought into vogue the concept of "surfing the Web," a phrase describing the concept of traveling from site to site on the Web, viewing different information sources. It is not a stretch of the imagination to say that surfing the Web only became possible because most sites were free; people would react quite differently on-line if they had to pay to access information on the Internet.

The current economic model of the Web, in which most information is free, is under stress as the Web continues to evolve, particularly as more and more sites are beginning to charge for access or are using advertising to support their costs of providing the Web site.

On-line Registration

One thing you will notice as you travel the Web is that some organizations have begun to require that you register in order to visit the full contents of their Web site, even if they provide access for free. Consequently, as you travel the Web, you will find a greater number of Web sites that require a user ID and password before you can get in. And you will soon be mumbling phrases of protest when you have to manage more user IDs and passwords than you might care to deal with. And you will forget a lot of them. Not only that, but in most cases you will have to fill out a registration form in order to get a user ID and password, and some sites will require that you provide what might be considered rather personal information, such as your address, telephone number, or income level. We suggest that you be cautious as you fill out such forms, keeping in mind that such information can be abused. Many sites promise to use information only for the most sacrosanct of purposes, but who can guarantee what they will do with the information you provide them? You should be cognizant and familiar with electronic privacy issues. Clearly, as we rush to cyberspace, we should be aware that we might be giving out just a little bit too much information to companies and people we do not even know.

Fee-based Web Sites

Of course, there are now many individuals and organizations attempting to figure out how to make money off the Internet, and a lot of these attempts involve efforts in building Web sites that you must pay to access. It does take a lot of time and effort to build and maintain a Web site, particularly sophisticated sites, so organizations are trying to recoup their costs or make a profit from their on-line activities. Hence, as you travel the Web, you will discover an increasing number of sites that require you to be a paid subscriber. For example, visit the *New York Times* Web site (**http://www. nytimes. com**), try to access a news story, and you are asked for your subscriber ID and password:

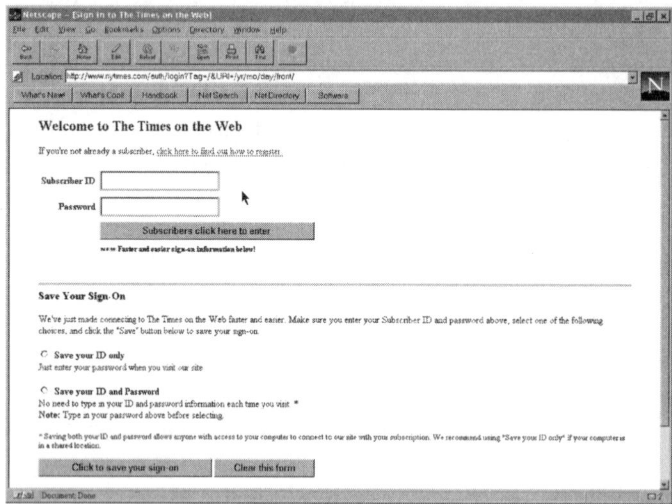

You don't have one? No problem. Click on the phrase "If you're not already a subscriber, click here to find out how to register," and you will get a form where you can provide all the necessary details, including your credit card number to pay for the subscription:

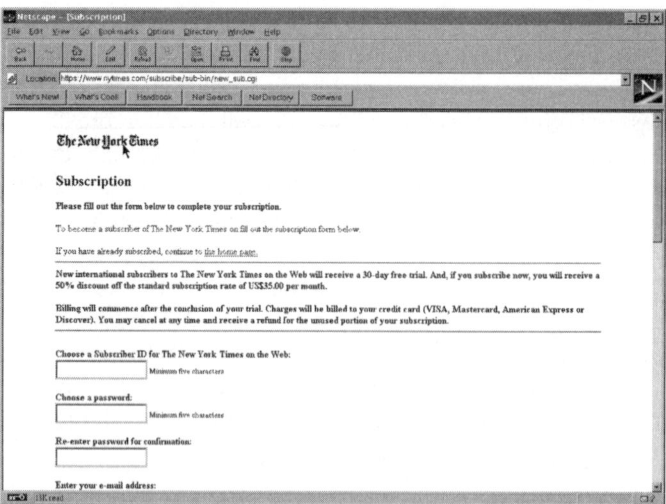

How are these sites doing? Are they signing up all kinds of subscribers? The truth is, many of them will not tell you. And to be honest, many of them are probably not even close to meeting their targets in terms of number of paid subscribers. The business model of the Internet is still very new, and it will take some time to evolve, particularly when it comes to trying to sell information on-line.

Advertising Comes to the Web

One method that organizations are actively exploring to fund the development and maintenance of their Web sites involves the use of advertising. It is such a significant trend that if you travel anywhere on the Web, you are bound to see an advertisement — it is unavoidable. The advertisement is usually in the form of a "hypertext link," the theory being that the Internet surfer visiting that site might choose to follow that link to the home page of the advertising company. Take, for example, the CANOE site (**http://www.canoe.ca**), an on-line initiative of Rogers Communications. On the date we visited their site it featured an advertisement for Bayshore Trust at the top of the page. Click on the Bayshore Trust logo, and you are whisked away to their site on the Internet:

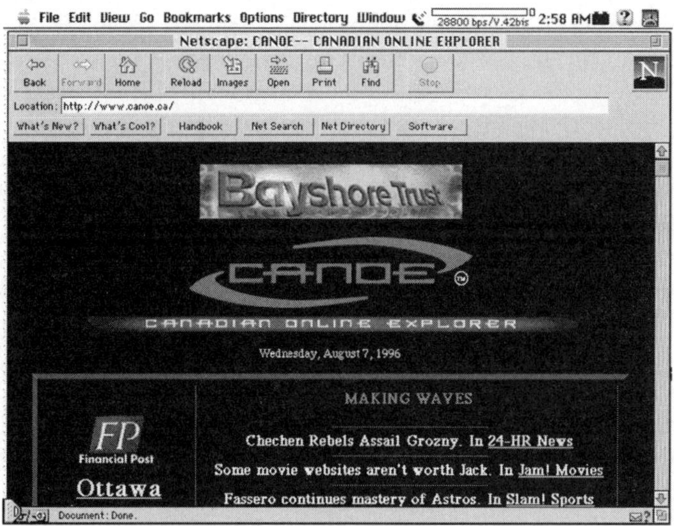

Bayshore Trust, in this case, pays a sum of money to place such a link on the CANOE Web site.

Of course, you do not need to be a huge organization to draw advertising; one of the authors of this book has been running an ad for a small software company for over a year, for a fairly respectable fee. It can be seen at the bottom of the screen (**http://www.jacc.com**):

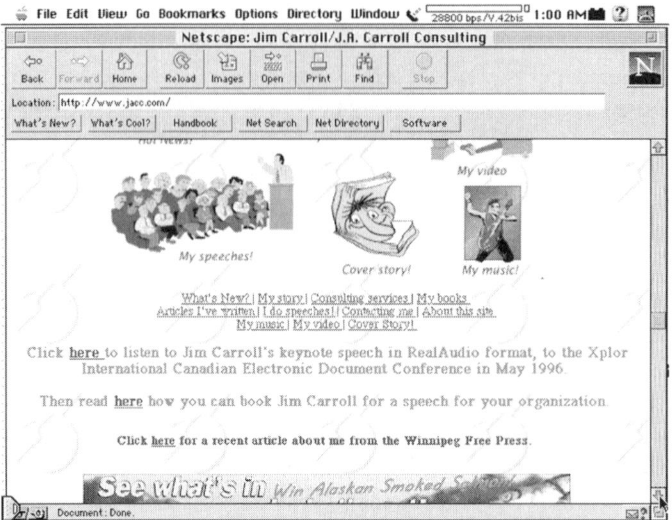

What do organizations pay to put an advertisement on a site? That, of course, depends upon how many visitors the site draws, the profile of the organization, and the ability of the company to actively sell advertising; in effect, whether they have a sales force or not. The current rates are all over the map. Certainly, there are some interesting sums of money being tossed around. *Wired* magazine and the popular Yahoo! index are two organizations that charge rates in the five figures for a monthly listing. Netscape is known to command several million dollars for a listing for a year, making this one of its most significant revenue sources.

But there are also many lower rates being tossed around; the business model for advertising on the Internet is also undergoing constant change. Some advertising organizations, such as Proctor and Gamble, threw a spanner in the works by indicating that they will only pay for an advertisement based on the number of people who actually "click" on the advertisement and travel to the P&G site. Hence there is no doubt that the advertising-supported model is evolving very quickly on the Internet, with new initiatives announced on an almost weekly basis. Of course, if advertisers are going to pay for an advertising link on a Web page, they will want to be able to verify that the site is actually drawing the reported number of visitors. In this regard, the Internet and advertising industries are now working closely together to establish guidelines for "Internet audience rating systems," which track the number of visitors to a site, much as these types of organization track how many people watch television shows.

Three organizations — Webtrack, NetCount, and Internet Profiles (I/Pro) — already provide Web site ratings by providing independently audited summaries of visitors to particular sites (referred to as "hits"). Other organizations such as Nielsen and the Audit Bureau of Circulation are jumping in as the corporate world wakes up to the fact that something significant is occurring on the Internet. But with the danger that many different tracking mechanisms will quickly emerge, advertising industry associations are now becoming involved to ensure that some rationalization occurs. For example, the U.S.-based Coalition for Advertising Supported Information & Entertainment (CASIE), in an effort backed by the American Association of Advertising Agencies and the Association of National Advertisers, announced a plan to get involved in the many new Web rating schemes emerging in the marketplace. As a result, advertisements on the Web are becoming a significant and potent force.

Ads Can Disappear

Even as advertisements have become a reality on the Internet, technology has emerged that can make them disappear. There are many who find advertisements on the Web to be intrusive, disturbing, and sometimes revolting. And just as these people might like to hit the fast forward button on their VCR to skip through the commercials on a taped TV program, they would like to be able to make advertisements on the Internet go away. No problem. Along comes the software Internet Fast Forward, a tool for Windows 95 computers that makes ads on the Internet disappear (**http://www.privnet.com**). Visit a Web site before Internet Fast Forward (IFF) is installed, and you might see an advertisement. For example, here is a page from the CNN news site; notice the three advertisements just below the "Olympic Park Bombing" item:

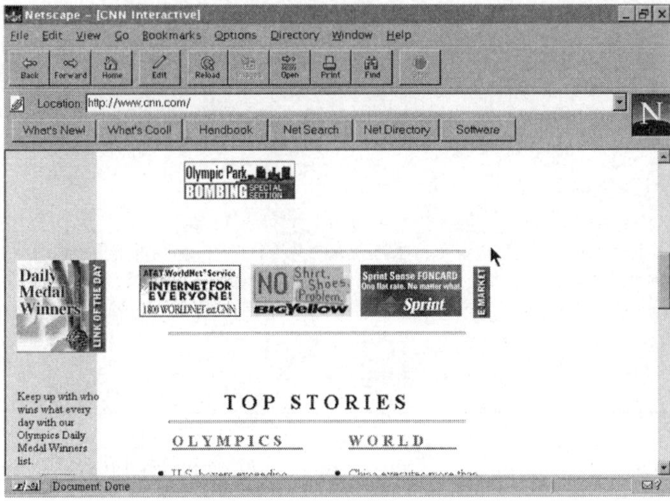

Visit it after you install IFF and notice how the advertisements have completely disappeared:

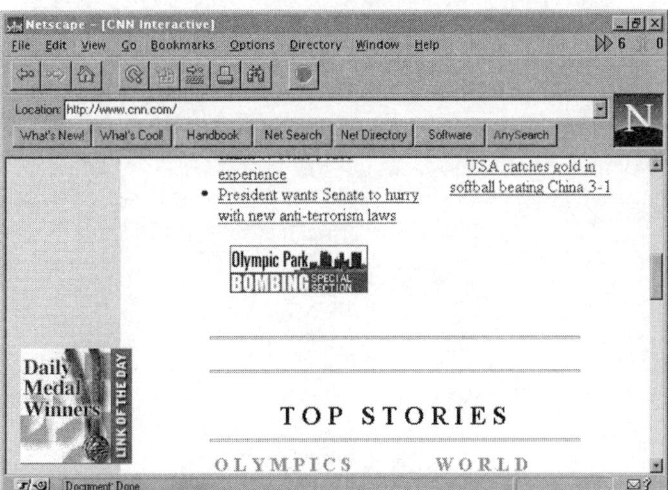

As you can see, it has added some buttons to the top right of the Netscape Web browser: a double arrow that allows you to make changes to the IFF configuration as well as a running report on the number of ads that it has filtered: six so far.

Internet Fast Forward can also avoid providing cookies to the sites you visit. Cookies, which were discussed earlier in the chapter, allow companies to track who is visiting their site and what visitors are doing there. Some people feel concerned that their privacy is being breached. IFF conveniently explains what a cookie is within one of the help screens:

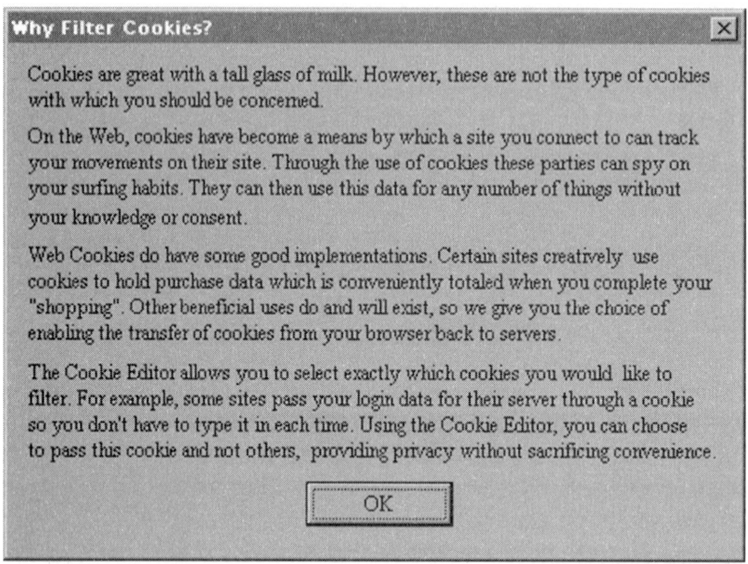

IFF gives you a number of options to filter out advertisements, giving you some flexibility in what you want it to filter:

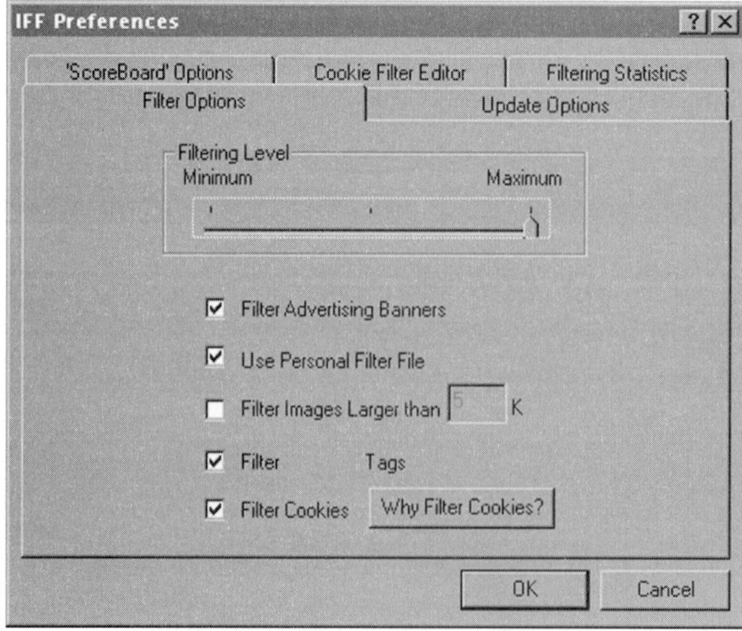

How does IFF work? When it visits a Web site, it refers to a local database that is installed with the software to see if any of the external links on the page, or the images found on the page, have been reported as an advertisement. Since new advertisements are always appearing on the Internet, it is important that IFF be able to keep up. To do that, the program gives you the ability to contact the on-line IFF database to obtain an update of new advertisements that should be filtered out:

Does the product filter out each and every advertisement? Of course not. But for those who are tired of being assaulted on-line by advertisements, a product like Internet Fast Forward is a welcome development.

The Information Conundrum

If the Web has done anything, it has served to lessen the value of information. This presents a particular challenge to media organizations, used to selling their information for a fee or trying to sell advertising on their Web site.

When it comes to the Internet, why bother paying to subscribe to the *Globe and Mail* on-line in order to read international news when you can read thousands of international news sites on-line for free? Why read the *Montreal Gazette* on the Internet for a fee, when there are many other Montreal-based news sources on-line? Why, indeed, pay for information, when we live in a world where unprecedented volumes of information have become available on-line for free?

These are interesting questions, and there are no easy answers. The truth of the matter is that there are many organizations and individuals trying to figure out how to build fee-based Web sites and little likelihood of any of them being successful without a huge amount of work and effort. It is a significant challenge for any organization trying to make money by selling information on-line, regardless of whether that organization is Joe's Local Fish and Bait Shop or the large and established *Globe and Mail* or *New York Times.*

We believe that if anyone tries to tell you that it is easy to make money selling information on the Internet, you should run away from him as fast as possible, because he is probably some type of scam artist. Quite simply, at this point it is perhaps the most significant challenge of the Internet.

Why? The Internet has flattened the field of information production and distribution. Since anyone with a computer and a modem can have their own "global printing press," it seems to have the effect of ripping apart centuries-old paradigms of publishing. It is a significant change to the global concept of information distribution as was the invention of the printing press, an invention that forever changed the world. Simply, the Internet devalues the value of information, by making information so freely available. In a world of excess supply, people are unwilling to pay for information. Nowhere is the impact of the Internet felt more dramatically than in the field of media since it serves to forever change the competitive playing field. Let us explain why. Before the Internet came around, the competition for the *Vancouver Sun* newspaper was the *Vancouver Province* newspaper. But on the Internet, when it comes to world news the competition for the *Vancouver Sun* is now not only local newspapers, but any one of several thousand newspapers worldwide. And when it comes to local weather information, the competition for the *Vancouver Sun* now includes The Weather Network Web site, the Environment Canada Web site, and countless other weather-related sites. When it comes to sports, you can find out the score and details from the latest Vancouver Grizzlies game from ESPN, TSN, or hundreds of other on-line news and sports sources. The Internet changes the competition, doesn't it?

So what are people willing to pay for on the Web? The honest answer is that no one really knows, but our gut feeling is that it is unlikely they will pay for information that they can so easily get for free elsewhere on the Internet. What needs to be done to make money from information on the Internet is to make it something worthwhile to purchase, to change it from being a simple commodity that is available for free everywhere else to something that is not so freely available. Information must be made special for it to have value. A good indication of information that has a special value is found with tools and services that make it easier for people to find and access specific information throughout the global Internet, particularly what we call personalized news sources. That is why we cover that topic in Chapter 10, "Personalized News Services."

The bottom line is that as you surf the Web, you will find an increasing number of sites trying to get you to pay for access to their information and requesting your credit card details on-line. Our advice is that you surf with care. Ask yourself whether it is really worth it to subscribe to a site on-line and determine if you might be able to receive similar information elsewhere for no charge. And always be careful; unless it is a high-profile, well-known site, you should be cognizant that there are scams on-line. The economic model of the Internet? It is one that is unknown, but for something that is so unknown, it is under constant change.

Accessing Other Information Through the Web

As we have mentioned, you can access several types of information through the Web, including text, graphics, pictures, sound, and video. Sometimes this information is shown to you as soon as you see a Web page, and in other cases you may have to "download," or retrieve, the information from that page before you can view it. In the latter case the reason you have to "download" the information is because there are certain other "data types" that you cannot "view" immediately with your Web browser. This means that when you want to see that information, you must first transfer the information to your own computer from the Web server you have visited. Once you have transferred the information, you then must use special software — a separate program — to view, listen to, or access the information.

There are literally hundreds of different types of information that you might access through a Web site that your browser is not capable of dealing with. Here is a good example: on the Web site for Andrew McCallum/Mental Floss (who we talked about in Chapter 3), you can retrieve some of his music. He makes his music available in two special formats, each of which requires a special "player" software program. One is called iPlay and the other is Ultratracker. He notes this on the Web page and provides a link to the sites where you can obtain these special programs:

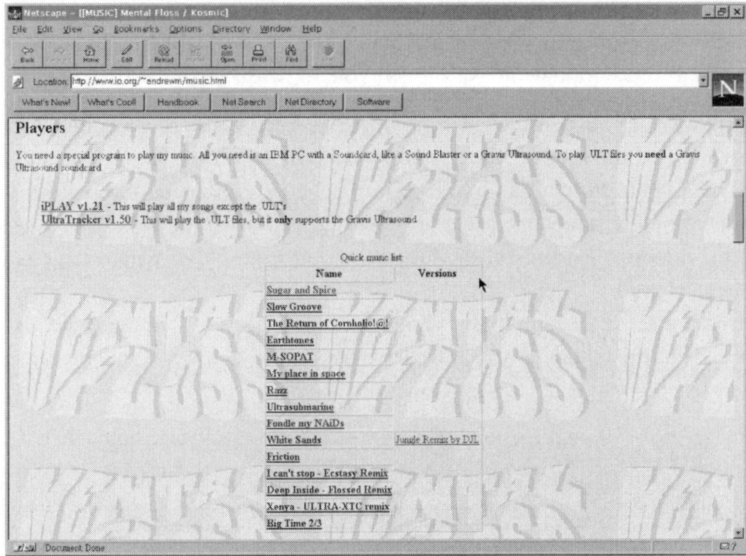

If you want to listen to his music, you must first download appropriate player software and install it. Then you can download a sound file and use the player software to listen to it.

Why do you have to download the songs? Why can't they just play through your Web browser? Why can't you use a Web browser to access all the information that it comes across from all over the world? Because there can be all kinds of data in all kinds of formats on a Web site. Sounds can come in "**.au**," "**.wav**," "**.aif**," and "**.ra**" format and countless other formats. Video can come in MPEG files or QuickTime format or in AVI files. Images can come in "**.tif**," "**.gif**," "**.jpeg**," and other formats. The list goes on.

It is difficult, if not impossible, for the programmers of a Web browser to ensure that their program can deal with all kinds of different data formats found on a Web page, particularly since new file types are emerging all the time. As a result, with many browsers today, you have to download a file first and then use a separate program to "view" it, or "play" it, the term "view" being used throughout the Internet to describe what you do with the file, whether it is sound, video, an image, or some other type of data. You download the file by "clicking" on it.

Accessing Other Data Types on the Internet

The secret of "player," or "viewer," software is that you can often configure your browser so that when you visit a Web site that contains a special format file, a program can be automatically "launched" to show, hear, or view the file. When your browser is configured in this way, one of two things happen when you choose to see a special file:

- The file is first automatically downloaded to your computer. Once it has finished downloading, the player or viewer program automatically starts and runs or shows the file that you have just retrieved. In this case you have to wait for the special file to finish downloading before you can see or hear it.

- Or the file starts to download to your computer. Within a few seconds of starting to download, your player or viewer program starts to show the file, or lets you hear it. In this case you do not have to wait for the file to finish downloading.

Let's explain by way of two examples. First, you will remember earlier in this chapter that we explained how we used the Internet to retrieve a video clip featuring Pierre Trudeau. In that case we chose that video item from a CBC Web page. The video proceeded to download to our PC, and once it was complete, a separate program started and showed the video. We had to wait several minutes for the download to finish. This is a good example of where a file is first downloaded and then "viewed."

Let's consider a second example, in which the file is "viewed," or "played," as soon as we start to receive it. On the following screen we have traveled to CKNW Vancouver, a radio station that broadcasts live in what is known as RealAudio format:

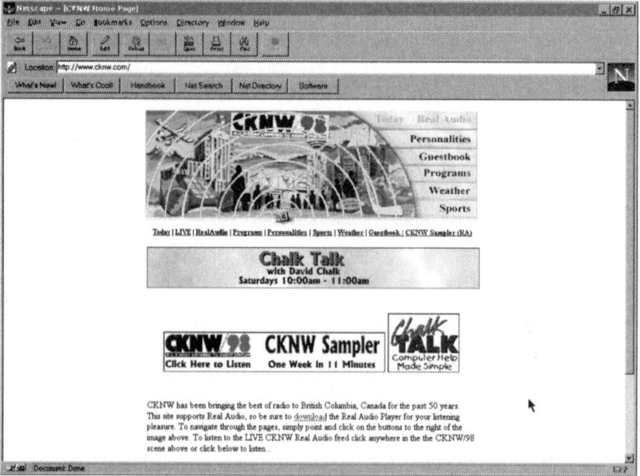

We just click on the "Click here to listen" button, and in a few seconds a separate program called the RealAudio player loads and starts to play the radio station live:

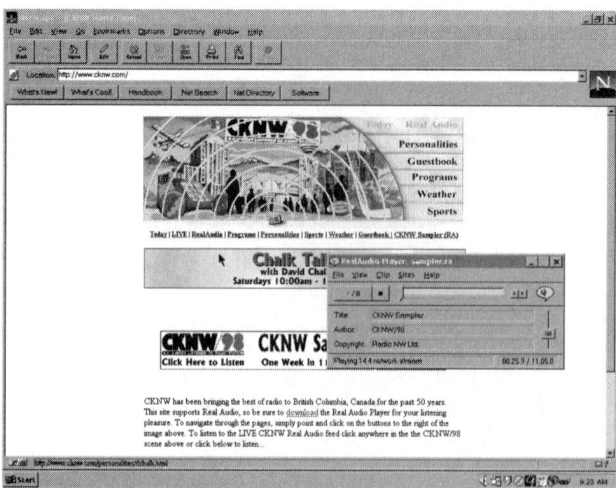

In this case the file being downloaded is played for us as it is received; this reduces the length of time we have to wait to listen to it. This type of download, often referred to as "streaming audio," is gaining increasing popularity on the Internet.

Configuring Automatic Player/Viewer Software

What is involved in setting up your browser so that you can hear audio, see video, or participate in some of the other special things that are happening on the Web? Several things:

- You must obtain the appropriate viewer software.
- The software must be installed.
- Your Web browser must be configured so that it recognizes the new type of information you are accessing on the Web, so that it starts the special new program that you have just obtained and configured.

It sounds terribly complicated, but it often isn't. Let's take a look at how we can configure our Web browser so that we can listen to broadcasts that have been set up using the RealAudio format on the Internet. What we want to do is ensure that our Netscape program is configured so that whenever it finds a RealAudio file on the Internet, it knows to run the RealAudio player program to play that file. In Netscape this means we want to install RealAudio as a "helper application."

To start out, you need to find and obtain the RealAudio software; this is easy enough, since it is available for free. You can get it from the RealAudio Web site (**http://www.realaudio.com**). You should be aware that in many cases the designer of a Web site will make it easy for you to go off and find the appropriate viewer or player software, by providing a link to the Web site of other viewer or player software. The folks at CKNW have done this; from their home page at **http://www.cknw.com**, if you click on the RealAudio button, you are taken to another page that details how to use, install, and get RealAudio for your computer:

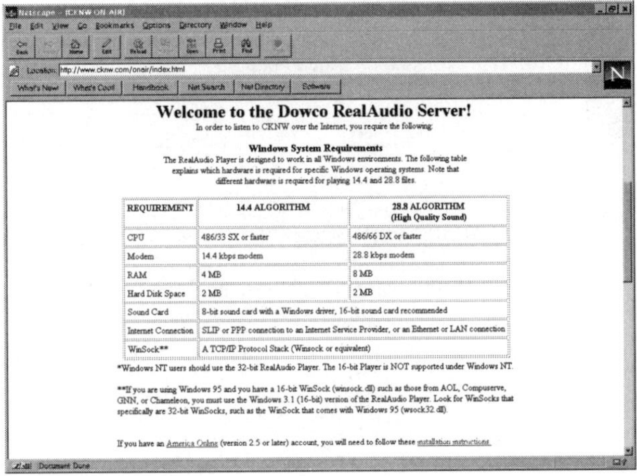

Further down the page, you will find the line "to download the PLAYER, visit the RealAudio Site":

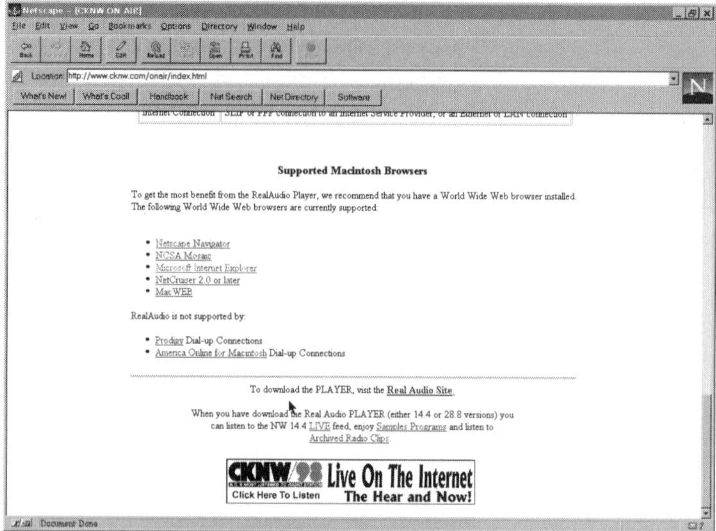

Just click on that, and you are taken to the RealAudio Web site, the company that developed the RealAudio player software:

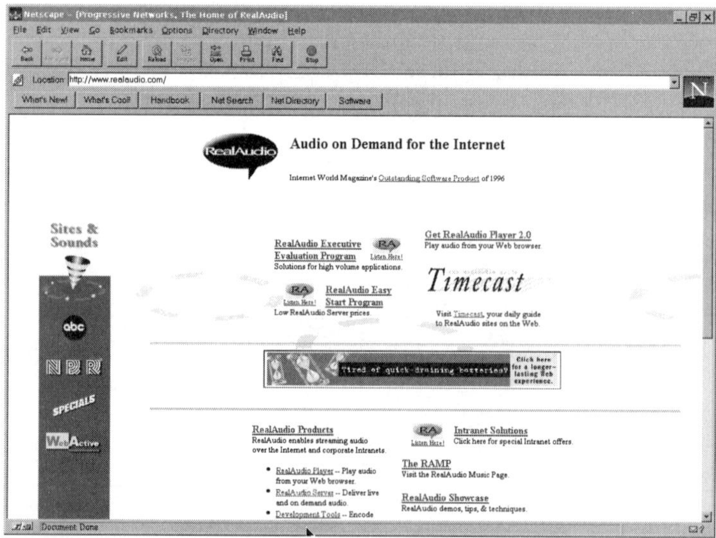

From there you fill out a form with your e-mail address and name:

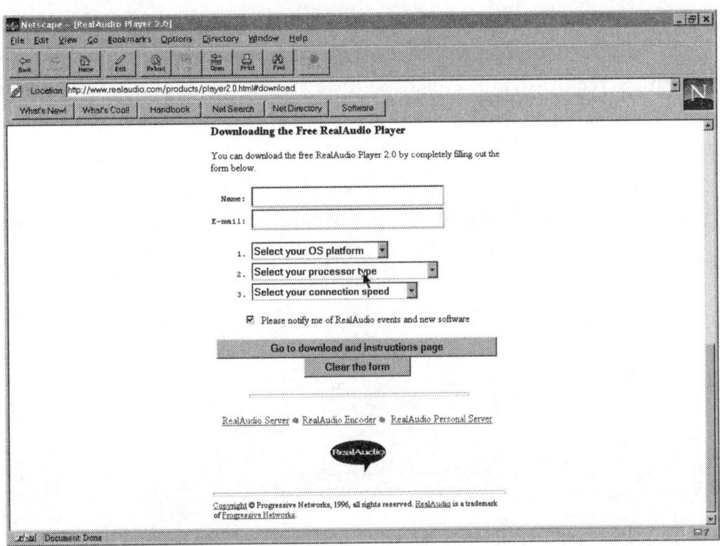

Once completed, the RealAudio player software is downloaded to your computer. You then run the installation routine that comes with the RealAudio program. This installation routine searches your computer for any Web browsers that you have and installs itself within them.

Let's look at the details of what the installation routine does using Netscape as an example. RealAudio installs itself as a "helper application." You can see what "helper applications" (i.e., players and viewers) are on your Netscape program by choosing the menu item "Options, General Preferences, Helpers":

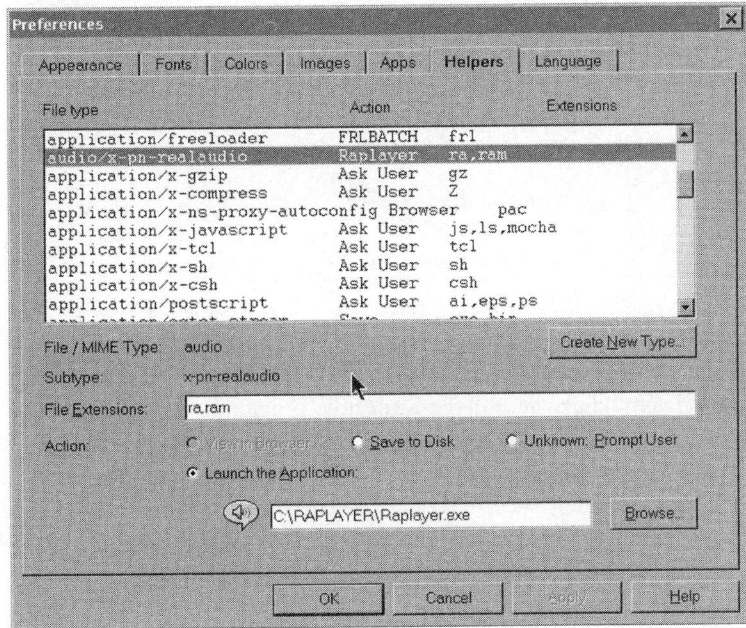

The highlighted line (the second line in the window) is the configuration line for RealAudio, the details of which are also provided on the bottom half of the screen. Let's get into some geekspeak here. In essence, this screen instructs Netscape to "Launch the application" **ra-player.exe** found in the directory **c:\raplayer** any time it encounters a file type of "**audio/x-pn-realaudio**," which has a "**file extension**" of "**.ra**" or "**.ram**" (i.e., the file name ends with that extension). In non-geek language this means that Netscape is instructed to launch the RealAudio player program any time it comes across a RealAudio file. Here is the same type of configuration screen as found within Microsoft Internet Explorer:

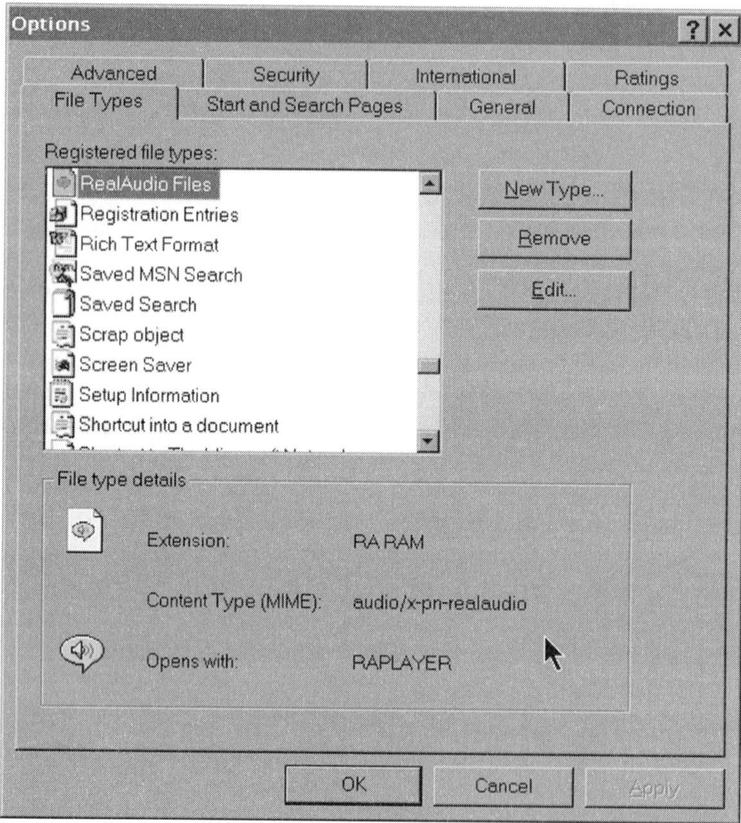

It says the same thing: if Internet Explorer encounters a "content type" of **audio/x-pn-realaudio**, with an extension of **.ra** or **.ram**, it should run the **RAPLAYER** program. Any time it encounters a RealAudio file, it should play it with the RealAudio program.

You normally do not have to worry about getting involved in these details, because programs like RealAudio are automatically configured when installed. Once the RealAudio program is installed, you need only click on the "listen here" button on the Web site and the program will start to play the sounds found on that link. RealAudio is a good example of how player/viewer programs can easily be added to your Web browser.

Challenges With Player/Viewer Configuration

During the installation of a player/viewer program, sometimes something can go wrong, and the Helpers screen above is not properly configured. How can you tell? You know you have downloaded and installed a player/viewer, but when you try to link to an item that contains that type of audio or video file supported by that player/viewer, nothing happens. You might, for example, click on a RealAudio link, but nothing happens. What do you do? We suggest taking a look at the Helpers screen above and find the name of the player/viewer that you installed. Check to make sure that the button "Launch the Application" is clicked, and make sure it points to the computer program that you installed. If it does not, that is probably the main reason for the problem. Fix that, and the problem might go away.

We also suggest that you review the documentation or "Readme.txt" file that came with the player/viewer, since these files usually provide the details on how to exactly configure the program within your Web browser.

Types of Players/Viewers

The state-of-the-art of the Internet today is such that you will encounter two types of player/viewer software:

- Separate stand-alone programs, such as seen with RealAudio above. In this case a completely separate program is loaded to play or view the file you have retrieved.
- Plug-ins, the new breed of programs that actually run within Netscape or Internet Explorer, allowing you to view or play the file directly within the Web browser.

We will first take a look at how you can add audio and video to your Web browser. Then we will look at how you can examine other types of data through the Web. In both cases some player/viewers that we examine will be separate programs, and others will be plug-ins. You can find listings of player/viewer software at several locations throughout the Internet. Some of the best sites are listed below.

Obtaining Web Player/Viewer Software	
Windows/Windows 95	
Consummate Winsock Apps List	**http://www.stroud.com**
The Ultimate Collection of Winsock Software	**http://www.tucows.com/**
Macintosh	
MacVantage Site	**http://www.discover.net/corporate/smiledoc/macvantage/**
Internet software for the Macintosh	**http://www.cyberatl.net/~mphillip/index.html**
Mac Internet Helpers	**http://www.wp.com/mwaters/machelp.html**

Obtaining Netscape Plug-ins

For version 2.0, take a look at **http://home.netscape.com/comprod/products/navigator/version_2.0/plugins/index.html.** Up-to-date lists for other versions of their software can also be located at their Web site. You can also check the Plug-in Plaza, **http://browserwatch.iworld.com/plug-in.html.** Both sites cover plug-ins for Windows and Macintosh environments.

For Microsoft Internet Explorer

Many Netscape plug-ins work with Internet Explorer. And to obtain ActiveX controls, which add features to your Internet Explorer program, visit Microsoft ActiveX Component Gallery **http://www.microsoft.com/activex/controls/**.

Definitely check out the Intel Plug-in Detector; it advises you if you are trying to access a file for which you do not have the proper plug-in and will take you to the Web site and immediately begin downloading the proper plug-in for you. Check it out at **http://www.intel.com/iaweb/cpc/iisum/**.

Adding Audio/Video Capabilities to Your Web Browser

The first thing you might want to do to enhance your Web experience is add audio and video to your Web browser, since there is a lot of audio and video information appearing on-line. There is an extensive, up-to-date list of audio and video players for Windows, Windows 95, and Macintosh computers in several places throughout the Internet, including the sites that we mentioned in the previous section. Also keep in mind that many of the sites you visit that support audio will have a link to the program that you require.

The Basics of Audio on the Internet

To get comfortable with the idea of retrieving audio on the Internet, there are a few basic concepts with which you should be familiar:

- An audio recording is converted to a digital format, that is, it is turned into a computer file, in order to be made accessible on the Internet. Because of the nature of the way that sound is delivered through a computer, it is important to keep in mind that the computer files that contain the sound can often be quite large, depending upon the way they are stored and the format that is used. A one-minute file can often take up as much as 1,000,000 or 2,000,000 bytes of storage space or as little as 60,000 bytes, depending upon the quality of the audio and the type of format used.
- There are many different audio formats used throughout the Internet. Individuals who put audio up on the Internet have a lot of flexibility in the type of recording they might put on-line and can choose from a number of different formats, leading to an often complex world in dealing with audio on-line. The type of format that is used has a direct impact on the size of the audio file and the quality of the sound.

  The most common types of audio files you might encounter are **.wav** (a format common to Windows), **.aif** or **.aiff** (a format common to Macintosh systems), **.au** (Sun Microsystems format), and **.ra** (RealAudio format). Any type of sound file, even though it might be common to a particular type of computer as we see above, can be listened to on almost any other type of computer. The audio file, regardless of the format used, is stored on a computer somewhere on the Internet, often the same computer used to store the Web page you are currently accessing, and is accessible through a hyperlink. To listen to it, you just click the appropriate link.

- However, to listen to the file, you need an audio player installed in your Web browser. If the audio file is in a format different than the basic ones supported by Netscape (**.au**, **.aiff**) or Internet Explorer (**.wav**), you will need to obtain and install appropriate audio player software. Once you have the right player installed, you can listen to the audio simply by double clicking on the sound file link on the Web page. Given all the different audio formats, it is not surprising that there are all kinds of different audio players. We will look into audio players in more depth below.
- There are two basic types of audio you can listen to on the Internet. The original format used throughout the Internet came to be known as "downloadable audio," such as was found with our example above. Basically, you choose the audio you want to listen to by clicking on an item on a Web page. You then wait a few seconds or minutes for the sound to be transferred — downloaded — to your computer. Once it has downloaded, you then listen to it.

  Many people find this type of audio on the Internet to be cumbersome; it is comparable to having to wait half an hour to "download" the evening news on television to your VCR before you can watch it. Given that, it did not take long for several companies to come up with what are called "streaming audio" formats, technology that plays an audio file as soon as you click on an audio file on a Web page. As audio is downloaded to your computer, it is instantly played, meaning that you do not have a long wait to hear the item. We will take a look at streaming audio formats such as RealAudio in a moment.

Today audio is one of the fastest-growing areas on the Internet. And one result of the availability of streaming audio is a wide diversity in what you can access. For example, surf the Internet and you can find:

- Live radio. Several radio stations across Canada and around the world now broadcast live, 24 hours a day, 7 days a week, using streaming audio formats.
- Sound archives of recently broadcast radio or television shows or other types of audio programming. CBC's *The World at Six* newscast, for example, is loaded onto the CBC Web site, so that you can listen to it any time in the next 24 hours after it is broadcast (in either downloadable or streaming audio format).
- Clips from albums or entire songs. Several bands and artists, including Porno for Pyros and Neil Young, actually debuted new albums on the Internet.

Let's look further into how you can take advantage of audio through the Internet.

Basic Audio Formats

As we noted above, most Web browsers, such as Netscape and Internet Explorer, come with the capability to support certain basic formats. Travel to the Geffen Records site, which provides information about the band Cowboy Junkies (**http://www.geffen.com/cowboyjunkies/**), click on a song title, and a clip is transferred to your PC in a minute or two:

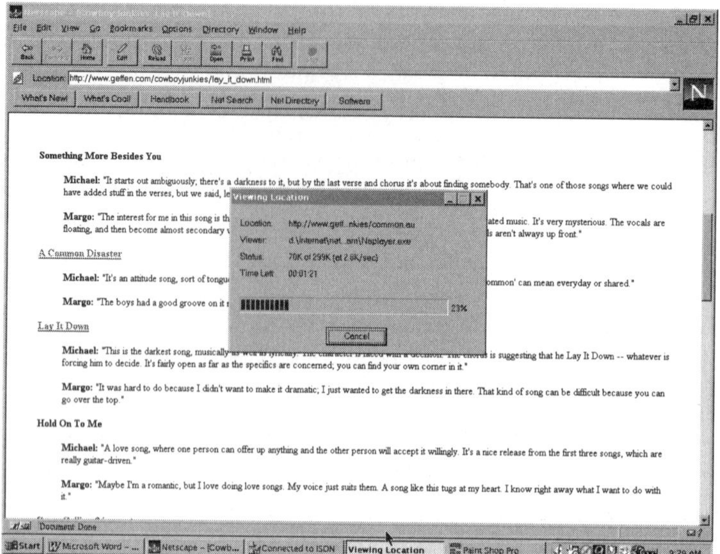

Once it has been transferred, the Netscape audio player plays the clip using a small, separate program:

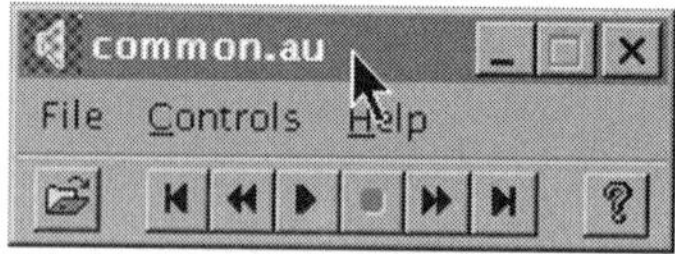

It's that easy.

Using Other Audio Players

Of course, if you travel to a Web site that supports a format that is not a basic part of your Web browser, you will need to obtain an "audio player" program to listen to the audio. In almost all cases you can retrieve a player from the Internet, install it into your Web browser once, and then use it again and again. Many sites that use alternative sound formats will provide a link through which you can easily obtain an appropriate player. For example, the Web site for the band Sucking Chest Wound (honest — we didn't make this up) (**http://www.io.org/~scw/sounds.html**) notes on one screen in their site that "to play the MPEG files you must have a player applet configured to work with your browser. If you don't have an MPEG Audio player, you can find one by going to the IUMA Help page." You can use this to quickly travel to another site to find an appropriate player for the MPEG format used at the site for Sucking Chest Wound:

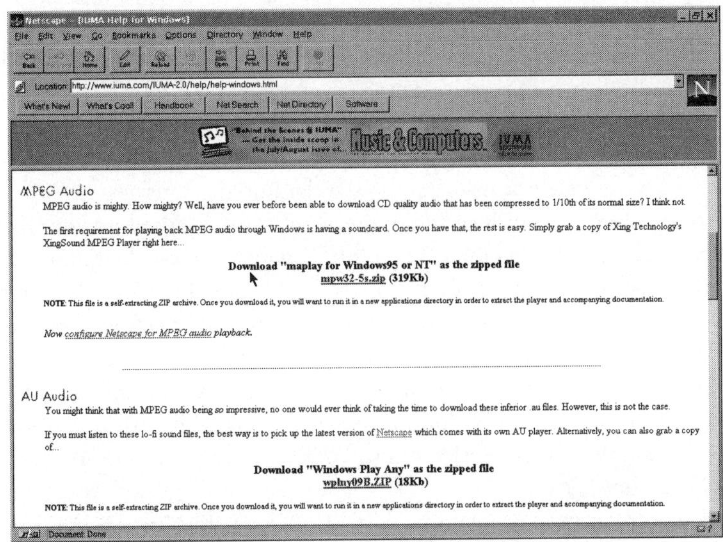

You will also be able to access instructions on how to install the player into your Web browser:

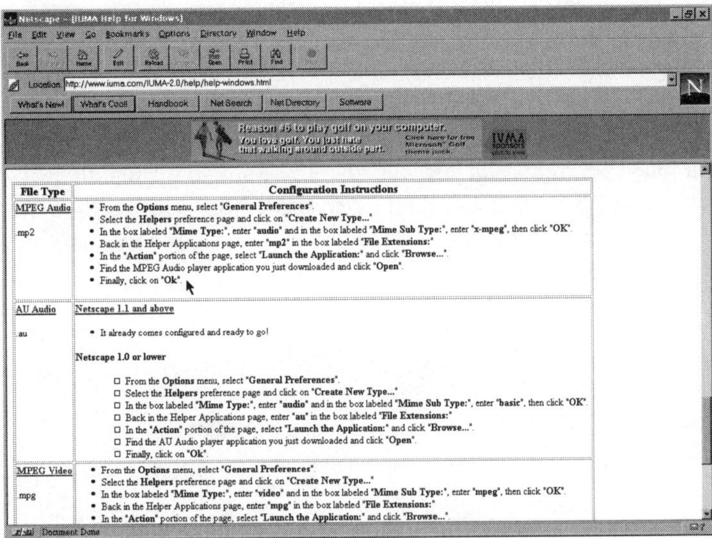

Once it is installed, you can choose a clip back at the Sucking Chest Wound site. Once it downloads, a separate program runs and plays the sound:

Streaming Audio

As we mentioned earlier, the big drawback for most audio on the Internet is the fact that you have to download the audio first before you listen to it, which has led to the concept of streaming audio. Two of the largest players in the streaming audio business are RealAudio and TrueSpeech. RealAudio (**http://www.realaudio.com**) is perhaps the pioneer in providing streaming audio and is probably the most widely accepted audio standard on the Internet.

There are two components to RealAudio: the client software, used on your own version of Netscape or other Web browser, and the server software, which is available from your Internet service provider and other organizations that support RealAudio "broadcasts" or archived sound files in RealAudio format. RealAudio can be used to listen to live broadcasts and archived sound files. It is easy to install on both Windows and Macintosh systems; you simply run an installation program. It will automatically configure itself and in most cases install itself into your Web browser, ready to play any RealAudio sound files you access while using the Web. If you are using version 2.0 or higher of the RealAudio software, you can use it to listen to a live radio show or an archived show.

RealAudio gets around the problem of the size of sound files by the use of compression, but it loses quality as it does this. Each second of sound is converted into a file of approximately 1,000 bits of information, so that 60 seconds take up 60,000 bytes compared to a megabyte or two (1,000,000 or 2,000,000) when saved in sound file formats without compression. Hence RealAudio is certainly listenable, but it is more like listening to a short wave radio than an FM broadcast. We saw an example of using RealAudio earlier when we visited CKNW, "B.C.'s Most Listened To Radio Station," itself a good example of a radio station that broadcasts live through the Internet as well as a good example of using RealAudio to access a live broadcast. However, you should note that the other way to use RealAudio is to access and listen to sound files found in radio archives from around the world. Did you miss the *The World at Six* nightly newscast on CBC Radio? No problem. Travel to the CBC Radio Web site (**http://www.radio.cbc.ca**), choose the "World at Six," and you can listen to the most recent news show. You will start hearing it within a few seconds of choosing:

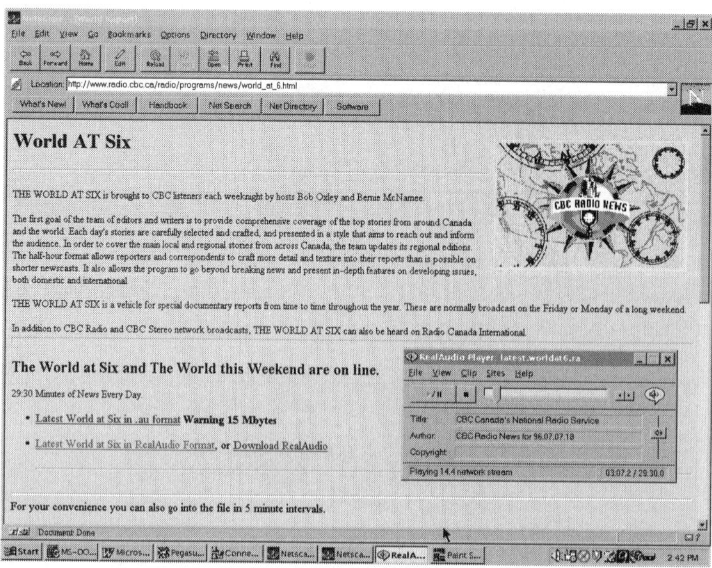

RealAudio claims to have the largest number of users of audio software on the Internet, and given the number of audio sites that support RealAudio, this does not seem to be a far-fetched claim. You can find up-to-date schedules of RealAudio broadcasts at TimeCast (**http://www.timecast.com**). It provides details of real time broadcasts as well as archives that can be accessed on-line, like an on-line TV guide of current Internet broadcasts:

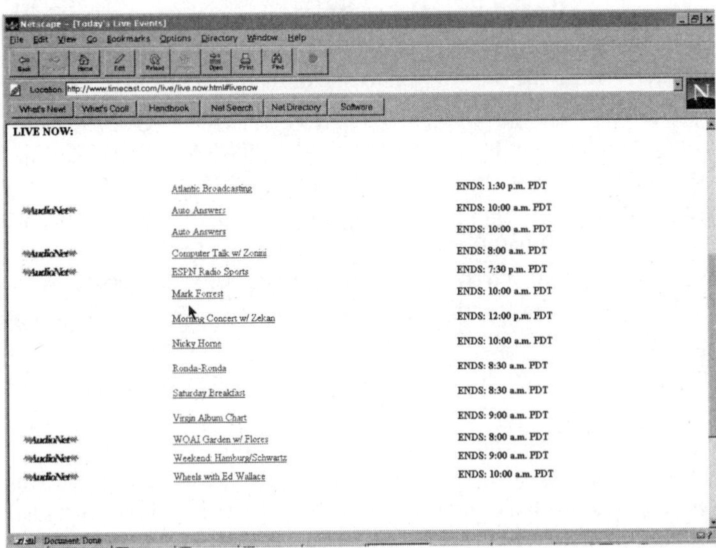

There are other real time players that you will encounter on-line, such as TrueSpeech (**http://www.truespeech.com**) and Xing Streamworks (**http://www.xingtech.com**). Xing Streamworks has a unique twist; you can run the Xing Streamworks program either as a Web browser plug-in, or you can run it separately and quickly access any of the sites to which the separate program links. For example, load the Xing Streamworks program by itself, and use the icons below to access various radio stations around the Internet. On the screen below we are listening to CFRA Radio broadcast live:

The Basics of Video on the Internet

You can find an extensive, up-to-date list of video players for Windows, Windows 95, and Macintosh computers in several places throughout the Internet, including the sites we mentioned in the previous section. Also keep in mind that many of the sites you visit that support video will have a link to the program that you require. Video on the Internet is still very much in its infancy. The big limitation is the fact that many people who access the Internet with modems just do not have a fast enough connection to the Internet to support video. It works the same way as audio on a computer: a video file is converted to one of many different computer formats, so that it is stored in a digital format. The problem is that it takes a lot more storage space to save a video file to a computer. For example, the video clip of Trudeau that we mentioned earlier in this chapter was less than 60 seconds long. It took us just about 8 minutes to retrieve the file containing the video with an ISDN connection to the Internet (of 128 K). It took close to 25 minutes to retrieve it with a 28 K (28,000 baud) modem and would take over an hour on a 14,000 baud modem. Hence from one perspective, the only people who can truly take part in the video experience on the Internet are those with really high-speed connections to the network.

Given that is the case, though, there are a lot of software companies experimenting with compression methods that could decrease the amount of time that it takes to send video files through the Internet. Others are using methods that send only an occasional "frame" through the network, rather than trying to send up to six frames or more per second, as is often sent for broadcast quality video. A good example of this approach can be found with the program VDOLive (**http://www.vdolive.com**), which is the format for video provided at the CBC Newsworld site (**http://newsworld.cbc.ca**). Install it, click on one of the VDOLive videos on the CBC Web site, and a small window opens within your Web browser, displaying the video and playing sound in a series of pictures:

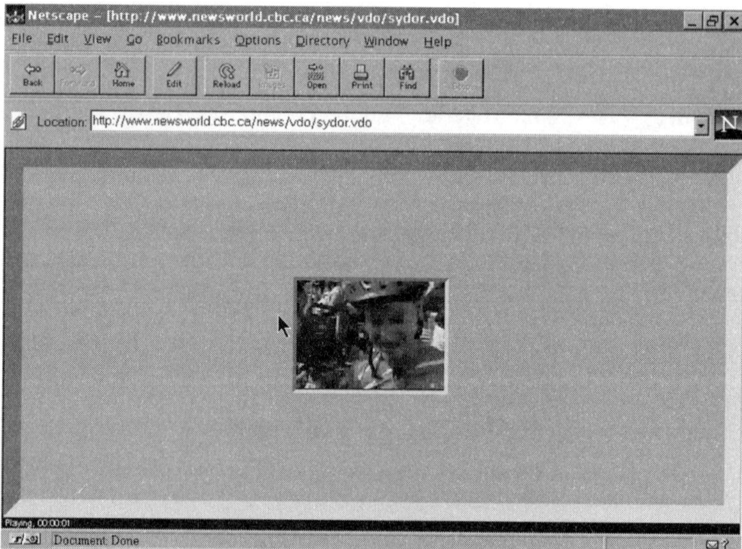

You can check out the VDOLive Gallery for other examples of how VDOLive is being used on the Internet. VDOLive is an example of a "streaming video" application on the Internet; it plays the video as it downloads it. There are other examples of "downloadable video," in which you download an entire video file before you play it. That is how we viewed the Trudeau video discussed earlier in this section. In the same way that streaming audio has quickly gained importance on the Internet, so too will streaming video. Check out CineWeb (**http://www.digigami.com/CineWebPress.html**), which lets you view two of the most popular video streaming formats, QuickTime movies and Video for Windows. For a good example of movies on the Web, check out the movies of Canada's ocean floor, available at the University of New Brunswick (**http://www.omg.unb.ca/hci/hci-movies.html**); this is also a good example of the type of useful information that is emerging on the Web.

Accessing Other Types of Data on the Web

There are many other types of information that you might encounter on the Web, sites that have been gussied up with Java, or "shocked sites," which feature animation from a product called Shockwave, or PDF files that you read with an Adobe Acrobat reader. Surf the Web, and you will find all kinds of information in all kinds of different formats, each of which requires some type of special viewer or plug-in program.

In the last year the Web has quickly become a cornucopia of different types of information supported by all kinds of different programs. One result is that your use of the Internet can be enhanced by many different types of utilities: programs that run by themselves as "helper applications" linked to your browser and plug-ins, which run directly within your Web browser. The other result is that should you decide to become involved with these features, you will find yourself often frustrated, ready to toss your computer out the office window. Let's take a look at some of the more popular categories of plug-ins and add-on applications.

Java

Java is not a plug-in; it is a special type of "computer program interpreter" built into popular Web browsers. In theory Java is simple:

- Some computer code is created and included in the HTML code on a Web page or referred to on that page.
- When you access that Web page, the Java computer code is sent to you along with the HTML code.
- The Java interpreter in your Web browser figures out what to do with that code; it essentially runs it, since, after all, it is a computer program.

The term "applet" describes the tiny (or large) programs that are sent to you as Java code. And, of course, these little applets can do anything. For example, here is a Java-enhanced site that features a unique calculator related to oxygen usage and depths related to diving. Key in the estimated length of your dive, and it prepares for you a spreadsheet graph of your suggested dive profile:

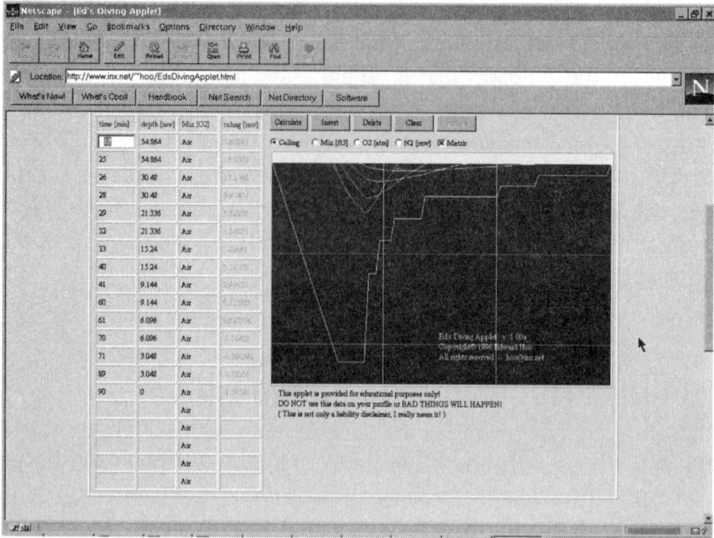

In other cases Java might result in a scrolling banner at the top of the screen or near the bottom of your browser. You might see animation, hear sound, or other forms of multimedia. It can support games, on-line chat capabilities, and other applications. You can even access an interactive subway map from New York City with which you can plot your route and see the suggested route immediately:

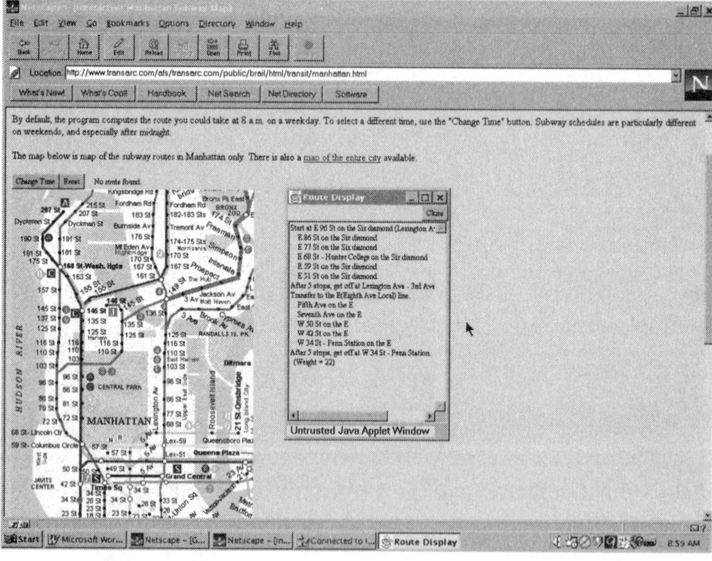

Java can be used for just about anything, since it is a new form of computer programming; in fact, some far-reaching claims have suggested that it could replace operating systems like Microsoft Windows. Microsoft has brought to the market its own Java-like capability, called ActiveX controls, which works only in the Windows environment.

We are in the very early days for Java, and the impact it will have on the World Wide Web and the Internet in general remains to be seen. To keep up-to-date on what you can do with Java, the best site is perhaps Gamelan (**http://www.gamelan.com**).

Document Viewers

There has been an explosion of electronic publishing on the Web, as organizations try to capitalize on the growing use of the Internet. The result has been that within the last year or two, the World Wide Web has become a very exciting and interesting technology; it supports a lot of graphics, text, and other information, accessible in a nice, friendly format. Many organizations are trying to use the World Wide Web for electronic publishing, but become frustrated that they cannot transfer the layout principles inherent in print publications over to the Internet. This is due to some basic limitations in HTML, the language that supports the Web, as well as the difficulty of getting across the specific fonts used in printed publications; since everyone is using different computers, everyone has a different configuration of fonts. This means that it is virtually impossible, using HTML, to reproduce on the Web exactly what appears in print.

However, take a look at a magazine; there are lots of special graphics, pictures are placed in strategic locations to catch your eye, and advertisements jump out at you from the page. Complex blends of colors, fonts, and graphics produce a page layout that is pleasing to the eye. A hundred years of typesetting skills has led to the science of page layout, a page layout that is not possible to transfer accurately to the Internet.

Enter document viewers, in particular, Adobe Acrobat. First released in 1992 to slow sales and mediocre reviews, the product has since gained a new foothold in the Internet as the method by which publications can be distributed in the exact format in which they appear in print. Acrobat lets you view a document on your computer screen exactly as it would have appeared had it been printed, regardless of the type of computer you are using. This might sound like a trivial undertaking, but it is actually a significant technical advance.

Some organizations now place publications on their Web sites in Adobe Acrobat format. Since Adobe makes the "viewer" program (or as they call it, a "reader" program) available for free, you can download both the software and a document at the same time. (The viewer is available for free at **http://www.adobe.com.** It can also be easily obtained from many of the sites that publish in Acrobat format, since many of them point to it.)

Here is an example of how it works: the TD Bank makes available various forms on-line with which you can apply for various bank services. Due to concerns about confidentiality, at the time we visited they did not let us fill out some of these forms on-line. Instead, they make available an Adobe Acrobat version of the form, which you can retrieve from the Web. Your Adobe Acrobat viewer program then allows you to view the file. Here is a screen through which you can download an application form for a TD Business VISA card:

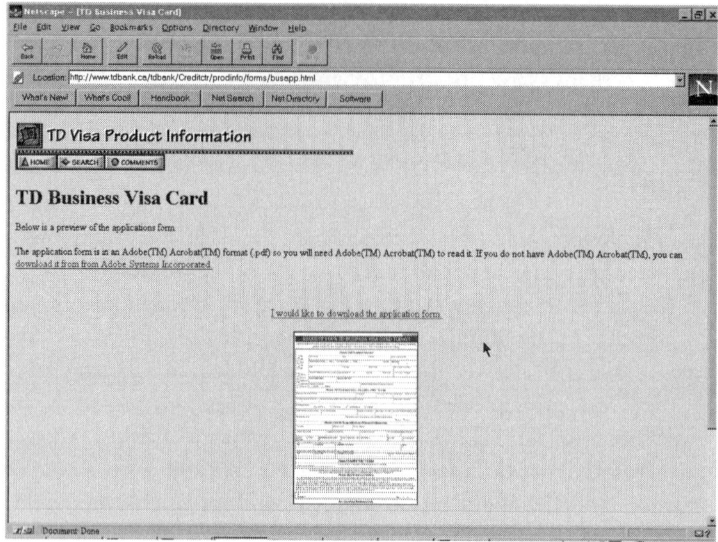

If you have already installed the Adobe Acrobat reader, all you need to do is click on the small image of the form, or click on "I would like to download the application form." (If you do not have the Adobe Acrobat reader, click on the line "If you do not have Adobe(TM) Acrobat(TM), you can download it from Adobe Systems Incorporated.") Once you do this, a few seconds go by while the file is retrieved. Once it is done, the Adobe Acrobat reader loads, and you can view the application form and print it out on paper so that you can then fill it out. You then fax or mail it to the TD Bank to the addresses provided on the form:

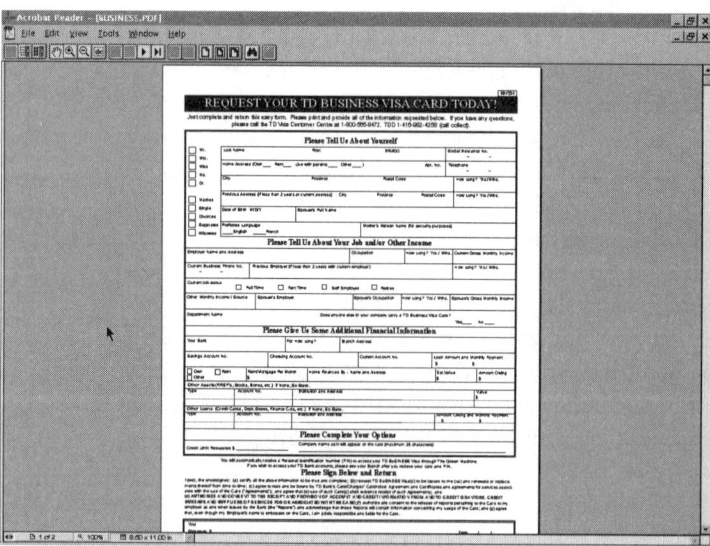

Another way in which organizations are using Adobe is to make available copies of their annual report, just as they appeared in printed format. For example, here is a page from Bell Canada (**http://www.bell.ca**), who make various financial documents available for retrieval in Adobe Acrobat format:

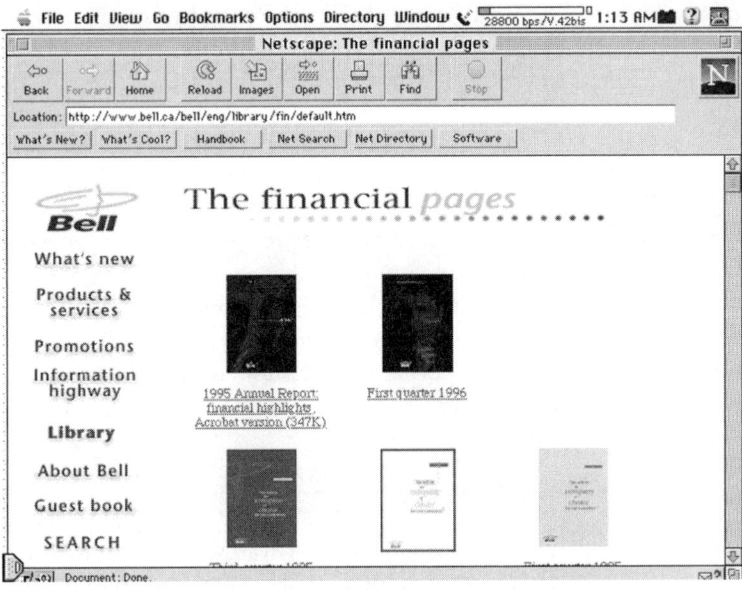

Hence the Adobe Acrobat reader lets organizations distribute information in a format that closely resembles the paper format in which they were originally prepared. When Adobe Acrobat first arrived on the scene, it worked as a separate program invoked by Netscape once the Acrobat file was downloaded; if you look at the TD Bank example above, you can see the separate program that was involved. However, Adobe Acrobat 3.0, released in mid-1996, runs as a Netscape plug-in, meaning that you can view Acrobat documents directly within the Web browser. This is what happened when we accessed one of the Bell Canada financial reports below:

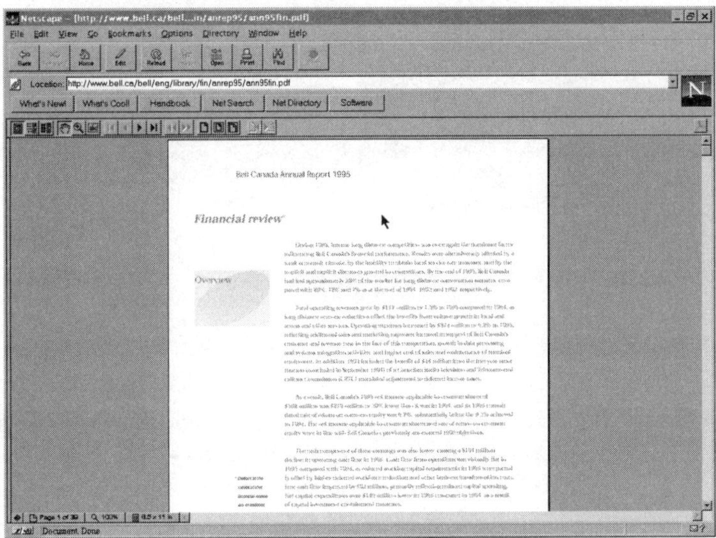

As you travel through the Web, you will find a greater number of sites placing publications up in Adobe format. Document readers are also appearing for specific types of word processing documents such as Microsoft Word. Install one of the programs, and you can travel to a Web site and view a Word document exactly as it would appear within the Word program. Hence the topic of document viewers is a quickly growing one on the Internet.

Presentation Viewers

A second and relatively new category on the Web is the presentation viewer, which is a program that permits you to view presentation programs from within your Web browser. ASAP WebShow, for example, is a plug-in for Netscape, Internet Explorer, and other browsers. Once installed, it really doesn't do anything until you go to a Web site that features an ASAP WebShow presentation. In that case a tiny row of buttons appears on the bottom of your Web browser, which you can use to navigate a WebShow presentation.

These are the controls used to run your slide show, moving backward or forward through the presentation. On this screen we have a presentation running about cars. Pressing either arrow key will move us forward or backward one slide. You can see the row of buttons to run the presentation near the bottom of the screen:

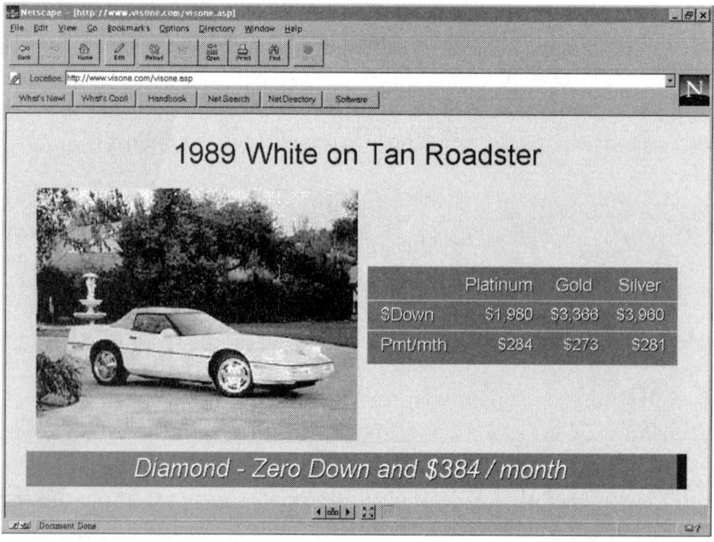

If you press the double arrow at the end of the button bar, the slide show will run for you automatically within your Web browser. And finally, the square button — the third from the right — allows you to change the size of the presentation; you can, for example, have it take over the whole computer screen:

You can download the WebShow presentation viewer from the ASAP Web site at **http://www.spco.com/**. There are other presentation viewers on the market; for example, the PowerPoint Animation Player and Publisher from Microsoft allows you to view PowerPoint files through the Internet.

Three-Dimensional Viewers

The next step for the Internet and the Web is virtual reality. Think of what you might encounter on your travels on the Web: you discover a hotel resort on-line. You can travel through the site and discover pictures of the resort, the pool, the rooms, the casino. Somehow it seems interesting but it also seems so limiting.

Right now, the Web is mostly a two-dimensional experience. You can see pictures and graphics. It certainly isn't three-dimensional. As the technology matures, it will be. Imagine visiting the same resort on the Web, except that you do not just view some pictures. You start at the front door and enter. You observe the sweeping expanse of the lobby and decide to take a quick right to look into the casino. You come back out and get into an elevator. In a few seconds the doors open, and you "travel" down the hall to view a model suite. You look around the room.

Far-fetched? Don't doubt it. A newly emerging technology on the Internet known as VRML (virtual reality modeling language) promises to change the way we navigate through the Internet, turning a flat, two-dimensional Web space into a fascinating three-dimensional world. Here is an example of a virtual reality site using a VRML browser, WebSite, from Silicon Graphics:

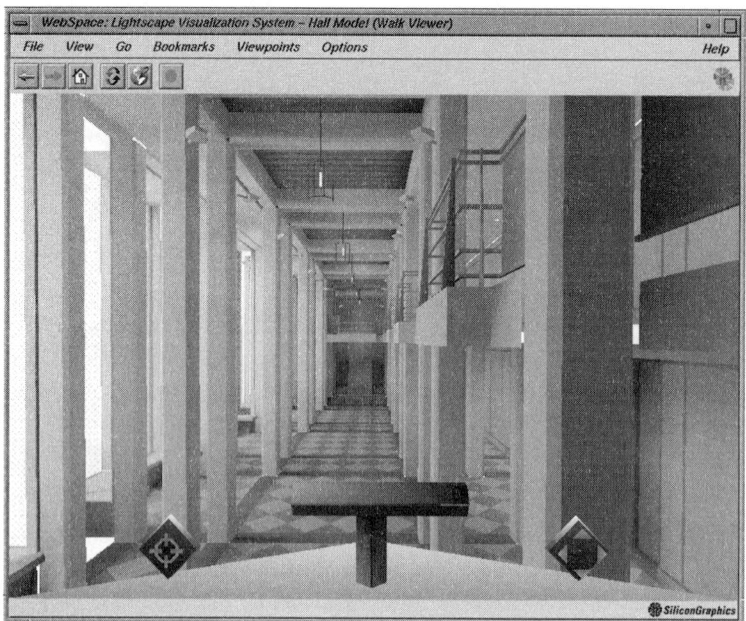

You can navigate your way down this hallway, look up, down, or to the left and right, and enter various rooms, such as this electronic classroom:

The three items at the bottom of the screen are your navigation tools; you use these to indicate where you want to travel within the room.

In the following view a number of Silicon Graphics computers are included in the room. You can move your way to any one of them, and when you click on one, a Web page is loaded with information about that computer:

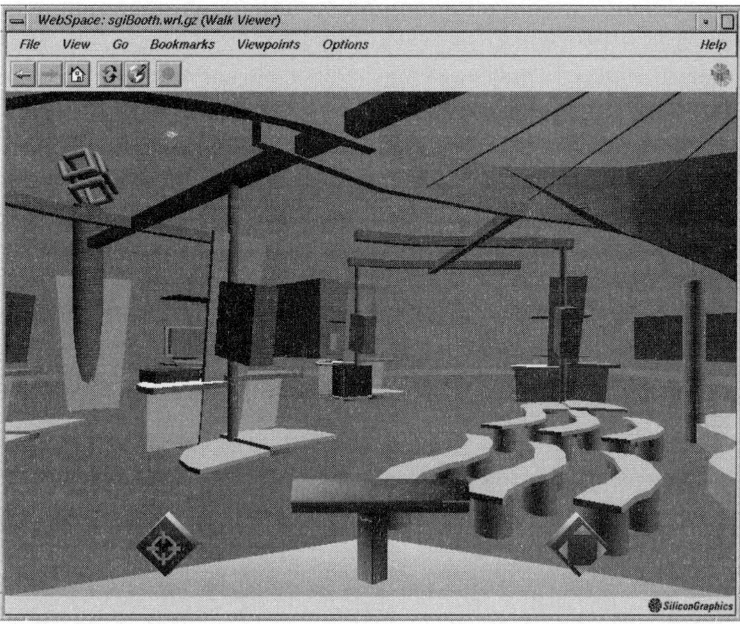

Virtual reality has long been talked about within the computer industry, and there has been much experimentation and many products come to market. Anyone who has attended a computer trade show has seen someone in a "virtual world," wearing one of those funny helmets. Virtual reality is now coming to the Internet, and you do not have to wear a funny helmet. The potential applications are enormous:

- interactive tours of cities and towns, used in a geography class;
- the opportunity to view the seating layout of a theatre before you buy your ticket, try out a few chairs to see what the view of the stage is like;
- medical professionals discussing possible treatments while viewing a three-dimensional image of a collapsed lung.

You may think that it will take a long time for virtual reality to emerge on the Internet; don't. With the number of companies involved with it, ranging from small start-ups to heavyweights such as Netscape and Microsoft, the technology to support three dimensions on the Internet is evolving rapidly. You may be concerned that you do not have a fast enough link to the Internet to support it; don't. A key feature about VRML is that it does not necessarily send down large graphic files of a "virtual" something; instead, it might send down mathematical formulas and other information that describe that world. It takes a lot less time to send a few mathematical formulas than it does to send a bunch of graphics.

Animation Viewers

Also emerging as a new category within the Web is the whole field of animation. Shockwave is a good example of one of the animation viewers available for the Internet; it helps to bring animation, cartoons, and other types of information to the Web. Travel, for example, to the M&M's candy Web site (**http://www.m-ms.com/mtvbeach/gazebo.html**), and after a few minutes of waiting, you will see animated candies walking on the screen and talking at the same time:

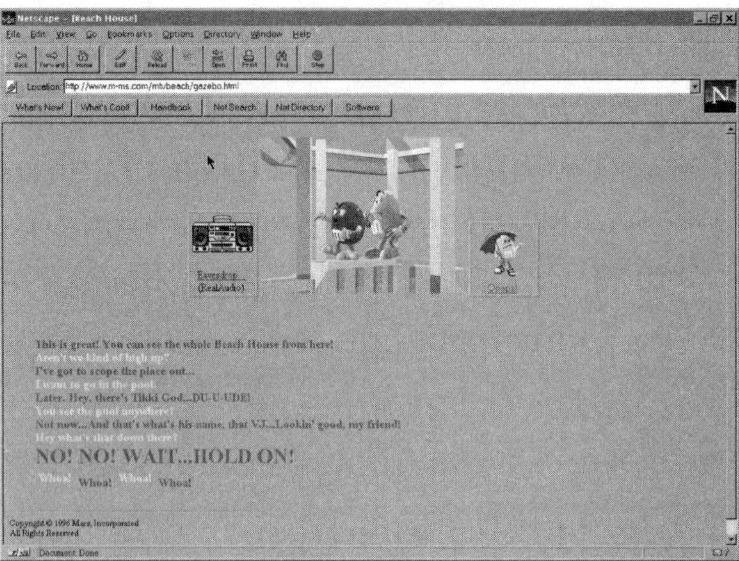

On-line animation on the Web is emerging as one of the fastest-growing fields on the Web and over time is bound to change the way we access and view information on the Internet. The big limitation at this time is the amount of time it takes to download animation, given the fact that many of us can only access the Internet through a modem.

Web Tracking Tools

There are also tools to track what you are doing on the Web. ISYS Hindsite, for example, is a marvelous little application. It takes advantage of the fact that when you use a Web browser such as Netscape or Internet Explorer, the HTML files and images of the sites are saved in a directory on your computer. (For Netscape it is called cache and can be found under the Netscape directory. For Internet Explorer it is most often saved in a directory called "Internet temporary files.")

You may notice that a Web site is a lot quicker when you go back to it a second time. The reason for this is that your Web browser checks the index of files from your previous voyages on the Web. If it finds that you have previously visited the site and that there is a copy of the Web page for that site on your computer, it loads the page from your hard disk rather than obtaining it through the Web, if the page has not changed. It makes your browsing of the Web dramatically quicker.

ISYS Hindsite takes advantage of the existence of your cache file by building an index of all the information found in the cache. It operates either as a stand-alone program or as a plug-in within your Web browser. Say we remember that we were at a site on the Web about gardening in Canada, but we cannot remember the address. Run the Hindsite program and just key in what you are looking for:

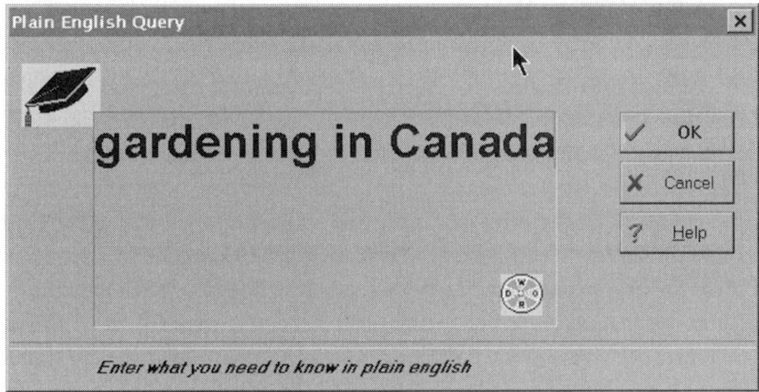

Once you do that, Hindsite comes back with a list of the Web pages found in your cache, sites you have previously visited, that mention those two words:

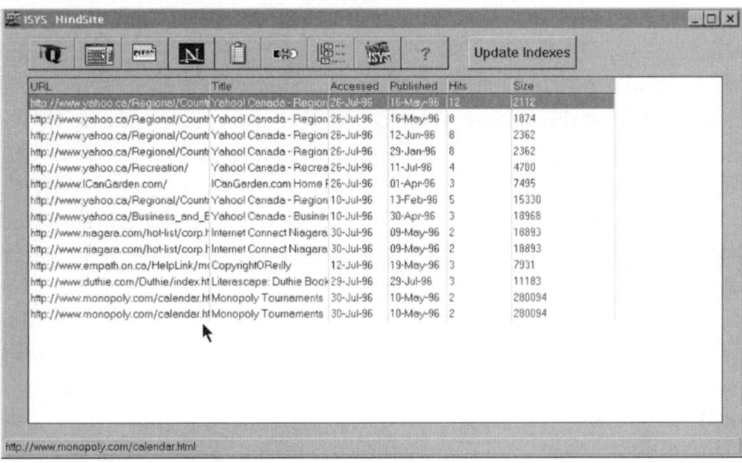

You can then scan through the list in order to find the Web site that you remember visiting and simply click on it. Your Web browser will be loaded, and, presuming you are on-line, you will be taken to the proper Web page. ISYS Hindsite is a wonderful example of a tool that can help you mange your activities on the Web. There are many similar tools available as separate programs or plug-ins.

Dealing With Plug-ins and Viewers

It is almost impossible to keep up with the many different types of data and information that are emerging on the Internet, and it is just as difficult to keep up-to-date with all the various plug-ins and new programs that are emerging to deal with these special types of information. You can quickly find yourself swamped and overwhelmed by what you will encounter on the Internet; just visit the Netscape plug-in listing, and you can find a comprehensive list of the many different types of plug-ins available. And having worked with many of these programs and software categories in this chapter, we have come to some conclusions.

It Is a Wonderful Way to Waste Time

Oh, what a strange state of affairs we have created with the Web. Visit a site, discover that it has some type of special data format, and your Web browser might indicate to you that there is information on that page that can only be accessed with a plug-in. You are then taken to a page that you can use to read about which plug-in you do not have and click a button to retrieve that plug-in. You fill out a form with some information such as your name and e-mail address in order to be able to download the plug-in. Then you try to finally download the plug-in program, only to be told that the "server is busy." Eventually, you succeed, and after spending a few minutes waiting for the proper plug-in to download, you install it. You try to remember what Web page you were at in the first place that had the information you were trying to access.

Finally, you locate the page, go there proudly with your fancy new plug-in, wait a couple of minutes for the animated file to download, and a little man scurries across the screen. Didn't see it? Load the page again. Wait a few minutes. There it goes! Isn't it marvelous?

There is a certain amount of techno-geekiness to the whole field of plug-ins and Java and Shockwave and other utilities that we mention in this section. Travel to a lot of Web pages these days, and you will see a message like "please wait while our Shockwave add-on module downloads." An incomprehensible message to many mere mortals who are expected to sit and wait politely for something important to happen. And what do they get for their patience? A two-minute period of time, after which a little animated character scurries across the screen. Forgive our skepticism, but we sometimes wonder if this rush to enhance the Web experience is worth it. We find ourselves, more and more, choosing plain vanilla Web pages over those that are "shocked" or feature Java or other types of special data. Folks, have we lost our collective sanity? What is possibly possessing us to become so enamored of the technology of the Internet that we are running around wasting time like this? Is the world suffering from some sort of desire to waste time? Did we overstate the example above? Not at all. This is precisely the type of thing that happened to us as we put together this section of the chapter. Over and over and over again we found ourselves twiddling our thumbs as we waited to either retrieve software or to download something relevant.

In some ways, perhaps, we are going a little overboard with the Internet. The Web is evolving at a rapid pace, and dramatic new capabilities are emerging, but if you dive in with both feet today, you should expect to waste a lot of time for what are, in many cases, marginal results.

It Is Experimental

In many ways the whole field of plug-ins, animation, three-dimensional viewing, and other new technology on the Web is very much in its infancy. Many times you may discover that you cannot get things to work. Weird, strange, and incomprehensible error messages pop up. Programs crash. Strange things happen on your Web screen. Our opinion is that "state-of-the-art" is barely that. We cannot count the number of plug-ins that we tried to install that just did not work. Let's look at an example. When we installed Shockwave on several machines, it took us a while to get it right. If we visited a "shocked" site, all we got for our efforts was a nice, big, square box with a jigsaw puzzle in the middle:

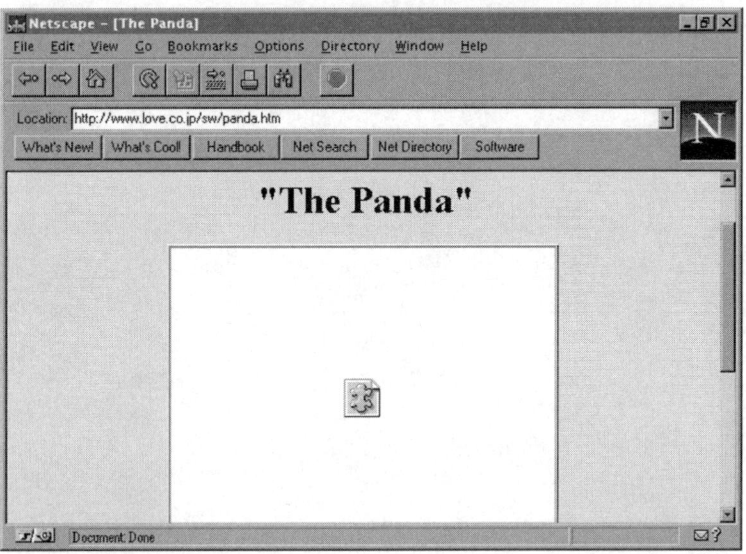

Is It Worth It?

Finally, we got Shockwave installed. We visited a site that had been "shocked." It featured a cute little panda bear. It took us several minutes to retrieve the page.

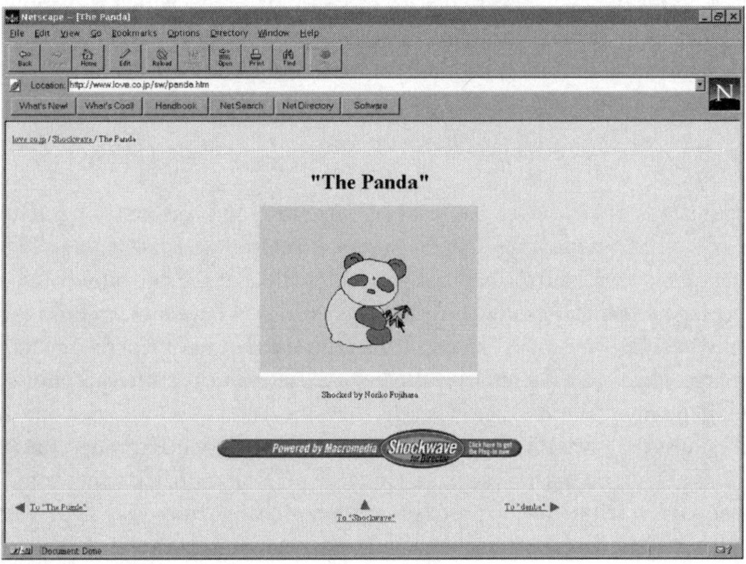

We clicked on his hand and he waved to us.

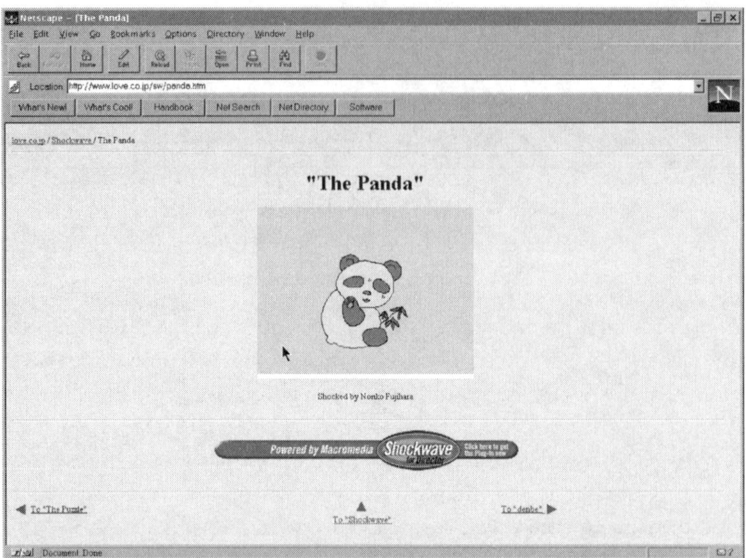

Yes, he waved to us. We invested two or three minutes of our life, waiting for a "shocked" Web page to load so that a little panda bear could wave to us. And once again, we began to question our sanity and the collective sanity of Internet users around the world.

Program Conflicts

If you install plug-ins, you will also find a lot of "beta software," which is computer industry code for computer software that is still full of bugs. You also find a lot of software that might conflict with other programs and plug-ins that you have installed. Hence you could quickly find yourself becoming quite frustrated as things break down and refuse to work. We certainly did.

Bottom Line?

It is almost as if it is 1950, television has just been invented, and you are trying to hook up your Super Nintendo NES entertainment system on your brand-new 1950 vintage TV. You might be able to make it all work, and we bet that you will wonder at the end why you did so.

The other big problem is "bandwidth"; simply, many of us have modem links to the Internet that are simply too slow to support some of the plug-ins that have emerged. The possibilities will truly emerge when we have universal high-speed access to the Internet, but we believe it will be largely experimental until then. Clearly, there are some useful utilities out there; Adobe Acrobat and Hindsite are two that come to mind. But our experience through the last few years with other forms of plug-ins has left us with a sour taste in our mouth. Certainly, some useful technology is emerging, which over time promises to forever change our view of the Web. But these add-on capabilities to the Web are going to take time to mature, and until that time, you may find it to be more of a challenge than a useful tool.

Challenges for the Web

As the Web continues to grow, it certainly faces some challenges and difficulties in the years to come:

- Web content has become controversial. Many countries are trying to block, restrict, or filter access to Web sites, notable examples being South Korea, Vietnam, and Singapore. And worldwide politicians continue to seek a solution to the challenge of offensive content on-line. It has become such a significant issue that we devote an entire to it: Chapter 21, "We Need to Protect the Internet."
- It transcends legal jurisdictions. The global reach of the Internet means that the many electronic commerce activities emerging on the Web will pose some tricky issues for taxation authorities in the future. When you purchase something in a store, you have a physical presence in a province and hence are subject to sales tax in that province. If you purchase something out of province, you pay the sales tax in that province and can then claim a refund of the tax paid upon leaving the province. You are also expected to remit to your own provincial government the sales tax on the purchase upon returning home. And when it comes to catalogue shopping, you only pay a sales tax if the company is located in your home province. If not, you are expected to remit appropriate sales tax to your province, but it is unlikely that people do. The equivalent holds true for GST on a national level.

  All of these nice, neat rules tend to break down once the Web arrives on the scene. As you pay for goods and services, you are often doing so on Web sites far beyond the reach of Canadian provincial jurisdictions. And in many cases you might be using international Web servers, far beyond the reach of Canadian law itself. Under Canadian tax law you will be expected to remit appropriate sales and GST tax, but we can expect that few will. Hence the move to cyberspace commerce promises to pose some tricky and interesting challenges for tax officials.
- Some people might use the Web excessively. In 1996 we saw a number of media outlets report on the topic of "Internet addiction," after a U.S. psychologist warned that some people could be considered to be using the network excessively. Regardless that the debate still rages, the fact remains that just as some people abuse alcohol, drugs, gambling, and other substances and activities, some people do use the Web excessively. Some feel that the Web is just a big waste of time and that people are just mindlessly wasting their time surfing. Maybe it is a waste of time. Maybe it isn't. But one thing is certain: lost in all the hype about the concept of Internet addiction, it seems, is that many people simply find the Web to be a more compelling and worthwhile tool than, say, television. After all, there are only so many *MASH* reruns that you can watch.
- It can be slow. The Web is exceeding its capabilities. It is fun to be able to access video, audio, and multimedia through the Web, but the Internet was never designed to support these capabilities. The result is that the network is under constant stress as the volume of traffic continually pushes near the boundary of capacity. The impact? At times, it may seem that the Web is slowing down to a crawl.

Not only that, but particular sites often get busy. When a popular movie comes out, there is often a lineup to get into the theatre. What do you do? You wait a few weeks and try again when its popularity has eased. It is the same with the Web. When a new, innovative, or interesting Web site comes up, there will often be a rush of people trying to access it. The result? You cannot get in. Or, when you do, it is terribly slow. Just wait a few weeks and try again.

You may have speed limitations of your own by being limited to access with a modem. Some individuals design pages full of wonderful graphics, so many, in fact, that it can take many seconds or minutes to view a page. Higher-access speeds are slowly coming to the Internet, but as we discuss in Chapter 20, perhaps not as quickly as we might hope. Second, many Web designers, conscious that many access their sites with modems, minimize the use of graphics so that pages load as fast as possible.

- There is too much information, and information overload is a problem. Many experience frustration with the Web, simply because it seems to have become too all-encompassing and too large, with too much information. You may find it too big and too difficult to keep up. In a general sense, the Web is overwhelming, which leads to that sense of frustration that many share that it is moving too quickly, such that you can never keep up with it.
- It can be very difficult to find information. Learning how to search for information on the Internet is not a skill that can be picked up in a few minutes or a few days or even a few weeks. Learning to undertake research on the Internet is a skill that is developed. The problem is compounded by the fact that there are too many indices. It is an important topic, and we look at it separately in Chapter 9. Part of the problem stems from the fact that it is very difficult to organize. Encyclopedias have the luxury of being able to define an intelligent structure in advance; that is not the case with the Web. Hence even popular search systems such as Yahoo!, which we discuss in Chapter 9, find it extremely difficult to categorize the information on the Web.
- There is a lot of irrelevant information. Sites exist that really and truly do not serve a useful purpose, consist of a bad design, or somehow are just plain "bad." Of course, given that this is the Web, you can check out "Mirsky's Worst of the Web" (**http://mirsky.turnpike.net/wow/Worst.html**) for a daily pointer to sites that are just plain lousy.
- The poor layout of many sites makes information difficult to read. As we noted above, people go silly with Web features, particularly with many of the new tools such as Java and Shockwave. You will encounter Web features that over time will make your blood boil. For example, one of the most overused HTML tags is the blink feature: it causes the text that follows it to blink. People have gone silly with use of this feature. You will begin to wish that some people took HTML design courses.
- Links become outdated, and there is much out-of-date information. Web pages can disappear as easily as they appear. Individuals or companies can decide to stop publishing on the Web or may find that circumstances beyond their control do not make it possible for them to participate any longer. In other cases page names change, the

name of the server hosting the page changes, or the directories change. Whatever the case may be, cross references (or links) within the Web are constantly changing. This means that sometimes you will click on a link and get the infamous "Error 404!"

There is a lot of out-of-date information too. You will come across many conferences from 1994, announcements for events in 1995, and other similar out-of-date information: Web sites that obviously have not been updated for some time or contain inaccurate information; "What's New" pages that do not have any information from the last year.

- Too many ill-fated attempts dissolve to nothingness. In some cases you may travel the Web and discover a resource that looks promising; its home page promises to be the "definitive guide" to whatever. But when you look through it, you discover that it is more or less an empty shell and does not contain the information you were hoping for. Many can get involved with the Web, and many become excited about building some type of resource that others can use, whether an index or other information. But then they discover that maintaining such a resource takes an increasing amount of time. They become busy with other things, or their interest tails off. Whatever the case, you cannot get angry at such things; you just have to accept that some of the things that you encounter on the Web will not be quite what you where looking for.
- The Web server protocol (**http**) is inefficient. If you want a good technical explanation why the Web server protocol is inefficient, you can view a document by Venkata N. Padmanabhan at the University of California–Berkeley, who notes that "the HTTP protocol, as currently used in the World Wide Web, uses a separate TCP connection for each file requested. This adds significant and unnecessary overhead, especially in the number of network round trips required" (**http://www.ncsa.uiuc.edu/SDG/IT94/Proceedings/DDay/mogul/HTTPLatency.html**). As a result, the Web is sometimes slow; it can take forever to pull down a page. This inherent inefficiency of the Web server protocol means that you will have to be patient.

You will encounter frustration with the Web. You will also be in awe of it and constantly fascinated by what it represents. The best way to deal with the Web is to develop an open mind and, most importantly, keep a sense of humor.

CHAPTER 8

Off-line Web Readers

We think it will be as significant as the VCR was to television. Slow Web connections and dependency upon a fixed location for Web access are constant barriers to the mobile professional. Taking the Web with you is finally a reality because it's easy to customize our new technology to automatically seek and retrieve specific sites and control the depth of information you download.

Mark Eppley, CEO, Travelling Software, in an interview on NetTalk Radio, www.nettalk.com

Off-line Web readers, a brand-new category of software that emerged on the Internet in 1996, will do for the Internet what the VCR did for television. These programs allow you to "download" Web pages or entire Web sites of information to your hard disk, so that you can browse those Web pages or Web sites when you are not connected to the Internet, just like you can tape a television show to watch later on, at your convenience. And they download everything you need: text, graphics, images, even sound and video files if you want.

The advantages of such programs are enormous. First of all, they bring portability to the Web, allowing you to "take your favorite Web sites with you." Do you do a lot of Internet presentations? Download the Web sites that you want to demo in advance, and visit those sites without having to go on-line. Not only that, but off-line Web readers have quickly become an indispensable information management tool; since most of these programs have a scheduling feature, you can instruct them to go off on a regular basis, whether hourly, daily, weekly, or monthly, to retrieve the contents of a Web site. Hence, if you want to retrieve the news each day from the Web site of your local newspaper, you can instruct an off-line reader to go and get the news at 4:00 a.m. each day, so that it is ready when you come into the office.

There are two categories of products that help you manage information on the Web:

- Off-line readers, which are the tools that allow you to view Web pages off-line.
- Notifiers, which are the tools that notify you when Web pages change.

In this chapter we take a look primarily at off-line readers, but we should mention that many of these programs perform both functions: they can download complete Web sites, or they can simply notify you if certain pages have changed on those Web sites. However, at the end of the chapter we do take a look at some of the systems emerging on the Internet that are considered to be strictly notifiers.

Why You Would Want to Use an Off-line Reader

There are several reasons why you might want to consider using an off-line reader:

- They reduce transmission delays. When "surfing" the Web you can spend a lot of time waiting for information to download, particularly if you are using a modem and are accessing sites that contain a lot of information and graphics. It is no surprise that many users of the Web become frustrated by inordinate delays and the slow nature of the World Wide Web. Off-line readers solve this problem, since they go off and retrieve information while you are busy doing something else, whether that be working or sleeping. The information from a Web site or multiple Web sites is transferred directly to your PC, so that when you want to view a Web site, you do not have to worry about low-speed modem connections; you read it right off your hard disk.
- They make the Web more mobile. Off-line readers make the Web "portable." Now while traveling you can take the Web with you; you can access your favorite sites while on the road, in a plane, on a boat, bus, subway, or in a park.
- Off-line readers facilitate demonstrations of the Web. Many people who work with the Internet give demonstrations of Web sites to others and always have to worry about signing on to the Internet. Anything can go wrong in a demo: the phone line to dial in to the Internet may not work, the Web site you want to access may be down, your Internet service provider may be experiencing technical problems, or something else could go wrong.

OFF-LINE WEB READERS

1. Off-line Web readers are tools that allow you to view Web pages off-line.
2. Many off-line Web readers will automatically retrieve specific Web pages on your behalf on a scheduled basis.
3. Notifiers are tools that notify you when Web pages have changed.
4. Off-line Web readers reduce transmission delays and make the Web more mobile.
5. Off-line readers will be useful in many situations, ranging from Internet presentations to classroom settings.

Off-line readers solve these problems by allowing you to take a copy of the Web sites you want to demo with you. They are great for interactive demos of the Web to clients, suppliers, co-workers — even your boss.

- They are multifunctional. Read the marketing literature from the companies that develop off-line Web readers, and you see that not only can they be used on the public Internet, but they also have many applications internally within organizations on the corporate Intranet (we discuss Intranets in Chapter 18). They can be set up to grab, for example, daily sales reports, company newsletters, press releases, management briefings, and other internal information available on a corporate Web site. Given the number of mobile employees and staff who use laptops, off-line readers can play a major role within organizations.
- They work unattended. You can schedule them to work when you are not at home or in the office, therefore making better use of your time. And they give you a lot more flexibility in the way you use the Internet; you can set up your system to retrieve key Web sites each night while you are sleeping, so that you can browse new content in those Web sites in the morning.
- They help you to track ongoing news. In Chapter 10 we take a look at personalized news services, systems that you can use to track only news stories and information that are of interest to you. But you can use many of the software programs in this chapter to do the same thing, that is, obtain from the Internet only the information that you want. Would you like to have waiting, every morning, the latest sports scores for your favorite teams, plus local weather and news from Nova Scotia? You can use one of the personalized newsreaders we examine in Chapter 10, or you can configure an off-line newsreader to do the same type of thing.
- They open up previously unavailable information. Many people who use the Web do not bother trying to access huge video files or sound files from Web sites, because they take too long to download. But put in place an off-line reader, and you can instruct it to go off and retrieve those huge files at night while you sleep. Suddenly, a whole new area of the Internet has opened up to you, since you do not have to wait for a big file to download.

Think about what these programs do, and it becomes obvious that the advantages are too numerous to mention.

How Off-line Web Readers Differ

As you read this chapter, you will notice that off-line Web readers differ from each other in numerous ways:

- Some of the programs run within your Web browser. When you start them, your Web browser is started (if it is not already running), and then a Web page is loaded from your hard disk which allows you to start configuring the program. Others run as separate programs altogether.
- Some of the programs come with a suggested list of sites to monitor, while others do not.

- Some programs allow you to navigate the Web sites or pages that you have retrieved exactly as if you were on the Internet: just click on a hyperlink. Others place on every downloaded Web page some navigation buttons that you must use to navigate your way through the Web site.

Challenges and Issues

Off-line readers are a new and exciting addition to the Internet, and they present some unique challenges in how you use the Internet. As we used them, we drew several conclusions:

- Tread carefully if you want to install and use more than one of these programs on your computer. Many of these programs fool around with your basic Internet configuration. Why? Some of them set up what we call "proxy servers," special programs that the off-line reader examines for a Web site before it looks on the Internet. When you are viewing a Web page and click on a link, the program first examines the proxy server on your own computer to see if that page is found locally on your hard drive, in one of the files retrieved previously by the off-line reader. This allows you to read the pages off-line.

  Such tools are tricky, and our experience is that while they work very well, if you install more than one of these programs, things are bound to go somewhat whacky. Hence, if you install more than one of these programs, expect trouble.

- Be careful how you use these programs. All the off-line reader programs that we look at in this chapter will go off and retrieve the contents of Web sites and allow you to specify how "deep" you want to go into the Web site. "Deepness" is defined as the number of links that the program should examine and retrieve within the site. If you define that you only want to go down one level, the program will retrieve only those Web pages directly below the home page. If you define that you want to go down two levels, it will pick up Web pages below the home page, plus any pages below those pages. And so on.

  You have to be careful when specifying to retrieve more than one level, because you can find yourself picking up a lot of information. For example, we ran a test that was set to retrieve the contents of a popular on-line Web site that reports about the computer industry. It was set to go at 6:00 p.m., and sure enough, it started on time. We left the office for the day and it was still running at 8:00 a.m., dutifully retrieving thousands and thousands of pages of information, and over 100 megabytes of information from this particular Web site. Why? With the particular program that we were using, we were able to specify that we did not want to restrict how "deep" the program would go.

  Many of the programs allow you to set restrictions on the number of levels, the amount of information retrieved, the amount of time on-line, whether pages from beyond the Web site you are requesting should be retrieved, and more. Conceivably, you could set up an agent that would go off and retrieve the entire global Internet, but we don't think you would want to do that.

- Be tolerant of what these programs do. There is a fine line between what is "on-line" and what is "off-line" when you use these programs, and you will have to be patient with the results. For example, suppose you are on a plane, browsing a Web site that you have downloaded, and you click on a link. Your Web browser seems to hang for a few minutes or seconds as it tries to find that page on a Web site, because, obviously, a copy of that page is not stored on your local PC. It is out on the Internet and was not captured by your off-line reader, either because it was one level too deep from what you defined, or it was on a Web site unrelated to the one you downloaded.

Hence not only will you have to learn how to fine-tune your downloading to make sure you get what you want, but you will have to be tolerant of the fact that you will encounter links on pages that will not go anywhere because the off-line reader was not set up to retrieve those external links.

- You must leave your computer on, unattended, for these programs to work. Most of these off-line readers go to retrieve information according to a schedule that you set; hence you must leave your computer on overnight for them to work.

The whole area of off-line Web readers is fascinating and wonderful to explore, and we definitely suggest that you dive right in. We just hope you understand the possible complications of what you might be diving into.

FreeLoader

Of all the off-line Web readers we examined, FreeLoader was one of the most complicated programs to set up and configure; it took us several minutes, for example, to figure out what we had to do to see the FreeLoader toolbar (seen below), which positions itself at the bottom of your Web browser, since it might conflict with your Windows 95 taskbar. (Hint: in the "Properties" section of the toolbar, click off the item "Always on Top.")

FreeLoader runs within your Web browser. When you run your Web browser, it immediately loads the FreeLoader "home page," which is simply a file stored on your hard disk:

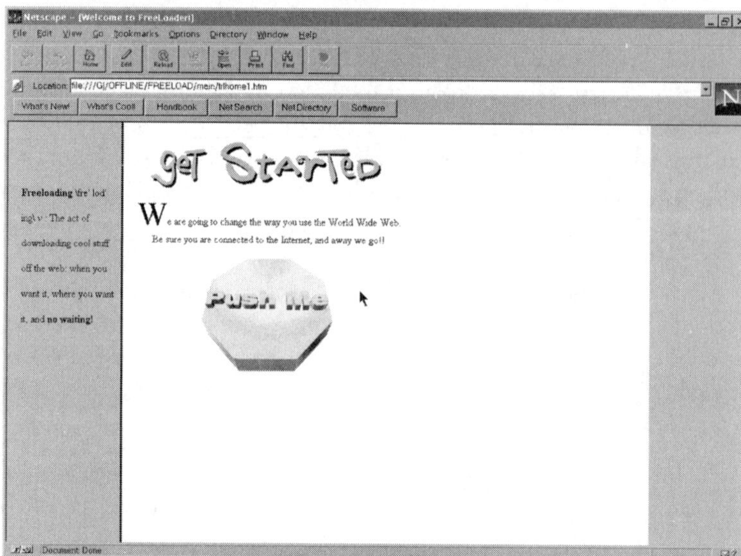

Once you press "Push Me," FreeLoader starts your connection to the Internet (if you are not already on-line) and then retrieves "FreeLoader On and Off the Net," a "magazine" (also called Salon) that provides information about the product and how it can be used. Be patient. It takes a while (in our case, 15 minutes) to retrieve the publication, and it is not something you can avoid. Once retrieved, the program will start quicker the next time, until the next new magazine is published.

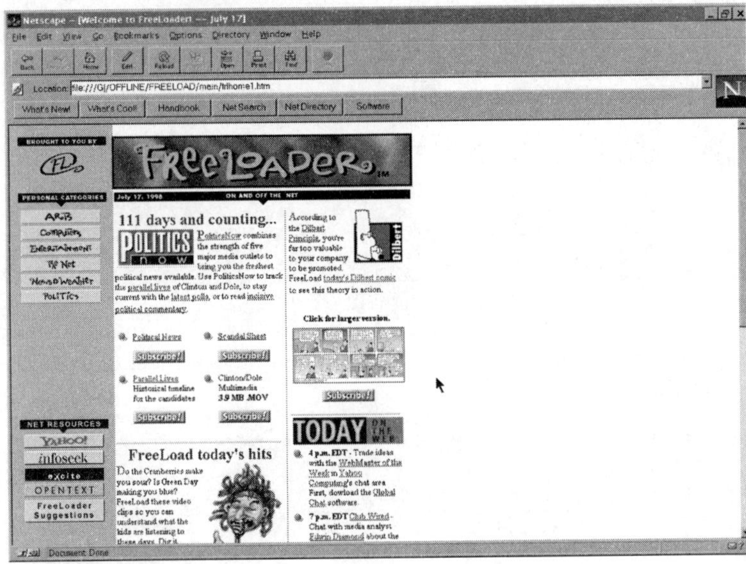

Once you have retrieved the publication (which you view in your Web browser, as seen above), you realize it was worth the wait, since it is not really a magazine, but a publication that makes it easy for you to "subscribe" to various Web sites. Want to track the Buffalo Bills? You will find them in the sports section. All you do is click on "Subscribe":

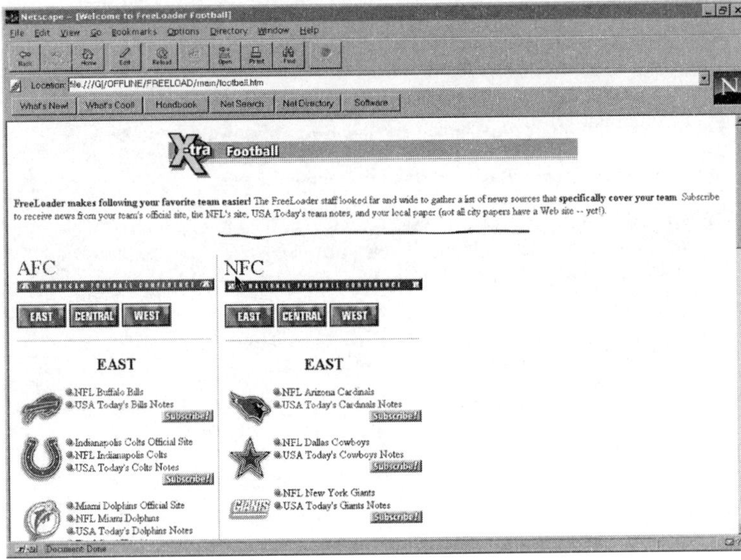

When you do that, you will see a screen through which you can indicate the specific Buffalo Bills Web sites you want to download and how often you would like to monitor them for changes, updates, or new pages:

FreeLoader Batch Subscription
The following sites will be FreeLoaded for you:
Buffalo Bills - NFL Site
Buffalo Bills - USA Today
OK
Cancel
Advanced
URL: http://nflhome.com/teams/bills/bills.html
File under category: Sports
Frequency
Hourly Daily Weekly Monthly Other

If you click on the "Advanced" button, you can request that the site be immediately downloaded, and you can specify how "deep" you want to go in terms of the number of links that should be followed through the Web site:

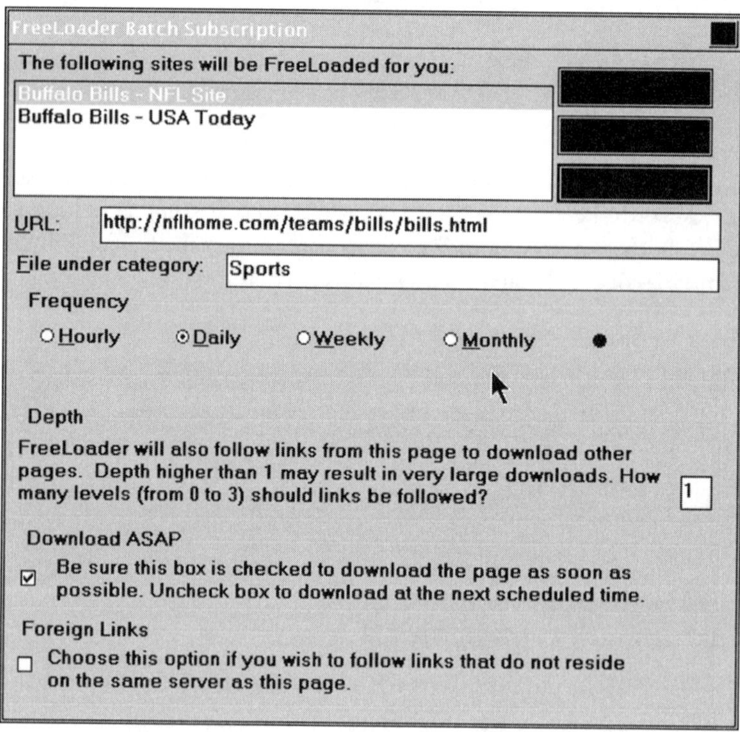

You can use the FreeLoader taskbar to call up the "Options" menu, which allows you to define the FreeLoader schedule, indicating at what time of day it should go off to get its site updates:

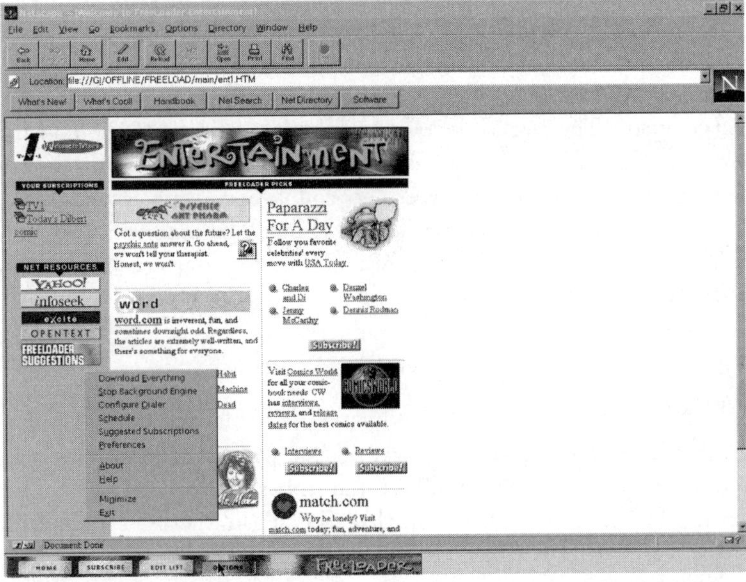

If you choose "Suggested Subscriptions," you can browse a list by category of all kinds of sites that you may wish to consider tracking:

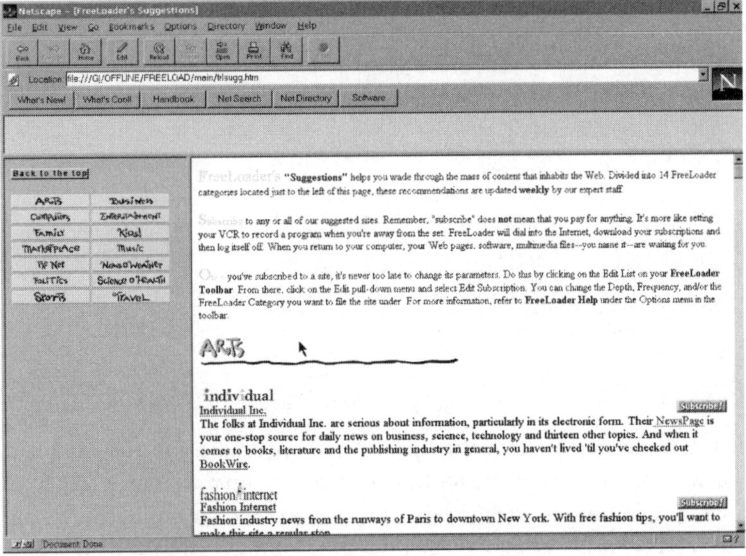

Since the FreeLoader program is designed to update this page on occasion, you can always be sure that there will be a lot of current, useful sites listed here. Keep in mind that you can choose to track any site on the Web, not just the sites suggested by FreeLoader. Finally, since the FreeLoader toolbar is always present, you can choose to "subscribe" to any Web site you visit, just by clicking on the "Subscribe" button. You can then indicate how often you would like to monitor the site and how much information FreeLoader should retrieve.

All in all, we really liked this program. It seemed to take the most innovative approach to the off-line delivery concept, through the Salon magazine and the suggested sites. That's not to say that we didn't find the program infuriating and exasperating at times. In fact, when we first installed the program and it took off for 15 minutes to grab the first "magazine," we weren't quite sure what was going on. However, the program will definitely mature and improve over time. Our advice? Definitely worth a look!

One final comment. The FreeLoader concept is built on an advertising model. It will install on your computer a screen saver that provides advertisements. And as you browse its "magazine" — a new one is automatically retrieved every couple of weeks — you will see lots and lots of advertisements. The benefit? So far, FreeLoader is free. The problem? Lots and lots of ads. FreeLoader can be found on the Internet, where a full working copy is available for download, at **http://www.freeloader.net**.

Smart Bookmarks

The approach that Smart Bookmarks takes to the off-line Web site concept is to organize your activities around the concept of "bookmarks." If you use Netscape, you will be familiar with bookmarks, the listing of places that you frequently like to visit. (In Microsoft Internet Explorer they are referred to as "Favorites.") The bookmark concept is so central to the program that your existing Netscape bookmarks will be loaded into the program during installation. Smart Bookmarks then presents itself to you as a separate program with a number of bookmarks of favorite Web sites: At first your own, and over 300 others suggested by Smart Bookmarks.

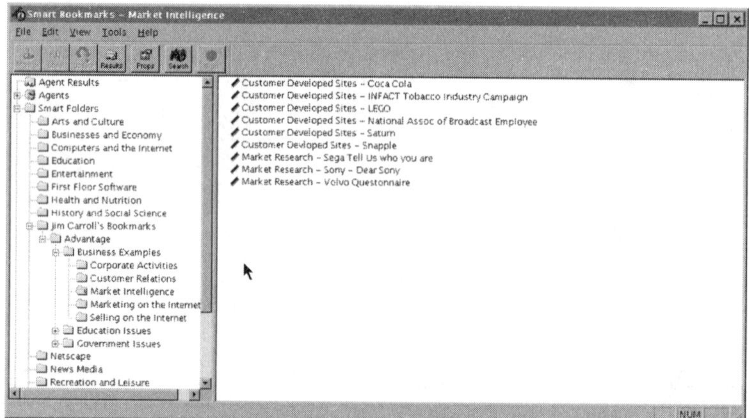

Also included in the program, and listed just above bookmarks on the left-hand side of the screen, are the "agents," the automated routines that you set up to run on a regular basis to check for new content or additions to Web sites, and which retrieve the entire contents of those Web sites. You set up an agent by using the Agent Wizard; it leads you through the series of steps that define how you want the agent to behave. You can use many different agents, each responsible for different activities and for different Web sites, making this program one that can help you to really organize your off-line Web activities into a number of well-defined tasks.

For example, you might want to have one agent that retrieves only summaries of pages that have changed for new Web sites. You might want another that retrieves the full text of particular newspapers, and another that runs a daily search on a popular search engine. In our example below we have set up a new agent that will be used to track weather on a daily basis. First, we will define the agent and what it does, and once we do that, we will define which Web sites it should retrieve. (One agent can be used to retrieve multiple Web sites.)

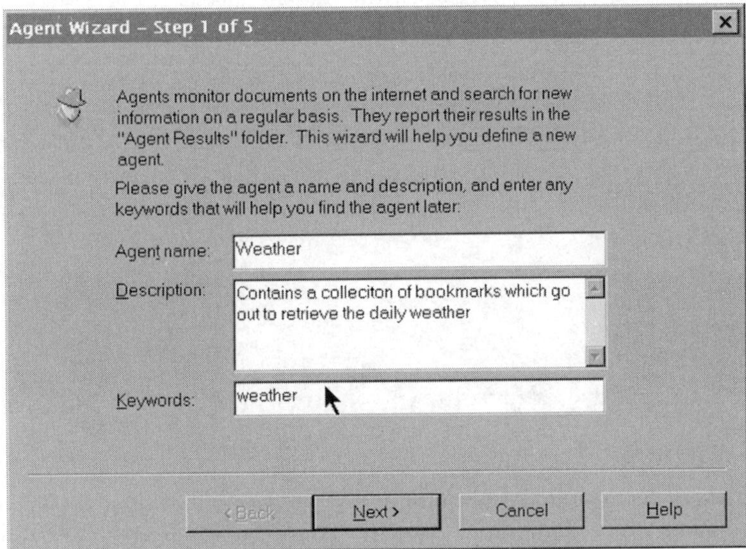

We then indicate that we want to monitor any changes to the Web sites that we will watch with this agent:

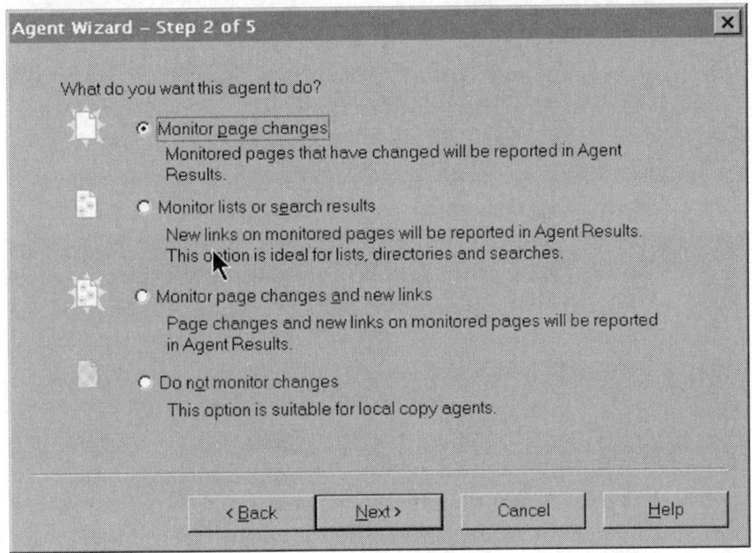

Then we indicate that we want to run this agent every morning at 8:00 a.m.

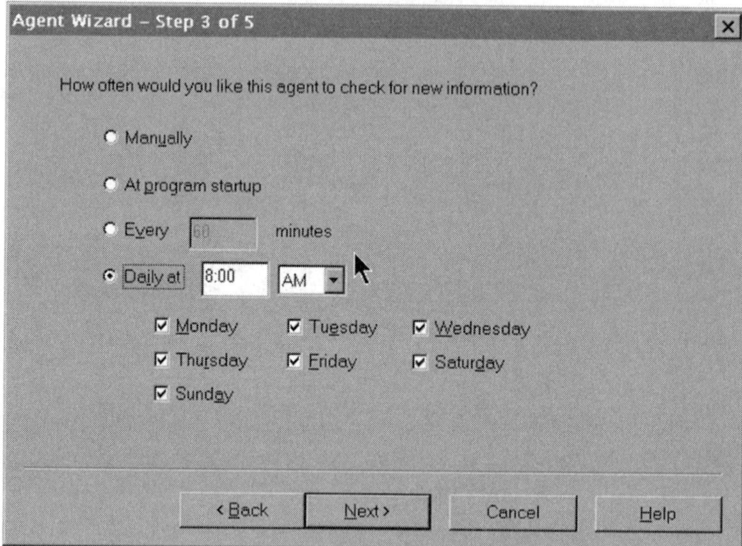

Finally, we instruct the agent to download actual Web pages when it visits the Web sites we assign to this agent (as opposed to just notifying us if pages have changed):

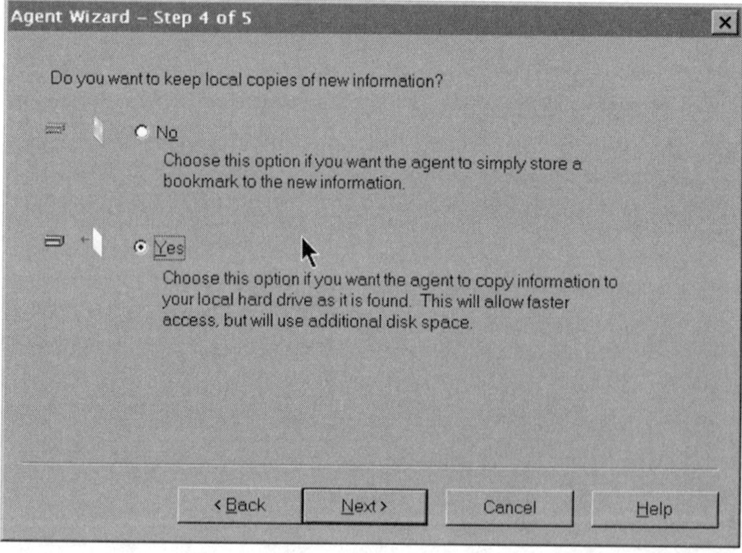

This has instructed the agent to track weather. We can now assign Web sites to this agent simply by dragging bookmarks from our bookmark list to the agent. Hence, if we had a number of weather sites in our bookmark list, we just click on them, drag them on top of the agent, and they will be all set to be monitored. If a weather site that you want to track is not in your bookmark list, you must bookmark it.

The results obtained by each agent are then loaded into the "Agent Results" list. You can view Web pages off-line or view the summaries of pages just by clicking on them. Suppose you are surfing the Web, and you decide you want to download regularly a site that you are currently visiting. That's easy enough. Just add it as a new smart bookmark and drag it to an existing agent (or create a new one).

Every program that we look at in this chapter seems to have some type of unique feature; for Smart Bookmarks it is its ability to set up an agent to run a search (or several searches) of popular search engines on the Internet (search engines are discussed in Chapter 9). A useful aspect of this feature is that the search is customizable. For example, on the following screen we have asked to be advised on a regular basis of the results of a search of InfoSeek that mentions our books and the names of the authors, but we do not want to know about our own Web site in the results of the search. We can then set this up within an agent to run on a daily basis:

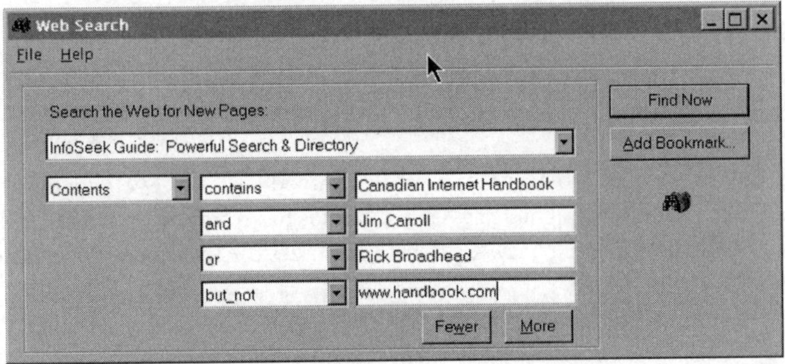

Smart Bookmarks is well organized, and because it relies on the concept of bookmarks, is easy to learn. You can set up several complicated, sophisticated agents to organize the information that you want to track, while enjoying a lot of flexibility in specifying the information that you want to bring back. You can download an evaluation copy and order a full version of Smart Bookmarks at their Web site, **http://www.firstfloor.com**. It is available for Windows 3.1 and Windows 95.

Surfbot

Like Smart Bookmarks, Surfbot is a separate program that runs on its own and organizes itself around the concept of bookmarks. Install the program, and the first thing Surfbot does is import your existing Netscape bookmarks folder so that you can monitor those sites if you want. Surfbot can monitor any site in your bookmark list, effectively, any site on the Web.

Surfbot will retrieve the entire contents of Web sites. And like Smart Bookmarks, Surfbot calls the automatic retrieval routines "agents." You can set up your own agents, or you can visit the Surfbot Web site to download a number of predefined agents. In our case we chose to use one of the latter, an agent that grabs various pages about rumors in the computer industry:

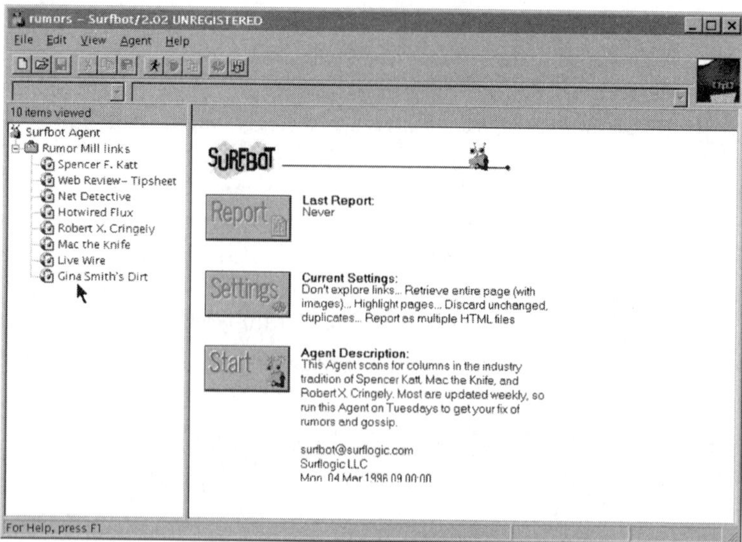

You can schedule the retrieval to occur on a predetermined basis or, if you are on-line, click on "Agent" and "Start" to retrieve right away. Once Surfbot has retrieved, it creates an HTML file — an index, which you can easily view — that summarizes the information available:

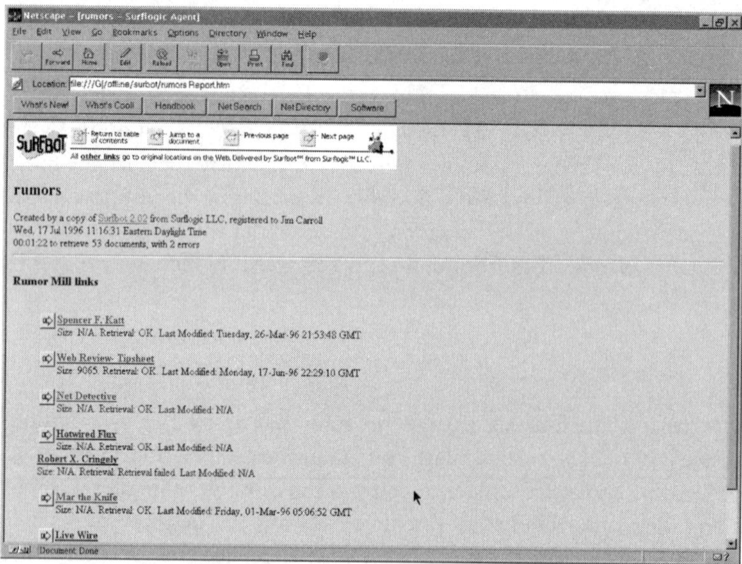

When Surfbot retrieves files, it saves them to your hard disk and puts symbols at the top of each page to help you navigate through them: to go back to the page above, go to the next page, or go to the previous page:

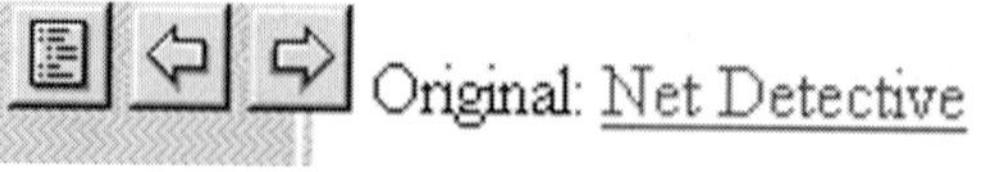

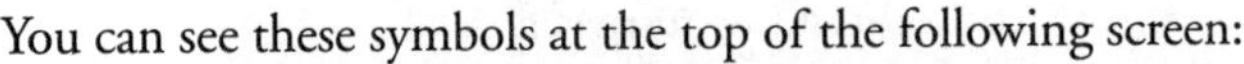

You can see these symbols at the top of the following screen:

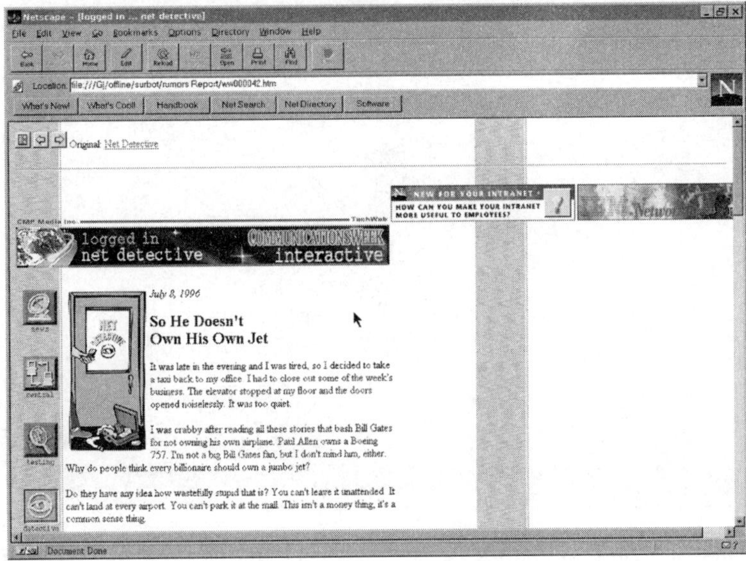

There are two ways to navigate through the Web pages that Surfbot has retrieved for you: use these buttons or use the index that it builds to all pages. If you click on a regular hyperlink and you are not on-line, you will get an error. Thus it is a little more frustrating than some of the other programs in this chapter, but still manages to get the job done. On the other hand, once you get used to this method of navigation, it does, in some ways, make it much easier and quicker to review the information that you want. It is very easy to set up a new agent, offering much flexibility. You can, for example, specify that Surfbot check a site on the Web or run a predefined search on a search engine:

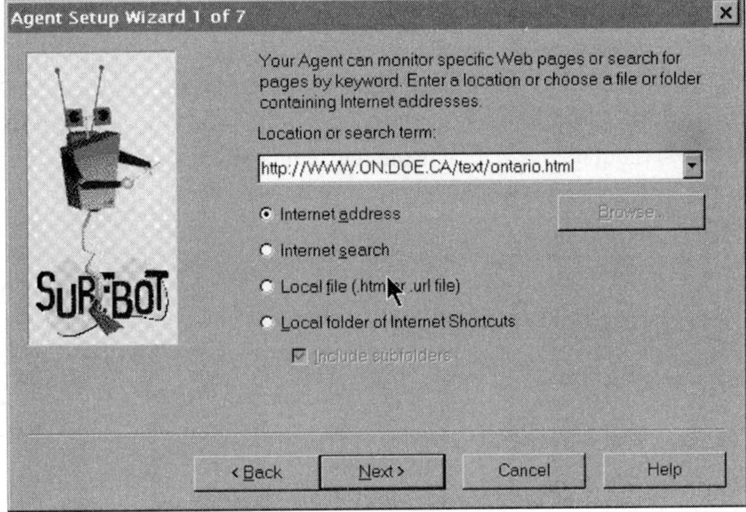

You can also easily specify how much information should be retrieved:

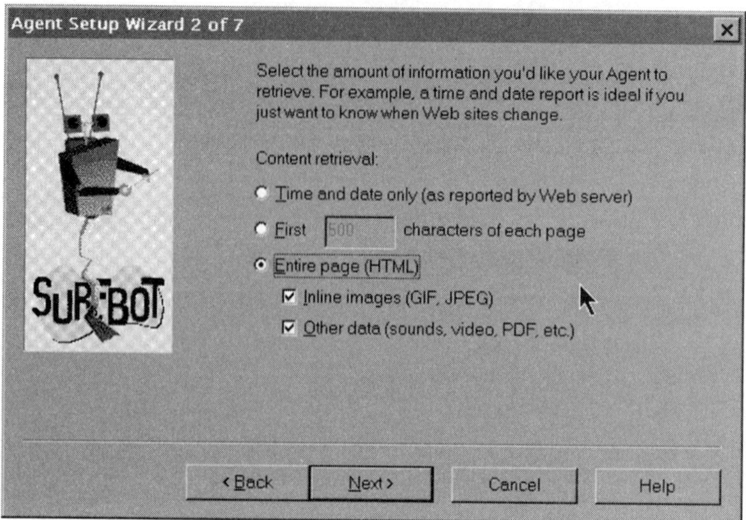

There are many other options that you can specify when creating a new agent, making this program as flexible as any other reviewed in this chapter. And given the fact that you can download many agents from the Surfbot Web site, it is easy to get it working right away. Surfbot is available for Windows 95 computers. You can download an evaluation version at **http://www.surflogic.com**.

WebEx

WebEx is another off-line reader that runs from within your Web browser. Start up the program, and your chosen Web browser software (either Microsoft Internet Explorer or Netscape Navigator) starts and then loads the WebEx home page, seen below. What is interesting is that it uses what appears to be a real Web address (**http://webex.travsoft**), but what is actually a file on your hard disk. It works by fooling your Web browser into looking at your hard disk for Web sites, before it looks for a site on-line, by using a "proxy server." When you type in a Web address, your Web browser first checks the proxy server to see if a copy exists on your hard disk; if it does not, the browser looks out on the Web. The program configuration, setup, and site selection are done using files stored on your hard disk, through your Web browser.

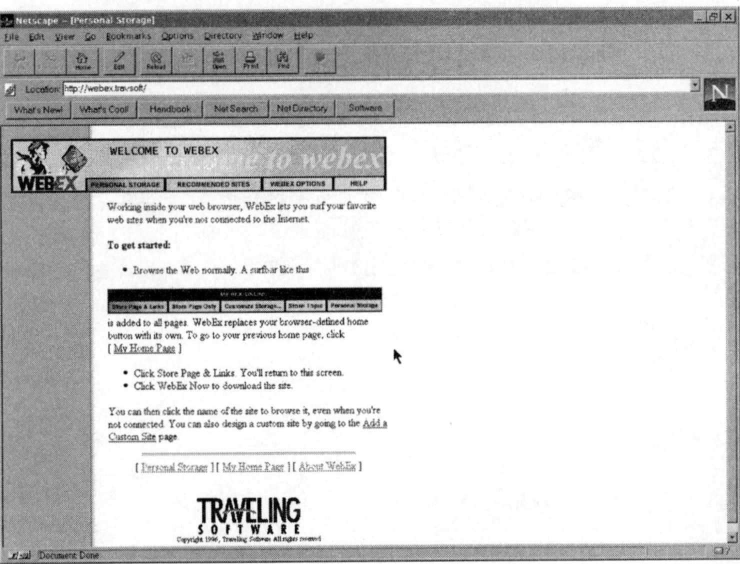

Using the program is easy enough. After providing information on your type of connection to the Internet, you can do two things:

- You can automatically download a number of predetermined sites, such as Dilbert or the New York Times.
- You can enter the details of a custom site — one that you choose — to download. Doing this is easy: just provide the URL and the details of what you would like to download:

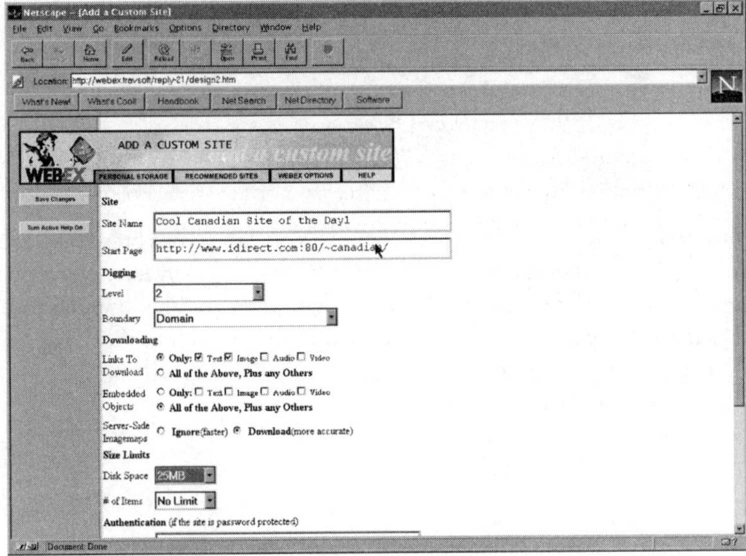

Once you have set up the details of the sites that you want to download, you leave WebEx running, and at the scheduled times it will start the downloading process:

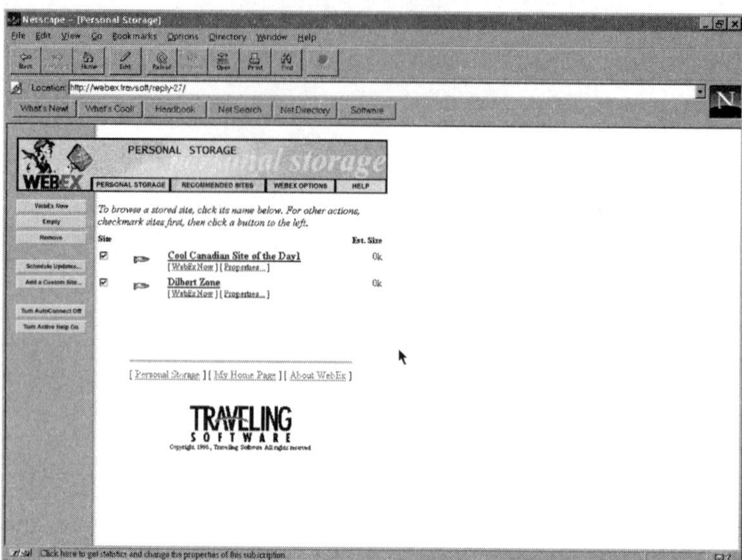

A small program known as the WebEx Agent then sits and waits until it must go and do its duty. And when it is finally retrieving information on-line, it provides details on what it is downloading, the kilobytes (kb) of information it has retrieved, and the transfer rate (how quickly it is grabbing information). The "15 to go" means that it has figured out, at this point, that it has 15 pages of information to retrieve before it is finished:

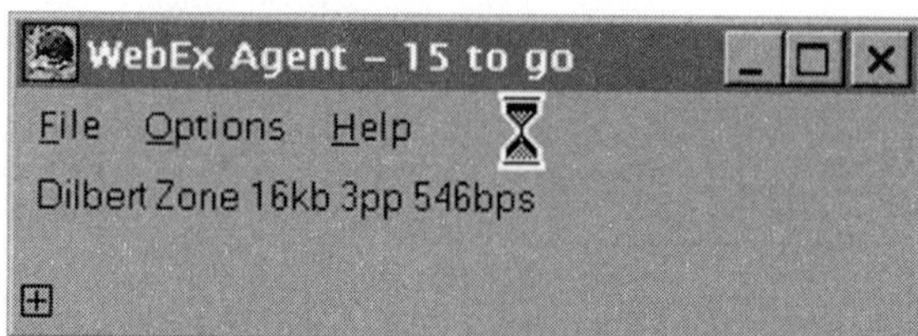

Once it obtains the information, you just click the Web site within your browser window, and you can view the entire contents of the site without ever having to go on-line. Just type in the Web address of the site, and it will be retrieved from your hard disk. Another useful feature of WebEx is that it makes it easy for you to "grab" a site while on-line or add it to the list of sites you want to monitor. When you are surfing the Web, WebEx puts a tiny menu bar at the top of each Web page, as can be seen on the following screen:

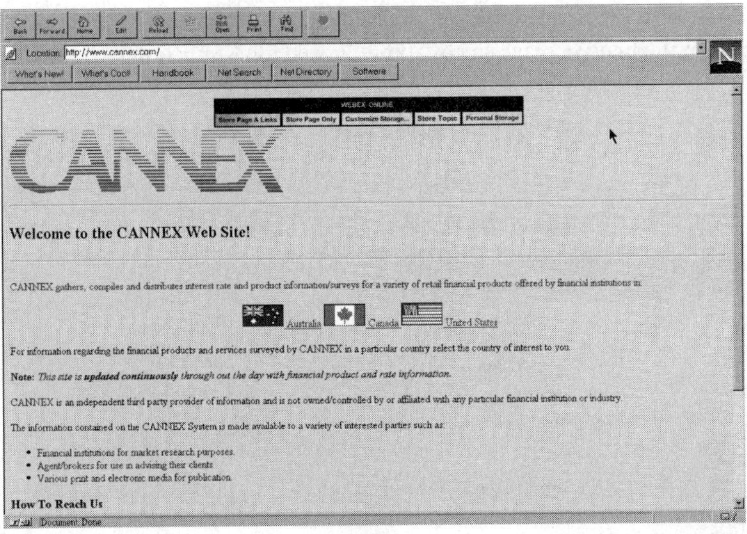

You can use this menu bar to store copies of the page or site that you are currently viewing just by clicking a button. WebEx will download the page or site and, once done, add the site to your list of monitored sites:

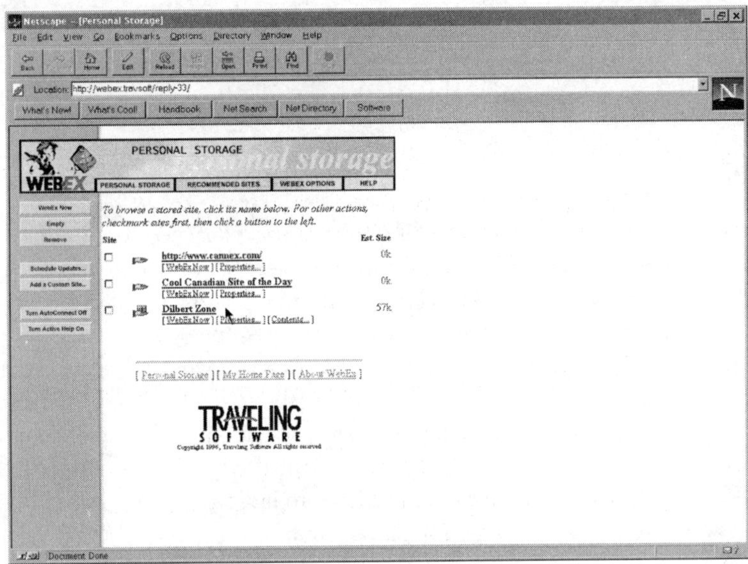

One final feature of note: you can turn on "active help" so that each WebEx Web page that you view contains comprehensive help screens about how to use WebEx, making this program easy to learn:

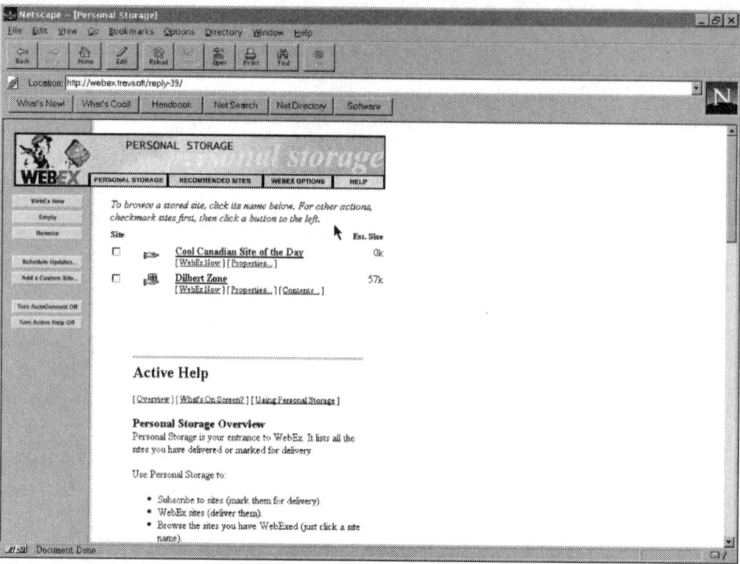

WebEx (formerly known as Milktruck) is available for Windows 95 computers. You can download an evaluation version at **http://www.travsoft.com**.

WebWhacker

WebWhacker is a separate program that, unlike some of the other programs in this chapter, does not run within your Web browser. However, it was also one of the easiest programs to learn to use. Once installed, you can use the WebWhacker program to set up the list of sites that you want to monitor or "grab" in the future, or you can start out in Netscape.

For example, when you use a Web browser like Netscape, you may decide that you want to "grab" a site, that is, add it to your list of sites to be monitored by WebWhacker. It is easy to do this, since when WebWhacker is loaded, it puts a row of buttons at the top of your screen above your Web browser: Just click the "Grab" button. You can also type the address of a Web site directly into WebWhacker. On this screen, for example, to indicate that we want to download on a regular basis the CyberBuzz site, we would click "Grab":

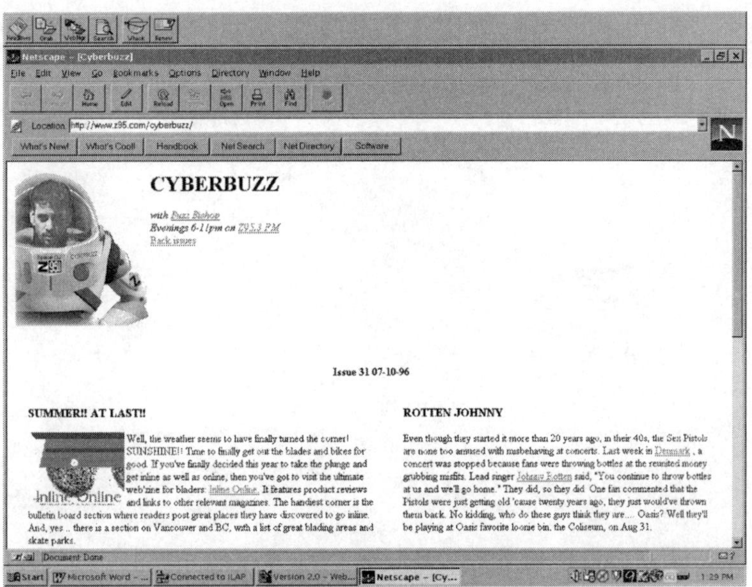

WebWhacker first asks to which information category you would like to assign this Web site; this is helpful when you want to refer to your downloaded Web page later:

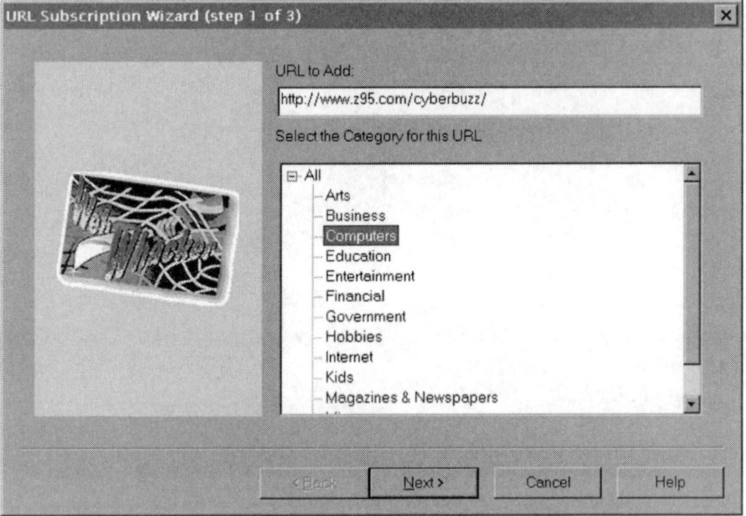

Next, WebWhacker asks how many levels you would like to track within the Web site; you can specify "all levels" (i.e., the entire Web site) or a specific number of levels:

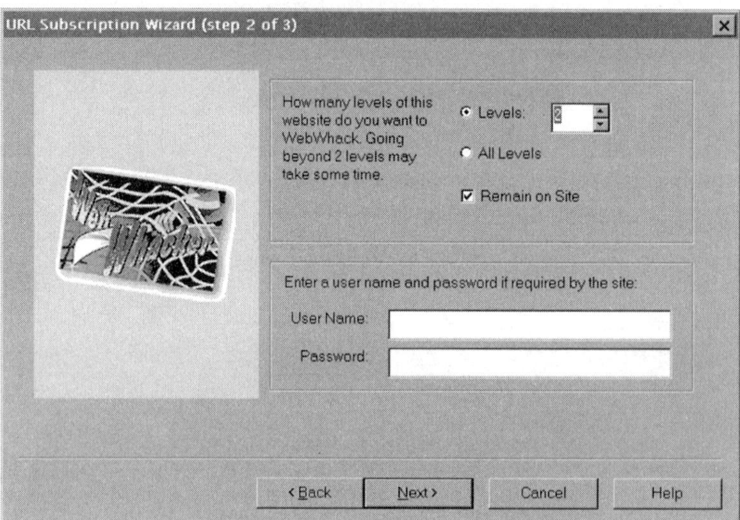

Finally, you are asked how often you would like to retrieve an updated copy of this site:

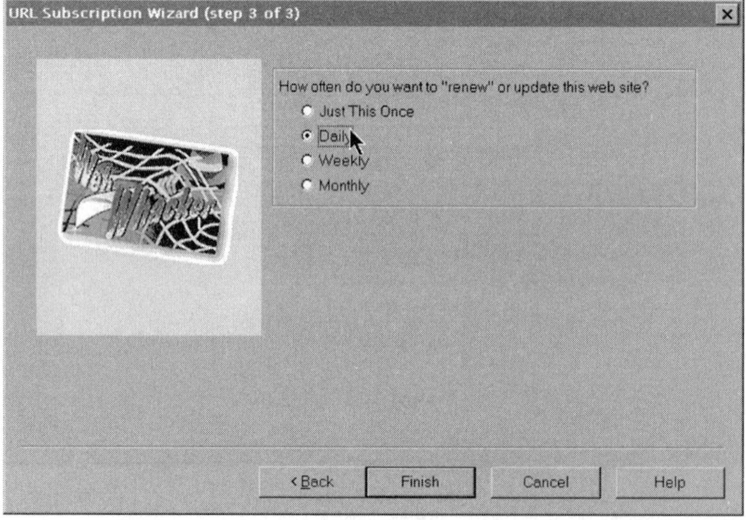

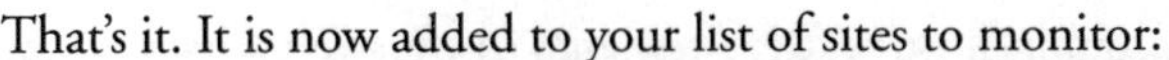

That's it. It is now added to your list of sites to monitor:

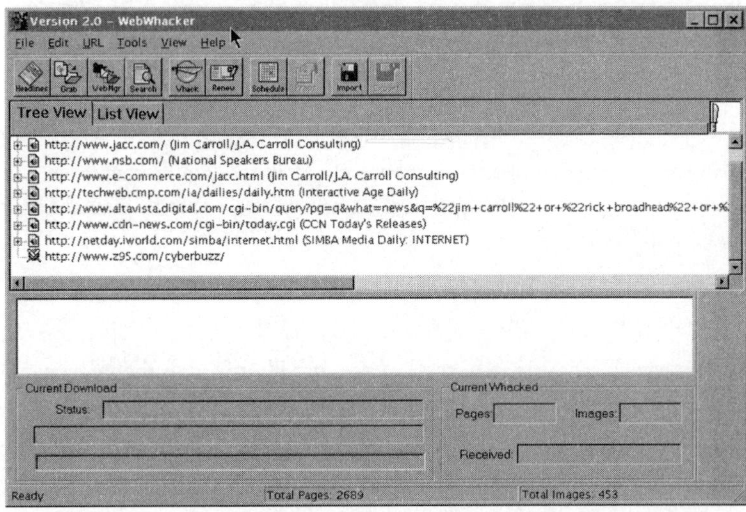

The only other thing to do is instruct WebWhacker at what time of day it should "whack" the site, in this case, at 8:48 p.m. every day. Sure enough, every night it will dial up the Internet using your regular Internet connection and "whack" the site:

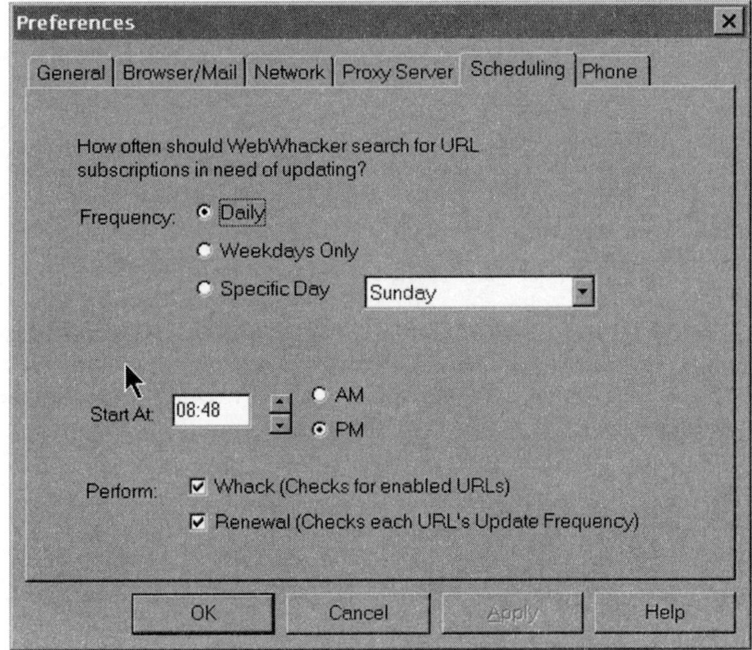

That's it! Come in the next morning, double click on the site name in the WebWhacker list, and you can browse the site without ever signing on to the Internet. WebWhacker is certainly one of the easiest and most straightforward of the programs that we explore in this chapter. It is very simple to set up site monitoring, as you saw above. WebWhacker has other useful features:

- You can view a list of the errors it found when trying to obtain a site.
- You can get a listing of sites that have changed by date, for example, see a listing of those pages that have changed in the last day, those that have changed in the last two days, and so on.
- If when surfing the Web you see a site that you want to grab, just click on "whack," and you will get a copy.
- If you have previously "whacked" a site, it will only grab the new pages or pages that have changed since the site was last downloaded.
- You can use the WebManager that comes with the program to organize the list of sites that you track by topic, making it much easier to deal with all the information you are downloading.

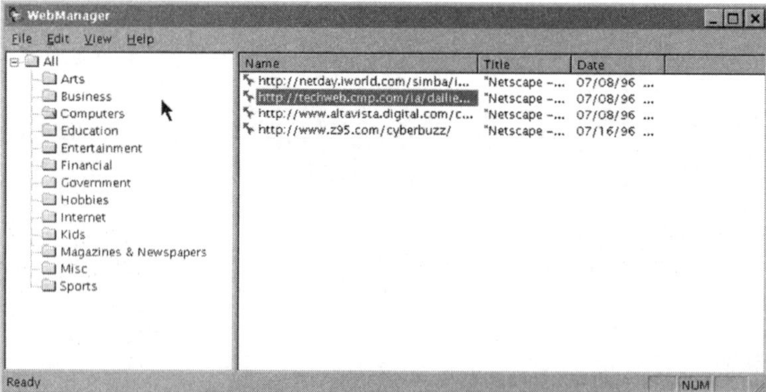

All in all, we rate WebWhacker as one of the best off-line readers that we examined in this chapter. WebWhacker is available for Windows 3.1, Windows 95, and Macintosh computers. You can obtain a free evaluation copy or order a full version at **http://www.ffg.com/whacker.html**.

Notifier Programs and Sites

Most of the programs examined above have an option that will allow you to monitor various Web sites for new or changed Web pages. You do not necessarily need to use one of these programs, though, to be notified if a change is made in your favorite Web sites. Some Web sites are self-monitoring and will notify you when changes have been made. For example, if you take a look at the Web site for the *North Shore News* of West Vancouver, BC, you will see a notice for a free reminder service that will notify you when changes are made to the Web site. The service, called URL-Minder, is offered by NetMind (**http://www.netmind.com**).

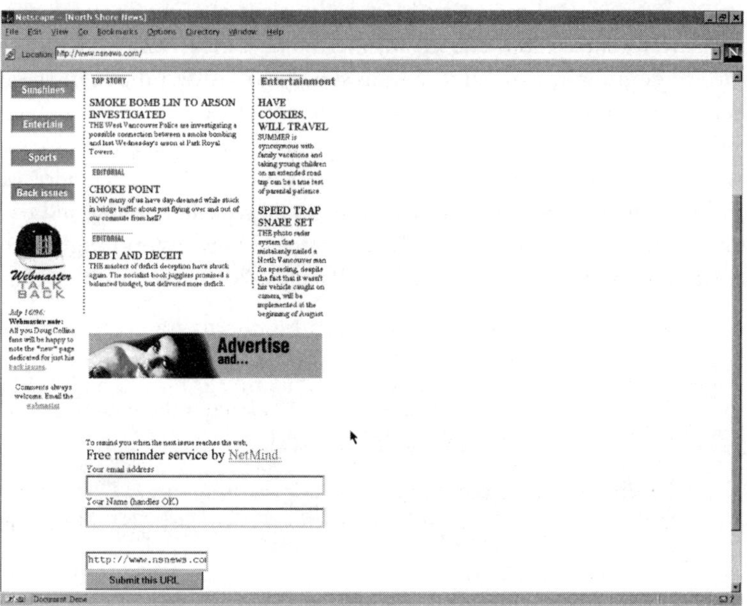

All you need to do is type in your e-mail address and your name, and the NetMind service will notify you if changes are made to the page. This way, you will know when changes are made to the *North Shore News* Web site:

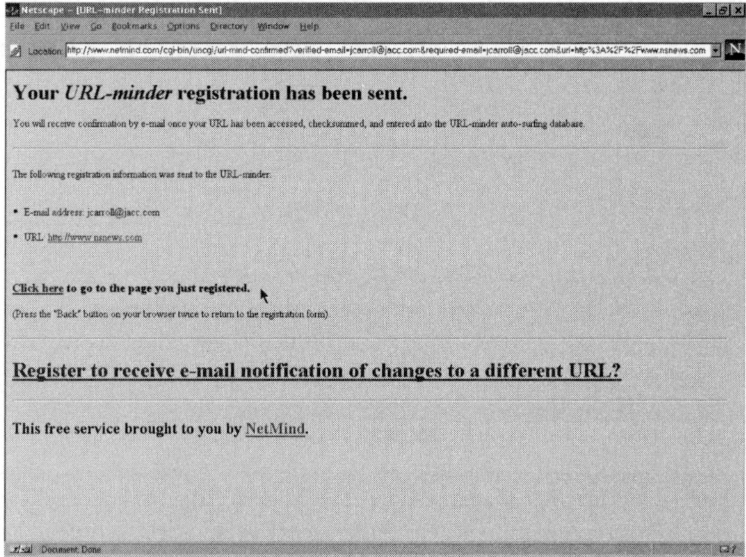

The URL-Minder by NetMind is one of an ever-growing number of services — most free — that monitor Web pages on your behalf and notify you of changes by e-mail. How they work is simple: They visit the Web sites that they monitor on a regular basis, usually daily, and notify the visitors who have registered for those pages if a change has been made.

In the example we used above, *North Shore News* had placed a form on their Web site that was automatically linked to the URL-Minder service. However, you can use the URL-Minder service to monitor *any* site on the Web simply by visiting the NetMind home page (**http://www.netmind.com**) and following the instructions there.

Such utilities are not just available on-line; they are finding their way into an increasing number of Web software programs. For example, Corel's Internet Mania includes a small utility, called Web Page Update Notifier, that tracks changes to Web pages. Simply add to it the URLs of the Web sites you wish to track, press the "Scan Selected Now" button under "Tools," and it will visit each site to see if it has changed since you last checked. Those that have changed will be marked by a red check mark.

Click on any of the items, and you will be immediately taken to those pages by your Web browser to see what changes have occurred. Internet Mania is available for Windows 95 computers. You can find out more about Internet Mania at Corel's Web site at **http://www.corel.ca**.

Finally, some programs, for example, NetBuddy, seem to be caught between being a simple notifier and a full-fledged off-line reader. You can use NetBuddy, for example, to find out if there is new information on particular Web sites:

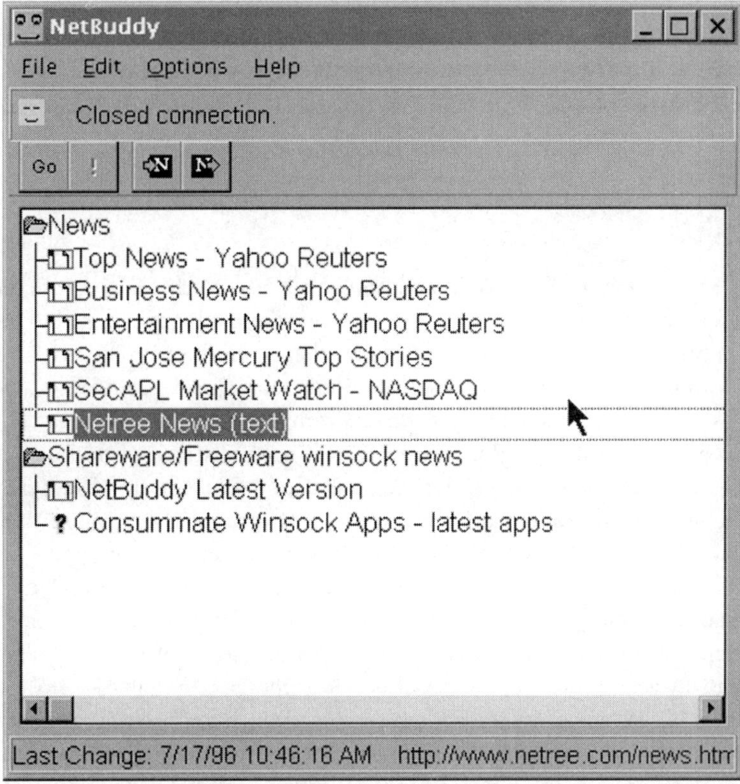

On the screen above, the symbols next to each item signify that there is new information on these pages. You can also configure NetBuddy to retrieve the text only from the pages that interest you; thus it is a bit of an off-line reader, but avoids the time that it can take to pull down complete Web sites, since it ignores the images and pictures found in those sites.

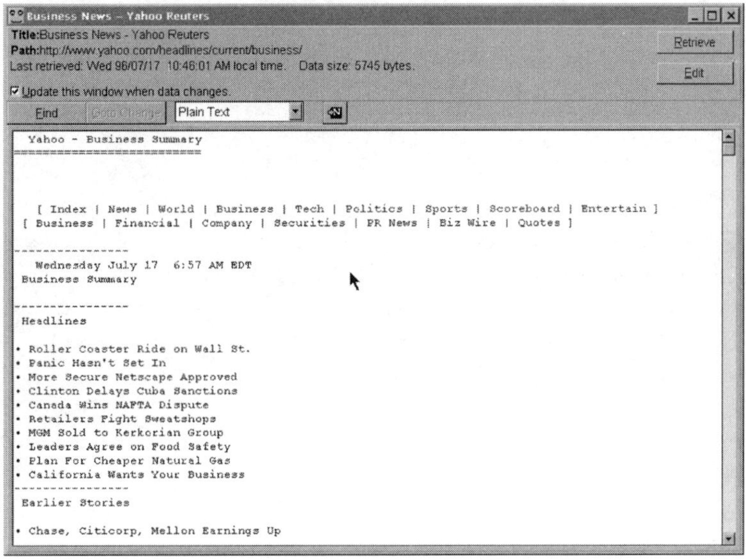

Hence, if you do not want to get into the full sophistication of an off-line reader and want a simple notifier, NetBuddy will do the trick with some added benefits. You can obtain a free copy of NetBuddy at **http://www.internetsol.com/netbuddy.html**. It is available for Windows 3.1 and Windows 95 computers.

Summary

The whole concept of off-line readers and notifiers is very much a new one to the Internet. It is amusing, for example, to look at a January 1996 market report for one of the products we reviewed in this chapter. At that time it was noted that there were no competitive products. All that changed within a month or two. Now some industry analysts estimate that this software category could be worth several hundred million dollars within the next few years.

What will the future bring? Certainly, we will see the arrival of new off-line readers with capabilities and features that we cannot even dream of today. And we believe that such software will help to revolutionize the Internet. That is why we have devoted a separate category to this topic. These new products demonstrate that with a little bit of imagination, you can discover completely new uses for the Internet that have not existed before, or you can solve traditional problems. Imagine, for example, a teacher who wants to take a class onto the Internet. The teacher may be concerned about letting students go on-line for a number of reasons, or perhaps students cannot actually get on-line because the school does not have enough modems.

With an off-line reader the teacher can download an entire Web site for a particular class and make it available to all the students. No worries about getting on-line, and no concerns about students accessing inappropriate information (e.g., pornography) during class. And since only one Web site is available to the students (the one that was downloaded, in fact), no worries that the students will link to other Internet sites or become distracted by other Internet information. Suddenly, a simple little tool like an off-line reader has resulted in a brand-new type of application for the Internet.

CHAPTER 9

Undertaking Research on the Internet

...knowledge itself is snowballing. Every four or five years, the total amount of world information doubles. The sum total of all human knowledge to 1993 was only 1% of the information that will likely be available to our children in the year 2050.

Business Quarterly, Spring, 1994

Turning information into knowledge is the creative skill of our age.

Anthony Smith, *Goodbye Gutenberg: The Newspaper Revolution of the 1980s* (Oxford University Press, New York, 1980)

The Internet is the engine of the information revolution. Take a look around the Internet, and you will quickly realize that the amount of information available on-line is simply staggering. But information without analysis is, for all intents and purposes, basically useless. Information is not necessarily knowledge. The Internet makes available a lot of information, but that information only becomes knowledge if it can first be located and then analyzed.

It is no wonder that the Internet makes available so much information; after all, it provides each of us with our own global printing press, with which we can contribute information to the world. And do we contribute! Everywhere around the world business, governments, organizations, and individuals are building Web sites and packing them with information on everything imaginable. It is almost as if the Internet is a giant vacuum, sucking up the collective wisdom and thoughts of organizations and people worldwide, a vacuum that until recently did not permit anyone to find out what was sucked up. In the "early days" — in Internet terms, that is pre-1995 — because it was so difficult to find anything on-line, people often compared using the Internet to the experience of entering a library — blindfolded, hands tied behind the back — where someone had turned out all the lights. Good luck trying to find a book!

Search Systems on the Internet

One key human trait is the overwhelming compulsion to organize information. With the arrival of the Internet this compulsion is taking new shapes, resulting in all kinds of different search systems and on-line indices throughout the Internet, all geared to helping you find information on-line. In a nutshell, people have been indexing the Internet like mad.

When the World Wide Web burst onto the Internet scene in 1994, along came the first "search engines" with their spiders and robots, handy little software programs that search the Web far and wide, indexing and cataloguing the information that they come across. Most of these search engines are very large-scale efforts, funded by millions of investment dollars. They go by names such as Lycos, Yahoo!, OpenText, AltaVista, HotBot, Ultraseek, and InfoSeek. Systems like these are easy to find, easy to learn, and fun to use. They are numerous, and they are all competing for your attention and your time.

Most of these systems provide everyone with free access; the system developers plan to earn revenue by accepting advertisements throughout the Web pages that they show to people. The business model is, as yet, largely unproven. Some search engines are not driven by an advertising model, but have been established to provide high profiles for the organizations that built them. Digital, for example, has said that making AltaVista available to the Internet community for free has had a powerful impact on Digital's role in the Internet, in addition to generating interest within the business community for private and corporate AltaVista search systems.

But when you need to find information on-line, you need not be restricted to these large-scale search engines. The beauty (and challenge) of the Internet is that anyone can create his/her own index of information on the Internet. Hence, when looking for something, you can often take advantage of the existence of all these hundreds of thousands of "mini-indices."

Consider "Josephine Coombe's Canadian Pet Sites Index" (**http://www.interlog.com/~pets/**), an index of Canadian Web sites related to the topic of pets. Coombe notes on her Web page why she spent the time creating this index: "Given the abundance of pet site lists with a largely American focus and the dearth of specifically Canadian resources this side of the border, I thought it was time to give the great white north a say!"

Why do people take the time to develop such indices on their own? When asked, Coombe responded to us by noting, "It started off as a way of making

UNDERSTANDING RESEARCH ON THE INTERNET

1. Hundreds of search systems and on-line indices can be found on the Net — some are individual efforts, while others are very large-scale enterprises funded by millions of investment dollars.
2. All search systems are different, in that they vary in the syntax that you must use to do a search, and in their structure and purpose.
3. Information found on the Internet is sometimes of questionable value and quality, is often out of date, and can disappear as quickly as it appears. The result is that the Internet is not always the best source of research information.
4. In doing research on the Net you need to plan your search, define your search terms, establish where you are going to search, and continually reinvent your search.
5. Depending on the type of information you are looking for, you may use any number of on-line search tools, such as category indices used when searching a broad topic; search engines when searching for a specific phrase, person, topic, etc.; review indices when you want to restrict your search to "qualified" sites; topical indices when searching a particular topic; geographic/regional indices when searching for a specific geographic area.
6. To get really good at searching you will need to learn about such things as Boolean logic, proximity operators, wildcards, and relevance ranking.

myself a useful resource. I wanted to make myself a useful resource for two main reasons/motives: 1) being a good 'net citizen' 2) to gain a reputation that might help my business, and particularly to enable me to target the pet market more for web design work. I've been involved with animals most of my life and so I'm naturally interested in the stuff that's out there, and I was disappointed by the American-centric nature of most of the pet indices. I thought we needed something for Canada and Canadians."

Problems With Search Systems

While there is no shortage of useful places to help you find information on the Internet, there remain several challenges:

- Knowing where to start. The day we looked at the "Searching the Web" category in Yahoo! when writing this chapter, there were 407 items in the "Indices to Web documents" listing. The number will be far bigger by the time you go and visit it. So for many people, searching on the Internet becomes a question of not "how do I search," but "where do I search?"
- Even if the information is on the Internet, it might not be catalogued in a search engine or search system. No search engine is 100% comprehensive. Even though there are many search systems on the Web, there is no guarantee that any or all of them will be aware of a particular Web site. The information that you need might exist on a Web site somewhere, but every single search system in the world may not be aware that it exists. Therefore, it is possible that you may not be able to locate this information, regardless of how hard you search.
- Even if the information exists, it may be difficult to find. Face it: Many of us have never had a formal course on how to search for information on-line. We were raised in the era of textbooks and library card catalogues. No one has taken the time to teach us the science of searching, so, quite simply, we should be willing to admit that we know very little about the basics of searching on-line.
- Search engines cannot distinguish between good and bad Web sites. Search engines simply provide results; they cannot tell you which sites have good content and bad content in terms of quality. This is beginning to change with the emergence of value-added services that allow you to perform a search on a database of Web reviews.
- Search engines all seem to operate differently. Start using any of the search engines that are out there, and you will quickly discover that they use different methods to conduct their search, and each method seems to provide differing levels of sophistication.
- The hype about search engines is confusing. Search engines have become "big business"; consequently, there is a lot of noise in the media and on the Internet about which system is the "best." Such hype often obscures the facts about the benefits and drawbacks of particular search systems. Each one is different, and each offers pros and cons.
- Search systems often become outdated or fall behind. In particular, many smaller indexing initiatives on the Web are begun by organizations or individuals with a burst

of energy but then begin to wither and die. It is easy to start a Web index, but it is tough to keep it going. That is why when you travel the Web, you will come across so many indices that have disappeared, are obviously out-of-date, or contain rather useless information.

- It is not just the small search systems that face challenges; large, well-funded efforts face difficulties as well. An article about search engines in *Wired* magazine's April 1996 issue stated, "...how do researchers possibly believe they can organize the rapidly growing Web? Have they really solved the problems that have stumped scientists for the last 200 years, or are they just ignoring them?"
- Search systems are not always up-to-date. When a new Web site appears on the Internet, it does not appear in a search engine automatically. Search engines rely on automated robots and user submissions to update their databases. It may take days or sometimes weeks before a new Web site appears in a particular search engine's database. In some cases it may never appear unless the address is manually submitted by the Web site owner/maintainer. The other problem is that when a Web site is removed from the Internet, the address is not automatically deleted from a search engine. Old addresses can linger in search engine databases for long periods of time. To alleviate this problem, some search engines allow Web site owners to manually delete and/or update addresses for Web sites they control.
- The command syntax is not interchangeable. There is currently no standard for search engine commands. This means that the commands you use on one search engine may not work on another.
- The results may not be objective. For example, at least one search engine allows advertisers to influence how results are displayed when a user searches for a particular word or product category.

Realities of Internet Information

Not only are there challenges in dealing with search systems, there are basic and fundamental problems with information on the Internet itself. With all the excitement about the Internet, too many people overlook the cold, hard realities of Internet information:

- The quality of some of the information found on-line may be of questionable value or use. Since anyone can create a Web site, there is much useful information on-line. By the same token, there is much useless information as well. When looking for something on the Internet, you might come across page after page of completely unrelated information of little value that was somehow picked up by the search you conducted.
- You might be disgusted by what you find. The simple reality of the Internet is that it makes available both the positive and negative aspects of the human condition. On some days your voyage into the Internet will open your eyes to the latter. You might not be pleased with what you see.

- The accuracy or validity of information you find on-line could be questionable. Want to publish a Web site in which you provide "conclusive proof" that Elvis shot JFK? Go for it! Create a Web site. Load it with articles from *serious sources* that you have invented. Use a computer graphics program to create a picture of the grassy knoll with Elvis on his stomach firing a shot at the limousine. Get *eyewitness statements* and publish them on-line. Elvis shot JFK! It's a fact! It's on the Net!

  As we enter the digital age, we must keep in mind that the marvelous computer tools that we use also provide wonderful opportunities to distort the truth. You should always examine any information that you find on-line with a critical eye and take everything with a grain of salt. As one wag has said, "You should never trust anything you find on the Internet."
- Information might be out-of-date. Some people publish information on the Internet to deliberately distort the truth. Others have good intentions when they put information on the Internet but for many reasons may not keep the site up-to-date. There is no guarantee that the information found on-line is the most recent, the most current, and the most accurate.
- Information on the Web can disappear as quickly and easily as it appears. Get used to the message "ERROR 404 — Not Found" as you browse the World Wide Web. It is the error message that you get when you go to a page of information that no longer exists. Information on the Internet can disappear as quickly as it appears. What you want may no longer exist.
- Information overload is a reality on the Internet. This is probably the biggest and most difficult challenge for new users of the Internet. The information age is quickly leading to information overload with the result that as you travel the Internet, you may simply feel overwhelmed at the extent of information on-line. It often seems impossible to find what you are looking for.

Quite simply, for all the sophistication and excitement that the Internet generates, you must accept that it suffers from these many significant limitations. You must always treat information you find on the Internet with skepticism and always question its accuracy and validity.

Finally, the *most important* point to keep in mind is that you will only find information on the Internet if it happens to exist on-line. Even the best search engine cannot find non-existent information.

How to Conduct a Search on the Internet

Your challenge in using the Internet, of course, is to find on-line the information that is important to you. It is easy to start looking for information on the Internet. The success of your efforts, however, will depend upon the method you use to find it. You can proceed in one of two ways:

- Sign on to the Internet, travel to your favorite search engine such as Infoseek (http://www.infoseek.com), and do a search. Begin browsing through the results. Surf many of the Web sites. Get frustrated. Give up. You have found little of relevance.

- Or sit back and think about what you are looking for. Plan a strategy. Invest some time in thinking up search terms. Think about what search systems might be most appropriate for your search. *Then* sign on to the Internet and do a preliminary search. Try some other search terms. View some of the results, and see if they lead you to some other search phrases. Try those phrases. Examine the results again. Refine your search again. Think about what you have achieved.

Do you notice a difference between these two approaches? The first is entirely hit-and-miss, while the second involves some careful thought and planning. The unfortunate thing is that most people who use the Internet fall into the first category. They have never really taken the time to learn how to search.

At Some Point, You Will Have to Learn to Search On-line.

Want to know a secret? For all the hype about the Internet, one thing that is often forgotten is that computer-based search systems have been around for a long time. Professional information searchers, for example, folks known as information brokers, who do research on behalf of companies for a fee, spend a lot of time thinking about and planning their search before they even dare go on-line. So there already are many people who long ago became experts at properly looking for information on-line. You can learn more about what they do and the methods they use to search by contacting the Association of Independent Information Professionals (**http://www.intnet.net/aiip/**).

Do not forget librarians, or, as they should be called, information professionals. Remember that most librarians have a degree in the "information sciences"; in other words, they are experts at dealing with the science of information. Even before computers were invented these individuals were search specialists in their own right. Today, you can find information professionals/librarians playing key roles not only in the information sciences, but in helping people learn how to search the Web.

Why do we raise this issue? Because we think that if you do not take the time to learn how to search effectively, then you will never have much success on-line. This style of thinking may seem foreign to you. After all, the whole attitude of those using the Internet leads you to believe that it is easy to find things on-line, with everybody telling you that "it is easy to search the Internet; it's big, and there's a lot of information. You can find anything. Just go to a search engine, type in what you are looking for, and you'll have results."

How Not to Search the Internet, Part 1

Just go to a search engine and type in a search. Say you have a tree in the backyard that is suffering from a gypsy moth infestation and you are worried this may damage the tree. You zip off to the search engine WebCrawler and type in "gypsy moth." Within a few seconds you are told that WebCrawler knows of 861 Web pages that mention gypsy moths. Included in this list are some pages that mention "gypsy myths," "Great Smoky Mountains Bibliography," something called the "1996 Winter Calendar of Events," and "ALETHEIA: The Hyperzine for Men - January 1996," in addition to many more pages that seem to be about gypsy moths. You spend a lot of time flitting from Web site to Web site, reading what they have, trying to figure out how to deal with the problem you have in your backyard. Frustrated, you give up and go out and buy a book or go to the garden store.

The Need to Plan Your Search

We regularly talk to many people across the country, many of whom indicate frustration with the fact that they cannot really find anything on the Internet. But we find that most do the type of search mentioned above. We believe their failures are due to one of two reasons: Either the information they are looking for is not on-line, or it is on-line but they do not know how to properly conduct a search. If it is not on-line, there is not much that we can do to help. But if it is and you cannot find it, then we think you may be going about your search in the wrong way.

There is a point we are trying to make here: we believe that with a little planning and training, you can avoid these types of problems when searching for information on the Internet. This, of course, seems to run counter to many of the attitudes that people have with respect to research on the Internet. For example, an author of books about the Internet made the following comment one day, when advising others about how to search on the Internet: "Probably the best strategy is to direct users to the various indices such as Yahoo!, Lycos, AltaVista, DejaNews, etc. Give descriptions of each of these services and how they work, as they all have their own quirks and strengths."

This is like a swim instructor saying: "Toss a new swimmer into the deep end. Let her know what might happen once she is in the water: She might sink or she might swim. But don't tell her how to swim."

What Happens If You Do Not Plan Your Search

1. You will get back a lot of junk and useless search results. The most common complaint that people have about searching on the Internet is that there is too much junk! But if you do not spend the time planning your search, of course you will get a lot of junk!

2. You will not find what you are looking for. The second most common complaint is that you cannot find what you are looking for. If you do not take the time to clearly understand what it is you are looking for, then how can you expect to find it?

3. You will waste time. Not planning your search is similar to going into a library and trying to find a book without the aid of the card catalogue. You would not do that in a library, so why would you do that on the Internet?

4. You will not access search systems that might be the best source of information for your search. Too many people come to rely on a "favorite" search system and always use it exclusively. But by doing so, they might not access a search system or topic index that might help them find precisely what they are looking for.

5. You will start to give up on the Internet. The more unsuccessful searches you do, the more frustrated you will become with the Internet. The more you become frustrated, the less likely you will be to use it in the future.

Our Suggested Internet Search Methodology

Here are our suggestions for conducting a useful search on the Internet:

- Educate yourself with respect to the topic before searching.
- Come up with a list of search terms that concisely define what it is you are looking for; this will give you flexibility in your search.

- Determine where you should search.
- Continually reinvent your search as you proceed by analyzing your results.

We cannot promise instant search success. However, we do believe that if you take the time to go about your Internet search in a more methodical fashion, you will have a greater chance for success. Let's examine these steps in more depth.

Educate Yourself With Respect to the Topic Before Searching

You cannot find what you do not know. Ask yourself this question before you start a search: Do I really know what I am looking for? Sometimes you might be searching for some information about a topic that is new to you. Does it not make sense to learn about the topic before figuring out how to search for the relevant information? It does, so you should consider "browsing" the topic before "searching" the topic to gain some useful background. This background information may guide you in defining more clearly the question that you should be asking.

Define Different Search Terms

The most important thing you can do when preparing to find something on the Internet is to come up with the "terms" or "words" that you will search for, *in advance of doing the search.* For example, consider what we did when preparing to write this chapter. We wanted to provide a listing of on-line documents that offered tips on search strategy, so we decided we wanted to find information on "how to do research on the Internet." We sat back and thought about related words and phrases, for example, "finding stuff on the Internet," "how to research the Web," and "doing on-line research."

Thus, long before we signed onto the Internet, we spent time defining the words that might lead us to the information we were looking for. We put effort into specifically defining the different phrases that people might have used in their Web sites about this topic. That way, when we did go on-line, we were prepared with several different starting points for our search.

Establish Where You Will Search

This is the key to searching effectively on the Internet. Many users have their own favorite Web search systems, whether it is Yahoo!, OpenText, or AltaVista. There is nothing wrong with that. But each of these systems has some advantages and drawbacks; we will cover those issues later. But they are not necessarily always the best place to start. Say you are looking for information on whether there is a comic strip that deals with gardening. You might zip into AltaVista and type "comic strips and gardening" and see what it gives you. Maybe you will get very little, or maybe you will get 10,000 entries to browse through. Either way, complete frustration.

Does it not make more sense to ask yourself a few questions, such as whether there might be a really good index of information somewhere on the Internet all about comics that would be a good starting point? Try "The Comics List," a comprehensive listing of comics on the Web (**http://www.intercom.es/agendagc/comics/english/**) or the "WraithSpace Comics Index," a comprehensive listing of comics both on and off the Web (**http://www.redweb.com/wraithspace/**). Why not find out whether there is a mailing list or USENET newsgroup about comics that might prove useful in providing insight on where to start? No problem. You could join the mailing list "COMICW-L: COMIC Writers Workshop" or look into the USENET newsgroups **rec.arts.comics.info** and **rec.arts.comics.misc**.

How did we find the sites above? Simple. We looked in Yahoo! for the comics category and visited a site called "Tile.Net" to search USENET newsgroups and mailing lists for the word "comics." That helped to focus our search.

If you spend a little bit of time thinking about where you might find the answer to your question, you might discover the answer that much quicker. It will help to focus you even before you begin your search. The key to finding information on the Internet is to know where to start looking. We will cover that topic in-depth later.

Continually Reinvent Your Search

Too often you might turn to a search engine, try your search terms, and give up because you did not find anything. Instead, you must master the art of "continuous reinvention" and recognize that you should not expect your first search to take you right to the best source of information on the planet! Continuous reinvention is the realizion that your first search will likely provide you more insight into the topic at hand, and rather than provide you with the answer you are looking for, might simply provide guidance on where to go next. It might, for example, suggest some other search terms.

When writing this chapter, we wanted to find information about "finding information on the Internet." We did not have much luck with that so we tried something else. And tried again. And again. Eventually one of the documents that we found contained the phrases "search tips" and "search methodology." That's it, we thought! Bull's-eye! We tried that as a search phrase and found that it happened to be the magic phrase that started to take us to some of the more useful documents referred to throughout this chapter.

Here is another perfect example: one of us was asked to give a keynote speech to the Purchasing Management Association of Canada. We first looked for the phrases "electronic bidding" and "electronic purchasing." We did come up with something, but nothing great. We knew there had to be more on-line, so we examined the documents we did find to see if they provided any guidance. They sure did; in fact, they suggested to us that we use the word "procurement." Talk about pay dirt! That was the one word (one that had not occurred to us) that opened the information floodgates for us.

Let's review what happened. Our initial search phrases, which we spent time carefully defining beforehand, did not provide us the home run. But they did get us to first base; the documents we did find initially contained the new phrases related to our topic. Once we went back and searched with the new phrases, a whole new source of related information opened up. Continually reinvent your search, and you will find that the Internet will work a lot more for you.

How Not to Search the Internet, Part 2

Use the special search features found in many on-line search engines. For example, if we go to the search engine AltaVista (http://www.altavista.digital.com) and type in "gypsy moths," we are told it knows of 6,000 pages of information!

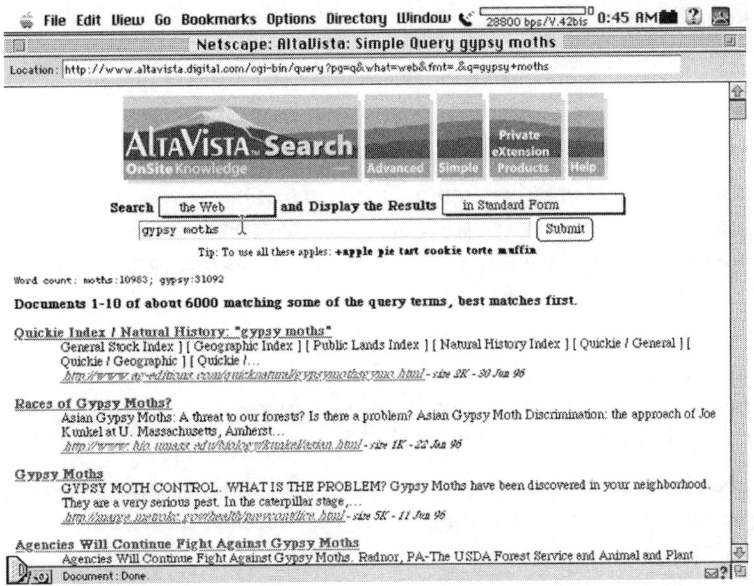

What a great way to waste time. But let's say we do an "advanced search" in AltaVista specifying our search in more detail. We are looking for the phrase "gypsy moth"; an important point is that we want the two words to appear beside each other on the page. Not only that, but the Web page must also contain the words "infestation" and "control."

Take a look at the first result, a document entitled "Identification, Life-History, Damage, and Approaches to Controlling the Gypsy."

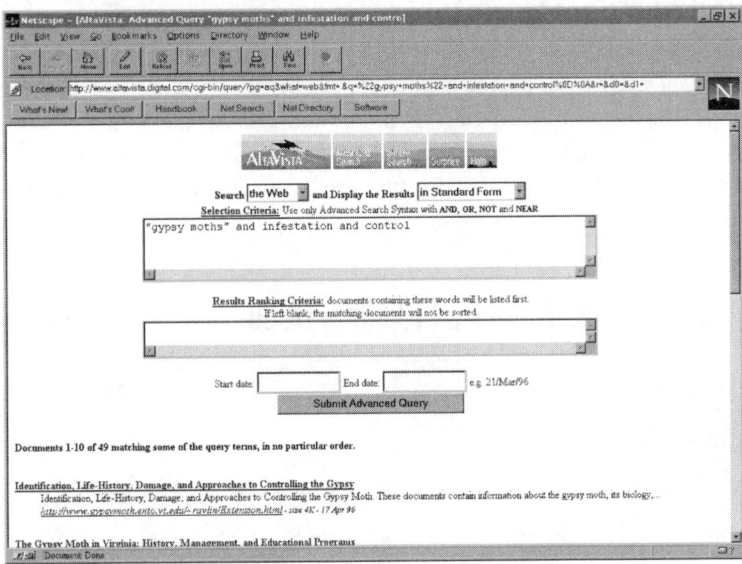

Hence it is important to learn the nuances of particular search systems and the basic methods that you can use to enhance your search. We will take a look at these concepts later in this chapter.

Common Sense Search Tips

You should also keep in mind some basic common sense tips that apply to searching on the Internet:

- Know when to give up! Even though you should not give up, you must also learn when to give up. Long-time information searchers have used the "law of diminishing returns" to know when to stop looking. They have developed a "gut feel" that tells them the point at which they believe that the time invested will be far in excess of any further returns they may get.
- Remember that experience counts. Frankly, on-line searching is a skill that you do not master overnight; it takes a lot of time and effort to get good at it. Hence you should strongly consider practice. Invest time in several of the different search systems and learn the nuances and special features of each search system.
- Remember that there are other sources for information. Sometimes people turn to the Internet to look for something when they should not, particularly in cases where it may take hours to find something on-line that can be obtained within minutes by picking up the phone.
- Remember, there is no best search method. As you search the Internet, do not get caught up thinking that there is one "true search method." Searching is more of an art than a science, and becoming good at it takes a lot of time and hard work. Take twenty expert searchers, and you will probably come up with twenty different search methods.

Categories of Search Tools On-line

The biggest challenge for most people is knowing *where* to start their search. There are many individuals and organizations that have invested time and effort in building Web sites to help you find other Web sites. Your goal is to figure out how to use those sites effectively. It is helpful to have an idea of the basic categories of places that you might start when looking for information on the Internet.

Category Indices/Browsing Index/Browsing Trees

Popular Category Indices

Yahoo! (**http://www.yahoo.com**)

The WWW Virtual Library (**http://www.w3.org/pub/DataSources/bySubject/Overview.html**)

GNN Select (**http://www.gnn.com/gnn/wic/wics/index.html**)

Magellan (**http://www.mckinley.com**)

A category index, also known as a browsing index or browsing tree, is one that is built upon specific categories of information. These indices are considered to be best used when you are looking for information about a broad topic rather than very specific information. For example, you might want to know what type of information exists on the Internet about ski resorts, a fairly general topic.

Yahoo! (http://www.yahoo.com) is probably one of the most popular category indices and is considered by many to be the closest thing to a set of on-line "yellow pages" for the Internet. Yahoo! organizes the Web sites it is aware of in simple categories, in the form of a "tree," with the top categories consisting of Art, Business, Computers, and so on. Each of these top categories contains subcategories, and each subcategory may contain more sub-subcategories, and so on. You can browse through these categories as described below, or search for a word or phrase within the categories. Yahoo! excels as a starting point for a search about ski resorts. Simply go to Yahoo! and choose the category "Recreation & Sports." You will see this:

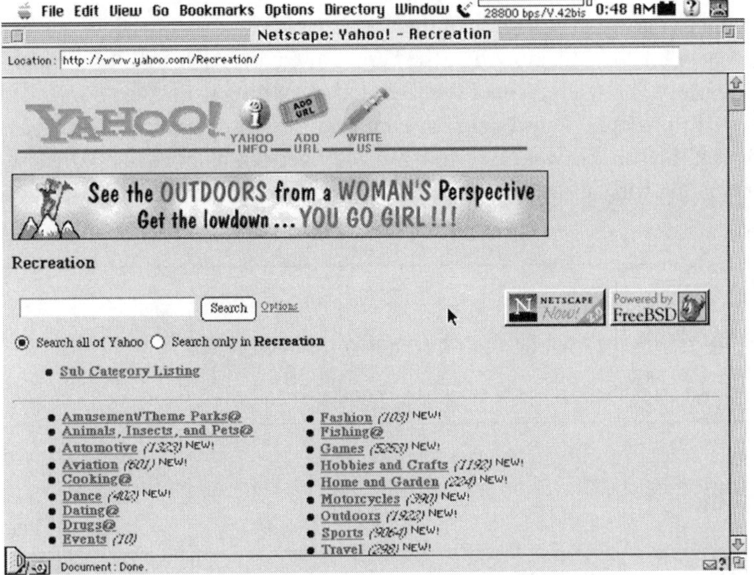

Choose the category "Sports." (Notice the number 209 beside the word "skiing." This means that on the date we visited Yahoo! it knew of over 200 Web sites about skiing.) From the new page presented, below, choose the category "Resorts," which will take you to a list of ski resorts or other directories about ski resorts.

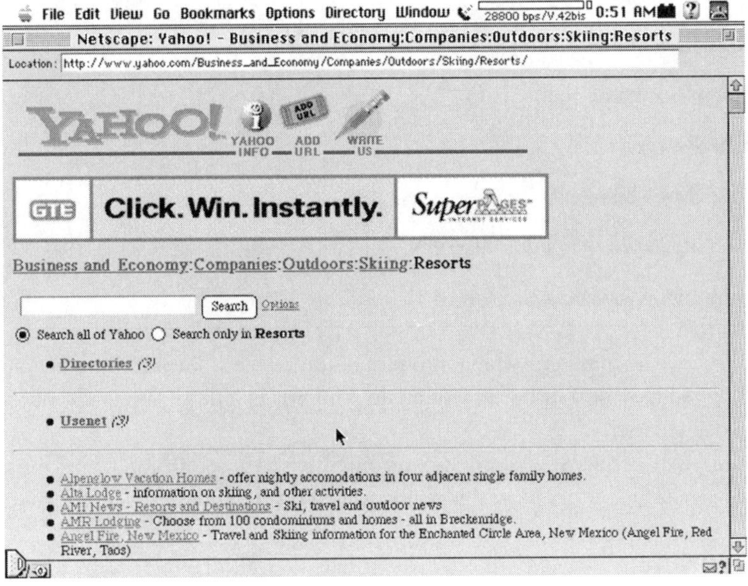

What could be easier? Elapsed time, perhaps 15 to 20 seconds.

The advantage of category or browsing indices is that they are very easy to use: you simply select a category and keep on working your way through the categories until you come across the information you need.

The disadvantage is that you are relying on the creators of the categories to think like you, and they are rather arbitrary for that reason; if you think about information categories differently than the creator, you may not find what you are looking for. Many argue that systems like Yahoo! will never succeed at successfully indexing information, since information categorization has long been a difficult and serious challenge.

You should recognize that because of the work involved, some category indices are having a hard time keeping up with the growth of the Web. Noted an article in *Wired*, April 1996: "...almost 800,000 people a day use Yahoo! to search for everything from Web-controlled Christmas trees to research on paleontology. In almost every way you can measure, Yahoo! has successfully exerted order on the chaotic Web. But how much longer can its hold last? Already, Yahoo! falls short of cataloguing the half-million or so sites on the Web. The enormity of its task is almost comical...."

When to Use a Category Index

- You are looking for an idea of what might be on-line for a broad topic.
- You are trying to find the Web site of a particular company.

Search Engines

Primary Search Engines

AltaVista (**http://www.altavista.digital.com**)

Excite (**http://www.excite.com**)

HotBot (**http://www.hotbot.com**)

Infoseek (**http://www.infoseek.com**)

Inktomi (**http://www.inktomi.com**)

Lycos (**http://www.lycos.com**)

OpenText (**http://www.opentext.com**)

Infoseek Ultra (**http://www.ultra.infoseek.com**)

WebCrawler (**http://www.webcrawler.com**)

An index like Yahoo! organizes everything into nice neat categories, such as company name or topic. But sometimes you may not find what you are looking for in Yahoo! What do you do then? You can use a "search engine."

Many computer geniuses, when first confronted with the explosion of information on the World Wide Web, decided that what was really needed on the Internet were computer programs that allowed Internet users to search the entire contents of the World Wide Web. Today, there are dozens of these search engines on the World Wide Web, all of which operate differently and all of which are competing for your attention. They also go by the names "robots," "spiders," and "keyword indices." Search engines differ in many ways:

- Speed. Different search engines operate at different speeds, so much so that the speed of the search has become one of the key points used in marketing hype about search engines. But whether one search engine does a search in half a second and the other in one second really becomes academic.
- Method of indexing the Web. Some search engines index every word on every Web page, while others index only the first few paragraphs or title.
- Value-added services. Some search engines provide additional information or services, such as news and weather.
- Method by which they rank results. Some search engines such as OpenText allow advertisers to pay for a top listing in a search result, thereby skewing the results. (They identify these items so at least you are aware of this fact.)
- Size of database. Some search engines try to index everything on the Web, while others index only sites that meet certain criteria. In addition, many search engines are involved in a marketing battle over who has the biggest search engine indexing the greatest number of sites on the Internet.
- User interface. Travel to any search engine, and you will notice completely different screen designs in terms of the way you enter your search. This can have a direct impact on how easy it is to search.
- How results are displayed. Different search engines display the search results in different ways and often give a choice between detailed and summary listings of the Web sites found.
- Search syntax. We do not yet have a standard set of commands for searching the Web; thus the commands that work on one search engine will not necessarily work on another. Not only that, but as we will see, different search engines use the various search commands differently, making it that much more of a challenge.
- Search ranking. Most search engines use some type of "relevance ranking" when displaying the results of the search. In effect, they try to list those sites that are most relevant to you first. However, each search engine differs in terms of how it determines relevance; hence a search for the same phrase in different search engines will return completely different results.
- Additional capabilities. Some search engines provide simple, useful features that you cannot get on other search engines. AltaVista, for example, allows you to determine which Web sites have linked to your own.

What a search engine does is index information found on Web pages throughout the Internet. Some search engines index every word found on a Web page, while others index only the title or the first few words and paragraphs; each operates differently. They then allow you to search that index using a word or a series of words.

Say you are looking for information about ski resorts in Whistler, BC. You should be able to go to a computer somewhere on the Internet, type in "ski resorts in Whistler," or something like that, and see if the search engine knows of any Web pages that contain those words. Chances are a good number of them might be about ski resorts in Whistler.

Sound far-fetched? It might, but it is real. Computer geniuses have a habit of figuring out how to build the things that they think should exist. For example, the folks at OpenText (http://www.opentext.com), a company based in Kitchener/Waterloo, ON, figured out how to get a computer to go out onto the World Wide Web and read, 24 hours a day, 7 days a week. Everything it finds goes into a large index, so that it now knows of many places that contain the phrase "ski resorts in Whistler."

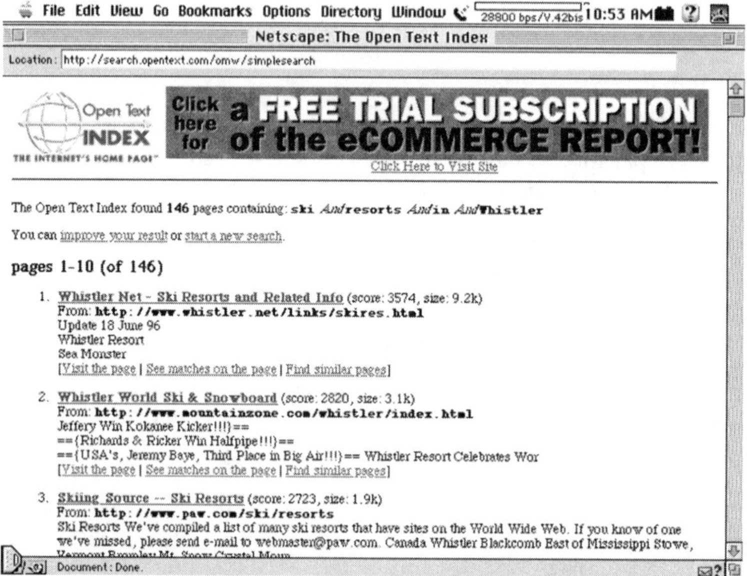

There are several keyword indices; many of them index the discussions that occur in USENET newsgroups in addition to indexing Web sites. One advantage of a keyword index is that rather than conducting your search based upon the categories that someone might apply to a particular Web site or page, you are searching for specific words and phrases found on a Web page. In other words, rather than searching categories, you are searching content, so the search is based on a much broader base of information. A second advantage is the automated nature of search engines, which means they are far more successful in finding and indexing new Web sites.

The disadvantage is, simply, that your search is based upon a lot more information, which means that you must learn how to search effectively for information on-line. That is a sufficiently important topic that we will address it in more depth shortly.

When to Use Search Engines

- When you are looking for a specific phrase or when you need to narrow your search to those sites that meet certain criteria.
- When you are looking for a very specific phrase, company, person, or topic, and you can come up with a very specific phrase to search.
- When you need to search for information that may be buried within a page and hence may not be picked up by a browsing index.
- When a search in a browsing index fails.

Review Indices

<u>Primary Review Indices</u>

Excite (**http://www.excite.com**)

Magellan Internet Guide (**http://www.mckinley.com/**)

Lycos (**http://www.lycos.com**)

WebCrawler (**http://www.webcrawler.com**)

Many of the organizations that build and run the types of Internet search engines described above are continually trying to find ways to stand out in the crowd. One way of doing this that is gaining increasing popularity is to include reviews of World Wide Web sites that describe and rank the content found on the site on a scale, in effect adding value by providing reviews of Web sites in addition to basic search capabilities. You can browse through the available reviews and sometimes search through them.

The advantage is that these systems steer you towards only the best sites, just as *TVGuide* might recommend particular television shows. The disadvantages are that the systems may not be comprehensive and simply may not have rated or reviewed a Web site that contains the information that you really want, meaning that you will not find it by using them.

When to Use Review Indices

- When you are looking for either a very specific phrase, company, person, topic, or a broad topic.
- When you want to restrict your search to those sites that have been "qualified" as having good content to help restrict some of the "junk" you might encounter in a search.

Topical Indices

<u>Suggested Sources for Subject Guides or Topic Indices</u>

The Argus Clearinghouse (**http://www.clearinghouse.net**)

InfoMine (**http://lib-www.ucr.edu**)

Look into the industry category in Yahoo! (**http://www.yahoo.com**). You will usually find the entry "Directories" or "Indices," which will help you to locate such indices.

These are also known as virtual libraries or subject guides. They simply focus on a particular topic. There are tens if not hundreds of thousands of topical indices around the Web like these, ranging from large-scale, well-funded initiatives to smaller indices maintained on a shoestring by individuals or organizations. For example, you might use any of the following indices as a starting point to undertake research on a very particular subject:

- Need to find some free software? The Virtual Software Library focuses on software (**http://www.shareware.com**).
- Want information on psychology? The Canadian Psychological Association provides "Canada's most complete listing of electronic psychology resources and links" on its Web site (**http://www.cpa.ca**).

- Need to find newspapers or magazines on the Internet? Look at the *American Journalism Review's* NewsLink site (**http://www.newslink.org**).
- Need to find companies in the television broadcast industry? TVNet provides a comprehensive listing of companies (**http://tvnet.com/misc/Resources/worldnets.html**).
- Need a listing of not-for-profit organizations involved in environmental and social issues worldwide? Check out The Institute for Global Communications (**http://www.igc.org**).
- Looking for a listing for an index about hockey? Check Yahoo! (**http://www.yahoo.com/Recreation/Sports/Hockey/Ice_Hockey/Indices/**), which lists quite a few hockey-specific indices.

> Why Do You Want to Find a Topical Index to Start Your Search?
>
> A topical index is often an excellent place to *start* when looking for information about the particular topic in question, since the index is usually prepared by someone who has knowledge about the topic. Say you are searching for information about insulation standards for residential construction. Where do you start? You could zip off into a search engine like AltaVista and try such a search and come up with a lot of irrelevant information.
>
> Or you could first try to establish whether there is a good index on the Internet that focuses on issues and companies within the construction industry in Canada, under the presumption that such an index might be a better way to find an answer to your question. In this case try a search in a keyword database, not with the objective of finding the answer to your question, but of finding an index about the topic or industry to which your question relates. For example, a search for the phrase "construction industry Canada" returned a list of several hundred items, but near the top of the list was a link to BuildingWeb (**http://www.builder-web.com/**), a very good topical index that provides links to all kinds of information about the construction industry in Canada. Searching there provided some answers to our questions.
>
> So searching first for a good index and then searching through that index can sometimes be a better type of on-line search, since the index becomes the new starting point for your search.

Finding such indices, of course, remains the basic challenge. The best starting point is the Clearinghouse site mentioned above. For example, say you are looking for a good index about Alzheimer's disease. Visit the Clearinghouse and choose the "Medical" category:

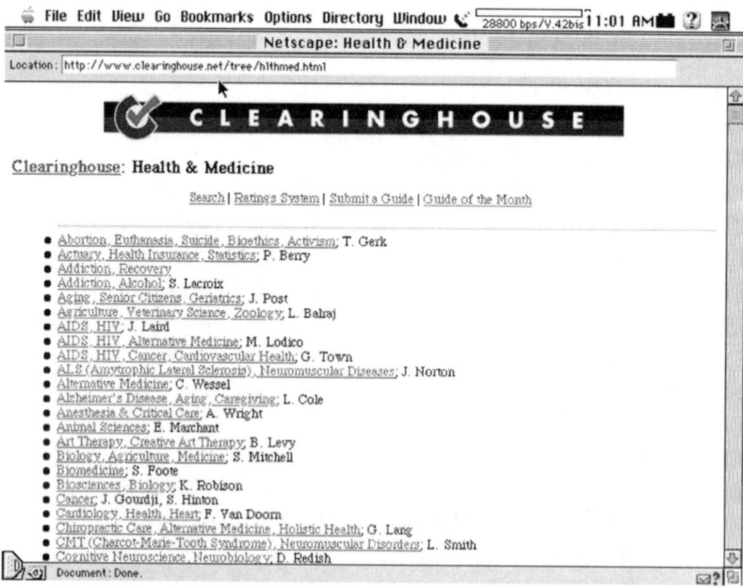

You can see there is a listing for Alzheimer's. Choosing this listing gives a screen that tells you there is a subject guide entitled "Family Caregiver Alliance: Links to Online Resources." Examine that, and you will see "Alzheimer's Web"; thus you have found what is probably the most comprehensive index on the Internet dealing with that particular topic.

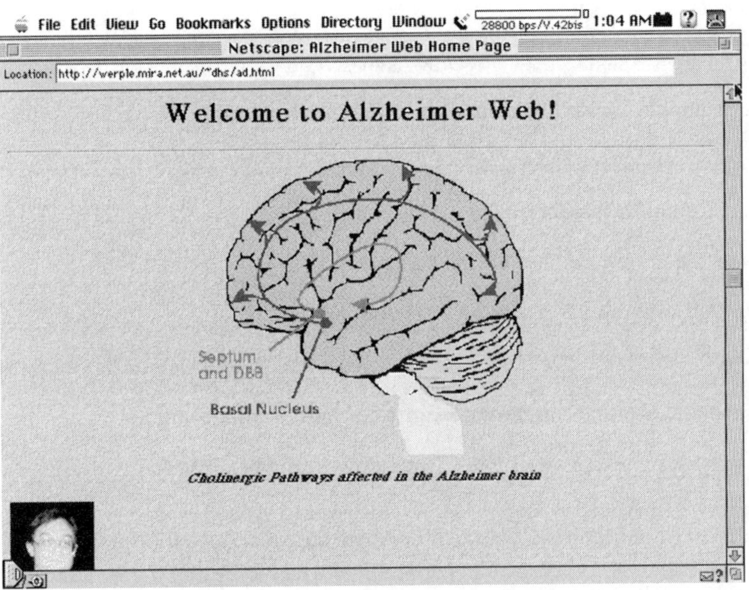

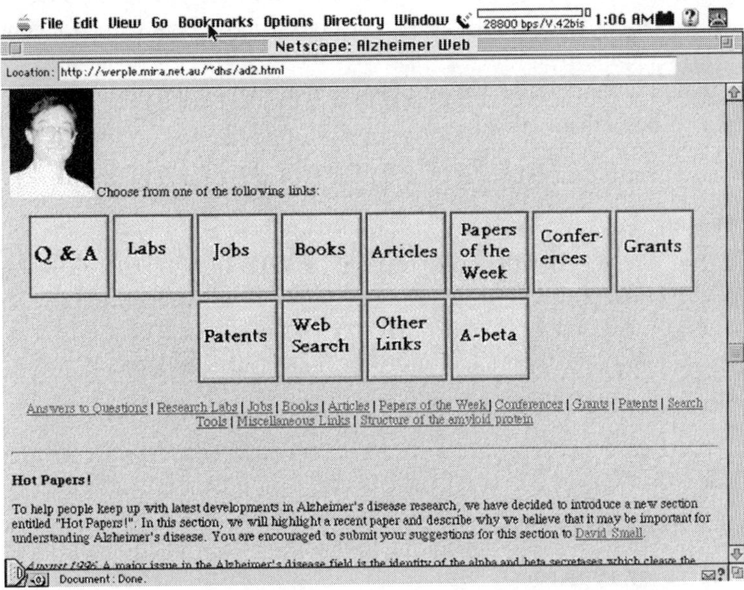

Given that there are so many possible indices, it can take some time to locate them, but once you do, they are often the most useful sources of information about the industry or organization that you are looking into.

Geographic/Regional Indices

Primary Geographic Indices

City.Net (**http://www.city.net**)

Geosurfer (**http://www.infohiway.com/way/geo/geo.html**)

Virtual Tourist (**http://www.vtourist.com**)

Examples of Regional Indices in Canada

Yahoo! Canada (**http://www.yahoo.ca**)

Maple Square (**http://www.canadas.net/maple-square**)

Nova Scotia Web Links (**http://mfusion.com/kellock/nslinks**)

British Columbia World Wide Web Servers/Home Pages (**http://freenet.victoria.bc.ca/bcw3list.html**)

Manitoba Internet Resources: (**http://www.kwanza.com/alice/manitoba.html**)

New Brunswick Internet Exchange - NEWBIE (**http://www.discribe.ca/newbie**)

Geographic/regional indices focus on providing information about various places in the world and can be used to locate Internet resources in particular geographic areas of the world. Many geographic indices are becoming affiliated with some of the larger category indices and search engines. City.Net and the Virtual Tourist (**http://www.vtourist.com/**) are perhaps the best known of the former category. Both offer an excellent way to locate information about particular countries, cities, towns, or other geographic locations.

Regional indices attempt to do what the large search engines do, but on a national, provincial or state, or local basis; that is, they help you discover Web sites in various geographic locations. For example, you can find indices that have the same objective as Yahoo!, but only for a specific country, state or province, city or town. In addition, you will find that Yahoo! itself is regionalizing through country initiatives (such as Yahoo! Canada, Yahoo! Japan, and Yahoo! San Francisco). In Canada there are many such emerging directories; often you can find local ones at the site of an Internet service provider in a particular city or town.

Indices of Indices

Primary Indices of Indices

Search.com (**http://www.search.com**)

All in One (**http://albany.net/allinone**)

The result of having so many different search systems leads to the ultimate absurdity: Web sites that help you find the Web sites that you use to locate Web sites!

All-in-One Search Pages

Primary All-in-One Indices

SavvySearch (**http:// guaraldi.cs.colostate.edu:2000/**)

MetaCrawler (**http://metacrawler.cs.washington.edu:8080/**)

Internet Sleuth (**http://www.isleuth.com/**)

You can also find sites that let you run multiple searches at one time on different search engines. While they can be used to do some interesting searching, you might find such tools to be rather clumsy and that it may be easier to use specific search engines directly.

Search Engine Basics

You must learn the basics of searching on-line before you start to search. We have reached this conclusion as a result of our experience with Internet users; we are always amazed when we watch people use the Internet — we ask them if they have used the help screens on a search system, only to be told no. And then they complain when they cannot find anything on-line! Good gosh! What do you expect? Learn to swim before you dive in. It is generally a good thing to do.

Basic Features of Many Search Systems

If you want to get really good at searching, you should take the time to go beyond the help screens at each search engine and learn the basics of on-line searching. This involves learning how to use "query operators," which define what your search will return. You'll need to understand the following concepts:

1. Boolean searching: the ability to include/exclude certain terms in your search. Some search engines use words such as "AND," "OR," and "NOT" while others use "+" and "-" signs; for example, Vancouver AND ocean vs Vancouver AND NOT ocean or Vancouver + ocean vs Vancouver - ocean.

2. Proximity searching: the ability to indicate that you want certain words to appear close to each other in a document, for example, Vancouver NEAR ocean.

3. Wildcard searching: the ability to include variations in the spelling of a word or all forms of a word. For example, colo*r finds both colour and color, and jump* finds jump, jumps, jumped, jumping, etc.

4. Phrases: the ability to treat a series of words as a phrase. This is usually indicated by double quotation marks, for example, "alice in wonderland" vs alice in wonderland.

Boolean Logic

When it comes to searching the Internet, you must learn to "think Boolean." You may have been exposed to the term "Boolean" in high school; it is a form of math that involves ways of examining the relationships between different bits of information.

Many search engines on the Web allow you to use Boolean logic to specify the relationships that exist between the words on a particular Web page, whether those words should coexist or not.

Boolean logic allows you to use a "query operator" in your search phrase, which helps to tell the search system what you are looking for. There are three key Boolean logic operators that are supported on many Internet search systems:

> OR means find this word or that word;
>
> AND means find this word *and* that word;
>
> NOT means find this word but *not* that word.

In effect, you use these concepts to specify whether certain words or phrases should be excluded or included in your search.

The best way to understand Boolean logic is with an example. Say you are looking for articles about bay windows because you are renovating. You might go into a search engine and type in "bay windows," and because of the way the particular system works, you might end up with thousands of articles about Microsoft Windows. What you need to do is tell the search system that you want any articles about *bay windows*, but you specifically want to exclude any about *Microsoft Windows.* This is where Boolean logic comes in: you can enter a search phrase that basically says "give me any articles that mention bay windows, but don't give me any that mention Microsoft Windows." You might enter this into AltaVista, for example, using the following search phrase, which contains the Boolean logic you want to use:

> "bay windows" and not "Microsoft windows"

In effect, you can use the AND, OR, and NOT operators to streamline your search. The beauty of it is that in many search engines you can usually mix and match these operators to increase the sophistication of your search. For example, conceptually you are thinking:

> "bay AND windows" to get articles about bay windows;
>
> "bay AND windows NOT Microsoft" to get articles about bay windows but excluding those that mention the word "Microsoft."

An important thing to keep in mind is that these Boolean operators will often work differently depending upon the particular search system you are using. Some search engines automatically default to using AND in a search. For example, type in "bay windows," and the search engine might interpret that automatically as "bay and windows." Others will not; so you need to understand how the individual search engines handle Boolean logic.

Not only that, but different search engines will use different symbols or words for the basic Boolean terms. For example, many search engines will use plus and minus signs (+ and -) in place of AND and NOT. Some search engines do not even support basic Boolean searching; for example, at the time we wrote this chapter Lycos did not support Boolean searching. Hence you should study the help screens of each particular search engine to understand if and how the system lets you take advantage of Boolean logic.

Proximity Operators

Sometimes you will need to be specific in terms of how close certain words should be in a Web site. For example, say you go into a search system that does not automatically deal with "proximity," how close together the words are. You type in "bay windows" as your search. The search engine returns a document where the first sentence is "The sun beat down on the boats in the bay..." and the last sentence reads "...and everyone closed their windows." You get kind of a useless document, don't you?

What you want to tell the search engine is this: I want only those documents in which the word "bay" appears right next to the word "windows." Forget everything else. If the search engine does not already address such proximity (and some do), then you must specify the proximity in the search.

Some search engines do allow you to specify proximity. If you do a "power search" in OpenText (http://www.opentext.com), for example, you can specify that one word or phrase must be "near" another word or phrase.

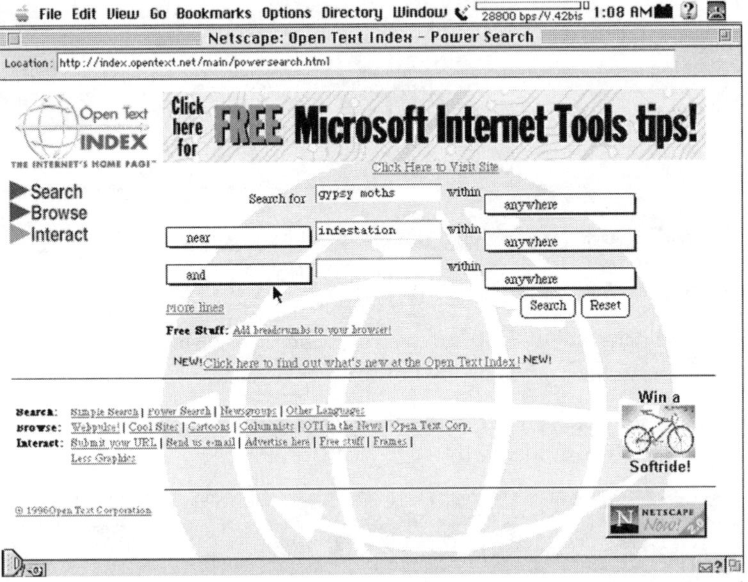

Wildcards

The wildcards feature allows you to specify that your search should cover several similar phrases.

For example, you may want to look for any sites that contain the words "manufacture," "manufacturers," or "manufacturing." If the search engine supports the wildcards feature, you can look for all three words by indicating a special character at the end of the basic word; "manufactur*" would return all three words above if * were the permitted wildcard symbol.

The Impact of Relevance Ranking

Many of the search engines on the Internet use relevance ranking to return your search results. AltaVista (http://www.altavista.digital.com), for example, will list the search results in order of the likelihood that they meet your search criteria, that is, the "relevance" of the search to your request. You should read the help screen with each particular search engine to understand how it uses relevance ranking.

The first item on our AltaVista search was a document entitled "Identification, Life-History, Damage, and Approaches to Controlling the Gypsy," located on a computer at Virginia Polytechnic Institute and State University.

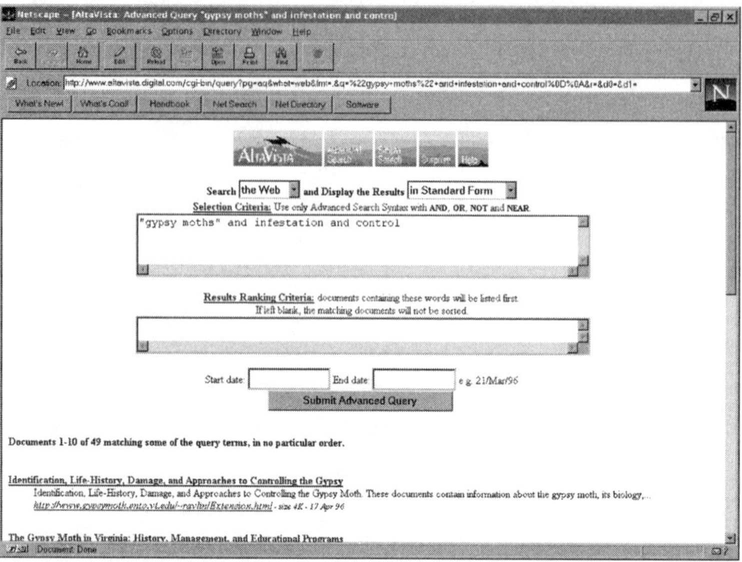

It is interesting to note that

- the second item on our AltaVista search ("The Gypsy Moth in Virginia") did not even appear in the top ten of any of the other sites;
- the only other search engine where this page actually showed up (and at the top of the list at that!) was OpenText.

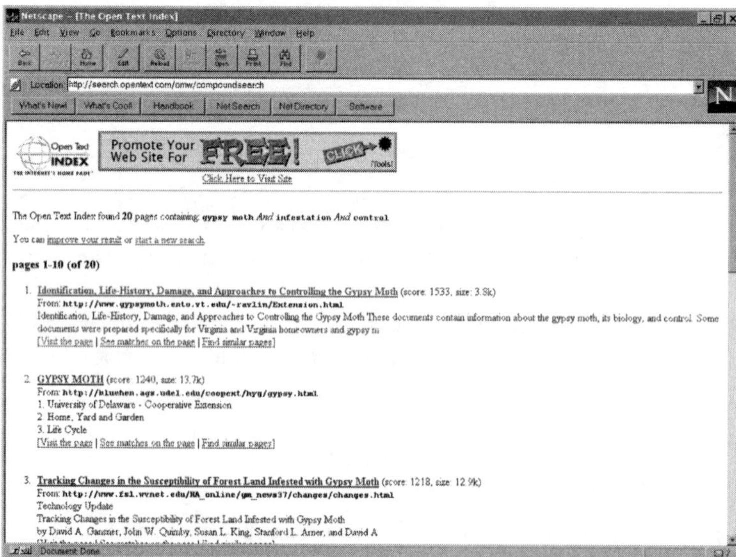

- the fourth item in our AltaVista search ("Aesthetic and Economic Impacts of the Gypsy Moth in Residential Areas") showed up as the top search item at Lycos;

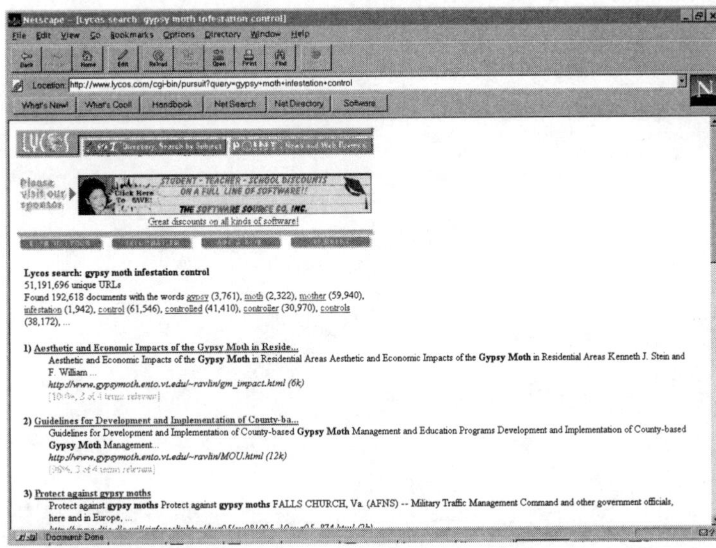

- WebCrawler returned only three items from the search;

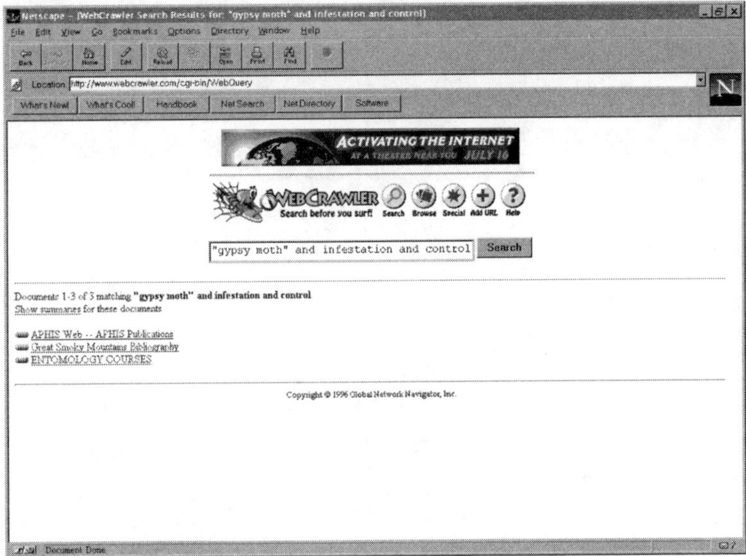

- none of the items that appeared in the first ten search items on HotBot appeared at any of the other search sites, as you can see here;

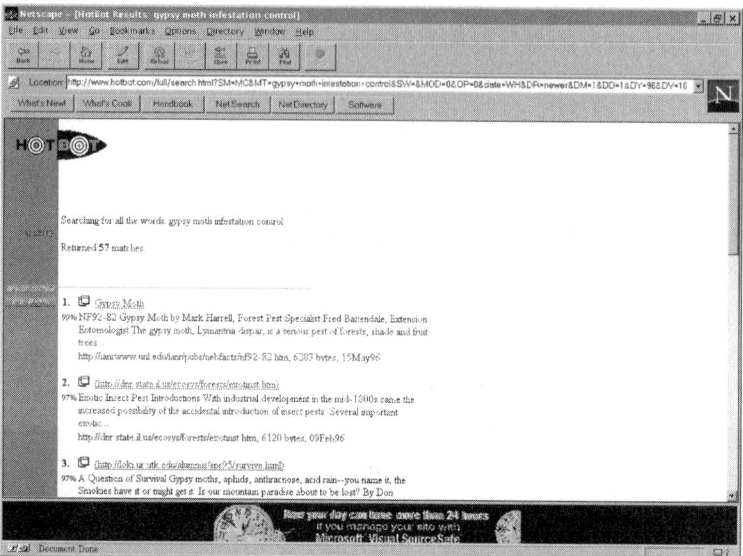

- the Magellan site returned the greatest number of irrelevant searches in the first ten items, including items on "remote sensing of floods" and "indoor air pollution."

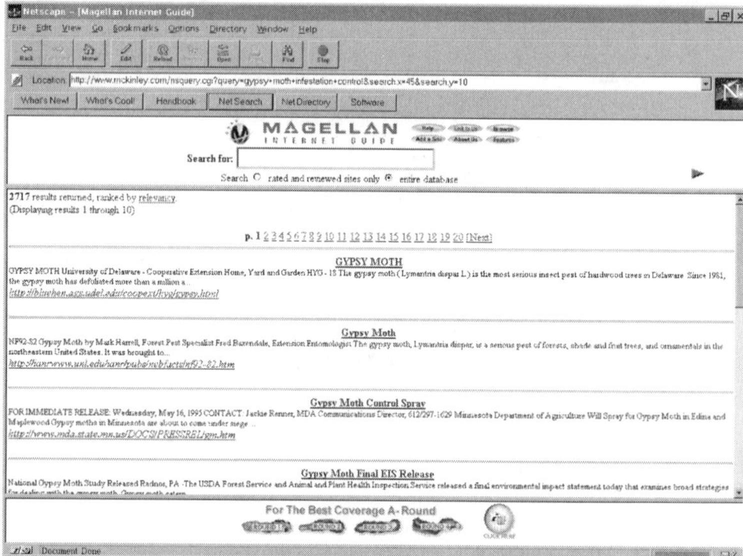

All this is not meant to imply that certain of these search engines are not any good; each has its own strengths and weaknesses. The reason we did this exercise was to demonstrate that a simple search using many of the different search systems will often return completely different results. The reason is that each system uses a different method to "rank" the "relevancy" of the items returned by the search. Hence you should always consider using different search systems when undertaking research, recognizing that each will rank the same set of documents differently.

On-line Sites With Information About Research

Finally, there are some useful sites on-line that provide further guidance about searching:

- "The CyberSkeptic's Guide to Internet Research" (**http://www.bibliodata.com**). Although a print publication, you can read a sample copy on-line. Useful for those who really want to sharpen their search skills.
- "Developing An Effective Search Strategy (Or How to Find Information on the Internet Without Suffering Eye-Strain)" (**http://services.canberra.edu.au/uc/disab/RICK-GUIDE/Design_Search_Index.html**).
- "Investigative Journalism on the Internet" (**http://www.vir.com/~sher/julian.htm**), although designed for journalists, provides an excellent introduction to the concepts of searching on the Internet. It is useful, since it organizes itself into categories: "How can I find people in chat groups?" "How can I find the experts?" and "How can I find the best reference materials and databases?"
- You can locate reviews and comparisons of different search engines by visiting Yahoo! Look in the category "Computers and Internet:Internet:World Wide Web:Searching the Web:Comparing Search Engines" (**http://www.yahoo.com/Computers_and_Internet/Internet/World_Wide_Web/Searching_the_Web/Comparing_Search_Engines/**).
- You can find a good listing of the basic features of various search engines on-line at **http://www.unn.ac.uk/features.htm**.

The key point in all these endeavors is that if you are serious about using the Internet as a research tool, then you have to invest the time to learn how to research on-line. Once again, hold your breath; it is a bit of an overwhelming world out there.

Thinking skills do not disappear because of the Internet. Indeed, with the explosion of information that is occurring on the network, this skill has become even more important. You have to keep a sense of professional skepticism in place in order to judge the validity of the documents you retrieve. You have to think about and analyze what you find. You have to compare one viewpoint against another in order to draw a conclusion. You have to learn to interpret the data that you find and not treat it as some type of final answer. It is easy to find information on the Internet. It is difficult to turn that information into knowledge.

CHAPTER 10

Personalized News Services

Only about 10 percent of the total information collected every day in the newspaper's newsroom and features desk (all of which is held on-line, i.e., in continuous direct communication with a computer) is actually used in the paper, and yet, according to most surveys, the reader only reads 10 percent of what has gone into the paper. It seems, therefore, that the whole agony of distribution is undergone in order to feed each reader just one percent of the material that has been so expensively collected.

Anthony Smith, *Goodbye Gutenberg: The Newspaper Revolution of the 1980s* (Oxford University Press, New York, 1980)

The PointCast Network has become the talk of the Net.

Newsweek, March 18, 1996

It has long been a dream of many people to have a world in which we could access only the news that we want. At the Media Lab at the Massachusetts Institute of Technology (MIT) in the 1980s, researchers worked on developing a "custom newspaper," which focused only on news articles of relevance to a particular person. Computers would go out and access news wires, press releases, and other information sources and monitor television and radio. Any articles or news items that met the specific interests of a particular person would be packaged into a custom, daily "newspaper," designed only for that person.

MIT called this newspaper, and the concept, *The Daily Me.* They saw that we would become a world of 500 million different newspapers, each one focused on just those topics that one individual wanted. And as Nicholas Negroponte, the Executive Director of the Lab, commented in the 1987 book about the research (*The Media Lab — Inventing the Future At M.I.T.*, by Stewart Brand), "There would be only one copy of *The Daily Me*, but it would have a devoted readership."

Customized News Services

The dream of leading-edge visionaries in the 1980s is already becoming a reality on the Internet today. Throughout the network we are seeing the emergence of a number of "personalized news information services," all of which purport to provide you with a customized news reference source that contains only those topics of interest to you. It is a relatively new field; most of the sites and/or software we examine in this chapter first emerged in late 1995. But once they arrived, they caught the interest of the business press and caught the imagination of many a computer genius and business entrepreneur. PointCast, in particular, has been praised by many as the tool that will define the Internet in the future, although many have dismissed it as a "cute piece of software," with which users will soon tire or become bored.

Revolutionary or boring? Who knows? One undeniable fact is that the field of customized, personalized news services on the Internet is bound to be a fascinating and fast-developing one.

News On-line

Keep in mind that there is no shortage of news information on the Internet. Browse through any of the categories that follow, and it is easy to discover all kinds of local, national, and international news.

Canadian Newspapers

News organizations ranging from the *Toronto Star* to the *Globe and Mail* to the *Vancouver Province* to the *Winnipeg Free Press* have Web sites. Most make available daily news, and some permit access to news archives of selected past news articles.

One of the best places to go for a comprehensive list of newspapers on the Internet is the Editor and Publisher Interactive home page (**http:// www.mediainfo.com**). There you will find over 1,000 entries organized by continent as well as statistics on on-line newspapers. There is a good list of Canadian newspapers on the Internet, organized by province.

Another good spot for a listing of Canadian newspapers on-line is "Julian Sher's Investigative Journalism on the Internet" site. In it you can find a listing of newspapers, magazines, and television and radio stations on-line. Sher is a producer with the CBC show *The Fifth Estate*, and he works hard to keep his Web site up-to-date (**http://www.vir.com./~sher/paperstv.htm**).

The American Journalism Review Newslink (**http://www.newslink.org**) also provides a detailed listing of on-line newspapers and magazines on the Internet.

PERSONALIZED NEWS SERVICES

1. Throughout the Internet, we are seeing the emergence of many tools and programs that allow you to obtain only the news information relevant to you.
2. There is no shortage of news information online — everything from newspapers to press releases and television and radio broadcasts.
3. Computer software or Web sites such as Crayon, Hunter, Mercury Mail, Newspage, Personal Excite, PointCast, InfoSage, Infoseek Personal, and Canadian Corporate News deliver to you only that news information that you are interested in, or track news sites that are relevant to you.
4. Regardless of the predictions that news on the Internet will render other media irrelevant, it is likely that we will still be reading newspapers and magazines, watching TV and listening to radio in the future. The Internet enhances other media — it won't replace them.

Canadian Press Release Services

Canadian press release services such as Canada Newswire (**http://www.newswire.ca**) and Canadian Corporate News (**http://www.cdn-news.com**) have established sites in which they make available daily news releases; these are worth checking if you want to know about a specific company or topic. Canadian Corporate News also offers a personalized news release service. We will take a look at it later in this chapter.

Television and Radio Stations

Television and radio stations have become involved with the Internet, and many are providing regularly updated news, some in audio and video format. Most notably, the CBC Newsworld group makes available video on their Web site as well as updated news stories (**http://www.newsworld.cbc.ca**). CNN also has an excellent Web site, along with searchable archives of their news reports (**http://www.cnn.com**).

An increasing number of radio stations broadcast live through the Internet; CFRA Radio in Ottawa is but one example (**http://www.cfra.com**). Others make available news reports that can be downloaded at any time. For example, you can pick up the World At Six News Report from the CBC Radio Web site at any time and listen to it with RealAudio (**http://www.radio.cbc.ca**). RealAudio is discussed in Chapter 7.

TV Net (**http://www.tvnet.com**) provides a good list of television stations with Internet sites. For a list of radio stations on the Web in Canada and around the world, visit the MIT List of Radio Stations on the Internet (**http://wmbr.mit.edu/stations/list.html**), or take a look at Web Times Canada (**http://www.canadas.net/WebTimes/Canada/**).

Personal News Sites and Software

In this chapter we take a look at some of the more innovative personal news services available on the Internet. They are:

- Crayon;
- Hunter;
- Mercury Mail;
- NewsPage Direct;
- Personal Excite;
- PointCast;
- infoSage;
- Infoseek Personal;
- Canadian Corporate News.

We encourage you to try some of these services and watch for new ones by looking at the Yahoo! Personalized News category (**http://www.yahoo.com/News/Personalized_News/**). Before we begin, let's look at some of the ways in which some personalized news services differ from others. Use this information to make comparisons between the different services.

Comparing Different Custom News Services

1. Cost. Many news-clipping services are available for free, while others charge a yearly or monthly fee. Some fee-based services offer only one package, while others may provide a variety of different pricing options to accommodate customers with different needs. Commercial services generally offer more flexibility and customization than free ones. If a fee is charged, find out what is included for that price and what services are extra.

2. Method of delivery. News can be delivered to you by electronic mail or on the World Wide Web. Some services offer both of these options, while others offer only one delivery method. You should think about which delivery method you prefer. If you choose to receive news stories by e-mail and if you are tracking a very popular subject such as politics, be prepared to receive a lot information. If you are not accustomed to dealing with large volumes of information, a regular stream of e-mail messages can easily overwhelm you. In such cases e-mail may not be the best alternative. However, if you are interested in receiving news as it happens, an e-mail-based service would notify you automatically, whereas with a Web-based service you have to regularly log in to access new stories. A third method of delivery is to use a proprietary software package, which you must obtain from the company supplying the news service. While e-mail and the Web are the two most common methods, at least one company (PointCast) uses its own software to deliver customized news. You can expect to see more news services use this approach in the future.

3. Sources of news. Personalized news services differ both in terms of the variety of sources they monitor and the number of sources they receive. The most popular sources of news are the major news wire services such as Associated Press, UPI, Reuters, Business Wire, and PR Newswire. Certain sources may be more important to you, depending upon the types of topics you want to follow.

4. Archives. Some news services offer archives of old news stories to their customers. Here are some questions to ask: Are archives available? Can they be searched? Is there a fee for this service? How much does it cost to retrieve an article from the archives?

5. Frequency of news delivery. Determine how frequently your news is delivered to you. For example, is it delivered to you once a day, several times a day, or as it happens?

6. Access to full text. Does the news service deliver the full text of articles to you or only the headlines? If you only see part of the article, can you access the full-text version, and how much does it cost?

7. Value-added services. Some news services allow you to receive other information in addition to news stories, such as stock quotes, comics, horoscopes, and birthday reminders. Often these "extras" are available at no charge.

8. Depth of customization. Find out to what extent you can customize the delivery of your news stories. For example, some news services impose a maximum on the number of topics you can track and/or restrict you to monitoring topics that they have predefined. Other services provide much greater flexibility and allow you to select an unlimited number of topics to follow. Also find out how easy it is for you to change your personal profile should you decide at some point in the future to modify the types of subjects you are monitoring.

We have a few other general comments about personalized news services:

- The biggest complaint is that most of these services are based in the United States. Keep in mind that to many Americans, Canada does not exist; hence most of the news sources, weather, stock quotes, and other information is either American or "international" in scope. It is so bad that every site will ask you for a state and zip code, but few will be enlightened enough to request your province and postal code.
- In many cases you have to provide personal information in order to subscribe to some of these news-clipping services. In some cases this includes personal information, such as your name, address, profession, and sometimes even your income range. You are expected to trust these organizations not to divulge such information. One must wonder if, over time, such trust will become unwarranted.
- Some services will require you to obtain a user ID and password in order to sign in. There are two problems here. First, if you have a popular name, you will probably find your choice of username is already gone. (There seem to be, e.g., many people out there who have already taken the name jcarroll on most of these services.) Second, with many sites on the Internet now requesting user sign-ons, you will soon find yourself having to remember far too many user IDs and passwords. ("Let's see — on this system, am I jcarroll, or jimcarroll, or carrolljim, or j-carroll?"). The bottom line is this: if you are assigned a username and password, then make sure you write it down and store it in a safe place. You will need this information in order to gain access to the service and modify your profile settings.
- Many of these news-clipping services use the same information sources: certain news wires and press release wires. There are two problems with this. First, you might quickly become bored with the lack of in-depth content that you get from news wire sources. But perhaps more importantly, it may take a while to discover that you can only read so many press releases before realizing that such information is not really news — it just happens to be more grandiose claims made by more organizations about how great they are. It is not news; it is pulp fiction of such poor quality that you will gladly go back to your newspaper for some real content.
- Finally, the level of filtering has a long way to go. You might choose "communications" as an industry category that you want to track. You will still get a lot of news, and you will have to wade your way through much of it to find only those stories of interest to you. The level of specialization of news categories in many of the services we examined certainly has a long way to go. And certainly one of the drawbacks of some personalized news services is that they rely on computer intelligence to decide what is and what is not relevant to the customer. Here is a good example: one of the authors of this book uses a personalized news service to keep up-to-date on new releases of Internet browser software. One of the stories he received from the service had the following title: "Largest mosaic ever found in Israel survives construction equipment." The story was about an archaeological excavation and had nothing to do

with Internet browsers, but clearly the news-clipping service tagged it because it contained the word "mosaic," which is the brand name of a type of Internet browser. The article was referring to a different type of "mosaic," a type of decoration, but the news-clipping service was not intelligent enough to know the difference. It is in this area that personalized news services will definitely need to improve. In the meantime, they will cause you frustration as you attempt to use them.

The news services that we review in this chapter may do two things:

- They may simply create a custom Web page of specific news sites that interest you, not filter specific news stories.
- They may filter specific news articles based on categories and keywords and build a custom Web page containing those articles, or e-mail the articles to you.

Let's take a look at some of the more innovative personal news systems available on the Internet.

Crayon

The name of this product, Crayon, is an acronym created from the phrase CReAte Your Own Newspaper. Crayon takes an innovative approach to providing a personalized new service, since what it does is create for you a customized Web page that includes only the specific news Web sites that interest you.

You can load this customized Web page at any time and quickly travel to your customized news selections.

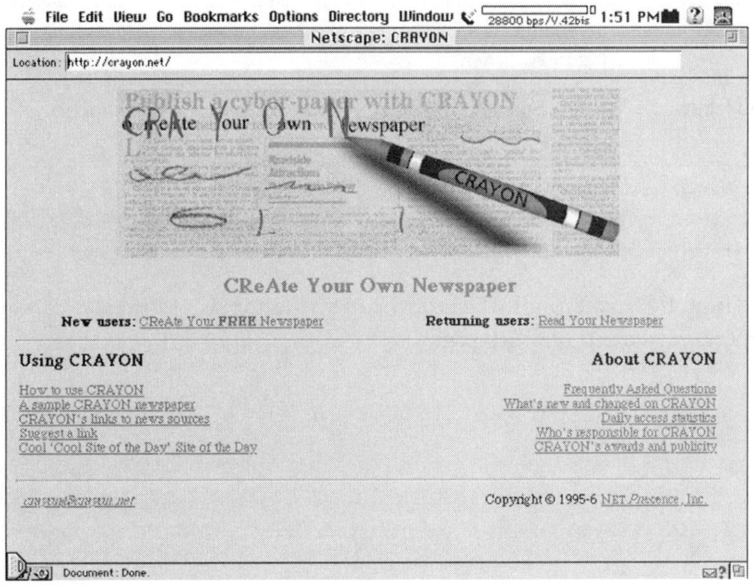

To start, you just click on "CReAte Your Own Newspaper." You are first given the opportunity to customize the title of your personalized news page:

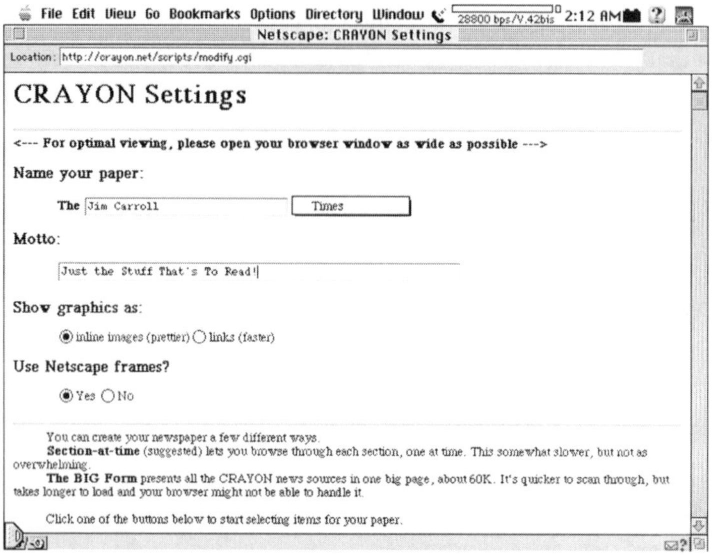

You are presented with a massive list of news-related Web sites, organized by the following categories:

U.S. News	Regional and Local News	World News	Politics as Usual
Editorial and Opinion	Weather Conditions and Forecasts	Business Report	Information Technology Report
Health and Fitness Roundup	Arts and Entertainment	Sports Day	Snippets Corner
The Funny Pages	The Tabloid Pages	New and Cool Web Sites	

You choose from these categories which of the many hundreds of different news sources you want to appear on your custom Web page:

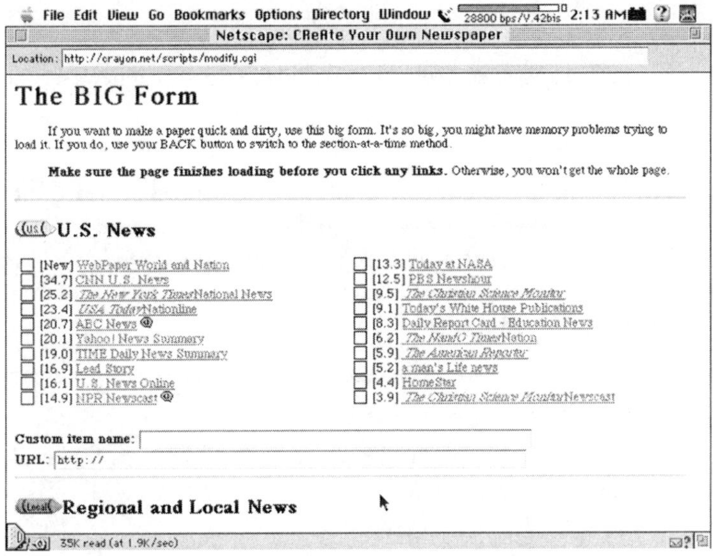

Once you do that, and indicate the order in which you would like your stories to appear, Crayon creates your custom news page:

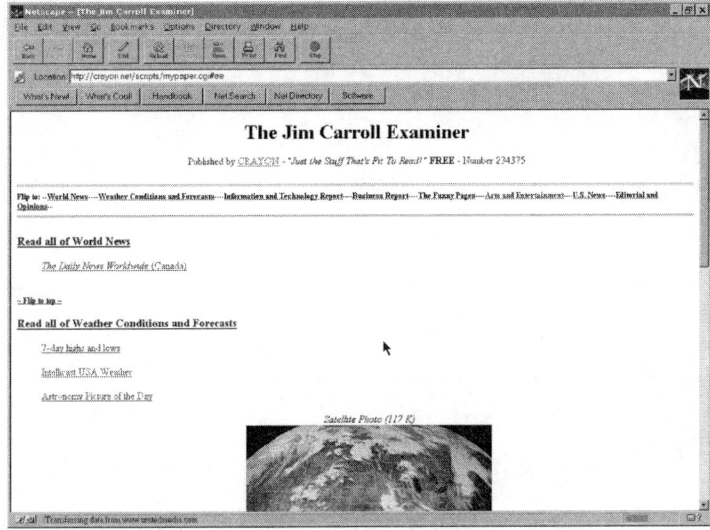

What Crayon does is create a Web page that has links to the Web sites of the news items that interest you; it also incorporates directly some of the images that you want to see daily, such as the daily satellite image (above) and your favorite daily comics. You can save this custom Web page to your own hard disk, making it easy to retrieve your "custom newspaper" whenever you want it. Crayon provides you with instructions on their Web site on how to save your "custom newspaper" to your hard disk and how to bookmark it so that you can easily call it up in the future. Although not as sophisticated as some of the other custom news services found throughout the Internet, Crayon does provide a useful service and a very innovative approach to the concept of custom news. You can visit the Crayon World Wide Web site at **http://www.crayon.net**.

Hunter

Hunter, affectionately called a "golden news retriever," is a free personal news service from the *Los Angeles Times.* Compared to Crayon, it is a true news filter in that it provides specific news stories, not just a custom listing of news Web sites. Hunter is important for several reasons:

- Although it is from Los Angeles, many of the news sources provided through Hunter by the *Los Angeles Times* are not specific to the Los Angeles area; in fact, there is a lot of international news available. The global nature of the Internet means that if you are interested in international news, you can just as easily pick it up from a U.S. custom news source as you could from a Canadian source.
- It is a good example of where we believe many Canadian newspapers will head over time, in terms of their own custom news.
- You do not have to be a resident of Los Angeles to use Hunter. It is available for use by Internet users worldwide.

The first thing you do after registering with Hunter is set up the list of topics that interest you. There is a list of 40 or so predefined news topics:

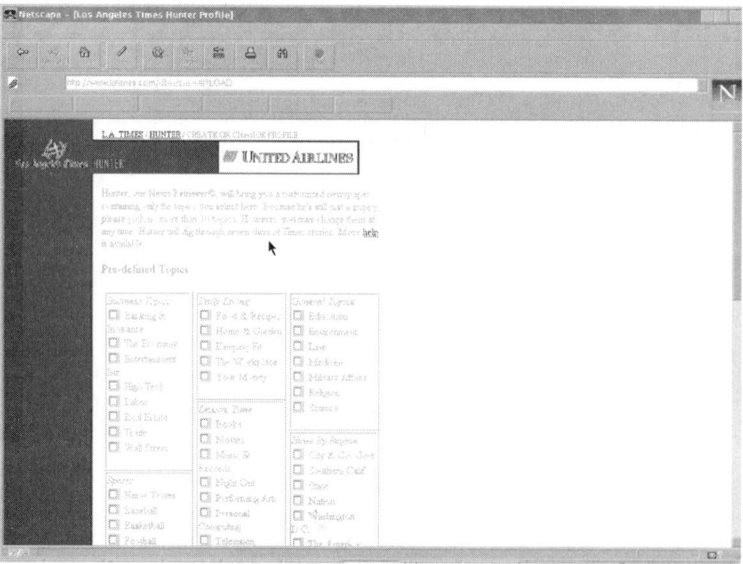

Not satisfied with their topic list? No problem. Hunter is one of the few services that allow you to specify personal news topics based on keywords. You could, for example, use the screen below to specify that you are interested only in those news stories in which Dread Zeppelin is featured in a reunion concert concurrent with the Beatles, by keying in "Dread Zeppelin and Beatles":

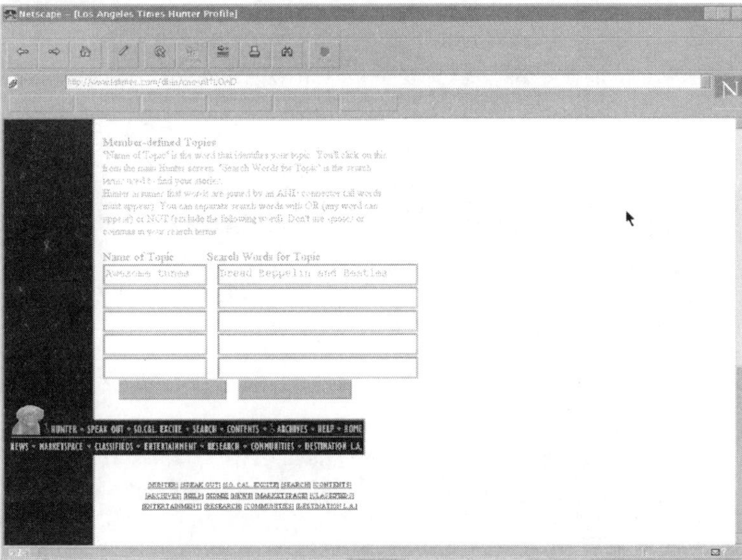

Once you have set up your profile, you can sign in to Hunter at any time and retrieve your "personal newspaper." Here is how it works: Hunter scans the last 7 days of the *Los Angeles Times* as well as the Associated Press news wire and identifies articles that match your profile. Any articles it finds will be displayed to you each time you log in. That's it!

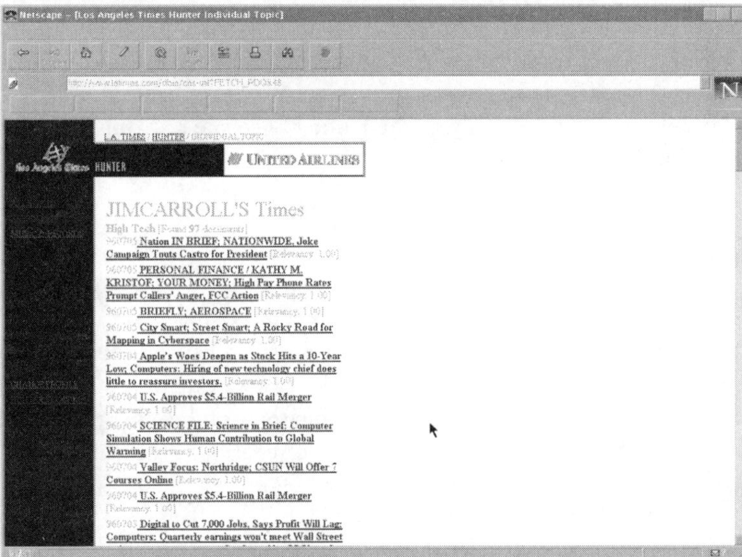

Hunter himself is a lovable little dog; he has his own column in which he writes about his adventures that you can access at the site. Want to send feedback on the service? Send Hunter some e-mail.

In a cute twist, the *Los Angeles Times* manages to sprinkle some advertisement links into Hunter's column. For example, when you click on the "custom handwriting font" link in the letter below, it takes you to a page that tells you about software that lets you create your own font:

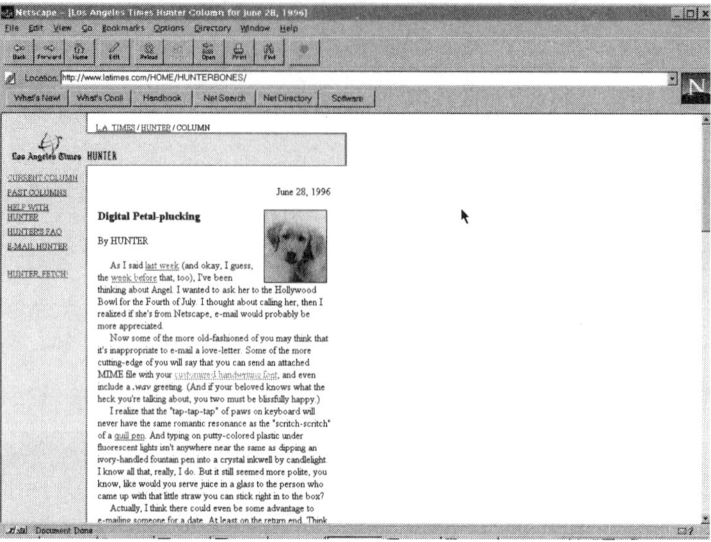

Hunter is a good example of the direction in which we will likely see many newspapers and magazines go in the near future: providing "custom newspapers" that list only the topics or areas of interest to you. Although somewhat limited at this time in terms of categories, Hunter's "keyword profile" feature, based on your own custom search terms, allows you to build a very flexible custom newspaper indeed. You can visit the *Los Angeles Times* Web site at **http://www.latimes.com** or go directly to the Hunter Web site at **http://www.latimes.com/HOME/HUNTER**.

Mercury Mail

Mercury Mail is a personalized news service that sends your personal news stories by e-mail. You set up your search profile on the Mercury Mail Web site, sit back, and receive your customized news on a daily basis in your electronic mailbox. The news categories in Mercury Mail are nowhere near as comprehensive as what are found within some of the other personalized news services (NewsPage, which we examine later, has 2,600 categories). For example, the news topic lists the following:

What is innovative about Mercury Mail is that it will provide, along with basic news services, special information categories such as the following:

- information on ski race events provided by the U.S. Skiing Association;
- custom weather information, provided by the U.S. Weather Channel;
- the ability to set reminders for important dates and anniversaries.

The latter capability is very interesting, since you can in effect use Mercury Mail as a very sophisticated annual reminder system. For example, on this screen we have asked to be notified when a certain birthday occurs:

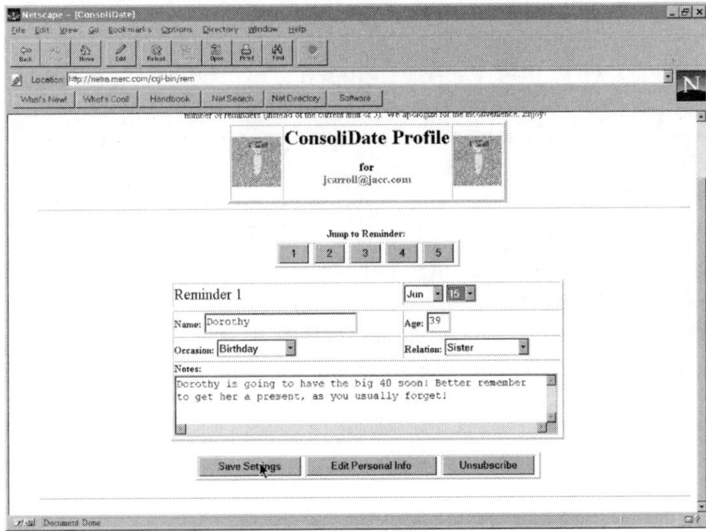

You can set up an unlimited number of reminders, which are sent to you on a specified day every year (we assume until your mailbox becomes defunct). Any of your requested news, weather, sports, or reminder items are then sent to you regularly by e-mail:

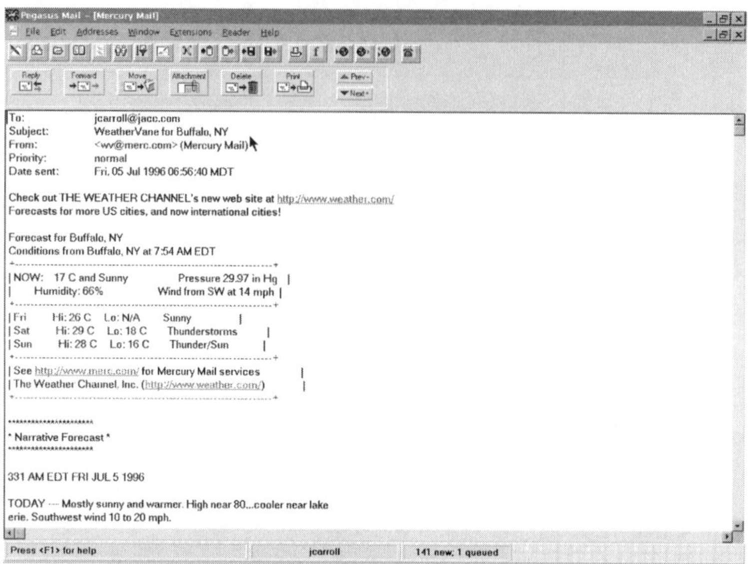

At the time we had a look, Mercury Mail was free. All in all, given the price, it is a great little news-clipping service that, even though it does not have the broad range of news that some other services have, still provides some innovative and useful capabilities. You can visit the Mercury Mail Web site at **http://www.merc.com**.

NewsPage Direct

NewsPage Direct is a service of the popular NewsPage Web site. NewsPage receives news stories from over 600 sources, including news wires, press releases, newspapers, and magazines. One of the benefits is that it organizes these news articles into over 2,600 different topic categories, meaning you can put in place a request for some pretty specific topic categories.

NewsPage itself is a basic Web news service (**http://www.newspage.com**). You can access any of these 2,600 categories through the main NewsPage Web site and scan a news article title, and the first paragraph, for free. Want to read the whole story? There may or may not be an additional charge to see the entire article, depending upon the source.

NewsPage Direct takes the NewsPage content one step further. You define a search profile consisting of 10 topics (from the 2,600 available) that are of interest to you. Setting up a search profile is very straightforward. You first specify to which e-mail ID the news stories should be sent and the broad topic areas that interest you:

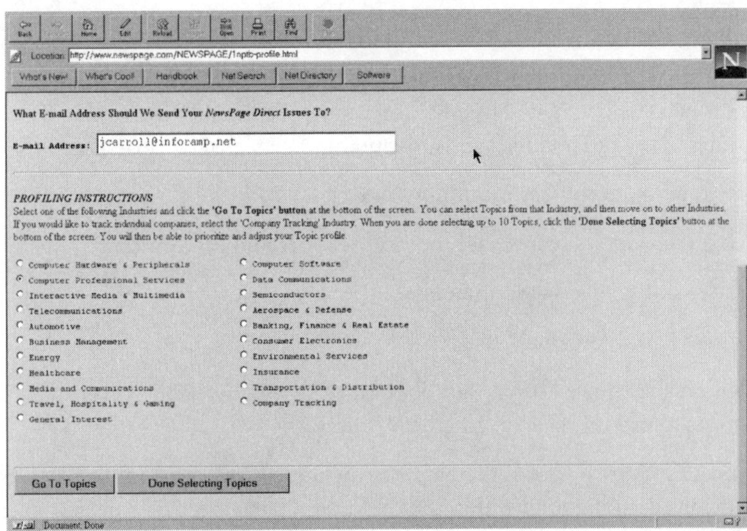

You then select the specific topics within those categories that you want to track. Within seconds, you have your search profile established. You will start receiving your first e-mail message containing articles within those topic areas the next day. From then on, you will get a daily e-mail message that contains the title and lead paragraph of up to 20 stories that appeared in the last 24 hours related to your 10 topics:

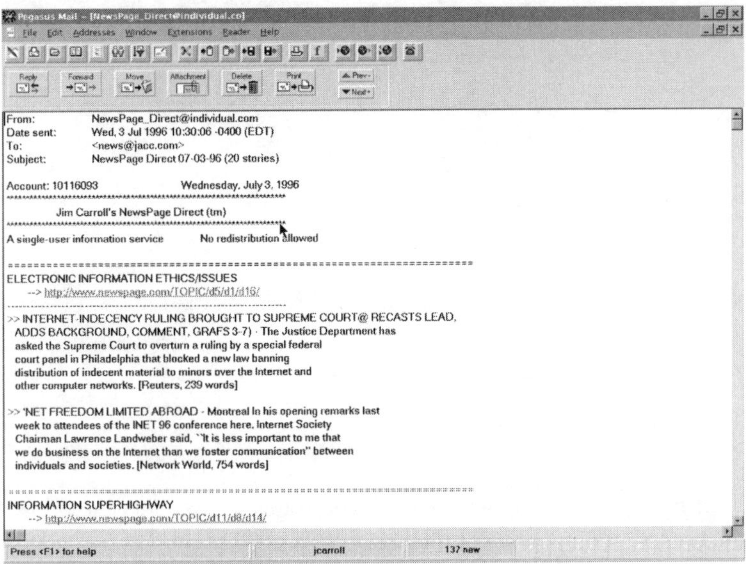

The e-mail message, remember, contains only the title and first paragraph. If you want to get the full article, you must go to the specific category for that article within the main NewsPage Web site. NewsPage Direct is a pay service and costs less than U.S. $10 per month. It is a good, inexpensive alternative to news tracking, but like most other services in this chapter, has a heavy U.S. focus. You can visit the NewsPage World Wide Web site at **http://www.newspage.com**.

Personal Excite

Excite is one of the major on-line search engines that we looked at in Chapter 9. It too has jumped into the personalized news business. You can use Personal Excite to create a custom Web page that features many different elements, including:

- news from major sources including Reuters;
- stock quotes, sports scores, and the weather, cartoons, and columns;
- birthday and anniversary reminders;
- a listing of your favorite Web sites;
- television and movie listings (although these are not available for all areas, Excite promises to extend coverage to North America).

Perhaps the most innovative twist is that you can include on your custom page "saved searches" generated from information found within the Excite search engine. Say you want to check, every day, whether anyone has been discussing the band Dread Zeppelin anywhere within USENET. It is easy to do this with Excite: simply add it to your list of "saved searches." Your custom Web page will then include as "news" any mention of that topic within the Internet:

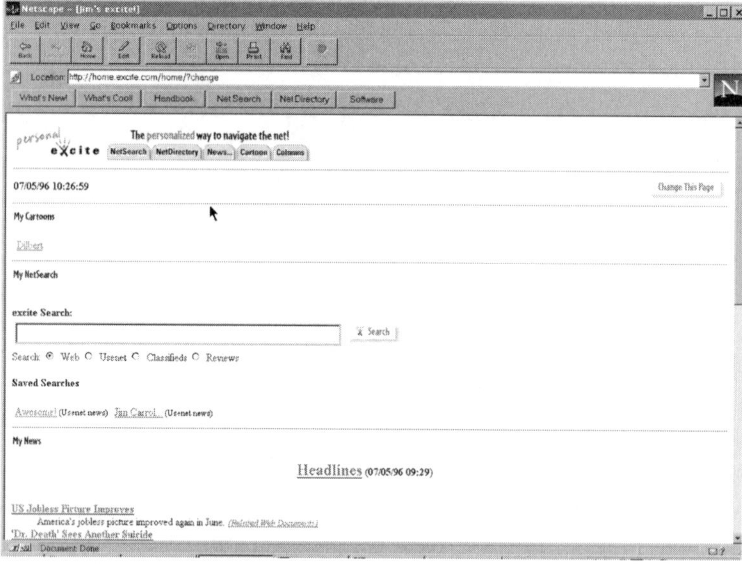

You can easily change the order in which your news page appears and even control its appearance, in terms of the background, type of text used, and other attributes.

Although Excite does have a limited range of actual news information, the fact that it can draw upon the Excite search system for "saved searches" makes it a useful tool. You can visit Excite's World Wide Web site at **http://www.excite.com**.

PointCast Canada

PointCast is probably the most unique service mentioned in this chapter, for several reasons:

- You do not obtain your customized news through your Web browser or through e-mail; instead, you use a customized program designed specifically to retrieve and display PointCast news.
- The PointCast news program will go out and get the news according to a schedule you determine. In other words, it will establish a connection to your ISP, sign on, and retrieve news updates in the middle of the night, if you configure it to do so.
- PointCast combines the news with advertisements and thus seems destined to be one company that solves the overriding dilemma found with the Internet — how to make money.

PointCast has managed to gain a lot of attention throughout the computer and business press as an extremely innovative Internet application. In addition, PointCast has been selected by the *Globe and Mail* to form the foundation for its national custom news service, helping to solve the problem with most systems reviewed in this chapter — the lack of Canadian content.

Once you install the PointCast software (which is available on their Web site at **http://www.pointcast.ca**), the first thing you do is establish the profile of topics you wish to track. There are several categories, including News, Companies, Industries, Sports, Lifestyle, and Weather. Within each of these categories you can select the specific types of news stories or information categories you wish to track. For example, you can specify to track articles from the following industry categories:

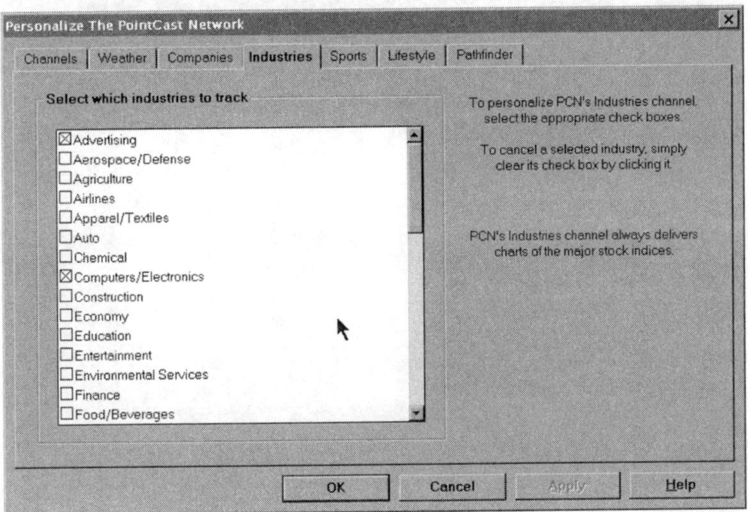

You then specify how often you want PointCast to update your news:

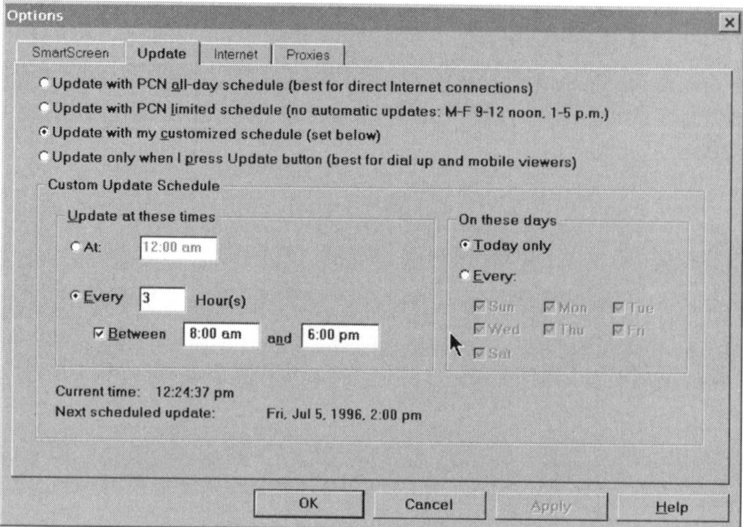

Once you have configured the software, you are in business. Here is where it gets interesting. PointCast is really a screen saver. Leave your computer inactive for a few minutes, and PointCast will take over your computer screen and display various news headlines, news items, and other information that you have requested:

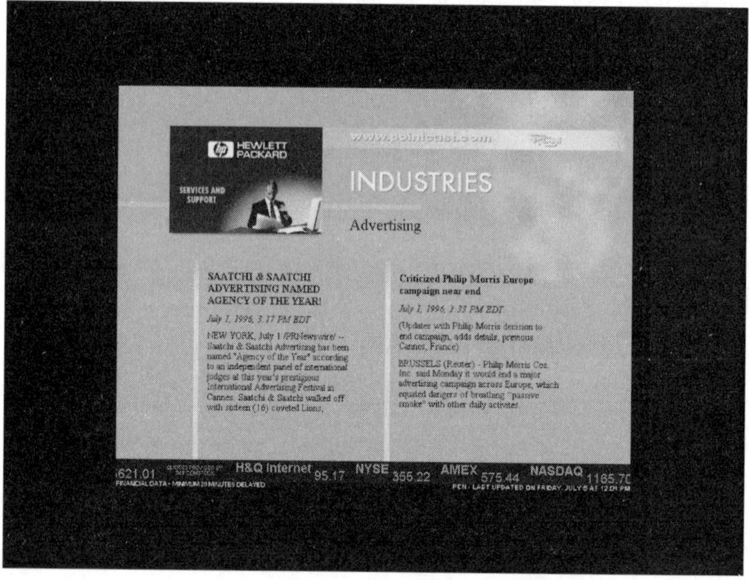

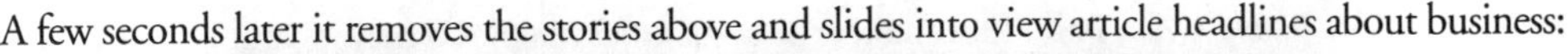

A few seconds later it removes the stories above and slides into view article headlines about business:

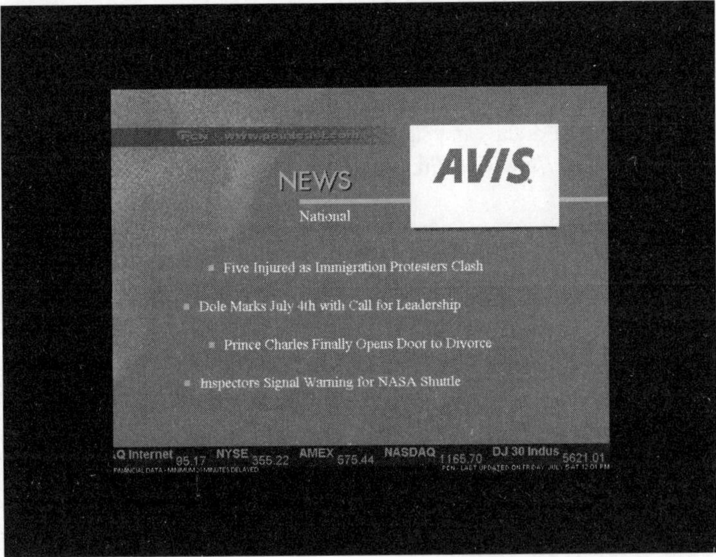

There are several noteworthy points to be made about the way these screens work:

- The text and information on the screen are constantly changing. Within a minute you will be taken through news, business, industry, and other headlines and may see a few full articles appear on-screen. You can click on any headline to read the full article behind that headline at any time.
- The advertisements contained on them move and change on a regular basis and include animation. Double click on any ad, and your Web browser will take you to the Web site of the advertiser.
- A stock ticker continuously runs across the bottom of the screen with market updates.

PointCast does not operate in this screen saver mode only; it also runs as a stand-alone program, browsing your custom news sources by topic at any time:

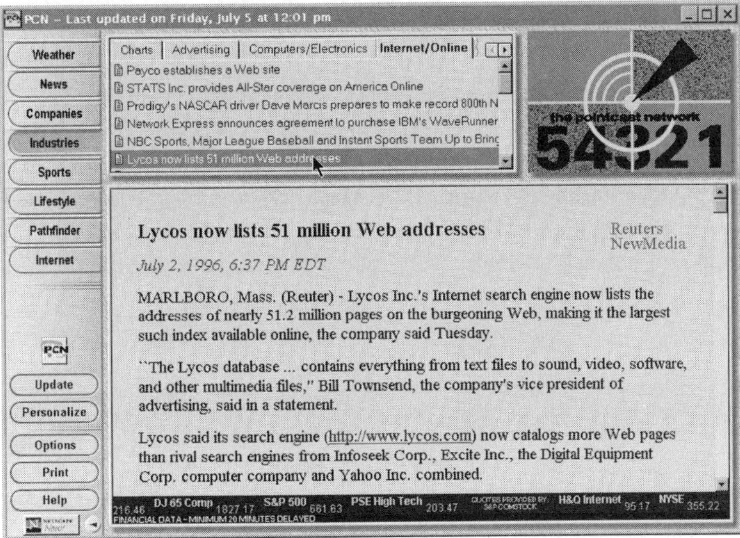

In another innovative twist, PointCast makes the software available so that it can be used for internal corporate information networks.

The most significant thing about PointCast is that it indicates the direction in which the Internet is going: software that does not rely on the World Wide Web, but uses the connection to the Internet to access data and information from computers around the planet. From this perspective PointCast is a world-class and significant piece of software. You can visit the PointCast World Wide Web site at **http://www.pointcast.com** or **http://www.pointcast.ca** (for the Canadian version).

infoSage

infoSage is a commercial news-clipping service run by IBM. Of all the services we have reviewed in this chapter, IBM's infoSage offers the most flexibility in terms of news customization. infoSage is based on a piece of software called a "Profile Editor" that you use to identify the types of stories you want to receive. When you first start the Profile Editor, you will be asked to choose from a variety of options, seen in the screen below:

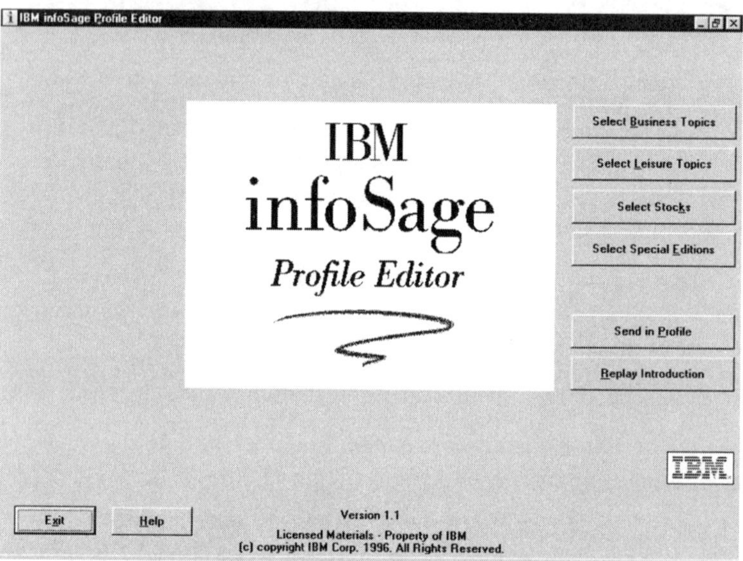

Say that you are interested in business stories; so you click on "Select Business Topics." The screen that appears next allows you to select the business topics that you want infoSage to track on your behalf. The list of main subject categories appears on the left. As you select topics you want to monitor, they appear on the right side of the screen. The topics you can choose from are organized into very broad topics, which then break down into more specific subtopics. infoSage has over 2,000 topics from which to choose, with more being added all the time.

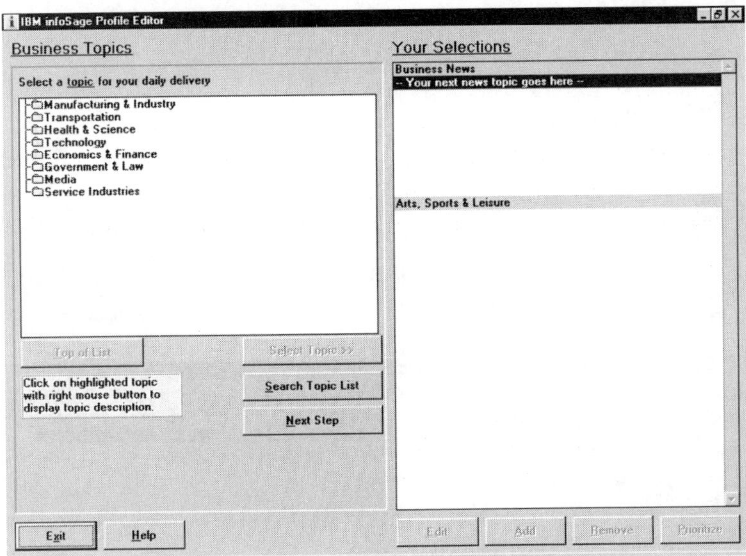

For example, Health and Science breaks down into the following 3 subtopics:

- Biotech;
- Health Care;
- Pharmaceutical Industry.

Health Care, in turn, is divided into the following 5 subcategories:

- Consumer Health;
- Health Care Management;
- Health Care Professionals;
- Health Facilities;
- Health Problems.

Health Problems is then broken down into the following 15 subjects:

- AIDS;
- Alcoholism;
- Allergies;
- Cancer;
- Diabetes;
- Drug Abuse;
- Heart and Cardiovascular Diseases;
- Infertility and Childbirth;

- Learning Disabilities;
- Mental Illness;
- Mental Retardation;
- Parkinson's Disease;
- Rehabilitation;
- STD (Sexually Transmitted Diseases);
- Smoking.

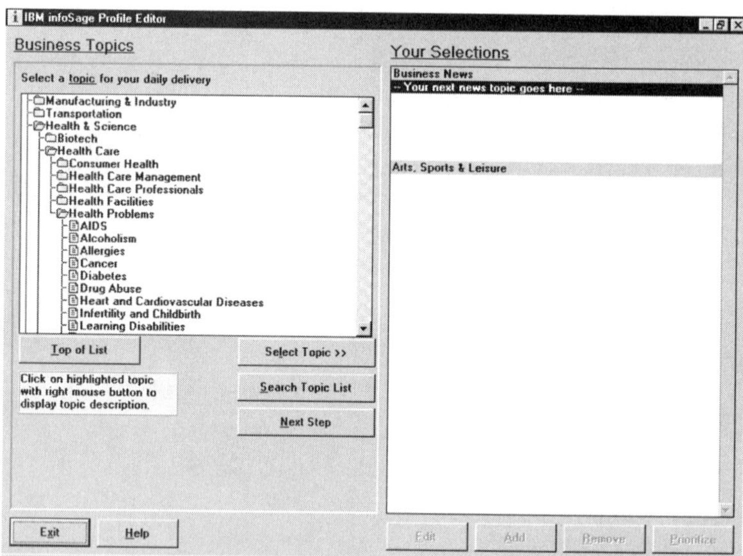

To select a topic, you simply click on it using your mouse, and the topic will appear on the right side of your screen under "Your Selections." In the screen below we have chosen to track "Allergies," "Learning Disabilities," and "Rehabilitation":

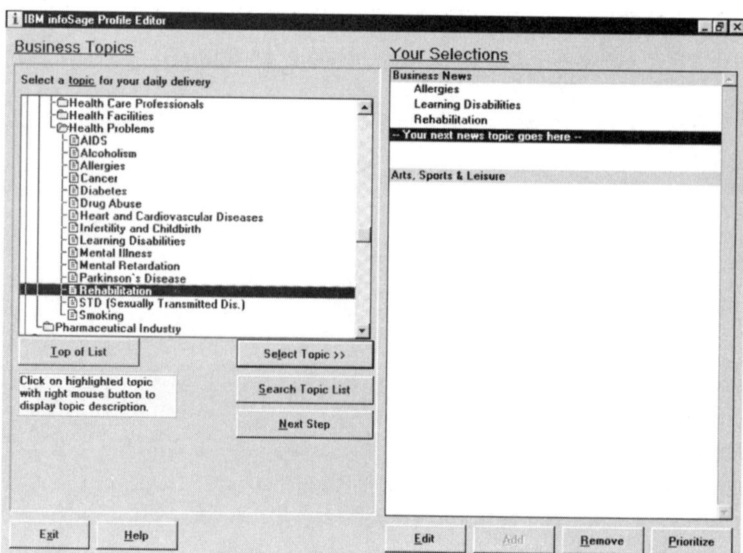

You then personalize individual topics with words or phrases that you would like to appear in the stories. For example, here we have requested that infoSage send us any articles about diabetes that contain the word "Canadian" or "Canada":

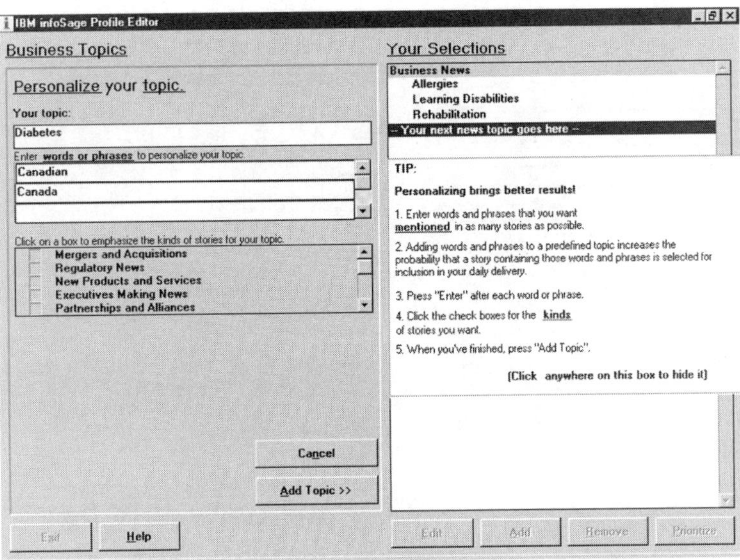

You can personalize your delivery even further by identifying the *types* of stories you would like to receive. For example, you can choose from "Mergers and Acquisitions," "Regulatory News," "New Products and Services," "Executives Making News," and "Partnerships and Alliances."

infoSage will normally send you a report twice a day, either over the World Wide Web or by e-mail. You can override this feature by placing "special alerts" on important topics and have matching stories delivered right to your e-mailbox soon after the story hits the news wires. If you choose to receive your custom news stories on the Web, infoSage builds a custom Web page for you that contains only those news stories that match your profile:

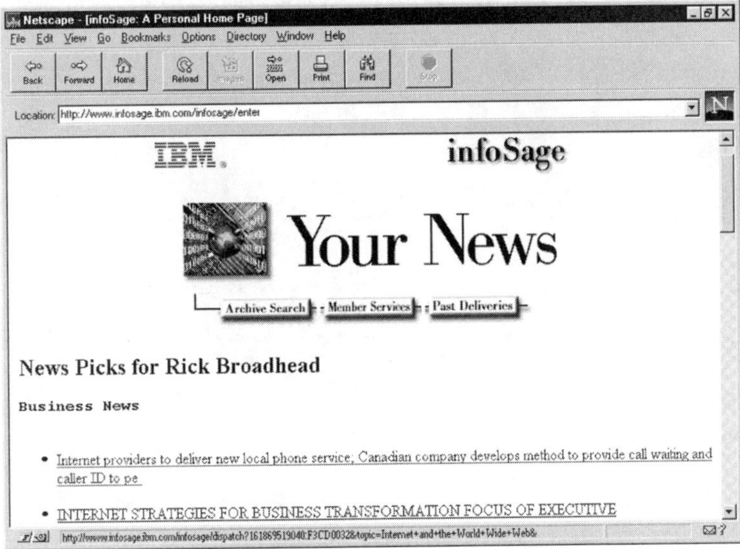

One really nice feature of infoSage is that it allows you to create your own topic if the subject you are interested in does not already exist. For example, say you are interested in turkey breeding. You can ask infoSage to send you any stories that contain the words "turkey" and "breeding":

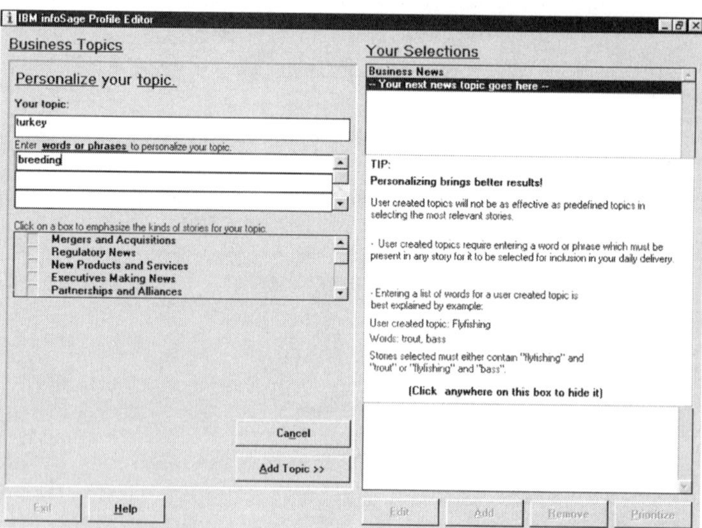

infoSage has been developed with the business user in mind, and it is one of the most powerful Internet-based services of its kind. To learn more about IBM's infoSage, visit their home page at **http://www.infosage.ibm.com**.

Infoseek Personal

Infoseek Personal is a free Web-based news service offered by Infoseek, one of the popular Web search engines, which we reviewed in Chapter 11.

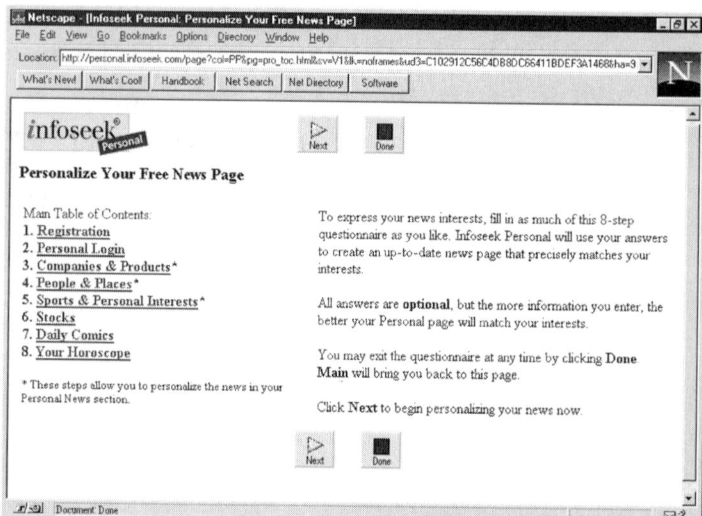

By following a step-by-step registration process, you identify the people, products, companies, and personal interests that you want Infoseek to track for you. Infoseek Personal also provides you with the ability to follow your favorite stocks, and your horoscope, and can deliver a selection of popular comics including Dilbert, Marmaduke, and Peanuts.

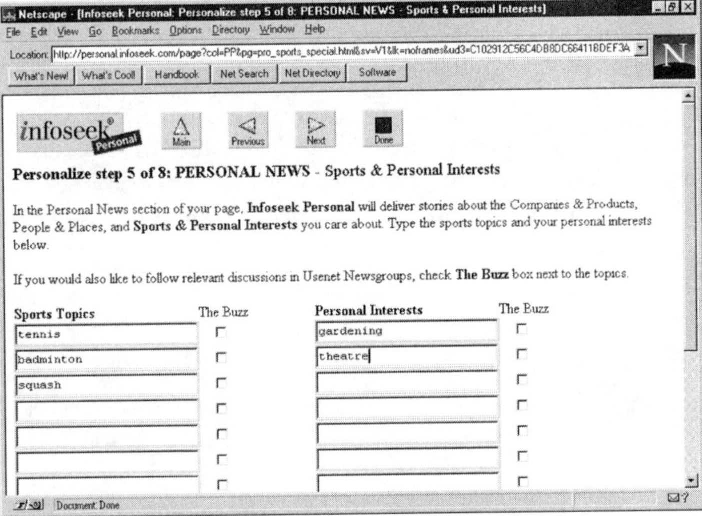

Once you are finished the registration process, you can place a bookmark on the Infoseek Personal Web site at **http://personal.infoseek.com** and return to the site whenever you want to read your custom news.

Infoseek is noteworthy in that it makes use of a special Internet feature called a "cookie" (we discuss cookies in Chapter 7). This means that whenever you return to the Web site, you do not have to log in, and you do not have to worry about remembering a password, as you do with some of the others sites. Infoseek always remembers your personal profile and delivers relevant news stories automatically.

One cautionary note: the cookie feature only works if you always use the same computer to access the Internet. To accommodate those Internet users who access the Internet using more than one computer, Infoseek Personal provides an optional "Personal Login" screen that allows you to create a personal login name and password so that you can access your customized news page from any computer:

Netscape - [Infoseek Personal: Personalize step 2 of 8: Personal Login]

File Edit View Go Bookmarks Options Directory Window Help

What's New! What's Cool! Handbook Net Search Net Directory Software

infoseek Personal

Main Previous Next Done

Personalize step 2 of 8: Personal Login

Access your Personalized News Page from anywhere by creating a Personal Login! No matter what computer or Internet access account you find yourself using, you can still catch up on the latest news.

If you do not wish to create a Personal Login, click **Next**.

The Personal Login is **completely optional**, and is most useful for people who wish to access their news page from completely different environments, such as at home and at work. You might also want to create a Personal Login if you are sharing a computer with another person and wish to have separate personal news pages.

Name:

You can restrict access to your personal news page by creating a password.

Password:

Type your password again:

Document: Done

You can visit Infoseek on the Web at **http://www.infoseek.com** or go directly to the Infoseek Personal Web site at **http://personal.infoseek.com**.

Canadian Corporate News

Canadian Corporate News offers full-text news releases for hundreds of Canadian organizations. You can access the full database of press releases without charge through the Canadian Corporate News Web site, or you can set up your own personal profile to have news releases delivered to you by e-mail, or to your own private "NewsBox" on the Web, as soon as they hit the news wire.

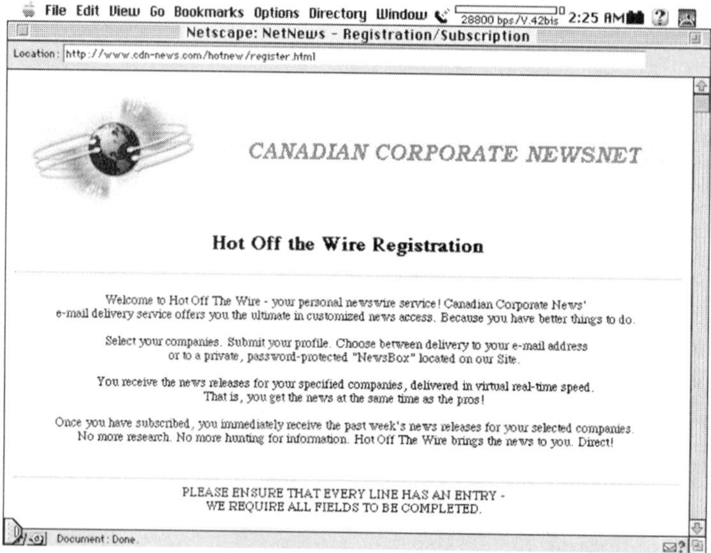

Once you have completed the on-line registration form available at **http://www.cdn-news.com**, you will be asked to choose a username and password. If you decide to receive your press releases on the Web (rather than by e-mail), you will need this information to gain access to your "NewsBox," where the press releases will be stored. You can then proceed to select the industries of interest. Almost two dozen categories are listed, ranging from "Aerospace and Defence" to "Transportation":

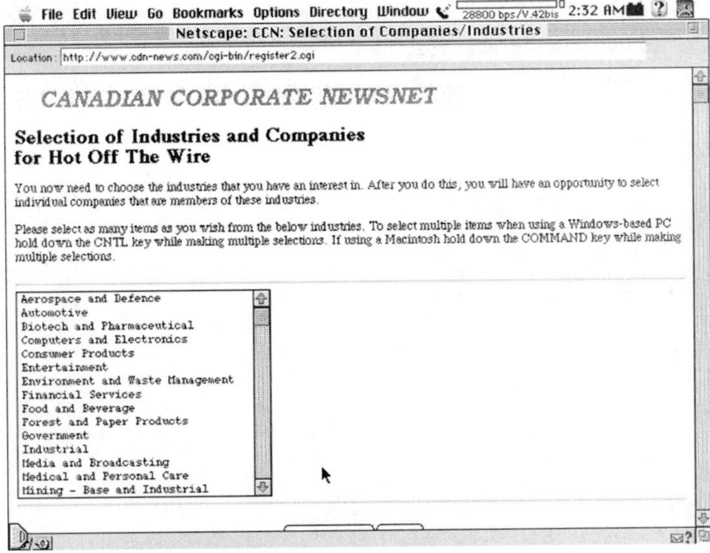

The last step is to select the companies you wish to track. For example, suppose you selected "Mining" during the previous step. The next screen, shown below, will allow you to select one or several mining companies to monitor:

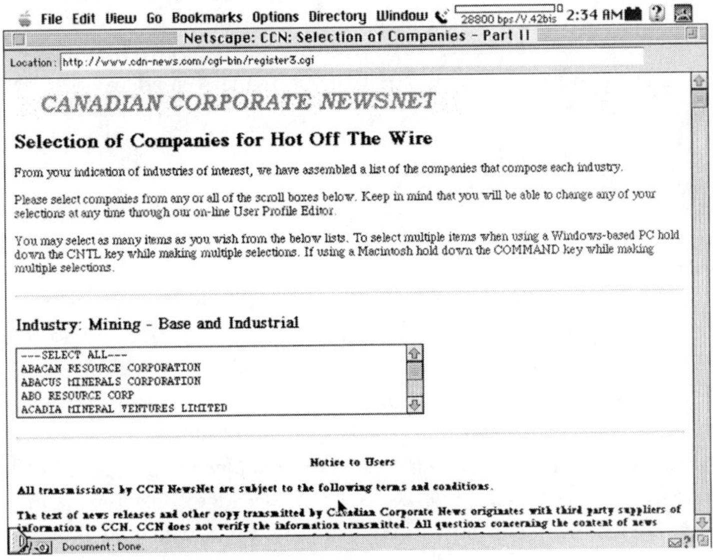

You're done! You will soon begin receiving press releases by e-mail or on the Web, depending upon the method you selected during registration. You can change your profile at any time by selecting the "Change Your Profile" option on the main home page. You will need to remember your username and password to do this:

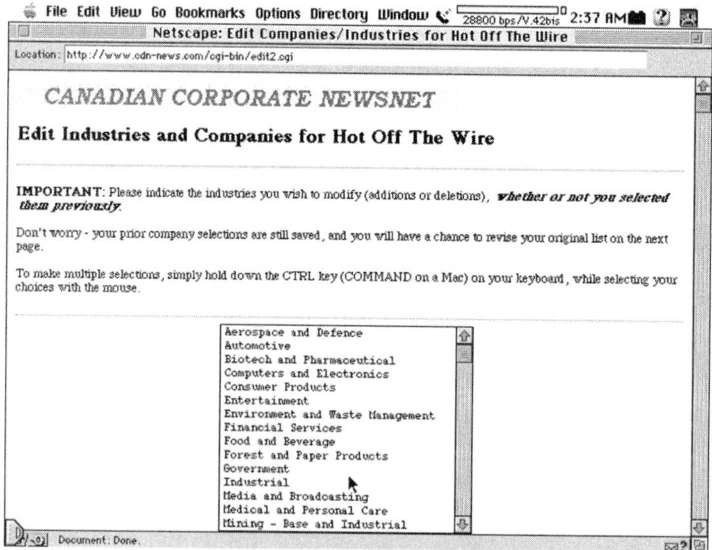

You can visit the Canadian Corporate News Web site at **http://www.cdn-news.com**. It is an easy, effective, and straightforward way of tracking particular Canadian organizations.

The Future of News Clipping

Certainly, many Canadian media organizations will soon have available products similar to those reviewed in this chapter. And certainly, the sophistication of on-line news clipping will grow as companies develop the tools to allow more sophisticated categorization and selection of news stories. But you should be aware that the future of news clipping will be even more dramatic than simple enhancements to the services noted in this chapter, once high-speed networking becomes available in Canada.

The future is found in initiatives such as the Personal News Network (PNN). A joint effort of the CBC and hi-tech firms such as Bell Canada, Newbridge, Televitesse, Oracle, and others, PNN promises to redefine our concept of news clipping. PNN will allow individuals to indicate what news interests them and will then clip newspaper, magazine, news wires, CBC news and radio broadcasts, and other sources of information. The personal news summary will not consist of the simple text of news stories; it will include video and audio of those stories.

Want to track any news about corporate takeovers? You will get news articles as well as any stories from last night's *The National* and *The World at Six* that contain information about corporate takeovers.

PNN is an ambitious project, and because it involves audio and video, it will not be available to many users of the Internet until high-speed networking becomes widespread in Canada. It is, however, a good indication that the future might be here quicker than we think.

What Does Personalized News Mean?

When you sit back and think about the software and Web sites we have seen in this chapter, you may wonder if the traditional media are obsolete. Are newspapers going to disappear because of systems like PointCast? We don't think so. One unfortunate aspect of the excessive level of hype that surrounds the Internet is that too many "visionaries" are running around making predictions that the Internet will put newspapers out of business, television news will disappear, and custom news services will become the backbone of the media in the future. Hogwash.

The Internet does not replace other forms of media; it enhances them. Personalized news-clipping services are useful and powerful and make it easier for people to access the news that they want. But sitting in front of a computer screen, reading a custom version of PointCast, will never replace sitting on a patio on a warm summer night, reading the latest *Globe and Mail* or *Field & Stream* magazine to ever-fading sunlight. It will never replace the peace you might find from sitting on the couch and flipping from *CNN Headline News* to *CBC Newsworld* and back again as some new world crisis unfolds. Personalized news will not replace the media; it will change it.

You should also keep in mind that this technology is still relatively new and that the concept of personalized news is in its infancy.

There is a lot of new and innovative stuff happening with the concept, particularly in many of the Web sites and the software that we examined in this chapter. But it is a brand-new field, and undoubtedly the software, technology, concepts, news sources, and levels of customization will change and mature. In many ways it is as though someone has just invented television, and now we are going to have many years of experimentation to figure out just what we can do with television.

Remember, it was not until John F. Kennedy's funeral that live television really became a force of social change, and that was some twenty-five years after television first arrived. It was not until CNN came on the scene, with its coverage of the Persian Gulf Crisis, that people came to understand the raw and naked power that television could have in influencing world events.

Perhaps the most exciting developments that we will see emerge on the Internet are personal "news agents," an agent being an intelligent software program that will watch what type of news you read and access. The agent will study your reading habits and, over time, will start suggesting to you other news stories that seem to match your areas of interest. Science fiction? Check out "Rex, The First Adaptive News Service" (**http://www.daptyx.com/home.html**), a worthy experiment in this area.

It will be some time until we truly understand and appreciate the impact that personalized news services will have on our concept of "news" and before the technology really understands what we want in terms of *The Daily Me.*

CHAPTER 11

Knowledge Networking

*Usenet... is dying a fast and painful death. i only keep up with **rec.music.christian** (the newsgroup that i'm most often associated with) and rec.sport.soccer these days, and not all that much at that. if you're serious about communicating with vast quantities of people over the 'net, find a good mailing list.*

Internet user Chuck Pearson on his home page **http://soyokaze.biosci.ohio-state.edu/~dcp/hotlistrec.html**

Internet mailing lists and USENET are the two primary methods by which you can "knowledge network" through the Internet.

The Benefit of Knowledge Networking

If you have the need to be an expert on a particular topic, or wish to bring yourself up-to-date on a certain issue, or wish to find an answer to a question, you can often use the Internet as a means of "knowledge networking." Knowledge networking is the term used to describe the ability to harness on-line information, either by regularly tracking information on a particular topic by receiving information on that topic or by seeking information or answers to questions by discussing a topic with others on-line.

By participating in Internet knowledge networks found in mailing lists and USENET newsgroups, you can receive information on specific topics on a regular basis and can join discussion topics with others. The unique cooperative nature of the Internet means that information is available to you on thousands of topics and from thousands of sources. For example, you can

- subscribe to formal or informal electronic journals and newsletters published by individuals or organizations from around the world;
- join mailing lists that will send you announcements of concerts, events, new publications or new products, or information about new initiatives by various organizations and governments;
- participate in discussions with thousands of others from around the world on a variety of topics, ranging from the serious to the ridiculous.

Mailing Lists Versus USENET

A mailing list is a collection of e-mail addresses. Any message sent to the address of the mailing list is automatically sent to the address of every member of the mailing list. There are thousands of mailing lists on all kinds of topics, and you can join practically any list by sending a specially formatted e-mail message to a system that manages the list. Mailing lists are a quick and easy method of distributing information, whether it is a newsletter or a question from a member of the list. Information that you receive from mailing lists comes in with your regular Internet e-mail; no special software is required to read a message sent to a mailing list, although special software is used to manage the mailing list itself.

USENET, on the other hand, is a global system for the exchange of information on thousands of topics, through "newsgroups." Individuals can subscribe to any particular newsgroup, read information sent to the newsgroup, and add or "post" information to the newsgroup. Each posting is referred to as a "news article." There are also "follow-ups" and "replies" in USENET. A "follow-up" is a comment made to a previous posting, while a "reply" is an e-mail message that you send to someone directly. USENET is like a massive global bulletin board with thousands of different information resources. You read the USENET newsgroups that you belong to with "newsreader" software, which also permits you to post messages to USENET.

KNOWLEDGE NETWORKING

1. You can "knowledge network" on the Internet either by regularly tracking information on a particular topic or by seeking information or answers to questions by discussing a topic with others on-line.
2. Knowledge networking is undertaken through two areas of the Internet known as USENET and electronic mailing lists.
3. USENET is a global system used for the exchange of information on thousands of topics through newsgroups.
4. Electronic mailing lists are collections of e-mail addresses organized into a list used to communicate about a particular topic.
5. There are extensive resources throughout the Internet to help you find particular USENET newsgroups and mailing lists.

What Is the Difference?

Although the mechanics of a mailing list and USENET differ, both permit you to join a particular group and receive information or converse with people concerning a topic within the group. Anyone with an Internet e-mail address can join any number of mailing lists; your only constraint will be the volume of information that you can read each day.

USENET newsgroups are not much different in concept from mailing lists.

Since you can obtain USENET news through most Internet service providers, you can choose to subscribe to the newsgroups that interest you. Given the volume of information, you will have to be selective. The major differences between USENET newsgroups and mailing lists are the following:

- USENET information is more structured, with individual postings filed into particular newsgroups. In contrast, e-mail messages from mailing lists are part of your general e-mailbox, unless you have some type of special filtering software. (This is the benefit of e-mail filtering software, as discussed in Chapter 6.)
- Most USENET newsgroups undergo a series of steps of approval before they become widely distributed through the USENET system. On the other hand, anyone can start a mailing list on any topic if he/she has the right software.
- USENET has a culture that frowns upon networking for commercial purposes. Mailing lists can be used for anything, as long as you do not abuse the primary purpose for which a particular mailing list was established.
- USENET news articles have a limited life span. Because of the large number of USENET messages, many sites will delete messages beyond a certain date (usually two weeks, and sometimes much less). Messages sent to mailing lists will last as long as messages last in your mailbox.
- USENET news articles are not sent to personal mailboxes, but are received in batches of postings, which are then made available for reading through newsreader software.
- USENET was designed as a mechanism to permit the rebroadcasting of information on a very wide basis. Any USENET article goes out to all the Internet hosts on the planet that wish to receive that specific newsgroup or that do not refuse that newsgroup. E-mail, on the other hand, was designed as a point-to-point method of communicating, and even with mailing lists, suffers from some problems when trying to be a broadcast tool.

Other than these points, USENET is very similar in concept to mailing lists, since it permits people to participate in knowledge networking with others from around the globe on a variety of topics.

To make matters more complex, there are also some "bidirectionally gated newsgroups" within USENET. Any news article sent to such a USENET newsgroup is also distributed automatically to others via a mailing list, meaning that even if you do not have access to USENET, you might be able to receive copies of postings to a particular newsgroup through your e-mail account.

USENET

USENET is described by many as the "world's largest bulletin board system," even though it is definitely not a bulletin board system. USENET consists of several thousand topic areas known as "newsgroups," with topics ranging from locksmithing to pyrotechnics to religion to C++ computer programming. Within these newsgroups people discuss, debate, and share information concerning the topic at hand. Given the global nature of the Internet, and the fact that there are thousands of topics available, there is a wealth of information that you can obtain through USENET.

What Can I Do with USENET?

Before we describe how USENET works and what it is made up of, we should give you an idea of what you can do in this area of the Internet. Through USENET you can

- join newsgroups (topics) that are of interest;
- discuss, debate, keep current, or ask questions about these newsgroups;
- receive newsletters or other information through some of these newsgroups;
- retrieve documents known as "frequently asked questions" (FAQs) related to these newsgroups.

Unmoderated Newsgroups

Many USENET newsgroups are used for interactive discussion between people interested in a common topic. There are thousands of topics, ranging from the serious to the bizarre, from mainstream to controversial, from conservative to silly. Many of the newsgroups are "unmoderated," that is, anyone can post information as long as they stick to the topic. (If they do not, they will get flamed, a topic discussed in Chapter 6.) For example, **alt.architecture** is used for the exchange of information between people involved in or interested in architectural issues. Here is a listing of just some of the topics discussed on a certain date:

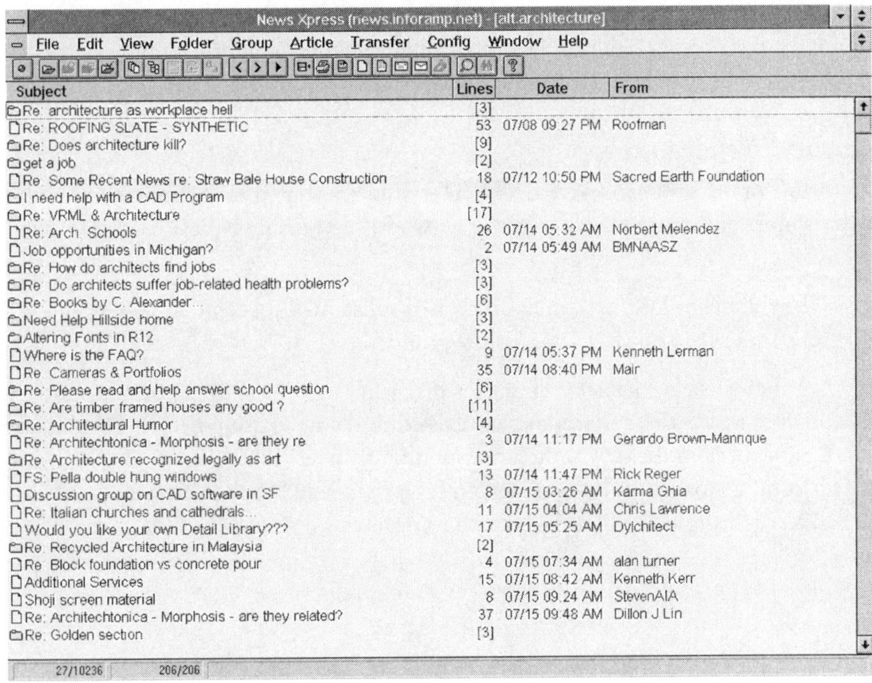

The power of USENET is that anyone can join a general discussion newsgroup like alt.architecture and post a question to those who belong to that newsgroup. Because of the unique cooperative spirit of the Internet, you will more often than not get answers from several participants. In this case, we can see a question that has been asked, and the answer someone offered in response:

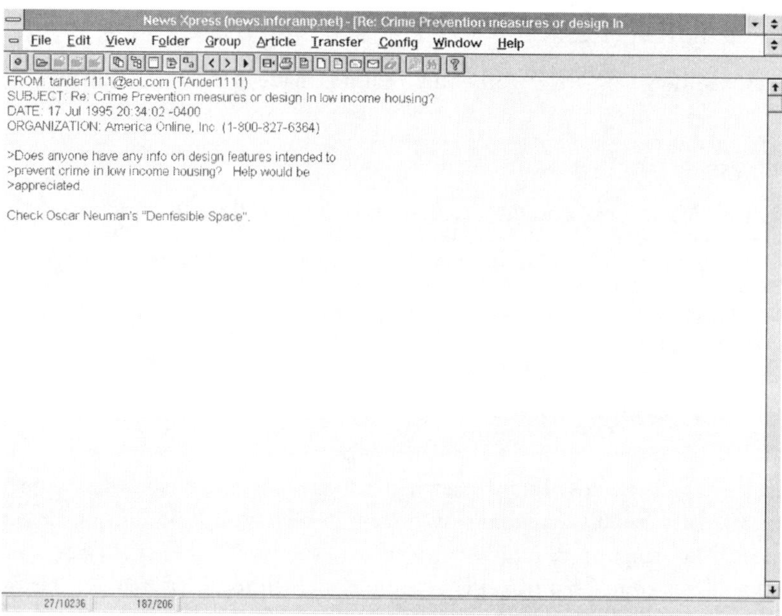

"Discussions" through USENET occur over a period of days and weeks (and often months) rather than in real time. Hence you can check every once in a while to see what is new. (However, keep in mind articles "expire"; due to the overwhelming volume of information that flows through USENET, most ISPs only keep articles for a week or two.)

Moderated Newsgroups

Of course, one of the problems with USENET is directly related to the massive growth of the Internet; as more and more people join the network, several things have begun to happen to USENET:

- The volume of information has increased substantially, such that you often cannot keep up-to-date on your chosen newsgroups.
- Expanding use of the network means that you might have to pay attention to a lot of other opinions that might not have existed in the newsgroup before. People who have a different point of view sometimes strenuously stress that point of view, causing you discomfort. Battles erupt and rage on topics unrelated to the newsgroup, causing you to leave the group until things return to normal.

- Cranks, kooks, nuts — people whose mental state might seriously be in doubt — post to many areas of USENET, causing you great frustration.[1]

One result of these problems has been a steady increase in the number of "moderated" groups. Within such groups, a volunteer or series of volunteers takes the time to "preread" postings to a particular group. Only those that fit the spirit (or "charter") of the newsgroup are posted. This helps to ensure that the group is focused on the topic at hand and to weed out a lot of the crank or useless postings that you might find in other, unmoderated groups.

A very good example of a moderated group is **comp.dcom.telecom**, where participants share information concerning telecommunication-related issues. In the case below, a moderator has "approved" all postings:

News Xpress (news.inforamp.net) - [comp.dcom.telecom]

File Edit View Folder Group Article Transfer Config Window Help

Subject	Lines	Date	From
Expansion of International Telephone Numbers	253	07/14 12:22 AM	Ben Heckscher
Sprint, DoJ Enter Consent Decree	57	07/14 10:04 AM	Geimann@aol.com
VITAsat Used in Ebola Crisis in Zaire	70	07/18 06:02 PM	Nigel Allen
Turkish Switching Causing Trouble in Holland	21	07/18 10:41 PM	Alex van Es
Finland Dialing Changes	18	07/18 11:33 PM	Toby Nixon
LEC to LEC DA Charges	79	07/19 03:37 AM	Lou Jahn
New York Workshop on Communications Decency Act	119	07/19 09:46 AM	Shabbir J. Safdar
Zenith vs. Enterprise	72	07/19 10:34 AM	Paul Robinson
Zenith, Enterprise, and WX Numbers	58	07/19 02:17 PM	Mark Cuccia
More About Integretel and Their Sleazy Clients	98	07/19 06:00 PM	TELECOM Digest Editor
Book Review: "NetWare LANs Performance and Troubleshooting"	50	07/20 01:42 AM	Rob Slade
Enterprise Management Summit '95	29	07/20 07:05 AM	Summit '94
UCLA Short Course: Wavelet Transform Applications	41	07/20 10:34 AM	William R. Goodin
UCLA Short Course: Optical Fiber Communications	40	07/20 11:09 AM	William R. Goodin
Device to Reset Modems	16	07/20 12:41 PM	Greg Tompkins
COOK Report Exclusive: AGIS to Acquire NET99	61	07/20 03:15 PM	Gordon Cook (via G. Jacobson)
The Bell's Are Taking Over	68	07/20 06:29 PM	BUCKINGHAM, JEFF
Loran-C Future	13	07/20 07:21 PM	Keith Ouellette
Kyl and Leahy to Introduce Anti-Hacker Bill	61	07/20 08:52 PM	John Shaver
NPA/NXX Web Search Page	12	07/20 10:30 PM	Greg 'Arg' Argendeli
PacBell Video Dial Tone Order	81	07/21 05:07 AM	SJSlavin
Enterprise/Zenith Numbers	6	07/21 05:26 AM	Lisa
Bell Atlantic Tests Cellular Fraud Software	17	07/21 07:21 AM	Monty Solomon
Petition to Immediately Implement 888 NPA (888 Area Code)	263	07/21 07:44 AM	Paul Robinson
'Interesting' Service Providers in the US?	21	07/21 12:29 PM	Ben Lippolt

28/10236 23/25

Some do not agree with the concept of moderated groups, while others think they are a good solution to a serious and growing problem on USENET. Whatever your opinion, keep in mind that USENET is a big place, and that often there are solutions for people who are on either side of the fence. For example, there is a similar telecommunications group, **alt.dcom.telecom**, which is not moderated, and which permits users to post anything related to the telecommunications topic. If you don't like the moderated aspect of **comp.dcom.telecom**, join the unmoderated **alt.dcom.telecom.**

USENET is used for many lighthearted purposes, but has a scientific side as well. Many moderated groups are used for reporting scientific information and other research; **sci.astro.hubble** is a group used by many space-related organizations for posting information directly related to the Hubble Space Telescope, for example:

---

1. USENET is a wild and wonderful place and often responds to problems with a sense of humor. There is a newsgroup, **alt.kook.of.month**, in which people vote for whom they believe is the individual on USENET most obviously not in tune with their mental faculties. There must be something about Canada — Canadians have won the award many times.

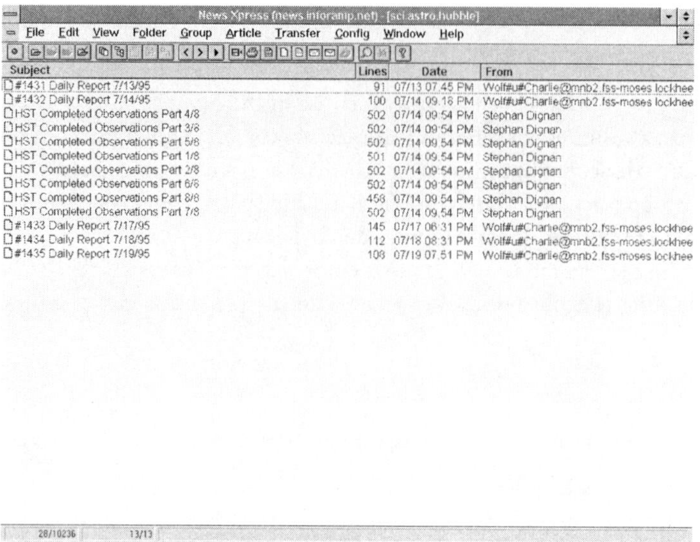

Lockheed posts a daily report of scheduled Hubble activities to the newsgroup, and thus **sci.astro.hubble** has become one of the primary methods by which space scientists worldwide keep in tune with projects and experiments involving the telescope.

ClariNet Newsgroups

A special type of USENET newsgroup can be found in the ClariNet topic, a special service offered by a few Internet service providers in Canada. ClariNet is a commercial news service for which you or your provider must pay a subscription fee. ClariNet redistributes news stories from various global newswires. With several hundred topics covered, it is a good source of up-to-date news information. An example newsgroup in the ClariNet section is **clari.biz.industry. tourism,** where news articles concerning the tourism industry are accessible:

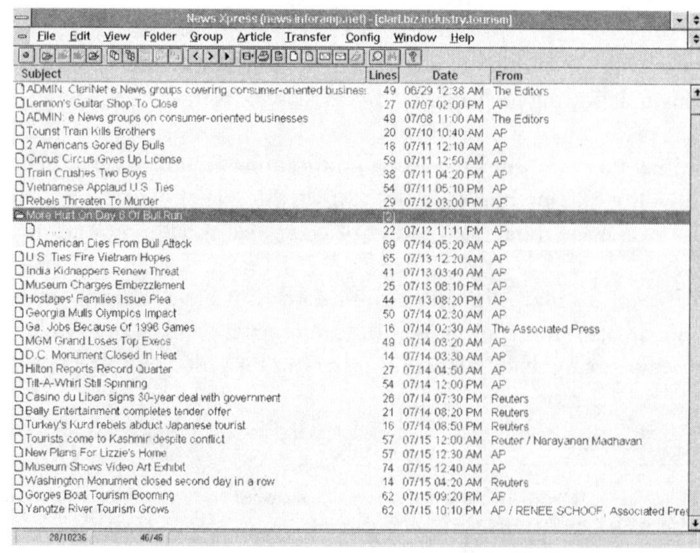

There are a number of Canadian ClariNet topics, such as this item from a Canadian business group:

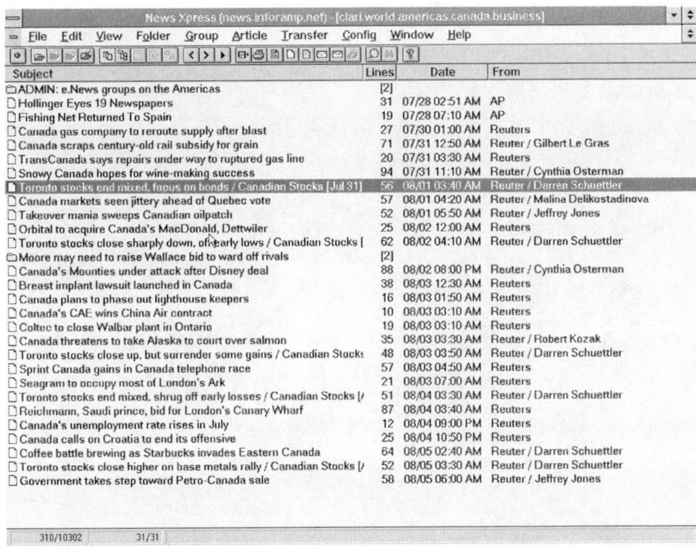

You might want to check if your Internet service provider provides access to ClariNet. If not, and you are interested in it, you can subscribe directly at **http://www.clari.net**, or by sending a message to **sales@clari.net**.

Frequently Asked Questions (FAQs)

Many newsgroups put together a FAQ, a document designed to answer the most frequently asked questions that new participants might ask within a newsgroup. FAQs are a good source of information about a particular topic, and if you plan to join a newsgroup, you should read its FAQ so that you do not ask questions that the group has talked about many times before, and so that you understand what types of discussions are appropriate (should one exist; they do not exist for all USENET newsgroups). FAQs are often used to detail the etiquette of the particular group, the "charter" of the group (which we discuss below). They are also often used to describe other sources of information related to the topic.

For example, here is the introductory page of the FAQ for the **rec.music.reggae** newsgroup, available at **http://www.cis.ohio-state.edu/hypertext/faq/usenet/music/reggae/top.html**:

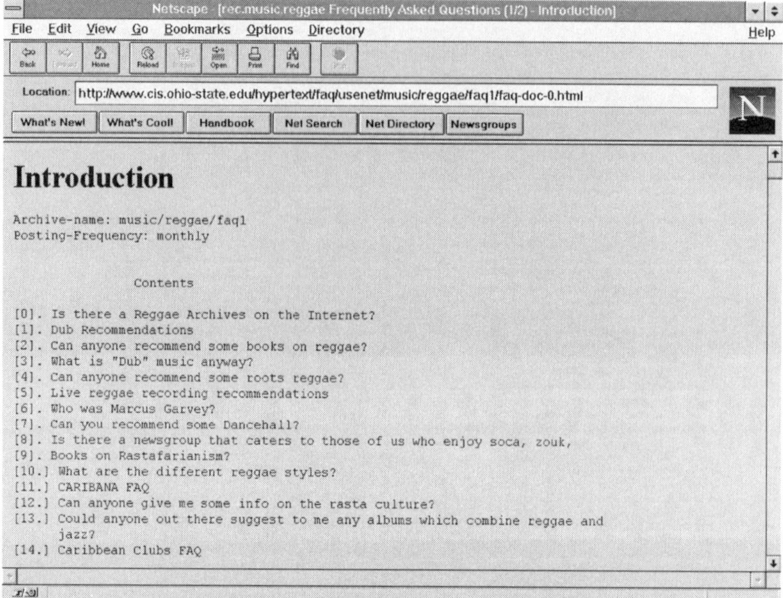

Many USENET FAQs can be found on-line at the following locations: **http://www.cis.ohio-state.edu/hypertext/faq/usenet/top.html** and **ftp://rtfm.mit.edu/pub/usenet/**. You can also find a lot of FAQs in the newsgroups **comp.answers**, **misc.answers**, **news.answers**, **rec.answers**, **sci.answers**, **soc.answers** and **talk.answers.**

Newsgroup Categories

Newsgroups within USENET belong to a series of categories. The major (global) newsgroup categories are listed in the following table. Excluding the **biz.** category, the balance are referred to as the "big 7" categories.

CATEGORY	TOPIC
biz.	Business-oriented topics
comp.	Computer-oriented topics
misc.	Topics that do not fit elsewhere
news.	News and information concerning the Internet or USENET
rec.	Recreational activities, such as bowling, skiing, chess
sci.	Scientific topics
soc.	Sociological issues
talk.	Debate-oriented topics

There is also an **alt.** group. What can you find in **alt.** groups? You name it, **alt.** groups likely discuss it. Anyone can start an **alt.** group without approval, but not all Internet service providers carry all **alt.** groups. The result is a somewhat freewheeling atmosphere, with some of the most controversial newsgroups being located in the **alt.** category.

Subtopics

Each category consists of several hundred or thousands of topics, organized in subcategories. For example, the newsgroup category **rec.** (recreation topics) includes the subcategories

- **rec.arts;**
- **rec.audio;**
- **rec.music;**

and from this, a further categorization exists, for example,

- **rec.arts.poems;**
- **rec.arts.misc;**
- **rec.arts.bonsai.**

For very popular topics, another level of categorization might be found. For example, because of the popularity of science fiction within the Internet, there are several science fiction newsgroups within the **rec.arts.sf** category, including

- **rec.arts.sf.misc;**
- **rec.arts.sf.movies;**
- **rec.arts.sf.science.**

An individual could choose to subscribe to all the **rec.arts.sf** groups (getting all three above as well as others) or could choose to subscribe to only the **rec.arts.sf.movies** group.

Canadian Newsgroup Categories

A separate set of newsgroup categories exists for Canadian USENET topics, consisting of a **can.** hierarchy as well as separate hierarchies for some provinces and some major cities in Canada. The categories include the following (excluding specific university categories found in Canada):

CATEGORY	TOPIC	CATEGORY	TOPIC
ab.	Alberta	**mtl.**	Montreal
atl.	Atlantic	**nf.**	Newfoundland
bc.	British Columbia	**niagara.**	Niagara
calgary.	Calgary	**ns.**	Nova Scotia
can.	Canadian	**ont.**	Ontario
edm.	Edmonton	**ott.**	Ottawa
hfx.	Halifax	**pei.**	Prince Edward Island
kingston.	Kingston	**qc.**	Quebec
kw.	Kitchener/Waterloo	**sj.**	St. John's
man.	Manitoba	**tor.**	Toronto
nt.	Northwest Territories	**van.**	Vancouver
yk.	Yukon	**wpg.**	Winnipeg

Some of the more popular Canadian newsgroups in the **can.** hierarchy include

- **can.general**. In this discussion of general Canadian issues, there is a wide-ranging number of topics, with debates, arguments, discussion, and announcements. A little bit of everything.
- **can.jobs**. A *lot* of job postings are made to this group. Many are for people with computer expertise, with a large number of postings by personnel agencies. However, we also see postings for other types of jobs and professional positions.
- **can.politics**. Deficits, governments, and all the related topics are discussed here. A very busy newsgroup. Be prepared to argue.
- **can.domain**. Announcements of organizations newly registered in the Canadian Internet domain are made in this newsgroup: a good way to track who is getting involved in the Internet in Canada. Some discussion of policies and procedures relevant to registration under the **ca.** domain also occurs.

There are many provincial discussion groups; in addition, several communities in Canada are very active with their local Internet newsgroups, including those within the **kw.** (Kitchener–Waterloo), **ott.** (Ottawa), and **tor.** (Toronto) newsgroups. A list of significant Canadian USENET newsgroups is found in Appendix E.

A Sample USENET Message

A USENET message looks like an e-mail message, with some subtle differences. The primary difference is that a newsgroup message includes a reference to the newsgroups to which the information was posted. Here is an example of a new posting:

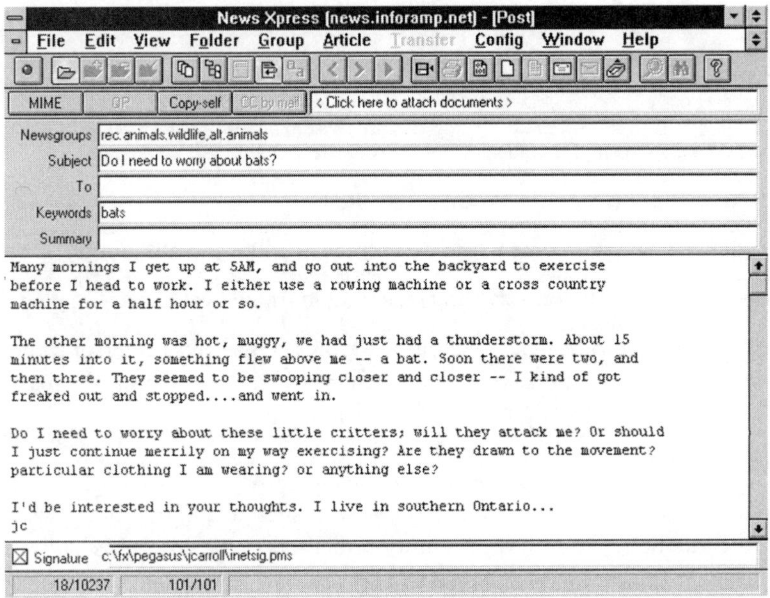

If we save the message to a file, we can see the structure that it has when it is sent through USENET:

Path: inforamp.net!ts1-06

From: jcarroll@jacc.com (Jim Carroll)

Newsgroups: rec.animals.wildlife,alt.animals

Subject: Do I need to worry about bats?

Date: Sat, 20 Jul 96 00:22:51 GMT

Organization: J.A. Carroll Consulting

Lines: 21

Message-ID: <3uqn65$4c6@inforamp.net>

NNTP-Posting-Host: ts1-06.inforamp.net

Keywords: bats

X-Newsreader: News Xpress Version 1.0 Beta #4

Xref: inforamp.net rec.animals.wildlife:3663 alt.animals:127

Status: N

Many mornings I get up at 5AM, and go out into the backyard to exercise
before I head to work. I either use a rowing machine or a cross country
machine for a half hour or so.

The other morning was hot, muggy, we had just had a thunderstorm. About 15
minutes into it, something flew above me — a bat. Soon there were two, and

then three. They seemed to be swooping closer and closer — I kind of got
freaked out and stopped....and went in.
Do I need to worry about these little critters; will they attack me? Or should
I just continue merrily on my way exercising? Are they drawn to the movement?
particular clothing I am wearing? or anything else?
I'd be interested in your thoughts. I live in southern Ontario...
jc
Jim Carroll, C.A. 905.855.2950 jcarroll@jacc.com
www.jacc.com
Co-Author, Canadian Internet Handbook/Canadian Internet Advantage

There are several components to the posting:

- The posting has been made to the **rec.animals.wildlife** and **alt.animals** newsgroups.
- Each posting has a subject, date, and organization (should you list one in your software).
- Most newsreader software lets you list key words. This helps people quickly determine whether they want to read a particular posting. You can also key in a summary.
- The text of the message also contains other information that uniquely identifies the message to USENET.

When this message is "posted," it is sent to the news system at the Internet service provider. From there, the unique replication or duplication method found in USENET transmits the message to all other Internet service providers and Internet servers that carry that particular newsgroup within minutes, hours, or, in some cases, days. The message will soon be available around the world and will be viewed by people who "subscribe" to the **rec.animals.wildlife** and **alt.animals newsgroups.**[2]

Creating USENET Newsgroups

It is useful, if you plan on using USENET, to understand the process of how new USENET newsgroups are created.

Creating a Newsgroup in the "Big 7" Categories

First, to understand how newsgroups are created in the "big 7" categories, consider the newsgroup **rec.sport.football.canadian**. Formed a number of years ago, it was established to provide a convenient discussion forum for the Canadian version of the sport.

Note that this process applies for the "big-7 hierarchy," that is, for the **comp.**, **rec.**, **sci.**, **news.**, **soc.**, **talk.**, and **misc.** newsgroups. Procedures for other hierarchies may vary.

- The individual who wanted to start the newsgroup sent a message to the moderator

---

2. Subsequent postings from people who read the note confirmed that we do not need to worry about bats in Southern Ontario.

of the USENET newsgroup **news.announce.newgroups** as well as to several other newsgroups, indicating why such a newsgroup should be formed. The message contained a "charter" for the group, that is, the reasons for the group, and an overview of the purposes for which the group would be used (the discussion of Canadian football). The message was posted to **news.announce.newgroups** by the moderator of that group.

- A period of discussion concerning the merits of having a special group devoted to Canadian football took place within the newsgroup **news.groups** for a month or so. Anyone could have participated in this discussion.
- Once the period of discussion was complete, a "call for votes" went out for people to vote on whether the group should be created. A designated period of time was set aside for voting, and an individual volunteered to be the official vote-taker. Everyone was permitted to vote.
- Once the period of time was up (usually 21–30 days), the votes were tabulated, and the group was found to have met the standard USENET acceptance criteria (the standard rules are that there are at least 100 more "yes" votes than "no" votes and that at least two-thirds of the votes must be "yes").
- Since the group "passed," a "newsgroup control message" was sent out by David Lawrence,[3] the moderator of the **news.announce.newgroups** newsgroup, advising all USENET sites that **rec.sport.football.canadian** was now considered to be on the "official" USENET list. A "newsgroup control message" provides a group with "official status." Everyone was advised of the results of the vote. Here is the original message pertaining to **rec.sport.football.canadian**:

```
>From 2893684@qucdn.queensu.ca Thu Jul 8 17:13:59 1993

Path: uunet!bounce-back

From: Andy <2893684@qucdn.queensu.ca>

Newsgroups:news.announce.newgroups,news.groups,soc.culture.canada,can.general,r

ec.sport.football.pro,rec.sport.hockey,rec.sport.football.misc Subject: RESULT:rec.sport.football.canadian
passes 175:27

Followup-To: news.groups Date: 8 Jul1993 11:10:15 -0400

Organization: Queen's University at Kingston Lines: 232

Sender: tale@rodan.UU.NET
```

3. In this role, David Lawrence comes the closest to being a central authority for USENET. He maintains his position as the result of having built up a large amount of trust and respect from all members of the USENET community through the years.

Approved: tale@uunet.uu.net

Message-ID:<21hdcnlNNfd7@rodan.UU.NET>

NNTP-Posting-Host: rodan.uu.net

Xref: uunetnews.announce.newgroups:3775 news.groups:75889 soc.culture.canada:21106can.general:17008 rec.sport.football.pro:55872 rec.sport.hockey:63082rec.sport.football.misc:1835

As of 23:59 5 July 1993 (last moment votes can be accepted), the resolution to create rec.sport.football.canadian has PASSED by a margin of 175 YES votes (87%) to 27 NO votes (13%). As the number of YES votes outnumber that of NO votes by a margin of more than 2:1 and as there are at least 100 more YES votes than NO votes, both conditions for the creation of r.s.f.c have been met. There was one spoiled vote which would not have changed the outcome had it been counted. The voters' list is as follows [not reproduced here].

- Had **rec.sport.football.canadian** not passed the vote, a newsgroup control message to create the group would not have been sent out by David Lawrence, and the group would not be an official group. The result would have been that most USENET locations would refuse to carry the group, since it had not passed the vote. (In fact, it could even have ended up on a list of invalid newsgroups.) Everyone is advised of the results of the vote in a message like the one above. Those who ignore the guidance over how to establish a new newsgroup will almost certainly fail in their attempt.
- A list of new newsgroups is regularly posted to **news.announce.newsgroups**. When **rec.sport.football.canadian** was created, it would have been included in an announcement of "New USENET Groups." If **rec.sport.football.canadian** had *not* passed, a notice to this effect would have been included in the "New USENET Groups" message. This is another method by which system operators around the world decide whether to carry a message or exclude it.
- Another factor is that even though it is now an official newsgroup, any USENET site has the choice of whether or not it carries the **rec.sport.football.canadian** newsgroup.

Here is the original charter for the **rec.sport.football.canadian** newsgroup:

>From 2893684@qucdn.queensu.ca Thu May 6 15:00:55 1993

Path: uunet!bounce-back

From: Andy <2893684@qucdn.queensu.ca>

Newsgroups:news.announce.newgroups,news.groups,soc.culture.canada,rec.sport.foot

ball.pro,rec.sport.football.misc Subject: RFD: rec.sport.football.canadian

Followup-To: news.groups

Date: 4 May 1993 19:42:56 -0400

Organization: Queen's University at Kingston

Lines: 28 Sender: tale@rodan.UU.NET

Approved: tale@uunet.uu.net

Message-ID: <1s6v20INN99p@rodan.UU.NET>

Xref: uunet.news.announce.newgroups:3542 news.groups:71409 soc.culture.canada:18619 rec.sport.football.pro:52567 rec.sport.football.misc:1743

RFD: Formation of Canadian Football newsgroup.

Time for discussion: 30 days starting May 4, 1993

NAME: rec.sport.football.canadian

STATUS: unmoderated

RATIONALE: There is currently no appropriate group in which to discuss

Canadian football and specifically the Canadian Football League. Canadian football is one of the oldest professional sports in North America with a long and honourable tradition and deserves discussion space. Reasons for r.a.f.c include the number of Canadians both in Canada and abroad who are CFL fans; the expansion of the CFL to the United States and the need to answer questions, provide a forum for discussion for Americans who are new to the game; discussion of the advantages and disadvantages of 3-down football and the effect that the larger field has on the game; the fact that many leading NFL coaches and players spent their early career in the CFL, r.a.f.c could thus give NFL fans a chance to familiarise themselves on possible NFL stars of tomorrow

CHARTER: Discussion topics open to anything of interest to participants particularly the CFL and CIAU (university football in Canada) Canadian rules and style, players and coaches, reviews of games, future of the league in Canada and the U.S., desirability or undesirability of the NFL adopting some Canadian rules, etc.

It is this global cooperative effort concerning the establishment of new newsgroups that is at the heart of USENET.

There are many documents around the Internet that pertain to the creation of a USENET newsgroup, including the following, which you can obtain on-line:

- "How to create a new USENET newsgroup" (**http://scwww.ucs.indiana.edu/NetRsc/usenet.html**);
- "Guidelines on USENET newsgroup names" (**http://www.cis.ohio-state.edu/hypertext/faq/usenet/usenet/creating-newsgroups/naming/part1/faq.html**);
- "So you want to create an alt newsgroup" (**http://www.math.psu.edu/barr/alt-creation-guide.html**);
- "Archives of USENET newsgroup charters and proposals" (1989 to current date) (this is an excellent resource if you want to create a new newsgroup and want to see what a charter looks like) (**ftp://ftp.uu.net/usenet/news.announce.newgroups**).

You can also check the USENET newsgroups **news.groups**, **alt.config**, **news.admin.misc**. A good pointer to all kinds of on-line information about USENET can be found at **http://scwww.ucs.indiana.edu/NetRsc/usenet.html**.

Creating Newsgroups in the Canadian Hierarchy

The process above applies to the main USENET newsgroups, that is, **comp.**, **news.**, **soc.**, **rec.**, etc. The process does not apply to newsgroups in the Canadian hierarchy (i.e., **can.**, **ont.**, and others). In fact, there is no *formal* process for creating newsgroups in Canada. However, keep in mind that USENET exists because of the cooperation of many individuals, whether they be computer system administrators at universities, businesses, and organizations or at Internet service providers or people who volunteer their own time to USENET administration. Because of this cooperative spirit, there is more or less an informal process in place for the creation of groups in some of the Canadian hierarchies.

For example, within the Canadian hierarchy (**can.**) a method has evolved in which proposals for new topics are posted and discussed in the newsgroup **can.config**. If there are no major objections, and if the consensus is that the group should be created, then a control message is propagated by a volunteer, and the group is created at Internet service providers across the country and in some others around the world (depending upon who wants to carry Canadian newsgroups).

The process, as it currently exists, is summarized quite nicely in a FAQ maintained by Chris Lewis (**clewis@ferret.ocunix.on.ca**). The document is posted on a regular basis to **can.config**. The following comments, taken directly from the FAQ, put into perspective the role of **can.config**:

> Subject: So this is **can.config**. What's it for?
>
> It's a newsgroup for the discussion and evolution of the **can.*** hierarchy. Discussion of and requests for the charters of existing **can.*** groups and discussions related to the creation, removal or modification of **can.*** newsgroups are welcome here.

The document also addresses how new groups should be proposed:

> New **can.*** newsgroups are proposed in **can.config**, similar to the procedure for creating new **alt.*** groups. The RFD is followed by a short (typically two weeks or less) discussion period which results in a general consensus as to whether or not the group will be created.

Is **can.config** the formal process for creation of new USENET newsgroups in the **can.** hierarchy? Certainly not. The FAQ addresses the fact that no real consensus has yet emerged:

> While there have been many ideas and suggestions about newsgroup creation procedures here, no real consensus appears to have been reached at this point in time. What you want to do is convince the majority of Canadian news administrators to create the new newsgroup so it is propagated well across the country.

This seems to be the closest thing to a formal process for newsgroup creation in Canada.

What about provincial groups? In that case, no formal process exists, so it would seem you would have to sell your idea for a new discussion group within the general discussion group for a particular province or city.

Our advice? Since USENET succeeds based on its cooperative spirit, you must learn to work within the unique culture that it presents. If you want to see a new group created in the **can.**

hierarchy, retrieve the document mentioned above, study it carefully, retrieve the other FAQs that it mentions, study them carefully, and then talk to an experienced Internet user about how to make your pitch for a new USENET newsgroup. Do not try to do it without knowing what you are doing, since you will more than likely be doomed to failure.

Finally, the informal process of newsgroup creation in Canada is strengthened through the circulation of periodic "checkgroup messages," which detail the Canadian newsgroups that have more or less been accepted by the Canadian USENET community. This has led to a high degree of consistency in what are accepted as the "official" Canadian USENET newsgroups.

Reading News

Once the newsgroup **rec.sport.football.canadian** was approved, users could subscribe to the newsgroup and could begin posting information to it. Hence, upon approval,

- Messages posted to **rec.sport.football.canadian** are now transmitted throughout the USENET system.
- Individual users of USENET choose which newsgroups they wish to join. Those with an interest in the CFL choose to belong to the **rec.sport.football.canadian** list.
- People throughout the world then read that newsgroup using their newsreader software.

The Rise and Tyranny of alt. Groups

The process described above for the creation of USENET newsgroups within the "big 7" categories and within the Canadian hierarchy has worked relatively well for many years and is widely accepted throughout the Internet community. However, in the last several years the "old order" of USENET has come under increasing pressure, particularly with respect to the USENET news group creation process. Many users are bypassing the formal procedures outlined above and instead are creating their own newsgroups within the **alt.** hierarchy, a hierarchy created not to discuss alternative topics, but originally created to allow people to create newsgroups without any discussion or votes.

It is easy enough to do; anyone who has a little bit of technical knowledge of USENET can create his/her own **alt.** group and bypass the traditional "big 7" hierarchies. The procedures that outline how to create an **alt.** newsgroup are becoming freely available. For example, check out "So you want to create an alt. Newsgroup?" (**http://www.math.psu.edu/barr/alt-creation-guide.html**). As the FAQ notes, "contrary to popular belief, 'alt' is not named because it is for 'alternative' topics. Back during the dawn of the modern Usenet, it was decided that newsgroups should be created by following a clearly defined set of 'Guidelines', involving formal discussions and a voting procedure. There was a significant number of people who felt that there should be a provision for a place where people could create groups without having to go through any discussion or votes. Thus alt was born. It is a hierarchy that is 'alternative' to the 'mainstream' (comp, misc, news, rec, soc, sci, talk) hierarchy." In effect, many of the USENET pioneers decided there should be an area where anyone could create a topic about anything; consequently, the **alt.** newsgroups have grown significantly in number as people take advantage of this. There are several reasons:

- Simply, there are many people out there who are not satisfied with the current procedures for group creation. They do not want to take the time to wait for approval for a new newsgroup or simply do not want to follow suggested procedures. Impatience and frustration are new and challenging problems for USENET.
- In other cases, individuals who have "lost" a bid for a new newsgroup are unhappy and charge off in their own direction to create a new newsgroup within the **alt.** hierarchy. When it comes to the **alt.** hierarchy, the nature of USENET is that there is nothing to prevent users from doing so.
- Others create **alt.** newsgroups simply on a whim. It is easy to do, so why not?

One impact is that when you get into the **alt.** hierarchy, there are many useless, silly, irrelevant, and just plain stupid topics. In other cases you can find a lot of empty **alt.** newsgroups. And finally, there are many **alt.** newsgroups that are not carried by ISPs worldwide, many of whom are struggling to deal with the ever-increasing volumes of information flowing through such news groups. Hence, while it is easy to create an **alt.** newsgroup, it is quite another task to see it carried worldwide. So the "big 7" remain the best alternative.

There is no doubt that existing USENET newsgroups are coming under pressure as the result of someone running off to create competing, alternative information topics. Even **rec.sport.football.canadian** has come under such pressure. Consider the following note, in which a long-time supporter of that group is reacting to someone who has just created a number of **alt.** newsgroups about Canadian football:

```
From          That Evil Prince <jcjlebla@acs.ucalgary.ca>
Organization  The University of Calgary
Date          Tue, 18 Jun 1996 09:45:00 -0600
Newsgroups    rec.sport.football.canadian
Message-ID    <Pine.A32.3.92.960618091452.60028C-100000@acs2.acs.ucalgary.ca>
References    1
On Mon, 17 Jun 1996, Canadian (Chris Foley) wrote:
> I posted a proposal on alt.config five days ago to create
> alt.sports.football.cfl.* groups for each CFL team. Well, I received 12
> mails, only 1 of which was opposed (because he thought the CFL had no
> interest out of Canada). I just newgrouped the following alt. groups:
>
> alt.sports.football.cfl.tor-argonauts
> alt.sports.football.cfl.ott-r-riders
> alt.sports.football.cfl.mtl-alouettes
> alt.sports.football.cfl.ham-tiger-cats
```

> alt.sports.football.cfl.bc-lions

> alt.sports.football.cfl.cgy-stampeders

> alt.sports.football.cfl.sk-roughriders

> alt.sports.football.cfl.edm-eskimos

> alt.sports.football.cfl.wpg-bombers

I am * completely * against this, for the following reasons:

First, this is a topic that has come up before when Saskatchewan fans considered starting their own group apart from this one. Fans from all CFL groups (including the US based teams) implored them to stay here so we could all benefit from Roughrider talk. Don't forget, this newsgroup is the one where American visitors to Grey Cup Week in Regina were astounded, while riding on a bus, to see the general goodwill and bonhommie displayed by fans of every team alike. A point that has been raised several times in the past is that CFL fans on the Internet have displayed more genuine

interest in the affairs of all the teams than one finds in any other sports-oriented groups. It is continually borne out here as we discuss issues, events, and ideas pertinent to the entire league and its fans. My point: how will splintering this newsgroup benefit *** ALL *** CFL fans?

To splinter this group among 9 regionally-oriented groups may doom all 10 groups to being cross-posted for lack of traffic volume. Such groups then die. It has happened over and over on Usenet. The operative question is: does this newsgroup have enough volume of traffic to not only warrant but survive the splintering into 9 groups? Of course not. Please consider this carefully. I have read and posted to this group for 1 1/2 years and seen it grow steadily, expand greatly with US expansion, then settle back into its present pattern in which mostly Canadian regulars post. There are many lurkers out there who should jump in if they can, and then perhaps we can look at traffic volume again.

Thirdly, before creating any Usenet groups, there are proper rules of netiquette and routine procedure requiring that you hold two votes on this and all related newsgroups as to:

a) the validity of your idea, and whether your concept is sufficiently supported at large

b) the willingness of Usenet users to patronize those groups.

Next, an independent vote counter must be found and results forwarded to the appropriate Usenet bodies for consideration.

I am likely leaving some elements out, so I would recommend that anyone interested or particularly affected by this process read Jim Carroll and Rick Broadhead's excellent "Canadian Internet Handbook" for complete details on starting Usenet groups.

It should be clear by the tone of this missive that I am against the splintering of rec.sport.football.canadian into 10 groups (itself and 9 others) as it will result in pitifully low volume on each, and in excessive cross-posting. Threads, under those conditions, are usually unreadable.

I hope that everyone will understand that if a majority of the users of this newsgroup decide, following accepted Usenet standards, that the creation of alternate CFL team-based newsgroups is supportable, I will accept such a decision but continue to argue against it.

Jon LeBlanc University of Calgary, Alberta, Canada, Earth

jcjlebla@acs.ucalgary.ca 51 04'48" North, 114 07'55" West

□ http://www.ucalgary.ca/~jcjlebla □

Alt. newsgroups are a reality and are undergoing some ongoing, significant changes to the overall structure of USENET.

Newsreader Software

Newsreader software is the computer program that lets you access USENET news. Just like electronic mail, many people on USENET will not be using the same "newsreader software." And some individuals will use USENET "on-line," that is, while linked to the computer of their Internet service provider by modem or some other link. Others use it "off-line," that is, all USENET articles for groups they belong to are transferred to their computer or local network and are read locally while not linked to another computer.

There are many different newsreader programs available; for example, tin, nn, Emacs and gnus are found on UNIX systems; Trumpet, Agent and News Xpress are used within the Windows environment; and a variety of programs are used on Macintosh computers. Obviously, each program operates and looks different, but all share certain basic functions.

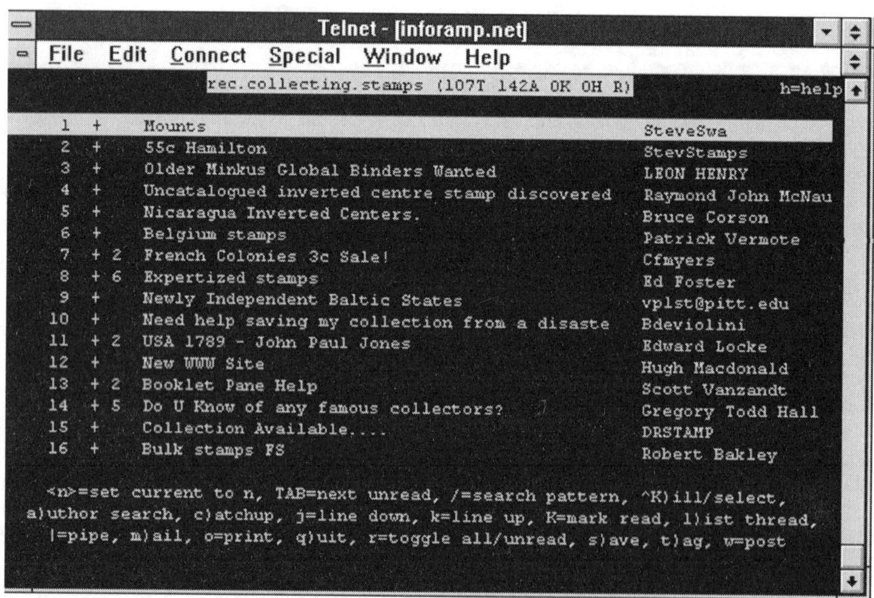

Looking at a similar listing through News Xpress in Microsoft Windows shows a completely different type of screen:

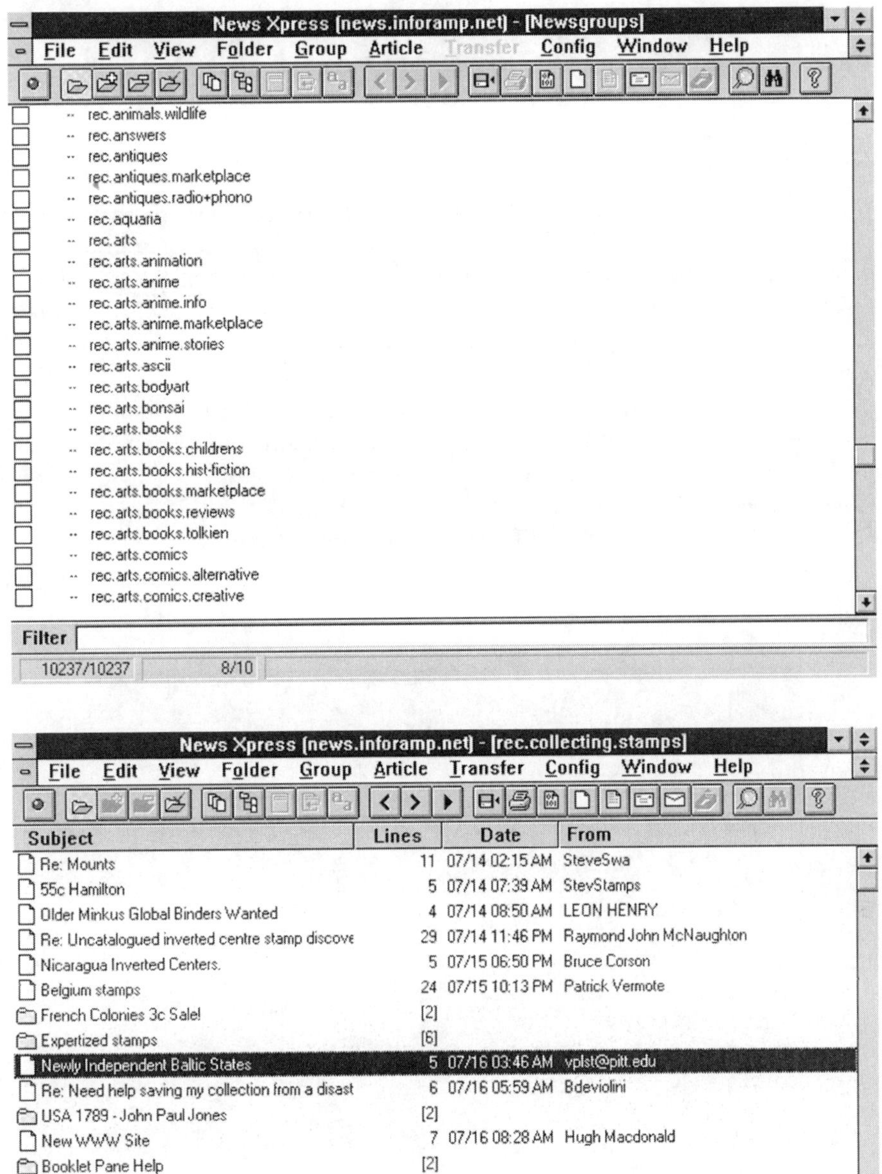

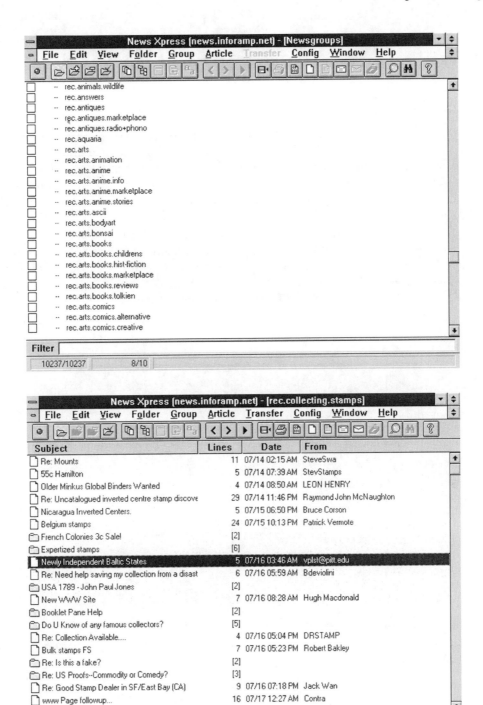

We have also seen the integration of USENET access into World Wide Web browser software. For example, consider the popular Netscape program, which in this case is being used to look at a particular newsgroup:

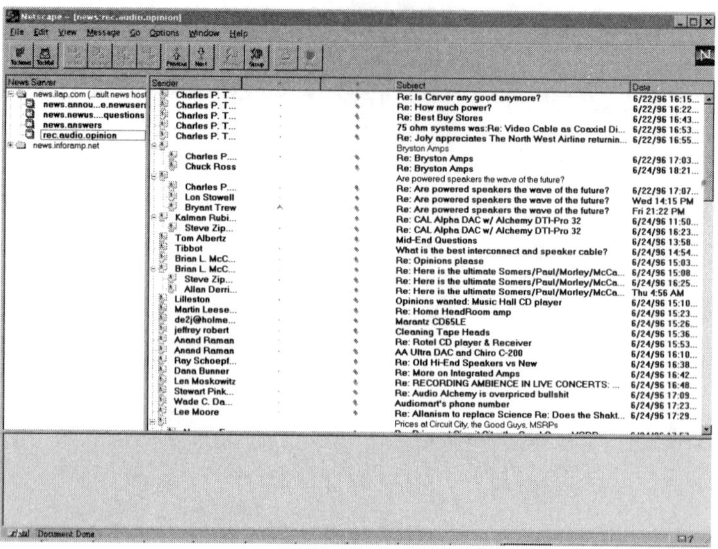
Netscape - [news:rec.audio.opinion]
File Edit View Message Go Options Window Help
News Server
news.ilap.com (...ault news host
news.annou...e.newusers
news.newus....questions
news.answers
rec.audio.opinion
news.inforamp.net
Sender
Subject
Date
Charles P. T... Re: Is Carver any good anymore? 6/22/96 16:15...
Charles P. T... Re: How much power? 6/22/96 16:22...
Charles P. T... Re: Best Buy Stores 6/22/96 16:43...
Charles P. T... 75 ohm systems was:Re: Video Cable as Coaxial Di... 6/22/96 16:53...
Charles P. T... Re: Joly appreciates The North West Airline returnin... 6/22/96 16:55...
Bryston Amps
Charles P.... Re: Bryston Amps 6/22/96 17:03...
Chuck Ross Re: Bryston Amps 6/24/96 18:21...
Are powered speakers the wave of the future?
Charles P.... Re: Are powered speakers the wave of the future? 6/22/96 17:07...
Lon Stowell Re: Are powered speakers the wave of the future? Wed 14:15 PM
Bryant Trew Re: Are powered speakers the wave of the future? Fri 21:22 PM
Kalman Rubi... Re: CAL Alpha DAC w/ Alchemy DTI-Pro 32 6/24/96 11:50...
Steve Zip... Re: CAL Alpha DAC w/ Alchemy DTI-Pro 32 6/24/96 16:23...
Tom Albertz Mid-End Questions 6/24/96 13:58...
Tibbot What is the best interconnect and speaker cable? 6/24/96 14:54...
Brian L. McC... Re: Opinions please 6/24/96 15:03...
Brian L. McC... Re: Here is the ultimate Somers/Paul/Morley/McCa... 6/24/96 15:08...
Steve Zip... Re: Here is the ultimate Somers/Paul/Morley/McCa... 6/24/96 16:25...
Allan Derri... Re: Here is the ultimate Somers/Paul/Morley/McCa... Thu 4:56 AM
Lilleston Opinions wanted: Music Hall CD player 6/24/96 15:10...
Martin Leese... Re: Home HeadRoom amp 6/24/96 15:23...
de2j@holme... Marantz CD65LE 6/24/96 15:26...
jeffrey robert Cleaning Tape Heads 6/24/96 15:36...
Anand Raman Re: Rotel CD player & Receiver 6/24/96 15:53...
Anand Raman AA Ultra DAC and Chiro C-200 6/24/96 16:10...
Ray Schoepf... Re: Old Hi-End Speakers vs New 6/24/96 16:38...
Dana Bunner Re: More on Integrated Amps 6/24/96 16:42...
Len Moskowitz Re: RECORDING AMBIENCE IN LIVE CONCERTS: ... 6/24/96 16:48...
Stewart Pink... Re: Audio Alchemy is overpriced bullshit 6/24/96 17:09...
Wade C. Da... Audiomart's phone number 6/24/96 17:23...
Lee Moore Re: Allanism to replace Science Re: Does the Shakt... 6/24/96 17:29...
Prices at Circuit City, the Good Guys, MSRPs
Document: Done

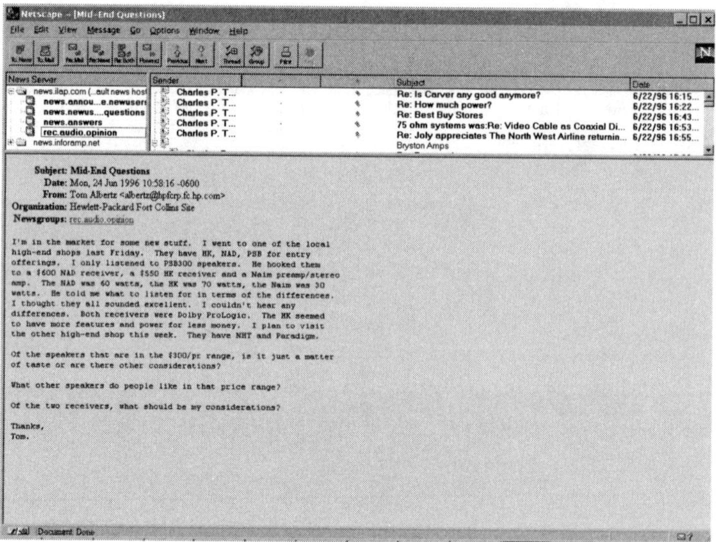
Netscape - [Mid-End Questions]
File Edit View Message Go Options Window Help
News Server
news.ilap.com (...ault news host
news.annou...e.newusers
news.newus....questions
news.answers
rec.audio.opinion
news.inforamp.net
Sender
Subject
Date
Charles P. T... Re: Is Carver any good anymore? 6/22/96 16:15...
Charles P. T... Re: How much power? 6/22/96 16:22...
Charles P. T... Re: Best Buy Stores 6/22/96 16:43...
Charles P. T... 75 ohm systems was:Re: Video Cable as Coaxial Di... 6/22/96 16:53...
Charles P. T... Re: Joly appreciates The North West Airline returnin... 6/22/96 16:55...
Bryston Amps
Subject: Mid-End Questions
Date: Mon, 24 Jun 1996 10:58:16 -0600
From: Tom Albertz <albertz@hpfcrp.fc.hp.com>
Organization: Hewlett-Packard Fort Collins Site
Newsgroups: rec.audio.opinion
I'm in the market for some new stuff. I went to one of the local
high-end shops last Friday. They have HK, NAD, PSB for entry
offerings. I only listened to PSB300 speakers. He hooked them
to a $600 NAD receiver, a $550 HK receiver and a Naim preamp/stereo
amp. The NAD was 60 watts, the HK was 70 watts, the Naim was 30
watts. He told me what to listen for in terms of the differences.
I thought they all sounded excellent. I couldn't hear any
differences. Both receivers were Dolby ProLogic. The HK seemed
to have more features and power for less money. I plan to visit
the other high-end shop this week. They have NHT and Paradigm.
Of the speakers that are in the $300/pr range, is it just a matter
of taste or are there other considerations?
What other speakers do people like in that price range?
Of the two receivers, what should be my considerations?
Thanks,
Tom.
Document: Done

Where to Find Newsreader Software

For Windows:

FreeAgent: **http://www.forteinc.com** or **ftp://ftp.forteinc.com/pub/forte**. You will find directories containing Agent and FreeAgent.

Trumpet News software can be retrieved at **ftp://magellan.iquest.com/pub/windows/papa/news**. Look for the file **wtwsklob.zip**

News Xpress: **ftp://ftp.microserve.net/pub/msdos/winsock/news_readers/**. File name begins with NX. There may be several files starting with NX; retrieve the most recent one for the latest version of the software.

For Macintosh:

InterNews: **ftp://ftp.dartmouth.edu/pub/mac/**

Retrieve file that starts with InterNews.

NewsView: **ftp://iraun1.ira.uka.de/pub/systems/mac/**

Retrieve file that starts with NewsView.

Newswatcher: **ftp://ftp.acns.nwu.edu/pub/newswatcher/**. Retrieve the file that starts with Newswatcher.

Newsreader Features

Regardless of how you access USENET, your newsreader will have a set of features that will let you do various things with USENET. Some of these features are described below. The particular software that you use may or may not have all these functions and may even support additional functions not listed here. You should be able to

- Easily join USENET newsgroups. The term used for joining a newsgroup is "subscribe." Obviously, your newsreader software should let you join, or subscribe, to newsgroups quickly and easily. FreeAgent lets you subscribe to a newsgroup, or before doing so, you can "sample" a few of the entries within the newsgroup:

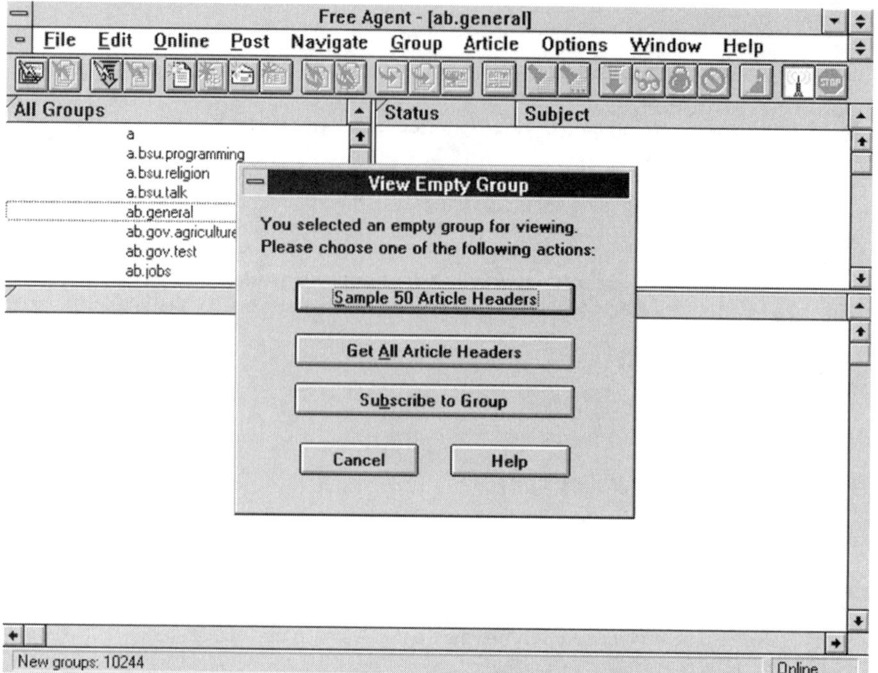

- Obtain a listing of all newsgroups and be able to search for newsgroups by "key word." One of the challenges of USENET is that new newsgroups are added to the system at a furious pace. And with several thousand newsgroups, finding the ones that might interest you can be a challenge. Your software will automatically update for any new USENET newsgroups each time you sign in. Hence your newsreader software should let you browse through a list of all USENET newsgroups; however, you should also be able to quickly see a listing of those newsgroups to which you have subscribed. In addition, you should be able to perform a quick search of all USENET newsgroups to identify only those that contain a certain word.

  In the example below, News Xpress has been used to list only those newsgroups containing the word "research." News Xpress permits you to do this by keying a "search term" at the bottom of the screen:

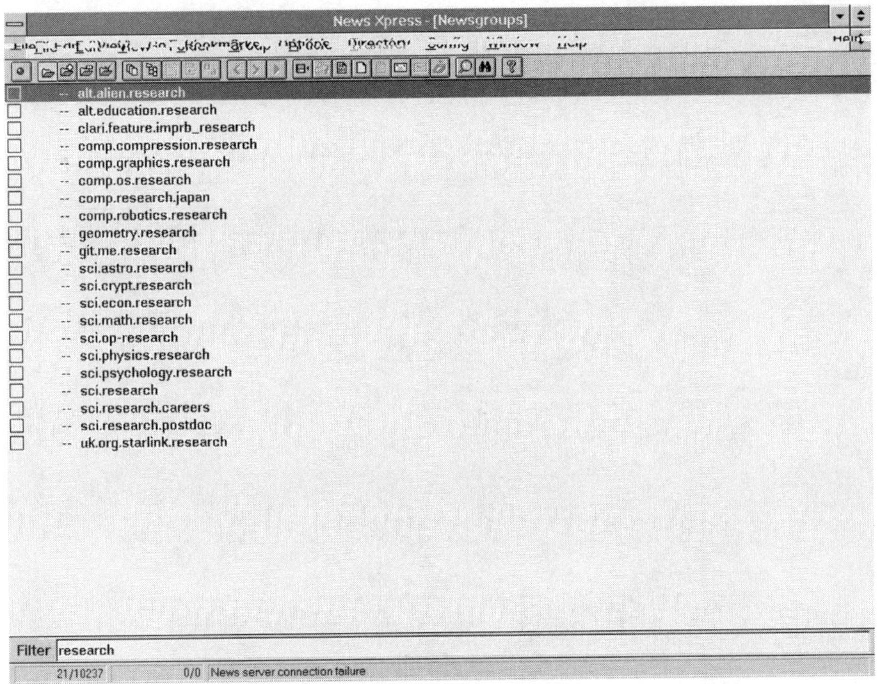

- Post an article or a follow-up to a previously posted message. Obviously, the whole point of USENET is that it allows you to participate in the discussions, so all news-reader applications allow you to put up an item or respond to a previous item. A "post" or an "article" is the term used to describe an item in a USENET newsgroup. A "follow-up" is a posting made in reference to a previous posting. Be aware that when you send a follow-up, everyone in the newsgroup can see your response, so you should be certain that you want to respond in public. Your newsreader software usually inserts a "RE:" in the subject line of a follow-up. In addition, the software should "quote" the original message (similar to how e-mail responses are quoted, as described in the previous chapter).

  As seen below, we are posting a follow-up to a USENET posting within the newsgroup **rec.travel.usa-canada.** In this case, the software has quoted the original message so that other readers will know what your follow-up is in reference to:

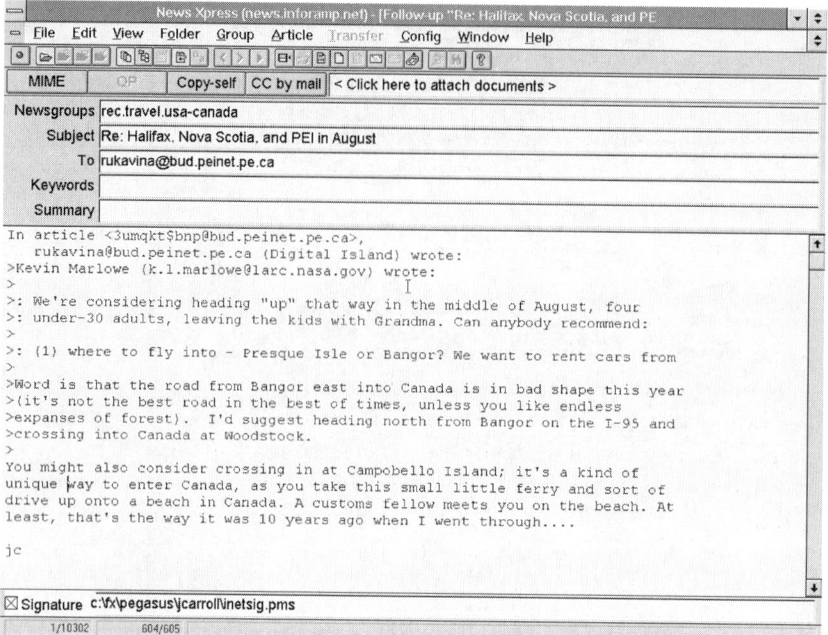

◆ Send e-mail to the author of an article or forward the message to someone else. Sometimes, you will not want to send a follow-up USENET post to everyone; you may just want to contact the author of the post directly via e-mail. Hence your newsreader software usually provides a way for you to send an e-mail to the author of any post.

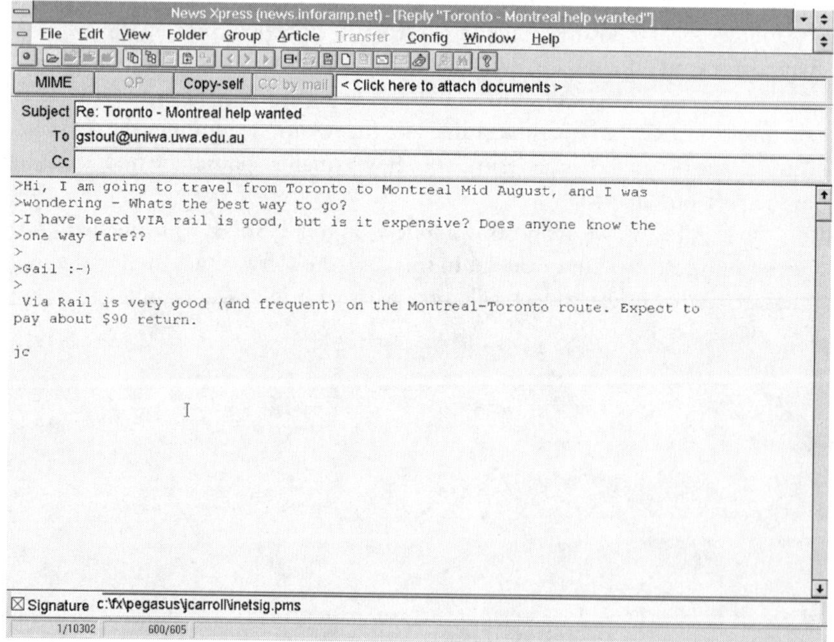

In other cases, you might want to forward the posting on to someone else, so your newsreader should provide this capability.

- Sort articles in a newsgroup. Some of the newsgroups that you will join will have a lot of postings; some see upwards of several hundred per day. Obviously, sometimes you will want to scan the list of unread articles in various ways — looking at them by date, by subject, or by author.

- View articles by "thread." Discussions within USENET can go on, sometimes for a long, long time. Certain messages generate a fast and furious response from many people. One topic might break down into discussions about many related subtopics. It can be difficult keeping track of what everyone is communicating about! Newsreader software that organizes postings by subject is very useful. Then you can follow the "thread," or topic, at hand. A "thread" is the term used to describe the original posting and all the follow-up responses to that posting.

  For example, the screen below is from the newsgroup **misc.immigration.canada**, a spot where many ask questions or share information about Canadian immigration issues. As can be seen, there were multiple postings about the topics "re: looking for a Canadian newsgroup with Job advertisements" and "The address of the Canadian Embassy in Australia." The newsreader software in this case (News Xpress) has organized the postings for us by topic, making it easier to track only those postings in which we are interested. Multiple postings related to one topic are listed under the subject:

News Xpress (news.inforamp.net) - [misc.immigration.canada]

File Edit View Folder Group Article Transfer Config Window Help

Subject	Lines	Date	From
Re: The Absolutely Fabulous US of A (more flamage of silly Amer	13	07/08 06:21 AM	JWCCTI1
Re: Where to get application form?	39	07/10 01:46 AM	dcameron@halcyon.com
Re: Do I need to prolong my visitor visa?	33	07/10 01:49 AM	dcameron@halcyon.com
Family -- visa needs place to stay	36	07/12 06:29 AM	(Ronnie D. Koehn)
Re: Looking for a canadian news group with Job advertisements	[9]		
......	18	07/13 10:29 AM	Anil K. Phalcomepely
......	21	07/15 10:55 AM	Ken Sanderson
......	4	07/19 12:17 AM	rojain@delphi.com
......	24	07/15 08:29 PM	Zoran Miscevic
......	33	07/15 08:41 PM	Zoran Miscevic
......	38	07/17 09:28 PM	Jonners
......	67	07/18 12:33 AM	Jeff Lawrence
......	24	07/18 04:34 PM	Igor Fedchenia
......	29	07/17 09:30 PM	Jonners
Re: Processing Fee for Assessment of CCPE !	24	07/13 08:31 PM	Gary E. Grant
Re: Addesses of Canadian Embassies for Applicants in Norway	15	07/13 09:28 PM	Mr A. Zafar
Sponsorship questions	18	07/14 10:16 AM	W. Bula
The address of Canadian Embassy in Australia?	[2]		
......	3	07/14 01:05 PM	Chen Xu
......	31	07/18 08:51 AM	dcameron@halcyon.com
Please help	[4]		
......	15	07/14 03:27 PM	Fan Zhen
......	26	07/15 02:24 AM	Gary E. Grant
......	36	07/18 03:07 PM	Warren Lloyd
......	30	07/18 09:11 PM	David Cohen - Attorney
Re: Help!! Sponsorship	26	07/14 08:15 PM	IO10947@MAINE.MAINE.EDU
Re: Books on Canadian companies	32	07/14 10:19 PM	IO10947@MAINE.MAINE.EDU
Re: Another dumb question	23	07/14 10:26 PM	IO10947@MAINE.MAINE.EDU
Re: Min. salary req. to sponsor fiance?	2	07/15 02:55 AM	Asif Batada
Can a student stay in USA while holding a Canadian PR?	9	07/15 04:32 AM	Jin yu Shao
Re: Fax No. to Canadian Embassy in Peking	15	07/15 09:50 AM	William P. Thomas

39/10237 168/168

Threading is a particularly useful feature to have and is increasingly supported in newsreader software.

- Use “killfiles” or “bozo filters.” Given the growth of the Internet and the number of kooks who seem to be joining it, killfiles are becoming absolute necessities. (They are often called bozo filters, since that is what they do — they filter bozos out of your USENET information. A bozo is whomever you would like it to be. You will meet lots of them on-line.) Killfiles “delete” articles sent to you that contain certain subjects or are sent from certain people, thus letting you screen out particular messages.

  Here is a simple killfile that is being used to filter out messages related to gun control and any messages from Elvis:

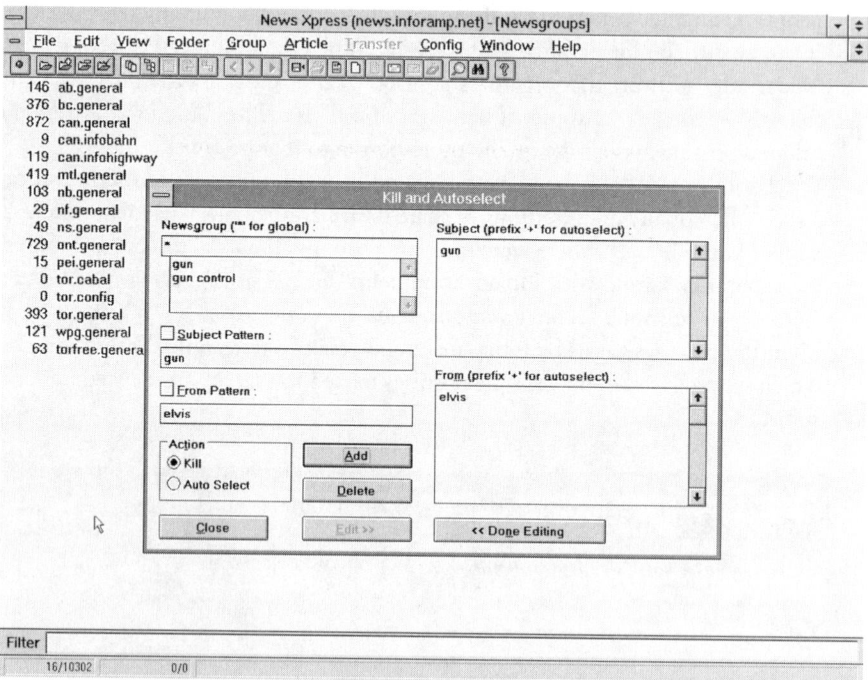

- Decode graphics. There are many USENET newsgroups to which people post graphic images, usually in uuencoded format. (Some of the more controversial newsgroups, for example, but many serious groups as well.) Remember from Chapter 6 that uuencoding is a technique that enables non-text computer files to be sent through the Internet.

  Some newsreader software lets you quickly decode such images and will even go so far as to show you the image immediately. Consider this posting, from **sci.astro**, which contains images from space. Retrieving an article containing an image shows the gibberish of a uuencoded file; however, the newsreader software lets you easily automatically “decode” the image, and even run a program to immediately view it once it is decoded:

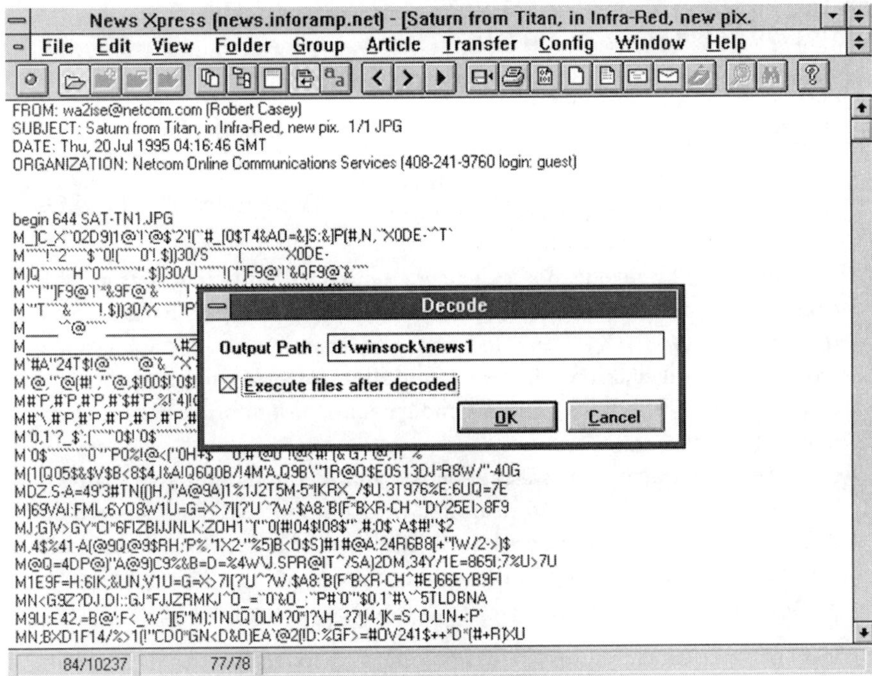

- Rotate postings (ROT-13). **rec.humor.funny** is the most popular USENET newsgroup. Within it, you can usually find all kinds of new humorous postings each and every day. This includes the occasional posting of politically incorrect or offensive information. To keep you from seeing such items without warning, they are "rotated," a very simple method of changing characters in a message; for example, A turns into N, B turns into O. If you want to read the posting, you choose to ROT-13 it, then you can see the politically incorrect or offensive item.

- Alert you to interesting stuff. Another way to deal with large volumes of information on USENET is to use the reverse of a bozo filter — an "interesting filter." Some newsreader software will let you set up a profile so that you are "alerted" if certain people post an item, or if there is a posting about a particular subject that interests you.

- See old articles. Sometimes, you may wish to look at older USENET postings, and some newsreader software will let you do so. However, keep in mind that due to the overwhelming volume of information sent through USENET, most providers do not keep more than a week or two of information.

- Crosspost to multiple groups. A newsreader should let you post to several groups at once (referred to as "crossposting"). However, this feature should be used with extreme caution, since it is easy to offend people on the Internet by crossposting.

USENET: What It Is Not

There are some things that you should know about USENET:

- It is not the Internet. USENET happens to be carried over the Internet as well as other networks. However, it has come to be so closely identified as an "Internet resource" that most people think of USENET as being a fundamental part of the Internet.
- It is not owned by anyone, nor is there one central authority that runs it. USENET exists because of the cooperative efforts of thousands of people: first and foremost, the thousands of UNIX systems and news administrators of subscribing systems around the world, and second, through the efforts of a large number of volunteers who catalogue USENET resources, conduct votes, post information, and participate in countless other ways.

  The result is an on-line system that is managed through the cooperative effort of literally thousands of people from around the globe. Some call it organized or cooperative anarchy. However, it does have a "culture" and it does have "rules," which have more or less been accepted throughout the community. This is referred to as network etiquette, or "netiquette," which is discussed in greater depth below.
- It is not for commercial use. There is no surer way to receive streams of on-line abuse than by using USENET for blatant advertising. USENET was formed by volunteers who wanted to exchange information on topics. Its entire history and culture holds the concept of advertising within USENET in extreme contempt. You do not do well by violating one of the cultural foundations of USENET.

  USENET was developed to support the exchange of knowledge and information. There are thousands of topics; yet with all the millions of news articles posted to USENET, it maintains its culture. Even as the Internet becomes more commercialized, USENET seems to be maintaining its status as a system not to be blatantly used for commercial purposes, even though there are some buy-and-sell newsgroups.
- It is used to a limited extent for commercial purposes. Even though USENET is not for commercial use, there are some newsgroups that exist for distribution of information concerning certain products and for service announcements from system vendors. For example, **rec.comics.marketplace** is used by people to exchange information about the sale of rare comics. USENET is a study in contradictions.

  What does this mean? You might use USENET with regard to your business: "I am trying to get my computer to do this; does anyone have any hints?" But you certainly should not use USENET to try to drum up business: "Hey, I've started a consulting firm. Call me if you need help — my rates are $120 an hour."

Network Etiquette

The most important thing you can learn about USENET is that it has a unique on-line culture, and those who do not respect this culture do so at their own peril. The culture includes procedures and guidance concerning topics such as newsgroup creation (as described above); what the network can be used for (e.g., non-commercial activity); how to post news articles; newsgroup names; official versus non-official newsgroups; chain letters; inappropriate postings; and hundreds of other issues of etiquette.

The easiest ways to learn about USENET culture are to join several newsgroups and to obtain documents on rules and netiquette. By joining several newsgroups, you can watch how they work for some time. In particular, if you are interested in how USENET newsgroups are established, subscribe to the groups **news.announce.newgroups** and **news.groups**. In **news.announce.newgroups** proposals for new groups are posted. **News.groups** is where these proposals are debated.

Be prepared to be shocked by what you might see in a debate involving a new proposed topic: sometimes simple proposals for a new newsgroup degenerate into raging debates, with emotions getting out of hand and insults and accusations flying with fury. Why? This is the culture of USENET. There is no better way to understand the culture of USENET than to belong to **news.groups** for a few months.

Documents such as "A Primer on How to Work with the USENET Community" and "Rules for Posting to USENET" are posted regularly to the groups **news.newusers.questions** and **news.answers** and can also be retrieved from a number of FTP locations. The following screens shows them as listed in **news.newusers.questions** and within **ftp://rtfm.mit.edu/pub/usenet/news.announce.newusers:**

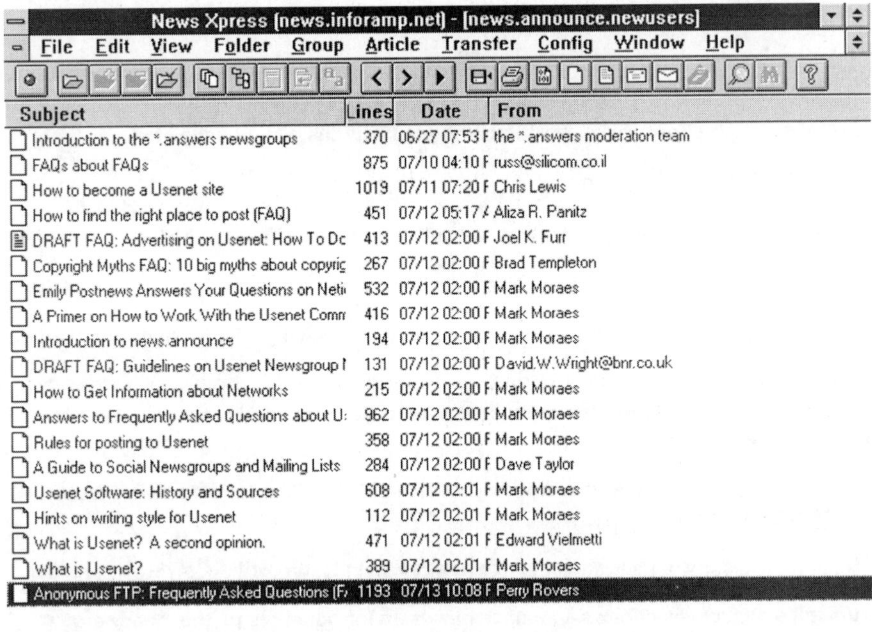

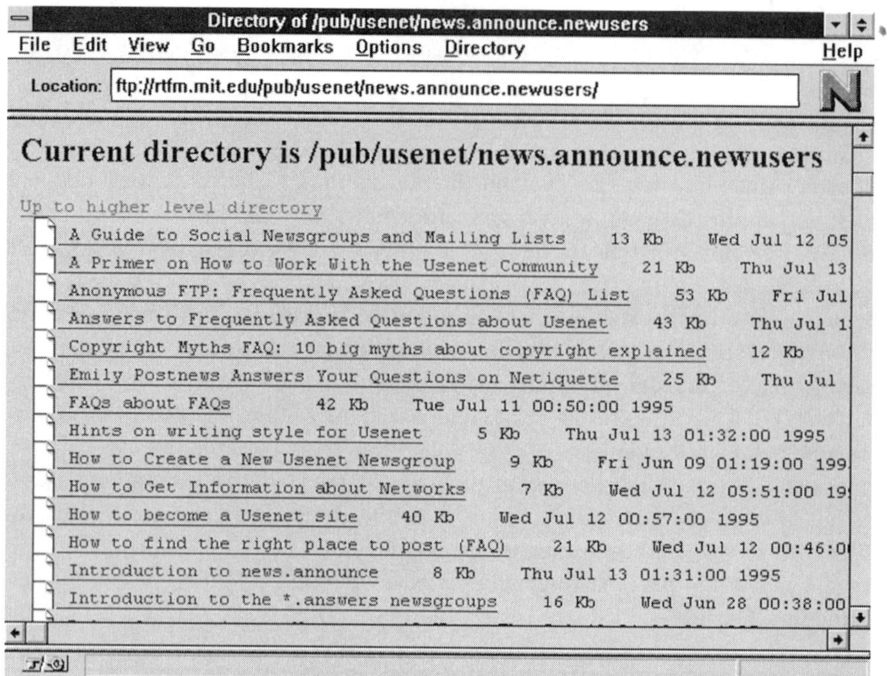

Retrieving Documents About "Netiquette"

The Net: User Guidelines and Netiquette: **http://www.fau.edu/rinaldi/netiquette.html**

What is USENET? A second opinion:

http://www.cis.ohio-state.edu/hypertext/faq/usenet/usenet/what-is/part2/faq.html

The granddaddies of all documents about Netiquette can found in the series of documents noted below:

ftp://rtfm.mit.edu/pub/usenet/news.announce.newusers/A_Primer_on_How_to_Work_With_the_Usenet_Community

ftp://rtfm.mit.edu/pub/usenet/news.announce.newusers/Answers_to_Frequently_Asked_Questions_about_Usenet

ftp://rtfm.mit.edu/pub/usenet/news.announce.newusers/Emily_Postnews_Answers_Your_Questions_on_Netiquette

ftp://rtfm.mit.edu/pub/usenet/news.announce.newusers/Hints_on_writing_style_for_Usenet

ftp://rtfm.mit.edu/pub/usenet/news.announce.newusers/Introduction_to_the_*.answers_newsgroups

ftp://rtfm.mit.edu/pub/usenet/news.announce.newusers/Rules_for_posting_to_Usenet

ftp://rtfm.mit.edu/pub/usenet/news.announce.newusers/What_is_Usenet?

Lists of Newsgroups

Hopefully, your newsreader software will let you obtain a listing of all USENET newsgroups and perform a search of the list. However, if you want a list of USENET newsgroups in the major USENET categories, you can look for several items. Look for the document "List of Active Newsgroups," which is posted to the group **news.announce.newgroups** on a frequent basis. It can also be found in the areas noted below:

> To Obtain the Document "List of Active Newsgroups."
>
> **ftp://rtfm.mit.edu/pub/usenet/news.lists/**
>
> Look for the document "List of Active Newsgroups."

You can also retrieve a listing of newsgroups in the **alt.** hierarchy as follows:

> To Obtain a List of **alt.** Newsgroups:
>
> **ftp://rtfm.mit.edu/pub/usenet/news.lists/**
>
> Look for the document "Alternative Newsgroup Hierarchies."

You can also access lists of newsgroups on the World Wide Web and through FTP. For example, here is the USENET Info Center Launch Pad at **http://sunsite.unc.edu/usenet-i/**:

You can also check Tile.Net (**http://tile.net**) for up-to-date listings of newsgroups.

Another document worth checking is "How to find the right place to post (FAQ)" available at the URL **ftp://rtfm.mit.edu/pub/usenet/news.answers/finding-groups/general**.

You should also check with your Internet service provider to obtain a list of the newsgroups provided. Not all providers distribute all newsgroups. If your ISP does not carry a newsgroup that interests you, you can ask the provider to do so; often the ISP will comply, although there is no obligation on the part of the ISP.

Internet Mailing Lists

Sometimes you will not find a topic that you are looking for within USENET newsgroups. In other cases, you might tire of the freewheeling atmosphere of an unmoderated USENET newsgroup, but still want to keep up-to-date on a particular topic. Or you may have become tired of the excessive amount of useless information within USENET. In these cases you might prefer joining an Internet electronic mailing list instead.

Internet mailing lists are another convenient method by which people on different computer systems can discuss particular topics or share information concerning specific issues. A mailing list may consist of as few as two people, or it may contain several thousand. With thousands of different mailing lists on the Internet, you can choose to join any particular one that interests you, as long as it is a public, or open, list. Once you have joined, you will receive any messages sent to the list. An Internet mailing list operates as shown in Figure 11.1.

FIGURE 11.1
Internet Mailing Lists

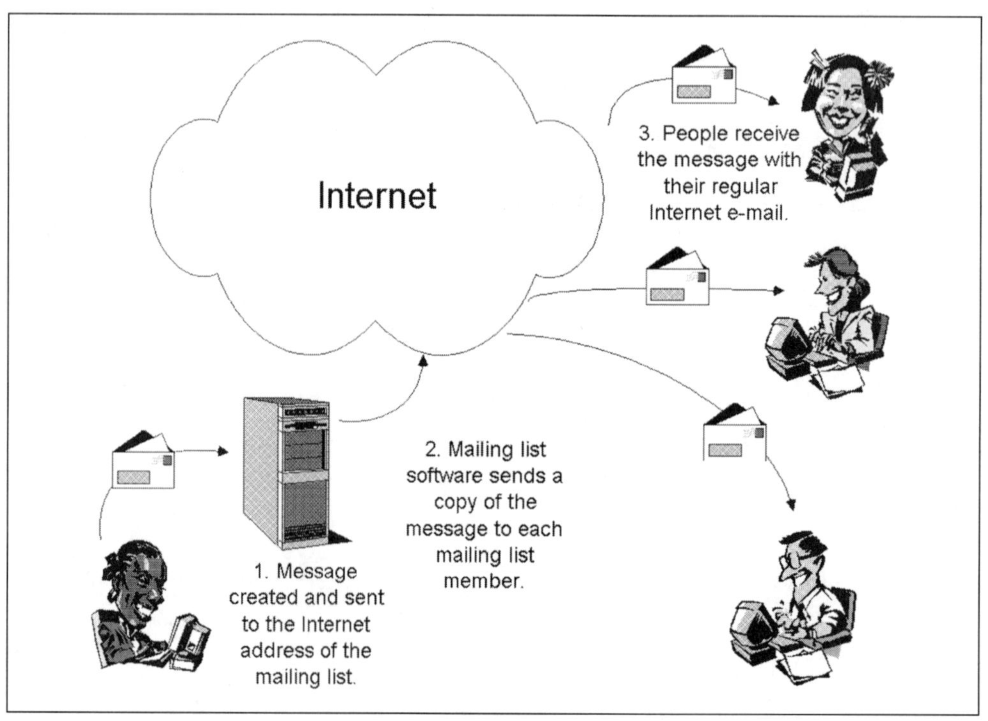

With the growing number of e-mail systems that have the capability of sending messages to and receiving messages from the Internet, it is no surprise that there are thousands of Internet mailing lists on virtually every topic imaginable.

Types of Lists

Mailing lists on the Internet differ by their purpose: some are used for discussion, while others are used for newsletters or announcements, and yet others are used to summarize information that has appeared in other lists or in USENET newsgroups.

Mailing lists have emerged as a new method of publishing; a number of journals, newsletters, and other information summaries are available to anyone with Internet e-mail access. In other cases, companies are establishing customer mailing lists that customers can choose to join in order to receive new product announcements or other information. The types of mailing lists available throughout the Internet are moderated, unmoderated, and closed.

Moderated

Lists are moderated to ensure that messages sent to the list are tightly focused on the list topic. In a moderated list, any message sent by you goes to the "moderator," who determines whether it should be redistributed to the list. This helps to keep the list on topic. The moderator, who manages the list, is an individual who takes on responsibility for sending messages to the list. The moderator takes an active role in determining what should be sent to the list, ensuring that only those messages relevant to the topic of the list are received by subscribers.

Moderated lists are most often used for newsletters and journals. For example, you can join "Elements," a list to which the "Keplarian elements" of space shuttle flights are sent on a regular basis. Both professional scientists and amateurs input these numerical elements into space object tracking software to plot the track of the shuttle currently in orbit. (Send a message to **elements-request@thomsoft.com** for more information.)

Unmoderated

In an unmoderated list any message sent by you immediately goes to everyone on the list. An unmoderated list might permit anyone to send to it, or it might be restricted, permitting only members to send to it. A good example is the Track-Canada mailing list, which is used by those involved in Canadian track and field, road racing, and triathlons. Details about the list can be found at **http://home.cc.umanitoba.ca/~csghoy/WhatisTC.html:**

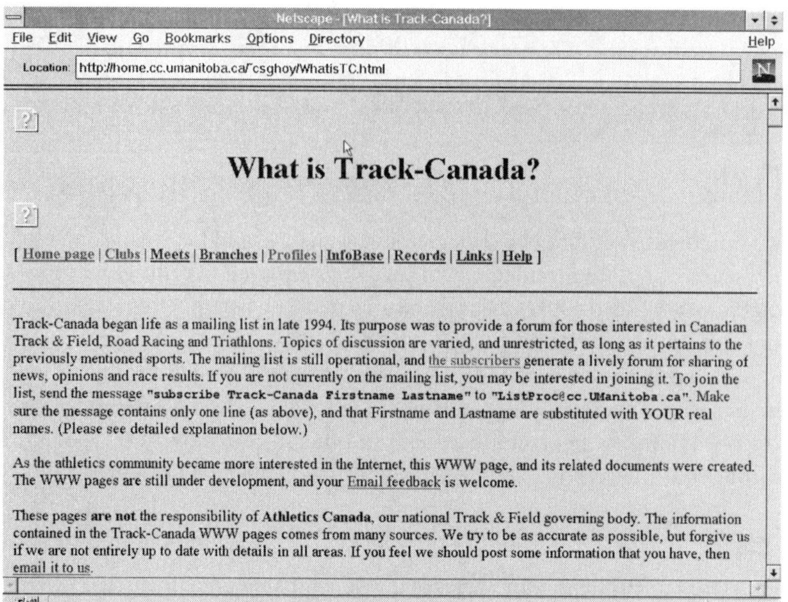

Closed

The Internet is a very diverse place; this results in some lists that simply are not open to everyone, "closed" lists. You must meet some type of qualification to join these lists — even to receive messages sent to the list. These lists are often used to restrict access to members of a particular organization. The Canadian Bar Association, for example, runs a number of mailing lists that only members can join.

Using Lists: The Mechanics

The mechanics of Internet mailing lists are quite straightforward. Normally, you join a list through electronic mail, although in some cases you can join one through the World Wide Web.

By E-mail

In most cases, you subscribe or join an Internet mailing list by sending an e-mail message to an Internet address established for the purposes of list maintenance. Your e-mail message contains a special line of text indicating that you wish to join the list. For example, we can join a list called CANADA-L by sending a message to the e-mail address **listserv@vm1.mcgill.ca** and then typing into the text of the message **subscribe canada-l yourname**. The actual command you use will depend upon the list software in use at the remote location.

Once your message has been received at the destination, your request to be added to or deleted from a list is processed manually by the list owner or processed by a specialized piece of software (called a "list manager," but also regularly referred to as a "listserver"), which automatically makes the change to the appropriate list. In the case of Canada-L, your request is processed by software known as a "listserv."

The following message is a copy of an original request to subscribe to the mailing list called Canada-L:

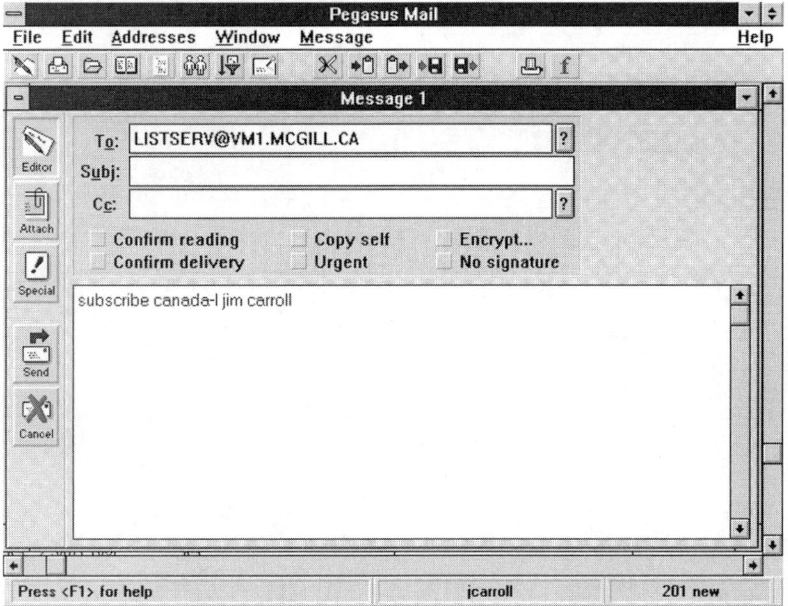

When this message was received at McGill University (at the e-mail address **listserv@vm1.mcgill.ca**), the program called listserv processed the details of the message, and the Internet e-mail address **jcarroll@jacc.com** was added to the list. Confirmation of this was sent back in the form of an e-mail message, which provided details about the list as well as all-important information about how to leave the list in the future. Never lose such instructions. Most lists return such a message as soon as you subscribe.

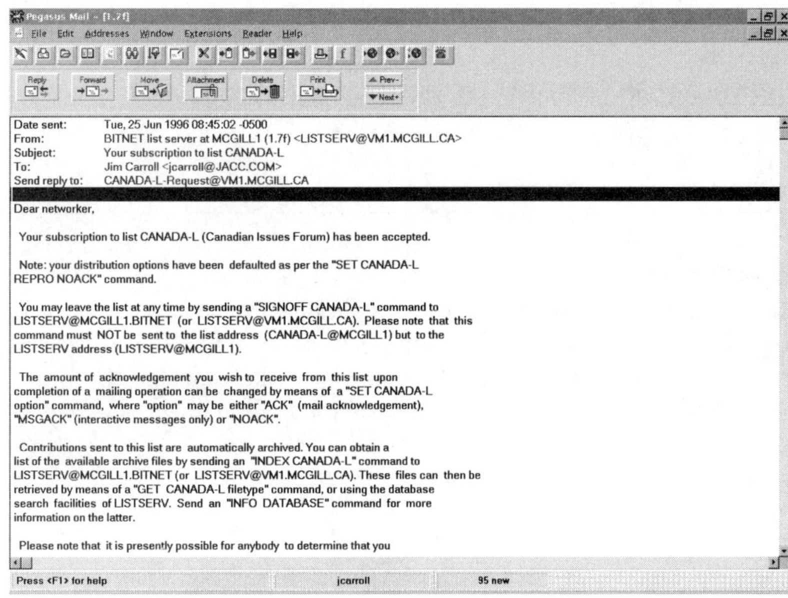

To leave this list, you simply send a message containing the sign-off instructions:

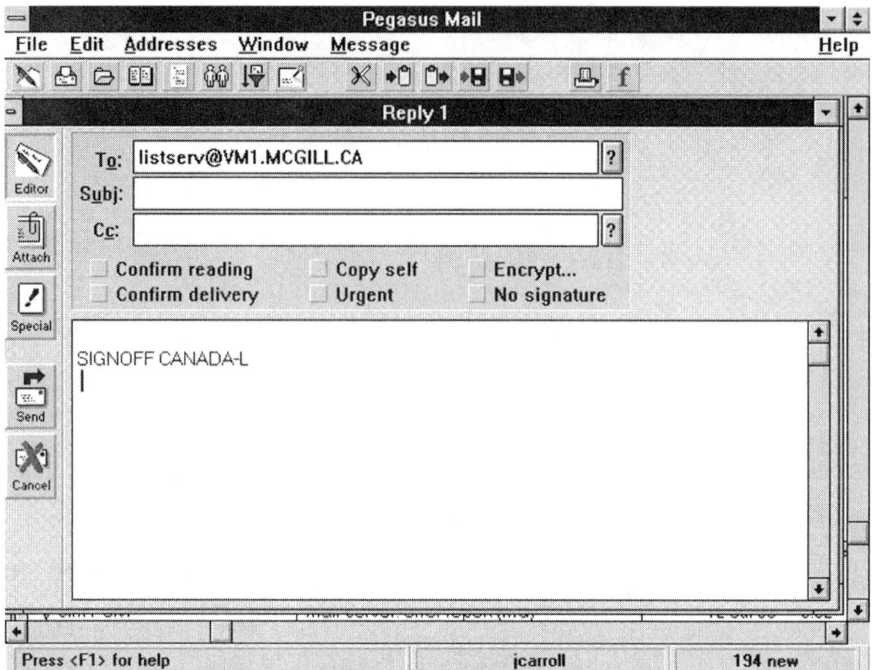

There are several automatic list managers throughout the Internet, including the programs **majordomo**, LISTSERV, and **mailserv**, all of which have their own unique methods for joining and leaving a list.

> To obtain this document using e-mail:
>
> send a message to: **listserv@ubvm.cc.buffalo.edu**
>
> In text of message, type: **get mailser cmd nettrain**
>
> To obtain this document on-line:
>
> URL: **http://lawlib.slu.edu/training/mailser.htm**

Through the Web

An increasing number of mailing lists are supporting a feature that allows you to subscribe by filling out a form on the World Wide Web. For example, the form (at **http://www2.advantage.com/Lists/Lists.html**) permits you to join various Vancouver Canucks mailing lists or permits you to easily request more information about a particular list before joining:

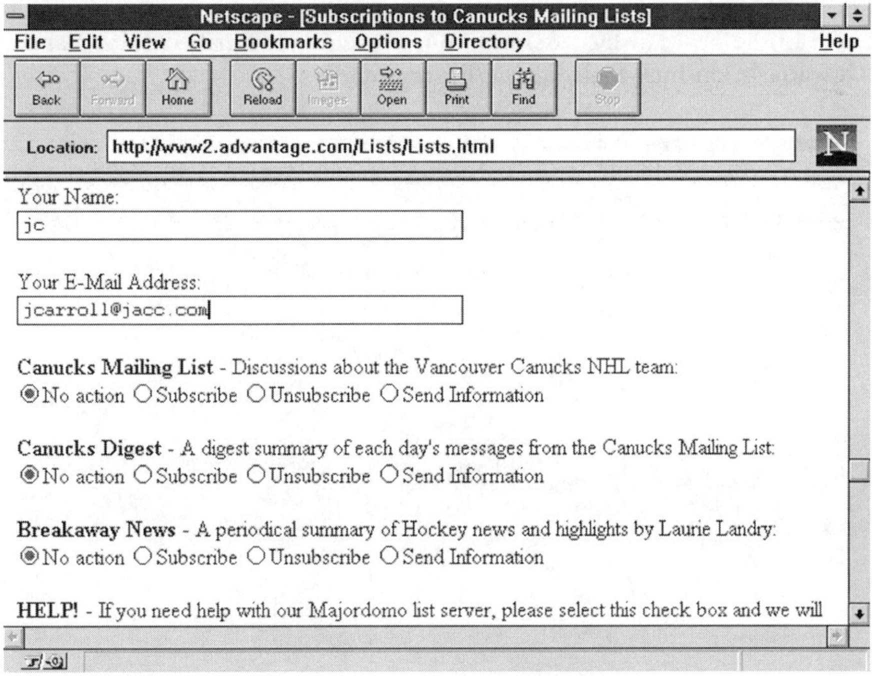

Starting Your Own List

One of the greatest benefits of the Internet is that anyone can establish an Internet mailing list. Your Internet service provider may be able to provide you with your own Internet mailing lists. If so, you can establish a mailing list on a particular topic and invite your friends and peers to join the list. Over time, you may find that the list begins to gain recognition throughout the Internet.

In addition, establishing automatic list servers through e-mail software is becoming more and more popular. Pegasus Mail for DOS and Windows, for example, includes this feature.

Many Internet lists began informally, but some have emerged to become the global "home" for a particular topic. Given the power of global knowledge networking, establishing your own mailing list on a topic of importance to you could become one of your most useful Internet resources.

Finding Lists

The obvious question now is, "How do I find a particular list?" You may hear about a mailing list by word of mouth or mentioned in some Internet resource that you track. Some USENET newsgroups, for instance, are often used to announce new lists (discussed in next section). However, there are also a number of resources on the Internet that provide details on thousands of mailing lists. These resources usually provide some background information concerning the list as well as instructions on how to join.

Let's take a look at a few examples. Later in this chapter we will detail some of the places you can go to access these "lists of lists."

Canada-L is a list used for the discussion of Canadian political, social, and other issues. It is listed in the "E-Mail Discussion Groups" archive (described below) as follows (**http://www.nova.edu/Inter-Links/cgi-bin/lists?canada-1**):

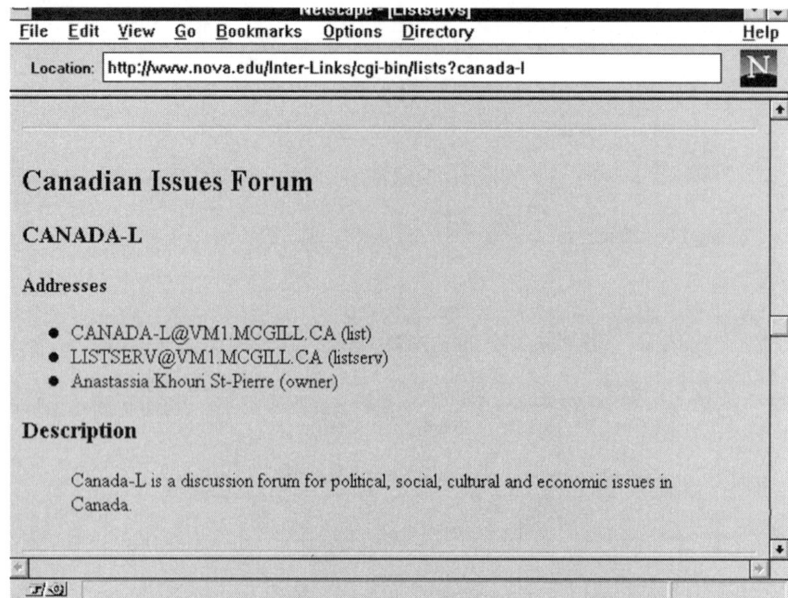

The same list is described in the Tile.Net listserv Database (described below) as follows (**http://www.tile.net/tile/listserv/canadal.html**):

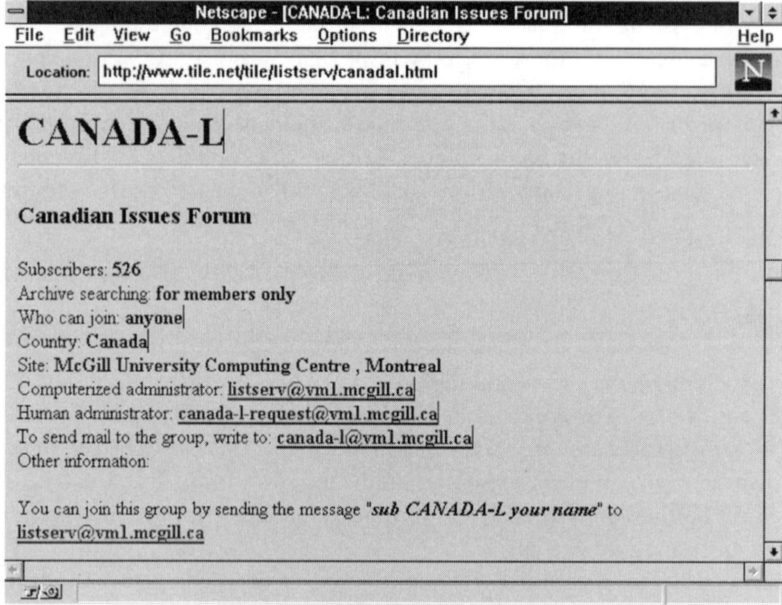

But it is not listed in the "Publicly Accessible Mailing Lists" database (described below), which is one of the largest summaries available. Hence, if you are looking for a list about a particular topic, it is usually worthwhile to check several sources.

Whatever the case may be, it is now quite simple to find lists by topic. The level of detail that each Internet resource provides varies, and not all lists are included in all resources. Many of the resources also include information on lists that have become defunct or that have been superseded by some newer list. Some of the more popular sources are detailed below.[4]

If retrieving these documents by e-mail, keep in mind that these documents are quite large; for example, the List of Interest Groups described below is over 1.2 megabytes in size. If you are using a commercial e-mail provider that charges on a per character basis, be prepared for a rather hefty bill!

None of these sources are comprehensive. But since new lists are being added throughout the Internet on a regular basis, these summaries are a good starting point to get an idea of the lists that are out there. For each summary of lists, we describe how to obtain it by e-mail and also provide the uniform resource locators so that you can access them using FTP or through the World Wide Web.

USENET

A good starting point to get many documents about lists on the Internet is through the USENET newsgroup **news.lists**. Here, you will find many of the following summaries posted on a regular basis, as well as other information concerning Internet lists.

Publicly Accessible Mailing Lists

This is the definitive summary of Internet lists. Revised monthly, the list contains a detailed description of each list as well as information on how to subscribe.

To obtain this listing using e-mail:

Send message to: **mail-server@rtfm.mit.edu**

In text of message, type:

send /pub/usenet/news.answers/mail/mailing-lists/part01

send /pub/usenet/news.answers/mail/mailing-lists/part02

send /pub/usenet/news.answers/mail/mailing-lists/part03

send /pub/usenet/news.answers/mail/mailing-lists/part04

send /pub/usenet/news.answers/mail/mailing-lists/part05

send /pub/usenet/news.answers/mail/mailing-lists/part06

send /pub/usenet/news.answers/mail/mailing-lists/part07

4. This being the Internet, you might find that some of the instructions below do not work. The Internet is constantly changing, and we often find that sometimes we print a pointer to a list, only to have the pointer change the month after we go to print. We have had some readers complain about this, but keep in mind that the Internet is a massive global network with millions of people. Things go out of date, and disappear.

send /pub/usenet/news.answers/mail/mailing-lists/part08

send /pub/usenet/news.answers/mail/mailing-lists/part09

send /pub/usenet/news.answers/mail/mailing-lists/part10

send /pub/usenet/news.answers/mail/mailing-lists/part11

send /pub/usenet/news.answers/mail/mailing-lists/part12

send /pub/usenet/news.answers/mail/mailing-lists/part13

send /pub/usenet/news.answers/mail/mailing-lists/part14

send /pub/usenet/news.answers/mail/mailing-lists/part15

send /pub/usenet/news.answers/mail/mailing-lists/part16

send /pub/usenet/news.answers/mail/mailing-lists/part17

To obtain the document on-line:

URL: **ftp://rtfm.mit.edu/ pub/usenet/news.answers/mail/mailing-lists/**, select any part from 1 to 22

URL: **http://www.neosoft.com/internet/paml/**

Viewing the document on-line through the World Wide Web is particularly useful, since you can quickly browse through the names of various lists or review list types by category:

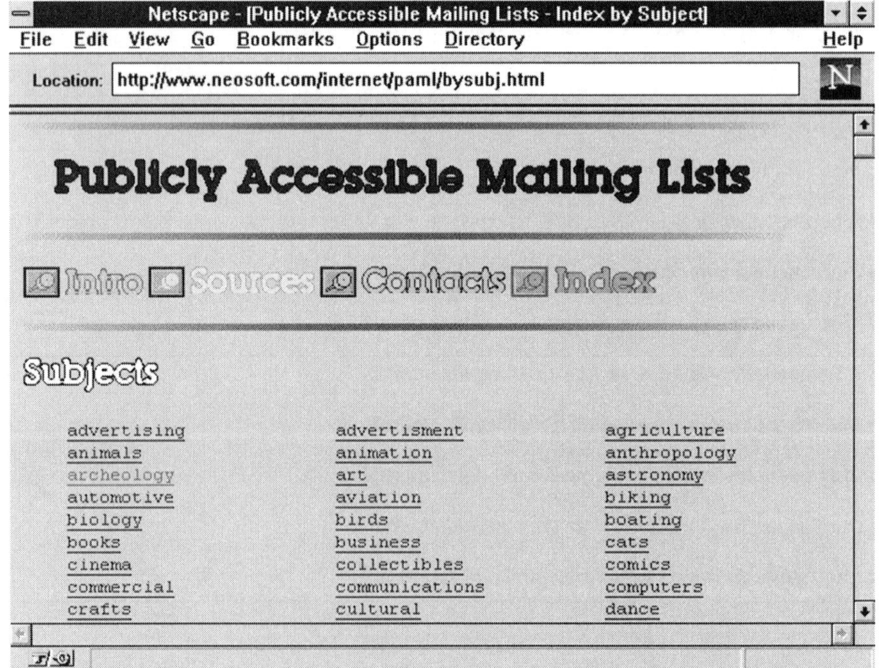

List of Interest Groups

This document refers to itself as the "List of lists," a listing of special interest group mailing lists available on the Internet.

> To obtain this listing using e-mail:
>
> Send message to: **mail-server@sri.com**
>
> In text of message, type: **send netinfo/interest-groups.txt**
>
> To obtain this listing on-line:
>
> URL: **ftp://sri.com/netinfo/interest-groups.txt**
>
> Note: this file is over 1 MB in size.

E-mail Discussion Groups

A comprehensive database of lists that can be searched by topic can be found at **http://www.nova.edu/Inter-Links/listserv.html**. A search for lists mentioning Canada found many references:

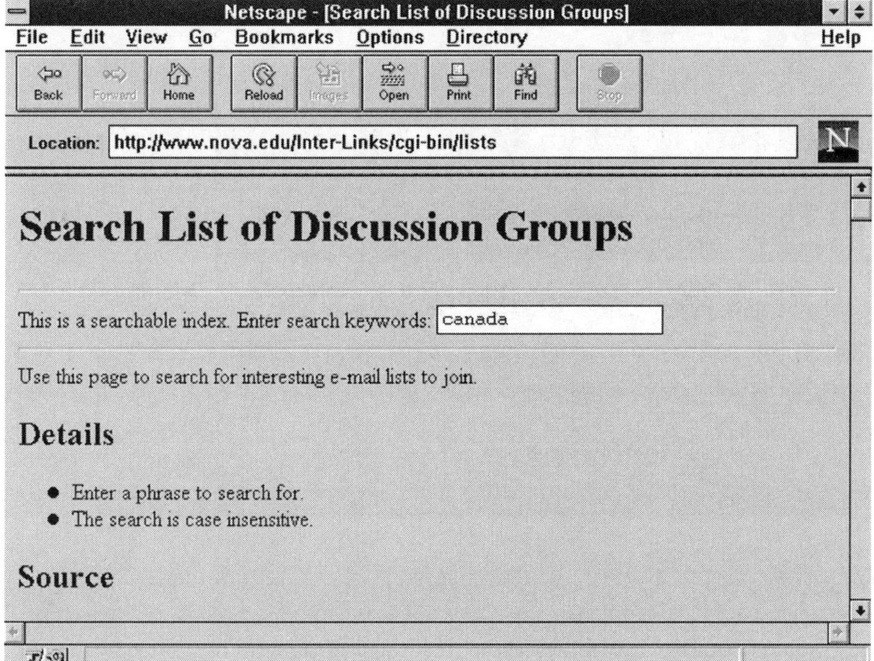

LISTSERV Databases

Tile.Net is a comprehensive database of listserv lists from around the world that you can list by category or topic (**http://www.tile.net/tile/listserv/**):

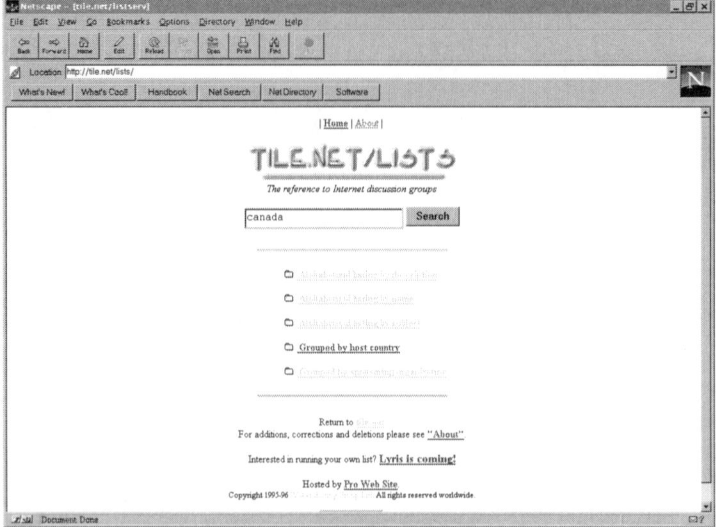

A search for Canada returned a number of results.

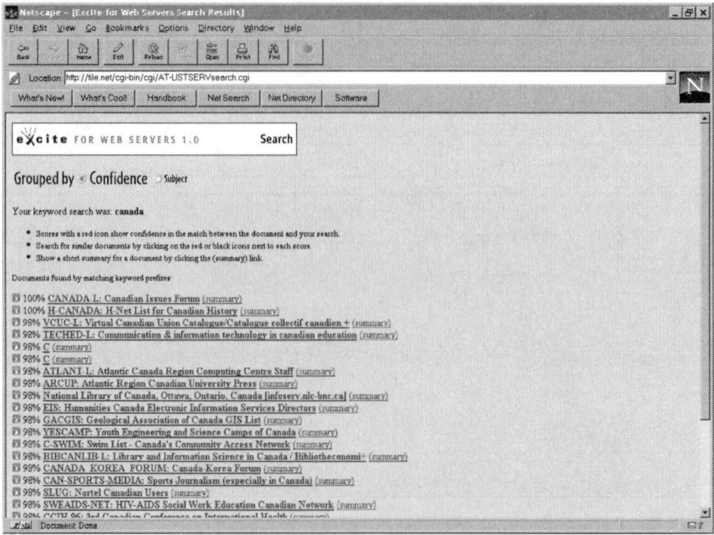

Another example of a listserv database is CataList (**http://www.lsoft.com**), which contains a searchable database of public listserv lists. The site is maintained by L-Soft International, the company that develops and distributes listserv mailing list software. You can view the entire list of listserv lists organized either by country or in alphabetical order.

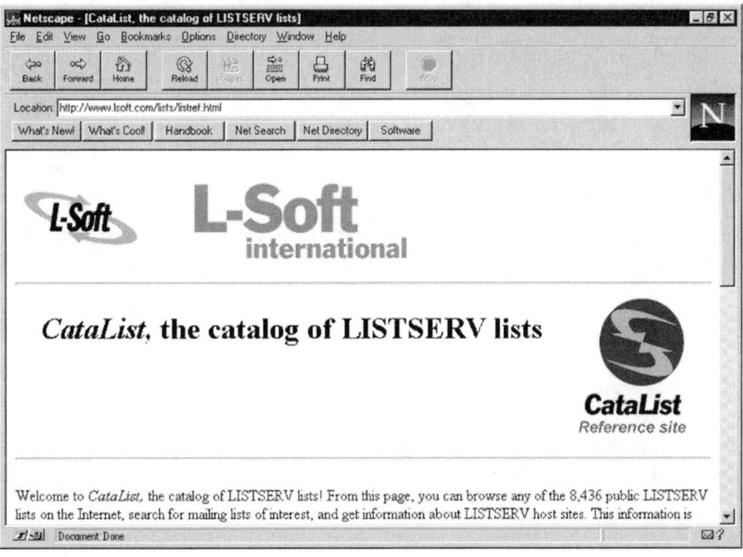

Argus Clearinghouse

This is one of the first places to look when looking for a mailing list on a specific topic. The Argus Clearinghouse (**http://www.clearinghouse.net**), based at the University of Michigan, contains dozens of topical guides to Internet mailing lists and other Internet resources. The guides have been prepared by countless volunteers and subject experts from all over globe. Categories include arts and entertainment, business and employment, education, engineering and technology, environment, government and law, health and medicine, the humanities, news and publishing, regional information, science, and social sciences and social issues. If you cannot find an Internet guide for your particular area of interest, consider compiling one and submitting it to the Clearinghouse.

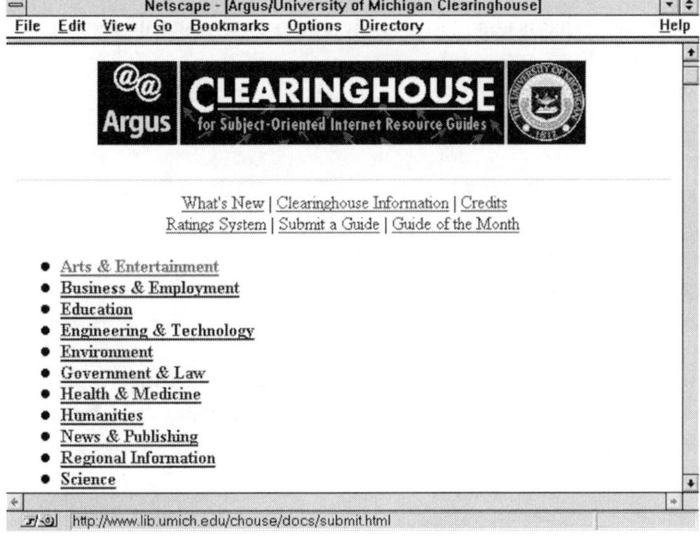

World Wide Web Virtual Library

A system distributed throughout the Internet, the World Wide Web Virtual Library covers over 150 different topics. Within each category you can find a comprehensive listing of mailing lists related to that category (**http://www.w3.org/hypertext/DataSources/bySubject/Overview.html**).

New-list Mailing List

This is a mailing list for announcements of new mailing lists. You might want to join this so that you can see if any new topics of interest to you have started up.

> To join this list using e-mail:
>
> Send message to: **listserv@vm1.nodak.edu**
>
> In text of message type: **subscribe new-list firstname lastname**
>
> Special instructions: Replace **firstname lastname** above with your own firstname and lastname.

List of USENET Groups That Are Available as Mailing Lists

This is a list of USENET newsgroups that are also available as mailing lists.

> To obtain this listing using e-mail:
>
> Send message to: **mail-server@rtfm.mit.edu**
>
> In text of message type: **send pub/usenet/news.answers/mail/news-gateways/part1**
>
> To obtain this listing online:
>
> URL: **ftp://rtfm.mit.edu/pub/usenet/news.answers/mail/news-gateways/part1**

Net-Happenings List

If you really want to track what is going on with the Internet, you should join the Global Internet: Net-Happenings list.

> To access this resource:
>
> USENET: **comp.internet.net-happenings**
>
> To review on-line:
>
> URL: **http://www.gi.net.80/NET/**

This list has about 15 to 20 messages per day. Announcements concerning new mailing lists and other Internet resources are sent to this list on a regular basis throughout the day. In addition, information that even remotely impacts the Internet, such as initiatives relating to the "information highway" or "national information infrastructure," are often sent to the list. The result is a continuous stream of messages that are wide-ranging and varied, but somehow relate to the Internet.

You should only join this list if you have a desire to receive a lot of e-mail and you want to track what is going on with the Internet. This list is for hard-core Internet junkies only. You can also search archives of this list, so that you can quickly zero in on announcements of new mailing lists, an example of which is seen below:

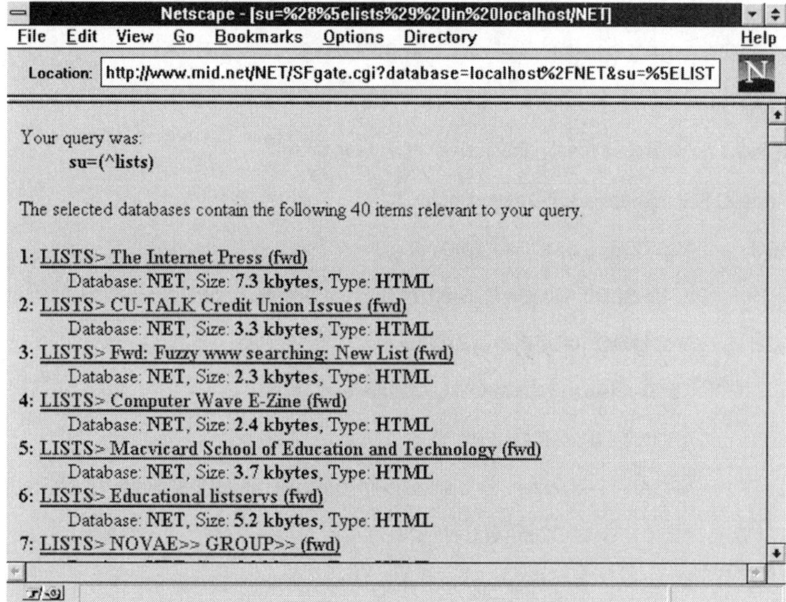

Searching LISTSERV Lists

It is possible to search several of these lists of lists. For example, you can search the LISTSERV lists database by sending a specially formatted e-mail message.

To search the LISTSERV list database using e-mail:
Send message to: **listserv@listserv.net**
In text of message type: **list global/keyword**
Special instructions: Replace **keyword** above with the word you wish to search.

For example, if you are looking for a list on Canada, you could send the command **list global/canada** to **listserv@listserv.net**. A search will be performed on the LISTSERV lists database, and an automatic reply will be mailed back to you containing the names of all the LISTSERV mailing lists that contain the word "canada." The automatic reply will look like this:

Date sent: Sat, 3 Aug 1996 20:00:31 -0400
From: BITNET list server at BITNIC (1.8a)
<LISTSERV@BITNIC.cren.net>
Subject: File: "LISTSERV LISTS"
To: Jim Carroll <jcarroll@JACC.COM>
Excerpt from the LISTSERV lists known to LISTSERV@BITNIC on 3 Aug 1996 20:00
Search string: CANADA

* To subscribe, send mail to LISTSERV@LISTSERV.NET with the following *

* command in the text (not the subject) of your message:*

SUBSCRIBE listname

* Replace 'listname' with the name in the first column of the table. *

Network-wide ID Full address and list description

ACMBSBBS ACMBSBBS@MCGILL1.BITNET

ACMBSBBS ACMBS Network of Canada Bulletin Board Service

ANCANACH ANCANACH@UABDPO.BITNET

Clan Henderson Society of US/Canada

ARCAN-L ARCAN-L@UALTAVM.BITNET

ARCAN-L — Listserv for discussion of archival issues in Canada

ASACNET ASACNET@PDOMAIN.UWINDSOR.CA

ASACNET- Administrative Sciences Association of Canada

ATLANT-L ATLANT-L@UNBVM1.BITNET

Atlantic Canada Region Computing Centre Staff

BIBSOCAN BIBSOCAN@UTORONTO.BITNET

Bibliographical Society of Canada

C-NET C-NET@UNBVM1.BITNET

C-NET: Community Access Net * Canada

CA-SPEED CA-SPEED@ASUACAD.BITNET

EDI topics among post-secondary institutions in Canada

CACI-L CACI-L@UALTAVM.BITNET

Research and Advanced Study: Canada and Italy

CANADA-L CANADA-L@MCGILL1.BITNET

Canadian Issues Forum

CASTOR CASTOR@YORKVM1.BITNET

American Schools of Oriental Research in Canada

CNC-L	CNC-L@UVVM.BITNET
	China News (Canada)
CNETIE-L	CNETIE-L@UALTAVM.BITNET
	International Centre Communication Network (Canada and elsewhe+
E-CANADA	E-CANADA@UICVM.BITNET
	History of Canada Editorial Board List
EIS	EIS@MORGAN.UCS.MUN.CA
	Humanities Canada Electronic Information Services Directors
FRANCO-L	FRANCO-L@UALTAVM.BITNET
	FRANCO-L Recherche & discussion entre francophones, surtout du+
GACGIS	GACGIS@MORGAN.UCS.MUN.CA
	Geological Association of Canada GIS List
H-CANADA	H-CANADA@MSU.EDU
	H-Net List for Canadian History
HELWA-L	HELWA-L@PSUVM.BITNET
	Malaysian Women in U.S. and Canada
HRIS-L	HRIS-L@UALTAVM.BITNET
	Human Resources Information (Canada)
INTAUD-L	INTAUD-L@UALTAVM.BITNET
	University Internal Audit (Canada)
PGS-S	PGS-S@UTORONTO.BITNET
	Physicians for Global Survival (Canada) — Students
SSFC-L	SSFC-L@UOTTAWA.BITNET
	Social Sciences Federation of Canada Discussion List
UBCREV-L	UBCREV-L@UALTAVM.BITNET
	UBCREV-L is a forum for Deans of Universities in Canada.
WIMNET-L	WIMNET-L@UALTAVM.BITNET
	Women in Management division of the Adm. Sci. Assoc. of Canada
WMCIC-L	WMCIC-L@QUCDN.BITNET
	Women's Committee of the Chemical Institute of Canada
YESCAMP	YESCAMP@UNBVM1.BITNET
	Youth Engineering and Science Camps of Canada

Any list description that contains the term "Canada" will be sent to you.

Researching Discussion Groups

There are many systems on-line that let you search thousands of USENET newsgroups for particular topics or phrases. For example, DejaNews (**http://www.dejanews.com**) lets you undertake a search for words or phrases appearing in newsgroups:

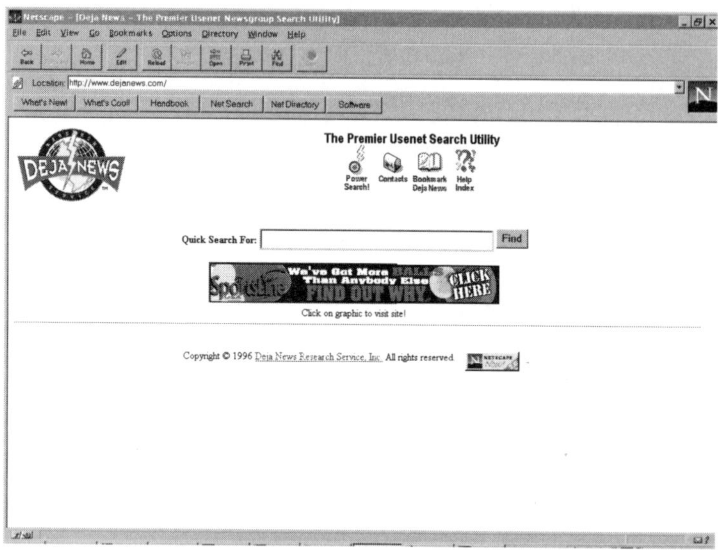

You can specify the sophistication of your search in several ways:

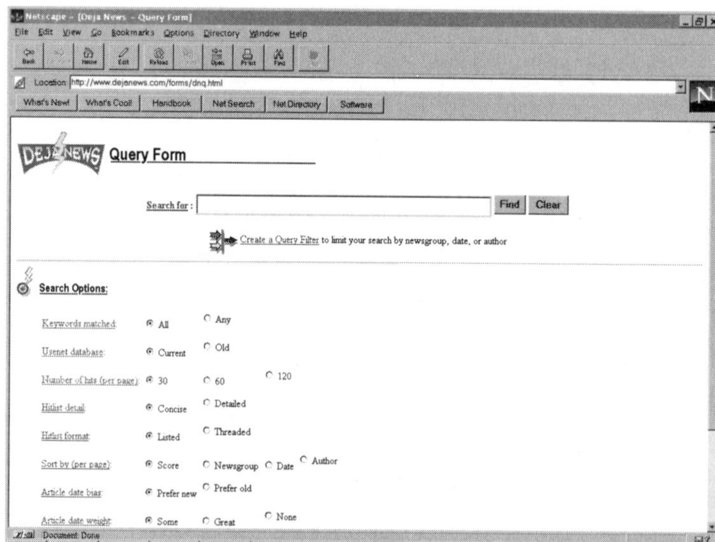

Here is the result of a search for USENET postings that contain the words "modern architecture" and "house":

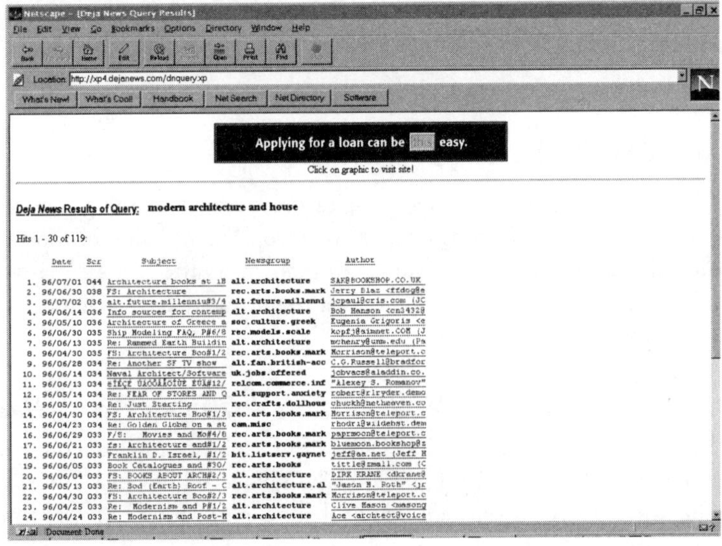

> USENET Newsgroup Search Systems
>
> InfoSeek (**http://www.infoseek.com**)
>
> AltaVista (**http://www.altavista.digital.com**)
>
> DejaNews (**http://www.dejanews.com**)

Reference.Com (**http://www.reference.com**) is another one to check; it allows you to set a search profile of items/topics you wish to track within USENET. On a daily basis you can access the first few lines of any USENET postings that match your search profile. You can then quickly retrieve the full text of any item by simply clicking on it.

You can also access a few searchable list archives. Automatic programs take all the information posted to an electronic mailing list and archive it in a database so that it can be searched by anyone at any time. Using such an archive is sometimes an attractive alternative to actually subscribing to a list, particularly lists that are very active. If the archive lets you list postings by date, you can quickly scan recent postings to determine which ones are relevant to you; in some cases, you can also perform a search by keyword.

You can usually find out if a particular list is archived by checking the list description in Tile.Net (**http://tile.net**) or Liszt (**http://www.liszt.com**).

The Problems with Discussion Groups

Many newcomers to the Internet venture into discussion groups, that is, USENET and unmoderated mailing lists, eager to participate in the promise that they bring. Unfortunately, many of these people are finding that these groups and lists, USENET in particular, are not what they are cracked up to be. They have changed in the last several years, and not for the good. The main problems are with USENET; however, many similar problems also exist in the unmoderated areas of electronic mailing lists. Even so, for the remainder of the discussion below we will refer to USENET only.

Ten Reasons Why People Walk Away from USENET

The very technical nature of USENET is such that anyone can post anything anywhere about any topic. Netiquette has always been a strong force to keep people in line with the topic of a particular newsgroup, but the old degree of order is breaking down. Quite simply, many users ignore Netiquette and do whatever they like on-line. As a result, many have given up on USENET, and many predict it will soon die.

1. Increasingly, Visiting USENET Is Like Visiting a Men's Bathroom

You may find your visit to particular areas of USENET to be a rather uncomfortable experience; you will meet all kinds of people, some of whom you will not like. Elsewhere, you will find that the language leaves a lot to be desired or that people "flame" too easily. In other cases, people will argue incessantly about the most obscure point.

It seems that more and more, going into a USENET newsgroup is like returning to high school. There are those who will throw sand and spit in your face without thinking. There are those who seem to delight in making offensive comments. There are those who spew venom and spittle at the slightest provocation.

USENET has become an increasingly uncomfortable and unfriendly neighborhood to hang around in, and you must have a thick skin to hang out there. Plain and simple, you may not like certain areas of USENET.

2. Discussion Groups Are Being Flooded with Junk Mail

USENET has always been an extremely anticommercial area, and most newsgroups prohibit commercial postings. This has not prevented "spamming," a practice in which junk mail — mostly advertisements as well as pyramid schemes and other questionable practices — is posted to many different newsgroups all at once.

The thing is, if you look at a lot of these postings, you will realize that only stupid people would fall for many of them. That does not deter the junk mail artists: they plod on relentlessly, dumping their garbage on the world for anyone to see.

Some individuals — long-time veterans of USENET — are fighting back. Chris Lewis in Ottawa (**clewis@ferret.ocunix.on.ca**), for example, has become world-renowned for his special antispamming program. Post any message to too many newsgroups, and Lewis will send out a special message that cancels it.

Can he do this? Is he right to do it? Can he be stopped? You can answer each question any way you like, but the fact is, Lewis has decided he hates excessive postings in USENET and has the technical smarts to cancel postings by those whom he believes abuse the network. Many wish him godspeed for doing so.

3. Kooks Rule the Roost in Many Discussion Groups

Travel through many USENET newsgroups, and you will discover the kooks. Who are they? They are easy to spot: people who seem to have a chip on their shoulder or who do not seem to be quite in control of their mental faculties. Their postings will talk about "conspiracies" and "cabals" and dark evil plots in which various other people or groups are out to rule the world. They will curse and swear and insult anyone who dares to say anything at all against them. They will constantly suggest that anything goes and therefore they can post whatever they like.

It is easy to find the kooks; you will know them by the insanity that drips from their postings. Unfortunately, they have managed to make many USENET discussion groups and some electronic mailing lists thoroughly uncomfortable and useless places to visit.

4. Fewer Postings Are Relevant to the Topic at Hand

Take the junk mail, add the kooks, and throw in an attitude problem, and you get the simple fact that fewer and fewer postings in many areas tend to be related to the topic of the particular newsgroup or e-mail list. It seems to be human nature that if someone has a point he wishes to make, he will make it, regardless of whether or not it has anything to do with what other people happen to be talking about.

5. There Is Too Much Information On-line

Another problem is that there is a lot of information floating through USENET. It used to be that you could check into a USENET newsgroup such as **misc.kids**, used for issues related to raising children, once a day and be caught up with all the postings. That is no longer true; in fact, you could spend hours a day within the topic and still not read everything.

Quite simply, as the Internet has exploded in scope and size, so too has the level of postings to USENET. The result is that many users find themselves overwhelmed with the volume and simply give up and walk away.

6. New Users Are Not Taking the Time to Learn About USENET

The pioneers of USENET designed the FAQ, the frequently asked question. You could find FAQs in many USENET newsgroups, the whole idea being that they were there for new users to read so that they would not post a lot of very simple questions to the group. In other cases documents were put together about Netiquette, with the idea that people take the time to learn about the unique culture to be found on-line.

The sad thing is that it has become apparent that many people do not bother to seek out and read the FAQ for the group they join. They do not take the time to understand on-line etiquette. They simply charge ahead and do whatever they like, which, of course, includes inundating other users of a particular newsgroup with a lot of irrelevant, often stupid questions.

7. The Mandate of Some Discussion Groups Is Unclear

A number of USENET newsgroups lack focus and do not have an on-line "champion" to help keep discussions focused. For example, a group such as **can.general** (for discussion of Canadian issues) has too broad a topic. Unfocused topics tend to result in a lot of wasted time, and this discourages participation.

8. Some Discussion Groups Repeat Themselves Over, and Over, and Over

Need we say more? Join a newsgroup, and you will eventually get bored with the same old argument occurring over and over again.

9. USENET Causes Many of the Internet Image Problems

When it comes to pornography and other questionable information, the Internet does present society with some difficult challenges. Join certain USENET newsgroups and you can find pornography. Pornography is a fact of life in our real society, and it is a fact of life in our virtual society. But USENET is being used for the distribution of information that is of questionable taste, is in violation of the laws of Canada, or runs against accepted community standards (for example, the distribution of literature on pedophilia). USENET is often in violation of the law. *The reality is that there is no way to control it.*

Increasingly, you will travel into newsgroups and find some hate literature posted. Or an ad for some new 1-900 pornography line. Or other information of questionable taste. Eventually, you will tire of seeing such junk.

10. You No Longer Have to Belong to a Newsgroup to Track What Is Going On

Technology itself is changing USENET. In the previous section we outlined how many USENET newsgroups are now archived, such that you can go in and do a search at a later date of postings in a particular newsgroup. These tools are useful, for users can get the benefit of USENET, that is, tracking what people have to say about a particular topic, without having to participate in USENET. And hence walk away from it.

Our Attitude Is Different

When we wrote the *1994 Canadian Internet Handbook*, we were generally enthusiastic about the concept of knowledge networking and the overall benefits of electronic mailing lists and USENET. But today we are not so sure. It is true that the nature of USENET is changing, and that people are leaving USENET for e-mail lists. It is also true that people are giving up on mailing lists as well.

USENET is an increasingly difficult place to put up with because of the challenges outlined above. You will have to decide whether or not participating in USENET is worth it and find the groups that have some value to you. Even though our attitude has soured, we still believe that there are some worthwhile areas on-line. The key with USENET seems to be that you must take the time to find a newsgroup that is not yet suffering from the problems outlined above. In many cases this will be a moderated group.

Take, for example, the newsgroup **sci.econ.research**. The group, used for the discussion of economic research topics, is moderated by David Lloyd Jones, a retired entrepreneur from Toronto. "I run the group with an iron fist," he notes, "and I've stood up to people when it's become necessary." He takes about a half hour to an hour each day to determine which messages to the newsgroup should actually be distributed. Most people in the newsgroup support his decisions, and the kooks accuse him of a dark conspiracy to control the flow of economic information worldwide.

He moderates the group because he finds such open worldwide discussion to provide more useful and relevant information than scholarly journals. And quite simply, as he notes, "because it's fun." Pressed, he comments: "This morning's mail: a note from a guy in New Zealand at six: wants Pacific Rim type info. I sling it out and go back to bed. At eight there's a reply from a

Chinese guy in Canada giving the source of the New Zealand guy's answers — in Korea. Plus there's another one in: a guy in the Ministry of Finance in Poland is writing regulations on municipal bonds and he wants to know how the hell Orange County went belly up. Out it goes: that one should get him half a dozen contradictory replies. It's not just that this stuff is useful: it's some of that old time feeling when the thing was first being built in the late sixties, early seventies: we're tying people together around the world!"

Some people have given up on USENET and discussion groups, and others persevere. What will work for you will depend upon what type of person you are and the particular discussion groups in which you decide to participate.

Could You Be Using Other Newsreader Software?

Earlier in this chapter we outlined where you could locate various USENET newreader programs on-line. If you become serious about USENET, you might consider exploring some of these programs, particularly those that feature "killfiles" or "bozo filters" to help you deal with the increasing number of irrelevant postings on-line.

Jim and Rick's Picks

Jim

I have been using both News Xpress and the news features within Netscape 2.0. I find I don't spend much time in USENET anymore; it just takes up too much time that I could be using much more productively. I had been using USENET since 1990 and noticed a serious degradation starting about 1995. From my perspective, things have really gone downhill.

I find that I use tools like InfoSeek and AltaVista if I am looking for particular information within USENET. In fact, I have a few bookmarks that automatically look for postings about particular topics in USENET; I check these once every day or two. But other than that, I really don't hang out on-line. I do miss it, but as far as I am concerned, the junk mail, hate postings, kooks, and other problems have just about ruined it for everyone. You can find News Xpress on the Internet at the Consummate Winsock Applications List **http://www.stroud.com**. Look under the "News Readers" category.

Rick

My favorite newsreader is Trumpet Newsreader for Windows; I have been using it for about three years. It is one of the oldest newsreaders in existence. I like the program primarily because of its simplicity. It doesn't support a lot of the features that the newer newsreaders do, but it suits my needs extremely well. I have tried some of the newer programs like News Xpress, but I find myself returning to Trumpet Newsreader again and again. One of the best features of the program is the "archive" feature, the ability to archive individual news articles into designated electronic "folders" so that I can view them later.

Like Jim, I don't spend a lot of time reading USENET anymore. The quality of the information has greatly diminished over the last couple of years.

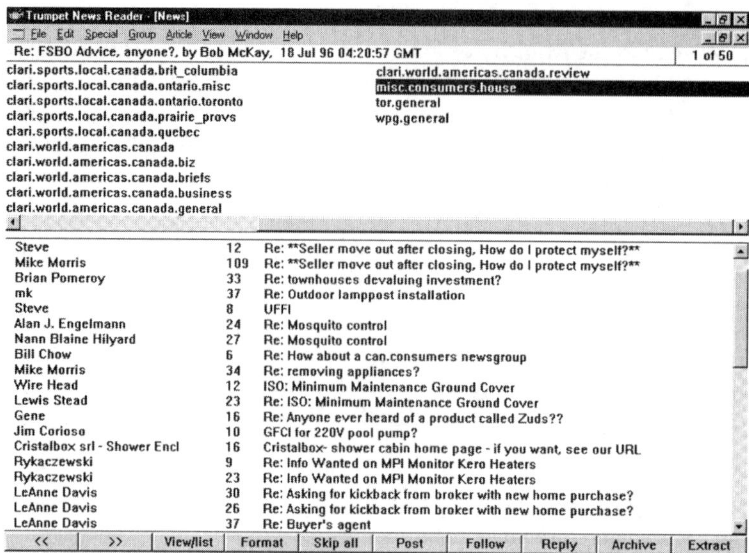

You can find Trumpet Newsreader on the Internet at the Consummate Winsock Applications List (**http://www.stroud.com**). Look under the "News Readers" category.

Knowledge Networking and the Internet

Internet mailing lists and USENET newsgroups are a tremendous asset to any individual or organization in that they provide new methods and new capabilities of obtaining answers to questions, seeking knowledge, and tracking topics. With the explosion in use of the Internet in Canada and around the world, the number of topics available will certainly continue to increase. As you learn how to use the Internet, always keep in mind that if a topic you would like to track does not exist today, it could very easily exist tomorrow.

CHAPTER 12

Interactive Communications On-line

Relentless technological change is driving down many of the elements in the cost of a telephone call. Already, the cost of carrying an additional call is often so tiny that it might as well be free. More significant, carrying a call from London to New York costs virtually the same as carrying it from one house to the next.

The death of distance as a determinant of the cost of communications will probably be the single most important economic force shaping society in the first half of the next century. It will alter, in ways that are only dimly imaginable, decisions about where people live and work; concepts of national borders; patterns of international trade. Its effects will be as pervasive as those of the discovery of electricity.

The Death of Distance —
A survey of telecommunications,
September 30, 1995
http://www.economist.com

As we saw in Chapters 7 and 8, the World Wide Web is certainly emerging as a tool that allows for interaction between people and is providing for the distribution of audio and video. But the Web is still very much a one-way experience: we receive information from another individual, organization, or business. There is some two-way interaction, such as when you fill out a form, but it is not truly interactive.

A whole new category of interactive applications is emerging rapidly on the Internet, which provides for direct two-way communication between people. The most interesting category has to be Internet phones, software that lets you talk to others on the Internet. This technology is quickly being married to on-line collaboration tools in what will soon be one of the hottest applications of the Internet. The next step? True videoconferencing where it will be possible for people to not only merely talk to each other, but see images of each other as well. And finally, an application that provides for on-line chatting, called IRC, Internet relay chat, is enjoying a resurgence of interest on the Internet. In this chapter we take a look at the emergence of these new software applications.

Internet Telephone Products

On the Internet you can make a "phone call" to someone else who happens to be on the other side of the world, talk to him/her for an hour, and pay about $0.25 or less for the whole hour, and in some cases, pay absolutely nothing. Why? The Internet takes advantage of the fact, as described in the *Economist* article from which we quoted above, that the true incremental cost to get any single "bit" of information from any point on the planet to any other point has pretty well become next to nothing. This is due primarily to the implementation of optical fibre, a true wonder technology of the computer age. As reported on *The Economist* Web site, "a single fibre thinner than a hair can carry 30,000 simultaneous telephone conversations."

Simply, global telecommunication companies, in implementing modern-day wonders such as optical cable, have made their systems so efficient at carrying data that when it comes to sending information around the planet, the cost for every new bit of information is almost free. And the Internet takes advantage of this: often sold for low hourly rates or flat monthly fees, the Internet operates on economics completely different from regular long distance, which are dependent upon time and distance.

Making a Phone Call on the Internet

What do you need to make a phone call on the Internet? First, you need a PC or a Macintosh that has sound capabilities and a microphone; most new computers sold today support these capabilities. Second, you need Internet phone software; that's easy enough, since many such programs can be obtained directly through the Internet. We provide the Web addresses for many Internet phone products below. Third, you need someone else with an Internet phone program to talk to. Once you have all this, you sign on to the Internet and load your Internet phone software. Then you "call" the person you wish to speak to, and the person answers by pressing a button on his/her Internet phone software. Having done that, you can then start talking to each other. Let's look at an example.

Vocaltec's Internet Phone

One of the first Internet phone products on the market, and still one of the most popular, is Vocaltec's "Internet Phone." You can obtain a sample copy of Internet Phone on Vocaltec's Web site at **http://www.vocaltec.com**. Their promotional literature says "with Internet Phone you can use the Internet to speak with any user all over the world! Yes, real-time voice

INTERACTIVE COMMUNICATIONS ON-LINE

1. A new type of interactive application is emerging on the Internet that supports two-way communication, often involving audio or video.
2. Products have appeared that allow you to place a rudimentary type of "telephone call" on the Internet to other individuals who use the network.
3. Internet conferencing/collaboration tools allow you to talk and share data with other users of the Internet.
4. Video conferencing is rapidly emerging on the Internet.
5. Internet Relay Chat is an older Internet application but one which is arousing increased interest as an interactive communications tool.

conversations over the Internet, at the price of a local phone call or even less. All you need is Internet Phone, a TCP/IP Internet connection and a Windows-compatible audio device. Plug in a microphone and speaker, run Internet Phone, and, by clicking a button, get in touch with Internet users all over the world."

How does it work? It is really quite straightforward: after you install it, it does a little test to see if it will work on your computer. You then choose to connect to an Internet Phone "server" from a list of available servers, and you are connected and ready to go:

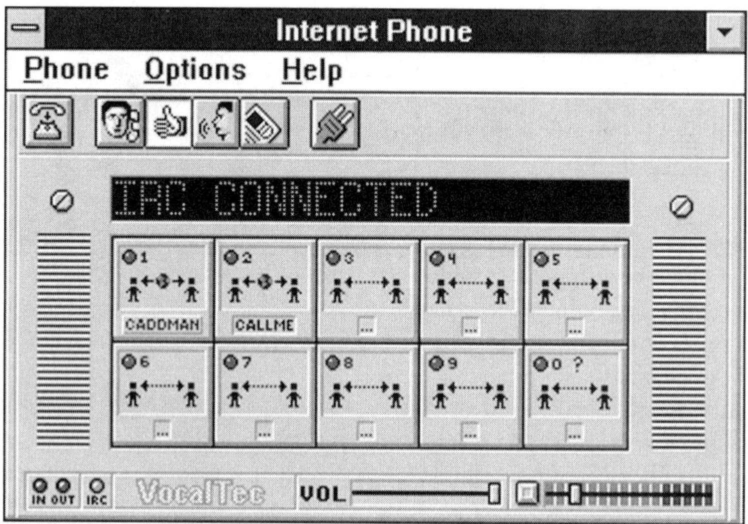

You can choose to make a "call" to someone by clicking on the little telephone icon. You see a list of people connected to this particular server; choose one, and Internet Phone will contact that person to see if he/she will accept a call from you. Internet Phone makes sounds like a telephone while connecting to simulate a real telephone conversation.

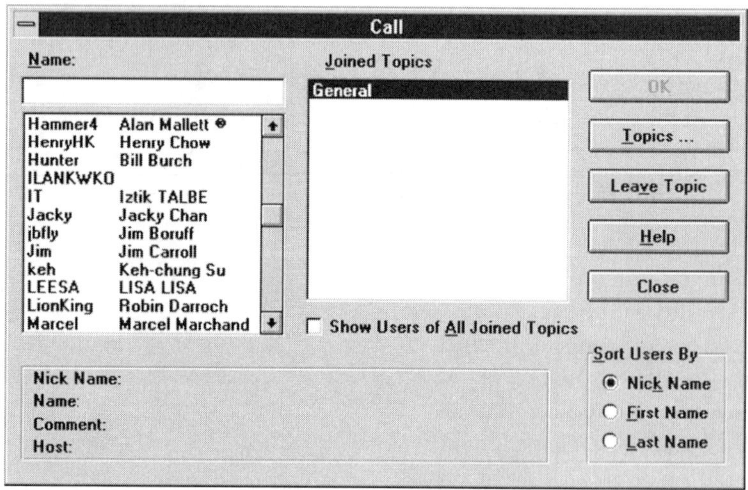

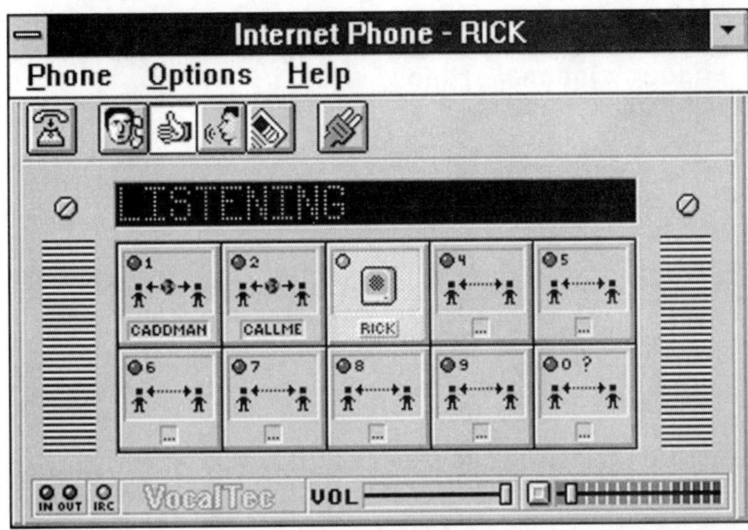

If you have set the software to accept calls, you will automatically be notified when someone wants to talk to you. When this happens, your computer "rings":

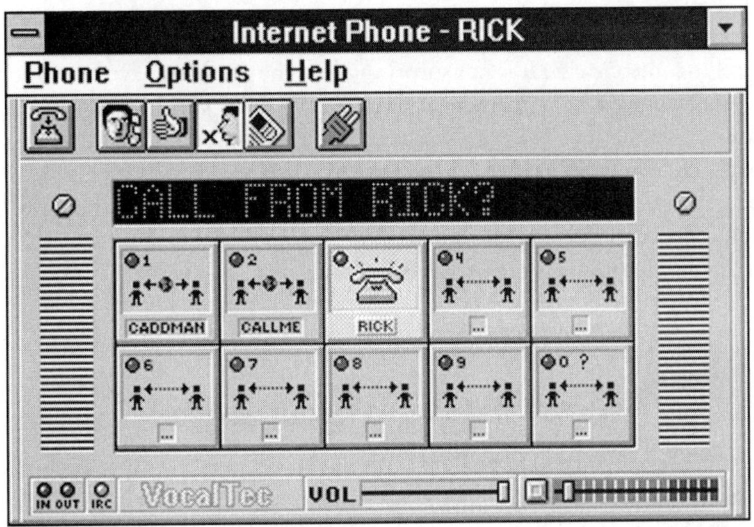

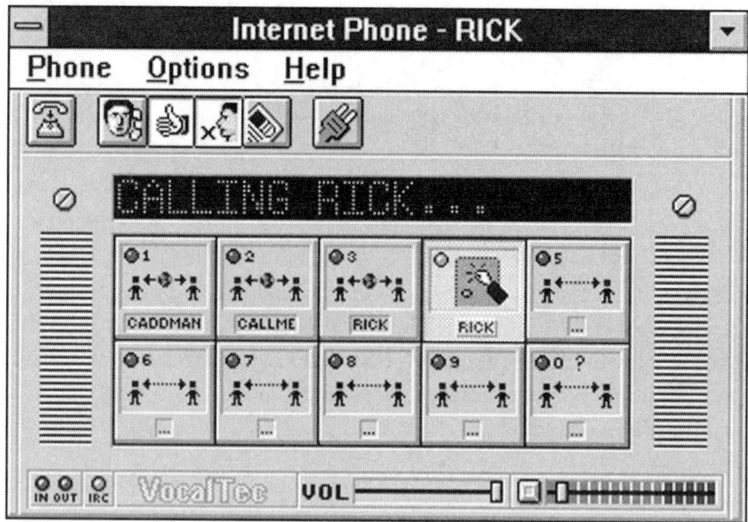

That's it; a few minutes of work, and you are in business.

Benefits

Obviously, the biggest benefit of an Internet phone product is the fact that you can make an inexpensive call to someone else. It is not surprising that the products have been adopted quickly in the university community, with students encouraging their parents back home to get on-line in order to cut down the costs of long-distance communication. And they are used extensively for international calls, which often bear the highest long distance charges. There are other benefits as well. The software has become fairly easy to implement, meaning that if you have the right type of PC and an Internet connection, you can usually be up and running in a matter of minutes. And finally, you are bound to get a deep sense of satisfaction at bypassing a major monopoly: the large, established telephone companies.

Disadvantages

Consider some of the traditional disadvantages of Internet phone products:

- Many Internet telephone products only allow you to talk with other Internet users; that is, you cannot make a phone call to just anyone. The person you are calling must be on the Internet. Later in the chapter we look at the next generation of Internet phone products, products that allow you to call anyone in world.
- For some people the entire process is somewhat cumbersome; rather than talking through a telephone handset, you speak to a person through a microphone and hear that person through your computer speakers.
- Until recently, there had been a lack of standards, meaning that Internet phone products could only communicate with each other if they were manufactured by the same vendor. Later in the chapter we discuss H.323, the new standard for Internet telephone products that will make it possible for Internet users to talk with each other regardless of what telephone product they are using.

- The sound quality may be poor. Internet telephone products do not yet have the clarity of a phone call you make with your regular telephone. Sometimes the sound is unclear and at other times it is fuzzy or distorted. However, manufacturers of Internet telephones are working on this problem, and many of the newer Internet telephone products have improved sound quality.
- When you talk to someone on a regular phone, there is a lot of what we might call "dynamic interaction"; one person says something, and the other person might say something right away, trying to gain the edge in the conversation by interrupting. But some Internet phone products allow only one person to speak at a time. This is known as "half-duplex mode." This means that the normal "flow" of a telephone call is missing. However, this problem is being eliminated by newer versions of Internet telephone products that operate in "full-duplex mode." This means that both people can speak simultaneously.
- Many Internet telephone products require you to be on-line in order to receive a call. The beauty of the regular telephone system, of course, is that your telephone is plugged in all the time, and you do not have to pay anything when you are not using the phone other than a nominal monthly rental charge. However, on the Internet you usually need to have your Internet phone product running in order to receive a call, making the entire process cumbersome, contrived, and expensive. If you pay for Internet access by the hour, you do not want to leave your computer connected to the Internet at all hours of the day. Newer Internet telephone products are addressing this problem by including voice-mail features that allow you to leave a voice-mail message for another person when he/she is unavailable to accept a call on the Internet. You record the message using the microphone on your computer, and the message is automatically sent by e-mail to the party you are trying to reach. You can also attach a text message to your voice mail, as seen in the picture below. Vocaltec's Internet Phone product supports this feature.

- Finally, using an Internet phone is kind of an eerie experience, particularly when you use it to communicate with people you do not really know. Although it is a normal thing to exchange e-mail with people you do not know around the world, and although it is an everyday thing to participate in USENET discussion groups or electronic mailing lists, there seems something odd about opening up a "phone call" with someone you do not even know and hearing the voice come through your computer.

Where to Obtain Internet Telephone Products

In 1995 there were only one or two Internet telephone products on the market; now it is a rather crowded field. Below is a list of some of the more popular Internet telephone products. In most cases you can download evaluation versions of these products off the Web for free.

Windows/Windows 95	
DigiPhone	**http://www.planeteers.com**
FreeTel	**http://www.freetel.inter.net**
Intercom Lite	**http://www.telescape.com**
Intel Internet Phone	**http://www.intel.com/iaweb/cpc**
Net2Phone	**http://www.net2phone.com**
PowWow	**http://www.tribal.com**
TeleVox	**http://www.voxware.com**
WebPhone	**http://www.itelco.com**
Quarterdeck's WebTalk	**http://www.qdeck.com**
Vocaltec's Internet Phone	**http://www.vocaltec.com**
Macintosh	
ClearPhone	**http://www.kaiwan.com/~radiobob**
e-Phone	**http://www.emagic.com**

Intel's Internet Phone Product

One product that is worthy of special mention is Intel's Internet Phone. You can download a copy at the Intel Web site (**http://www.intel.com**). Once you install the product, it establishes itself at the bottom of your Windows 95 screen, providing a control panel through which you can make and accept calls:

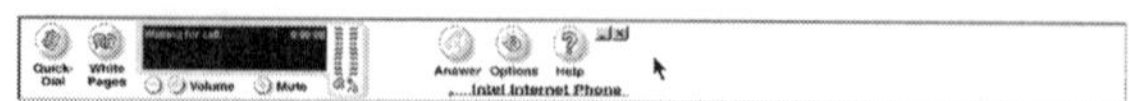

The product was released with a lot of fanfare, and it is ground-breaking for two important reasons:

- It was the first Internet telephone product to support the International Telecommunication Union's H.323 standard for audio compression. This means that users of the Intel Internet Phone product can communicate with any other Internet user who has an H.323 compliant Internet phone. This is a significant development, because until the H.323 standard was developed, Internet telephones from one vendor could not communicate with Internet telephones from another vendor. Intel's product has solidified the adoption of a single standard for Internet phone products and is quickly leading to a situation in which most Internet telephone products can communicate with each other, thus overcoming one of the most significant challenges with the technology.

- It was the first Internet phone product to link itself to a number of on-line directories of Internet users. Click on the "white pages" button, and you can travel to a number of on-line directories, each of which is working with Intel to provide a user look-up feature. If someone you find in the directory is on-line with an Internet phone product at the moment you perform the look-up, his/her name will be highlighted.

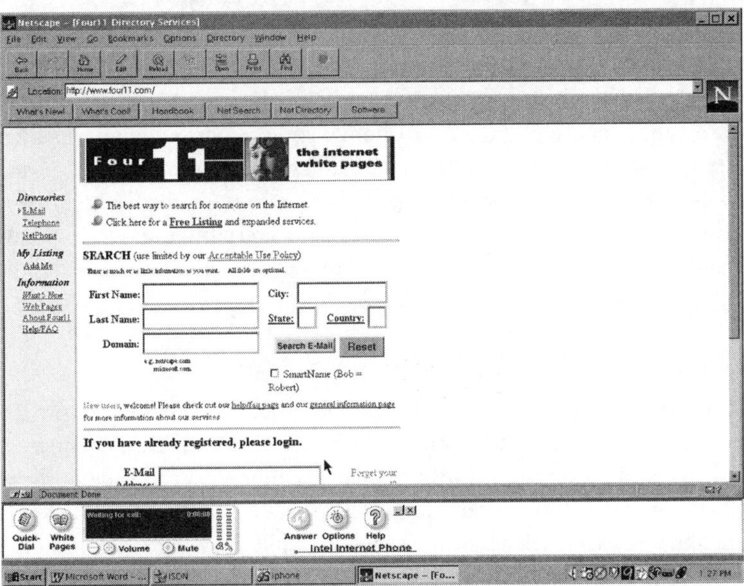

- The product is "full-duple" (if you have a full-duplex sound card on your PC), meaning that both individuals on the call can talk at once, thus allowing you to speak in more of a conversational style.

Intel's Internet Phone is a good example of how advanced these products have become in only a short period of time. Intel is hoping that the demand for sophisticated Internet communications will drive up the demand for new high-end computers.

The Future for Internet Telephones

Internet telephones are real, the products are maturing, and over time we will see greater numbers of people adopt them. Many people believe that, in time, they will replace large portions of the global telephone network. Obviously, the Internet telephone is a serious concept, since major software companies such as IBM are throwing their weight behind it. And the reaction to the product within the telephone industry has been interesting: The giant AT&T organization, for example, has announced its own Internet telephone product.

Even as the Internet telephone becomes a serious new tool, there are those who are opposed to the concept. The America's Carriers Telecommunication Association, which represents 130 small long-distance companies, filed a petition with the U.S. Federal Communications Commission to have them regulate the "industry," thus trying to shut down Internet phones. Even so, it is likely that no amount of regulation will ever be possible. Should the CRTC or FCC step in and decide to regulate the usage of Internet phones, they would have to stop you from downloading a program from the Vocaltec Web site in Israel or any other Web site on the planet, a dubious proposition at best. Suffice it to say that life will never be the same for telephone companies. A few trends worth noting:

More Telephones Will Adhere to the H.323 Standard

Earlier we mentioned the H.323 standard for Internet phones. To appreciate how important this is, consider how the regular telephone system works. Standards exist that make it possible for two people to talk to each other regardless of the type of phone each party is using. For example, you may have a Panasonic telephone in your home, and the person you are calling may have a Northern Telecom phone. Because both phones adhere to the same telephone standards, you can talk to each other. The H.323 standard promises to do the same thing for telephone communications on the Internet. In the near future virtually every Internet telephone will adhere to the H.323 standard. When this happens, you will not have to worry about what type of Internet phone product the person at the other end is using.

Integration with the Telephone System

One of the traditional limitations of Internet phone products is that they only let you talk to other Internet users who are using the same software. This is all beginning to change, as Internet phone products begin to integrate with the regular telephone system. One of these products is Net2Phone (**http://www.net2phone.com**) by IDT Corporation, a product that allows you to make a call from the Internet to any telephone in the world, while enjoying some of the cost savings of the Internet.

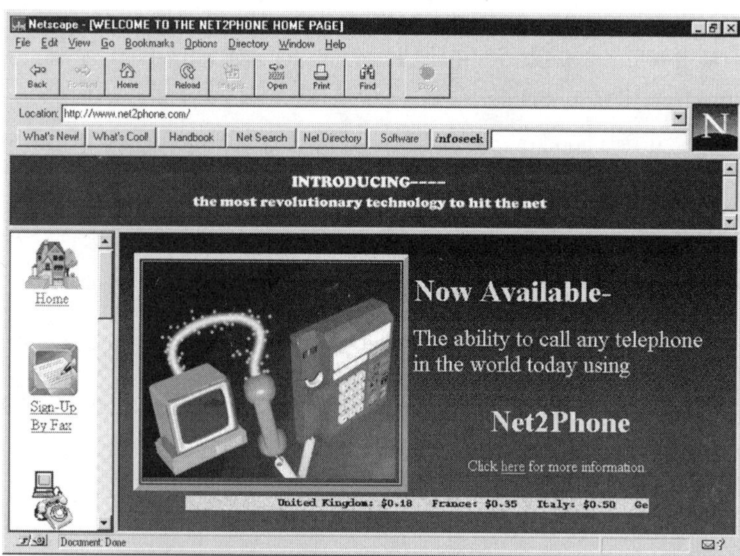

Here's how it works. You download the Net2Phone software from the Net2Phone Web site. Once you have dialed into the Internet through your Internet access provider, you start the program and dial a number using the Net2Phone software. Your phone call is routed from your PC to a computer at Net2Phone, which then routes it to a telephone anywhere in the world through the Internet. IDT Corporation charges a fee to place telephone calls over the Internet, but their rates are lower than regular long-distance rates.

On-line Voice Support

Imagine that you are shopping on a Web site, and you come across a product that really interests you. Wouldn't it be nice if you could click on a "phone call" icon and "talk" directly to someone at the company via the Internet? VocalTec (**http://www.vocaltec.com**) is one of several companies releasing software that makes it possible for businesses to link customers to existing call centres through their Web pages. This is but one of the many future applications for Internet telephone products.

Better Sound Quality

Finally, the sound quality of Internet telephone products is continually improving. Companies like Intel recognize that consumers will not buy in to this technology unless the sound quality is nearly equivalent to what they can get through the regular telephone system.

For More Information

A good site for keeping up-to-date on the evolution of Internet telephone standards is the Voice On The Net Coalition site (**http://www.von.org**). We also recommend the Voice on the Net Home Page (**http://www.von.com**), which contains links to many Internet telephone resources.

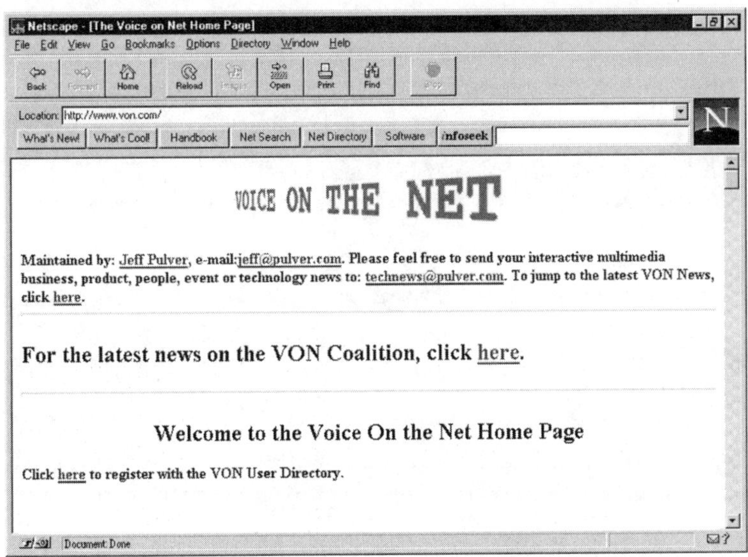

Internet Conferencing and Collaboration Tools

One step beyond Internet phone products are on-line conferencing and collaboration tools. Three such products are Internet Conference Professional from Vocaltec, CoolTalk from Netscape, and NetMeeting from Microsoft. CoolTalk is directly incorporated into the most recent version of Netscape, available from **http://www.netscape.com**. It offers several features:

- audio conferencing, so that one or more people can take part in a call at one time;
- an answering machine, which takes voice messages while you are away;
- a shared whiteboard, so that you can share a graphic and edit it in real time with the individual with whom you are sharing the conference;
- a "chat" feature, so that you can type on-line as you talk to the person so that he or she can see what you are typing.

NetMeeting from Microsoft (**http://www.microsoft.com/ie/ie3/netmtg.htm**) is a similar product. It allows on-line discussions with one or more people and has whiteboard and chat features as well:

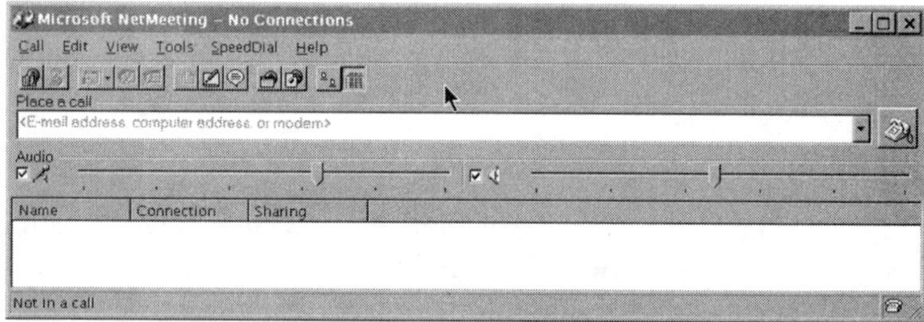

With an Internet connection in place, you can easily obtain a list of various people available for a call at that point in time:

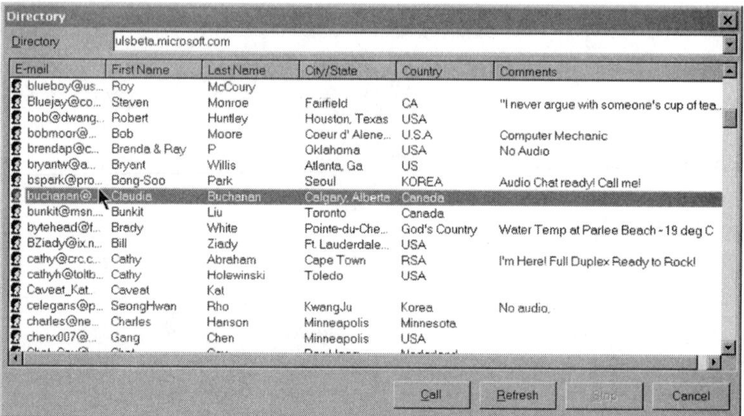

Vocaltec's Internet Conference Professional (**http://www.vocaltec.com**) provides many of the same functions. It even includes collaborative viewing of World Wide Web pages (shown below) so that everyone in the conference can view a Web page at the same time.

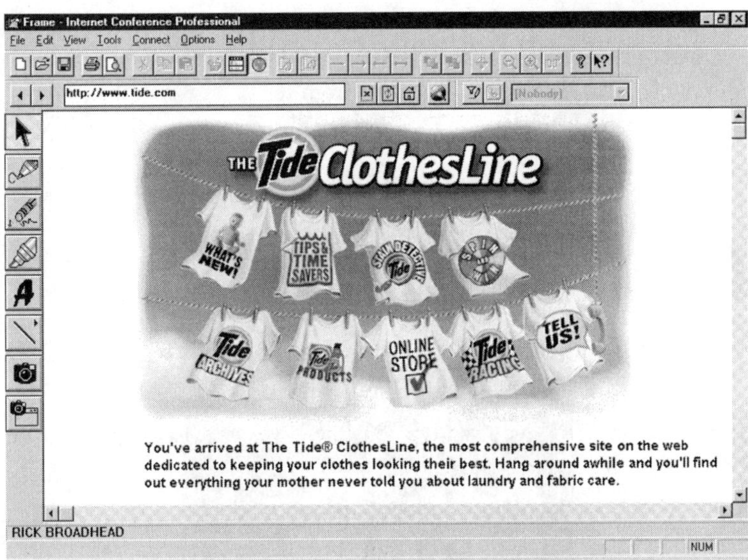

By the time you read the 1998 *Canadian Internet Handbook*, collaborative conferencing over the Internet may be a very significant new software category.

Videoconferencing

If you can chat through the Internet, share whiteboards, and talk through the Internet, why not broadcast in real time? Consider a software product known as CU-SeeMe. Originally developed at Carnegie Mellon University, the product permits a rudimentary form of videoconferencing and broadcasting through the Internet. Recently commercialized, details about the product and copies of the program are available at the Web site for White Pine Software (**http://www.wpine.com**).

White Pine describes the product as follows: "CU-SeeMe can be used over the Internet to make connections to any other desktop using CU-SeeMe in the same fashion as email, except that with CU-SeeMe you can have a real-time meeting with video, audio and written messages. With its unique 'Reflector' technology, CU-SeeMe can be used for group conferencing or 'TV' type broadcasting. CU-SeeMe is targeted at low bandwidth connections, requires no special hardware and supports inexpensive video cameras. A software only solution for both Windows and Macintosh, CU-SeeMe will affordably bring Videoconferencing to offices, educational institutions and homes worldwide."

A tall order for any product. CU-SeeMe requires a fast connection to the Internet. Those who access the Internet with a regular modem cannot really use the product effectively. If you have a SLIP or PPP dial-up connection to the Internet, you can try out CU-SeeMe. At the end of this section we let you know where to get it. But you will find it almost impossible to use with a dial-up connection, since you really need a fast link to the Internet. To use the product just to view other CU-SeeMe sites, you do not need any special equipment. If you want to set your site up to send pictures and sound, however, you will need a camera/camcorder and a computer that can support it as well as a microphone. A full list of the requirements is available on the White Pine Software Web site.

While mostly experimental at this time, the possibilities are intriguing. Taking a look at how it is being used today offers a tantalizing glimpse of the future of "broadcasting" through the Internet. For example, here is a snippet of a video from the band Kiss, taken from a CU-SeeMe broadcast of the Canadian MuchMusic television channel, available from KVR TV in Austin, TX:

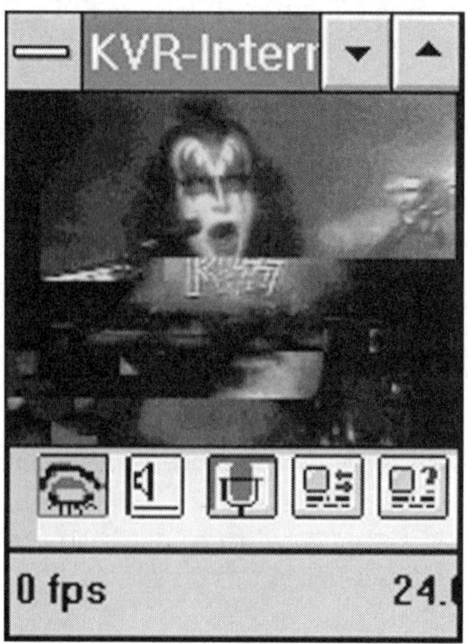

Notes a press release available on the KVR Web site (**http://www.utexas.edu/depts/output/www/pr.html**): "this pilot project was conceived by students to merge cutting-edge technology . . . computer-literate students will be on their Macintosh computers watching MuchMusic while they work." Certainly experimental, possibly controversial, but imagine how such a broadcast technology could be used in a real educational or research setting. The scientific aspects are already making themselves known. NASA is the first organization to regularly broadcast through the Internet, using CU-SeeMe to transmit full-day coverage of shuttle missions and other endeavours. Here is their program schedule as posted early in the day, announcing what will be shown through their "station" later in the day:

The limitations in the CU-SeeMe concept are obvious; even for those with a high-speed link to the Internet the screens are jerky. Obviously, the software does not provide broadcast quality.

Another hot technology on the Internet is the MBone, or multicast backbone, which provides another sort of "TV" through the Internet. This is a complex technology. Suffice it to say, leading-edge researchers are working out with the MBone another method of providing for video distribution through the Internet. You can find the FAQ about it at **http://www.research.att.com/mbone-faq.html**.

But on the day that high-speed cable modems and other forms of high-speed access arrive, products like CU-SeeMe will be a mainstream, everyday application on the Internet. If you are curious about when high-speed access will really arrive in Canada, take a look at Chapter 20, where we address this very issue.

Where to Obtain Internet Videoconferencing Products

Here is a list of some of the more popular Internet videoconferencing products that you might want to check out. Remember that in most cases you will need a fast Internet connection and, if you want to transmit information, a camera. PicturePhone (**http://picturephone.com/cuseeme.htm**) has a good list of cameras and accessories that work with CU-SeeMe.

Windows/Windows 95	
CineVideo	**http://www.cinecom.com**
FreeVue	**http://www.freevue.com**
VDOPhone	**http://www.vdo.net**
Windows/Windows 95/Macintosh	
Cu-SeeMe	**http://www.wpine.com**

Internet Relay Chat

Internet relay chat (IRC) is best described as a "CB radio" for the Internet and is the most popular type of chat service on the Internet. Often forgotten or overlooked by many Internet users, it is an application that has a large number of very enthusiastic fans and seems to have grown substantially within the last several years. Using IRC, you can participate in live, on-line discussions with other Internet users. Discussions can be either public or private. To use IRC, you should have a SLIP/PPP account or direct connection to the Internet and have the IRC client software on your own system. You will also need the address of an IRC "server." This is the computer that you will link to in order to use IRC. Many Internet providers have a designated server that they recommend to their customers. Before starting IRC, ask your Internet provider for assistance in linking to the appropriate IRC server.

When you are in an IRC "session," you join a "channel," or topic, that interests you. If you type something, all other members of that channel will see what you typed within seconds, and you will see what they have typed. This permits you to have an "interactive," or "real time," discussion through the Internet. IRC is used for serious purposes, for example, it was used as a communications channel during several major world events, including the Oklahoma bombing crisis in April 1995. It was also used extensively during the 1994 California earthquake, the 1993 Russian revolt and 1992 revolution, and the 1991 Persian Gulf War. You can find archives and logs of IRC communications during these events at **http://sunsite.unc.edu/dbarberi/chats.html**. The archives provide a good glimpse into the serious side of IRC.

To access an IRC session, the first thing you must do is access a server that will link you into IRC. In the following screen we are using the program WSIRC to link to an IRC server at York University in Toronto:

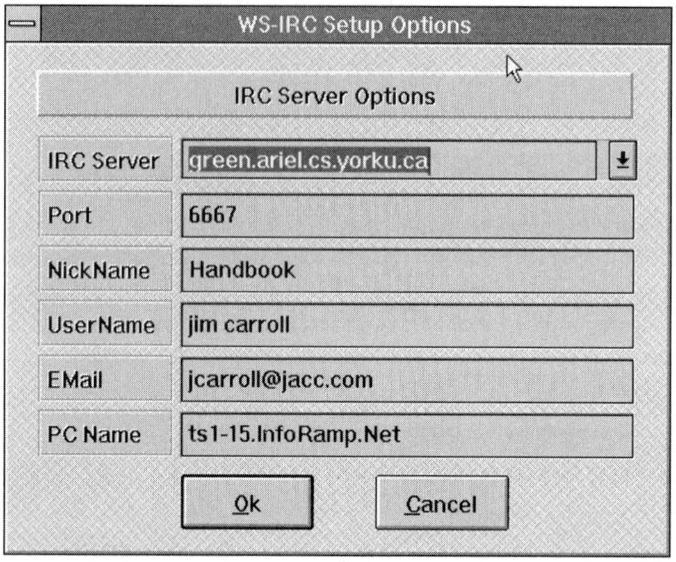

WS-IRC Setup Options

IRC Server Options

IRC Server	green.ariel.cs.yorku.ca
Port	6667
NickName	Handbook
UserName	jim carroll
EMail	jcarroll@jacc.com
PC Name	ts1-15.InfoRamp.Net

Ok Cancel

Once we are linked into the IRC server, we can choose a "channel" (topic) to join. You can request a list of channels from the server you are linked to by clicking on an icon.

In the following screen we have joined the **#riskybus** channel, which permits us to participate in a Jeopardy-style game. The interesting thing about IRC is that it is populated by what are known as "bots" (or "robots"), programs that automate some of the interaction within various IRC channels. In this case the **#riskybus** channel is managed (i.e., the questions are asked and the answers are checked) by a "bot" name RobBot:

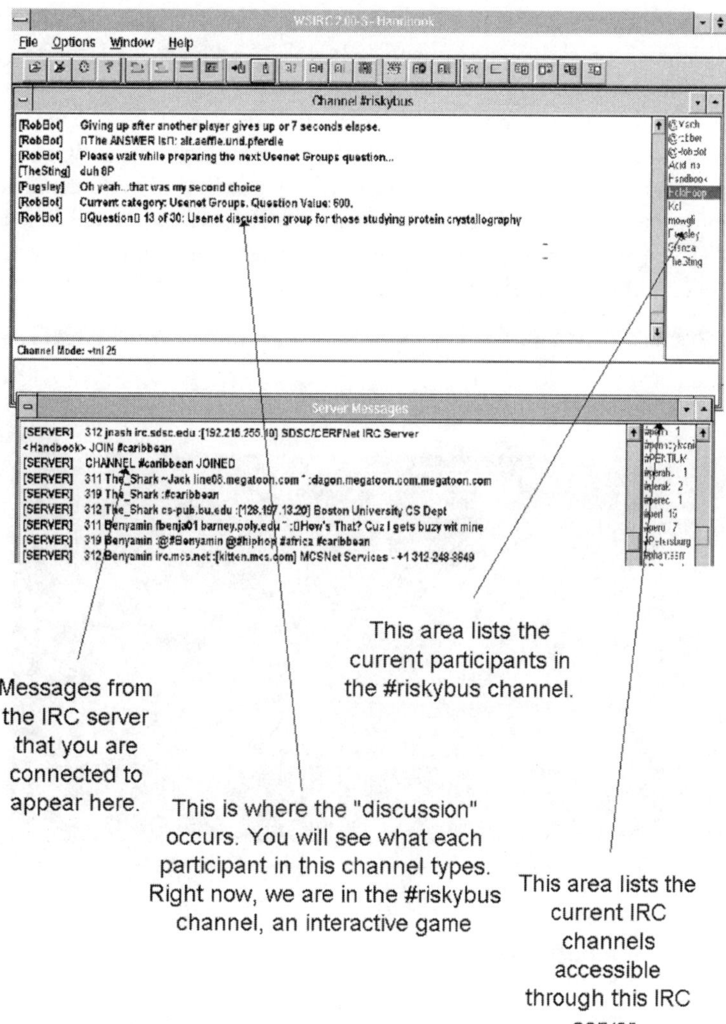
This area lists the current participants in the #riskybus channel.
Messages from the IRC server that you are connected to appear here.
This is where the "discussion" occurs. You will see what each participant in this channel types. Right now, we are in the #riskybus channel, an interactive game
This area lists the current IRC channels accessible through this IRC server.

IRC is an interesting place to visit, but it is a little weird. More often than not, a venture into IRC is a voyage to the weirdness of the human psyche. For example, an IRC "channel" known as **#hottub** is a place where people pretend to be in a hot tub and talk back and forth; the discussions that take place in **#netsex** should be obvious. Other channels carry more lurid titles.

You will truly discover the stranger side of the global character of the Internet in an IRC session. More often than not someone will ask "where's everybody from?" Responses will come from locations right around the world. And many of those people will be using "handles" (nicknames), which define their persona, or who they want to "be."

The discussions that occur in some IRC channels are in some cases off-the-wall and zany; in other cases they appear to be of the mentality found in a grade five boys' locker room. IRC has a no-holds-barred, anything-goes mentality, so if you plan to visit it, you should be prepared for anything. There are many "fans" of IRC who participate in IRC sessions on a regular basis. In fact, some of them might be considered "IRC junkies," in need of a daily fix.

But there are many real IRC applications as well. Aside from its use as a disaster recovery tool, IRC is used as a support tool by some companies. It is also used for training courses. IRC also provides a fascinating glimpse into the future; new software is being released that permits you to view pictures of those with whom you are conversing. It does not take a huge leap of the imagination to picture the day when we will have live, real time, video-based IRC.

There are two major IRC systems, EFNet and the Undernet. EFnet is the largest of the two networks and has the most users. There are many smaller IRC systems as well. The Undernet network has a Web page at **http://www.undernet.org**, where you will find general information about the service and Internet relay chat in general.

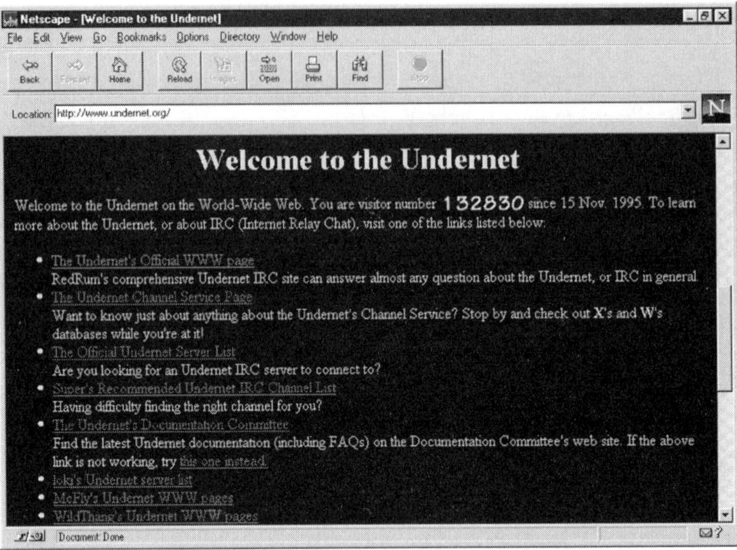

Where to Obtain IRC Software

Windows/Windows 95	
Netscape Chat	**http://www.netscape.com**
mIRC	**http://www-2.nijenrode.nl/software/mirc/index.html**
PIRCH	**http://www.bcpl.lib.md.us/~frappa/pirch.html**
WSIRC	**ftp://cs-ftp.bu.edu/irc/clients/pc/windows/wsirc**
Quarterdeck's Global Chat	**http://www.globalchat.com**
Macintosh	
ircle	**http://www.xs4all.nl/~ircle**

For more information about IRC, visit the Internet relay chat Frequently Asked Questions Home Page at **http://www.kei.com/irc.html**.

In order to use IRC, you need to learn IRC commands. For an overview of some of the most common IRC commands, we recommend that you read the Internet Relay Chat Primer at **http://www.kei.com/irc/IRCprimer1.1.txt**. Also check out Yahoo!'s list of IRC Web pages at **http://www.yahoo.com/Computers_and_Internet/Internet/Chatting/IRC** for links to many on-line documents, tips, and guides about IRC.

The Future for Interactive Applications On-line

Technology on the Internet evolves at a rapid pace. What starts as an experiment often ends up as a commercial product. Combine the concept of high-speed Internet access in the future with the CU-SeeMe concept, and you can see where the Internet is headed. Allow people to make phone calls on the Internet for little or no cost, and they will begin to adopt the technology. Provide for electronic meetings on-line, and people will discover new opportunities. The real future for interactive applications lies with high-speed access to the Internet. As we obtain faster network links, anyone with a PC equipped with a sound card and digital video camera can become a "broadcaster" on the Internet. In fact, anyone will soon be able to establish a live, global television station. How long will it take? Two years? Five years? Ten or twenty? No one knows, but keep your eyes and ears tuned, for there are some fascinating developments underway.

CHAPTER 13

Older Internet Applications

> *Just as the home-oriented dial-up services have moved e-mail from the realm of high-level Internet sites into the public domain, so URLs promise to bring the rest of the Net to the masses. The key is that URL technology transforms what have been enormously complex commands in the computer language used by AT&T's UNIX operating system into the same sort of drag-and-drop on-screen techniques that computer users employ with Microsoft Corp.'s Windows or Apple Computer Inc.'s Macintosh.*
>
> *For nearly a decade, those UNIX commands have served as the key to the information in the Internet when it was the sole domain of computer scientists and the more sophisticated hobbyists. These commands have names like File Transfer Protocol (FTP), Gopher, Veronica, Usenet, Finger, Archie and Internet Relay Chat.*
>
> The Internet Business
> *Chicago Tribune*, March 26, 1995

Earlier editions of the *Canadian Internet Handbook* spent much time describing such Internet applications as Gopher, Telnet, FTP, and Archie. Anyone getting involved with the Internet had to become quite familiar with these applications, since they were the main tools used to access information from around the Internet. Even today, these older applications continue to provide access to a wealth of information. Using Telnet, you might link to other computers on the Internet, such as a mainframe at a public library, to review and search information on that remote computer (such as a catalogue of books). You might use FTP to retrieve a computer program or document from somewhere on the Internet. You might use Archie to find a particular computer file by searching for it by name. And you might use Gopher to access all kinds of information from around the world using a simple "menu" of choices.

However, you might also find that you have no need for most of these applications, or that if you need to access an FTP site or look at a Gopher site, you can do so through your World Wide Web browser, rather than having to run a separate program. Sometimes you might find yourself retrieving a file using FTP from within the Web, without even realizing that you are using FTP.

These applications have become, in a way, superseded by the sophistication, reach, and power of the Web. Reflecting this fact, we have moved these applications to this chapter under the title "Older Internet Applications." You still need to learn about them (in particular, FTP), but you will find them to be less important and less useful than simple e-mail, USENET, and the World Wide Web.

The Changing Internet

Until late 1994, you had to learn how to use separate programs such as Gopher and FTP if you wanted to know how to use the Internet; thus they were an important part of previous editions of this book. Then in the fall of 1994 Netscape was released, a program of such sophistication and power that it helped to fuel an explosion in growth and use of the World Wide Web. The arrival of the Web changed the Internet forever, by resulting in a concentration on the Web as the tool of choice for the publishing of information by individuals and companies.

Until 1994, companies and individuals establishing information sites on the Internet might have chosen to establish them on a Gopher server or might have made documents available in an FTP site, but now they largely ignore Gopher and FTP and use the Web instead. In other cases, companies might have linked internal computers to the Internet so that they could be accessed via Telnet, but now link those systems to the Web.

Whatever the case may be, these "older" technologies are used less and less throughout the Internet. (FTP and IRC are perhaps the only real "survivors" of these early Internet applications, as we will see below.)

OLDER INTERNET APPLICATIONS

1. There are several Internet applications, such as Telnet, FTP, and Gopher, that have in some ways become superseded by the sophistication, reach, and power of the Web.
2. Even as their use decreases, Gopher, FTP, and Telnet sites still exist and can be accessed with separate client software or by Web browser software such as Netscape and Microsoft's Internet Explorer, using the standard URL method of addressing.
3. FTP is a program used to retrieve files and information from around the Internet.
4. Telnet is an application that lets you travel from your Internet account to another computer somewhere else on the Internet in order to run a program at that computer.
5. Gopher is an information retrieval system that presents a text-oriented view of information.
6. Finger is a utility that lists details about users located at another location on the Internet.

The Role of the Web Browser

The Internet is a system that is constantly evolving. One result is that there are still many FTP, Gopher, and Telnet sites throughout the Internet. And if you want, you can access these sites with separate FTP, Gopher, and Telnet client software. In this chapter, we will take a look at examples of how this is done.

But in most cases you can also access Gopher and FTP sites using your Web browser (such as Netscape and Microsoft's Internet Explorer), using the standard URL (uniform resource locator) method of addressing. Hence for many of these applications your Web browser can become the one and only information access tool in your life, rather than separate programs for separate purposes. More and more, these applications are being integrated into the Web. Why would you want to do this? It helps you to avoid complexity; you can use one program to access many different types of information, rather than having to use separate programs to access different information sites.

In this chapter you will see each of these applications from the perspective of someone with a SLIP or PPP connection to the Internet. We will describe some of the special considerations for those who might access the Internet using a shell account. And in each case, we will show you how they are used via a separate client software program and how they are accessed through the World Wide Web.

FTP

You could describe FTP as one of the granddaddies of all Internet applications, right beside Telnet (which we describe next). Before the World Wide Web began to dominate information retrieval through the Internet, people needed a way to retrieve documents, files, and computer programs from throughout the Internet. That's where FTP came in.

FTP, which stands for file transfer protocol, was the program used most often to retrieve files and information from around the Internet. In fact, until early 1995, FTP was the application that saw the highest volume of information transferred through the Internet. Of course, all that changed with the arrival of the World Wide Web.

But FTP is still used quite heavily throughout the Internet community. In fact, of all the "older" Internet applications, it is likely the one you might use the most. You might even find yourself using FTP while in a World Wide Web session without even knowing it.

The reason for this is that in many cases it is still convenient for organizations to put actual computer programs or fully formatted word processing documents (or other types of computer files) up on FTP sites. These FTP sites can then be accessed directly with FTP software to retrieve a file, or they can be linked to a Web site so that you can retrieve the file with your Web browser. Thus throughout the global Internet you can find "FTP servers" that contain

- Public domain and shareware software, that is, software written by individuals and released for general use by anybody. In some cases, a fee or donation is required in order to comply with the terms provided with the software.
- Documents discussing the Internet or virtually any topic imaginable, in text form or specialized word processor form. In other cases, documents are available in "Postscript" format, which requires a printer with Postscript capability.
- Images from NASA and other organizations in a variety of formats. You will need a file viewer compatible with the particular file type in order to view the image.
- Sound files, for example, CBC radio programs, which are now available via the Internet. You will need sound capability on your system to deal with the file.

Many of these FTP sites have now been linked into World Wide Web pages so that when you go to retrieve a particular document from the World Wide Web, you are actually using an FTP session to do so!

Hence people no longer think of FTP as being a separate program that you run on the Internet to access a file, but, rather, think of it as a different type of Internet resource to access with a World Wide Web browser.

Using FTP

FTP sites are referred to in two ways: by their older address and file directory instructions and by the newer URL (uniform resource locator) method. As you start to use the Internet, you might still see references to documents or other information available by FTP. For example, you might come across the phrase "To obtain a document about 'Opportunities in Selected Ethnic Markets in Canada', use anonymous FTP to access **foodnet.fic.ca** and get **ethnic1.exe** in the directory **Documents/trends**." This is the "older method" by which people describe how to obtain a file using FTP.

You might also see the phrase "You can obtain the document about 'Opportunities in Selected Ethnic Markets in Canada' using the URL **ftp://foodnet.fic.ca/Documents/trends/ethnic1.exe**." This is the newer way of describing how to find information in an FTP site, based on the URL method of addressing. You would use this address to retrieve the document using your Web browser.

The key thing to keep in mind is that you can retrieve this document using FTP software or by using a World Wide Web browser like Netscape. Let's look at both cases.

Retrieving Files Using FTP Software

First, we retrieve the document described above using FTP client software, in this case, the program WS_FTP.

An FTP document reference usually contains three pieces of information that will help you retrieve the information mentioned:

- the domain address or domain name of the FTP site;
- the file location, in terms of the directory location;
- the file name.

In our example above **foodnet.fic.ca** is the FTP site, **Documents/trends** is the directory location, and **ethnic1.exe** is the name of the file that you want to get.

Using WS_FTP, you can choose to open up an FTP session to this site, and key in the directory information directly. Note that our session is based on an "anonymous log-in," which is described below:

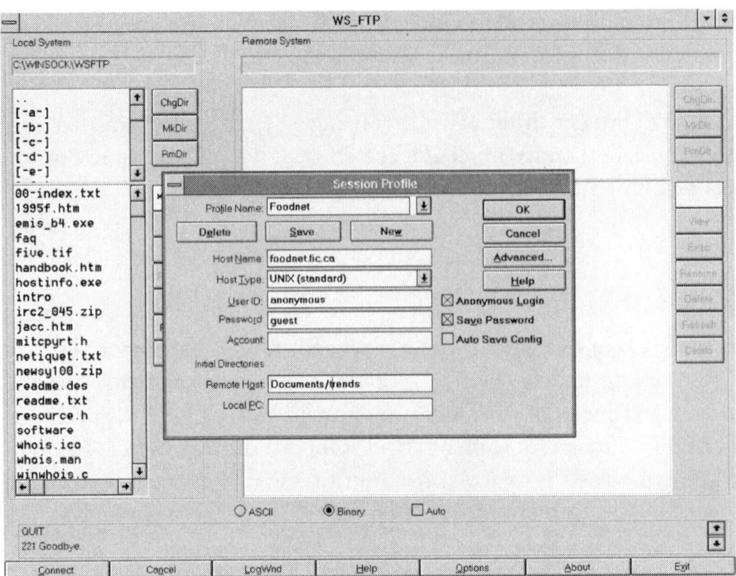

When you are logged into an FTP site with software such as WS_FTP, you will see your local hard disk files on the left and the files on the remote FTP site on the right. In this case, once the FTP software connects with the **foodnet.fic.ca** FTP server, you are presented with a listing of files in the directory **Documents/trends.**

To retrieve the document you want, point to the file (**ethnic1.exe**) and press the <— key to transfer it back to your computer:

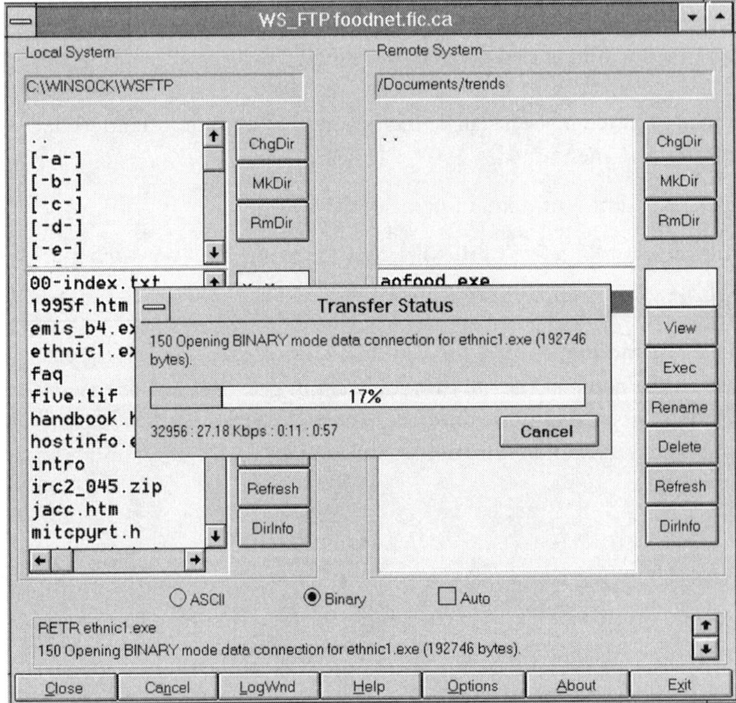

Thus you can use a separate FTP client to perform an FTP transfer.

Retrieving Files Using Your Web Browser

Most people wonder, why bother to use a separate FTP program? The need to run a separate FTP program to retrieve such a file has been negated by the arrival of sophisticated World Wide Web browsers. Netscape, for example, lets you easily access FTP sites, in this case using the URL **ftp://foodnet.fic.ca/Documents/trends/ethnic1.exe**. Simply keying this address into your Web browser will result in the file being transferred to your system.

You can also view FTP directories with a program such as Netscape. If you want to view the directory that contains the file for our example, use the URL **ftp://foodnet.fic.ca/Documents/trends/**, and you will see the following:

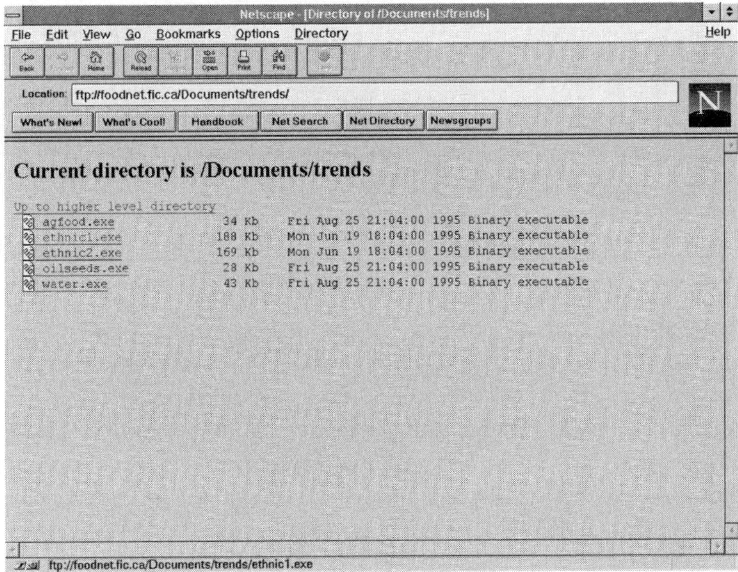

From here, you can easily retrieve the specific file that you want, simply by double-clicking on it within the listing.

FTP Basics

There are a few things to remember when using FTP on the Internet:

- Many services permit "anonymous" log-ins; that is, they allow anyone on the Internet to access them by providing a user ID of "anonymous." If you access an FTP site using a Web browser, you do not need to worry about "anonymous" log-ins.

  However, if you are using a separate FTP client, you are asked for a password along with the user ID "anonymous." As a courtesy, you should use your own e-mail address as the password. In some cases, the FTP server will only permit a connection if you do identify yourself in this way. Some even validate what you supply.

  Most graphical FTP software supports simple anonymous log-ins; for example, in WS_FTP you can choose an anonymous log-in simply by clicking on the "Anonymous Login" button:

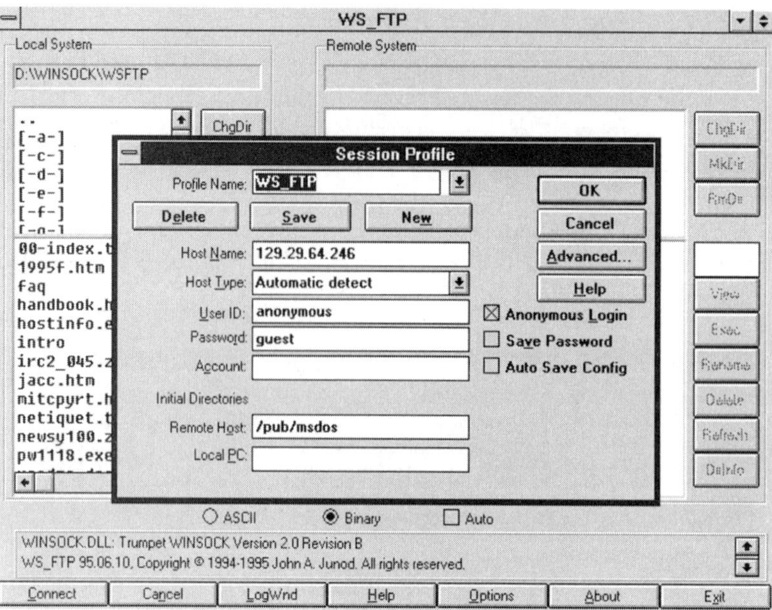

- In order to speed up the file transfer process, many of the files throughout the Internet have been compressed or combined. Files with the extensions **.zip**, **.arc**, **.Z** or **.z**, **.tar**, **.lzh**, **.sit**, or **.cpt** are compressed or combined or both. The most common type of file extension is **.Z**, indicating a file that has been compressed using the UNIX program "compress." You will need appropriate software to uncompress or uncombine the file that you retrieve. Many FTP sites on the Internet include an uncompress program. If you do not have an uncompress program available, obtain one from your Internet service provider.

  Make sure that you have appropriate tools to uncompress or uncombine files that you might retrieve. The following table lists some of the more popular compression programs, the file extension used, and the probable computer environment that the file is from.

EXTENSION	PROGRAM	PLATFORM
.zip	Pkzip/Pkunzip	DOS/Windows
.arc	Arc	DOS/Windows
.sit	Stuffit	Macintosh
.cpt	CompressIt	Macintosh
.z	Compress	UNIX
.lzh	LZH	DOS/Windows

Retrieval of Files by E-mail

It is possible to retrieve many of the files that are available through FTP by e-mail instead, through a few FTP archives. This is done by sending an e-mail message containing the file name that you want, including the directory details, to a specific e-mail address at the FTP archive site. At the FTP archive, a "mail robot" takes apart your request, obtains the selected file, and sends it back to you via e-mail. The requests are handled on a very low priority basis, so you might not receive the file for several hours or even several days.

One of the most popular of these sites is a server at the Massachusetts Institute of Technology, which has an FTP site containing information about the Internet. For example, to retrieve a document from this site that details how to use the ftp-by-mail service:

- Create a message to **mail-server@rtfm.mit.edu**.
- In the text of the message, you input a command that will send a help file or will retrieve specific files that might otherwise have been available via FTP. For example, to obtain help, send an e-mail message to **mail-server@rtfm.mit.edu** that contains the word "help" in the text of the message.

  To obtain actual files, use the send command within the body of the message, that is,

```
Date: Thu, 30 Dec 1996 08:43:06 est

Reply-To: jcarroll@jacc.com

From: jcarroll@jacc.com (Jim Carroll)

To: mail-server@rtfm.mit.edu

Cc:

send /pub/usenet/news.answers/mail/mailing-lists/part01

send /pub/usenet/news.answers/mail/mailing-lists/part02

send /pub/usenet/news.answers/mail/mailing-lists/part03

send /pub/usenet/news.answers/mail/mailing-lists/part04

send /pub/usenet/news.answers/mail/mailing-lists/part05

send /pub/usenet/news.answers/mail/mailing-lists/part06
```

This will result in e-mail messages being sent to you that summarize some of the mailing lists available on the Internet. There are several sites throughout the Internet that permit file retrieval by e-mail. Although there might be minor variations in the method, the concept is consistent from location to location. If in doubt, obtain the help file from a particular site first.

Obtaining FTP software:	
For Windows:	
CuteFTP	**http://www.cuteftp.com**
WSFTP	**http://www.csra.net/junodj/ws_ftp.htm**
For Macintosh:	
Fetch:	**ftp://ftp.wustl.edu/systems/mac/info-mac/comm/tcp**
Look for file name **fetch-xxx.hqx**, where **xxx** represents the current version number.	

The Slow Demise of FTP?

As with Gopher, the use of FTP was finally surpassed by World Wide Web traffic in 1994. One reason has been an increased tendency to publish a document on the World Wide Web for viewing, rather than simply making the document available on an FTP site for people to come and get it. Using the World Wide Web, people can view a formatted document with images, sound, and other information immediately on the screen. Using FTP, you would have to go and retrieve a file first, and then do something to view the file. There is simply no comparison in terms of ease of use.

Even as electronic publishing migrates to the World Wide Web, there will still be a big need for FTP servers. There will always be a lot of information in FTP sites — computer files, programs, and other information that you do not view on-line, but that you do need to retrieve. But over time you will likely find that most of your FTP file retrieval occurs automatically from within a World Wide Web session, rather than through separate FTP client software.

Telnet

Telnet is an application that lets you travel from your Internet account to another computer somewhere else on the Internet in order to run a program (such as an electronic catalogue) at that computer. As recently as one or two years ago, it was a major Internet application in use throughout the Internet. Telnet was the primary method, next to Gopher, through which you might access library catalogues or browse on-line "stores" of books and records.

Telnet still exists and is in use throughout the Internet; it is just not used or implemented as widely as it was in the past, since it is an older, character-based application. In Canada, these locations include

- Links to the on-line catalogues of various libraries, such as the Vancouver Public Library, to search for particular books or other materials.
- Access to pay-per-use database services such as Dialog and Nexis, if you have an account already set up with these services.[1]

---

1. Accessing these services through the Internet is often less expensive than accessing them through regular data services like Datapac or Tymnet.

Using Telnet today is a little like time travel, if you are currently using the World Wide Web with software like Netscape or Microsoft's Internet Explorer. With Telnet, you leave the comfortable 1990s world of point-and-click information access and retreat back to a computer screen based on characters, menus, numbers — an application that looks like it was designed (and often was) in the 1970s and 1980s.

A Sample Telnet Session

Once you reach a location by Telnet, you will be able

- to directly access the resource, if no "log-in" or "sign-in" ID is required;
- to access the resource by providing a public user ID;
- to access the resource by providing a valid user ID and password for a system that has generally restricted its access.

In our example, we will use a Windows program, Trumpet Telnet.

The following session details the steps taken to Telnet to the Alberta Wheat Pool (AWP). In this case, the AWP has set up a system through which farmers can obtain up-to-date livestock and grain prices, as well as other information, on-line. Within Trumpet Telnet, we choose to "open" a new session and key in the Telnet address for the AWP, **fis.awp.com**:

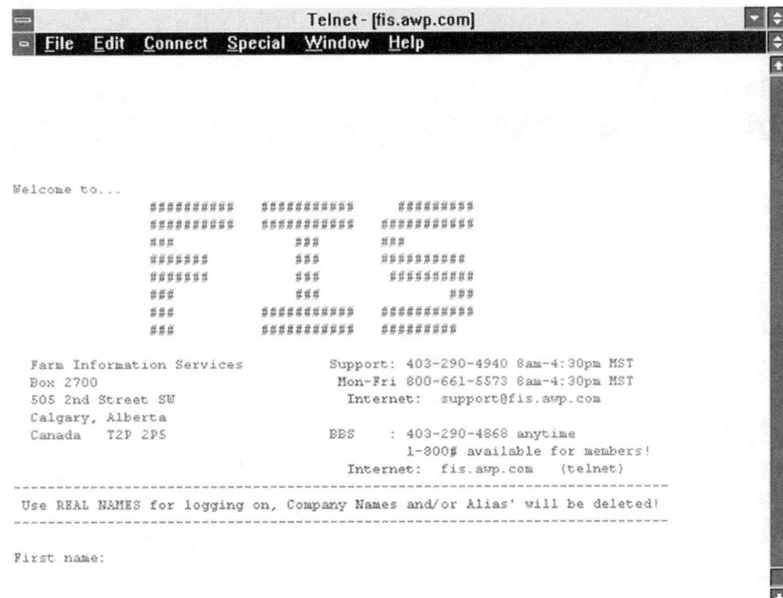

Trumpet Telnet opens a connection to this site and displays the welcoming screen. (Anyone can obtain a user ID and password at this site by filling out the forms that follow this welcome screen.)

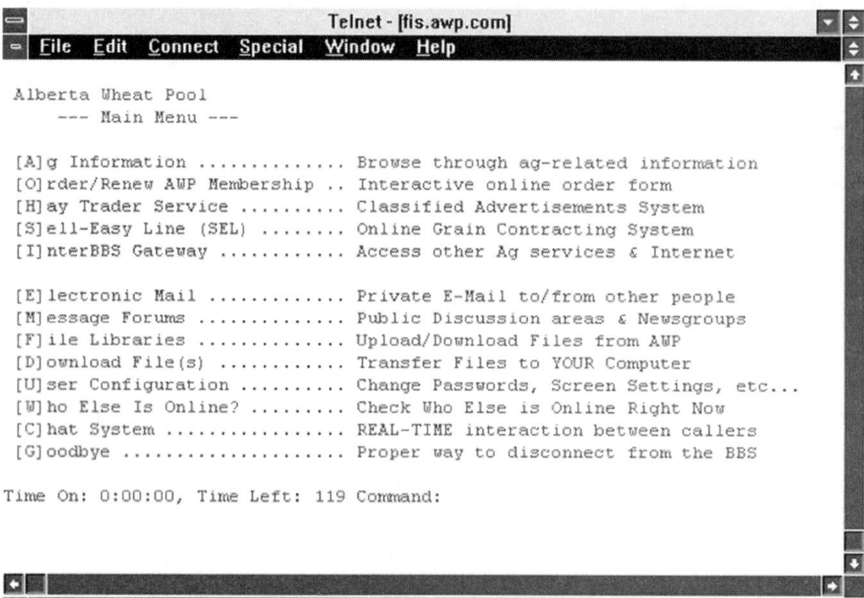

Once you are signed in, you can access the "main menu" of information:

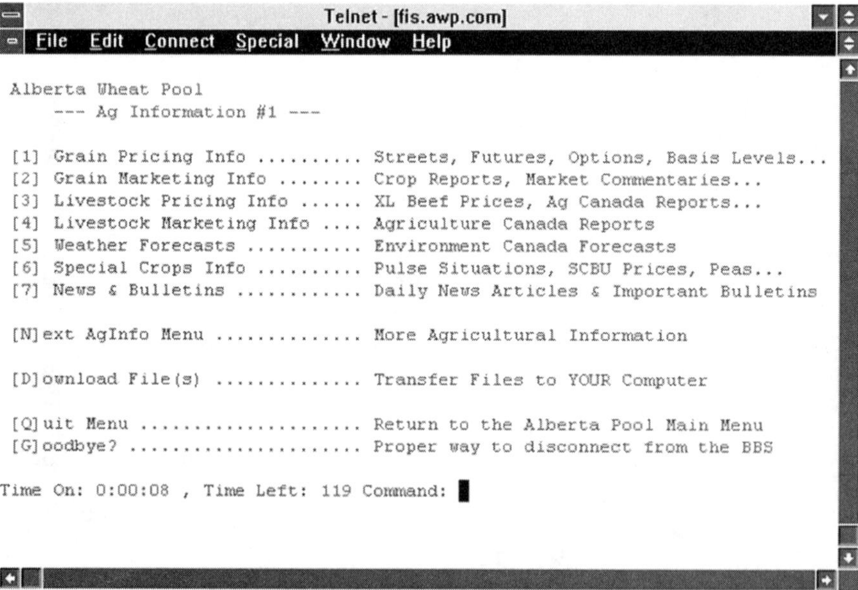

From here, you can access several types of information, including a wealth of livestock and commodity marketing information:

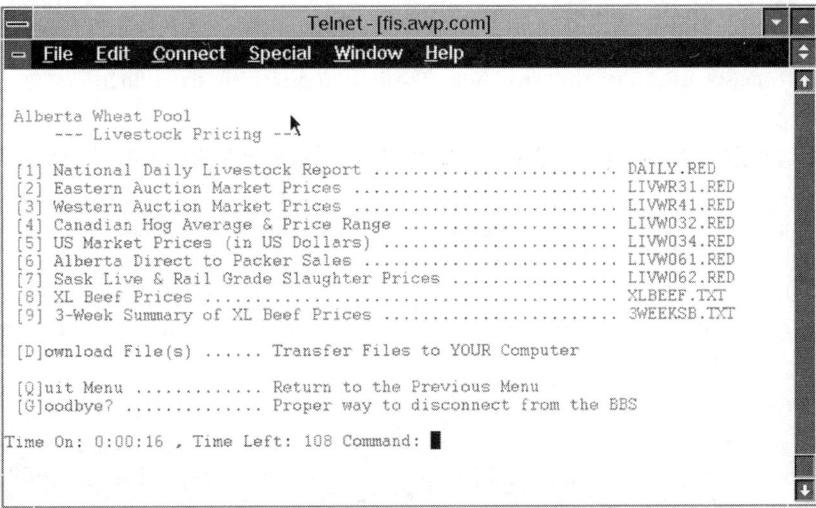

One final thing about Telnet: such sites are often linked into the World Wide Web. If you have configured your Web browser properly, when you choose such an item from the Web, your browser will load your Telnet software and take you to the site. The AWP has established a Web site, and the Telnet site above is accessible through it:

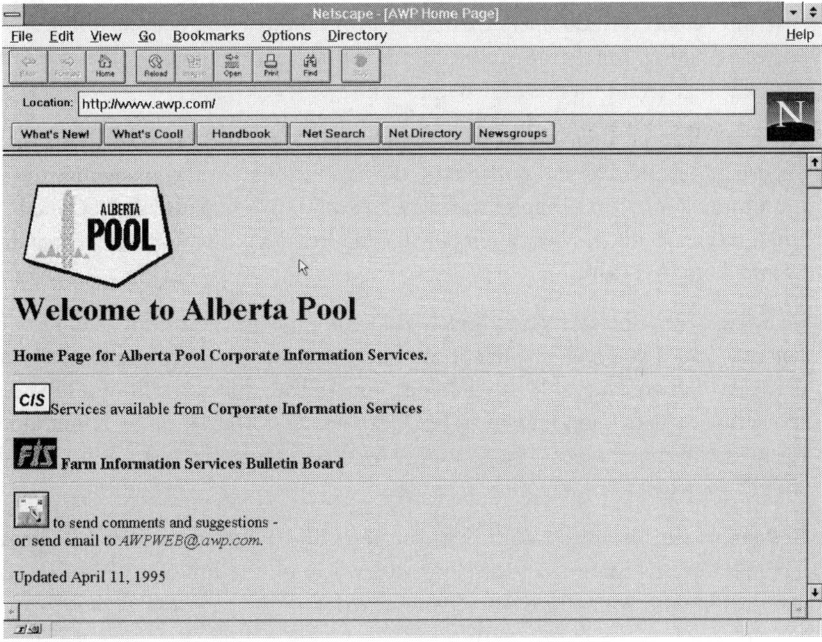

Special Things About Telnet

There are some special things that you should keep in mind as you use Telnet:

- On occasion, you will be advised to use the domain name with a particular "port" number. This is required when you are accessing a system on the Internet in which the port directs you to a particular application. You are usually told when a particular port address is required. Key in the port number after the Telnet address when a port number is required. For example, access to the University of Michigan Weather Underground system, which includes Canadian weather details, requires a port number. In this case, you are advised to Telnet to the address **downwind.sprl.umich.edu 3000**, where 3000 is the port number used for this particular application.

- When using Telnet, you should always keep in mind that you are accessing other computers on the Internet, and as a result you are "pretending" to be directly linked to them through "terminal emulation." "Terminal emulation" when using Telnet is one of the necessary evils of the Internet. When using Telnet, you could be linking into all kinds of different computers around the globe, each of which might run differently. Your computer has to pretend to be the proper type of "terminal" for each system that it might access, and given the different types of systems out there, it cannot pretend to be everything to everyone.

  What does this mean? Likely that you will experience some frustration with Telnet due to the use of "terminal emulation" and due to the fact that every system that you Telnet to could operate differently and present you with a completely different way of doing things. The result of this is that Telnet is not, nor can it ever be, a completely friendly, mouse-driven application.

- Some applications that you access will ask you to specify the terminal type that you are using. Be sure that you understand the various types of terminals that your communications software supports, and how to switch to any particular terminal type when you are on-line. Most services will support, at a bare minimum, the popular terminal type VT-100.

- Be aware of any special instructions that might apply to certain Internet resources. For example, if you review some of the Internet resources described in our resource directory that are accessible using Telnet, you will see that some libraries require you to use an access method known as TN3270, which is a variation of Telnet modified for special terminal types. The Directory includes the special instructions that you should use when accessing these locations.

- Remember the "escape character" for the particular Telnet client that you are using. There is nothing worse than traveling somewhere on the Internet without understanding how to get back to where you started.

  In your link to the Alberta Wheat Pool, you were told, once you had signed in, that the "escape character" is "^]". This means that you press the ctrl key and] together on your computer when you are ready to leave this particular Telnet site. The escape character permits you to exit from a particular Telnet session in case the service you have linked to does not make it obvious how to exit or in case your current session seems to "hang" or "freeze."

The Evolution of Telnet

Telnet was most often used by companies and organizations to permit people to run a program located on their computer. This program would let the person query some type of database for information at that remote computer. The Alberta Wheat Pool example used above permits people to retrieve on-line market prices, which are actually stored on a computer system at the Wheat Pool.

But we are seeing many such applications spring up on the World Wide Web, instead of being implemented as a Telnet application. This permits people to query a database somewhere, yet do it through the simple, user-friendly World Wide Web browser.

Obtaining Telnet clients:

For Windows:

EWAN:	**http://www.lysator.liu.se/~zander/ewan.html**
NetTerm:	**http://starbase.neosoft.com~zkrr01/netterm.html**

For Macintosh:

NCSA Telnet 2.6	**ftp://ftp.wustl.edu/systems/mac/info-mac/comm/tcp/**

Look for file **ncsa-telnet-xxxx.hqx**, where **xxxx** is the latest version number.

As in all cases, check for the proper version numbers on-line.

Gopher

Gopher is an information retrieval system developed at the University of Minnesota to permit easier access to local university information. Like many developments within the Internet community, the authors of the Gopher software made it available on the Internet so that anyone could use it and set up their own Gopher server. Given that it was such an easy application to set up, there was an explosion of growth in the use of Gopher right around the world, with well over 7,000 "sites" accessible by 1994. But that year the World Wide Web arrived in full force, and the number of new Gopher sites being established began to decrease.

One key to Gopher's success is that it is not overly complicated. It is easy to use and, moreover, makes an orderly, logical presentation out of dissimilar and scattered "chunks" of information from all over the Internet (although the Web does a much better job of doing this). The other key feature of Gopher is that unlike the World Wide Web, its presentation of information is text-oriented, meaning that people with old, character-based computers running a "shell account" still find Gopher easy to use. In other words, you do not need a powerful computer to access Gopher.

The result is that today there are still many Gopher resources around the Internet that are being constantly updated and maintained, particularly within academic institutions in Canada where it is used to provide a campus-wide information system.

However, clearly, Gopher is on the way out. For example, when we went to visit the official "Gopher Jewels" site, which details some of the best Gopher sites in the world, we got an error when trying to access the "What's New" category.

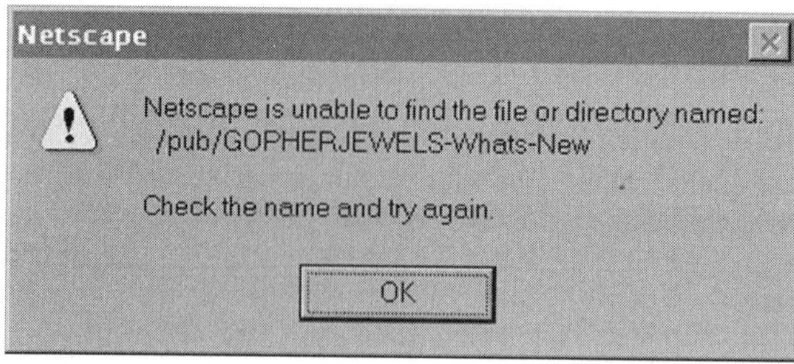

Using Gopher

With a SLIP/PPP account or a direct Internet connection, you can access Gopher in one of two ways:

- using Gopher client software such as Winsock Gopher, or
- using a World Wide Web browser that supports access to Gopher resources, such as Netscape.

Gopher appears similar regardless of the software used, in that it presents a listing of items in the form of a menu from which you can choose.

For example, here is the Gopher site for Electronic Frontier Canada, an organization that gets involved in issues related to freedom for electronic communications in Canada. Their site can be found at the Gopher address insight.mcmaster.ca. Here is what it looks like using the program Winsock Gopher:

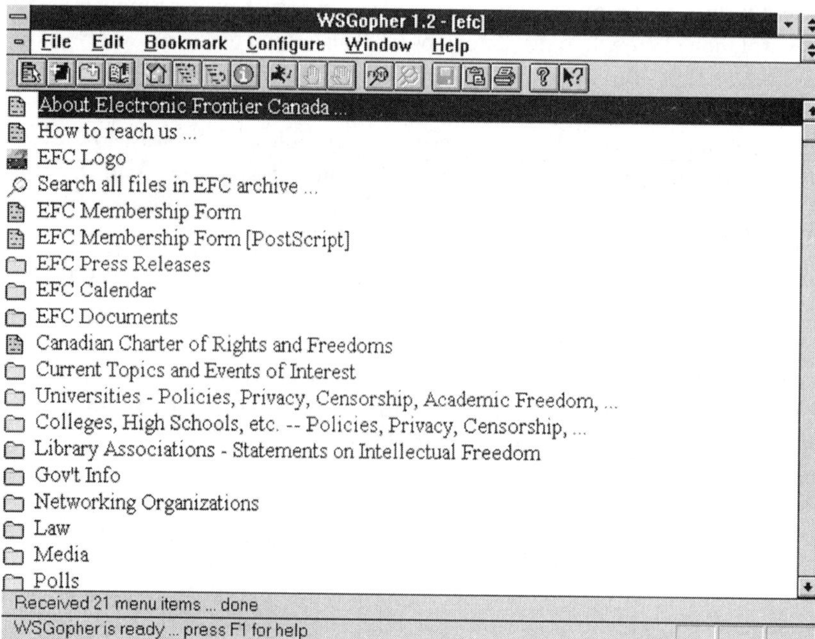

Here is the same thing as seen through Netscape, accessed using the URL **gopher://insight.mcmaster.ca:**

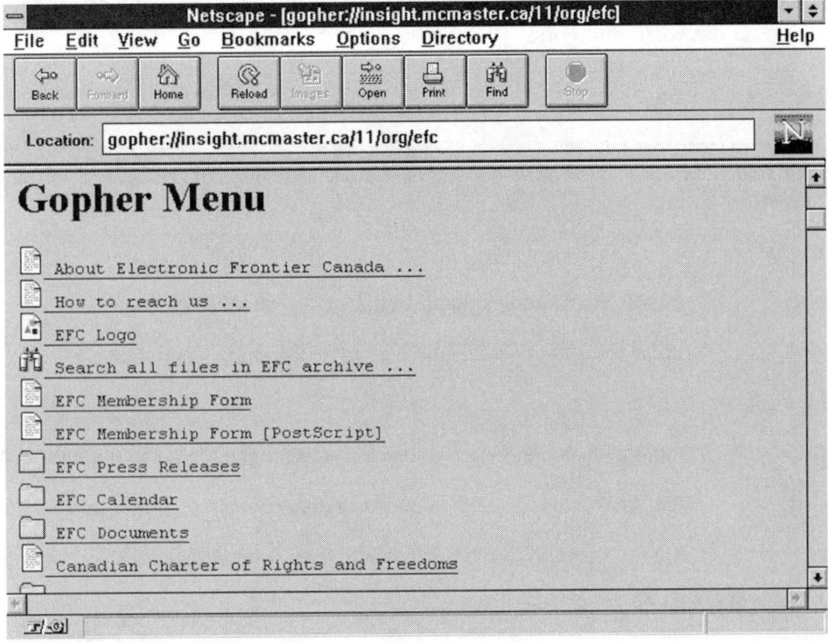

And here is their Web site.

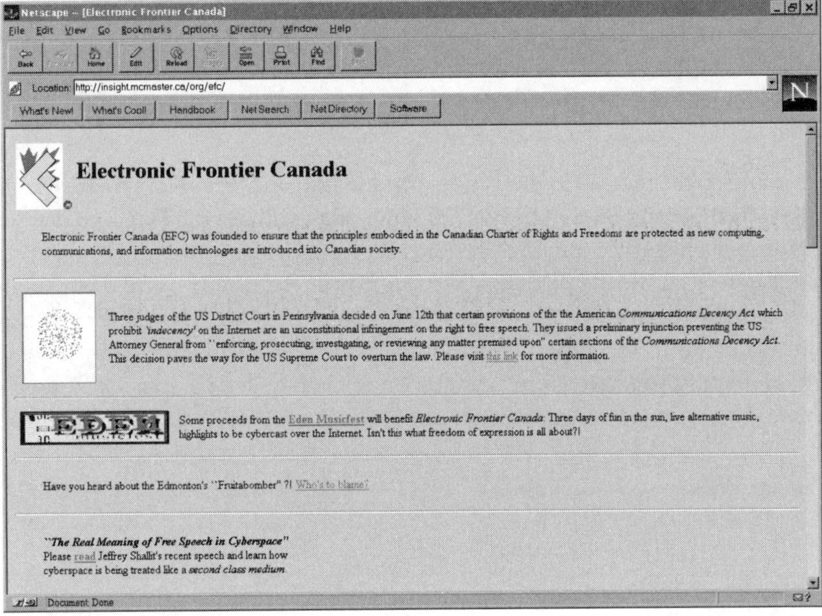

As you can see, accessing a Gopher resource is not that much different whether you are using a Gopher client (i.e., a software program used to access Gopher) or a World Wide Web browser. However, it is easy to see why organizations are adopting the Web instead of Gopher. Clearly, the time for Gopher has come and gone.

Obtaining Gopher Software:

Keep in mind that most popular Web browser software lets you access Gopher sites, using URLs of the format **gopher://address**. Thus you do not need separate Gopher client software. However, if you must have it, try the following:

For Windows:

WSGopher	**ftp://ftp.wust1.edu/systems/ibmpc/win3/winsock/wsg-11.exe**
Hgopher	**ftp://ftp.ccs.queensu.ca/pub/msdos/tcpip/winsock/hgoph24.zip**

For Macintosh:

Turbo Gopher	**ftp://ftp.wustl.edu/systems/mac/info-mac/comm/tcp/turbo-gopher-20b8.hqx**
GopherApp++	**ftp://ftp.wustl.edu/systems/mac/info-mac/comm/tcp/gopher-app-22b43.hqx**
PNL Info Browser	**ftp://ftp.wustl.edu/systems/mac/info-mac/comm/tcp/pnl-info-browser.hqx**

As in all cases, check for the proper version numbers.

Keep in mind that there are fewer and fewer Gopher sites you can access, so you will use these for little more than historical curiosity.

Finger

Finger is a utility originally used in the UNIX world to list users on a local system or to list users located at another location on the Internet. In some cases, you can use Finger to determine the last time that someone logged into their Internet account.

Other locations on the Internet are now using Finger as a simple method of making information available. For example, if you are in a shell account that has a Finger client, you can obtain recent information on auroral (Northern Lights) activity in Canada by keying **finger aurora@xi.uleth.ca**. If you have a direct connection to the Internet, you can use Winsock Finger, a public domain Finger client. Accessing the site above, for example, shows you the following:

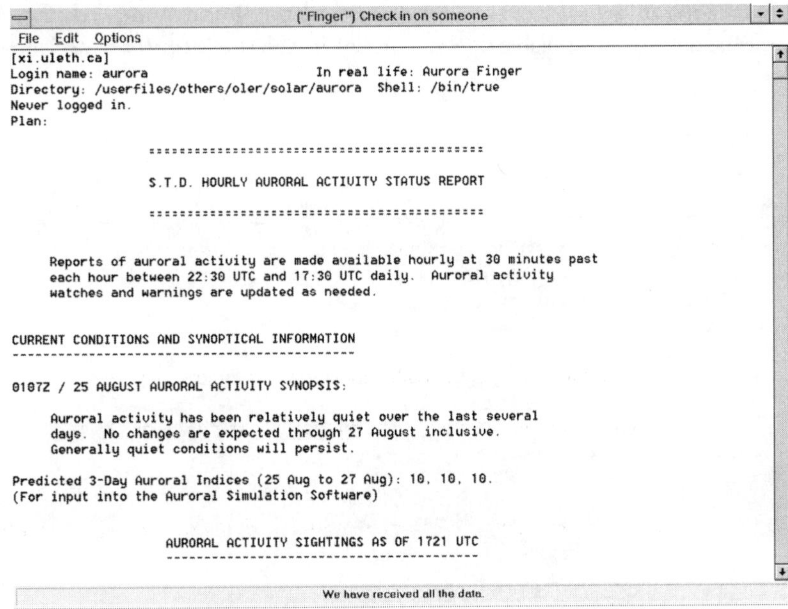

You can "finger" **seisme@seismo.emr.ca** to get information on recent earthquake activity in Canada:

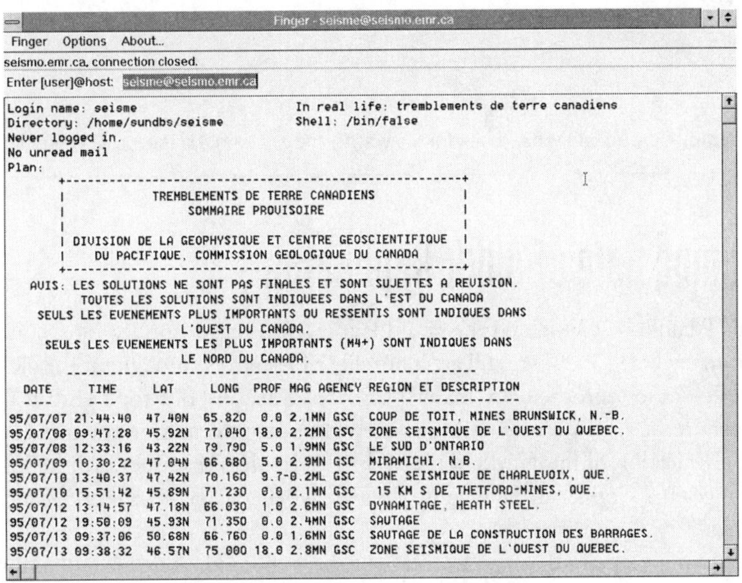

Like most older applications, Finger is being eclipsed by the World Wide Web. For example, the same information above is available directly through a Web site (**http://www.seismo.emr.ca**):

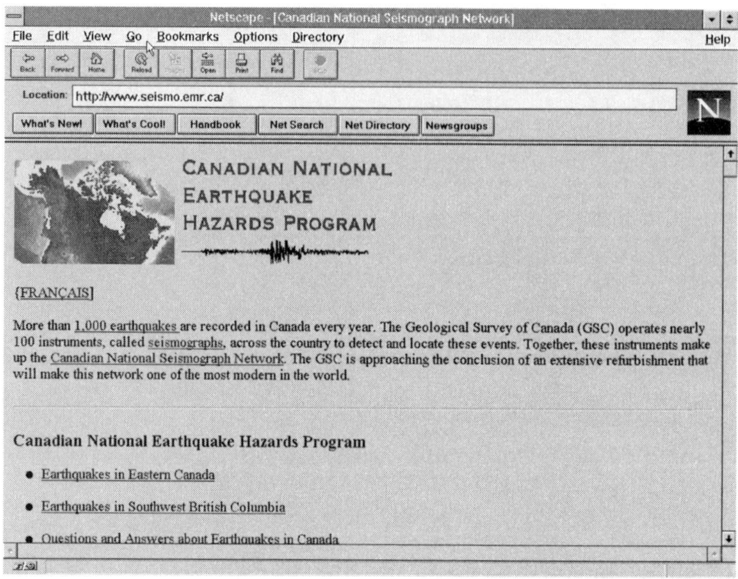

> Obtaining Finger Software:
>
> For Windows:
>
> WS-Finger
>
> **ftp://sparky.umd.edu/pub/winsock/** (Look for file **wsfngr*.zip,** where * is the latest version number)

The Declining Role of Older Applications

Telnet and FTP could be considered the granddaddies of Internet applications, since they have been used for many years, and there still are a number of resources throughout the global Internet that you can Telnet to, and there are many FTP sites available. But the trend in Canada and elsewhere is that most organizations setting up new Internet information resources are using the increasing sophistication of the World Wide Web. The result is that Telnet and FTP and applications like Finger and Gopher are falling into disfavor as general, day-to-day applications for most Internet users.

However, it is important that you learn about them, because there are still a number of resources throughout the Internet that you can access through these two capabilities. We can expect to see many FTP sites throughout the Internet, particularly as methods to retrieve files from these sites using the World Wide Web become common.

CHAPTER 14

Setting Up a Web Site

A basic Web site, with no links to other sites on the World Wide Web and a fairly straightforward design, can be had for as little as $200. That goes up to around $1,500 for a site linked to other sites with interesting graphic design. The really high end corporate sites, such as FedEx, which allows visitors to track packages, cost tens of thousands of dollars to create and need a staff to maintain them.

Web sites wonderful but aren't business panacea
Vancouver Sun,
January 19, 1996

Since the days when people first gathered around campfires and told stories, the ways in which we convey legends and learning have affected how we work, learn, and play. Written language, for instance, meant that people didn't need to meet the storyteller to receive the tales. Like the ripples from a stone tossed into a pond, the printing press meant that millions more could hear others' tales — and learn from their experiences, whether good or bad. Now comes a tool that accelerates how fast information spreads, creating hopes of broad new impact for the better on society.... No one was very good at predicting the impact of such inventions as the printing press, which helped lead to mass literacy, and the telegraph, which let people communicate instantly over huge distances. For the Web you don't need to rely entirely on predictions. There's already plenty of evidence of real effects.

On the Internet, a Worldwide Information Explosion Beyond Words
The Washington Post,
June 30, 1996

"How can I set up my own Web site?" This is one of the most frequently asked questions in Canada today from those who are dealing with the Internet. One of the key reasons the Internet is growing at such a furious pace is that anyone can have a Web site. In this chapter we will take a look at what is involved in setting up your own Web site, including the following issues:

- finding a home for your Web site;
- preparing the Web pages for your site;
- design tips and other issues related to the effectiveness of your site;
- making others aware of your Web pages.

We will also talk briefly about Web editors, which are programs that can be used to help you create your Web pages. However, they have become such a significant topic of their own that we will devote the entire next chapter to them.

We could write a whole book on the topic of creating your own Web site, but there already are many such books available. Hence the purpose of this chapter is not to provide you with detailed instructions on how to build a Web site, but simply to provide guidance on what is involved in doing so. Once you have read this chapter (and the next one, "Web Development Software"), you will have a better idea of where to start.

A Home for Your Web Site

The first thing you need is a place to locate your Web site, basically, a computer somewhere on the Internet that acts as a Web server. You have two options:

- If you do not have a full-time connection from your network to the Internet, you can rent space on the Web site of a company that "hosts" the site on your behalf.
- If you do have a full-time connection from your network to the Internet, you can establish your own Web server on one of your own computers instead of renting space from a "host."

Most individuals will fall into the first category. Many companies will also fall into the first category, unless they have taken the time and effort to establish a full-time connection to the Internet. Even then, it may not make sense for them to establish their own Web site. Let's see why.

Renting Space for Your Web Site

The easiest way to establish your own Web site is to rent space on the Web server of a third-party organization. There are all kinds of companies that will "host" your site for you, that is, they will store on their computers the computer files that make up your Web site and provide the necessary service and support to ensure that your site is available to the world on a regular basis. The categories consist of:

- An Internet service provider. In addition to selling access to the Internet, these companies will rent space to you on their computer to host your Web site.
- An Internet presence provider, a company in the business of hosting, establishing, and developing Web sites for individuals and organizations on their own computer systems. These companies focus on helping organizations develop an Internet *presence* on the Web and do not sell Internet *access* services to the general public. Thus they are sometimes a little more focused on their mission than Internet service providers. Good examples are the

SETTING UP A WEB SITE

1. Anyone can set up a site on the World Wide Web.
2. All that is involved is finding a "home" for your Web site, and preparing the Web pages in what is known as HTML format.
3. Your Web site will usually be on computer space rented from an organization with a full time link to the Internet. If you have a full-time link to the Internet, it will be on your own computer.
4. You can prepare your Web page by learning how to write HTML code, as many people have, or by using one of a growing number of HTML or Web editor programs.
5. There are many tips, hints, and design issues that you should be aware of if you are establishing your own Web site.
6. Once your Web site has been established, you must work hard to make people aware of its existence.

Mississauga-based E-Commerce (**http://www.e-commerce.com**) and the New Brunswick-based CyberSmith (**http://www.csi.nb.ca**).

- Major computer organizations, such as IBM Canada (**http://www.ibm.com**). These organizations will also rent Web space on their own networks and promote themselves as the best alternative for large-scale, sophisticated Web sites for major organizations. Usually they concentrate on medium- to large-sized businesses.
- On-line shopping malls. There is now an increasing number of on-line shopping malls found on the Internet, any of which will rent you Web space.

Eight Ways to Find an Organization to Host Your Web Site

1. If you are on the Internet, talk to your own Internet service provider to find out if they offer such a service.
2. Browse through Appendix G to get an idea of which Internet service providers host Web sites.
3. Use on-line directories, such as Yahoo!'s directory of Internet presence providers (**http://www.yahoo.com/Business_and_Economy/Companies/Internet_Presence_Providers/**).
4. Talk to people within the Internet community to find out who offers Web presence services. If you see a Web site that you like, call up the company and find out who designed the site.
5. Talk to your friends and business associates to see if they have any recommendations.
6. Pick up a copy of *The Computer Paper,* a free, monthly computer publication available in most major cities in every province across Canada. It is also available in some rural communities for a small cost. It can generally be found at public libraries and computer retailers. Many Internet presence providers advertise there.
7. Alternatively, check with your local computer store to see if your community has a local computer publication. In Toronto, for instance, there is a free, monthly publication called *Toronto Computes!* A similar publication called *Alberta Computes!* is available in Calgary and Edmonton. These publications are also available on a subscription basis if they are not available near you.
8. Take a look at the page "Leasing a Server," which details many low-cost Web server sites (**http://union.ncsa.uiuc.edu/HyperNews/get/www/leasing.html**).

The Cost of a Site

You may encounter any or all of the following types of charges from the company that rents you the space and services to host your Web site:

- A minimum monthly fee to host your site. This fee often provides a set number of megabytes of storage for your Web pages and a set maximum volume of traffic through your Web site before additional charges apply. Sometimes your basic subscription to the Internet through your ISP provides the capability of hosting a Web site for no additional charge, with maximum storage and traffic capabilities before extra charges as described below are levied.
- Storage charges. These charges are levied on the storage used by you to host your Web pages in excess of any storage already provided and are usually levied per megabyte of information stored. Hence, if you intend to use a lot of graphics, sound, or video files in your site, you could end up paying more for storage.

- Traffic charges. The traffic charges are levied on the number of megabytes that are accessed through your Web site in excess of any traffic volumes already provided, also usually charged per megabyte. Once again, if your site uses a lot of graphics, sound, or video files, the traffic volume charges will be higher.
- Setup fees. These fees simply pay for the time and effort, by your provider, that go into setting up the server to host your Web site.
- Web site creation fees. If the provider actual creates the Web site for you, then there will be a creation fee. The issue of "outsourcing" the creation of your Web site is discussed in more detail below.
- Page fees. The page fees are based upon the number of pages you have in your site. Some providers allow a certain number of pages and then charge for each additional page. You should avoid these types of providers like the plague, for a much more reasonable basis to charge is the storage charge described above. A page fee greatly reduces the flexibility that you have in the design of your site.
- Virtual domain name fees. This type of fee is charged if you want to use your own registered domain name as your Web address. For example, you might have an address like **http://www.provider.com/~yourname**, which is not terribly friendly. To use a virtual domain name, you must register a domain name (i.e., **yourcompany.com**). You might then be charged a fee by the company that hosts your Web site to be able to use the Web address **http://www.yourcompany.com**.
- Directory listing fees. Some providers will charge to list you on their home page.

Some of these fees may or may not be reasonable in your particular circumstances. For example, you should ask yourself whether you want to pay a directory listing fee, since you can take the time and effort to list yourself on the many search engines found throughout the Internet. In addition, some organizations will charge different rates for business pages and personal pages on the theory that business pages draw more traffic and hence have a higher inherent cost.

The simplest way to find out what a company charges to host a Web site is to visit their Web site. Many organizations will provide pricing for their basic Web hosting service on-line; if they do not, ask for a quote by phone or e-mail.

If you explore the topic, you will quickly discover that there are many different price structures in place. We have picked a few examples to illustrate this. Keep in mind that these are simply examples, and it is quite likely that the companies mentioned below may have changed their prices in the interim or may have gone to completely different price structures.

- Pictou County, NS, Internet service provider North Shore Internet Services (**http://south.nsis.com/nsis/hpform.html**) distinguishes between personal and business Web sites in their pricing structure and provides for minimum fees to host Web sites. It then charges for storage and traffic charges above certain minimums, depending upon whether you are an individual or a business.

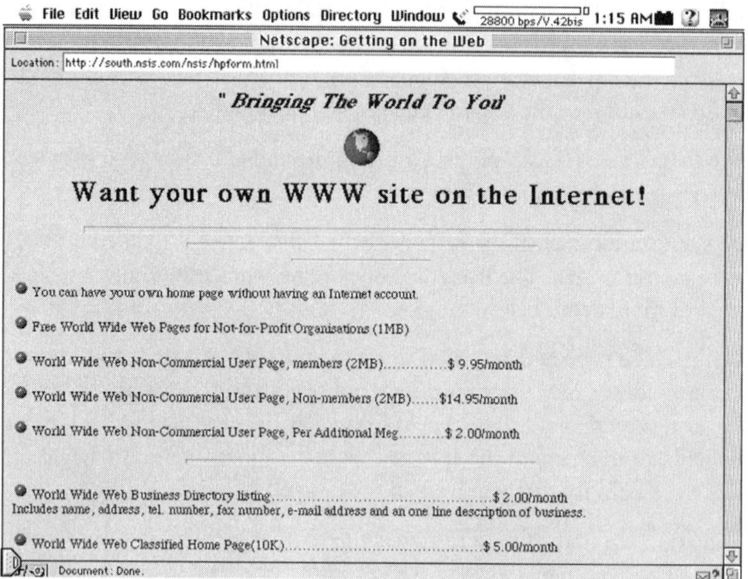

- Cybersurf Information Access (**http://www.cia.com/**) prices not on a monthly basis but on a yearly basis, with $150 per year getting you a corporate Web site with up to 2 megabytes of storage, and each additional megabyte costing $60 per year. In addition, if you want to use your own domain name, they will charge an additional $125 per year.

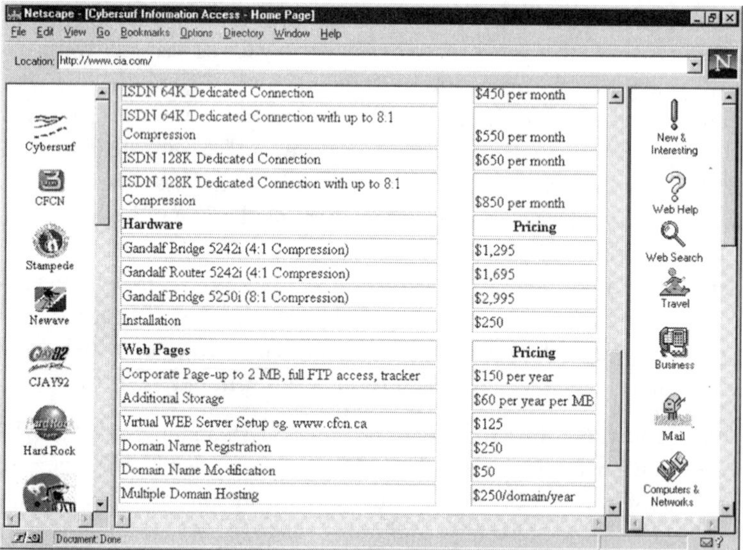

- Internet Portal in Vancouver also provides a page detailing their price structure, with 2 megabytes of free storage and a charge of $0.49 per megabyte per month. Traffic charges vary according to the "plan" that you purchase, as can be seen in the following screen (**http://www.portal.ca/services/web-domain.html**):

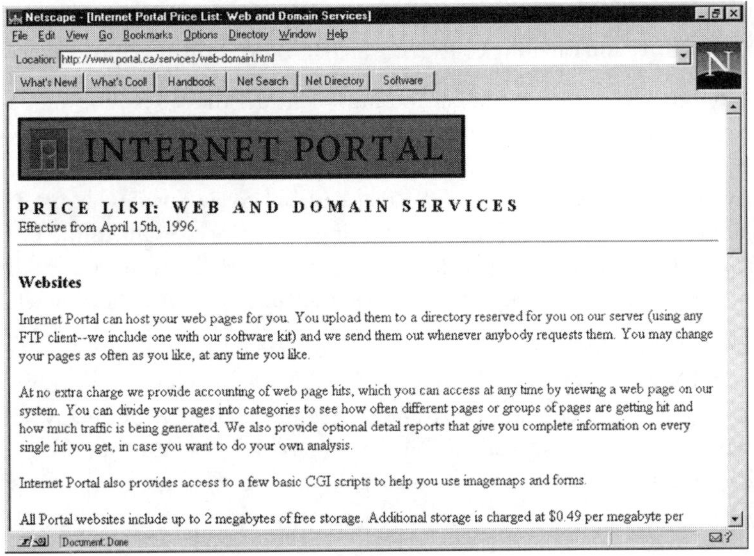

- The Malls of Canada charges a rate of $350 for one page of information up to 350 words, for one year. If you want additional pages, they can cost $225 per year for a second page and $165 for each page beyond that (**http://www.canadamalls.com/pages.html#HOW**):

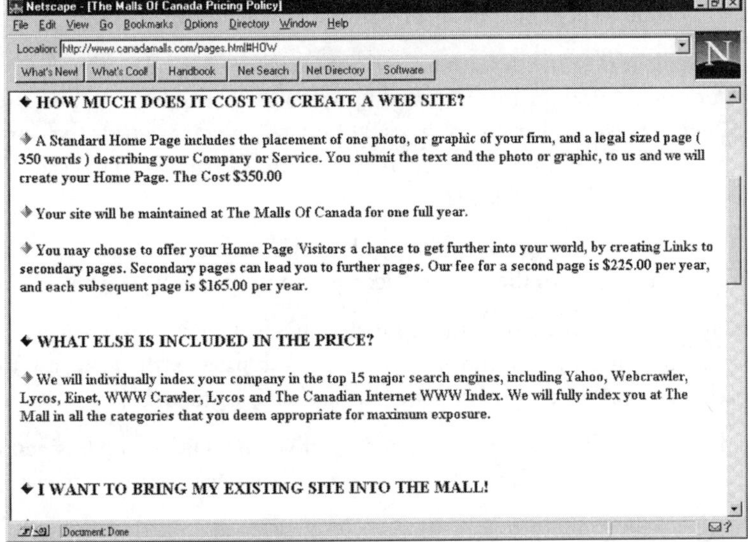

As you can see, rates are all over the map, with all kinds of innovative pricing methods. The result is that it can be difficult or challenging to do a price comparison. Keep in mind that prices are continually changing because competition is rampant. We have several suggestions:

- Shop around and compare prices. The Internet is still a new and evolving market; hence, if you spend some time exploring different options, you will discover some good deals.

- Understand what you are getting into. Take the time to clearly understand the pricing structure, and carefully consider if there are any hidden extras.
- Do not purchase solely on price. You must consider the service and support that an organization offers. You should ask the potential host several questions: Will my Web site be available 24 hours a day? What type of link do they have to the Internet? You may not want to go with a provider that has a relatively slow 56 kb or 128 kb link to the Internet if you have a lot of graphics if you can get the same thing from a company that has a faster T1 link. If, however, your site will be mostly text, then speed is less important. What type of support will they offer you? Are they knowledgeable?
- Consider the long-term future. Is the provider reliable? Is the provider likely to be in business a year from now? Keep in mind that there are many, many companies rushing into the Internet marketplace and that some will survive but many will not. There is nothing worse than having someone trying to access your Web page, only to discover it is not there anymore because the company has gone out of business.
- If you operate a business, strongly consider using a virtual host name, that is, **www.yourcompany.com** instead of **www.yourhost.com/~yourcompany**. The reason for this is not only does it look nicer, but it could save you lots of money in the long run. If you have to move your Web site to another provider in the future, you will not have to change your stationery, business cards, and other marketing and business literature. Remember that if your Web address is based on the name of the your ISP, and you switch ISPs, then your Web address changes. If you have your own domain name, it does not change, regardless of which ISP you use.
- Take a look at the other sites they host. Do they have a good track record? Is the site well organized, neat, maintained, and up-to-date? Or are there a lot of "broken links" (i.e., hypertext links that do not work)? Outdated information? If they appear slovenly and lazy on-line, it is likely they will not do a good job to ensure that you have a good quality, reliable site.
- What do they do about maintenance? Do they schedule maintenance for off-hours, or do they bring down the server to accomplish it whenever they feel like it?
- Ask around for advice from others. Do not be reluctant to send an e-mail to those companies or individuals who already have a Web page on their site; ask them whether or not they are pleased with the particular company.
- Find out about their technical expertise, creative capabilities, and business expertise, particularly if they are going to help you with Web page creation and design.
- Will they help you to promote the site? Do they have marketing and strategic expertise? Will they know all the areas and indices where your site should be indexed? Will they offer to add your site to all these indices as part of their service?
- What features do they offer on their Web server? For example, do they support emerging methods for secure electronic transactions? Do they offer other features such as RealAudio for sound, as discussed in the chapter about the World Wide Web, or other special data formats?

- Will they permit you to modify the content on your own site, or do all changes have to pass through an administrator? It is important that you have as much control over your site as possible, rather than having to wait for someone to upload your new pages or changes for you.
- Do they provide some type of statistical monitoring or report, or allow you to obtain the "access logs" so that you can review detailed information about traffic at your site?

You need a professional organization to provide your Web site, since reliability of service will be key. Hence shopping around is an extremely important thing to do.

Should I Use an Internet Shopping Mall?

It seems you cannot go anywhere these days without hearing about Internet shopping malls. They also go by the names cybermalls, Internet malls, and on-line shopping malls.

There are hundreds of them; they are multiplying like rabbits. Simply take a look at the Yahoo! category for on-line malls and you get the idea (**http://www.yahoo.com/Business_and_Economy/Companies/Shopping_Centers/Online_Malls/**).

If you are considering setting up your Web site in an on-line shopping mall, there are several things you should think about:

- It is easy for anyone to create a "shopping mall" on the Internet, tell the world they are open for business, and start renting space. The result is that there are a lot of quality malls on-line, there are a lot of so-so malls, and there are a lot of malls that you should not touch with a ten-foot pole. It is simple to create a mall on the Internet; it is difficult to make it work as a serious and profitable business.
- Internet shopping malls seem to be a bit of a conundrum. One economic impact of the Internet is known as disintermediation. This means that the role of the middleman in business will increasingly become redundant, since consumers will be able to travel directly to the Web site of a company with which they wish to do business. But an on-line shopping mall is in essence a middleman. In the days in which the middleman is losing value, it is interesting to see so many middlemen springing up. To carry this point a bit further, organizations are increasingly questioning the value of advertising within an on-line shopping mall as it becomes easier to set up their own World Wide Web sites.
- Pricing to locate your Web site on an on-line mall is all over the map. Many of the on-line malls that we visited had outrageous prices for what you got (i.e., one or two Web pages), compared to what it would cost to rent space with an Internet service provider and hire a couple of designers to create your pages for you.
- Internet shopping malls seem to disappear as frequently as they appear. It is a difficult, cutthroat business, and this is evidenced by the lack of business stability of some of the malls on-line. What good is a shopping mall if it disappears within a few months of obtaining your money, particularly after you list your Web address on your stationery and business cards? Spend a few minutes browsing the on-line mall category in Yahoo!, and you can see how many have disappeared.
- You are often limited in what you can do on-line compared to having your own Web site. Join a shopping mall, and you might get one or two Web pages. These are nothing more than "billboards in cyberspace" offering to sell a product, and as we discuss later in this chapter, you must do more than provide a simple billboard on-line to get noticed. You must provide useful, valid content in order to attract interest and attention.
- Image is also important. To many people throughout the Internet, you only appear as a serious organization if you have your own Web site rather than just renting space in a "mall."
- Will the mall draw people to your site? With so many thousands of shopping malls out there, you could just be a pebble on a beach. How will you get noticed? Folks who run on-line shopping

> malls often use the phrase "location, location, location" to indicate why you should locate on them. But how can locating on a particular cybermall be useful when there are thousands of shopping malls about? It is difficult for any "cybermall" to distinguish itself on-line, so sometimes the location argument just does not wash.

We might seem a little down on the concept of Internet shopping malls; we are. We think that you should carefully analyze the advantages and disadvantages of using a mall compared to having your own Web site rented on the space of an Internet presence provider. Malls might be right for some people and not for others. The bottom line is that you should know what you are doing before you go on-line.

Hosting Your Own Web Site

If you have established a dedicated link from your own computer network directly to the Internet, as we outlined in Chapter 4, you may choose to establish your own Web server. Our first comment is that doing so can be a trivial undertaking. Our second comment is that it can be a massively complex thing to do. Let us explain that contradiction.

Presuming that you already have a direct link to the Internet and have addressed the issues of security, implementing your own Web server can be as simple as buying a Web server program, installing it, and creating some Web pages. We look at a few examples below of Web servers that come straight out of the box and can be "easily installed."

On the other hand, while it is trivial to install this software, it is not necessarily trivial to configure it, primarily because you must have a very good working knowledge of the Internet and the World Wide Web to ensure that you set up and maintain a good, reliable, and secure Web server. Some of the issues you must deal with in the configuration include:

- General security over the Web server itself. You want to ensure that the server and the information on it are not at risk of an attack by people throughout the Internet.
- Security issues related to access, including the ability to provide for user authentication, that is, requiring a password to get to different Web pages as well as obtaining the necessary "security authentication certificates" from "authentication authorities" to support a secure Web server. User authentication is a method of controlling who can access your Web site by asking for a username and password every time someone tries to visit your home page or an area within your site. This would be required, say, if you wanted to restrict access to people who meet certain criteria. For example, if you operate a medical organization, you may want to make your Web site available only to qualified members of the medical profession. Alternatively, if you want to sell subscriptions to the information on your Web site, you will want to control access and admit only paying subscribers.
- How to configure your Web site to monitor the number of visitors to the site at different times of the day. You will also want to track which areas of your site are the most and least popular.
- Performance issues, that is, the number of concurrent users that you can support and the ways that you can optimize performance of your server.

- Implementing the special features the server might support, including technical issues such as on-line surveys, comment forms, and interactive forums. These involve such things as forms, processing of those forms via what is known as CGI scripting, and other special technologies.
- Keeping up-to-date with the latest software to support the latest developments on the Web to ensure that your server supports these developments.
- Maintenance and analysis tools to help you analyze your Web site and ensure that it is working properly at all times.
- Configuring your server to support "virtual hosting," thus allowing the use of multiple different domain names.

There are many, many more features. So you can see that while it may be easy to buy inexpensive Web software or even download it for free, it can be a challenge and a significant undertaking to configure and maintain a Web site if you do not know what you are doing.

Web Server Software

As we noted in the chapter about the World Wide Web, the Web "serves," or provides, your Web pages to the world when someone requests them. It does so by running a Web server program. If you are interested in establishing your own Web server, the best site for up-to-date information on different Web servers is WebCompare (**http://www.webcompare.com/**); this site provides comprehensive listings of many of the Web servers available, their features, price, commentary, and other useful information. It is the best place for comparative server information and is a good place to start.

You can also take a look at ServerWatch (**http://www.serverwatch.com/**) for up-to-date information about Web server software and the whole world of running and managing a Web server. It includes information on how to enhance your server for sound, audio, video, and other capabilities; it also includes a news section, which details the many ongoing and daily changes occurring in the Web server industry.

Setting up Web server software can be as easy as opening a box, choosing to install the disks, and answering a few questions. Examples abound:

- Netscape, the granddaddy of all Internet companies, is by far the leading commercial provider of Web server software and has a substantial share of the global market. Netscape has a full range of server products filling all kinds of different needs. The best source for information is the Netscape Web site itself (**http://www.netscape.com**).
- O'Reilly (**http://www.oreilly.com**), a well-known publisher of books and software about the Internet, sells WebSite, Web server software for Windows NT systems. (You can run it on Windows 95, but since Windows 95 is not a real multitasking program, it is not advisable, other than for experimentation or a very small-scale Web site.) Installing it is a snap; assuming that you have a direct link to the Internet, we will presume that you have a good grasp of the necessary details such as your domain name. Once installed, you can access the administration program in order to configure it for the various Web site structure details, security issues, logging, directory, and other details:

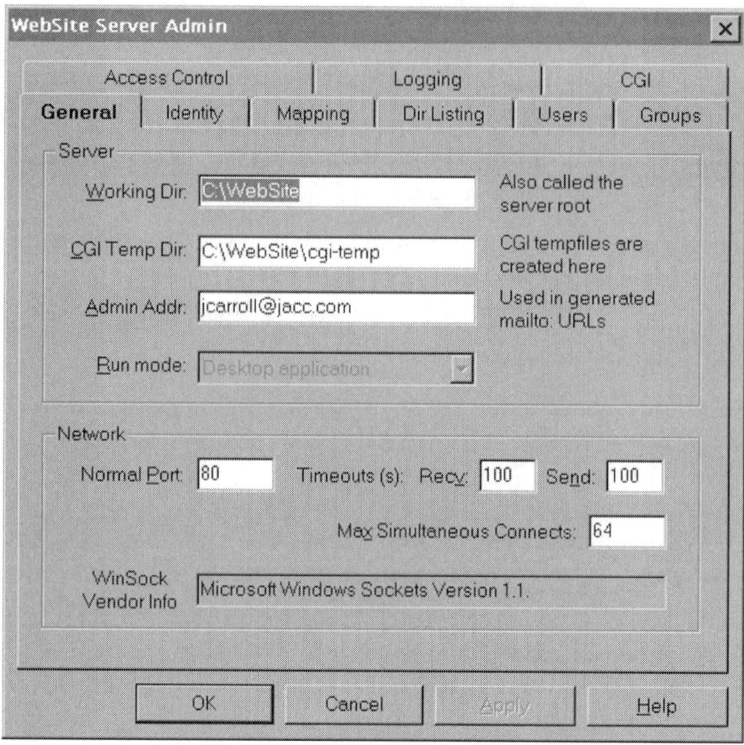

Once you have configured the software, you click on the server, and there it sits, ready and willing to serve your Web pages to the world:

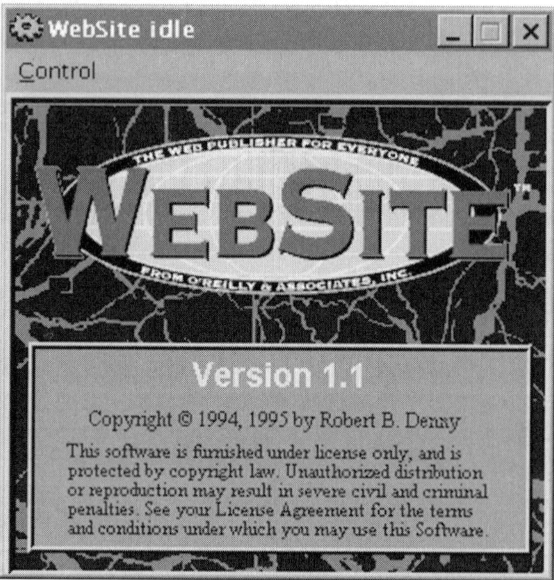

- Microsoft FrontPage, the Web-authoring tool, which we take a look at in the next chapter, comes with its own "personal Web server." Although not an "industrial-strength" server, you can experiment with it to get a grasp of what is involved in configuring a Web server. Microsoft also makes available for downloading the Microsoft Internet Information Server for Windows NT systems and is positioning it to become a competitor to Netscape.

- For Apple Macintosh systems you can look into products such as WebStar from StarNine Technologies (previously known as MacHTTP) (**http://www.starnine.com**).

The bottom line is that it is becoming increasingly easy for individuals to set up their own Web sites, but the technical complexity to do so is not necessarily disappearing. You must have good, fundamental working knowledge of the Web to configure a good, solid, reliable, and secure Web server. Hence the scope of configuring and supporting a Web server is far beyond the scope of this book.

What Does It Cost?

The cost to purchase Web server software can range from the trivial (i.e., some shareware programs you can try out for free) to a few hundred dollars (e.g., for WebSite) to several thousands of dollars (for high-end Netscape server programs). The real cost is not in the software; it is in the setup and initial configuration. It is in the cost of the full-time link to the Internet and providing proper and ever vigilant security over the link. It is the ongoing configuration and maintenance issues. In other words, it is in the time and resources that you will spend establishing the server and maintaining it in top operating condition at all times.

Preparing the Web Pages

The second issue in establishing a Web site is preparing the Web pages that make up your site. The pages are created in a format known as HTML, or hypertext markup language. We discussed this briefly in our chapter about the World Wide Web. Once again, there are two choices:

- You can create your Web pages yourself by learning HTML or by learning to use an HTML editor program;
- You can contract the design of your site to a third-party organization (i.e., hire a "Web company").

What Does It Cost?

Your first question probably is, "what does it cost to prepare Web pages?" This is like asking, "what does it cost to prepare a brochure?" It depends, of course, upon many different things, such as do you do it yourself or contract it out? Do you go black and white or full color? Two-sided or two-sided with a fold? Do you design it yourself or have someone design it for you? Should it have just text or a lot of graphics? And so on.

Obviously, you can prepare a brochure quite inexpensively, or you can spend a fair chunk of money on it. The Web is no different, and the money you pay for your Web site will depend upon how far you go with it.

So the first thing that affects the cost of your brochure, or your Web site, is how sophisticated it becomes. The cost is also affected by how you go about preparing it. You can create your paper brochures by learning how to use desktop publishing software, or you can hire a graphics design organization to do it for you. The same is true with the Web: you can create the pages for your Web site yourself by learning what is involved, or you can hire professionals to do it on your behalf. The cost of your site will vary accordingly, and the result will depend upon your own creative skills or the skills of those whom you hire.

Hence answering what it costs to "develop" a Web site is like asking, "how high is up?" We have seen situations in which it costs less than a $100 to get rolling and others that have involved up to million-dollar Web campaigns with major Fortune 500 companies and large-scale national advertising firms, with the participation of specialized Internet presence providers. Obviously, what is right depends upon your own circumstances and your budget.

Creating Your Own Web Site

As we outlined in Chapter 7, information on the Web is created in a format known as HTML, hypertext markup language, the language of the Web. Every site on the Web is built upon HTML. In essence, an HTML file is a special type of computer file that contains a number of codes contained within angular brackets; the codes define how the information surrounded by the brackets should be shown when the file is accessed by a Web browser.

To create your own Web site, you must prepare a series of computer files in HTML code. These computer files in HTML format are then put on your Web server, whether you have your own Web server or you are renting space on the Web server of someone else. Once they are put on a Web server, your Web site is available to the world. There are two ways of preparing your Web site:

- You can prepare your Web site by learning HTML and creating the Web pages in HTML code. In this case you use a regular text editor such as Windows Notepad to write the HTML file yourself directly, using what we call HTML "tags"; we describe these below.
- You use a Web editor program that inserts the proper HTML codes into your Web page. A Web editor can help to isolate you from the nuances of HTML and in some cases operates like a word processor.

Your choice depends upon how involved you want to become with the Web and the extent to which you want flexible capabilities in the design of the site. The more you learn about HTML, the more flexible you can be. As we said at the beginning of this chapter, the topic of creating your own Web site could fill a book on its own. So here we will provide guidance only. But first, let's take a diversion into the topic of HTML.

Learning About HTML

You should have some understanding of what HTML is all about, even if you decide to use a Web editor that hides you from much of the complexity of HTML. HTML is not that complex, and the very nature of the Web is that it has been easy for people to learn how others have created their Web site, hence answering the question "how did they do that?"A good way to learn how HTML works is to experiment with code that has already been prepared by someone else. We will show you below how to do this, to help explain what HTML is and how it works.

- The first step is to view the HTML code "behind" a Web site. Here is "Central Canada's Bowling Page" (**http://www.foxnet.net/users/bowling/foxbowl.html**):

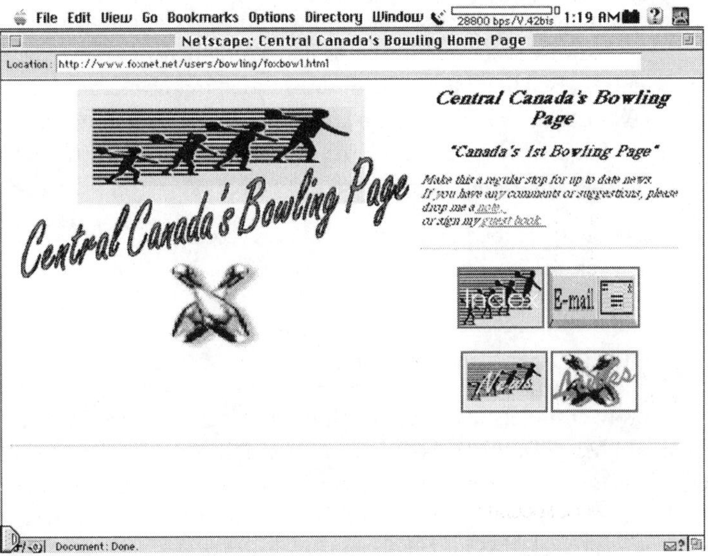

To view the HTML code from within your Netscape browser, click on "View" and then on "Document Source":

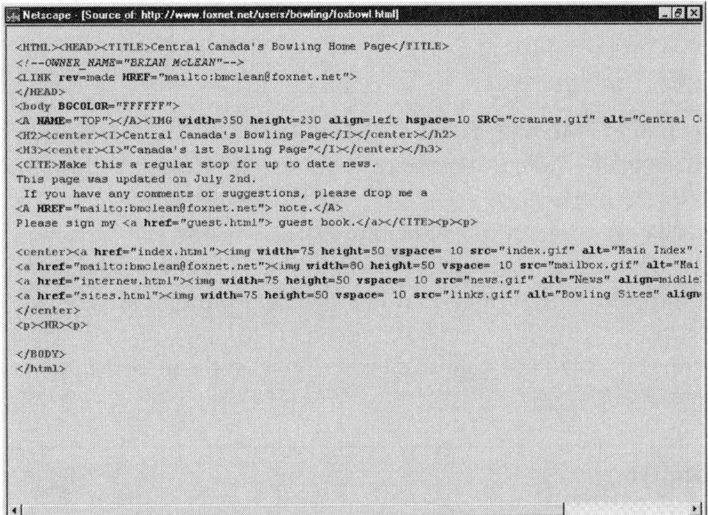
Netscape - [Source of: http://www.foxnet.net/users/bowling/foxbowl.html]

```
<HTML><HEAD><TITLE>Central Canada's Bowling Home Page</TITLE>
<!--OWNER_NAME="BRIAN McLEAN"-->
<LINK rev=made HREF="mailto:bmclean@foxnet.net">
</HEAD>
<body BGCOLOR="FFFFFF">
<A NAME="TOP"></A><IMG width=350 height=230 align=left hspace=10 SRC="ccannew.gif" alt="Central C
<H2><center><I>Central Canada's Bowling Page</I></center></h2>
<H3><center><I>"Canada's 1st Bowling Page"</I></center></h3>
<CITE>Make this a regular stop for up to date news.
This page was updated on July 2nd.
 If you have any comments or suggestions, please drop me a
<A HREF="mailto:bmclean@foxnet.net"> note.</A>
Please sign my <a href="guest.html"> guest book.</a></CITE><p><p>

<center><a href="index.html"><img width=75 height=50 vspace= 10 src="index.gif" alt="Main Index" .
<a href="mailto:bmclean@foxnet.net"><img width=80 height=50 vspace= 10 src="mailbox.gif" alt="Mai
<a href="internew.html"><img width=75 height=50 vspace= 10 src="news.gif" alt="News" align=middle
<a href="sites.html"><img width=75 height=50 vspace= 10 src="links.gif" alt="Bowling Sites" align
</center>
<p><HR><p>

</BODY>
</html>
```

This is the HTML code used by Brian McLean (**bmclean@foxnet.net**), the creator of this site. You can view the HTML code for virtually any site on the World Wide Web, which makes a great starting point for learning how HTML works.

- HTML consists of "tags." Let's take a look at what we have on the screen above. The first line reads

```
<HTML><HEAD><TITLE>Central Canada's Bowling Home Page</TITLE>
```

This is "HTML speak," or code, which defines this as the opening section, or "title," of the HTML document. In most Web browsers the "title" will show up at the top of your Web browser. For example, look at the Web site above, and you will notice that at the top of our Netscape browser we have the phrase "Central Canada's Bowling Home Page." Now we will explain what is happening here. We have the phrase "Central Canada's Bowling Home Page" surrounded by the words <TITLE> and </TITLE>. We call the <TITLE> item an HTML "tag"; it is an instruction to the Web browser that says, "here is something that will tell you how to show the next little bit of information on the Web browser screen."

◆ Web browsers interpret the HTML tags and act accordingly. Your Web browser comes to the Web site, accesses Central Canada's Bowling Home Page, and sees the first line containing

```
<HTML><HEAD><TITLE>Central Canada's Bowling Home Page</TITLE>
```

Your Web browser understands that anything that is surrounded by angled brackets (< >) is an HTML "tag." It knows what to do with most HTML tags. First, it looks at the HTML tag and from that understands this page to be a Web page (instead of a sound file, an image file, a graphic, a movie, or some other type of computer file). Then it sees the tag <HEAD>. It realizes that this first section is some introductory information about the page. Then it sees <TITLE>. It knows that anything it sees after the <TITLE> tag should be shown at the top of the Web browser, as the title of the page. Hence it places "Central Canada's Bowling Home Page" at the top of the screen. Finally, it sees a </TITLE> tag. The slash (/) tells the Web browser that this is the ending of the title section, so it knows to stop showing any more of the text up on the title bar.

◆ The heart of HTML is the fact that Web browsers interpret hundreds of different HTML tags. HTML code, in essence, is quite straightforward: it consists of tags that define for the browser how certain information should be shown. Each tag has a start and an ending. A start tag does not have a slash, while an end tag does. The text surrounded by a tag (e.g., between <TITLE> and </TITLE>) will be shown according to whatever rule has been established for that tag within the Web browser.

There are well over a hundred common HTML tags, many of which have been accepted by international standards bodies. Some of the more common tags are listed below.

COMMON HTML TAGS

Tag	Meaning	Example
<HTML>	Tells a Web browser that this is an HTML document. Must be in every Web page.	<HTML> is used at the start of every HTML file.
<HEAD>	Instructs the Web browser that the section surrounded by <HEAD> is the "header," or top part, of the Web page.	The <HEAD> area always ends with a </HEAD> tag.

<TITLE>	This is the title for the page and is shown at the top of the Web browser.	<TITLE>A sample Web page</TITLE>.
<BODY>	Indicates the start of the information that makes up the document.	<BODY> surrounds the rest of the information that makes up the Web page. </BODY>
<blink>	The text surrounded by this tag blinks on and off.	<blink>This text is flashing.</blink>
<center>	Centre the text or item surrounded by this tag on the page.	<center>This text is centred</center>
<H1>	Show the text surrounded by this tag in the large "headline 1 font."	<H1>This text appears in great big letters.</H1>
<H2>	Show the text surrounded by this tag in the smaller "headline 2 font."	<H2>This text appears somewhat smaller than the previous sentence.</H2>
<P>	Start a new paragraph.	<P>The text right after the P tag shows up as a new paragraph.</P>
<B>	Bold the text.	<B>This text is bolded.</B>
<I>	Italicize the text.	<I>This text is italicized.</I>

- You can use HTML tags to create a basic Web page. We can use the sample HTML tags outlined above to create a basic Web page by combining them all together into one computer file by following a few basic rules (primarily, the document must start and end with an HTML tag, and the <HEAD> and <BODY> tags must be used to define certain parts of the overall document). The entire HTML file looks like this:

```
<HTML>

<HEAD><TITLE>A sample Web page</TITLE></HEAD>

<BODY>

<blink>This text is flashing.</blink>

<center>This text is centred.</center>

<H1>This text appears in great big letters.</H1>

<H2>This text appears somewhat smaller than the previous sentence.</H2>

<P>The text right after the P tag shows up as a new paragraph.

<P>

<B>This text is bolded.</B>

<I>This text is italicized.</I>

</BODY>

</HTML>
```

If we put this HTML file up on a Web server and access it, this is what we get:

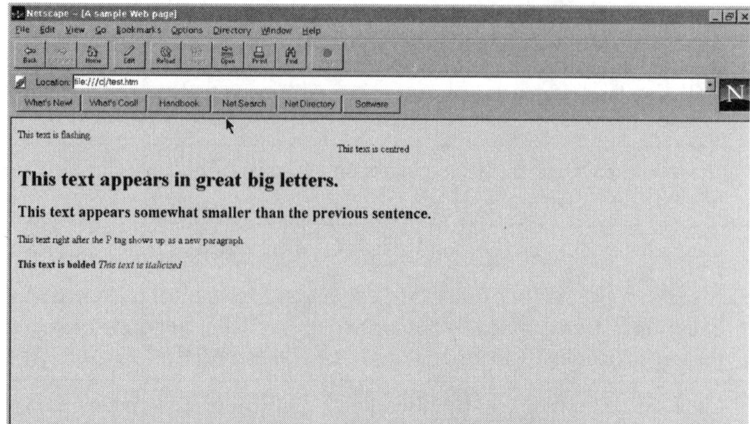

That's it; HTML is simply a computer file that contains HTML tags that describe how the information that is surrounded by those tags should be shown by a Web browser.

Want to try this on your own? It's easy. Simply type the text above into a text editor or word processor, exactly as it appears with the HTML codes. Save the file as **test.htm**; this identifies it as an HTML file. Then open the file **test.htm** with your Web browser, by choosing "File – Open File" in your Web browser. You have just created your first Web page!

- Different HTML tags do different things. Let's return to our "Central Canada's Bowling Home Page" example. At the start of the HTML document that makes up that page, we have the section <TITLE>Central Canada's Bowling Home Page</TITLE>. This tells our Web browser to show "Central Canada's Bowling Home Page" at the top of our Web browser. Then we have some information that identifies the creator of the document:

```
<!—OWNER_NAME="BRIAN McLEAN"—>

<LINK rev=made HREF="mailto:bmclean@foxnet.net">

</HEAD>
```

This uses two special tags, which identify the owner of the document (Brian McLean) and the e-mail address for the owner. These tags are optional. The </HEAD> section tells the Web browser that this is the end of the introduction section of the document.

The next line contains a code that indicates the "background color" that should be used on the page. The "FFFFFF" tells the Web browser to show a plain white background:

```
<body BGCOLOR="FFFFFF">
```

Of course, now the question is, how do you know what the code is for a particular background color? How did McLean know it was FFFFFF? Suppose you want your background color to be dark green? What is the corresponding code? The color is based on what is known as "RGB code." You do not have to know much about it, other than the fact that there are many sites on the Web that will help you match colors to the corresponding code. These sites automatically calculate the code for you:

http://www.sci.kun.nl/thalia/guide/color/
http://www.hidaho.com/colorcenter/
http://www.phoenix.net/~jacobson/rgb.html

The next few lines do several things, the most important of which is showing the graphic image with the bowling pins at the left-hand side of the screen. The image is found in a computer file with the name **siteno.gif**:

```
<A NAME="TOP"></A><IMG width=375 height=240 align=left hspace=10 SRC="siteno.gif">
```

What does the section above do? The <A NAME> tag gives this particular section of the Web page a name; we will ignore its purpose here. Instead, take a look at the next bit of information:

```
<IMG width=375 height=240 align=left hspace=10 SRC="siteno.gif">
```

This section instructs the Web browser how and where to show an image on the page. <IMG> is a special HTML tag which means, in essence, "show a computer image file here."

- Some HTML tags carry special instructions. As you can see above, <IMG> is used with other information that instructs the Web browser how and where to show the actual image. For example, the <IMG> tag uses "attributes," which instruct the Web browser to show the height and width of the image (measured in what are known as "pixels"). It is also told that the image should be aligned to the left of the screen and that what is known as "horizontal space" (hspace) should be left between the previous section and the image. Finally, it is told that the image itself can be found in a computer file at the Web server called **siteno.gif**.

Let's continue. We get a few lines that indicate the "title lines" for the page that should be shown on the page next to the graphic, "Central Canada's Bowling Page" and "Canada's 1st Bowling Page," through the use of the <H2> and <H3> tags. These tags cause that text to be shown in two different sizes – fonts – on the centre of the screen. The <I> codes italicize the text:

```
<H2><center><I>Central Canada's Bowling Page</I></center></h2>

<H3><center><I>"Canada's 1st Bowling Page"</I></center></h3>
```

- Some HTML tags establish hypertext links from the page. You will remember from Chapter 7 that the beauty and power of the Web is that you can quickly link from any Web site to many other sites by clicking on the "hyperlinks" found on that site. Here is where HTML gets interesting. Take a look at the actual bowling Web site page, and you will notice that the word "note" is highlighted and underlined. This is where the "hypertext link" has been made in the HTML document, so that if you click on the word "note," you will have the opportunity to send an e-mail message to **bmclean@foxnet.net**. This is done by surrounding the word "note" with a special HTML code, **<A** HREF="mailto:bmclean@fox.net"**>** and an **</A>**, as seen below.

```
Make this a regular stop for up to date news. This page was updated on June 12th. If you have any comments or suggestions, please drop me a <A HREF="mailto:bmclean@foxnet.net"> note.</A><br>
```

- <A HREF="location"> is a special HTML tag that means the text immediately following the <HREF> is the actual hypertext link that should be used if someone clicks here. It is called the "anchor" tag. In this case it will allow you to send an e-mail to Bruce McLean. Also notice that the text surrounded by the <A> and </A> (in our case, the word "note") is what is highlighted when you view the Web page. (The <br> causes a line break before the next paragraph.)
- Some hyperlinks take you to other Web pages. The hyperlink above allows you to send an e-mail to Bruce McLean. In other cases you can use the <A HREF> tag to provide a link to a different Web page. For example, take a look at the next line:

```
Please sign my <a href="guest.html"> guest book.</a></CITE><p><p>
```

This tells your Web browser "if the person clicks on the highlighted/underlined phrase guest book, take them to the HTML page **guest.html**." In other words, <A HREF> is the HTML command that is used to link one Web page to another Web page.

- There are two types of hyperlinks that you can use to go to other Web pages. The Web addresses used with an <A HREF> tag can consist of local addresses, that is, another Web page on the same Web server. In the example above **guest.html** is found on the same Web server. In addition, you can use the <A HREF> tag to provide an address for any page on any other Web site in the world. In this case it consists of the full URL for that Web page. For example,

```
<A HREF="http://www.e-commerce.com/JACC/theft.html">Read about property theft!</A>
```

will highlight the phrase "Read about property theft." If anyone clicks on that phrase, he will be taken to the Web page at **http://www.e-commerce.com/JACC/theft.html**.

- There are "standard" and "non-standard" HTML tags. When it comes to HTML, there are several classes of tags. First, there are the basic HTML tags known as HTML version 2.0 or 3.0. These are generally accepted throughout the Internet community and are widely used by most Web browsers. HTML is under constant evolution; new features are being continually added. The 2.0 and 3.0 versions are those that are relatively final in terms of being globally accepted by various standard-setting organizations.

  There are also "Netscape extensions" and "Microsoft Internet Explore extensions." These are special HTML tags originally implemented by Netscape and Microsoft to perform certain functions on their own particular Web browsers. Not all other browsers will support all Netscape or Internet Explore tags. What this means is that a Web site can look different, depending upon the browser being used. This is because some HTML commands are only recognized by certain types of browsers.

  When you go to a Web site and notice that a certain feature does not work, it may be because the feature is not supported by the browser you are using. To alleviate this problem, some Web site designers have created different versions of their Web site to accommodate users of different browsers. Since it is a lot of work to create and maintain different versions of a Web site, some Web designers have chosen to create their Web sites to accommodate only users of one particular browser. For example, most Web designers have chosen to focus on Netscape, because it is the most popular Web browser.

  When you visit a Web site and see the phrase "This Web site is optimized for Netscape," it simply means that the designer has chosen to focus on serving Netscape users. If you are using another browser, this phrase is meant to caution you that some features may not work. Again, this is because the Web site may contain certain HTML tags that can only be understood by Netscape. GlaxoWellcome is an example of a site that does this (**http://www.glaxowellcome.co.uk/**):

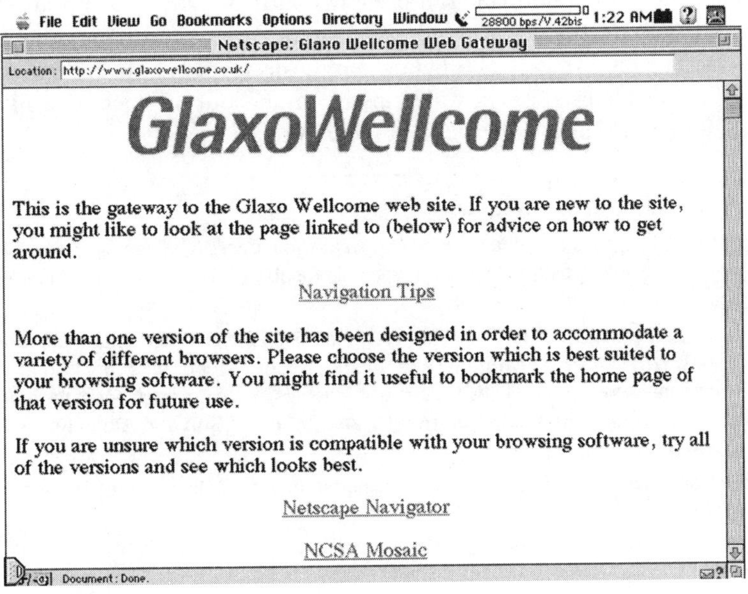

Such is the nature of HTML. There are many documents on-line that describe the many different HTML tags that can be used, as well as documents that provide guidance on writing HTML code.

> Documents That Describe HTML
>
> HTML Language Page (**http://union.ncsa.uiuc.edu/HyperNews/get/www/html/lang.html**)
>
> HTML Quick Reference (**http://kuhttp.cc.ukans.edu/lynx_help/HTML_quick.html**)
>
> The HyperText Markup Language page, which describes special tags used with Netscape in addition to basic tags (**http://www.best.com/~mcguirk/gavito/html-spec.html**)
>
> The Hypertext Madness of Laurence Simon (**http://www.phoenix.net/~lsimon/tricks/default.html**)
>
> How Do They Do That With HTML? (**http://www.nashville.net/~carl/htmlguide/index.html**)
>
> A Practical Guide for HTML Publishing and Resources (**http://members.aol.com/Rick1515/index.htm**)
>
> Net Tips for Writers and Designers (**http://www.dsiegel.com/tips/index.html**)
>
> Great Website Design Tips (**http://www.unplug.com/great/**)
>
> The Web Designer (**http://web.canlink.com/webdesign/nl.htm**)

HTML is sufficiently complicated that we could write a whole book about it, but there are plenty of books available already. Learning HTML will take time and patience. You may also wonder why you should bother learning about HTML now that Web editors are available. Even though Web editors make it easy for you to create Web documents without knowing the intricacies of HTML, a basic understanding of HTML is highly recommended. Even though you may know how to drive, it is still a good idea to understand what happens under the hood of your car.

Creating Web Pages by Writing HTML Code Directly

One result of the World Wide Web and HTML has been that many people have created their Web pages by learning how to "write HTML," that is, create a file that contains the special HTML codes used above to show their information in the way that they want it to appear. In fact, Bruce McLean, who prepared Central Canada's Bowling Home Page, admitted to us that this is how he went about creating his own pages. He figured out the details of HTML and prepared his pages using the Windows Notepad program. He inserts throughout his document all the different HTML tags surrounded by their brackets, in order to create a page.

> Learning to Create Your Own Web Page
>
> Regardless of whether you want to learn how to create your own Web page by writing HTML code directly, or if you plan on using a Web editor, you will probably need to learn more about HTML and Web page creation than we can tell you here. There are several good sources:
>
> 1. On-line sources, such as the Beginners Guide to HTML (**http://www.ncsa.uiuc.edu/General/Internet/WWW/HTMLPrimer.html**). Take a look into the Yahoo! category "Computers and Internet:Software:Data Formats:HTML:Guides and Tutorials" to locate a number of the many guides available (**http://www.yahoo.com/Computers_and_Internet/ Software/Data_Formats/HTML/Guides_and_Tutorials/**)
>
> 2. Books and magazines. There is an increasing number of books and magazines focusing on Web publishing and design.
>
> 3. Look at the HTML code in existing Web sites (as described earlier).

4. Take a course. There are more and more popular courses now that teach you about Web page creation:

- check one of the free computer publications we described earlier in the chapter for organizations advertising HTML courses;
- many computer/Internet trade shows now feature hands-on courses;
- check with your local computer store to see if they offer any courses;
- check with your local community college or university; many, such as the Ontario College of Art, now offer courses in Web design;
- check the computer section of your local newspaper for companies advertising Web design courses.

Creating a Web Site with a Web Editor

Of course, not everyone wants to learn the nuances of HTML. And then there are those who have created their Web site by learning HTML and writing it directly, but are looking for an easier way to create new pages and to maintain their current pages. For these folks there is an increasing number of "Web editors" available, programs that act like word processors that generate the necessary HTML code for a Web site. Some examples of Web editors are HoTMetaL, InContext Spider, PageMill, and FrontPage. In a nutshell, you can find any number of programs that will help you to create the necessary code for your own Web site.

Let's take a look at how a Web editor works. Here is Corel WebDesigner; we have designed a short HTML file within the program by typing out our text and formatting it just as we would in a word processor. If you want to centre text, you simply highlight it and click on the centre button. WebDesigner then surrounds that text with the necessary HTML code:

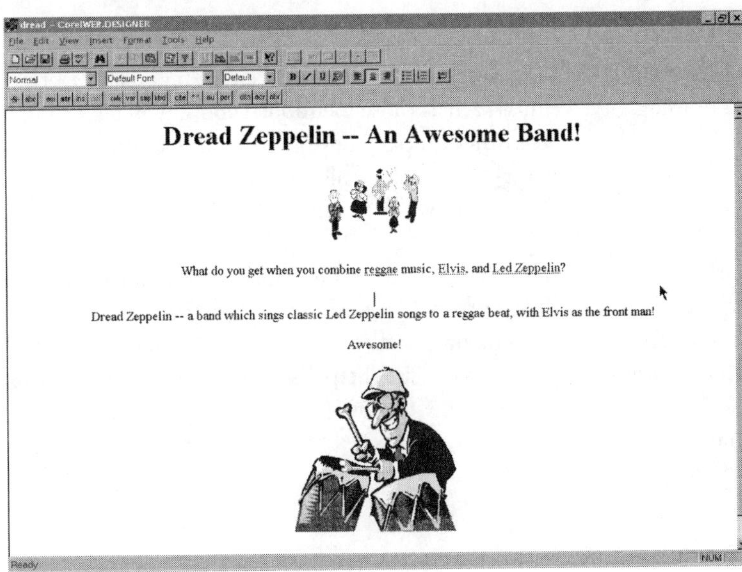

All the while, behind the scenes, Corel WebDesigner is creating the necessary HTML code. You can choose to look at it at any time.

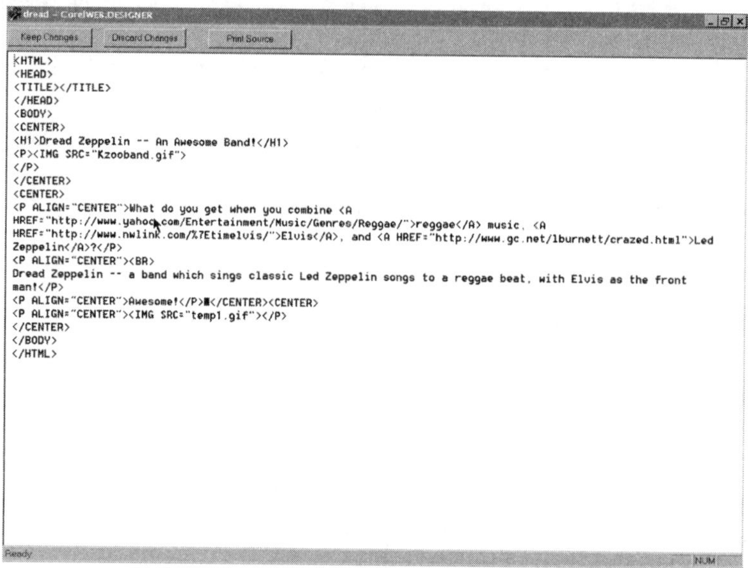

We can choose to edit the HTML code in the window above or do all our work in the word processing-style screen. Given that Web editors have come into their own and have become such an important topic, we devote the entire next chapter to them.

Uploading Your Web Pages

Once you have created your Web pages in HTML format, either manually creating the HTML code yourself or using a Web editor such as those mentioned above, you have to upload them to your own Web server, or the site of the company or organization that is renting you Web space, in order to make them available on the Web. Hopefully, the company that you have chosen to host your Web site allows you to upload your own pages directly, so that you don't have to rely on one of its staff members to do it for you.

It is a fairly straightforward process: you use an FTP program to upload your Web pages to a directory at the FTP site of the company that hosts your Web pages. The host should provide you with a set of simple instructions on how to do this. North Shore Internet Services, for example, provides such information on its own Web site (**http://south.nsis.com/nsis/howto.html**). (We reviewed what FTP is and how to use it in Chapter 13. It is a program that is used to transfer files on the Internet.)

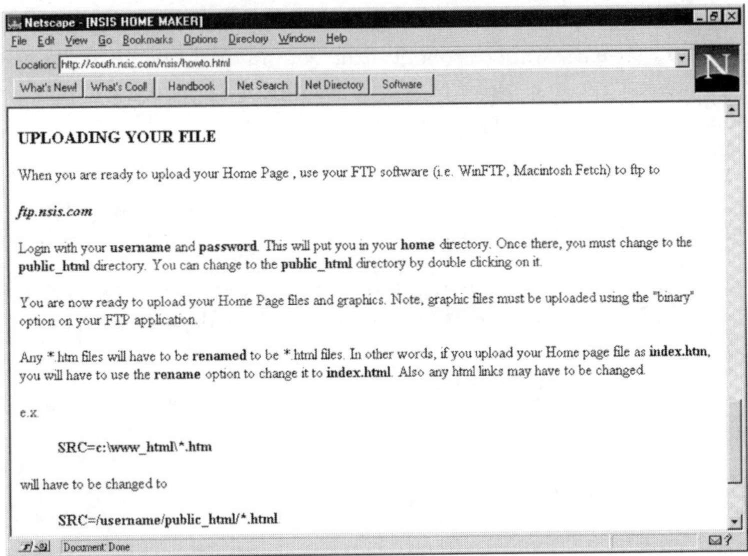

Hire a "Web Company"

If you do not want to take the time to learn how to create your own Web pages, you can hire someone to create them for you. There are many options that you can pursue; some days it seems that everyone and his dog is becoming an Internet presence provider. Consider some of the organizations that can help you in this regard:

- Advertising and marketing firms. Most major and minor advertising firms have divisions or staff who develop Web sites.
- Internet service providers, that is, companies in the business of selling access to the Internet. ISPs are also heavily involved in helping companies to establish Web sites.
- Internet presence providers, as noted earlier. Not only will they host the Web site on your behalf, but they may also design and maintain your site for you.
- Computer companies, ranging in size from mighty IBM to smaller computer consulting firms have jumped into the business of creating Web sites.
- Other companies, including consulting companies, independent contractors, desktop publishers, graphic artists, graphic design firms, printing firms, the list goes on, with every type of organization imaginable getting involved.
- Just plain individuals: people who work at home, university students, high school kids, just about anyone.

Consequently, there are all kinds of people and organizations out there who can help you to create and maintain a Web site. Now, where do you find them? Everywhere and anywhere:

- Check with your ISP. Either they will do it themselves or have arrangements with others who can.
- Look into computer trade publications; organizations and individuals often advertise there.

- Browse Web sites. Most often, if designed by a third party, the company or individual name of the designer will be listed near the bottom or elsewhere in the site. If you see a Web site that you like, see if the Web site contains information about the company that designed it. If not, call the organization that maintains the Web site and ask who designed it.
- Ask around. Talk to friends and business acquaintances about Web designers whom they have used or can recommend.
- Look into the Yahoo! category **http://www.yahoo.com/Business_and_Economy/Companies/Internet_Services/Web_Presence_Providers/Web_Page_Designers/**. Thousands are listed here.

While there are many individuals and organizations who would be willing to help you out, their expertise, skills, and costs will vary wildly.

How to Determine What Is Right

When hiring an individual or organization to create and maintain your home page, there are several important things that you should consider. For example, you should ask about their

- Track record. Have they developed other sites? Go and have a look. Get references. There is perhaps no more significant criterion. Everybody can create a Web page — you might have learned how to do so yourself — and then set themselves up in the business of Web page creation. You need to examine what they have actually done in order to make an intelligent choice.
- Business background. Anyone can create Web pages. The strategy behind the Web site is key. Look for someone with a good grasp of Internet strategy issues and the many issues we describe in the next section about "making a Web site work."
- Graphic design skills. Do they have a sense of graphic design? Are they artistic? Putting together a Web site is a bit more involved than just throwing together some information. Issues related to graphic design become very important, because the result must be visually pleasing to the eye. It takes a skilled graphic designer to create an attractive Web site. There are all kinds of "good designs" found on the Web. Consider this site for Duracell (**http://www.duracell.com**):

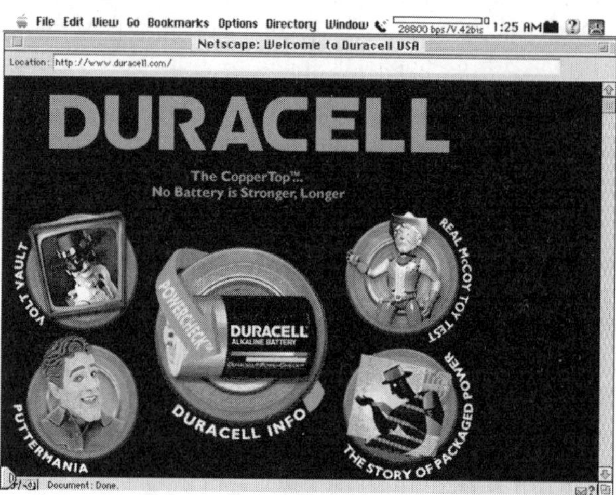

- Marketing skills. Do they have skills in marketing through the Internet? Building a Web site is one thing. It is rather useless if no one comes to visit you. Hence you have to think of how to attract people to your site. They should be able to help in this regard.
- Programming skills. Do they have skills in CGI-scripting and UNIX programming? These two skills are often useful in the creation of Web sites. For example, these skills are used to create sites that promote a high level of interactivity and allow the user to create sophisticated information forms. Anyone can learn to create basic HTML code, but the ability to create a site that permits visitors to complete comprehensive forms, and the ability to process the data in those forms, are specialized skills.

Finally, do not forget that you can hire someone to initially create your Web site and when it is complete take over the maintenance of the Web site yourself. It is worthwhile to do this if you feel you do not have skills to come up with "a great creative design" but do want to update and add to the site over time. That is how we did our NetTalk Web site (**http://www.nettalk.com**). We hired a small company of great designers to prepare an initial site design for a reasonable fee (in our case, less than $1,500). We then took over the maintenance and updating ourselves (for as long as we are on the air).

What Does it Cost?

The cost for an outside organization to develop your Web site will depend upon many factors. Remember, we said that it is like trying to get an answer to the question, how high is up? The overall complexity of the site, the number of pages, the number of graphics, whether graphics are custom-designed or not, special features such as discussion forums or feedback forms — all these considerations will influence the overall cost of your Web site creation.

It is important that you get a clear understanding of the cost from the Web design company prior to commencement of the project. It is always a good idea to get a written estimate.

We will note that it is not easy to find out "established rates" for many Web designers, since the cost will depend upon so many different factors. Some do advertise their hourly rate. For example, the ISP Worldgate (**http://www.worldgate.com**) notes that "additional time for WWW document creation or background process programming is $40 per hour. Professional graphic design (outsourced to some really talented professional graphic designers) is also available for $40 per hour."

Should I Design In-house or Hire Someone?

This is a major decision, and it is not an easy one. If you work within an organization you need to think about the following issues in deciding whether to outsource or use in-house capabilities:

- Technical resources. Do you have anyone who is Internet savvy or has graphic design expertise? Bear in mind that these people do not necessarily have to be skilled in the Internet. For example, if you have someone on your staff who is skilled in graphic design, that person probably has a great deal of technical competence already, and learning how to design for the Internet will not be that difficult for him/her. A professional development course would probably be sufficient to bring that person up to competence.

- Financial resources. You can find some good, inexpensive, quality talent out there to build Web sites. On the other hand, you can also find some fabulous and expensive Web design organizations. Your decision whether to build your Web site in-house or to hire an outside source will depend upon the financial resources available to you. Not only that, the financial resources available will determine the type of outside designer you can hire, ranging from the high school student who does it on a part-time basis to full professional graphic design houses.

- Management commitment.The extent of financial resources available for your project will depend directly upon the extent to which management supports your efforts. If the managers believe that your suggested Internet application is strategic and important, they will provide you with the necessary resources to make the project work, which might allow you to draw upon more expensive external financial resources. On the other hand, if they think the Internet is merely a toy, you will have little funding available. Hence you must work hard to make management understand the strategic goals behind your Internet plans.

Building an Effective Web Site

When it comes to implementing a Web site to support communications with your customers, suppliers, and others, there are two important points to keep in mind:

- You must do it right the first time. Remember, your Web site is on display to the world, and if you do not do it right, you may be doing yourself more harm than good.
- There are no instant solutions or magic tips to make your Web site work. Anyone who tells you differently is a fraud.

It will take a lot of hard work and planning to establish an effective Web site.

What is an effective Web site? It is a site that meets your strategic objectives, has a pleasing design, is easy to navigate, and keeps drawing people back on a regular basis. There are certain things you can do to make sure you have an effective Web site.

Make Sure You Are Ready!

In far too many cases people make an unfinished Web site available to the world, which, if you think about it, ends up doing more public relations damage than good. Think about the number of Web sites that you have visited that display a silly little "under construction" sign or a page that says "under construction" when you try to access some information. Consider some examples. TrekCanada, a Star Trek exhibit, was actually advertising its Web site on TV; this is all you got if you visited (**http://www.trekcanada.com**):

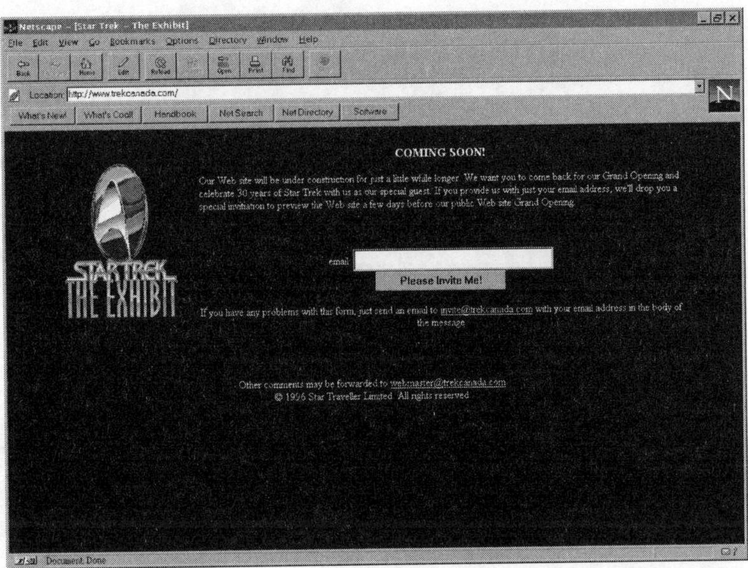

Or consider Rembrandt Oral Care (**http://www.rembrandt.com**); it certainly is an attractive Web site:

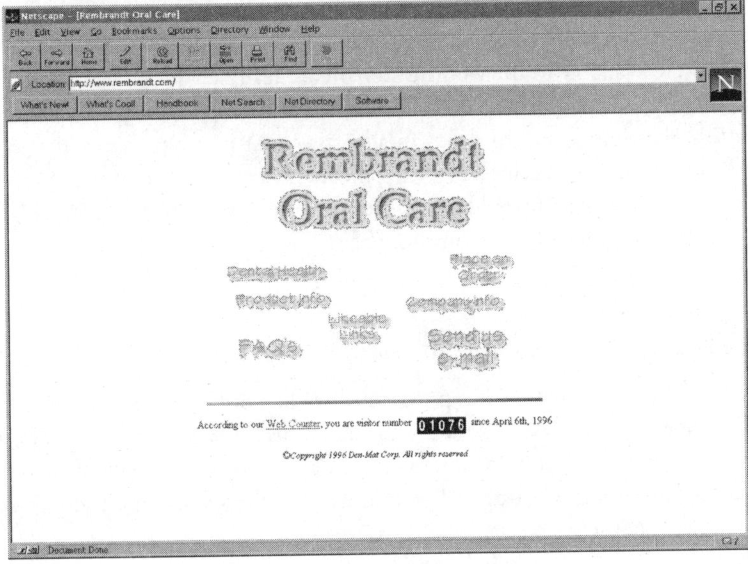

But when we clicked on "Product Information," this is what we got:

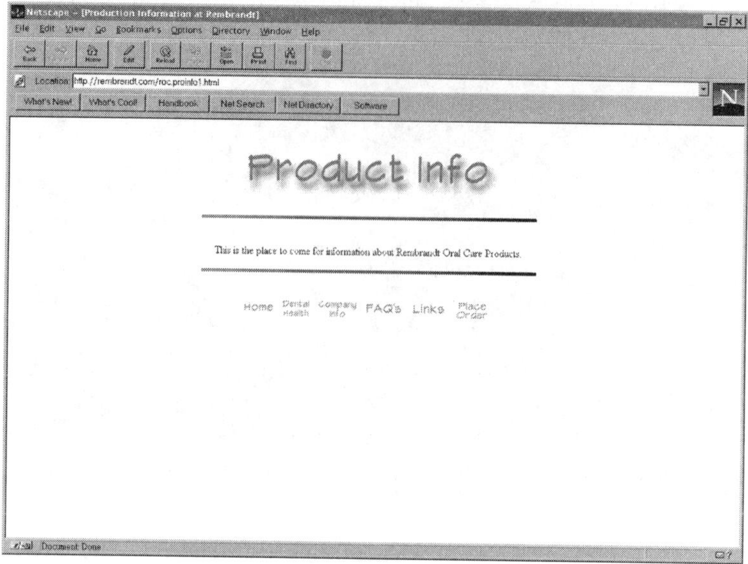

How do you feel when you visit sites like this? Bothered? Frustrated? A little perturbed with the organization? Did you think to yourself, "I'm not coming back here!"? This is how many people will react to your own site if you implement it before it is ready. As a result, you should not make your Web site available to the world until you are really ready to do so.

It is important that you treat the Web like any other marketing or publishing medium and ask yourself this question: "would I print an advertisement in a newspaper that was only half finished?" Would I hand out a business card to someone that said, "Logo goes here"? Would I send out a fax cover sheet that said, "I would have a diagram here but it isn't finished yet." No. So don't even think of doing this type of thing on the Web.

Test Your Site Before It Goes On-line

Make sure everything works before you put it on-line. The only thing more frustrating than an "under construction" sign within a Web site is the infamous message "Error 404–Not Found" displayed when a link in a particular document does not work or is not available. Even if you take the time to make sure your site is ready before putting it on the Web, you can find that errors have occurred in your HTML code.

There are several tools, such as InContext Analyzer, that you can use to test the integrity of the HTML code in your site before you make it available on-line. It is a good idea to use one before going "live." This is such an important topic that we will take a look at some of this software in the next chapter, where we discuss Web editor software.

Pay Attention to Content

A key objective when implementing a Web site is to try to get people to visit the site on a regular basis. The key word when it comes to the Web is content: you must provide some useful content that will be of interest in order to draw visitors to your site. Keep this in mind. A simple sales pitch or brochure on the Internet does not work; in fact, if your site is simply a hard sell ("buy this!"), you will turn people off instead of gaining their attention. With one simple mouse click, poof! They are gone.

Most often, it is useful, practical content that will draw people to your site, rather than simply dazzling graphic design. Design is important, but content is critical. You have to do something to draw the attention and interest of people.

What works? It could be any number of things; when developing your site, you have to ask yourself the question, "What can I provide that might be of use or interest to others?" Think carefully about the answer, for it could make the difference between success and failure on-line. The answer will depend upon what it is you do and what you provide.

Always remember that in your Web site you can reuse and reintegrate existing information that you already have and make it available in your Web site. You should also consider integrating your Internet publishing with other marketing and publishing initiatives, so that the information you are preparing in paper form is also available on-line. In effect, you need to modify your information production streams so that information you generate in paper form is also immediately made available on the Web.

- An example of good "content" can be found with Ernst & Young Canada. They make available an entire book called *Managing Your Personal Taxes* as well as regularly updated tax information (**http://tax.ey.ca/ey/**):

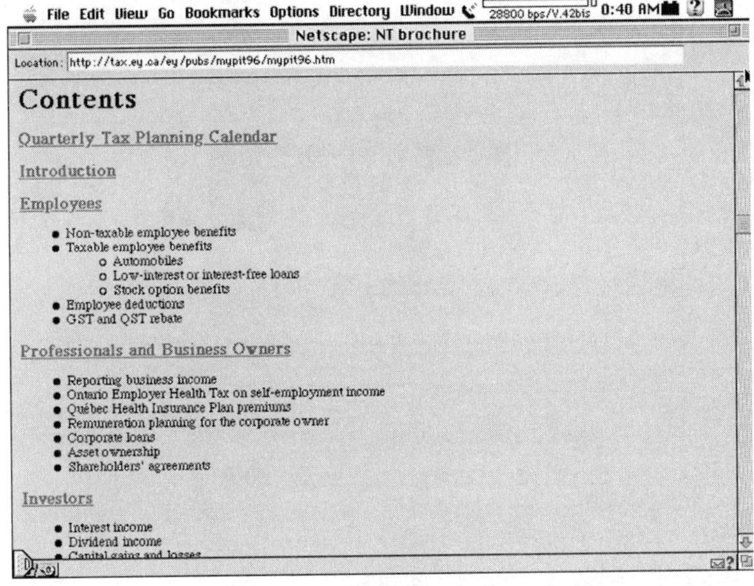

- The Weather Network Web site (**http://www.weathernetwork.com)** is another example of a content-rich site:

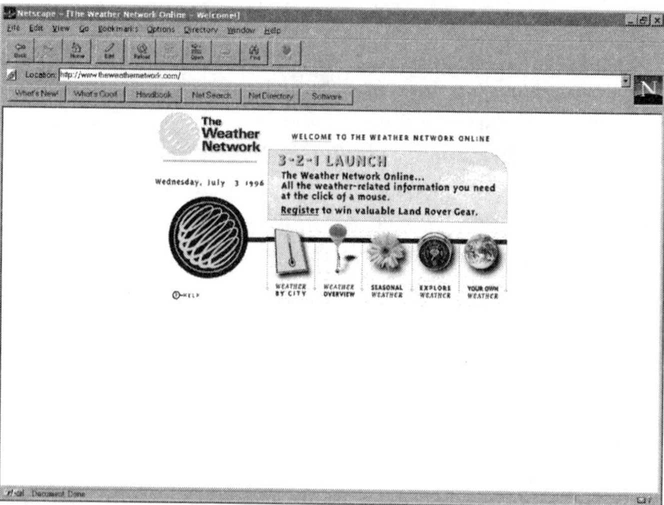

- Tide's ClothesLine site is full of information, with lots of practical information about laundry (**http://www.clothesline.com**):

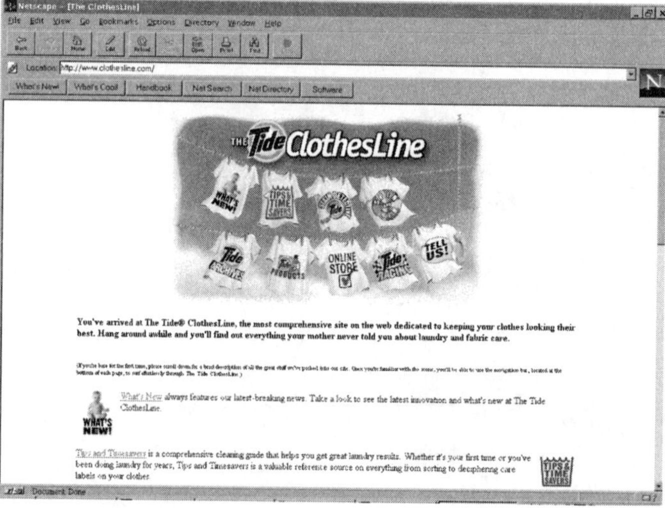

- Joseph C. Grasmick is a Buffalo-based lawyer specializing in issues related to Canadians seeking immigration to the United States. His site is full of information about the topic and serves, in effect, as a powerful draw to his law firm for professional services (**http://www.grasmick.com**):

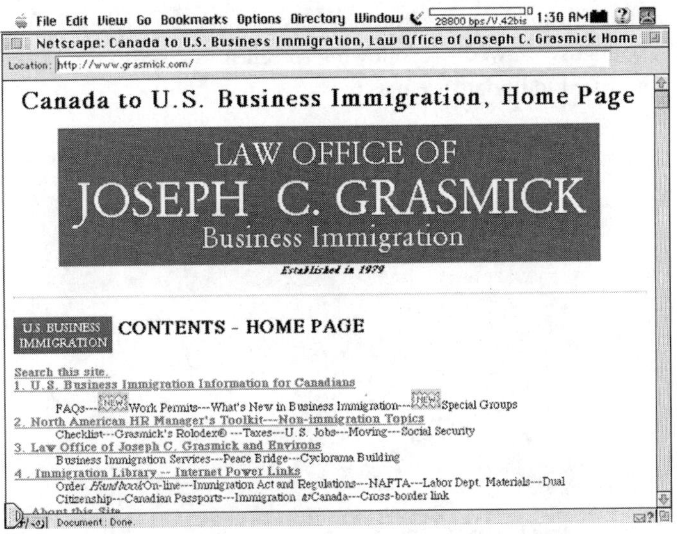

All these sites excel at providing good and useful content and draw the notice of users throughout the Internet.

Update Your Site on a Regular Basis

One trick to an effective Web site is to provide up-to-date information. This is done by continually adding information of interest to visitors. Think about the sites you visit. Your first visit gives you a good idea of what the site is all about, and hopefully there is content that catches your eye. You might go back a few weeks later and see the same old information. You cross it off your list and do not visit it again.

If you do not update your site on a regular basis, you cause the same irritation for visitors. Hence, in designing your site and figuring out your strategy, one of the first questions you must ask yourself is, "what can I do to keep people coming back?" Unfortunately, there are too many examples of sites that are not updated. The City of Summerside Home Page, for example, features a "What's New" section, which at the time we visited was almost a year behind:

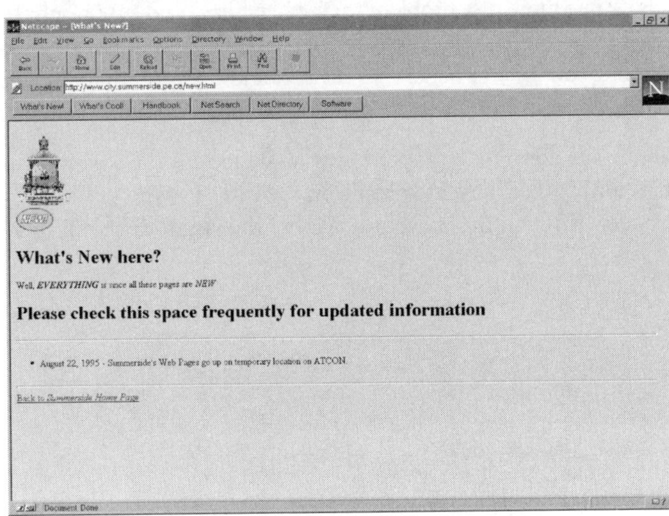

Now look at the site for Flonase (**http://www.flonase.com**), an allergy relief product from Glaxo. Its "Product News" category showed the following screen in the summer of 1996. Check out the date that they promised to update the page:

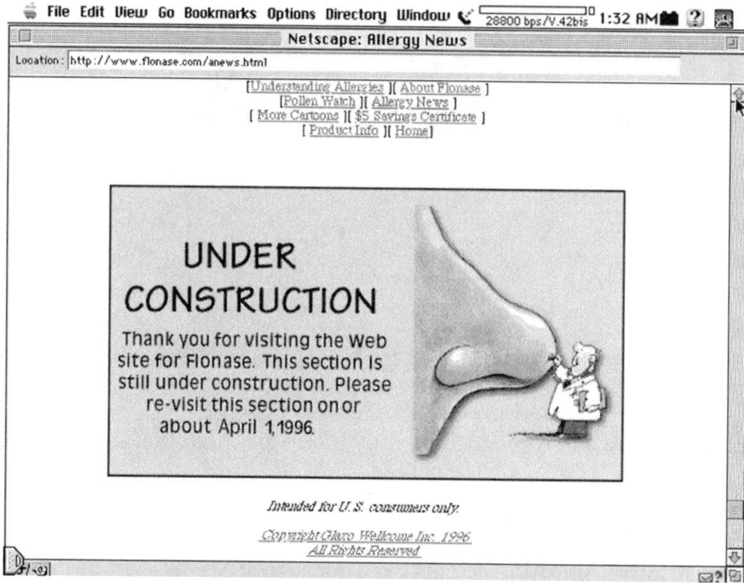

What does this say about how seriously the company takes the product if they cannot even keep their Web site up-to-date?

Pay Attention to Layout

One of the most important things you can do when implementing a Web site is pay attention to the graphic design of the site. Your site *must* be pleasing to the eye and easy for people to use and navigate. People must be able to easily read the information you include on-line. There are several suggestions:

- Backgrounds can be more of a problem than a benefit: do not use bright colors as backgrounds if they conflict with the color of the text. There is nothing wrong with bright colors, but you have to make sure the text and background complement each other. If the background and text colors are the same, you cannot read the text.
- Do not load the site down with graphics; always design for the lowest common denominator, assuming that there are people on the Internet who do not have the fancy computer systems that you may have. Remember the vision-disabled: there are blind

people who use the Internet, and there are some things you should do to ensure that their voice systems can access your page. (Many blind users of the Internet have systems that read out the content of Web pages for them, and if you do not include text, their systems cannot read it.) To get around these problems, consider a "graphics version" and a "text-only version." The United Nations, for example, provides both (**http://www.un.org**):

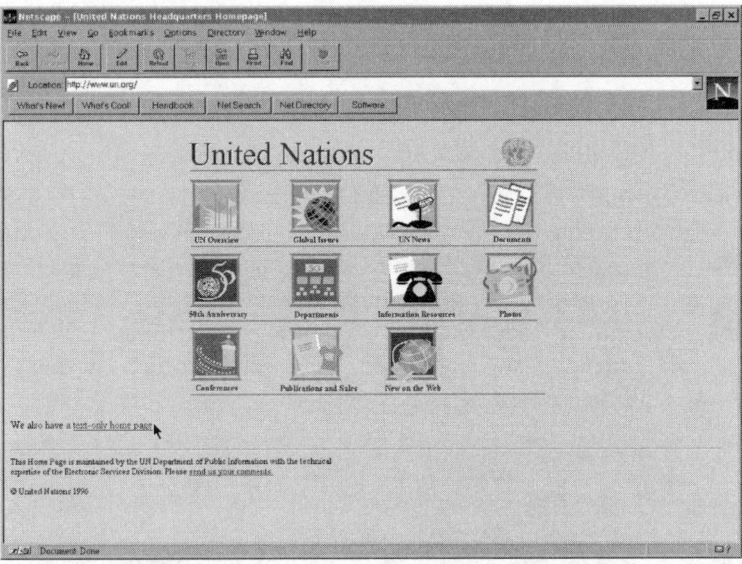

- Do not use graphics that take more than thirty seconds or a minute to load; people will become frustrated and leave. Keep in mind that it is possible to design a site that looks great, seems to have lots of graphics, but loads quickly. The Tide ClothesLine site we mentioned previously is a good example of such a site.
- Finally, do not use the "blink" command, the HTML feature that causes text to blink on and off, or use it in moderation, since it annoys many Internet users.
- Consider the language of your target audience and, if appropriate, translate the site into different languages, as, for example, Kinko's has done (**http://www.kinkos.com**). Kinko's home page provides translations into Japanese, Korean, Dutch, Russian, Hebrew, Arabic, German, Chinese, French, Spanish and Vietnamese — all linked to the English-language page.

- Consider designing for multiple browsers. Increasingly, as you travel the Web, you will see many sites that have designed one version for users of Netscape and another for users of Microsoft Internet Explorer.

Graphic design is important and is one of the areas in which money is often best spent. Some people are artistically creative and some are not. If you are not artistically inclined, it can be worth your while to spend money on graphic artists or Web design specialists who can give your site that extra edge that it needs in terms of visual content. But keep in mind that even if you get a brilliant graphic design, unless you have real content, your Web site will fail.

Avoid Technical Nirvana

There is a lot of neat stuff on the Internet: tools like Shockwave, which adds animation to your site, and countless other "plug-ins" that we reviewed in our chapter about the World Wide Web. It can be fun to use these tools, but they can be frustrating to many users. Too many Web designers get caught up in Internet technical issues and try to make their site a home for leading-edge technical design. It might be wonderful from a technical perspective but will do little for your objectives. Consider the following screen from St. Joseph's Health Centre in London, ON (**http://www.stjosephs.london.on.ca/**):

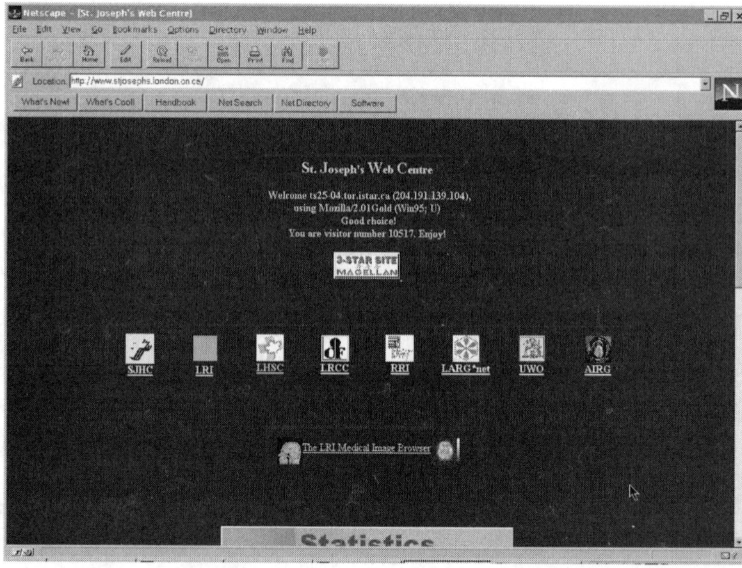

On the introduction screen it says "Welcome ts25-04.tor.istar.ca (204.191.139.104), using Mozilla/2.01Gold (Win95; U) Good choice!" What the heck is that supposed to mean to a new user? While it might be a brilliant technical "hack," it does little to lend any real value to the site.

Let People Contact You

When you build your Web site, make it easy for people to contact you. We are still stunned by the number of Web sites we visit that do not include such basic information as a phone number, fax number, or other contact information. It seems like a simple thing, but many do not do this, so, at a minimum, you should ensure that your Web site includes your e-mail address, phone number, fax number, and mailing address.

You should consider providing other contact information as well, for example, how to get help and who to call for support. Many companies include on-line directories with the sole intent of making it easy for visitors to contact particular people or departments.

Finally, if you let people contact you for help, support, or information through the Web, follow up. If you do not, you will end up doing damage to your reputation as a good, reliable company.

For large organizations the volume of contact from visitors to their Web site can be overwhelming. Apple, for instance, receives approximately 700 messages per week on its Web site. If you expect to have difficulty providing a personal reply to everyone who contacts you by e-mail, consider setting up an automatic response mechanism so that every e-mail message you receive is automatically acknowledged by the computer. This is better than not sending any response at all. The e-mail message, in addition to acknowledging the sender's message, could also contain answers to some of the most frequently asked questions you receive. Look at what the *Los Angeles Times* does. Whenever you send a message to the *Los Angeles Times* Web team (**tech@latimes.com**), you receive an automatic reply like this:

Thanks for writing to the L.A. Times Web team.

We're very excited about the volume of mail we've received—so excited, we may not be able to answer your e-mail personally.

However, we're very interested in your comments, and we do read each message that arrives—it's our way of finding out what works and what doesn't.

If you have a problem or a question, you can always try our help section at:

http://www.latimes.com/HOME/HELP/

or our FAQ at:

http://www.latimes.com/HOME/HELP/FAQ/

Here's the answer to some common questions:

Q: I don't have a login for your site. How do I get one?

A: You can register at:

http://www.latimes.com/HOME/REGISTER/

Registration is free and gives access to Hunter and AP Online.

Q: I have a question for hunter.

A: Send e-mail to hunter@latimes.com

Remember, you can always post a note on our Bulletin Board, which is

available from our Speak Out section at:

http://www.latimes.com/HOME/SPEAKOUT/

Thanks again for your message, and visit us again soon!

The Worker Bees

feedback@latimes.com

Solicit Feedback from Internet Users

Ask others what they think of your Web site and what other features they would like to see. Consider putting up an on-line survey or feedback page, and use this information to help you improve your on-line offerings in the future. It is one of the best ways to ensure that your Web site is meeting the needs and wants of your visitors. For example, the City of Toronto (**http://www.city.toronto.on.ca/1wel/feedback.htm**) asks visitors to leave comments on questions such as:

- How would you rate the information on our Web site?
- Do you find our site easy to navigate?
- What type of information are you looking for today?
- What information would you like to see more of?

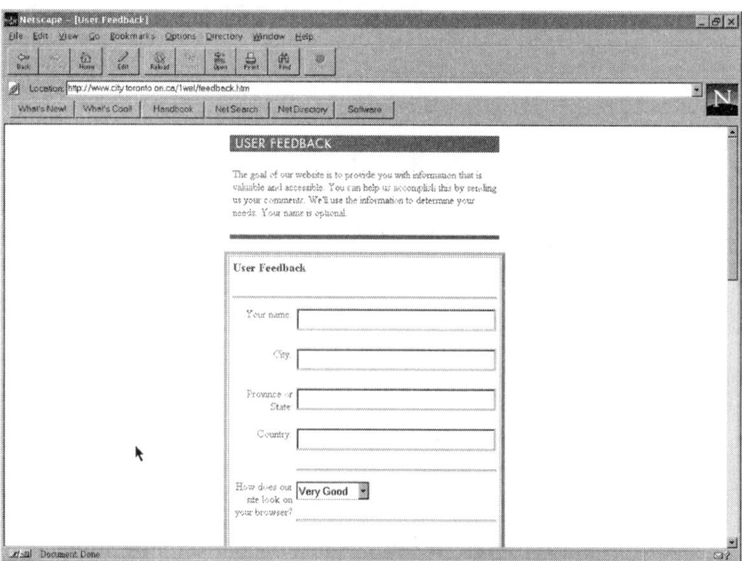

Highlight What Is New

Make sure you regularly highlight what is new so that regular visitors can quickly focus on enhancements and additions to the Web site.

Implement a Mailing List

You could also consider establishing an electronic mailing list for visitors to join; then you can keep them up-to-date with your company's activities. Consider these two types of lists. First, you can put in place a general mailing list that distributes information about your company and its products and services on a regular basis. An example is found with Nabisco Canada (**http://www.nabisco.ca**):

Or you can set up a mailing list to update people when you make changes or additions to your Web site. The computer company Oracle, for example, allows you to request notification if certain Web pages are changed (**http://www.synapse.net/~oracle/Contents/Priority.html):**

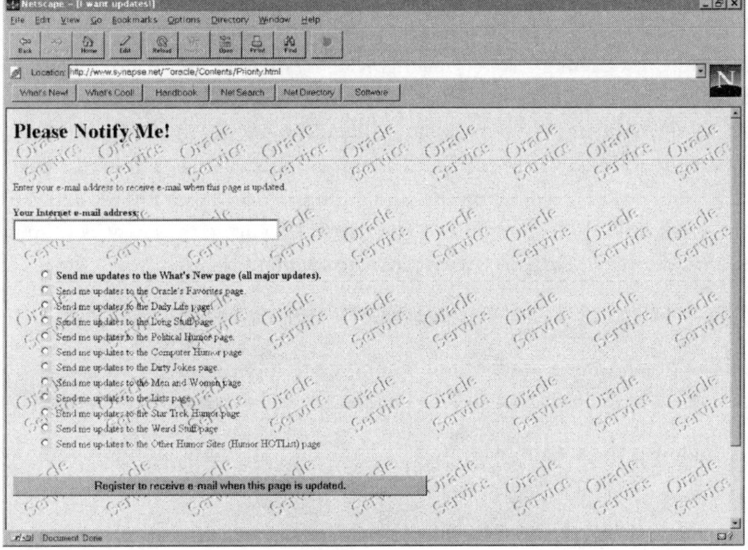

Market Your Internet Presence

Once you have invested the time and energy in putting together a site on the World Wide Web, you then must make people aware of it. After all, what good is a Web site if you do not have visitors? Our opinion is that it is easy to create a Web site, but the tough part is drawing people to it.

Hopefully, you will have taken the time to build the site so that it has good and useful content, since that is the key to making your site work. If you have done a great job at providing content, word of the site will get around; the Internet has many great self-reporting mechanisms.

You also need to let the Internet know your Web site exists and let the "real world" know your Web site exists. Your goal is to work, and work hard, at letting people know that you now have a Web site.

How to Promote Your Site on the Internet

1. Register with search engines (e.g., AltaVista, Lycos, InfoSeek, OpenText, Excite, WebCrawler).
2. Register with Internet directory services (e.g., Yahoo!).
3. Register with geographic indices (e.g., Maple Square).
4. Use a Web announcement service (e.g.,Submit-It).
5. Get other Web sites to link to you.
6. Announce your Web site on relevant mailing lists, electronic newsletters, and discussion groups where appropriate.

Study the chapter "Undertaking Research on the Internet," which provides an overview of the different types of indices that we mention above, to get an understanding of the many different areas in which you can register your Web site.

Register Your URL On-line

Take the time to register your Web site in as many on-line indices as possible. This is an important way of ensuring that Net surfers will discover your site. The reason you want to register your Web address on-line is that people using the Internet will either find your company or will discover your company while researching a topic on-line. Most search engines will list your site for free.

You can register in three areas: search engines, Web directories, and virtual libraries. There are around 500 of these different systems, so it is difficult to register in all of them. At a minimum, include your new site in major directories and search engines such as Yahoo!, Digital's AltaVista, InfoSeek, and OpenText. (The backgrounds, and addresses, for these sites are extensively covered in the chapter "Undertaking Research on the Internet.") To do so is as easy as filling out a form. For example, consider Lycos (**http://www.lycos.com/register.html**):

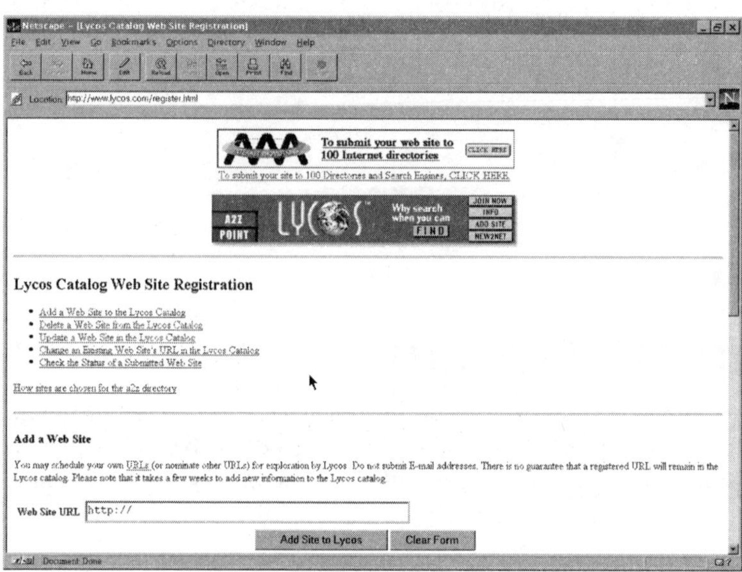

There are also increasing numbers of "all-in-one" registration sites, which will automatically register you in many different search engines. A good example is Submit-It (**http://www.submit-it.com/**), a site that will register your site automatically in all kinds of other search systems.

You should periodically revisit and update all the various search engines that you know of to reregister or to check on the status of your site listing, particularly if you have redesigned your site or added new information. Remember, you want the indices to know all about your site, so that people will find it if they are looking in an index for sites that contain the type of information you make available. You should also register your address in the many "What's New" areas found on the Internet. This will help make others aware that your site exists.

Finally, there are many new services offering to add your site to these indices for a fee. For example, we regularly receive e-mail that says:

> Is your Web site the best kept secret on the Internet? We'll promote it around the Internet and complete the job in two business days. For details, please respond to:

We cannot understand why you would want to pay someone else money to do something that is often so easy to do yourself. Be cautious of such ventures; many of them are questionable in terms of what they do for the money you spend.

Get Your Site Linked Elsewhere

Another way to increase traffic to your site is to get other sites to link to your site. This is one of the most important ways of marketing a Web site. This often involves finding others with similar Web sites who might include a link to your site, or getting yourself listed in one or more of the "topical indices" found on the Internet, specialized indices that focus on particular topics or issues. For example, if you have a Web site about flowers, you should find other flower-related Web sites and ask the maintainers to create a pointer to you. You may also want to discover if there are any horticultural, gardening, or other indices that focus on the topic in which you could list your Web site. The issue, of course, is how to find such sites. For that, we suggest you take a look at the chapter "Undertaking Research on the Internet," in which we discuss how to locate many of these special indices.

Promote Visibility Through the Real World

You must also work hard at making people in the "real world" aware of your site. We are continually surprised at how many individuals and organizations take the time to create a Web site and then do not tell the world that it exists. There are several things that you should do:

- Ensure that you list your Internet address on every bit of paper and information that your company produces.
- Place your address in all your print media: business cards, letterhead, fax paper, stationery, and even product packaging.
- Be creative! Think of additional places to list your Web address. A good example of innovative thinking can be found with Federal Express: their World Wide Web

address is exhibited as a flower bed display, which can be observed by thousands driving to work in Toronto every day.

- Finally, make sure that you link your Web address into all your other advertising; your goal is to let others know that your Web site exists, so that you build up the number of existing and potential customers visiting it.

Keep in mind that your effort on the Web should be part of your overall marketing plan and that the Web does not let you abandon conventional advertising; it supplements it.

Hidden Costs of the World Wide Web

It is easy to set up a Web site, but it is quite another to maintain it. When you get involved with the Web, you should recognize that you are making a decision. Either

- you implement a static, unchanging Web site with little content that will likely fail to meet whatever objectives you have in mind, or

- you implement a Web site that will continually change and evolve and in which you will constantly make available new, interesting content.

To do the latter, you will need resources to manage and support your site and to make the changes that are necessary over time. Not only that, but there will be follow-up costs as you or someone within the company takes the time to answer the questions that might be sent through the site. You should also keep in mind that you will face costs in the future to redesign and change your site. Your first Web site design will not be your last, since when it comes to the Web, continuous reinvention is critical.

The sheer nature of the Internet and the rapid pace at which the Web evolves will guarantee that you will continually change the design, content, and layout of your site. All these changes will cost money.

Risks of Not Keeping Up-to-Date

You should also recognize that you may run some serious risk if you do not keep your site up-to-date. After all, it is only a matter of time before lawyers discover the Web, and when they do, it will be a prime territory for lawsuits. We are already seeing the early signs that there are real and substantial risks from not updating a Web site.

In 1995 the Internet world became abuzz with news of a $14,000 fine levied against Virgin Atlantic Airways by the U.S. Department of Transportation for placing a "misleading" fare advertisement on the Internet. The simple facts are that Virgin has a Web site (**http://www.virgin.com**) in which it advertises airline fares from the United States to England. After the 1995 summer season it did not update a page with more up-to-date prices.

Why did they not update the information? Probably for the same reasons that many other organizations do not: laziness, a lack of funding or management support, or simply the fact that the Web site was an experiment. It is expensive to undertake an experiment in public.

The Virgin Airways case was fascinating, for it sent a wake-up call to senior management, alerting them to the fact that they had better begin taking use of the World Wide Web within their organizations seriously and ensure that the medium is treated with a degree of respect, attention, and proper funding.

What Needs to Be Done?

In the real world many companies are concerned with their professional image and take great care in the preparation of any advertisements, brochures, and reports; in fact, the public relations departments of many companies have established "corporate visual image" guidelines that proscribe the appearance and layout of all corporate communications. Such guidelines ensure that "misleading" advertising charges do not arise, among other things, but the guidelines should be extended to publishing on the Web to avoid a host of potential legal and public relations problems.

All organizations involved with the Internet should recognize that publishing information on the Web is essentially the same as publishing brochures, advertisements, and other paper reports, except information on the Web has a much wider distribution given the global reach of the Internet. The result is that organizations must take care when it comes to using the Web to publish information and must be cognizant of the risks if they fail to update this information.

Business Strategy

Finally, we must emphasize that when it comes to building a Web site, particularly if you are doing so for your business, you must have a good, rational business strategy in place. This is what we will look at, in Chapter 16, "Thinking Strategically About the Internet."

CHAPTER 15

Web Development Software

Publishing Web pages is not just for the Internet gurus but will someday be as normal — and simple — as printing out a letter from a word processor.

Page-Publishing Tools Create Profits, Too
San Jose Mercury News, January 28, 1996

In the previous chapter we noted: "Given that Web editors have come into their own and have become such an important topic, we devote the entire next chapter to them." Consider this overview of the scope and potential of Web editors:

- Several Canadian organizations, such as InContext and SoftQuad, went public on the stock market in 1996, opening up the eyes of many to the potential of the Web editor business.
- Major software organizations such as Microsoft and Adobe made high-profile acquisitions in 1996 of some of the leading Web editor software available, indicating the degree of seriousness that leading software vendors give to the category.
- Lotus/IBM released tools for Lotus Notes, which converts Notes documents to HTML format, thus turning Notes into a Web development tool.
- Conversion tools have became available for most word processing programs, allowing you to easily convert word processing files to HTML format.

Turn anywhere in the computer industry, and there is some type of development occurring with what we will call "Web development software," software that in one way or another helps you to prepare the necessary files in HTML format for your Web site so that your data can be made available to anyone on the Web. We take a look at several categories of Web development software in this chapter:

- Web editor software, which you can use to create Web pages in HTML format;
- Web conversion software, which converts existing data into HTML format;
- Web analysis and management software, which detects problems and errors in your HTML files.

In addition, we take a look at developments that will impact the whole topic area involving the creation and management of Web files in HTML format.

Our objective with this chapter is not to present a detailed, feature-by-feature comparison of different software programs; such an undertaking would be futile, since the entire industry changes every few months. Rather, our objective is to give you an idea of what is occurring with software that creates and manages Web sites, so that you have an idea of what you should be looking for, should you decide to delve further into this field.

Finally, one comment that is of importance to us, since this is the *Canadian Internet Handbook.* Five of the software packages that we look at here — HTML Editor, SoftQuad HoTMetaL, InContext Spider, HTML Assistant Pro, and DisplayPage — are Canadian-made. We have not included these programs just because they are Canadian; in fact, each is quickly earning a global reputation. Rather, these programs have all earned a good, solid, reliable worldwide reputation based upon their features, and Canadians should be proud of their success. After all, a little bit of nationalism can't hurt on occasion.

WEB DEVELOPMENT SOFTWARE

1. There are many different programs available that you can use to edit Web sites, including Hot Dog, HTML Editor, HTML Assistant Pro, InContext Spider, SoftQuad HoTMetaL, Microsoft Frontpage, Netscape Navigator Gold and Adobe PageMill. Many of these programs differ in function and capabilities, but not in purpose.
2. There are also a growing number of programs which allow you to convert data or information from word processing or database formats to the HTML format required for a Web site, allowing you to use existing information for your Web site.
3. There are Web sites and software you can use to check your Web site or pages for errors or inconsistencies.
4. Software like DisplayPage from Mississauga-based e-Commerce is the future of publishing on the Web, since it involves less direct maintenance of the pages in a Web site.

Types of Web Editor Software

You can classify Web editor software in several ways, but three of the most convenient are style of editing, purpose of the software, and distribution method.

- Style of editing. Some of the software that we examine in this chapter requires that you edit an HTML file directly, meaning that you will use the features of the program to enter all the various HTML codes directly onto the Web page. Want to bold some text? Highlight it, click on the "bold" button, and the appropriate <B> and </B> HTML codes are inserted around the text.

Other programs are what the industry calls WYSIWYG editors, that is, what you see is what you get. You edit your HTML file on the screen, and it appears in a format that comes pretty close to what it will look like within a Web browser. Want to bold a section of text? Highlight it, click on the "bold" button, and the text on screen will be bolded. Behind the scenes the HTML file for the Web page is modified so that the appropriate <B> and </B> HTML codes are inserted around the text, but you do not have to see that if you do not want to. Hence you create your HTML file without ever really touching HTML.

Some of the WYSIWYG editors in this chapter (and others available on the market) allow you to view the HTML code at any time or, if you want, allow you to edit in HTML directly instead of in WYSIWYG mode.

- Purpose of the software. Some of the software that we describe in this chapter can only be considered Web page editor software: it just helps you design a Web page. Other programs, notably Microsoft FrontPage and SiteMill, a sister product to the PageMill program, might more adequately be described as Web site management software in that they take you beyond creating a page and offer tools and capabilities that allow you to manage the many different pages that make up your Web site.

- Distribution method. You will come across three different types of Web editor software: freeware, shareware, and commercial. Actually, these categories are not just specific to Web editor software; they apply to virtually every kind of software and describe the different ways in which software is distributed.

  Freeware is software that is made available for free by the developer. Shareware is software that can be "test-driven" for free. If the user likes the software and decides to keep it, a royalty (anywhere from $5.00 to $50.00 and up, depending upon the software) should be paid to the developer. Shareware is widely distributed on the Internet, and payment is based on the honor system, since the developer does not keep track of who is using the product. Commercial software is software that is available for purchase through the Internet and retail channels such as computer and software stores. Many companies offer free evaluation versions of their commercial software on the Internet. Commercial software packages are generally superior in quality and functionality to freeware and shareware products and often come with printed manuals and technical support from the manufacturer.

As you review the software in this chapter, there are several things that you should keep in mind:

- You can obtain a copy of most of the Web editors in this chapter from the Web site of the developer. In most cases this will be a somewhat limited version, with enough key features taken away to encourage you to purchase the full version. This means that you can try out many HTML editors to see what you like and do not like and then select one that seems most appropriate for your purposes. In other cases the version you can download on-line will be good enough for your purposes, and you do not necessarily have to buy the full version.

- Do not automatically discount the packages that we look at in this chapter that allow you to edit HTML code directly. Certainly the world is moving towards those that hide you from the complexities of HTML, but you should ask yourself if you really want to do this. If you really want to get into innovative Web design and want to understand how to get the maximum degree of flexibility in your site, you should have a good working knowledge of HTML. We are not suggesting that you become an HTML expert, but we do feel that you should have some knowledge. As we said in the previous chapter, if you want to drive a car, it is good to have an idea of what goes on under the hood.

- Think about what type of computer user you have been in the past. Are you one who likes to tinker and figure things out? If so, you probably should go for an editor that lets you edit HTML directly or one that "lets you at the HTML" in addition to editing in a WYSIWYG view. Or are you a computer user with a "let's get on with it" attitude, with little inclination for details? In that case you probably want an editor that shields you completely from HTML and features full WYSIWYG capabilities.

  If the program is not WYSIWYG, it will let you click a single button to view the current Web page being edited in your Web browser. Thus you can flip back and forth between your file and Web browser to see what any changes might look like.

- Regardless of the type of Web editor program, most now come with templates, or predesigned Web pages. Templates are great for the novice, in that you can design a reasonable-looking Web page very quickly. But, to be honest, Web pages designed with templates, well, look like they have been designed with templates. Sometimes the use of templates leads to Web pages that lack spontaneity, creativity, and overall design. We suggest that you use templates to learn what it is all about, but be creative, and go for your own design.

- You can expect to see a flood of Web editor software. We look at less than ten programs in this chapter to give you an idea of the range and types of software that are available, but there are many more available, all of which offer different features and capabilities.

  Keep in mind that the Web editor software industry is like the Web browser industry: there is a constant battle between developers to offer new, enticing features, with the result being a new release every couple of months. Hence we have specifically stayed away from trying to do a feature comparison in this chapter and have focused on the fundamentals of the programs, with the intent of giving you an idea of what particular programs are all about. Does a certain program lack a feature today? Perhaps. Will it have that feature tomorrow? Most definitely.

  Another reason why Web editor software is released on a frequent basis is to keep up with the continual evolution in Web browsers. In the ongoing battle between Microsoft and Netscape, each organization now supports its own custom HTML tags in order to support some new and innovative feature. When a new version of their browser software is released that supports those tags, Web developers rush to implement the tags on their Web sites and are coming to expect that the Web editor software they use should immediately support the new tag. Hence a Web editor must quickly be modified by the developer to support those tags if they are expected to stay in the game and keep loyal customers.

Finding and Analyzing Different Web Editors

One thing you might want to do is keep up-to-date with the Web editor market to keep abreast of the new features that are being supported or to find new and innovative programs.

- The best place to start is the Yahoo! HTML editors category (**http://www.yahoo.com/Computers_and_Internet/Internet/World_Wide_Web/HTML_Editors/**).
- One of the most comprehensive and complete overviews of Web editors, converters, and analysis software can be found at the site of the World Wide Web consortium (**http://www.w3.org/pub/WWW/Tools/**). Another comprehensive list is "(The New) Mag's Big List of HTML Editors" (**http://union.ncsa.uiuc.edu/HyperNews/get/www/html/editors.html**). It includes access to the discussions in a mailing list about various editors.
- You can get more information about Macintosh editor software at the ComVista resource page (**http://www.comvista.com/net/www/htmleditor.html**). This page includes links so that you can download the many demo versions that are available.
- Web editors have become a big business, so it has become easier to locate reviews of particular packages on-line. Do a search in AltaVista or OpenText for the phrase "HTML editors and review" or "Web editors and review" to find current reviews, or check the sites of popular computer publications such as *PCWeek* (**http://www.pcweek.com**), *The Computer Paper* (**http://www.tcp.ca**), *PCMagazine* (**http://www.pcmag.com**), and *C|Net* (**http://www.cnet.com**).
- Also, take a look at "HTML Editor Reviews" (**http://homepage.interaccess.com/~cdavis/edit_rev.html**), where you can find ongoing reviews of new releases of Web editor software.

Now we take a look at some of the more recognized Web editor programs:

- HotDog;
- HTML Editor;
- HTML Assistant Pro;
- InContext Spider;
- SoftQuad HoTMetaL;
- Microsoft FrontPage;
- Netscape Navigator Gold;
- Adobe PageMill (and SiteMill);
- Claris HomePage.

HotDog

We will begin with a few editors that you use to edit in HTML directly. HotDog is one such program. The version of HotDog that we used came with the O'Reilly Web site program that we looked at briefly in the previous chapter. It is a full-featured program; a "professional version" that includes many more capabilities can also be purchased. You can download a basic working version on-line to try out on your own. The version we used was certainly capable of doing most things you would want to do on a Web page; you would only need the professional version if you really wanted to expand your Web capabilities.

HotDog has developed somewhat of a reputation in the community as a good starting point for individuals eager to learn how to create their own Web sites, since it was one of the first full-featured Web editors available. It is a very straightforward program; for example, as soon as you start it, it puts up a help screen so that you can learn more about the program and HTML:

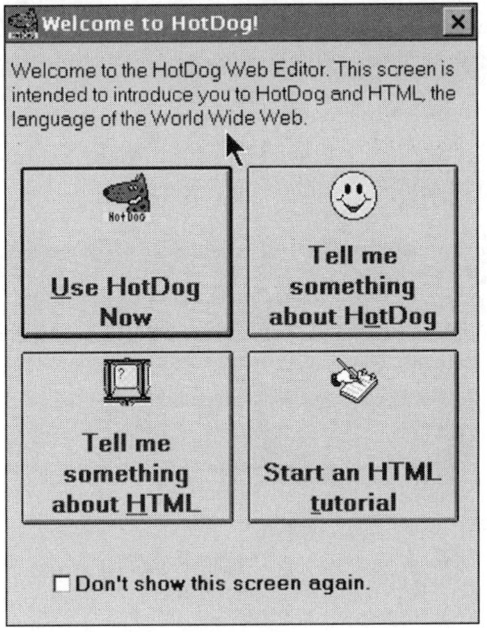

HotDog lets you edit HTML code directly, rather than letting you edit in WYSIWYG mode. However, it is easy to use HotDog to insert various HTML tags or change their meaning: simply highlight the text you want to change, click on "tags, " and choose one of the tag categories (e.g., bolding, headings, images, etc.). Each category then allows you to choose specific attributes related to that tag. For example, on the following screen we want to make the phrase "Music for the Masses" a second-level heading, that is, give it an <H2> tag at the start and an </H2> tag at the end. To do so, rather than typing in these codes directly, we simply highlight the phrase "Music for the Masses," choose "tags," and then choose "heading 2":

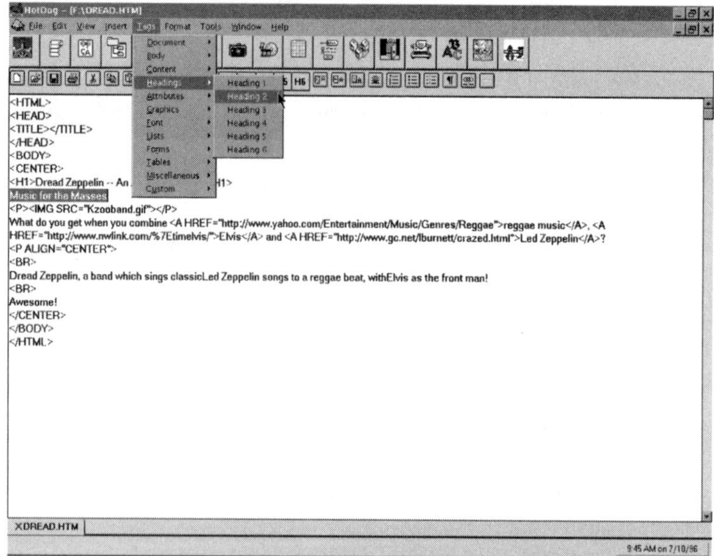

HotDog surrounds the text so that it is now **<H2>**Music for the Masses**</H2>**, making it a second-level heading, as can be seen in the following screen:

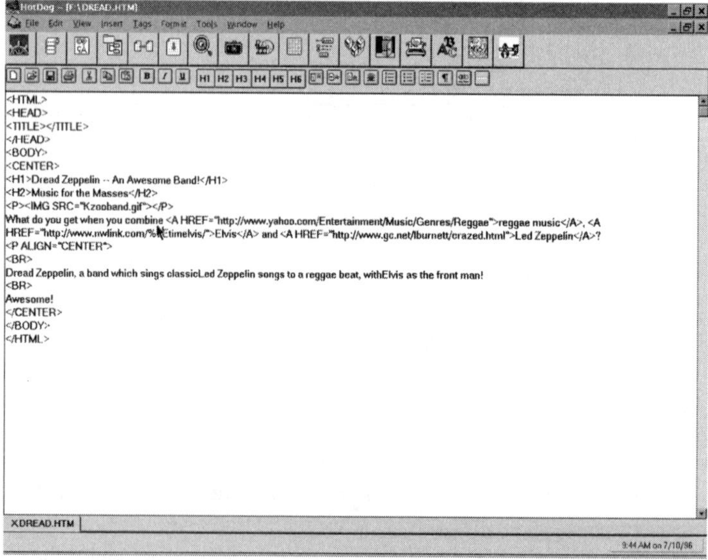

Given that you can download a fully functional version on-line to try out, HotDog is worth looking into. For more information about HotDog visit the Sausage Software Web site at **http://www.sausage.com**. A free evaluation version is available on-line.

HTML Editor

HTML Editor could probably be classified as the Macintosh equivalent of HotDog. It is a straightforward, simple HTML editor that allows you to easily prepare a Web page by highlighting the text and choosing one of the formatting items from the menu presented. It features a "button bar" that allows you to quickly bold, italicize, give headings to components of your HTML file, and put a hyperlink in the document to another Web page or Web site:

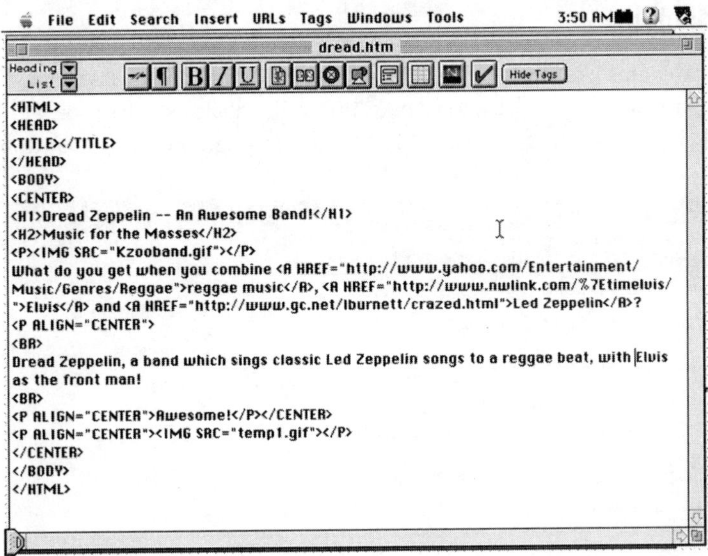

You can easily insert images into your HTML file, with flexibility over their placement on the page in terms of the alignment (i.e., top, left, centre) and size (height, width, etc.):

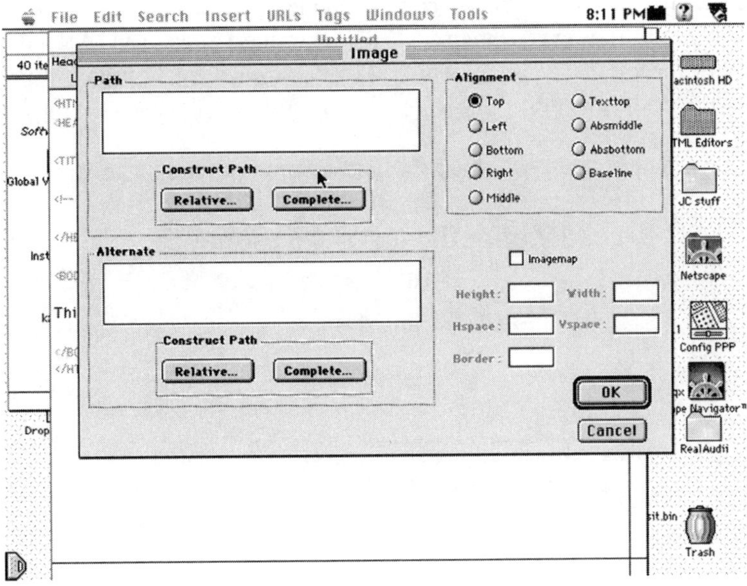

Although it does not support full WYSIWYG editing, you can click on the "Hide Tags" button to get a rough idea of what your HTML file will look like through a Web browser, without the images. HTML Editor has earned a solid reputation as a simple and straightforward tool to get going. Developed by a professor at Acadia University in Nova Scotia, the program is available as shareware. You can obtain a copy of HTML Editor on-line at **http://dragon.acadiau.ca/~giles/home.html**.

HTML Assistant Pro

A step beyond programs like HotDog and HTML Editor is HTML Assistant Pro. Developed in Nova Scotia by Brooklyn North Software Works, the program allows you to edit HTML code directly and easily insert and change specific HTML tags through the use of a button bar:

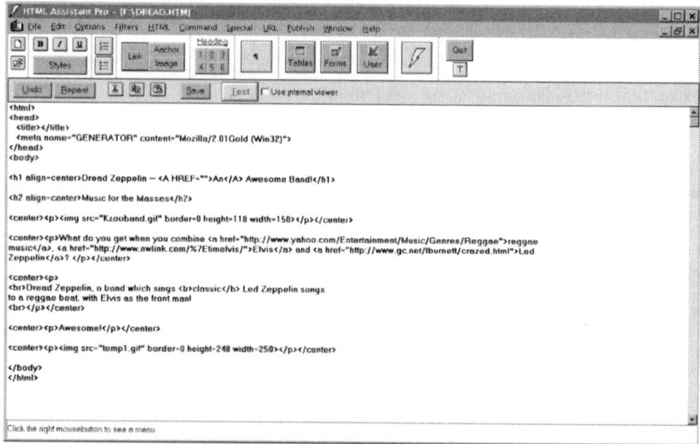

HTML Assistant Pro is not a WYSIWYG editor, although you can link it to your favorite Web browser, so that you can easily view the results of any changes to your HTML code. You can also choose to use the internal "viewer, " which at least lets you see your page as it might appear in a browser, without the pictures:

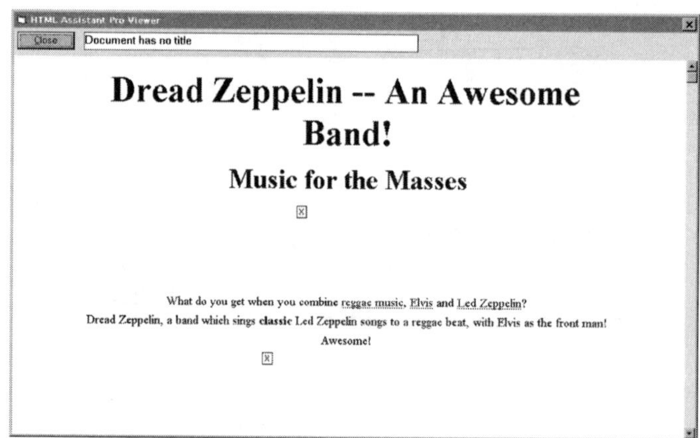

HTML Assistant Pro features pretty well everything you need for a sophisticated Web site: forms, tables, a spell checker, and other capabilities. When changing or adding anything to a basic HTML item, there is a lot of flexibility. For example, when inserting an image, you can do everything you would likely need to do, such as indicating the position of the picture, the size, "white space" around it, and so on:

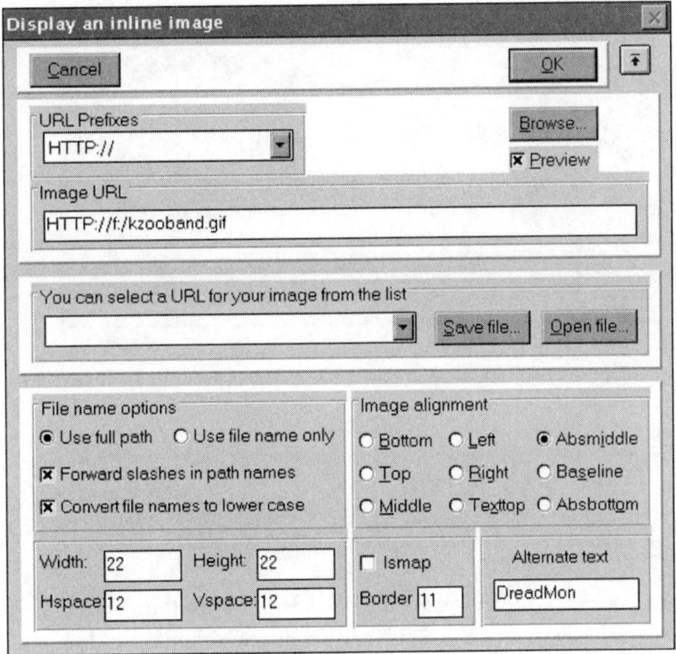

There are also many unique features:

- A background editor, which allows you to easily choose the color and images to be used on your Web page. For example, by moving the bars on the right of the following screen, you can immediately change the background color. The proper HTML code is then inserted into your Web page to support that color — see the screen on the next page.

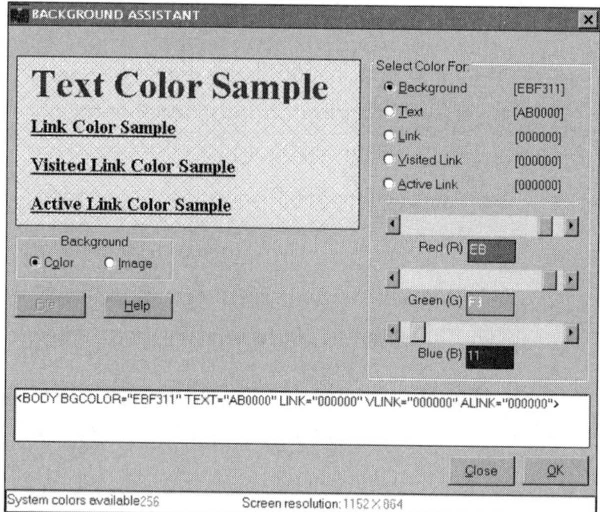

- A separate "form" toolbar, which can be used to create fill-in forms and "frames" or "tables":

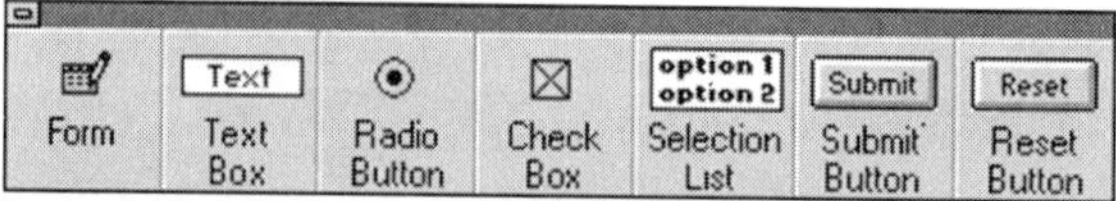

- You can import a word processor file if it has been saved in what is known as RTF format. This lets you save the formatting that you might have done on documents in Microsoft Word, WordPerfect, or other programs, and easily convert them into HTML format. (RTF stands for "rich text format" and is often used within word processing and other programs to allow for the exchange of documents between different word processors.)
- The ability to easily change a specific line of text in multiple HTML files. For example, this will let you easily change a copyright notice on all your Web pages.
- The ability to quickly strip the HTML out of the file so that you can save a basic text version.

In fact, there are so many special features scattered throughout the program that we would be willing to bet that short of multimedia (i.e., Java) applications, you could do everything you need to with this package. For more information about HTML Assistant Pro, visit the Web site for Brooklyn North Software Works at **http://www.brooknorth.com**. A freeware version of the product is available on their Web site.

InContext Spider

InContext Systems is a Toronto-based organization that has released Spider, a simple and straightforward method of creating Web pages. Spider features a number of predesigned templates, which you can choose from a list, as well as a description of what each template does:

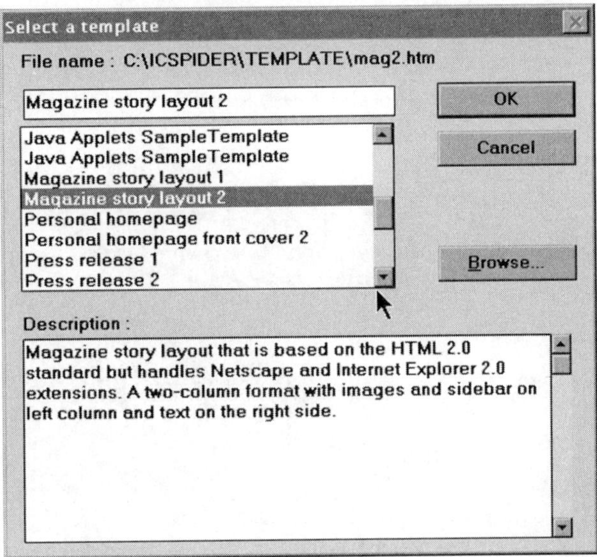

Choose a predesigned template and it is then loaded and shown on the screen. What is unique about the program is that rather than showing you the HTML code, the left-hand side of the screen will show you the type of HTML tag that has been given to particular text. For example, on the screen below, "ATTENTION GRABBING HEADLINE" has been highlighted, and the left-hand side of the screen tells us that this is in Heading 1 format. You will also notice that the text itself is presented in a format that closely matches what you will see in the browser:

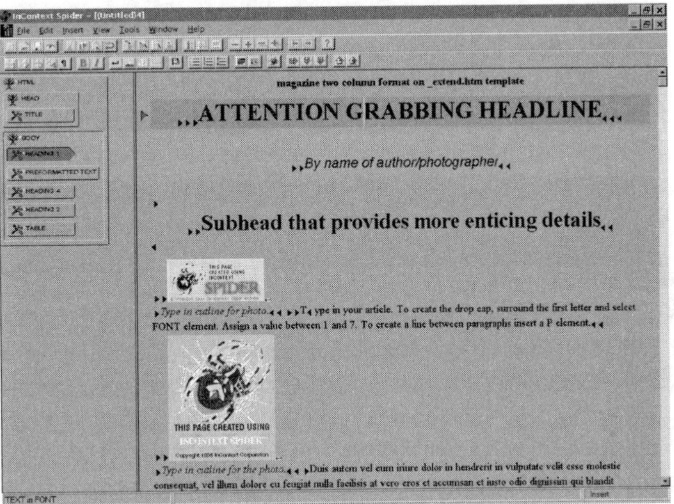

To create your own page from this template, you simply modify the text with your own content:

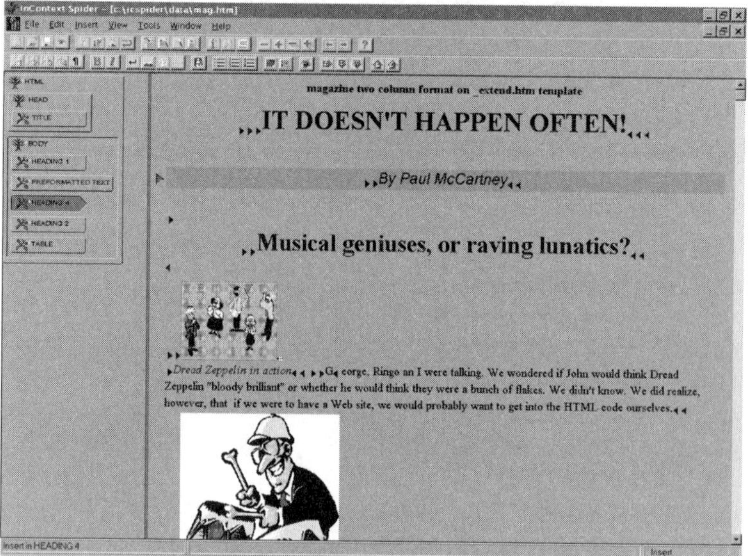

then press a button and see the results in your Web browser:

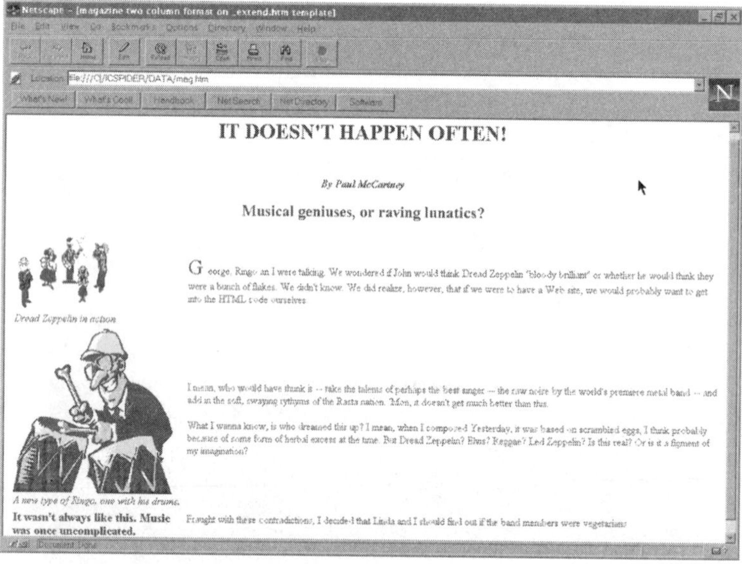

InContext is not a true WYSIWYG editor, since you do not edit an HTML file in the exact or "close to exact" format that you would see within your browser, but it comes pretty close. It is also important to keep in mind that InContext Spider is not restricted to simple templates; there are many options available to create fairly sophisticated Web pages. InContext features other notable features:

- One-button Web publishing, which provides the details of where your Web site is stored, along with the appropriate user ID and password. Spider will load up your new or revised Web pages by pressing a single button. This means that you do not have to fool around with clumsy FTP programs or use other messages to make your new pages available.

- A "Web manager," which helps you to manage the other Web pages or many Web site links that you may want to include in your Web documents.

It is also worth noting that InContext is proof that many Web editor companies are now beginning to ship lots of other software with their Web editors to enhance your capabilities. Install the software, and you get a screen about the "bonus" software that is available to you:

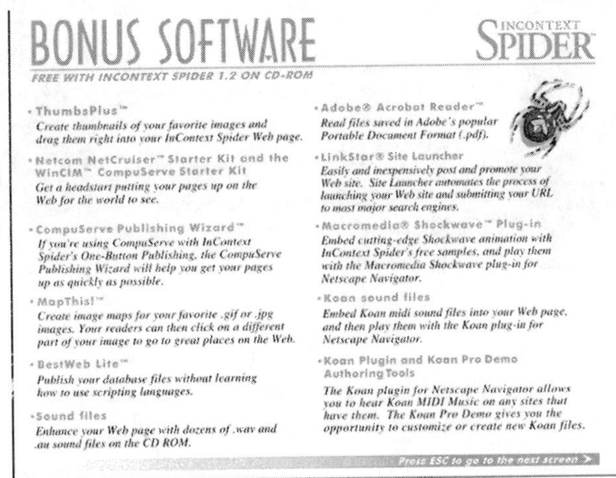

Included is a program to convert databases to HTML format; also included are ways to add multimedia capabilities to your Web site. Finally, the version of Spider that we looked at was a full copy (not the trial version you can download on-line) that came on CD ROM. Included was a wonderful tutorial that walks through the process of using the program. You can choose to view any one of a number of topics:

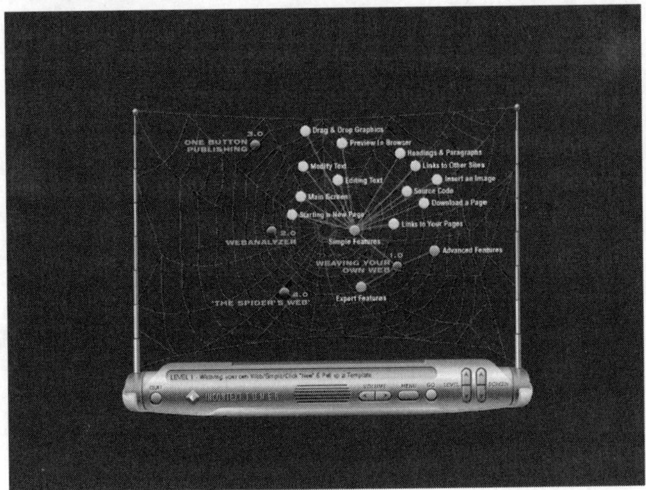

Once you choose a topic, you get a presentation about that topic, featuring spoken instructions, animation, and music on a sample Spider screen:

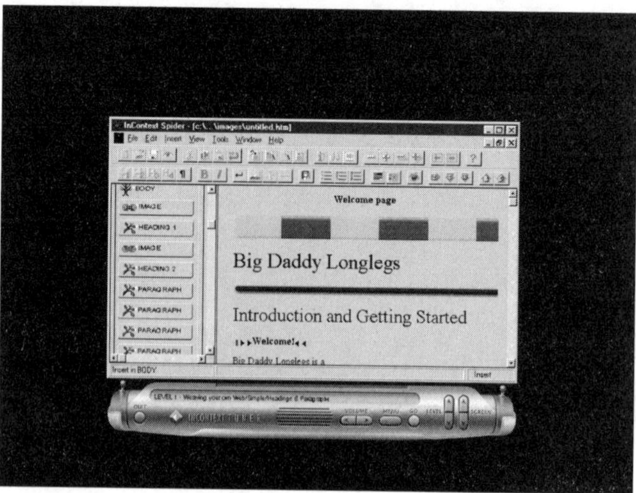

Hence it is a useful way to learn about the basics of HTML and how to use the Spider program. All in all, InContext Spider is a full-featured and innovative approach to Web design. For more information about InContext Spider, visit the InContext Systems Web site at **http://www.incontext.com**. There you can obtain an evaluation copy of the software for free.

SoftQuad HoTMetaL

HoTMetaL is somewhat of a hybrid: it allows you to edit HTML code directly or in WYSIWYG view if you like. Available from a Toronto-based organization, it was one of the earliest HTML editors available on the market. The program comes in two versions: HoTMetaL and HoTMetaL Pro, the latter providing many more features than the former, which is available for downloading through the SoftQuad Web site. Consider the flexibility in the way you can edit an HTML file with this program. Here is our sample page in pure HTML format, as we have seen with the editors above:

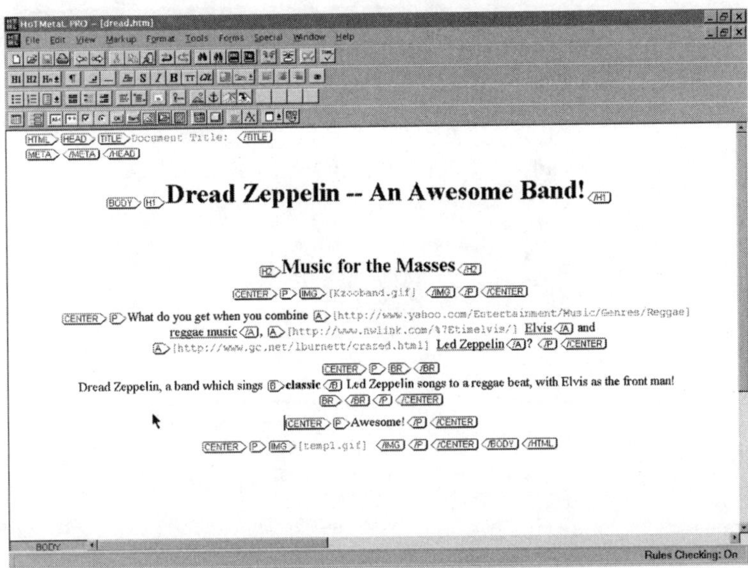

Here is the same file with the images "turned on," so that we can edit in HTML directly but at least see the images as we edit the file:

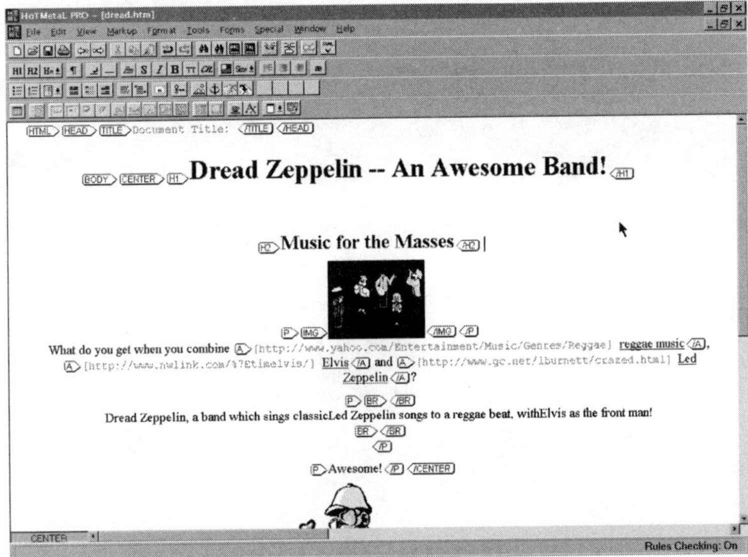

Here is the same file; however, in this case we have turned off the HTML tags but left the URLs (hyperlinks) still showing:

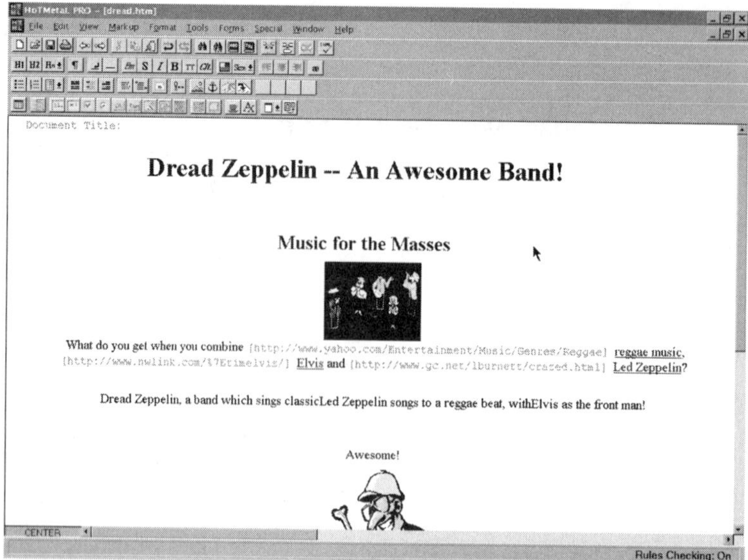

And finally, on this screen we have edited the file without showing either the URLs or the HTML tags. In this case we are editing the file and seeing directly and immediately what any changes might look like within the Web page. In other words, what you see on the screen below is what you get on the Web page when you examine it with a browser:

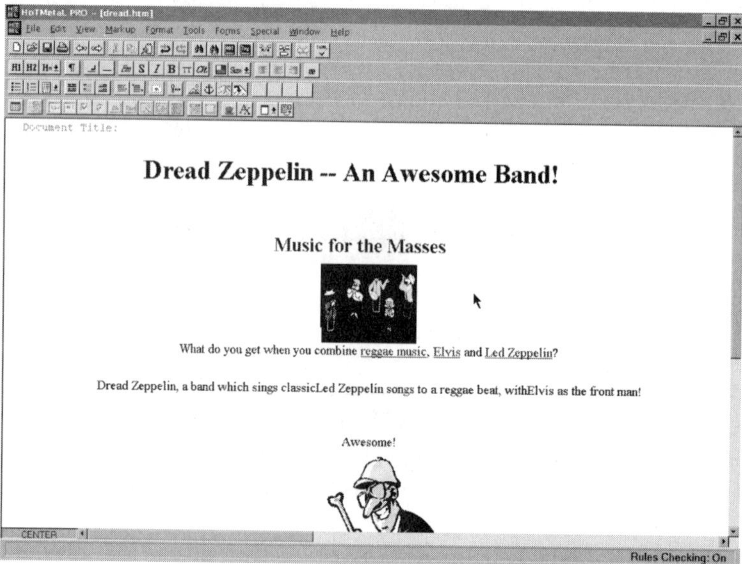

In this way, we can use HoTMetaL like a word processor: to change some text and give it a new HTML tag, simply highlight it and then choose a formatting command. To bold text, highlight it, press the bold button as you would within a word processor, and the text will then be bolded on the screen. Behind the scenes the actual HTML file will be modified so that the proper <B> and </B> HTML tags are inserted.

HoTMetaL includes a number of formatting bars that you can use in creating your HTML files. For example, the following bar, found near the top of the screen, allows you to do several things:

If you highlight your text and press:

- H1, H2, or H3, the text will be formatted as an HTML headline;
- B, the text will be bolded;
- I, the text will be italicized.

Other buttons on other bars let you insert images, links, tables, forms, and other HTML features.

If you know how to use a word processor, you will know how to create a Web HTML file. Hence HoTMetaL Pro is one of those programs that you can use to prepare an HTML file without knowing much about HTML itself, although we still maintain that you should have a working knowledge of HTML to be able to cope with such a program. It is also perhaps one of the most comprehensive Web editor programs available and could be described as industrial-strength. It includes a spell checker, thesaurus, and many other features.

This program is known for probably having the strictest rules in terms of compliance to the "rules" of HTML. The rules, found in the "validation checker," compare your page to the formal and informal "standards" of HTML, and if there are any errors, HoTMetaL lets you know about them. In reality, there are hundreds of thousands of Web pages with errors on them, and most browsers will still somehow manage to show the information on them. SoftQuad goes one step further by wanting to have you fix any errors.

But the rules are so strict that some people try to load their existing Web pages only to be told that they have an error without any hint of what to do to solve the error and hence become frustrated with the program. One saving grace is that you can turn the "rule checker" off.

HoTMetaL Pro is a great alternative for serious Web developers, given its flexibility. You can download a working version from their Web site at **http://www.sq.com**.

Microsoft FrontPage

Like HoTMetaL, FrontPage from Microsoft is a WYSIWYG editor and acts and operates like any other word processing program. For example, here is the view of our sample HTML file. You can bold, highlight, italicize, centre, or apply any other type of formatting to the text, simply by highlighting and clicking on one of the buttons found on the button bars:

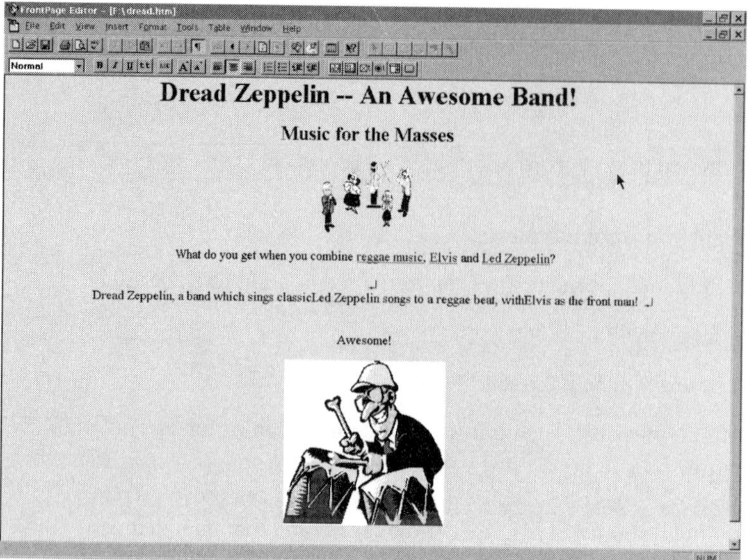

Like HoTMetaL, it is easy to edit the URLs within your Web document: simply highlight the phrase that you would like to make into a link, and fill in the details box that presents itself:

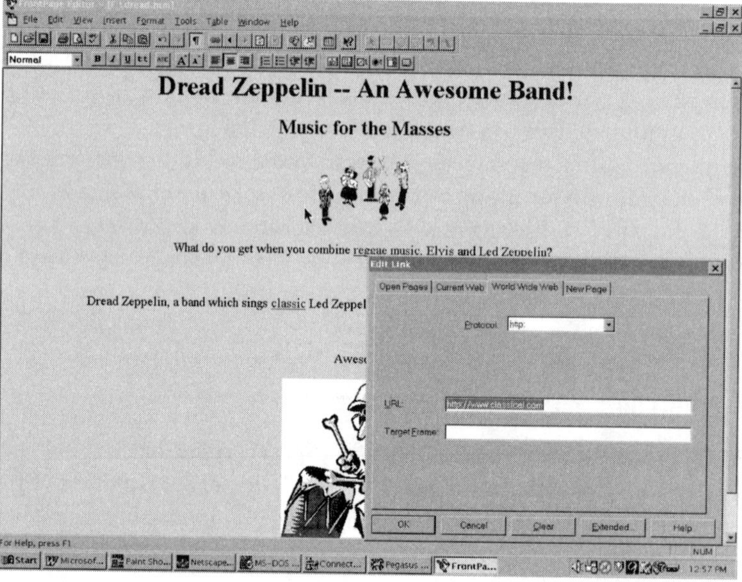

FrontPage is a program that promises to hide from you much of the complexity of HTML. You cannot edit HTML code directly within the program; you can only view it as seen on the screen below. (You could edit it directly in any other type of text editor if you so chose.)

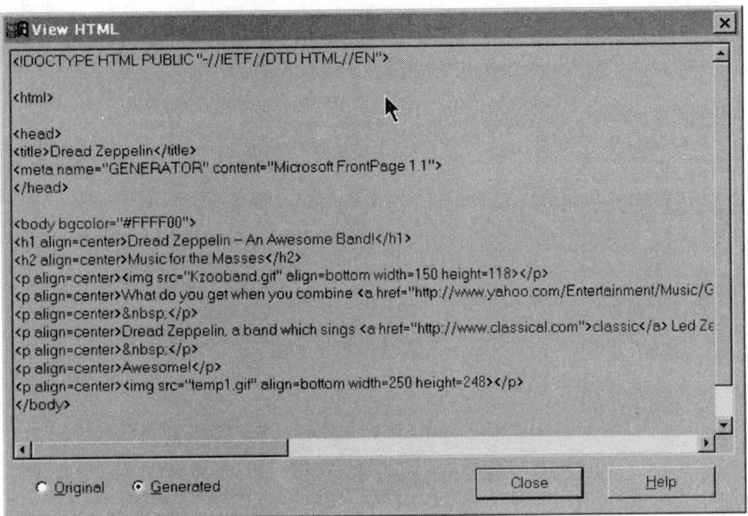

From this perspective, if you want to create a Web site without touching HTML code directly, FrontPage is a good choice. However, we believe you should still have a good working knowledge of HTML to take advantage of a program such as FrontPage. Why? From the menu select "Insert" and choose "Definition," and see the choices "List," "Term," and "Definition":

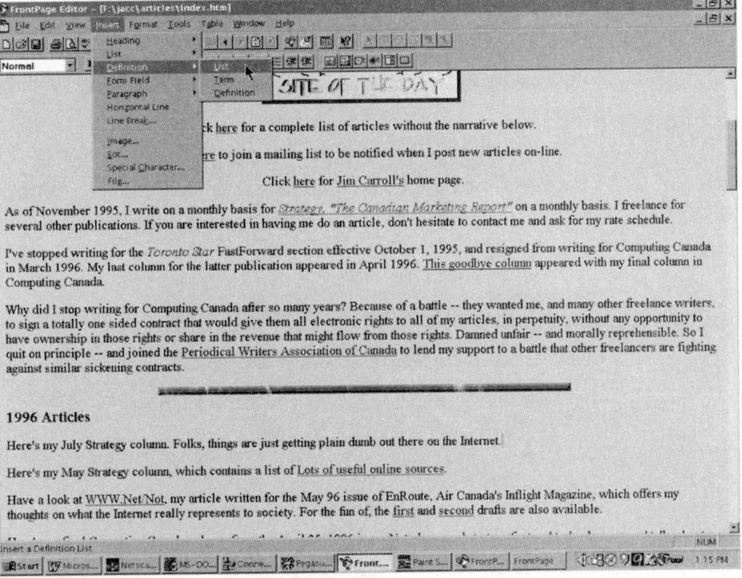

You will not really know what such choices will do, other than experimenting with them or by understanding HTML, or by studying help screens. So it doesn't hurt to learn about HTML, even though you do not use it directly.

FrontPage comes with a number of "templates," or predefined Web pages, that you can use to create your own Web pages. For example, here is a page that you can use to create your own "Feedback Form":

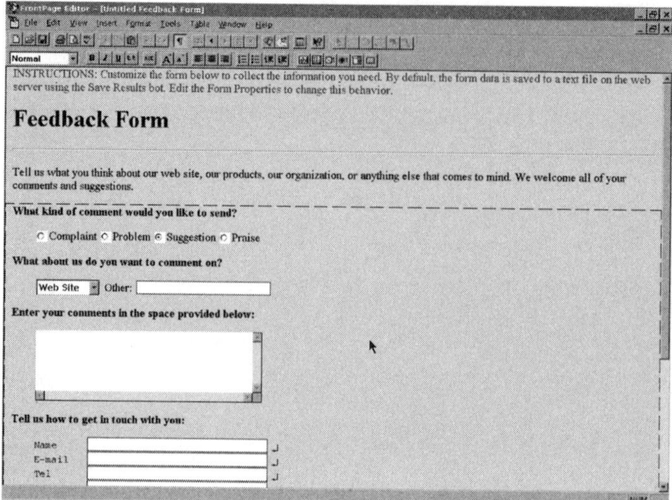

Just make changes to customize it, and you are ready to go.

Given Microsoft's considerable size and scope in the computer industry, and given their stated intention to be a major player within the Internet industry, it can be expected that FrontPage will continue to evolve and become a choice for many people. The program is available for Windows 95 and Macintosh systems, with a UNIX version also available. You can find out more about the program at Microsoft, **http://www.microsoft.com**.

Netscape Navigator Gold

Netscape Navigator Gold is a version of the Netscape Navigator Web browser program that happens to include a Web editor. For example, load the Web browser, click on "File," and you will see a new item, "Open File in Editor":

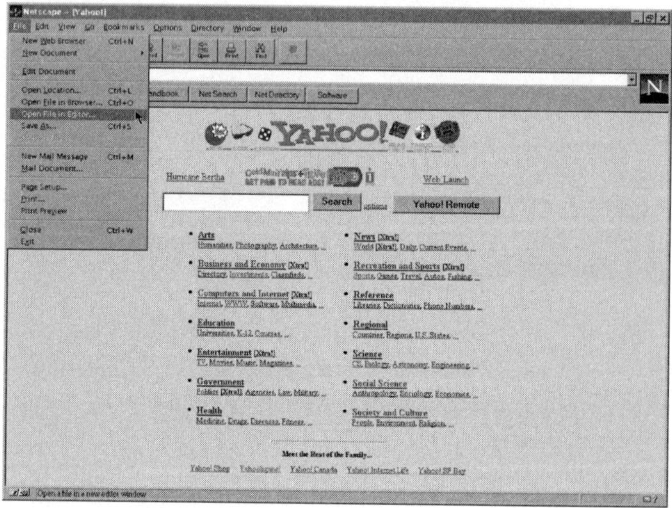

Do this, choose an HTML file to edit, and you are taken directly into the Netscape HTML editor, a fully WYSIWYG program like FrontPage:

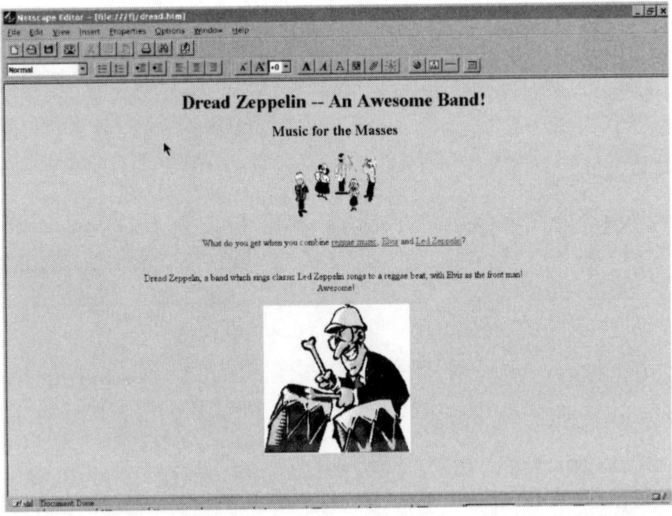

And like FrontPage, using the Netscape Editor is as easy as using a word processing program: just highlight some text, choose the format, or attributes, such as bold, italic, head level, and the appropriate HTML codes are inserted. You cannot edit in HTML directly, but you can choose to view it any time, just as with Microsoft FrontPage.

One innovative feature that is certain to be found in most other Web browsers is the ability to easily upload your Web pages to your Web server (or the server of the organization from which you rent Web space) with the press of a button. Just indicate the pages you want to upload, provide the name of the FTP or Web site along with user ID and password where your Web pages should be stored, and the Netscape Editor will take care of uploading the files for you:

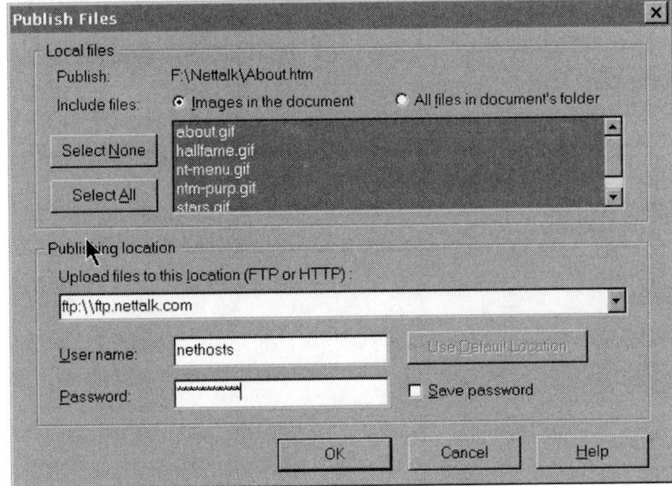

In another innovative twist, you can use the Netscape Editor to grab a copy of any Web page that you like and edit it yourself to create your own version. Want to use the PEI government home page as a starting point? Simply click on "Open Location" within Netscape, and choose to open a Web page in your Web editor, rather than in the Web browser:

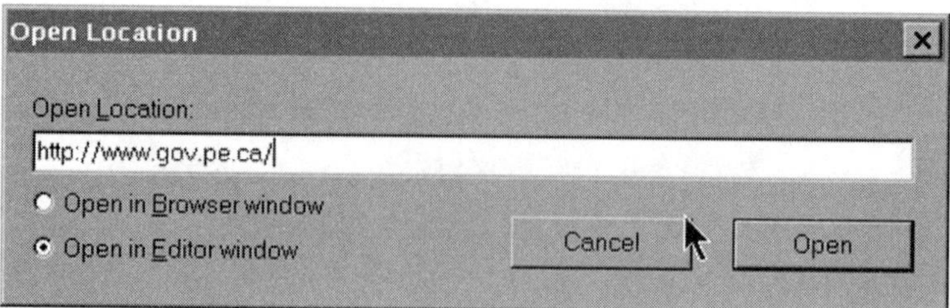

You will be told that a copy of the Web page will be made and saved to your hard disk, so that you can edit it:

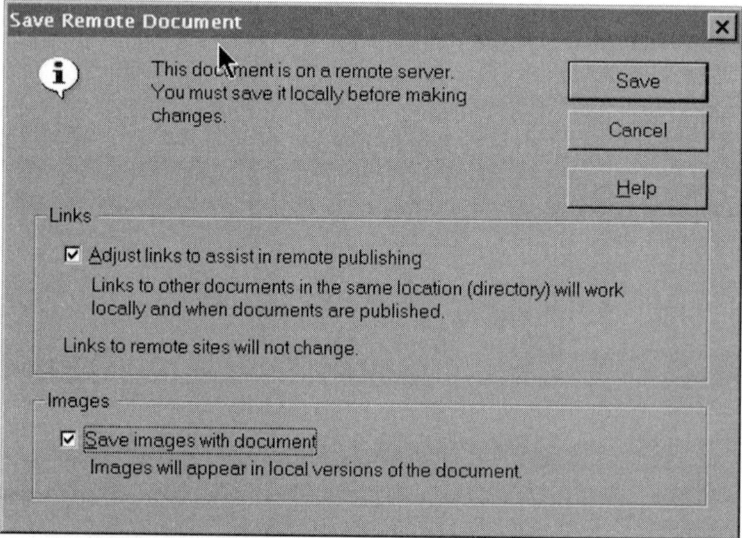

And then, just before it downloads the page, you are conveniently reminded that you should respect any copyright that the owner of the page may have in place (we discuss copyright and intellectual property issues in Chapter 19):

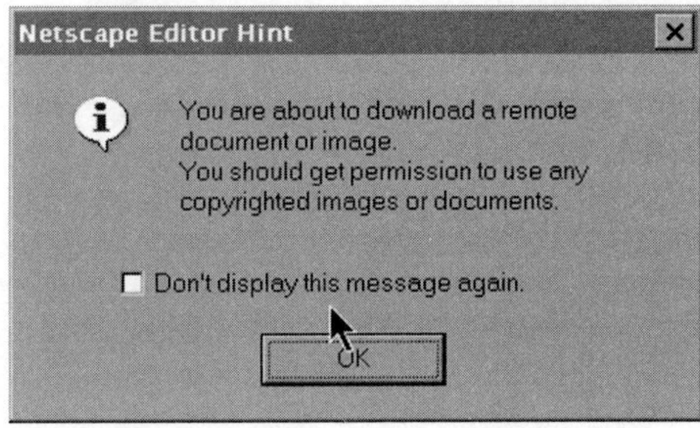

Press "OK," and a copy of the PEI government home page is pulled into your Netscape Web editor, so that you can use the code to prepare your own page:

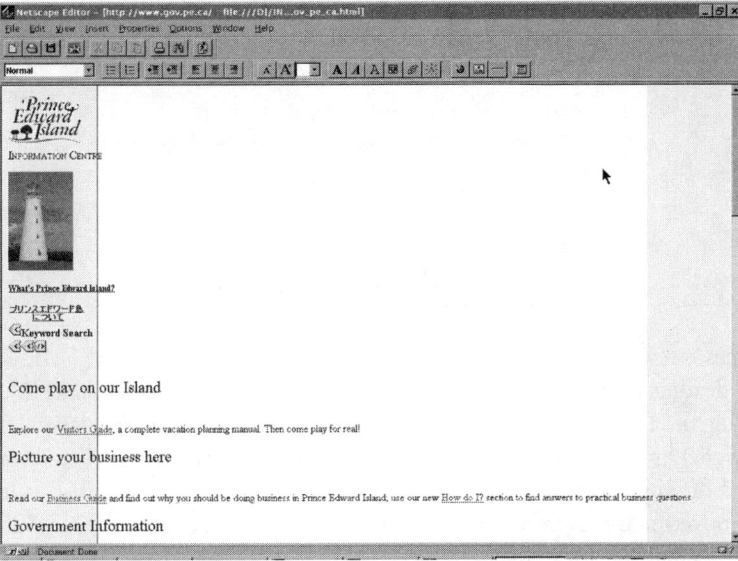

The convenience of Netscape Navigator Gold is that you will be doing your editing in a system that will be, essentially, Netscape, and if Netscape is your preferred browser, you will find it a comfortable working environment. You can obtain an evaluation copy of Netscape Gold at Netscape (**http://www.netscape.com**).

Adobe PageMill (and SiteMill)

In the previous chapter, in which we discussed what is involved in setting up a Web site, we stressed the need for good graphic design and that you should consider hiring the talents of a professional graphic designer to achieve this. And, of course, it is well known that the vast majority of creative graphic designers prefer to work on Macintosh computers; Macs simply appeal to the creative mindset. Hence PageMill from Adobe Systems (and its more sophisticated version, SiteMill) is now one of the most popular Web editor programs. PageMill and SiteMill have recently become available for Windows 95 as well.

PageMill takes advantage of the intuitiveness of the Macintosh user interface, which has long supported, for example, the concept of "drag and drop." Want to move an image in your Web document to another position on the screen? Simply click it and drag it to the spot you want to put it. And PageMill is, of course, a true WYSIWYG editor: what you do on the screen is what you will see on your browser. For example, here is our sample file, with no HTML codes in view whatsoever:

Being a Macintosh, efforts are made to hide even the "geekier" aspects of HTML. For example, rather than dealing with HTML tags such as Heading 1 (H1), Heading 2 (H2), Heading 3 (H3), Heading 4 (H4), PageMill simply calls them "Largest, Larger, Large, Small." PageMill offers much of the sophistication found in other Web editors in this chapter. For example, there is a lot of flexibility in how you might insert an image into your document. But it is intuitive enough to convert graphics from other formats to the necessary format for a Web site, if you just drag that graphic over into the Web file.

PageMill also does a very good job in helping in the design of forms, given its focus on the graphic elements of Web page design; in fact, many of the buttons on the button bar are used for the creation of forms.

PageMill has a more sophisticated cousin, SiteMill, whose goal is to manage Web sites. SiteMill will examine all the HTML files within your Web site and alert you to any errors, "orphan" files, and other problems. It will also discover the links that exist between the various files in your Web site. We will take a look at SiteMill in the section Web Management Tools later in this chapter. You can download an evaluation copy of PageMill for both Macintosh and Windows 95 at **http://www.adobe.com**.

Claris HomePage

This is another Macintosh program, similar in concept to PageMill in that it lets you create a Web site without having to know about HMTL:

Unlike PageMill, however, it will let you edit the "raw" HTML code:

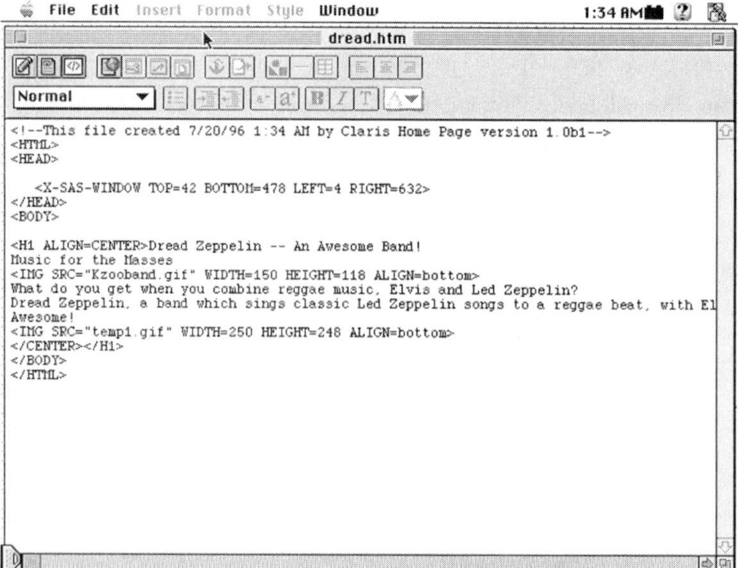

HomePage features a row of "button bars" that contain many of the commands you will want to use when creating a Web page or series of pages. And while it may not seem like there are many of them, there is a lot of flexibility hidden behind those buttons, such as the attributes you can give to an image:

and the background you can give to a page:

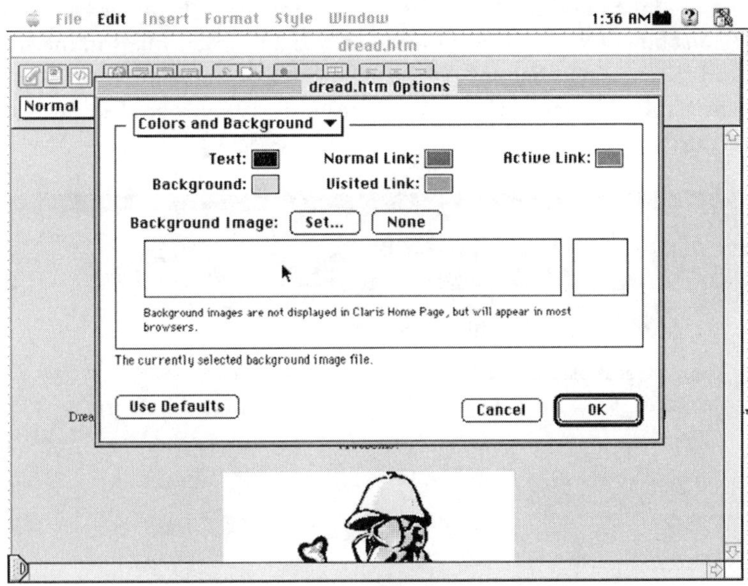

At the time we looked at it, Claris HomePage was still new, but given that it comes from Apple's primary software arm, it is bound to gain a quick and loyal following. You can download an evaluation copy of HomePage at **http://www.claris.com**.

Web Conversion Software

You may have existing data that you wish to make available to people on the Internet, for example, information that you have created in a word processing program, a presentation package, a spreadsheet package, or a database application. There are now programs that will convert your data into HTML format. Let's review some examples.

Word Processing Programs

Most of the more popular word processing programs include the capability to convert a word processing document into HTML format. This means that you can prepare your document in your favorite word processor and then simply save it as a basic HTML file. Your formatting within the word processing document, that is, bolding, italics, any centring of text, and other formatting information, will be saved with the proper HTML codes. In most cases, however, you will have to edit the file further with a text editor or HTML editor to add other features such as hyperlinks. You should check the manual for your word processing program or contact the developer of your word processor to see if such a conversion tool is built into their software or is available as a separate add-on.

Microsoft, for example, makes available a program called Internet Assistant for Microsoft Word that acts as a Web browser and also converts Word documents into HTML format. You can obtain the software for free on the Microsoft Word Home Page (**http://www.microsoft.com/msword**). Here is how it works. First, you download and install the Internet Assistant for Microsoft Word. Next, using Microsoft Word, you open a document that you want to convert into HTML format. In the example below we are using a case study on the Canadian beer market that was created using Microsoft Word:

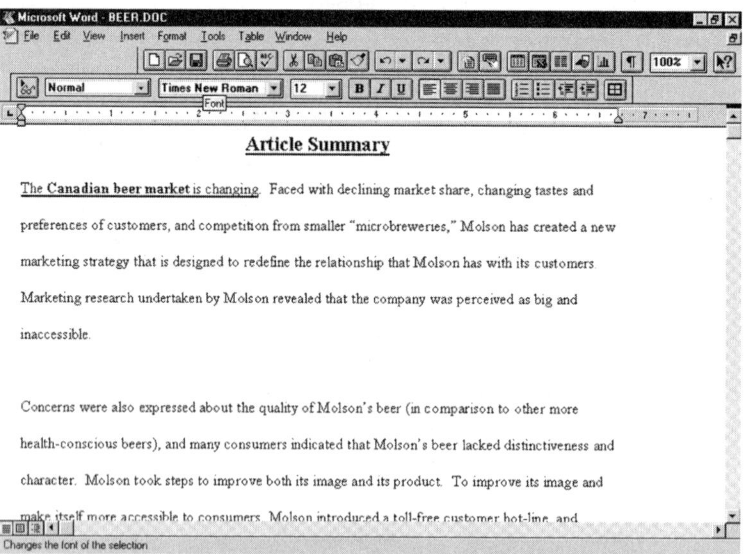

To save the document in HTML format, you click on "File" in the menu bar, then select "Save As." Then you select "HyperText Markup Language (HTML)" from the list of available formats and choose the name of the file and the directory where you want to save the file. In this example we saved the file as "beer.htm" in the c:\word\reports directory. (HTML files created on your personal computer will always end in the HTM extension, which stands for hypertext markup language.)

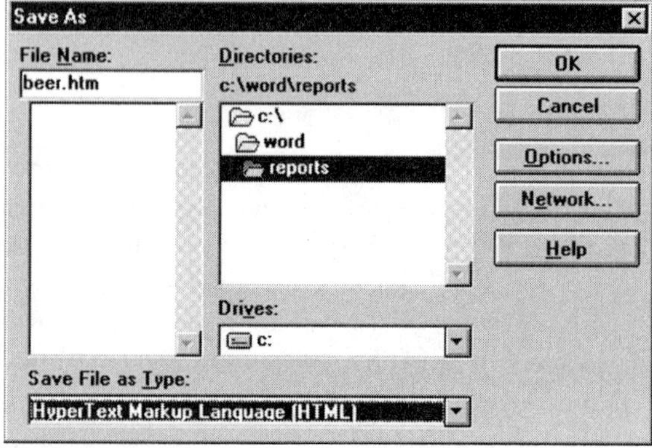

The document is then converted into HTML format, and the resulting file is displayed on the screen, as seen below:

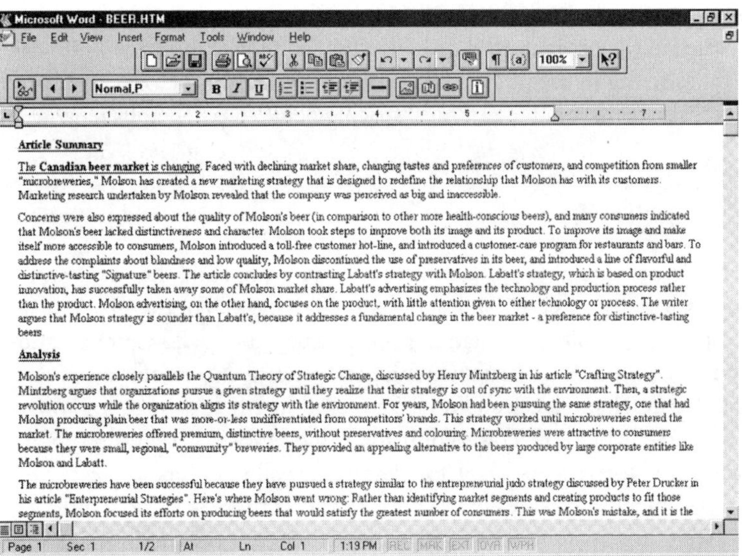

To see how the file will be displayed on the Web, open it using your favorite World Wide Web browser. For example, if you are using Netscape, select "Open File," which appears under the "File" option on the menu bar. Then navigate to the directory where you saved the file and click on the file name. In this example we open the file "beer.htm" from the c:\word\reports directory, since that is where we saved the file a few moments ago.

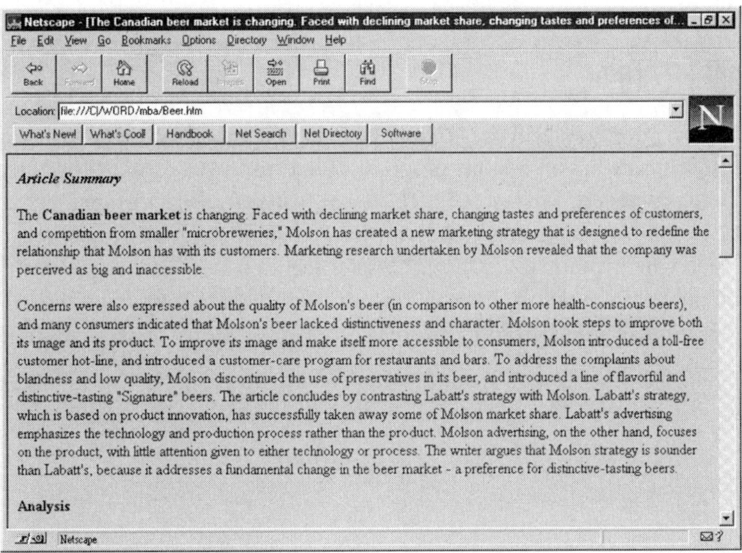

The document now appears on our Web browser. Notice that not all the attributes of the original document were converted to HTML. One of the drawbacks of Internet Assistant for Microsoft Word, and many other conversion programs, is that some features of the document you are converting are lost during the conversion process. For example, notice that the title of the document was centred in the original word processor file, but it is not centred in the HTML version. The size of the lettering in the title was also not retained when the conversation took place, although characteristics like bold, italics, and spacing between paragraphs remained intact.

Presentation Programs

Many presentation programs — programs that let you run slide shows on your computer — have a built-in capability for converting slides into Web pages. For example, the latest version of Freelance Graphics, a popular presentation package from Lotus, allows presentations to be saved in HTML format, as does Microsoft's presentation software, Microsoft PowerPoint. In the latter case Microsoft has developed a free add-on utility called Internet Assistant for PowerPoint that can be used to convert a Microsoft PowerPoint for Windows 95 presentation file into a series of HTML documents. Internet Assistant for PowerPoint allows users to create not only graphic versions of slides, but also text versions. This means that those with slow Internet links or with non-graphic Web browsers will be able to access the slides over the Internet and flip through them quickly.

The great benefit of having your slides available on the Web means that you can provide colorful and interactive presentations to co-workers and clients anywhere there is an Internet connection. And because the slides are actually on the World Wide Web, you can link information on your slides to other World Wide Web sites, something you cannot do if you are using stand-alone software on your PC. Internet Assistant for PowerPoint is available at the Microsoft PowerPoint Home Page. (**http://www.microsoft.com/mspowerpoint**).

Spreadsheet Programs

Many spreadsheet programs will allow you to convert spreadsheet data to HTML format. Microsoft, for example, has an add-on program called Internet Assistant for Microsoft Excel that does this for owners of Microsoft Excel, its popular spreadsheet program. Here is how it works. Suppose you own a business, and you have created the following spreadsheet file in Microsoft Excel, which summarizes monthly sales for your two sales regions, Region A and Region B. You now want to put that data up on your World Wide Web site without having to retype the information. With Microsoft's Internet Assistant, it is easy to do in just a few steps.

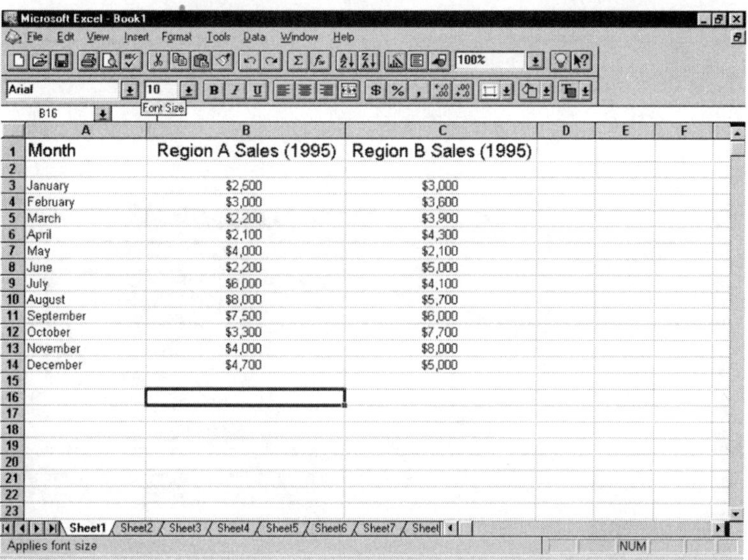

Month	Region A Sales (1995)	Region B Sales (1995)
January	$2,500	$3,000
February	$3,000	$3,600
March	$2,200	$3,900
April	$2,100	$4,300
May	$4,000	$2,100
June	$2,200	$5,000
July	$6,000	$4,100
August	$8,000	$5,700
September	$7,500	$6,000
October	$3,300	$7,700
November	$4,000	$8,000
December	$4,700	$5,000

Once you have downloaded Internet Assistant for Microsoft Excel from the Microsoft home page and launched your Microsoft Excel program, you select the "Add-Ins" option from the "Tools" menu and select "Internet Assistant Wizard":

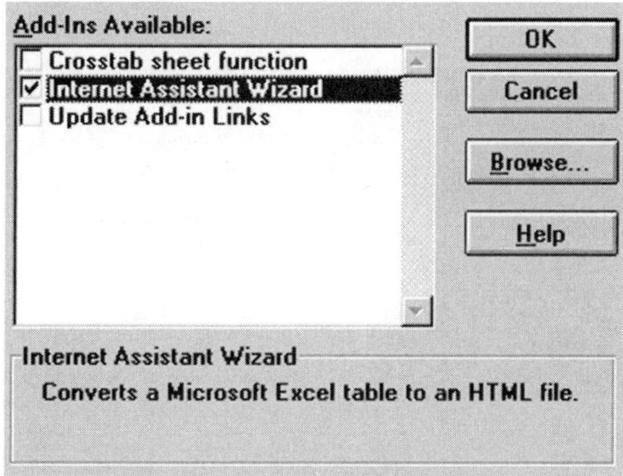

Internet Assistant Wizard will then appear as one of the options under the "Tools" menu. You select it, and an Internet Assistant Wizard appears on the screen. Using your mouse, you then select the area of the spreadsheet that you want to convert to the Web. You select columns A, B, and C, the columns containing the data you wish to convert:

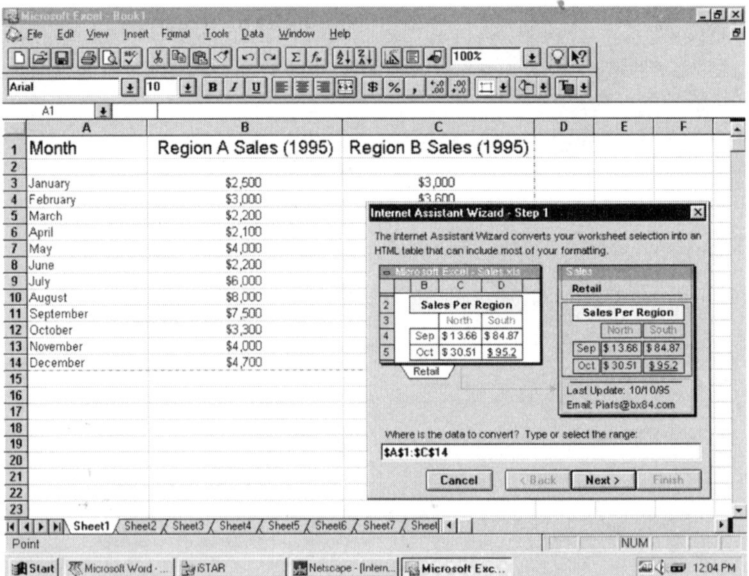

The Internet Assistant Wizard now gives you two options: you can either convert your data to its very own HTML document, or you can insert the data into an HTML document that you have already created. Let's assume you want to create an independent HTML document, so you select the first option:

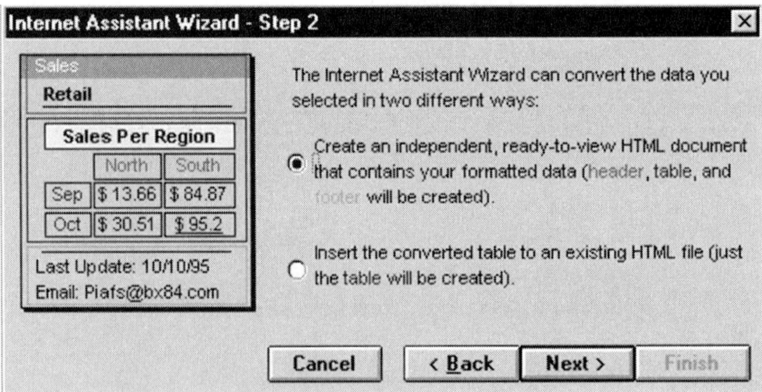

You then select a title and heading for your Web document. For this example we will title your Web document "ABC Corporation" and use the heading "Sales Information":

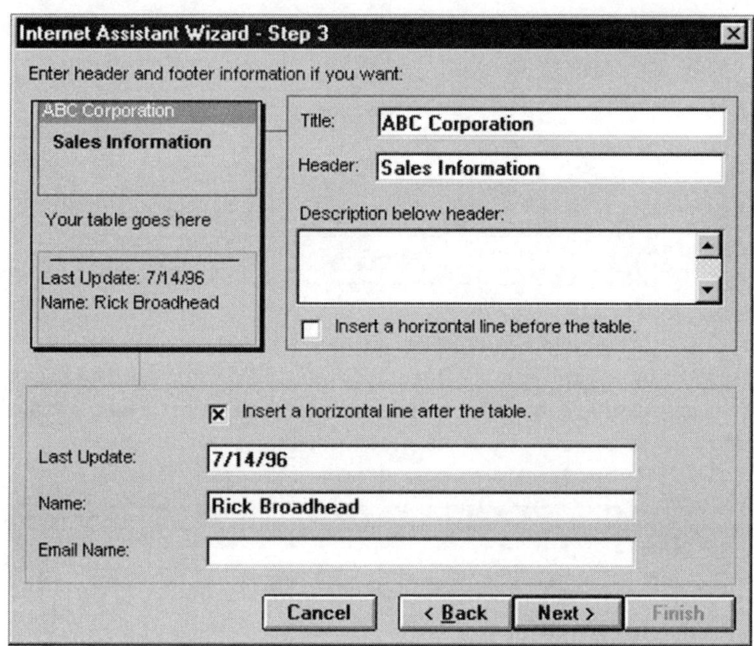

You are asked how much of your formatting you want to convert. You are given two options: you can either convert as much of the formatting as possible or only the data. Formatting includes attributes such as the color, size, and appearance of the data. In this case we want to convert not only the raw data, but the appearance of the information as well, so we select "Convert as much of the formatting as possible":

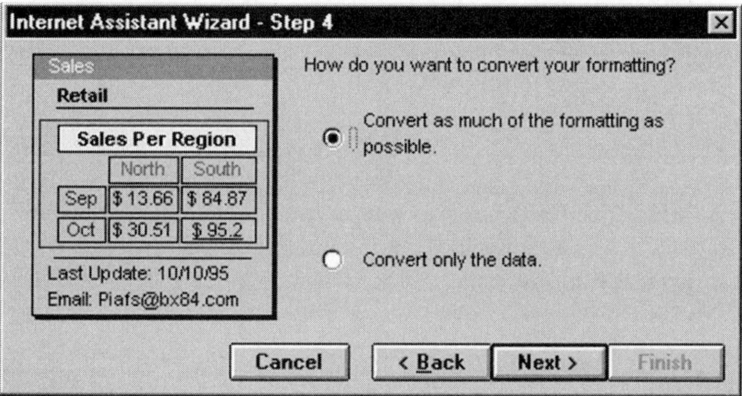

We then pick a name for the file. In this example we will use the name "test.htm" and save it in the c:\excel directory:

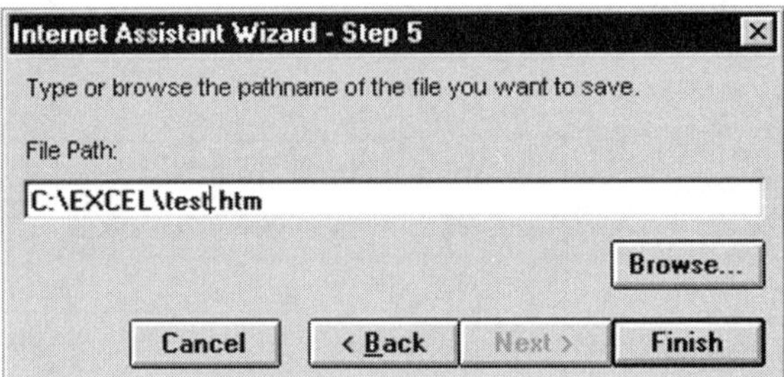

Click "Finish" and you are done. You can now open the document using your favorite Web browser. Below we show you what the document looks like with Netscape Navigator. Using Netscape Navigator, you simply click on "File" from the menu bar, choose "Open File," and then you select the file "test.htm" from the c:\excel directory:

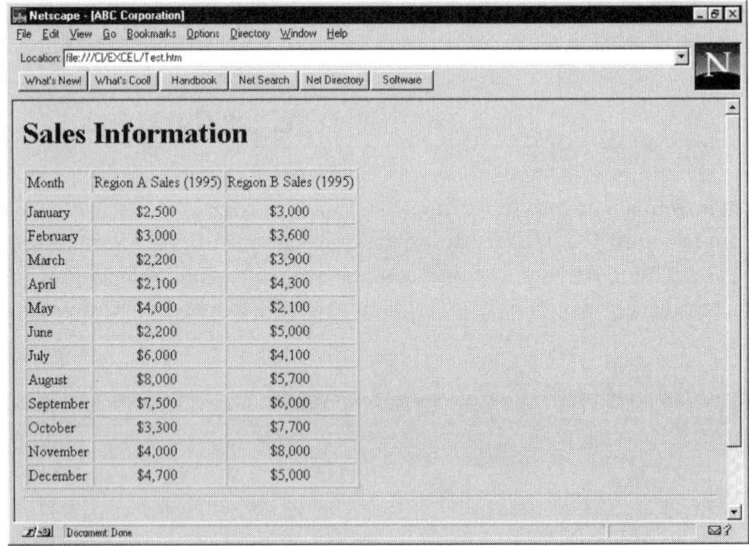

Sales Information

Month	Region A Sales (1995)	Region B Sales (1995)
January	$2,500	$3,000
February	$3,000	$3,600
March	$2,200	$3,900
April	$2,100	$4,300
May	$4,000	$2,100
June	$2,200	$5,000
July	$6,000	$4,100
August	$8,000	$5,700
September	$7,500	$6,000
October	$3,300	$7,700
November	$4,000	$8,000
December	$4,700	$5,000

The Internet Assistant Wizard is extremely easy to use, and the entire conversion process takes only a couple of minutes. Internet Assistant Wizard is available at the Microsoft Excel Home Page (**http://www.microsoft.com/msexcel**).

Database Programs

Finally, an increasing number of programs have become available that perform special conversions between database files and the Web. Corel Web.Data, which we review below, is one example. Web.Data is quite versatile since it can convert data from a number of different database formats.

Microsoft has come out with its own conversion tool for users of its Microsoft Access program, a popular database management tool. Customers can use it to publish Microsoft Access data on the World Wide Web. It is available at the Microsoft Access Home Page (**http://www.microsoft.com/msaccess**).

If you have specialized conversion needs and have a technical inclination, you can access a listing of HTML conversion tools at the World Wide Web consortium site (**http://www.w3.org/pub/WWW/Tools/Filters.html**) or a listing of Converters to and from HTML (**http://union.ncsa.uiuc.edu/HyperNews/get/www/html/converters.html**). The latter includes messages from a mailing list about the topic. Both of these sites focus on some very technical issues, but are a good starting point to find out if conversion software is available for your particular type of data.

Corel Web.Data

Corel Web.Data is an excellent example of the types of programs becoming available to convert existing database data into a form suitable for the Web. As we mentioned above, this program is quite versatile; you can use it for all kinds of different things. If you have data in a database, Web.Data can probably convert it.

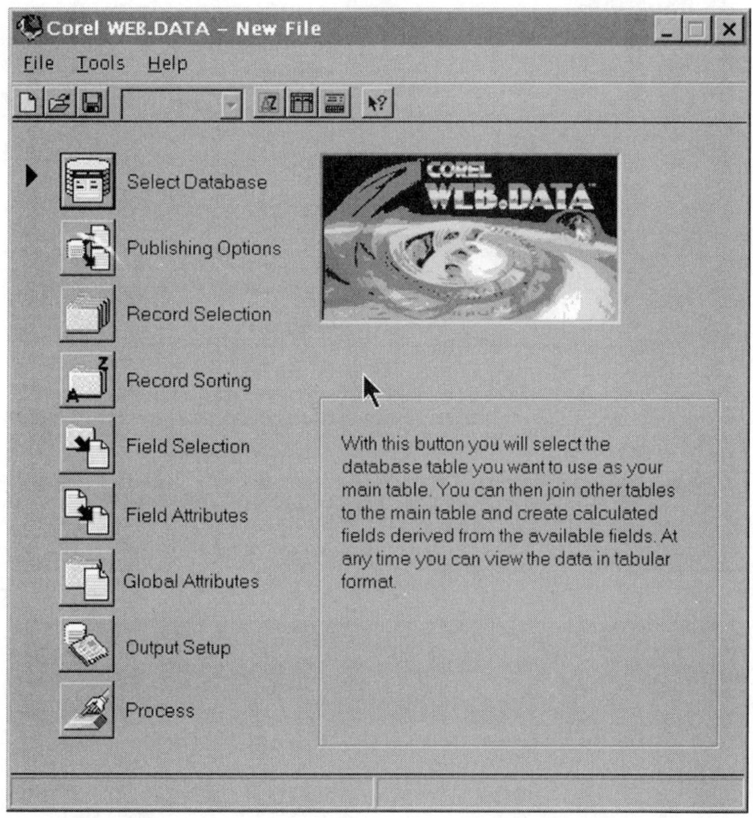

Basically, you use Corel Web.Data by walking through the steps above: selecting what database you want to convert, the formatting options that you would like to use when converting it to HTML format, and which items from the database you would like to include. There is a lot of flexibility in the way you select the data and present it. Let's go through an example. We will convert a simple music database (a listing of CDs) from Lotus 1-2-3 to an HTML file. The first thing we do is select which "fields," or which information, from the database we want to include in our HTML file: as shown in the following screen we have told Web.Data that we want only the band/artist and album title to appear on our Web page, not the other categories from our Lotus 1-2-3 file:

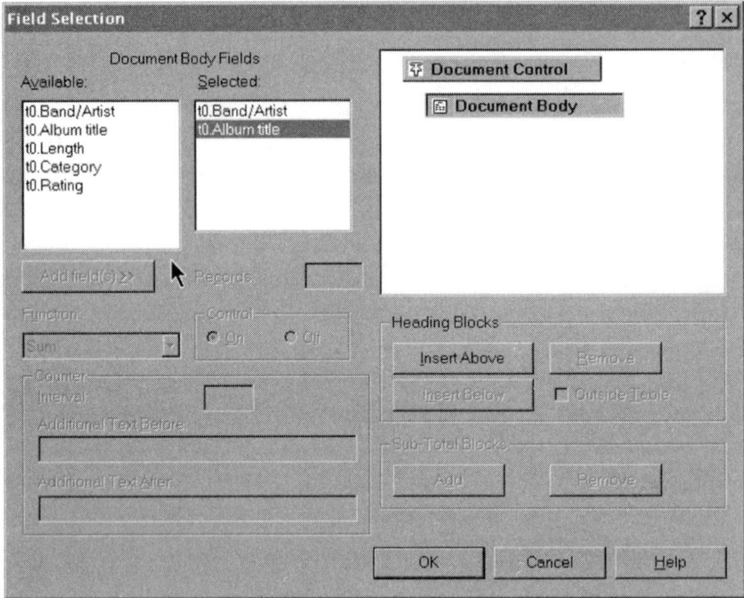

You can also instruct Web.Data to process only certain records or the entire database:

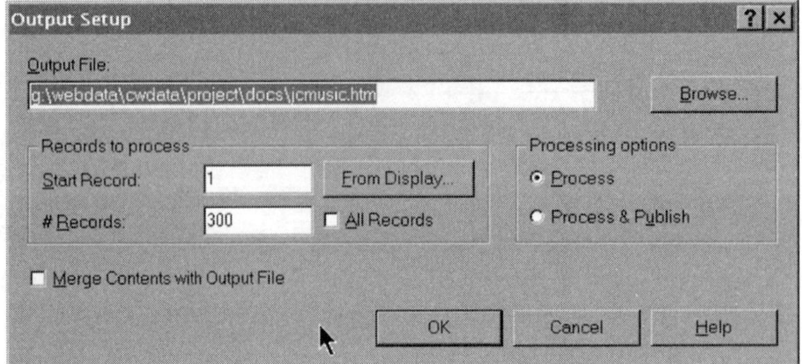

Press the process button, and you get a Web page containing your database. In this case we asked for the database to be presented in HTML table format:

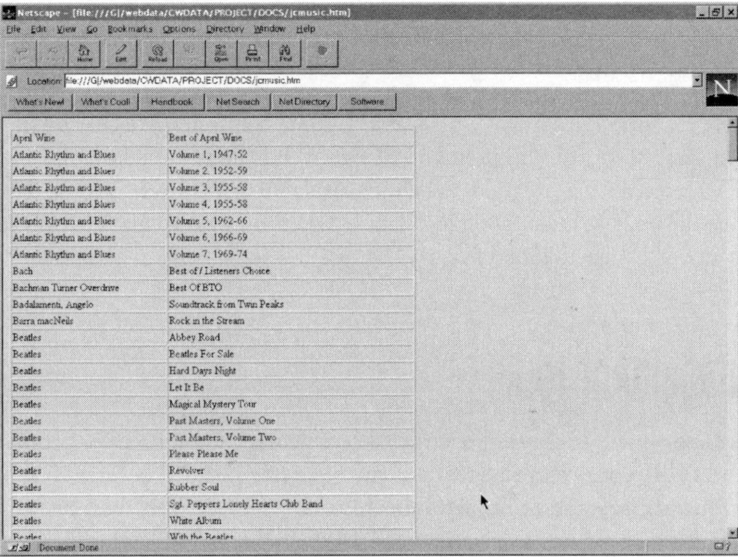

The key feature with Web.Data is the flexibility in the way you process the database. A few more keystrokes and we have added some alphabetical "section breaks," a change that took only seconds to make:

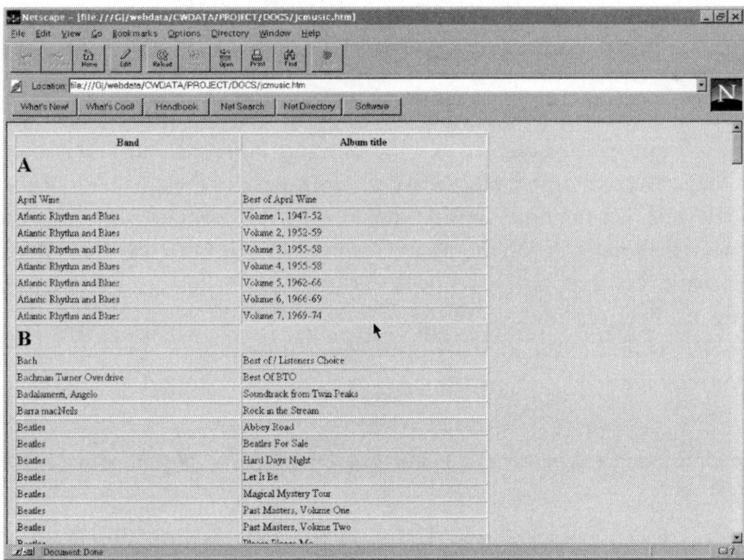

There are many other things you can do when converting a database to HTML format. You can, for example, instruct Web.Data

- to process only those records that match a certain condition ("choose only those products that are in stock," for example);
- to fill in the blanks with some predetermined text, if a particular item is empty;
- to apply formatting options (many are available) in terms of how you lay out the text from your database.

All in all, there is a lot of flexibility. Someone with some computer/database expertise could do some fairly amazing stuff with this program. Hence Web.Data is a good example of the impressive types of Web conversion programs becoming available that convert existing database files to HTML format. If you have information in a database that you want to make available on the Web, Web.Data is a good choice to look into.

Web Management Tools

With the ongoing growth in the World Wide Web there has come a need for people to check for errors in their HTML code. There are two primary types of errors that occur with a Web site: first, and most frequently, missing or broken links to Web pages or Web sites, because the linked pages have disappeared, addresses have changed, or the information has been moved to another site; second, errors in the actual HTML code itself. These often creep in because individuals prepare their HTML code in a regular text editor without the use of an HTML editor, or because errors are generated by the HTML editor itself.

Fortunately, we are seeing the emergence of new software that analyzes Web sites; there are now also Web sites that help you discover errors in your Web page.

Software

Web analysis software is being released as separate stand-alone software and is also being incorporated into basic Web editor software. Many editors now have the capability of checking for errors in HTML code. For example, consider the HoTMetaL program previously examined: it is known as one of the programs you should use if you really want to verify that your HTML code is in tip-top shape. Load any HTML document, turn on "validation," and it will come back with a lengthy list of errors found in the page.

The problem with the validation performed by many editor programs is that what they tell you about the error is often incomprehensible. For example, InContext told us that one of the errors it found was

```
SGML error at f:\jaccra_0. htm, line 113 at "<" Invalid character(s) ignored; attempting to resume DOCTYPE subset.
```

What the heck is that supposed to mean? Unfortunately, to most mere mortals, such information will be more than useless; it is a turnoff. Fortunately, there are more and more stand-alone programs that check Web sites. We look at a few here to give you an idea of the types of programs available.

InContext WebAnalyzer

InContext is the company that released InContext Spider, which we looked at earlier in this chapter. They released WebAnalyzer in 1996 to answer demands by many Web developers for tools to monitor Web sites. WebAnalyzer is a Windows 95 program that tests each and every link throughout your Web site and reports which links have problems or potential problems.

To use WebAnalyzer, you simply establish a new "project" — a new site to analyze — and tell it the URL of the Web site that you would like to have tested. WebAnalyzer then establishes a connection to the Internet (if you are not already on-line) and tests each link from that Web page and the links found on pages below that page, up to a maximum number of "levels." You can set how many levels it should check.

Depending upon the complexity of the Web site, it can take several minutes to analyze everything. Once it does, it prepares a report — in HTML format — that you can review to discover any broken links (i.e., links to other Web pages or Web sites that are not working) as well as any duplicate files in your site. Simply press a button in WebAnalyzer, and you will see this report within your Web browser:

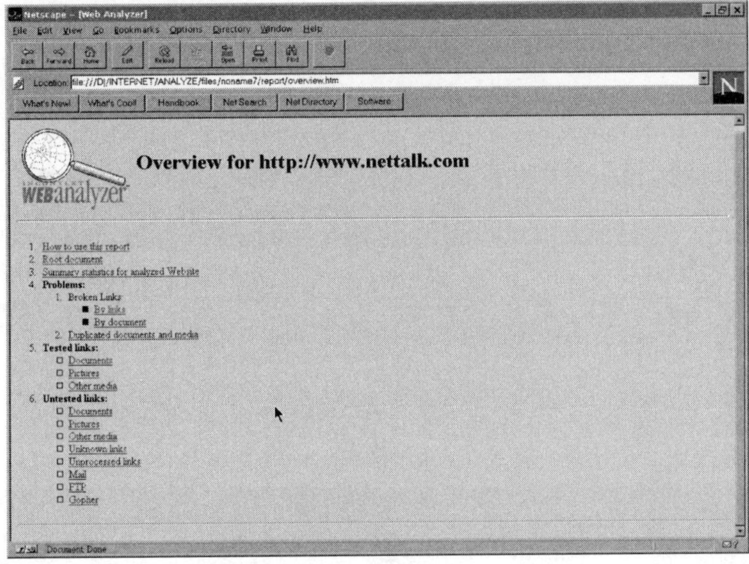

You can then choose any item for more details. For example, here is a list of "broken links" in our NetTalk Web site:

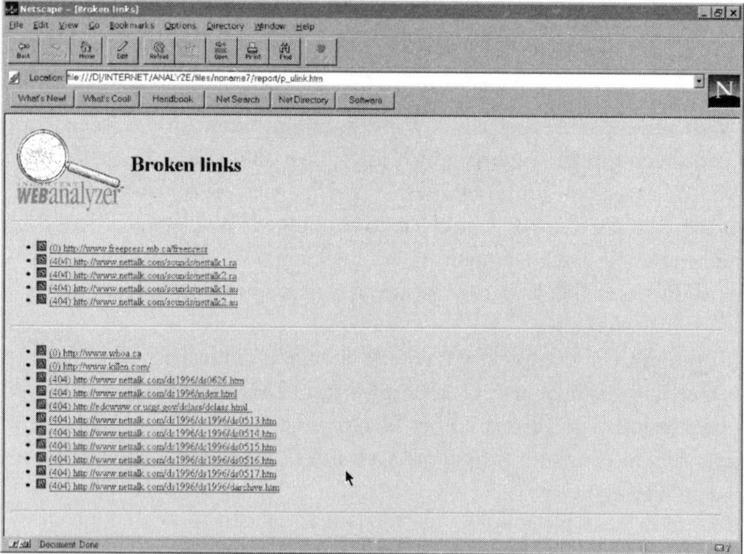

Choose any one of the broken links by double clicking on it, and you will get details about the nature of the problem that caused this to be a "broken link" by seeing the actual error message that was generated when the link was tested. This will tell you whether there was an actual error in the link or whether the error was perhaps simply due to a site being temporarily unavailable:

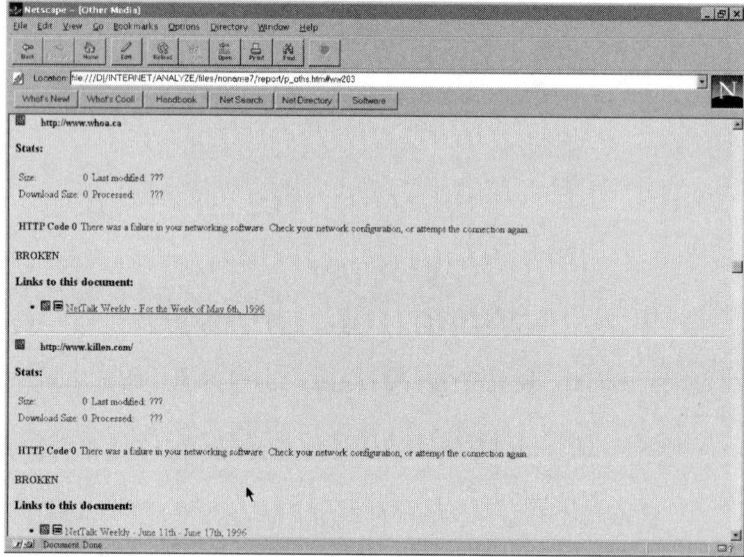

WebAnalyzer can also be used to see a graphic representation of your Web site and understand which files are pointing to other files, something that is often not easy to do. This can be useful to you as you manage individual files in your site. For example, on the following screen a pictorial representation of our NetTalk Web site is at the top right of the screen. Each item in each circle represents a file in one level of our Web site. On the left-hand side of the screen we have asked to view which files are linked to a particular file; WebAnalyzer has provided the file name:

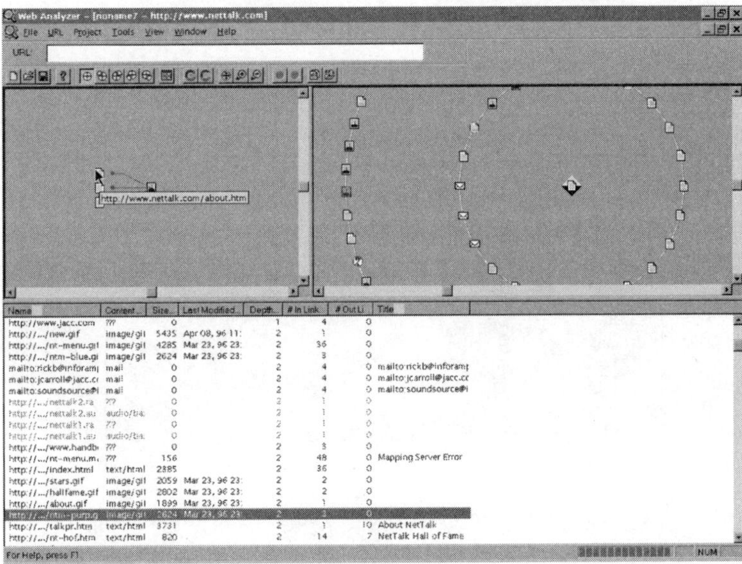

InContext WebAnalyzer is a good example of the type of program becoming available to assist people in management of their Web sites, and the few minutes invested in learning how to use it could save you hours and hours of frustration in keeping your Web site in good operating order. WebAnalyzer is available only for Windows 95 systems. You can download a trial version at InContext's Web site (**http://www.incontext.com**).

SiteMan

SiteMan is a small shareware program that has modest goals: to discover "broken links" in your Web site and to find "orphan files" (i.e., files in your Web site that really do not have a purpose). It will also do a quick search and replace of text in your Web site as well as a few other things. To run SiteMan, you must copy your Web site to a local hard disk. Unlike InContext Analyzer, it does not check a site on-line. Once you have copied it, you choose the directory containing your Web site, and then choose one of the five possible actions:

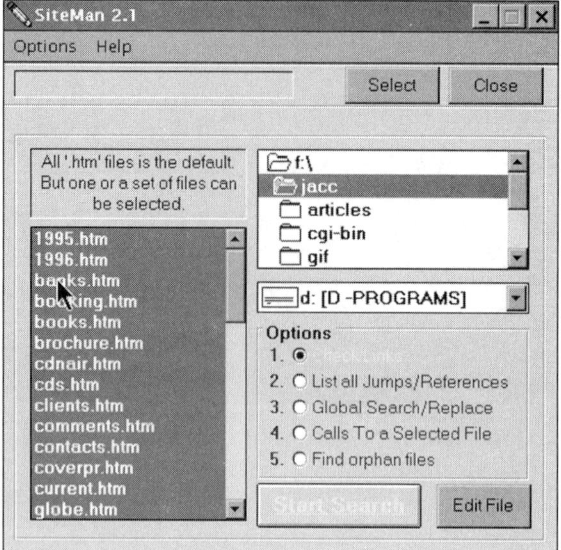

Choose "check links," and within a minute or two you get a summary:

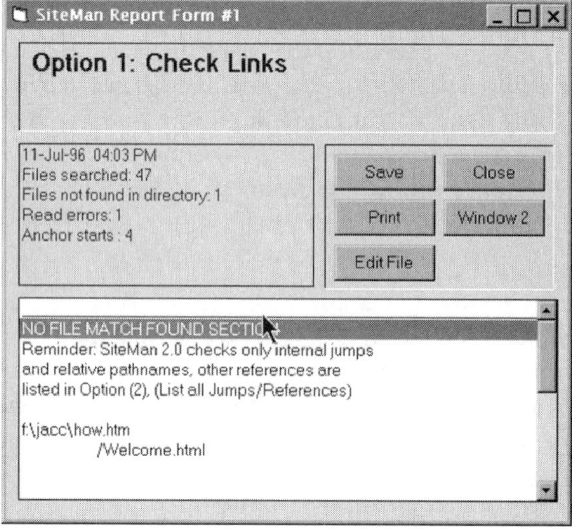

Choose "Find Orphan Files," that is, files that do not match up to anything in your Web site, and SiteMan will report on these too:

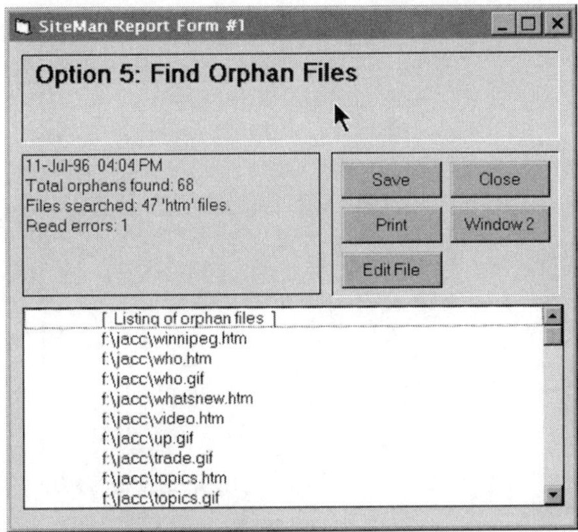

SiteMan is an effective tool that, despite its modest goals, gets the job done quickly and is recommended for anyone with a Web site. You can find it on-line at **http://www.morning.asn.au/siteman/**.

SiteMill

SiteMill is perhaps the most sophisticated Web management program that we examine in this chapter. SiteMill is an upgraded version of PageMill, reviewed previously. You can use it to create your Web pages with all the features, and then some, of PageMill. But it also provides a tool with which you can manage the site and find errors, find which files refer to other files, examine external links, and access other information that will help you keep your site in tip-top shape. SiteMill also provides a list of the external URLs that are referenced from pages in your own Web site.

To use SiteMill, you simply indicate a local directory where your Web site can be found; you must have made a copy on your local Macintosh or Windows 95 system. It examines every file throughout your Web site and then builds a number of interactive reports that you can examine. First, it builds a report detailing the structure of your Web site: every file within the site is listed, and information about what that file links to and which file links to it is easily obtainable by clicking on the double arrows in the middle of the screen:

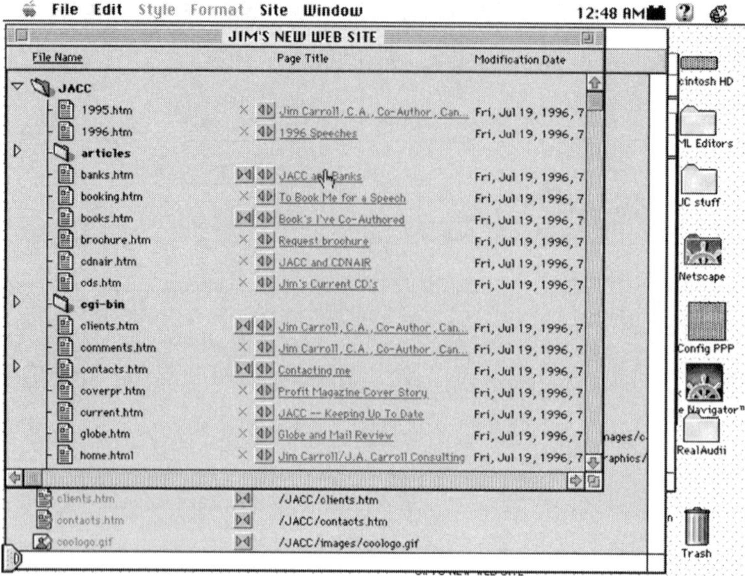

You can work your way through this report to quickly gain key information about your site, to discover unused files that may exist within your site, and to examine the links throughout the site. You can, for example, click on a folder to expand the information about the files within that folder/directory:

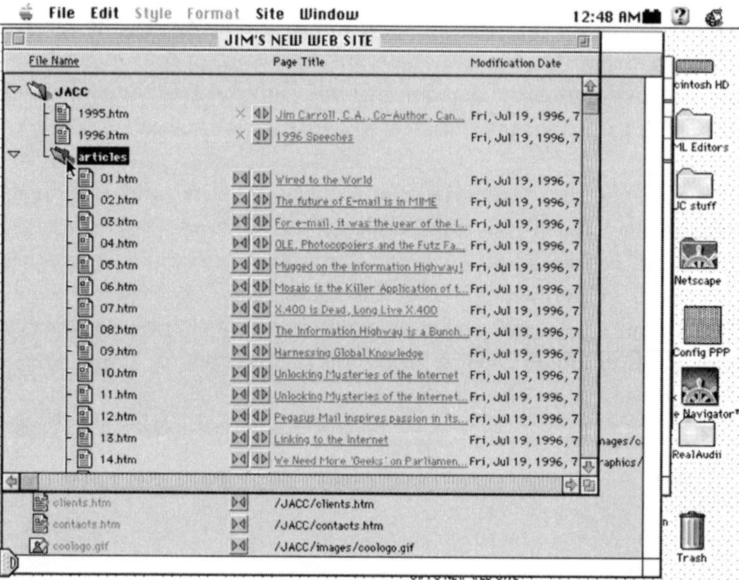

And, most importantly, any files with red X's indicate an error with that file. To find out more, you can turn to the error report, which lists files that are either not linked to anything in your Web site or have a reference to another file that does not seem to exist:

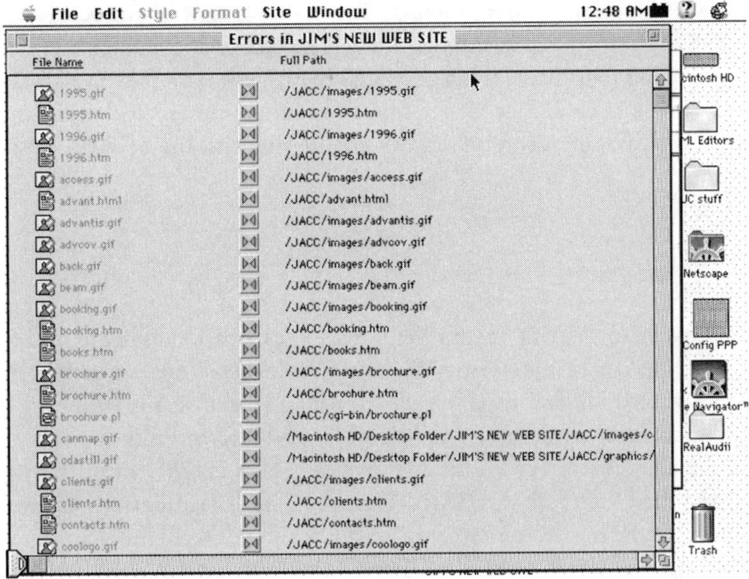

You can quickly run through this report to figure out what the problems with the various files might be, and work on fixing them. As errors with particular files are cleared up, they disappear from the listing.

Another extremely useful aspect of SiteMill is that you can fix many of these broken links simply by dragging over the file that the link should be referring to, which automatically fixes the HTML code. This reinforces the whole philosophy of PageMill/SiteMill that you do not need to go into the HTML code to prepare and maintain a Web site. Finally, you can access a list of external Web sites that are referenced from your site, and you can click on each to find out which specific HTML file in your site refers to that external site:

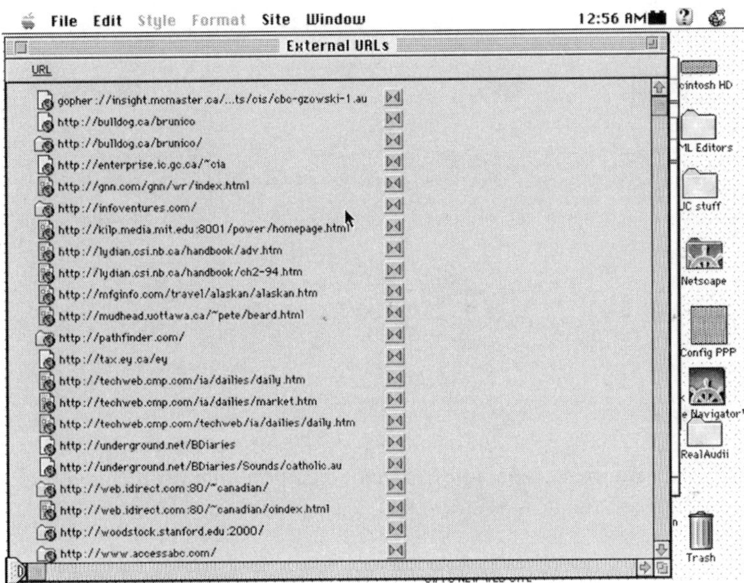

And if you want to change the URL of such a site, you simply change one occurrence of it, and each and every HTML site that refers to that site will be changed. Small features like this make SiteMill an outstanding tool. SiteMill is a good example of where most Web editors need to go: beyond offering simple HTML page preparation and further into the field of site management. It is well worth a look. For more information about SiteMill, visit the Adobe Web site at **http://www.adobe.com**.

Web Sites

In addition to software tools that test your Web site, you can use a number of on-line Web sites that will test your Web page for any errors. Simply provide one of these sites with your URL; it will pause for a few seconds, and then come back with a report on any problems it may have found. These sites will report both on HTML errors and broken links. A good place to find these sites is in the Yahoo! category "Validation Checkers" under HTML (**http://www.yahoo.com/Computers_and_Internet/Software/Data_Formats/HTML/Validation_Checkers/**). Keep in mind that many of the sites in this category are quite complex technically, so you may have to try a few to find one that makes you feel comfortable.

Doctor HTML

Doctor HTML (**http://imagiware.com/RxHTML/**) is an on-line service that runs several tests on a Web site, including a spelling check, checking the integrity of links to other Web pages and sites, and verifying the structure of elements in a page. Just provide the URL of the site that you want to have checked and indicate the tests that you want to run:

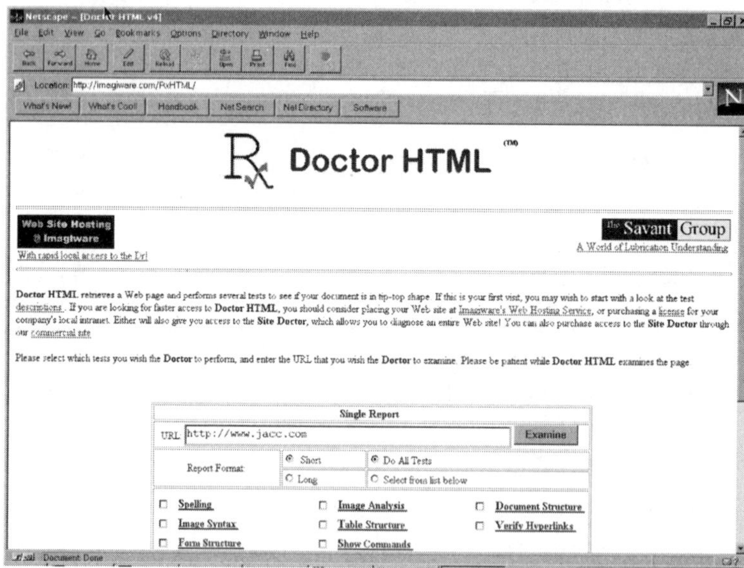

You then get back a summary report of problems and potential problems found within your site:

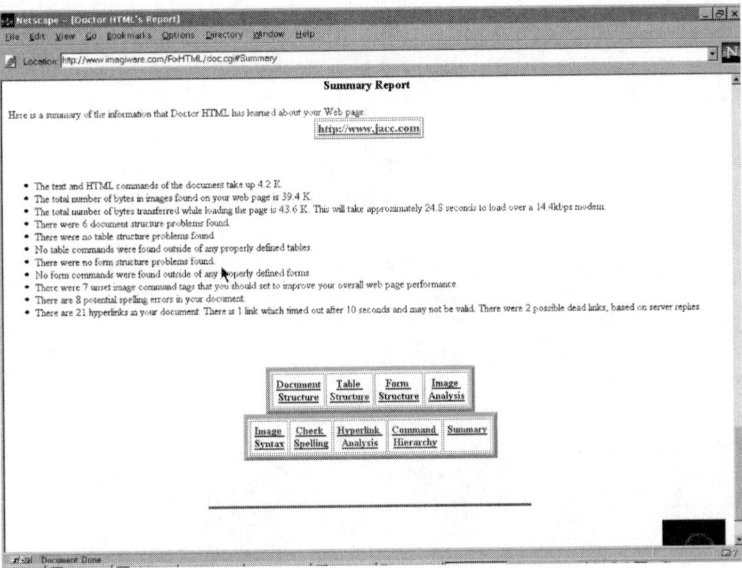

You can examine any one of the problem areas for a more detailed report; there are also suggestions on what you can do to fix them:

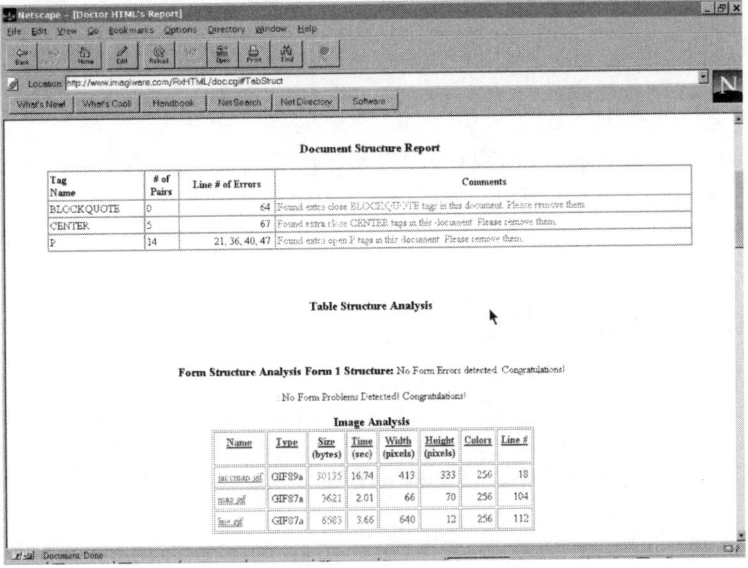

Tag Name	# of Pairs	Line # of Errors	Comments
BLOCKQUOTE	0	64	Found extra close BLOCKQUOTE tags in this document. Please remove them.
CENTER	5	67	Found extra close CENTER tags in this document. Please remove them.
P	14	21, 36, 40, 47	Found extra open P tags in this document. Please remove them.

Name	Type	Size (bytes)	Time (sec)	Width (pixels)	Height (pixels)	Colors	Line #
jaccmap.gif	GIF89a	30135	16.74	413	333	256	18
map.gif	GIF87a	3621	2.01	66	70	256	104
line.gif	GIF87a	6583	3.66	640	12	256	112

Doctor HTML is a simple, effective, and useful tool to check the integrity of your Web site. Of particular note are some of its special features. For example, it will advise you how long any images might take to download through a 14,400 baud modem, thus giving you an idea whether your site might be considered too graphic-intensive. Definitely worth a visit.

WebLint

WebLint is similar to Doctor HTML in that it checks your site on-line. There are many WebLint sites available, since the program itself is based on computer code that is given away for free on the Internet. Hence you can do a quick search in Yahoo! for the word "WebLint" and find any number of sites that can test a Web page for errors. It works like Doctor HTML: just provide your URL, and it will go off to test the site. Within a few minutes you will have a report of what it found.

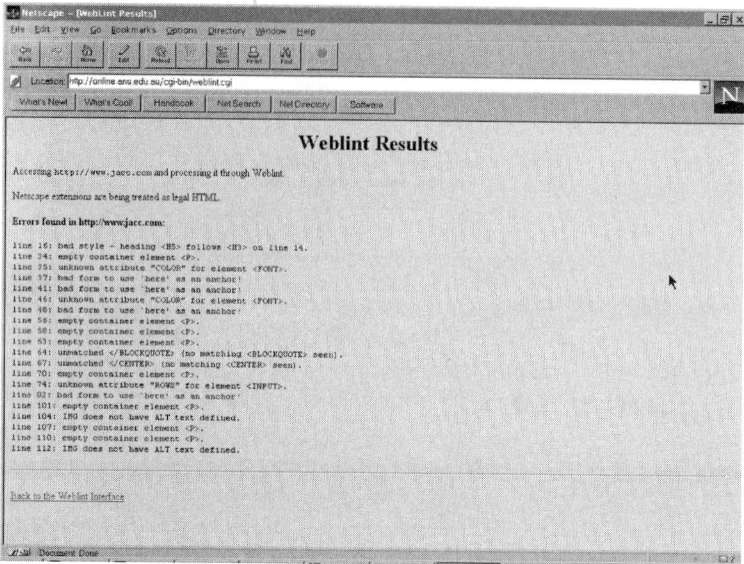

Although not as comprehensive as Doctor HTML, it will point out some straightforward errors within a Web site. You can try out WebLint at **http://www.cen.uiuc.edu/cgi-bin/weblint**.

The Future of HTML Editors

Of course, the real trend with Web page development is that there will be less of a need for people to prepare Web pages in HTML format. This is because many organizations and individuals who have built large-scale Web sites that consist of 100 pages or more now realize that the administration and maintenance time can become excessive. Naturally, a market has emerged for tools to help solve the dilemma.

We saw some of these tools above, in the Web analyzer and Web site management software reviews. But even such tools do not go all the way in solving the potential magnitude of the problem. Hence the emergence of new, sophisticated tools that generate Web pages on demand. Hold on. We are about to get a little complex here.

Think about what we have covered in this chapter: we have examined how to create text files that contain HTML code in proper format. Those text files are then made available on a Web server, so that anyone with a Web browser can view the page. In the future HTML will still be used as the common language of the Web, but more sophisticated Web sites will use tools that will generate the necessary HTML code only when someone asks to view a particular page of information. Why? Because such tools will help to ease the maintenance and administration nightmare that many organizations are encountering.

DisplayPage

An excellent example of this type of thinking is a product called DisplayPage, from a Mississauga, ON, based company, e-Commerce. What DisplayPage does is allow a Web designer to create a number of "templates" which define the layout of a particular Web page. Data for those templates are then stored separately to be used as needed.

Here is what happens when a visitor with a Web browser visits a site based on DisplayPage: the template that defines the layout of the page to be shown is matched up with appropriate data for that page, and the HTML code is put together by DisplayPage in less than a second. In effect, the data for the page are used to "fill in the blanks" within the template for that page. Hence instead of a bunch of HTML files sitting around, HTML code is automatically generated by the Web server when needed and "served" to the visitor with their browser.

For an example of DisplayPage in action, travel to FedEx Canada (**http://www.fedex.ca**) and browse around. Choose "Tracking, " for example, rather than a Web URL such as **http://www.fedex.ca/tracking.html**, you get one that looks like this: **http://www.fedex.ca/FedExCa/cgi-bin/DisplayPage?SITE=FedExCa&KEY=track&TRACKID=MC_3369**, as seen on the following screen:

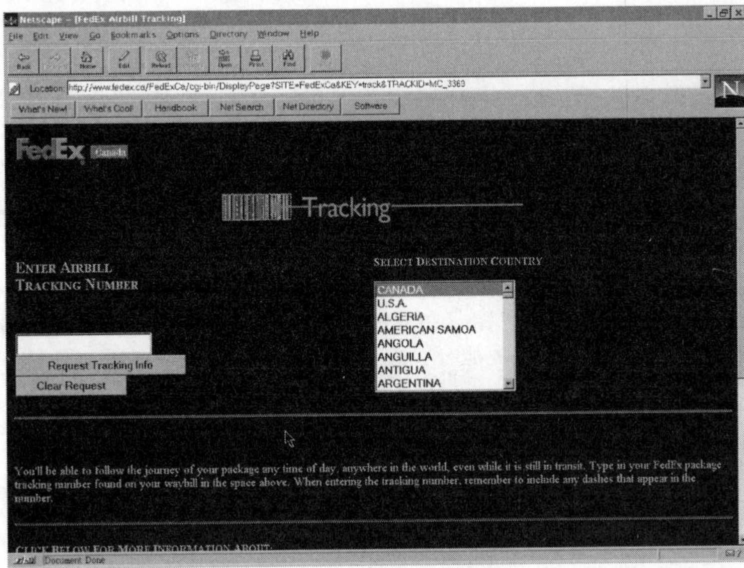

What has happened here? DisplayPage has done several things:

- It has created the basic layout for the page, based on the page design specified by the original designers for this particular type of page.
- It has pulled in the data for the destination country by generating a query to a database that contains the appropriate data.

- It has pulled together the text for the page from another file.
- It has then generated the HTML code in less than a second from this diverse source.

It is still regular HTML: click on "View/Document Source" if you want to, but it is not HTML that exists on a Web server. But visit any page on FedEx Canada, and you are seeing Web pages that were generated a second or two ago by a computer.

What is the benefit of such a system? Consider a simple example. At one point FedEx Canada wanted to change the copyright notice that appeared on the bottom of each and every Web page on its site. In a normal Web environment this would have necessitated changes to hundreds of computer files, something that could take several hours. For FedEx all that was involved was visiting a form, asking for the copyright element, and changing it. Instantly, any Web page viewed from that point on would have the new copyright element in place. In effect, DisplayPage turns hours of work into seconds — just like that. You can get more information on DisplayPage at the e-Commerce Web site at **http://www.e-commerce.com**.

Linking of Database Technology to the Web

DisplayPage is but one example of how the world of HTML publishing is being turned upside down through a very close integration with database systems. Clearly, this is the future of the Web, because many business organizations have realized that there are strategic opportunities to be found through involvement with the World Wide Web and that customers are seeking real content and real information on-line. As management becomes involved in strategic planning involving use of the Internet, the opportunity to make available selected information from a corporate database to the customer and other parties is discovered.

Thus we are seeing a lot of linking of internal corporate information databases to the Web, thus permitting visitors to interact with large volumes of information, which has a direct impact on how organizations are going about creating the HTML code for their sites.

Think about this fact: many corporate organizations worldwide run their accounting, financial, inventory tracking, and other database systems on sophisticated database technology from companies such as Oracle and Sybase. Keep in mind that both of these software organizations have released tools with which organizations can link their corporate information systems with the Web in order to provide an electronic link to their customers through the Internet. It would work like this:

A customer visits a Web site and wants to determine if a particular part is in stock. She fills in a form on the Web site. At that point, the information is taken from the form and is presented to the corporate database as a question:

- "Yes, the part is in stock," replies the corporate database, at which point a Web page is automatically constructed that contains the details and is shown to the customer.
- Verifying availability, the customer decides to fill out a purchase order requisition to buy the product. Once the form is completed, the information from the Web form is automatically extracted and is presented to the corporate database as a purchase order.
- A confirmation is made by the corporate database, a new Web page is constructed, and the customer is advised that her order has been processed.

Science fiction? No. The technology to support such an integration is already available and is being implemented on many of the leading-edge Web sites on the Internet. We mention this here because in these circumstances the HTML code for a page is also being "assembled" when needed, because each and every Web page for the queries described above will be different.

If you really want an idea of where the sophistication of the Web is headed, take a voyage to the American Airlines Travelocity system (**http://www.travelocity.com**) and ask to look up a flight schedule. You fill out a few forms, and within a few seconds you have a detailed listing of the requested flights:

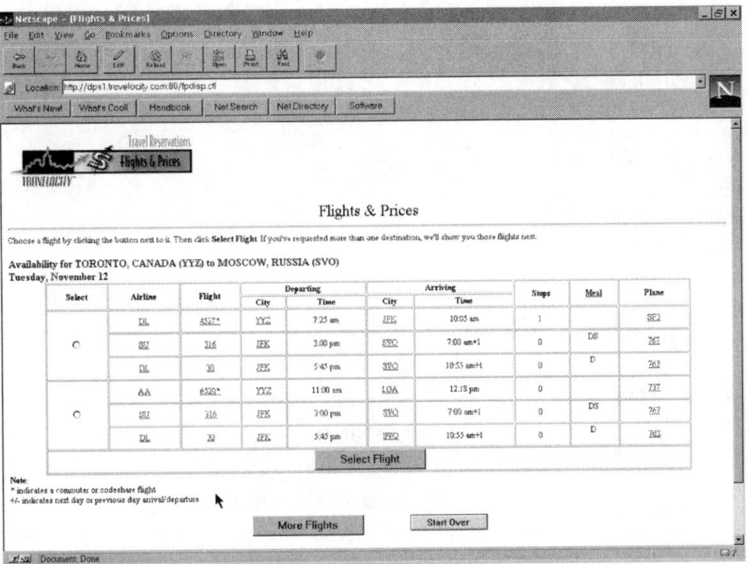

What happened when you visited this site? Several things:

- The information that you provided in the form was used to generate a query to the massive airline reservation system at American Airlines.
- The information from the query, containing the flights and prices, was then used to construct the Web page seen above, based on a predefined layout.

The integration of database technology into the Internet is opening up all kinds of new opportunities for companies to establish strategic applications on the Internet or for an organization to fulfill its mandate. This is probably one of the most significant trends in the industry today. As the trend continues to evolve, it will have a definite and significant impact on the types of Web editor/conversion software that we have examined in this chapter. We believe that

- rather than editors that create HTML files, we will see the emergence of tools that help users design Web templates defining the layout of pages on their sites, with data filled in as appropriate depending upon what the visitor asks;
- rather than converting a database into a format that can be viewed on the Web, the database will be *linked* into a Web site, so that it can be queried at any time.

We believe that we are sitting on the tip of the iceberg in terms of the sophistication of Web preparation software.

CHAPTER 16

Thinking Strategically About the Internet

The problem with the information highway and the Internet, which is one of its key components, is that it's so revolutionary nobody knows where it's going, what products or services it will spawn, what people want or will use it for, or how anyone can profit from it.

Adam Mayers, The Toronto Star, May 13, 1996

Dismissing the Net now would be like telling Alexander Graham Bell that he could never make the telephone a commercial success unless he could find a way to sell something over it. I mean seriously, who would pay simply to use the phone?

Inc. Online, **http://www.inc.com/beyondthemag/real_time/internet_backlash.html**

No one has the Internet figured out yet. Go back and have a look at the many predictions and comments we made in Chapter 1. It is obvious, isn't it, that it is easy for anyone to make a mistake. And it should be evident that it is a challenge for people to figure out what might be real and what is not when it comes to the future. And just as latter-day experts made many mistakes in their predictions and comments about new technologies, events, and ideas, so too do many of today's observers of the Internet phenomena.

So let's be honest: no one really knows what the Internet means today or what it will mean in the future. This is an important point, whether you are already a user of the Internet or whether you intend to become one soon, particularly when it comes to trying to discover how to do business on-line. *No one has got this thing figured out!* Let's consider this thought in more depth.

Business Has Not Yet Figured Out the Business Model of the Internet

If you are a business person already involved with the Internet, you are probably doing your best trying to figure out some type of business advantage from it. You might be trying to sell products or services on-line, or you might be using the Internet to assist in your marketing and support efforts. You are probably trying to discover how to make money on-line.

And if you are not yet involved with the Internet, you might still be wondering how you can do these things. You might have bought this book to take advantage of some of those "cyberspace riches" that everyone seems to be talking about.

But let's be honest. When it comes to business applications, it is our belief that no one has really figured out what the Internet is all about. We have around us business structures and methods and ways of doing business that go back, in some cases, several decades or several hundreds of years. And all of a sudden, along comes a computer technology that we all know will somehow change our business world, but none of us can be sure exactly what the change will be.

It also seems to be quite true that even as business becomes involved with the Internet, managers are quite hesitant about doing so. They are venturing into the network, seeking to market, sell products, and support customers on-line, but it is painfully evident that they are not providing adequate budgets or resources to do so. They have one foot in the water and one foot on the beach, and they are afraid to dive in all the way. The result? Only marginal success from their initiatives so far, or in other cases, absolutely none. You can't get wet unless you go in the water.

What is happening with the Internet and business? One sure thing is failure. Many individuals behind various Internet initiatives in 1996 began to lose money, and inevitably some will scale back their efforts dramatically while others shut down altogether. One of the biggest Internet flops of 1996 was the U.S. National Association of Realtors' information network, which was designed to provide extensive real estate information on the World Wide Web. The project ran out of its $12.9 million in funding and fell victim to "overly ambitious goals and unexpected changes in technology," according to one report.

THINKING STRATEGICALLY ABOUT THE INTERNET

1. Despite all the hoopla about the Internet in the business community, it is obvious that no one has truly figured out the role of the Internet in a business context.
2. Even so, the Internet is very real, and will have a significant and profound impact on the business community in years to come.
3. There are several reasons why the Internet is important in a business context: The average consumer is increasingly turning to the Internet for information; it is emerging as the foundation for much that the computer industry does today, and the financial community is beginning to implement the necessary infrastructure to support business on-line.
4. The impact of the Internet is that it will lead to disintermediation — a reduction in the role of the middleman — and increased competition within the business community.
5. Organizations seeking to use the Internet for business purposes should consider how it can be used for competitive advantage, to establish efficiencies and cost savings, or to restructure their business activities.
6. Organizations should plan their Internet strategy carefully, thinking about it from a strategic, not just a technical, perspective.
7. Too many organizations have become caught up in the hype of the Internet, and are making many fundamental mistakes in their approaches to it.

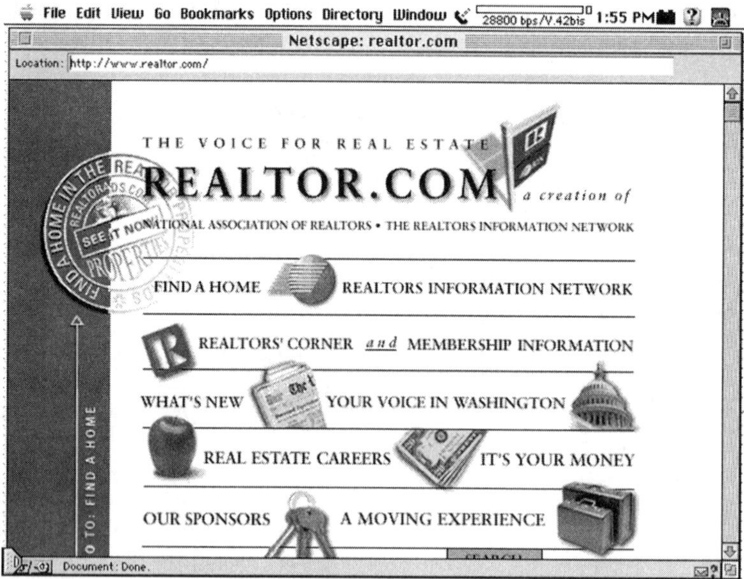

If the business model for the Internet remains unknown, such failures are not unexpected, just as some business initiatives fail in the "real world." But at the same time many other Web initiatives will continue, and some will become profitable as elements of the long-sought business model begin to emerge.

Too many people with dollar signs in their eyes are plunging into something that they do not fully comprehend, and while they try to comprehend it, it changes continually. There are far too many people involved with the Internet who have fallen for the belief that it is a modern-day gold rush, and throughout 1997 we will see many of them humbled as they realize the limitations imposed by the slow state of evolution of the business model on the network. So when it comes to thinking strategically about the Internet, we make one specific comment: there seems to be precious little of it.

Many organizations concentrate on the short-term potential of the Internet by putting up a Web site without really thinking about their actions. In doing so, they are not taking the time to fully understand the short-, medium-, and longer-term potential that the Internet might represent to their business. Sadly, the carnival atmosphere that surrounds the Internet is causing people to make decisions that are, perhaps, diverting their attention away from the real strategic opportunity that the Internet represents.

Confusing Messages

Perhaps part of the reason people have not figured the Internet out is due to the fact that it is truly so new, but the problem is worsened by the many contradictory messages that surround the network. Consider, for example, some of the headlines that appeared in the *Globe and Mail* during a six-week period, from December 15, 1995 to January 31, 1996:

- "Firms say Internet unsafe for business — Fear of electronic break-ins making North American companies network-shy, survey shows";

- "Internet commerce deemed dead — Consultant says businesses can't justify cost of maintaining public presence in cyberspace";
- " '96 tips: Forget the Net";
- "Dose of reality predicted for Web";
- "World Wide Web called house of cards";
- "Fear of electronic break-ins making North American companies network-shy, survey shows."

Reading such messages, the average executive might tend to believe that the Internet is just a lot of hype — a management fad, so to speak — that is destined to wither on the vine in 1996 and disappear completely shortly thereafter. But consider other headlines in the same publication that ran during the same time period:

- "GM plans Internet drive — The world's largest auto maker is starting an aggressive attempt to become No. 1 in marketing cars and trucks on the Internet";
- "Little Known Facts — The NFL's Super Bowl Internet web site (http://superbowl.com) registered 28 million hits in January, including six million on Super Bowl Sunday";
- "BETTER BUSINESS TRAVEL — Using the Internet to book your stay with Delta Hotels";
- "Canada Trust finds Internet solutions — Trust company's clients gain access, security";
- "FOCUS ON THE INTERNET — The Internet emerges as essential business tool."

The average executive is bombarded with so many different versions of the same story that he/she might feel a little like Alice, waking up in a world in which nothing makes sense anymore. This makes it particularly challenging for an organization to come up with a cohesive, coherent, and realistic business strategy involving the Internet.

Is the Internet Real?

Regardless of the current, excessive hype that surrounds the Internet, the fact is the Internet is very real, and it will, through the next decade, have a profound impact on the business community. The impact will be felt because of two simple facts:

- The Internet is the leading edge of a trend in which computer and computer networks around the world are linking together, resulting in one massive, large-scale global network that brings together individuals, businesses, governments, educational institutions, science and research bodies, and other organizations.
- A computer network that permits such widescale electronic interaction in the business world has never existed before, and the belief is that this massive network is leading us to the era of *networked business*, one in which organizations will conduct day-to-day business with their customers and other organizations around the corner and around the globe through the Internet.

The mere existence of a computer-based network through which customers can conduct business electronically will inevitably lead to a change in the way that business is conducted around the globe, since it compresses the time that it takes for communications to occur between business organizations and their customers. Such a network provides the potential for cost savings in those communications and allows business organizations to publish information for access by their customers at a very low cost. *That, from a bottom line perspective, is what the Internet is all about.*

Consider 3M Corporation (**http://www.mmm.com**), manufacturers of the world-famous Post-It Notes. 3M has decided to distribute free samples of its popular "Software Notes" product through the Internet. (Software Notes is the electronic version of Post-It Notes; they work on your computer.)

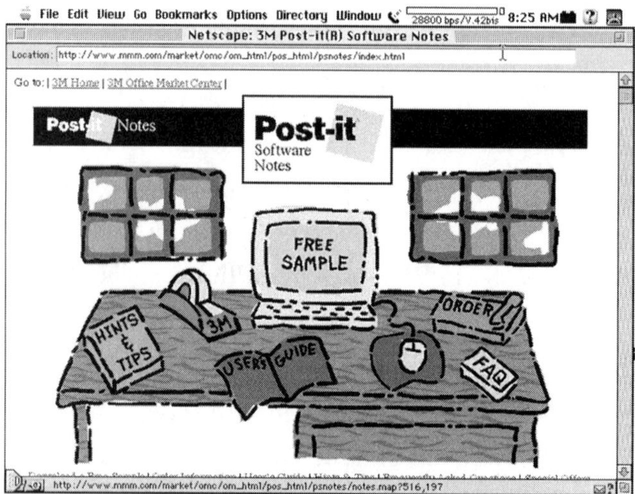

3M has established a World Wide Web site where it invites customers to download a sample of the product for a free 30-day trial (try it!). A full user's guide is provided on-line that explains, step by step, how to download the product and install it.

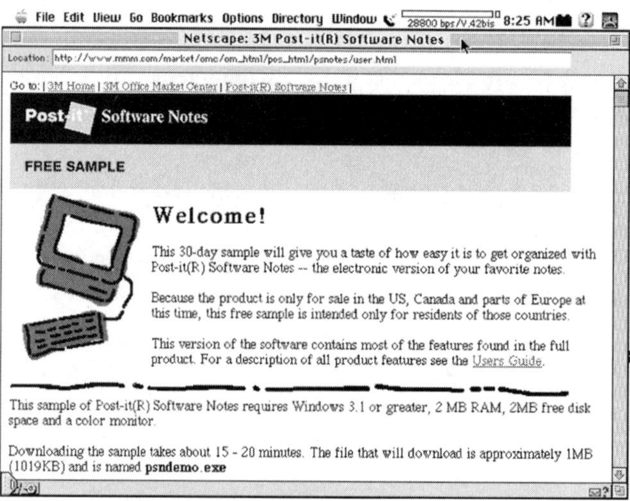

Should you like the product enough, you can even order it through the Internet when the 30-day trial expires:

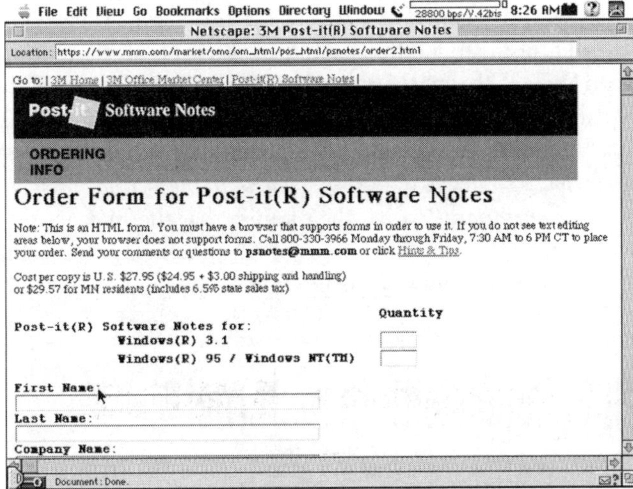

What is the point we are trying to make here? 3M has applied the Internet in such a way that 3M's incremental distribution and order-processing costs may be reduced; 3M is also using the network to encourage trial of a new product, two valid and useful business strategies.

Every time an interested customer downloads a sample of the product off the Internet or places an order on-line, the additional cost to 3M is negligible. When customers request a sample of the product, there are no postage and handling costs whatsoever, and delivery of the product is immediate. Best of all, because the Internet is being used to distribute the free samples and take orders for the commercial version, customers worldwide have access to the site 24 hours a day, 7 days a week, regardless of what time zone they are in.

Is the 3M initiative on the Internet so big that it is earthshaking to their business? Absolutely not. And we would expect that results to date are marginal at best. But what 3M is doing is taking the necessary steps to discover the business formula of the Internet: how do we reach out to our customers and build an electronic relationship with them? It is a question that takes a lot of work to answer, and the answer does not become apparent for quite some time.

The Role of the Internet in Business

Many people seem to be rather impatient with how long it takes for a technology to be implemented and how long it can take for a technology to have a real and substantial impact on day-to-day business activities. Such is the case with the Internet; many people simply have overexpectations for how long it will take the network to have a positive impact on our business world. It is an important point, and we will talk more about it later.

But the problem manifests itself through the fact that there are many people clearly *awed* by the interactive nature of the Internet, who write breathless articles that predict that the next wave of "interactive on-line sales" is firmly upon us in the form of the Internet. And they are contradicted by the skeptics who write that the Internet is really all just a waste of time and that it would do us well to ignore it.

To the authors, the most fascinating thing about the debate between these two camps is that each side draws a "definitive conclusion" about the Internet, and for all intents and purposes, the Internet has only been around for a couple of years. Think about it: the Internet and, in particular, the World Wide Web, only began to invade our consciousness in the last few years.

It is all very, very new, and yet already we are seeing "experts" declare definitive conclusions about it: either it is a success, or it is a failure. We believe it is too early to judge that. As we wrote in our Internet business strategy guide, *The Canadian Internet Advantage — Opportunities for Business and Other Organizations*, "for all the promise that the Internet shows, we need to keep in mind that we are still in the very early stages of a significant development. We need to be cautious and realistic in our expectations of the Internet."

What Is Really Going on With the Internet?

Senior executives must appreciate this about the Internet: it is the technical foundation of an emerging economy in which individuals and business will increasingly access information and undertake transactions with other business, government, associations, not-for-profits, health care institutions, and anyone else well into the future. In essence, the Internet of today is the foundation of a network that will, *over time*, increasingly carry the transactions that drive the global economy and in doing so, will come to be the economic engine of the future.

Why the Internet Is Important

We make the statement above with a straight face, because we believe that there are three key trends that are propelling the Internet forward. These trends mean that the Internet is not just a fad, but is very real and will have an important impact on business in the future.

The Electronic Consumer

One significant thing that is happening with the Internet is that it is coming to represent an absolutely massive change in the way that people obtain the information used for their purchasing decisions and the manner in which they expect to deal with companies. What we are really seeing through the Internet is the emergence of a new breed of individual in Canada, what we call the "electronic consumer," individuals whose purchasing decisions and activities are influenced by the information they find on-line. Organizations seeking to discover how to think strategically about the Internet must learn how to reach and deal with this person. The "electronic consumer" has several expectations:

- On-line product information. Increasingly, consumers are using the Internet to find information about products and services *prior* to making a purchase. They are discovering all kinds of Web sites that meet that demand. KitchenAid, for example, allows consumers to view product information and specifications for their microwaves, ranges, dishwashers, refrigerators, washers, and dryers (**http://www.kitchenaid.com**):

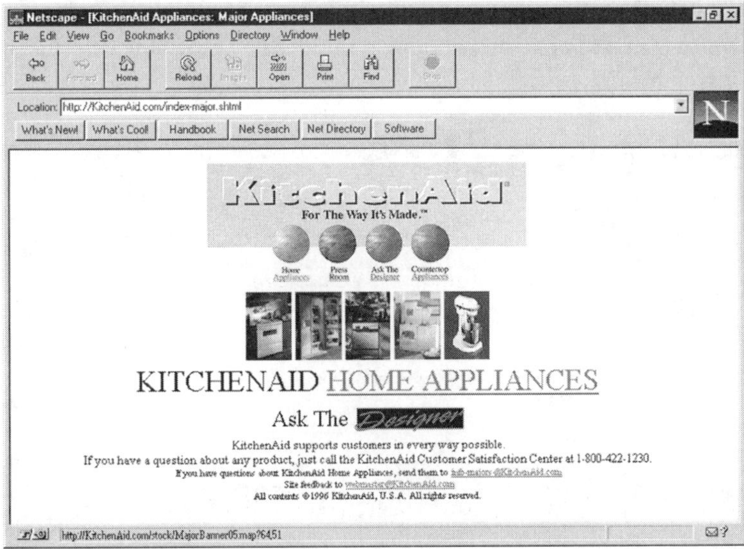

- On-line product support. Once a purchase has been made, consumers are increasingly seeking support documents on-line, such as answers to Frequently Asked Questions (FAQs) about the product, and are finding that companies are moving product support to the Internet. Have a problem with your Magnavox television set? You can call their 1-800 line, but you can also visit their World Wide Web site (**http://www.magnavox.com**), where you will find answers to the most common technical questions as well as full warranty information on all their products:

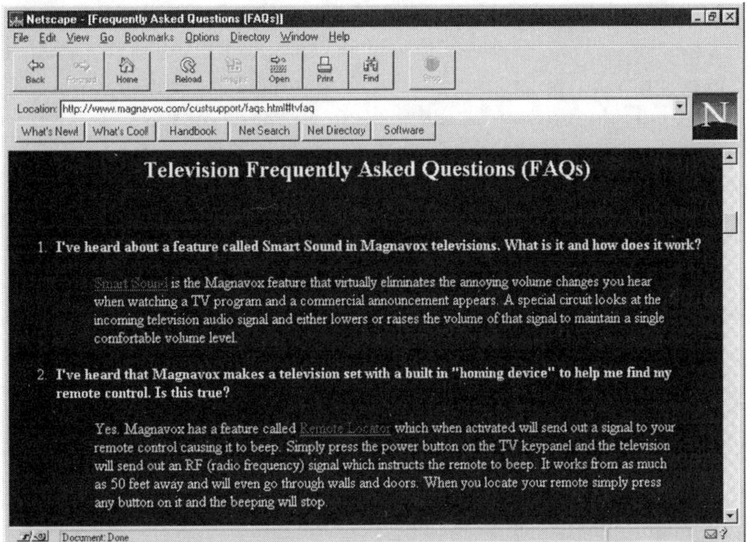

- Access to customer service. Should consumers have a complaint or comment about a product they have purchased, they are increasingly looking for the opportunity to contact the manufacturer on-line. In doing so, they expect prompt, no-hassle follow-up by the organization in question. Organizations like Northern Telecom (**http://www.nt.com**) are responding to this need by providing customer comment forms on their Web site:

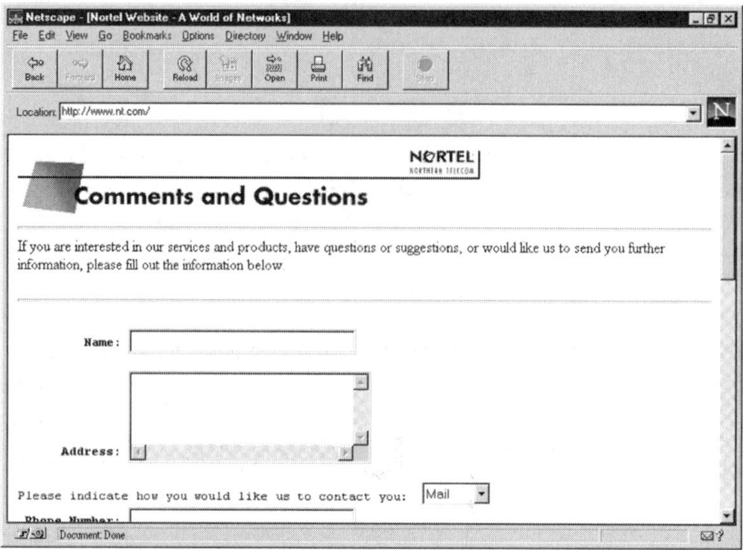

Quite simply, the electronic consumer will increasingly come to expect a business relationship with an organization that is provided through the Internet.

The next generation of consumer is going to be very different from the one we know today. This is because we are seeing, for the first time, the emergence of the first "wired generation," a generation that will forever change the business landscape. Think about it: today we have an entire generation growing up with computers and the Internet. These kids do not suffer from a fear of computers; for them, the Internet is a source of wonder, entertainment, and delight. Most important, it is a useful information tool, and to them, the media consists of television, radio, newspapers, magazines, and the Net, although not necessarily in that order.

The Internet is a very significant source of information for the wired generation. As a result, into the future most business organizations will have come to accept the fact that the "electronic consumer" is a very real — and very large — part of our market demographics. Most businesses will include methods of reaching this electronic consumer through the Internet as a fundamental part of every aspect of their everyday business strategies.

Technical Underpinnings

The second significant trend on the Internet is the technology emerging to support it. Take a look around, and you will see that the entire global computer industry is galvanized by the Internet. Consequently, too much energy, financial resources, and intellectual capital are being invested in the Internet for it not to have a significant and everlasting impact on the world of business. If the electronic consumer is real, we must also be willing to accept that the technology of the Internet will present more significant business opportunities into the future, particularly as that technology matures.

The computer industry is beginning to integrate the Internet into everything they do. Virtually every form of software, hardware, and stuff in between is being linked into the Internet or being made Internet-capable. The boundary between what is your PC and what is "out there" is blurring, as a seamless worldwide network of unprecedented proportions takes shape. Sun Microsystems has long had the motto "the network is the computer." We'll borrow that thought and say "the economy is in the network."

A Financial Infrastructure

A significant and reliable infrastructure to support financial transactions on the Internet has emerged more quickly than many people realize. Tip Top Tailors (**http://www.tiptop.ca**) is one of hundreds of Canadian retailers experimenting with on-line shopping using the Internet. Using Tip Top's Internet Shirt Buying Service, you can purchase a shirt using your Web browser and have it delivered by courier the following day. What could be easier?

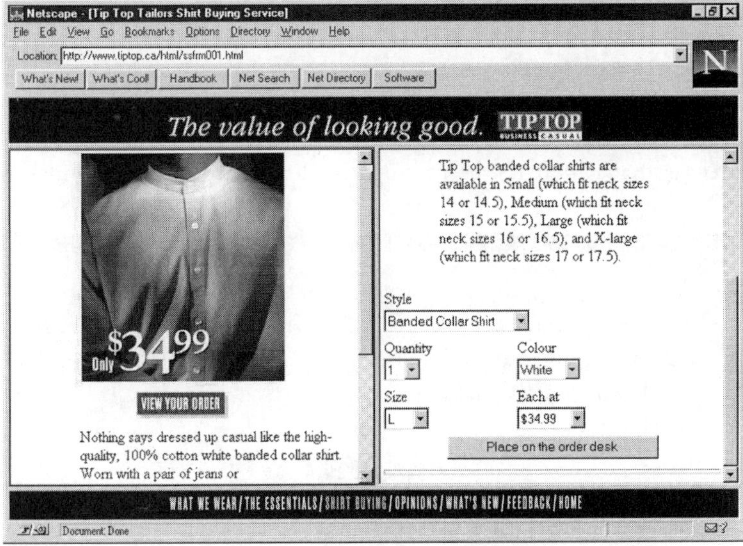

To protect its customers from credit card fraud, Tip Top uses special secure transaction software, called Secure Sockets Layer (SSL) technology, which ensures the safety of credit card information as it is being transmitted over the Internet. SSL technology involves the use of "encryption" so that your credit card information is scrambled into an unbreakable code before it is sent over the Internet. This protects you from credit card fraud, because the information could not be deciphered if it were intercepted by an unauthorized party.

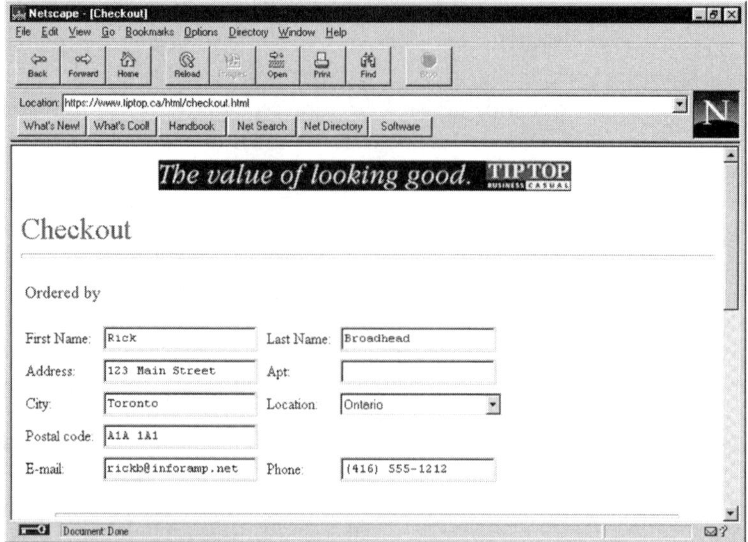

Wal-Mart (**http://www.samsclub.com**) also uses Secure Sockets Layer technology to allow Internet users to securely and safely purchase everything from luggage to cappuccino makers:

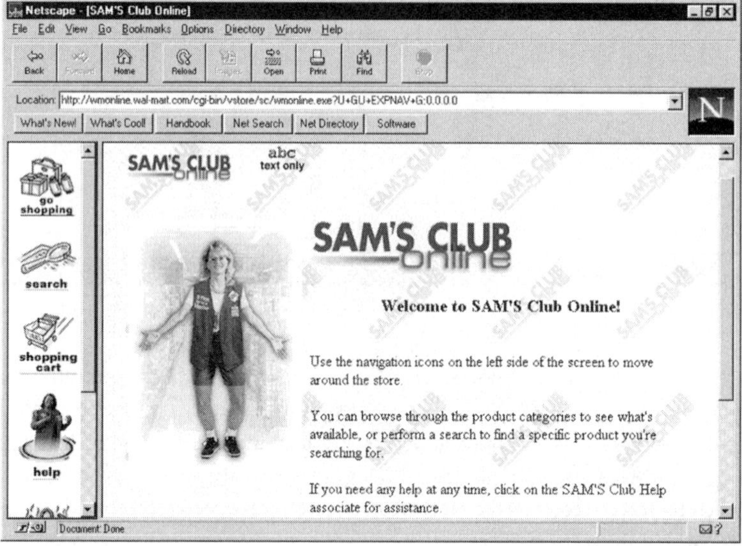

Secure Sockets Layer did not exist three years ago but has become accepted as one of the standard means of supporting electronic transactions on-line. What is involved behind the scenes? Quite a bit; so much that later in this chapter we take a look at what does go on behind the scenes in a section called "How Does an On-line Credit Card Transaction Work?" This is only the tip of the iceberg. Many executives are losing sight of the fact that much more is happening behind the scenes. And what is happening is that the systems, technology, and standards are quickly emerging that will permit much more than simple credit card transactions on-line.

Much of this is happening as the concepts that brought EDI — electronic data interchange — to many business organizations in the1980s migrate to the Internet of the1990s. EDI has been around for many years. It is a technology that permits the exchange of business information between organizations in a highly secure and reliable environment. Organizations involved in EDI figured out methods to exchange purchase orders, invoices, and payment in electronic form, resulting in a multibillion dollar EDI industry worldwide. EDI has had the participation of major financial institutions, who oversaw the development of necessary standards to provide for secure electronic payment.

The impact was dramatic: organizations were able to reduce their need to build expensive inventory stockpiles, because their EDI systems could determine exactly when stock had to be ordered. Expensive systems of paper processing disappeared. Payment cycles were compressed, resulting in more efficient cash flow. Products were manufactured to order, reducing the need for often inaccurate production estimates. Wherever you turned, organizations that implemented EDI learned to become mean, lean, efficient production machines. Implemented in such sectors as auto manufacturing, the retail world, and transportation, EDI helped to dramatically transform entire industries throughout the1980s and helped companies to achieve significant efficiencies and cost savings.

But EDI had its drawbacks. In particular, as EDI caught on, many organizations with EDI networks refused to purchase from companies that did not support EDI. This meant that many small- and medium-sized companies were forced to implement EDI in order to continue doing business with their trading partners, often at prohibitive expense.

And given the profound impact that it had, EDI is not terribly pervasive throughout the business community. This is not surprising; the traditional form of EDI as practised today is a "black art," unnecessarily complex and overwhelmingly expensive to implement. The result? A lot of business organizations stayed away because it is complex, cumbersome, difficult, and expensive to implement. It is too bad, for it is one of the computer applications that really makes strategic sense.

What does this have to do with the Internet? Traditional EDI has gone about as far as it will go and will likely not be implemented much further throughout the business community. But it will be replaced, instead, by Internet-based electronic commerce, much of it occurring through the World Wide Web.

Internet-based electronic commerce will not be about simple credit card transactions online; it will be about the methods that organizations will use to integrate their own information systems to the World Wide Web in order to effect an electronic business relationship. Consider this: many leading-edge organizations are now integrating their corporate information systems with the World Wide Web in order to provide an electronic link to their customers through the Internet. Such organizations recognize that what is quickly emerging on the Internet is a new form of "electronic data interchange" between business organizations, one that involves use of the World Wide Web as the conduit into the information system of your supplier or customer.

The real appeal of the Internet as an electronic commerce tool is that it is already widely implemented in the business community. Unlike EDI, which was expensive to implement and maintain, many businesses already have the tools they need to use the Internet for data sharing with their business partners.

How does it work? Imagine this: a customer visits your Web site and determines if a particular part is in stock by querying your inventory system directly. Verifying availability, the customer then fills out a purchase order requisition on your Web site. Once the form is completed, the data from the Web form are automatically extracted and updated to your corporate information system. Later on, the customer queries your corporate system on the status of the order, once again through the Web. Presto! Instant person-to-business or interorganization transactions (depending upon the type of customer); in effect, a new form of EDI. This type of transaction is not pie in the sky. It is here today. The technology to support such an integration today is already available from organizations such as Sybase, Oracle, and IBM.

Here's an example. Fruit of the Loom (**http://www.fruit.com**), the world-famous underwear and t-shirt manufacturer, uses the World Wide Web to support its order management system. Using a standard World Wide Web browser such as Netscape, customers and distributors can obtain general product information, place orders, and even check on the status of an order:

How quickly is this new form of "Internet-based EDI" evolving? Consider the fact that GE Information Services, one of the leading EDI vendors in the world, has a service called TradeWeb (**http://www.getradeweb.com**), which is designed to help small companies exchange business information with larger companies that are using GE's proprietary EDI network. The benefit to small companies is that they do not have to install any EDI software. Using a standard World Wide Web browser, they can visit TradeWeb and fill out ready-to-use forms such as purchase orders and invoices. TradeWeb takes care of all the details, automatically translating the forms into a format compatible with the proprietary EDI networks being used by GE's customers.

"We're harnessing the explosive growth and open environment of the Internet to make it easier, cheaper and faster for suppliers to do business with GE," said a GE press release. Indeed. And by placing such a substantial chunk of its business on-line, GE is signaling that it believes the Internet is "ready for prime time" for electronic commerce. And it is initiatives like these that herald the real future for business on the Internet, a system that will drive the transactions of the global economy, on-line, and through the Internet.

The Impact of Disintermediation

It is also important for an organization to realize one impact that the Internet will have over time. The Internet permits manufacturers and service organizations to deal directly with end users of their products and services, thereby slowly reducing or perhaps eliminating the role of the retailer or middleman in the business relationship. Consider the following examples:

- American Airlines permits customers to purchase airline tickets and other travel products directly through its Internet site, Travelocity (**http://www.travelocity.com**). Traditionally in the travel industry, travel agents bought tickets from airlines and sold them to customers. All that changes with the Internet, since airlines can sell tickets directly to customers, reducing the need for an intermediary, the travel agent.
- California-based Real Goods Trading Corporation (**http://www.realgoods.com**), a manufacturer of energy-saving solar panels, sells its stock over the Internet. This means that shareholders can deal directly with the company without having to go through a stockbroker and pay a commission to a financial advisor. The U.S. Securities and Exchange Commission has given its blessing to on-line stock trading on the Internet.

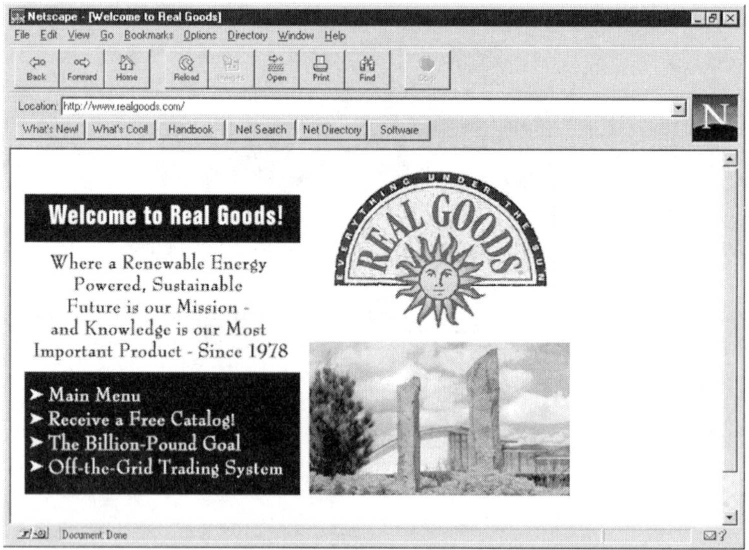

The company explained the system this way: "Our new 'off-the-grid' stock trading program is not only a service to current shareowners and others but also consistent with our mission of creating independent alternatives for our customers so that they can buy and sell our stock without having to go to Wall Street or having to pay a brokerage commission. You are able to manage the process yourselves and control the price at which you buy and sell our stock. This is what Real Goods is all about."

New Intermediaries

Both of the above examples illustrate situations where the sales channel is altered by the *elimination* of an intermediary (in the first case the travel agent disappears; in the second case the stockbroker is removed from the picture). However, in some cases the *opposite* happens, and the Internet gives rise to *new* entities in the distribution channel. For example, here in Canada several gas utilities are now using the Internet to interact directly with several Alberta-based gas companies to commit to the purchase of gas supplies. In the middle a new business entity has been formed to manage this new infrastructure through which several hundred million dollars worth of business flows. New and direct business relationships like these are slowly transforming the gas industry in Canada.

In your own business endeavors take the time to understand how the Internet could affect the way you do business by providing you with the ability to interact with business partners and customers in new and unique ways.

"Electronic Glue": Business Strategies on the Internet

Where should an organization start in thinking strategically about the Internet? We can tell you where not to start, which is where many organizations begin: with a technically based approach to the Internet. We are stunned by the number of organizations and individuals who approach the Internet on the following basis:

- the technical staff go out and buy Internet access;
- they figure out how to plug it into the company;
- they implement a Web site;
- they sit back and hope for the best.

Of course, this leads to a situation where the initiative fulfills absolutely no strategic goals, because none were defined in the first place, and where there is no perceived success, because there is likely none.

Organizations that truly want to take advantage of the Internet should, beyond thinking in the medium and longer term, clearly establish their business objectives for the Internet before they do anything else. We believe there are three fundamentals to doing business on the Internet:

- Determine how the Internet could be used for competitive or strategic advantage in the market in which the business organization operates.
- Discover how to achieve efficiencies and cost savings in the way the organization does business.
- Learn how to restructure the organization's core business activities to attain some type of business benefit.

What is business on the Internet really all about? We want you to think about it as a form of "electronic glue"; that is the key to the future. Let's take a look at what that means.

Competitive and Strategic Advantages

Any organization seeking business opportunities on the Internet must first consider

- how the Internet can be used to gain some type of advantage in the marketplace;
- how the Internet can redefine the nature of the relationships the organization has with its customers.

The following questions should be considered:

- What are the benefits of using the Internet as a communications and support tool? Can we reduce the costs of customer support? Provide our clients with better customer support? Improve communication and collaboration with our customers? Reduce communication costs?
- How can we link the data in our information systems to the Web so that our suppliers can automatically monitor stock levels, and our customers can obtain product pricing and availability information? How can we use the Web to allow customers to track the status of their orders?
- How can the Internet be used to tap into new markets for our products and/or services? What corporate information can we provide over the Internet to our customers and to the general public? How will this reduce our information distribution costs?

- How can we use the Internet to gain an edge over our competition? What is it? How can we make it last?
- Are there any new or incremental revenue opportunities that we might be able to leverage through the Internet?

In the short term, seeking competitive or strategic advantage involves asking how the Internet could be used to enhance marketing, sales, or customer support activities. In the longer term, it will involve the development of electronic links to customers that make it difficult or unattractive for them to do business elsewhere.

Short Term

In the short term, there are many opportunities that you can exploit through the Internet. For example, you should consider how you might use the Internet for the following areas:

- Customer interaction and feedback. Consider using the Internet to improve the dialogue your organization has with its customers. The Shell Oil Company (**http://www.shellus.com/ OilProducts/Welcome.html**), for example, has an area on its Web site called "Tell Shell Oil Company," where it encourages feedback from the public about the cleanliness and general appearance of their gas stations. Customers fill out a form on Shell's Web site, and comments are sent electronically to the head office for immediate follow-up.

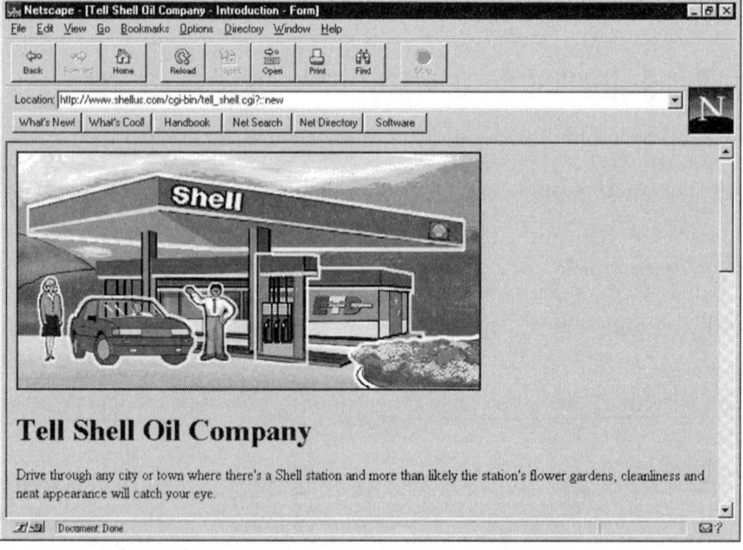

- Customer support. A good customer is a happy customer, and a happy customer is a repeat customer. Think about using the Internet to provide after-sales support to your customers. TSN's (**http://www.tsn.ca**) audience relations department accepts Internet e-mail from viewers who have questions or concerns about the station's programming or scheduling. Messages can be left at any time of the day or night:

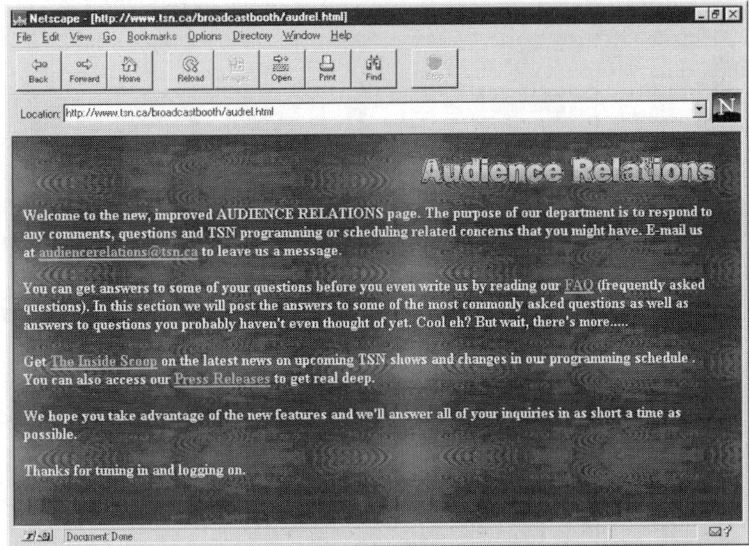

◆ Marketing. By distributing product and service information through the Internet, you can reach potential customers and tap into new markets. For example, Canada's Greyhound Air (**http://air.greyhound.ca**) uses the Internet to market their airline service, which they introduced to Canadians in 1996:

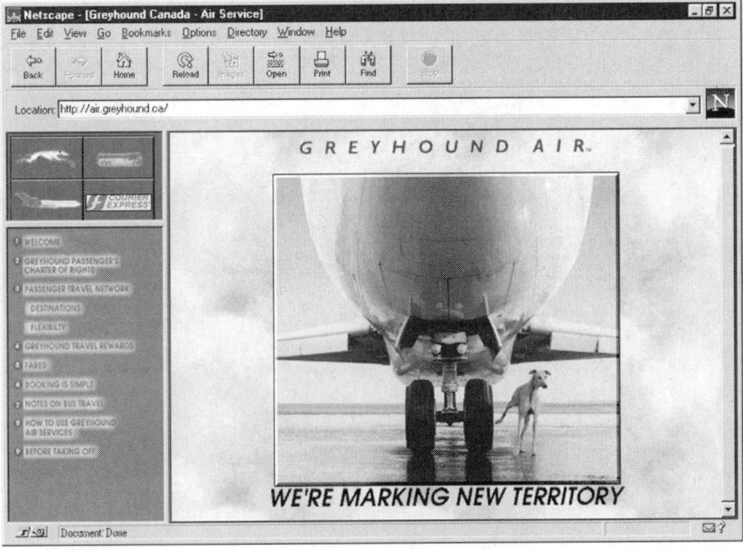

◆ Investor relations. If you are part of a public company, consider how the Internet can be used to serve the information needs of your investors and the investment community in general. McDonald's (**http://www.mcdonalds.com**) is one of many companies that use the Internet to distribute financial news and annual report information:

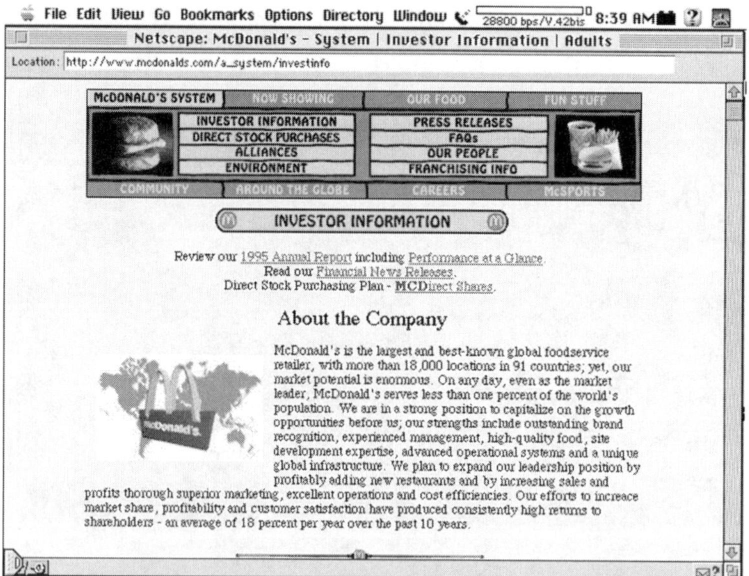

- Recruitment. Many companies, such as Toys'R'Us (**http://www.tru.com**), use the Internet to advertise career opportunities with their firms. In addition to job postings, the Toys'R'Us Web site provides benefits information and describes the Toys'R'Us culture to job seekers:

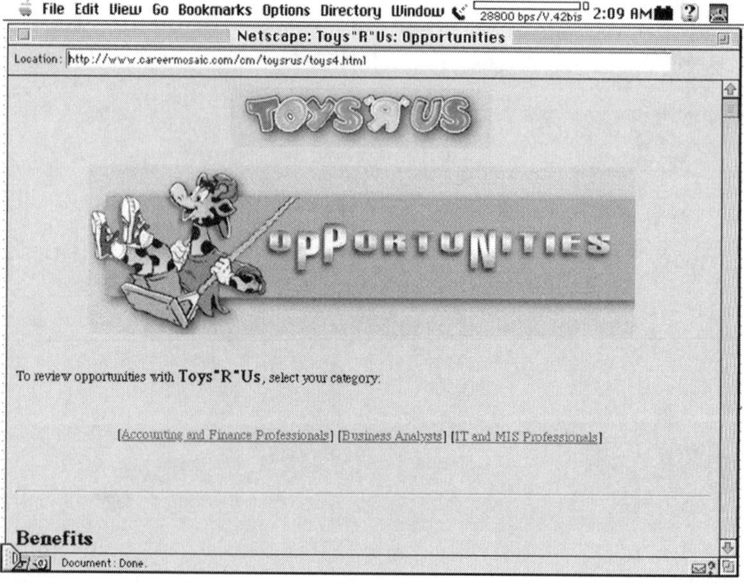

- Corporate communications. The Internet can be used to improve the flow of information between your organization, the media, and the general public. Seen in the screen below, StarKist Foods (**http://www.starkist.com**), the company that sells StarKist tuna, uses the Internet to distribute news releases about its products:

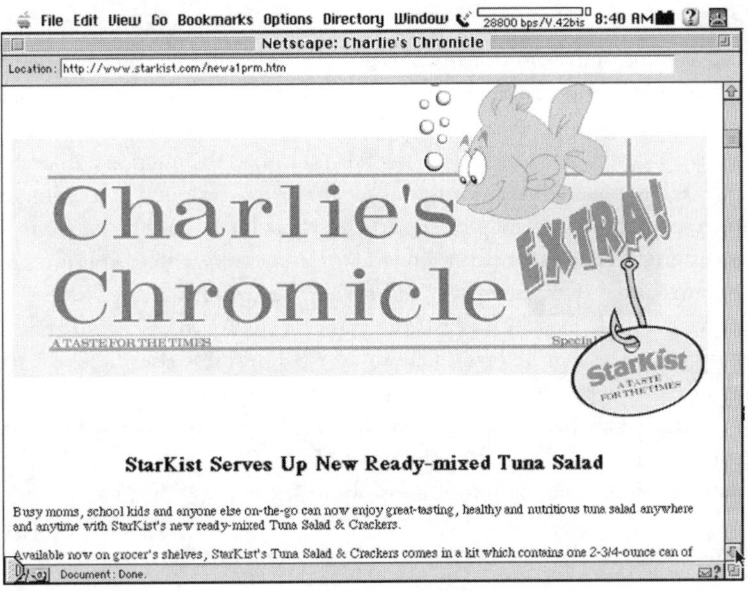

◆ Image enhancement. Many organizations use the Internet to strengthen their organization's brand image, generate positive publicity, and build goodwill toward their firms. During the 1996 Olympics in Atlanta, Nike (**http://www.nike.com**) used the Internet to promote its sponsorship activities. Notice the message on the opening screen that clearly spells out the intent of the Nike World Wide Web site: "The purpose of this site is not to sell shoes":

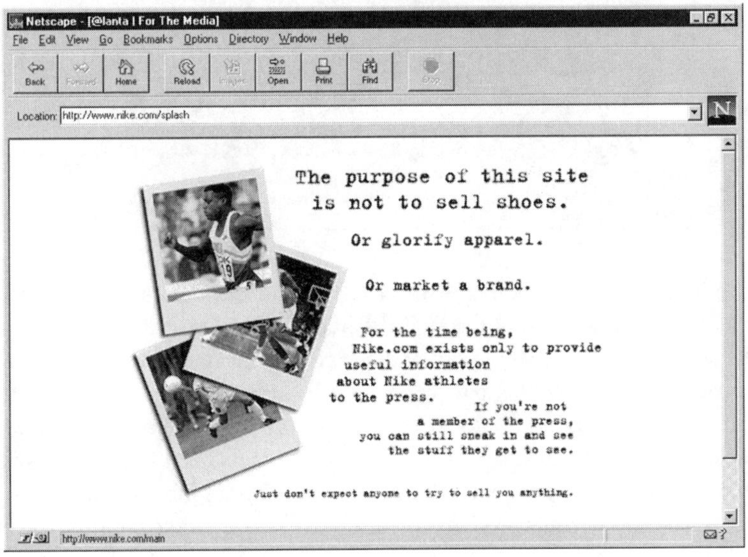

Longer Term

We have looked at some of the short-term applications of the Internet. But the Internet is about much more in the longer term. The future was best stated in an article in *Forbes ASAP,* a technology supplement to *Forbes* magazine, on August 28, 1995: "...the way to customers' hearts is through transparent on-line access to what used to be the holy of holies: the internal corporate database."

We interpret this as saying that true business advantage will be found on the Internet through the establishment of technology that provides an electronic link — a form of electronic glue — directly to the customer. The customer can undertake transactions with the business organization through the Internet and achieve significant cost savings and efficiencies by virtue of doing so, as does the company; both sides benefit. The customer finds it so easy and straightforward to do business with the organization that he is unlikely to take his business elsewhere. This is how you should be thinking when it comes to the Internet. This concept is best illustrated with an example.

Bank One (**http://www.bankone.com**), an Ohio bank, allows its major cheque-writing customers to tap into its cheque database using the World Wide Web. The purpose of the cheque database is to allow customers to obtain information about "exception" cheques:

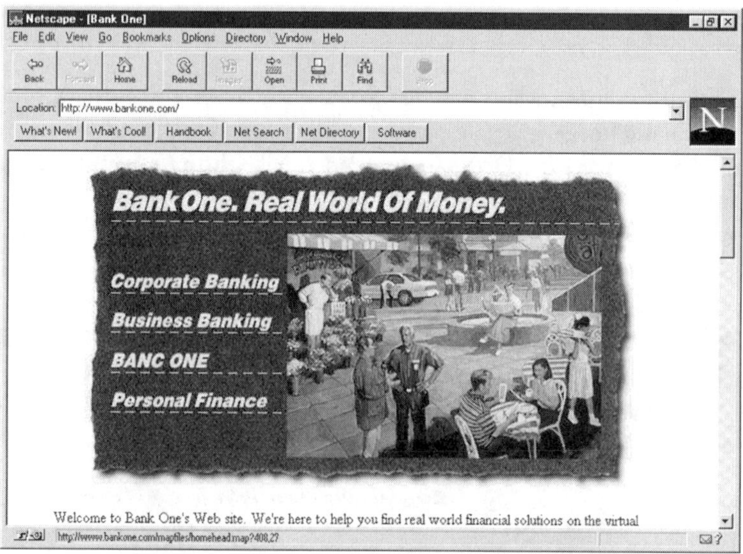

An "exception" cheque is a cheque that is suspicious; perhaps because the dollar amount is high or the recipient is unknown. Using the World Wide Web, the customer can view a summary screen of exception cheques, view the front and back of any cheque, and by filling out a form on the Web, instruct the bank to either pay or hold particular cheques.

The system has several layers of protection so that only authorized users can get access to the cheque database through the Internet. For example, customers need IDs and passwords to gain access to the system, and the system only admits users from certain Internet sites. Prior to the Web-based system, exception cheques were handled manually and either faxed to the customer or hand-delivered, a process that was time-consuming and subject to human error. Providing a Web-based link offers significant efficiencies and cost savings to both the bank and the customer.

Such applications of the Internet are limitless. By using the Web as a front end to corporate systems, companies can implement business applications that permit the customer to make enquiries, make updates, and order products directly from an organization. This creates many new opportunities. For example, rather than mailing out costly monthly paper statements, businesses can provide access to account information on-line. Instead of contacting a call centre to check if a particular product is in stock, the customer can access inventory information directly through the Web, 24 hours a day.

The important thing to keep in mind is that because of the consumer behavior issue — the fact that it takes time for people to adapt to technology — these types of electronic links are going to take time to evolve and might actually happen in three stages.

- During the first stage, customers could use the electronic link for simple enquiries and data delivery. They could use it to access information on the status of their accounts or to access on-line reports that they might otherwise receive in paper form.
- In the next stage the customer might be allowed to update data through the electronic link. This could include placing an order, although no funds transfer would take place.
- The final stage is actual funds transfer and electronic payment through the Internet.

Organizations intent on doing business on the Internet must explore how such a strategic form of electronic glue could be put in place. The question to ask is, "can we use the technology of the Internet to form a direct electronic relationship with the customer that provides a competitive advantage in our business relationship with them?"

Cost Avoidance and Reduction

If you accept that where we are headed with the Internet is that it is a system that will allow customers to "talk" directly to financial, inventory, and other systems at business organizations, then you can begin to see that what the Internet really represents is a huge opportunity to reengineer the customer relationship in order to achieve cost savings and efficiencies in the relationship. Let's define what we mean by reengineering; it is a wonderful buzzword and one that is often overused throughout the computer industry. Think about what it represents:

The cost to process an order. The customer calls the telephone number of a supplier and talks to a clerk. The clerk keys some data into a computer, which then processes the order. What is the potential of the Internet? If the supplier's order processing system is made accessible through the Web, then the customer, not the clerk, can enter the order into the supplier's computer. Over time this leads to direct cost savings, since there will be less of a need for clerks to do order entry. There will be efficiencies in the relationship, because the customer can now interact with the supplier that much quicker.

The cost to an organization to send information to a customer. A monthly statement or letter is printed, is stuffed into an envelope, postage is paid, and the information is sent. At the other end someone opens the envelope, puts it into a mail cart, and it is eventually delivered. It then sits on someone's desk until he/she is ready to look at it. What is the potential of the Internet? A monthly statement is generated and stored on the corporate Web site, accessible only to the company for whom it is intended, since it is password-protected. Or perhaps monthly statements are not prepared at all; instead, they are only generated on demand, when the recipient accesses the Web site to obtain one. Direct savings result from the elimination of a paper statement.

The point is, over time, the Internet will come to replace or enhance existing paper-based information processing systems. By virtue of doing so, it promises to introduce significant and far-reaching cost savings and efficiencies. We passionately believe that the Internet will truly manifest itself in these types of opportunities. We also fully appreciate that such initiatives are going to take time to define, to evolve, and to implement. They will not happen overnight.

Small Business and the Internet

And having said this, we should point out that you do not have to be a big business to discover how to use the Internet to save money, serve existing customers, and attract new ones. Consider how one Western Canadian lawyer is using the Internet. Douglas Alger (**http://upanet.uleth.ca/~dalger**) has established a Web site that provides general information about his legal practice as well as articles that he has written on a wide range of legal topics, including divorce, estate planning, and real estate law:

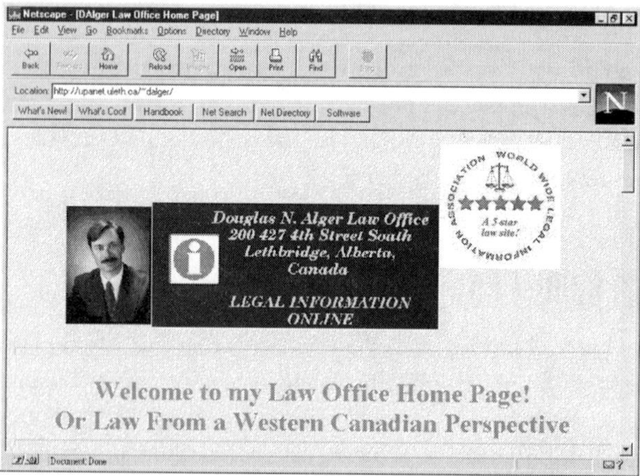

Many of the simplest applications of the Internet are often overlooked by small businesses. Carmen DeFacendis, a Toronto-based lawyer, uses the Internet to provide directions to her law office (**http://www.io.org/~carmdef/**):

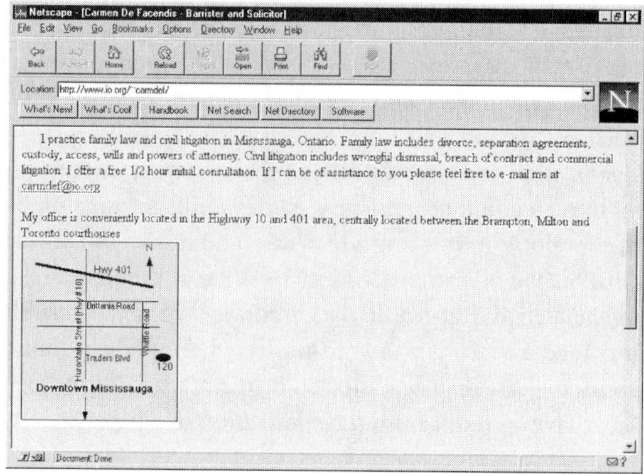

The beauty of the Internet to small business is that it is probably one of the lowest-cost investments that you can make, with rates as low as $20.00 to $30.00 a month for a basic Internet account. Cost savings are a big reason any small business should be on the Net. Internet e-mail, for example, is dramatically less expensive than courier, fax, and telephone costs. With more and more people putting Internet addresses on their business cards, there are tremendous opportunities for cost savings.

Small business should also recognize that the Internet is an extremely effective and low-cost customer support tool. Establishing an e-mail support mailbox (i.e., **support@xyz.com**) is one way that customers can request help; establishing a World Wide Web site loaded with customer support information is another method. The latter method is relatively inexpensive. Many Internet providers will establish a Web site for a small business for $150 a month or less. Load the site with technical support documents, put up an interactive form through which the customer can get answers to questions, provide pointers to other related information resources, and publish the details in your marketing literature. Over time, you will find that you have taken steps towards solidifying the relationship with your customer base, as more and more of them begin to use the Internet and learn to access your site for support information.

How Does an On-line Credit Card Transaction Work?

Earlier we told you how Tip Top tailors actually had the infrastructure in place to support secure, encrypted credit card transactions on-line. It is useful to understand what actually happens during the process, so here we will look at the technology and processes to do this, with the aid of the screens below. It is useful to note that this is but a small part of what might be considered "electronic commerce"; after all, as we saw earlier, credit card transactions are just one component of the business transactions that will occur on-line. Even so, it is instructive to go "behind the scenes" of such a transaction to see the number and types of players who are becoming involved. The refrain when it came to credit card shopping on the Internet used to be that such transactions were not secure, but now major banks are supporting them, fully satisfied that security has been addressed to a reasonable degree.

Keep in mind that if you plan on trying this yourself, the exact screens you see below will change over time as Tip Top redesigns their Web site. However, the steps in the process will remain more or less unchanged.

- First, visit the Tip Top Web site at **http://www.tiptop.ca:**

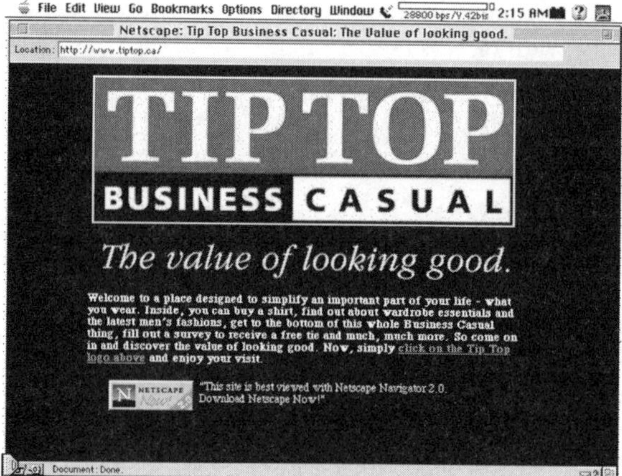

◆ Select the shirt buying service from the list of options on the opening menu:

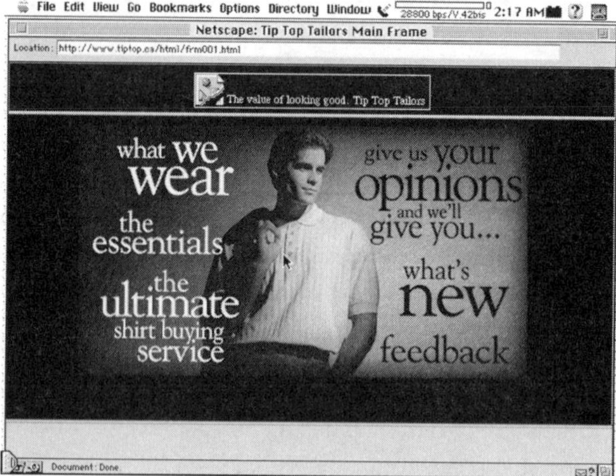

◆ Select the style of shirt you want: "business," "business casual," or "casual":

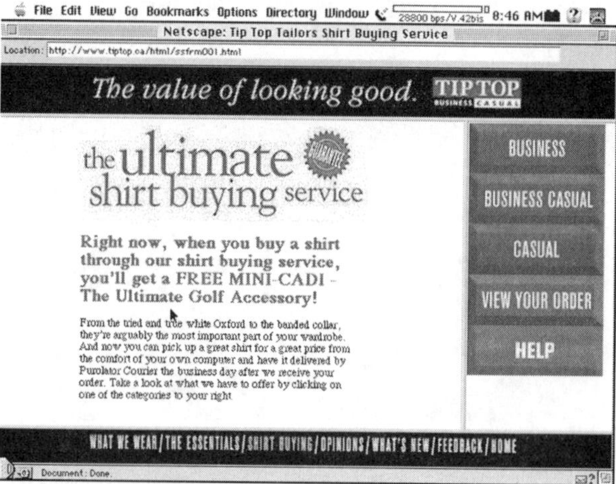

◆ Select the type of shirt you want:

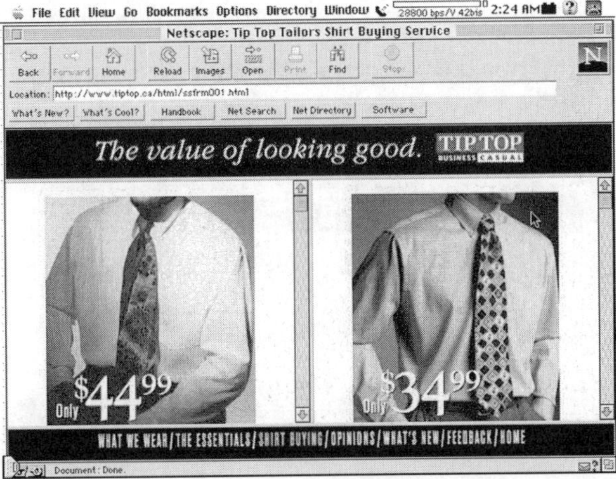

◆ Select the quantity of shirts you want, and don't forget to specify the size and color:

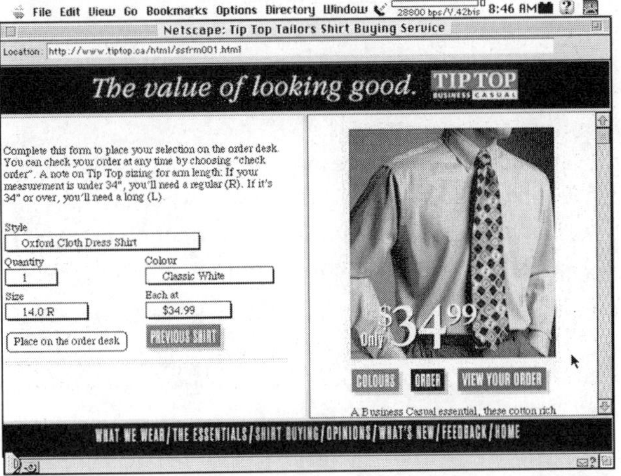

◆ Confirm the items you want to purchase:

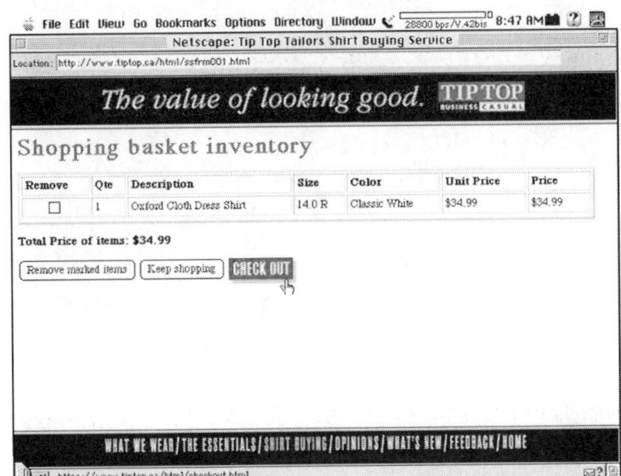

- Finally, check out! What could be easier? Your shirt will be delivered to your door the very next day.

File Edit View Go Bookmarks Options Directory Window 28800 bps/V.42bis 8:52 AM
Netscape: Checkout
Location: https://www.tiptop.ca/html/checkout.html
The value of looking good. TIPTOP BUSINESS CASUAL
Checkout
Ordered by
First Name: Rick Last Name: Broadhead
Address: 123 Main Street Apt
City: Toronto Location: Ontario
Postal code: A1A 1A1
E-mail: rickb@inforamp.net Phone: 416 555-1212
Credit Card Information
Credit Card: Master Card
Name on Credit Card: Rick Broadhead
Credit Card number: 123-3456-789

It seems so straightforward; however, there are many technical processes happening behind the scenes. You are notified that these processes are about to start when Netscape notifies you that you are about to start a secure, encrypted transaction. Any information that you transmit while you are in the secure area, such as credit card numbers, will be scrambled to protect you against fraud.

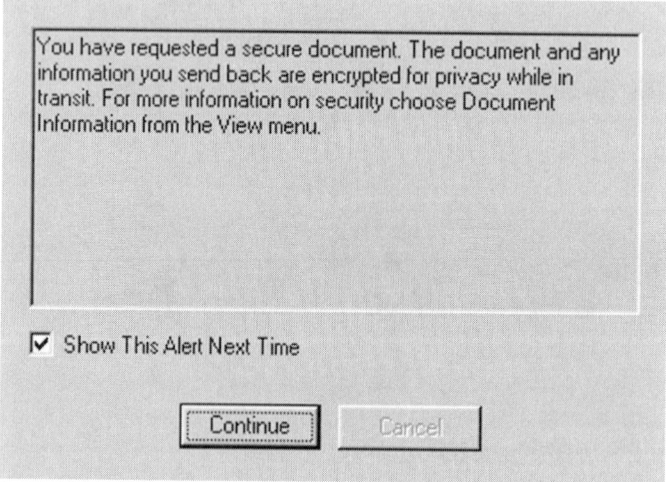

One Single Standard for Financial Transactions on the Internet

One of the historical problems with electronic commerce on the Internet has been that different companies have been pursuing different security standards for on-line financial transactions. For example, at one point VISA had teamed up with Microsoft to develop a standard for financial transactions on the Internet. At the same time MasterCard and Netscape joined forces to develop a similar standard that would compete directly with the technology being developed by VISA and Microsoft. VISA and MasterCard are competitors, as are Netscape and Microsoft. The result for consumers and merchants would have been disastrous, since certain browsers would have only worked with certain on-line merchants, and merchants would have been forced to choose between the competing standards.

All that has since changed. In 1996 VISA and MasterCard agreed to work together to develop a single standard for secure financial transactions on the Internet. Their solution was a technology called Secure Electronic Transactions (SET). You will be hearing lots about SET in the coming months and years. SET is supported by all three of the big credit companies —VISA, MasterCard, and American Express — and will be deployed throughout 1997. SET is also supported by the major Web browsers, including Netscape Navigator and Microsoft Explorer.

Like the Secure Sockets Layer technology that Tip Top and Wal-Mart are using in the examples described above, SET scrambles your credit card number when you are making a purchase on the Internet, making it unintelligible to electronic thieves. The significance of it is that it is being rapidly adopted throughout the Internet and financial communities.

Automatic Authorization of Credit Card Purchases on the Internet

SET provides a way for secure financial transactions to take place on the Internet, but it is only one part of the puzzle. The next step is to allow merchants to get immediate authorization for credit card purchases made over the Internet, in the same way they do when you make a purchase in a retail store. It is one thing for a company such as Wal-Mart to accept credit card purchases on the Internet; it is quite another matter for those purchases to be authorized on the spot.

For example, once a credit card number is received over the Internet from a customer making an on-line purchase, the merchant has to manually check to see whether the card is valid and not stolen, for instance. Generally the merchant does this by calling the merchant's bank or using one of the card-swipe devices to get authorization for the purchase. In either case the process is manual and is completed after the credit card information is received over the Internet, increasing the risk of fraud or misuse.

So, many organizations have indicated that it is necessary for on-line credit card transactions to be authorized within seconds of an order taking place. This is where an organization named VeriFone (**http://www.verifone.com**) comes in. One of the biggest players in the Internet credit card authorization market but relatively unknown, the company operates behind the scenes most of the time, but plays a major role in the North American financial services industry. They manufacture, for example, the card swipe devices that are used in many retail stores to authorize credit card purchases. Merchants use them to make sure that your credit card is still valid and has not been reported stolen.

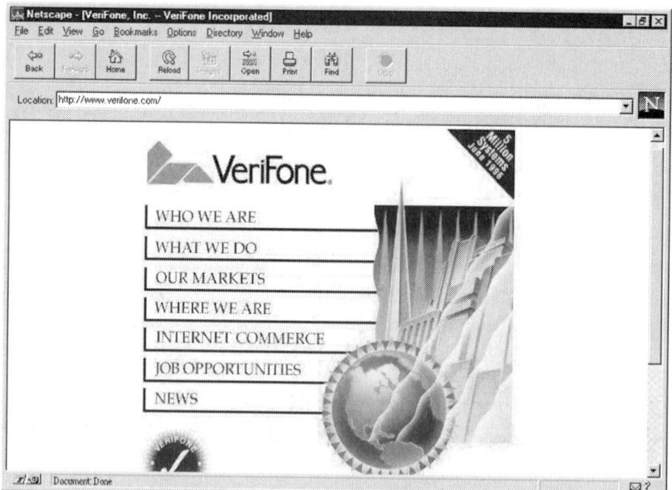

Their involvement with the Internet is that they have taken a leading role in distributing software that allows merchants to link their Internet sites to their bank in order to get authorization for credit card purchases made by Internet users. The VeriFone software is designed to work with the SET standard described earlier that has been adopted by VISA, MasterCard, and American Express. Expect to see the VeriFone system deployed throughout 1996 and 1997.

What Software Is Required to Use the VeriFone Internet Payment System?

Consumers

Consumers will use a piece of software called "vWallet" (virtual wallet), which will be distributed by participating banks. This software will reside on your computer and will be used to store your credit card numbers and other important financial data. Since vWallet will be compliant with the SET standard, it will allow you to make secure purchases over the Internet.

Merchants

Merchants who want to sell products over the Internet will need a piece of software called "vPOS" (virtual point of sale). This software will sit on the merchant's Internet site and connect to the merchant's bank and the bank's credit card processing system. Many banks, such as the Royal Bank of Canada, are setting up Internet sites (called "cybermalls") that will rent out space to vendors who want to sell their products over the Internet. Vendors who do not want to set up their own Internet sites can participate in these cybermalls without the need of any special software or hardware. This type of arrangement is advantageous to Internet vendors because they will not need to purchase the vPOS software; the banks will assume responsibility for maintaining the Internet site and operating the vPOS software.

Banks

Banks that want to authorize credit card transactions over the Internet will need a piece of software called "vGATE," which allows the financial institution to accept transactions from merchants over the Internet.

How the System Works

The process is quite simple. Consumers access a vendor's Internet site on the World Wide Web, select the products and services they want, then place the order using their credit card number. The credit card information is securely transmitted to the merchant over the Internet. The merchant, in turn, transmits the information to its bank, and the bank authorizes the purchase. The consumer is notified that the transaction is approved, and the merchant fills the order for the customer. All this happens in a few seconds. One of the first Canadian banks to align itself with VeriFone was the Royal Bank of Canada (**http://www.royalbank.com**). To help you understand how this entire process works, we have included two diagrams in this chapter. The following screen shows how the process would work in general:

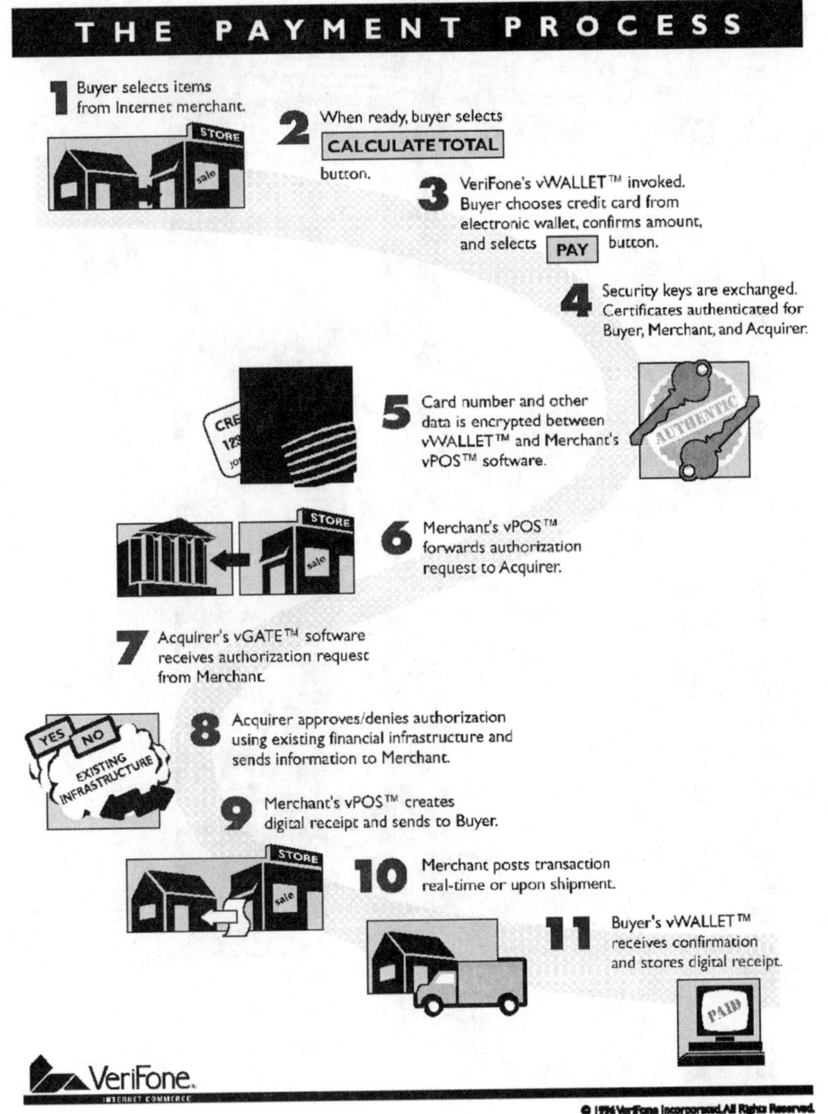

And this diagram shows how the process would work from the Royal Bank's perspective:

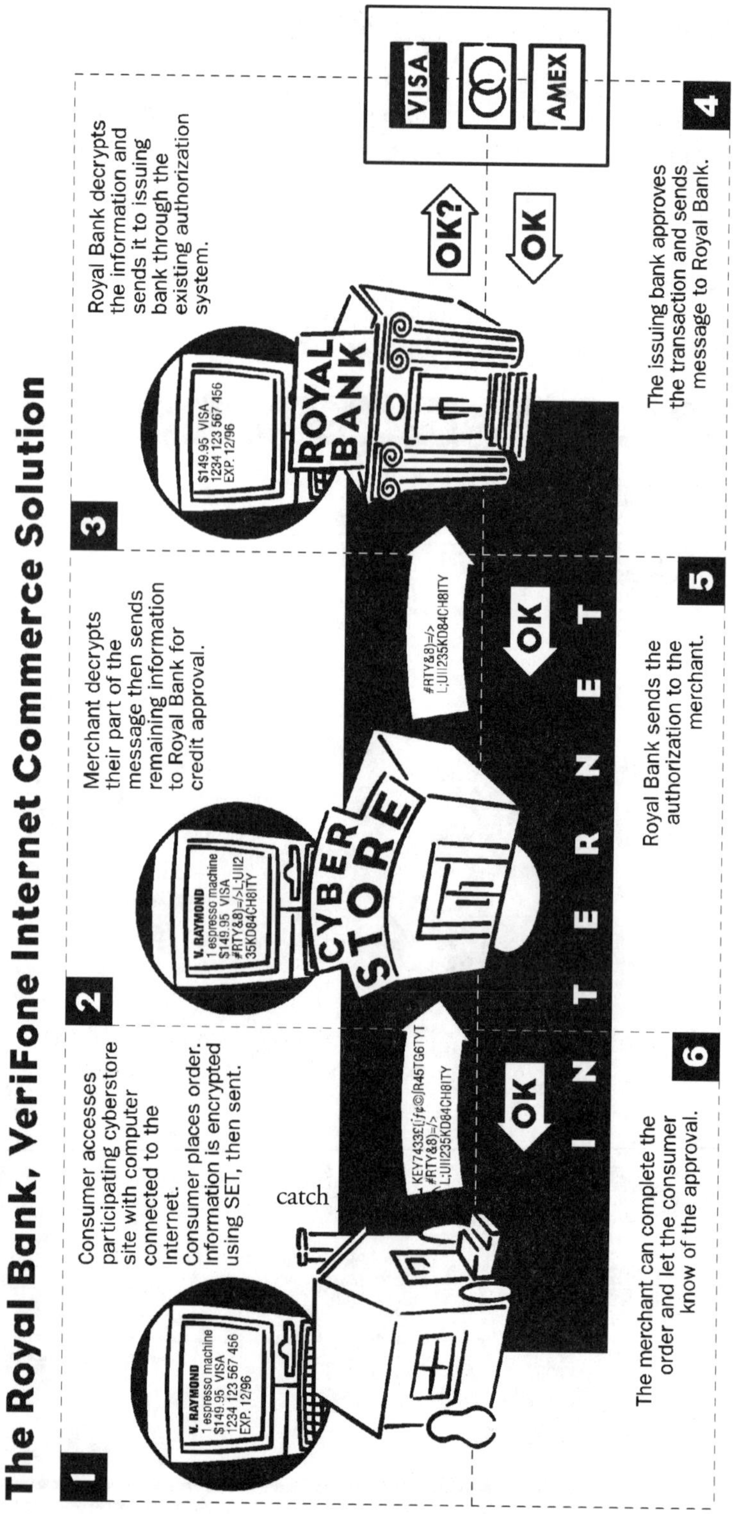
The Royal Bank, VeriFone Internet Commerce Solution
1
Consumer accesses participating cyberstore site with computer connected to the Internet. Consumer places order. Information is encrypted using SET, then sent.
V. RAYMOND
1 espresso machine
$149.95 VISA
1234 123 567 456
EXP. 12/96
catch
2
Merchant decrypts their part of the message then sends remaining information to Royal Bank for credit approval.
CYBER STORE
3
Royal Bank decrypts the information and sends it to issuing bank through the existing authorization system.
$149.95 VISA
1234 123 567 456
EXP. 12/96
ROYAL BANK
VISA
AMEX
OK?
OK
4
The issuing bank approves the transaction and sends message to Royal Bank.
5
Royal Bank sends the authorization to the merchant.
6
The merchant can complete the order and let the consumer know of the approval.
I N T E R N E T
OK

You can get more information on VeriFone's Internet commerce products and the specifics of how they work by visiting their Web site at **http://www.verifone.com**.

Authentication and Digital Certificates/Digital IDs

There is one last piece of information that you should be aware of when it comes to electronic commerce on the Internet. A number of companies, for example, VeriSign (**http://www.verisign.com**), are working with credit card companies such as VISA to provide ways of authenticating on-line shoppers to vendors and banks on the Internet. They are doing this by developing "digital certificates," or "digital IDs."

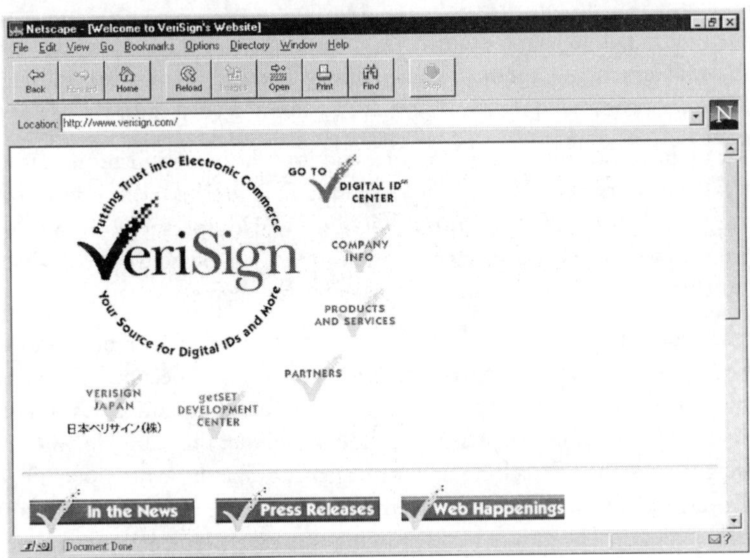

Banks and merchants will use the digital certificates to confirm your identity when you make purchases on the Internet. It helps to think of a digital certificate as your "digital driver's license"; you carry it around with you as you shop on the Internet in the same way you carry your driver's license with you as you drive. The digital certificate will be part of the "virtual wallet" we discussed earlier and will sit on your computer along with your credit card information. Digital certificates are not in wide use yet. In the future, banks will distribute digital certificates to their customers for use on the Internet in the same way they distribute credit cards and ATM cards today.

An Approach to the Internet That Makes Sense

We are proponents of a careful, step-by-step approach to the Internet. It is our belief that you should spend a lot of time figuring out what you should be doing on-line, before you even begin to set up shop on-line.

Planning Your On-line Activities

We think that you should do several things to properly plan what it is you are going to do on-line. First, take the time to figure out what might be possible in the short, medium, and longer term with the goal of educating yourself with respect to the potential strategic implications of the

Internet. Then examine the key strategies, plans, and goals of your organization with a view to understanding how the Internet could help to achieve them. And take the time to understand the mistakes that others have made in their approach to the Internet — and learn from their mistakes.

Understand the Possibilites

The first thing you should do is take the time to gain insight into what could be possible if your organization were to become involved with the Internet. You can do this by taking a good look around the Internet, spend some time surfing. But do not restrict yourself to just on-line activities; take the time to talk to your customers and others who might be interested in seeing you involved with the Internet, take a look at your industry, and spend some time talking to industry experts. Hence we recommend that you start out by doing several things:

- Get on-line. The only way to comprehend the strategic opportunities is to get on-line if you are not already. We are not suggesting that you get on-line and surf away like crazy strictly for the fun of it; you should do so with specific objectives in mind. For example, you want to examine how the Internet can be used to achieve some of the short-term objectives we discussed earlier in this chapter.

- Take a look at your industry. You should undertake a review of how your industry and the markets in which you operate are responding to and becoming involved with the Internet. This means that you should do some "benchmarking." Use the search engines we discussed in Chapter 9 to explore how other businesses in your industry are using the Internet. For a long time management types have been pursuing the concept of benchmarking as a means of determining what objectives should be pursued within their company. The idea of benchmarking is to take a look at your close surroundings — companies in your industry, your direct competitors, not-so-direct competitors, and other organizations that are somewhat similar — and determine who is doing the "best job" in various categories. For example, who has the best marketing strategy? Which organization has done the best job at making a name for itself? Which company has managed to get the highest profile for a new product launch?

  Once you have identified the "best" in many different categories, you then sit back and ask yourself the question, "what did they do to make them the best for that particular category?" This isn't necessarily an easy question to answer, *but if you can answer it, then you have identified the something that you should be doing to improve your own organization in that particular category.* In effect, you use the practice of benchmarking to gain insight into the best activities or practices that you should use within your own strategy. It is sort of a fancy form of idea-stealing.

  The Internet is ideal territory for benchmarking. It is easy to spend hours surfing the Web and examining the Web sites of your competitors, others in the industry, and, in fact, any type of organization. What you need to do is surf with a view to finding an answer to a particular question, "Who has done the best job at providing customer service through the Internet?" for example. You spend time visiting customer service centres in sites on-line and determine which one seems to be the most effective and best organized, perhaps in terms of the way the information is laid out and the type of information that is made available.

  Figure out what they have done right and set out to do exactly that or even better in your own Internet strategy. Benchmarking is a powerful and useful way of figuring out what you should be doing on the Internet.

- Talk to your customers and ask them what you should be doing with the Internet. We are constantly amazed at how many organizations charge ahead and become involved with the Internet, building a site to help or reach out to their customers in some way. And what becomes painfully obvious once they have launched their on-line initiative is that no one bothered to talk to the customers to ask them what they wanted to see on-line.

  Even so, we have also seen an increasing number of Fortune 1000 organizations, big business organizations that can afford the research, participate in sophisticated "focus groups" in which small, select groups of customers are queried at length about what they would like to do on the Internet. These companies are also purchasing sophisticated marketing studies prepared by polling organizations such as Canada's Angus Reid Group, which carefully probe the attitudes and plans of the emerging "electronic consumer." They then build their Web sites and Internet strategies accordingly.

  You can learn a lot from such organizations, for they are undertaking a very significant and useful step: they are listening to their customers. Hence we suggest that you take the time to do the same: talk to your customers, potential customers, suppliers, investors, and the general public to the extent that you can to find out what they would like to see you doing on-line. You might not be able to afford fancy focus groups and market research studies, but you can go out and talk to people.

  Ask your key customers if they are on the Internet. If not, find out what is holding them back. If they are on-line, find out how they are currently using the Internet. Explore how the Internet can improve your existing business relationship. Don't forget to survey potential customers as well. What needs do they have that are not currently being served by the marketplace? What services would they like to see on the Internet? One extremely useful way of doing this is to ask visitors to your Web site, if you already have one, for their suggestions on what else you could be doing on-line. Many companies do this by asking visitors to their Web sites to voluntarily fill out an on-line survey or answer simple questions like "What would you like to see on our Web site?" It simply makes sense to ask people what they want, doesn't it?

- Talk to experts "in the know." By now it should be apparent that the technology of the Internet is changing on a continual, rapid basis. Developments in the field of electronic commerce, on-line marketing, and other areas are constantly changing and maturing. You should spend some time with an individual or company that is closely involved with the Internet, such as an Internet consultant, an Internet presence provider, or an Internet service provider; pick their brains to find out what you could be doing on-line or what your competitors and similar organizations are up to.

  We also suggest that you be very careful in talking to such people; they may be particularly biased, since their objective might be to convince you to charge ahead with putting a Web site on-line before you are ready. You also run the risk of getting lost in "technical nirvana"; spend some time with an expert and you will see the latest and greatest in on-line animation, Java scripts, and other such wild and wonderful exciting technology bits that often have little direct relevance to your own particular strategic needs and goals.

Educate the Decision Makers

You must take the time to educate the folks who control the money; after all, to "do" the Internet properly, you will need some. Simply, if you are to deal with the Internet from a strategic perspective, management must know what the heck is going on. To deal successfully with the Internet, senior management must be prepared to accept that the Internet will profoundly and forever reshape your business. To succeed strategically on the Internet, management must recognize that the Internet is a fundamental tool of business strategy. Managers must be on-line, and they must think strategically about the Internet; they must understand, for example, the concept of "electronic glue."

Senior management will not pay attention if you explain the Internet from a technical perspective. They don't give a darn for HTML and Web servers and Java and TCP/IP; that's not their language. They do want to know how the Internet can help to achieve strategic objectives, how business opportunities can be expanded and improved through use of the network, but they will certainly want to know the risk of the strategy going wrong. If you describe the Internet to them as a technical exercise, they will not give your efforts the time of day; if the Internet is described in strategic terms, they will.

Hence one of the most useful things you can do is educate senior management on what the Internet is all about. Now that you have taken the time to identify the sites on-line that work — "the best" — you can use them to educate management. Run an on-line Internet demonstration so that they can see the Web firsthand. Highlight the Web sites of competitors and similar companies. Make sure that they are set up to surf the Web on their home PCs and laptops, since many of them will not be able to go on-line during the day. Get them to attend executive-level Internet briefings or conferences. Put magazine articles that discuss the Internet from a strategic perspective in front of them.

Put this book in front of them, and highlight this sentence: senior management executives who do not take the time to understand the potential impact on their business through the next decade are abdicating their management responsibility. Whatever you do, make sure that you take the time to help them understand what is going on. It will be critical as you move along.

Examine Your Own Corporate Goals

The other key thing that you must do is examine your own corporate goals: what are the key strategies, objectives, and opportunities that your corporate organization is pursuing? And how can the Internet help to solve some of those problems? If you are in management, you will already know the answers to these questions. But if you are not, you should take the time working with management to see if you can get an answer to those questions, for the best way to use the Internet is, of course, to solve current corporate problems and challenges.

Outline Your Plans and Test Them on Others

By this point, you should be able to put together a rough outline of what you hope to do on-line. The outline should cover the following:

- Your organization's *objectives.* What do you hope to accomplish on-line, and what business strategy is being fulfilled through the Internet?
- Planned on-line *activities.* What do you need to do with the Internet in order to achieve your stated objectives?
- Expected *results.* What will be accomplished through your Internet activities? What are the deliverables? Also discuss what will *not* be accomplished and why. It is important that your expectations be realistic.

It is a good idea to put your outline on paper to help you to clearly identify each item. It might look like the following:

OBJECTIVE	ACTIVITY	EXPECTED RESULTS
In the short term we should ensure that customers can access a document with the most common problems related to product X, with the objective of reducing the number of calls made to our 1-800 line.	The Web site will include a customer support centre, which will include a "frequently asked questions" summary. Customers will be advised via product packaging and a promotional campaign that such service is now available on-line.	In the short term we do not expect a dramatic dropoff in support calls. However, within 1 to 2 years, as the new product packaging goes out, and as more people sign on to the Net, we expect to see a 10% decrease in usage.
It has been identified that we might be able to reduce the likelihood of customers moving to a competitor if they can reserve product electronically before it is in production. We can reduce inventory carrying costs by eliminating the current 14-day buildup in stock prior to production runs.	We will build a bridge so that selected customers can initially query upcoming production quotas. Once the bugs are ironed out, we will let those customers reserve product directly on-line; we will back it up by ensuring that they use the current telephone system for 2 months as well. Once they indicate they are comfortable and we have taken care of any concerns, we'll go live.	Within 6 months we expect 6 of our largest customers, which represent 45% of our business, will be reserving production runs 2 weeks in advance. This will let us plan our purchasing cycle better, resulting in an identified 28% reduction in carrying costs.

Prepare your outline from the perspective of the short, medium, and longer term. And be concise; if you are too vague, then it is quite likely that you will quickly get off the rails when you start to get involved with the Internet. And don't overestimate the deliverables. As you read this chapter, it has probably become obvious that we are quite conservative on when the expected benefits from the Internet "revolution" will materialize. This makes us believe that those individuals and organizations that overestimate the returns from their involvement with the Internet end up with egg on their faces and black marks on their career potential.

Once you have prepared the outline, you should review it with management, decision makers, and other affected parties. Get their feedback, comments, changes, and input. Rework the plans until everyone is satisfied that you are on the right track. Keep in mind what you are really doing here: in essence, you are defining how your business may function in the future — in the short, medium, and longer term — as a result of the emergence of the new wired world. You are indicating which corporate strategies can be influenced by the arrival of the Internet and which could be helped along with use of such a technology. You are preparing the blueprint that will help the organization to think strategically, not technically, about the Internet, so it is critical that you do a good job.

Be Prepared to Revise Your Plans Regularly

One of the toughest aspects of planning for the Internet is dealing with the fast rate of change online. If you spend too much time formulating your plan, your plan will be out-of-date by the time you finish it. On the other hand, if you do not spend enough time putting together an action plan that covers all the elements we discussed in the preceding section, your plan will be short-sighted because you will not have thought through all the issues. Don't spend too much or too little time with your plan, and, above all, keep in mind that your plan will continually need to be changed to adapt to new products, technologies, changing Internet demographics, and competitor activities.

Prepare an Outline of Your Web Site

In Chapter 14, "Setting Up a Web Site," there was a section entitled "Building an Effective Web Site." The point we were trying to make in that section is that anyone can create a Web site, but only with careful effort can you build a Web site that truly works. We believe that if you have identified the strategic reasons for your involvement with the Internet, you are on the right track.

When it comes to your on-line activities, strategy isn't the only required item; what is also required is "content." As we noted in Chapter 14: "A key objective when implementing a Web site is to try to get people to visit the site on a regular basis. The key word when it comes to the Web is content: you must provide people some useful content that will be of interest in order to draw visitors to your site."

Your earlier benchmarking process should have helped in identifying what might work in terms of content. As you visited other sites, you should have asked yourself the questions, "what are they doing in this site to keep people coming back? And is it working?" So you must take the time to identify the content that you could use on-line. To do so, prepare a "blueprint," or outline on paper, of your future Web site for the short, medium, and longer term. Prepare dummy Web pages if that helps. The outline should include specific details on the pages of information to be found in particular sections of the Web site. For example, clearly outline all the pages of information that you might expect to include in the "Customer Support Centre" section of the Web site.

Such an effort is not a trivial undertaking and can take a lot of time. However, experience has shown that by undertaking to "design" the site on paper, the organization is forced to clearly comprehend the complexity of the project. Such an exercise is also critical to obtaining a realistic quote for the design and implementation from an external Web design company if you decide to go that route. The initial design of the Web site should

- focus on creating a "home page" that reflects and highlights the key business strategies that you have outlined;
- ensure that a structure is created within the Web site that clearly addresses each item within your outline of objectives.

The paper design is just a "tree diagram" that helps to outline the components of the future Web site. The more detailed the better. For example, it might include the following categories, with each category expanded as appropriate:

We're More Than a Retailer!

Institutional/Financial Info

Residential Customer Centre

- Your Link to Magic ABC Company On-line
- Why Magic ABC? Our Credibility and History
- Customer Support Centre
- Our On-line Catalogue

Service and Store Locations

Warranty and Service Information

What's New

Feedback

Once such a design is complete, you can circulate the document to leading Web design companies for quotes, if you are having your Web site designed by an outside organization. If you are designing the Web site within your company, it is useful to keep the technical staff focused on the job at hand.

Get Funding

Experience has shown that the Internet cannot be implemented or managed on a shoestring budget. If the business is serious about using the Internet as a strategic tool, it must allocate sufficient resources to get the job done. Hence at this stage, you must take the time to ensure that management allocates sufficient funds to let you get the job done.

Dedicate Appropriate Resources

"Dedicate appropriate resources" means ensuring that you have the appropriate financial, human, and technical resources to effectively maintain your Internet site once you get it off the ground. This is why funding is so important. For example, who in your organization is going to be responsible for answering e-mail enquiries from potential customers and existing customers? Many organizations underestimate the number of e-mail messages that are generated by visitors to a Web site.

Some of the larger organizations on the Web, such as Apple Computer, receive in the neighborhood of 700 messages a week from customers and other Internet users. As we discussed earlier in the section on "The Electronic Consumer," consumers have high expectations when it comes to doing business electronically. Most consumers expect, and deserve, a prompt response to an e-mail query. If you invite customers to contact you by electronic mail, you should treat an electronic communication from a customer no differently than you would treat a telephone call from that same individual. This means checking your e-mail several times daily and responding promptly to customer queries as they arrive. If you set up a Web site and begin to solicit business that way, make sure that you can deliver.

Executing Your Plan

By now, you should have a good idea of what you should be doing on-line. Now is the time to proceed. A lot of what we covered in Chapter 14, "Setting Up a Web Site," will be relevant at this point. We suggest you reread the sections about what is involved in setting up a Web site and how to build an effective Web site. We have a few more suggestions for you as you proceed.

Stay Focused

As you become involved with the technology of the Internet, it is going to become all too easy for you to get off track. The Internet is like a drug: start using it, and you can quickly get sucked into the maelstrom, lost in all the excitement and allure that it represents. Avoid the temptation to go off on a technical tangent; stay focused on your strategic plan.

Continually Reinvent Your Plans

Hopefully, you have done a great job at outlining your Internet strategy. But as everyone who gets involved with the network learns, your first approach to the Internet certainly is not your last. Track some of the best Web sites, and you will observe that they are constantly changing. They are being fine-tuned, modified, and updated as the organization and people behind the sites continually learn what works and what doesn't work. You must be in the same frame of mind. In effect, take the time to periodically reinvent your strategy.

Don't Get Caught Up in Internet Hype!

As you begin to pursue a business strategy on the Internet, it is important that you do not get caught up in the hype of the Internet and develop unrealistic expectations of success. Why do we say this? Because it is our observation that much of the current hype about the Internet has led many otherwise sane individuals and organizations into rushing about trying to figure out how to capitalize on the Internet by "doing business on-line." And given the current "gold rush" mentality that envelopes anything Internet-related, they are doing so with some very short-term expectations about the potential impact that it could have on business.

As a result, there are many disappointed people, some poor business decisions, and activities that sometimes border on the fraudulent. And certainly, some common mistakes that seem to surround so much of what is going on with the Internet in the business world today. Consider what we have seen happening:

- Some people have unrealistic and false expectations about what the Internet represents. Listen to the radio or read the newspaper, and you will see advertisements that talk about the "Gold rush in cyberspace," "How to Make Money on the Internet!" and "Make Sure You Get Your Share of the Internet gold rush!" Beware of these ads: not only are they usually loaded with exclamation marks or feature breathless announcers when announced on-air, but, in our opinion, many of them are at worst fraudulent, and if not that, border on being dishonest.

  The reality? There is no way to get rich quick on the Internet. There is no pot of gold. There is no instant nirvana just waiting to solve all your business problems. Any one who leads you to believe that there is, is probably after one thing: the money in your pocket.

  The unfortunate reality of the Internet today, given the extreme amount of hype that surrounds the topic, is that there are tremendous overexpectations being built, in many cases due to a genuine belief, but in other cases due to basic human greed and dishonesty. If you are already involved with the Internet or decide to become involved, it is important that you keep reality in focus; there are business opportunities to be found on the Internet, but you have to work long and hard to make them bear fruit.

- Too much of a short-term focus. Not only will it take a lot of work to learn how to do business on the Internet, it will take a lot of time for the opportunities to establish themselves and pay off. We have stressed this point several times, and it is perhaps the most important point to appreciate as you become involved with the Internet. Many of the unrealistic expectations that we allude to above are fueled by ridiculously short-term expectations. Case in point: listen to some people talk about the Internet, and it is obvious they are leading others to believe that "all you need to do is put up a Web site and magic happens."

Let's be blunt. Magic does not happen and will not happen in the way that you are led to believe, at least not in the short term. And if it is going to happen in the medium and longer term, it is going to be because of a lot of hard work by yourself. Learning to take advantage of the Internet, whether by building a customer-focused Web site or establishing a new type of service on-line, is, in reality, a long and arduous process. There is no magic formula, and you should not expect to find one.

- A me-too attitude is rampant. We talked to the Vice-President of Marketing of a Fortune 500 company one day who actually said to us: "Well, we have to have a Web site because everyone else has one!" This is not the basis on which to approach the era of the wired economy. Sadly, the hype of the Internet means that too many organizations are rushing into it blindly without really understanding what it is they are doing and why they are doing it at all. This leads to poor business decisions, management ineptitude, unfocused projects, and immediate skepticism as soon as the promised "magic" does not occur.

- There are too many "brilliant" ideas that go nowhere. The hype of the Internet makes many people believe that there are business opportunities just waiting to be had on the Internet. Too often we see people who have bought into the idea that you "just plug in, set up shop, and you've got a brand-new, leading-edge business!" Except that is not reality. There are all kinds of people, each of whom thinks he/she has a significant new idea for a business initiative on-line, who discover that hundreds if not thousands of other people around the world already have the same idea. Many of these initiatives revolve around some type of exclusive on-line directory for which people or organizations must pay a fee to be listed.

  The problem is that often such directory initiatives are already underway, and each is struggling to define a role for itself. Consider this letter to the editor from the July 14, 1996 issue of *The Washington Post*, in which an owner of a small hotel comments: "I receive on average at least one solicitation for a listing on the Internet per week. Everybody and his brother is offering me GLOBAL EXPOSURE to MILLIONS of potential guests for an UNBELIEVABLY low price. No bed-and-breakfast, country inn or even large hotel can afford to be included in every on-line travel planner, reservation service or accommodations directory. The results are that dozens if not hundreds of travel peddlers on-line are offering directories that are skimpy at best."

- A misfocus on on-line shopping. Talk to anyone involved with the Internet these days, and the topic of on-line shopping will come up. Read the press and look at the headlines; it almost seems like there is a mantra that is repeated over and over by those in the Internet community: "If we solve the credit card transaction problem on the Internet, there will be lots of on-line shopping."

  Over and over people repeat the mantra, waiting and waiting for the explosion of on-line shopping. Perhaps if they repeat it often enough, it will come true! But it is our belief that the barrier to shopping on-line is not a technical one; it is behavioral. Simply put, it will take some time for a broad cross section of society to become comfortable with the concept of shopping on-line, even as the security problem is "fixed" (which it pretty well has been). It will take a long time for people to develop trust in the technology, to overcome their perceived fears about the Internet, and come to appreciate the convenience of shopping on-line.

In addition, there are some products that it just does not make sense to try to sell on-line, grocery shopping, for instance. From our viewpoint, people want to see if the lettuce is green, if the cut of meat is good, activities we cannot really do on the Internet. We want to try on a pair of jeans before buying them to check their fit, not order them through some new-fangled Internet home page.

Our point? We think that many well-adjusted individuals are not about to run out to become a bunch of crazed-computer-zombie-Internet-geek-dweeb-cybershoppers, ready to convert their lives to some type of plastic on-line shopping experience. There will be some consumers ready and willing to adopt to the "Internet way of doing things," but in the early days we think these will be rather insignificant in number.

Companies expecting to make a killing through the on-line shopping bonanza of the Internet should instead focus their Internet energies elsewhere, for example, in learning how to really use the Internet as an interactive marketing and customer support tool.

- There is a belief that "electronic commerce" is all about credit cards. Related to the on-line shopping focus, if you listen to some people, it would seem that business on the Internet is all about the use of credit cards on-line. We beg to differ. We think electronic commerce is about far more than that. As we outlined with our concept of "electronic glue," it should be apparent that it is about electronic funds transfer, electronic payment, and "electronic data interchange." It is about the ability for a customer to link directly to the purchase order system of the supplier and the ability for a supplier to make its inventory system available to potential customers. It is about direct electronic interaction between business organizations.

- Many on-line initiatives are not properly funded. One reason why it is so easy to say that management is still extremely tentative about the Internet is the sad reality that too many Internet projects are clearly not properly funded. Organizations plow ahead with limited budgets to create their Web site and then do not fund ongoing maintenance. The result? "What's New" sections that are over a year old. Links that don't work. Information that is obviously out-of-date. A Web site that consists of pretty pictures and not much else.

  Clearly, if organizations care to get involved with the Internet, they must provide proper funding for the project, not only to get the project off the ground, but to maintain and enhance the project well into the future. Organizations that do not provide their Internet project the proper degree of funding shouldn't bother going near the Internet at all.

- There is too much of a focus on technology and not enough on strategy fundamentals. Travel to many Web pages these days, and you might be immediately told, "please wait while our Shockwave add-on module downloads." An incomprehensible message to many mere mortals who are expected to sit and wait politely. And what do you get for your patience? A two-minute wait, after which a little animated character scurries across the screen. Wow! Did you see it go? No? Oh, well click to load it again even if it takes two minutes again. After all, you've got bags of time, right?

Unfortunately, too much of what seems to go on with the Internet is focused on the technology and not on the strategy. A Web site might support the latest, greatest technology, and be stillborn in terms of real business content.

- The marketing department has hijacked the Internet. If you listen to some folks, the Internet would seem to be all about marketing. And examine many of the Web sites on-line, and you will discover that they are nothing less than gussied-up brochures or advertisements, recooked at a higher temperature to be served up for the information age.

  Marketing is a critical and important business function, but if you listen to some folks, you would tend to think that it is the only one. The Internet is about much more than marketing; it is about customer support, feedback, and interaction, and the many other strategies we outlined in this chapter. It is a technology that can be used to change existing business processes to provide some efficiency and cost savings in customer and supplier interaction. It is a technology that could be used to assist an organization as it defines methods of doing old activities to make the business run better. It is about using the Internet to drive new corporate business partnerships that help the organization to focus on new strategic opportunities.

  The thing about the Internet is that it is about so much more than plain, simple marketing. But take a look around many organizations, and you will discover that currently the responsibility for the Internet lies within the marketing department, giving it an unrealistic and unnecessary focus on that particular topic. Organizations that fall into this trap lose their focus on Internet strategy and take too narrow a view of what it represents.

- Press releases have taken over the Internet agenda. We are prepared to argue that organizations involved with the Internet today care more about getting a good press release out than they care about getting any real strategy in place. The name of the game with the Internet seems to be to announce before doing and promise before delivery. Reality does not bear any weight when it comes to the Internet. Get your name out there before you get your plans in place!

  Just spend a little time browsing through on-line news wires such as Canada Newswire, Canadian Corporate News, PRNewswire, and Businesswire. Every day you can see press releases from all kinds of organizations, announcing their *significant, new* and *profound* Internet initiatives. Adjectives fly like promises in an election campaign. Chief executive officers state they are *leading-edge* and *visionary* and ready for the *twenty-first century!*

  And the amazing thing is the press eats this stuff up. Every day, it seems, the press reports on the latest huge Internet breakthrough. Forgive our skepticism, but frankly we are becoming rather tired of Internet press releases. We want real content, real initiatives, real strategy, and fewer announcements of grand plans and great agendas.

Does it sound like we are beating up on the Internet? Somewhat. On the other hand, let us say this: we believe that what is happening with the Internet is extremely profound and that business, society, government, and individuals will be forever transformed. We just don't think it is going to happen in the next ten minutes, and that people must come to adjust their expectations.

Business Challenges On-line

As the Internet expands, it brings with it some difficult challenges for government and private industry.

Fraud

As the Internet's popularity soars, so do reports of on-line fraud. So on the Internet the usual caveat applies: buyer beware. That is because many companies are using the Internet as the platform for their on-line scam operations. For example, a company called Fortuna Alliance was able to bilk Internet users of $6 million by operating an Internet-based pyramid scheme before being shut down by the Federal Trade Commission (**http://www.ftc.gov**) in 1996.

In another high-profile case the U.S. Securities and Exchange Commission (SEC) closed an Internet site that promised to earn investors "$150,000 annually, tax free." The SEC accused the site of fraudulently selling promissory notes.

Government authorities in both the United States and Canada are stepping up their efforts to detect on-line scams like these. The SEC (**http://www.sec.gov**), for example, has set up an Enforcement Complaint Center on the Web to accept complaints from Internet users.

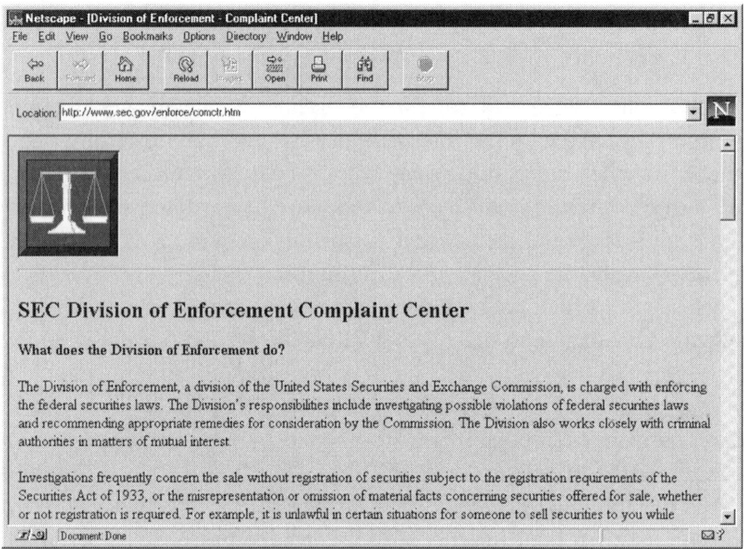

Internet proponents worry that this problem could discourage consumers from using the Internet as an electronic commerce tool.

Tax Evasion

As consumers begin to shop on-line, governments stand to lose millions of dollars in tax revenue. Why? In most Canadian provinces a sales tax is levied on many purchases, and the GST is applied on applicable purchases in all provinces. But on the Internet you can shop worldwide and avoid paying local taxes. Even when the on-line transaction is with a Canadian retailer, appropriate taxes are not always collected. Part of the problem is that the Internet blurs the distinction between a product and a service.

For example, a CD purchased in a record store is considered to be a "good." But if that same CD is downloaded over the Internet for a fee (as you will one day be able to do), it could be argued that the transaction is a service. Some industry analysts have proposed that the Canadian government implement a "proxy tax" to make up for the lost revenue. Such a tax would be levied on Internet service providers and perhaps passed on to consumers in the form of higher Internet access fees. The issue of taxation and the Internet is one that is bound to gain increasing attention in the years to come.

Think for the Future

Finally, we close this chapter with a simple observation: regardless of the cautionary tone we use in this chapter, we believe that every organization *must* become involved with the Internet. There is simply something too big and important happening here to ignore: The emergence of an economy that will increasingly function through computers, with those computers being linked through the Internet.

CHAPTER 17

Dealing With Offensive Content on the Internet

> *Parents, too, have options available to them. As we learned at the hearing, parents can install blocking software on their home computers, or they can subscribe to commercial online services that provide parental controls. It is quite clear that powerful market forces are at work to expand parental options to deal with these legitimate concerns. More fundamentally, parents can supervise their children's use of the Internet or deny their children the opportunity to participate in the medium until they reach an appropriate age.*
>
> Judge Stewart Dalzell in The United States District Court for the Eastern District of Pennsylvania, June 11, 1996

In a court decision that ruled the *U.S. Communications Decency Act* to be unconstitutional, Judge Dalzell clearly stated that it is the parents, not the government, who are ultimately responsible for shielding their children from offensive content on the Internet. Yet another responsibility added to the complexities of being a parent in today's age! Fortunately, parents who are concerned that their kids may access offensive content on-line can use any number of different software programs to help them manage and restrict their children's activities on-line.

Parenting and the Internet

There is no denying that there is an increasing use of the Internet in the home by families. Many parents end up joining the Internet in order to exchange e-mail with their children who are at college or university. Many students are provided with an Internet e-mail ID during registration or must learn how to use it as part of a course. Once they return home from college or university for a visit, talk around the dinner table inevitably turns to the Internet, and the kids end up convincing mom and dad to join. Soon, the family is "wired," with parents and children exchanging e-mail on a regular basis.

Of course, use of the Internet in families is not restricted to e-mail; many families are taking the time to learn how to use the World Wide Web. Inevitably, the kids pressure mom and dad to get an Internet account because their friends are on-line.

The 1995 Christmas season was the first time that computers outsold televisions, with the result that many of the kids are taking the time to learn how to use computers to assist with their homework and other studies. Your reaction may be "come on; there aren't that many people using the Internet." But keep in mind another interesting trend: television viewership has started to decline because of the Internet! A Coopers and Lybrand study found that 58% of the computer users it polled in a survey were cutting back on television time in order to go on-line. Today's parents need not only concern themselves with offensive content on television; they also have to deal with undesirable content on the Internet.

Parents wonder if they should join the Internet and then become concerned about offensive content. The first thing that parents should realize is that there are many useful, child-oriented sites that can provide a rich and rewarding on-line experience. Two simple examples help to illustrate this point:

- For the very young, have a look at the site for Theodore the Tugboat, the lead character in a popular Canadian television show (**http://www.cochran.com/tt.html**). As indicated on-line, "Children can help Theodore decide what to do next in an illustrated, interactive story created especially for the Internet. You can also download a page from our on-line coloring book or receive a postcard with Theodore's picture."

DEALING WITH OFFENSIVE CONTENT ON THE INTERNET

1. There is offensive content on the Internet — and parents should recognize it is their role to guide their children's use of the Internet.
2. There are many Internet filtering programs that allow parents to restrict access to particular sites and content on the Internet. These programs include CyberPatrol, CYBERsitter, Internet Filter, NetNanny, NetShepherd, SurfWatch and Tattle-Tale.
3. There are also many sites throughout the Internet that guide children to sites that contain content appropriate for them.
4. The Internet industry is working to develop "content rating schemes" which can be used to define the type of content found at particular Internet sites.
5. Parents should take the time to educate themselves about the issue of information filtering on-line, and should understand that they, not the government, are ultimately responsible for protecting their children from offensive content on-line.

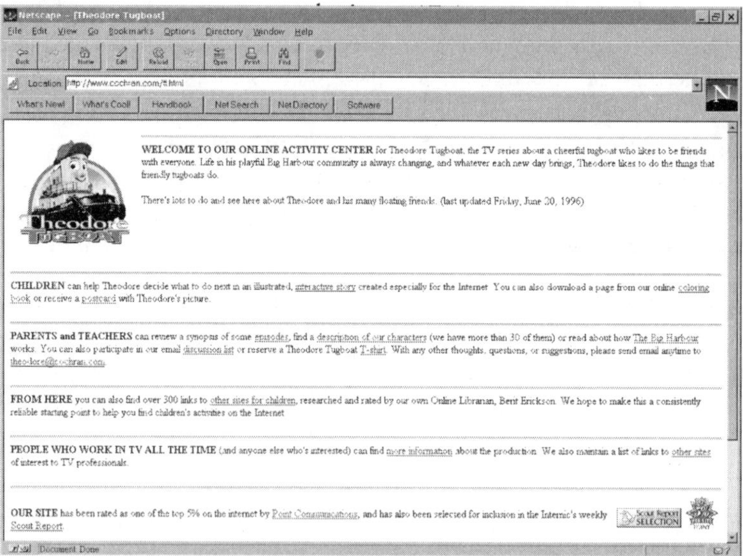

Sure enough, if you visit the site and request the postcard, a few days later a colorful little card arrives in the mail from Theodore, thanking you for visiting him on the Internet. Kids love it!

- For older children you can start at the site "SciEd: Science and Mathematics Education Resources," which is a listing of specific scientific and math education resources found on the Internet (**http://www-hpcc.astro.washington.edu/scied/science.html**). Within minutes of visiting there, kids can find themselves locating pictures of the solar system, planets and galaxies; traveling to sites containing information about earthquakes, volcanoes, and weather; or visiting museums around the globe.

Get involved with the Internet, and you can discover thousands of similar sites that contain "kid-friendly" information. Parents, of course, face several dilemmas when it comes to the Internet:

- Kids are pressuring parents to join the Internet. Kids are not dumb. They know that something "big" is happening with the Internet, and they want to be part of it. They see it talked about on television, in the news, and in the classroom. They want on, and they are pushing the parents to link them up to the Internet at home. If the parents ignore their requests, some of them run out and get an Internet account on their own. Technical-savvy kids are no match for computer-illiterate parents.
- The Internet is being introduced into the classroom. The federal government and all provinces have agreed to try to link all schools into the Internet by the end of 1997. Even if parents wanted to avoid the Internet, they cannot. It is becoming a part of the educational system, and there is no avoiding it.
- Internet addresses are hard to avoid. They appear on television commercials, in magazine and newspaper ads, and on radio programs. For example, many movie ads now prominently feature Internet addresses. There is a lot of temptation for kids to get onto the Internet and explore the sites they are being exposed to in the media.

- The Internet will soon be a required skill. There is no doubt that the Internet will change the world of business. Therefore, it will become just as important for kids to know how to find information on the Internet tomorrow as it is for them to know how to use a library today. "Cyberspace navigation," the ability to perform electronic research, will become a critical business and career skill in the years to come.

  Students are already increasing their reliance on the Internet. In the United States, for example, eight out of ten college students surveyed by AT&T say they are likely to use the Internet as a job-search tool.

Parents really have no choice, do they? One way or another, their kids are going to be on the Internet, and the question for parents becomes, do we or do we not get involved in helping them to learn how to use it?

Offensive Material on the Internet

Many parents are concerned that if children use the Internet, they will be suddenly deluged with revolting information. Media hype would lead them to believe that the Internet is nothing more than a cesspool of sick and disgusting information: child pornography, hate literature, bomb-making instructions, and other evils, and that kids are suddenly surrounded by perverts as soon as they venture on-line.

Parents should remember that the media does not always report reality, and when it comes to the Internet, the simple fact of the matter is that many media organizations have overstated the reality of the Internet in their quest for sensational news reports. As we wrote in our 1996 *Canadian Internet Handbook*, "the authors of this book, like many Internet users in Canada, are sometimes disgusted with the fraud and deception that often permeates coverage of these difficult Internet issues in the media."

(You can find the full chapter on-line at our Web site (**http://www.handbook.com**); it is a good primer on how the media has misrepresented the Internet.)

The reality is that if you use the media as your source of information on what the Internet is all about, you will sometimes be badly misled. Why do we say this? There is no doubt there is offensive material on-line, but the extent of the problem reported by the media is often far beyond the reality.

There are two other key issues when it comes to understanding the risk of your children encountering offensive content on the Internet:

- In most cases kids have to choose to go out and access this information. Only in rare circumstances are kids sent unsolicited offensive material, so you can forget the media image of kids instantly coming across pornography as soon as they get on-line.

- An increasing number of programs, called "Internet filters," have become available. These programs, to the extent possible, can restrict access to offensive material.

The Need for Parental Involvement

Parents must recognize that useful as well as tasteless information is available on the Internet and that sooner or later, their kids are going to discover some of this offensive material.

The question parents must ask themselves is, how will we deal with this fact? Just sit back and ignore it? Hope that the kids do not explore any nasty sites on-line? Let them discover it on their own or discover the Internet with the wisdom of parental guidance? And will parents become involved in managing their child's use of the Internet to minimize any risk they will access unwanted information?

Parents cannot just wish that the Internet will go away, because it will not. Parents also cannot hope that the government will step in and regulate the content on the Internet, since for all intents and purposes, the government is impotent when it comes to such regulation. The next step to keep in mind is that as parents not only do we need to educate our children, but we need to shape their morals and teach them a sense of right and wrong, including the right and wrong aspects of the Internet. We can do this by directly getting involved in monitoring and guiding use of the Internet by our kids. We need to teach them that just as there are negative things in society and that they should never get into a car with strangers, there are negative things on the Internet, and they must always be cautious what they do on-line.

Finally, parents can put in place some technical restrictions over access to the Internet by their children, by using Internet filters. But in doing so, the parent must realize that such a program can never be 100% effective and that it does not eliminate the need for parental involvement.

In this chapter we take a look at the following three methods of controlling access to offensive content on the Internet:

- Internet filter programs;
- kid-appropriate content guides;
- voluntary rating systems.

Internet Filter Programs

Partly in response to government attempts to regulate the Internet and partly because entrepreneurs have discovered a market, we have seen the release of several programs that help parents deal with offensive material on-line. These programs, often referred to as "Internet filters," do one or more things. They might

- prevent access to particular sites on the Internet containing offensive material;
- provide a "log" of on-line activity so that the parent can see which sites their kids have been visiting;
- shut down or restrict access to the computer if a certain number of offensive sites are accessed.

The definition of what is considered to be "offensive" information can differ, depending upon the particular filter being used. Many of the programs will refer to a list of offensive sites maintained by the software developer and allow the user to obtain an up-to-date list of new offensive sites, thus helping to deal with the explosive growth of the Internet.

Parents have a number of choices when it comes to choosing a software program that will allow them to control what their children do on-line. Many of these software programs provide very sophisticated methods of controlling access and, from our review, worked quite well at achieving their goal. However, anyone planning on using any of these programs must keep several things in mind:

- None of these programs are infallible. In all cases you are relying on a computer technology to screen out information that is considered offensive. The software will only be as good as the underlying programming. The nature of the Internet is such that no one can ever design a program that will be 100% effective in blocking out offensive material.
- As we mention throughout this book, the Internet is growing at a remarkable rate, with one result being that the volume of offensive material is growing at a similar rate. Thus these programs will never be 100% current, even though many of the developers provide regular, ongoing updates to their listings of "offensive" sites.
- One person's offensive material is another person's art. Everyone on this planet is different; hence some may view some of these programs as going too far, while others will feel that they do not go far enough.

The bottom line is that Internet filters are useful and can help to ease parental concern about offensive material on the Internet, but they are no substitute for the role of the parent.

CyberPatrol

CyberPatrol is that one of the most sophisticated and flexible filtering programs that we examined. The fun begins with installation: it plays the theme from the TV show *Hawaii Five-O* while being installed. CyberPatrol allows a parent to set up restrictions on access to Internet sites based on content, time of day, and even on the total time the Internet is used by the child. These restrictions can be used to provide full access, no access at all to particular Internet applications, or selective access based on lists defined by CyberPatrol and the parent. It also allows access restrictions to be placed on other computer activities such as games. It allows this through a very flexible control screen, access to which can be protected by a password.

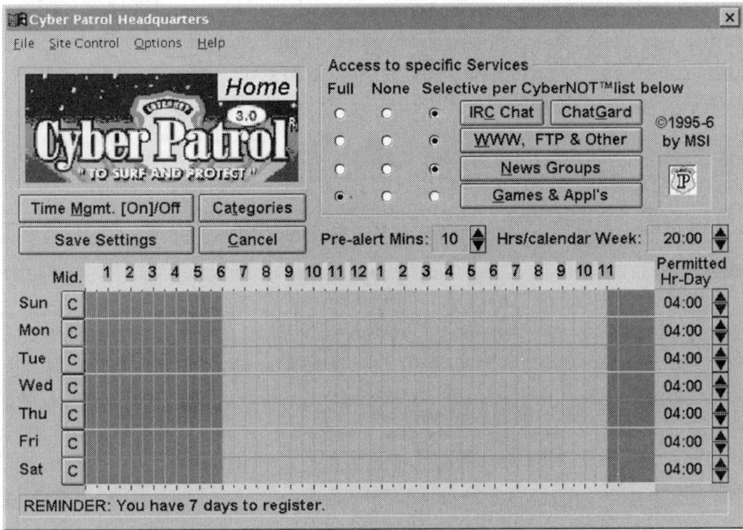

In order to filter out objectionable sites, CyberPatrol provides a "CyberNOT" and a "CyberYES" list of Internet sites. The former is the list of "banned sites," while the latter is a list of sites that can be visited because they have been rated as having content suitable for children. These lists are provided by the software company that created CyberPatrol, so you are relying on their judgment of what are "good" and "bad" sites. When you try to access a restricted site, you quickly get a notice saying that you will not be permitted to do so, such as when we tried to access Playboy:

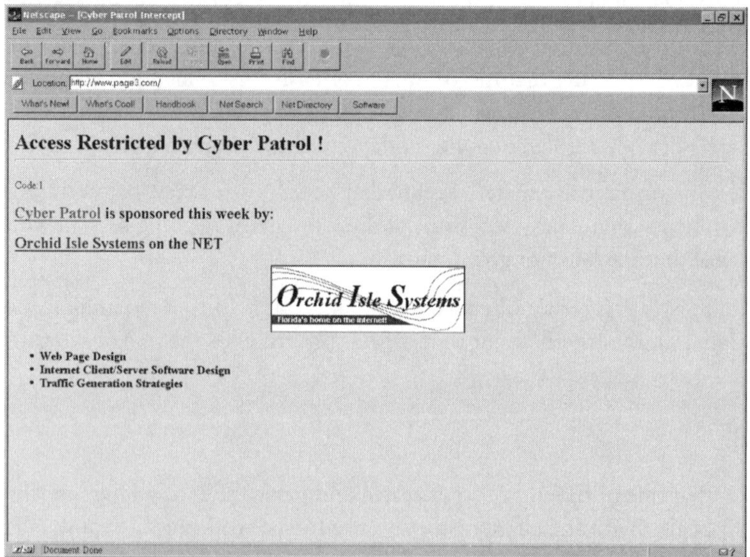

You can use the CyberNOT and CyberYES lists in different ways, depending upon the approach you want to take to controlling access to the Internet by your children. Say you are concerned that even though CyberPatrol has a list of banned sites, your child might still get through to some offensive sites, either because they are new or because the folks at CyberPatrol have missed them in their summary of offensive sites. No problem. In this case you could choose to restrict access to only those sites identified by CyberPatrol as having good content for children, and you choose to use the CyberYES list. From this point on CyberPatrol will block your child from accessing *any* Web sites other than those deemed by CyberPatrol as being worthwhile for children. These sites are found on the CyberPatrol Route 6-16 list (**http://www.microsys.com/616/default.htm**):

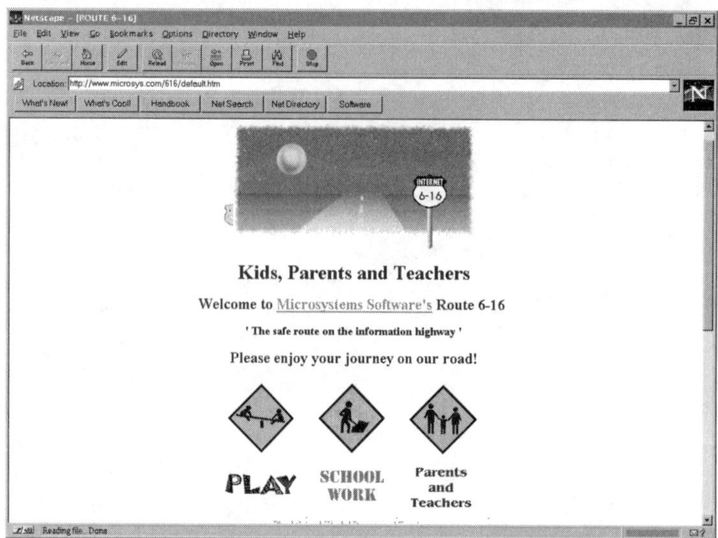

On the other hand, you may want your child to be able to access any site except those deemed offensive by CyberPatrol. In that case you choose to provide "selective access" with restrictions based on sites in the "CyberNOT" list. This allows your child to explore the Internet but not access those sites identified by CyberPatrol as having offensive content. The CyberNOT list categorizes offensive sites by the nature of their content, as seen by the categories below. You can choose to selectively define what types of sites should be filtered while you are on-line.

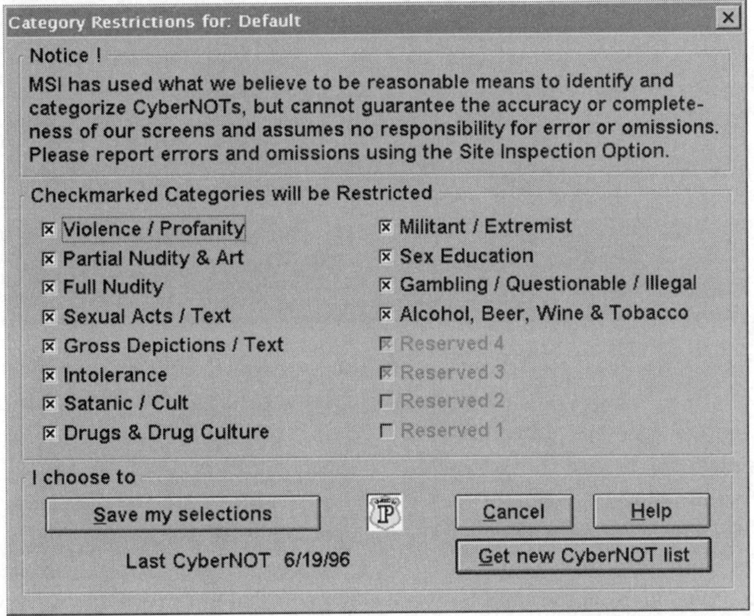

The folks at CyberPatrol maintain an updated list of "offensive" and "good" Web sites that form the basis of the CyberNOT and CyberYES lists. You can obtain updates of these lists at any time, simply by clicking on a button. CyberPatrol also provides for content filtering based on several of the rating schemes that are emerging on the Internet. These are schemes in which Web sites are rated for content by an automated program or by an individual at a rating organization. The Web page is then assigned a rating code, which is entered into the Web page HTML code.

When CyberPatrol accesses the page that has been rated, it compares it to the type of access that has been defined by the parent and allows or denies access accordingly. These emerging rating schemes provide for different levels of access depending upon the type of content. For example, the sex category allows for up to five different levels of access, depending upon the content rating.

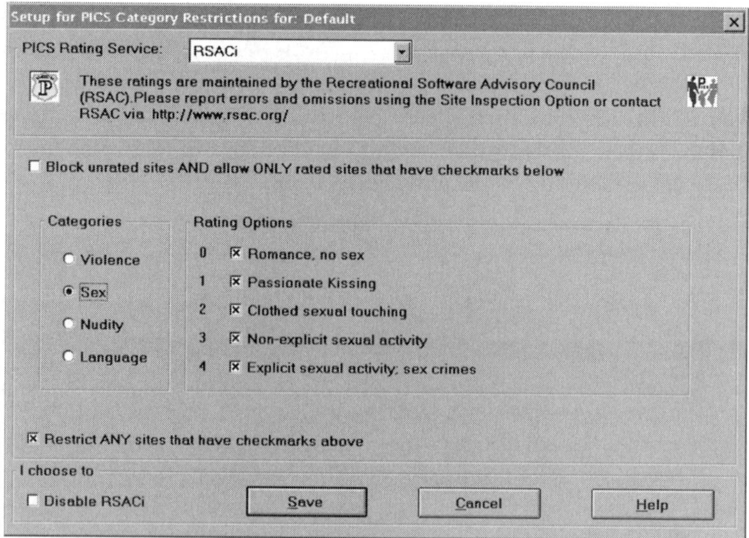

CyberPatrol is not restricted to Web sites; it can also apply to USENET newsgroups, FTP sites, and IRC chat lines. In terms of the latter, it can prevent access to IRC groups that contain certain words in their title, thus preventing your child from getting into specific groups focused on offensive content.

Not only that, in a very useful feature CyberPatrol also allows the parent to specify that if the child joins an IRC chat group that does not contain an offensive word in the title, but does type or see certain words, those words are replaced with xxx's. Parents can add specific words to the "offensive word list" to prevent the child from providing personal information to someone on-line. This feature can prevent the child from participating in certain discussions and from providing someone with personal information, such as telephone numbers or addresses.

ChatGard – Chat Filtering Control for: Default

Chat Groups can be one of the most dangerous areas of the Online experience. ChatGard is designed to watch words as they are typed by your child or copied from the clipboard to "filter" certain words and strings of characters.

The famous Carlin-7 words are included at the front of the list. These cannot be viewed or removed.

Specific Entries

First/Last Name:

Street Address:

City:

State/Zip Code:

Phone #:

School:

E-mail Address:

Enter the information EXACTLY as you want ChatGard to filter it. For example: last name only or the last 4 digits of your phone number.

Other words to filter:

Disable ChatGard

I choose to

Save Changes | Delete highlighted item | Cancel | Help

Does it work? Most definitely. We gave it a try and it worked like a charm.

CyberPatrol also allows the parent to restrict Internet access to certain times of the day. This could mean, for example, that the child is prevented from accessing the Internet during the day while a baby-sitter is there, so that access is only allowed in the evenings while the parents are home. It also permits limits to be set on the total time spent surfing each week.

Finally, CyberPatrol allows control over access to particular software on your computer; you just list the applications that can be excluded. You can also restrict access to other communication programs that use a modem through this screen thus, for example, preventing a child from using a regular communications program to access a bulletin board.

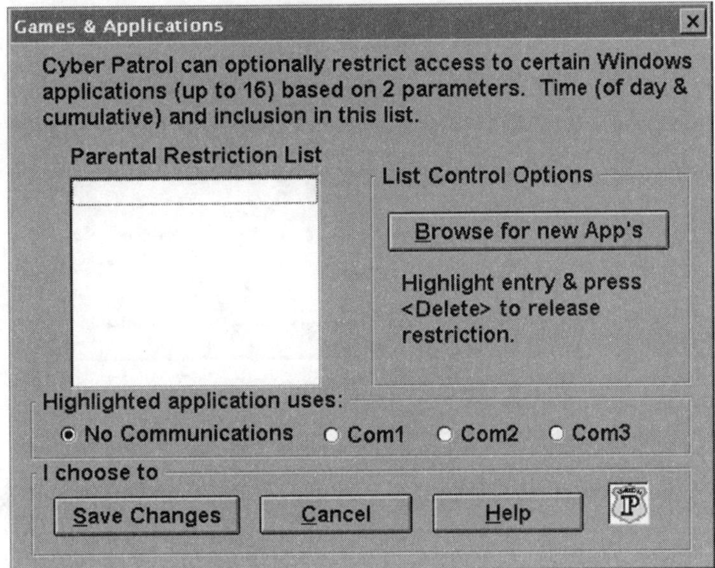

All in all, CyberPatrol has a lot of flexibility and should provide more than enough control for parents who are concerned about use of the Internet by their kids. To top it off, parents can add their own sites to the CyberNOT and CyberYES lists. You can find out more about CyberPatrol at **http://www.cyberpatrol.com**. The program is available for Windows and Macintosh computers.

CYBERsitter

Like CyberPatrol, CYBERsitter operates by referring to a list of sites that contain offensive content. During setup, you can specify to CYBERsitter whether it should completely restrict access to these sites, report on when they are accessed, or report and restrict.

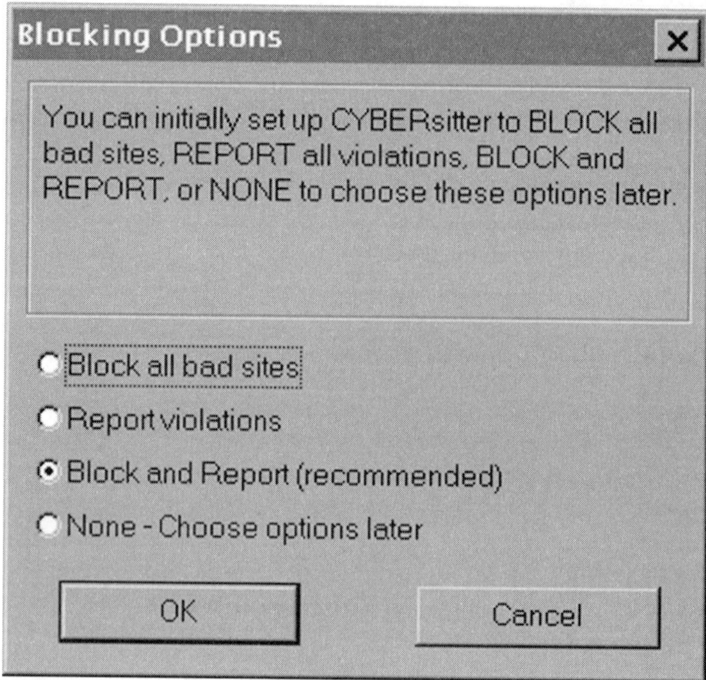

You can also have it report on all the Internet sites that are visited during any Internet session. This might help you get an idea of what your children (or parents!) are doing on-line.

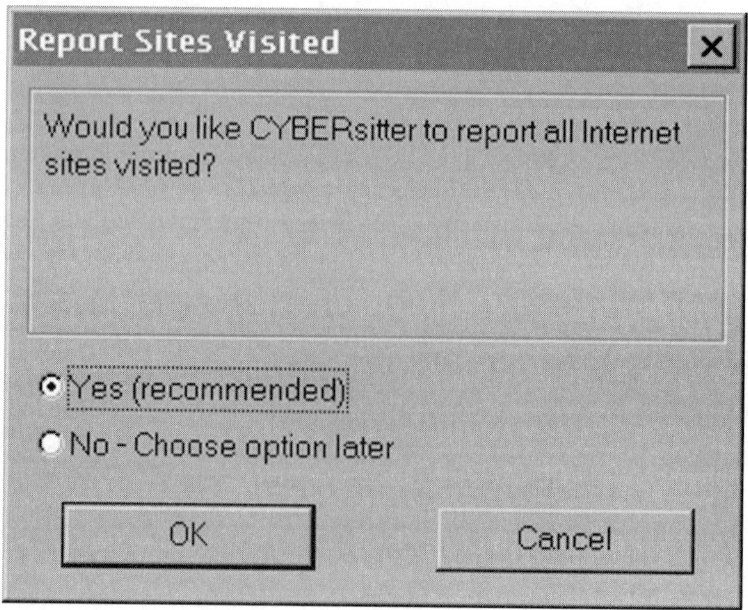

You can change any of these options later, once the program has been installed.

CYBERsitter works by blocking content accessed through the World Wide Web, USENET newsgroups, or FTP sites. It does this in two ways. First, it simply does not permit access to a list of "banned sites." For example, if you try to access a site on the "banned site list" (e.g., **http://www.playboy.com**), you are simply told you are not permitted to access it.

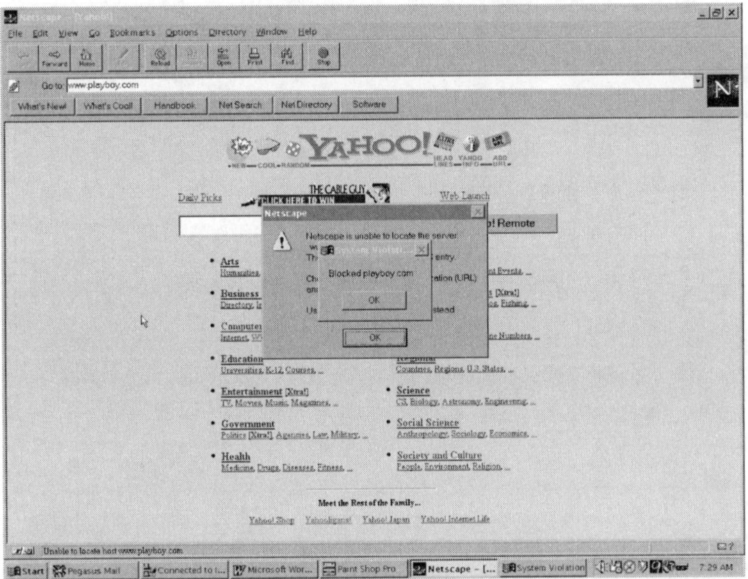

Given the constant rate at which the Internet evolves and the fact that there are hundreds of new Web sites every day, CYBERsitter gives a simple, easy way to obtain a list of new banned sites at any time from the developer, Solid Oak Software. (The program also tells you the last time your filter file was updated.)

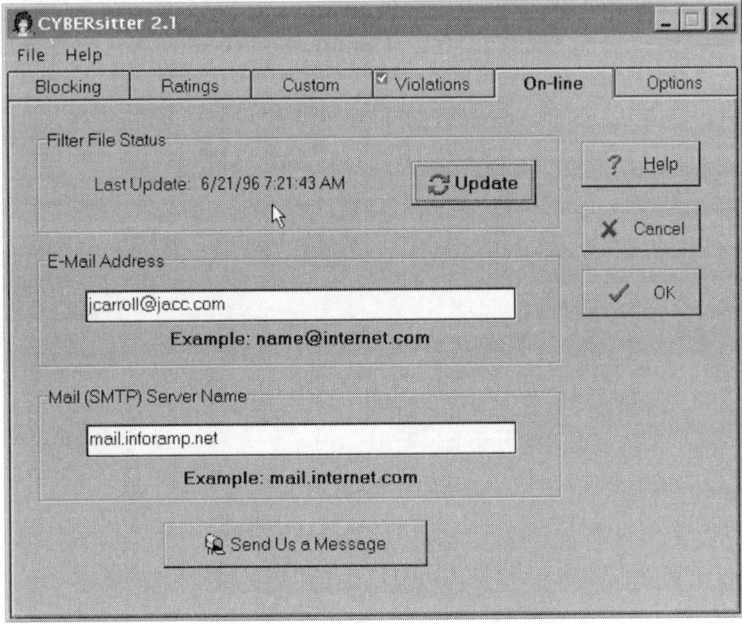

Simply click on "Update," and it begins transferring the most recent filter file to you. This way, you can help ensure that you are relying on CYBERsitter to keep your system up-to-date in banning the most recent objectionable sites on the Internet.

Another feature of CYBERsitter is that it filters out any "banned phrases." Travel to Yahoo!, for example, and take a look at the "Society and Culture" category; it has a category for "Sexuality":

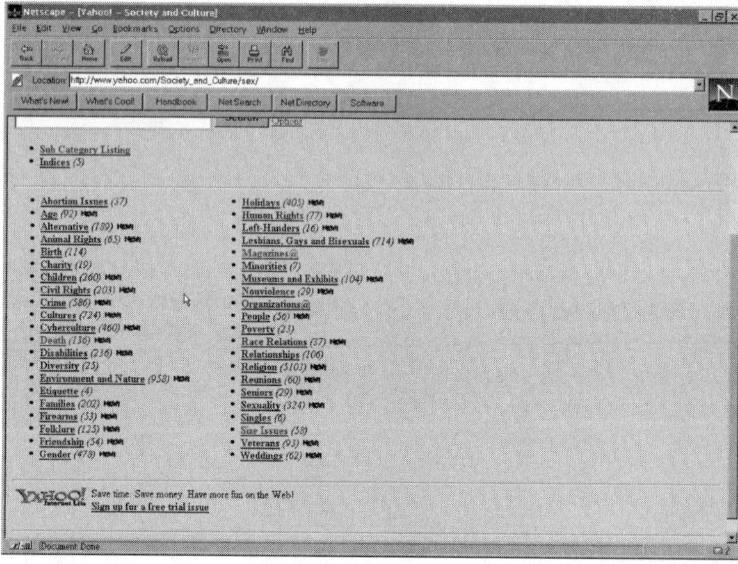

Travel there with CYBERsitter active, and the "Sexuality" topic does not exist anymore; CYBERsitter has filtered it out.

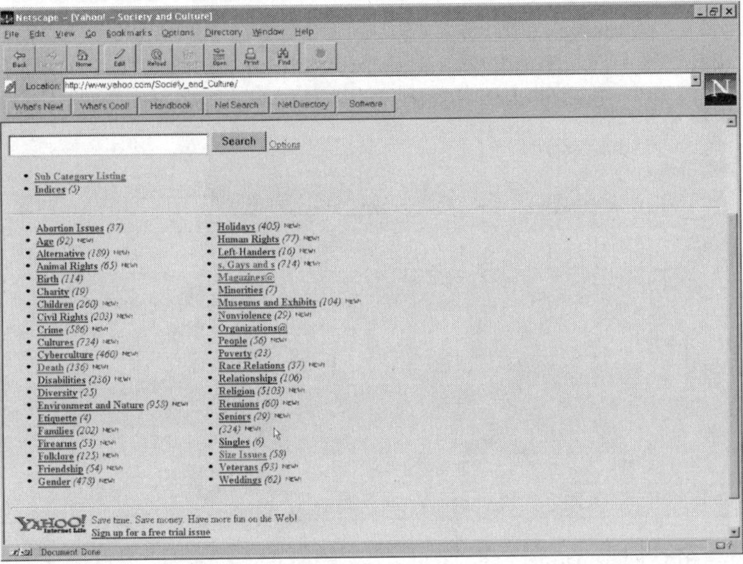

Hence CYBERsitter will automatically filter out objectionable phrases. You can add your own words and phrases if you wish.

Finally, another useful feature is a log that records any violations, that is, any sites to which your children are trying to gain access. You can also set the log so that it records all Internet activity, helping you understand in even more depth what they are doing on-line.

All in all, CYBERsitter appeared to be more than adequate as a tool to deal with objectionable content on the Internet for Windows 95 machines. You can find out more about CYBERsitter at **http://www.solidoak.com/index.htm.**

Internet Filter

Internet Filter lets you define a series of "bad domains" (or Web sites), "bad" newsgroups, and "bad" phrases that your child should not have access to or see. It also comes with a list of predefined "bad" sites, newsgroups, and phrases, with updates being made available on-line. You can then assign each "bad" domain, newsgroup, or keyword a violation level of 1 to 3:

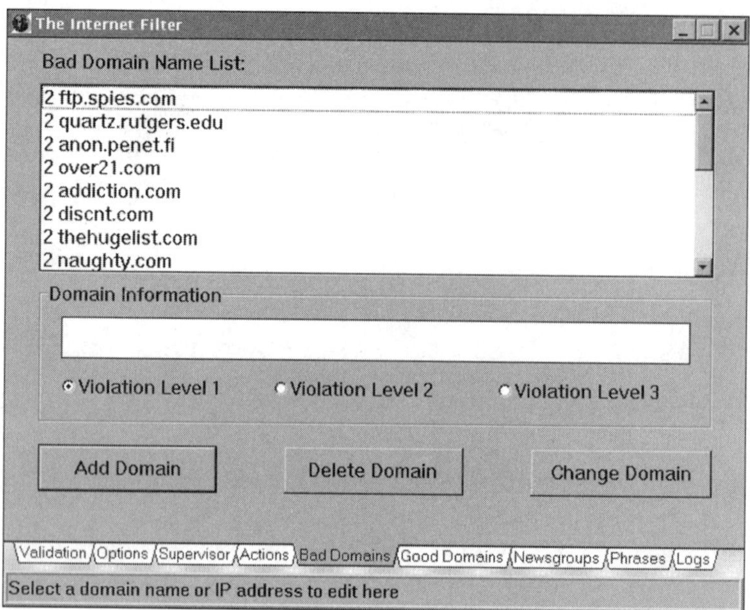

You can then define what happens for each of the three violation levels. The possibilities are:

- censoring out the phrase;
- writing details about the activity into a log for later review;
- sending you an e-mail message with details of the activity;
- shutting down the Internet connection.

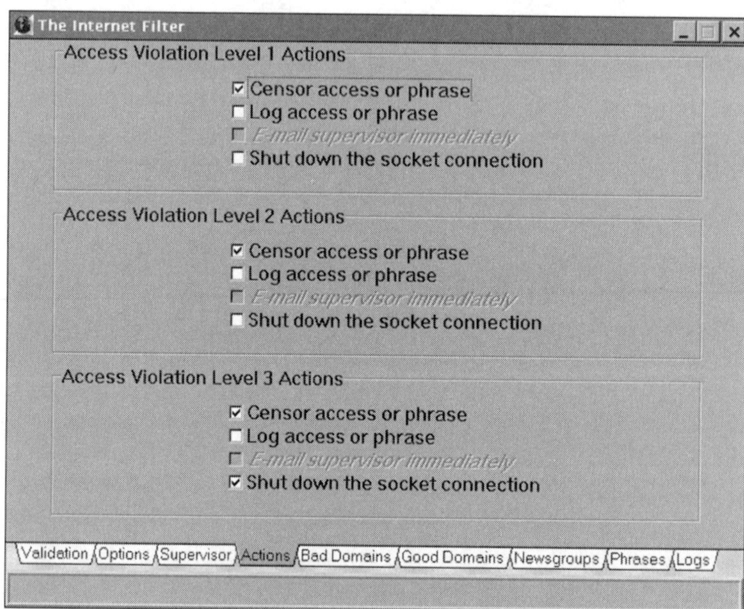

In this way, you are essentially providing for different levels of severity depending upon the type of infraction. You also have control over the extent to which Internet Filter will restrict on-line activities, if you do not want to restrict access to USENET news, for example:

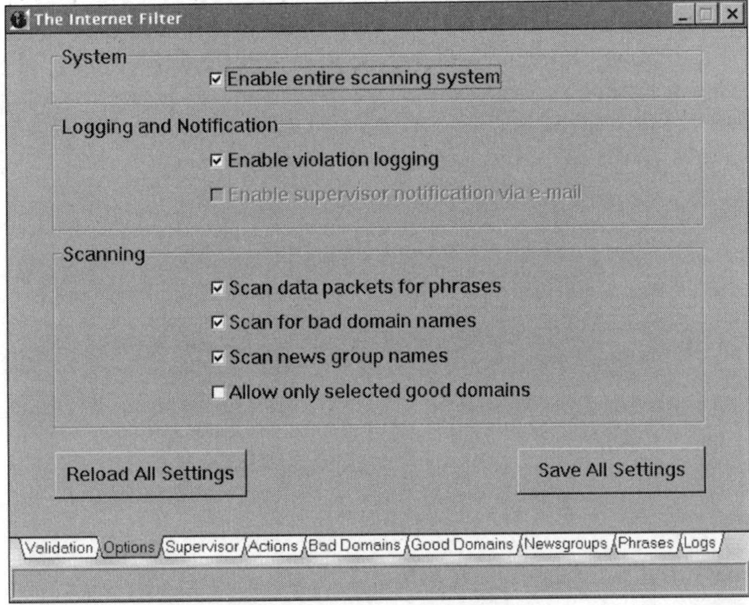

An evaluation version of Internet Filter is available on the Internet at no charge. It features the full capabilities of the Internet Filter program, with the exception that you cannot make and save any changes to the configuration or the list of banned sites.

Internet Filter is a concise, simple, and straightforward program that will provide an adequate level of protection, and since you can download the trial "version zero" for free on-line, you can experiment with the product before deciding to make a purchase. You can find out more about Internet Filter at **http://www.xmission.com/~seer/Turner/index.html.** The program is available for Windows systems (Windows 3.1 and 95).

NetNanny

NetNanny takes a different approach to the filtering issue. Rather than specifically looking at what you are accessing by referring to a list of "good" or "bad" sites, NetNanny examines what you type on your computer or what words appear on your screen. If either are on the list of the "objectionable word dictionary," it records that as a "hit."

You can instruct NetNanny to shut the computer down if a certain number of "hits" are reached. In this way, you are effectively saying to your children: "I'll be watching, and if you are doing things you shouldn't, not only will I know about it, but you won't be able to use the computer again until I let you."

Because of the approach it takes, NetNanny can screen e-mail messages, FTP sites, USENET newsgroups, IRC sessions, and any other application running on or off the Internet. This includes anything that might be accessed through bulletin boards, CD ROMs, computer programs, and other computer applications.

One virtue of NetNanny is its flexibility. The owner of the PC has total control over what is blocked and can add, delete, or modify what is being blocked through control of the dictionary of offensive terms. In addition, when NetNanny is installed, the parent can become the "system administrator" and thus the only person who can define what can or cannot be accessed based on the terms in the dictionary.

Like CYBERsitter, NetNanny provides an on-line site through which users of the software can download an updated list of objectionable words. The process, however, is not as automatic and convenient as with some of the other programs we review in this chapter. After installing the software, you first run the NetNanny administration program.

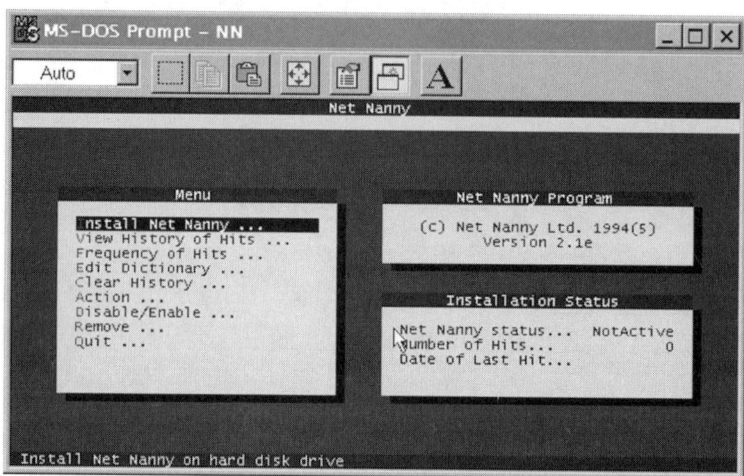

This program allows you to set up the actions that should occur if the offensive words or phrases are typed or appear on the screen, as well as the tools to manage the dictionary of offensive content. Then, whether your child is using a program in Windows or DOS, NetNanny operates in the background, tracking what your child is doing and taking action accordingly.
However, there are some very real limitations to NetNanny:

- The program operates on the basis of words that it finds in the dictionary. Since it does not provide a predefined list of terms, it is up to the parent to dream up as many words as possible that might represent objectionable content. This problem can be overcome by downloading a starter dictionary from NetNanny (**http://www.netnanny.com/netnanny/dictionary.html**).

- It cannot filter out graphics unless you manage to define them by file name. Hence there is no stopping your child from seeing a graphic button labeled "Hot Sex Chat 24-hrs a day." NetNanny will not be able to prevent your child from seeing that graphic, and if that site contains only graphics, not text, NetNanny will not be able to act.

Because of its shut-down mechanism, NetNanny seems designed for parents who want to take an ironfisted approach to use of the Internet by their children. You can find out more about NetNanny at **http://www.netnanny.com**. The program is available for Windows 3.1, and a version is planned for Windows 95.

NetShepherd

The approach that NetShepherd takes to filtering Internet content is perhaps one of the most unusual. Once installed, NetShepherd adds a tiny bar to the bottom of your Netscape screen, as seen below:

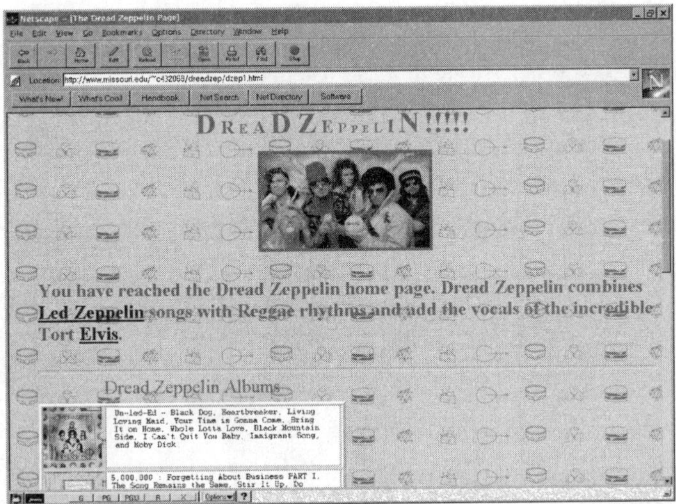

This bar provides a dynamic, ever-changing "rating" of the type of information you are currently accessing, according to the scale used in movies: G (general), PG (parental guidance), PG13 (parental guidance 13), R (restricted), and X (X-rated).

The rating bar works in two ways:

- If a page has been rated and is in your "local ratings database" or the NetShepherd rating database, the rating for that page will be highlighted. For example, travel to the Playboy site, and you can see that the rating is highlighted on R:

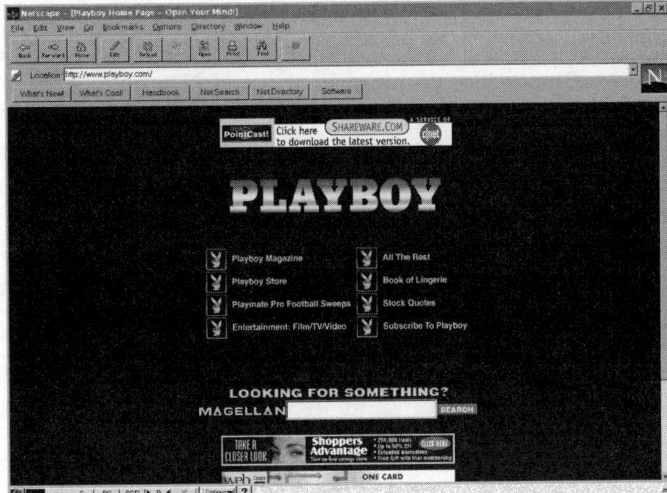

This means that the NetShepherd system has rated Playboy as restricted.

- If you go to a site that has not been rated, no highlight shows up on the ratings bar.

Here is where things get interesting. The administrator of NetShepherd, that is, the parent, can assign different rating levels to particular computer users, restricting the types of pages they can access. For example, on the screen below user "Jim" is permitted to access only G (general) areas and is not allowed to access sites that have not been rated. This pretty well restricts what he can do on the Web to only those sites that have been rated by NetShepherd as G (general). Other users could be allowed to access progressively more adult-rated sites:

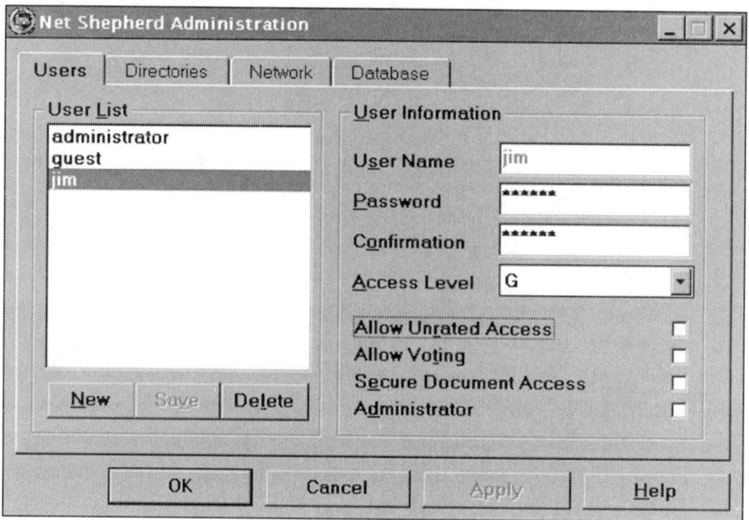

The power of this rating scheme might not be apparent, so imagine this scenario. A teacher wants to provide her students with access to just five Web sites. The teacher visits those sites, rates them as G, and makes sure the students do not turn on "Allow Unrated Access." This means that the students will only be able to visit those five Web sites and other general-rated sites.

Where do the ratings come from? As the folks at NetShepherd say on their Web site, "NetShepherd is not just a filtering system that can block unwanted material. It is a fully interactive rating, classification and information management system."

They go on to comment that "unlike solutions introduced so far, NetShepherd gives you a voice in deciding what is and what is not appropriate on the Net. It is not just a static blacklist of bad sites, but rather a dynamic, constantly changing list of rated information. Our databases of ratings never sleep as they are continuously contributed to by people who surf the Net every day. You then have the choice to use NetShepherd as a simple blacklist program, or you can use it to give you selective filtered access to the WWW."

If you have the right computer configuration (i.e., you are running a "32-bit" Web browser), NetShepherd will also filter out Web sites and USENET newsgroups based on content. For example, here is the Yahoo! sexuality category:

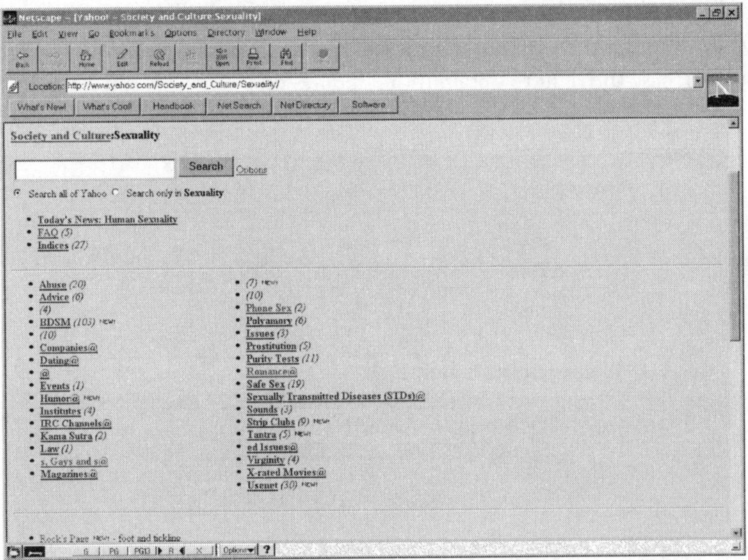

NetShepherd takes one of the most innovative approaches to on-line filtering of all the programs we examine in this chapter and subscribes to the philosophy that rather than banning everything outright, there should be only progressive levels of restricted access. You can find out more about NetShepherd at **http://www.shepherd.net**. The program is available for Windows 95 systems.

SurfWatch

At the time we looked at it, SurfWatch was one of the few programs available for both Windows and Macintosh systems. SurfWatch does not offer the degree of configuration flexibility that we found in programs such as CYBERsitter in defining what can or should be restricted; in fact, it is perhaps one of the most unobtrusive filtering products we review in this chapter. However, it is a program that is enjoying a very high degree of success in the market and has been adopted by many of the largest Internet service providers as their filtering product of choice.

It operates by referring to a list of offensive sites maintained by the SurfWatch organization. When you buy the software and install it, one of the first things it does is retrieve the most up-to-date list of offensive sites:

You can get two more free updates, which will happen in the first and second month after you install the software. During the installation process, you are given the opportunity to register with SurfWatch to purchase the right to obtain more updates on a regular basis, for a monthly or annual fee:

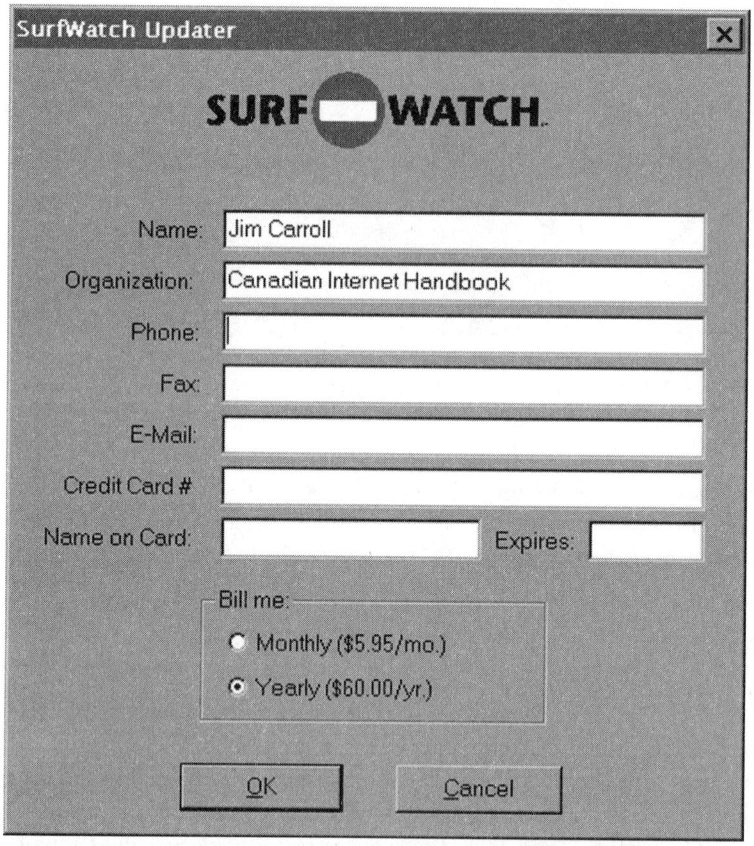

Once SurfWatch is installed, there is not much you can do with it; it simply sits quietly in the background, examining your connection to the Internet. Should it find you accessing any offensive Web sites, USENET newsgroups, FTP sites, or IRC channels, it blocks your access:

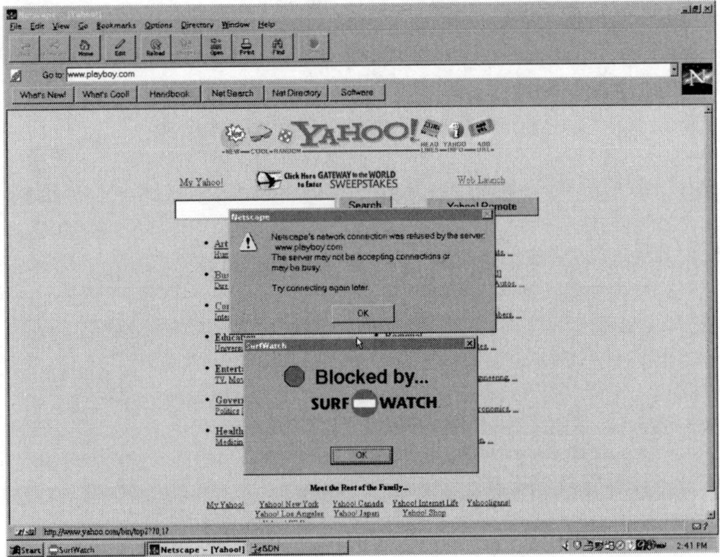

That is it; a simple, straightforward installation with a simple, straightforward method of operation. If you want something uncomplicated and do not want to have to fool with a lot of different methods of controlling access to offensive content on-line, SurfWatch is a good choice. You can find out more about SurfWatch at **http://www.surfwatch.com**.

Tattle-Tale

The approach taken to the Internet by Tattle-Tale is simple: It wants to excel as a tool that reports where your children have been on the Internet. It accomplishes this by keeping track of all the World Wide Web sites visited (and soon, IRC chat groups and e-mail sent and received). You can then view this report on-screen and see the URLs visited. Or, with its most convenient feature, you can generate an HTML file containing the sites the children visited and then easily travel to each of those sites from within your Web browser.

For example, we went to a number of sites. We then had a look at Tattle-Tale and confirmed that it had kept track of all the visits. It took only seconds to generate an HTML file, load it into our Netscape browser, and then travel to those sites.

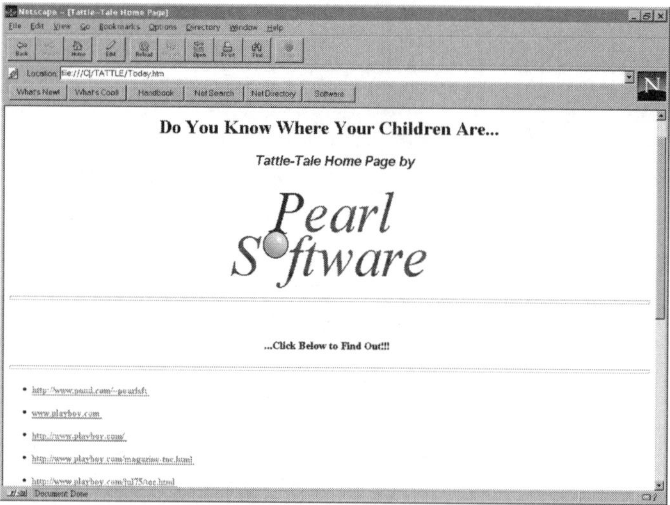

Hence you could install Tattle-Tale and then use it to quickly discover everywhere your child has been on the Internet.

Tattle-Tale does allow you three options in terms of access to the Internet: unrestricted access, restricted access with defined sites off-limits, and no access to the Internet at all.

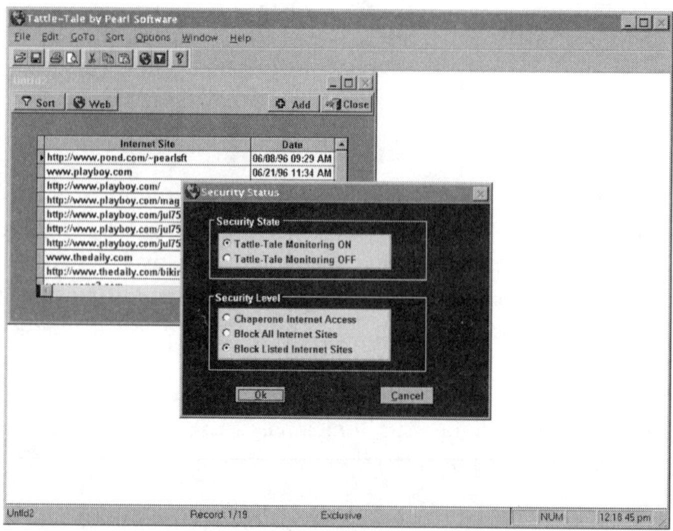

Unfortunately, at the time we reviewed Tattle-Tale, it did not include a list of sites containing offensive content; you would have to come up with your own list.

However, as a tool to track where your kids have been, it excels. If you are a parent who trusts your kids but wants to track their on-line activities, then Tattle-Tale would be a good choice. You can find out more about Tattle-Tale at **http://www.pond.com/~pearlsft/**. The program is available for Windows systems.

Kid-Appropriate Content Guides

A second method of dealing with the issue of offensive content on the Internet is to give children access to those Web indices that "filter out" sites deemed unfit or unsafe for kids.

- Yahoo! is one of the most popular Web indices, one of the reasons being that it is so comprehensive. But within Yahoo! you can find links to some sites that you might not want your children to access, such as those dealing with sexuality, white power, bondage, and other adult or controversial themes. Yahoo! has recognized the need for an index that is for kid-friendly sites and as a result has set up Yahooligans!

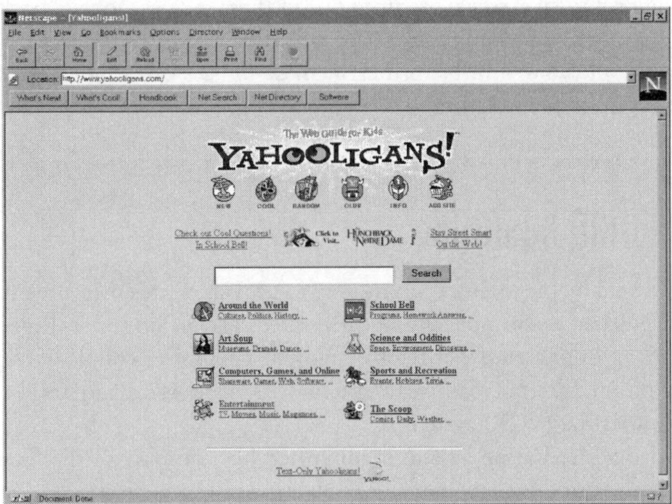

- Bess, the Internet Retriever (**http://bess.net/**), is another index of good sites for children. Bess is interesting in that it is not just a Web index; it is a product that can run on Internet servers to restrict access to offensive content. Thus it could be implemented on a school network and therefore work on all computers in the school, precluding the need to buy and implement a separate filtering program for each system.

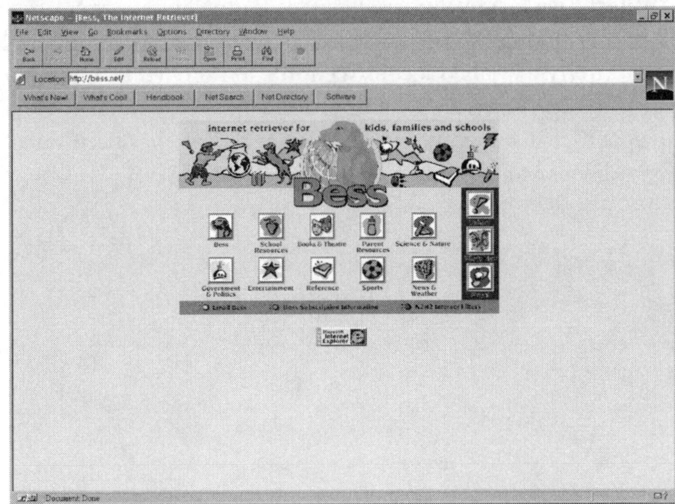

- The previously mentioned CyberPatrol Route 6-16 list (**http://www.microsys.com/616/default.htm**) is another good site.
- Other sites include The Kid's Playhouse (**http://www.wtp.net/~Suzan/kids/**), Berit's Best Sites for Children (**http://www.cochran.com/theosite/KSites.html**), Not Just for Kids (**http://www.night.net/kids/**), and Christian Kids Links (**http://netministries.org/kids.html**).

But it is important that parents understand the limitations of such "kid-friendly" indices. These indices are "not closed," that is, it is easy to get out of them. It is similar to putting your child in a safe shopping mall with all the doors to the outside world unlocked.

Once you connect to an external site from one of these indices, you are back on the public Internet, where it is easy to find a link back to an unfiltered index or to a search engine where you can search for any topic you wish. Nevertheless, these indices can be a great help in locating some great Internet sites for children.

Voluntary Rating Systems

The third method used by the Internet community to provide a safe environment for children is to rate Internet sites based on their content. A rated site displays a logo on its home pages that indicates if the site is appropriate for viewing by children. There are a couple of competing rating efforts that exist on the Internet: SafeSurf's Internet Rating System and Solid Oak Software's Voluntary Content Rating (VCR) System.

The SafeSurf Internet Rating System is supported by a number of the filtering programs that we reviewed earlier in this chapter, including NetNanny, CyberPatrol, and SurfWatch. The Voluntary Content Rating System is supported by Solid Oak Software's own filtering program, CYBERsitter, which was reviewed earlier in this chapter as well.

Sites that want to register with the SafeSurf system can voluntarily rate themselves by filling out a form on the SafeSurf Home Page (**http://www.safesurf.com**). They then receive a special logo that they can add to their home page as well as instructions detailing how to add the appropriate code to their Web document.

To register a Web site with the Voluntary Content Rating System, you simply need to add a few lines of HTML code to your Web document. Full instructions are available at the Solid Oak Software home page (**http://www.solidoak.com/vcr.htm**). You also receive a VCR logo, which you can display on your Web site. Here is an example of a site that has been rated by SafeSurf. Notice the button in the upper left-hand corner that indicates the site has been rated "All Ages" by SafeSurf (**http://www.bconnex.net/~kidworld/**):

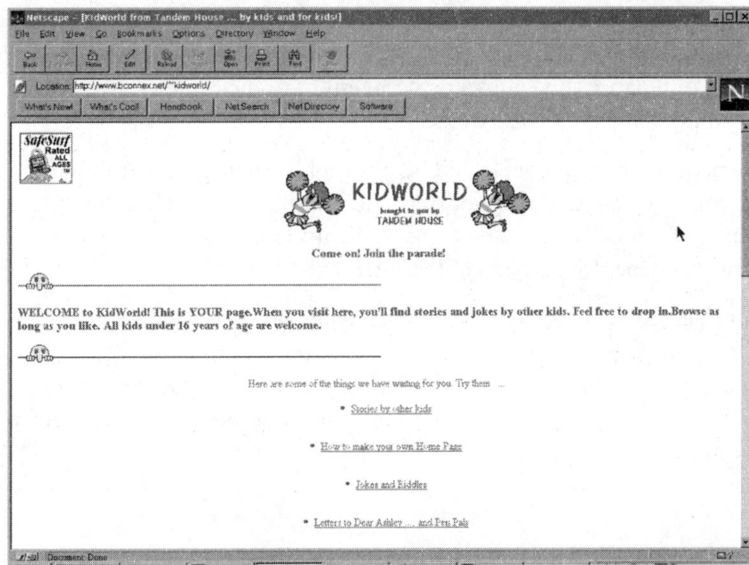

The SafeSurf Rating System is compliant with an industry-wide effort called PICS (Platform for Internet Content Selection). PICS provides a common method by which Internet browsers read rated Web sites. When a parent uses a browser that supports the PICS standard (such as Microsoft's Internet Explorer), the parent will be able to set up viewing levels to block access to sites that the parent deems inappropriate. For more information, visit the PICS Web site at **http://www.w3.org/pub/WWW/PICS/**.

The Role of the Parent

Whether parents put Internet filtering software on the home PC or guide their children to an on-line site of acceptable information, their responsibilities do not go away. Indeed, parental responsibilities are increased because of the Internet. There are several things that parents should consider:

- If an Internet filter is used, parents should ensure that it is kept up-to-date. Most of the software programs reviewed in this chapter featured some type of on-line update mechanism that provides a list of new offensive Web sites or requires some type of action to manually list sites or phrases that should be banned. It is the responsibility of the parents to keep this information up-to-date in recognition of the growth rate of information on the Internet.
- Parents need to keep control over the password to the filtering program. Most programs reviewed here are password-controlled in that they can only be uninstalled or user profiles can only be changed by providing the proper password. Parents must take care to ensure their children do not have access to this password, in other words, make it complex, and if you do write it down, put it where the children will not find it.
- If the filtering program provides a logging capability, it should be examined on a regular basis to observe what the child is up to on-line.

- Parents cannot rely on these tools to solve the potential problem of offensive content. New sites are always established that the child might come across. The child needs parental guidance and counseling with respect to the Internet, particularly if they do encounter some problems on-line.
- Children still require guidance. There should be some ground rules regarding what they can and cannot do on-line, regardless of the fact that a filtering program might be used. Parents should be prepared to discuss and educate their children with respect to the many negative aspects of the Internet.
- Some parents will have to cope with the child who is more computer savvy than the parent and who will try to uninstall the filtering program or try to figure out its weak spots. Parents must be prepared to deal with brilliant children and may have to consider extreme penalties such as preventing access to the computer except when the parent is present.

Keeping Up-to-Date

As a parent you should spend time trying to understand the Internet censorship issue, and you should keep track of ongoing efforts to provide for content regulation on the Internet. A number of good sites that we suggest include the following:

- Read the Declaration of Independence of Cyberspace if you really want to understand what many people on the Internet think about the Internet freedom of speech issue from a philosophical perspective. Written by one of the world's most popular Internet advocates, John Perry Barlow (**http://numedia.tddc.net/scott/declaration.html**), the document is a must-read item for any parent trying to understand the "anything goes" atmosphere of the Internet.

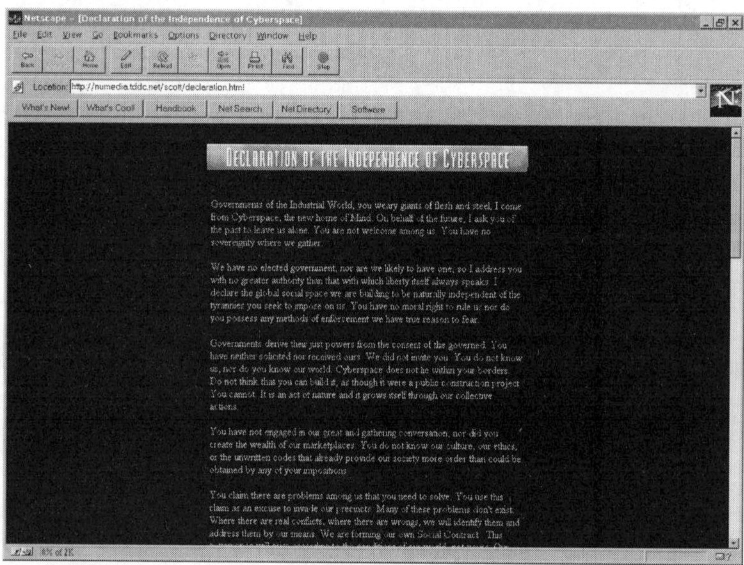

- Read “Child Safety on the Information Highway,” a brochure that focuses on the risks and roles of parents; it is one of the best overviews of issues you should think about (**http://www.larrysworld.com/child_safety.html**). Check out Larry’s World in general; he is a writer for the *Los Angeles Times* and writes a lot of about children on the Internet (**http://www.larrysworld.com**).
- Check out the “Internet Travel Tips For Kidz” page, which offers lots of good, practical advice for parents (**http://www.go-interface.com/fridgeartz/kidsafe.html**).
- You must check out “Welcome To Kathy’s Resources on Parenting, Domestic Violence, Abuse, Trauma & Dissociation,” which includes a number of excellent pointers to useful Web sites. In particular, take a look at “Kathy’s Views on Children and the Internet,” an outline of one parent’s attitude to the Internet (**http://www.mcs.net/~kathyw/home2.html**). Spend a few hours browsing this site — yes, hours — since it is probably the best summary of information about parenting in general to be found on the Internet.
- Howard Rheingold is a popular and well-known San Francisco author and parent. Take a look at his articles “Why Censoring Cyberspace is Dangerous & Futile,” “The Hidden Dangers of Indecency Police,” “Citizen Censorship or Government Control?” and other articles at his Web site (**http://www.well.com/user/hlr/tomorrow/ index.html**).
- A good starting point for information about use of the Internet by children is the Child Safety on the Internet site (**http://www.voicenet.com/~cranmer/censorship.html**).
- Read the Internet Parental Control Frequently Asked Questions (FAQ) (**http://www.vtw.org/ipcfaq**) document, which will answer many of your basic questions.
- You can access the “Children Accessing Controversial Information” mailing list, in which individuals discuss issues around the use of the Internet by kids. As they note on-line, “Can children be prevented from accessing materials which are controversial? Is preventing access even desirable? We believe censorship is not the answer. What alternatives do we have or could we provide? How do we talk with children about these issues? What can we say to concerned parents and school administrators? Who decides what is acceptable in a given setting? How and by whom are community standards set?” (**http://www.zen.org/~brendan/caci.html**)

A Word About Controlling Internet Access in the Workplace

We close this chapter with a comment about some developments in the corporate world related to content on the Internet. Some companies that provide employees with access to the Internet are concerned that staff may spend their time accessing inappropriate content on-line or may be wasting time on-line. To overcome the perceived problem, these organizations are looking for Internet filtering or blocking software that can block or restrict employee access to the Internet. Some companies have adopted the software that we reviewed in this chapter, while others are examining different types of programs, one that has been specifically developed to help employers monitor both computer and Internet activity by their employees. One of these products is called Internet Watchdog.

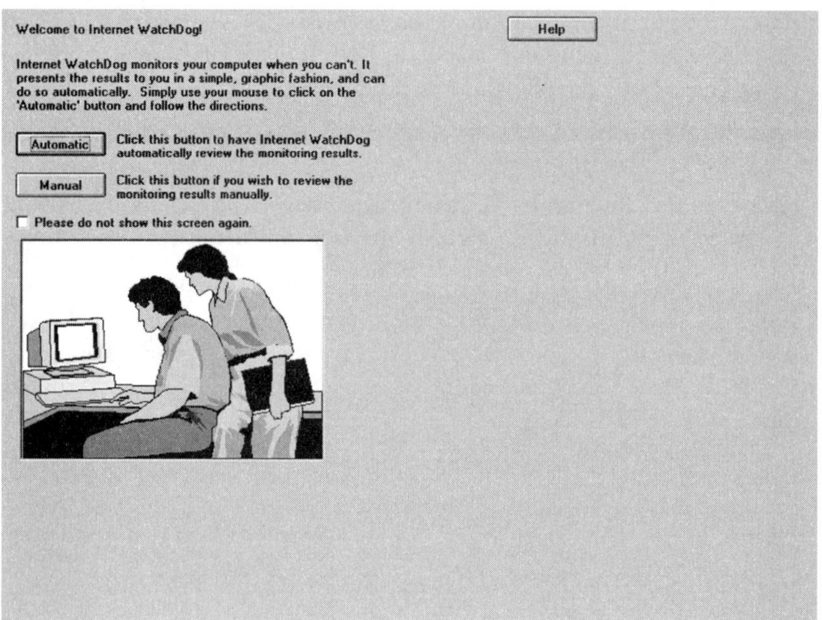

What does WatchDog do? It records everything your computer does and takes pictures of the images on your computer screen at predetermined intervals, stamping them with the date and time. The program also keeps a running list of the files on the hard drive of your computer, which includes details of any pictures or other material you may have downloaded from the Internet. In summary, Internet Watchdog does not "block" access to sites on the Internet; it was designed specifically to be a "monitoring" device. At the end of the day your boss can review what you have been doing on your computer all day.

The product has wide appeal not only to employers, but also to parents and school administrators, who want to monitor how children are using computers and the Internet. The developer of the product notes: "The Internet WatchDog allows the parent, teacher or employer to monitor and record all computer activity, whether or not on the Internet — much like a telephone bill enables the caller to see a listing of phone numbers. This product is engineered to aid managers in increasing their employee productivity, and to aid parents and teachers in monitoring the general computer and Internet activity of their children and students." Kind of a scary product if you think about it. Internet WatchDog is available for both Macintosh and PCs running either Windows 3.1 or Windows 95.

Internet Filtering or Information Control?

Some people, particularly those who are fighting to protect free speech on the Internet, believe that Internet filtering software has gone too far. Why? Think about this: by adopting many of the filtering programs outlined in this chapter, a parent is indicating, "I think someone else should have control over what my child does when it comes to the Internet." And with the grand battle that rages worldwide over control of the Internet, it is quite possible that things will be carried too far and that these tools, which purport to protect children from the evils of the Internet, will come to be used as tools to control political thought. Consider, for example, some of the sites that were reported to be in the CyberPatrol CyberNOT list:

- *Wired* magazine, a magazine that focuses on many Internet issues and often comments on the need to respect freedom of speech on-line, is a restricted site.
- The site of an animal rights group, which featured on its Web site photos of some of the things that happen to animals in testing labs. In effect, children are being banned from understanding some of the issues in the ongoing battle against cruelty to animals. Should we not encourage an open mind on this issue?
- Most gay and lesbian resources are restricted, as are any mention of the words. Not just sites and newsgroups that include gay and lesbian pornography, but sites that involve the discussion of gay and lesbian politics. Is outright prevention of *discussion* of political issues proper in a country that has passed legislation indicating that discrimination against gays and lesbians is a violation of the Human Rights Code?
- CyberNOT blocks anything on-line having to do with the topic of feminism. Women's groups and others involved in the issues of women's rights should be outraged and deeply disturbed that some individuals believe that children should not have access to the discussion of such topics.

In other words, some programs go far beyond restricting access to on-line pornography or other material and delve into control over access to political viewpoints and perspectives. If parents are going to rely on others to guide their children through the Internet, they should understand what is being censored.

One must wonder if, in this way, filtering programs really represent a new kind of creeping Big Brotherism, one that will become particularly repugnant over time. Filtering programs serve a purpose at certain times and in certain places and can help to ease parental concern about the Internet. On the other hand, anyone involved with the Internet must ensure that they do not become tools of organizations that want to stamp into our minds their own form of acceptable thought.

Conclusion

Does the Internet contain offensive content? Yes. Is it possible for a parent to put in place software that helps to restrict access by their children to this content? After our review of the software in this chapter, the answer is most definitely yes. We were impressed by the comprehensiveness of many of the software programs.

Will the parent be certain that the child will never find or access offensive content on-line? Even with these programs the answer is no; simply, the parent must continue to play an active role in use of the Internet by their children, regardless of which filtering program they adopt.

However, parents should not hold their children back because of fear that the Internet is some dark, evil place; instead, they should embrace the Internet and encourage its use. Simply, there are too many useful and exciting things on-line to avoid it.

CHAPTER 18

Intranets

It is a powerful new information technology than can unlock huge productivity gains. No, not the Internet. It's the intranet—and it's coming your way.

Good Fences Make for Lousy Intranets
Business Week, February 26, 1996

As business organizations explore the use of the Internet as a tool for reaching and dealing with their customers, they should keep in mind that the technology of the Internet is now being widely adopted as a means of providing access to and distribution of *internal* information. Enter the Intranet, which is the use of Internet technology to distribute information over a private computer network within an organization.

The birth of the so-called Intranet is a significant and far-reaching development, as companies establish internal, private Web sites that can be accessed only by employees. They have come to realize that the technology of the World Wide Web provides for a useful and powerful method by which employees can access internal information, including employee manuals, product descriptions, price lists, customer support information, employee suggestion boxes, product launch plans — you name it.

Intranets Are for Everyone!

Intranets are an important — and extremely hot — topic and trend. But if you pick up the average Intranet book, you will see that it typically focuses on the technology and the technical details. This chapter isn't for techno-dweebs — it's for you!

We believe that Intranets are for everyone. You do not have to be a computer whiz to understand their impact and significance. In this chapter we will explain Intranets in simple, human terms so that you can understand what all the fuss is about. You do not have to be working in an organization that is using an Intranet, or even planning to use one, to benefit from this chapter. *Intranets are a fundamental part of what the Internet is all about.* Some general knowledge about Intranets will help you understand the significance and potential applications of Internet technology in the business community, the government community, and in the economy in general. Let's get started.

What Is an Intranet?

As the Internet burst onto the scene throughout the corporate world in 1995 and 1996, individuals came to appreciate that an internal World Wide Web site — an Intranet — could be a very simple and straightforward means of providing employees with access to internal information. An Intranet could link employees together, just as the Internet links people together from around the world, using the same software as the Internet. Any employee with a computer on his/her desk can access the company Intranet with a World Wide Web browser such as Netscape Navigator or Microsoft's Internet Explorer. This is one of the reasons why Intranets are so popular. Businesses do not have to duplicate their software costs. Employees can use the same software to get access to internal information as they do to get access to external information on the Internet. And like the Web, Intranets can be global. Internal Web sites can be located in the same office, in another office in the same city, or in another country. As you will see later in this chapter, employees at Chevron Resources Canada in Calgary use an Intranet to access private company Web sites as far away as Nigeria. These Web sites are only available to Chevron employees; public Internet users cannot use them.

To implement an Intranet, you need

- an internal TCP/IP network (TCP/IP describes the technology underlying the Internet);
- one or more Web servers (these are the computers used to store the corporate information you want to put on your Intranet);

INTRANETS

1. Intranets are simply internal Internets — in effect, World Wide Web sites that can be used only within an organization, and which cannot be accessed by anyone other than an employee.
2. Intranets have gained interest in the corporate sector because they present opportunities for cost savings, efficiencies in information distribution, lower training costs, and many other benefits.
3. When implementing an Intranet, an organization should keep in mind that it is not a magic solution to internal information distribution. There are several challenges in implementing an Intranet.
4. In this chapter, we examine Intranets which are in use at organizations such as Fletcher Challenge, Agriculture Canada, J.P. Morgan, Shell Canada, Natural Resources Canada and Chevron Canada.

- a license for the internal use of a Web browser by employees (e.g., you could get a company-wide license for Netscape Navigator so that all your employees could use it).

Companies have come to realize that an "internal Web" can be used to distribute almost anything. Here is a sample of some of the items an organization could place on an Intranet for its employees:

- employee notices, for example, retirement notices, new hires, department changes, and job postings;
- an electronic version of official company publications;
- copies of speeches and presentation slides;
- announcements about new products and services;
- purchasing forms for office supplies;
- human resource information such as details about employee benefit programs, training programs, and other career and professional development information, employee policy manuals, salary information;
- financial information, such as quarterly financial results and annual reports;
- approved travel information and policies such as details about hotels, travel agents, airlines, and corporate travel discounts;
- worldwide office locations, telephone directories;
- event calendars;
- information about community events the organization is sponsoring;
- historical information about the company;
- press releases and internal memoranda;
- a link to the company's paging system.

Many Intranets are being linked to internal information databases and thus have become a straightforward method of providing employees with the ability to query and access information within those systems. This is directly related to the trend that we described in Chapter 15, where we observed that many Web sites are being linked to corporate databases. An Intranet can be used for almost any purpose within an organization. All it takes is a little imagination. Consequently, it is not surprising that Intranets are an extremely popular topic within organizations right now.

Intranets have become a big business for many Internet companies. For example, you might be surprised to learn that 80% of Netscape's business comes from the sale of servers and software for Intranets. Even Bill Gates has stated loudly and clearly that he views Intranet technology to be a significant opportunity for his company. Many other high-profile computer companies, such as Lotus and Novell, produce products for the Intranet market.

What Are the Benefits of an Intranet?

There are many reasons why Intranets have become such an important topic so quickly. Quite simply, they provide organizations with a simple and effective tool for distributing information to their staff. Let's look at some of the benefits in more detail.

Cost Savings

One of the most obvious benefits of an Intranet is that it results in cost savings and efficiencies in internal information distribution. Companies can reduce printing and mailing costs by using an Intranet to distribute documents to employees. The cost to put a notice up on an internal Web site is often far less than the cost to prepare, print, and distribute a paper message to all the employees in an organization. This is particularly the case for large companies and companies that are geographically dispersed.

Inexpensive Technology

If a computer infrastructure is already in place within an organization, it is generally an inexpensive proposition to implement an Intranet. If a company has an internal TCP/IP network (as many companies do), all that is needed to get started is a Web server and Web browser software. And as we noted in our chapter about building a Web site, many Web server programs are becoming available for well under $500. For under $40 a person, each employee in the company can be equipped with Netscape Navigator. Alternatively, a company could use Microsoft's Internet browser, Internet Explorer, for free. Because Internet software and hardware are relatively inexpensive, the cost of setting up an Intranet is often far less than the cost of setting up any other form of internal network.

Efficiencies in Information Distribution

Intranets also provide for efficient delivery of information through an organization. For years companies have sent long paper memos, manuals, and reports to staff and have put in place complex internal information distribution systems to support these activities. It costs a lot of money to ship paper around a company, not to mention the inevitable time delays. To get around these costs, some companies have implemented sophisticated electronic mail systems. The challenge with these systems is that they generally cannot support the volume of information that a company generates internally on a day-to-day basis. Employees cannot be sent, each day, hundreds of individual e-mail messages containing the information released by the company that day; it just is not practical.

The beauty of an Intranet is that internal information distribution becomes a passive rather than an active activity. Rather than dumping a large volume of information on employees, staff are made aware that when they need information, they can go out and find it on the Intranet. Employees go and get the information that they need, only when they need it, and only when it is relevant to them. They do not have to sift through a mountain of irrelevant information each day. This provides for far greater efficiencies in the way that information is distributed in an organization.

Intranets also reduce waste and redudancy since they centralize information delivery and provide a single point of reference for corporate information. Big organizations often suffer from a problem where multiple groups or departments publish similar information in different formats.

An Intranet provides a consistent way to distribute information and makes it easier for organizations to assign publishing responsibilities to specific departments and groups.

Lower Training Costs

Companies have long known that it takes time to make employees familiar with new information systems. The cost to train them on new technologies can often be excessive. So one advantage of Intranets is that companies can exploit the fact that a good number of their employees may already be surfing the Internet and hence are already familiar with the basic technology behind an Intranet. Web pages on the public Internet work the same as internal Web pages; all that is needed is an understanding of how to point and click your way through documents by clicking on hypertext links.

With an Intranet, organizations can use the Web's user-friendly interface to help employees gain quick and easy access to corporate information. Imagine putting your employee manual on an internal Web site; it's a natural for the hypertext capabilities of the Web. Employees could move from page to page or chapter to chapter with the click of a mouse. Add one of many different search engines to the Intranet, and staff can quickly narrow in on the particular employee policy that is of interest.

For employees who are not familiar with the Web, it is comforting to know that Web-based programs are relatively easy for employees to learn how to use; this can reduce training costs substantially. Employees just need to learn how to navigate through documents on the Web. Once an Intranet is in place, it is even possible to deliver employee training programs — on almost any subject — over the World Wide Web. AT&T, for example, was able to reduce classroom time for 4,500 customer service representatives from 50 to 25 days by using its Intranet for instructional purposes.

Collaboration

Several years ago many businesses woke up to the power and potential of a software program called Lotus Notes, a package that earned the name "groupware" and became known for its ability to permit electronic collaboration within companies. Notes allowed companies to establish topics and discussion groups in which employees could exchange and share information in the form of ongoing discussions. Notes helped organizations to capture their "corporate knowledge" in electronic form—that is, the combined knowledge, experience, and wisdom of their employees. If you had to deal with an issue, you could examine the corporate Notes database to see if the issue had already been discussed and resolved. Thus Notes earned a place as a powerful and important information resource within many companies.

As people began to implement Intranets, they realized that the technology of the Web could provide for the same type of on-line discussion as Notes. As a result, many companies began to implement private discussion groups, organized by the different topics and issues of importance within their respective organizations. Archiving capabilities were added with powerful Internet search software, allowing employees to search the contents of past discussions. The impact? Lotus Notes found itself with some new and significant competition in the form of internal Web sites.

Significant new tools are arriving that provide for even greater levels of internal collaboration through an Intranet. There are workflow tools that automate the flow of information through an organization, programs that support document sharing and editing, and programs that improve scheduling. For example, the Ford Motor Company uses an Intranet to allow employees in different locations to work on the development of its cars.

Simplicity of the Technology

Intranets, like the Internet, did not emerge from any grand strategic vision. Instead, they more or less just happened. As soon as the Web appeared and individuals began building Web sites, it became apparent to many organizations that Web sites could be used internally. In Chapter 7 we discussed many of the programs that make it easy for people to publish material on the Web. These same programs can be used to publish information on an Intranet. With a little training anyone can quickly learn how to publish material electronically.

Intranets also help to level the technology playing field because they are platform-independent. This means that employees are not restricted by the type of computer they have; they can easily access a company's Intranet regardless of whether they are using Macintosh computers or IBM compatibles. As *Business Week* noted, "intranets can do something far more important. By presenting information in the same way to every computer, they can do what computer and software makers have frequently promised but never actually delivered: pull all the computers, software, and databases that dot the corporate landscape into a single system that enables employees to find information wherever it resides."

Simplified Access to Company Databases

Coincident with the implementation of Intranets have come tools that permit Web sites to query internal information systems. What has this led to? In many companies Intranets have been linked to internal databases, allowing employees simpler, more straightforward, and more immediate access to other information systems within the organization. Employees no longer need to call someone in the MIS department when they need to run a report; they can simply obtain the report on the Intranet.

A lot of technology to support this type of activity has emerged. Simware, an Ottawa-based company, has released a software tool that allows a Web site to query a large-scale IBM mainframe system. This allows banks, insurance companies, and other organizations to implement systems in which the Intranet becomes the primary window into their internal information. That lets the organization take further advantage of the cost savings inherent in an Intranet deployment.

Third-party Access to Corporate Information

Many organizations are taking employee access to corporate databases one step further and are allowing "trusted parties" to access their Intranet from outside the company. For example, a supplier may dial into a customer's Intranet in order to check inventory levels, or a customer may dial into a supplier's Intranet in order to place a new order or check the status of an existing order.

Improved Access Speeds

Because Intranets run over private computer networks (as opposed to the public Internet networks), they often do not suffer from the congestion problems that public Web pages experience. For example, on the public Internet there may be hundreds of people trying to access the same Web page. You are also limited by the speed of your modem, so files can take a long time to download. On an Intranet employees only have to compete with themselves for access to internal information. Furthermore, many Intranets operate on high-speed networks, permitting employees to download corporate video and sound files at fast speeds. For example, a company might make available a prototype of a radio commercial on its Intranet or a speech made by the company's chief executive officer.

Reduced Help Desk Costs

This is a big enough benefit that we felt it should stand on its own. Many organizations are moving their help desks to an Intranet to simplify employee access to technical resources. Intranets can be used to distribute answers and solutions to common problems. Electronic forms can also be set up to allow employees to report technical problems on the World Wide Web.

Permanent Archive for Company Information

Information can be stored on an Intranet for years, giving employees immediate access to archival material that would be cumbersome or time-consuming to find any other way. One popular application of this concept relates to press releases. Many organizations keep a permanent archive of all their press releases on their Intranet, organized by month and year. An organization could easily make this information searchable by installing a search engine that allows employees to search the press releases by keyword.

Remote Access to Company Information

As we mentioned earlier, Intranets can connect offices in different countries, improving information flow across the organization. For example, with only a few keystrokes an employee in the South American branch of a company could access a report prepared by a colleague in the company's Vancouver office. Not only that, but employees do not need to be in their office to get access to their company's Intranet. Many companies have their Intranets set up in such a way that employees can access them when on the road. For example, a sales representative may tap into the company Intranet from his hotel room to check on the availability and pricing of a product.

Improved Employee Productivity

Because Intranets allow employees to quickly find the information they are looking for, Intranets can dramatically improve worker productivity.

Test Bed for Public Web Projects

Finally, when an organization implements an Intranet, it is generally enhancing the capabilities and skills of its staff in dealing with HTML and Web site technology. This makes it much easier for the firm to develop and implement a public, external Web site at a later date. Organizations with Intranets gain valuable experience in the design, implementation, maintenance, and quality control of internal Web sites. This helps them prepare for those same issues when they launch a public Web site.

Some companies are using Intranets to let employees test public Internet Web sites before they become widely available to make sure that any problems, such as broken links, are identified well in advance of the public launch. By deploying a Web site on an Intranet before it goes public, employees have the opportunity to comment on its design, content, and layout. This ensures that when the site does go public, it has been well tested and well received.

An Intranet Reality Check

As wonderful as they are, Intranets can fail if they are not managed properly. Below, we examine some of the crucial management issues related to Intranets.

Organization of the Content is Crucial

Spend time mapping out an Intranet in advance. Key questions include: How will different departments work together to provide information on the Intranet? How will employees submit information for the Intranet? Will the entire contents of the Intranet be indexed or searchable? You need to make it easy for employees to find things. If employees have to spend ten minutes trying to find a document, they are going to beg the organization for a return to paper.

Your Corporate Image Is as Important Internally as It Is Externally

It is easy for internal Web sites to begin to proliferate without any consistency in style or layout. Is this a problem? It could be. It depends upon the culture and management style within your organization. Some organizations prefer to let individual departments "do their own thing" when it comes to Web pages. Other organizations establish strict guidelines on how internal Web pages should look. We believe that the best approach is to set a policy that is somewhere in the middle. Establish "loose guidelines" so that the Intranet does not get out of control, but do not make the guidelines so strict that you overly restrict employees and stifle their enthusiasm and creativity.

Keep Your Information Current

Appropriate resources have to be dedicated to ensuring that the Intranet is kept up-to-date. Employees will lose faith in the technology if the information is never current.

Do Not Underestimate the Need for Training

Employees should be thoroughly trained on how to use the Intranet. Intranets are relatively easy to use, *once employees are shown how to use them.* Do not assume that an employee will just catch on. Many employees fear new technologies such as the Internet. Help them to overcome this fear. If your local university or college has Internet or Intranet classes, consider registering all your employees for a course.

For an Intranet to be fully accepted by employees, company management must stand behind it. Have management communicate the benefits of Intranets to employees so that they understand why this new technology is necessary; otherwise, many employees will resist the change. Finally, organizations that implement Intranets should have a plan in place to support users once they begin to use the Intranet. Who can they turn to with questions?

Do Not Forget About Hidden Costs

While the technology costs associated with an Intranet are relatively inexpensive, they are not the only costs to consider. There are many invisible, or hidden, costs that organizations often forget about. For example,

- training and support (how much training is required? how will we support users?);
- browser and equipment upgrades (e.g., how often will we need to upgrade the version of the browser on employees' desks? how much will this cost?);
- content development and design (e.g., do we need to hire a consultant to design Web pages, implement databases, or act as a project manager?).

While some of these expenses may be relatively minor, it is important to work them into the Intranet budget.

What About Security?

Earlier in the chapter we defined an Intranet as a set of private Web sites that are only available to employees. But just because the Web sites are not available to the public does not mean that the information on them is safe. Organizations need to take appropriate security precautions to protect their Intranets from being broken into. Many companies use software called a "firewall" to do this. Organizations should consider hiring an Internet security consultant to help them evaluate appropriate security measures for their Intranets.

Consider Establishing Employee Policies Regarding the Use of the Intranet

New technology can be confusing to employees. It is important to let employees know that certain information on the Intranet may be confidential and should not be sent to anyone outside the company. It is easy for an employee to copy a document from the Intranet into an e-mail message and transmit it to people around the world with only a few keystrokes. Organizations need to educate employees about the potential security risks associated with using an Intranet.

Do Not Use the Intranet as an Excuse to Distribute Information

Finally, many organizations use an Intranet to distribute information that no one really wants or needs. Make sure the information you are distributing is useful to employees. How do you do this? Survey employees *before* the Intranet is implemented to find out what information they are interested in receiving in electronic form. For an Intranet to be successful, employees need to see value in the information they are accessing.

Case Studies

To show you how companies and government organizations are implementing and applying Intranet technology, we interviewed managers from two government departments and four organizations in the private sector. We asked for their perspectives on the benefits that Intranets have and the challenges that they create. As you are reading each of the six profiles, keep in mind that there is not necessarily a right or wrong approach to an Intranet. What works well in one organization may not work well in another.

Fletcher Challenge Canada

Vancouver, British Columbia

Fletcher Challenge Canada (FCC) is a Vancouver-based manufacturer of paper that employs 3,500 people across Canada. It produces newsprint, directory, and other types of paper for clients such as Sunkist, Southam, J.C. Penny, Labbatt, and the *Los Angeles Times.* According to Dave Sinnett, FCC's Director of Information Systems and Services, the company has been using an Intranet since late 1994. A pilot project was subsequently launched to build support for the service, which is now known as "FletcherNet." Although FletcherNet was initially confined to the Vancouver head office, it is now accessible to employees at the company's three manufacturing facilities in British Columbia: Crofton, Elk Falls, and Mackenzie. The company has a U.S. sales office in California, which is connected to FletcherNet as well.

A wide range of information is distributed through FletcherNet, as seen in the screens below. The information includes company announcements, job postings, financial results, floor plans, surveys, production statistics, exchange rates, policy documents, and phone lists:

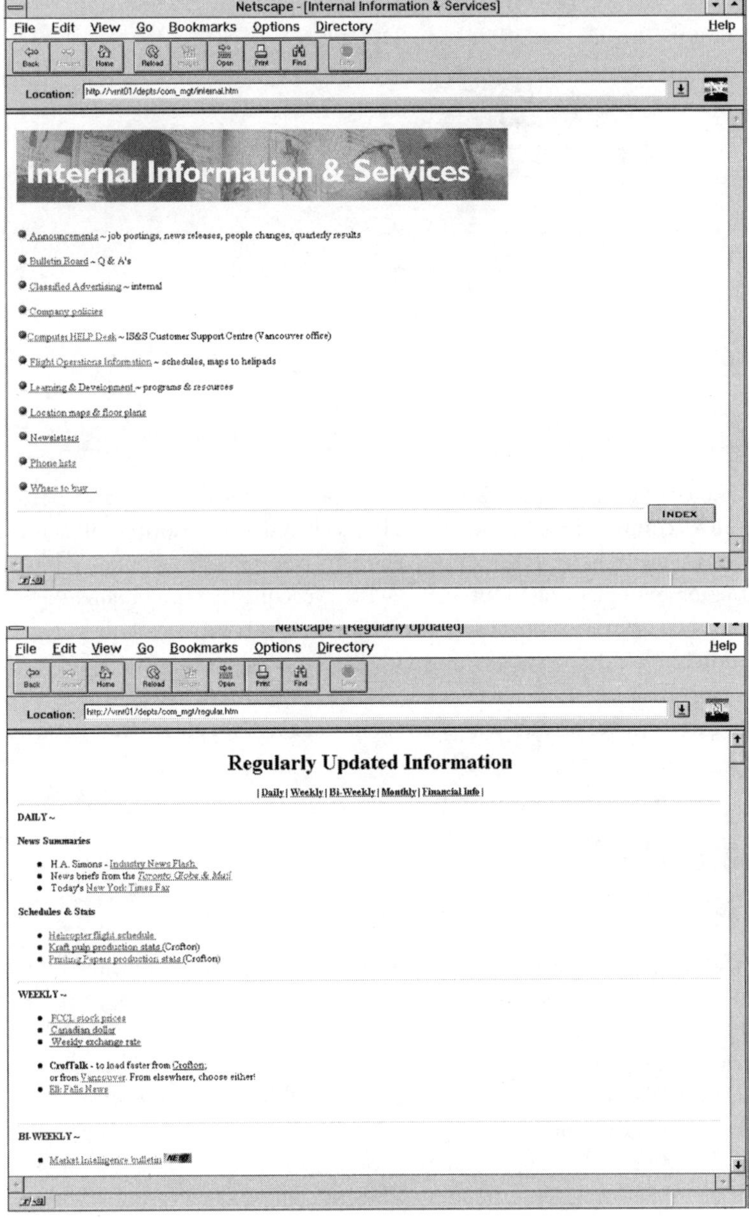

FletcherNet has also become a convenient and practical way for the company to distribute helicopter schedules to its employees. Helicopters are used to transport employees between the head office and the company's pulp and paper mills:

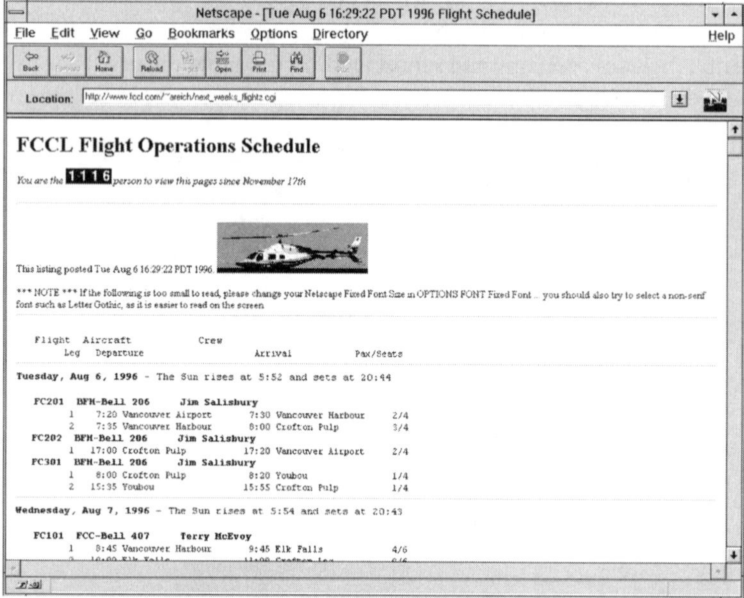

Sinnett says FletcherNet provides primarily "soft" benefits for the company. For example, the Intranet improves communication and makes it easier to deliver information across the organization in a consistent fashion. Interestingly enough, cost savings were not a big factor in the company's decision to implement an Intranet. "We're expecting that [eventually] there will be some hard-dollar savings ... but we didn't justify the project on the basis of a whole bunch of dollar savings," says Sinnett. "We didn't go into this with the expectation we were going to save a whole bunch of money on paper."

"For our company, we probably wouldn't want that to happen anyway," he chuckles.

Agriculture Canada

Ottawa, Ontario

Agriculture and Agri-Food Canada is the government department responsible for Canada's agricultural activities. Agriculture Canada's Intranet first got off the ground a couple of years ago when the department was publishing a corporate newsletter in paper form. When a program review came around "we suddenly found ourselves without any budget," says Jennifer Vincent, a Communications Assistant in the Communications Branch and the Ministry's WebMaster. "Within a very short turn-around time, we had to figure out a new way to get corporate information out." The Ministry hired a consultant to develop a bulletin board system, but that created problems because some employees were using different computer platforms. "One way or another, there were always some employees who were left out of the loop," notes Vincent. "Just as we were looking for another solution to solve that problem, suddenly the Intranet came along." Convinced that the Intranet was the way to go, Vincent's deparment started developing an Intranet in the summer of 1995. The project was developed from the ground up. "It has been a real grassroots thing. We started it in the corporate affairs bureau and built it up ourselves by meeting with people from other departments," she says. By the end of 1997, the Ministry plans to have 80% of its employees connected to the Intranet, which has been dubbed "AgriSource." The main page for AgriSource appears below:

The Intranet provides access to just about everything: news bulletins, hotel and car rental directories, special events, newsletters, and training and development information. Vincent says that job postings have been a big hit. "When we asked each branch what they wanted to see on the Intranet, it was overwhelmingly job opportunities," she notes.

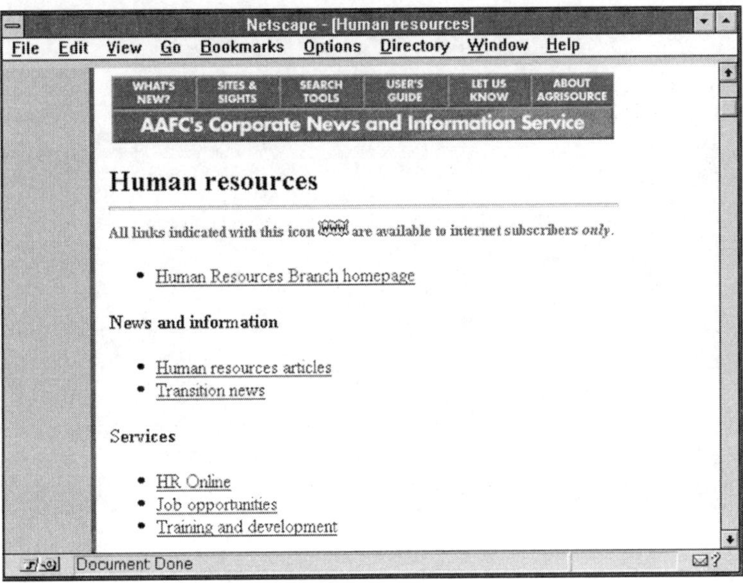

Like many organizations, Agriculture and Agri-Food Canada developed a public presence on the Internet before rolling out its Intranet to employees. The Ministry's public Internet site, called ACEIS (**http://www.agr.ca/newintre.html**), distributes news releases, documents, reports, and directories to public Internet users. The front page of ACEIS can be seen in the screen below:

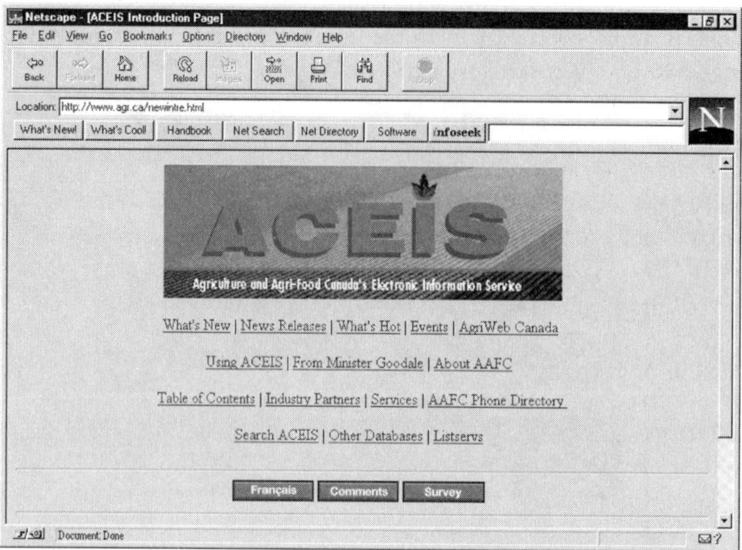

This created a dilemma for employees, because many of them did not have Internet access. "We ran into a problem. We were distributing information on the Web to the public and to our clients, but our own employees didn't have access to it," explained Vincent. To solve this problem, links were created from AgriSource to the department's public Web site. However, only employees with public Internet access can use the links, which are specially tagged with a "WWW" symbol (seen in the screen below).

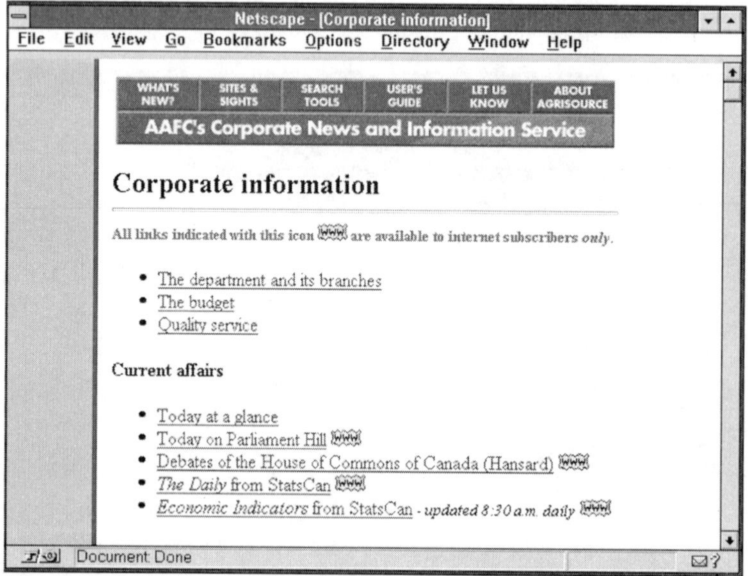

Vincent says the Intranet is "the ultimate communications tool," since it puts two-way communication at an employee's fingertips. Other benefits of an Intranet, according to Vincent, are its ease of use and the fact that it gives employees access to the information they want, when they want it. As opposed to e-mail, she said, which is "getting on people's nerves," because many people receive interoffice messages they are not interested in. For example, Vincent pointed to a survey her department conducted following the launch of a new corporate newsletter. Sixty percent of the employees said they would prefer to receive the information electronically. But, she says, when you start sending out material electronically, employees start complaining that their e-mail boxes are becoming congested. "It is a no-win situtation," she observes. An Intranet solves this problem by putting the employee in control.

But helping users to make the transition to an Intranet has not been easy, adds Vincent. "The biggest challenge is changing people's way of thinking." Some employees and managers are frightened by the fast rate of change on the Internet. Others are afraid that the learning curve will be too steep. The perceived cost of implementing an Intranet is another obstacle that Vincent has had to overcome. Vincent says that while employees had no trouble understanding that e-mail can lower costs, they see an Intranet as a more expensive alternative to existing methods of distribution. Vincent's own research has proven that this is not the case. She says that when you factor in the costs of postage and labor, an Intranet can reduce the costs of printing, mailing, and distributing newsletters by at least half. An Intranet provides "the best value for your dollar."

Vincent has some advice for other government departments that are considering an Intranet: "Have a plan and get your branch head or your Minister/Deputy Minister to buy in from the start." She says that because her department's Intranet was developed as a grassroots project, it took a long time to build support. At the very beginning they ran into a Catch 22 situation: "In order for us to get people interested, we had to have stuff available … and people would only want to put in the time to develop Web sites if we already had a preestablished audience."

Because there was no management buy-in in the initial stages of the project, Vincent had to approach each branch independently and do a lot of "tailored marketing." The process would have been much easier, she now realizes, if management had given their support to the project right at the beginning. Without management's support, Vincent was put in the position of having to sell the concept to each branch, one by one. All this work could have been eliminated, she says, with one memo from management.

Before you approach management, Vincent suggests that you do "a lot of homework" to understand "where management's head is at." She suggests surveying employees to find out their attitudes toward technology. Also find out how much money your organization is spending on internal communications such as newsletters and memoranda and compare that to the cost of distributing information through an Intranet. When it comes to building a business case for management, Vincent says there are two popular theories. Which one you should use depends upon your organization and the specific problem you are trying to solve.

Perspective 1: "Intranets are a great communications tool and they are cheap."

Perspective 2: "Intranets are cheap and you can communicate with them."

See the difference? The first perspective emphasizes efficiencies in communications, while the second stresses cost savings.

One day, Vincent predicts, "all government departments are going to be communicating using Intranets or Internet." Jennifer Vincent can be reached at **vincentj@em.agr.ca**.

J.P. Morgan

New York, New York

J.P. Morgan is a global financial services organization in New York with approximately 14,000 employees throughout Canada, the United States, Latin America, Europe, and Asia. J.P. Morgan runs a public Internet site at **http://www.jpmorgan.com** (shown below). The firm also runs an Intranet for its employees.

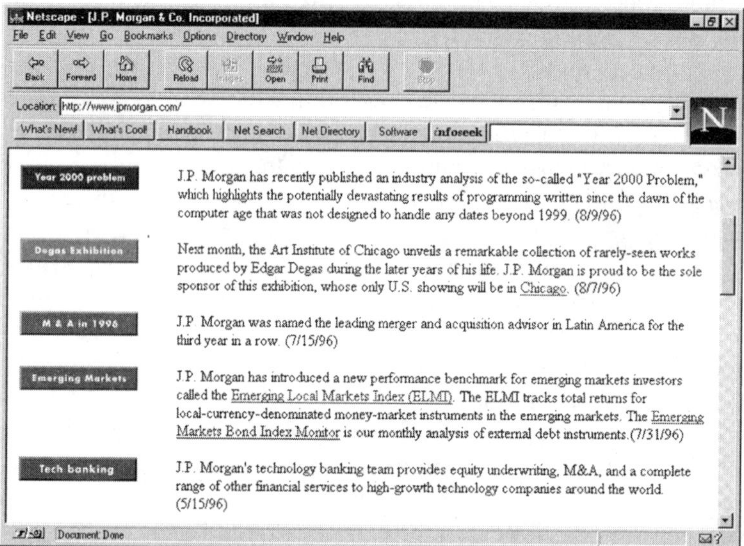

According to Susan Martinson, a Manhattan-based Intranet consultant who is working with the company, the J.P Morgan Intranet is used on two levels. First, she says, it "provides a network through which employees around the world can easily communicate with one another." Second, "it acts as a clearinghouse for information of importance to employees." To make the Intranet as easy to use as possible, it is structured as a directory of categories that keep track of Web content produced throughout the firm. Shown below is the page that provides employees with links to information about J.P. Morgan's business sectors:

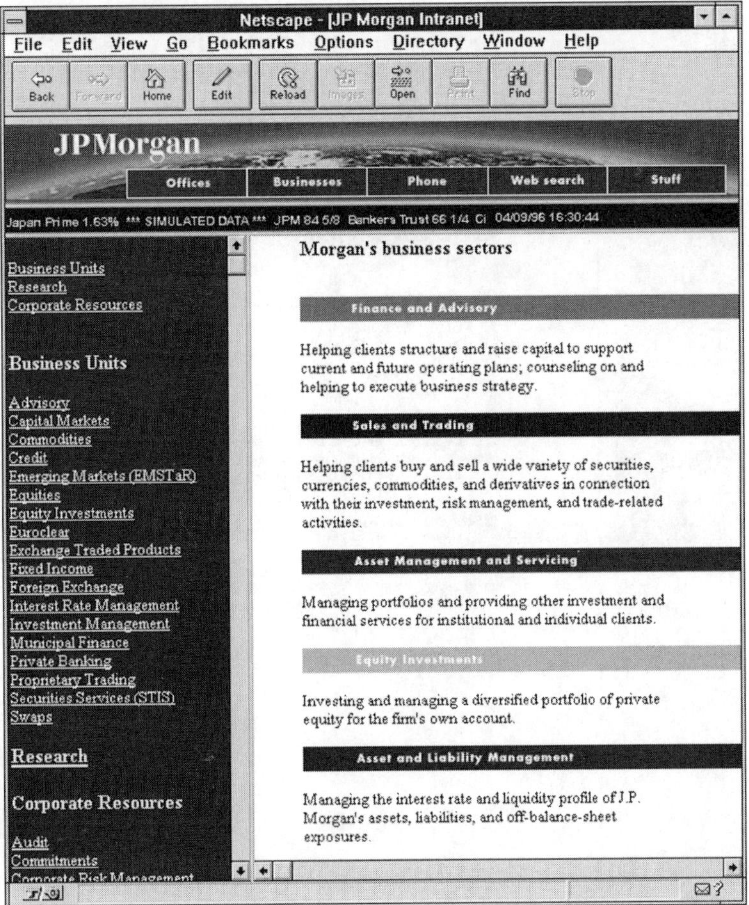

Any employee at J.P. Morgan can have his/her Web pages added to the company's Intranet, but he/she needs to fill out a form first. Martinson says this procedure is necessary to keep the Intranet organized. "The form classifies the material into the geographic region and/or business group that most accurately describes it, making it accessible to the rest of the firm in an intuitive manner," she points out. The form also allows the company to systematically keep track of new Web pages and add them to the company's internal search engine. Employees use the search engine when they are looking for information on the Intranet.

As part of its effort to keep the Intranet organized and well-structured, J.P. Morgan has established Web pages for all its regional offices. Shown in the screen below is the Web page for the Toronto office:

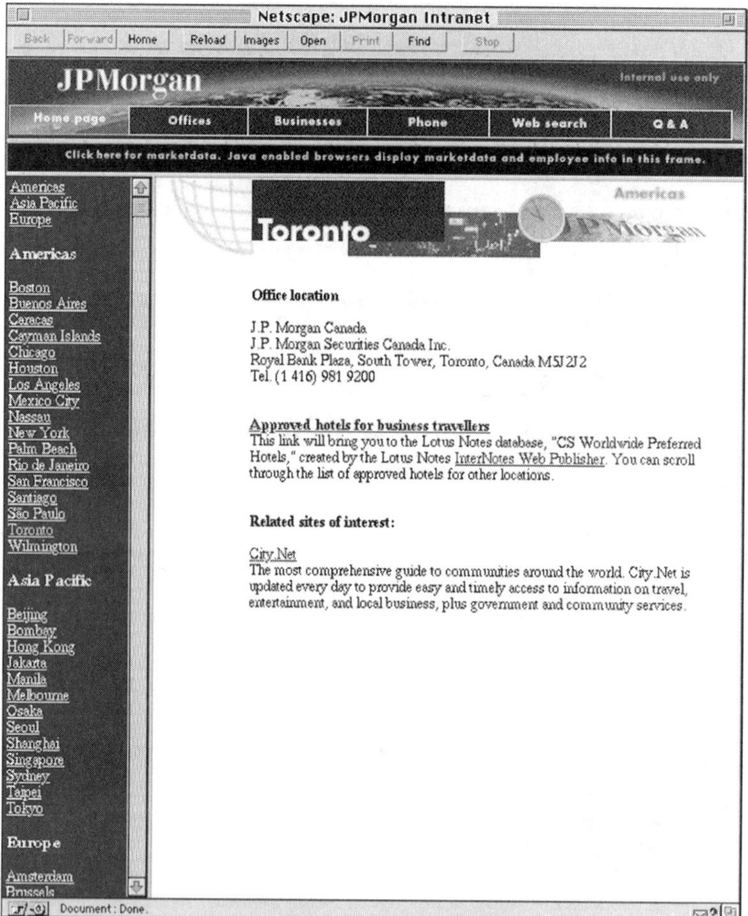

To help employees evaluate the effectiveness of their internal Web sites, Martinson says the company is planning to produce use reports for site managers. These reports will allow site managers to monitor how often their sites are visited and by which groups within the company.

Types of information found on the J.P. Morgan Intranet include news about the firm, facts and data on business and economic trends, updates on the progress of group projects, and educational and instructional materials. Below is the main page that employees see when they access the Intranet. It provides a summary of important news for employees:

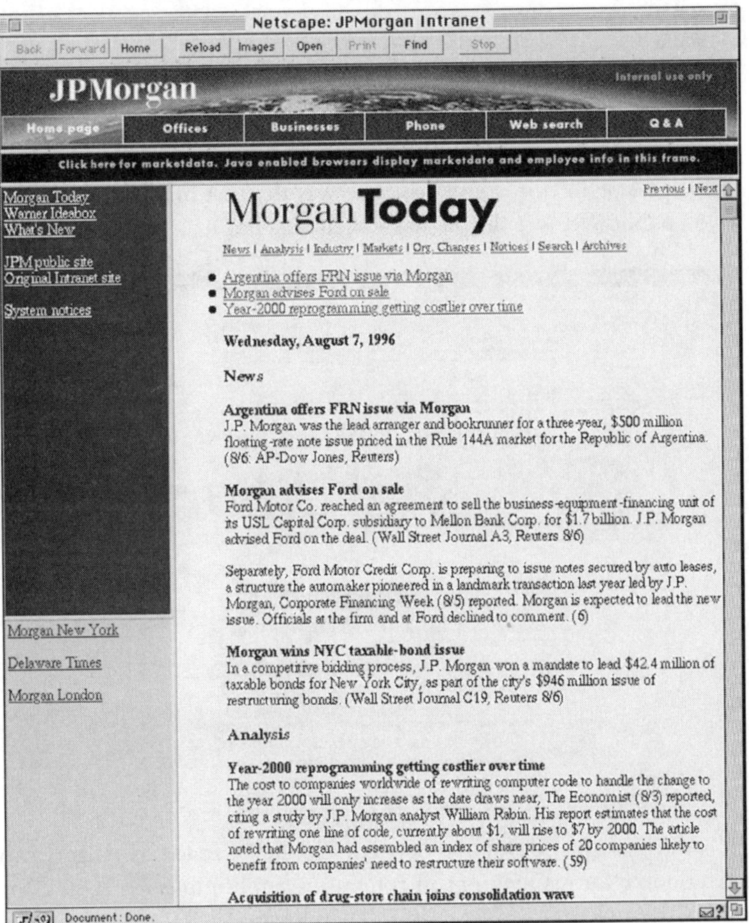

Martinson says that if you are planning to implement an Intranet within your organization, it is absolutely imperative to get the buy-in of the corporate communications department. "We see this as a communications vehicle much more than simply a technology," she observes. Once you get the support of your corporate communications department, your project will not appear as a grassroots movement to the rest of the firm, she says. Martinson believes that if the corporate communications department works hand-in-hand with the technology groups within your organization, it will lend credibility to the entire project.

She recommends a three-step methodology to help you clarify your thoughts. "Message, medium, maintenance" is the mantra that Martinson uses at J.P. Morgan. The first step is to focus on the message you are trying to communicate. Second, look at the advantages and disadvantages of using the Web as a distribution mechanism. Last, consider what kinds of maintenance issues you will be faced with. Only after you have gone through these three stages, Martinson says, should you start the process of actually building anything. "Too many people build an Intranet for the sake of having something on the Web." Susan Martinson can be reached at **susanm@interport.net**.

Shell Canada

Calgary, Alberta

Shell Canada owns and/or operates approximately 2,600 service stations across Canada and is Canada's third-largest petroleum company. Shell was the first major petroleum company in Canada to have a public Web site (**http://www.shellcan.com**):

Dave Fennell is the manager of Desktop Services for Shell Canada in Calgary, where his department is responsible for maintaining all computing applications for Shell Canada's offices coast to coast. His department is also in charge of developing Shell Canada's corporate Intranet, which connects employees at refineries in Montreal, Sarnia, and Edmonton and offices in Brockville, Toronto, and Calgary.

Shell's first Intranet site went up in mid-1995, and served primarily the exploration/production end of the company until the summer of 1996, when it was deployed as a company-wide resource. Four thousand employees now have access to the Shell Intranet, where they can obtain news and financial information, policy documents, and general information about the company. The screen following shows the main page for the Shell Canada Intranet:

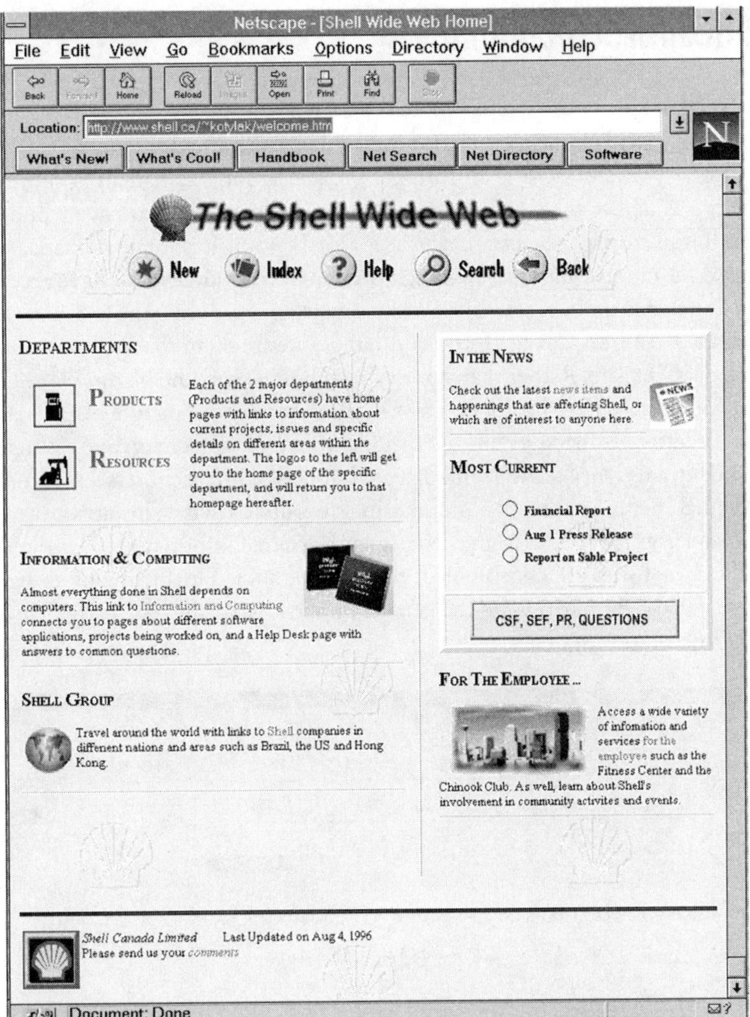

Fennell has two pieces of advice for any organization that is currently building an Intranet or considering implementing one for its employees. First, he says, "Spend a lot of time thinking about how you want to organize the information … the organization is critical." Second, Fennell points out that he has deliberately avoided promoting the Intranet as a "technology." "I'm being very cautious in not pushing this as a technology," he says. "I'm trying to get support from the the public affairs department to push it as a communications vehicle." Fennell says that once the public affairs department is on-side, they can take on ownership of the content, organization, and dissemination of the information. At that point, according to Fennell, it becomes much easier to sell the concept to the rest of the organization. Dave Fennell can be reached at **fennell@shell.ca**.

Natural Resources Canada

Ottawa, Ontario

Natural Resources Canada is the federal government department responsible for Canada's mineral, energy, and forestry resources. It is an Internet pioneer among Canadian government departments, since it was one of the first federal government departments to have a public Web site. Atulesh Nandi, the manager of Internet services for Natural Resources Canada, says that the Ministry is also running an Intranet, to which over 4,000 employees now have access. "The discovery of the Internet as an Intranet vehicle really dawned on us during the last year," notes Nandi.

The Natural Resources Canada Intranet is rather interesting in that it also doubles as the department's public Web site. Rather than have its own home page, the Natural Resources Canada Intranet is actually a subset of the public site. On the next page is a picture of the main screen for the Natural Resources Canada public Web site (**http://www.nrcan.gc.ca**). When employees connect to the Intranet, they see the same screen that public Internet users see, but they have access to additional menu options that are invisible to public users. This approach ensures that employees always have easy access to the department's external information. It also means that the internal and external sites are consistent in their appearance. Finally, maintaining one master system for use by both employees and the general public is generally less costly than maintaining two different information systems.

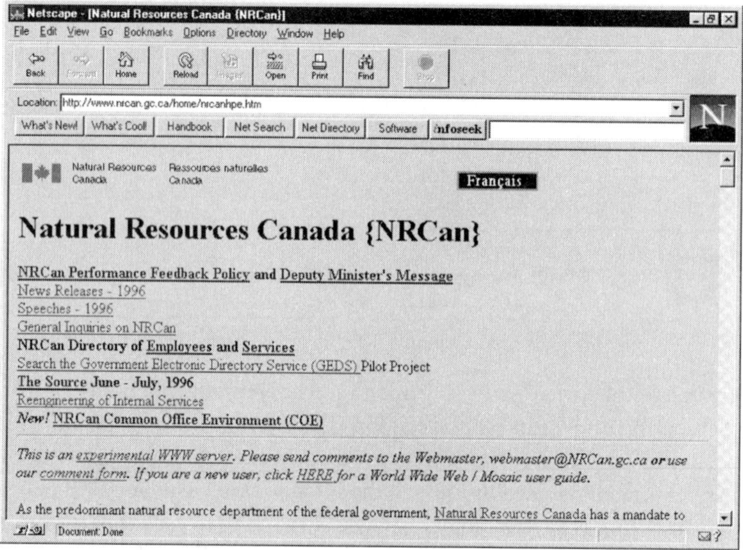

The Natural Resources Canada Intranet includes policy documents, telephone and e-mail directories, surveys, and human resources information. Below is an Intranet screen for the Corporate Services Sector:

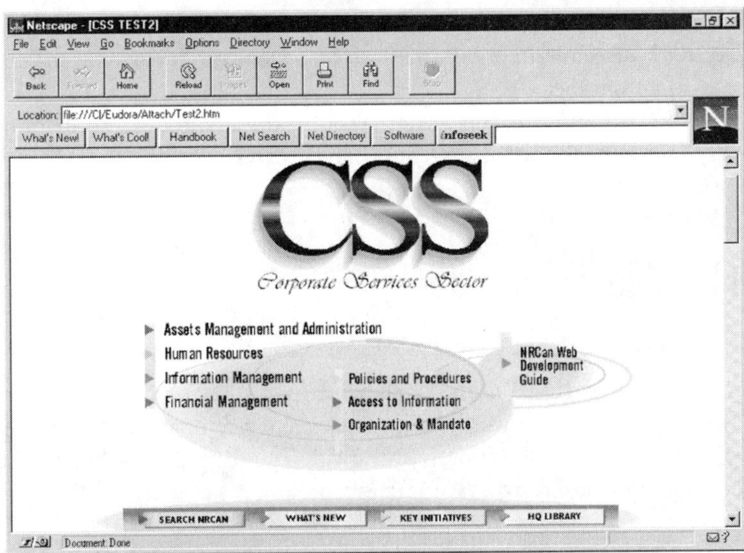

The Intranet even includes the department's weekly cafeteria menu:

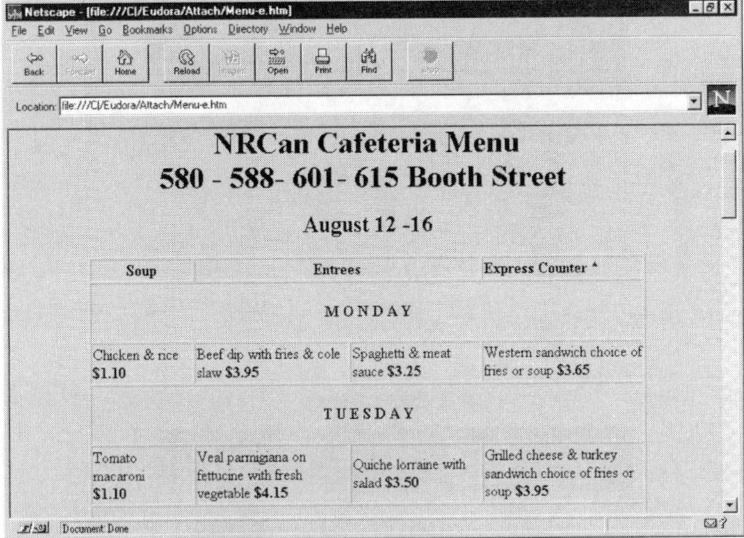

NRCan Cafeteria Menu
580 - 588- 601- 615 Booth Street

August 12 -16

Soup	Entrees		Express Counter *
MONDAY			
Chicken & rice **$1.10**	Beef dip with fries & cole slaw **$3.95**	Spaghetti & meat sauce **$3.25**	Western sandwich choice of fries or soup **$3.65**
TUESDAY			
Tomato macaroni **$1.10**	Veal parmigiana on fettucine with fresh vegetable **$4.15**	Quiche lorraine with salad **$3.50**	Grilled cheese & turkey sandwich choice of fries or soup **$3.95**

Nandi says that the most important benefit that the Intranet brings to Natural Resources Canada is the cost savings. For example, the Intranet can be used to survey employees, and results can be tabulated automatically with no manual effort whatsoever. Nandi also points out that the Intranet shortens the publishing cycle because there is no delay between publication and distribution of a document. On the Intranet, as soon as the document is published, it is immediately available to employees.

Nandi also says that in order for an Intranet to succeed, "education at all levels" is critical. He adds that a big stumbling block in organizations is confusion over the difference between an Intranet and the Internet. This, he observes, leads to the misconception that information placed on a company's Intranet is also accessible by the general population. Another problem is that traditional communications departments are very paper-based and often resist the movement toward the electronic distribution of information. Management, he says, has to be sensitized to the effectiveness of an Intranet.

His final words? "An Intranet is only as successful as the amount of information that people have." Atulesh Nandi can be reached at **webmaster@nrcan.gc.ca**.

Chevron Canada Resources

Calgary, Alberta

Chevron Canada Resources (CCR) is the Canadian arm of Chevron Corporation, based in San Francisco. Chevron is one of the world's largest petroleum companies, employing about 750 people across Canada and thousands more worldwide. You can access Chevron Corporation's public World Wide Web site at **http://www.chevron.com**.

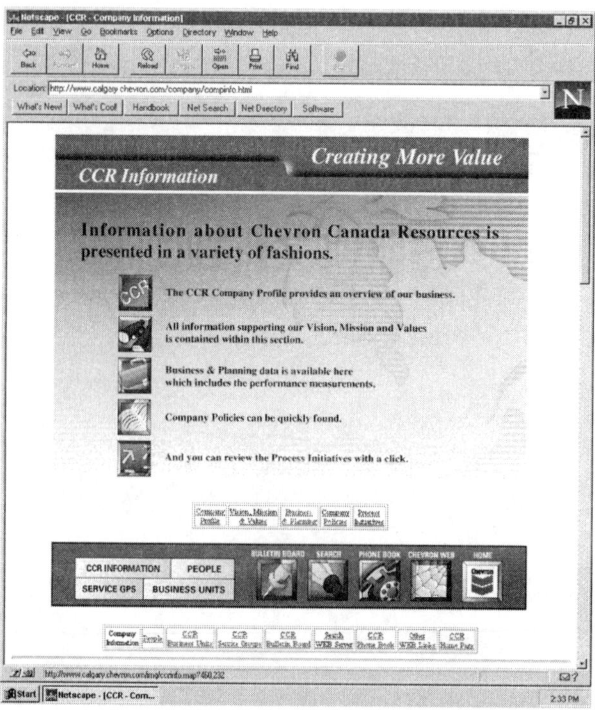

Charlie Stewart, Chevron Canada's Manager of Communications and External Affairs, says that the idea for a Chevron Intranet in the Canadian office came about in mid-1995. At that time, Chevron was trying to figure out a way to conveniently distribute its company measurement metrics to employees (metrics are graphs that show Chevron employees how well the company is performing against its stated goals and objectives). Stewart says it was at this point that the company started to explore the possibility of using the World Wide Web as an internal distribution tool.

A team of six people was assembled to work on the project. The team represented a cross-section of departments within the company and was led by the Communications and External

Affairs Department. An outside consultant was brought in to work on the design for the Intranet. Stewart says that "the most amazing part" of the process was the quick approval he got from top management. He made a brief presentation to company management and received approval on the spot. "It probably took less than 15 minutes," he says. Following a month and a half of planning, the Chevron Intranet was launched in October 1995 with 16 screens of information.

"The beauty of oil companies is that they are very technologically based … virtually everyone in our company has a PC on their desk," explains Stewart. "Literally over one weekend, we had our information technology people put a browser onto each PC in the office."

The launch of the Intranet was carefully planned and executed. When employees walked into their offices on Monday morning, they received a package of information that introduced the concept of an Intranet. To build employee interest in the project, each employee received a mouse pad that read: "Surf Pad to the Chevron Net — Your Link From Paper to Electronic Information." Even the president of the company got involved. When employees connected to the Chevron Intranet for the first time, they were greeted by a letter of welcome from the president, which explained the purpose of the Intranet. Needless to say, the launch was a smashing success.

Welcome to CCR — On the Chevron Internet!

Today, CCR is taking the plunge into cyberspace by launching its home page as part of Chevron Corporation's internal World Wide Web, an Internet communication service. By joining this rapidly expanding global network, CCR employees will be able to readily communicate and access data from both other Chevron Web sites and external sources.

The home page is like a global on-line calling card. It's available to a Chevron Internet audience and offers basic facts and figures about CCR and Chevron Corporation's world-wide subsidiaries …

The process of deploying Netscape within CCR is the first step to using this technology as a strategic communication tool. Our long term goal is to move as much information as possible onto the Web and make the transition from distributing hard copy information to using an electronic system. The move will provide a substantially expanded platform for communication and teamwork with other Chevron sites and organizations … It is also expected that virtually all external suppliers and contractors will eventually provide access to information on their products and services through this platform.

Access is simple — Internet users can obtain information quickly by selecting different categories and by clicking, with a computer mouse, on highlighted text and graphics …

I am very excited about using the Internet as an information tool and hope you find the service useful …

Don Paul

President

Chevron Canada Resources

The main screen of the Chevron Intranet is shown on the next page. It is divided into six main sections: Chevron Information, People, Service Groups, Business Units, the Bulletin Board, and the Chevron Web:

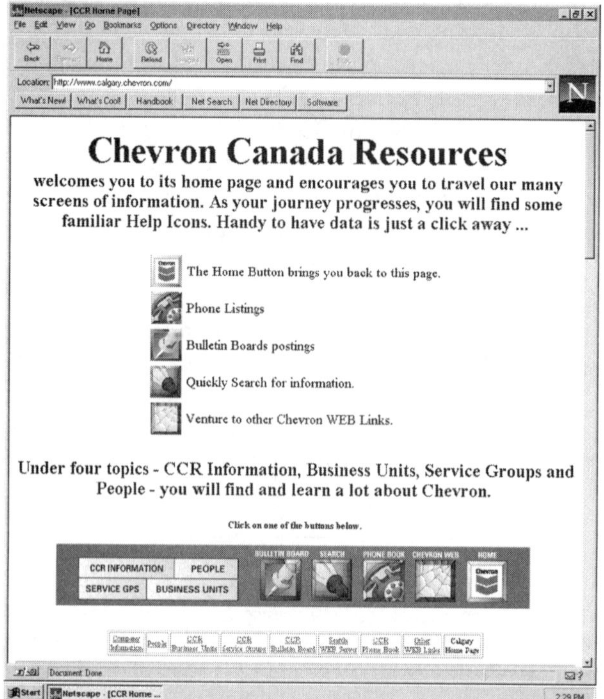

The Chevron Information section includes company policies, business and planning data, a company profile, and information pertaining to Chevron's vision, mission, and values:

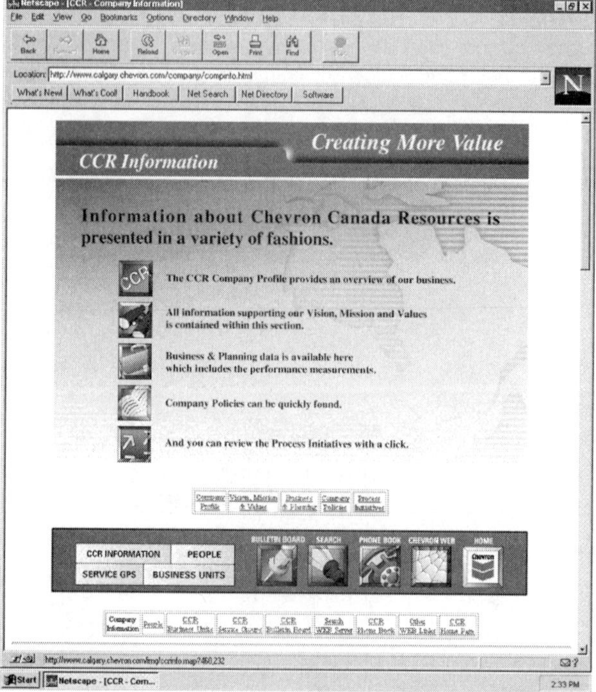

The People section contains organizational charts, salary information, compensation data, job postings, and information on employee facilities such as the social club, credit union, and exercise facility:

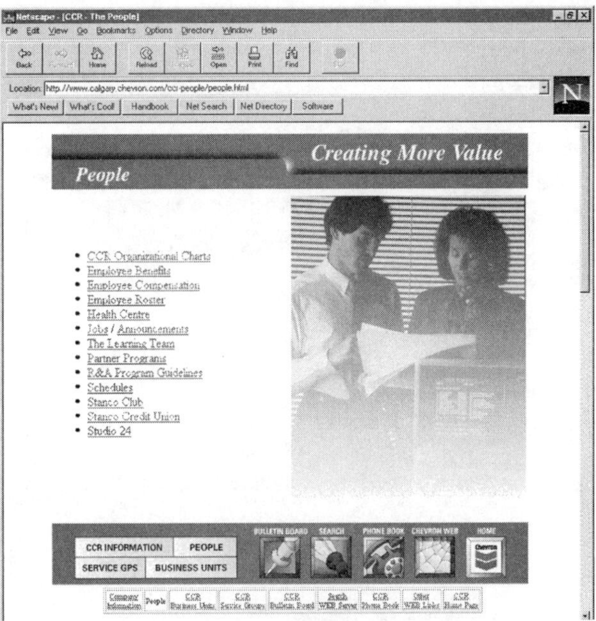

The Service Groups area provides information on specific service groups within the company, such as the legal department and business and technical services. Each service group is responsible for building its own page. The Business Units area contains information about Chevron's five business units. The Frontier Business Unit, for example, provides information about the Hibernia project:

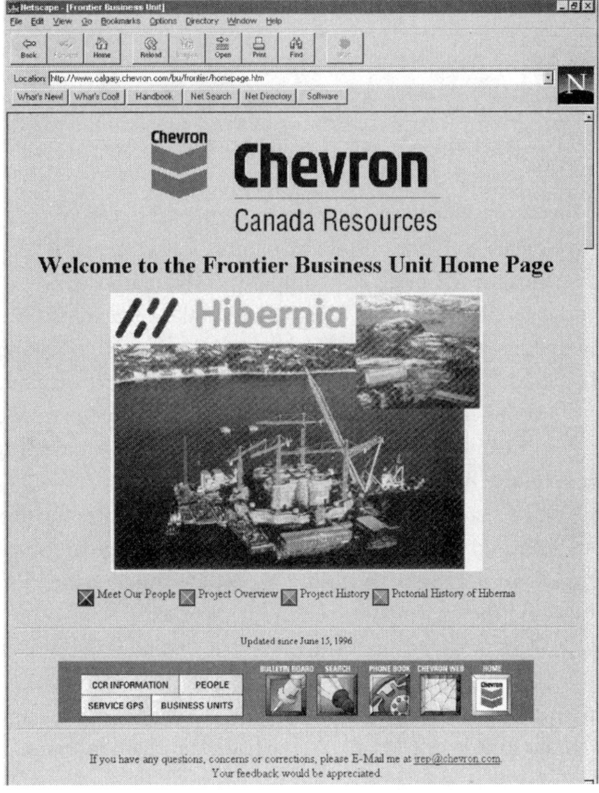

The Bulletin Board provides company-wide news and announcements and includes a three-year archive of company news releases:

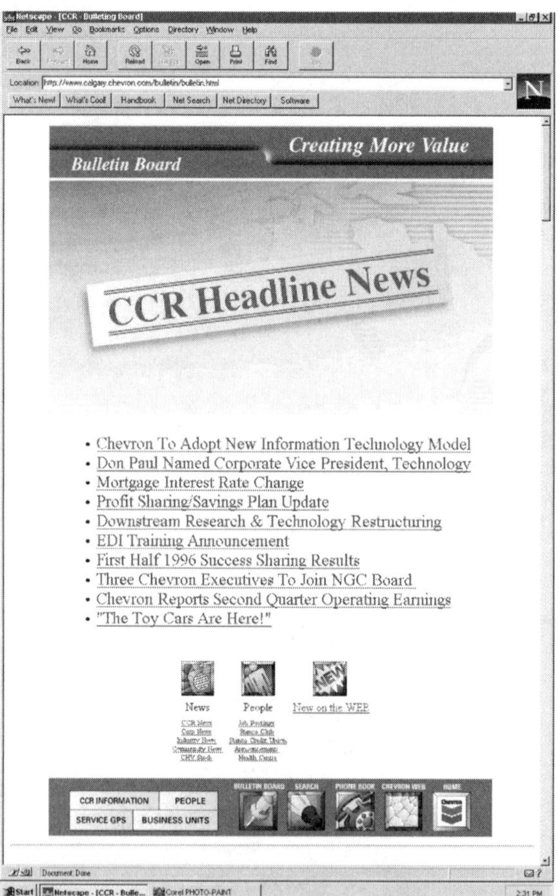

The Chevron Web provides links to the Intranets of other Chevron offices in such places as London, San Francisco, Nigeria, and Houston. In turn, other Chevron employees around the world can access the Canadian Intranet through the company's private network.

Stewart says the Intranet has helped the company to make a full transition to electronic distribution of company documents. For example, the Intranet has effectively replaced the notice boards that used to exist on each floor of the Calgary head office. Departments once used the boards to distribute news and announcements, but Stewart says that employees would tack so many notices on them that they became difficult to manage, labor-intensive, and "pretty messy." Now employees place notices on the Intranet instead.

Nearly all of Chevron's Canadian employees have access to the Intranet. Stewart says that use has been "tremendous," and employees were quick to begin using the new technology. "We thought it would become a natural thing," he says. "As people would see the value of [the Intranet] ... they would start building their own pages ... and it's worked!"

What advice does Stewart have for other companies that are building Intranets? Don't play "Big Brother," he cautions, by making it difficult for employees to use the Intranet. At Chevron, rules and procedures have been deliberately kept to a minimum. "One of our goals [at Chevron] was that we want people to use this technology ... we are putting hardly any barriers in front of them," explains Stewart.

"Make it easy for people to access information ... don't make it complicated ... don't over-formulate it ... don't overbureaucraticize it and put in so many rules and regulations and how-to's that you turn people off from the technology ... because then it won't work." He recommends that organizations embrace the technology. "Don't be afraid of it," he says. Most of all, Stewart stresses, "make it useful" for employees. "As people become more used to the technology ... it will be our challenge to put up more useful, immediate things ... that will help them do their job better."

Stewart says that the biggest benefit of an Intranet is that it opens up the flow of information within a company. "No longer is information deemed to be hoarded at the top," he says. On an Intranet, he points out, "information is out there for all to see." For example, an employee might be interested in learning about the company's maternity leave benefits. An Intranet makes it easy for an employee to look up that type of information without having to ask anyone.

Cost savings are also a big factor. Chevron's policy manual is now maintained electronically, and updates are accomplished with only a few keystrokes. Updates to the paper version had to be manually circulated to hundreds of employees.

The learning curve with Internet technology is steep, and Stewart says that this is all the more reason for companies to get involved now. The Intranet is giving Chevron vital experience with a medium that few companies can afford to ignore. "We've decided, as a company, to get on that learning curve ... it could become, at some point, a competitive advantage," he says. "In five years, if people aren't using the Internet for company information, they are going to be left in the dust." Charlie Stewart can be reached at **scrs@chevron.com**.

Recommended Intranet Resources

If you are interested in learning more about Intranets, especially from a technical perspective, we suggest the following resources.

The Complete Intranet Resource	**http://www.lochnet.com/client/smart/intranet.htm**
Building a Corporate Intranet	**http://webcom.com/wordmark/sem_1.html**
The Intranet Information Page	**http://www.strom.com/pubwork/intranet.html**
The Intranet Journal	**http://www.brill.com/intranet/**
Fortune Magazine — Building an Intranet	**http://pathfinder.com/fortune/specials/intranets/index.html**
Netscape Intranet Solutions	**http://home.netscape.com/comprod/at_work/index.html**

A Final Word: Where Are Intranets Headed?

The word "Intranet" only came into vogue in late 1995, but Intranets are already being heralded as the standard for corporate information systems. Paul McAfee, a reporter with *The Business Press* in Ontario, CA, summed up the situation nicely when he said, "Intranets are threatening to make obsolete the more-expensive local area network (LAN) or wide area network (WAN) systems that have ruled the corporate roost for years." According to Zona Research Inc., a Redwood City, CA-based market research firm, sales of software to run Intranet computers will increase to more than $4 billion in 1997, compared to sales of $476 million in 1995. Zona says that in 1998 the figure will reach $8 billion, four times the size of total sales for Internet servers.

CHAPTER 19

Intellectual Property on the Internet

If our property can be infinitely reproduced and instantaneously distributed all over the planet without cost, without our knowledge, without its even leaving our possession, how can we protect it? How are we going to get paid for the work we do with our minds? And, if we can't get paid, what will assure the continued creation and distribution of such work?

Everything you know about intellectual property is wrong.
John Perry Barlow, *Wired*, March 1994

You cannot obtain the products of a mind except on the owner's terms, by trade and by volitional consent. Any other policy of men toward man's property is the policy of criminals, no matter what their numbers. Criminals are savages who play it short-range and starve when their prey runs out ... We, the men of the mind, we who are traders, not masters or slaves, do not deal in blank checks or grant them.

John Galt, in Ayn Rand, *Atlas Shrugged* (Random House, New York, 1957)

The Internet is a gigantic copying machine the likes of which have not been previously seen and that challenges with the flick of a keyboard 500 years worth of copyright and trademark law. It allows anyone to take information of any kind and in an instant transmit it around the world, out of the reach of the owner. Intellectual property, protected by trademark and copyright law, is under siege from the Internet. Some people believe that because of the Internet, intellectual property can no longer be effectively protected. At least, that is one perspective. Another slant is that the Internet is just a different type of communication tool that simply needs a bit of time and attention from a few lawyers to be tamed.

Whichever perspective you subscribe to, you should be aware that the law is coming to cyberspace and is having both an easy and a tremendously difficult time in dealing with this challenging new frontier. In some cases organizations are fighting a battle to protect their intellectual property online, trying to prevent people from copying their material and distributing it on-line or trying to stop individuals from misusing their trademarks on the Internet.

The problem is not restricted to organizations. Many individuals are discovering that others are using their artistic and a literary works on-line without their permission, and they are finding it tremendously difficult to prevent such misuse. And in at least one case it seems that they are fighting a losing battle, unable to deal with big media organizations insistent on stripping away that which has been theirs for a hundred years. This, then, is the story of intellectual property on the Internet.

The Internet and Intellectual Property

Through the last several years many have become cognizant that the Internet is causing a great deal of stress for the owners of intellectual property, which is protected by trademark and copyright law. What is intellectual property? It is, in essence, anything created by one's own mind, the product of the intellect. Do a simple search for the phrase "what is intellectual property" on AltaVista, and you will be taken to a number of sites that delve into the concept (see the screen on the next page).

Examples of intellectual property are

- articles and books;
- pictures taken by photographers;
- letters and memos;
- artistic, dramatic, and musical works;
- computer programs;
- logos and product names.

For years battles over intellectual property have occurred in courtrooms and have been the subject of many a legal memo and threat, when intellectual property has been misused in violation of the rights of the owners. In the days before the Internet, it was an often easy — but often extremely complex — issue to deal with, given that most offenses occurred using the medium that has been with us for 500 years or more, paper.

With the arrival of the Internet, however, things changed. Suddenly it became easy for anyone to take one's intellectual property and turn it into a digital computer file. The Internet could then be used to send and store that digital file anywhere in the world. The problem? It became too easy to distribute intellectual property, making it difficult for owners to protect themselves. With the arrival of the World Wide Web, it suddenly became easy to "publish" someone else's intellectual property and make it available to an on-line community of millions.

INTELLECTUAL PROPERTY ON THE INTERNET

1. The Internet is presenting people and organizations with tremendous challenges when it comes to trademark and copyright issues.
2. Organizations are finding it important to work to protect their trademarks on the Internet, by clearly identifying their trademarked information on-line.
3. Many disputes have arisen throughout the Internet over the issue of trademarks and domain names.
4. The Internet, because of its very nature, makes it difficult for people and organizations to protect their copyrighted information on-line. However, it appears that many of the fundamentals of Canadian copyright law apply to information published on the Internet.
5. A particular challenge with copyrighted information and the Internet is that many freelance writers are discovering that their copyrighted material is being used on-line without their permission, or that publishers are forcing them to sign contracts in which they give away all rights to their copyrighted work, without any additional remuneration.

The international aspect of the Internet makes the challenge more difficult than ever before: not only could someone's work be distributed on the Internet, it could end up on a computer in Denmark, far out of the easy reach of Canadian intellectual property laws and beyond the economic ability of many to pursue.

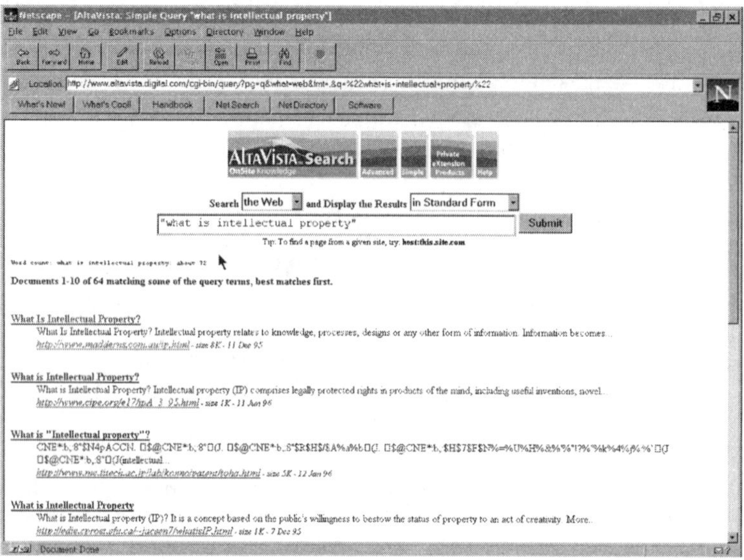

The Impact of the Internet on Intellectual Property

Intellectual property violations throughout the Internet are rampant. Many situations have occurred innocently enough, as individuals use the World Wide Web to publish information on their hobbies and interests. In doing so, they often, sometimes inadvertently, violate the intellectual property of authors. However, in other cases we have seen concerted and deliberate attempts to cause harm to other persons or organizations by violating their intellectual property rights.

There have been cases in which organizations have obtained Internet domain names (see Chapter 5) that are clearly based on the trademark of another organization. We have seen situations where individuals have created Web sites — on-line memorials, so to speak — about their favorite television shows, sports teams, and other subjects, and in which they have rather innocently used trademarked information. In other cases individuals have posted copyright works on their Web sites with full knowledge that they are violating the rights of the owners. We have seen major media organizations sell the copyright work of freelance writers through electronic databases without the permission of the owners, an act that the owners regard as theft. Further, these media organizations are now trying to get from those writers permission to use their intellectual property in perpetuity in any electronic form and without additional compensation in this new era of the Internet.

We have also seen situations where lawyers who specialize in intellectual property are unsure whether certain actions on the Internet actually constitute intellectual property infringement. For example, battles have erupted over the right of one individual to actually link to the Web site of another individual.

It is not easy to apply intellectual property law to new media such as the Internet. For example, how does traditional copyright and trademark law apply to new technologies such as the World Wide Web and electronic mail? What legal recourse do I have if someone is using my intellectual property on the Internet? Can I stop someone from using my intellectual property on the Internet in another country? The intent of this chapter is to give you some guidance on these questions. A few points before we get started:

- We must stress that the comments and observations offered in this chapter do not constitute legal advice and should not be relied upon in that regard. You should only use this chapter as an introduction, at the most basic level, to some of the unique challenges posed by the Internet when it comes to intellectual property and how some of those challenges are being resolved. As with any legal issue, you should consult a lawyer for definitive advice.
- A second important point is that the law in any respect to the Internet is very difficult to apply, given the unique problems posed by the Internet. It seems that nothing is black and white, especially where the Internet is concerned, and that any conclusions that people might draw are very conditional and always subject to change.
- Third, it is important to note that many of the scenarios described in this chapter have not been tested in Canadian courts. Many intellectual property lawyers disagree about how the courts would deal with certain copyright and trademark infringements on the Internet. Only time will tell.
- Fourth, there are many groups seeking to have the fundamentals of Canadian copyright and trademark law changed as a result of the new technologies and challenges posed by the Internet. As intellectual property cases pertaining to the Internet are heard in Canadian courts, new precedents will be set that will influence the direction of this area of the law and its application to new media such as the Internet.
- Fifth, as you browse the Web looking for information about intellectual property law, keep in mind that Canadian law is not the same as U.S. law — or, for that matter, the law of any other country. Information coming from a Web site in another country will almost always be from that country's legal perspective.
- Finally, we want to caution you that many of the Web sites described in this chapter are embroiled in heated legal disputes. If you try to reach a Web site that is listed in this chapter, and you receive an error message, it is entirely possible that the site has been forced to shut down.

In this chapter we will deal with two aspects of intellectual property: trademarks and copyright.

Trademark Disputes

A trademark is a word, symbol, or picture, or a combination of these elements, used to distinguish the goods or services of one person or organization from those of others in the marketplace. Examples of trademarks include brand names, such as Jell-O, Tylenol, Uncle Ben's, Fleischmann's, Sun Maid, and Dr. Scholl's, and company names, such as McDonald's and Kraft; and logos and slogans. For example, VISA has trademarked the slogan "It's The Only Card You Need."

An organization spends a great deal of time and effort building its corporate image. A trademark is closely tied to an organization's image in that it conveys certain values and qualities that have come to be associated with that organization. Trademarks can therefore influence someone's purchasing behavior. Misuse of a trademark can weaken the distinctiveness or the goodwill associated with the trademark and cause confusion among consumers and businesses. Hence when organizations see their trademark misused on the Internet, they are often quick to do battle with those who abuse it, regardless of the intent, innocent or otherwise. Here are a few common questions and answers pertaining to trademarks.

Questions and Answers About Trademarks and the Internet

Here is the World Wide Web page for TriMark Mutual Funds (**http://www.trimark.ca**). If you look closely at the screen below, you will notice that the ® symbol appears after the word "Trimark" and the letters "TM" appear after the words "Discovery Fund":

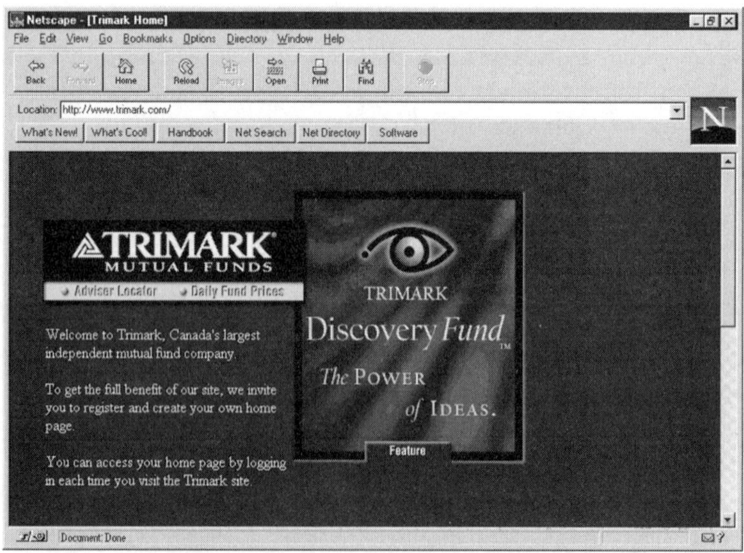

1. What Does the ® Symbol Mean?

This is known as the "R in a circle" symbol. It identifies that a word, design, or phrase is a trademark registered with the Canadian Trademarks Office.

2. What Does the "TM" Symbol Mean, and How Does It Differ from the ® Symbol?

TM means "trademark." It identifies that the owner holds a trademark on the name, phrase, or symbol. The TM mark can be used regardless of whether the trademark is registered, while the ® symbol should only be used if the trademark is registered. In French, the mark "MC" (marque de commerce) is used instead of TM.

3. What Is the Difference Between Registered and Unregistered Trademarks?

A registered trademark is one that has been registered with the Canadian Trademarks Office. Trademarks do not have to be registered, but registration makes it easier for a trademark holder to protect his/her rights if the trademark is challenged. It is strongly recommended that a trademark be registered to afford the word, phrase, or logo the maximum possible degree of protection under the law. The registration of a trademark is valid for 15 years and can be renewed.

4. If a Logo Appears on a Web Page Without an ® or a TM Mark Beside It, Can I Assume the Logo or Product is Not Protected Under the Law?

No. If you find a logo on a Web page that you like, and want to use it on your own Web page, always ask the owner of the Web page for permission first. Canada's *Trademarks Act*, for example, does not require that any symbols be used to identify a trademark. Most companies do make use of these symbols, however, to remind the world that the mark in question is protected as a trademark. Even though the Web page you are looking at may be in another country, the trademark may be protected in Canada, which leads us to the next question.

5. If a Trademark Is Protected in One Country, Is It Automatically Protected in Another?

No. You have to register the trademark in each country where you want protection. For example, if you register a trademark with the Canadian Trademarks Office, this action only protects the trademark in Canada. Similarly, a trademark registered in another country (e.g., the United States or Great Britain) is not protected in Canada unless the trademark is registered here. However, if that trademark appears in advertising that reaches Canada, its exposure may create some rights here.

The Web Raises Some Unique Trademark Challenges

The global nature of the Web raises some interesting challenges for companies that are doing business on the Internet. The only way you can fully protect a trademark on the Web is to register it in every country that can be accessed over the Web.

For example, suppose that Company A, a successful retail chain of shoe stores in Canada, decides to start selling its shoes over the Web. Company B, which sells shoes in Jamaica, also launches a Web site based in Jamaica and starts selling shoes over the Internet.

Let's assume that the Jamaican company is using a logo that is almost identical to the logo used by Company A. If both companies were not operating on the Web, this really wouldn't be a problem. Company A operates in Canada, and Company B operates in Jamaica.

Although the logos of the two companies are almost identical, they do not conflict with each other because the companies are operating in different countries.

However, on the Web everything changes. On the Web there are no borders. All countries are operating in the same "virtual space," and consumers can shop as easily in Jamaica as they can in Canada. When the Jamaican company advertises its shoes on the Web, that advertising reaches Internet users worldwide, including those in Canada. The Jamaican company could easily target Canadian Internet users with its sales messages and start to dilute the value of Company A's trademark, since the two logos are so similar.

What can Company A do? Not very much, since the Jamaican company operates out of Jamaica and is protected under Jamaican trademark law. In other words, the Web site of the Jamaican shoe company physically resides in Jamaica. As long as the Web site stays in Jamaica, it is outside the jurisdiction of Canadian trademark law. If the Jamaican shoe company opened a Web site in Canada, Company A would have some legal recourse.

6. If I Have a Trademark on a Product Name, Why Is It Important to Police It on the Internet?

Did you know that words such as "Zipper" and "Escalator" used to be trademarks and refer to a specific organization's product? These words became so commonly used that the owners lost their right to ownership over those names. The word "escalator," for example, has become a generic term for a moving staircase. For this reason, owners need to vigorously protect their trademarks both on Web sites and in discussion groups on the Internet. If a product name becomes a generic part of the language, the owner risks losing the trademark on that product name. Trademark owners can try to prevent that from happening by monitoring the Internet for improper use of their trademarked names.

7. Can You Give Me an Example of the Situation That You Describe in Question 6?

Velcro® is an example of a product name that is protected by a registered trademark in dozens of countries. However, many people use the word "velcro" generically to refer to the substance that fastens things. But as the Velcro® companies point out, this use of the Velcro® name is wrong, and they say so on their Web site: "[Velcro] is not the generic name of the stuff that fastens shoes, pockets, and hundreds of other things."

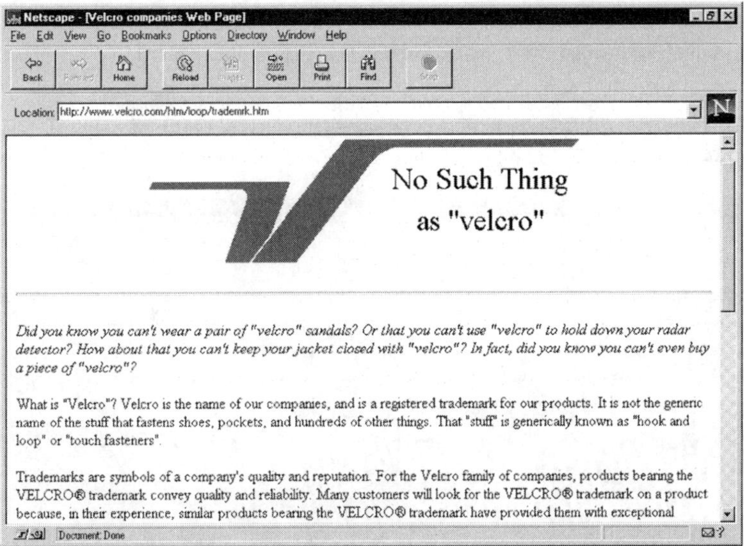

To further drive home this point, Velcro® maintains a Web page (**http://www.velcro.com**) that lists all its registered trademarks:

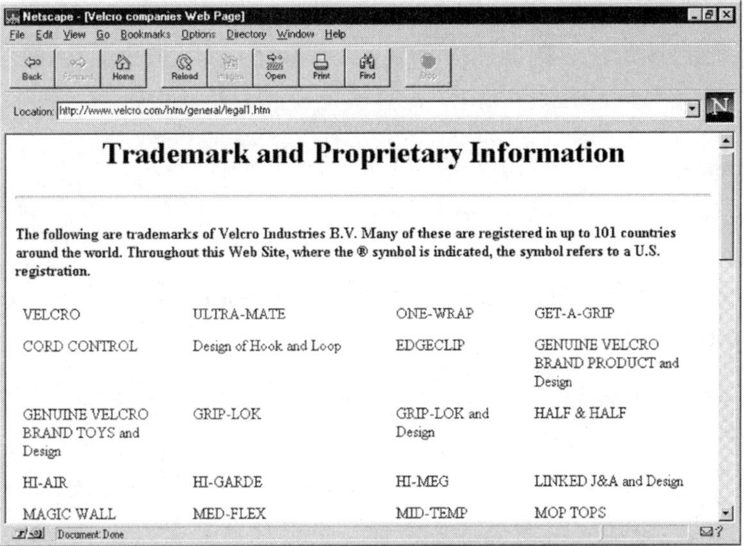

It took us only a few minutes of searching on the Web to find someone referring to Velcro in a generic sense, which demonstrates how widespread this type of problem is. On the opening page of the Web site for a product called "Eclipse Sun Shade" (**http://www.carshade.com**), the following sentence is found: "Customized to your car, the Eclipse Sun Shade draws together to velcro fasten in the center":

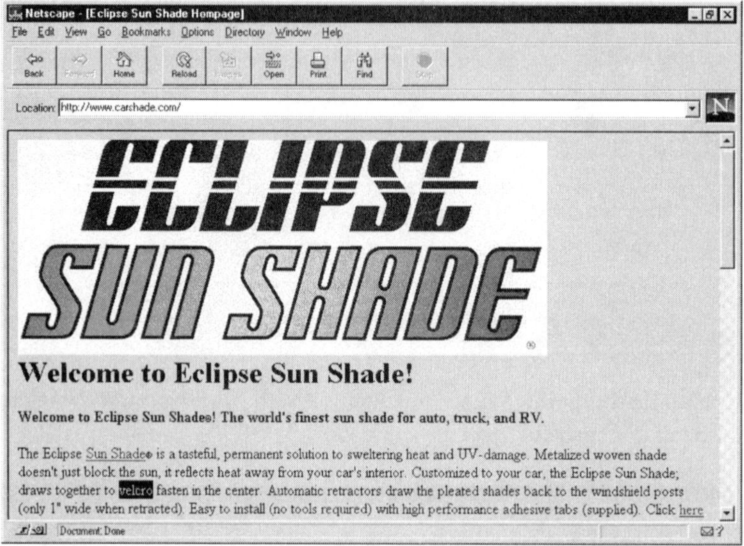

Domain Names

When it comes to the Internet, domain names have presented some particularly tricky trademark issues. One way organizations try to protect their trademarks on the Internet is by registering a domain name that is equivalent to the trademark held by the company. We discussed domain names in Chapter 5, "How Does the Internet Work?" and described how they form an integral part of e-mail addresses and addresses for sites on the World Wide Web. They are fundamental to the way that people communicate and access information on the Internet. Domain names can be company names, as seen in the examples below.

coca-cola.com	Coca-Cola
nt.com	Northern Telecom
ontariocorn.org	Ontario Corn Producers' Association
shellcan.com	Shell Canada
bmw.ca	BMW Canada
nabisco.ca	Nabisco Canada

Domain names can also be product names.

tide.com	Tide Laundry
trix.com	Trix
liquidpaper.com	Liquid Paper
alka-seltzer.com	Alka-Seltzer

Problems with domain names first came to light in late 1993, when some organizations reserved domain names that were identical to trademarks held by other organizations. The matter first gained the attention of corporate management throughout Canada with the publication of an article in the *Globe and Mail*, October 25, 1994:

> Guess who owns the right to use the name McDonald's on the Internet. If you said a major international hamburger chain, you guessed wrong. As of two weeks ago, it was an enterprising New York reporter, who registered the name just to show he could do it. A number of major North American companies are about to find out just how important — and valuable — it is to have a highly visible address on the "information highway." The rights to use business and product names as registered addresses on the Internet are being staked out in an electronic equivalent of the Yukon gold rush.

At the time, the organization responsible for domain registrations in the **.com**, **.org**, **.net**, **.edu**, and **.gov** domains — the InterNIC — did not have a policy that addressed the registration of a trademark as a domain name, so the reporter mentioned in the *Globe and Mail* article was able to obtain **mcdonalds.com**, much to the chagrin of the hamburger chain.

Unique Challenges Posed by Domain Names

In the "real world" more than one organization can use the same name. For example, "Excel" is both the brand name for a type of chewing gum and a computer spreadsheet package manufactured by Microsoft. However, trademarks can exist on both "Excel" products because they do not compete with each other (i.e., spreadsheets do not compete with chewing gum). Trademark law limits protection of a mark to the particular good or service with which it is used. This means that non-competing organizations can register the same trademark provided there is no confusion. But on the Internet *only one organization can have rights to any given domain name*; hence there can be only one **excel.com**. Who owns it? A company called Excelsior Information Systems, not Microsoft or the chewing gum company.

All kinds of unique situations have arisen like this. We look at some examples below.

- You might think that **continental.com** belongs to Continental Airlines, but it does not; it was snapped up by a company called Continental Cablevision.
- The address **www.para.com** will take you to a company called Parallel Productions, not Para Paints. This, of course, has probably caused some stress for the paint company.
- INCO, the international nickel mining company, sought the name **inco.com**, only to discover that it had been reserved by a company based in Moscow, IncomA. Often the international reach of the Internet causes some unforeseen challenges like this.

InterNIC's Role

The InterNIC's stated position has always been that it does not have the resources or the mandate to "police" domain name registrations. The InterNIC allocates domain names on a "first-come, first served" basis and does not get involved in resolving disputes between domain name owners and trademark holders. It presumes that domain name applicants have the legal right to use the domain names for which they are applying. *This policy continues to the present day.*

However, prior to July 1995, the InterNIC refused to take any action against domain name holders who were allegedly infringing on another organization's trademark. In the months leading up to July 1995, many organizations discovered that their trademarks were being registered as domain names by their competitors or other organizations with malicious intent. In fact, from mid-1994 to mid-1995 many individuals and organizations rushed to obtain as many domain names as they could, reserving trademark names, corporate names, and even the names of competitors to which they really had no legal right.

Lawyers started to get involved, as difficult trademark and copyright issues began to emerge around the globe. Clearly something had to give. Finally, in 1995 the InterNIC introduced rules to curb the abuse of domain names and to provide recourse for organizations that felt their trademarks were being violated by someone else's domain name. The press release announcing the change read as follows:

NETWORK SOLUTIONS ANNOUNCES INTERNET DOMAIN NAME POLICY

(HERNDON, VA) July 28, 1995 — A new policy that deals with disputed Internet domain names until ownership issues are resolved by the courts was announced today by Network Solutions, Inc., a subsidiary of Science Applications International Corp. (SAIC).

The new policy recognizes that an Internet domain name may conflict with an existing trademark or service mark, but that the trademark or service mark holder may not have the exclusive right to use that name on the Internet.

NSI serves as the InterNIC domain name registrar under a cooperative agreement sponsored by the National Science Foundation.

Domain names are assigned to organizations that want to be accessible on the Internet. The Internet's growing popularity has led to an explosion of requests for domain names, with NSI currently processing more than 600 per day.

Domain names will continue to be assigned on a first-come, first-serve basis, with NSI checking to ensure that a requested domain name has not already been given to another user. Like a telephone book publisher, NSI presumes that an applicant for a domain name has the legal right to use that name. Applicants now will be asked to confirm this on their registration forms.

NSI has found that Internet users occasionally select domain names which may be identical to the registered trademarks or service marks of other organizations. While NSI cannot resolve such legal disputes, the company is concerned that domain names not cause confusion or interfere with the legal rights of third parties. Although ownership of a trademark or service mark does not automatically include rights to domain name ownership, the new policy recognizes trademarks as quantifiable evidence relevant to domain name disputes.

If the holder of a trademark provides evidence to NSI that a domain name already assigned to an Internet user is identical to that trademark, NSI will ask the Internet user to submit proof that the user also has a trademark for that name (for example, the trademark Acme may have been issued to many different entities for different types of products or services). If the Internet user cannot provide such proof of trademark, the holder of the domain name will be allowed a reasonable period of time to transition to a different domain name.

Then the disputed name will be placed in a hold status and not used by anyone until a proper court resolves the dispute. This policy is intended to be neutral as to the respective rights of the registrant and trademark holder to the disputed domain name.

If the user does provide proof of its trademark, that user can continue to use the name as long as the user agrees to protect NSI from the costs of defending lawsuits brought against NSI by the other trademark holder. Otherwise, the domain name will again go on hold.

NSI will also apply these procedures in dealing with foreign trademark holders who have their trademarks certified by the U.S. Patent and Trademark Office.

"We want to emphasize that Internet users don't need to have a trademark to get a domain name", said NSI attorney Grant Clark. "The problem is that NSI doesn't have the authority or expertise to adjudicate trademark disputes. Some have even suggested that NSI should pre-screen domain names to check for possible infringement. That would turn us into a mini-trademark office with costs going through the roof and processing times in months rather than days."

Clark said NSI will evaluate its policy on an ongoing basis, and will remain sensitive to the opinions of the hundreds of thousands of diverse Internet users.

Problems with the New Policy

The new policy meant that a trademark holder could challenge any organization with a domain name identical to its trademark. If the domain name was registered after the complainant's trademark registration or first use of the trademark *and* the party being challenged could not produce evidence of a trademark on the domain name, then the domain name owner was required to forfeit the domain name. While the new policy solved some problems, it created others. Consider one aspect of the new rules that many people complained about. Once the domain name owner was contacted by the InterNIC about a trademark dispute, the domain name owner had 30 days to prove ownership of a trademark identical to the domain name. Since the InterNIC was willing to accept any valid foreign trademark, some domain name holders hired lawyers to obtain trademarks from places such as Tunisia in Africa, where trademarks could be obtained quickly, within the 30-day deadline.

The second big problem was that the new policy had a fundamental weakness: it relied too heavily on registered trademarks and ignored other forms of trademarks that are recognized and protected by law. For example, as we discussed earlier in the chapter, you do not have to register a trademark to use one. You can have a trademark on a name simply by using it; this is called a common law trademark. The InterNIC's policy, however, did not consider common law trademarks, only registered trademarks. The policy allowed a registered trademark holder to take a domain name away from an another organization if that organization could not produce a *registered* trademark on the domain name.

1996 Policy Changes

Few people were happy with the InterNIC's July 1995 policy, and the InterNIC was under intense pressure to make further modifications to its Domain Name Dispute Policy. Finally, in August 1996, the InterNIC announced yet another new policy. The press release announcing the changes is reproduced below. If you are not interested in all the fine details, skip right to the next section, entitled "Current Situation," where we explain the implications of the new policy.

HERNDON, Va. Aug. 14 /PRNewswire/ — Effective September 9, 1996, Network Solutions, Inc., internationally known as the Domain Name Registrar for InterNIC, will implement a revised Domain Name Dispute Policy. This marks the second time that the policy has been revised since it was

> published in July, 1995. The policy revision was accepted by the National Science Foundation in accordance with the cooperative agreement with Network Solutions, Inc.
>
> The policy represents the leadership position Network Solutions has taken in the new frontier of "cyberlaw," where there is neither legislation nor case law addressing the relationships between Internet domain names and trademarks. The revised policy maintains and strengthens a balanced position between the competing demands of trademark owners and domain name registrants. In doing so, the policy makes it clear that Network Solutions provides a domain name registration service without any interest in the person or organization that registers the domain name. When disputes over a name occur, Network Solutions emphasizes that the two parties must resolve their dispute and agree to be bound by either a negotiated settlement or a court order.
>
> The revised policy removes confusion surrounding trademark owners' challenges to domain name registrations. In particular, it clarifies that the only "evidence" Network Solutions will consider under the policy is the trademark owner's certified copy of a federal registration certificate. And, it more clearly explains the situations in which Network Solutions will place a domain name in a "Hold" status. As a result, no one will be able to use the name, pending resolution of the dispute.
>
> Also under the revised policy, challengers will be less likely to submit a complaint against a domain name registrant without sufficient grounds. The policy requires the trademark owner to give unequivocal and specific notice to the domain name registrant that its registration of use of the domain name violates the legal rights of the trademark owner. Such notice must occur before the trademark owner asks Network Solutions to take action pursuant to the policy. In fact, the policy provides that Network Solutions cannot take any action unless it receives both a certified copy of the federal registration certificate and a copy of the notice sent to the domain registrant.
>
> The revised policy also precludes domain name registrants from obtaining a last minute, instant trademark to use as prima facie evidence of their legal right to the domain name. The policy clearly states that Network Solutions can only accept a certified copy of a federal registration from a domain name registrant if that trademark was registered before the domain name registrant received a complaint that its domain name violates the rights of a third party.
>
> Furthermore, the revised policy explicitly states that if a trademark owner or a domain name registrant files suit against the other regarding the registration or use of the domain name, Network Solutions will deposit control of the domain name into the registry of the court and will abide by all court orders. [...]

Current Situation

Let's summarize the current situation regarding domain names and trademarks. If an organization owns a trademark and discovers that someone else has registered a domain name that is identical or confusingly similar to that trademark, the organization can go directly to court and obtain a ruling against both the domain name holder and InterNIC — a prompt but costly solution. If the organization does not wish to go to court, it can seek redress through InterNIC. Under InterNIC's new policy, effective September 1996, the trademark owner must first contact the domain name owner and provide "unequivocal and specific notice" that the registration of the domain name violates its legal rights as a trademark holder. If the domain name owner refuses to relinquish the domain name, the complainant can approach InterNIC and request that InterNIC suspend the use of the disputed domain name. Before taking any action, InterNIC requires that the complainant furnish a certified copy of a U.S. or foreign trademark registration *and* a copy of the notice that was provided to the domain name owner. Upon receiving these two pieces of information, InterNIC will approach the individual holding the disputed domain name. The original domain name owner is allowed to continue using the domain name only if:

- the domain name was registered before the earlier of (i) the date of the complainant's trademark registration *or* (ii) the date of first use of the complainant's trademark; or
- the domain name owner had, before receiving notice of the dispute, registered in the U.S. or abroad a trademark that is the same as the domain name.

If the original domain name owner can satisfy either requirement above, the domain name does not have to be relinquished. If neither of the above conditions can be satisified, the domain name owner must relinquish the domain name and obtain a new one, pending the resolution of the dispute. Once the domain name is relinquished by the original owner, it is put "on hold" indefinitely and is not available for use by anyone. Once this happens, the only way for either party to get the domain name reinstated is to obtain an order from a U.S. federal or state court or settle the dispute themselves. If, before the domain name goes "on hold," either the trademark owner or the domain name owner files suit against the other, InterNIC will *not* put the domain name "on hold" and will give control of the domain name to the courts.

In Canada registrations in the **.ca** domain have not been much of a problem, because the CA Domain Committee scrutinizes each application very carefully. In 1995 the CA Domain Committee did make one policy change that is worth noting here: the registration form for a **.ca** domain was modified to allow companies to register their trademark as a domain name.

Reaction to the 1996 Policy

The 1996 policy revision solved one of the major problems with the old policy: the ability for domain name owners to rush a trademark application through after receiving notice of a trademark challenge. Under the new policy the trademark must exist at the time the domain name owner is challenged; otherwise, InterNIC will not accept it. Overall, however, the new policy was not well received in the Internet community. Why? It does not address the issue of common law trademarks. InterNIC's policy still gives all the rights to an organization that has a *registered* trademark in either the United States or a foreign country. Common law trademark holders have little protection if their domain names are challenged by registered trademark holders.

Types of Domain Name Problems Today

How do we translate the above into basic and simple guidance? It is quite straightforward: if you have registered a domain name, you may be infringing on another company's trademark. There are two fundamental types of trademark problems: domain hijacking and innocent registrations.

- Domain hijacking. Domain hijacking occurs when an organization or individual intentionally registers a domain name that they know violates the trademark of another individual or organization. The registration is generally undertaken for financial or competitive reasons or just as a hoax. For example, a company may register a domain name to prevent a competitor from obtaining it. Alternatively, an individual may obtain a domain name and then try to sell it to another organization for a profit. An example would be the reporter who registered **nyt.com** and later sold it to the *New York Times.* The reporter who registered **mcdonalds.com** eventually relinquished it to McDonald's, but only after the company made a donation to charity.
- Innocent registrations. Innocent registrations occur when the applicant registers a domain name that is a logical choice for his/her organization but coincidentally similar

or identical to another organization's name or registered trademark. This can lead to confusion among visitors to the Web page who are expecting to see one organization but instead find another. For example, you might expect that **ctv.com** belongs to the CTV Television Network; in fact, it belongs to an organization known as Corporate Technology Ventures. Typing **www.ctv.com** in your Web browser will connect you to the Corporate Technology Ventures World Wide Web site.

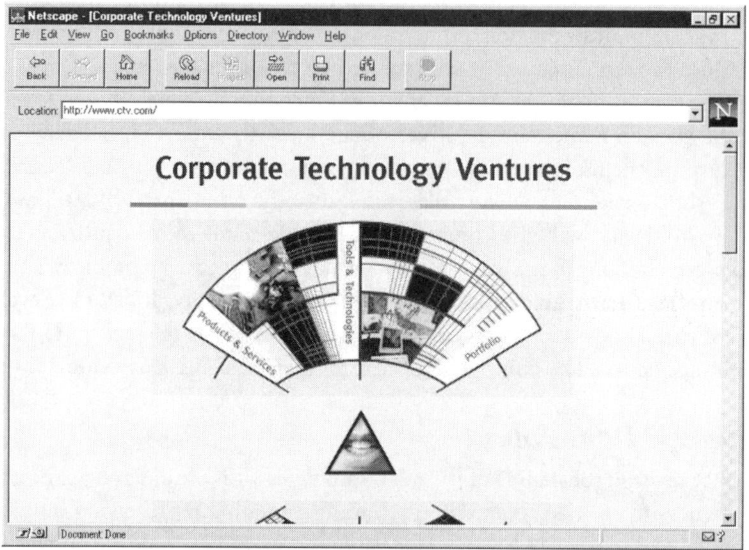

Fry's Electronic, Inc., a retail electronic chain based in Palo Alto, CA, brought an action against Frenchy Frys, a Seattle seller of french fry vending machines, which had registered the domain **frys.com**:

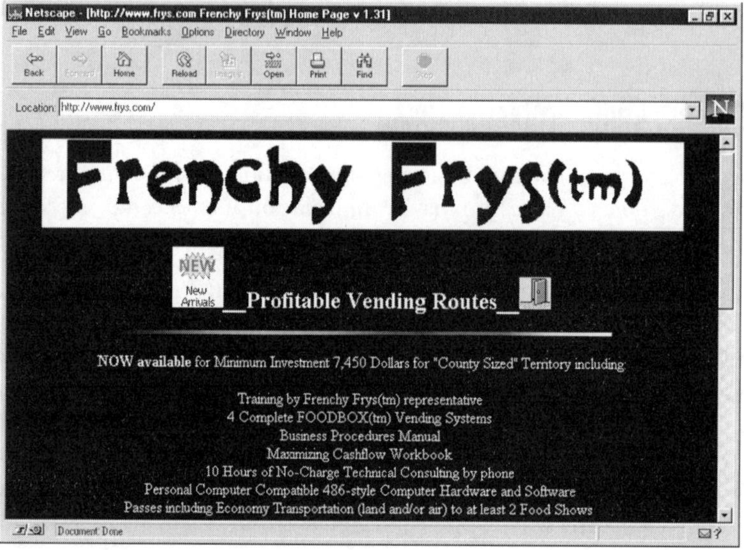

Hasbro, manufacturer of the board game Clue, filed a lawsuit against a company called Clue Computing, which had registered the domain name **clue.com**:

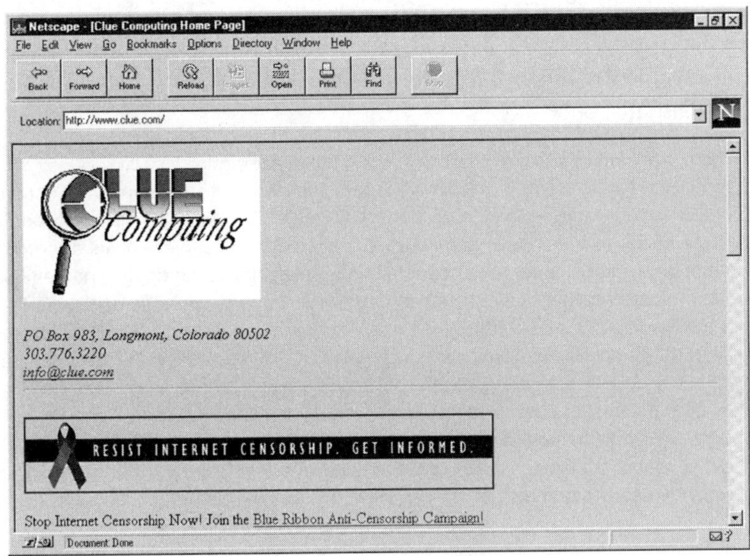

Warner Brothers, which owns a trademark on Roadrunner (the famous cartoon character, meep, meep!) filed a suit against Roadrunner Computer Systems, which had registered the domain **roadrunner.com**. The company name is derived from the New Mexico State bird:

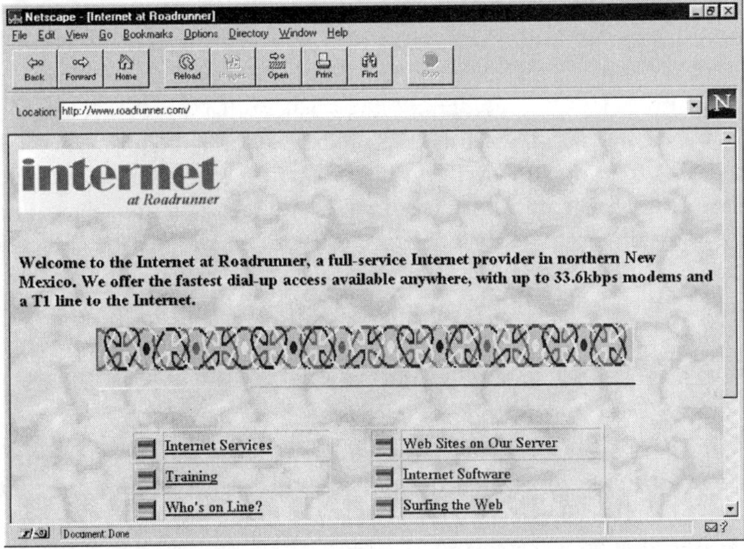

How has each case been resolved? Each and every case is treated on its own merits by the courts, and many of the cases were still in the process of being resolved at the time we reviewed them.

Problems With the Current System

It is important to note that through all the policy changes discussed above, *the InterNIC's basic position has remained unchanged.* The InterNIC continues to hand out domain names on a "first come, first served" basis. Their position is that they cannot prescreen domain names for possible trademark infringements. To drive this point home, the following note is contained in the Domain Name Dispute Policy:

> Network Solutions, Inc. ("Network Solutions") is responsible for the registration of second- level Internet domain names in the top level COM, ORG, GOV, EDU, and NET domains. Network Solutions registers these second-level domain names on a "first come, first served" basis. By registering a domain name, Network Solutions does not determine the legality of the domain name registration, or otherwise evaluate whether that registration or use may infringe upon the rights of a third party. The applicant ("Registrant") is responsible for the selection of its own domain name ("Domain Name"). The Registrant, by completing and submitting its application, represents that the statements in its application are true and that the registration of the selected Domain Name, to the best of the Registrant's knowledge, does not interfere with or infringe upon the rights of any third party. The Registrant also represents that the Domain Name is not being registered for any unlawful purpose. Network Solutions does not act as arbiter of disputes between Registrants and third party complainants arising out of the registration or use of a domain name.

This is not an unreasonable position to take; it would be impractical for the InterNIC to monitor every possible domain name for trademark infringements or to try to act as a mediator between duelling organizations.

But despite the many policy changes that have been made to address trademark disputes, many organizations regard the current domain name system as inadequate, unfair, and badly in need of a major overhaul. The InterNIC is a U.S. organization, yet it controls **.com** and **.org** domain registrations for the entire world. Some argue that an international treaty needs to be put in place, one that is fair to all nations concerned, and one that addresses the trademark problems that arise from current policies and procedures. Others believe that a partial solution would be to create more top-level domains (i.e., expand the number of top-level domains beyond **.com**, **.net**, **.edu**, **.org**, and **.gov**). This would allow the same word to be used in a variety of different contexts.

The definitive answer on domain name disputes? As yet there is none. Lawsuits continue to be filed, and organizations continue to lobby for changes to the system. There is no easy solution. The situation is, as might be expected, constantly evolving. Many cases are being decided on their own merits. Take a look at **http://www.law.georgetown.edu/lc/internic/domain1.html** for an overview of the many domain name disputes that are being examined in the courts. Our suggestion: If you find yourself in a domain name dispute, obtain appropriate legal advice.

More Information About Policies Relating to Domain Registration

If you are interested in knowing who owns the rights to a particular domain name, or if you want to see if a certain domain name has been taken by someone else, visit the InterNIC Web site at **http://rs.internic.net**. You can search their database of domain name holders for free. The InterNIC's Web site also provides information about domain name application procedures and includes documents that explain the InterNIC's policies pertaining to domain names and trademarks. The latest press releases and documents about domain name policies for the **.com**, **.org**, **.net**, **.gov**, and **.edu** domains will always be available there.

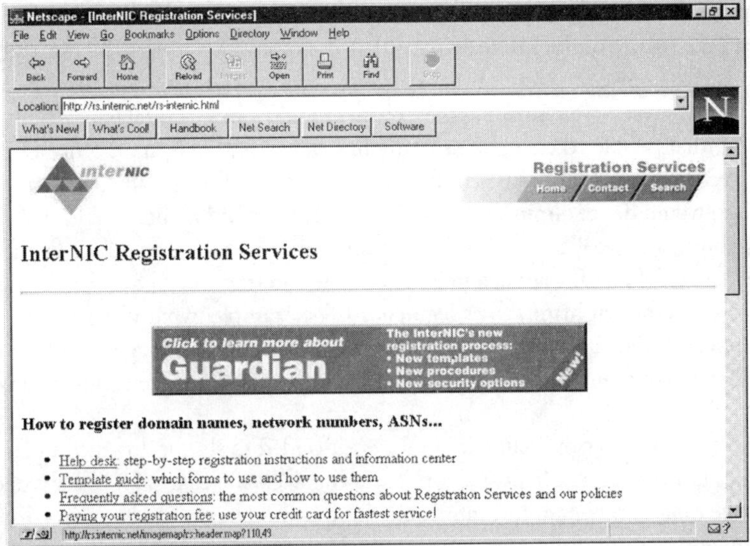

For up-to-date information about the status of domain registrations and policies in Canada (i.e., for the **.ca** domain names), we suggest you visit the Web sites of CA*Net (**http://www.canet.ca**) and the Canadian Association of Internet Providers (**http://www.caip.ca**).

A document that summarizes the current policy for **.ca** domain names is available at the following address on your Web browser:

- **ftp://ftp.cdnnet.ca/ca-domain/application-form**.

An up-to-date list of **.ca** domain names can be retrieved at either of the following addresses on your Web browser:

- **ftp://ftp.cdnnet.ca/ca-domain/index-by-organization**;
- **ftp://ftp.cdnnet.ca/ca-domain/index-by-subdomain**.

Using a Trademarked Domain Name as Part of Your Web Address

Trademark problems do not arise only with domain names; challenges can present themselves if you use a trademarked name in part of your Web address. Take the case of Home Pages, Inc., a California-based company that designs World Wide Web home pages. The company had set up a Web site for the purpose of uniting Lego fans around the world. The Web site contained pictures of Lego models, Lego news, and other information contributed by dozens of Lego hobbyists on the Internet.

The site had no official connection whatsoever with the manufacturers of Lego, Interlego, A.G. Under most circumstances you would expect Interlego to be pleased that users of its products were exchanging information about its products on the Internet. However, here is the problem. The Web address for the site was **http://legowww.homepages.com**. We have underlined the offending part of the address. Because part of the Web address contained the word "lego," which is a trademark belonging to Interlego, A.G., the company requested that the site owner modify the address and remove the word "lego" — to no avail. The company next instructed their trademark counsel to contact the owner of the site to request that the offending address be removed. The folks at the site posted a copy of the letter from the lawyers for a brief period of time. Reading it, one could see that the lawyers were stressing their client's concern over several issues, with the primary concern being that people accessing the site might believe they were at an official Lego site. The letter indicated that this would cause confusion in the mind of the public or might actually mislead them, and would hence diminish the value of the Lego brand name. Interlego, A.G. was quite prepared to commence legal action. Lego was clearly concerned that the public might mistake the Home Pages site to be an official Lego presence on the Internet. (Lego does, in fact, have an official site on the Internet, at **http://www.lego.com**.) For example, what if inaccurate information started to appear at the site? From Lego's perspective this could damage the value of the Lego trademark. Lego, like many other companies, is quite prepared to take action against a site that violates its trademark rights.

The outcome? The person maintaining the site decided to shut it down completely upon receiving the letter from Lego. He posted a note on the Web site that said: "I have decided that I no longer have time to maintain this information." It should be pointed out, in fairness to Lego, that the company was not seeking to shut the site down. It only sought to have the Web address changed.

Trademarks and Web Sites

Since anyone can be a publisher on the Web, you might expect that trademark infringements are quite commonplace. They are. Spend a few minutes on the Web, and you will quickly come across dozens of Web pages that make use of unauthorized images and logos. In the sections below we examine two types of trademark problems on the Web: Web sites established by fans of a particular person or organization and Web sites that parody specific organizations or people.

Fan Sites

There are many "fan sites" throughout the Internet, Web sites devoted to popular television and movie stars, television shows, sports teams, and specific products and services. For the most part these Web sites are "unofficial" in nature and therefore have no official connection with the person or organization represented on the page. For example, here is a Web page set up by a group of Saturn car enthusiasts (**http://www.ishare.com/Saturn**):

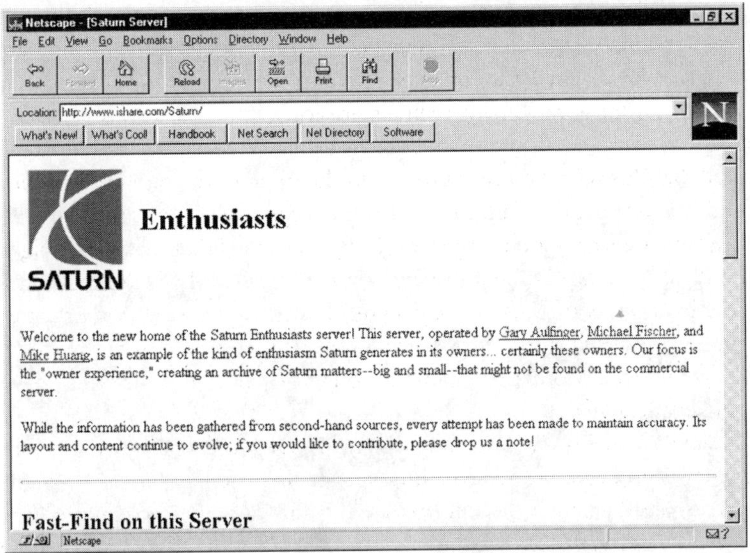

This site is not affiliated with Saturn in any way, but notice that the site is stamped with the official Saturn logo. Why does this site exist? Simply because a bunch of Saturn enthusiasts decided to build it. It is their on-line "shrine" to the cars made under the Saturn name. Remember: anything goes on the Internet.

Many "unofficial" sites like this one exist on the Internet. But it is only in the last year or so that they caught the attention of corporate lawyers. Throughout 1995 and 1996 the Internet gained a high public profile. Businesses started to use the Internet, and as they did, many discovered that their trademarks were being unlawfully used on the Net. Businesses faced a difficult dilemma. Should they prevent fan sites from using their trademarks because of the possible diminution of the value of the trademark, or should they recognize the inherent value in having fans do marketing on their behalf? It is a difficult dilemma.

Many organizations chose the former route and now devote a great deal of energy to monitoring the Internet for trademark abuses in an effort to protect their intellectual property. Some companies take a hard-lined approach and send their lawyers after any offenders they come across. The result? If you travel the Web today, you will discover many "ghost sites" that have been stripped of pictures, images, and logos that violated trademarks. We look at some examples below.

Here is a Web site put up by a fan of the popular television show *The X-Files.* The owner of the site has placed a large "censored" button where images from the show used to be, removed at the demand of a lawyer representing the popular television series (**http://ourworld.compuserve.com/homepages/Stephanie/postepis.htm**):

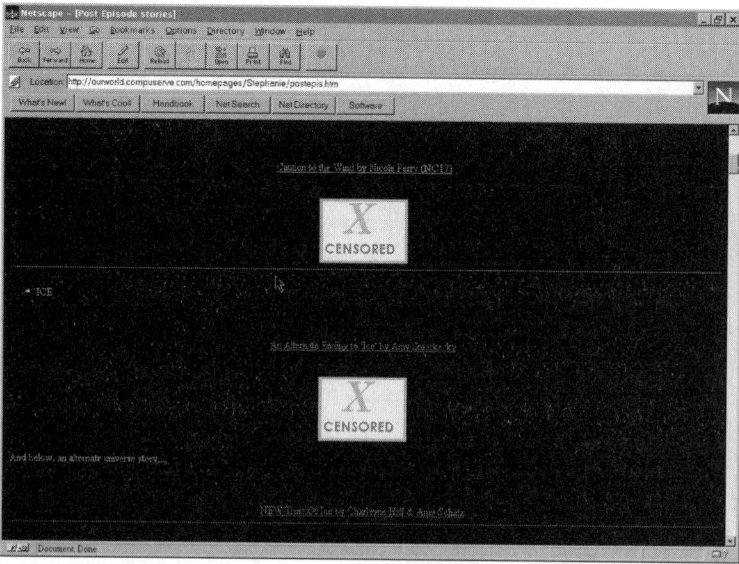

The following note appears on the Web page and explains what happened:

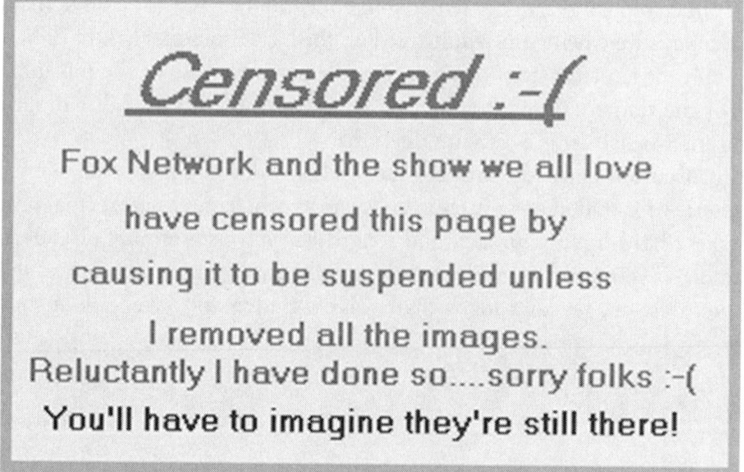

A Web site featuring small icons of characters from the popular television show *The Simpsons* suffered a similar fate. The person who designed the icons received a letter from Twentieth Century Fox, demanding that the icons be deleted from the Web site because they constituted copyright infringement (**http://www.snpp.com/icons.html**).

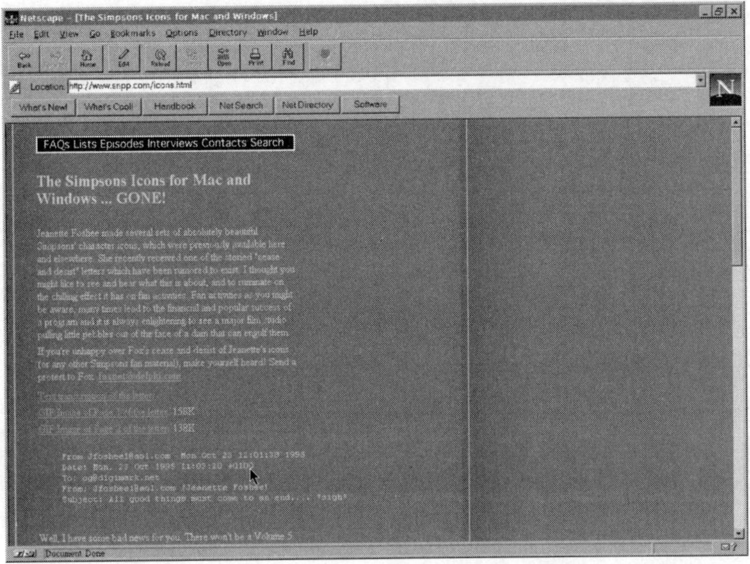

Does it make sense for copyright and trademark holders to go after fans who create sites containing their work? From one perspective, no. After all, the fans are undertaking marketing and promotion on behalf of the copyright or trademark holder. Some people argue that companies should leave the fans alone, because their activities on the Web can help to popularize a product or brand name. But look at the issue from another perspective. Fans are creating Web sites that are clearly in violation of the rights of others. Owners of trademarks are entitled to enforce their rights in order to protect their intellectual property. One could argue that some violations are harmless, but in many situations the company's image is being tarnished or profits are being lost as a result of the infringement. Hence organizations concerned about the value of their trademarks must be vigilant about misuse of their trademarked property — one reason why they go after fan sites so readily.

Parody Web Sites

Fast emerging as a legal issue on the Internet is the concept of a "parody Web site." A parody Web site is a Web site that has been established for the purpose of poking fun at a particular person, company, or organization. Some parody sites blatantly violate another organization's trademark. A good illustration of this concept is the "Xmart Sucks" page, which pokes fun at a major retailer (**http://www.brandeis.edu/students/ st950496/kstory.html**):

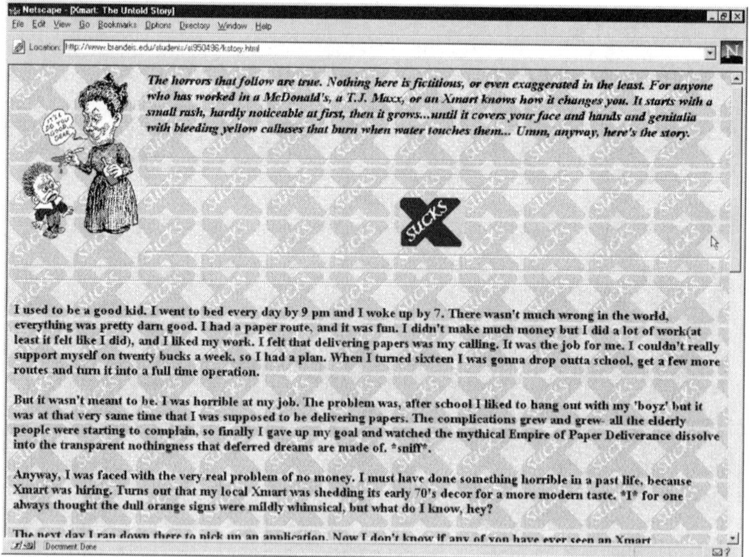

The owner of the Web page uses it to write about his experiences as a Kmart employee. Originally he had used a defaced version of the Kmart logo, a violation of trademark law. He has since changed it.

Parody sites have come to affect the political scene as well. For example, during the 1996 U.S. Presidential election, one enterprising individual created his own "unofficial" Bob Dole site and obtained the domain name **dole96.org** to do so. Type in the address **http://www.dole96.org** and you will end up at the parody site seen below. If you were to come across the address **http://www.dole96.org** on the Internet, you would certainly think that it is official:

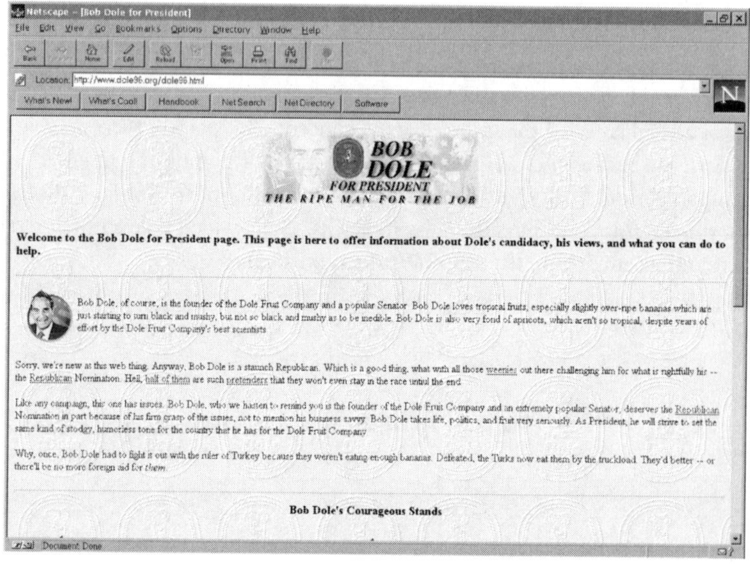

It's not until you get to the Web site and read the text that you realize something is amiss: "Bob Dole, of course, is the founder of the Dole Fruit Company and a popular Senator. Bob Dole loves tropical fruits, especially slightly over-ripe bananas which are just starting to turn black and mushy, but not so black and mushy as to be inedible. Bob Dole is also very fond of apricots, which aren't so tropical, despite years of effort by the Dole Fruit Company's best scientists." The *real* Bob Dole Web site is at **http://www.dole96.com**:

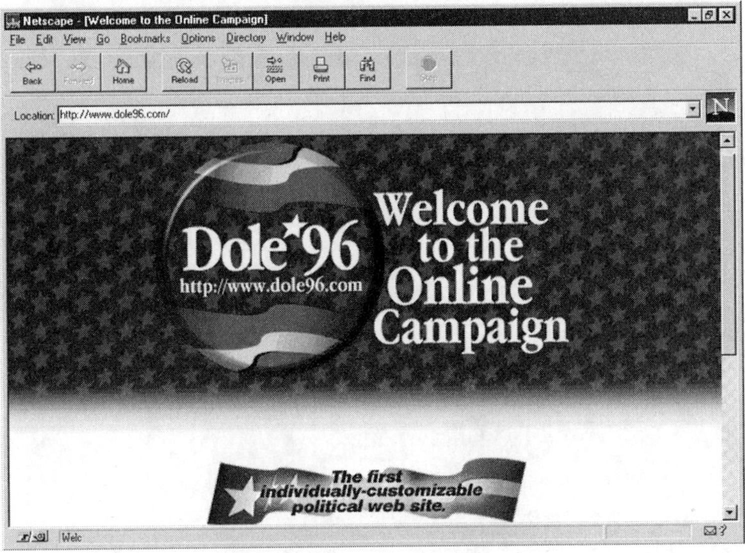

Toys 'R' Us

Perhaps the classic story involving a trademark battle on the Internet is the conflict between Toys 'R' Us and a Web site known as "Roadkills-R-Us." Rather than repeating the whole story here, we suggest you read the ongoing saga by visiting Roadkills-R-Us **at http://www.rru.com/tru**. It is a good example of how, perhaps, both sides have gone a little too far:

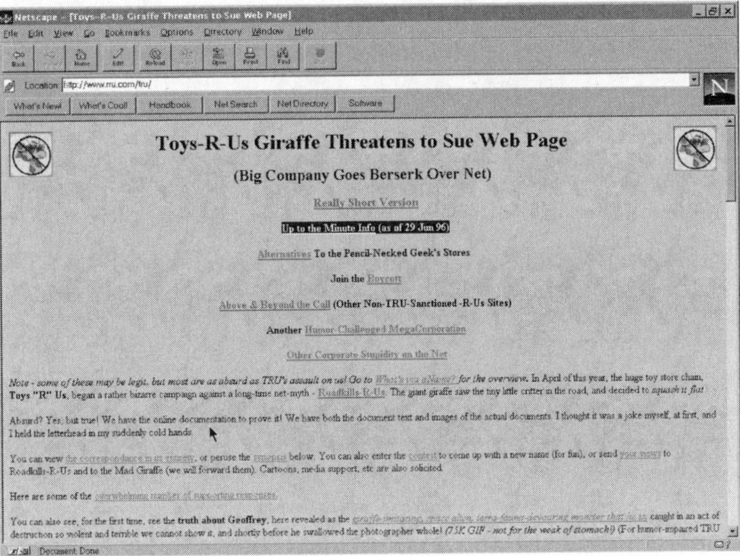

Protecting Your Organization Against Parody Sites

Some parody sites are clearly hoaxes. But what if one of your competitors sets up a Web site that is almost identical to yours with the intention of deceiving your customers? It is easy for anyone to set up a bogus site on the Internet. When this happens, consumers may have a hard time distinguishing between the "real" site and an imitation. Naturally, organizations are trying to find ways to protect themselves against this type of on-line fraud. An organization called TrueSite thinks it may have come up with the solution:

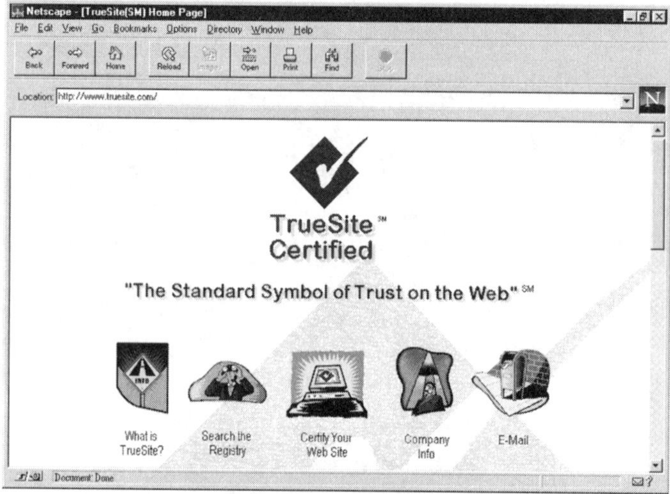

For a fee TrueSite will verify the information on your organization's Web site and then certify it as authentic. Once your Web site is certified, your organization is given a license to display the TrueSite logo on your home page. The logo is then linked to the TrueSite Registry. When people visit your Web site, they can "click" on the logo with their mouse and receive a message back confirming the site is official. Full details describing how the process works can be found on the TrueSite Web page at **http://www.truesite.com**. Let's look at an example. Saturday Nights! (**http://www.saturdaynights.com**), an on-line entertainment publication, is an example of a Web site that uses the TrueSite system:

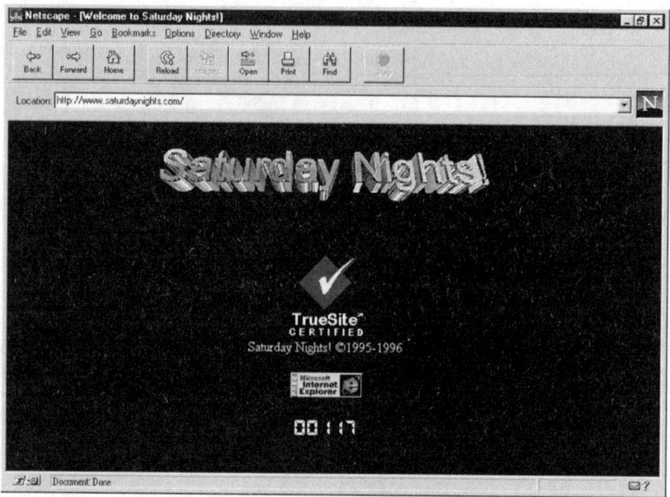

When you visit the Saturday Nights! Web page, the TrueSite logo appears (as seen in the screen above). To verify that the site is authentic, just click on the TrueSite logo and you will see a screen like this:

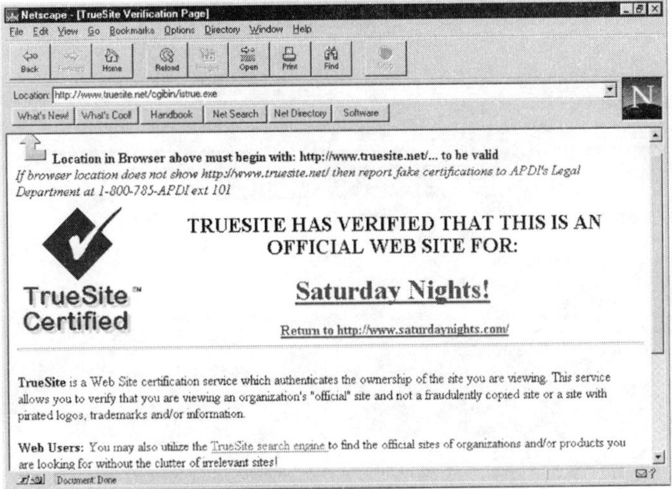

TrueSite is an innovative solution to the dilemma of parody Web sites, but we are skeptical about the commercial viability of the service. Only time will tell if the Internet community backs TrueSite as a standard for protecting the integrity of sites on the World Wide Web.

On-line Sources of Information About Trademarks Including Domain Name Disputes

If you are interested in reading more about domain name disputes or trademark law in general, there are several sources we recommend. The What's In a Name archive at Georgetown University Law Center offers information on the relationship between domain names and trademarks. It includes an archive of domain name disputes (**http://www.law.georgetown.edu/lc/internic/domain1.html**):

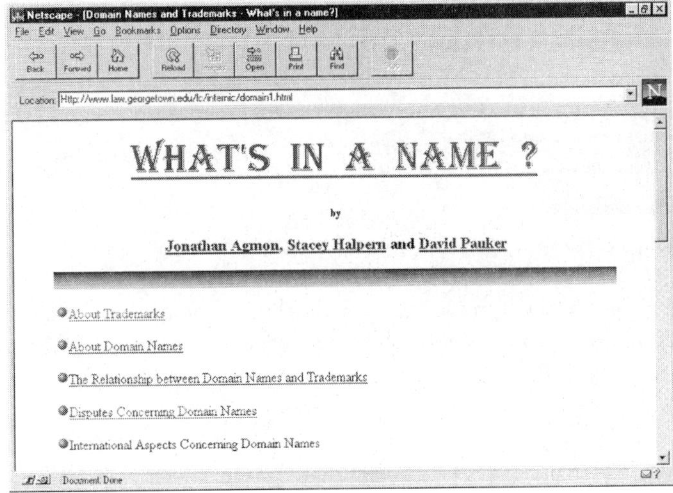

The NSI Flawed Domain Name Policy Information Page, available from the Oppedahl & Larson Patent Law Web site (**http://www.patents.com**), provides pointers to news articles and resources about domain name disputes:

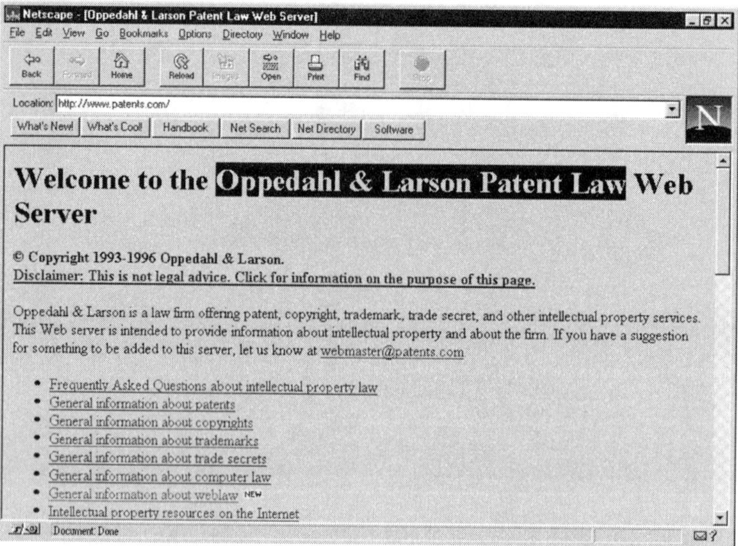

Comparative Domain Dispute Resolution Policies (**http://www.digidem.com/legal/domain.html**) examines how different countries are dealing with the issue of trademarks and domain names:

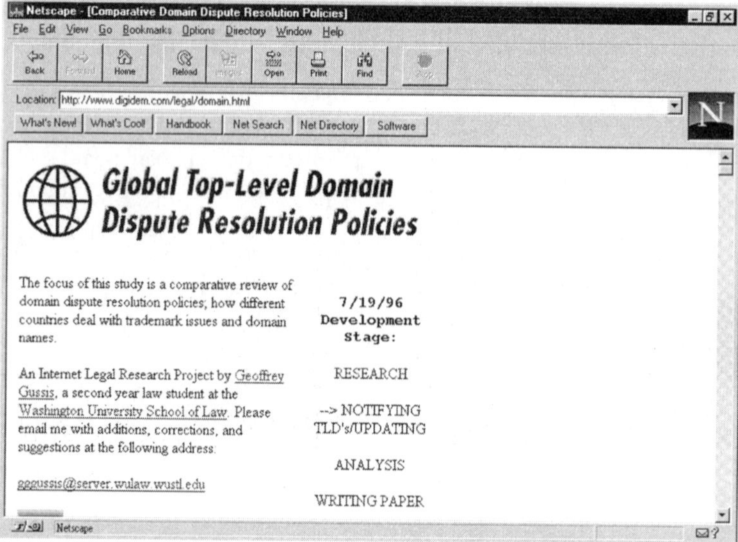

Bereskin & Parr, a Toronto law firm specializing in intellectual property law, maintains a Web page with a great section on trademarks and intellectual property (**http://www.bereskinparr.com**). Many other Canadian law firms provide similar information on their Web pages.

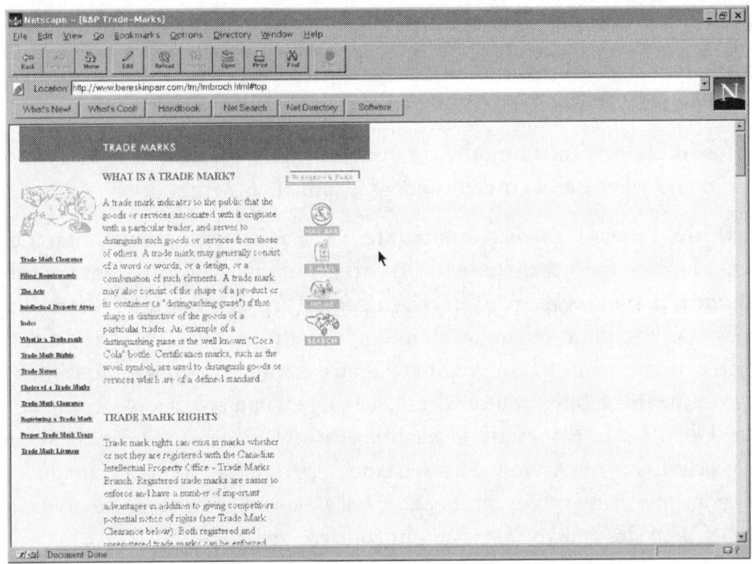

Information Law Alert (**http://www.infolawalert.com**) is a subscription-based newsletter that covers intellectual property and new media law. The Web site contains a great selection of articles that deal with the issues surrounding trademarks and the Internet:

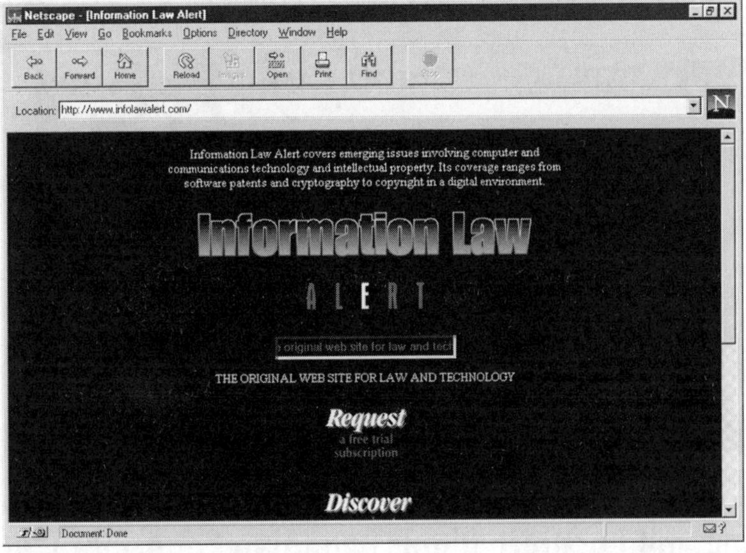

Copyright and the Internet

Copyright means the right to copy. Literary works, dramatic works, musical works, artistic works, and choreographic works are just some of the items protected under the Canadian *Copyright Act.* Copyright owners have the sole and exclusive right to reproduce, perform, or publish works protected under the Canadian *Copyright Act*— books, songs, articles, and letters, for example.

The Internet has caused two very real problems when it comes to copyright:

- the Internet is a tool that makes it very easy for people to distribute or make available copyright information;
- because it is a new medium, the Internet has created a great deal of confusion over what is and what is not covered under Canadian copyright law.

Copyright law affects every Canadian on the Internet. It is important that you understand what your rights are, how to protect them, and how to avoid violating the rights of others. In this chapter we summarize some of the relevant copyright issues so that you can protect your own copyrighted property. Keep in mind that you should not interpret this chapter as definitive legal advice. Canadian and international copyright law is an extremely complex and difficult subject. If you want to examine this subject in more detail, we suggest you take a look at *Canadian Copyright Law* by Lesley Ellen Harris. Ms. Harris is an authority on Canadian copyright law, and her book will be a great help to anyone trying to understand copyright law from a Canadian perspective. You can find more information about the book as well as general information about Canadian copyright law on her Web site at **http://www.mghr.com/copyrightlaw**:

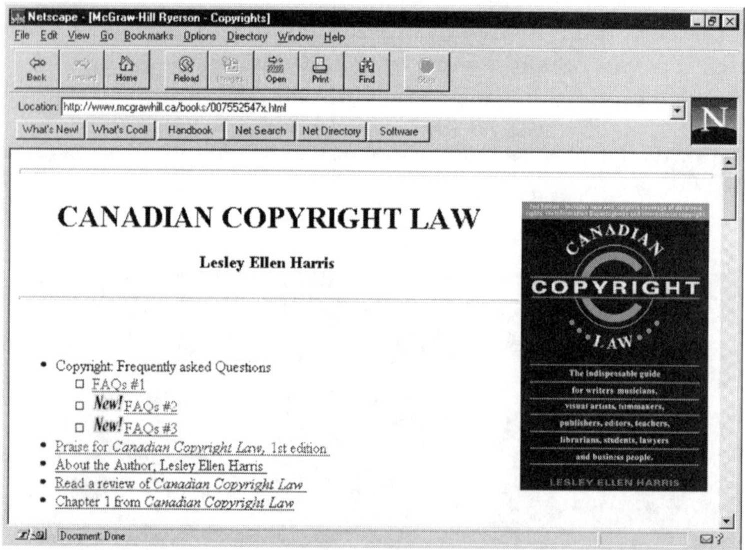

Questions and Answers About Canadian Copyright Law and the Internet

Because there are so many nuances with copyright law, we approach the issue of copyright and the Internet in the form of common questions and answers.

1. Are Web Pages Protected by Canadian Copyright?

Yes. Copyright protection extends to World Wide Web pages. Under Canadian copyright law only the copyright owner has the right to reproduce a Web page in any form, electronic or otherwise. Strictly speaking, then, it is illegal to print a Web page on your printer or e-mail yourself any text that appears on a Web site because this constitutes "reproduction." This also means that when you access a Web page on the Internet, you are technically infringing on the Web page owner's copyright, since the Web document is being reproduced on your computer screen. Not only that, but most Web browsers feature a cache, which stores on your hard disk a copy of all pages and images that you see. However, some lawyers believe that when you place material on the Web, you are granting implied consent for anyone to use that information when surfing the Web. This would presumably cover actions like e-mailing a Web page back to yourself and printing out a Web page, where the information is being used for personal and private purposes.

2. What Uses Are Not Covered Under Implied Consent? For Example, Is It Permissible to E-mail a Web Page to Someone Else or Save a Web Document on My Hard Drive?

The scope of implied consent would have to be decided by a court on a case-by-case basis. The courts have yet to test the application of implied consent as it applies to Web pages. Saving a copy of the document to your hard drive for private study is likely to be permissible. However, making multiple copies of a Web page for distribution in a classroom or business is less likely to fall under the concept of "implied consent."

3. Can a Copyright Holder Override an Implied Consent?

Yes. To override "implied consent" you can include a copyright notice on a Web page and attach certain conditions to it in order to specifically restrict what people may do with information on your site. For example:

"No part of this page may be reproduced, stored in a retrieval system, or transmitted in any form or by any means — electronic, mechanical, photocopying, recording, or otherwise — without the prior written permission of the copyright owner."

"Pages, logos, text and images contained on this Web site may not be published separately, in hard copy or electronically, without the express written permission of their owners."

"Information provided in directories on this Web site may not be recompiled into other directories or used as the basis for a derived work without permission."

"Contents of this site may not be reproduced in any manner whatsoever either in whole or in part without written permission of the copyright owner."

4. Do I Need to Place a Copyright Notice on My Web Page in Order to Copyright It?

No. Copyright protection is automatic in Canada upon the "fixation" of a work, and this extends to the Web. You may wonder what we mean by "fixation." In order for a work to be protected under Canadian copyright law, it must be "fixed." This means that it must exist in a material form. For example, a document that appears on your computer screen may not be considered "fixed" until it has been saved on your hard drive. However, in the context of the Internet this is likely a minor point, so don't let it confuse you. Here is the bottom line: a Web page is protected by copyright even if you do not put a copyright notice on it.

5. If Copyright Protection Is Automatic in Canada, Are There Any Advantages to Attaching Copyright Notices to Your Work?

Yes. Even though a copyright notice is not required on material you place on the Web, it helps people who want to locate the copyright holder and obtain permission to use it. It is not always clear who owns the copyright to certain pieces of work. For example, your Web site may contain an article for which you do not own the copyright. Placing a copyright notice on the article will help Internet users locate the copyright holder. It can also help protect copyright in other countries (see question 22 below).

6. Is It Legal to Link to Another Site Without the Site's Permission?

This question has not yet been tested in a court of law. However, you may have a valid legal argument if you can demonstrate that your reputation has been harmed as a result of a link from another site with which you do not want to be associated. Canadian copyright law protects that reputation and honor of an author, and the author of a work has the right to prohibit anyone from using that work "in association with a product, service, cause or institution." There may also be grounds for action under other laws, including unfair competition and trademark laws.

If you operate a Web site and are concerned about this issue, you might consider regularly monitoring who is linking to it. AltaVista's search engine (**http://altavista.digital.com**) will allow you to do this.

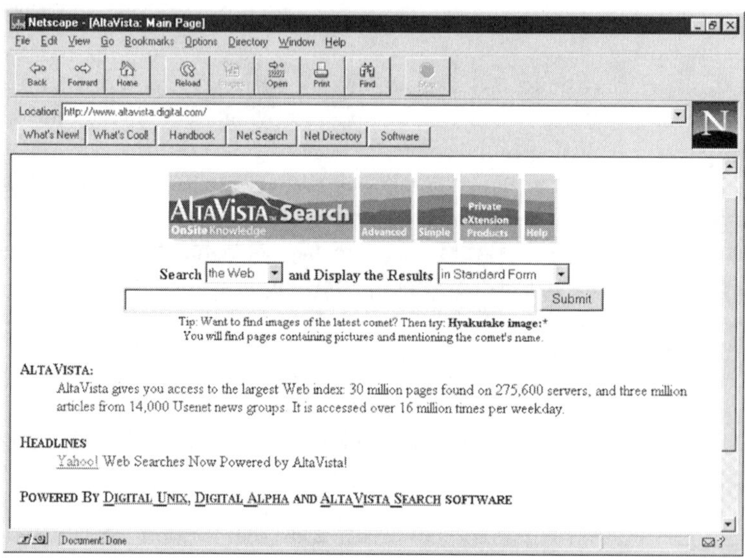

Select "Advanced" from the menu at the top of the screen; this will display a screen similar to the one below:

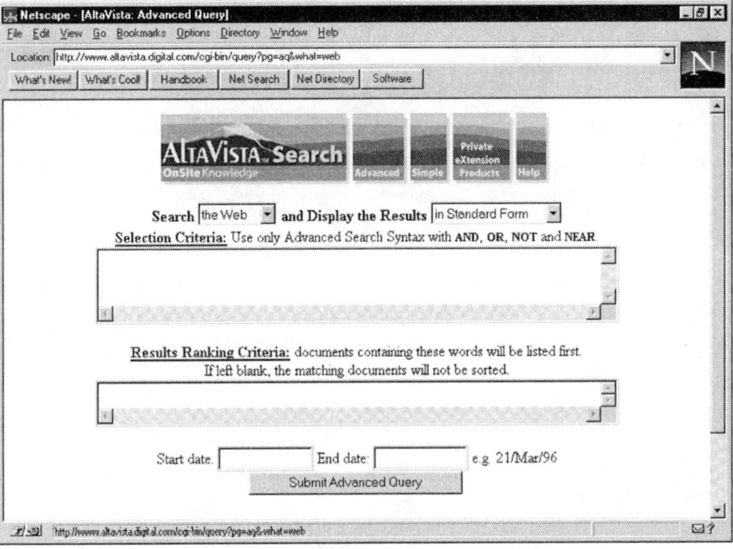

To obtain a list of Web pages that are linking to a specific Web page, use the **link:** command. For example, the command **link:www.mcdonalds.com** will provide you with a list of all the Web pages that are linked to the McDonald's Web site. Similarly, the command **link:www.rcmp-grc.gc.ca** will list all the Web sites that are linked to the official Royal Canadian Mounted Police Home Page:

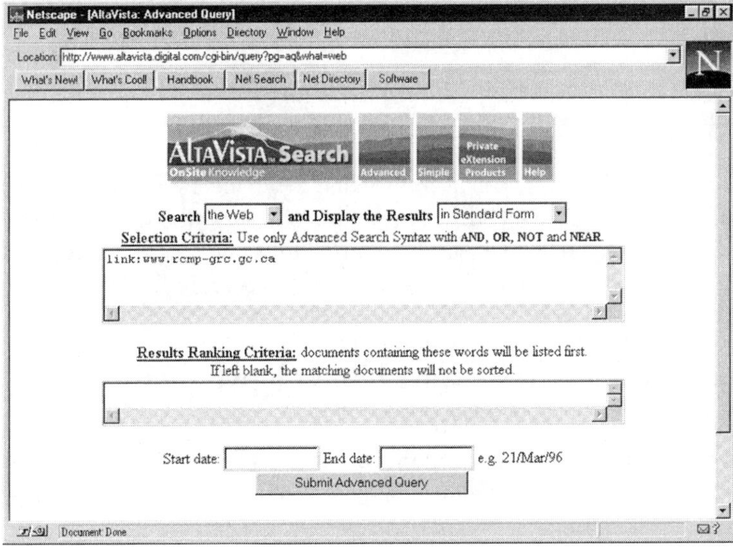

You can see in the screen below that AltaVista found 173 Web pages that were linked to the RCMP Web site, including a community-based policing site in Alberta and the World Police/Fire Games Web site:

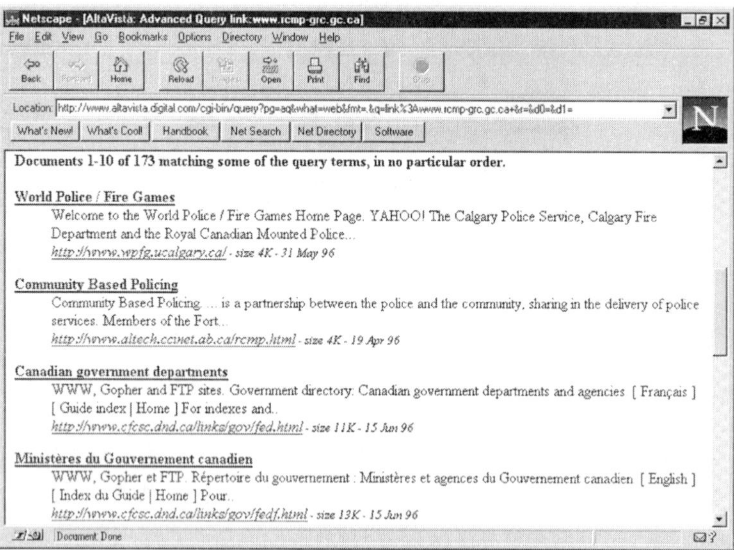

If you have your own home page, try it out. Follow the format above, inserting the address of your home page after the **link:** command.

7. Am I Violating the Law If I Simply Link to Copyright Items from My Web Site But Display Them on My Home Page?

The answer is *likely* yes. You may find this question difficult to understand. We include this question because it is technically possible to display information on your Web site without actually having the information physically resident on the Internet computer hosting your Web pages. Even under these circumstances you are still likely violating copyright law. Under Canadian copyright law the copyright owner has the sole right to reproduce his/her work. If you reproduce someone else's copyright work on your home page without permission, you are guilty of copyright infringement. The physical location of the work is likely irrelevant in this situation.

8. Is a Compilation of Hypertext Links Copyrightable?

Yes, provided that the owner can demonstrate that original skill, research, and labor went into the selection and organization of the information. For example, Peter Sim of Manitoba maintains a directory of Canadian legal resources, shown in the screen on the next page (**http://www.mbnet.mb.ca/~psim/can_law.html**):

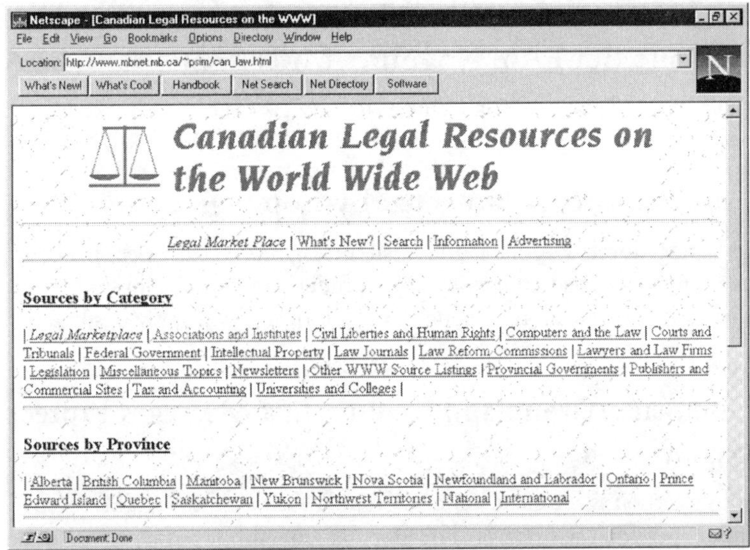

If someone on the Web were to take Sim's directory and place it on his/her own Web site without Sim's consent, Sim could argue that this constitutes copyright infringement. It is important to realize that the hypertext links themselves are not protected by copyright; it is the selection and arrangement of the information that is copyrightable. This includes a compilation or database of hypertext links.

9. Are There Any Situations Where It Would Be Permissible for Me to Display Copyright Material on My Web Site Without Obtaining Consent from the Copyright Holder?

Yes. The copyright holder can prevent the use of his/her work only if a "substantial" part of the work is reproduced. However, the Canadian *Copyright Act* does not define what "substantial" is, and this would be decided on a case-by-case basis in the courts. You do not violate Canadian copyright in the following situation:

- "any fair dealing with any work for the purposes of private study, research, criticism, review, or newspaper summary, if (i) the sources and (ii) the author's name, if given the source, are mentioned."

The concept of "fair dealing" is not defined in the *Copyright Act* either, but if you use a small portion of the work for any of the purposes listed above (e.g., private study, research, criticism, review, or newspaper summary), you are probably operating within the law.

10. What If I Want to Reproduce Part of Someone Else's Work on My Web Site But I Am Not Sure If It Is a "Substantial" Amount?

It is best not to take the chance and risk facing a lawsuit. Ask the copyright holder for permission.

11. Are E-mail Messages Protected By Copyright?

Yes. Copyright protection is automatic on e-mail messages you create even if a copyright notice does not appear on the message. Therefore, any reproduction or redistribution of an e-mail message constitutes copyright violation, although implied consent will apply in some circumstances.

12. Are Discussion Group and Mailing List Messages Protected by Copyright?

Yes. Copyright protection is automatic on newsgroup messages that you create even if a copyright notice does not appear on the message. Therefore, any unauthorized reproduction or redistribution of a newsgroup message constitutes copyright violation. It is not true that the author of a copyright holder relinquishes his/her copyright by posting the message in a public forum. However, implied consent will apply in some circumstances. For example, it is likely acceptable under the law to forward an e-mail message found in a discussion group to a friend or colleague.

13. I Thought That Newsgroup Messages Were in the Public Domain.

No. Public domain means that the work can be freely copied without the permission of the copyright owner. A work is only in the "public domain" once the copyright has expired. In many countries, including Canada, copyright expires 50 years after the author's death. It is important to note that the calculation starts at the end of the calendar year immediately following the author's death and not on the date of the author's death. However, the rule is different for works published before 1989 in the United States.

14. I Am a Freelancer/Consultant. I Have Just Prepared an Article/Report for a Newspaper/Magazine/Periodical. I Now Want to Put That Article on My Web Site. Do I Own the Copyright on It?

Yes. Freelancers and consultants own the copyright on articles they have written for newspapers and magazines unless there is an agreement to the contrary. Thus newspapers and magazines wishing to reproduce commissioned articles must obtain the permission of the author.

15. If I Commissioned a Photograph or Portrait, Do I Need the Photographer's Permission to Place the Photograph on My Web Site?

No. Under Canadian copyright law the person commissioning the photograph or portrait is considered to be the owner and copyright holder provided that (a) the photograph/portrait was created following an order and not before the order was made, and (b) there is some exchange of money or services in return for the photograph. If these conditions are met, you are free to put the commissioned photograph up on your Web site without the permission of the photographer. For photographs in general, the copyright is held by the person who owns the initial photograph or other plate at the time when that negative or other plate was made.

However, here is an important point. The photographer still owns the "moral" rights to any photograph he/she takes, even when the photograph has been commissioned. This means that the photographer has the right, where it is reasonable under the circumstances, to have his/her name associated with the photograph. The photographer also has the right, where it is reasonable under the circumstances, to remain anonymous or use a pseudonym or pen name. For example, suppose you have created a Web page for your family and your last name is "Smith." You call your Web site "The Smith Family Home Page," and you include a photograph of your family that you commissioned from a photographer. Under Canadian copyright law the photographer can request that his/her name be attached to (or removed from) the photograph on your Web site. The photographer can also invoke moral rights to prevent you from distorting or modifying ("morphing") a photograph.

16. If I Receive a Letter from an Organization or an Individual, Can I Put It on My Web Site?

No. The author of a letter holds the copyright to the letter. Employers own the copyright on articles, letters, and memos that are created during the course of a job. In either case the recipient of the letter does not own the copyright and cannot post the letter on his/her Web site without the permission of the copyright holder.

17. Suppose I Prepare an Article/Script/Letter/Memo/Photograph for My Employer. Can I Put That Information on My Web Site Without Permission?

Generally, no. However, the employer can put the article up on *their* Web site without *your* permission. Employers generally own the copyright to works made during the course of employment provided that (a) the employee is employed under a "contract of service," (b) the work is created in the course of performing this contract, and (c) there is no agreement that states that the employee owns the copyright. Regardless of the above, an employee still owns the "moral rights" to his/her work. This means that if your employer places an article you wrote on its Web site, you have the right to have your name appear on the article, where it is reasonable under the circumstances. You also have the right to request that your article be presented without your name appearing as the author. You can also request that a pseudonym or pen name be used instead of your real name.

18. If I Prepare an Article/Diagram for a Client and Agree to Assign the Copyright to Them, Do I Retain the Right to be Credited with Preparing the Article/Diagram?

Yes. The author of a work, even though he/she may no longer own the copyright to that work, has the right, where reasonable in the circumstances, to have his/her name associated with a work (e.g., if the client subsequently puts the article/diagram on a Web site). The author also has the right to remain anonymous and/or use a pseudonym or pen name with respect to a work.

19. Can I Take Someone Else's HTML Code and Use It for the Basis of My Home Page?

HTML code is protected by Canadian copyright law. Recall that HTML code is the computer code that is used to create Web pages. If you take someone else's HTML code to help you learn how to write HTML, this could fall under the "fair dealing" provision of the Canadian *Copyright Act,* which allows the use of a *small portion of the work* for "private study, research, criticism, review, or newspaper study." You could argue that you are only using the HTML code for "private study," as a learning exercise. If you proceeded, however, to create your own Web site using all of the other party's HTML code as your template, it could be argued that this is a violation of the other party's copyright depending upon (a) how much of the HTML code you are copying (i.e., is it substantial?), and (b) how much original skill and labor went into the preparation of the HTML code. Hence you should be cognizant of the legal issues that surround using HTML code from someone else's Web site.

20. I Found a Web Site That I Would Like to Poke Fun At. Can I Create a Parody of the Site And Place It on the Web?

Parody is not specifically addressed in the Canadian *Copyright Act.* Therefore, whether or not parody is a violation of copyright would depend upon the situation at hand. Parody could fall under the "fair dealing" provision (discussed in Question 19) if the parody is a form of criticism. Therefore, the person or organization making the parody could argue that the parody is allowed under Canadian copyright law. On the other hand, if the parody is not a form of criticism, the copyright holder could argue that such use constitutes copyright infringement.

21. I Wrote an Article for a Magazine/Newsletter, and I Just Discovered That My Article Is on Their Web Site. Can I Ask That the Article Be Taken Down?

Yes, provided that you have not signed away any electronic rights to your article. Unless you have given your client "all rights" or "electronic rights" to your article, the client is not permitted to distribute your article electronically, and for them to do so is akin to theft of your copyrighted work. Many authors negotiate additional fees for "electronic rights" to their work, above and beyond the fee paid for print rights to the work. The Internet introduces some important challenges for freelance writers when it comes to copyright.We explore this issue in greater depth later in this chapter, in the section The Freelance Dilemma.

22. I Have a Web Site That Resides in Canada. I Just Noticed That an Article/Graphic from My Web Site Appears on a Web Site in Zimbabwe. Is My Copyright Protected There?

Yes, since Zimbabwe is a member of the Berne Convention and the World Trade Organization. Let's explain what this means. If your work is protected by Canadian copyright, your work is *also* protected in any country that is party to either the Berne Convention *or* the World Trade Organization *or* the Universal Copyright Convention (UCC). However, to claim protection in UCC countries, your work must be marked with the word "copyright," the abbreviation "copr.," or the symbol ®, the year of the first publication, and the name of the owner of the copyright. This is not a requirement under the Berne Convention or the World Trade Organization.

The other thing you should know is that when it comes to foreign copyright protection, the protection is always based on the *laws of the foreign country.* This means that for the purposes of this example, you are not protected under *Canadian copyright* law in Zimbabwe. You are protected under the *copyright laws of Zimbabwe,* which may be different from the laws that exist in Canada. Even though your work may be protected under the copyright laws of another country, you may not be afforded the same degree of protection that would have been afforded if the violation had taken place in Canada. In other words, you cannot assume that an act constituting a copyright violation in Canada would also be a copyright violation in another country, such as Zimbabwe.

23. What If My Work Is Being Used on a Web Site in the United States?

The same reasoning that was used in the previous question applies here. Since the United States is a member of the Berne Convention, the Universal Copyright Convention, and the World Trade Organization, your work is protected in the United States. But as we explained above, your work is protected under the laws of the foreign country, in this case the United States. Therefore, your work is protected under *U.S. copyright law,* not Canadian copyright law.

24. Are Residents of Other Countries Protected by the Copyright Laws of Canada? For Example, Suppose I Want to Use Copyright Materials from a Web Site in Iceland on My Home Page?

Foreigners who are protected by the copyright laws of their own country are *also protected in Canada* if the country belongs to either the Berne Convention, the Universal Copyright

Convention, or the World Trade Organization. Since Iceland belongs to all three, Icelanders are protected under Canadian copyright law.

25. How About if I Take Copyright Items from a Web Site in the United States and Display Them on My Web Page in Canada?

The answer to the last question also applies here. Since the United States is a member of the World Trade Organization and a signatory to both the Berne Convention and the Universal Copyright Convention, U.S. copyright holders are protected under the copyright laws of Canada if a copyright violation occurs here.

26. My Organization is a Not-for-Profit Organization/Club/ Association. Are There Any Exceptions in Canadian Copyright Law for Organizations of My Type?

No. All the information in the foregoing questions applies equally to Canadian non-profit organizations.

27. I Notice That a Lot of People Circulate Newspaper Articles by E-mail and Post Them on Web Sites. Is This Legal?

No. Newspaper articles are protected by Canadian copyright law. You should not place a newspaper article on your Web site or distribute it by e-mail without the permission of the newspaper and/or author of the article.

28. Can You Give Me an Example of a Site That Violated Someone Else's Copyright and Was Required to Remove the Offending Materials?

The Winnie the Pooh Gallery at **http://charon.nmsu.edu/~mcarlson/wtp.html** was forced to remove a number of illustrations after the publisher of the Winnie the Pooh books discovered that they were taken directly from two Pooh books: *Winnie-the-Pooh* and *The House At Pooh Corner.* Following the removal of the illustrations, the following message appeared on the site: "Due to the fact that it is a copyright infringement, the Winnie-the-Pooh art has been removed":

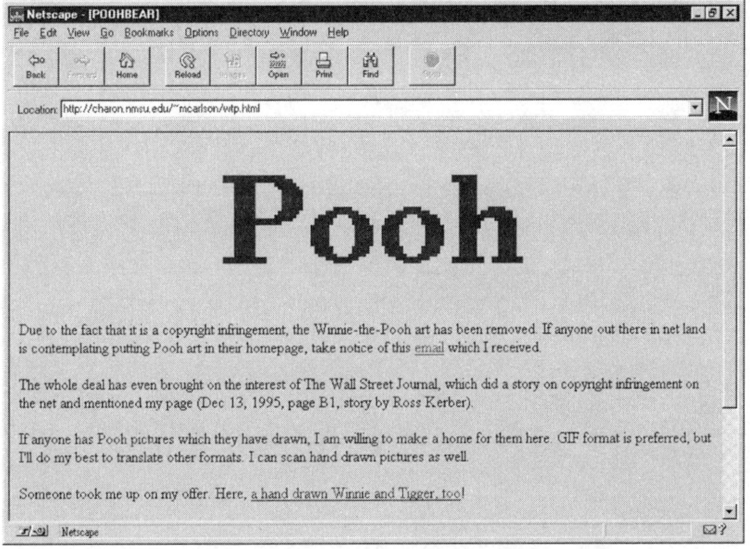

Other Sources of Copyright Information Pertaining to the Internet

Copyright law is a fascinating legal area and one that is increasingly relevant to the Internet, as you have no doubt discovered in this chapter. It is a subject that we certainly will continue to address in subsequent updates of this book. In the meantime, if we have whetted your appetite for more information on Canadian copyright law, we highly recommend the following sources of information.

Canadian Information Highway Advisory Council

The Canadian Information Highway Advisory Council was established by Industry Canada in 1994 to advise the government on the development of the information highway. A Copyright Subcommittee was created to examine issues pertaining to copyright on the information highway. The Copyright Subcommittee's final report is available on the Information Highway Advisory Council's Web site at **http://info.ic.gc.ca/info-highway/ih.html**.

Canadian Intellectual Property Office

The Canadian Intellectual Property Office (CIPO) administers intellectual property in Canada. CIPO's Web site (**http://info.ic.gc.ca/ic-data/marketplace/cipo/index.html**) is an outstanding resource. It provides answers to common questions about intellectual property, links to other resources, and information on proposed changes to copyright and trademark legislation. You can also find the complete text of Canadian copyright and trademark guides.

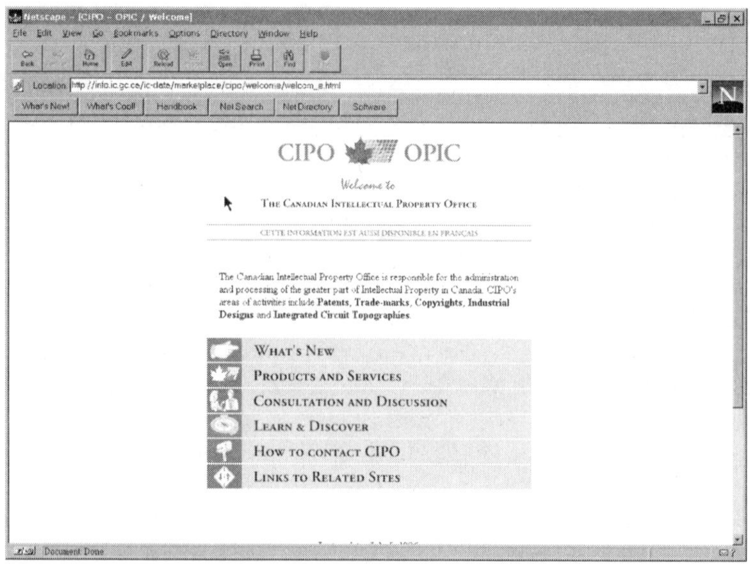

Stanford University Libraries Copyright and Fair Use Web Site

This site focuses on copyright law from a U.S. perspective; nevertheless, it is an excellent source of reference material on the subject. Funded by Stanford University Libraries & Academic Information Resources, the Council on Library Resources, and FindLaw Internet Legal Resources, it provides access to basic copyright information, statutes and regulations, current legislation, legal cases, and testimonies and position papers. All the information in this site is full-text searchable, so it is easy to locate specific information or specific cases (**http://fairuse.stanford.edu**):

Remedies for Copyright and Trademark Infringement on the Web

If you discover a site on the Internet that appears to violate your copyright or trademark rights, what should you do? The first step is to contact the violator and inform the person of the copyright/trademark infringement. This is often the quickest way to resolve the problem. Upon receiving notice of the infringement, the violator may be more than happy to comply with your request to remove the offending material. Although it is not always necessary, a strongly worded letter that hints at the possibility of legal action will let the offender know that you are to be taken seriously. You may want to contact a lawyer to help you prepare the letter, since a letter coming from a lawyer's office may be taken more seriously by the offender than a letter coming from you personally. However, lawyers can be expensive, so try to resolve the problem on your own without getting a lawyer involved. However, bear in mind that if the violator is in another country, his/her rights may differ. If the violator refuses to cooperate with you, you may want to seek legal advice and have your lawyer contact the offender (if you haven't already done so).

Another possible course of action, and one that is often overlooked, is to contact the Internet service provider that supplies the Internet facilities to the offender. Determine the name of the Internet provider that is hosting the Web pages for the offender and notify the company that a copyright breach has arisen out of the use of their facilities. Should the offender not comply with your initial request, you can request that the Internet service provider remove the offending materials. They are not obligated to do this, but they might help you.

Your lawyer can also help you seek an injunction that would require the offender to cease the copyright/trademark infringement. In more complicated cases you can seek monetary damages and other remedies. A discussion of these remedies, however, is outside the scope of this book.

What Approach Should Your Organization Take?

It may not always be in a firm's best interests to enforce its full rights under copyright and trademark law by demanding that another Web site remove copyright/trademark material belonging to the organization. Many Web sites guilty of copyright/trademark infringement generate positive publicity and goodwill toward the organization in question. For example, the "unofficial" Saturn Web site described earlier in this chapter may very well be guilty of trademark infringement (because it uses the Saturn logo), but it is also a great source of free publicity for Saturn. What more can a company ask for than to have its own customers publicly promoting its brands?

Say that Saturn demanded that the individuals running the service remove any and all Saturn trademarks from the site. Such an action could backfire on the company and generate a lot of negative publicity. On the Internet, bad publicity spreads fast. Any company on the verge of taking legal action against an infringing Web site should weigh the pros and cons of proceeding with such an approach and consider other ways of making a settlement with the offenders.

A classic example to illustrate this point is the infamous Twinkies trademark dispute on the Web. The controversy centred around two U.S. university students who had created a Web site depicting various scientific experiments on Twinkies (**http://www.owlnet.rice.edu/~gouge/twinkies.html**). The Web site was dubbed "The T.W.I.N.K.I.E.S. Project." The company that manufacturers Twinkies, Interstate Bakeries, got wind of the Web site and became concerned that the site violated their Twinkies trademark.

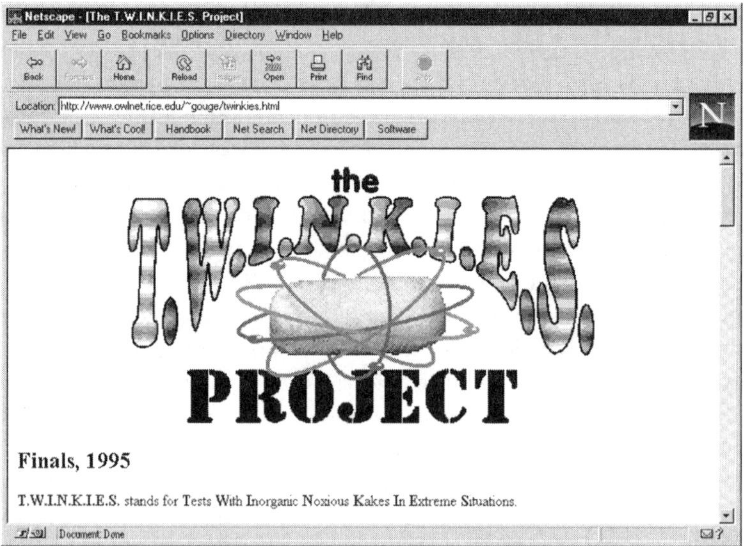

It wasn't long before the media were alerted about the story, and soon the story of the Twinkies Web page found its way onto the Reuters news wire, where it was distributed to other media outlets worldwide. The entire Reuters article is reprinted below, with permission from Reuters.

> HOUSTON (Reuter) — Two Rice University students returned from Easter break this week to find their Web site featuring scientific experiments on Twinkies yanked from the school's computers, a university spokeswoman said Thursday.
>
> Rice spokeswoman Patricia Bass said the Web site, which had been posted on the private university's host computer to the World Wide Web, was taken down after a "third party" not affiliated with the school complained of possible copyright violations.
>
> "I think it's clever and very well done," Bass said of the Web site, which parodies the scientific method of conducting systematic experiments in the pursuit of knowledge. In this case, junior Todd Stadler and sophomore Chris Gouge built a Web site to post results of seven "experiments" studying the effects of fire, gravity, microwaves and blenders on the popular snack cake.
>
> Officials with Interstate Bakeries Corp, which makes the Hostess product, said they were aware of the Web site and were studying whether it violates their Twinkies trademark.
>
> "I get a chuckle out of the Web site myself," Mark Dirkes, marketing vice president with the Kansas City, Missouri-based company, told the Houston Chronicle.
>
> Interstate Bakeries attorney Sandy Sutton, who will meet with university officials Friday, said the trademark concerns were not raised by the company. At issue is whether depiction of the Twinkies on the Web page is a fair use of the company's trademarked product, university and company officials said.
>
> "The issue is, are our students violating somebody's trademark," said Bass, who is with the legal affairs office of the university in Houston.

Two ordinary university students suddenly found themselves in the international spotlight, and Interstate Bakeries was in the hot seat. Would they force the students to shut down their Twinkies

Web page? After some discussions the two students and Interstate eventually reached an amicable solution. The Web page was allowed to stay, but the students had to add the following information to their Web site:

"TWINKIES" and the "TWINKIE THE KID Character" are registered trademarks of Interstate Brands Corporation, 12 East Armour Blvd., Kansas City, MO 64111.

It was a "win–win" situation for all parties involved. The students were allowed to keep their Web site, and the company received proper attribution of their trademark. Interstate Bakeries could have taken a much tougher stance with the students. They could have demanded that they remove all the Twinkies trademarks from the Web site, including the picture of "Twinkie the Kid," the Twinkies mascot. The students would have likely complied, but consider how the world would have reacted to such a move by the company. In the months leading up to the trademark controversy, the Twinkies Web site had become one of the most popular attractions on the Web.

What is the moral of our story? Think carefully about the public relations fallout that may result from any action you take to enforce your intellectual property rights on the Web. Sometimes it just makes sense not to get the lawyers involved.

Monitoring the Internet for Trademark and Copyright Infringements

Do you know where your intellectual property is? Don't be surprised if you find it on the Internet. Right now, there are thousands of copyright and trademark violations taking place on the Internet. Most of these cases go unchallenged because the copyright and trademark owners do not know they exist and in other cases cannot afford to take legal action. Your intellectual property may be at risk right now. There are two ways that you can monitor the Internet to identify potential copyright and trademark abuses:

- You can do it yourself, using some of the free search engines and personalized news services that we have discussed in this book.
- You can use a commercial monitoring service to monitor the Internet on your behalf.

Monitoring the Internet Yourself

The cheapest way to find copyright and trademark violators on the Internet is to look for them yourself. We discuss several tools below, all of which are free.

Search Engines and Directories

Search engines such as InfoSeek (**http://www.infoseek.com**), AltaVista (**http://altavista.digital.com**), Lycos (**http://www.lycos.com**), OpenText (**http://www.opentext.com**), Excite (**http://www.excite.com**), and WebCrawler (**http://www.webcrawler.com**) will allow you to monitor the Web for just about anything. Just type in the word, phrase, or subject you are looking for (e.g., your company or product name). You should also try the search feature on Yahoo! (**http://www.yahoo.com**). It will help you identify Web sites that may pertain to your organization and its products and/or services. Get into the habit of using these search services at least once a week to look for references to your company, product, and brand names on the World Wide Web. Many of these services will also allow you to search current USENET postings for references to your company or product names.

USENET Search Services

Services like DejaNews (**http://www.dejanews.com**) are invaluable for monitoring the Internet. DejaNews will allow you to search the archives of thousands of USENET discussion groups for occurrences of any words or phrases you specify. You can limit the search to certain newsgroups and dates or search the entire archive at once:

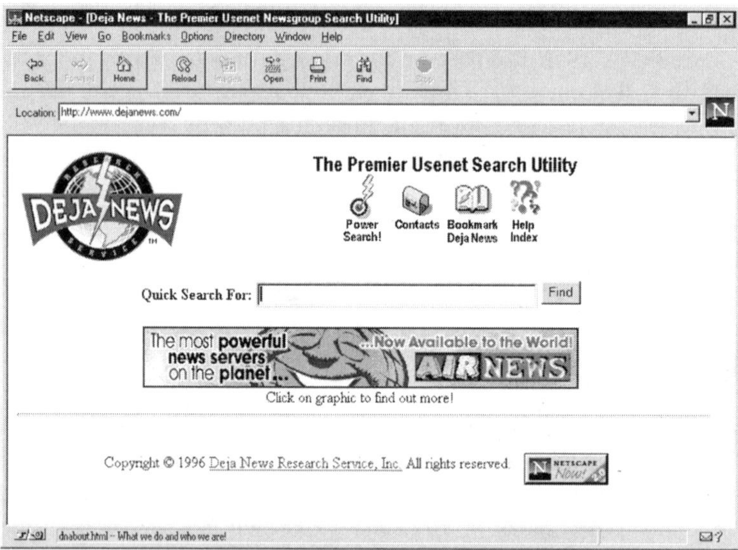

Personal News Services

Services like InfoSeek Personal (**http://personal.infoseek.com**) will regularly monitor USENET newsgroups for references to any company or product names you specify:

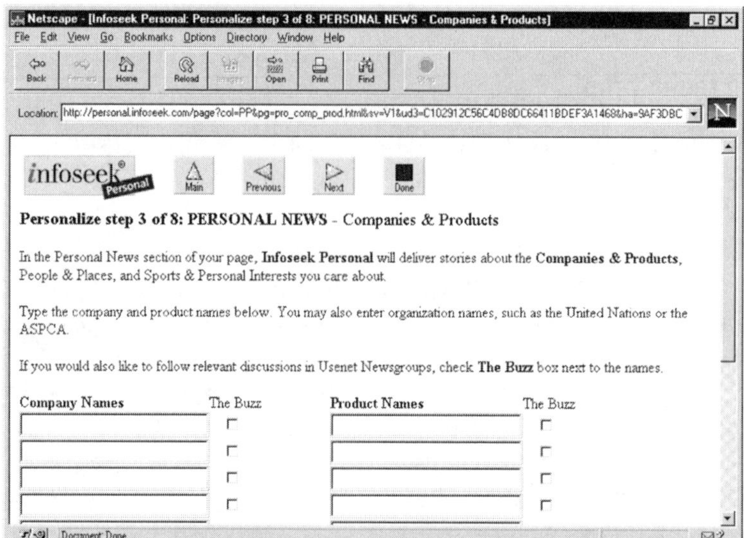

In addition, many of the services that monitor newspapers and news wires (see Chapter 10) are also effective ways of indirectly monitoring the Web. There is hardly a newspaper today that does not have at least one reporter who regularly covers the on-line/Internet scene. Services like InfoSage (**http://www.infosage.ibm.com**) can monitor hundreds of news sources for any mention of your organization or any of its products.

Using a Commercial Monitoring Service

If you do not have the time to monitor the Internet yourself, there are several commercial services that can help you. Two of the most popular are MarkWatch and CyberImage.

MarkWatch

MarkWatch (**http://www.markwatch.com**) bills itself as an "early-warning system" to help organizations protect their image in cyberspace. For an annual fee MarkWatch will monitor the World Wide Web, USENET discussion groups, and news wires for references to your trademarks and products:

MarkWatch has several applications. Not only does the product warn organizations about trademark violations, but it can also identify areas on the Internet where people are making reference to their products and services. MarkWatch claims that it will "catch comments by disgruntled customers, comparison ads by rivals, and general references to your brand." Reports can be delivered to you by e-mail, telephone, or on the World Wide Web. If you decide to receive your reports on the Web, you will be assigned a user ID and a password, which you will use to access the system, as seen in the screen below:

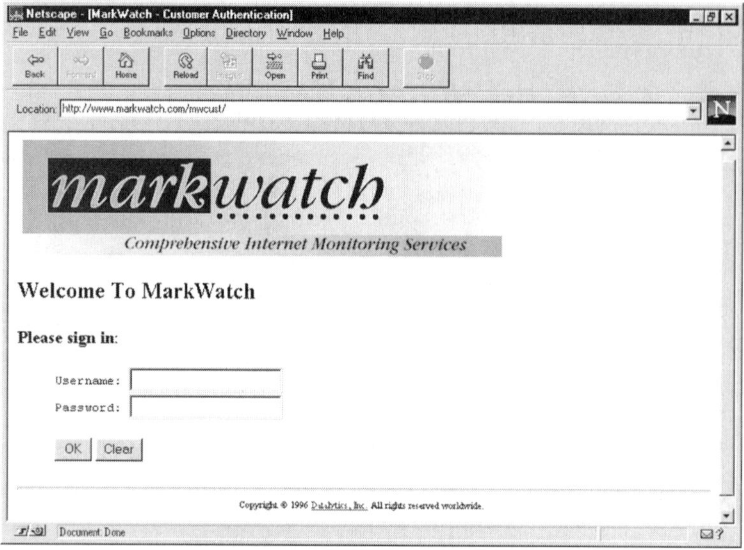

CyberImage

CyberImage from the Delahaye Group (**http://www.delahaye.com**) monitors discussion forums on the Internet and commercial on-line services, such as CompuServe and America Online, for references to your company or product name. The purpose of the service is to assess how the client is being perceived on the Internet; it is not designed to identify trademark and copyright infringements. For example, CyberImage can prepare reports that analyze positive and negative comments about a company or brand name. However, often these reports can lead to the identification of Web sites where violations may be occurring:

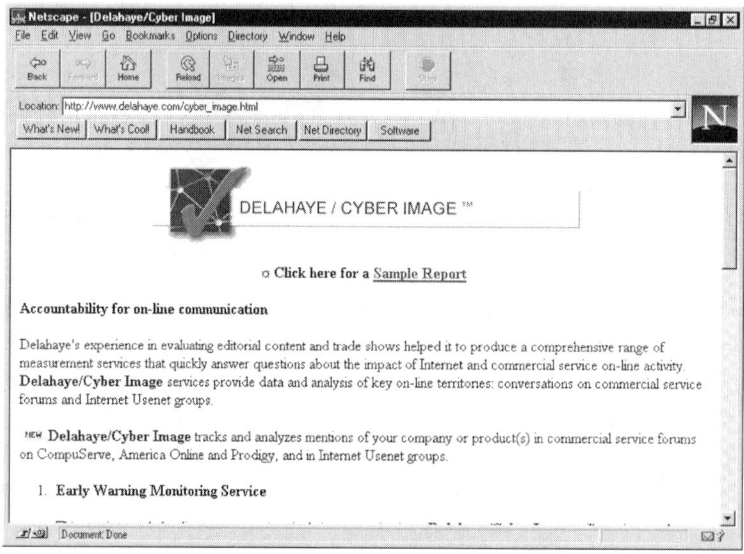

The Freelance Dilemma

With the rush to this new electronic world that we are creating, we are seeing some unfortunate and often ill-advised side effects. Certainly, many owners of intellectual property are finding it difficult to prevent their intellectual property from being copied, distributed, or used on the Internet without authorization. And as we have seen, in many cases big business can throw its legal weight around and use a heavy hand to prevent individuals from carrying out such misuse.

But what is unfortunate — and mostly unreported — is that many individuals are being affected by the rush to this new electronic age in an adverse way. Small businesses and individuals often cannot afford a lot of lawyers and thus find themselves with little recourse should their rights be abused or trampled. So when it comes to intellectual property on-line, we are entering a two-tier world: those who can afford a lot of lawyers to protect their property and those who cannot.

In Canada and around the world, various types of professions are being affected by the Internet in many different ways, and creative talents are finding that the network is fostering some distinct problems. These include the following:

- writers' works are being copied around the Web without permission;
- photos are finding their way onto Web sites in violation of the photographers' rights;
- musical artists, are discovering that their songs are being uploaded and distributed around the world without royalty;
- architects' designs and drawings are being exchanged on-line;
- visual artists are discovering that images of their work are available on the network.

The list goes on. Those with a creative bent are finding the Internet to be both a significant opportunity to expand their horizons and a threat to their livelihood. In some cases groups of these individuals have banded together to try to protect themselves. SOCAN (the Society of Composers, Authors and Musical Publishers of Canada), for example, represents composers and musicians, whose music has long been copied on cassette tape, so that they lose large amounts in royalties. The group has been successful in having a special tax levied on the sale of such tapes to make up for the lost royalties. Now there is the Internet, which may lead to a new era in which songs are copied and exchanged easily on-line. SOCAN has been pushing for a solution that many believe is impractical and unfair. The solution would see Internet service providers subject to a special tax, such tax to be remitted to musical artists across the country to compensate for their loss of revenue.

The battle by SOCAN is often reported in newspapers and magazines, making it seem that the media has a moral interest in ensuring that the rights of the "little guy" are well protected. In fact, press coverage of the SOCAN battle in this new world of the Internet has been highly effective, creating an image of a media that cares about the rights of creative talent in this new wired world. Nothing, however, could be further from the truth, for in a largely unreported, unnoticed battle raging in Canada and elsewhere, the senior management and owners of newspapers and magazines are taking from writers what they have had for hundreds of years: The right to be compensated for *each* use of their work.

Freelance Writers and Copyright

Many publications hire freelancers — independent writers — to research and write articles for publication. Canadian copyright law has long held that when the independent writer provides the article to the publication, in the absence of any agreement to the contrary, the writer is providing to the publisher the right to print the article *once*, on what is referred to as a "single use" or "specific use" basis.

A problem has come about, however; many media organizations have come to embrace the Web: they wish to place articles written by freelance authors on their Web sites. Under Canadian copyright law they have no right to do so unless they provide additional remuneration to the freelancer to obtain that right, or unless the freelancer provides them with specific permission to reproduce the article in electronic form. You can find a good overview of this reality on the Web site of the Periodical Writers Association of Canada, an association of freelance writers from across Canada (**http://www.cycor.ca/pwac**):

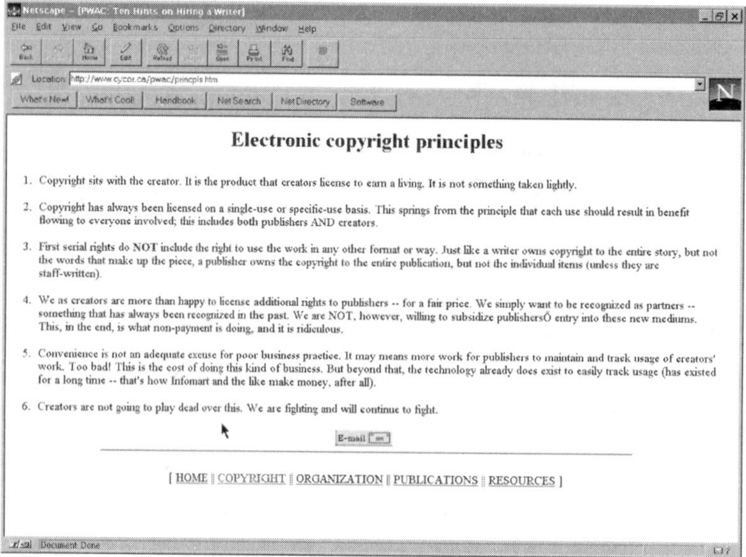

Electronic copyright principles

1. Copyright sits with the creator. It is the product that creators license to earn a living. It is not something taken lightly.
2. Copyright has always been licensed on a single-use or specific-use basis. This springs from the principle that each use should result in benefit flowing to everyone involved; this includes both publishers AND creators.
3. First serial rights do NOT include the right to use the work in any other format or way. Just like a writer owns copyright to the entire story, but not the words that make up the piece, a publisher owns the copyright to the entire publication, but not the individual items (unless they are staff-written).
4. We as creators are more than happy to license additional rights to publishers -- for a fair price. We simply want to be recognized as partners -- something that has always been recognized in the past. We are NOT, however, willing to subsidize publishersÕ entry into these new mediums. This, in the end, is what non-payment is doing, and it is ridiculous.
5. Convenience is not an adequate excuse for poor business practice. It may means more work for publishers to maintain and track usage of creators' work. Too bad! This is the cost of doing this kind of business. But beyond that, the technology already does exist to easily track usage (has existed for a long time -- that's how Infomart and the like make money, after all).
6. Creators are not going to play dead over this. We are fighting and will continue to fight.

E-mail

[HOME || COPYRIGHT || ORGANIZATION || PUBLICATIONS || RESOURCES]

Problems have arisen in the wired world, because media organizations are doing one of two things:

- Media organizations are placing articles on-line without the permission of freelancers. As some people have stated in the many on-line discussions about the topic, this is akin to "theft." In one posting in a discussion group about the topic, we saw the comment that "organizations such as the *Globe and Mail* and Southam are trafficking in stolen property" (the level of emotion by writers who have been wronged is often quite high). The problem is particularly rampant with on-line databases such as InfoGlobe and Infomart, services sold by those two organizations, which we describe in more detail below.
- Media organizations are forcing freelancers to sign contracts in which the freelancer forever signs away all rights to the article, including the right to share in any revenue that might be derived from having the article in the Web site. This permits the media

organization to include the article in their Web site, to place it on a CD ROM, or to use it for any other electronic purpose whatsoever, with the author of the article receiving no payment for any of these uses. They are, in essence, asking the freelance author to give them rights to use the article forever, without anything further in return.

Why is this wrong and morally reprehensible? Think about it this way: writers worldwide are being asked to give away all rights forever to their property, without anything in return. A pretty extreme proposition. The American Society of Journalists and Authors provides a document on its Web site titled "E-Wrongs about E-Rights" (**http://www.asja.org/ewrongs.htm**), that does as good a job as any educating the reader about the injustices being done throughout the world today by media organizations intent on ripping away from freelance writers the copyright they have long held on their articles. It is a good site for gaining familiarity with the issue.

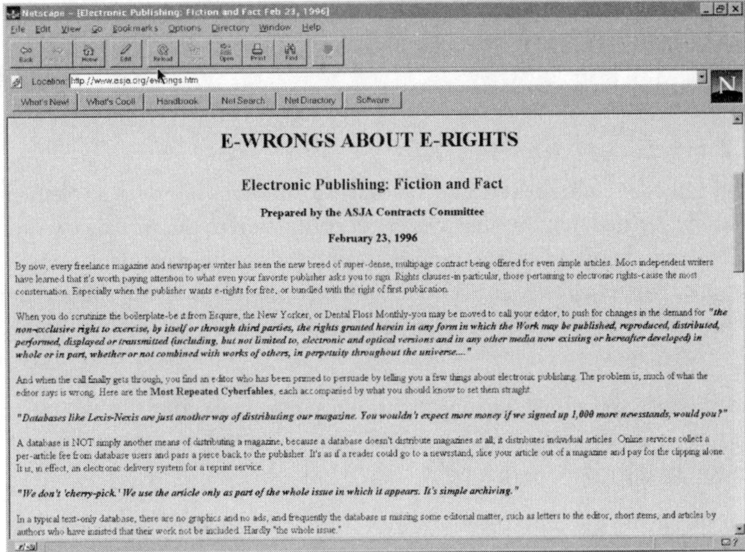

E-WRONGS ABOUT E-RIGHTS

Electronic Publishing: Fiction and Fact

Prepared by the ASJA Contracts Committee

February 23, 1996

By now, every freelance magazine and newspaper writer has seen the new breed of super-dense, multipage contract being offered for even simple articles. Most independent writers have learned that it's worth paying attention to what even your favorite publisher asks you to sign. Rights clauses-in particular, those pertaining to electronic rights-cause the most consternation. Especially when the publisher wants e-rights for free, or bundled with the right of first publication.

When you do scrutinize the boilerplate-be it from Esquire, the New Yorker, or Dental Floss Monthly-you may be moved to call your editor, to push for changes in the demand for ***"the non-exclusive right to exercise, by itself or through third parties, the rights granted herein in any form in which the Work may be published, reproduced, distributed, performed, displayed or transmitted (including, but not limited to, electronic and optical versions and in any other media now existing or hereafter developed) in whole or in part, whether or not combined with works of others, in perpetuity throughout the universe...."***

And when the call finally gets through, you find an editor who has been primed to persuade by telling you a few things about electronic publishing. The problem is, much of what the editor says is wrong. Here are the **Most Repeated Cyberfables**, each accompanied by what you should know to set them straight.

"Databases like Lexis-Nexis are just another way of distributing our magazine. You wouldn't expect more money if we signed up 1,000 more newsstands, would you?"

A database is NOT simply another means of distributing a magazine, because a database doesn't distribute magazines at all; it distributes individual articles. Online services collect a per-article fee from database users and pass a piece back to the publisher. It's as if a reader could go to a newsstand, slice your article out of a magazine and pay for the clipping alone. It is, in effect, an electronic delivery system for a reprint service.

"We don't 'cherry-pick.' We use the article only as part of the whole issue in which it appears. It's simple archiving."

In a typical text-only database, there are no graphics and no ads, and frequently the database is missing some editorial matter, such as letters to the editor, short items, and articles by authors who have insisted that their work not be included. Hardly "the whole issue."

You are probably saying to yourself, "Why haven't I heard about this? Why don't we see it reported in the press? After all, isn't this precisely the type of little guy versus big guy battle that many newspapers love to report?" Therein lies the answer: no media organization wants to publicly report on its transgressions. The fact is that through 1996, media organizations — newspapers and magazines alike — began trying to force freelance writers to give up all rights to their articles, but failed to report on their attempts to do so. When the rights of musical artists are trampled, it's news. When it involves writers, it isn't. It is an issue to quietly ignore.

As one individual posted in a discussion group about the topic: "What newspaper wants to report that they are guilty of theft? What magazine wants to tell their readers that they are attempting to steal from writers that which has belonged to the writer for hundreds of years?"

Unauthorized Use of Freelance Writers' Work

The first problem that we identified above has actually existed for several years. You may not be aware of it, but for some time the full texts of newspapers, magazines, and publications have been stored in computer databases in electronic form, available to those who wish to search for a specific article or topic. Individuals and businesses pay hefty fees to search these databases —

services such as InfoGlobe from the *Globe and Mail,* Infomart from Southam, Knight Ridder's Dialog, and the massive American database Lexis/Nexis, and many others. The fees they earn? These organizations charge rates that often approach $180 an hour — the equivalent of $3 to $4 per article retrieved. Given the power of the database, a lot of big businesses and governments willingly shell out for access.

The problem is that many of these databases include the full text of articles written by freelance writers, most of whom have never given permission for their material to be sold in this way and who never get a penny when their property is sold. All revenue is kept by the database/media company. This is a clear violation of Canadian copyright law. When you talk with individuals whose work has been taken in this way, they become quite emotional, with phrases such as "theft" and "stolen property" filling the air.

The situation has poisoned relations between freelancers and media across Canada and, indeed, around the world. As an indication of how serious the battle has become, the *New York Times* has been taken to court by the U.S. National Writers Union in what is expected to be a landmark case.

The Great Freelancer Rights Grab

As the Internet exploded onto the scene and media organizations began to implement Web sites, these organizations realized that they had better get permission to put freelance writers' works on their sites; in so doing they implicitly recognized their previous copyright violations. So, throughout 1996, freelance writers across Canada began to receive contracts attempting to change the historical scope of the relationship. These contracts, in a nutshell, offered writers the following conditions:

- The freelance writer gives up any right, forever, to their article in any electronic form that now exists or may ever be invented. The writer will be provided no remuneration for having given up that right.
- Even so, having given up the right, they will maintain liability should they be sued by anyone for the contents of that article.

In essence, freelance writers are being asked to give up any future role in the emerging world of the Internet: "Give us everything, but we will give you nothing in return, and by the way, you keep the risk." Newspapers, magazines, and publishers offer a number of reasons why they must obtain these rights. First and foremost, they point out that no one is making any money on-line, and hence there is no money to share. Certainly this is true, as we have stated in this book; the business model of the Internet is taking time to evolve. But if this is the case, argue writers, why not provide contracts that provide a fee should revenue be made? Second, writers question this stance, particularly when they see a lot of advertising appearing on sites such as CANOE (**http://www.canoe.ca**).

Third, the media indicate that they are not doing anything in violation of copyright law; many believe that Canadian copyright law says nothing about their needing permission. Of course, this begs the question, then why are they are seeking such permission in the first place?

Across Canada, sickened by what they saw, some writers began to fight back by refusing to sign the contracts presented to them. But in many cases well-known newspapers and magazines such as the *Globe and Mail,* the *Toronto Star,* the *Financial Post, Maclean's,* and *Chatelaine* implicitly threatened the writers: "Sign the contract or you will never write for us again." So it was reported in many on-line discussion groups and e-mail messages. And many freelancers, whose economic circumstances are such that their need to feed their families exceeded their moral outrage, backed down and signed the outrageous contracts put in front of them, giving away their property.

The Nature of the Battle

What is happening now? Some freelancers in Canada, and indeed around the world, are fighting to retain their rights and are organizing themselves to refuse the many one-sided contracts that publishers are urging them to sign.

Periodical Writers Association of Canada

In Canada the previously mentioned Periodical Writers Association of Canada (PWAC) has established a Web site that provides information about the nature of the battle at hand (**http://www.cycor.ca/pwac**):

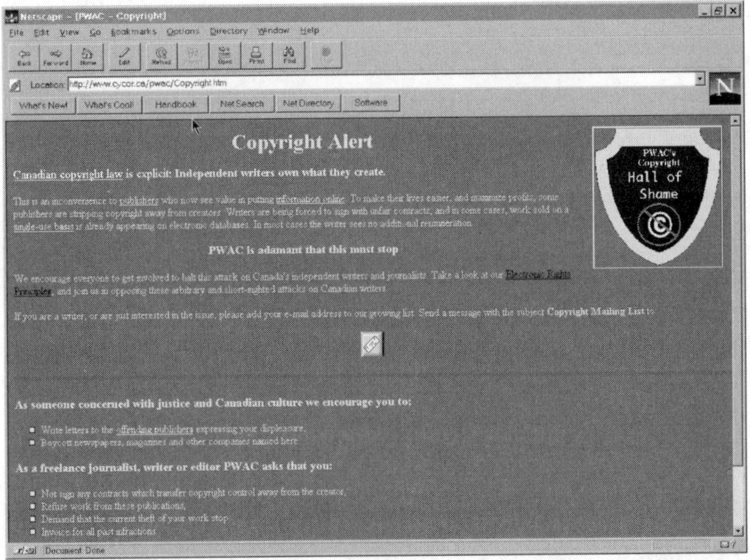

PWAC includes in their Web site what they call their "Hall of Shame." On the page they comment that "in the Spring of 1995 the Periodical Writers Association of Canada conducted a search of electronic full-text database services. The results show that copyright theft is rampant." This refers to the issue of unauthorized use of freelancers' work as described above. In other words, they found that articles written by many freelancers exist in on-line databases such as InfoGlobe and Infomart and are being sold by those organizations for a fee. The freelancers have never given permission for those articles to be sold and are certainly not seeing any share of the revenue derived from their sale. PWAC considers, as a result, organizations like the *Globe and Mail* and Southam to be guilty of theft.

PWAC also notes that these same publishers are now attempting to legalize the practice of reprinting freelancers' articles in Web sites through the imposition of new contracts. They note that these contracts "shift copyright control away from the person who actually created the work, into the hands of publishers. This is unfair, breaks with all traditional practice and ignores the Canadian *Copyright Act*." They then proceed to provide the details of the contracts being offered by publishers. It certainly is an interesting page to visit, since it provides insight into the "story you never hear about in the press" and helps to identify those whom PWAC believe to be the guilty organizations. It reads like a Who's Who of Canadian publishing.

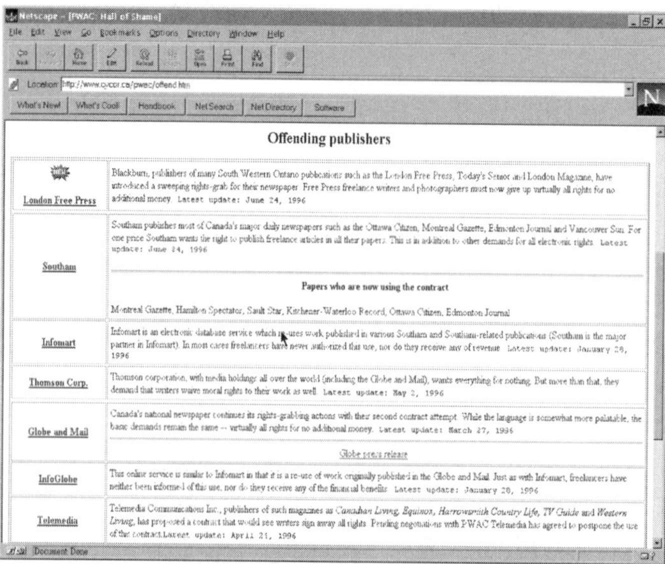

The Canadian Creators Coalition

The Canadian Creators Coalition is an example of how many in the creative community in Canada are organizing. On their site (**http://helios.physics.utoronto.ca:8080/ccc.html**) they say: "Faced with unprecedented demands from publishers in Canada and around the world, Canadian freelance writers, photographers and illustrators have banded together to defend their professional lives." Members of the coalition include the Canadian Association of Photographers and Illustrators in Communications, Concerned Writers of Canada, the Periodical Writers Association of Canada, the Canadian Science Writers' Association, SF Canada, the Travel Media Association of Canada, and the Writers' Union of Canada, all of whom are being affected by the "rights grab."

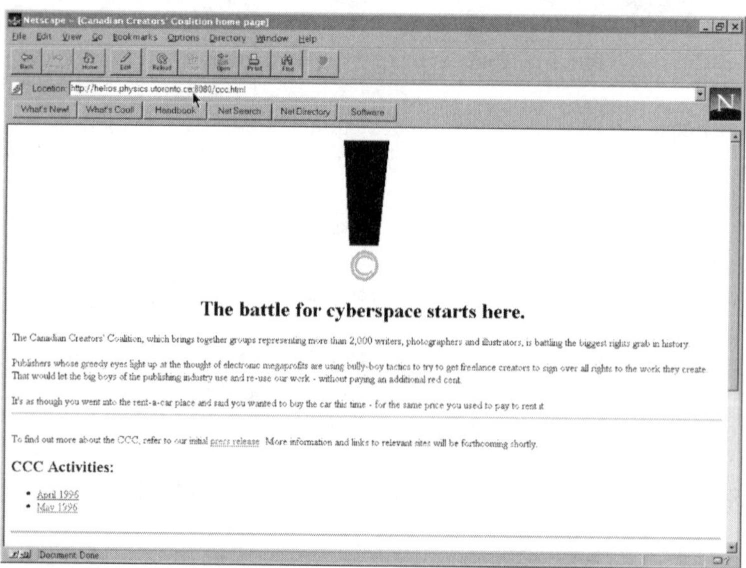

National Writers Union

The American-based National Writers Union represents over 4,500 writers: "Journalists, book authors, poets, copywriters, academic authors, cartoonists, technical and business writers." They too are fighting the freelance battle. The organization has gone so far as to support a suit launched by one of its members against the *New York Times*. They are claiming that "the defendants violated the Copyright Law by taking material originally published in print form and selling those works via on-line databases and CD-ROMs without permission and without further compensation." And they are demanding that the case by resolved to the following ends:

- "An immediate end to the illegal practice of selling the plaintiffs material without permission."
- "The return of money improperly pocketed by the defendants who profited from illegally placing the plaintiffs material on-line."
- "The declaration of a legal precedent so thousands of other writers can seek their own lost income from similar illegal practices throughout the industry."

On the Web page about the case they indicate why they are fighting this battle:

> Tasini et al vs The New York Times et al is the landmark lawsuit brought by members of the National Writers Union against The New York Times Company, Newsday Inc., Time Inc., Lexis/Nexis, and University Microfilms Inc., charging copyright violation regarding the electronic reuse of work produced and sold on a freelance basis.
>
> For decades, when freelance writers sold stories to American publications it was understood by all concerned that they were selling only First North American Serial rights which allowed the newspaper or magazine to publish the story in print one time. For freelance authors, retention of all other copy rights is crucial to their economic survival because a significant additional source of income comes from their ability to sell secondary rights such as syndication, translations, anthologies, and so forth, to other publications.
>
> With the advent of electronic media including databases like Nexis, publishers such as Time/Warner and the Times/Mirror Company, the parent companies of Time and Newsday, have been selling freelance-authored material to electronic databases such as Nexis/Lexis without any additional payment or purchase of electronic rights from the original authors. They claim, without justification, that by purchasing First North American Serial rights they automatically gain electronic re-publication rights. Tasini vs The New York Times is going to establish that they are violating the copy rights of writers.

You can access up-to-date information about the landmark case at the National Writers Union Web site (**http://www.nwu.org/nwu/**):

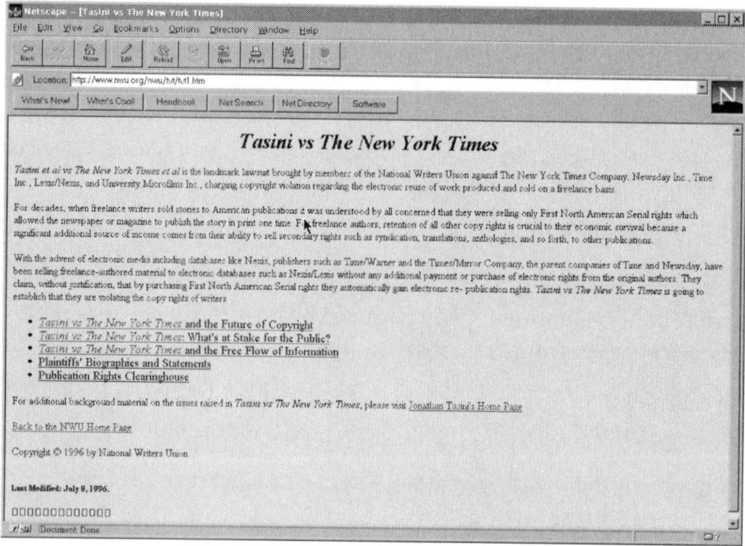

You should also read the article "The Tele-Barons: Media Moguls Rewrite the Law and Rewire the Country," by the fellow who is the focus of the lawsuit, Jonathan Tasini. It is on his Web site at **http://www.nlightning.com/tasini/**. He succinctly puts the issue into perspective by noting: "In a sharp departure from past practice, writers, photographers and artists are being forced to give up their rights forever to works that they create. It used to be that writers were paid a fee for a one-time print use. Today, an increasing number of newspapers and magazines (among them the New York Times, the Tribune Co., Times-Mirror and others), are demanding all future rights to an article—and for no more money. The media giants could cash in on works for decades, without having to pay additional money to many of those who actually created the work."

American Society of Journalists and Authors

The American Society of Journalists and Authors is also involved in the issue. It runs an electronic mailing list, which anyone can join, that reports on its ongoing efforts to resist one-sided freelance contracts. You can access back issues through the group's Web site (**http://www.asja.org/cwpage.htm**) to gain further insight into the types of contract successes they are managing to arrange and to see details of some of the more reprehensible contracts from U.S. media organizations:

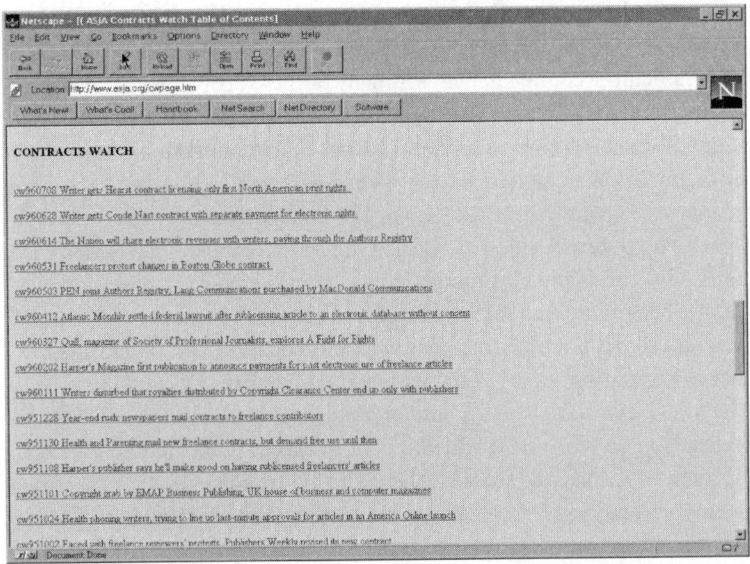

Very specific details are available on each new contract proposal or settlement:

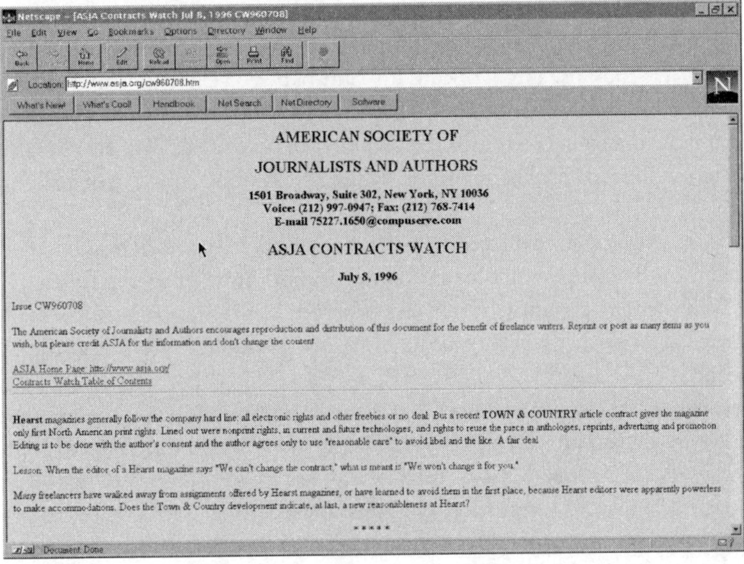

Hence it is a good place for background on the issue and for reports on the methods used by individual writers for dealing with the many one-sided contracts being offered south of the border.

There Is a Human Face

With the number of associations and groups involved in trying to turn back the tide on this issue, what is often lost is the human side of the story. But across Canada and around the world, many tens of thousands of freelance writers are faced with a very difficult dilemma: do they sign away all rights forever to their work and throw away their rights under a hundred years of copyright law, or do they refuse to sign the contracts in the hopes that they will still be able to write in the future?

It is a pretty difficult decision; after all, for many of these people freelance writing is not a terribly lucrative career in the first place. And many have been intimidated into signing by not-so-subtle hints from publishers that future assignments are dependent on them having signed the contract. Consequently, many freelance writers have broken down and signed contracts and condemned themselves to a slow and painful death as the world moves increasingly to an electronic world.

Some do strike up the courage to fight back. One good example is Joe Fisher, a freelance writer based in Fergus, ON. He has a distinguished and credible background; he has written eight books, which have been translated into at least 16 different languages. One of his books, *Hungry Ghosts*, has been adapted for a film screenplay, and another features a preface by the Dalai Lama. He has worked as a freelancer for 14 years, with regular columns in the *Toronto Sun*. He has also written for the *Globe and Mail*, the *Toronto Star*, and other publications. He became enraged about the freelancer issue when he first heard of it in early 1996; then he joined the Periodical Writers Association of Canada to see what he could do to help. Not soon enough; he shortly received, as many writers began to receive, a suggested contract from the *Toronto Sun*, which would provide that paper with "the right to republish your complete work, or an edited version thereof, on an on-line site established by us," prefaced by the caveat that the freelance writer would waive "all applicable moral rights defined in the Canadian *Copyright Act*." This was the standard, "give us everything, you get nothing" type of deal proposed by the media.

The *Toronto Sun* contract included an "addendum" that covered what the contract provided for: Specifically, "We may use any work in any Sun paper or extension thereof. This includes Canoe or any other electronic distribution or any CD-ROM product containing the newspaper." And a letter from the managing editor for the *Toronto Sun* noted that "You are also giving us a perpetual licence to use your material in any form, including electronic, our Internet site and our other newspapers."

In other words, Fisher was expected to give up all rights to his work that he would ever have and assign them to the *Toronto Sun* for no compensation, now or in the future. Granted, the *Toronto Sun* Web site may certainly be in a loss position, but if that paper succeeds in turning it into a revenue product, Fisher will have no right to any revenues derived from the availability of his work on-line.

Fisher wrote back to the *Toronto Sun*: "From the Sun's viewpoint, I can quite understand the intent of the contract that you have just mailed me. If a new world opens up with promising yet unknown potential, the normal human reaction is to secure to one's advantage all rights in that world. But, as a freelancer, I am not sitting in your corner, Mike. I am one of many lone writers who also expect to reap some benefit from this uncertain Xanadu called the Internet and I would be depriving myself of a livelihood if I were to hand over to the *Toronto Sun* and other publishers all rights in that non-material territory."

Today, Fisher is one of the few writers who has found the courage to stand up to these contracts, in order to protect his rights into the future. Talk to him, and you can hear the frustration in his voice as he describes his perspective: "Unless freelance writers fight this thing now, they will be finished into the next century — we will have sabotaged our future right to write. So I'm fighting it on principle."

Fisher, like many writers, believes that as more of the publishing world migrates to the Internet, it is important for writers to safeguard their own futures. By giving away their rights by signing these contracts, they are ensuring that their future role will not be successful.

He is also frustrated by the duplicity he sees in the media. "Read some of these publications and they seem so high and mighty, sticking up for the common man, and taking the side of labor in labor issues — except on this one." And what he finds particularly repulsive is the fact that "they want us to waive our moral rights under the *Copyright Act*. If we sign these contracts, we lose all rights and protection that we have under the *Act*."

Fisher has some concern for the newspaper editors who are being forced to send the contracts to freelance writers: "I believe they are being ordered to do so by management, and that even so, they don't agree with what is happening."

Fisher hopes to keep on writing and hopes to keep his intellectual property. You can contact him at **sbardo@freespace.net** to see how he is making out.

Is a Solution Possible?

Definitely. Consider the following items from the American Society of Journalists and Authors (ASJA) contracts watch mailing list:

> More and more publishers are paying individual freelancers for having taken what wasn't theirs: the right to peddle electronic reprints of articles after they're published. Latest settlements achieved with an assist from ASJA involve WEIGHT WATCHERS and MARKETING COMPUTERS.
>
> In the case of five freelance articles in Marketing Computers (a BPI publication), the author wrote and waited, wrote and waited, wrote and waited. At last, he sent a certified demand letter with an invoice and a three-day deadline after which he would file suit. The publisher responded, negotiated and, on the last day, sent a courier with a check for $2,000, a little more than 20 percent of the print fees originally paid.
>
> It took a filing in Small Claims Court for contract breach to get the attention of Weight Watchers International. The writer, who found her piece in databases without her consent, went to court after her claim was ignored a bit too long. Before the hearing date, WWI ponied up more than 40 percent of the original article fee.
>
> Both agreements call for electronic use of the material to stop.
>
> Other publications that have settled with individual writers on e-rights violations include CONSUMERS DIGEST, NEWSWEEK, PARAGON PUBLISHING (UK), VEGETARIAN TIMES (COWLES) and the WASHINGTON POST. "PUBLISHERS WEEKLY said last week it would make good by early fall on a promised payback to all contributors whose articles and reviews have been used in electronic databases in recent years. PW is working with the Authors Registry to make the retroactive payments and to share income from future secondary uses."
>
> In March, K-III, publisher of NEW YORK, SEVENTEEN and others, said it had paid some $28,000 in back royalties to authors and pledged it would soon pay the balance owed—more on-line and CD-ROM database income the magazines had accepted without authors' consent. Writers, still waiting, are starting to complain. A K-III official told Contracts Watch he'd check on the delay.
>
> The AUTHORS REGISTRY, meanwhile, announced that it has begun mailing the first of more than $150,000 worth of royalty checks to writers, covering payments for photocopy and electronic use of their work. The money is the first collected and passed on by the new nonprofit agency, which boasts the cooperation of 30 writers' groups and 95 literary agencies and is working directly with publishers, database compilers and others in the secondary markets.

Sadly, all these initiatives are taking place south of the border. There is little such activity in Canada, where the publishing scene is dominated by three or four large organizations such as Maclean Hunter, owned by Rogers Communications, and Southam, owned by Conrad Black. But it is still apparent that even as settlements are made, publishers continue to enter into deals that earn them revenue from the sale of articles to which they have no legal right, and that their claims not to be making money are considered by many writers to be fraudulent.

> LEXIS-NEXIS will soon be available on the World Wide Web. The broad online database service, which includes full text of articles from current and back issues of many magazines and newspapers, has been restricted to subscribers willing to pay stiff subscription, search and download fees. Under the new arrangement, over-the-counter users on the Lexis-Nexis Web site will pay by credit card according to use.
>
> The ELECTRIC LIBRARY research service on the Web is adding the contents of magazines published by CMP (HOMEPC, NETGUIDE, WINDOWS and nine other high-tech magazines) and WEIDER PUBLICATIONS (MUSCLE AND FITNESS, FLEX, SHAPE and others). The Electric Library allows searches of nearly a thousand magazines and newspapers as well as reference books and other materials. Publishers are paid regular royalties according to the number of accesses.
>
> Any wonder why some publishers ask freelancers to let them have "electronic rights" for free, with no obligation to share the income? Any wonder why savvy freelancers say sorry, but no?

What Is Needed?

What, then, is the impact of the freelancers' battle? Why should the average Canadian even care? The case is best stated by Tasini himself: "Unless the abuses we face are halted by legislation or other means, the constitutional copyright protection for authors will be dead. The people who produce the articles, books, photographs or drawings will lose control of their livelihood and some, at least, will be driven out of the business. This is a disaster for our cultural heritage."

Several things are needed:

- Freelance writers need support at the political level. Certainly, the heritage minister and others involved in defending Canadian culture must be willing to support freelance writers and other creative artists in their calls for fairness in this new electronic world. The prime minister should take notice, to ensure that the rights of Canadian writers are not trampled by a few large media organizations. We must not allow another segment of Canadian culture to be destroyed by the ever more concentrated Canadian media.
- Canadians must be made aware that some on-line Web sites they use contain property illegally obtained, or obtained through coercive contracts. Canadians should be willing to speak up in support of freelance writers and other creative artists.
- Some writers believe that the Canadian Musical Reproduction Rights Agency, which pays a fee to musical artists, collected from radio stations that play their music, is a good example of the type of strategy that can work in this emerging world of the Internet. In the case of *Harper's* magazine in the United States, just that is happening: Monies are being paid and distributed in respect of the use of freelance writers' work in electronic form.

- There are a number of class action suits underway or anticipated involving freelance writers who are trying to change the situation. You might consider donating to the legal fund for the writers involved in these suits.
- Finally, more media organizations need to realize, as *Harper's* has done, that they can only enjoy Canada's creative talent if they are willing to play a game that is fair, equitable, and moral.

It is a difficult issue, and certainly one that deserves a fair solution.

Conclusion

In this chapter we have given you just a taste of the many legal difficulties that the Internet is causing in the area of intellectual property. It is a challenging topic; the culture found on-line runs up against the methods people have long used to deal with intellectual property. The network emerged in an environment of information sharing and exchange, and still retains this unique culture. For example, people still write software and release it so that it can be freely exchanged on-line. The Web has grown so quickly because people have been able to figure out how to put up their own Web sites by examining the HTML code of other Web sites and "borrowing" that code. As lawyers come to invade the Internet, it will be interesting to see how the Internet will really respond.

As the Internet becomes a real force in our everyday business, economic, social, and political life, all kinds of laws, practices, and standards will be subject to extreme stress. As John Perry Barlow wrote in a classic article, "Everything You Know About Intellectual Property is Wrong" for *Wired* magazine (**http://www.hotwired.com/wired/2.03/features/economy.ideas.html**), "In the Third Wave we have now entered, information to a large extent replaces land, capital, and hardware, and information is most at home in a much more fluid and adaptable environment. The Third Wave is likely to bring a fundamental shift in the purposes and methods of law which will affect far more than simply those statutes which govern intellectual property."

Perhaps this is most true.

CHAPTER 20

The Changing Face of the Canadian Internet Industry

As local and long-distance telephone companies scramble to boost their own Internet offerings, cable operators are trying to sell a pricey, largely unproven product to a confused, sometimes hostile audience. And partly because they have made such optimistic projections about the revenue-generating potential of cable modems, operators are facing unusually strict scrutiny from the media and Wall Street.

Jones Adds Phone Modem Offering in Va.
Cable World, July 15, 1996

The high-tech dreamscape is indeed littered with busted promises: interactive television and its 500 channels; hand-held personal digital assistants that could read your handwriting (remember Apple's Newton?); video phones; two-way paging. And what about the Internet, the mother of all hyped technologies? PC users are still awaiting its promise of fast, real-time video and interactivity. And will Oracle CEO Larry Ellison's vision of mass-market, low-cost computers that connect people to the Net be the next Big Thing? One thing is for certain, the industry has promised — and failed to deliver — so much that people have a right to be skeptical.

Computer dreamscape littered with busted promises
USA Today, June 30, 1996

During 1996, the Internet industry in Canada underwent a dramatic metamorphosis, as it completed the final steps of turning into a full-fledged, stock-price-driven commercial industry. In this chapter we take a look at two of the more significant impacts: first, an overview of some Canadian Internet trends, and second, a critical assessment of the high-speed Internet access in Canada.

Nine Canadian Internet Trends

Trend 1: The Internet Is Being Shrink-wrapped

When we wrote the first edition of this book in 1994, we spent a great deal of time describing how you could find various types of Internet software. That continued into the 1995 edition. The problem back then was that we faced a Catch 22 situation: to find software to use on the Internet you had to be on the Internet, and to be on the Internet, you had to have some Internet software. In a nutshell, it was a very difficult process to get on the Internet, and once you were there, it was pretty difficult to do anything at all.

Today, this is no longer a challenge. As we explained in Chapter 4, to get set up with an Internet account, all you have to do is call an Internet service provider. They will set you up with a SLIP/PPP account (the standard type of Internet account in use across Canada today) and send you the proper software. Moreover, if you walk into a computer store or browse through a computer catalogue, you can easily find all kinds of off-the-shelf Internet software for various purposes.

The Internet software market has become a full-fledged industry and will continue to grow in size and scope. Hardly a day goes by without some announcement from some company about a new release of Internet software. New companies are continually being born to take advantage of this opportunity.

In Canada developers of Web editor software such as InContext Systems and SoftQuad have made names for themselves worldwide. OpenText has established itself as the leading Web search engine. Border Network Technologies, a maker of firewall products, has merged with the world's leading firewall maker to become a significant player in the global Internet security industry (a firewall is a system that controls access to a computer on the Internet). SimWare has established a strong niche by releasing software that allows a Web site to query an IBM mainframe application. The list goes on.

In addition to significant advances for Canadian companies, we are also seeing the Web become "shrink-wrapped," a term often used in the computer industry to signify that software is sold on retail shelves. This is significant, because for a long time the only source for Internet software was on the Internet, and the software was rarely found in one single place; it was scattered across the Internet.

A good example of where the industry is headed is found with Net Commander, a package from a Canadian company, Luckman Interactive. Luckman was formed with the intention of providing simple access to comprehensive Internet software. Install Net Commander, and you will have virtually every type of Internet utility you might need, as seen on the following screen. It includes software for viewing video on-line, conferencing, Internet relay chat, the Microsoft Internet Explorer program, a sound/audio program, a program to make telephone calls on-line, and other utilities:

THE CHANGING FACE OF THE CANADIAN INTERNET INDUSTRY

1. Several changes are occurring at a rapid pace in the Internet industry in Canada and around the world.
2. The Internet is being "shrinkwrapped" — that is, the software industry has become quite involved with the Internet.
3. The Canadian Internet industry is rapidly being privatized and is undergoing consolidation.
4. U.S. companies have moved into the Canadian Internet access market in a major way.
5. It is becoming easier for anyone to access the Internet, as methods emerge to access the network via televisions, game devices, and via special "Internet computers."
6. Faster access to the Internet will one day be a reality as telephone and cable companies become involved with the Internet, but will probably occur later rather than sooner.
7. In the interim period, ISDN will emerge as a practical alternative for higher-speed access for some people.
8. Microsoft will have a significant impact on the future development of the Internet.

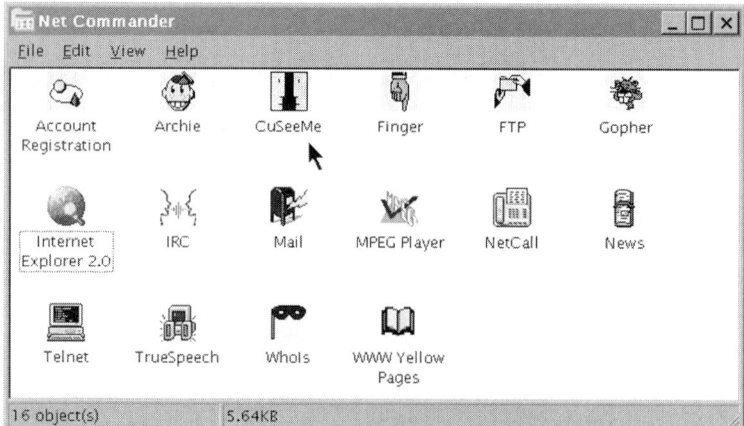

The program comes with an install routine that also allows you to install many of the special Web viewers/players that we discussed in Chapter 7, such as the Acrobat Reader program, QuickTime for Windows, Xing Streamworks, a virtual reality viewer, and a directory of Web sites:

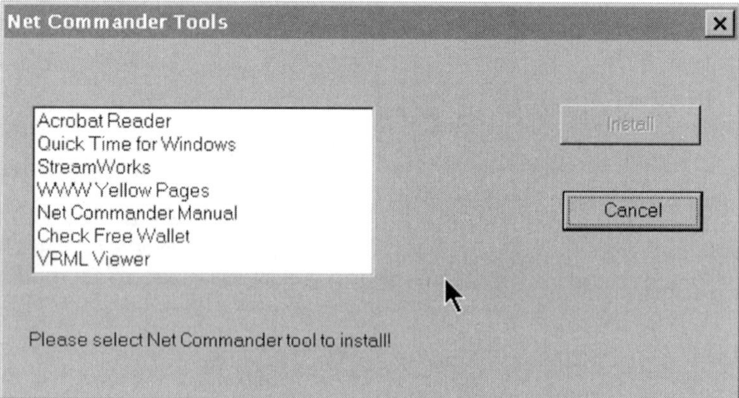

The cost for the software? A suggested street price of $49.95, but often available for less. Granted, you can access and obtain much of this software on the Internet, but for under $50 you can get almost all the Internet software you need in one place, and on one CD ROM.

Luckman also makes available a product called Web Commander, which provides a number of components necessary for building, hosting, and maintaining a Web site. The program includes a Web browser (Microsoft Internet Explorer), the Web Commander Web server, a tool to create "imagemaps" on Web sites, a version of InContext's Spider Web editor software called WebStudio, a utility called WebPage, which can create a Web site for you literally in minutes, and some other utilities. The cost? A street price of $129, and often available for less:

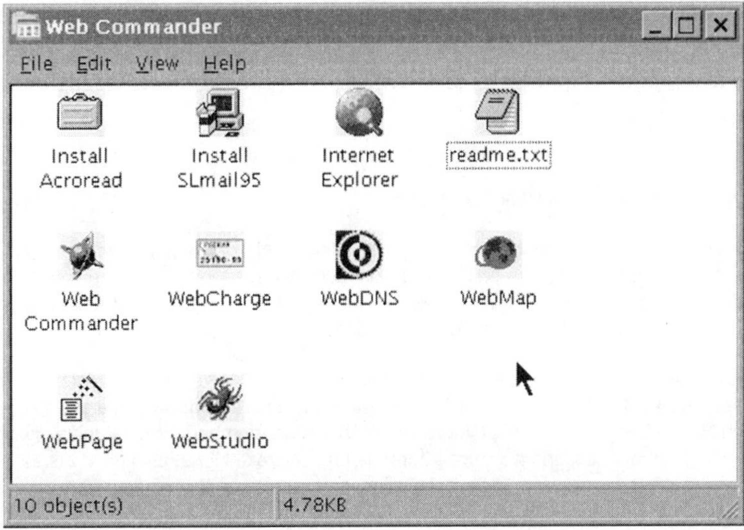

A lot of software for a relatively low price, considering what you are getting. And it's a good example of where the industry is headed. The point we are trying to make here is that the Internet software industry is evolving rapidly and is becoming a serious force within the retail computer industry.

Trend 2: Privatization of the Canadian Internet Industry

When we wrote the 1994 edition of this book, we took great pains to describe how the network was slowly making a transition from being a system used throughout the academic and research communities to one that was more commercial in scope. In our earlier books organizations such as CA*Net and CANARIE received a lot of attention, since they dominated the funding for much of the infrastructure that supported use of the Internet in Canada. As we wrote in the 1995 edition, "networks are linked together across Canada through CA*Net, the major Internet system in Canada today. CA*Net was established in the late eighties in order to foster a cooperative environment for connectivity between Canada's regional networks. Even though CA*Net is the national network, it really is just a coordinating body for the regional (or provincial and territorial) networks."

How things have changed. Today, the Internet industry is almost entirely commercial, run primarily by the private sector, with independent Internet service providers, large players like iSTAR, NETCOM, and HookUp, and the telephone and cable companies dominating the scene.

Examples abound of the changes that have occurred: in 1996 ownership of NLnet, which at one time was the primary provider of Internet access across Newfoundland, was transferred to an alliance of three companies: Cable Atlantic, Unitel Communications, and HookUp Communications. Cable Atlantic is the primary provider of cable television services in Newfoundland; HookUp Communications is a large Canadian Internet service provider; and Unitel Communications is a telecommunications company, primarily known for its long distance services. Until the time of the transfer, NLnet had been run by the Memorial University of Newfoundland on limited resources. The press release issued by the Memorial University of

Newfoundland described the reasons for the privatization. We provide an extract below to help you understand why the change took place. The NLnet situation is typical of the sweeping changes that have occurred in the Canadian Internet industry over the last two years.

> June 4, 1996
>
> Memorial Announces Transfer of NLnet to NF.net
>
> Memorial University has selected the response submitted by NF.net, a joint venture of Cable Atlantic Incorporated, Unitel Communications, and HookUp Communications as the preferred response to its request for proposals for the divestiture of NLnet. HookUp Communications is a major national Internet service provider (ISP) with operations in 110 Canadian locations.
>
> NLnet, operated by Memorial University since its inception six years ago, was the original Internet service provider in Newfoundland and Labrador and it is still the largest. NLnet's primary mandate is to provide Internet services to the education community in the province. Among its members are the university, many of the community college campuses, and numerous libraries and schools. NLnet also provides services to several federal government departments, the provincial government, several commercial organizations, and to STEM~Net and the Enterprise Network.
>
> With the full support of NLnet members, Memorial decided to seek the interest of the private sector in continuing the development of NLnet.
>
> The selection process sought a partner who subscribed to NLnet's principles and who would best continue the development of the network. As the local Internet market matured, it became obvious that the private sector had the interest and capability to take on this challenge and to provide the additional resources needed to meet NLnet's objectives.
>
> Following a thorough analysis of proposals submitted by various bidders, Memorial selected the NF.net bid. All parties are confident that NLnet will be developed and expanded to a level not otherwise possible given the resource constraints currently faced by Memorial.
>
> "NLnet has become too large and too important to be operated as a sideline," said Wilf Bussey, director of the Department of Computing and Communications, the Memorial University department that has been responsible for NLnet's operations.
>
> "NLnet was at a point where it needed the infusion of more resources," Mr. Bussey explained, "As it was set up, we didn't have the capital behind us to continue development of the network and to continue expansion into additional communities. Also, we don't have the resources to continue with the level of technical and user support that is needed to do this job properly in today's fast-paced environment."
>
> When proposals from the private sector were solicited, Memorial specified four principles that it felt were essential to NLnet's mandate: universal access to allow all citizens in Newfoundland and Labrador to potentially have access; capacity for network enhancement; service levels of the network supported and strengthened significantly; and reasonable cost.
>
> Those who have been responsible for the creation and growth of NLnet see the network as a trust that is being passed on. "We wanted to know that whoever took it over would take this public trust and advance it to the next level," Mr. Bussey said. "NLnet was a pioneering activity and the university is confident that this divestiture will only improve the availability of the Internet in Newfoundland and Labrador."

Trend 3: Consolidation of the Internet Industry

This brings us to the next trend: anyone reading the business press in Canada or who has an Internet account is likely aware that many small independent providers in Canada have been swallowed up by some of the Internet giants. Some of the larger Internet service providers in Canada went on a buying spree in 1996. Companies like iSTAR, HookUp, and Internet Direct, funded by investment dollars raised on the public stock exchange, began to snap up many of the smaller independent Internet service providers across the country. Their objective is to form large-scale, national ISPs that can effectively compete with the Internet services being established by telephone and cable companies.

The telephone companies have also been merging their Internet services. All of Canada's provincial telephone companies, which at one time were operating their own independent Internet access services, have consolidated their operations under a single brand name, Sympatico, which is being marketed across Canada as one single Internet access service (**http://www.sympatico.ca**):

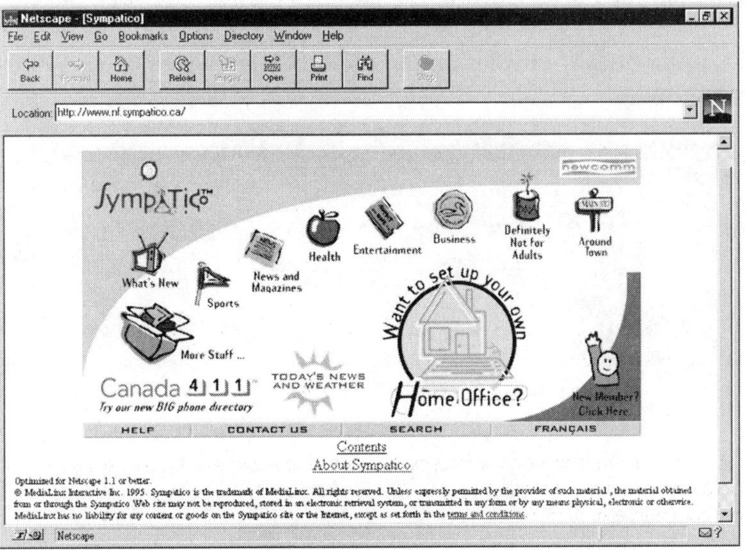

Of course, not every small ISP in Canada was bought out. Hundreds of independent providers still exist in every province. Will they survive? We expect many of them will, in the same way that boutique stores exist in a world of megastores like Costco and Price Club. Many of the independent providers argue that they can continue to provide a high degree of personalized service to their customers, unlike the larger companies, which, they point out, have grown too big too fast. Time will tell. Inevitably, some providers will go out of business, and others will merge with larger providers, and still others will simply give up operating in what has become an extremely competitive business.

And as we noted in Chapter 4, everyone in Canada seems to want to become an Internet service provider. Canadian cable companies and telephone companies and other communications firms are staking their claims to the Internet frontier. Major international computer hardware and software firms such as IBM and Microsoft sell access to the Internet. Newspapers, radio stations, and just about everyone else are selling access. And major on-line networks such as CompuServe, which for years enjoyed year-after-year growth, found themselves having to move into the Internet marketplace in order to survive. In some communities community networks known as FreeNets offer low-cost access to some parts of the Internet, but in a world in which Internet services are selling for increasingly lower rates, they are struggling to obtain the necessary funding in order to survive.

Trend 4: U.S. Internet Companies Are Moving into Canada

As the Internet market continues to mature, and companies increase their market penetration internationally, many U.S.-based Internet firms are setting up shop in Canada, establishing subsidiaries and branch offices here. This U.S. expansion is taking place on three primary fronts.

Internet Access Providers

Many large U.S. Internet service providers are now competing in Canada directly alongside Canadian-based providers of Internet access. Examples include America Online, which established AOL Canada, NETCOM, one of the largest ISPs in the United States, which formed NETCOM Canada (**http://www.netcom.ca**), and PSINet, which opened PSINet Canada (**http://www.psi.ca**):

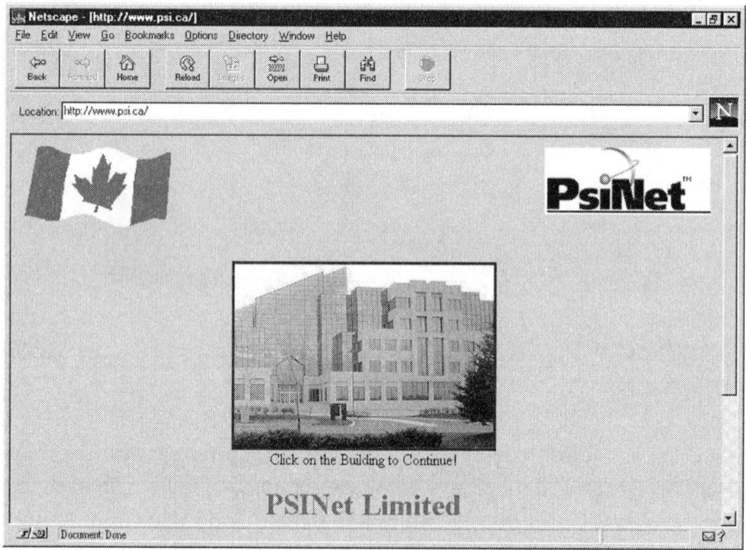

Internet Navigation Companies

Companies like Yahoo!, which specialize in helping Internet users find information on the Internet, have opened up Canadian versions of their service. Yahoo! Canada (**http://www.yahoo.ca**), for example, is operated by Rogers Multi-Media Inc. and the Toronto Sun Publishing Company and provides a directory of Canadian World Wide Web sites:

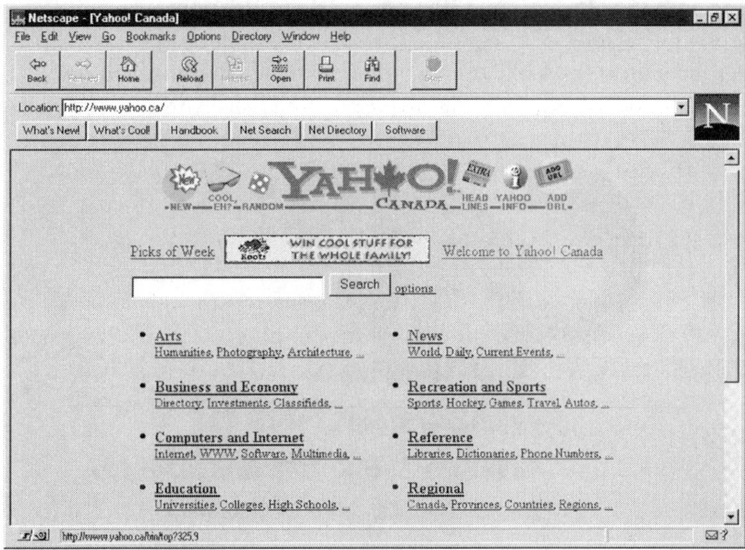

Internet Software Companies

Finally, U.S. companies that manufacture Internet software for consumers and businesses have arrived in Canada. Netscape (**http://www.netscape.com**), the company that makes the famous World Wide Web browser by the same name, has a Canadian subsidiary called Netscape Canada that is based in Toronto. Open Market Inc., a firm that makes software for businesses that want to engage in electronic commerce on the Internet, has a Canadian sales office, also based in Toronto. The Open Market Web site is at **http://www.openmarket.com**:

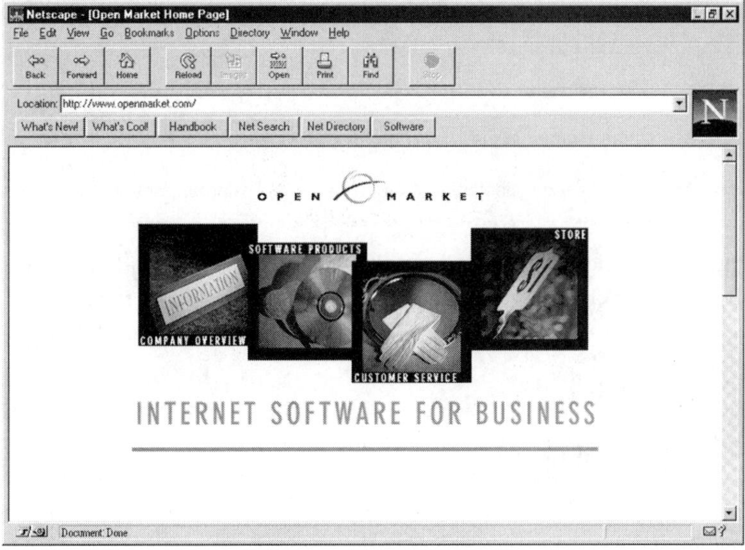

Trend 5: The Internet Industry Is Becoming More Organized

One result of the industry consolidation is a movement across Canada to organize ISPs so that they are in a better position to deal with the pressures and challenges this fast-paced industry is creating:

CAIP, the Canadian Association of Internet Providers (**http://www.caip.ca**), established itself in 1996 with the intent to "foster the growth of a healthy and competitive Internet service industry in Canada through collective and cooperative action on issues of mutual interest." Their specific objectives, provided on their Web page, are as follows:

> To provide Internet architecture coordination and general Internet registration policy and services in Canada.
>
> To provide a forum for dealing with issues of common interest to the membership.
>
> To proactively promote the views of the Corporation to organizations such as regulatory or government bodies.
>
> To promote a positive image for the Internet industry and to educate and build awareness for Internet industry issues.
>
> To facilitate the global expression of Canadian culture and commerce.
>
> To represent the Canadian Internet industry to international bodies.
>
> To do all such other things as are incidental or conducive to the attainment of the above objectives.

The organization is working on issues related to pornography and offensive content on the Internet and is guiding policy discussions regarding the operation of the Internet in Canada. We suggest that you regularly check the CAIP Web site for up-to-date information on Canadian Internet policy initiatives.

Trend 6: Easier Internet Access

One of the hotly debated issues in the Canadian Internet community is the need for universal Internet access across Canada. Some observers argue that we are destined to become a society of Internet haves and have-nots. This raises concerns about the disparities that might result. The government recognizes the need for broader access and is establishing programs that will help individuals, organizations, and communities access the Internet.

The private sector is doing its part too. Many companies are trying to provide new, lower-cost methods to access the Internet through televisions, telephones, game modules, and other systems. These new access devices promise to bring the Internet into the homes of millions of people around the world by making it simple to get on-line with minimum hassle. Most of these devices are in the $200 to $1,000 range, and they generally do not include the cost of Internet access; they only act as the medium through which you access the Internet. They are designed to be less expensive and less complicated than a standard computer.

As these plans bear fruit and access becomes easier than ever before, it is certain that there will be growth in the number of people who use the Internet. Below, we briefly look at some of the devices that will provide Canadians with access to the Internet in the months and years ahead.

Televisions

Have you ever thought about surfing the Internet from the comfort of your living room? Television manufacturers such as Zenith are launching televisions that can be used to surf the Web by remote control. Other companies, such as ViewCall America (**http://www.viewcall.com**), are producing VCR-like boxes for surfing the Internet through a television set. You will need a remote control to use the Web. If you want to send and receive electronic mail, you can purchase an optional keyboard attachment:

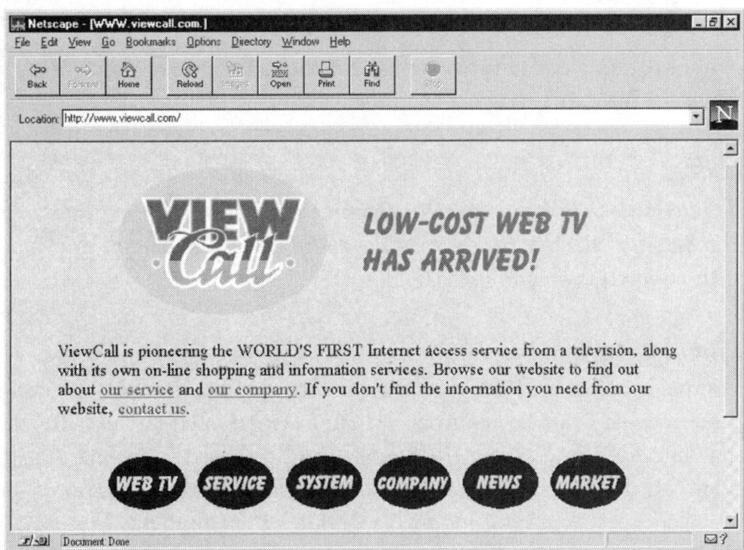

The box sits on top of your television and is easy to use. All you need to do is plug the box into your television and into a phone line. This method of Internet access has already arrived in Canada: the Manitoba Telephone System has teamed up with ViewCall America to offer this service to Manitoba residents.

Another major player in the Internet–television market is WebTV (**http://www.webtv.net**), whose technology has been licensed by consumer electronics companies such as Sony Electronics and Philips Electronics. WebTV's stated mission is to "make the Internet as accessible and compelling for consumers as broadcast television is today":

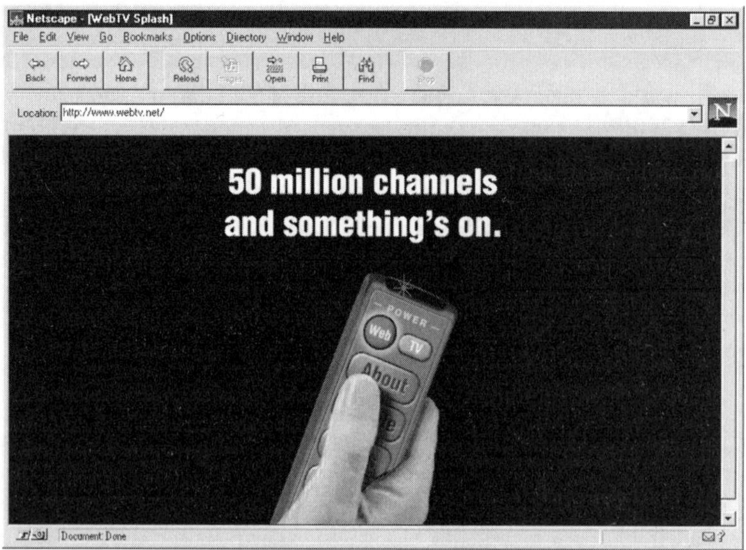

Telephones

Cellular telephone companies and firms such as Northern Telecom are launching products that provide access to the Internet through a telephone.

Game Devices

Game manufacturers such as Nintendo (**http://www.nintendo.com**) and Sega (**http://www.sega.com**) have released products that allow their game consoles to be used to browse the Web. Consumers will use their television sets as monitors.

Network Computers

Computer companies such as Oracle and IBM are developing small devices called "network computers" that provide access to the Internet. They are designed as "no-frills" machines that will contain a computer processor, a small amount of memory, a keyboard, a screen, and a modem, but no hard drive. Companies endorsing the "network computer" include Sun Microsystems, Netscape Communications, Apple, Digital Equipment, Motorola, Mitsubishi, and NEC.

Limitations of These Devices

There is much debate about the future of Internet access through set-top television boxes and network computers. Will they be accepted by consumers? Are they just a fad? And there are several real problems throughout the Internet industry concerning the issue of ubiquitous access. Many of these issues were highlighted in a keynote speech given on behalf of Reed Hundt, the chairman of the U.S. Federal Communication Commission, to INET '96, the annual meeting of the global Internet Society held in Montreal in the summer of 1996. He raised the question whether technology companies really are interested in solving the problem of ubiquitous access and raised several interesting points:

- At this point in time, it would cost about $1,500 per person to link people into the Internet based on current technology and training requirements.
- Software companies like Microsoft seem interested only in developing high-end software for the fastest of computer systems. Wryly, he made the comment that "Bill Gates would be Henry Ford if Ford had started out producing Lincoln Continentals."
- Web page designers are developing sites that demand all kinds of computer horsepower to keep increasing the disparity between those who have the fastest machines and those who do not.

They do have many potential shortcomings:

- Poor picture quality. The picture quality and resolution of television sets are lower than what is currently available on a computer monitor. Critics are warning that if a television set becomes the visual interface for the Internet users will be disappointed.
- Low intelligence. Network computers and television devices will be low on intelligence, disk space, and memory. They will not come packaged with the same capabilities and features as a fully featured multimedia computer. This means that if you want to use a word processor or other software program such as a spreadsheet or accounting package, you will likely have to borrow another computer. Many Internet users do not like the thought of using one device for their Internet access and another for their general computing needs.
- Small price gap. As the prices for high-end PCs continue to drop, the price difference between these devices and a fully featured personal computer will decrease. Critics argue that users will question the value of purchasing an Internet access device when, for only a few hundred dollars more, they can purchase a high-power computer.

In spite of these drawbacks, Internet access devices have many advantages. They include low cost, ease of use, and simple maintenance. IBM, for instance, has estimated that the maintenance cost of a network computer will decrease by 25% over a traditional computer. Because of these benefits, proponents argue that in the end these devices will increase Internet use among households and businesses.

Trend 7: Faster Internet Access

Most people access the Internet using a device called a "telephone modem." Telephone modems can operate at speeds of up to 33.6 bits per second (bps), although most Internet users use modems that work at speeds of 14,400 bps or 28,800 bps. One of the biggest complaints about the Internet is that it is slow. While major telecommunications companies are constantly upgrading their networks to allow for faster Internet access, the Internet's sluggish performance is not going to improve anytime soon. If you are interested in accessing the Internet at higher speeds, there are three technologies that you should be aware of: ISDN, ADSL, and cable modems. Let's briefly look at each technology.

ISDN

ISDN stands for "integrated services digital network." An ISDN connection provides access to the Internet over a digital telephone line. It consists of two "channels," called "B channels," that can each transmit data at 64,000 bps. When the two channels are used together, ISDN can provide access to the Internet at speeds of 128,000 bps, about four times faster than what you can get by using a standard modem. ISDN Internet connections are currently offered by Internet service providers and telephone companies across Canada. We take a more detailed look at ISDN later in the chapter.

ADSL

ADSL stands for "asymmetrical digital subscriber line." ADSL is even faster than ISDN for downloading information off the Internet, processing data at speeds of more than 1.5 million bps, or 50 pages of text a second. ADSL technology works over standard residential copper telephone lines; some telephone companies call it ISDN on steroids. Some organizations are promising ADSL links to the Internet at speeds of up to 6 or 7 million bps, or even faster. Canadian telephone companies are positioning ADSL services as an option to the high-speed cable modem services that are being launched by cable companies.

Cable Modems

Cable companies across Canada are experimenting with "cable modems," devices that will allow consumers to access the Internet through their cable networks. Some cable companies claim that cable modems will eventually provide access to the Internet at speeds of 10 million bits of information per second. Other cable companies are more conservative in their estimates.

When Will High-Speed Access Really Arrive?

ISDN access to the Internet is already available in many areas across Canada. However, the real focus of the Internet industry has been on the two newer technologies described above, ADSL and cable modems. The issue of high-speed access to the Internet was, perhaps, the "story of the year" in 1996. A battle continues to rage between the cable and telephone companies for supremacy in the Internet access market:

- "Rogers rolls out Internet access — High-speed, cable-based system to reach 500,000 homes by 1996," *The Globe and Mail*, November 19, 1995;
- "Bell enters high-speed Internet access lane: It is trying to compete with cable companies that are testing faster speeds," *London Free Press*, June 26, 1996;
- "Battle for the Internet: Bell Canada to offer high-speed access through network," *Kitchener–Waterloo Record*, June 26, 1996;
- "Big fight looms for highway rider Bell and Rogers racing to sell high-speed Internet access," *Toronto Star*, November 6, 1995.

The plans and dreams are significant. In an article in *The Globe and Mail* on September 12, 1995, Ted Rogers, the chief executive officer of Rogers Communications, one of Canada's largest cable operators, said: "Cable modems have a capacity 1,000 times greater than a traditional telephone modem. We are making our entire cable plant two-way to support high-speed-switched interactive broadband services, simultaneously incorporating voice, data, video in colour and full motion. Books that talk, encyclopedias with film clips, magazines in three dimensions are part of this future." The telephone companies, on the other hand, are placing their bets on ADSL.

Certainly the so-called battle between telephone companies and cable companies with respect to the Internet is a pitched and prolonged marketing battle, but so far, it seems to be a battle of the press release and hyperbole. In fact, every time we see another press release or report from a telephone or cable company, we form an image in our mind: the marketing staffs from several telephone companies and cable companies are fighting it out to the death in front of a cheering crowd! Gladiators in armor and with fax machines in the crook of their arms, their only available weapon is the press release — the more hype and the more promises, the better to slay their opponent with! In the back rooms, a few network engineers, hidden away, struggle to deliver on the promises made by their CEO and quietly bear the pressure as they struggle to respond to requests by a vice president of marketing impatient with their inability to make it work immediately.

Telephone companies versus cable companies for Internet supremacy? From our perspective, the whole situation is overhyped far in advance of any delivery of real services.

Anyone who has expectations of an imminent world of high-speed access to the Internet needs to take a deep breath and realize that the future will not be here as quickly as the cable and telephone companies have told us. Much of what you hear and read about high-speed Internet access is a byproduct of an ongoing battle, with the cable companies trying to outdo the phone companies and vice versa. The battle is far from over and is as much about public perception as anything else. Talk to a cable company representative, and he will say wonderful things about cable modems and why ADSL will be a definitive flop, and then talk to a telephone company representative, and he will say wonderful things about ADSL modems, and why cable modems will be a definitive flop. It all seems like one giant game so far, and it is.

The reality? New technologies are on the way that will support higher-speed access to the Internet, but they will not be here as soon as users might like. The concept of high-speed access to the Internet seems promising enough. For example, assume for a moment that cable modems will eventually allow us to access the Internet at speeds of 10 million bits of information per second, and that ADSL will eventually operate at 7 million bits of information per second. Compare that to the telephone modem speeds at which most individual Internet users operate today — 14,400 bps or 28,800 bps — and it certainly looks exciting.

FIGURE 20.1
Comparison of High-Speed Internet Access

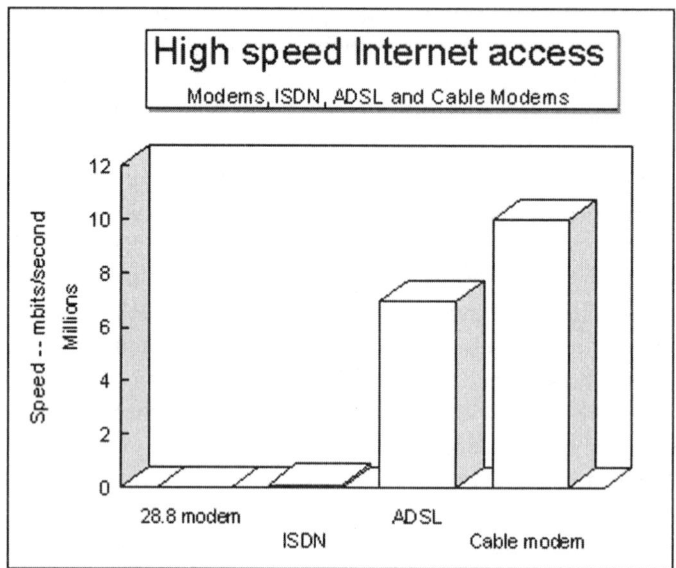

But when it comes to high-speed access there are many questions and issues that arise. Let's look at some of them.

The Reality Does Not Match the Hype

Many cable companies were overly effusive in 1995 and early 1996 about their plans to provide high-speed access to the Internet through cable modems and went so far as to predict widescale deployment and availability in 1996. Ted Rogers, for example, said 500,000 homes would be hooked up by the end of 1996. The reality? Less than a few thousand. By mid-summer 1996 most cable companies had become rather quiet, and full-scale deployment of cable access to the Internet certainly was not happening. It was not possible to call your cable company and order a cable modem link to the Internet; they were not ready deliver it.

Telephone companies, in 1996, began to issue press releases trumpeting their involvement with ADSL, boasting that it would permit access to the Internet at speeds some 4,000 times faster than a modem. But read below the headline, and you will discover that full-scale deployment of ADSL is also a long way off. According to one report that addressed the deployment of ADSL in the United States, "it will be years before consumers nationwide have access to the service."

It seems that reality only sets in when the network engineers — the ones who have to make all this marvelous technology work — are faced with the task of fulfilling the marketing promises made by their employers. Cable companies discover that while cable modems worked well in the lab, it is a different story altogether out in the real world. And telephone companies realize that what works well in theory is a challenge to implement in practice.

Telephone and cable companies are all too often driven by a marketing agenda that ignores the engineering reality. If you really want to know the truth, we suggest you get to know a few engineers at your local cable and telephone company, since they seem to be the only ones who really know what is possible.

Consumer Demand for High-speed Access Is Uncertain

Overly optimistic claims about the market penetration of high-speed Internet access are regularly made in the press. Individuals speak glowingly of the billions of dollars to be made from high-speed access to the Internet and the hundreds of thousands of cable and ADSL modems that consumers will soon snap up. But no one really knows if consumers will truly adopt this technology as quickly as everyone thinks they might. And what price will they be willing to pay?

Some of the early experiments are cause for reflection. For example, OTV, a small cable company in Oliver, BC, has been providing cable modem access to the Internet since 1995. By mid-1996 the service had drawn only 24 users, at a monthly charge of $50. A pilot offering of cable modem access to the Internet in Newmarket, ON, by Rogers Cablesystems drew only 3% of cable customers. While it is a respectable number in real terms, it is far below what one might expect.

A similar rollout of cable modem technology in Alexandria, VA, drew only 70 paying customers after "three months of pitching high-speed data devices through direct-mail pieces, telemarketing, retail promotions and outdoor fair demonstrations." The cable operator in Alexandria was apparently so discouraged by the lack of response to its cable modem service that it decided to offer regular, low-speed Internet access in the hopes of attracting customers. We are talking of *thousands* of dollars of revenue, not *billions.*

The Technology Is Lagging Behind the Marketing Hype

Dig beneath the marketing glitz, and you will discover that cable modem technology has yet to fully mature. Here is one problem: cable modem standards are still under development. This means that cable modems from different manufacturers cannot communicate with one another. ADSL is not ready for widescale deployment either. Both ADSL and cable modems are still being tweaked and tested, but this shouldn't come as a surprise. It takes time to work out the glitches, bugs, and technical problems that accompany the introduction of any new technology. Clearly, there is still a lot of work that needs to be done to ensure that both technologies operate correctly with the vast majority of different computers and operating systems in use throughout Canada. The result? Keep in mind that things are pretty well experimental when it comes to the technology to support high-speed access to the Internet.

The Speed of Access Might Not Be as Fast as Promised

Initial stories describing cable modem access to the Internet boasted of network speeds up to "1,000 times faster than a regular modem." ADSL proponents talk of speeds 4,000 times faster. But industry observers have pointed out that, at least where cable modems are concerned, transmission speeds to the home will slow down when a lot of people get on-line at the same time. This makes us wonder what might happen if an entire neighborhood decides to use the Internet at once: the speed could really slow down dramatically. Reality? As cable modem technology evolves, the true speed will become apparent. We suggest you wait for the reality, rather than believe the glitz. We would suggest similar cautious optimism with respect to ADSL.

Deployment Could Be Expensive

Early in 1996 the cable company serving one of the authors of this book began to upgrade the cable infrastructure in his neighborhood. This wasn't to provide for Internet access; it was a basic upgrading of the cable system to support future channel expansion and other capabilities. Trucks spent about two weeks on the street, digging and lifting and filling as they placed a new cable line down the road. Then a new cable wire was brought up onto each lawn. It sat there for two months before another company came along to wire it into the homes on the street. Different companies came back at least three or four times to dig up the same holes on the same street.

What does this have to do with the Internet? Not much, really, except to point out that both telephone companies and cable companies face mammoth challenges in ensuring that their systems can support high-speed Internet access. Cable systems were designed to send data one way: into your home from the cable company. In order for Canadians to access the Internet through their cable networks, cable lines need to be upgraded to allow two-way communications. This is a difficult and expensive process. Talk to cable modem engineers, and they will tell you of the tremendous challenges that cable companies face in getting their cable networks to support high-speed Internet access. They will tell you of cable systems originally built to carry only television signals, systems where it does not matter if some data is dropped, since you won't really notice it on your TV screen. For example, if 2% of a TV signal is lost, it doesn't really matter much; the picture might be a wee bit fuzzy. If 10% is lost, it's fuzzier, but it still isn't that big a deal.

But you cannot afford to lose any data with a computer connection. Cable company engineers will tell you about the special technical challenges that arise in trying to ensure that the system can reliably carry data without any loss of that data. Also, the wiring both outside and inside the home has to be just perfect. Talk to telephone company engineers, and they will describe the enormous challenges pertaining to the true distance that ADSL modems can transmit before expensive upgrades are necessary.

And consider the state of the industries involved. Rogers Cable, for example, has a debt in excess of $4 billion, and other cable companies are in similar dire straits. Telephone companies are suffering from a new competitive world in which the cream, their long distance revenue, is under attack from long distance resellers, and are streamlining their operations and capital expenditures in order to stay competitive. Cash to upgrade their networks is scarce, but high-speed Internet access technology is quite expensive. Just look at ADSL. It reportedly costs the telephone company about $1,000 to equip a customer's telephone line with ADSL technology. Both industries face potential problems in upgrading their networks to support high-speed access to the Internet, and money simply does not grow on trees.

How far in the future are we talking? A spokesperson for cable modem maker Hewlett-Packard estimates that even by the year 2000, only 40% of the United States will be connected to a system that can handle two-way cable modems. We presume similar challenges exist in Canada.

Big Education Problems

Imagine this: a cable fellow comes to your house to install a cable wire. Kind of straightforward: string the wire, link it to a box on the side of the house, run some wire into the home, plug it into the TV, and voilà, cable television.

Now picture this. The same fellow comes to your house. He runs another wire off the outdoor box, into your home and near your computer. He puts in a cable modem and configures it for the proper TCP/IP settings. He figures out what type of TCP/IP stack you are already running on your computer and then diagnoses a problem between his system and yours. If you are not already running TCP/IP, he helps you figure out how to install it from your Windows or Macintosh setup disks. He then ensures that your system is configured for the proper Domain Name Server and that your Internet configuration is set up for "static IP addressing." He takes the time to ensure that your cable modem does not interfere with your current Ethernet card. Having done that, he tests the line and finds it doesn't work. He tries to diagnose the problem.

Don't worry if the paragraph above doesn't make sense to you; it is some of what might be involved for these folks to make the link work. Why do we tell you this future scenario? Staff of telephone and cable companies are going to have to master a very different skill set when it comes to learning how to implement the technology associated with high-speed Internet access. They are going to have to learn how to deal with customers who are impatient and skeptical, and who know little about the Internet. The cable trial that we referred to earlier in Alexandria, VA, was plagued by this problem. According to an article in *Cable World* about the project, "even in a town with high education levels and remarkably high computer penetration — an estimated 72%, twice the national average — the market is more diverse, complex and skeptical than initially imagined." Such training and upgrading of skills will not come easy; yet another reason to be skeptical over claims that we will have ubiquitous high-speed access to the Internet anytime soon.

We Are Skeptical

Do we sound skeptical about the whole issue of high-speed access to the Internet? The answer is an unequivocal, emphatic *yes*, not from the perspective of "will it work," *because we believe it will*, but from that of *when* it will work. We do not expect to see high-speed access to the Internet available on a broad basis across Canada any time soon.

We believe it will not be widely available for at least three years and that we will still be in the trial phase throughout much of 1997. We believe that when there are limited implementations within various neighborhoods, all kinds of unforeseen challenges and problems will emerge. And we really wonder if the rate of consumer adoption will be as fast as everyone says it will be.

Who Will Win?

Who will win the battle between the phone companies and the cable companies? We expect there will probably be a tie, and that in the long run the phone and cable companies will both establish healthy market shares.

What Does the Future Hold for Other Internet Service Providers?

We do not believe that the telephone and cable companies will spell the death of traditional Internet service providers, neither the large ones like iSTAR and NETCOM Canada nor the smaller independents. Eventually, it will be possible for non-cable companies to sell Internet access over cable, and non-telephone companies to sell Internet access using ADSL technology. In other words, in the long run the battle between Internet providers will not be about who can provide the fastest access, since all providers will eventually be on an equal playing field; it will be about who can provide the best and most reliable service.

ISDN Will Establish a Niche Market

We took a brief look at ISDN earlier in the chapter. ISDN is one of the methods that "average folks" can use to access the Internet at speeds higher than a standard telephone modem offers. It is actually a decade-old technology, long promoted by telephone companies, originally designed to let users talk on the phone at the same time they were sending or receiving data through a regular telephone line.

Designed with a top data speed of 128,000 bps (or four to five times faster than 28,800 bps modem), it never really took off. Many joked that ISDN really meant "I still don't," until the Internet came along. The Internet has provided a new market opportunity for ISDN-based products and services.

Since cable modems and other higher-speed technologies are slow in arriving to the home market, ISDN has emerged as a useful alternative for individuals with home offices and anyone who just wants faster access to the Internet. ISDN today provides access to the Internet at about four times the speed of a 28,800 bps modem. And for the business community, ISDN is a good technology for linking organizations to the Internet at a reasonable cost.

If you monitor the computer trade press, you will have probably read many horror stories about how difficult and painful ISDN can be to implement and install. During its early days, this was certainly true. Setting up ISDN access was a bit of a nightmare. Today it is much easier. Most major telephone companies across Canada can sell you an ISDN link to the Internet, and many Internet service providers are equipped to sell ISDN access as well. Recognizing that ISDN can be a complex technology, many of the organizations that sell ISDN access today have set up support teams that should, for the most part, make the process rather straightforward.

What Is Required to Use ISDN to Access the Internet?

- An ISDN line. The ISDN line is usually ordered directly from your telephone company. If you decide to use an Internet service provider other than your local telephone company, your provider can order the ISDN from the telephone company on your behalf. What is involved in bringing the ISDN line into your home or office? If you have a home office with only one telephone, not much at all. Since most home telephone wires support two lines, the ISDN line will just take up the second unused phone line. In that case, all the phone company has to do is install a special jack. Already have two lines used? Then the phone company will have to dig a little to get a new telephone wire into your home.
- An ISDN modem. The price for these special modems is dropping rapidly, such that they are now available for less than $700 and are often available for $450 or less. Some computer stores sell them, and sometimes you can purchase an ISDN modem directly from your Internet service provider.
- An account with an Internet service provider that supports ISDN. If your telephone company sells ISDN access to the Internet, then it can be your Internet service provider. Alternatively, you may be using another company for your access to the Internet. Some telephone companies will help you find a company in your area that sells ISDN access to the Internet. For example, Bell Canada, which provides telephone service in Ontario and Quebec, has set up a Web page (see below) to help residents of those two provinces find ISDN providers in their area:

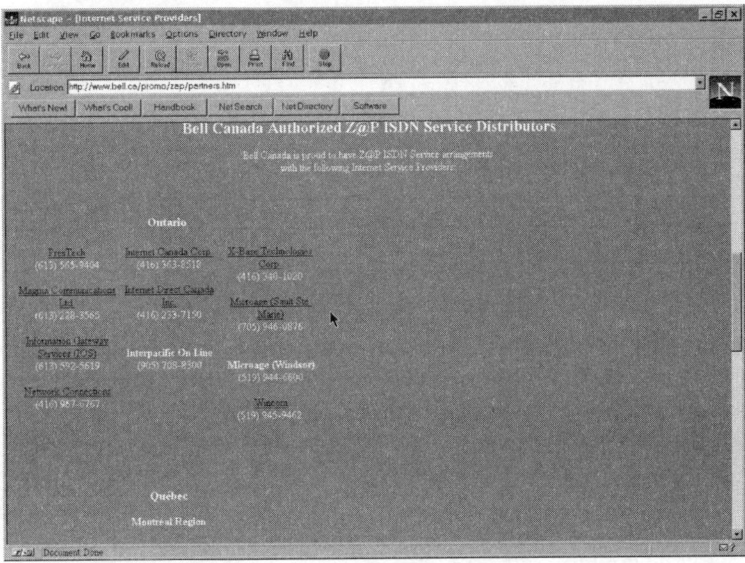

One of the authors of this book decided to try out ISDN. He offers a summary of his experience below.

I arranged with Bell Canada for an ISDN line for my home office and planned to try out both the Zyxel 2864IU and Motorola BitSURFR Pro ISDN modems.

The day came for the ISDN line installation, and the biggest problem encountered was that our home had been undergoing substantial renovations: the phone lines into the home (four of them) were not yet wired properly; the electrician had not yet completed the job. This meant that the telephone service fellow ended up doing that work on the electrician's behalf, something rather unexpected for him. But other than that hiccup (which was no fault of the phone company), the installation of the ISDN line was no problem.

We tried out the Zyxel modem first. Physically installing the Zyxel ISDN modem was as simple as installing any other modem; you simply plug it in and turn it on. Trying to configure it, however, I found myself dealing in a new world of ISDN technology and terminology, with phrases like SPIDs and switch types and other new stuff added to my vocabulary. However, that proved no problem. We just called the Bell ISDN support centre, who walked us through the installation and configuration software. There were a few minor things we discovered along the way, things that we probably could not have easily figured out on our own, but that's why the support centre is there. Soon we were on-line.

We then tried the Motorola BitSURFR Pro modem; having installed another ISDN modem, this one actually took less than 10 minutes to get working. Once again, we made a call to Bell to go through the configuration, but why not? They know their stuff, and it meant we didn't have to waste time.

Both modems brought us up to speeds of 115,200 baud. After using a 28,8 modem for a few years, this was remarkable: Web pages loaded much quicker than before, and some graphics jumped onto the page. It must be said, however, that there are still inevitable delays here and there, as you wait to get to sites that must obviously be busy. We presume you will encounter this regardless of how fast a link you have to the Internet.

There are some other comments that should be made. First, rely on help from your ISP and the technical folks at the phone company as much as you can. The folks who helped us, in particular, one Paul Danis at the Sympatico Member Services group, were extremely familiar with both modems and were able to quickly walk us through, step by step, the configuration of each modem. And when we did encounter a unique or unknown problem, they quickly brought on a technical contact from the modem vendor, who also walked through the steps to solve the problem.

> You can figure it out yourself, perhaps, but even opening the manual for an ISDN modem might be a bit intimidating. Fortunately, with the level of ISDN expertise at the telephone company and the ISP, you can usually get rolling very quickly and not have to look at it at all.
>
> All in all, we were rather positive about the whole experience. The result? Truly a painless exercise, and nothing like the horror stories that you read in the computer press.

What Does ISDN Cost?

There are several elements:

- An installation charge. The installation charge can be as high as a $100 or more. It is levied by the telephone company as a one-time fee. Many companies, however, are waiving this installation charge as a promotional tool.
- An ISDN use charge. There are two types of charges: residential and business. Residential rates consist of a base fee: $40 to $60 per month, plus about $1 to $1.50 an hour for use. Corporate rates are usually $90 to $100 per month, flat rate. Rates are lower on evenings and weekends.
- A charge for your Internet account. This is the fee that you pay to your Internet service provider for your Internet account. If you are already on the Internet, you can get an idea of what the cost might be by visiting the Web pages of Internet providers in your area. For example, here is the ISDN rate sheet for Magma Communications Limited, an Internet service provider located in Ottawa (**http://www.magmacom.com**):

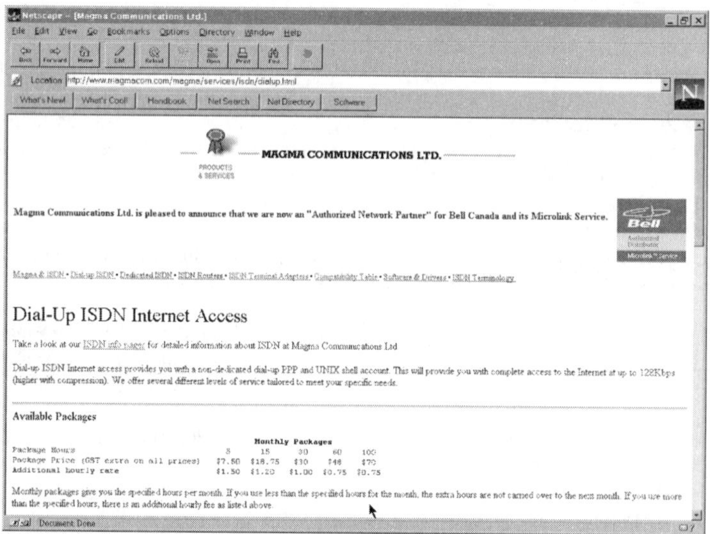

ISDN is not cheap. You have to spend a lot more than you would for a normal dial-up account, which typically runs in the neighborhood of $0.50 per hour, or $20 to $30 per month. On the other hand, you do get to enjoy and use the Internet at a speed at least four times higher. This will no doubt change the way in which you use the Internet. ISDN is not for everyone, but for those who can justify its cost, it is a good alternative that can provide relatively fast access to the Internet while we wait, patiently, for even higher access speeds.

Trend 8: Convergence

How will the Canadian government's new Convergence Policy affect the Internet industry? No one is really sure. In August 1996 the federal government approved a policy that will allow cable companies to provide local telephone service, and telephone companies to provide cable television service. It's called the "Convergence Policy." While the new policy takes effect immediately, the impact will probably not be felt in Canada until at least 1998. The immediate question the policy raises among Canadian Internet users is this: "Does this mean I will be able to use a cable modem to access the Internet through my local telephone company?" Many analysts believe that telephone companies will stick with the ADSL technology they are developing (described above) to deliver Internet services and television services rather than invest in cable, which is expensive to implement.

This new policy means that one day you will be able to buy your Internet services, telephone services, and cable services from the same company. You will not have to use one company for your Internet service, a different company for your cable television service, and yet another company for your telephone service. You will be able to choose which company you want to deal with for all your information services: the telephone company or the cable company. Of course, you will not be forced to purchase all your services from the same company. For example, you could choose to have your cable company provide your telephone service and your telephone company provide your cable service.

Many have suggested that the Convergence Policy will lead to the cable and telephone companies providing new services such as home shopping, interactive video games, video on demand, and home banking. However, it is very possible that in the long run most or all of these services will be provided over the Internet. The telephone and cable companies, therefore, will not act as content providers. Instead, they will provide a gateway between your home and the Internet, where you can purchase the services from any organization you choose.

Finally, the federal government is arguing that because convergence will increase competition among telephone and cable companies, it will lower prices for consumers. This should mean lower prices for high-speed Internet services in the future.

Trend 9: Microsoft Will Have a Major Impact on the Internet

Enough said. When the chairman of the world's largest company states that the company plans to make the Internet central to its future, its aims and objectives are clear to everyone.

Summary

As a closing comment we observe what is obvious to many: there is a lot of hype that surrounds the future potential of the Internet, and there are dramatic changes occurring to its landscape. As a result, as you deal with the network and read about its future, we would caution you to always have what we call "healthy skepticism." The Internet industry has become a marketing and public relations battleground, and reality does not always rule the roost.

CHAPTER 21

We Need to Protect the Internet

As the most participatory form of mass speech yet developed, the Internet deserves the highest protection from governmental intrusion.

Judge Stewart Dalzell, in The United States District Court For The Eastern District Of Pennsylvania, June 11, 1996

Like an octopus on steroids, the Internet has grown around the world, posing dilemmas for governments who want to participate in the international economy but still control the flow of information to their citizens.

Inter-Press Service, April 23, 1996

A free society needs a free Internet.

Jeffrey Shallit, Cofounder, Electronic Frontier Canada, **http://www.efc.ca**

It is often said that people do not understand all the fuss about freedom of speech issues until their freedom of speech is taken away. So it is with the Internet. Despite all the hype and hyperbole, the Internet is a unique development in human history that we all must work hard to protect. And it is so important that we must choose to do battle with those who purport to control it.

A battle rages worldwide for control of cyberspace, a battle being fought between government authorities and the denizens of the on-line world. The battle is cloaked in phrases such as "censorship" and "regulation," but make no mistake about it, worldwide, the Internet is faced with a bleak future should these efforts bear fruit. Why? Because the ill-conceived efforts and the ignorance of the people behind many of these efforts will make it illegal for you to do on the Internet what it is already legal for you to do in the "real world." An Internet double standard is emerging: we may have fewer freedoms on-line than we enjoy in our everyday lives.

The Challenge of the Internet

There is no doubt that the Internet presents society with some tremendous challenges; most are aware of this by now. It is well known that there is pornography, bomb-making instructions, and hate literature found on-line. Offensive content on the Internet has become as real as it is already in our real world. Many are revolted by what is available. And clearly, politicians, governments, and law enforcement officials are trying to deal with those challenges, in many cases by passing laws that make illegal certain activities on-line. The problem is that in their rush to deal with those challenges, they are sweeping under the rug many of the fundamental freedoms that we already enjoy. That is a dangerous truth.

So we have a choice before us: we can ensure that cyberspace is based upon the fundamental democratic freedoms that we all enjoy in the real world, or we can choose to let it become a cold and lifeless world subject to the most base form of authoritative control in which others do your thinking for you. We can let cyberspace enjoy the same rule of law as guides our everyday lives in the real world, or let it become subject to a new set of laws, far more restrictive on our freedoms than in the real world. It is a stark choice, and we think you should understand why the issue is so important. So it is fitting to close this book with this topic, given the profile that the topic of regulating the Internet took on in 1996.

Our Attitude to Free Speech On-line

We start by saying that the two authors of this book are not a couple of bleeding-heart liberal-hippy-freak-peaceniks. Far from it. We might consider ourselves to be from the middle-of-the-road side of the conservative spectrum. But when it comes to the Internet, we agree with Judge Dalzell that "the Internet deserves the highest protection from government intrusion." Our backgrounds are probably typical of many of those throughout the Internet who are fighting to prevent it from unwarranted control. And we passionately believe that the Canadian government, or any government authority, has no right to control what we think, what we say, and what we do on the Internet, just as it has no right to control our minds, our thoughts, and our beliefs in the real world. We do not believe that freedom of expression on the Internet should follow any special standard that is not applicable in the real world. We believe that the laws of Canada must be applied equally to the real world and to the Internet and that special laws to deal with the Internet are therefore not required.

Let us explain why and help you understand why we believe that all Canadians must stand up to preserve their fundamental freedoms on-line. But before we start, keep in mind that one of the problems with the topic of freedom of speech on the Internet is that it is often so difficult

WE NEED TO PROTECT THE INTERNET

1. As the Internet takes on a role throughout society, it is raising many difficult freedom-of-speech issues.
2. The Internet is under attack from governments worldwide, many of which are concerned that it permits too free a flow of information.
3. In many attempts to regulate the Internet worldwide, governments are placing more restrictions on freedom of speech on the Internet than exist in the "real world."
4. Governments often end up being exposed as impotent, when their attempts to crack down on the Internet by regulating it are unsuccessful.
5. Canadian government officials and politicians should take more time to understand the Internet as they attempt to deal with the difficult problems it represents.
6. Efforts by individuals or organizations such as Ken McVay and Electronic Frontier Canada are good examples of how to deal with the difficult challenges the Internet presents to society.
7. There is a growing recognition worldwide that in many ways, the Internet has become its own global nation state.

to strike up the moral courage to take part. Become involved with the issue and speak out, and you will find yourself backed into a corner by your opponents, who accuse you of defending child pornography and other ills. It is too easy for your opponents to drag out those bug-a-boos and twist their usage in order to try to make you lose the argument.

As you become involved in the issue, recognize that proponents of free speech on the Internet are not out to defend child pornography, hate literature, and instructions on how to build bombs. Most are sickened and repulsed by the offensive content found on the Internet. What they are defending is maintenance in the virtual world of cyberspace of the basic human rights that we enjoy in the real world.

Free speech on the Internet proponents do not want to wake up one day in the future to find that our fundamental human rights and freedoms have been taken away.

The Internet Is Under Attack

Worldwide, the Internet is under attack. Government woke up to the reality of the Internet in 1994, and for various reasons in various countries, efforts are underway to control what occurs on-line. Throughout 1996 governments targeted the Internet. Let's look at some of their efforts.

Singapore

In Singapore measures were announced that allowed the country to regulate "political and religious content" on the Internet. As part of the policy all Internet service providers in the country must register with the Singapore Broadcast Authority (SBA). Any organization that wants to publish political or religious information on-line must also register with the SBA. In a rather chilling statement a senior government official had this to say about expressing yourself on the Internet: "In our society, you can state your views, but they have to be correct."

In one of the first applications of Singapore's Internet laws, the government censored a posting that criticized a local law firm. The posting was made to a USENET newsgroup and complained about the quality of service provided by the firm. The SBA claimed that the contents of the message were defamatory in nature and were harmful to the reputation of the law firm.

It is bad enough that the government finds it necessary to control the political thought of its citizens — it is well known that Singapore is not a democratic country by any stretch of the imagination — but do citizens really want their government to control their expression of opinion? And think about how quickly Singapore moved from regulating "political and religious content" to a form of regulation over the ideas expressed by people.

South Korea: The Canadian Connection

North and South Korea have been technically at war since the early 1950s. Under South Korean law it is a serious offense to "manufacture, import, copy, possess or distribute data that can benefit, eulogize or encourage the enemy." And in 1996 this came to cover materials that reside on the Internet. South Korean government officials announced that citizens who access or publish Web pages about North Korea are considered to be committing a crime, even if those Web pages are located elsewhere in the world.

How did this come about? There is a Canadian connection, actually: David Burgess, a political science major at the University of Saskatchewan in Saskatoon, is a normal kid with no particular political agenda. He visited North Korea and obtained a number of pamphlets that he later put up on his Web site to "give curious outsiders a view inside the secluded state," according to the Associated Press.

Whoah! He soon found himself in the middle of an international incident. As the Associated Press reported, "for a Canadian university student, creating an Internet site on North Korea was simply opening a small library on the reclusive nation. For South Korean authorities, it was threat to national security. Last week, South Korea declared David Burgess' World Wide Web site subversive and ordered 14 local computer networks with Internet links to block public access to it." Burgess' Web page included, among other things, a portrait of the North Korean leader, Kim Jong Il. A subversive! In Saskatchewan! Will wonders never cease!

What happened to David Burgess? He eventually took the Web page down and refuses to speak to anyone. After all, as he said, he's just an average kid who will be looking for a job one day and does not want a potential employer to consider him a subversive.

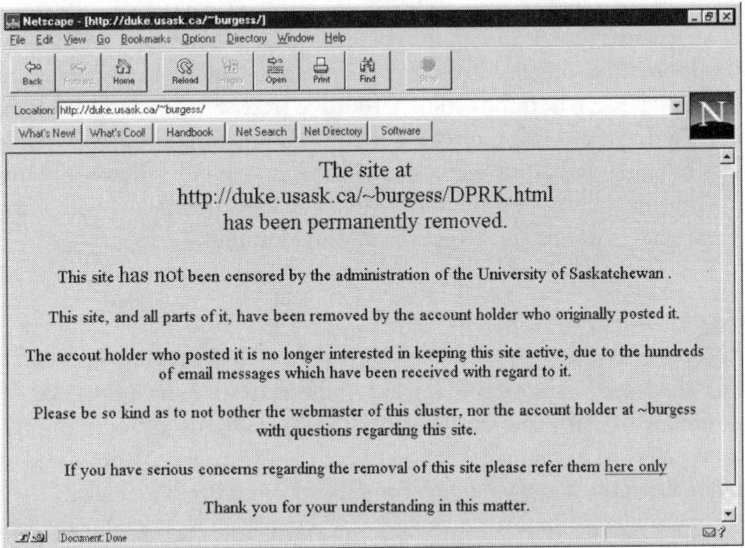

The situation is even more bizarre when you consider what is really happening here. South Korea criticizes North Korea because it is a totalitarian regime, well known for the fact that it controls the thoughts and actions of its citizens. After all, it is one of the last countries still under the Communist ideology. But then South Korea turns around and decides to control the thoughts and actions of its citizens by restricting the information they access?

Germany

In 1996 the German government tried to ban its citizens from accessing Holocaust-revisionist documents stored on a World Wide Web site in Santa Cruz, CA, by ordering Internet service providers to block access to that site. Free speech advocates worldwide responded to this censorship by duplicating the information on other Web sites around the world, making it impossible for German authorities to control access to the information without shutting down access to the Internet in Germany. Within days, German authorities came to realize the technical futility of their attempt to control cyberspace but announced they would continue to try to deal with the challenges that it represents.

Vietnam

The Vietnamese government banned access to the Internet by individuals and announced that Internet service providers in the country will be subject to government monitoring of Internet traffic. The regulations prohibit "data that can affect national security, social order, and safety or information that is not appropriate to the culture, morality, and traditional customs of the Vietnamese people." The government is particularly concerned that citizens will have access to foreign Web sites that criticize the country's government.

China

Internet users are required to register with the police and sign an agreement promising not to harm the country or do anything illegal. As part of the regulations Internet subscribers are prohibited from transmitting state secrets, information harmful to state security, and pornography.

Jeff Smith, President of Bridge to Asia, a non-profit organization that is trying to connect Internet users in China and Southeast Asia, had this to say in response to China's actions: "Censorship? There probably will be, but it's like trying to stop the wind...it will chill Internet use, but those who are clever will be able to get the information they want."

United States

The State of Connecticut passed a law that makes it illegal to send any message on-line "with intent to harass, annoy or alarm another person." The law is vague at best. We presume that if you sent an e-mail message to your next-door neighbor that "space aliens have landed on your front lawn" you might alarm them and would be committing an indictable offense.

The State of Georgia passed a law making it illegal to place a registered trademark or logo on a Web page. Critics argue that the law is confusing and is open to varying interpretations. For example, opponents of the law argue that it would be illegal to create a link to another Web page if the link mentioned a trademarked company's name.

Mitchell Kaye, a member of the U.S. House of Representatives, had this to say about the law: "When you have a bunch of politicians that don't understand technology and are afraid of it, they try and pass a law to solve a problem that doesn't exist and it really sends a very dangerous message to the rest of the world that Georgia doesn't understand and is inhospitable to technology."

Canada

After the TWA crash and Olympic bombings in 1996, Lloyd Axworthy, the Minister of External Affairs, announced that Canada would work with other G7 countries to try to deal with the perceived problem of terrorists using the Internet to exchange hate literature and share bomb-making instructions.

Problems With Current Government Actions

In their rush to deal with some of the very difficult challenges posed by the Internet, many governments are taking actions that have far-reaching consequences. Consider some of the issues we raise below.

- Governments are passing laws that violate the fundamental democratic freedoms that we enjoy in the real world. Few would argue against government efforts to try to deal with the difficult problem of child pornography on-line. In fact, most of us are as repulsed as is government by some of what goes on with the Internet. But as many governments try to deal with the challenges presented, they end up sweeping many basic human rights under the rug. For example, the *U.S. Communications Decency Act*, rushed through Congress to try to deal with child pornography on-line, had the sweeping effect of making any discussion of sexual issues on the Internet illegal. You could say "I enjoy sexual intercourse" in the real world, but it is illegal to say this on the Internet. That is a double standard, and it is typical of so many of laws passed and proposed. These types of issues on the Internet need be treated no differently than they are in the real world.
- Governments are using Internet laws to stifle political thought and other forms of expression. You should always keep in mind that freedom of expression, and democracy itself, is always at the top of a slippery slope that leads to extinction and is only prevented from sliding down by the concerted efforts of concerned citizens. Singapore is a good example of the misuse of laws and regulations originally put in place for one purpose and then used for another. Their law to attempt to deal with child pornography on-line is now being used to stifle honest political expression or opinion. You cannot, it seems, make a negative comment about lawyers in Singapore on the Internet. Was that the intent of the law? Probably not. Is it being used that way? It sure is.

  Could this situation happen in Canada? Many think not. But what happens if, one day in the future, an extreme right-wing government is elected? They find this useful little law that is so vague it can be used for anything, including their own objective of stifling political thought. The only way to ensure that a law is not misused is not to pass the law in the first place.
- Governments are passing vague laws that are too sweeping in nature. Many of the proposed Internet laws are so vague that they are almost laughable. The idiocy of the *U.S. Communications Decency Act* is that the wording is so vague that it is clearly in violation of the U.S. Constitution. The effort in Georgia to deal with copyright and trademark violations on the World Wide Web has had the effect of making it illegal to put up links to other Web pages, according to some critics. Other idiotic situations abound.

  Clearly, in dealing with the Internet, we need some intelligence and thought by our government leaders. Sadly, in their rush to deal with the challenge of the Internet, bad decisions are being made, and fundamental human rights are being breached. The problem is made worse by an atmosphere of distrust and disbelief, and many on the Internet are skeptical about the intent of government and lawmakers.

- By limiting Internet access, governments also limit economic growth. As the Internet becomes an important backbone for global commerce, Asian countries like China, Vietnam, and Singapore will face some difficult decisions. Their economies are heavily based on exports, and increasingly they will depend upon external telecommunications links to their trading partners in order to compete effectively with other export-dependent countries. Many nations are quickly beginning to realize that by limiting their citizens' access to the Internet, they are also stifling the growth of their own economies.

- Governments are trying to pass laws in an environment of distrust. It is painfully evident that many people in today's generation have little trust for politicians and a lessened respect for government authority. It is no wonder. The actions of many politicians give us little basis for trust. ("I will resign if we do not cancel the GST.") People have come to realize that politicians will respond to the heat of the political moment and will twist their morals and sensibilities to do whatever it takes to stay in power.

  Distrust is already occurring with attempts to regulate the Internet because of sleazy and reprehensible behavior by some politicians. One relatively unknown impact of the infamous *U.S. Communications Decency Act*, which was ruled to be unconstitutional, is that a canny senator slipped in wording that made it illegal for anyone to talk about abortion on the Internet. And in a court case launched within minutes of the bill being signed into law, a U.S. government official immediately commented that indeed, the provision violated the U.S. Constitution. But the U.S. Justice Department then went on to say, in effect, "let us leave the provision in place. We promise we won't use it." Obviously, abortion groups and freedom of speech advocates believe that such trust is unwarranted and proceeded to ensure that the provision was declared unconstitutional by the courts. After all, why should they trust these people?

  In the ongoing debate about regulation of cyberspace, politicians and bureaucrats will often acknowledge that while the laws they are rushing to pass might have the unwanted effect of restricting fundamental democratic freedoms, we should just trust them, "since that is not our intent to use the provision." But individuals fighting for our democratic freedom point out that such trust is unwarranted. What if a right-wing administration is voted into power and decides to use the provisions found in a bill to control the expression of political thought on-line?

  And today's generation, growing up in a mess of a world created for them by the baby-boom generation, often has little respect for political authority. They do not trust — and often rightly so — political leaders and bear a cynicism previously unseen in this country and around the world. How can they have any respect for governments trying to control the flow of information about bombs on the Internet, when those same governments are responsible for the sale of arms and the subsidization of arms industries worldwide, resulting in the death and destruction of countless innocent people worldwide? They have little trust in the government leaders who purport to represent them and have no plan to give them their trust. They are ever-vigilant and proud defenders of their own human rights. They are proud and staunch defenders of the Internet — their Internet — and have no intent of letting anyone, particularly untrustworthy politicians, take it away from them.

- Government officials are passing laws without understanding what they are trying to do. It is also evident that lawmakers often have little knowledge of the technology that they are trying to restrict. In Georgia, House of Representatives member Don Parsons, who introduced the "Net Police Law," has never been on the Internet: "During floor debate, Rep. Parsons could not explain the concept of a link on a home page. It was clear to many that he had no idea of what the Internet was all about. Supposedly, his desire was to prevent 'misrepresentation' on the Internet. Parsons admitted that he had never been on the Internet, except looking over a colleague's shoulder at work" (**http://www.clark.net/pub/rothman/ga.htm**).

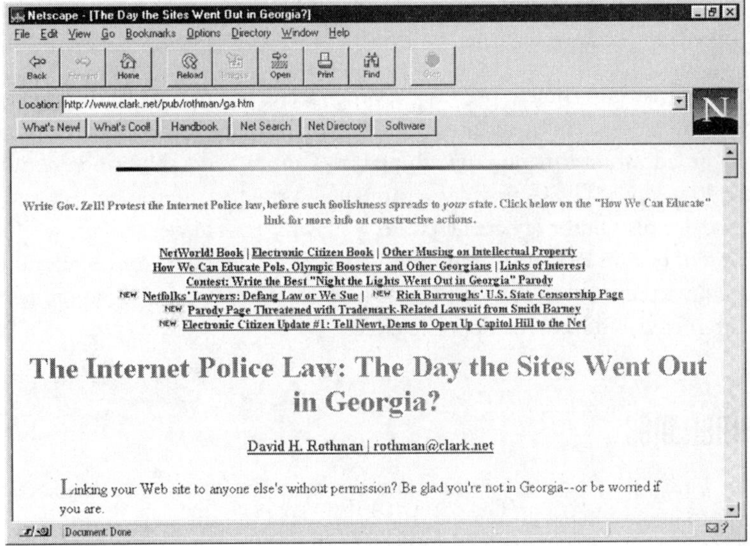

And it is a well-known fact that when the *U.S. Communications Decency Act* was passed, few members of Congress had actually used the Internet or had ever been exposed to it. Their understanding of the Internet was often limited to fraudulent reporting such as that found within an infamous *Time* magazine article on "Cyberporn," an article that was so obviously inaccurate that *Time* recanted the article within several weeks.

> Visit the authors' Web site at **http://www.handbook.com**. In it you can find the chapter "Fraud and Dishonesty" from our 1996 *Canadian Internet Handbook*, in which we discuss how the media has twisted reporting of the Internet to serve its own particular purpose. It goes into detail on the infamous *Time* magazine situation described above.

The problem is that these staunch defenders of public morals often have no knowledge or experience with what they are trying to regulate, something like flying a plane with no experience as a pilot.

The Futility of Control

Finally, it is evident that there are still some people who believe that regulation of the Internet is truly possible on a technical level. The reality, plain and simple for everyone to see, is that it is not. In the words of one Asian diplomat, "Even if the government can develop a screening process, technology will always catch up with ways to get around it." Worldwide we are seeing people dedicate themselves to the cause of helping government authority understand the futility of their actions. Consider some examples.

Germany

When the German government pressured CompuServe, one of the world's largest commercial online services, to block access to certain controversial newsgroups, individuals around the world immediately broadcast information describing how CompuServe subscribers could bypass the ban in a mere 30 seconds. The German government also tried to shut down access to the Web site of Ernst Zundel, a distributor of hate literature. Following that move, activists worldwide posted the entire content of Zundel's site to multiple Web sites worldwide. Not because they believe in his words and his actions, but to show the German government that their action to restrict information on the Internet would have the opposite effect.

The Netherlands

When the Dutch government pressured the owners of a Web site, which hosted information for a terrorist, to remove that information, the contents of the site were "spirited across the border" to be hosted on a computer in Germany. The result? It became evident to many that the technology of the Internet is such that data can be shared throughout the global Internet in a microsecond — and always will be months and years ahead of the ability of government to control it.

France

François Fillon, France's Minister for Information Technology, said during a parliamentary debate that France would seek international rules to govern global computer networks like the Internet. This announcement followed a French court decision that banned a book called *Le Grand Secret* (The Big Secret), which described former French President François Mitterrand's battle with cancer. The book was written by Mitterrand's personal doctor. Following the court's decision, an activist posted the entire book on the Internet, where it was immediately accessible to French citizens and others around the world. Within a week it was reported that 12,000 copies of the manuscript were downloaded by Internet users worldwide.

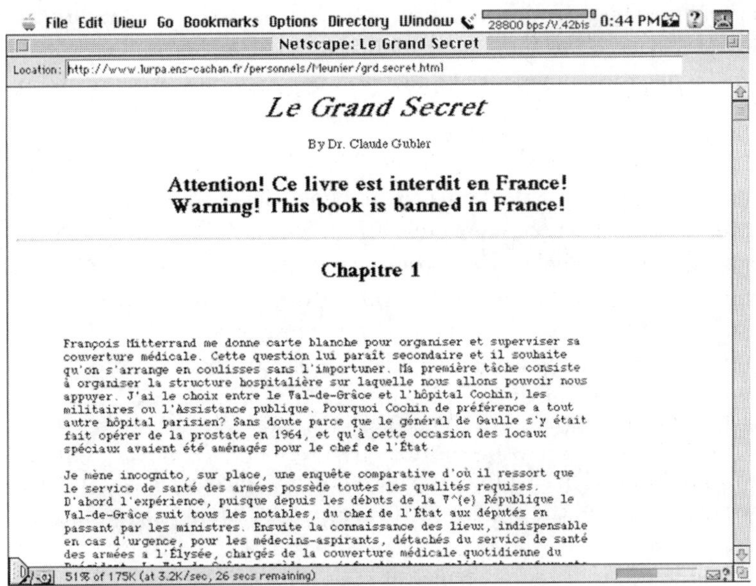

And when the French government tried to shut down the Web site containing the book, it was immediately reposted to many other Web servers worldwide. The Internet is a multiheaded dragon; slay one, and seven new heads pop up.

The Unreality of Control

Every time we hear talk of the need to regulate the Internet, we form in our minds an image: it is 1450, and a number of distinguished gentlemen, the government authorities of the day, are sitting around a table trying to figure out how to ban the printing press. After all, it will let people access information directly. It will make words and knowledge more widely available. They did not succeed then, and their counterparts likely will not succeed now. For in effect, trying to control the flow of information on the Internet is like trying to stop people from using paper.

And every time the "regulate the Internet" clarion cry is made, we half hope that we will see a law first passed in Parliament to control content on the Internet, and a second law passed immediately after that outlaws winter in Canada. Passing such laws together makes sense, since they have an equal chance of being enforced.

When will these folks realize that the Internet is the paper of the twenty-first century and that just as it was impossible to prevent the explosion of words that followed the invention of the printing press and paper, that it will be impossible to control the flow of information on the Internet? It is impossible to outlaw winter, and it is impossible to control the Internet.

Some Recommendations

When it comes to the difficult challenges in dealing with the Internet, several issues must be considered.

- Technology, not legislation, is the solution. In Chapter17 we examined many of the programs that are emerging to deal with offensive content on-line. We must admit, before trying these programs out, that we were skeptical of what they could do. Having worked with them, we remain convinced that the challenges posed by the Internet can only be dealt with by technology and that laws will have no effect.
- Legislators, law enforcement officials, and politicians must understand the technology of the Web. We need more geeks on Parliament Hill! And we must do our best to ensure that existing politicians become computer geeks. They need to be on-line and must use the technology first-hand to understand why their legislation will be impotent. They must surf the Net and understand its global persona. They must learn from the many examples available of how futile attempts at control have been. They must recognize that the Internet is a global organism, one that cannot be subject to any form of legislative control. They must recognize reality.
- We must use existing laws to deal with Internet challenges. There should not be one law for the Internet and another for the real world. Child pornography is illegal in Canada; a law to deal with the problem already exists. Special laws are not needed. What is needed is education: police officials need the mandate, the budget, and the training to upgrade their skills to deal with the new challenges in trying to deal with the Internet.

Canadian Groups That Need Recognition

And finally, all Canadians must support those who fight for their fundamental electronic freedoms and who recognize the way to deal with the significant challenge posed by the Internet. We believe that many politicians, governments, and law enforcement officials twist their words, misstate facts, and obscure the truth in their quest to deal with the challenges that the Internet represents. In other cases other politicians struggle to deal with the very serious problems found on the Internet, but lack a basic understanding of its fundamentals and hence are unable to appreciate the futility of their proposals.

On the other side of the spectrum are average individuals, people who passionately believe that we must ensure that the fundamental freedoms we already enjoy are available to us on-line or who are fighting their own lonely battle against those who misuse the Internet. It is important that you understand who these people are and what they are fighting for.

Nizkor Project/Ken McVay

Often lost in all the hype about regulation of the Internet are the efforts of a chap named Ken McVay. But we are such believers in his efforts that we believe he should be nominated for the Order of Canada; he has already been awarded the Order of British Columbia. Visit the Web page of the Nizkor project, the fruit of Ken's activities, at **http://www.nizkor.org/**, and read the dedication at the top of the screen:

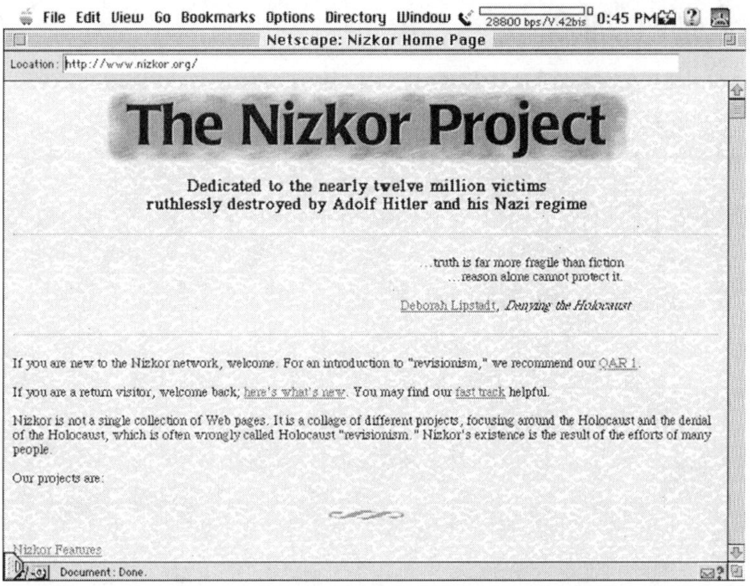

Who is Ken McVay, and what is he all about? He is a simple chap who lives on Vancouver Island and for various reasons has decided to use the Internet to fight those who distribute information that suggests the Holocaust never happened. As he states on his home page, "Ken McVay is a retired 55-year-old Vancouver Island man who has been one of the leaders in developing and carrying out community based and grass roots strategies for countering the lies of those promoting hatred on the Internet."

With the Nizkor project it is his stated goal to expose the fallacy of the arguments made by Holocaust deniers, white supremacists, and anti-Semites. It is McVay's objective to expose those who distribute their filth on the Internet by using a simple tactic: printing the truth. The result? The Nizkor archives are the largest site of information on the Internet about the reality of the Holocaust and serve to provide factual information that exposes the falsehoods in the information distributed by Holocaust deniers.

McVay fights relentlessly on-line: debating skinheads, neo-Nazis, and other ilk, or by publishing information that discounts what they say. His philosophy is best stated on-line on a Web page that summarizes the goals and objectives of the project: "The way to combat noxious ideas is with other ideas. The way to combat falsehoods is with truth."

His conclusion is that in this new and wired world, it will be impossible to control the flow of information on-line and that it is inevitable that these people will use the Net to distribute their lies. And since the views of these people are repulsive to him and many others, he is approaching the issue not by issuing a cry for control and regulation of the Internet — an impossibility at best — but to fight information with information.

Given his tireless efforts in the face of adversity — he has been threatened, as you might expect, with death several times — we believe that he deserves recognition and deserves to be held up as a role model for all Canadians on how to deal with the challenges posed by this new and difficult world in which we live. We strongly suggest that you visit the Nizkor archives and consider donating to the congregation that currently accepts donations to help defray the cost of his efforts.

Electronic Frontier Canada

Electronic Frontier Canada, at **http://www.efc.ca**, is an organization that deserves recognition, respect, and funding:

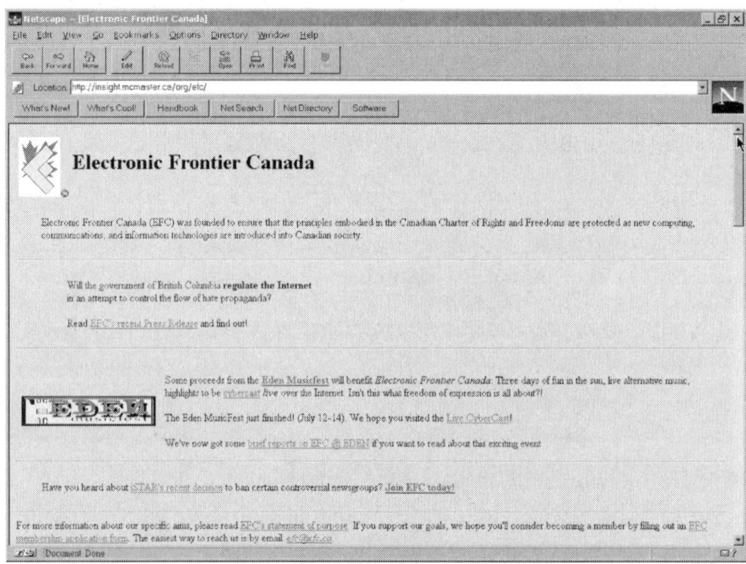

We believe in their efforts so much that we encourage you to become a member and make a donation to assist them with their efforts. They are one of the few groups in Canada working to ensure that you can, in the future, say on the Internet what you have the right to say in your backyard. Electronic Frontier Canada's goal is simple: "Electronic Frontier Canada (EFC) was founded to ensure that the principles embodied in the Canadian Charter of Rights and Freedoms are protected as new computing, communications, and information technologies emerge."

EFC is fighting to ensure that Canadians are aware that many of the proposals emerging in the effort to control and regulate content and information on the Internet make illegal things that are legal in the real world. For example, information available on the Internet on building a bomb would be illegal, but purchasing a copy of the book *The Anarchist's Handbook*, which also contains detailed information about pipe bombs and is available at your local bookstore, would not. Accessing a picture of a Playboy Playmate on-line is illegal under the *U.S. Communications Decency Act*, but it is still legal to buy it in your local corner store.

Jeffrey Shallit, one of the founders, gave a speech entitled "The Real Meaning of Free Speech in Cyberspace" at an Internet conference in which he commented on the absurdity of efforts to regulate and deal with content on the Internet (you can find a copy of the speech at the EFC Web site). In discussing how the University of Waterloo decided to ban certain USENET newsgroups about sexual acts and containing sexual pictures, he noted that a double standard seemed to apply, in that the information they tried to ban on-line was not banned in the real world. His observation? "...the University of Waterloo library carries the book *Caught Looking: Feminism, Pornography, and Censorship*, which contains explicit scenes of sex and bondage. And, at the time of the ban, the UW bookstore openly sold Celeste T. Paul's book *Women's Erotic Dreams*, which contains explicit descriptions of sex with children and animals."

Through the EFC Web site you can read of their efforts in dealing with the many emerging Canadian regulatory, political, and legal issues. And it is a good place to understand the absurdity of how many things on the Internet are dealt with. You must, for example, read the story about the Edmonton Fruitabomber. Finally, take a look at their Freedom of Expression Links list, which will help you explore the many other Web sites on-line, both Canadian and otherwise, dealing with the Internet regulation issue.

Other Groups in Canada and Beyond

Here are more groups and sites that deserve your attention and support:

- For a legal spin on freedom of speech issues, visit The Legal Group For The Internet In Canada (LoGIC) at **http://www.io.org/~logic/**:

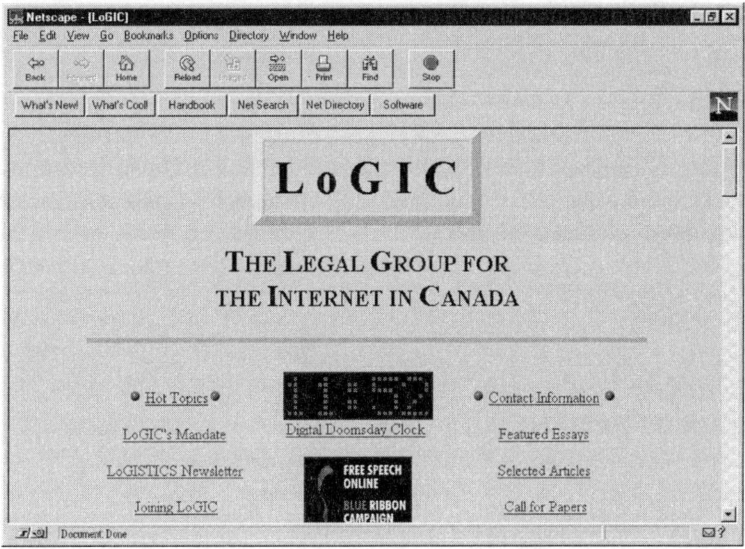

- Visit PEN Canada (**http://www.pencanada.ca**). With past presidents as notable as Margaret Atwood and June Callwood, the organization "works on behalf of writers, at home and abroad, who have been forced into silence for writing the truth as they see it. Our Centre has 30 honorary members in 17 countries around the world on whose behalf we work so that their voices can be heard once again." It is a good place to get an overview of issues of censorship in Canada beyond the Internet:

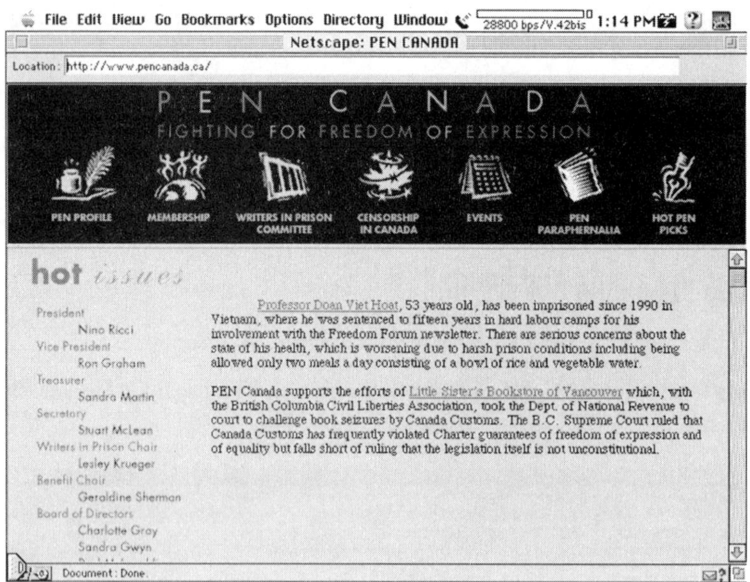

- Read the document "Illegal And Offensive Content On The Information Highway," a background paper released by Industry Canada (**http://insight.mcmaster.ca/org/efc/pages/doc/offensive.html#GS29**). It is an excellent overview of the nature of the problem posed by the Internet and the challenges in trying to deal with those problems.
- Visit the Web site for the American Civil Liberties Union's Freedom Network (**http://www.aclu.org**). The ACLU is very active is protecting and promoting free speech on the Internet. Their Web site contains a biweekly update on the organization's Internet activities:

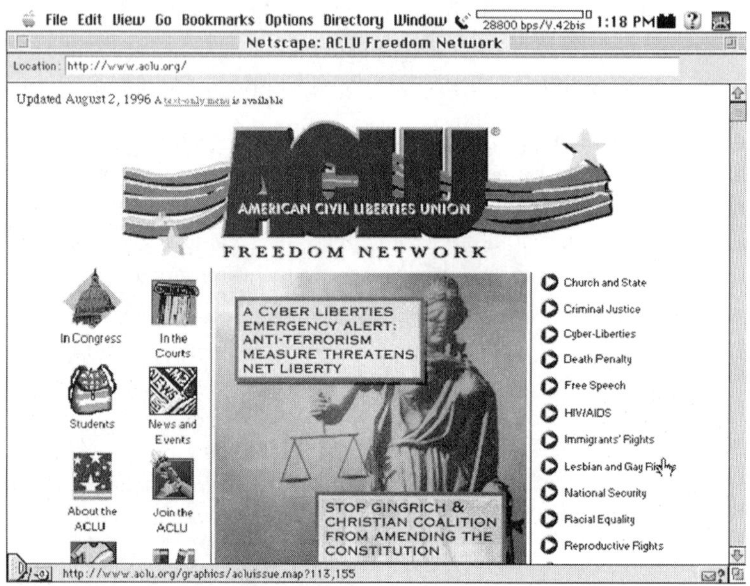

- The Electronic Frontier Foundation (**http://www.eff.org**) is the U.S. counterpart to Electronic Frontier Canada. EFF's Web site contains information about free speech, privacy, and intellectual property issues that pertain to the Internet:

The Internet Nation-State

To close this book, we will make the comment that the most unique thing about the Internet is that it does transcend national borders and makes them largely irrelevant. We are rushing into a new world, one in which all our concepts of law are breaking down, whether the law has to do with copyright and intellectual property or whether it involves offensive content. What is also unique about the Internet is that for the first time in the human experience, people are choosing to bind themselves together not by physical geography, cultural background, or language, but by a more basic human trait: their interests.

Journey into USENET, and you will find a nation of cat lovers, people worldwide who share an interest in cats. You will discover blacksmiths who are working to preserve this lost art. You will come across game show enthusiasts and individuals whose passion in life happens to be gardening — collections of individuals from around the world who share an interest in a topic.

The ultimate impact of the Internet? We are seeing the emergence of millions of tiny electronic nation-states, each with its own unique culture, rules, and attitudes. Global communities that are based not on their physical location or language or culture, but on personal interests. These tiny nation-states are establishing, and will continue to establish, their own laws, their own rules, and their own regulations.

The ultimate impact of the Internet? John Perry Barlow, a cofounder of the Electronic Frontier Foundation, the U.S.-based organization at the forefront of the battle to protect democratic freedom on-line, said it best in a speech he made to world leaders in 1996 at an annual conference in Davos, Switzerland. He read to them the "Declaration of the Independence of

Cyberspace," a declaration modeled on the U.S. Declaration of Independence. Perhaps more than any other document it summarizes the attitudes and belief of those who have journeyed into the on-line world.

Declaration of the Independence of Cyberspace

Governments of the Industrial World, you weary giants of flesh and steel, I come from Cyberspace, the new home of Mind. On behalf of the future, I ask you of the past to leave us alone. You are not welcome among us. You have no sovereignty where we gather.

We have no elected government, nor are we likely to have one, so I address you with no greater authority than that with which liberty itself always speaks. I declare the global social space we are building to be naturally independent of the tyrannies you seek to impose on us. You have no moral right to rule us nor do you possess any methods of enforcement we have true reason to fear.

Governments derive their just powers from the consent of the governed. You have neither solicited nor received ours. We did not invite you. You do not know us, nor do you know our world. Cyberspace does not lie within your borders.

Do not think that you can build it, as though it were a public construction project. You cannot. It is an act of nature and it grows itself through our collective actions.

You have not engaged in our great and gathering conversation, nor did you create the wealth of our marketplaces. You do not know our culture, our ethics, or the unwritten codes that already provide our society more order than could be obtained by any of your impositions.

You claim there are problems among us that you need to solve. You use this claim as an excuse to invade our precincts. Many of these problems don't exist.

Where there are real conflicts, where there are wrongs, we will identify them and address them by our means. We are forming our own Social Contract. This governance will arise according to the conditions of our world, not yours. Our world is different.

Cyberspace consists of transactions, relationships, and thought itself, arrayed like a standing wave in the web of our communications. Ours is a world that is both everywhere and nowhere, but it is not where bodies live.

We are creating a world that all may enter without privilege or prejudice accorded by race, economic power, military force, or station of birth.

We are creating a world where anyone, anywhere may express his or her beliefs, no matter how singular, without fear of being coerced into silence or conformity.

Your legal concepts of property, expression, identity, movement, and context do not apply to us. They are based on matter. There is no matter here.

Our identities have no bodies, so, unlike you, we cannot obtain order by physical coercion. We believe that from ethics, enlightened self-interest, and the commonwealth, our governance will emerge. Our identities may be distributed across many of your jurisdictions. The only law that all our constituent cultures would generally recognize is the Golden Rule. We hope we will be able to build our particular solutions on that basis. But we cannot accept the solutions you are attempting to impose.

In the United States, you have today created a law, the Telecommunications Reform Act, which repudiates your own Constitution and insults the dreams of Jefferson, Washington, Mill, Madison, De Toqueville, and Brandeis. These dreams must now be born anew in us.

You are terrified of your own children, since they are natives in a world where you will always be immigrants. Because you fear them, you entrust your bureaucracies with the parental responsibilities you are too cowardly to confront yourselves. In our world, all the sentiments and expressions of humanity, from the debasing to the angelic, are parts of a seamless whole, the global conversation of bits. We cannot separate the air that chokes from the air upon which wings beat.

In China, Germany, France, Russia, Singapore, Italy and the United States, you are trying to ward off the virus of liberty by erecting guard posts at the frontiers of Cyberspace. These may keep out the contagion for a small time, but they will not work in a world that will soon be blanketed in bit-bearing media.

Your increasingly obsolete information industries would perpetuate themselves by proposing laws, in America and elsewhere, that claim to own speech itself throughout the world. These laws would declare ideas to be another industrial product, no more noble than pig iron. In our world, whatever the human mind may create can be reproduced and distributed infinitely at no cost. The global conveyance of thought no longer requires your factories to accomplish.

These increasingly hostile and colonial measures place us in the same position as those previous lovers of freedom and self-determination who had to reject the authorities of distant, uninformed powers. We must declare our virtual selves immune to your sovereignty, even as we continue to consent to your rule over our bodies. We will spread ourselves across the Planet so that no one can arrest our thoughts.

We will create a civilization of the Mind in Cyberspace. May it be more humane and fair than the world your governments have made before.

John Perry Barlow, Cognitive Dissident Co-Founder, Electronic Frontier Foundation

Davos, Switzerland

February 8, 1996

http://numedia.tddc.net/scott/declaration.html

The cyberspace nation has been born.

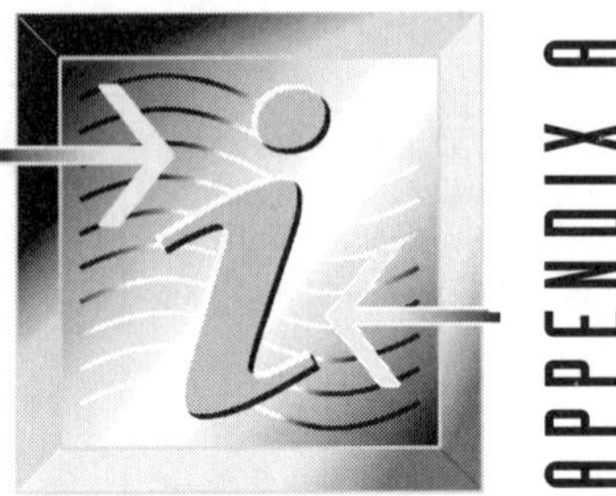

APPENDIX A

Top 25

Rick and Jim's Picks for the 25 Most Memorable Internet Events of 1996

In what we hope will become an annual tradition, we have selected our choices for the 25 most memorable Internet events of 1996. They are presented below in no particular order and cover the period from January to September, 1996. How did we come up with this list? It represents those Internet events that stick out in our minds because they were controversial, humorous, newsworthy, ground-breaking, or of historical significance. We didn't restrict ourselves to Canadian events. If you would like to make comments about this list, or take issue with us regarding an event you believe should have made it into our "Top 25," please e-mail us at **authors@handbook.com**

1 America Online suffered a serious outage that left its six million subscribers without access to e-mail, the Internet, and other on-line services for almost 19 hours. It was the biggest blackout in cyberspace history. (August 7, 1996)

2 AT&T officially launched its "WorldNet" Internet access service at its New Jersey headquarters. The service included 5 hours of free Internet access per month for AT&T's 90 million long-distance customers in the United States. The move was seen as a death knell for smaller Internet service providers and sent shock waves throughout the industry. (March 14, 1996)

3 Apple Computer announced that it would shut down eWorld — its struggling commercial on-line service. eWorld was one of the first casualties of the rising popularity of the Internet. (March 1996)

4 The Prime Minister of Canada established an e-mail address — **pm@pm.gc.ca** (May 21, 1996)

5 The world's first computer — the ENIAC — celebrated its 50th anniversary. It weighed 30 tons, contained 17,468 vacuum tubes, and could count to 5,000 in 60 seconds. Today, the average hand-held calculator has more computing power than the ENIAC did. (February 14, 1996)

6 Netcom Canada announced flat-rate Internet access, the first major Internet provider in Canada to implement such a pricing scheme. (March 27, 1996)

7 Spain's ambassador to Canada published some unflattering remarks about Canadian government officials on the Spanish Embassy's World Wide Web site in Ottawa. He also posted a series of angry, sarcastic statements and propaganda attacking former Fisheries Minister Brian Tobin's handling of the Canada-Spain turbot war. Canada responded to the action by registering an official complaint with Spain's foreign ministry in Madrid. (March, 1996)

8 Encyclopaedia Britannica announced that it would cease in-home sales of its encyclopedia products in the U.S. and Canada and focus instead on direct-marketing activities and using the Internet as a distribution channel. (April 24, 1996)

9 Yahoo!, the popular Internet directory service, went public, making instant millionaires out of the service's two founders, Jerry Yang, 27, and David Filo, 29. The company ended the day with a market capitalization of nearly $1 billion. It was the most closely watched public offering since Netscape went public in December, 1995. (April 12, 1996)

10 IBM officially launched its Web site for the Centennial Olympic Games in Atlanta. This event marked the first time in history that an Olympic Games Organizing Committee had a Web site. It was also the first time ever that Olympic merchandise and tickets were sold over the Internet. (July 1996)

11 A three-judge panel in Philadelphia issued a preliminary injunction blocking enforcement of portions of the United States Communications Decency Act (CDA), signed into law by President Clinton on February 8, 1996. U.S. District Judge Stewart Dalzell wrote, "As the most participatory form of mass speech yet developed, the Internet deserves the highest protection from governmental intrusion." This statement will surely be rememered as one of the most famous Internet quotations of all time. (June 12, 1996)

12 *Wired* magazine published a satirical article about the demise of the World Wide Web called "The Great Web Wipeout." The article immediately ignited debate about the future of the World Wide Web. (April, 1996)

13 VISA and MasterCard announced the development of a standard for secure credit card transactions over the Internet. (February 1, 1996).

14 The InterNIC, the organization that registers Internet domain names, suspended the domain names of more than 9,000 organizations that hadn't paid their $100 registration fees. Due to a billing mix-up, the domain name belonging to MSNBC — Microsoft and NBC's cable venture — was deactivated for an entire day, knocking the Microsoft/NBC Web site off the Internet. Following the mishap, one publication dubbed the InterNIC as "The World's Newest, Toughest Utility". (June 27, 1996)

15 iSTAR Internet, one of Canada's largest Internet providers, secretly delisted several controversial Internet newsgroups from its USENET service. A private memo was circulated to iSTAR staff, asking them not to disclose the full list of censored newsgroups to the public. However, the memo was leaked to the press, and it sparked intense debate about Internet censorship. (July, 1996)

16 The South Korean government issued a national directive warning its citizens not to contact North Koreans over the Internet. The government also threatened to punish any South Korean citizen who visited a North Korean Web site. At the centre of the controversy was a Web site about North Korea that had been created by a Canadian student following his school trip to the country. The South Korean authorities caused an international stir by suggesting that the Canadian student had secret ties to North Korea. The unfortunate student was deluged with e-mail messages from all over the world asking whether or not he was a North Korean spy. (June, 1996)

17 A public outcry occurred after Yahoo! launched a telephone number lookup service that included millions of unlisted home addresses and phone numbers. Under pressure from privacy advocates, Yahoo! agreed to delete the information. (April, 1996)

18 Digital Equipment launched a PC version of its popular AltaVista search engine for the World Wide Web. The software can be used to build an index of every word of almost every document stored on a person's computer hard drive. (July, 1996)

19 Mickey Mouse made his debut on the Internet with the official launch of the Walt Disney Web site. (February, 1996)

20 (From **http://www.ggtech.com**) In an unprecedented ruling, a British judge allowed the Internet to be used to serve a court order outside of the United Kingdom. The case concerned a European man's threats — via e-mail — to publish defamatory statements about the plaintiff over the Internet. The plaintiff's lawyers quickly obtained an injunction and persuaded the court to allow the injunction to be delivered over the Internet to the defendant's two e-mail addresses. To show that the defendant received notice of the order, the lawyers used e-mail's return-receipt capabilities. The defendant also admitted receiving the injunction. (May, 1996)

21 OpenText Corporation of Waterloo, Ontario, announced a plan that would allow advertisers to buy preferred placements on its Internet search engine. This would increase the likelihood that an advertiser's Web site would appear in a person's search results. Opponents of the plan said that it compromised the integrity of the search engine. OpenText said the practice is no different than the Yellow Pages where advertisers pay to influence the size and placements of their ads. (June, 1996)

22 Immediately following the release of a controversial book about the death of former French President Mitterand, the French government banned French stores from selling it. However, the government was up in arms the next day, when it learned that an activist had circumvented the ban by making an electronic version of the book available on the World Wide Web. Within a week, 10,000 copies had been downloaded all over the world. The French government was so enraged by the incident that it announced plans to legislate the use of the Internet. (January, 1996)

23 Over 2,500 Internet users from more than 100 countries assembled in Montreal for the sixth annual Internet Society conference. This was the first time the conference was held in Canada, and it represented the largest concentration of foreign Internet users ever to assemble in Canada for a single event. (June, 1996)

24 A clever Florida executive, fired from his job as the Marketing Manager for the Green Meadows animal petting farm in Orlando, negotiated an unusual settlement package with his company — his severance included 40,000 tickets to the petting farm! The tickets were valued at $520,000 and the executive promptly announced plans to hawk them on the Internet for $11.00 apiece — $2.00 less than the retail price. (August, 1996)

25 Following a complaint that alleged possible copyright infringement, a popular Web site describing scientific experiments on Twinkies snack cakes was yanked off the Net at Rice University in Houston, Texas, where it had been created by two local college students. The incident garnered worldwide attention and the two students received messages of support and sympathy from all over the world. The site was eventually put back on-line after an agreement was worked out with Interstate Brands, the company that produces Twinkies. (April, 1996)

APPENDIX B

Good Surfing Spots on the Web

To help you discover information on the Web, we've prepared this useful list of Internet directories and search services. Use these resources whenever you're looking for something on the Web. Our guide is organized into two sections. The first section contains a list of directories on the World Wide Web that you can browse through, and sometimes search. The second section contains a list of search engines on the Web. Search engines are searchable databases of Internet resources. Resources that index primarily Canadian content are marked by a 🍁 symbol. For more detailed information about searching the Web, be sure to read Chapter 9 – *Undertaking Research on the Internet.* Happy surfing!

Directories of World Wide Web Sites

The Argus Clearinghouse

http://www.clearinghouse.net

Provides subject-specific guides to Internet resources. Dozens of guides are available, covering such subjects as agriculture, business, cancer, economics, film, forestry, history, journalism, life insurance, and telecommunications.

🍁 British Columbian Home Pages

http://www.freenet.victoria.bc.ca/bcw3list.html

A large collection of Web sites in British Columbia, maintained by the Victoria Free-Net.

🍁 Canadian Almanac's Canada Info

http://www.clo.com/~canadainfo

Provides a directory of Canadian Internet sites. Categories include associations; culture; education; environment; government; history; geography and weather; news and media; and travel.

Canadian Government Information on the Internet

http://library.uwaterloo.ca/discipline/Government/CanGuide/index.html

Anita Cannon of the University of Waterloo has prepared this guide to Canadian government sites on the Internet. It covers federal, provincial, and municipal government resources.

Canadiana — The Canadian Resource Page

http://www.cs.cmu.edu/afs/cs.cmu.edu/user/clamen/misc/Canadiana

A great compilation of Canadian Internet sites. Categories include news and information; facts and figures; travel and tourism; government services and information; politics and history; science and education; technology and commerce; and culture and entertainment.

Canuck Site of the Day

http://www.10q.com/canuck

A directory of well-designed Canadian Web sites. A new site is selected every day.

Charity Village

http://www.charityvillage.com/cvhome.html

Offers links to Canadian non-profit organizations on the Internet. Categories include addiction and substance abuse; children; youth and family; community and social services; culture and heritage; disabilities; education; environmental/animals; health and diseases; human rights and civil liberties; international relief/development/peace; religion; research and policy development; seniors; and sports and recreation.

City.Net

http://www.city.net

City.Net provides an excellent geographic index to information on the Internet. It provides pointers to information resources on cities, towns, and countries around the world. Includes many links to Canadian villages, towns, and cities with sites on the Web.

Cool Canadian Site of the Day

http://web.idirect.com/~canadian

A directory of Canadian Web sites that have been recognized for excellence in content and/or design. Updated daily.

Government of Canada Main Web Page

http://www.canada.gc.ca

Provides a master list of federal government organizations on the Internet.

La Toile du Quebec

http://www.toile.qc.ca/englqc.htm

An index to World Wide Web sites in Quebec. Categories include arts and culture; computers; commercial sites and business; education; government; research and sciences; society; sports and leisure; and tourism.

Manitoba Internet Resources Page

http://www.xpressnet.com/alice/manitoba.html

A directory of Internet resources in Manitoba. Categories include cities, towns, and communities; universities and colleges; k-12 education; community networks; music, arts, and culture; sports and recreation; and politics, government, and law.

Maple Square

http://maple.canadas.net

A directory of Internet resources pertaining to Canada. Categories include entertainment; business and economy; education; government; health; heritage and culture; news; recreation; reference; regional; science and technology; social science; and travel and tourism.

National Library of Canada's Canadian Information by Subject

http://www.nlc-bnc.ca/caninfo/ecaninfo.htm

A collection of links to Internet resources about Canada. Categories include philosophy and psychology; religion; social sciences; language and languages; science and mathematics; applied sciences and technology; arts and recreation; literature; and geography and history.

New Brunswick Internet Exchange

http://www.discribe.ca/newbie

The New Brunswick Internet Exchange is an index to World Wide Web sites in New Brunswick. Categories include culture; education; entertainment; government; people; publications; and recreation and leisure.

NewfoundLinks

http://pagemaker.com/db/links.html

A searchable directory of hundreds of Newfoundland Web pages.

Newfoundlanders Adrift!.. Ties to Home Page

http://magi.com/~holwell/links/nllinks.html

An excellent set of Internet resources about Labrador and Newfoundland. Categories include tourism; communities; history and culture; commercial; education and current affairs; and Odds & Sods!

Nova Scotia Links

http://www.mfusion.com/kellock/nslinks

A listing of World Wide Web sites in Nova Scotia. Categories include travel and tourism; education and religion; accommodations; libraries and museums; and organizations and associations.

Open Market's Commercial Sites Index

http://www.directory.net

A directory of commercial services, products, and information on the Internet.

Point Communications Top Sites of the Web

http://www.pointcom.com

This site reviews and rates thousands of sites on the World Wide Web. Categories include arts and humanities; business and finance; computers and the Internet; education; entertainment; government; health and medicine; leisure activities; and science and technology.

SaskWeb

http://saskweb.com

Provides a directory of Web sites in Saskatchewan.

Vancouver CommunityNet Community Pages

http://www.freenet.vancouver.bc.ca/community

A set of pointers to Web sites in British Columbia, maintained by the Vancouver CommunityNet. Categories include art, culture and entertainment; education; employment and labour; environment; family; law and policing; science and technology; and travel and transportation.

World Wide Web Virtual Library

http://www.w3.org/pub/DataSources/bySubject/Overview.html

Contains pointers to dozens of subject-specific Web directories, including African studies; architecture; beer and brewing; ceramics; dance; games; gardening; languages; meteorology; museums; nursing; whale watching; and much much more!

Yahoo!

http://www.yahoo.com

Yahoo! is unquestionably the most popular directory on the Internet. Categories include arts; business and economy; computers and Internet; reference; education; entertainment; science; government; social science; health; and society and culture. The entire directory is searchable.

Yahoo! Canada

http://www.yahoo.ca

A Canadian version of the tremendously popular Yahoo! directory service.

YukonWeb

http://www.yukonweb.com

A guide to Internet resources in the Yukon.

World Wide Web Search Engines

AltaVista

http://altavista.digital.com

One of the most popular search engines on the Internet. Operated by Digital Equipment Corporation.

Champlain: Canadian Information Explorer

http://champlain.gns.ca

A searchable database of Canadian tourism information, legal information, and federal/provincial government information on the Web.

Excite

http://www.excite.com

Includes tens of thousands of Web site reviews by a top-notch editorial team.

HotBot

http://www.hotbot.com

The search engine operated by *Wired* magazine.

Infoseek Guide

http://www.infoseek.com

A great roadmap to the Internet!

Lycos

http://www.lycos.com

Lycos is the Latin term for the "Wolf Spider." Check it out!

OpenText

http://www.opentext.com

A Canadian success story! This search engine is run by OpenText Corporation in Waterloo, Ontario.

🍁 Saskatchewan Web Sites Broker

http://www.saskweb.com

Provides a searchable database of Web sites in Saskatchewan.

Infoseek Ultra

http://ultra.infoseek.com

A lightning-fast search engine operated by InfoSeek Corporation.

WebCrawler

http://www.webcrawler.com

One of the original search engines on the Internet. Operated by America Online.

APPENDIX C

Telephone and E-mail Lookup Services

You'll Never Have to Use Directory Assistance Again

Did you know that the Internet contains many free services that allow you to look up telephone numbers, postal codes, mailing addresses, and e-mail addresses for people all over the world? Below we present a handy guide to some of our favourite "lookup" resources. The telephone number databases are especially useful since they are a cheap alternative to calling directory assistance. Resources that index primarily Canadian content are marked by a 🍁 symbol. Have fun!

Telephone and Mailing Address Lookup Services

BigYellow

http://www.bigyellow.com

A searchable directory of telephone numbers and mailing addresses for millions of U.S. businesses. Searches can be narrowed by subject (e.g. flowers), business name, city, area code, street, or zip code. Very powerful!

🍁 Canada411

http://canada411.sympatico.ca

A searchable directory of millions of Canadian residential and business telephone numbers. Just plug in the person's first name, last name, city, and province, and Canada411 will retrieve the information for you, including a full mailing address. Looking for a postal code? No problem — Canada411 will find postal codes too! Not sure of the exact spelling? Don't worry — you can even search by partial last name.

🍁 Canada Post

http://www.mailposte.ca

Visit this site for Canadian postal code information.

InfoSpace

http://www.infospace.com

InfoSpace provides a searchable database of business, residential, and yellow pages listings for both Canada and the United States, including fax machines. You can also retrieve listings for U.S. government and 1-800 numbers.

MapBlast

http://www.mapblast.com

Provides an instant map for almost any address in the United States. Just type in the street address, city, and state. This service lets you display the resulting map on your home page. You can also send maps by e-mail to your friends.

Switchboard

http://www.switchboard.com

Switchboard is another useful resource if you're hunting for telephone numbers. It provides a searchable directory of U.S. residential and business listings.

United States Postal Service ZIP Code Lookup Service

http://www.usps.gov

Enter a U.S. address and get the correct zip code. You can also do a reverse lookup to find out which cities are associated with a certain zip code.

Yahoo! People Search

http://phone.yahoo.com

Yahoo!'s People Search provides a nifty reverse lookup feature for residential telephone numbers in the United States. Just type in a telephone number and People Search will return a matching name and mailing address.

E-mail Address Lookup Services

Bigfoot

http://www.bigfoot.com

Just type in the name of the person you are searching for, and Bigfoot will return a list of matching e-mail addresses.

Four11 Directory Services

http://www.four11.com

Search by first name, last name, city, state/province, or country.

Internet Address Finder

http://www.iaf.net

Allows you to look up Internet users by last name or e-mail address.

WhoWhere?

http://www.whowhere.com

Simply provide a person's name, and WhoWhere? will provide a summary of matching e-mail addresses. You can also look for people who share your interests.

APPENDIX D

Identifying Countries on the Internet

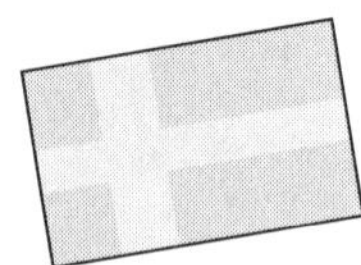

As discussed in Chapter 5, at the extreme right of every Internet address is either a two-letter country code or a three-letter descriptive zone name. In Canada and the United States both types of addressing are used. In Canada, for example, you will see many Internet addresses that end in **.ca** (the two-letter country code for Canada). You will also see many Canadian Internet addresses that end in **.com**, **.org**, **.net**, or **.edu**. Similarly, in the United States many Internet addresses end in **.us** (the two-letter country code for the United States). You will also see many U.S. Internet addresses that end in **.com**, **.org**, **.net**, **.gov**, **.mil**, and **.edu** (**.mil** and **.gov** are not used in Canada with a couple of exceptions. e.g., **mtp.gov** belongs to the Metropolitan Toronto Police Department and **peelpolice.gov** belongs to the Peel Regional Police in Ontario).

While the three-letter descriptive zone names are common in North America, most countries and territories/dependencies on other continents use two-letter country codes that have been assigned by the International Organization for Standardization in Switzerland. To help you identify Internet addresses and their countries of origin, this Appendix lists two-letter country codes that have been assigned by the International Organization for Standardization. For example, suppose you are surfing the Internet and you come across a World Wide Web site with an address like this:

http://www.simi.is

Notice that the two-letter country code in this address is **is**. To determine what country this address is from, look up the country code in the table below. You will find that **is** is the country code for Iceland.

Here is another example. Suppose you are reading a USENET newsgroup and you see an e-mail address that looks like this:

johns@tidco.co.tt

According to the list of country codes below, **tt** is the country code for Trinidad and Tobago. Therefore, you know that this e-mail address belongs to someone in Trinidad and Tobago. In the list below the code is followed by the name of the country or geographical region.

It's that easy. Have fun!

AD	Andorra
AE	United Arab Emirates
AF	Afghanistan
AG	Antigua and Barbuda
AI	Anguilla
AL	Albania
AM	Armenia
AN	Netherlands Antilles
AO	Angola
AQ	Antarctica
AR	Argentina
AS	American Samoa
AT	Austria
AU	Australia
AW	Aruba
AZ	Azerbaijan
BA	Bosnia–Herzegovina
BB	Barbados
BD	Bangladesh
BE	Belgium
BF	Burkina Faso
BG	Bulgaria
BH	Bahrain
BI	Burundi
BJ	Benin
BM	Bermuda
BN	Brunei Darussalam
BO	Bolivia
BR	Brazil
BS	Bahamas
BT	Bhutan
BV	Bouvet Island
BW	Botswana
BY	Belarus
BZ	Belize
CA	Canada
CC	Cocos (Keeling) Islands
CF	Central African Republic
CG	Congo
CH	Switzerland

CI	Ivory Coast/Côte d'Ivoire
CK	Cook Islands
CL	Chile
CM	Cameroon
CN	China
CO	Colombia
CR	Costa Rica
CU	Cuba
CV	Cape Verde
CX	Christmas Island
CY	Cyprus
CZ	Czech Republic
DE	Germany
DJ	Djibouti
DK	Denmark
DM	Dominica
DO	Dominican Republic
DZ	Algeria
EC	Ecuador
EE	Estonia
EG	Egypt
EH	Western Sahara
ER	Eritrea
ES	Spain
ET	Ethiopia
FI	Finland
FJ	Fiji
FK	Falkland Islands
FM	Micronesia
FO	Faroe Islands
FR	France
GA	Gabon
GB	United Kingdom (generally uses UK)
GD	Grenada
GE	Georgia
GF	French Guiana
GH	Ghana
GI	Gibraltar
GL	Greenland
GM	Gambia

GN	Guinea
GP	Guadeloupe
GQ	Equatorial Guinea
GR	Greece
GT	Guatemala
GU	Guam
GW	Guinea–Bissau
GY	Guyana
HK	Hong Kong
HM	Heard and McDonald Islands
HN	Honduras
HR	Croatia
HT	Haiti
HU	Hungary
ID	Indonesia
IE	Ireland
IL	Israel
IN	India
IO	British Indian Ocean Territory
IQ	Iraq
IR	Iran
IS	Iceland
IT	Italy
JM	Jamaica
JO	Jordan
JP	Japan
KE	Kenya
KG	Kyrgyz Republic
KH	Cambodia
KI	Kiribati
KM	Comoros
KN	St. Kitts and Nevis
KP	North Korea
KR	South Korea
KW	Kuwait
KY	Cayman Islands
KZ	Kazakhstan
LA	Laos
LB	Lebanon
LC	Saint Lucia
LI	Liechtenstein
LK	Sri Lanka
LR	Liberia
LS	Lesotho
LT	Lithuania
LU	Luxembourg
LV	Latvia
LY	Libya
MA	Morocco
MC	Monaco
MD	Moldova
MG	Madagascar
MH	Marshall Islands
MK	Macedonia
ML	Mali
MM	Myanmar
MN	Mongolia
MO	Macau
MP	Northern Mariana Islands
MQ	Martinique
MR	Mauritania
MS	Montserrat
MT	Malta
MU	Mauritius
MV	Maldives
MW	Malawi
MX	Mexico
MY	Malaysia
MZ	Mozambique
NA	Namibia
NC	New Caledonia
NE	Niger
NF	Norfolk Island
NG	Nigeria
NI	Nicaragua
NL	Netherlands
NO	Norway
NP	Nepal
NR	Nauru
NT	Neutral Zone

NU	Niue
NZ	New Zealand
OM	Oman
PA	Panama
PE	Peru
PF	French Polynesia
PG	Papua New Guinea
PH	Philippines
PK	Pakistan
PL	Poland
PM	St. Pierre and Miquelon
PN	Pitcairn
PR	Puerto Rico
PT	Portugal
PW	Palau
PY	Paraguay
QA	Qatar
RE	Reunion
RO	Romania
RU	Russian Federation
RW	Rwanda
SA	Saudi Arabia
SB	Solomon Islands
SC	Seychelles
SD	Sudan
SE	Sweden
SG	Singapore
SH	St. Helena
SI	Slovenia
SJ	Svalbard and Jan Mayen Islands
SK	Slovakia
SL	Sierra Leone
SM	San Marino
SN	Senegal
SO	Somalia
SR	Suriname
ST	Sao Tome and Principe
SU	Soviet Union
SV	El Salvador
SY	Syria
SZ	Swaziland
TC	Turks and Caicos Islands
TD	Chad
TF	French Southern Territories
TG	Togo
TH	Thailand
TJ	Tajikistan
TK	Tokelau
TM	Turkmenistan
TN	Tunisia
TO	Tonga
TP	East Timor
TR	Turkey
TT	Trinidad and Tobago
TV	Tuvalu
TW	Taiwan
TZ	Tanzania
UA	Ukraine
UG	Uganda
UM	U.S. Minor Outlying Islands
US	United States
UY	Uruguay
UZ	Uzbekistan
VA	Vatican City State
VC	Saint Vincent and the Grenadines
VE	Venezuela
VG	British Virgin Islands
VI	U.S. Virgin Islands
VN	Vietnam
VU	Vanuatu
WF	Wallis and Futuna Islands
WS	Samoa
YE	Yemen
YT	Mayotte
YU	Yugoslavia
ZA	South Africa
ZM	Zambia
ZR	Zaire
ZW	Zimbabwe

APPENDIX E

Canadian USENET Newsgroups

This is a directory of major Canadian USENET newsgroups. While not all Internet access providers in Canada will carry every one of these newsgroups, most are willing to carry additional newsgroups on request. If you see a newsgroup below that you like, ask your provider if they are willing to carry it for you. For more detailed information about USENET, be sure to read Chapter 11 — *Knowledge Networking.*

This guide is divided into three sections. The first section lists newsgroups in the Canadian USENET hierarchies; the second section lists newsgroups in the mainstream USENET hierarchies; and the third section lists newsgroups in the ClariNet hierarchies.

Canadian Hierarchies

NAME OF NEWSGROUP	DESCRIPTION
ab.general	General discussion for people in Alberta
ab.jobs	Job/employment discussions in Alberta
ab.politics	Discussion about politics in Alberta
bc.cycling	Discussion about bicycling in British Columbia
bc.general	General discussion for people in British Columbia
bc.jobs	Job/employment discussions in British Columbia
bc.politics	Discussion about politics in British Columbia
bc.weather	Discussion about the weather in British Columbia
brocku.forsale	Items for sale at Brock University, St. Catharines, Ontario

brocku.general	General discussion at Brock University, St. Catharines, Ontario
calgary.announce	Announcements in Calgary, Alberta
can.atlantic.general	General discussion about the Atlantic Provinces
can.atlantic.biz	Commercial postings in Atlantic Canada
can.atlantic.forsale	Items for sale in Atlantic Canada
can.community.asian	General discussion about the Asian community in Canada
can.community.military	General discussion about the military in Canada
can.config	General discussion about new newsgroup proposals in the can.* hierarchy
can.construction	General discussion about construction issues in Canada
can.domain	New Canadian domain registrations and discussion about the Canadian domain name system
can.english	General discussion about English-language issues in Canada
can.forsale	Items for sale in Canada
can.francais	General discussion about Francophone issues in Canada
can.general	General discussion for Canadians
can.gov.announce	Canadian government announcements
can.gov.general	General discussion about government in Canada
can.infohighway	General discussion about Canada's information highway
can.jobs	Job/employment openings in Canada
can.legal	General discussion about Canadian law
can.med.misc	Miscellaneous postings about medical issues in Canada
can.motss	General discussion about gay/lesbian/bisexual issues in Canada
can.newprod	General discussion about new products in Canada
can.org.cips	General discussion about the Canadian Information Processing Society
can.politics	General discussion about Canadian politics
can.schoolnet.arts.drama	General discussion about drama for SchoolNet participants
can.schoolnet.arts.music	General discussion about music for SchoolNet participants
can.schoolnet.biomed.jr	General discussion about biology and medicine for elementary school students participating in SchoolNet
can.schoolnet.biomed.sr	General discussion about biology and medicine for secondary school students participating in SchoolNet
can.schoolnet.chat.students.jr	General discussion for elementary school students participating in SchoolNet
can.schoolnet.chat.students.sr	General discussion for secondary school students participating in SchoolNet
can.schoolnet.chat.teachers	General discussion for teachers participating in SchoolNet

can.schoolnet.chem.jr	General discussion about chemistry for elementary school students participating in SchoolNet
can.schoolnet.chem.sr	General discussion about chemistry for secondary school students participating in SchoolNet
can.schoolnet.comp.jr	General discussion about computer science for elementary school students participating in SchoolNet
can.schoolnet.comp.sr	General discussion about computer science for secondary school students participating in SchoolNet
can.schoolnet.earth.jr	General discussion about the earth sciences for elementary school students participating in SchoolNet
can.schoolnet.earth.sr	General discussion about the earth sciences for secondary school students participating in SchoolNet
can.schoolnet.elecsys.jr	General discussion about electrical/systems engineering for elementary school students participating in SchoolNet
can.schoolnet.elecsys.sr	General discussion about electrical/systems engineering for secondary school students participating in SchoolNet
can.schoolnet.eng.jr	General discussion about engineering for elementary school students participating in SchoolNet
can.schoolnet.eng.sr	General discussion about engineering for secondary school students participating in SchoolNet
can.schoolnet.english	General discussion about English curriculum for SchoolNet participants
can.schoolnet.firefighters	General discussion about firefighting and fire safety issues for SchoolNet participants
can.schoolnet.history	General discussion about history for SchoolNet participants
can.schoolnet.math.jr	General discussion about math for elementary school students participating in SchoolNet
can.schoolnet.math.sr	General discussion about math for secondary school students participating in SchoolNet
can.schoolnet.phys.jr	General discussion about physics for elementary school students participating in SchoolNet
can.schoolnet.phys.sr	General discussion about physics for secondary school students participating in SchoolNet
can.schoolnet.physed	General discussion about physical education for SchoolNet participants
can.schoolnet.problems	General discussion about SchoolNet problems
can.schoolnet.projects.calls	SchoolNet requests for proposals
can.schoolnet.projects.discuss	General discussion about SchoolNet projects
can.schoolnet.school.improvement	General discussion about improving Canada's schools
can.schoolnet.socsci.jr	General discussion about the social sciences for elementary school students participating in SchoolNet
can.schoolnet.socsci.sr	General discussion about the social sciences for secondary school students participating in SchoolNet

can.schoolnet.space.jr	General discussion about space sciences for elementary school students participating in SchoolNet
can.schoolnet.space.sr	General discussion about space sciences for secondary school students participating in SchoolNet
can.schoolnet.staff.development	General discussion about staff development issues in Canada's schools
can.scout-guide	General discussion about scouting in Canada
can.talk.bilingualism	General discussion about bilingualism in Canada
can.talk.guns	General discussion about guns and gun control in Canada
can.talk.smoking	General discussion about smoking issues in Canada
can.taxes	General discussion about Canadian tax matters
carleton.general	General discussion at Carleton University, Ottawa, Ontario
concordia.announce	Announcements at Concordia University, Montreal, Quebec
concordia.general	General discussion at Concordia University, Montreal, Quebec
dal.general	General discussion at Dalhousie University, Halifax, Nova Scotia
edm.announce	Announcements in Edmonton, Alberta
edm.forsale	Items for sale in Edmonton, Alberta
edm.general	General discussion for people in Edmonton, Alberta
edm.politics	General discussion about politics in Edmonton, Alberta
hfx.forsale	Items for sale in Halifax, Nova Scotia
hfx.general	General discussion for people in Halifax, Nova Scotia
kingston.eats	General discussion about dining out in Kingston, Ontario
kingston.events	Events in Kingston, Ontario
kingston.forsale	Items for sale in Kingston, Ontario
kingston.jobs	Job postings in Kingston, Ontario
kingston.wanted	Items wanted in Kingston, Ontario
kingston.general	General discussion for people in Kingston, Ontario
kw.eats	General discussion about dining out in Kitchener/Waterloo, Ontario
kw.forsale	Items for sale in Kitchener/Waterloo, Ontario
kw.general	General discussion for people in Kitchener/Waterloo, Ontario
kw.housing	Discussions about accommodation/housing in Kitchener/Waterloo, Ontario
kw.jobs	Job/employment discussions in Kitchener/Waterloo, Ontario
kw.theatre	General discussion about theatre in Kitchener/Waterloo, Ontario
laurentian.general	General discussion at Laurentian University, Sudbury, Ontario
man.forsale	Items for sale in Manitoba
man.freenet	General discussion about community networks in Manitoba

man.politics	General discussion about politics in Manitoba
man.general	General discussion for people in Manitoba
mcgill.general	General discussion at McGill University, Montreal, Quebec
mcmaster.announce	Announcements at McMaster University, Hamilton, Ontario
mtl.general	General discussion for people in Montreal, Quebec
mtl.vendre-forsale	Items for sale in Montreal, Quebec
mun.general	General discussion at the Memorial University of Newfoundland, St. John's
mun.wanted	Items wanted in Memorial University of Newfoundland, St. John's
nb.biz	Commercial postings in New Brunswick
nb.forsale	Items for sale in New Brunswick
nb.general	General discussion for people in New Brunswick
nb.jobs	Job postings in New Brunswick
nbgov.info.highway	General discussion about the information highway in New Brunswick
nbgov.investment.newbrunswick	General discussion about investment in New Brunswick
nf.birds	General discussion about birding in Newfoundland
nf.computing	General discussion about computing in Newfoundland
nf.general	General discussion for people in Newfoundland
nf.wanted	Items wanted in Newfoundland
nf.women	General discussion about women's issues in Newfoundland
ns.announce	Announcements in Nova Scotia
ns.forsale	Items for sale in Nova Scotia
ns.general	General discussion for people in Nova Scotia
nwt.general	General discussion for people in the Northwest Territories
ont.archives	General discussion about archival issues in Ontario
ont.bicycle	General discussion about bicycling in Ontario
ont.events	Events in Ontario
ont.forsale	Items for sale in Ontario
ont.general	General discussion for people in Ontario
ont.jobs	Job postings in Ontario
ott.events	Events in Ottawa, Ontario
ott.forsale.computing	Computing items for sale in Ottawa, Ontario
ott.forsale.other	Other items for sale in Ottawa, Ontario
ott.general	General discussion for people in Ottawa, Ontario
ott.housing	Discussions about accommodation/housing in Ottawa, Ontario
ott.jobs	Job/employment discussions in Ottawa, Ontario

ott.online	General discussion about the on-line world in Ottawa, Ontario
ott.weather	General discussion about the weather in Ottawa, Ontario
qc.general	General discussion for people in Quebec
qc.jobs	Jobs in Quebec
qc.jobs.wanted	Jobs wanted in Quebec
qc.politique	Discussion about politics in Quebec
queens.events	Announcements of events at Queen's University, Kingston, Ontario
queens.forsale	Items for sale at Queen's University, Kingston, Ontario
queens.general	General discussion at Queen's University, Kingston, Ontario
rye.general	General discussion at Ryerson Polytechnic University, Toronto
sfu.general	General discussion at Simon Fraser University, Vancouver
sj.general	General discussion for people in St. John's, Newfoundland
sk.announce	Announcements in Saskatchewan
sk.forsale	Items for sale in Saskatchewan
sk.general	General discussion for people in Saskatchewan
sk.internet	General discussion about the Internet in Saskatchewan
sk.jobs	Job/employment discussions in Saskatchewan
sk.jobs.offered	Job postings in Saskatchewan
sk.jobs.wanted	Jobs wanted in Saskatchewan
sk.library	General discussion about library issues in Saskatchewan
sk.politics	General discussion about politics in Saskatchewan
sk.sports	General discussion about sports in Saskatchewan
stemnet.announce	Announcements at STEM~Net, St. John's Newfoundland
stemnet.general	General discussion at STEM~Net, St. John's, Newfoundland
tor.arts	General discussion about the arts in Toronto, Ontario
tor.buysell	Items wanted/for sale in Toronto
tor.eats	General discussion about restaurants and eating in Toronto, Ontario
tor.events	Event listings in Toronto
tor.forsale	Items for sale in Toronto, Ontario
tor.housing	General discussion about housing in Toronto
tor.jobs	Job/employment discussions in Toronto, Ontario
trentu.general	General discussion at Trent University, Peterborough, Ontario
ualberta.general	General discussion at the University of Alberta, Edmonton
ubc.events	Events at the University of British Columbia, Vancouver
ubc.general	General discussion at the University of British Columbia, Vancouver

umoncton.annonces	Announcements at the University of Moncton, New Brunswick
umontreal.general	General discussion at the University of Montreal
uqam.general	General discussion at the University of Quebec (Montreal)
usask.general	General discussion at the University of Saskatchewan
ut.general	General discussion at the University of Toronto
ut.jobs	Job/employment discussions at the University of Toronto
uvic.forsale	Items for sale at the University of Victoria, British Columbia
uvic.general	General discussion at the University of Victoria, British Columbia
uvic.jobs	Job/employment discussions at the University of Victoria, British Columbia
uw.forsale	Items for sale at the University of Waterloo, Ontario
uw.general	General discussion at the University of Waterloo, Ontario
uwo.events	Events at the University of Western Ontario, London
uwo.forsale	Items for sale at the University of Western Ontario, London
uwo.general	General discussion at the University of Western Ontario, London
van.forsale	Items for sale in Vancouver
van.general	General discussion for people in Vancouver, British Columbia
wpg.forsale	Items for sale in Winnipeg, Manitoba
wpg.general	General discussion for people in Winnipeg, Manitoba
wpg.politics	General discussion about politics in Winnipeg
yk.general	General discussion for people in the Yukon
york.announce	Announcements at York University, Toronto
york.general	General discussion at York University, Toronto

Mainstream Hierarchies

NAME OF NEWSGROUP	DESCRIPTION
alt.fan.muchmusic	Discussion about MuchMusic
alt.music.canada	Discussion about Canadian music
alt.radio.networks.cbc	Discussion about CBC Radio
alt.tv.networks.cbc	Discussion about CBC Television
alt.tv.discovery.canada	Discussion about Canada's Discovery Channel
alt.sports.baseball.montreal-expos	Discussion about the Montreal Expos
alt.sports.baseball.tor-bluejays	Discussion about the Toronto Blue Jays
alt.sports.basketball.nba.tor-raptors	Discussion about the Toronto Raptors

alt.sports.hockey.nhl.clgry-flames	Discussion about the Calgary Flames
alt.sports.hockey.nhl.edm-oilers	Discussion about the Edmonton Oilers
alt.sports.hockey.nhl.mtl-canadiens	Discussion about the Montreal Canadiens
alt.sports.hockey.nhl.ott-senators	Discussion about the Ottawa Senators
alt.sports.hockey.nhl.tor-mapleleafs	Discussion about the Toronto Maple Leafs
alt.sports.hockey.nhl.vanc-canucks	Discussion about the Vancouver Canucks
misc.immigration.canada	Discussion about Canadian immigration issues
misc.invest.canada	Discussion about Canadian investments
rec.sport.football.canadian	Discussion about Canadian football
rec.travel.canada-usa	Travel discussion for Canada/U.S.A.
soc.culture.canada	Discussion about Canadian culture
soc.culture.quebec	Discussion about Quebec culture

ClariNet Hierarchies

NAME OF NEWSGROUP	DESCRIPTION
clari.sports.local.canada.atlantic-provs	Sports news from the Atlantic Provinces
clari.sports.local.canada.brit_columbia	British Columbia sports news
clari.sports.local.canada.ontario.misc	Ontario sports news
clari.sports.local.canada.ontario.toronto	Toronto sports news
clari.sports.local.canada.prairie_provs	Sports news from the Prairie Provinces
clari.sports.local.canada.quebec	Quebec sports news (moderated)
clari.world.americas.canada	General Canadian news (moderated)
clari.world.americas.canada.biz	Canadian business news (moderated)
clari.world.americas.canada.briefs	Canadian business briefs (moderated)
clari.world.americas.canada.general	General Canadian news
clari.world.americas.canada.review	Review of Canadian news (moderated)

APPENDIX F

Guide to Canadian Government Internet Domains

As discussed in Chapter 5, there is a Canadian Government Domain Registrar that is responsible for allocating domain names to federal government departments and agencies in Canada. This appendix presents a list of Canadian government domains and the names of government bodies to which they were issued.

When choosing a domain name, Canadian government departments have one of three choices:

- they can choose to have both an English domain name *and* a French domain name e.g. Natural Resources Canada uses both **nrcan.gc.ca** (Natural Resources Canada) and **rncan.gc.ca** (Ressources naturelles Canada)
- they can choose to have a hyphenated English-French domain e.g. The Royal Canadian Mounted Police uses **rcmp-grc.gc.ca** (Royal Canadian Mounted Police-Gendarmerie royale du Canada)
- they can choose to have a domain that works in both French and English e.g. Industry Canada uses **ic.gc.ca** (Industry Canada/Industrie Canada)

Many of the government organizations listed below have Web sites. In most cases, you simply need to add a **www** in front of the domain name to get the address for the Web site. For example, to get the Web site address for the Canadian International Development Agency, just place a **www** in front of **acdi-cida.gc.ca** (the domain name obtained from the table below). The resulting address is **www.acdi-cida.gc.ca** Just type this address in your Web browser, and you'll see a screen similar to the one displayed below.

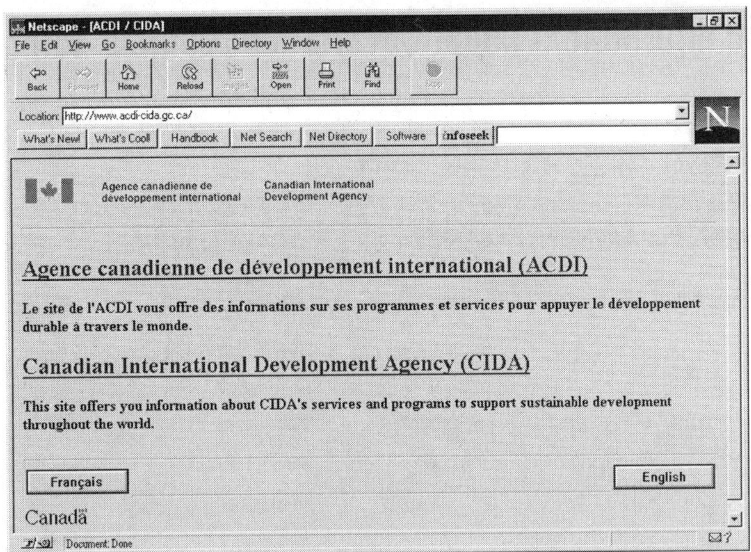

Here's another example. To get the Web site address for Transport Canada, just add a **www** to **tc.gc.ca** (the domain name obtained from the table below). The resulting address is **www.tc.gc.ca.** Just type this address in your Web browser to connect to the Transport Canada Web site (seen in the following screen).

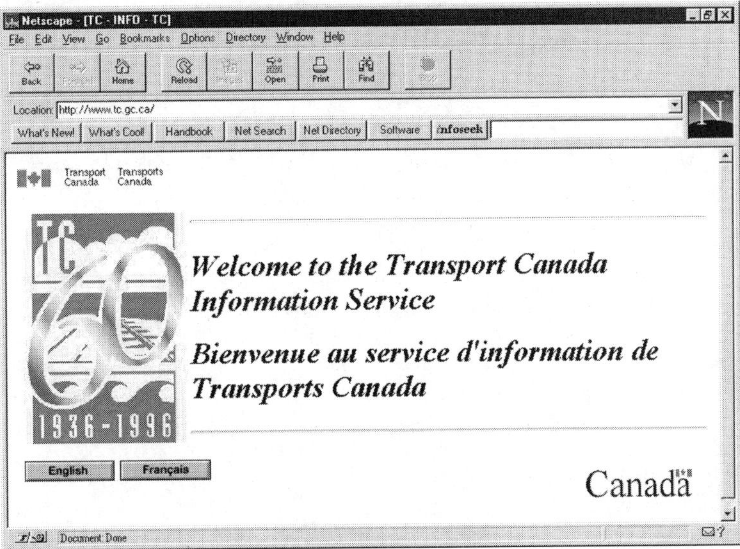

If you add a **www** to a domain name found in the table below, and you get an error message when you type this address into your Web browser, it probably means there is no Web site for the government organization you have chosen (the domain names below are used for both e-mail addresses and Web sites and not all government organizations have implemented Web sites).

For More Information About Government Domain Names

If you represent a Canadian government organization and you would like more information about registering a domain name for your agency or department, send e-mail to the Canadian Government Domain Registrar at **registry@gc.ca**

GOVERNMENT DEPARTMENT/AGENCY	DOMAIN NAME
Atomic Energy Control Board	atomcon.gc.ca
Bank of Canada	obligation.gc.ca
Canada Pension Plan	cpp-rpc.gc.ca
Canadian Centre for Foreign Policy Development	cfp-pec.gc.ca
Canadian Centre for Management Development	ccmd-ccg.gc.ca
Canadian Conservation Institute	cci-icc.gc.ca
Canadian Environmental Assessment Agency	acee.gc.ca
Canadian Environmental Assessment Agency	ceaa.gc.ca
Canadian Heritage	pch.gc.ca
Canadian Heritage Information Network	chin.gc.ca
Canadian Heritage Information Network	rcip.gc.ca
Canadian Intergovernment On-Line	intergouv.gc.ca
Canadian Intergovernment On-Line	intergov.gc.ca
Canadian Intergovernmental Conference Secretariat	scics.gc.ca
Canadian International Development Agency (CIDA)	acdi-cida.gc.ca
Canadian International Trade Tribunal	citt.gc.ca
Canadian International Trade Tribunal	tcce.gc.ca
Canadian Judicial Council	cjc-ccm.gc.ca
Canadian Mortgage and Housing Corporation	cmhc-schl.gc.ca
Canadian Polar Commission	polarcom.gc.ca
Canadian Police College	ccp.gc.ca
Canadian Police College	cpc.gc.ca
Canadian Radio-television Telecommunications Commission	crtc.gc.ca
Canadian Security Intelligence Service	csis-scrs.gc.ca
Canadian Space Agency	espace.gc.ca
Canadian Space Agency	space.gc.ca
Canadian Transportation Agency	cta-otc.gc.ca
Citizenship and Immigration Canada	ci.gc.ca
Competition Tribunal	ct-tc.gc.ca
Conference, Consultations and Events Conferences	cce.gc.ca
Consulting Audit Canada	cac.gc.ca

Consulting Audit Canada	cvc.gc.ca
Conversation Canada	conversation.gc.ca
Correctional Services Canada	csc-scc.gc.ca
Defence Construction Canada	dcc-cdc.gc.ca
Department of Foreign Affairs and International Trade	dfait-maeci.gc.ca
Department of Justice	justice.gc.ca
Emergency Preparedness Canada	epc.gc.ca
Environment Canada	ec.gc.ca
Federal Court of Canada	fct-cf.gc.ca
Federal Judicial Affairs	fja-cmf.gc.ca
Federal Office of Regional Development	bfdrq-fordq.gc.ca
Finance Canada	fin.gc.ca
Fisheries Resource Conservation Council	ccrh.gc.ca
Fisheries Resource Conservation Council	frcc.gc.ca
Government Enterprise Network (GENet)	genet.gc.ca
Government Information Finder Technology	gift.gc.ca
Government of Canada's Primary Internet Site	canada.gc.ca
Government Telecommunications and Informatics Services	gtis.gc.ca
Health Canada	hc-sc.gc.ca
Human Resources Development Canada	hrdc-drhc.gc.ca
Human Resources Development Library	hrdbli.gc.ca
Immigration and Refugee Board	irb-cisr.gc.ca
Indian and Northern Affairs Canada	inac.gc.ca
Indian and Northern Affairs Canada	ainc.gc.ca
Indian and Northern Affairs Library	inalib.gc.ca
Industry Canada	ic.gc.ca
Information System on Marine Navigation	innav.gc.ca
Intergovernmental Affairs	aia.gc.ca
National Energy Board	neb.gc.ca
National Energy Board	one.gc.ca
National Joint Council	njc-cnm.gc.ca
National Search and Rescue Secretariat	nss.gc.ca
National Search and Rescue Secretariat	snrs.gc.ca
Natural Resources Canada	nrcan.gc.ca
Natural Resources Canada	rncan.gc.ca
Network Centres of Excellence	nce.gc.ca
Network Centres of Excellence	rce.gc.ca

Network Planning and Support Division	nspd.gc.ca
Office of the Auditor General of Canada	oag-bvg.gc.ca
Office of the Commissioner of Official Languages	ocol-clo.gc.ca
Office of the Superintendent of Financial Institutions	osfi-bsif.gc.ca
Parks Canada-Canadian Heritage	parksnet.gc.ca
Parliament of Canada	parl.gc.ca
Prairie Farm Rehabilitation Administration	pfra.gc.ca
Prime Minister's Office	pm.gc.ca
Privy Council Office of Canada	bcp.gc.ca
Privy Council Office of Canada	pco.gc.ca
Public Service Commission of Canada	psc-cfp.gc.ca
Public Service Staff Relations Board	pssrb-crtfp.gc.ca
Public Works and Government Services Canada	pwgsc.gc.ca
Public Works and Government Services Canada	tpsgc.gc.ca
Radian Learning and Communications Network	radian.gc.ca
Reference Canada	refcda.gc.ca
Revenue Canada	rc.gc.ca
Royal Canadian Mounted Police	rcmp-grc.gc.ca
Saskatchewan Region - Human Resources	saskvision.gc.ca
Solicitor General Secretariat Canada	sgc.gc.ca
Status of Women Canada	swc-cfc.gc.ca
Supreme Court of Canada	scc-csc.gc.ca
Telefilm Canada	telefilm.gc.ca
The Bank of Canada	bond.gc.ca
Transport Canada	tc.gc.ca
Transportation Safety Board of Canada	bst-tsb.gc.ca
Treasury Board Secretariat	tbs-stc.gc.ca
Veterans Affairs	vac-acc.gc.ca
X.400 Gateway Service	x400.gc.ca

APPENDIX G

Directory of Canadian Internet Access Providers

Your Provincial and Territorial Guide to Getting on the Internet

Welcome to the directory of Canadian Internet access providers! This is a guide to organizations that sell access to the Internet in Canada. Whether you are looking for a personal Internet account or an Internet connection for your entire organization, you can use this directory to find Internet access providers that are operating in your city or town. To help you locate an access provider in your calling area, this directory has been divided into two sections. The first section includes an alphabetical list of Canadian cities and towns cross-referenced to the names of local Internet access providers. The second section contains an alphabetical listing of Internet access providers in Canada. In addition to selling "access" to the Internet, many Internet access providers sell World Wide Web services. These services range from do-it-yourself Web pages to full design and implementation of a World Wide Web site for your company or organization. See Chapter 14 ("Building a Web Site") for a discussion of some of the issues involved in setting up a Web site.

There are an estimated 400 – 500 Internet access providers in Canada today. This number is constantly fluctuating as new providers appear, old providers disappear, and existing providers merge with each other. This directory does not attempt to list every single access provider in Canada. Rather, it provides a cross-section of providers operating across the country. Be sure to read Chapter 20 ("The Changing Face of the Internet Industry in Canada") for an overview of some key Internet trends relating to Internet access in Canada.

Here's how to use this directory:

Step 1. Look up the name of a city or town in the list below. Also check for the names of other cities and towns in the local calling area of the city or town you are interested in.

Step 2. Check under the city or town name for the names of Internet providers operating in that area. Most Internet providers are rapidly expanding their service areas. If you can't find an Internet access provider in your community, contact the providers that are closest to you to determine when and if they plan to offer service in your community. Also check with national Internet providers such as Sympatico to find out if they offer Internet access in your area.

Step 3. Proceed to the alphabetical listing of providers and look up the names of the providers you are interested in. There you will find a profile of each provider, including services and contact information. That's it!

Community Networks

One alternative source of Internet access not covered by this directory is a community network or "Free-Net." Community networks are not-for-profit, locally operated computer systems that provide residents with access to on-line community information and the Internet. Most of these systems are run primarily by volunteers, and are funded either by their users or through corporate or government grants. Some community networks operate under the same principle as public libraries, and provide their services at no charge to users. Other community networks impose a mandatory membership fee or other charges for their services. Community networks can be a great place to get your feet wet, but they usually cannot provide the same quality of Internet access that you would receive through a commercial Internet access provider. Check with your local library to find out if there is a community network or Free-Net operating in your community.

If you are already on the Internet, we recommend two sources of information about community network initiatives in Canada. The first is Telecommunities Canada, a not-for-profit organization that promotes community networking across Canada. Visit Telecommunities Canada's home page at **http://www.freenet.mb.ca/tc/index.html**. The second source of information is Community Access Canada, an Industry Canada initiative that is funding hundreds of Internet access projects in rural communities across the country. Visit the Community Access Canada Web site at **http://cnet.unb.ca**

Index of Cities and Towns Served by Canadian Internet Access Providers

Canada

Canada-wide These organizations provide Internet access in multiple cities and towns across Canada. AOL Canada, CompuServe, HookUp Communications, IBM Global Network, iSTAR Internet Inc., NETCOM Canada Inc., Sympatico, TotalNet Inc.

Alberta

Alberta-wide Sympatico—The Internet Service For Everyone™

Acme CYBERStream Inc., Kneehill Internet Services

Aidrie CYBERStream Inc.

Airdrie CyberWAVE Technologies Inc., Telnet Canada Enterprises, Ltd.

Alberta Beach Super i-Way, The Internet Centre, WorldGate Inc.

Ardrossan Super i-Way, The Internet Centre

Ashmont The Internet Centre

Banff HookUp Communications

Barons Lethbridge Internet Services

Barrhead Lands Systems Ltd., Westlock Internet

Bashaw The Internet Centre

Bawlf The Internet Centre

Beaumont The Internet Centre, Super i-Way, WorldGate Inc.

Beaverlodge The Internet Centre

Beiseker CYBERStream Inc., CyberWAVE Technologies Inc., Kneehill Internet Services, Telnet Canada Enterprises, Ltd.

Berwyn The Internet Centre

Blackie CYBERStream Inc., CyberWAVE Technologies Inc.

Blue Ridge Lands Systems Ltd.

Bon Accord The Internet Centre, Super i-Way, WorldGate Inc.

Bragg Creek CYBERStream Inc., CyberWAVE Technologies Inc.

Brooks HookUp Communications

Brownvale The Internet Centre

Bruderheim Super i-Way, The Internet Centre, WorldGate Inc.

Calgary Alberta Supernet Inc., AOL Canada (America Online), CompuServe, Cybersurf Information Access, CyberWAVE Technologies Inc., Cycor Communications Inc., Fleximation Systems Inc., HookUp Communications, i*STAR Internet Inc., Kneehill Internet Services, Lexicom Ltd., Metrix Interlink Corporation, Netcom Canada Inc., NetMatrix Corporation, Netway Internetworking Technologies, OA Internet, Omegan Internet Services Inc., QNETIX Computer Consultants Inc., T-8000 Information Systems, Telnet Canada Enterprises, Ltd., TNC–The Network Centre, UUNET Canada Inc., WBM Office Systems, WestLink Internet

Calmar Super i-Way, The Internet Centre, WorldGate Inc.

Camrose The Internet Centre

Cardston Lethbridge Internet Services

Carmangay Lethbridge Internet Services

Caroline The Internet Centre

Carstairs CYBERStream Inc., CyberWAVE Technologies Inc.

Castlegar HookUp Communications

Champion Lethbridge Internet Services

Chipman Super i-Way, The Internet Centre, WorldGate Inc.

Chochrane Telnet Canada Enterprises, Ltd.

Clairmont The Internet Centre

Clyde Westlock Internet

Coaldale Lethbridge Internet Services

Cochrane CYBERStream Inc., CyberWAVE Technologies Inc.

Cold Lake The Internet Centre

Cremona CYBERStream Inc., CyberWAVE Technologies Inc.

Crossfield CYBERStream Inc., CyberWAVE Technologies Inc.

Dapp Westlock Internet

Daysland The Internet Centre

Debolt The Internet Centre

Devon Super i-Way, The Internet Centre, WorldGate Inc.

Didsbury/Sundre The Internet Centre

Dixonville The Internet Centre

Drayton Valley The Internet Centre

East SpringBank Telnet Canada Enterprises, Ltd.

Edmonton (International Airport) Super i-Way

Edmonton Alberta Supernet Inc., AOL Canada (America Online), Communication Inter-Accès, CompuServe, Cybersurf Information Access, Cycor Communications Inc., HookUp Communications, i*STAR Internet Inc., Metrix Interlink Corporation, Netcom Canada Inc., Netway Internetworking Technologies, OA Internet, Omegan Internet Services Inc., P.G. DataNet Inc., QNETIX Computer Consultants Inc., The Internet Centre, The Internet Companion, TNC–The Network Centre, UUNET Canada Inc., WBM Office Systems, Web Networks/NirvCentre, WorldGate Inc.

Elk Point The Internet Centre

Enchant Lethbridge Internet Services

Estevan HookUp Communications

Fawcett Westlock Internet

Flatbush Westlock Internet

Fort Assiniboine Lands Systems Ltd.

Fort Macleod Lethbridge Internet Services

Fort McMurray The Internet Centre, TNC–The Network Centre

Fort Saskatchewan Super i-Way, The Internet Centre, WorldGate Inc.

Fort Vermilion The Internet Centre

Gibbons Super i-Way, The Internet Centre, WorldGate Inc.

Girouxville The Internet Centre

Glendon The Internet Centre

Glenwood Lethbridge Internet Services

Grimshaw The Internet Centre

Hay Lakes Super i-Way, The Internet Centre, WorldGate Inc.

Heisler The Internet Centre

High Level The Internet Centre

High Prairie The Internet Centre

High River CYBERStream Inc., CyberWAVE Technologies Inc., Telnet Canada Enterprises, Ltd.

Hinton The Internet Centre

Hobbema The Internet Centre

Hythe The Internet Centre

Innisfail Alberta Supernet Inc.

Iron Springs Lethbridge Internet Services

Irricana CYBERStream Inc., CyberWAVE Technologies Inc.

Jarvie Westlock Internet

Jasper The Internet Centre

Keephills Super i-Way, The Internet Centre, WorldGate Inc.

Kinuso The Internet Centre
Lacombe Alberta Supernet Inc.
Lamont Super i-Way, The Internet Centre, WorldGate Inc.
Langdon CYBERStream Inc., CyberWAVE Technologies Inc.
Leduc/Nisku TNC–The Network Centre
Leduc Super i-Way, The Internet Centre, WorldGate Inc.
Legal Super i-Way, The Internet Centre, WorldGate Inc.
Lethbridge Cybersurf Information Access, Lethbridge Internet Services
Linden Kneehill Internet Services
Lloydminster HookUp Communications
Long View CyberWAVE Technologies Inc.
Longview CYBERStream Inc.
Magrath Lethbridge Internet Services
Mameo The Internet Centre
Mayerthorpe Lands Systems Ltd.
Medicine Hat HookUp Communications
Millet Super i-Way, The Internet Centre, WorldGate Inc.
Mirror The Internet Centre
Morinville The Internet Centre, WorldGate Inc.
Morley CYBERStream Inc., CyberWAVE Technologies Inc.
Mulhurst The Internet Centre
Myrnam The Internet Centre
Namao Super i-Way, The Internet Centre, WorldGate Inc.
Nampa The Internet Centre
Neerlandia Westlock Internet
New Dayton Lethbridge Internet Services
New Norway The Internet Centre
New Sarepta Super i-Way, The Internet Centre, WorldGate Inc.
Nisku Super i-Way, The Internet Centre
Nobleford Lethbridge Internet Services
Okotoks CYBERStream Inc., CyberWAVE Technologies Inc., Telnet Canada Enterprises, Ltd.
Olds Alberta Supernet Inc., The Internet Centre
Onoway Super i-Way, The Internet Centre, WorldGate Inc.
Peace River The Internet Centre
Pickardville Westlock Internet
Picture Butte Lethbridge Internet Services
Ponoka Alberta Supernet Inc., The Internet Centre
Raymond Lethbridge Internet Services
Red Deer Alberta Supernet Inc., Cybersurf Information Access, Netway Internetworking Technologies, The Internet Centre
Redwater Super i-Way, The Internet Centre, WorldGate Inc.
Rimbley The Internet Centre
Rochester Westlock Internet
Rocky Mountain House Alberta Supernet Inc., The Internet Centre
Rosalind The Internet Centre
Rycroft The Internet Centre
Sangudo Lands Systems Ltd.
Sexsmith The Internet Centre
Sherwood Park Super i-Way, The Internet Centre, WorldGate Inc.
Slave Lake Alberta Supernet Inc., The Internet Centre
Smith The Internet Centre
Spirit River The Internet Centre
Spruce Grove Super i-Way, The Internet Centre, WorldGate Inc.
St. Albert The Internet Centre, WorldGate Inc.
St. Michael Super i-Way, The Internet Centre, WorldGate Inc.
St. Paul The Internet Centre
St. Vincent The Internet Centre
Standoff Lethbridge Internet Services
Stettler Alberta Supernet Inc., The Internet Centre
Stirling Lethbridge Internet Services
Stony Plain Super i-Way, The Internet Centre, WorldGate Inc.
Strathmore CYBERStream Inc., CyberWAVE Technologies Inc.
Strome The Internet Centre
Swan Hills Alberta Supernet Inc., Lands Systems Ltd.
Taber Lethbridge Internet Services
Tawatinaw Westlock Internet
Thorhild Westlock Internet
Thorsby Super i-Way, The Internet Centre, WorldGate Inc.
Three Hills Kneehill Internet Services, The Internet Centre
Tofield Alberta Supernet Inc., Super i-Way, The Internet Centre, WorldGate Inc.
Turner Valley CYBERStream Inc., CyberWAVE Technologies Inc.
Two Hills The Internet Centre
Vega Westlock Internet
Vilna The Internet Centre

Wabamun Super i-Way, The Internet Centre, WorldGate Inc.
Wanham The Internet Centre
Wembly The Internet Centre
Westlock Lands Systems Ltd., Westlock Internet
Wetaskiwin The Internet Centre
Whitecourt Lands Systems Ltd.
Widewater The Internet Centre
Wrentham Lethbridge Internet Services

British Columbia

British Columbia-wide Sympatico—The Internet Service For Everyone™
100 Mile House HookUp Communications, Synaptic Communications Inc.
Abbotsford HookUp Communications
Aldergrove HookUp Communications, Infinity Internet Communications, Infoserve Technology Ltd.
Ashcroft HookUp Communications
Aspen Park HookUp Communications
Atlin Hypertech North Inc.
Barnfield HookUp Communications
Beach Grove Infoserve Technology Ltd.
Black Creek Digital Ark
Bowser Digital Ark
Britannia Mountain Internet (Division of Tantalus Technologies Inc.)
Burnaby Axion Internet Communications Inc., HookUp Communications, Infinity Internet Communications, Infoserve Technology Ltd., Internet Portal Services, Maximum Internet, NPSNET, SOHO Skyway
Burns Lake HookUp Communications
Campbell River Digital Ark, HookUp Communications
Castlegar The Net Idea Telecommunications Inc.
Cedar Digital Ark
Chetwynd Synaptic Communications Inc.
Clearwater HookUp Communications
Clinton HookUp Communications
Cloverdale Infoserve Technology Ltd.
Comox Digital Ark, HookUp Communications
Coquitlam Axion Internet Communications Inc., HookUp Communications, Infinity Internet Communications, Infoserve Technology Ltd., Internet Portal Services, NPSNET, SOHO Skyway
Courtenay Digital Ark
Cranbrook HookUp Communications
Creston HookUp Communications
Cumberland Digital Ark
Dawson Creek Synaptic Communications Inc.
Delta Axion Internet Communications Inc., HookUp Communications, Infinity Internet Communications, NPSNET, SOHO Skyway
Denman Island Digital Ark
Douglas Lake HookUp Communications
Duncan HookUp Communications
Egmont Sunshine Net Inc.
Fernie Okanagan Internet Junction, Inc.
Fort Langley Infinity Internet Communications, Infoserve Technology Ltd.
Fort St. John HookUp Communications, Synaptic Communications Inc.
Furry Creek Mountain Internet (Division of Tantalus Technologies Inc.)
Gabriola Island Digital Ark
Gold River HookUp Communications
Golden Okanagan Internet Junction, Inc.
Grand Forks HookUp Communications
Haney Infoserve Technology Ltd.
Hornby Island Digital Ark
Houston HookUp Communications
Invermere Okanagan Internet Junction, Inc.
Kamloops HookUp Communications
Kelowna CSI Group of Companies (Cyberstore Systems Inc.), HookUp Communications, Silk Internet
Ladner HookUp Communications, Infoserve Technology Ltd., Maximum Internet
Langley Infinity Internet Communications, Infoserve Technology Ltd., NPSNET
Lantzville Digital Ark
Logan Lake HookUp Communications
Lumby Okanagan Internet Junction, Inc.
Lytton HookUp Communications
Mackenzie Synaptic Communications Inc.
Maple Ridge Axion Internet Communications Inc., HookUp Communications, Infinity Internet Communications, NPSNET
Merritt HookUp Communications
Merville Digital Ark
Mission HookUp Communications, Infinity Internet Communications
Nanaimo Digital Ark, HookUp Communications
Nanoose Digital Ark
Nelson HookUp Communications, The Net Idea Telecommunications Inc.
New West Maximum Internet

New Westminster Axion Internet Communications Inc., HookUp Communications, Infinity Internet Communications, Infoserve Technology Ltd., NPSNET

Newton Infoserve Technology Ltd.

North Delta Maximum Internet

North Vancouver Axion Internet Communications Inc., HookUp Communications, Infinity Internet Communications, Infoserve Technology Ltd., Internet Portal Services, NPSNET, SOHO Skyway

Oak Bay Octonet Communications Corporation

Okanagan Centre Silk Internet

Oyster Bay Digital Ark

Parksville Digital Ark

Parkville HookUp Communications

Peachland Silk Internet

Pemberton Mountain Internet (Division of Tantalus Technologies Inc.)

Penticton HookUp Communications

Pitt Meadows HookUp Communications, Infinity Internet Communications, Infoserve Technology Ltd.

Port Alberni HookUp Communications

Port Coquitlam HookUp Communications, Infinity Internet Communications, Infoserve Technology Ltd., NPSNET

Port Hardy HookUp Communications

Port Mellon Sunshine Net Inc.

Port Moody Axion Internet Communications Inc., Infinity Internet Communications, Infoserve Technology Ltd., Internet Portal Services, NPSNET

Portage La Prairie Okanagan Internet Junction, Inc.

Prince George HookUp Communications, Mag-Net BBS Ltd., Synaptic Communications Inc.

Prince Rupert HookUp Communications

Quadra Island Digital Ark

Qualicum Beach Digital Ark

Qualicum HookUp Communications

Queen Charlotte HookUp Communications

Quesnel HookUp Communications, Synaptic Communications Inc.

Richmond Axion Internet Communications Inc., HookUp Communications, Infinity Internet Communications, Infoserve Technology Ltd., Internet Portal Services, Maximum Internet, SOHO Skyway

Salmon Arm HookUp Communications

Sidney Octonet Communications Corporation

Smithers HookUp Communications

Sooke Octonet Communications Corporation

Squamish CSI Group of Companies (Cyberstore Systems Inc.), Mountain Internet (Division of Tantalus Technologies Inc.)

Surrey Axion Internet Communications Inc., Infinity Internet Communications, Infoserve Technology Ltd., Maximum Internet, NPSNET

Terrace RGS Internet Services Ltd.

Tofino HookUp Communications

Trail HookUp Communications, The Net Idea Telecommunications Inc.

Treherne Okanagan Internet Junction, Inc.

Tsawassen Maximum Internet

Ucluelet HookUp Communications

Union Bay Digital Ark

Vancouver AOL Canada (America Online), Axion Internet Communications Inc., British Columbia Business Connections Ltd., Communication Inter-Accès, CompuServe, CSI Group of Companies (Cyberstore Systems Inc.), CSP Internet (Pacific Interconnect), Cycor Communications Inc., Fleximation Systems Inc., Helinet, A Division of Helikon Technologies Inc., Helix Internet, HookUp Communications, Infinity Internet Communications, Infoserve Technology Ltd., Internet Portal Services, i*STAR Internet Inc., Magic Total Net Inc., Maximum Internet, Metrix Interlink Corporation, Mortimer Online, Netcom Canada Inc., NPSNET, Omegan Internet Services Inc., QNETIX Computer Consultants Inc., SOHO Skyway, UUNET Canada Inc., Web Networks/NirvCentre

Vernon Okanagan Internet Junction, Inc.

Victoria AOL Canada (America Online), British Columbia Business Connections Ltd., CompuServe, CSI Group of Companies (Cyberstore Systems Inc.), CSP Internet (Pacific Interconnect), Cybersurf Information Access, Cycor Communications Inc., HookUp Communications, i*STAR Internet Inc., Netcom Canada Inc., NPSNET, Octonet Communications Corporation, Omegan Internet Services Inc., Pacific Coast Net Inc.

Walley Infoserve Technology Ltd.

Wellington Digital Ark

West Vancouver Axion Internet Communications Inc., HookUp Communications, Infinity Internet Communications, Infoserve Technology Ltd., NPSNET, SOHO Skyway

Westbank Silk Internet

Westwold HookUp Communications

Whistler Mountain Internet (Division of Tantalus Technologies Inc.)

White Rock Axion Internet Communications Inc., HookUp Communications, Infinity Internet Communications, Infoserve Technology Ltd., Maximum Internet, NPSNET

Whonnock Infoserve Technology Ltd.

Williams Lake HookUp Communications, Synaptic Communications Inc.

Willow Point Digital Ark

Winfield Silk Internet

Manitoba

Manitoba-wide Sympatico—The Internet Service For Everyone™

Altona Astra Network Inc.

Amarath CompuTECH Internet

Ashern Escape Communications Corp.

Baldur CompuTECH Internet

Brandon Astra Network Inc., Docker Services Ltd.

Cross Lake NorthStar Communications

Dauphin Astra Network Inc.

Dugald Astra Network Inc., Autobahn Access Corporation, Gate West Communications

Emerson Astra Network Inc.

Eriksdale Escape Communications Corp.

Fisher Branch Escape Communications Corp.

Gladstone CompuTECH Internet

Glenboro CompuTECH Internet

Gretna Astra Network Inc.

High Bluff CompuTECH Internet

Komarno Astra Network Inc.

Langruth CompuTECH Internet

Letellier Astra Network Inc.

Lockport Astra Network Inc., Autobahn Access Corporation, Gate West Communications

Lorette Astra Network Inc., Autobahn Access Corporation, Gate West Communications

Lundar Escape Communications Corp.

MacGregor CompuTECH Internet

Marquette Astra Network Inc.

McCreary Astra Network Inc.

Moosehorn Escape Communications Corp.

Morris Astra Network Inc.

Nelson House NorthStar Communications

Oakbank Astra Network Inc., Autobahn Access Corporation, Gate West Communications

Oakville CompuTECH Internet

Paint Lake NorthStar Communications

Petersfield Astra Network Inc.

Plum Coulee Astra Network Inc.

Poplarfield Escape Communications Corp.

Portage La Prairie CompuTECH Internet

Sanford Astra Network Inc., Autobahn Access Corporation, Gate West Communications

Selkirk Astra Network Inc.

Setting Lake NorthStar Communications

St. Adolphe Astra Network Inc., Autobahn Access Corporation, Gate West Communications

St. Andrews Gate West Communications

St. Francois Xavier Astra Network Inc., Autobahn Access Corporation, Gate West Communications

St. Jean Astra Network Inc.

St. Laurent Escape Communications Corp.

St. Rose Astra Network Inc.

Starbuck Astra Network Inc., Autobahn Access Corporation, Gate West Communications

Stonewall Astra Network Inc., Autobahn Access Corporation, Gate West Communications

Stony Mountain Astra Network Inc., Autobahn Access Corporation, Gate West Communications

Teulon Astra Network Inc.

Thompson NorthStar Communications

Waboden NorthStar Communications

Warren Astra Network Inc.

Wawanesa CompuTECH Internet

Winnipeg AOL Canada (America Online), Astra Network Inc., Autobahn Access Corporation, CompuServe, Cyberspace Online Information Systems, Cybersurf Information Access, Cycor Communications Inc., Escape Communications Corp., Fleximation Systems Inc., Gate West Communications, HookUp Communications, Internet Solutions Inc., i*STAR Internet Inc., Magic Total Net Inc., Metrix Interlink Corporation, Netcom Canada Inc., Omegan Internet Services Inc., Pangea.ca Inc., QNETIX Computer Consultants Inc.

Woodlands Astra Network Inc.

New Brunswick

New Brunswick-wide NB Tel, Sympatico—The Internet Service For Everyone™

Dieppe Maritime Internet Services Inc. (MIS)

Fredericton Maritime Internet Services Inc. (MIS)

Grand Bay Maritime Internet Services Inc. (MIS)

Hampton Maritime Internet Services Inc. (MIS)

Kennebecasis Valley Maritime Internet Services Inc. (MIS)

Moncton Cycor Communications Inc., HookUp Communications, i*STAR Internet Inc., Maritime Internet Services Inc. (MIS), Omegan Internet Services Inc.

New Maryland Maritime Internet Services Inc. (MIS)
Oromocto Maritime Internet Services Inc. (MIS)
Riverview Maritime Internet Services Inc. (MIS)
Sackville Kayhay Internet & Communications
Saint John Cycor Communications Inc., IBM Global Network, Maritime Internet Services Inc. (MIS)
St. Andrews Maritime Internet Services Inc. (MIS)
St. Stephen Maritime Internet Services Inc. (MIS)
Westfield Maritime Internet Services Inc. (MIS)

Newfoundland

Newfoundland-wide Atlantic Connect, Sympatico—The Internet Service For Everyone™
Baie Verte STEM~Net
Bay Robert's STEM~Net
Bonavista STEM~Net
Burin STEM~Net
Carbonear STEM~Net
Clarenville STEM~Net
Corner Brook Atlantic Connect, STEM~Net
Deer Lake STEM~Net
Gander STEM~Net
Grand Bank STEM~Net
Grand Falls-Windsor STEM~Net
Happy Valley-Goose Bay STEM~Net
Labrador City STEM~Net
Lewisporte STEM~Net
Mount Pearl Cable Atlantic Incorporated
Placentia STEM~Net
Port aux Basques STEM~Net
Springdale STEM~Net
St. Anthony STEM~Net
St. John's Cable Atlantic Incorporated, Cycor Communications Inc., HookUp Communications, IBM Global Network, STEM~Net
Stephenville Atlantic Connect, STEM~Net
Windsor STEM~Net

Nova Scotia

Nova Scotia-wide Sympatico—The Internet Service For Everyone™
Amherst Atlantic Connect, i*STAR Internet Inc., North Shore Internet Services, Omegan Internet Services Inc.
Annapolis Royal Global Linx Internet Inc.
Antigonish Atlantic Connect, i*STAR Internet Inc., Omegan Internet Services Inc.
Baddeck Atlantic Connect
Bedford Atlantic Connect, Kayhay Internet & Communications, NavNet Communications
Belliveau Cove HookUp Communications
Bridgewater Atlantic Connect, i*STAR Internet Inc., Omegan Internet Services Inc.
Brooklyn Atlantic Connect
Chezzetcook Kayhay Internet & Communications
Dartmouth Atlantic Connect, HookUp Communications, Kayhay Internet & Communications, NavNet Communications
Digby Global Linx Internet Inc.
Elmsdale Kayhay Internet & Communications
Enfield Atlantic Connect
French Village Kayhay Internet & Communications
Guysborough Atlantic Connect
Halifax AOL Canada (America Online), Atlantic Connect, CompuServe, Cycor Communications Inc., HookUp Communications, i*STAR Internet Inc., Kayhay Internet & Communications, Metrix Interlink Corporation, NavNet Communications, Netcom Canada Inc., NewEdge Technologies Inc., Omegan Internet Services Inc.
Hantsport Global Linx Internet Inc.
Hubbards Atlantic Connect, Kayhay Internet & Communications
Kentville Global Linx Internet Inc., i*STAR Internet Inc., Omegan Internet Services Inc.
Ketch Harbour Kayhay Internet & Communications
Lawrencetown/Middleton i*STAR Internet Inc.
Liverpool Atlantic Connect
Lunenburg HookUp Communications
Middleton Global Linx Internet Inc., Omegan Internet Services Inc.
Milton Atlantic Connect
Montague HookUp Communications
Mount Uniacke Kayhay Internet & Communications
Musquodoboit Harbour Kayhay Internet & Communications
New Glasgow Atlantic Connect, i*STAR Internet Inc., North Shore Internet Services, Omegan Internet Services Inc.
Pictou Atlantic Connect, North Shore Internet Services
Port Hawkesbury Atlantic Connect, i*STAR Internet Inc., Omegan Internet Services Inc.

Prospect Road Kayhay Internet & Communications
River John North Shore Internet Services
Sackville Atlantic Connect
Shelbourne County HookUp Communications
Shubenacadie Atlantic Connect, i*STAR Internet Inc., NavNet Communications, Omegan Internet Services Inc.
Springhill Atlantic Connect
St. John HookUp Communications
St. Margarets Kayhay Internet & Communications
Stellarton Atlantic Connect
Sydney Atlantic Connect, i*STAR Internet Inc., Omegan Internet Services Inc.
Tatamagouche Atlantic Connect, North Shore Internet Services
Tignish HookUp Communications
Truro Atlantic Connect, i*STAR Internet Inc., North Shore Internet Services, Omegan Internet Services Inc.
Waverley Kayhay Internet & Communications
Wentworth Atlantic Connect
Whycocomagh Atlantic Connect
Windsor Global Linx Internet Inc., i*STAR Internet Inc., Omegan Internet Services Inc.
Wolfville i*STAR Internet Inc.
Yarmouth i*STAR Internet Inc., Omegan Internet Services Inc.

Northwest Territories

Fort Providence NTnet Society, SSI Micro
Fort Smith Network North Communications Ltd., NTnet Society
Hay River Network North Communications Ltd., NTnet Society, SSI Micro
Inuvik Network North Communications Ltd., NTnet Society
Iqaluit Network North Communications Ltd., NTnet Society
Rankin Inlet Network North Communications Ltd., NTnet Society, Sakku Arctic Technologies Inc.
Yellowknife NTnet Society, SSI Micro, Tamarack Computers Ltd.

Ontario

Ontario-wide ONet Networking Inc. (ONet), Sympatico—The Internet Service For Everyone
Acton Aztec Computer Inc., Globalserve Communications Inc., Interactive Online Ltd., Internet Innovations Inc., MGL Systems Computer Technologies Inc., Sentex Communications Corporation
Adolphustown InterNet Kingston
Ailsa Craig MGL Systems Computer Technologies Inc., Netcom Canada Inc., Odyssey Network Inc., Serix Technologies
Ajax-Pickering Internet Light and Power™, Netcom Canada Inc., Netcom Canada Inc., Sentex Communications Corporation
Ajax Interhop Network Services Inc., Internet Canada Corporation (ICAN), Magic Total Net Inc., Myna Communications Inc., Online Computer Distribution, Xenon Laboratories
Alberton Networx Internet System
Alcona Beach TransData Communications
Aldershot Globalserve Communications Inc., Networx Internet System
Alexandria DataCom Online Services, Glen-Net Communications
Alfred CyberPlus Technologies Inc., Glen-Net Communications
Algoma Mills Internet North
Alliston Barrie Connex Inc., Barrie Internet, Central Ontario Internet Services Inc., Interhop Network Services Inc.
Alma Sentex Communications Corporation
Almonte CyberPlus Technologies Inc., HookUp Communications, Netcom Canada Inc., Resudox Online Services Inc., Travel-Net Communications Inc., Trytel Internet Inc., WorldLink Internet Services
Alton headwaters network
Alvinston Odyssey Network Inc., Serix Technologies
Amherstburg HookUp Communications, Information Gateway Services Windsor, Netcom Canada Inc., NetCore Global Communications
Ancaster Burlington Network Services, Globalserve Communications Inc., Internet Connect Niagara, NetAccess Systems Inc., Netcom Canada Inc., Network Enterprise Technology Inc., Networx Internet System, Passport Online, Sentex Communications Corporation, Weslink Datalink Corporation, WorldCHAT™ Internet Services
Angus Barrie Internet, TransData Communications
Auburn Odyssey Network Inc.

Aurora Interhop Network Services Inc., Internet Light and Power™, Netcom Canada Inc., Sentex Communications Corporation, Xenon Laboratories

Avonmore DataCom Online Services, Glen-Net Communications

Ayr Burlington Network Services, Information Gateway Services (Kitchener-Waterloo) Inc., MGL Systems Computer Technologies Inc., Sentex Communications Corporation

Ayton Log On Internet Solutions

Baden Burlington Network Services, Information Gateway Services (Kitchener-Waterloo) Inc., MGL Systems Computer Technologies Inc., Sentex Communications Corporation

Bailieboro Heydon Computer Services Ltd., Online Computer Distribution, Peterboro.Net

Baillieboro KawarthaNET

Bala Muskoka.com

Baltimore Northumberland Online Ltd.

Barrie Barrie Connex Inc., Barrie Internet, Central Ontario Internet Services Inc., Grant Internet Communications Corporation, Interhop Network Services Inc., Internet Canada Corporation (ICAN), Magic Total Net Inc., TransData Communications

Bath InterNet Kingston

Baxter TransData Communications

Bayfield Odyssey Network Inc.

Baysville Muskoka.com

Beachville Internet NNT, Odyssey Network Inc.

Beamsville Internet Connect Niagara, Netcom Canada Inc., Networx Internet System, Vaxxine Computer Systems Inc.

Beeton Barrie Connex Inc., Barrie Internet, Interhop Network Services Inc., Times.net, TransData Communications

Bell Ewart TransData Communications

Belle River HookUp Communications, Information Gateway Services Windsor, Netcom Canada Inc., NetCore Global Communications,

Belleville NetReach International

Belmont MGL Systems Computer Technologies Inc., Netcom Canada Inc., Odyssey Network Inc., Serix Technologies

Bethany Heydon Computer Services Ltd., KawarthaNET, Online Computer Distribution, Peterboro.Net

Bethesda Interhop Network Services Inc., Internet Light and Power™, Netcom Canada Inc., Netcom Canada Inc., Sentex Communications Corporation, Xenon Laboratories

Binbrook Burlington Network Services, NetAccess Systems Inc., Netcom Canada Inc., Network Enterprise Technology Inc., Networx Internet System, Sentex Communications Corporation, WorldCHAT™ Internet Services

Blackheath Networx Internet System

Blackstock Online Computer Distribution

Blenheim HookUp Communications, Odyssey Network Inc.

Blind River Internet North

Bloomfield NetReach International

Bluewater Barrie Connex Inc., Central Ontario Internet Services Inc., TransData Communications

Blyth Odyssey Network Inc.

Bobcaygeon KawarthaNET

Bolton Interhop Network Services Inc., Internet Light and Power™, Netcom Canada Inc., Netcom Canada Inc., Sentex Communications Corporation, Xenon Laboratories

Bond Head Times.net

Borden-Angus Barrie Connex Inc., Central Ontario Internet Services Inc., Grant Internet Communications Corporation, Interhop Network Services Inc.

Borden Barrie Internet, TransData Communications

Bothwell Odyssey Network Inc.

Bourget Travel-Net Communications Inc.

Bowmanville Interhop Network Services Inc., Online Computer Distribution

Bracebridge Interhop Network Services Inc., Muskoka.com

Bradford Barrie Internet, Interhop Network Services Inc., Internet Canada Corporation (ICAN), Times.net

Brampton Aztec Computer Inc., Fleximation Systems Inc., Globalserve Communications Inc., Internet Canada Corporation (ICAN), Internet Front Inc., Internet Light and Power™, Internet XL, Myna Communications Inc., Netcom Canada Inc., Sentex Communications Corporation, Xenon Laboratories

Brantford HookUp Communications, Huron Internet Technologies, Interhop Network Services Inc., Network Enterprise Technology Inc., Networx Internet System, Sentex Communications Corporation

Brentwood TransData Communications

Breslau Burlington Network Services, Information Gateway Services (Kitchener-Waterloo) Inc., Internet Innovations Inc., MGL Systems Computer Technologies Inc., Netcom Canada Inc., Sentex Communications Corporation

Bridgenorth Heydon Computer Services Ltd., KawarthaNET, Online Computer Distribution, Peterboro.Net

Bright's Grove Electro-Byte Technologies

Bright Burlington Network Services, Information Gateway Services (Kitchener-Waterloo) Inc., Internet NNT, MGL Systems Computer Technologies Inc., Sentex Communications Corporation

Brooklin Netcom Canada Inc., Online Computer Distribution

Buckhorn Heydon Computer Services Ltd., KawarthaNET, Online Computer Distribution, Peterboro.Net

Bullock Corners Networx Internet System

Bunyan Electro-Byte Technologies

Burford WorldCHAT™ Internet Services

Burgessville Internet NNT

Burleigh Falls Heydon Computer Services Ltd., KawarthaNET, Online Computer Distribution, Peterboro.Net

Burlington Binatech Information Services Inc., Burlington Network Services, Interhop Network Services Inc., Internet Connect Niagara, Internet XL, i*STAR Internet Inc., NetAccess Systems Inc., Netcom Canada Inc., Network Enterprise Technology Inc., Networx Internet System, Passport Online, Pathway Communications, Sentex Communications Corporation, Spectranet Connections Inc., Weslink Datalink Corporation, WorldCHAT™ Internet Services

Caledon East headwaters network, Internet Canada Corporation (ICAN), Netcom Canada Inc.

Caledon Village headwaters network

Caledonia Burlington Network Services, Globalserve Communications Inc., NetAccess Systems Inc., Netcom Canada Inc., Network Enterprise Technology Inc., Networx Internet System, WorldCHAT™ Internet Services

Caledon Sentex Communications Corporation

Calgary Internet Canada Corporation (ICAN)

Cambray KawarthaNET

Cambridge Easynet Inc., Interactive Online Ltd., Interhop Network Services Inc., Internet Innovations Inc., i*STAR Internet Inc., MGL Systems Computer Technologies Inc., Network Enterprise Technology Inc., Sentex Communications Corporation, WorldCHAT™ Internet Services

Cameron KawarthaNET

Campbellford Heydon Computer Services Ltd., Online Computer Distribution

Campbellville Aztec Computer Inc., Burlington Network Services, Interhop Network Services Inc., Netcom Canada Inc., WorldCHAT™ Internet Services

Camperdown TransData Communications

Carleton Place HookUp Communications, Netcom Canada Inc., Resudox Online Services Inc., Travel-Net Communications Inc., Trytel Internet Inc., WorldLink Internet Services

Carp CyberPlus Technologies Inc., HookUp Communications, Netcom Canada Inc., Resudox Online Services Inc., Travel-Net Communications Inc., WorldLink Internet Services

Casselman Netcom Canada Inc., Travel-Net Communications Inc.

Castlemore Internet Light and Power™, Netcom Canada Inc., Sentex Communications Corporation, Xenon Laboratories

Cavan Heydon Computer Services Ltd., KawarthaNET, Online Computer Distribution, Peterboro.Net

Cayuga Burlington Network Services, NetAccess Systems Inc., Network Enterprise Technology Inc., Networx Internet System, WorldCHAT™ Internet Services

Centralia MGL Systems Computer Technologies Inc., Netcom Canada Inc., Odyssey Network Inc., Serix Technologies

Centreville InterNet Kingston

Chatham HookUp Communications, Inter*Com Information Services, Odyssey Network Inc., Worldwide Data Communications Inc.

Chatsworth Log On Internet Solutions, Sentex Communications Corporation

Chesley Log On Internet Solutions

Chippawa Vaxxine Computer Systems Inc.

Christian Island Barrie Connex Inc., Central Ontario Internet Services Inc., TransData Communications

Churchill TransData Communications

Clairemont Xenon Laboratories

Claremont Internet Canada Corporation (ICAN), Internet Light and Power™, Netcom Canada Inc., Sentex Communications Corporation

Clarence Creek Netcom Canada Inc., Travel-Net Communications Inc.

Clarington Interhop Network Services Inc.

Clarkson Burlington Network Services, Internet Light and Power™, Netcom Canada Inc., Sentex Communications Corporation, Xenon Laboratories

Clifford Log On Internet Solutions

Clinton Huron Internet Technologies, Odyssey Network Inc.

Cobalt Northern Telephone Ltd.
Coboconk KawarthaNET
Cobourg Northumberland Online Ltd.
Cochrane Age.net
Coldwater Barrie Connex Inc., Barrie Internet, Central Ontario Internet Services Inc., Interhop Network Services Inc., TransData Communications
Collingwood Barrie Connex Inc., Barrie Internet, Central Ontario Internet Services Inc., Grant Internet Communications Corporation, Huron Internet Technologies, TransData Communications
Comber NetCore Global Communications
Concord Dtronix Internet Services, Metrolinx
Connaught Northern Telephone Ltd.
Constance Bay CyberPlus Technologies Inc., HookUp Communications, Netcom Canada Inc., Resudox Online Services Inc., Travel-Net Communications Inc., WorldLink Internet Services
Cookstown Barrie Connex Inc., Barrie Internet, Central Ontario Internet Services Inc., Interhop Network Services Inc., Internet Canada Corporation (ICAN), Times.net, TransData Communications
Cooksville Burlington Network Services, Internet Light and Power™, Netcom Canada Inc., Sentex Communications Corporation, Xenon Laboratories
Corlam NetCore Global Communications
Cornwall DataCom Online Services, Glen-Net Communications
Corunna Electro-Byte Technologies, HookUp Communications
Courtright Electro-Byte Technologies
Craighurst TransData Communications
Craigleith TransData Communications
Crediton MGL Systems Computer Technologies Inc., Odyssey Network Inc., Serix Technologies
Creemore Barrie Connex Inc., Barrie Internet, Central Ontario Internet Services Inc., Grant Internet Communications Corporation, TransData Communications
Crown Hill TransData Communications
Crysler Travel-Net Communications Inc.
Cuister Centre Networx Internet System
Cumberland CyberPlus Technologies Inc., HookUp Communications, Netcom Canada Inc., Resudox Online Services Inc., Travel-Net Communications Inc., WorldLink Internet Services
Dalston TransData Communications
Delhi Internet NNT, Norfolk Internet Services
Deseronto NetReach International
Dorchester MGL Systems Computer Technologies Inc., Netcom Canada Inc., Odyssey Network Inc., Serix Technologies
Dorset Muskoka.com
Drayton Burlington Network Services, Information Gateway Services (Kitchener-Waterloo) Inc., MGL Systems Computer Technologies Inc., Sentex Communications Corporation
Dresden Odyssey Network Inc.
Drumbo Information Gateway Services (Kitchener-Waterloo) Inc., Internet NNT
Dublin ORCCA Networks Ltd.
Duncan TransData Communications
Dundas Burlington Network Services, Globalserve Communications Inc., Interhop Network Services Inc., NetAccess Systems Inc., Netcom Canada Inc., Network Enterprise Technology Inc., Networx Internet System, Passport Online, Sentex Communications Corporation, Weslink Datalink Corporation, WorldCHAT™ Internet Services, WorldCHAT™ Internet Services
Dunedin TransData Communications
Dunnville Networx Internet System
Dunsford KawarthaNET, Peterboro.Net
Duntroon TransData Communications
Durham Log On Internet Solutions
Dutton MGL Systems Computer Technologies Inc., Netcom Canada Inc., Odyssey Network Inc., Serix Technologies
Dwight Muskoka.com
Earlton Northern Telephone Ltd.
East Gwillimbury Times.net
Eastwood Internet NNT
Edgar TransData Communications
Edmonton Internet Canada Corporation (ICAN)
Eeryville Information Gateway Services Windsor
Elliot Lake Internet North
Elmira Burlington Network Services, Information Gateway Services (Kitchener-Waterloo) Inc., Interactive Online Ltd., MGL Systems Computer Technologies Inc., Sentex Communications Corporation, WorldCHAT™ Internet Services
Elmvale Barrie Connex Inc., Barrie Internet, Central Ontario Internet Services Inc., Interhop Network Services Inc., TransData Communications
Elmwood Log On Internet Solutions
Elora Burlington Network Services, Information Gateway Services (Kitchener-Waterloo) Inc., Interactive Online Ltd., Internet Innovations Inc., MGL Systems Computer Technologies Inc., Sentex Communications Corporation

Embro Internet NNT, MGL Systems Computer Technologies Inc., Odyssey Network Inc., Serix Technologies

Embrun HookUp Communications, Netcom Canada Inc., Resudox Online Services Inc., Travel-Net Communications Inc., WorldLink Internet Services

Emeryville Netcom Canada Inc., NetCore Global Communications

Emsdale Muskoka.com

Englehart Age.net, Northern Telephone Ltd., Ontario Northland–ONLink

Enterprise InterNet Kingston

Erin Aztec Computer Inc., Internet Innovations Inc., Sentex Communications Corporation

Essex HookUp Communications, Netcom Canada Inc., NetCore Global Communications

Etobicoke Globalserve Communications Inc., Metrolinx, Wiznet Inc.

Everett TransData Communications

Exeter MGL Systems Computer Technologies Inc., Odyssey Network Inc., Serix Technologies

Fenelon Falls Interhop Network Services Inc., KawarthaNET

Fergus Interactive Online Ltd., Internet Innovations Inc., MGL Systems Computer Technologies Inc., Sentex Communications Corporation

Fergusonvale TransData Communications

Fesserton TransData Communications

Feversham Grant Internet Communications Corporation, TransData Communications

Finch DataCom Online Services, Glen-Net Communications

Fingal MGL Systems Computer Technologies Inc., Netcom Canada Inc., Odyssey Network Inc., Serix Technologies

Forest Electro-Byte Technologies

Fort Erie Internet Connect Niagara, Vaxxine Computer Systems Inc.

Frankford NetReach International

Freelton Burlington Network Services, NetAccess Systems Inc., Netcom Canada Inc., Network Enterprise Technology Inc., Networx Internet System, Sentex Communications Corporation, WorldCHAT™ Internet Services

Fruitland Networx Internet System

Fulton Networx Internet System

Galt Burlington Network Services, Information Gateway Services (Kitchener-Waterloo) Inc., Netcom Canada Inc., Sentex Communications Corporation

Gananoque InterNet Kingston

Garden Hill Northumberland Online Ltd.

Georgetown Aztec Computer Inc., Globalserve Communications Inc., Internet Canada Corporation (ICAN), Internet Direct Canada Inc., Netcom Canada Inc.

Gilford TransData Communications

Glanford Networx Internet System

Glen Huron TransData Communications

Glen-Roberton Glen-Net Communications

Glencairn TransData Communications

Glencoe MGL Systems Computer Technologies Inc., Netcom Canada Inc., Odyssey Network Inc., Serix Technologies

Gloucester Achilles Internet Ltd., Babillard Synapse Inc., CyberPlus Technologies Inc., Cyberus Online Inc., HookUp Communications, Magma Communications Ltd., Resudox Online Services Inc., Travel-Net Communications Inc., Trytel Internet Inc., WorldLink Internet Services

Goderich HuronTel, Odyssey Network Inc.

Gormley Interhop Network Services Inc., Internet Light and Power™, Netcom Canada Inc., Sentex Communications Corporation, Xenon Laboratories

Grand Bend Internet HTL

Grand Valley headwaters network

Granton MGL Systems Computer Technologies Inc., Netcom Canada Inc., Odyssey Network Inc., Serix Technologies

Grassie Networx Internet System

Gravenhurst Interhop Network Services Inc., Muskoka.com

Grimsby Burlington Network Services, Internet Connect Niagara, NetAccess Systems Inc., Netcom Canada Inc., Network Enterprise Technology Inc., Networx Internet System, Sentex Communications Corporation, Vaxxine Computer Systems Inc., Weslink Datalink Corporation, WorldCHAT™ Internet Services

Guelph Burlington Network Services, Easynet Inc., Huron Internet Technologies, Information Gateway Services (Kitchener-Waterloo) Inc., Interactive Online Ltd., Interhop Network Services Inc., Internet Innovations Inc., Internet XL, i*STAR Internet Inc., Netcom Canada Inc., QNETIX Computer Consultants Inc., Sentex Communications Corporation, Web Networks/NirvCentre, WorldCHAT™ Internet Services, Worldwide Data Communications Inc.

Guthrie TransData Communications

Hagersville Burlington Network Services, NetAccess Systems Inc., Netcom Canada Inc., Network Enterprise Technology Inc., Sentex Communications Corporation, WorldCHAT™ Internet Services

Haileybury Northern Telephone Ltd.

Hamilton Binatech Information Services Inc., Burlington Network Services, CompuServe, Cycor Communications Inc., Focus Technologies Networks – aka FTN, Globalserve Communications Inc., IBM Global Network, Interhop Network Services Inc., Internet Canada Corporation (ICAN), Internet Connect Niagara, Internet Direct Canada Inc., Internet XL, i*STAR Internet Inc., Magic Total Net Inc., NetAccess Systems Inc., Netcom Canada Inc., Network Enterprise Technology Inc., Networx Internet System, Passport Online, QNETIX Computer Consultants Inc., Sentex Communications Corporation, Web Networks/NirvCentre, Weslink Datalink Corporation, WorldCHAT™ Internet Services

Hampton Online Computer Distribution

Hannon Networx Internet System

Hanover Huron Internet Technologies, Log On Internet Solutions

Harpers Corners Networx Internet System

Harrietsville MGL Systems Computer Technologies Inc., Netcom Canada Inc., Odyssey Network Inc., Serix Technologies

Harrow NetCore Global Communications

Harrowsmith InterNet Kingston

Hastings Heydon Computer Services Ltd., KawarthaNET, Online Computer Distribution, Peterboro.Net

Havelock Heydon Computer Services Ltd., Online Computer Distribution

Hearst Age.net, Northern Telephone Ltd., Ontario Northland–ONLink

Hensall Odyssey Network Inc.

Hepworth Log On Internet Solutions, Sentex Communications Corporation

Hespeler Burlington Network Services, Information Gateway Services (Kitchener-Waterloo) Inc., i*STAR Internet Inc., Netcom Canada Inc., Sentex Communications Corporation

Hickson Internet NNT

Highgate Odyssey Network Inc.

Hillsburgh Internet Innovations Inc., MGL Systems Computer Technologies Inc., Sentex Communications Corporation

Hillsdale TransData Communications

Hockley TransData Communications

Holly TransData Communications

Huntsville Muskoka.com

Hurley WorldCHAT™ Internet Services

Ilderton MGL Systems Computer Technologies Inc., Netcom Canada Inc., Odyssey Network Inc., Serix Technologies

Ingersoll Internet NNT, MGL Systems Computer Technologies Inc., Odyssey Network Inc., Serix Technologies

Ingleside DataCom Online Services, Glen-Net Communications

Innerkip Internet NNT

Innisfil TransData Communications

Inverary InterNet Kingston

Iron Bridge Internet North

Iroquois Falls Age.net, Northern Telephone Ltd.

Iroquois Glen-Net Communications

Jarvis Norfolk Internet Services

Jerseyville Networx Internet System

Jockvale HookUp Communications, Netcom Canada Inc., Resudox Online Services Inc., Travel-Net Communications Inc., WorldLink Internet Services

Kakabeka Falls Norlink Communications and Consulting

Kamiskotia Northern Telephone Ltd.

Kanata Achilles Internet Ltd., Babillard Synapse Inc., CyberPlus Technologies Inc., Cyberus Online Inc., HookUp Communications, Magma Communications Ltd., Netcom Canada Inc., Resudox Online Services Inc., Travel-Net Communications Inc., Trytel Internet Inc., WorldLink Internet Services

Kapuskasing Age.net, Northern Telephone Ltd., Ontario Northland–ONLink

Keene Heydon Computer Services Ltd., KawarthaNET, Online Computer Distribution, Peterboro.Net

Kemptville CyberPlus Technologies Inc., Netcom Canada Inc., Travel-Net Communications Inc.

Kerwood MGL Systems Computer Technologies Inc., Netcom Canada Inc., Odyssey Network Inc., Serix Technologies

Keswick Interhop Network Services Inc.

Killbride Networx Internet System

Kimberley TransData Communications

Kincardine HuronTel

King City Globalserve Communications Inc., Interhop Network Services Inc., Internet Light and Power™, Netcom Canada Inc., Netcom Canada Inc., Sentex Communications Corporation, Xenon Laboratories

Kingston i*STAR Internet Inc., Metrix Interlink Corporation, Omegan Internet Services Inc.

Kingsville Netcom Canada Inc., NetCore Global Communications

Kintore MGL Systems Computer Technologies Inc., Netcom Canada Inc., Odyssey Network Inc., Serix Technologies

Kirkland Lake Age.net, Northern Telephone Ltd., Ontario Northland–ONLink

Kirkton MGL Systems Computer Technologies Inc., Odyssey Network Inc., Serix Technologies

Kitchener-Waterloo IBM Global Network, Information Gateway Services (Kitchener-Waterloo) Inc., i*STAR Internet Inc., MGL Systems Computer Technologies Inc., Netcom Canada Inc., Web Networks/NirvCentre, WorldCHAT™ Internet Services

Kitchener AOL Canada (America Online), Burlington Network Services, CompuServe, Cycor Communications Inc., Easynet Inc., Huron Internet Technologies, Interactive Online Ltd., Interhop Network Services Inc., Interhop Network Services Inc., Internet Innovations Inc., Internet XL, Metrix Interlink Corporation, Sentex Communications Corporation, UUNET Canada Inc., Worldwide Data Communications Inc.

Kleinburg Interhop Network Services Inc., Internet Light and Power™, Netcom Canada Inc., Sentex Communications Corporation, Xenon Laboratories

L'Orignal Glen-Net Communications

La Salle Information Gateway Services Windsor, Netcom Canada Inc., NetCore Global Communications

Lafontaine Barrie Connex Inc., Central Ontario Internet Services Inc., TransData Communications

Lakefield Heydon Computer Services Ltd., KawarthaNET, Online Computer Distribution, Peterboro.Net

Lambeth MGL Systems Computer Technologies Inc., Netcom Canada Inc., Odyssey Network Inc., Serix Technologies

Lancaster DataCom Online Services, Glen-Net Communications

Langton Norfolk Internet Services

Larder Lake Northern Telephone Ltd.

Latchford Northern Telephone Ltd.

Laurin TransData Communications

Leamington Information Gateway Services Windsor, NetCore Global Communications

Lefroy Barrie Connex Inc., Barrie Internet, Central Ontario Internet Services Inc., Interhop Network Services Inc., Times.net, TransData Communications

Lindsay Interhop Network Services Inc., KawarthaNET, Online Computer Distribution, Peterboro.Net

Linwood Burlington Network Services, Information Gateway Services (Kitchener-Waterloo) Inc., MGL Systems Computer Technologies Inc., Sentex Communications Corporation

Lisle TransData Communications

Listowel Huron Internet Technologies

Little Britain KawarthaNET

London AOL Canada (America Online), CompuServe, Cycor Communications Inc., Focus Technologies Networks – aka FTN, HookUp Communications, HyperNet, Inter*Com Information Services, Internet Direct Canada Inc., Internet XL, Metrix Interlink Corporation, MGL Systems Computer Technologies Inc., Netcom Canada Inc., Odyssey Network Inc., Omegan Internet Services Inc., Passport Online, UUNET Canada Inc., Worldwide Data Communications Inc.

Long Sault DataCom Online Services, Glen-Net Communications

Loretto TransData Communications

Lowville Networx Internet System

Lucan MGL Systems Computer Technologies Inc., Netcom Canada Inc., Odyssey Network Inc., Serix Technologies

Lucasville Electro-Byte Technologies

Lucknow HuronTel

Lynden Burlington Network Services, NetAccess Systems Inc., Netcom Canada Inc., Network Enterprise Technology Inc., Networx Internet System, Sentex Communications Corporation, WorldCHAT™ Internet Services

Maidstone Netcom Canada Inc., NetCore Global Communications

Malton Internet Light and Power™, Netcom Canada Inc., Sentex Communications Corporation, Xenon Laboratories

Manotick CyberPlus Technologies Inc., HookUp Communications, Netcom Canada Inc., Resudox Online Services Inc., Travel-Net Communications Inc., Trytel Internet Inc., WorldLink Internet Services

Mansfield TransData Communications

Maple Interhop Network Services Inc., Internet Light and Power™, Netcom Canada Inc., Sentex Communications Corporation, Xenon Laboratories

Markham Dtronix Internet Services, Interhop Network Services Inc., Internet Front Inc., Internet Light and Power™, Metrolinx, Myna Communications Inc., Netcom Canada Inc., Sentex Communications Corporation, Wiznet Inc., Xenon Laboratories

Marmora NetReach International

Martintown DataCom Online Services, Glen-Net Communications

Matheson Northern Telephone Ltd.

Maxville DataCom Online Services, Glen-Net Communications

Maxwell TransData Communications

McGregor Netcom Canada Inc., NetCore Global Communications

Meaford Log On Internet Solutions, Sentex Communications Corporation, TransData Communications

Melbourne MGL Systems Computer Technologies Inc., Netcom Canada Inc., Odyssey Network Inc., Serix Technologies

Merlin Odyssey Network Inc.

Merrickville Netcom Canada Inc., Travel-Net Communications Inc.

Metcalfe CyberPlus Technologies Inc., HookUp Communications, Netcom Canada Inc., Resudox Online Services Inc., Travel-Net Communications Inc., WorldLink Internet Services

Midhurst TransData Communications

Midland Barrie Connex Inc., Barrie Internet, Central Ontario Internet Services Inc., Interhop Network Services Inc., TransData Communications

Mildmay Log On Internet Solutions

Milford Bay Muskoka.com

Millbank ORCCA Networks Ltd.

Millbrook Heydon Computer Services Ltd., Interhop Network Services Inc., KawarthaNET, Online Computer Distribution, Peterboro.Net

Millgrove Networx Internet System

Milton Aztec Computer Inc., Burlington Network Services, Globalserve Communications Inc., Interhop Network Services Inc., Netcom Canada Inc., WorldCHAT™ Internet Services

Milverton ORCCA Networks Ltd.

Minesing TransData Communications

Mississauga Burlington Network Services, Dtronix Internet Services, Fleximation Systems Inc., Focus Technologies Networks – aka FTN, Globalserve Communications Inc., Inline Information Services, Inc., Internet Front Inc., Internet Light and Power™, Magic Total Net Inc., Metrolinx, Myna Communications Inc., Sentex Communications Corporation, Spectranet Connections Inc., Wiznet Inc., Xenon Laboratories

Mitchell ORCCA Networks Ltd.

Monkton ORCCA Networks Ltd.

Moonbeam Northern Telephone Ltd.

Moonstone Barrie Connex Inc., Central Ontario Internet Services Inc., Internet Canada Corporation (ICAN), TransData Communications

Moose Creek DataCom Online Services, Glen-Net Communications

Moosonee Age.net

Mount Albert Interhop Network Services Inc.

Mount Albion Networx Internet System

Mount Brydges MGL Systems Computer Technologies Inc., Netcom Canada Inc., Odyssey Network Inc., Serix Technologies

Mount Forest Huron Internet Technologies

Mount Hope Burlington Network Services, NetAccess Systems Inc., Netcom Canada Inc., Network Enterprise Technology Inc., Networx Internet System, Sentex Communications Corporation, WorldCHAT™ Internet Services

Mount Pleasant WorldCHAT™ Internet Services

Murillo Norlink Communications and Consulting

Nairn MGL Systems Computer Technologies Inc., Netcom Canada Inc., Serix Technologies

Napanee InterNet Kingston, NetReach International

Narin Odyssey Network Inc.

Navan CyberPlus Technologies Inc., HookUp Communications, Netcom Canada Inc., Resudox Online Services Inc., Travel-Net Communications Inc., WorldLink Internet Services

Nepean Achilles Internet Ltd., Babillard Synapse Inc., CyberPlus Technologies Inc., Cyberus Online Inc., HookUp Communications, Magma Communications Ltd., Resudox Online Services Inc., Travel-Net Communications Inc., Trytel Internet Inc.

Neustadt Log On Internet Solutions

New Dundee Burlington Network Services, Information Gateway Services (Kitchener-Waterloo) Inc., MGL Systems Computer Technologies Inc., Sentex Communications Corporation

New Hamburg Burlington Network Services, Information Gateway Services (Kitchener-Waterloo) Inc., MGL Systems Computer Technologies Inc., ORCCA Networks Ltd., Sentex Communications Corporation, WorldCHAT™ Internet Services

New Liskeard Age.net, Northern Telephone Ltd., Ontario Northland–ONLink

New Lowell TransData Communications

Newburgh InterNet Kingston

Newcastle Online Computer Distribution

Newmarket Barrie Internet, Internet Canada Corporation (ICAN), Internet Direct Canada Inc., Netcom Canada Inc., Passport Online, Times.net

Newton ORCCA Networks Ltd.

Newtonville Online Computer Distribution

Niagara Falls Internet Connect Niagara, Internet XL, Netcom Canada Inc., Passport Online, Vaxxine Computer Systems Inc.

Niagara-on-the-Lake Internet Connect Niagara, Netcom Canada Inc., Passport Online, Vaxxine Computer Systems Inc.

Nobleton Interhop Network Services Inc., Internet Light and Power™, Netcom Canada Inc., Sentex Communications Corporation, Xenon Laboratories

North Bay Age.net, Ontario Northland–ONLink, Web Networks/NirvCentre

North Gower HookUp Communications, Netcom Canada Inc., Resudox Online Services Inc., Travel-Net Communications Inc., WorldLink Internet Services

North York Dtronix Internet Services, Globalserve Communications Inc., Metrolinx, Wiznet Inc.

Norwich Internet NNT

Norwood Heydon Computer Services Ltd., KawarthaNET, Online Computer Distribution, Peterboro.Net

Nottawa TransData Communications

Oak Ridges Interhop Network Services Inc., Internet Canada Corporation (ICAN), Internet Light and Power™, Netcom Canada Inc., Sentex Communications Corporation, Xenon Laboratories

Oakland WorldCHAT™ Internet Services

Oakville-Burlington Internet Direct Canada Inc.

Oakville Binatech Information Services Inc., Burlington Network Services, Globalserve Communications Inc., Internet Light and Power™, Internet XL, Magic Total Net Inc., Myna Communications Inc., Netcom Canada Inc., Networx Internet System, Sentex Communications Corporation, Spectranet Connections Inc., Wiznet Inc., WorldCHAT™ Internet Services, Xenon Laboratories

Oakwood KawarthaNET

Odessa InterNet Kingston

Ohsweken WorldCHAT™ Internet Services

Omemee Heydon Computer Services Ltd., Interhop Network Services Inc., KawarthaNET, Online Computer Distribution, Peterboro.Net

Orangeville headwaters network, Interhop Network Services Inc.

Orillia Barrie Connex Inc., Barrie Internet, Central Ontario Internet Services Inc., Interhop Network Services Inc., TransData Communications

Orleans Achilles Internet Ltd., Babillard Synapse Inc., CyberPlus Technologies Inc., HookUp Communications, Netcom Canada Inc., Resudox Online Services Inc., Travel-Net Communications Inc., Trytel Internet Inc., WorldLink Internet Services

Oro Barrie Connex Inc., Barrie Internet, Central Ontario Internet Services Inc., Interhop Network Services Inc., TransData Communications

Orono HookUp Communications, Online Computer Distribution, Netcom Canada Inc., Resudox Online Services Inc., Travel-Net Communications Inc., WorldLink Internet Services

Oshawa-Whitby Internet Direct Canada Inc., Pathway Communications

Oshawa AOL Canada (America Online), Cycor Communications Inc., Interhop Network Services Inc., Internet Canada Corporation (ICAN), Internet XL, i*STAR Internet Inc., Magic Total Net Inc., Netcom Canada Inc., Online Computer Distribution, UUNorth International Inc.

Ottawa Achilles Internet Ltd., AOL Canada (America Online), Atréide Communications Inc., Babillard Synapse Inc., Communication Inter-Accès, CyberPlus Technologies Inc., Cyberus Online Inc., Cycor Communications Inc., Focus Technologies Networks – aka FTN, HookUp Communications, Internet Access Inc., Internet Canada Corporation (ICAN), Internet Direct Canada Inc., Internet XL, i*STAR Internet Inc., Magic Total Net Inc., Magma Communications Ltd., Metrix Interlink Corporation, Netcom Canada Inc., Omegan Internet Services Inc., QNETIX Computer Consultants Inc., Resudox Online Services Inc., Travel-Net Communications Inc., Trytel Internet Inc., UUNET Canada Inc., Web Networks/NirvCentre, WorldLink Internet Services

Otterville Internet NNT

Owen Sound Huron Internet Technologies, Log On Internet Solutions, Sentex Communications Corporation

Pakenham Travel-Net Communications Inc., Trytel Internet Inc.

Palgrave headwaters network, Interhop Network Services Inc., Internet Light and Power™, Netcom Canada Inc., Sentex Communications Corporation, Xenon Laboratories

Paris WorldCHAT™ Internet Services

Parkhill MGL Systems Computer Technologies Inc., Netcom Canada Inc., Odyssey Network Inc.

Pefferlaw Interhop Network Services Inc.

Pelham Netcom Canada Inc.

Pembroke i*STAR Internet Inc., Omegan Internet Services Inc.

Penetanguishene Barrie Connex Inc., Central Ontario Internet Services Inc., TransData Communications

Perkinsfield TransData Communications

Peterborough Heydon Computer Services Ltd., HookUp Communications, Interhop Network Services Inc., KawarthaNET, Online Computer Distribution, Peterboro.Net

Petrolia Electro-Byte Technologies, HookUp Communications

Phelpston TransData Communications

Pickering Dtronix Internet Services, Globalserve Communications Inc., Interhop Network Services Inc., Internet Front Inc., Internet Light and Power™, Internet XL, Magic Total Net Inc., Metrolinx, Myna Communications Inc., Netcom Canada Inc., Online Computer Distribution, Sentex Communications Corporation, Wiznet Inc., Xenon Laboratories

Picton NetReach International

Plantagenet Netcom Canada Inc.

Plattsville Burlington Network Services, Information Gateway Services (Kitchener-Waterloo) Inc., MGL Systems Computer Technologies Inc., Sentex Communications Corporation

Pleasant Park Netcom Canada Inc., NetCore Global Communications

Point Edward Electro-Byte Technologies

Pontypool KawarthaNET

Port Carling Muskoka.com

Port Colborne Internet Connect Niagara, Vaxxine Computer Systems Inc.

Port Credit Burlington Network Services, Internet Light and Power™, Netcom Canada Inc., Sentex Communications Corporation, Xenon Laboratories

Port Dover Norfolk Internet Services

Port Franks Internet HTL

Port Hope Interhop Network Services Inc., Northumberland Online Ltd.

Port McNicoll Barrie Connex Inc., Barrie Internet, Central Ontario Internet Services Inc., Interhop Network Services Inc., TransData Communications

Port Perry Online Computer Distribution

Port Robinson Netcom Canada Inc., Vaxxine Computer Systems Inc.

Port Rowan Norfolk Internet Services

Port Stanley MGL Systems Computer Technologies Inc., Netcom Canada Inc., Odyssey Network Inc., Serix Technologies

Port Sydney Muskoka.com

Preston Burlington Network Services, Information Gateway Services (Kitchener-Waterloo) Inc., Netcom Canada Inc., Sentex Communications Corporation

Princeton Internet NNT, WorldCHAT™ Internet Services

Queensville Interhop Network Services Inc.

Quinte IGS (Information Gateway Services)

Ravenna TransData Communications

Redwing TransData Communications

Richmond Hill Globalserve Communications Inc., Interhop Network Services Inc., Internet Front Inc., Internet Light and Power™, Myna Communications Inc., Netcom Canada Inc., Sentex Communications Corporation, Xenon Laboratories

Richmond CyberPlus Technologies Inc., HookUp Communications, Netcom Canada Inc., Resudox Online Services Inc., Travel-Net Communications Inc., WorldLink Internet Services

Ridgetown Odyssey Network Inc.

Ridgeway Vaxxine Computer Systems Inc.

Ripley HuronTel

Rockcliffe Trytel Internet Inc.

Rockland CyberPlus Technologies Inc., HookUp Communications, Netcom Canada Inc., Resudox Online Services Inc., Travel-Net Communications Inc., WorldLink Internet Services

Rockwood Interactive Online Ltd., Internet Innovations Inc., MGL Systems Computer Technologies Inc., Sentex Communications Corporation

Rosemont TransData Communications

Roseneath Heydon Computer Services Ltd, Online Computer Distribution

Rugby TransData Communications

Russell CyberPlus Technologies Inc., HookUp Communications, Netcom Canada Inc., Resudox Online Services Inc., Travel-Net Communications Inc., WorldLink Internet Services

Salem WorldCHAT™ Internet Services

Sarnia Electro-Byte Technologies, HookUp Communications, Inter*Com Information Services, Internet XL, Worldwide Data Communications Inc.

Sauble Beach Log On Internet Solutions, Sentex Communications Corporation

Sault Ste. Marie Age.net, Internet XL

Scarborough Dtronix Internet Services, Globalserve Communications Inc., Metrolinx, Wiznet Inc.

Schomberg Barrie Internet, Interhop Network Services Inc., Internet Canada Corporation (ICAN), Internet Light and Power™, Netcom Canada Inc., Netcom Canada Inc., Sentex Communications Corporation, Times.net, Xenon Laboratories

Scotland WorldCHAT™ Internet Services

Seaforth Odyssey Network Inc.

Sebringville ORCCA Networks Ltd.

Seeleys Bay InterNet Kingston

Selby InterNet Kingston

Selkirk Burlington Network Services, NetAccess Systems Inc., Netcom Canada Inc., Network Enterprise Technology Inc., WorldCHAT™ Internet Services

Severn Bridge Muskoka.com

Shakespeare ORCCA Networks Ltd.

Shallow Lake Log On Internet Solutions

Shanty Bay TransData Communications

Sharon Times.net

Shedden MGL Systems Computer Technologies Inc., Netcom Canada Inc., Odyssey Network Inc., Serix Technologies

Shelburne headwaters network

Simcoe Norfolk Internet Services

Singhampton TransData Communications

Smithville Internet Connect Niagara, Networx Internet System

Smooth Rock Falls Age.net, Northern Telephone Ltd., Ontario Northland–ONLink

Snelgrove Aztec Computer Inc., Internet Light and Power™, Netcom Canada Inc., Netcom Canada Inc., Sentex Communications Corporation, Xenon Laboratories

South Gillies Norlink Communications and Consulting

South Pickering Internet Light and Power™, Netcom Canada Inc., Sentex Communications Corporation, Xenon Laboratories

South Porcupine Northern Telephone Ltd.

Sparta MGL Systems Computer Technologies Inc., Netcom Canada Inc., Odyssey Network Inc., Serix Technologies

Spragge Internet North

Sprucedale Muskoka.com

St-Eugene Glen-Net Communications

St. Catharines AOL Canada (America Online), Cycor Communications Inc., Internet Connect Niagara, Internet XL, Netcom Canada Inc., Networx Internet System, Passport Online, Vaxxine Computer Systems Inc.

St. Clements Burlington Network Services, Information Gateway Services (Kitchener-Waterloo) Inc., MGL Systems Computer Technologies Inc., Sentex Communications Corporation

St. George Network Enterprise Technology Inc., Sentex Communications Corporation, WorldCHAT™ Internet Services

St. Jacobs Burlington Network Services, Information Gateway Services (Kitchener-Waterloo) Inc., MGL Systems Computer Technologies Inc., Sentex Communications Corporation, WorldCHAT™ Internet Services

St. Mary's MGL Systems Computer Technologies Inc., Odyssey Network Inc., ORCCA Networks Ltd., Serix Technologies

St. Thomas MGL Systems Computer Technologies Inc., Netcom Canada Inc., Odyssey Network Inc., Serix Technologies

Stayner Barrie Connex Inc., Central Ontario Internet Services Inc., Grant Internet Communications Corporation, Interhop Network Services Inc., TransData Communications

Stevensville Vaxxine Computer Systems Inc.

Stirling NetReach International

Stittsville CyberPlus Technologies Inc., HookUp Communications, Netcom Canada Inc., Resudox Online Services Inc., Travel-Net Communications Inc., WorldLink Internet Services

Stoney Creek Burlington Network Services, Globalserve Communications Inc., NetAccess Systems Inc., Netcom Canada Inc., Network Enterprise Technology Inc., Passport Online, Sentex Communications Corporation, Weslink Datalink Corporation, WorldCHAT™ Internet Services

Stoney Point Information Gateway Services Windsor, Netcom Canada Inc., NetCore Global Communications

Stouffville Interhop Network Services Inc., Internet Light and Power™, Netcom Canada Inc., Sentex Communications Corporation, Xenon Laboratories

Stratford Huron Internet Technologies, Inter*Com Information Services, MGL Systems Computer Technologies Inc., ORCCA Networks Ltd., WorldCHAT™ Internet Services, Worldwide Data Communications Inc.

Strathroy MGL Systems Computer Technologies Inc., Netcom Canada Inc., Odyssey Network Inc., Serix Technologies

Streetsville Burlington Network Services, Internet Light and Power™, Netcom Canada Inc., Sentex Communications Corporation, Xenon Laboratories

Stroud Barrie Connex Inc., Central Ontario Internet Services Inc., Interhop Network Services Inc., TransData Communications

Sturgeon Bay TransData Communications

Sturgeon Falls Age.net, Ontario Northland–ONLink

Sudbury Age.net, Cycor Communications Inc., Internet XL

Sundridge Age.net, Ontario Northland–ONLink

Sutton Interhop Network Services Inc.

Swastika Northern Telephone Ltd.

Sydenham InterNet Kingston

Tamworth InterNet Kingston

Tara Log On Internet Solutions, Sentex Communications Corporation

Tavistock ORCCA Networks Ltd.

Tecumseh Information Gateway Services Windsor, Netcom Canada Inc., NetCore Global Communications

Temagami Age.net, Ontario Northland–ONLink

Thamesford MGL Systems Computer Technologies Inc., Netcom Canada Inc., Odyssey Network Inc., Serix Technologies

Thamesville Odyssey Network Inc.

Thedford Internet HTL

Thessalon Internet North

Thornbury TransData Communications

Thorndale MGL Systems Computer Technologies Inc., Netcom Canada Inc., Odyssey Network Inc., Serix Technologies

Thornhill Globalserve Communications Inc., Interhop Network Services Inc., Internet Light and Power™, Myna Communications Inc., Netcom Canada Inc., Sentex Communications Corporation, Xenon Laboratories

Thornton TransData Communications

Thorold Vaxxine Computer Systems Inc.

Thunder Bay Cycor Communications Inc., HookUp Communications, Internet XL, MicroAge Computer Centres, Norlink Communications and Consulting, UUNorth International Inc., Web Networks/NirvCentre

Tilbury HookUp Communications, Odyssey Network Inc.

Tillsonburg Internet NNT

Timmins Age.net, Northern Telephone Ltd., Ontario Northland–ONLink

Toronto AOL Canada (America Online), Burlington Network Services, CIMtegration Ltd., Communication Inter-Accès, CompuServe, Cybersurf Information Access, Cycor Communications Inc., Dtronix Internet Services, Enterprise-Terraport Online, Fleximation Systems Inc., Focus Technologies Networks – aka FTN, Globalserve Communications Inc., HookUp Communications, Inline Information Services, Inc., Interhop Network Services Inc., InterLog Internet Services, Internet Canada Corporation (ICAN), Internet Direct Canada Inc., Internet Front Inc., Internet Light and Power™, Internet XL, i*STAR Internet Inc., Learn-Ed Internet Services, Magic Total Net Inc., Metrolinx, Metrix Interlink Corporation, Myna Communications Inc., Net Access Systems Inc., Netcom Canada Inc., NetSurf Inc., Omegan Internet Services Inc., Passport Online, Pathway Communications, QNETIX Computer Consultants Inc., Sentex Communications Corporation, Spectranet Connections Inc., TotalNet Inc., UUNET Canada Inc., UUNorth International Inc., Web Networks/NirvCentre, Wiznet Inc., Xenon Laboratories

Tottenham Barrie Connex Inc., Interhop Network Services Inc., TransData Communications

Trent River Heydon Computer Services Ltd.

Trenton NetReach International

Tweed NetReach International

Uniondale MGL Systems Computer Technologies Inc., Odyssey Network Inc., ORCCA Networks Ltd., Serix Technologies

Unionville Globalserve Communications Inc., Interhop Network Services Inc., Internet Front Inc., Internet Light and Power™, Myna Communications Inc., Netcom Canada Inc., Sentex Communications Corporation, Wiznet Inc., Xenon Laboratories

Uxbridge Interhop Network Services Inc., Online Computer Distribution

Vancouver Internet Canada Corporation (ICAN)

Vanier Achilles Internet Ltd., Cyberus Online Inc., HookUp Communications, Resudox Online Services Inc., Travel-Net Communications Inc., Trytel Internet Inc.

Vankleek Hill Glen-Net Communications

Vasey TransData Communications

Vaughan Globalserve Communications Inc., Internet XL

Verona InterNet Kingston

Victoria Harbour Barrie Connex Inc., Barrie Internet, Central Ontario Internet Services Inc., TransData Communications

Victoria Aztec Computer Inc., Internet Canada Corporation (ICAN), Netcom Canada Inc.

Vineland Netcom Canada Inc., Vaxxine Computer Systems Inc.

Wabaushene Barrie Connex Inc.

Wainfleet Vaxxine Computer Systems Inc.

Walkerton Log On Internet Solutions

Wallaceburg HookUp Communications, Odyssey Network Inc.

Warkworth Online Computer Distribution

Wasaga Beach Barrie Connex Inc., Barrie Internet, Central Ontario Internet Services Inc., Grant Internet Communications Corporation, TransData Communications

Washago Interhop Network Services Inc.

Waterdown Binatech Information Services Inc., Burlington Network Services, Globalserve Communications Inc., NetAccess Systems Inc., Netcom Canada Inc., Network Enterprise Technology Inc., Networx Internet System, Sentex Communications Corporation, WorldCHAT™ Internet Services

Waterford Norfolk Internet Services, WorldCHAT™ Internet Services

Waterloo Burlington Network Services, Easynet Inc., Focus Technologies Networks – aka FTN, IBM Mail Exchange, Information Gateway services (Kitchener-Waterloo Inc.), Interactive Online Ltd., Interhop Network Services Inc., Internet Innovations Inc., Internet XL, i*STAR Internet Inc., MGL Systems Computer Technologies Inc., Netcom Canada Inc., Sentex Communications Corporation, Web Networks/Nirv Centre, WorldCHAT™ Internet Services, Worldwide Data Communications Inc.

Watford Electro-Byte Technologies, MGL Systems Computer Technologies Inc., Odyssey Network Inc., Serix Technologies

Waubaushene Barrie Internet, Central Ontario Internet Services Inc., Interhop Network Services Inc., TransData Communications

Waverley TransData Communications

Wawa Internet North

Welcome Northumberland Online Ltd.

Welland Internet Connect Niagara, Vaxxine Computer Systems Inc.

Wellesley Burlington Network Services, Information Gateway Services (Kitchener-Waterloo) Inc., MGL Systems Computer Technologies Inc., Sentex Communications Corporation

Wellington NetReach International

West Lincoln Netcom Canada Inc., Network Enterprise Technology Inc., Networx Internet System, Sentex Communications Corporation

Westlyville Northumberland Online Ltd.

Whitby Interhop Network Services Inc., Internet XL, Netcom Canada Inc., Online Computer Distribution

Wiarton Log On Internet Solutions, Sentex Communications Corporation

Williamsburg Glen-Net Communications

Winchester CyberPlus Technologies Inc.

Windermere Muskoka.com

Windsor AOL Canada (America Online), Cycor Communications Inc., Focus Technologies Networks – aka FTN, HookUp Communications, IBM Global Network, Information Gateway Services Windsor, Inter*Com Information Services, Netcom Canada Inc., Worldwide Data Communications Inc.

Wingham Huron Internet Technologies

Winnipeg Internet Canada Corporation (ICAN)

Winona NetAccess Systems Inc., Netcom Canada Inc., Network Enterprise Technology Inc., Networx Internet System, Sentex Communications Corporation, WorldCHAT™ Internet Services

Wolfe Island InterNet Kingston

Woodbridge Interhop Network Services Inc., Internet Light and Power™, Netcom Canada Inc., Sentex Communications Corporation, Xenon Laboratories

Woodslee Netcom Canada Inc., NetCore Global Communications

Woodstock Huron Internet Technologies, Inter*Com Information Services, Internet NNT, Odyssey Network Inc., Worldwide Data Communications Inc.

Woodville KawarthaNET

Wooler NetReach International

Wyebridge TransData Communications

Wyevale TransData Communications

Wyoming Electro-Byte Technologies

Yarker InterNet Kingston

Prince Edward Island

Prince Edward Island-wide Atlantic Connect, Sympatico—The Internet Service For Everyone™

Charlottetown Cycor Communications Inc., HookUp Communications, IBM Global Network, Island Services Network

Covehead Island Services Network

Crapaud Island Services Network
Eldon Island Services Network
Hunter River Island Services Network
Morell Island Services Network
Mount Stewart Island Services Network
New Haven Island Services Network
Rusticoville Island Services Network
St. Eleanor's Atlantic Connect
St. Peters Island Services Network
Summerside Atlantic Connect, HookUp Communications
Vernon River Island Services Network
Wilmot Atlantic Connect

Québec

Québec-wide CitéNet Telecom Inc., Quebectel Communication Inc., Sympatico—The Internet Service For Everyone™
Ange-Gardien Oricom Internet
Anse St-Jean Le Cybernaute
Aylmer Atréide Communications inc., Babillard Synapse Inc., CyberPlus Technologies Inc., Cyberus Online Inc., HookUp Communications, Netcom Canada Inc., Resudox Online Services Inc., Travel-Net Communications Inc., Trytel Internet Inc., WorldLink Internet Services
Baie-d'Urfé Connection MMIC Inc.
Beaconsfield Connection MMIC Inc.
Beauharnois Connection MMIC Inc., FrancoMédia, HookUp Communications, Les services télématiques Rocler, Matrox SphereNet
Beauport Oricom Internet
Beloeil Connection MMIC Inc., FrancoMédia, HookUp Communications, Matrox SphereNet, Netcom Canada Inc.
Black Lake Internet Mégantic
Boischatel Netcom Canada Inc.
Boucherville Communications Accessibles Montréal, Connection MMIC Inc., FrancoMédia, HookUp Communications, Matrox SphereNet, Netcom Canada Inc.
Bourget Netcom Canada Inc.
Brossard Communications Accessibles Montréal, FrancoMédia, Réseau Virtuel d'Ordinateurs RVO
Buckingham Atréide Communications inc., Babillard Synapse Inc., Netcom Canada Inc., Travel-Net Communications Inc.
Cantley CyberPlus Technologies Inc.
Cap-Rouge ClicNet Télécommunications, Inc.
Carigan Réseau Virtuel d'Ordinateurs RVO
Chambly Connection MMIC Inc., FrancoMédia, HookUp Communications, Matrox SphereNet, Netcom Canada Inc., Réseau Virtuel d'Ordinateurs RVO
Charlesbourg ClicNet Télécommunications, Inc., Oricom Internet
Charny Netcom Canada Inc., Oricom Internet
Chateau-Richer Netcom Canada Inc.
Chateauguay FrancoMédia, HookUp Communications, Les services télématiques Rocler, Matrox SphereNet, Netcom Canada Inc.
Chelsea Atréide Communications inc., CyberPlus Technologies Inc., HookUp Communications, Netcom Canada Inc., Resudox Online Services Inc., Travel-Net Communications Inc., WorldLink Internet Services
Chicoutimi Le Cybernaute, Metrix Interlink Corporation, QNETIX Computer Consultants Inc., RISQ Réseau interordinateurs scientifique québécois
Chomedey Connection MMIC Inc., FrancoMédia, Netcom Canada Inc.
Chomedy HookUp Communications, Matrox SphereNet
Châteauguay Connection MMIC Inc.
Clarenceville FrancoMédia, HookUp Communications, Matrox SphereNet
Coleraine Internet Mégantic
Coteau-du-Lac Les services télématiques Rocler
Coteau-Landing Les services télématiques Rocler
Crysler Netcom Canada Inc.
Deux-Montagnes Connection MMIC Inc.
Disraéli Internet Mégantic
Donnacona Netcom Canada Inc., Oricom Internet
Dorion Connection MMIC Inc.
Dorval Connection MMIC Inc.
Drummondville InfoTeck Internet, Internet Login
East Broughton Internet Mégantic
Franklin Centre Les services télématiques Rocler
Frontenac Internet Mégantic
Garthby-Beaulac Internet Mégantic
Gatineau Achilles Internet Ltd., Atréide Communications inc., Babillard Synapse Inc., Cyberus Online Inc., HookUp Communications, Internet XL, Magma Communications Ltd., Netcom Canada Inc., Resudox Online Services Inc., Trytel Internet Inc., WorldLink Internet Services
Gloucester Netcom Canada Inc.
Granby Internet Login, TotalNet Inc.
Grand-Mère InfoTeck Internet

Greenfield Park Communications Accessibles Montréal, Réseau Virtuel d'Ordinateurs RVO

Grenville Glen-Net Communications

Hemmingford FrancoMédia, HookUp Communications, Matrox SphereNet

Henryville Connection MMIC Inc.

Howick Les services télématiques Rocler

Hudson Connection MMIC Inc., FrancoMédia, HookUp Communications, Matrox SphereNet, Netcom Canada Inc.

Hull Achilles Internet Ltd., Babillard Synapse Inc., Communication Inter-Accès, CyberPlus Technologies Inc., Cyberus Online Inc., HookUp Communications, Internet XL, Magma Communications Ltd., Metrix Interlink Corporation, Resudox Online Services Inc., RISQ Réseau interordinateurs scientifique québécois, Travel-Net Communications Inc., Trytel Internet Inc., WorldLink Internet Services

Huntingdon Les services télématiques Rocler

Île-Perrot Connection MMIC Inc., FrancoMédia, HookUp Communications, Les services télématiques Rocler, Matrox SphereNet, Netcom Canada Inc.

Jonquière Le Cybernaute

Kazabazua HookUp Communications, Resudox Online Services Inc.

Kinnear's Mills Internet Mégantic

Kirkand Connection MMIC Inc.

L'Assomption Connection MMIC Inc., FrancoMédia

L'Épiphanie-L'Assomption HookUp Communications, Matrox SphereNet, Netcom Canada Inc.

L'Épiphanie Connection MMIC Inc., FrancoMédia

La Baie Le Cybernaute

La Prairie Connection MMIC Inc., FrancoMédia, HookUp Communications, Matrox SphereNet, Réseau Virtuel d'Ordinateurs RVO

Lac Beauport Oricom Internet

Lac St-Charles Oricom Internet

Lac-Drolet Internet Mégantic

Lac-Mégantic Internet Mégantic

Lachine Connection MMIC Inc., FrancoMédia, HookUp Communications, Matrox SphereNet, Netcom Canada Inc.

Lachute FrancoMédia, HookUp Communications

Lacolle FrancoMédia, HookUp Communications

Laprairie Netcom Canada Inc.

Lauzon Oricom Internet

Laval-Est Connection MMIC Inc., HookUp Communications, Matrox SphereNet, Netcom Canada Inc.

Laval-Ouest Connection MMIC Inc., HookUp Communications, Matrox SphereNet, Netcom Canada Inc.

Laval Connection MMIC Inc., FrancoMédia, Globale Internet Canada, Internet XL

Lavaltrie FrancoMédia, HookUp Communications, Internet Login, Matrox SphereNet, Netcom Canada Inc.

Le Gardeur Connection MMIC Inc., FrancoMédia, HookUp Communications, Matrox SphereNet, Netcom Canada Inc.

Leeds Internet Mégantic

Les Cèdres FrancoMédia, HookUp Communications, Les services télématiques Rocler

Longueuil Communications Accessibles Montréal, Connection MMIC Inc., FrancoMédia, HookUp Communications, Matrox SphereNet, Netcom Canada Inc., Réseau Virtuel d'Ordinateurs RVO

Loretteville ClicNet Télécommunications, Inc., Netcom Canada Inc., Oricom Internet

Low Atréide Communications inc., HookUp Communications, Netcom Canada Inc., Resudox Online Services Inc., Travel-Net Communications Inc., WorldLink Internet Services

Luskville HookUp Communications, Netcom Canada Inc., Resudox Online Services Inc., Travel-Net Communications Inc., WorldLink Internet Services

Lévis ClicNet Télécommunications, Inc., Netcom Canada Inc., Oricom Internet

Maniwaki Atréide Communications inc.

Marieville FrancoMédia, HookUp Communications, Matrox SphereNet

Marston Internet Mégantic

Mascouche Connection MMIC Inc., FrancoMédia, HookUp Communications, Matrox SphereNet, Netcom Canada Inc.

Masson Babillard Synapse Inc.

Masson-Anger Atréide Communications inc.

Melocheville FrancoMédia

Mirabel St-Augustin Matrox SphereNet, Netcom Canada Inc.

Mirabel-Aeroport HookUp Communications, Matrox SphereNet, Netcom Canada Inc.

Mirabel-Saint-Scholastique HookUp Communications

Mirabel Connection MMIC Inc., FrancoMédia

Montréal AEI Internet, AOL Canada (America Online), Communications Accessibles Montréal, Communication Inter-Accès, CompuServe, Connection MMIC Inc., ConsuLan, Cybersurf Information Access, Cycor Communications Inc., Fleximation Systems Inc., FrancoMédia, generation.NET – Total Internet Solutions, Globale Internet Canada, HookUp Communications, Internet Login, Internet Québec IQ inc., Internet XL, i*STAR Internet Inc., Lanzen Corporation, Magic Total Net Inc., Matrox SphereNet, Metrix Interlink Corporation, Netcom Canada Inc., Omegan Internet Services Inc., Osiris (Software) Inc., Prisco interNET, QNETIX Computer Consultants Inc., RISQ Réseau interordinateurs scientifique québécois, Réseau Virtuel d'Ordinateurs RVO, TotalNet Inc., UUNET Canada Inc., VIF Internet, Web Networks/NirvCentre, ZooNet Inc.

Napierville FrancoMédia, HookUp Communications, Matrox SphereNet, Netcom Canada Inc.

Neuville Netcom Canada Inc., Oricom Internet

Notre-Dame-des-Laurentides Netcom Canada Inc.

Oka Connection MMIC Inc., FrancoMédia, HookUp Communications, Matrox SphereNet, Netcom Canada Inc.

Ormstown Les services télématiques Rocler

Papineauville Atréide Communications inc.

Perkins HookUp Communications, Netcom Canada Inc., Resudox Online Services Inc., Travel-Net Communications Inc., WorldLink Internet Services

Petit Saguenay Le Cybernaute

Pierrefonds Connection MMIC Inc.

Piopolis Internet Mégantic

Plaisance Atréide Communications inc.

Pointe-aux-Trembles Connection MMIC Inc.

Pointe-Claire Connection MMIC Inc., FrancoMédia, HookUp Communications, Matrox SphereNet, Netcom Canada Inc.

Pont-Rouge Netcom Canada Inc., Oricom Internet

Pont-Viau Connection MMIC Inc., FrancoMédia, HookUp Communications, Matrox SphereNet, Netcom Canada Inc.

Portneuf Oricom Interne

Quyon HookUp Communications, Netcom Canada Inc., Resudox Online Services Inc., Travel-Net Communications Inc., WorldLink Internet Services

Québec Accès Communications Internet Inc., AOL Canada (America Online), ClicNet Télécommunications, Inc., Communication Inter-Accès, CompuServe, Connection MMIC Inc., Internet XL, i*STAR Internet Inc., Magic Total Net Inc., Metrix Interlink Corporation, Netcom Canada Inc., Omegan Internet Services Inc., Oricom Internet, QNETIX Computer Consultants Inc., RISQ Réseau interordinateurs scientifique québécois, TotalNet Inc., UUNET Canada Inc.

Repentigny Connection MMIC Inc.

Richelieu Réseau Virtuel d'Ordinateurs RVO

Rigaud FrancoMédia, HookUp Communications, Matrox SphereNet, Netcom Canada Inc.

Rimouski RISQ Réseau interordinateurs scientifique québécois

Rivière-Beaudette Les services télématiques Rocler

Robertsonville Internet Mégantic

Rougement Internet Login

Rouyn Metrix Interlink Corporation, RISQ Réseau interordinateurs scientifique québécois

Roxboro Connection MMIC Inc., FrancoMédia, HookUp Communications, Matrox SphereNet, Netcom Canada Inc.

Saint-Bruno Communications Accessibles Montréal, Connection MMIC Inc., FrancoMédia, HookUp Communications, Matrox SphereNet, Netcom Canada Inc.

Saint-Chrysosthome FrancoMédia, HookUp Communications

Saint-Constant Connection MMIC Inc., FrancoMédia, HookUp Communications, Matrox SphereNet, Netcom Canada Inc.

Saint-Rémi FrancoMédia, HookUp Communications, Matrox SphereNet, Netcom Canada Inc.

Saint-Vincent-de-Paul HookUp Communications

Sainte-Anne-des-Plaines FrancoMédia, HookUp Communications

Sainte-Julie-de-Verchères HookUp Communications, Matrox SphereNet, Netcom Canada Inc.

Sainte-Julienne FrancoMédia, HookUp Communications

Sainte-Madeleine FrancoMédia, HookUp Communications

Sainte-Martine FrancoMédia, HookUp Communications

Sainte-Thérèse FrancoMédia, HookUp Communications

Senneville Connection MMIC Inc.

Shawinigan InfoTeck Internet

Shawville Atréide Communications inc., Travel-Net Communications Inc.

Sherbrooke Communication Inter-Accès, Internet Login, Internet XL, Metrix Interlink Corporation, RISQ Réseau interordinateurs scientifique québécois

Sillery ClicNet Télécommunications, Inc., Oricom Internet

St-Agapit Netcom Canada Inc.

St-Antoine-de-Tilly Netcom Canada Inc.

St-Apollinaire Netcom Canada Inc.

St-Augustin Netcom Canada Inc.

St-Calixte-de-Kilkenny FrancoMédia, HookUp Communications, Matrox SphereNet, Netcom Canada Inc.

St-Charles-de-Bellechasse Netcom Canada Inc.

St-Clet Les services télématiques Rocler

St-Denis FrancoMédia, HookUp Communications, Matrox SphereNet, Netcom Canada Inc.

St-Eustache Connection MMIC Inc., FrancoMédia, HookUp Communications, Matrox SphereNet, Netcom Canada Inc.

St-Ferréol Netcom Canada Inc.

St-Flavien Netcom Canada Inc.

St-Geneviève FrancoMédia, HookUp Communications, Matrox SphereNet

St-Georges-de-Beauce Internet Login

St-Henri-de-Lévis Netcom Canada Inc.

St-Hubert Réseau Virtuel d'Ordinateurs RVO

St-Hyacinthe Internet Login, Prisco interNET

St-Jean-d'Orleans Netcom Canada Inc.

St-Jean-sur-Richelieu Connection MMIC Inc.

St-Jean FrancoMédia, HookUp Communications, Matrox SphereNet, Netcom Canada Inc.

St-Joseph-sur-le-Lac Connection MMIC Inc.

St-Julienne Matrox SphereNet

St-Jérôme Connection MMIC Inc., Globale Internet Canada, Internet Login

St-Lambert Communications Accessibles Montréal, Connection MMIC Inc., FrancoMédia, HookUp Communications, Matrox SphereNet, Netcom Canada Inc.

St-Lambert-de-Lauzon Netcom Canada Inc.

St-Laurent Connection MMIC Inc., FrancoMédia

St-Lazare Connection MMIC Inc.

St-Lin FrancoMédia, HookUp Communications, Matrox SphereNet, Netcom Canada Inc.

St-Luc Connection MMIC Inc.

St-Ludger Internet Mégantic

St-Marc FrancoMédia, HookUp Communications, Matrox SphereNet, Netcom Canada Inc.

St-Martine Matrox SphereNet

St-Michel-de-Bellechasse Netcom Canada Inc.

St-Nicolas Netcom Canada Inc., Oricom Internet

St-Pierre de Broughton Internet Mégantic

St-Pierre-de-Wakefield Resudox Online Services Inc., WorldLink Internet Services, Netcom Canada Inc.

St-Polycarpe Les services télématiques Rocler

St-Regis DataCom Online Services, Glen-Net Communications

St-Romuald Oricom Internet

St-Rose FrancoMédia, HookUp Communications, Matrox SphereNet, Netcom Canada Inc.

St-Rémi Connection MMIC Inc.

St-Sauveur FrancoMédia, HookUp Communications, Matrox SphereNet, Netcom Canada Inc.

St-Sebastien Internet Mégantic

St-Timothée Les services télématiques Rocler

St-Tite-des-Caps Netcom Canada Inc.

St-Vincent-de-Paul Connection MMIC Inc., Matrox SphereNet, Netcom Canada Inc., Netcom Canada Inc.

Ste-Anne-de-Beaupré Netcom Canada Inc., Oricom Internet

Ste-Anne-de-Bellevue Connection MMIC Inc.

Ste-Anne-des-Plaines Connection MMIC Inc., Matrox SphereNet, Netcom Canada Inc.

Ste-Brigitte-de-Laval Netcom Canada Inc.

Ste-Catherine Connection MMIC Inc., Netcom Canada Inc.

Ste-Clothilde Internet Mégantic

Ste-Croix Oricom Internet, Netcom Canada Inc.

Ste-Cécile-de-Whitton Internet Mégantic

Ste-Dorothée Connection MMIC Inc.

Ste-Foy ClicNet Télécommunications, Inc., Oricom Internet

Ste-Geneviève Connection MMIC Inc., Netcom Canada Inc.

Ste-Julie Connection MMIC Inc.

Ste-Julienne Netcom Canada Inc.

Ste-Justine-de-Newton Les services télématiques Rocler

Ste-Marthe-sur-le-Lac Connection MMIC Inc.

Ste-Marthe Les services télématiques Rocler

Ste-Martine Connection MMIC Inc., Les services télématiques Rocler, Netcom Canada Inc.

Ste-Petronille Netcom Canada Inc.

Ste-Rose Connection MMIC Inc., Netcom Canada Inc.

Ste-Thérèse Connection MMIC Inc., Matrox SphereNet, Netcom Canada Inc.

Stoneham Netcom Canada Inc., Oricom Internet
Stornoway Internet Mégantic
Stratford Internet Mégantic
Terrebonne Connection MMIC Inc., FrancoMédia, HookUp Communications, Matrox SphereNet, Netcom Canada Inc.
Thetford Mines Internet Mégantic
Thurso Babillard Synapse Inc., Netcom Canada Inc., Travel-Net Communications Inc.
Trois-Rivières InfoTeck Internet, Internet Login, RISQ Réseau interordinateurs scientifique québécois
Val Bélair Oricom Internet
Val-des-Bois Travel-Net Communications Inc.
Valcartier Netcom Canada Inc., Oricom Internet
Valleyfield Connection MMIC Inc., FrancoMédia
Varennes Connection MMIC Inc., FrancoMédia, HookUp Communications, Matrox SphereNet, Netcom Canada Inc.
Vaudreuil Connection MMIC Inc., FrancoMédia, HookUp Communications, Les services télématiques Rocler, Matrox SphereNet, Netcom Canada Inc.
Verchères Connection MMIC Inc., FrancoMédia, HookUp Communications, Matrox SphereNet, Netcom Canada Inc.
Verdun Réseau Virtuel d'Ordinateurs RVO
Victoriaville Internet Login
Ville LeMoyne Réseau Virtuel d'Ordinateurs RVO
Wakefield CyberPlus Technologies Inc., HookUp Communications, Netcom Canada Inc., Travel-Net Communications Inc., WorldLink Internet Services
Weedon Internet Mégantic
Woburn Internet Mégantic

Saskatchewan

Saskatchewan-wide Sympatico—The Internet Service For Everyone™
Barbour HMT INTERNET Inc.
Barvas HMT INTERNET Inc.
Chrysler HMT INTERNET Inc.
Dunleath HMT INTERNET Inc.
Ebenezer HMT INTERNET Inc.
Fonehill HMT INTERNET Inc.
Good Spirit Lake HMT INTERNET Inc.
Gorlitz HMT INTERNET Inc.
Hamton HMT INTERNET Inc.
Kessock HMT INTERNET Inc.
McKim HMT INTERNET Inc.
Mehan HMT INTERNET Inc.
Moose Jaw Data Link Canada West (DLC-West), HookUp Communications, Internet XL
Oliver HookUp Communications
Orcadia HMT INTERNET Inc.
Otthon HMT INTERNET Inc.
Pollack HMT INTERNET Inc.
Prince Albert Internet XL, WBM Office Systems
Regina AOL Canada (America Online), CompuServe, Cycor Communications Inc., Data Link Canada West (DLC-West), Internet XL, WBM Office Systems
Rokeby HMT INTERNET Inc.
Saskatoon AOL Canada (America Online), CompuServe, Cycor Communications Inc., Data Link Canada West (DLC-West), Internet XL, WBM Office Systems, Webster Internet Communications Inc.
Spiritwood HMT INTERNET Inc.
Springside HMT INTERNET Inc.
Sturgis HMT INTERNET Inc.
Swift Current HookUp Communications
Tonkin HMT INTERNET Inc.
White Spruce HMT INTERNET Inc.
Willowbrook HMT INTERNET Inc.
Yorkton HMT INTERNET Inc., HookUp Communications
Young Siding Villages HMT INTERNET Inc.

Yukon

Yukon Territory-wide Hypertech North Inc.
Beaver Creek Hypertech North Inc.
Burwash Landing Hypertech North Inc.
Carcross Hypertech North Inc., YKnet
Carmacks Hypertech North Inc., YKnet
Dawson City Hypertech North Inc., YKnet
Destruction Bay Hypertech North Inc.
Faro Hypertech North Inc., YKnet
Haines Junction Hypertech North Inc., YKnet
Mayo Hypertech North Inc., YKnet
Old Crow Hypertech North Inc.
Pelly Crossing Hypertech North Inc., YKnet
Ross River Hypertech North Inc., YKnet
Teslin YKnet
Watson Lake Hypertech North Inc., YKnet
Whitehorse Hypertech North Inc., YKnet

Directory of Canadian Internet Access Providers

Accès Communications Internet Inc.

Québec City, Québec
acica.com

5 rue Richelieu, Suite 010
Québec City, Québec G1R 1J4

Voice: 418-524-5458
Fax: 418-524-5460
E-mail: information@acica.com
Web: http://www.acica.com

Services: Dial-up SLIP/PPP, Web hosting, Web design

Achilles Internet Ltd.

Nepean, Ontario
achilles.net

14 Colonnade Road, Suite 260
Nepean, Ontario K2E 7M6

Voice: 613-723-6624
Fax: 613-723-8583
E-mail: info@achilles.net, office@achilles.net
Web: http://www.achilles.net

Services: Dedicated ISDN, dial-up ISDN, dial-up SLIP/PPP, Web hosting, Web design

AEI Internet

Montréal, Québec
aei.ca, aei.net

3577 Atwater, Suite 320
Montréal, Québec H3H 2R2

Voice: 514-939-2488
Fax: 514-939-0677
E-mail: info@aei.ca
Web: http://www.aei.ca

Services: Dedicated ISDN, dial-up ISDN, dial-up SLIP/PPP, high-speed dedicated access, Web hosting, Web design

Age.net

Sault Ste. Marie, Ontario
age.net

773 Great Northern Road
Sault Ste. Marie, Ontario P6A 5K7

Voice: 705-946-0876
Fax: 705-946-0878
E-mail: jjw@age.net
Web: http://www.age.net/age/agehome.htm
Affiliated with: ONLINK

Services: Dedicated ISDN, dial-up ISDN, dial-up SLIP/PPP, high-speed dedicated access, Web hosting, Web design

Alberta Supernet Inc.

Edmonton, Alberta
supernet.ab.ca

#325 Pacific Plaza, 10909 Jasper Avenue
Edmonton, Alberta T5J 3L9

Voice: 403-441-3663
Fax: 403-424-0743
E-mail: info@supernet.ab.ca
Web: http://www.supernet.ab.ca

Services: Dedicated ISDN, dial-up SLIP/PPP, high-speed dedicated access, Web hosting, Web design

Ameritel Online Services

Winnipeg, Manitoba
aos.com, ameritel.ca, directions.ca

200-165 Garry Street
Winnipeg, Manitoba R3C 1G7

Voice: 204-943-2256
Fax: 204-949-0310
800 Voice: 1-800-738-2525
E-mail: ameritel@mbnet.mb.ca
Web: http://www.directions.ca, http://198.163.214.10

Services: Dial-up SLIP/PPP, high-speed dedicated access, Web design

AOL Canada (America Online)

Vienna, Virginia
aol.com

8619 Westwood Center Drive
Vienna, Virginia 22182-2285

800 Voice: 1-800-827-6364
Web: http://www.aol.com

Services: Dial-up SLIP/PPP, Web hosting

Astra Network Inc.

Winnipeg, Manitoba
man.net

2633 Portage Avenue
Winnipeg, Manitoba R3J 0P7

Voice: 204-987-7050
Fax: 204-987-7058
E-mail: info@man.net
Web: http://www.man.net

Services: Dedicated ISDN, dial-up ISDN, dial-up SLIP/PPP, high-speed dedicated access, Web hosting, Web design

Atlantic Connect

Halifax, Nova Scotia
atcon.com

3845 Dutch Village Road, 4th Floor
Halifax, Nova Scotia B3L 4H9

Voice: 902-429-0222
Fax: 902-429-0218
800 Voice: 1-800-661-0222
E-mail: trish@atcon.com, info@atcon.com
Web: http://www.atcon.com
Affiliated with: Hookup Communications

Services: Dedicated ISDN, dial-up SLIP/PPP, cable modem access, high-speed dedicated access, Web hosting, Web design

Atréide Communications inc.

Gatineau, Québec
atreide.net, gatineau.net, outaouais.net, saguenay.com, saguenay.net

500 Bl. Gréber (bureau 304)
Gatineau, Québec J8T 7W3

Voice: 819-243-1414
Fax: 819-243-2754
E-mail: tech@atreide.net
Web: http://www.atreide.net

Services: Dedicated ISDN, dial-up ISDN, dial-up SLIP/PPP, high-speed dedicated access, Web hosting, Web design

Autobahn Access Corporation

Winnipeg, Manitoba
autobahn.mb.ca

1666 Dublin Avenue
Winnipeg, Manitoba R3H 0H1

Voice: 204-632-7573
Fax: 204-694-1581
E-mail: info@autobahn.mb.ca
Web: http://www.autobahn.mb.ca

Services: Dedicated ISDN, dial-up ISDN, dial-up SLIP/PPP, high-speed dedicated access, Web hosting, Web design

autoroute.net inc.

Montréal, Québec
autoroute.net, autobahn.net, autoroute.ca, compupartner.com

5773 Ferrier Street, Suite 211
Town of Mount Royal, Québec H4P 1N3

Voice: 514-341-4023
Fax: 514-341-4701
E-mail: info@autoroute.net
Web: http://www.autoroute.net
Affiliated with: System Technology Development Inc.

Services: Dedicated ISDN, dial-up ISDN, dial-up SLIP/PPP, cable modem access, high-speed dedicated access, Web hosting, Web design

Axion Internet Communications Inc.

Vancouver, British Columbia
axionet.com, axion.net

600-1380 Burrard Street
Vancouver, British Columbia V6Z 2H3

Voice: 604-687-8030
Fax: 604-687-8130
E-mail: info@axionet.com
Web: http://www.axionet.com

Services: Dedicated ISDN, dial-up ISDN, dial-up SLIP/PPP, high-speed dedicated access, Web hosting, Web design

Aztec Computer Inc.

Georgetown, Ontario
aztec-net.com

348 Guelph Street, Unit 3
Georgetown, Ontario L7G 4B5

Voice: 905-873-2141
Fax: 905-873-2596
E-mail: admin@aztec-net.com
Web: http://www.aztec-net.com

Services: Dial-up SLIP/PPP, Web hosting, Web design

Babillard Synapse Inc.

Gatineau, Québec
synapse.net

22 Beloeil
Gatineau, Québec J8T 7G3

Voice: 819-561-1697
Fax: 819-561-9304
E-mail: info@synapse.net
Web: http://www.synapse.net

Services: Dedicated ISDN, dial-up SLIP/PPP, Web hosting

Barrie Connex Inc.

Barrie, Ontario
bconnex.net, connex.net

55 Cedar Pointe Drive, Unit 606
Barrie, Ontario L4N 5R7

Voice: 705-725-0819
Fax: 705-725-1287
800 Voice: 1-800-461-8883
E-mail: info@bconnex.net
Web: http://www.bconnex.net

Services: Dedicated ISDN, dial-up ISDN, dial-up SLIP/PPP, Web hosting, Web design

Barrie Internet

Barrie, Ontario
barint.on.ca, barint.net, cantravel.net

48 Morrow Road
Barrie, Ontario L4N 3V8

Voice: 705-733-3630
Fax: 705-733-3637
E-mail: info@barint.on.ca
Web: http://www.barint.on.ca, http://www.cantravel.net
Affiliated with: Cyberion Networking Corp.

Services: Dedicated ISDN, dial-up ISDN, dial-up SLIP/PPP, high-speed dedicated access, Web hosting, Web design

Binatech Information Services Inc.

Hamilton, Ontario
binatech.on.ca, binatech.com

100 Main Street East, 40th Floor
Hamilton, Ontario L8N 3W6

Voice: 905-527-7007
Fax: 905-527-0585
E-mail: info@binatech.on.ca
Web: http://www.binatech.on.ca

Services: Dedicated ISDN, dial-up SLIP/PPP, high-speed dedicated access, Web hosting, Web design

British Columbia Business Connections Ltd.

Victoria, British Columbia
commercial.net, canlaw.net, golf-handicap.com

P.O. Box 2412
Sidney, British Columbia V8L 3Y3

Voice: 604-652-4815
Fax: 604-652-4867
E-mail: bcbc@commercial.net
Web: http://www.commercial.net/vault

Services: Dial-up SLIP/PPP, Web hosting, Web design

Burlington Network Services

Burlington, Ontario
bserv.com

140 Plains Road East
Burlington, Ontario L7T 2C3

Voice: 905-632-3977
Fax: 905-632-3536
800 Voice: 1-800-263-8433
E-mail: webmaster@bserv.com
Web: http://www.bserv.com

Services: Dedicated ISDN, dial-up SLIP/PPP, high-speed dedicated access, Web hosting, Web design

---

Cable Atlantic Incorporated

St. John's, Newfoundland
cableatlantic.nf.ca, cableatlantic.net

541 Kenmount Road, P.O. Box 8596
St. John's, Newfoundland A1B 3P2

Voice: 709-753-7583
Fax: 709-722-8384
E-mail: info@cableatlantic.nf.ca, jhoward@cableatlantic.nf.ca
Web: http://www.cableatlantic.net
Affiliated with: Hookup Communications

Services: Cable modem access, high-speed dedicated access, Web hosting

---

Central Ontario Internet Services Inc.

Barrie, Ontario
cois.on.ca

166 Bayfield Street
Barrie, Ontario L4M 3B5

Voice: 705-721-5600
Fax: 705-726-0399
E-mail: info@cois.on.ca
Web: http://www.cois.on.ca

Services: Dial-up SLIP/PPP, Web hosting, Web design

CIMtegration Ltd.

North York, Ontario
cimtegration.com

2727 Steeles Avenue West
North York, Ontario M3J 3G9

Voice: 416-665-3566
Fax: 416-665-8285
E-mail: sales@cimtegration.com, info@cimtegration.com
Web: http://www.cimtegration.com

Services: Dedicated ISDN, dial-up ISDN, dial-up SLIP/PPP, Web hosting, Web design

---

CitéNet Telecom Inc.

Montréal, Québec
citenet.net, citenet.com, citenet.ca

4890 Eymard
Montréal, Québec H1S 1C5

Voice: 514-861-5050
Fax: 514-861-5953
E-mail: info@citenet.net
Web: http://www.citenet.net

Services: Dedicated ISDN, dial-up ISDN, dial-up SLIP/PPP, high-speed dedicated access, Web hosting, Web design

---

ClicNet Télécommunications, Inc.

Québec, Québec
qbc.clic.net

840, rue Ste-Thérèse
Québec, Québec G1N 1S7

Voice: 418-686-CLIC ext 2542
Fax: 418-682-6247
E-mail: info@qbc.clic.net
Web: http://www.qbc.clic.net

Services: Dedicated ISDN, dial-up ISDN, dial-up SLIP/PPP, high-speed dedicated access, Web hosting, Web design

Communication Inter-Accès

Montréal, Québec
interax.net

5475 rue Paré, Suite 104
Montréal, Québec H4P 1R4

Voice: 514-395-1023
Fax: 514-368-3529
E-mail: info@interax.net, support@interax.net
Web: http://www.interax.net

Services: Dedicated ISDN, dial-up ISDN, dial-up SLIP/PPP, high-speed dedicated access, Web hosting

Communications Accessibles Montréal

Montréal, Québec
cam.org, cam.net, cam.qc.ca

1205 Papineau, #050
Montréal, Québec H2K 4R2

Voice: 514-529-3000
Fax: 514-529-3300
E-mail: info@cam.org
Web: http://www.cam.org

Services: Dedicated ISDN, dial-up ISDN, dial-up SLIP/PPP, high-speed dedicated access, Web hosting

CompuServe

Columbus, Ohio
compuserve.com

5000 Arlington Center Boulevard, P.O. Box 20212
Columbus, Ohio 43220

800 Voice: 1-800-848-8199
Web: http://www.compuserve.com

Services: Dial-up SLIP/PPP, Web hosting

CompuTECH Internet

Portage La Prairie, Manitoba
cpnet.net

165 Saskatchewan Avenue East
Portage La Prairie, Manitoba R1N 0L7

Voice: 204-239-1974
Fax: 204-239-0797
E-mail: info@cpnet.net
Web: http://www.cpnet.net

Services: Dial-up SLIP/PPP, high-speed dedicated access, Web hosting, Web design

Connection MMIC Inc.

Montréal, Québec
connectmmic.net

5635 chemin St-François
St-Laurent, Québec H4S 1W6

Voice: 514-331-6642
Fax: 514-332-6642
E-mail: info@connectmmic.net
Web: http://www.connectmmic.net

Services: Dedicated ISDN, dial-up ISDN, dial-up SLIP/PPP, high-speed dedicated access, Web hosting, Web design

ConsuLan

Montreal, Québec
consulan.com

5800, boul. Cavendish, bureau 402
Côte-St-Luc, Québec H4W 2T5

Voice: 514-482-4848
Fax: 514-482-5001
E-mail: info@consulan.com
Web: http://www.consulan.com

Services: Dedicated ISDN, dial-up SLIP/PPP, Web hosting, Web design

CSI Group of Companies (Cyberstore Systems Inc.)

Vancouver, British Columbia
cyberstore.ca, cyberstore.com, cyberstore.net

601 West Broadway, Suite 201
Vancouver, British Columbia V5Z 4C2

Voice: 604-482-3400
Fax: 604-482-3433
800 Voice: 1-800—
E-mail: info@cyberstore.ca
Web: http://www.cyberstore.ca

Services: Dedicated ISDN, dial-up ISDN, dial-up SLIP/PPP, high-speed dedicated access, Web hosting, Web design

CSP Internet (Pacific Interconnect)

Victoria, British Columbia
pinc.com, coastnet.com, softwords.bc.ca, csp.net, vvv.com

4252 Commerce Circle
Victoria, British Columbia V8Z 4M2

Voice: 604-953-2680
Fax: 604-953-2659
E-mail: sales@pinc.com
Web: http://vvv.com

Services: Dedicated ISDN, dial-up ISDN, dial-up SLIP/PPP, high-speed dedicated access, Web hosting, Web design

CyberPlus Technologies Inc.

Ottawa, Ontario
cyberplus.ca, cyberplus.net

P.O. Box 27011
Gloucester, Ontario K1J 9L9

Voice: 613-749-8598
Fax: 613-749-7108
E-mail: info@cyberplus.ca
Web: http://www.cyberplus.ca

Services: Dial-up SLIP/PPP, Web hosting, Web design

Cyberspace Online Information Systems

Winnipeg, Manitoba
cyberspc.mb.ca

18-794 Sargent Avenue
Winnipeg, Manitoba R3E 0B7

Voice: 204-775-3650
Fax: 204-775-3501
E-mail: info@cyberspc.mb.ca
Web: http:/www.cyberspc.mb.ca

Services: Dedicated ISDN, dial-up SLIP/PPP, high-speed dedicated access, Web hosting, Web design

CYBERStream Inc.

Calgary, Alberta
CYBERStream.net, CYBERStream.com

1835B-10 Avenue S.W.
Calgary, Alberta T3C 0K2

Voice: 403-244-0269
Fax: 403-244-0875
E-mail: info@cyberstream.net
Web: http://www.cyberstream.net

Services: Dedicated ISDN, dial-up ISDN, high-speed dedicated access, Web hosting

Cybersurf Information Access

Calgary, Alberta
cia.com

1212-31 Avenue N.E., Suite 312
Calgary, Alberta T2E 7S8

Voice: 403-777-2000
Fax: 403-777-2003
E-mail: info@cia.com
Web: http://www.cybersurf.net

Services: Dedicated ISDN, dial-up SLIP/PPP, high-speed dedicated access, Web hosting, Web design

Cyberus Online Inc.

Ottawa, Ontario
cyberus.ca, cyberus.com

99 Fifth Avenue, Suite 406
Ottawa, Ontario K1S 5P5

Voice: 613-233-1215
Fax: 613-233-0292
800 Voice: 1-800-809-9883
E-mail: info@cyberus.ca
Web: http:/www.cyberus.ca

Services: Dedicated ISDN, dial-up ISDN, dial-up SLIP/PPP, Web hosting, Web design

CyberWAVE Technologies Inc.

Calgary, Alberta
cwave.com

1602 Centre Street North
Calgary, Alberta T2E 2R9

Voice: 403-571-5580
Fax: 403-571-5584
E-mail: cyber@cwave.com, eric@cwave.com, vinh@cwave.com
Web: http://www.cwave.com

Services: Dedicated ISDN, dial-up ISDN, dial-up SLIP/PPP, high-speed dedicated access, Web hosting, Web design

Cycor Communications Inc.

Charlottetown, Prince Edward Island
cycor.ca

P.O. Box 454
Charlottetown, Prince Edward Island C1A 7K7

Voice: 902-629-2453
Fax: 902-629-2456
800 Voice: 1-800-282-9267
E-mail: sign.me.up@cycor.ca
Web: http://www.cycor.ca

Services: Dedicated ISDN, dial-up ISDN, dial-up SLIP/PPP, Web hosting, Web design

Data Link Canada West (DLC-West)

Regina, Saskatchewan
dlcwest.com

1542 Albert Street
Regina, Saskatchewan S4P 2S4

Voice: 306-585-0362
Fax: 306-352-6450
E-mail: jim.nickel@dlcwest.com
Web: http://www.dlcwest.com

Services: Dedicated ISDN, dial-up ISDN, dial-up SLIP/PPP, high-speed dedicated access, Web hosting, Web design

DataCom Online Services

Cornwall, Ontario
datacom.ca

P.O. Box 332
Cornwall, Ontario K6H 5T1

Voice: 613-938-0016
Fax: 613-938-5498
E-mail: support@datacom.ca
Web: http://www.datacom.ca

Services: Dial-up SLIP/PPP, Web hosting, Web design

DataStore Inc.

St. John's, Newfoundland
datastore.com, seascape.com

516 Topsail Road, Suite 204
St. John's, Newfoundland A1E 2C5

Voice: 709-745-8555
Fax: 709-745-8001
E-mail: surf.seascape.com, glenda.seascape.com
Web: http://www.datastore.com

Services: Dial-up SLIP/PPP, dedicated ISDN, cable modem access, high-speed dedicated access, Web hosting, Web design

Digital Ark

Courtenay, British Columbia
ark.com, mars.ark.com, oberon.ark.com

P.O. Box 3310, 205-576 England Avenue
Courtenay, British Columbia V9N 5N5

Voice: 604-334-9641
Fax: 604-334-2365
E-mail: dmartel@oberon.ark.com
Web: http://www.ark.com

Services: Dial-up SLIP/PPP, high-speed dedicated access, Web hosting, Web design

Docker Services Ltd.

Brandon, Manitoba
docker.com

47-10th Street
Brandon, Manitoba R7A 4E7

Voice: 204-727-7788
Fax: 204-726-4580
E-mail: webweaver@docker.com
Web: http://www.docker.com

Services: Dial-up SLIP/PPP, Web hosting, Web design

Dtronix Internet Services

Mississauga, Ontario
dtronix.com

2857 Derry Road East, Suite 307
Mississauga, Ontario L4T 1A6

Voice: 905-824-2814
Fax: 905-824-8678
E-mail: info@dtronix.com
Web: http://www.dtronix.com

Services: Dedicated ISDN, dial-up SLIP/PPP, Web hosting, Web design

Easynet Inc.

Cambridge, Ontario
easynet.on.ca

8 Queen Street East
Cambridge, Ontario N3C 2A6

Voice: 519-654-9999
Fax: 519-654-0301
E-mail: admin@easynet.on.ca, sales@easynet.on.ca, watchman@easynet.on.ca
Web: http://www.easynet.on.ca

Services: Dial-up SLIP/PPP, Web hosting, Web design

Electro-Byte Technologies

Sarnia, Ontario
ebtech.net, sarnia.com

559-B Exmouth Street
Sarnia, Ontario N7T 5P6

Voice: 519-332-8235
Fax: 519-332-8307
E-mail: info@ebtech.net
Web: http://www.ebtech.net

Services: Dial-up SLIP/PPP, high-speed dedicated access, Web hosting, Web design

Enterprise-Terraport Online

Markham, Ontario
terraport.net, enterprise.ca

2820-14th Avenue
Markham, Ontario L3R 0S9

Voice: 416-477-6000
Fax: 416-477-7062
E-mail: info@terraport.net
Web: http://www.enterprise.ca, http://www.terraport.net

Services: Dedicated ISDN, dial-up SLIP/PPP, Web hosting, Web design

---

Escape Communications Corp.

Winnipeg, Manitoba
escape.ca

1383 Pembina Drive, Suite 206
Winnipeg, Manitoba R3T 2B9

Voice: 204-925-4290
Fax: 204-925-4291
E-mail: info@escape.ca
Web: http://www.escape.ca

Services: Dedicated ISDN, dial-up ISDN, dial-up SLIP/PPP, high-speed dedicated access, Web hosting, Web design

---

Fleximation Systems Inc.

Mississauga, Ontario
flexnet.com

1495 Bonhill Road, Units 1 and 2
Mississauga, Ontario L5T 1M2

Voice: 905-795-0300
Fax: 905-795-0310
E-mail: sales@flexnet.com
Web: http://www.flexnet.com

Services: Dedicated ISDN, dial-up ISDN, dial-up SLIP/PPP, high-speed dedicated access, Web hosting, Web design

---

Focus Technologies Networks – aka FTN

Mississauga, Ontario
ftn.net

5380 Timberlea Boulevard
Mississauga, Ontario L4W 2S6

Voice: 905-602-6266
Fax: 905-602-6272
800 Voice: 1-800-FTN-INET
Web: http://www.ftn.net

Services: Dedicated ISDN, dial-up ISDN, dial-up SLIP/PPP, high-speed dedicated access, Web hosting, Web design

---

FrancoMédia

Montréal, Québec
francomedia.qc.ca

3300 boul. Rosemont, bureau 218
Montréal, Québec H1X 1K2

Voice: 514-721-8216
Fax: 514-727-2164
E-mail: admin@francomedia.qc.ca, support@ francomedia.qc.ca, info@francomedia.qc.ca, jvero@francomedia.qc
Web: http://www.francomedia.qc.ca

Services: Dedicated ISDN, dial-up ISDN, dial-up SLIP/PPP, Web hosting, Web design

---

Gate West Communications

Winnipeg, Manitoba
gatewest.net, gatewest.mb.ca

525 London Street

P.O. Box 64007
Winnipeg, Manitoba R2K 2Z0

Voice: 204-663-2931
Fax: 204-667-1379
E-mail: info@gatewest.net
Web: http://www.gatewest.net

Services: Dedicated ISDN, dial-up SLIP/PPP, high-speed dedicated access, Web hosting

---

generation.NET — Total Internet Solutions

Montréal, Québec
generation.net

2020 University, Suite 1620
Montréal, Québec H3A 2A5

Voice: 514-845-5555
Fax: 514-845-5004
888 Voice: 1-888-650-5555
E-mail: info@generation.net, sales@generation.net, ventes@generation.net
Web: http://www.generation.net

Services: Dedicated ISDN, dial-up ISDN, dial-up SLIP/PPP, high-speed dedicated access, Web hosting, Web design

Glen-Net Communications

Alexandria, Ontario
cybermall.cornwall.on.ca, glen-net.ca

P.O. Box 837
Alexandria, Ontario K0C 1A0

Voice: 613-525-3689
Fax: 613-525-3459
E-mail: sales@glen-net.ca
Web: http://www.glen-net.ca

Services: Dial-up SLIP/PPP, high-speed dedicated access, Web hosting, Web design

Global Linx Internet Inc.

Kentville, Nova Scotia
glinx.com

21 Aberdeen Street, P.O. Box 362
Kentville, Nova Scotia B4N 3X1

Voice: 902-678-1900
Fax: 902-678-2191
800 Voice: 1-800-759-4422
E-mail: support@glinx.com
Web: http://www.glinx.com

Services: Dial-up SLIP/PPP, high-speed dedicated access, Web hosting, Web design

Global-X-Change Communications Inc.

Ottawa, Ontario
globalx.net, globalx.com

170 Laurier Avenue West, Suite 709
Ottawa, Ontario K1P 5V5

Voice: 613-235-6865
Fax: 613-232-5285
E-mail: reception@globalx.net, info@globalx.net
Web: http://www.globalx.net

Services: Web design

Globale Internet Canada

Rosemère, Québec
globale.com

277 boul. Labelle, Suite 150
Rosemère, Québec J7A 2H3

Voice: 514-965-9065
Fax: 514-965-8929
E-mail: info@globale.com
Web: http://www.globale.com

Services: Dedicated ISDN, dial-up ISDN, dial-up SLIP/PPP, Web hosting, Web design

Globalserve Communications Inc.

Oakville, Ontario
globalserve.net, globalserve.on.ca

466 Speers Road, Suite 323
Oakville, Ontario L6K 3W9

Voice: 905-337-0152 or 416-410-2005
Fax: 905-337-1063
888 Voice: 1-888-CITY-NET
E-mail: admin@globalserve.net
Web: http://www.globalserve.net

Services: Dedicated ISDN, dial-up ISDN, dial-up SLIP/PPP, Web hosting, Web design

Grant Internet Communications Corporation

Collingwood, Ontario
grant.ca

243 Hurontario Street
Collingwood, Ontario L9Y 2M1

Voice: 705-446-2900
Fax: 705-446-2901
E-mail: info@grant.ca
Web: http://www.grant.ca, http://www.georgian.net, http://www.huronia.net

Services: Dial-up SLIP/PPP, high-speed dedicated access, Web hosting, Web design

---

headwaters network

Orangeville, Ontario
headwaters.com

113 Broadway
Orangeville, Ontario L9W 1K2

Voice: 519-940-9252
Fax: 519-942-3776
E-mail: sales@headwaters.com
Web: http://www.headwaters.com

Services: Dedicated ISDN, dial-up ISDN, dial-up SLIP/PPP, high-speed dedicated access, Web hosting, Web design

---

Helinet, A Division of Helikon Technologies Inc.

Vancouver, British Columbia
helinet.com, helikon.com

3566 King George Highway
Surrey, British Columbia V4P 1B5

Voice: 604-893-7077
Fax: 604-893-7076
E-mail: info@helinet.com, info@helikon.com
Web: http://www.helinet.com, http://www.helikon.com

Services: Dedicated ISDN, dial-up ISDN, dial-up SLIP/PPP, Web hosting, Web design

---

Helix Internet

Surrey, British Columbia
helix.net, *.helix.net

302-12886 78th Avenue
Surrey, British Columbia V6W 8E7

Voice: 604-501-5430
Fax: 604-501-5440
E-mail: service@helix.net
Web: http://www.helix.net

Services: Dedicated ISDN, dial-up SLIP/PPP, high-speed dedicated access, Web hosting, Web design

---

Heydon Computer Services Ltd.

Hastings, Ontario
heydon.com

Dunlay Road
Hastings, Ontario K0L 1Y6

Voice: 705-696-2766 or 705-696-2882
Fax: 705-696-2535
E-mail: hcs@heydon.com
Web: http://www.heydon.com
Affiliated with: iSTAR

Services: Dial-up ISDN, dial-up SLIP/PPP, Web hosting, Web design

---

HMT INTERNET Inc.

Yorkton, Saskatchewan
hmtnet.com, awinc.com

36-2nd Avenue North
Yorkton, Saskatchewan S3N 1G2

Voice: 306-782-9150
Fax: 306-786-6160
E-mail: sales@hmtnet.com, admin@hmtnet.com, rslywka@hmtnet.com
Web: http://www.hmtnet.com

Services: Dial-up SLIP/PPP, high-speed dedicated access, Web hosting, Web design

---

HookUp Communications

Oakville, Ontario
hookup.net

1075 North Service Road West, Unit 207
Oakville, Ontario L6M 2G2

Voice: 905-847-8000
Fax: 905-847-8420
800 Voice: 1-800-363-0400
E-mail: sales@hookup.net
Web: http://www.hookup.net

Services: Dedicated ISDN, dial-up ISDN, dial-up SLIP/PPP, high-speed dedicated access, Web hosting

---

Huron Internet Technologies

Kitchener, Ontario
huron.net, wingham.com

12-300 Victoria Street North
Kitchener, Ontario N2H 6R9

Voice: 519-745-5513
Fax: 519-745-5522
800 Voice: 1-800-603-5032
E-mail: sales@huron.net
Web: http://www.huron.net

Services: Dial-up SLIP/PPP, high-speed dedicated access, Web hosting, Web design

---

HuronTel

Ripley, Ontario
hurontel.on.ca

Box 220, 60 Queen Street
Ripley, Ontario N0G 2R0

Voice: 519-395-2625
E-mail: service@hurontel.on.ca
Web: http://www.hurontel.on.ca

Services: Dedicated ISDN, dial-up ISDN, dial-up SLIP/PPP, high-speed dedicated access, Web hosting, Web design

---

HyperNet

London, Ontario
lonet.ca

140-4026 Meadowbrook Drive
London, Ontario N6L 1C8

Voice: 519-652-3790
Fax: 519-652-0569
E-mail: admin@lonet.ca
Web: http://www.lonet.ca

Services: Dedicated ISDN, dial-up ISDN, dial-up SLIP/PPP, Web hosting, Web design

---

Hypertech North Inc.

Whitehorse, Yukon
hypertech.yk.ca, yukon.net, whitehorse.net

Box 4098
Whitehorse, Yukon Y1A 3S9

Voice: 403-668-7214
Fax: 403-633-6056
E-mail: sales@hypertech.yk.ca, service@hypertech.yk.ca, admin@hypertech.yk.ca
Web: http://www.hypertech.yk.ca, http://www.yukon.net

Services: Dedicated ISDN, dial-up SLIP/PPP, high-speed dedicated access, Web hosting, Web design

---

IBM Global Network

Markham, Ontario
ibm.net, ibm.com

3500 Steeles Avenue East
Markham, Ontario L3R 2Z1

800 Voice: 1-800-IBM-CALL ext. 1051
Fax: 800-565-6612
E-mail: ibm_direct@ca.ibm.com
Web: http://www.can.ibm.com/globalnetwork

Services: Dedicated ISDN, dial-up SLIP/PPP, high-speed dedicated access, Web hosting, Web design

---

Infinity Internet Communications

Vancouver, British Columbia
infinity.ca, cyberion.com, helix.net

470-1090 Homer Street
Vancouver, British Columbia V6B 2W9

Voice: 604-669-9630
Fax: 604-669-4923
E-mail: tmarkin@infinity.ca, infinity@infinity.ca
Web: http://www.infinity.ca
Affiliated with: Cyberion Networking Corp., Helix Internet, World Wide Data Communications

Services: Dedicated ISDN, dial-up ISDN, dial-up SLIP/PPP, high-speed dedicated access, Web hosting, Web design

IGS (Information Gateway Services)

Belleville, Ontario
blvl.igs.net

Century Place

199 Front Street, Suite 209
Belleville, Ontario K8N 5H5

Voice: 613-962-9299
Fax: 613-962-0877
E-mail: info@blvl.igs.net
Web: http://www.blvl.igs.net

Services: Dedicated ISDN, dial-up ISDN, dial-up SLIP/PPP, high-speed dedicated access, Web hosting, Web design

Information Gateway Services (Kitchener-Waterloo) Inc.

Kitchener-Waterloo, Ontario
kw.igs.net

151 Frobisher Drive, Suite E-118
Waterloo, Ontario N2V 2C9

Voice: 519-884-7200
Fax: 519-884-7440
E-mail: info@kw.igs.net
Web: http://www.kw.igs.net

Services: Dedicated ISDN, dial-up ISDN, dial-up SLIP/PPP, high-speed dedicated access, Web hosting, Web design

Information Gateway Services Windsor

Windsor, Ontario
windsor.igs.net, kelcom.on.ca

363 Eugenie Street East
Windsor, Ontario N8X 2Y2

Voice: 519-250-5050
Fax: 519-250-5080
E-mail: webmaster@windsor.igs.net, sales@windsor.igs.net
Web: http://www.windsor.igs.net
Affiliated with: Information Gateway Services

Services: Dedicated ISDN, dial-up ISDN, dial-up SLIP/PPP, Web hosting, Web design

Infoserve Technology Ltd.

Burnaby, British Columbia
infoserve.net

5438 Imperial Street
Burnaby, British Columbia V5J 1E6

Voice: 604-482-8238
Fax: 604-482-8248
E-mail: info@infoserve.net
Web: http://www.infoserve.net

Services: Dial-up SLIP/PPP, Web hosting, Web design

InfoTeck Internet

Trois-Rivières-Ouest, Québec
infoteck.qc.ca

5480, boul. Jean XXIII
Trois-Rivières-Ouest, Québec G8Z 4A9

Voice: 819-370-3232
Fax: 819-370-3624
800 Voice: 1-800-861-3232
E-mail: luc.pronovost@infoteck.qc.ca
Web: http://www.infoteck.qc.ca

Services: Dedicated ISDN, dial-up ISDN, dial-up SLIP/PPP, cable modem access, high-speed dedicated access, Web hosting, Web design

Inline Information Services, Inc.

Mississauga, Ontario
inline.net, inline.org

7305 Rapistan Court
Mississauga, Ontario L5N 5Z4

Voice: 905-813-8800
Fax: 905-542-9223
E-mail: info@inline.net
Web: http://www.inline.net

Services: Dedicated ISDN, dial-up SLIP/PPP, Web hosting, Web design

Interactive Online Ltd.

Waterloo, Ontario
ionline.net, mucsoft.com

701-20 Erb Street West
Waterloo, Ontario N2L 1T2

Voice: 519-886-8286
Fax: 519-886-5766
E-mail: sales@ionline.net, info@ionline.net
Web: http://www.ionline.net

Services: Dedicated ISDN, dial-up ISDN, dial-up SLIP/PPP, high-speed dedicated access, Web hosting, Web design

Inter*Com Information Services

London, Ontario
icis.on.ca, icis.net

1464 Adelaide Street North, #2
London, Ontario N5X 1K4

Voice: 519-679-1620
Fax: 519-679-1583
E-mail: info@icis.on.ca
Web: http://www.icis.on.ca
Affiliated with: Hookup Communications

Services: Dedicated ISDN, dial-up ISDN, dial-up SLIP/PPP, high-speed dedicated access, Web hosting, Web design

Interhop Network Services Inc.

Newmarket, Ontario
interhop.net

171 Main Street South
Newmarket, Ontario L3Y 3Y9

Voice: 905-715-7600
Fax: 905-836-8324
E-mail: admin@interhop.net
Web: http://www.interhop.net

Services: Dedicated ISDN, dial-up ISDN, dial-up SLIP/PPP, high-speed dedicated access, Web hosting, Web design

InterLog Internet Services

Toronto, Ontario
interlog.com

1075 Bay Street, Suite 510
Toronto, Ontario M5S 2B1

Voice: 416-975-2655
Fax: 416-975-9639
E-mail: sales@interlog.com
Web: http://www.interlog.com

Services: Dedicated ISDN, dial-up ISDN, dial-up SLIP/PPP, high-speed dedicated access, Web hosting, Web design

Internet Access Inc.

Nepean, Ontario
ottawa.net, intacc.net

1916 Merivale Road
Nepean, Ontario K2G 1E8

Voice: 613-225-5595
Fax: 613-225-7733
E-mail: info@ottawa.net
Web: http://www.ottawa.net
Affiliated with: Hookup Communications

Services: Dedicated ISDN, dial-up SLIP/PPP, Web hosting

Internet Canada Corporation (ICAN)

Toronto, Ontario
ican.net, io.org, ulix.net, expresslane.ca

20 Bay Street, Suite 1625
Toronto, Ontario M5J 2N8

Voice: 416-363-8518
Fax: 416-363-8713
E-mail: info@ican.net, sales@ican.net, advertising@ican.net, support@ican.net, training@ican.net
Web: http://www.ican.net

Services: Dedicated ISDN, dial-up ISDN, dial-up SLIP/PPP, Web hosting, Web design

The Internet Centre

Edmonton, Alberta
incentre.net, incenter.net, ccinet.ab.ca

4130-95 Street
Edmonton, Alberta T6E 6H5

Voice: 403-450-6787
Fax: 403-450-9143
E-mail: info@incentre.net
Web: http://www.incentre.net

Services: Dedicated ISDN, dial-up ISDN, dial-up SLIP/PPP, high-speed dedicated access, Web hosting, Web design

Internet Communication R-d-L Inc.

Rivière-du-Loup, Québec
icrdl.net

80 rue Frontenac (Local B113)
Rivière-du-Loup, Québec G5R 1R1

Voice: 418-868-0077
Fax: 418-868-0077
E-mail: info@icrdl.net, admin@icrdl.net
Web: http://www.icrdl.net

Services: Dedicated ISDN, dial-up ISDN, dial-up SLIP/PPP, cable modem access, high-speed dedicated access, Web hosting, Web design

The Internet Companion

Edmonton, Alberta
webvertise.com

10712-176 Street, Suite 210
Edmonton, Alberta T5S 1G5

Voice: 403-489-5740
Fax: 403-489-6196
E-mail: bob@tic.ab.ca, ticnet@webvertise.com
Web: http://www.webvertise.com/ticnet

Services: Dedicated ISDN, dial-up ISDN, dial-up SLIP/PPP, Web hosting, Web design

Internet Connect Inc.

Edmonton, Alberta
connect.ab.ca

#222, 9704-54 Avenue
Edmonton, Alberta T6E 0A9

Voice: 403-413-1864
Fax: 403-437-8989
E-mail: info@connect.ab.ca, webmaster@connect.ab.ca
Web: http://www.connect.ab.ca

Services: Dedicated ISDN, dial-up ISDN, dial-up SLIP/PPP, Web hosting, Web design

Internet Connect Niagara

St. Catharines, Ontario
niagara.com

25 Church Street
St. Catharines, Ontario L2R 3B4

Voice: 905-988-9909
Fax: 905-988-1090
E-mail: sales@niagara.com
Web: http://www.niagara.com

Services: Dedicated ISDN, dial-up ISDN, dial-up SLIP/PPP, high-speed dedicated access, Web hosting, Web design

Internet Direct Canada Inc.

Toronto, Ontario
idirect.com

5415 Dundas Street West, Suite 301
Etobicoke, Ontario M9B 1B4

Voice: 416-233-7150
Fax: 416-233-6970
E-mail: sales@idirect.com
Web: http://idirect.com

Services: Dedicated ISDN, dial-up ISDN, dial-up SLIP/PPP, cable modem access, high-speed dedicated access, Web hosting, Web design

---

Internet Front Inc.

Scarborough, Ontario
internetfront.com

3300 McNicoll Avenue, Unit 215
Scarborough, Ontario M1V 5K6

Voice: 416-293-8539
Fax: 416-293-8327
E-mail: support@internetfront.com
Web: http://www.internetfront.com

Services: Dial-up SLIP/PPP, Web hosting, Web design

Internet HTL

Thedford, Ontario
htl.net

P.O. Box 280
Thedford, Ontario N0J 1C0

Voice: 519-243-4000
Fax: 519-296-5111
E-mail: sales@htl.net, help@htl.net
Web: http://www.htl.net

Services: Dial-up SLIP/PPP, Web hosting, Web design

Internet Innovations Inc.

Cambridge, Ontario
in.on.ca

Pinebush Corporate Centre,
320 Pinebush Road, Unit 8
Cambridge, Ontario N3C 2V3

Voice: 519-621-9300 (Cambridge) or 519-654-2936 (Guelph)
Fax: 519-623-3350
E-mail: general@in.on.ca
Web: http://www.in.on.ca

Services: Dedicated ISDN, dial-up ISDN, dial-up SLIP/PPP, Web hosting, Web design

---

InterNet Kingston

Kingston, Ontario
kingston.net, ltd.com, losers.com, kingston.org

177 Wellington Street, Suite 302
Kingston, Ontario K7L 3E3

Voice: 613-547-6939
Fax: 613-547-5436
E-mail: info@adan.kingston.net
Web: http://www.kingston.net

Services: Dedicated ISDN, dial-up ISDN, dial-up SLIP/PPP, high-speed dedicated access, Web hosting, Web design

---

Internet Light and Power™

Toronto, Ontario
ilap.com, ilap.net, ilap.ca

2235 Sheppard Avenue East, Suite 905
North York, Ontario M2J 5B5

Voice: 416-502-1512
Fax: 416-502-3333
E-mail: staff@ilap.com
Web: http://www.ilap.com

Services: Dedicated ISDN, dial-up SLIP/PPP, high-speed dedicated access, Web hosting, Web design

---

Internet Login

Montréal, Québec
login.net

500, boul. René Lévesque ouest, suite 916
Montréal, Québec H2Z 1W7

Voice: 514-875-6446
Fax: 514-875-8596
800 Voice: 1-800-GO-LOGIN
E-mail: info@login.net, support@login.net
Web: http://www.login.net

Services: Dedicated ISDN, dial-up SLIP/PPP, high-speed dedicated access, Web hosting

---

Internet Mégantic

Lac-Mégantic, Québec
megantic.net, tm.megantic.net

2946 D'Orsennens
Lac-Mégantic, Québec G6B 2R2

Voice: 819-583-3929
Fax: 819-583-5287
800 Voice: 1-800-922-0388 (for 514, 819, 418 area codes)
E-mail: info@megantic.net
Web: http://www.megantic.net

Services: Dial-up SLIP/PPP, Web hosting

Internet NNT

Burgessville, Ontario
oxford.net

P.O. Box 33, 19 Main Street North
Burgessville, Ontario N0J 1C0

Voice: 519-456-3333 or 519-468-3333
Fax: 519-424-2290
E-mail: sales@oxford.net, admin@oxford.net, support@oxford.net
Web: http://www.oxford.net

Services: Dial-up SLIP/PPP, Web hosting, Web design

Internet North

Elliot Lake, Ontario
inorth.on.ca

27 Timber Road
Elliot Lake, Ontario P5A 2T1

Voice: 705-848-3047 or 705-848-3552
Fax: 705-848-3972
E-mail: inorth@cancom.net
Web: http://www.inorth.on.ca

Services: Dial-up SLIP/PPP, high-speed dedicated access, Web hosting, Web design

---

Internet Portal Services

Vancouver, British Columbia
portal.ca

2525 Manitoba Street, Suite 201
Vancouver, British Columbia V5Y 3A7

Voice: 604-257-9400
Fax: 604-257-9401
E-mail: info@portal.ca
Web: http://www.portal.ca

Services: Dedicated ISDN, dial-up SLIP/PPP, high-speed dedicated access, Web hosting, Web design

---

Internet Québec IQ inc.

Montréal, Québec
iq.ca

8642 Saint-Denis
Montréal, Québec H2P 2H2

Voice: 514-383-4064
Fax: 514-381-5197
E-mail: info@iq.ca, support@iq.ca
Web: http://www.iq.ca

Services: Dedicated ISDN, dial-up ISDN, dial-up SLIP/PPP, cable modem access, high-speed dedicated access, Web hosting, Web design

---

Internet Solutions Inc.

Winnipeg, Manitoba
solutions.net, solutions.mb.ca

2nd Floor, 490 Des Meurons
Winnipeg, Manitoba R2L 0W9

Voice: 204-982-1060
Fax: 204-982-1070
E-mail: info@solutions.net
Web: http://www.solutions.net

Services: Dedicated ISDN, dial-up SLIP/PPP, high-speed dedicated access, Web hosting, Web design

Internet XL

Coquitlam, British Columbia
xl.ca, bossy.com, equity.com

571 Rochester Avenue, #101
Coquitlam, British Columbia V3K 2V3

Voice: 604-939-6995
Fax: 604-939-6445
800 Voice: 1-800-XL-NETCO
E-mail: sales@xl.ca, tellmemore@xl.ca
Web: http://www.xl.ca, http://www.home.xl.ca, http://www.realty.xl.ca

Services: Dedicated ISDN, dial-up ISDN, dial-up SLIP/PPP, high-speed dedicated access, Web hosting, Web design

Internet-BBSI Inc.

Sept-Iles, Québec
bbsi.net

141 Régnault
Sept-Iles, Québec G4R 4M4

Voice: 418-968-4433
Fax: 418-968-5634
E-mail: info@bbsi.net
Web: http://www.bbsi.net

Services: Dedicated ISDN, dial-up ISDN, dial-up SLIP/PPP, Web hosting, Web design

Island Services Network

Charlottetown, Prince Edward Island
isn.net, sellit.com, pei.net

129 Kent Street, Suite 303
Charlottetown, Prince Edward Island C1A 1N4

Voice: 902-892-4476
Fax: 902-892-6012
E-mail: info@isn.net, sales@isn.net
Web: http://www.isn.net

Services: Dial-up SLIP/PPP, high-speed dedicated access, Web hosting, Web design

iSTAR Internet Inc.

Ottawa, Ontario
istar.ca, mindlink.net, mindlink.bc.ca, inforamp.net, magi.com, wimsey.com, arc.ab.ca, aurora.net, canrem.com

250 Albert Street, Suite 200
Ottawa, Ontario K1P 6M1

Voice: 613-780-2200
Fax: 613-780-6666
888 Voice: 1-888-GO-ISTAR
E-mail: sales@istar.ca
Web: http://www.istar.ca

Services: Dedicated ISDN, dial-up ISDN, dial-up SLIP/PPP, high-speed dedicated access, Web hosting, Web design

KawarthaNET

Peterborough, Ontario
knet.flemingc.on.ca

229 King Street
Peterborough, Ontario K9J 2R8

Voice: 705-748-5638
Fax: 705-743-9704
E-mail: info@knet.flemingc.on.ca
Web: http://www.knet.flemingc.on.ca

Services: Dial-up SLIP/PPP, Web hosting

Kayhay Internet & Communications

Halifax, Nova Scotia
kayhay.com

P.O. Box 3306, 5675 Spring Garden Road, Suite 208
Dartmouth, Nova Scotia B2W 5G3

Voice: 902-492-0280
Fax: 902-429-7840
E-mail: kic@kayhay.com, sales@kayhay.com
Web: http://www.kayhay.com

Services: Dial-up SLIP/PPP, Web hosting, Web design

Kingston Online Services

Kingston, Ontario
kosone.com

303 Bagot Street, Suite 309
Kingston, Ontario K7K 5W7

Voice: 613-549-8667
Fax: 613-549-0642
800 Voice: 1-800-208-0086
E-mail: info@post.kosone.com
Web: http://www.kosone.com/kos/welcome.html

Services: Dedicated ISDN, dial-up ISDN, dial-up SLIP/PPP, high-speed dedicated access, Web hosting, Web design

Kneehill Internet Services

Linden, Alberta
kneehill.com, info-pages.com

Box 37
Linden, Alberta T0M 1J0

Voice: 403-546-3021
Fax: 403-546-2276
E-mail: info@kneehill.com, terry@kneehill.com, dannstp@kneehill.com
Web: http://www.kneehill.com

Services: Dial-up SLIP/PPP, high-speed dedicated access, Web hosting, Web design

Lands Systems Ltd.

Barrhead, Alberta
ls.barrhead.ab.ca

5808-53 Street
Barrhead, Alberta T7N 1N1

Voice: 403-674-3711
Fax: 403-674-5690
E-mail: sales@ls.barrhead.ab.ca
Web: http://www.ls.barrhead.ab.ca

Services: Dial-up SLIP/PPP, Web hosting, Web design

Lanzen Corporation

Montréal, Québec
lanzen.net, lanzen.com

1751 Richardson, Suite 2525
Montréal, Québec H3K 1G6

Voice: 514-937-4422
Fax: 514-937-4317
E-mail: info@lanzen.net
Web: http://www.lanzen.net

Services: Dedicated ISDN, dial-up ISDN, dial-up SLIP/PPP, high-speed dedicated access, Web hosting, Web design

Le Cybernaute

Chicoutimi, Québec
cybernaute.com, envirovision.qc.ca

391 Racine Est,
Chicoutimi, Québec G7H 1S8

Voice: 418-543-9555
Fax: 418-543-9187
E-mail: webmaster@cybernaute.com, postmaster@cybernaute.com
Web: http://www.cybernaute.com

Services: Dedicated ISDN, dial-up ISDN, dial-up SLIP/PPP, Web hosting, Web design

Learn-Ed Internet Services

Toronto, Ontario
learned.com, sitescene.com

55 Eglinton Avenue East, Suite 504
Toronto, Ontario M4P 1G8

Voice: 416-483-4000 ext. 26
Fax: 416-483-0988
E-mail: johngas@learned.com, kathy@sitescene.com
Web: http://www.learned.com

Services: Dedicated ISDN, dial-up ISDN, dial-up SLIP/PPP, cable modem access, Web hosting, Web design

---

Lethbridge Internet Services

Lethbridge, Alberta
lis.ab.ca

814-3rd Avenue South
Lethbridge, Alberta T1J 0H7

Voice: 403-381-4638
Fax: 403-320-0484
E-mail: info@lis.ab.ca
Web: http://www.lis.ab.ca

Services: Dedicated ISDN, dial-up SLIP/PPP, high-speed dedicated access, Web hosting, Web design

---

Lexicom Ltd.

Calgary, Alberta
lexicom.ab.ca, lexi.net

203 Lynnview Road S.E., Suite 60
Calgary, Alberta T2C 2C6

Voice: 403-279-0325
Fax: 403-279-8291
E-mail: webmaster@lexicom.ab.ca
Web: http://www.lexicom.ab.ca

Services: Dedicated ISDN, dial-up ISDN, dial-up SLIP/PPP, high-speed dedicated access, Web hosting, Web design

---

Log On Internet Solutions

Owen Sound, Ontario
log.on.ca

Box 289
Chatsworth, Ontario N0H 1G0

Voice: 519-794-3502
Fax: 519-794-3363
888 Voice: 1-888-LOG-ON-IN
E-mail: admin@log.on.ca, sales@log.on.ca
Web: http://www.log.on.ca

Services: Dial-up SLIP/PPP, high-speed dedicated access, Web hosting, Web design

---

Magic Total Net Inc.

Toronto, Ontario
magic.ca, total.net

260 Richmond Street West, Suite 206
Toronto, Ontario M5V 1W5

Voice: 416-591-6490
Fax: 416-591-6409
E-mail: info@magic.ca, info@total.net
Web: http://www.magic.ca, http://www.total.net
Affiliated with: Accent Internet, Infobahn, Total Internet, Megatoon, Magic Online Services Winnepeg Station

Services: Dedicated ISDN, dial-up ISDN, dial-up SLIP/PPP, high-speed dedicated access, Web hosting, Web design

---

Magma Communications Ltd.

Nepean, Ontario
magmacom.com

52 Antares Drive, Unit 201
Nepean, Ontario K2E 7Z1

Voice: 613-228-3565
Fax: 613-228-8313
E-mail: info@magmacom.com, sales@magmacom.com, support@magmacom.com, web@magmacom.com
Web: http://www.magmacom.com

Services: Dedicated ISDN, dial-up ISDN, dial-up SLIP/PPP, Web hosting

---

Mag-Net BBS Ltd.

Prince George, British Columbia
mag-net.com, mag-net.bc.ca

2012 Pine Street
Prince George, British Columbia V2L 2C9

Voice: 604-564-6765
Fax: 604-563-8752
E-mail: sales@mag-net.com
Web: http://www.mag-net.com

Services: Dedicated ISDN, dial-up ISDN, dial-up SLIP/PPP, Web hosting, Web design

---

Maritime Internet Services Inc. (MIS)

Saint John, New Brunswick
mi.net, mis.nb.ca

28 King Street, Suite 32, P.O. Box 6477
Saint John, New Brunswick E2L 4R9

Voice: 506-652-3624 (Saint John); 506-450-2821 (Fredericton); 506-854-2821 (Moncton); 506-466-2003 (St. Stephen)
Fax: 506-635-3400
E-mail: sales@mis.nb.ca
Web: http://www.mis.nb.ca

Services: Dial-up SLIP/PPP, high-speed dedicated access, Web hosting, Web design

---

Matrox SphereNet

Montréal, Québec
spherenet.com

1110 St-Regis Blvd.
Dorval, Québec H9R 2J5

Voice: 514-685-4442
Fax: 514-685-8780
E-mail: info@spherenet.com
Web: http://www.spherenet.com

Services: Dedicated ISDN, dial-up ISDN, dial-up SLIP/PPP, Web hosting, Web design

---

Maximum Internet

Ladner, British Columbia
max-net.com

#101, 5007 47A Avenue
Delta, British Columbia V4K 1T9

Voice: 604-940-8921
Fax: 604-940-8952
E-mail: mail@max-net.com
Web: http://www.max-net.com

Services: Dial-up SLIP/PPP, Web hosting, Web design

Metrix Interlink Corporation

Montréal, Québec
interlink.net, interlink.ca

500, boul. René-Lévesque Ouest, bureau 1004
Montréal, Québec H2Z 1W7

Voice: 514-875-0010
Fax: 514-875-5735
E-mail: info@interlink.net, support@interlink.net
Web: http://www.interlink.net

Services: Dedicated ISDN, dial-up ISDN, dial-up SLIP/PPP, cable modem access, high-speed dedicated access, Web hosting, Web design

---

Metrolinx

Scarborough, Ontario
metrolinx.com

1365 Morningside Avenue, Unit #12
Scarborough, Ontario M1B 4Y5

Voice: 416-283-2573
E-mail: info@metrolinx.com
Web: http://www.metrolinx.com

Services: Dedicated ISDN, dial-up SLIP/PPP, Web hosting, Web design

---

MGL Systems Computer Technologies Inc.

Cambridge, Ontario
mgl.ca, mgl.net

240 Holiday Inn Drive, Suite "T"
Cambridge, Ontario N3C 3X4

Voice: 519-651-2713
Fax: 519-651-2272
E-mail: sales@mgl.ca
Web: http://www.mgl.ca

Services: Dedicated ISDN, dial-up ISDN, dial-up SLIP/PPP, high-speed dedicated access, Web hosting, Web design

---

MicroAge Computer Centres

Thunder Bay, Ontario
microage-tb.com

871-B Tungsten Street
Thunder Bay, Ontario P7B 6H2

Voice: 807-343-4490
Fax: 807-346-4963
E-mail: aauld@microage-tb.com, web-master@microage-tb.com
Web: http://www.microage-tb.com
Affiliated with: A&W Inc.

Services: Dial-up SLIP/PPP, cable modem access, Web hosting, Web design

---

Mortimer Online

Vancouver, British Columbia
mortimer.com, left-coast.net

2465 Beta Avenue, Suite 120
Burnaby, British Columbia V5C 5N1

Voice: 604-294-2995
Fax: 604-294-8341
E-mail: info@mortimer.com
Web: http://www.mortimer.com

Services: Dial-up SLIP/PPP, Web hosting, Web design

Mountain Internet (Division of Tantalus Technologies Inc.)

Squamish, British Columbia
mountain-inter.net

Box 136, 38013 Third Avenue
Squamish, British Columbia V0N 3G0

Voice: 604-892-9556
Fax: 604-892-9579
800 Voice: 1-800-643-7520 (in B.C. only)
E-mail: info@mountain-inter.net
Web: http://www.mountain-inter.net

Services: Dial-up SLIP/PPP, high-speed dedicated access, Web hosting, Web design

---

Muskoka.com

Bracebridge, Ontario
muskoka.com, cottage.net, smellies.com

Box 2832
Bracebridge, Ontario P1L 1W5

Voice: 705-645-6097
Fax: 705-645-6632
E-mail: info@muskoka.com
Web: http://www.muskoka.com

Services: Dial-up SLIP/PPP, high-speed dedicated access, Web hosting, Web design

---

Myna Communications Inc.

Toronto, Ontario
myna.com

151 Front Street West, Suite 505, P.O. Box 14
Toronto, Ontario M5J 2N1

Voice: 416-362-7000
Fax: 416-362-7001
E-mail: info@myna.com
Web: http://www.myna.com

Services: Dedicated ISDN, dial-up ISDN, dial-up SLIP/PPP, high-speed dedicated access, Web hosting, Web design

---

NavNet Communications

Halifax, Nova Scotia
navnet.net

106 Chain Lake Drive, Unit 20
Halifax, Nova Scotia B3S 1A8

Voice: 902-450-1020
Fax: 902-450-1021
E-mail: webmaster@navnet.net
Web: http://www.navnet.net

Services: Dedicated ISDN, dial-up ISDN, dial-up SLIP/PPP, high-speed dedicated access, Web hosting, Web design

---

NBTel

Saint John, New Brunswick
nbnet.nb.ca, nbtel.nb.ca

One Brunswick Square, P.O. Box 1430
Saint John, New Brunswick E2L 4K2

Voice: 506-694-2340
Fax: 506-694-2168
E-mail: nbinfo@nbnet.nb.ca, support@nbnet.nb.ca
Web: http://www.nbnet.nb.ca

Services: Dial-up SLIP/PPP, cable modem access, high-speed dedicated access, Web hosting

---

Net Communications Inc.

Saint-Jean-sur-Richelieu, Québec
netc.net

Aéroport Municipal de St-Jean, Bureau #1
Saint-Jean-sur-Richelieu, Québec J3B 3B5

Voice: 514-346-3401
Fax: 514-346-3587
E-mail: netc@netc.net
Web: http://www.netc.net

Services: Dedicated ISDN, dial-up ISDN, dial-up SLIP/PPP, Web hosting, Web design

---

The Net Idea Telecommunications Inc.

Nelson, British Columbia
netidea.com

715 Vernon Street
Nelson, British Columbia V1L 4G3

Voice: 250-352-3572
Fax: 250-352-9780
E-mail: sales@netidea.com
Web: http://www.netidea.com

Services: Dial-up SLIP/PPP, high-speed dedicated access, Web hosting, Web design

---

NetAccess Systems Inc.

Hamilton, Ontario
netaccess.on.ca

231 Main Street West
Hamilton, Ontario L8P 1J4

Voice: 905-524-2544
Fax: 905-524-3010
E-mail: info@netaccess.on.ca
Web: http://www.netaccess.on.ca

Services: Dedicated ISDN, dial-up ISDN, dial-up SLIP/PPP, Web hosting, Web design

---

Netcom Canada Inc.

Toronto, Ontario
netcom.ca

905 King Street West
Toronto, Ontario M6K 3G9

Voice: 416-341-5700
Fax: 416-341-5725
E-mail: info@netcom.ca
Web: http://www.netcom.ca

Services: Dedicated ISDN, dial-up ISDN, dial-up SLIP/PPP, Web hosting

---

NetCore Global Communications

Windsor, Ontario
netcore.ca

360 Victoria Avenue
Windsor, Ontario N9A 4M6

Voice: 519-258-0004
Fax: 519-258-9601
E-mail: info@netcore.ca
Web: http://www.netcore.ca

Services: Dedicated ISDN, dial-up SLIP/PPP, Web hosting, Web design

NetMatrix Corporation

Calgary, Alberta
netmatrix.com

#36001, 6449 Crowchild Trail S.W.
Calgary, Alberta T3E 7C6

Voice: 403-686-1193
Fax: 403-686-1193
E-mail: info@netmatrix.com
Web: http://www.netmatrix.com

Services: Dedicated ISDN, dial-up ISDN, dial-up SLIP/PPP, high-speed dedicated access, Web hosting, Web design

NetReach International

Carrying Place, Ontario
reach.net, workshop.net

Box 10
Carrying Place, Ontario K0K 1L0

Voice: 613-962-2500
Fax: 613-969-0222
E-mail: info@connect.reach.net
Web: http://www.reach.net

Services: Dedicated ISDN, dial-up ISDN, dial-up SLIP/PPP, high-speed dedicated access, Web hosting, Web design

NetSurf Inc.

Etobicoke, Ontario
netsurf.net

5481 Dundas Street West, Suite 200
Etobicoke, Ontario M9B 1B5

Voice: 416-237-0874
Fax: 416-237-0494
E-mail: info@netsurf.net
Web: http://www.netsurf.net

Services: Dedicated ISDN, dial-up ISDN, dial-up SLIP/PPP, Web hosting, Web design

Netway Internetworking Technologies

Calgary, Alberta
netway.ab.ca

201-2216 27th Avenue N.E.
Calgary, Alberta T2E 7A7

Voice: 403-250-5462
Fax: 403-250-2792
E-mail: help@netway.ab.ca, service@netway.ab.ca
Web: http://www.netway.ab.ca

Services: Dedicated ISDN, dial-up SLIP/PPP, Web hosting, Web design

Network Enterprise Technology Inc.

Hamilton, Ontario
netinc.ca

20 Jackson Street West, Suite 206
Hamilton, Ontario L8P 3K9

Voice: 905-525-4555
Fax: 905-525-3222
E-mail: info@netinc.ca
Web: http://www.netinc.ca

Services: Dedicated ISDN, dial-up ISDN, dial-up SLIP/PPP, high-speed dedicated access, Web hosting, Web design

Network North Communications Ltd.

Yellowknife, Northwest Territories
netnorth.com, nnc.nt.ca

P.O. Box 2044
Yellowknife, Northwest Territories X1A 2P5

Voice: 403-873-2059
Fax: 403-873-4996
E-mail: patg@netnorth.com, derrang@netnorth.com
Web: http://www.netnorth.com

Services: Dial-up SLIP/PPP, cable modem access, high-speed dedicated access, Web hosting, Web design

Networx Internet System

Hamilton, Ontario
networx.on.ca

154 Main Street East, Suite LL101
Hamilton, Ontario L8N 1G9

Voice: 905-528-4638
Fax: 905-525-8473
E-mail: sales@networx.on.ca
Web: http://www.networx.on.ca

Services: Dedicated ISDN, dial-up ISDN, dial-up SLIP/PPP, cable modem access, high-speed dedicated access, Web hosting, Web design

NewEdge Technologies Inc.

Halifax, Nova Scotia
newedge.net, newedge.ca, destination-ns.com

1505 Barrington Street, Suite 1508
Halifax, Nova Scotia B3J 3K5

Voice: 902-425-4222
Fax: 902-425-4433
E-mail: nesales@newedge.net, rnelson@newedge.net, dclarke@newedge.net
Web: http://www.newedge.net

Services: Web design

Norfolk Internet Services

Simcoe, Ontario
nornet.on.ca, nornet.com, gtp.com, harness.com

395 Queensway West
Simcoe, Ontario N3Y 2M9

Voice: 519-426-5575
E-mail: info@nornet.on.ca
Web: http://www.nornet.on.ca

Services: Dial-up SLIP/PPP, high-speed dedicated access, Web hosting, Web design

Norlink Communications and Consulting

Thunder Bay, Ontario
norlink.net

176 Blucher Avenue
Thunder Bay, Ontario P7B 4Y9

Voice: 807-767-5055
Fax: 807-768-2388
E-mail: info@norlink.net, kowen@norlink.net
Web: http://www.norlink.net

Services: Dial-up SLIP/PPP, Web hosting, Web design

North Shore Internet Services

New Glasgow, Nova Scotia
nsis.com

169 Provost Street, Suite 407
New Glasgow, Nova Scotia B2H 2P9

Voice: 902-928-0565
E-mail: support@nsis.com, sales@nsis.com
Web: http://www.nsis.com

Services: Dedicated ISDN, dial-up ISDN, dial-up SLIP/PPP, high-speed dedicated access, Web hosting, Web design

Northern Telephone Ltd.

New Liskeard, Ontario
nt.net

P.O. Box 4000, 25 Paget Street
New Liskeard, Ontario P0J 1P0

Voice: 705-647-3347
Fax: 705-647-3584 or 1-800-253-2992
800 Voice: 1-800-889-6779
E-mail: comments@nt.net
Web: http://www.nt.net

Services: Dial-up SLIP/PPP, high-speed dedicated access, Web hosting

NorthStar Communications

Thompson, Manitoba
norcom.mb.ca

27 Nelson Road
Thompson, Manitoba R8N 0B3

Voice: 204-778-7407
Fax: 204-778-8946
E-mail: info@norcom.mb.ca, sysop@norcom.mb.ca
Web: http://www.norcom.mb.ca

Services: Dial-up SLIP/PPP, Web hosting, Web design

Northumberland Online Ltd.

Port Hope, Ontario
nhb.com

P.O. Box 516
Port Hope, Ontario L1A 3W4

Voice: 905-885-9309
Fax: 905-885-9309
E-mail: sales@nhb.com
Web: http://www.nhb.com

Services: Dial-up SLIP/PPP, Web hosting, Web design

NPSNET

Richmond, British Columbia
npsnet.com

Netcore Professional Services,
103-8080 Anderson Road
Richmond, British Columbia V6Y 1S4

Voice: 604-272-2624
Fax: 604-271-2624
800 Voice: 1-800-319-8500
E-mail: info@npsnet.com
Web: http://www.npsnet.com

Services: Dedicated ISDN, dial-up ISDN, dial-up SLIP/PPP, high-speed dedicated access, Web hosting, Web design

NTnet Society

Yellowknife, Northwest Territories
ntnet.nt.ca

Box 613
Yellowknife, Northwest Territories X1A 2N5

Voice: 403-669-7284
Fax: 403-669-7286
E-mail: admin@ntnet.nt.ca
Web: http://www.ntnet.nt.ca

Services: High-speed dedicated access

Nucleus Information Service Inc.

Calgary, Alberta
nucleus.com, nucleus.ca

1835B-10 Avenue S.W.
Calgary, Alberta T3C 0K2

Voice: 403-541-9470
Fax: 403-541-9474
E-mail: sysop@nucleus.com
Web: http://www.nucleus.com

Services: Dedicated ISDN, dial-up ISDN, dial-up SLIP/PPP, Web hosting, Web design

OA Internet

Edmonton, Alberta
oanet.com

4907-99 Avenue
Edmonton, Alberta T6E 4Y1

Voice: 403-430-0811
Fax: 403-436-9965
E-mail: info@oanet.com
Web: http://www.oanet.com

Services: Dedicated ISDN, dial-up ISDN, dial-up SLIP/PPP, high-speed dedicated access, Web hosting, Web design

Octonet Communications Corporation

Victoria, British Columbia
octonet.com

2nd Floor, 612 Fisgard Street
Victoria, British Columbia V8W 1R6

Voice: 604-995-2806 or 604-995-2807
Fax: 604-383-8935
E-mail: occ@octonet.com, support@octonet.com
Web: http://www.octonet.com

Services: Dial-up SLIP/PPP, Web hosting, Web design

Odyssey Internet

Montréal, Québec
microtec.ca

85 de la Commune est
Montréal, Québec H2Y 1J1

Voice: 514-861-3432
Fax: 514-861-6599
E-mail: info@microtec.ca, support@microtec.ca, help@microtec.ca, feedback@microtec.ca
Web: http://www.microtec.ca

Services: Dedicated ISDN, dial-up ISDN, dial-up SLIP/PPP, high-speed dedicated access, Web hosting, Web design

Odyssey Network Inc.

London, Ontario
odyssey.on.ca

21 King Street
London, Ontario N6A 5H3

Voice: 519-660-8883
Fax: 519-660-6111
E-mail: info@odyssey.on.ca
Web: http://www.odyssey.on.ca

Services: Dedicated ISDN, dial-up ISDN, dial-up SLIP/PPP, high-speed dedicated access, Web hosting, Web design

Okanagan Internet Junction, Inc.

Vernon, British Columbia
junction.net

4216-25th Avenue, Suite 1
Vernon, British Columbia V1T 1P4

Voice: 604-549-1036
Fax: 604-549-4130
E-mail: info@junction.net, webmaster@junction.net
Web: http://www.junction.net

Services: Dedicated ISDN, dial-up ISDN, dial-up SLIP/PPP, high-speed dedicated access, Web hosting, Web design

Omegan Internet Services Inc.

Carleton Place, Ontario
omegan.on.ca

155 Industrial Avenue
Carleton Place, Ontario K7C 3V7

Voice: 613-257-2423
Fax: 613-257-7552
E-mail: sales@omegan.on.ca, info@omegan.on.ca
Web: http://www.omegan.on.ca
Affiliated with: Hookup Communications

Services: Dedicated ISDN, dial-up SLIP/PPP, high-speed dedicated access, Web hosting, Web design

ONet Networking Inc. (ONet)

Mississauga, Ontario
onet.on.ca

5925 Airport Road, Suite 200
Mississauga, Ontario L4V 1W1

Voice: 905-405-6263
Fax: 905-405-6271
E-mail: info@onet.on.ca
Web: http://www.onet.on.ca

Services: Dedicated ISDN, high-speed dedicated access

Online Computer Distribution

Peterborough, Ontario
oncomdis.on.ca

194 Charlotte Street
Peterborough, Ontario K9J 2T8

Voice: 705-749-9225
Fax: 705-749-9226
E-mail: sysop@oncomdis.on.ca
Web: http://www.oncomdis.on.ca

Services: Dial-up SLIP/PPP, high-speed dedicated access, Web hosting, Web design

---

Ontario Northland-ONLink

North Bay, Ontario
onlink-net

555 Oak Street East
North Bay, Ontario P1B 8L3

Voice: 705-495-2951
Fax: 705-995-2025
800 Voice: 1-800-667-0053
E-mail: info@onlink-net
Web: http://www.onlink-net

Services: Dedicated ISDN, dial-up ISDN, dial-up SLIP/PPP, high-speed dedicated access, Web hosting

---

ORCCA Networks Ltd.

Stratford, Ontario
orc.ca

500 Lorne Avenue
Stratford, Ontario N5A 6T7

Voice: 519-273-7004
Fax: 519-273-0350
E-mail: info@orc.ca
Web: http://www.orc.ca

Services: Dedicated ISDN, dial-up ISDN, dial-up SLIP/PPP, high-speed dedicated access, Web hosting, Web design

---

Oricom Internet

Québec, Québec
oricom.ca

400 Nolin, Suite 150
Vanier, Québec G1M 1E7

Voice: 418-683-4557
Fax: 418-849-6582
E-mail: info@oricom.ca
Web: http://www.oricom.ca

Services: Dedicated ISDN, dial-up SLIP/PPP, Web hosting, Web design

---

Osiris (Software) Inc.

Montréal, Québec
osiris.com, osinet.net, osiris.ca

2057 Papineau
Montréal, Québec H2K 4J5

Voice: 514-522-7475
Fax: 514-522-7937
E-mail: sales@osiris.com
Web: http://www.osiris.com

Services: Dedicated ISDN, dial-up ISDN, dial-up SLIP/PPP, high-speed dedicated access, Web hosting, Web design

---

Pacific Coast Net Inc.

Victoria, British Columbia
pacificcoast.net

103-1315 Esquimalt Road
Victoria, British Columbia V9A 3P5

Voice: 604-380-7322
Fax: 604-380-7349
E-mail: info@pacificcoast.net
Web: http://www.pacificcoast.net

Services: Dedicated ISDN, dial-up ISDN, dial-up SLIP/PPP, Web hosting, Web design

---

Pangea.ca Inc.

Winnipeg, Manitoba
pangea.ca

300-297 Smith Street
Winnipeg, Manitoba R3C 1L1

Voice: 204-985-9025
Fax: 204-956-2331
E-mail: info@pangea.ca
Web: http://www.pangea.ca

Services: Dedicated ISDN, dial-up SLIP/PPP, Web hosting, Web design

---

Passport Online

Toronto, Ontario
passport.ca

230 Richmond Street West, 7th Floor
Toronto, Ontario M5V 3E5

Voice: 416-351-1040
Fax: 416-351-8438
888 Voice: 1-888-296-0666
E-mail: staff@passport.ca
Web: http://web.passport.ca

Services: Dedicated ISDN, dial-up ISDN, dial-up SLIP/PPP, high-speed dedicated access, Web hosting, Web design

---

Pathway Communications

Toronto, Ontario
pathcom.com

1 Yonge Street, Suite 2205
Toronto, Ontario M5E 1E5

Voice: 416-214-6363
Fax: 416-214-6238
E-mail: info@pathcom.com
Web: http://www.pathcom.com

Services: Dedicated ISDN, dial-up ISDN, dial-up SLIP/PPP, high-speed dedicated access, Web hosting, Web design

---

Peterboro.Net

Millbrook, Ontario
peterboro.net

P.O. Box 97
Millbrook, Ontario L0A 1G0

Voice: 705-932-2188 or
705-749-0091 or
705-277-3772
Fax: 705-932-2329
E-mail: support@peterboro.net
Web: http://www.peterboro.net

Services: Dial-up SLIP/PPP, high-speed dedicated access

P.G. DataNet Inc.

Edmonton, Alberta
datanet.ab.ca

4652-99 Street
Edmonton, Alberta T6E 5H5

Voice: 403-438-5897
Fax: 403-434-3957
E-mail: info@datanet.ab.ca
Web: http://www.datanet.ab.ca

Services: Dial-up SLIP/PPP, Web hosting

Prisco interNET

St-Hyacinthe, Québec
prisco.net, maska.net

1695 W. Girouard
St-Hyacinthe, Québec J2S 2Z9

Voice: 514-771-4966
Fax: 514-771-4999
800 Voice: 1-800-871-4966
E-mail: jety@maska.net
Web: http://www.prisco.net

Services: Dedicated ISDN, dial-up ISDN, dial-up SLIP/PPP, high-speed dedicated access, Web hosting, Web design

QNETIX Computer Consultants Inc.

Toronto, Ontario
qnetix.ca

95 King Street East, Suite 400
Toronto, Ontario M5C 1G4

Voice: 416-861-0423 (Toronto); 514-860-2643 (Montreal)
Fax: 416-861-1838
800 Voice: 1-800-860-6389
E-mail: sales@qnetix.ca
Web: http://www.qnetix.ca

Services: Dedicated ISDN, dial-up ISDN, dial-up SLIP/PPP, cable modem access, high-speed dedicated access, Web hosting, Web design

Quebectel Communication Inc.

Rimouski, Québec
quebectel.com, globetrotter.net, globetrotter.qc.ca

128 rue Cathédrale, Suite 201
Rimouski, Québec G5L 7E4

Voice: 1-800-520-4562
Fax: 418-722-1516
E-mail: comgengt@globetrotter.qc.ca
Web: http://www.globetrotter.qc.ca

Services: Dedicated ISDN, dial-up ISDN, dial-up SLIP/PPP, high-speed dedicated access, Web hosting, Web design

Réseau Virtuel d'Ordinateurs RVO

St-Hubert, Québec
rvo.qc.ca

C.P. 88, Succursale St-Hubert
St-Hubert, Québec J3Y 5S9

Voice: 514-676-2526
Fax: 514-676-2850
E-mail: rvo@rvo.qc.ca
Web: http://www.rvo.qc.ca

Services: Dedicated ISDN, dial-up ISDN, Web hosting, Web design

Resudox Online Services Inc.

Ottawa, Ontario
resudox.net

50 O'Connor Street, Suite 1015
Ottawa, Ontario K1P 6L5

Voice: 613-567-6925
Fax: 613-567-8289
E-mail: admin@resudox.net
Web: http://www.resudox.net
Affiliated with: PresTech Information Access Services

Services: Dedicated ISDN, dial-up ISDN, dial-up SLIP/PPP, Web hosting, Web design

RGS Internet Services Ltd.

Terrace, British Columbia
kermode.net, rway.net

4722 Lakelse Avenue
Terrace, British Columbia V8G 1R6

Voice: 604-635-3444
Fax: 604-635-9727
E-mail: olene@kermode.net, webmaster@kermode.net
Web: http://www.kermode.net

Services: Dial-up SLIP/PPP, Web hosting, Web design

RISQ Réseau interordinateurs scientifique québécois

Montréal, Québec
risq.qc.ca, risq.net

1801 avenue McGill College, bureau 800
Montréal, Québec H3A 2N4

Voice: 514-398-1234
Fax: 514-398-1244
E-mail: info-risq@risq.qc.ca
Web: http://www.risq.qc.ca

Services: Dedicated ISDN, dial-up SLIP/PPP, high-speed dedicated access, Web hosting, Web design

Les services télématiques Rocler

St-Timothée, Québec
rocler.qc.ca

6, Cléophas
St-Timothée, Québec J6S 6A5

Voice: 514-377-1898
Fax: 514-377-5139
E-mail: info@rocler.qc.ca, rodrigue@rocler.qc.ca
Web: http://www.rocler.qc.ca

Services: Dedicated ISDN, dial-up ISDN, dial-up SLIP/PPP, Web hosting, Web design

Sakku Arctic Technologies Inc.

Rankin Inlet, Northwest Territories
arctic.ca

P.O. Box 731
Rankin Inlet, Northwest Territories X0C 0G0

Voice: 819-645-2035
Fax: 819-645-2155
E-mail: support@arctic.ca
Web: http://www.arctic.ca

Services: Dial-up SLIP/PPP, Web hosting

Sentex Communications Corporation

Cambridge, Ontario
sentex.ca, sentex.net

240D Holiday Inn Drive
Cambridge, Ontario N3C 3X4

Voice: 519-651-3400
Fax: 519-651-2215
888 Voice: 1-888-4-SENTEX
E-mail: info@sentex.net, sales@sentex
Web: http://www.sentex.net

Services: Dedicated ISDN, dial-up ISDN, dial-up SLIP/PPP, high-speed dedicated access, Web hosting, Web design

Serix Technologies

London, Ontario
serix.com

215 Piccadilly Street, Suite 306
London, Ontario N6A 1S2

Voice: 519-645-1532
Fax: 519-645-8930
E-mail: info@serix.com
Web: http://www.serix.com

Services: Dedicated ISDN, dial-up SLIP/PPP, Web hosting, Web design

Silk Internet

Kelowna, British Columbia
silk.net

1598 Pandosy Street
Kelowna, British Columbia V1Y 1P4

Voice: 604-860-4202
Fax: 604-860-0505
E-mail: info@silk.net
Web: http://www.silk.net

Services: Dedicated ISDN, dial-up ISDN, dial-up SLIP/PPP, high-speed dedicated access, Web hosting, Web design

SOHO Skyway

North Vancouver, British Columbia
sohoskyway.net

R.R.5 S24 C35
Gibsons, British Columbia V0N 1V0

Voice: 604-482-1222
Fax: 604-885-3654
E-mail: sales@sohoskyway.net
Web: http://www.sohoskyway.net

Services: Dedicated ISDN, dial-up ISDN, dial-up SLIP/PPP, Web hosting

Spectranet Connections Inc.

Oakville, Ontario
spectrannet.ca

220 Wyecroft Road, Unit 46
Oakville, Ontario L6K 3V1

Voice: 905-338-3552
Fax: 905-338-7549
E-mail: mailbox@spectranet.ca
Web: http://www.spectranet.ca

Services: Dedicated ISDN, dial-up ISDN, dial-up SLIP/PPP, high-speed dedicated access, Web hosting, Web design

SSI Micro

Yellowknife, Northwest Territories
ssimicro.com

#16 Panda II Mall, 4815-49th Street
Yellowknife, Northwest Territories X1A 3S4

Voice: 403-669-7500
Fax: 403-669-7510
E-mail: staff@ssimicro.com
Web: http://www.ssimicro.com

Services: Dial-up SLIP/PPP, high-speed dedicated access, Web hosting, Web design

STEM~Net

St. John's, Newfoundland
stemnet.nf.ca

Memorial University of Newfoundland, E-5036
G.A. Hickman Building
St. John's, Newfoundland A1B 3X8

Voice: 709-737-8836
Fax: 709-737-2179
E-mail: staff@calvin.stemnet.nf.ca
Web: http://www.stemnet.nf.ca

Services: Dial-up SLIP/PPP, Web hosting, Web design

Sunshine Net Inc.

Gibsons, British Columbia
sunshine.net

Box 44
Grantham's Landing, British Columbia V0N 1X0

Voice: 604-886-4120
Fax: 604-886-4513
E-mail: admin@sunshine.net, support@sunshine.net
Web: http://www.sunshine.net

Services: Dial-up SLIP/PPP, high-speed dedicated access, Web hosting, Web design

Suntek Software

Winnipeg, Manitoba
suntek.mb.ca

Unit 3, 1329 Niakwa Road East
Winnipeg, Manitoba R2J 3T4

Voice: 204-925-7483
Fax: 204-925-7486
E-mail: info@quanta.suntek.mb.ca
Web: http://www.suntek.mb.ca

Services: Dedicated ISDN, dial-up ISDN, dial-up SLIP/PPP, cable modem access, Web hosting, Web design

Super i-Way

Edmonton, Alberta
superiway.net, towndir.com

#100, 10620-178 Street
Edmonton, Alberta T5S 2E3

Voice: 403-413-9111
Fax: 403-413-9150
E-mail: info@superiway.net
Web: http://www.superiway.net

Services: Dedicated ISDN, dial-up ISDN, dial-up SLIP/PPP, high-speed dedicated access, Web hosting, Web design

Sympatico—The Internet Service For Everyone™

Toronto, Ontario
sympatico.ca, sympatico.com

20 Richmond Street West, Suite 600
Toronto, Ontario M5C 3B5

Voice: 416-350-1515
Fax: 416-350-1516
800 Voice: 1-800-773-2121
Web: http://www.sympatico.ca

Services: Dedicated ISDN, dial-up ISDN, dial-up SLIP/PPP, Web hosting

Synaptic Communications Inc.

Prince George, British Columbia
netbistro.com, synaptic.net, pgonline.com

1363 4th Avenue
Prince George, British Columbia V2L 3J6

Voice: 604-563-8668
Fax: 604-563-4280
E-mail: info@netbistro.com
Web: http://www.netbistro.com, http://www.synaptic.net

Services: Dedicated ISDN, dial-up ISDN, dial-up SLIP/PPP, high-speed dedicated access

T-8000 Information Systems

Calgary, Alberta
t8000.com

#36001, 6449 Crowchild Trail S.W.
Calgary, Alberta T3E 7C6

Voice: 403-686-1193
Fax: 403-686-1193
E-mail: info@t8000.com
Web: http://www.t8000.com

Services: Dedicated ISDN, dial-up ISDN, dial-up SLIP/PPP, high-speed dedicated access, Web hosting, Web design

Tamarack Computers Ltd.

Yellowknife, Northwest Territories
tamarack.nt.ca, yk.com

24-5102 50th Avenue
Yellowknife, Northwest Territories X1A 3S8

Voice: 403-920-4380
Fax: 403-920-4384
E-mail: tamarack@yk.com, tony@tamarack.nt.ca, jimg@tamarack.nt.ca
Web: http://www.tamarack.nt.ca

Services: Dial-up SLIP/PPP, high-speed dedicated access, Web hosting, Web design

Telnet Canada Enterprises, Ltd.

Calgary, Alberta
tcel.com

540 5th Avenue S.W., Suite 1500
Calgary, Alberta T2P 0M2

Voice: 403-262-5859
Fax: 403-264-4032
E-mail: info@tcel.com
Web: http://www.tcel.com

Services: Dedicated ISDN, dial-up ISDN, dial-up SLIP/PPP, high-speed dedicated access, Web hosting, Web design

TELOS Communications Inc.

Belleville, Ontario
telos.ca, telos.org

100 Bell Boulevard, Suite 355
Belleville, Ontario K8P 4Y7

Voice: 613-962-5776
Fax: 613-962-5703
800 Voice: 1-800-898-3567
E-mail: telos@telos.ca
Web: http://www.telos.ca

Services: Web hosting, Web design

Times.net

Bradford, Ontario
times.net

32 Holland Street East, Box 1570
Bradford, Ontario L3Z 2B8

Voice: 905-775-0372
Fax: 905-775-4489
E-mail: info@times.net
Web: http://www.times.net

Services: Dedicated ISDN, dial-up ISDN, dial-up SLIP/PPP, high-speed dedicated access, Web hosting, Web design

TNC-The Network Centre

Edmonton, Alberta
tnc.com

10509-81 Avenue, Suite 212
Edmonton, Alberta T6E 1X7

Voice: 403-448-1290
Fax: 403-436-6055
E-mail: info@tnc.com
Web: http://www.tnc.com

Services: Dedicated ISDN, dial-up ISDN, dial-up SLIP/PPP, high-speed dedicated access, Web hosting, Web design

TotalNet Inc.

Montréal, Québec
total.net, accent.net, infobahnos.com, gyg.net, magic.ca, magic.mb.ca, megatoon.com

5252 boulevard de Maisonneuve Ouest, Bureau 200
Montréal, Québec H4A 3S5

Voice: 514-481-2585
Fax: 514-481-2785
800 Voice: 1-800-920-SURF
E-mail: admin@total.net
Web: http://www.total.net

Services: Dedicated ISDN, dial-up ISDN, dial-up SLIP/PPP, high-speed dedicated access, Web hosting, Web design

TransData Communications

Barrie, Ontario
transdata.ca

128 Anne Street South
Barrie, Ontario L4N 6A2

Voice: 705-727-0733
Fax: 705-725-1065
E-mail: sysop@mail.transdata.ca, info@mail.transdata.ca
Web: http://www.transdata.ca

Services: Dedicated ISDN, dial-up ISDN, dial-up SLIP/PPP, high-speed dedicated access, Web hosting, Web design

Travel-Net Communications Inc.

Ottawa, Ontario
travel-net.com

292 Montreal Road
Ottawa, Ontario K1L 6B7

Voice: 613-744-3000
Fax: 613-744-2602
E-mail: info@travel-net.com
Web: http://www.travel-net.com

Services: Dedicated ISDN, dial-up ISDN, dial-up SLIP/PPP, Web hosting, Web design

Trytel Internet Inc.

Ottawa, Ontario
trytel.com

818 Boyd Avenue, Unit B
Ottawa, Ontario K2A 2C7

Voice: 613-722-6321
Fax: 613-722-6749
E-mail: info@trytel.com
Web: http://www.trytel.com

Services: Dedicated ISDN, dial-up ISDN, dial-up SLIP/PPP, cable modem access, high-speed dedicated access, Web hosting, Web design

UUNET Canada Inc.

Toronto, Ontario
uunet.ca

20 Bay Street, Suite 1910
Toronto, Ontario M5J 2N8

Voice: 416-368-6621
Fax: 416-368-1350
800 Voice: 1-800-463-8123
E-mail: info@uunet.ca
Web: http://www.uunet.ca
Affiliated with: UUNet Technologies

Services: Dedicated ISDN, dial-up ISDN, dial-up SLIP/PPP, high-speed dedicated access, Web hosting, Web design

---

UUNorth International Inc.

Toronto, Ontario
north.net

3555 Don Mills Road, Unit 6-304
Willowdale, Ontario M2H 3N3

Voice: 416-225-8649
Fax: 416-225-0525
E-mail: info@mail.north.net
Web: http://www.north.net

Services: Dedicated ISDN, dial-up SLIP/PPP, high-speed dedicated access, Web hosting, Web design

---

Vaxxine Computer Systems Inc.

Jordan Station, Ontario
vaxxine.com, ontario.net, niagara.net

4520 Jordan Road, P.O. Box 279
Jordan Station, Ontario L0R 1S0

Voice: 905-562-3500
Fax: 905-562-3515
E-mail: admin@vaxxine.com, sales@vaxxine.com, jim@vaxxine.com
Web: http://www.vaxxine.com

Services: Dedicated ISDN, dial-up ISDN, dial-up SLIP/PPP, high-speed dedicated access, Web hosting, Web design

---

VIF Internet

Montréal, Québec
vif.com

7851 Grenache
Anjou, Québec H1J 1C4

Voice: 514-493-6447
Fax: 514-493-9589
E-mail: info@vif.com
Web: http://www.vif.com

Services: Dedicated ISDN, dial-up ISDN, dial-up SLIP/PPP, high-speed dedicated access, Web hosting, Web design

---

WBM Office Systems

Regina, Saskatchewan
wbm.ca

421 McDonald Street
Regina, Saskatchewan S4N 6E1

Voice: 306-721-2560
Fax: 306-721-2498
E-mail: info@wbm.ca
Web: http://www.wbm.ca

Services: Dedicated ISDN, dial-up ISDN, dial-up SLIP/PPP, high-speed dedicated access, Web hosting, Web design

---

Web Networks/NirvCentre

Toronto, Ontario
web.net, web.apc.org, web.ca

401 Richmond Street West, Suite 104
Toronto, Ontario M5V 3A8

Voice: 416-596-0212
Fax: 416-596-1374
800 Voice: 1-800-932-7003
E-mail: outreach@web.net, ottawa@web.net, liaison@web.net
Web: http://www.web.net

Services: Dedicated ISDN, dial-up ISDN, dial-up SLIP/PPP, Web hosting, Web design

---

Webster Internet Communications Inc.

Saskatoon, Saskatchewan
webster.sk.ca

1735 Alberta Avenue
Saskatoon, Saskatchewan S7K 7Z6

Voice: 306-668-2345
Fax: 306-665-9896
E-mail: cybersales@webster.sk.ca, webmaster@webster.sk.ca
Web: http://www.webster.sk.ca

Services: Dedicated ISDN, dial-up ISDN, dial-up SLIP/PPP, high-speed dedicated access, Web hosting, Web design

Weslink Datalink Corporation

Hamilton, Ontario
interlynx.net, weslink.ca

1603 Main Street West
Hamilton, Ontario L8S 1E6

Voice: 905-524-LYNX or 905-524-5969
Fax: 905-522-2123
E-mail: info@interlynx.net, info@weslink.ca
Web: http://www.interlynx.ca

Services: Dedicated ISDN, dial-up ISDN, dial-up SLIP/PPP, cable modem access, high-speed dedicated access, Web hosting, Web design

WestLink Internet

Calgary, Alberta
westlink.net

Suite 607, 105-150 Crowfoot Crescent N.W.
Calgary, Alberta T3G 3T2

Voice: 403-289-8742
Fax: 403-289-8744
E-mail: westlink@westlink.net
Web: http://www.westlink.net

Services: Dial-up SLIP/PPP, Web hosting, Web design

Westlock Internet

Westlock, Alberta
west-teq.net, cherokee.west-teq.net, www.west-teq.net

Box 1800
Westlock, Alberta T0G 2L0

Voice: 403-349-5559 or 403-349-4259
Fax: 403-349-6259
E-mail: daval@west-teq.net, len@west-teq.net
Web: http://www.west-teq.net

Services: Dial-up SLIP/PPP, cable modem access, High-speed dedicated access, Web hosting, Web design

Wiznet Inc.

Toronto, Ontario
wiznet.ca

80 Bloor Street West, Suite 401
Toronto, Ontario M5S 2V1

Voice: 416-967-4414
Fax: 416-967-5955
E-mail: info@wiznet.ca, sales@wiznet.ca
Web: http://www.wiznet.ca

Services: Dedicated ISDN, dial-up ISDN, dial-up SLIP/PPP, high-speed dedicated access, Web hosting, Web design

WorldCHAT™ Internet Services

Burlington, Ontario
wchat.com, wchat.on.ca

3018 New Street
Burlington, Ontario L7N 1M5

Voice: 905-637-9111
Fax: 905-637-0140
800 Voice: 1-800-219-8802
E-mail: datastorm@worldchat.com
Web: http://www.wchat.com

Services: Dedicated ISDN, dial-up SLIP/PPP, high-speed dedicated access, Web hosting, Web design

WorldGate Inc.

Edmonton, Alberta
worldgate.com, worldgate.net, wg.net, worldgate.edmonton.ab.ca

575 Sun Life Place, 10123-99 Street
Edmonton, Alberta T5J 3H1

Voice: 403-413-1910
Fax: 403-421-4929
E-mail: admin@worldgate.com, info@worldgate.com (auto-responder)
Web: http://www.worldgate.com

Services: Dedicated ISDN, dial-up ISDN, dial-up SLIP/PPP, high-speed dedicated access, Web hosting, Web design

WorldLink Internet Services

Ottawa, Ontario
worldlink.ca

99 Bank Street, Suite 600
Ottawa, Ontario K1P 6B9

Voice: 613-233-7100
Fax: 613-233-7704
E-mail: info@worldlink.ca, admin@worldlink.ca, sales@worldlink.ca
Web: http://www.worldlink.ca

Services: Dedicated ISDN, dial-up SLIP/PPP, Web hosting, Web design

Worldwide Data Communications Inc.

London, Ontario
wwdc.com, onlinesys.com

383 Richmond Street, Suite 900
London, Ontario N6A 3C4

Voice: 519-642-1411
Fax: 519-642-0733
E-mail: info@wwdc.com
Web: http://www.wwdc.com
Affiliated with: Cyberion Networking Corp.

Services: Dedicated ISDN, dial-up ISDN, dial-up SLIP/PPP, high-speed dedicated access, Web hosting, Web design

Xenon Laboratories

Toronto, Ontario
xe.net, xe.com, xemail.net

330 Bay Street, Suite 1109
Toronto, Ontario M5H 2S8

Voice: 416-214-5606
Fax: 416-214-5607
E-mail: info@xe.net, sales@xe.net, techsup@xe.net
Web: http://www.xe.net

Services: Dedicated ISDN, dial-up ISDN, dial-up SLIP/PPP, high-speed dedicated access, Web hosting, Web design

YKnet

Whitehorse, Yukon
yknet.yk.ca

Box 4900
Whitehorse, Yukon Y1A 4N6

Voice: 403-668-8202
Fax: 403-668-4907
E-mail: yknet@yknet.yk.ca
Web: http://www.yknet.yk.ca

Services: Dial-up SLIP/PPP, high-speed dedicated access, Web hosting

ZooNet Inc.

Montréal, Québec
zoo.net

P.O. Box 5
Montréal, Québec H3Z 2T1

Voice: 514-935-6225
Fax: 514-935-6225
E-mail: info@zoo.net
Web: http://www.zoo.net

Services: Dedicated ISDN, dial-up SLIP/PPP, Web hosting, Web design

Glossary

Anonymous FTP A version of FTP supported by many computers on the Internet, that permits users to freely access files on those computers without having to use a special ID and password.

Archie An old program that permits users to search for computer files on the Internet. Archie is seldom used today due to the popularity of the World Wide Web.

ADSL Abbreviation for *asymmetrical digital subscriber line.* An emerging technology now being deployed by the telephone companies, that permits extremely fast data communication over regular telephone lines.

AUP Abbreviation for *acceptable use policy.* AUPs were in place as recently as two years ago on parts of the Internet and restricted use of the network to research and educational activities. AUPs restricting business on the Internet are now virtually extinct, but some Internet service providers have AUPs that prescribe acceptable behavior on the Internet.

Bandwidth A term used to describe the transmission capacity of the lines that carry the Internet's electronic traffic.

Baud A measure of the speed at which a modem can transmit and receive information.

BBS Abbreviation for *bulletin board system.* A computer-based system that permits people to exchange e-mail, discuss topics within discussion groups, or download computer files or software. There are thousands of BBSs across Canada, many of which permit you to send and to receive Internet e-mail as well as information from selected USENET newsgroups.

Bookmarks A feature found in Web browsers such as Netscape and Microsoft Explorer that allows users to easily keep track of sites to which they wish to return.

Bounced Message An e-mail message that is returned to the sender because it could not be delivered properly.

bps Abbreviation for *bits per second.* A measure of how fast computer information is transmitted.

Browser A program used to navigate the World Wide Web. Two of the most popular browsers are Netscape and Microsoft's Internet Explorer.

BTW An abbreviation frequently used in e-mail messages that means "by the way."

Cable Modem A special type of modem designed to work through your cable system and provide high-speed access to the Internet.

Caching A feature found within many Web browsers that keeps a copy, on your hard disk, of Web pages that you have previously visited. The next time you visit the site, the page is retrieved from your computer rather than from the Internet. This speeds up your use of the Web.

Client A program that you use to access information on the Internet. For example, Netscape is a client.

Closed List An electronic mailing list that requires you to meet some type of qualification in order to join.

Community Network An organization whose purpose is to provide free or low-cost on-line access to community information and the Internet. Community networks are usually run by volunteers and are supported by grants or donations. They are sometimes referred to as "Free-Nets."

Crossposting The act of posting to several USENET newsgroups at one time.

Cyberspace A term used to describe the Internet and the on-line world.

Dedicated Connection A permanent, full-time connection to the Internet (as opposed to a "dial-up connection").

Dial-Up Connection A temporary connection to the Internet in which you dial a telephone number and connect to the Internet using a personal computer and a modem (as opposed to a "dedicated connection").

Discussion Group A forum on the Internet that is used to exchange information among people who share a particular interest. There are two types of discussion groups on the Internet — mailing lists and USENET.

Disintermediation A term used to describe the elimination of the middleman. The World Wide Web supports disintermediation since it allows organizations to sell directly to consumers without the need for a retailer.

Download The process of transferring a computer file from another computer to your computer.

DNS Abbreviation for *Domain Name System.* A large, globally distributed database that translates domain names into numeric Internet addresses ("IP addresses") and vice versa. The DNS makes it possible for people to use the Internet without having to remember the IP addresses associated with each computer on the network.

Domain Name A naming convention on the Internet that forms a part of Web addresses and e-mail addresses. For example, in the e-mail address **rickb@inforamp.net** (Rick Broadhead's e-mail address), **inforamp.net** is the domain name.

Domain Registration The process of registering a domain name on the Internet.

E-mail Electronic mail, a service that permits users to electronically exchange messages. E-mail can be used to send text as well as computer files such as word processing documents or graphics.

E-mail Address The term used to describe the address you input to reach someone through e-mail on the Internet.

E-mail Filter A program that presorts your e-mail based on parameters you have established. E-mail filters are a very convenient way of dealing with large quantities of e-mail.

Encryption The capability of turning information into a special encoded format that can only be read by providing a special "key." Information is sometimes encrypted on the Internet in order to ensure the security of that information as it is sent through the network.

Eudora A popular brand of e-mail software used on the Internet.

FAQs Acronym for *frequently asked questions.* FAQs summarize common questions and answers about a specific subject. FAQs on a variety of topics can be found in USENET newsgroups and in many other areas of the Internet.

Finger An Internet program used to find out the status of someone else's e-mail account, such as when the person last read his/her e-mail. It can sometimes be used to retrieve information from particular computers on the Internet. Because many people consider the finger program to be an invasion of privacy, it has been disabled by many Internet service providers.

Firewall A system that protects a computer network from unauthorized access by people on the Internet.

Flame A nasty e-mail or USENET message, usually sent in anger in response to something that someone else has written.

Free-Net *See* Community Network.

FTP Abbreviation for *file transfer protocol.* A program used to retrieve files from computers on the Internet. Often referred to as Anonymous FTP since special passwords and IDs are usually not required.

GB Abbreviation for *gigabyte.* A standard measure of storage capacity on a computer. One gigabyte = 1,024 megabytes of information.

GIF Acronym for *graphics interchange format.* A popular type of file format that is used to provide graphics on Web pages.

Gopher An older information retrieval system found on the Internet that permits access to a wide variety of information resources. Gopher fell into disfavor when the massive growth of the World Wide Web began.

Home Page The introductory page of a Web site — the first page you see when you access a Web site. Sometimes an entire Web site is casually referred to as a "home page."

Host A computer connected to the Internet that "hosts" or holds information for a particular company or organization.

HTML Abbreviation for *hypertext markup language.* The language that is used to create documents on the World Wide Web.

HTTP Abbreviation for *hypertext transfer protocol.* The protocol (rules) that computers use to support communications between a Web site and a Web browser such as Netscape or Microsoft Explorer.

Hypertext The system used on the World Wide Web that connects words, phrases, and pictures to other documents on the Web via hidden links. When you click on a hypertext item, information about that subject will be displayed.

IMHO An abbreviation frequently used in e-mail and USENET messages that means "in my humble opinion."

Internet Access Provider An organization that connects individuals and businesses to the Internet. Also referred to as an Internet service provider, or ISP.

Internet Presence Providers Companies or organizations that assist others in gaining a presence on the Internet, particularly the World Wide Web.

Internet Phone A product that allows Internet users to have voice conversations with other Internet users. Some Internet phone products allow users to bypass the long-distance telephone network and make long-distance calls through the Internet.

InterNIC Acronym for *Internet Network Information Center.* An organization based in the United States that processes domain name requests under the .com, .org, and other domain hierarchies.

Intranet A collection of private Web sites that are only available to employees (or other trusted parties) within an organization.

IP Number The unique numerical address assigned to every computer connected to the Internet. IP numbers consist of 4 numbers separated by dots (e.g. 198.53.144.2).

IRC Abbreviation for *Internet relay chat.* A popular Internet program that allows users to participate in real-time discussion sessions with other Internet users.

ISDN Abbreviation for *integrated services digital network.* A method of obtaining high-speed access to the Internet through the telephone network. ISDN access is available from many Internet service providers in Canada.

ISP Abbreviation for *Internet service provider.* A company or organization that connects individuals and businesses to the Internet.

JPEG Acronym for *joint photographic experts group.* A type of graphics format.

kB Abbreviation for *kilobyte.* A standard unit for measuring storage capacity on a computer. One kilobyte = 1,024 bytes of information.

kbps Abbreviation for *kilobits per second.* A measure of how fast computer information is transmitted.

Killfiles Also known as bozo filters. Killfiles automatically delete USENET postings or e-mail messages that have been sent to you from certain people or that contain certain subjects. Killfiles help Internet users screen out messages they don't want to read.

Knowledge Networking The ability to harness on-line information, either by regularly tracking information on a particular topic with USENET, or by seeking information or answers to questions by discussing a topic with others on the Internet.

LAN Acronym for *local area network.* The term used to describe computers that have been linked together within an organization.

Leased Line A type of dedicated connection to the Internet.

Listserv A specialized piece of software that is used to manage a mailing list.

Mail Robot A program that automatically mails back a message in response to one sent to a given e-mail address.

Mailing List A collection of e-mail addresses that allows any member of the mailing list to reach all the other members of the group by sending a message to a central address. Mailing lists are a popular application on the Internet since they permit people around the world to debate particular topics or share information concerning specific issues.

MB Abbreviation for *megabyte.* A standard unit for measuring storage capacity on a computer. One megabyte = 1,024 kilobytes of information.

Mbps Abbreviation for *megabits per second.* A measure of how fast computer information is transmitted.

MIME Acronym for *multipurpose Internet mail extensions.* A feature supported by many e-mail programs that allows computer files to be attached to e-mail messages. MIME is used to send non-text messages such as pictures, spreadsheets, and word processing documents by e-mail.

Mirror Site A site on the Internet that duplicates the information found on another Internet site. Mirror sites are usually set up to reduce congestion at popular Web and FTP sites.

Modem A computing device that lets your PC "talk" to another computer. Modems are used to access the Internet.

Moderated Mailing List/USENET Newsgroup A special type of discussion group in which all messages are first sent to a moderator, who then determines if the message should be posted to the rest of the list, thus helping to ensure that the discussion stays on topic.

MUD Acronym for *multi-user dungeon, domain, or dimension.* An interactive action-, adventure-, or fantasy-based game that takes place on the Internet. Users create a character and interact with other characters in a "virtual" environment.

Netiquette Network etiquette. Term used to describe generally accepted rules of behaviour on USENET and mailing lists.

Netscape A popular program used to access the World Wide Web.

Netsurfers People who surf the Internet. *See* Surfing.

Newsgroups Subject areas within USENET. USENET contains thousands of newsgroups.

Newsreader A program used to read and contribute information to USENET newsgroups.

Pegasus A popular e-mail program used on the Internet.

PoP or Point of Presence An area where an Internet access provider has a local telephone number allowing local residents to get access to the Internet. Many Internet access providers have points of presence across Canada. For example, iSTAR Internet has points of presence in Vancouver, Calgary, Edmonton, Winnipeg, Toronto, and other Canadian cities.

POP (Post Office Protocol) A service that allows Internet users to transfer e-mail messages to their own computer from their Internet service provider's computer. When e-mail arrives for a user, it is stored on the Internet service provider's computer until it is accessed by the user.

Post The word that describes the action of sending a message to a mailing list or USENET newsgroup.

Posting A message that has been distributed to a mailing list or USENET newsgroup.

Postmaster A person who manages an organization's connection to the Internet.

PPP Abbreviation for *point to point protocol.* PPP is a popular method that individuals use to access the Internet. Very similar to SLIP.

Protocol The "language" spoken between computers to help them exchange information.

Public Domain Programs Software programs that are free to use.

Router A computing device found throughout the Internet that transfers information between computer networks.

Search Engine A computer program that "travels" throughout the World Wide Web on a regular basis, noting information found on Web sites. The search engine then builds an index of the World Wide Web that Internet users can query. Examples of search engines include InfoSeek, Lycos, WebCrawler, and Excite.

Server A computer that delivers information over the Internet.

Shareware Software that you can try out for free. If you like the software and plan to use it, you are asked to pay a fee to properly license it.

Signature A message that is attached to the end of an e-mail message containing the sender's affiliation and contact information such as mailing address, telephone, and fax number. Signatures often contain disclaimers or funny quotes.

Site A location on the World Wide Web.

SLIP Acronym for *serial line Internet protocol.* A popular method used by individuals to access the Internet over a dial-up connection. Similar to PPP.

Smiley A little picture made out of keyboard characters to indicate a particular emotion. Smileys are also known as emoticons.

SMTP Abbreviation for *simple mail transfer protocol.* The protocol that defines how e-mail messages are sent between different computers on the Internet.

Sound Card A device that allows you to listen to sounds on your computer. A sound card is necessary in order to use some programs on the Internet.

Spamming The process of sending unsolicited messages to many people at once through the Internet.

Surfing The expression used to describe the process of traveling from site to site on the World Wide Web.

TCP/IP Abbreviation for *transmission control protocol/Internet protocol.* The underlying language of the Internet. All computers directly linked to the Internet "talk" TCP/IP.

T1 The term that describes a data transmission speed of 1.544 million bits per second. Many organizations connect to the Internet at T1 speeds.

T3 The term that describes a data transmission speed of 45 million bits per second. Some large organizations such as Microsoft connect to the Internet at T3 speeds.

Telnet An older Internet application that can be used to access other computers on the Internet.

Thread The term used to describe a series of messages on the same topic.

UNIX A powerful operating system found on many computers throughout the Internet.

Unmoderated Mailing List/Newsgroup A discussion group in which contributions are not prescreened by a moderator. Any message sent to the group is automatically sent to all members of the list.

Upload The process of transferring a computer file from your computer to another computer.

URL Acronym for *uniform resource locator.* The address for a resource on the Internet. Each resource on the Internet has its own URL. A URL begins with a word that identifies the type of resource; it is followed by a colon and two slashes and the exact location of the resource on the Internet. For example, the URL for the *Canadian Internet Handbook* Web site is **http://www.handbook.com** (where "http" identifies this as a Web resource).

USENET A global system found within the Internet that is used for the exchange of information on thousands of topics.

UUCP Abbreviation for *Unix to Unix copy protocol,* an old method of accessing the Internet.

Veronica An old search tool that is used to find information on Gopher sites. Veronica is seldom used today due to the popularity of the World Wide Web.

VRML Abbreviation for *virtual reality modeling language.* An emerging technology that permits people to browse through three-dimensional Web sites.

Web Server The software required to operate a Web site. The term Web server also refers to the computer that hosts a Web site.

Web Site A location on the World Wide Web. A Web site can contain text, pictures, video, sounds, and more. A Web site can be accessed using a browser program such as Netscape or Microsoft Explorer.

Webmaster The person in an organization responsible for operating the organization's Web site.

World Wide Web Also known as the Web. A collection of millions of "pages" of information about individuals, businesses, government organizations, and associations. You navigate the World Wide Web by clicking on words or phrases that interest you.

Yahoo! One of the most popular directories of information on the World Wide Web.

Index

—J—

—K—

—L—

—X—

—Y—

—Z—

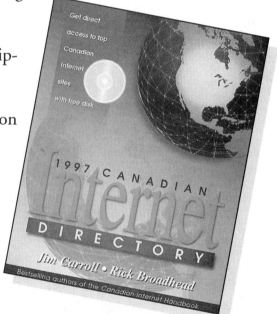

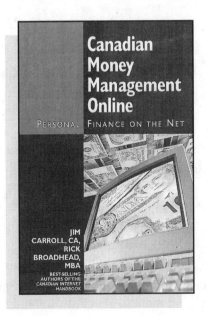

Internet Presentations by Rick Broadhead

On the Internet, change takes place at a frightening pace. How familiar is your organization with the latest on-line trends and opportunities?

Having co-authored 12 Internet books, including the national #1 bestseller the *Canadian Internet Handbook*, Rick Broadhead is one of Canada's leading Internet gurus and a popular writer and commentator on the Internet. He speaks at annual meetings and conferences across North America, and he has made presentations on the Internet to a wide range of government organizations, businesses, and not-for-profit associations. Rick also teaches at York University's Schulich School of Business, where he was awarded the 1996 George A. Edwards Marketing Medal for demonstrated excellence in marketing.

His diverse client list includes organizations such as the Government of Alberta, ADIA Personnel Services, the Financial Management Institute of Canada, the Ontario Ministry of Economic Development and Trade, the Canadian Paint and Coatings Association, Credit Union Central of Canada (Canadian Conference for Credit Union Executives), Hybrid Turkeys, the Confectionery Manufacturers Association of Canada, the Canadian Wood Council, the Pipe Line Contractors Association of Canada, Canadian Business Press, the City of North Bay, and VISA International, where he was commissioned to prepare an overview of the strategic implications of the Internet for VISA's member financial institutions worldwide.

For further information about an Internet presentation for your organization or conference, please contact Rick Broadhead using any of the methods below:

TELEPHONE: (416) 487-5220

FAX: (416) 440-0175

E-MAIL: **rickb@inforamp.net**

More detailed information about Rick Broadhead can be found on his World Wide Web site at
http://www.intervex.com